THE WYETH AND WYTHE FAMILIES OF AMERICA

Seven Generations of the Descendants of
~ NICHOLAS WYETH ~

Compiled and Written by
CHRISTINA WYETH BAKER

Based on the Research of
JEFFREY MICHEAL WYETH and
CHRISTINA WYETH BAKER

Foreword by **JAMES BROWNING "JAMIE" WYETH**

HERITAGE BOOKS
2019

HERITAGE BOOKS
AN IMPRINT OF HERITAGE BOOKS, INC.

Books, CDs, and more—Worldwide

For our listing of thousands of titles see our website
at
www.HeritageBooks.com

Published 2019 by
HERITAGE BOOKS, INC.
Publishing Division
5810 Ruatan Street
Berwyn Heights, Md. 20740

International Standard Book Number
Paperbound: 978-0-7884-5897-2

15th Century Baptismal Font in All Saints Church
Saxtead, Suffolk County, England
Photograph taken by Christina Wyeth "Tina" Baker on 12 Jul 2008

"We all shine on like the moon and the stars and the sun."

~ John Winston Lennon

DEDICATION

This history is dedicated to one of the brightest lights of my life... my brother, Sidney James Wyeth (28 Aug 1956 - 24 Dec 2014). The memories of the nights we spent playing hide and seek with only the moon to light our way, of gazing at the stars in the vast country sky, of holding jars of lightning bugs under our blanket while trying to stay awake until the sunrise... those thoughts remain in my mind in bright Technicolor. When his light darkened on that heartbreaking silent night, it gave me even more empathy for the sisters and brothers, mothers and fathers, and sons and daughters who fill these pages. In Sid's honor, I have diligently tried to make their black and white stories glitter with a dash of color. All those who went before us, continue to shine on through us.

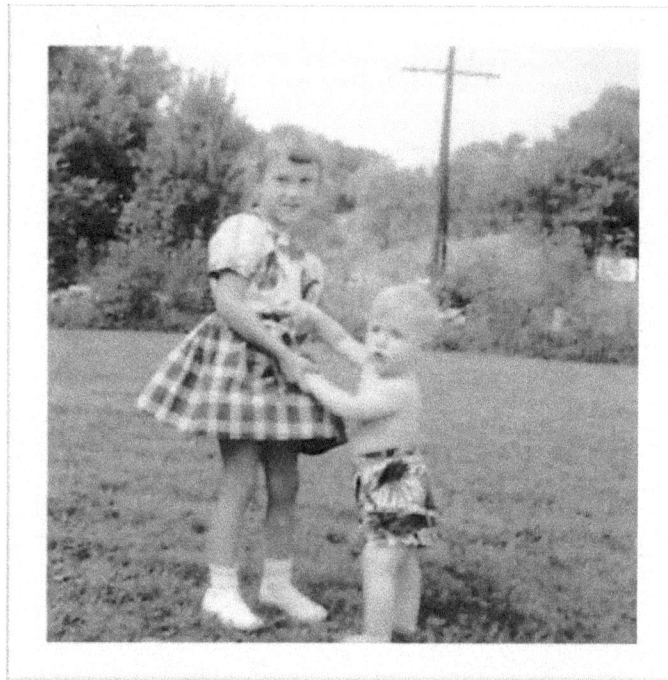

Tina and Sid Wyeth in the front yard of their childhood home at the foot of Roley Hill, on State Route 13, in Licking County, Ohio. The photograph was taken by their uncle Scott Harmon Wyeth.

CONTENTS

FOREWORD

Many distinguished Wyeths are listed in these pages. Because I am a descendant of two of them, artists Newell Convers "N. C." Wyeth and Andrew Newell Wyeth, Tina asked me to write the foreword to this book.

Although I never knew my grandfather, I do know he was fascinated with our remarkable family history. The adventures of the daring Oregon Trail pioneer, Nathaniel Jarvis Wyeth, particularly inspired N. C. in his work.

Portraits of my third great grandparents, Captain Job Wyeth and Lydia Convers Francis, as well as

Photo taken 16 Feb 1992 of Jamie and his distant cousin, Marc Wyeth, at Jamie's Point Lookout Farm that straddles the Delaware and Pennsylvania state line.

their son, John Bound Wyeth, still hang in the dining room of N. C.'s home. John, my third great uncle, accompanied Nathaniel part of the way on his first expedition to Oregon.

My aunt Carolyn Wyeth, who taught me to draw, said, "Pa believed all the Wyeths in America are related."

Tina's book does much to substantiate my grandfather's claim.

~ James Browning "Jamie" Wyeth
Point Lookout Farm, Chadds Ford, 2016

ACKNOWLEDGMENTS

Simply put, this book would have been impossible without the painstaking research of my brother, Jeff Wyeth. He has spent countless hours slogging through cemeteries, patiently viewing incalculable rolls of microfilm, calling Wyeth phone numbers from directories in every city he visits, inspecting census reports, and interviewing relatives. As soon as he hears of a new birth or a wedding in the family, he is on the case diligently recording the facts in his ever-present ledger book.

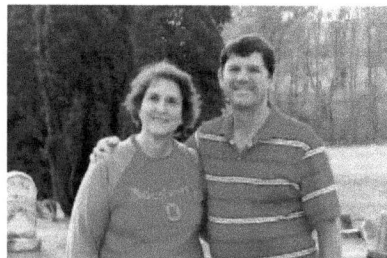

Christina "Tina" Baker and
Jeffrey Micheal "Jeff" Wyeth

In 1977, while stationed with the U.S. Army in Hanau, Germany, Jeff began writing letters to his extended family. Helpful information came from these individuals who are no longer with us:

Lula Browning, Joan Wyeth Carpenter, Milton Dirst, Clara Wyeth Emmons, Edna Schroeder Evans, Helen Wyeth Bright Hampson, Patricia King Harms, Lucy Snow Wyeth Hoffman, Erma Lockwood Hutchman, Naoda Hungerford Little, Ann Wyeth McCoy, Donna Hampton McKinney, Walter and Jean Linden McNamee, Margaret Wyeth Seekins, Margo Julia Wyeth Stratford, Marvel June Wyeth Ucen, Effie May Wyeth Winn, Ace Wyeth, Anna May Souva Wyeth, Charles Leon Wyeth, Donald Elwyn Wyeth, Grace Gann Wyeth, Irving Rudolph Wyeth, Jack Mitchell Wyeth, Jackson Wyeth, John Allan Wyeth Jr., John Churchill Wyeth Jr., John Woodfall Wyeth, Juanita Vogt Wyeth, Kurt Nicholas Wyeth, Laurabelle Boehme Wyeth, Leonard Jarvis Wyeth V, Marion Sims Wyeth Sr., Richard DeAngeles Wyeth, Richard Kent Wyeth, Robert Calvin Wyeth, Sidney James Wyeth, Stella Kluesner Wyeth, Stuart Mac R. Wyeth, Wallace H. Wyeth, and Willard Hiram Wyeth Sr.

Over four decades later, help still comes from family members all over the United States and Canada. In an effort to properly acknowledge our current contributors for their valuable input and suggestions, Jeff and I assembled a list of them for Appendix 1 of this book. Hopefully, we have not inadvertently overlooked thanking anyone who sent photos, informational letters, emails, Bible records, stories or family data forms. If we did, please email us at WyethBaker6@gmail.com.

The generous contributions to this book of my distant cousin, James Browning "Jamie" Wyeth, my daughter, Traci Michelle Baker Kerns, and my longtime friend, Susan Gerhardt Lyle, deserve special thanks. Amazingly, on the day before Jamie responded about writing the foreword to this book, I read from a fortune cookie, "Someone important will soon recognize your good work." Indeed. To my precious Traci, a high school history teacher, I am immensely grateful for all her insightful suggestions. To my dear friend Susan, who provided Traci with her first baby bed, I greatly appreciate Susan's time and the fresh set of eyes she put on this manuscript.

I acknowledge last, for emphasis, the enormous contribution of my husband, Arthur Allen Baker. Not only is Art a veteran of the U.S. Air Force, but he is a student of the Civil War and World War II. His understanding of the military was particularly helpful as I wrote the *Heroism and Sacrifice* section in part one of this book. I would not have attempted this massive book-writing endeavor without Art's support and encouragement. When I wake him at 5:00 am excited about a new Internet research discovery I just made, sometimes he falls back asleep while I am in mid-sentence. However, usually he cannot go to sleep again and turns out of bed to start his day. Art has taken over the cooking, the wash, the dusting, doing the dishes and the shopping. He does, however, draw the line at cleaning the bathrooms.

To **everyone** who contributed to this book – thank you, thank you, thank you.

For Natalie and Richard,
Art, Traci and Tricia,
Jack and Dylan.

"Tho' I know I'll never lose affection
For people and things that went before,
I know I'll often stop and think about them,
In my life I love you more."

~ John Lennon and Paul McCartney

PREFACE

Because my husband and I have a keen interest in history, we planned each and every vacation since our daughters, Traci and Tricia, were born around a historical location. As the Boston area is one of the most emblematic centers of American history, we visited there many times and learned many things about my Wyeth ancestors.

On our first trip in 1979, we rode the subway from Boston to Cambridge to find the Old Burying Ground in Harvard Square where Nicholas Wyeth was buried in 1680. Then being young and energetic, we walked all the way to Mt. Auburn Cemetery, at the border of Cambridge and Watertown, to see a monument erected by Jonas Wyeth 2[d] to Nicholas' memory.

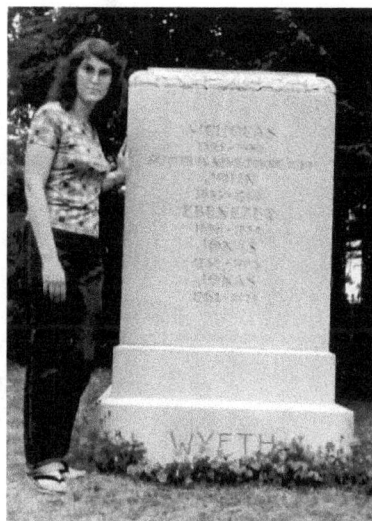

On another trip, we saw Joshua Wyeth's name on a diorama at the Old South Meeting House. It was so exciting to push a button next to his name and hear of his participation in the 1773 Boston Tea Party. A few years later at the newly built Boston Tea Party

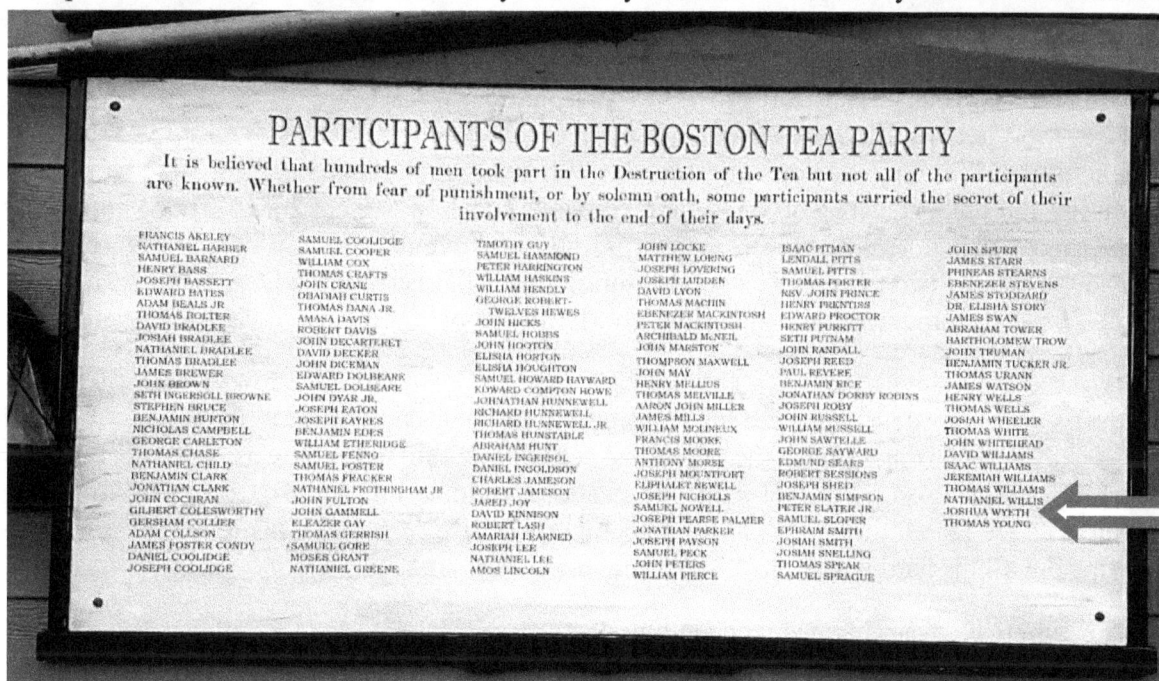

PARTICIPANTS OF THE BOSTON TEA PARTY

It is believed that hundreds of men took part in the Destruction of the Tea but not all of the participants are known. Whether from fear of punishment, or by solemn oath, some participants carried the secret of their involvement to the end of their days.

FRANCIS AKELEY	SAMUEL COOLIDGE	TIMOTHY GUY	JOHN LOCKE	ISAAC PITMAN	JOHN SPURR
NATHANIEL BARBER	SAMUEL COOPER	SAMUEL HAMMOND	MATTHEW LORING	LENDALL PITTS	JAMES STARR
SAMUEL BARNARD	WILLIAM COX	PETER HARRINGTON	JOSEPH LOVERING	SAMUEL PITTS	PHINEAS STEARNS
HENRY BASS	THOMAS CRAFTS	WILLIAM HASKINS	JOSEPH LUDDEN	THOMAS FOSTER	EBENEZER STEVENS
JOSEPH BASSETT	JOHN CRANE	WILLIAM HENDLY	DAVID LYON	REV. JOHN PRINCE	JAMES STODDARD
EDWARD BATES	OBADIAH CURTIS	GEORGE ROBERT-	THOMAS MACHIN	HENRY PRENTISS	DR. ELISHA STORY
ADAM BEALS JR.	THOMAS DANA JR.	TWELVES HEWES	EBENEZER MACKINTOSH	EDWARD PROCTOR	JAMES SWAN
THOMAS BOLTER	AMASA DAVIS	JOHN HICKS	PETER MACKINTOSH	HENRY PURKITT	ABRAHAM TOWER
DAVID BRADLEE	ROBERT DAVIS	SAMUEL HOBBS	ARCHIBALD MCNEIL	SETH PUTNAM	BARTHOLOMEW TROW
JOSIAH BRADLEE	JOHN DECARTERET	JOHN HOOTON	JOHN MARSTON	JOHN RANDALL	JOHN TRUMAN
NATHANIEL BRADLEE	DAVID DECKER	ELISHA HORTON		JOSEPH REED	BENJAMIN TUCKER JR.
THOMAS BRADLEE	JOHN DICKMAN	ELISHA HOUGHTON	THOMPSON MAXWELL	PAUL REVERE	THOMAS URANN
JAMES BREWER	EDWARD DOLBEARE	SAMUEL HOWARD HAYWARD	JOHN MAY	BENJAMIN RICE	JAMES WATSON
JOHN BROWN	SAMUEL DOLBEARE	EDWARD COMPTON HOWE	HENRY MELLUS	JONATHAN DORBY ROBINS	HENRY WELLS
SETH INGERSOLL BROWNE	JOHN DYAR JR.	JOHNATHAN HUNNEWELL	THOMAS MELVILLE	JOSEPH ROBY	THOMAS WELLS
STEPHEN BRUCE	JOSEPH EATON	RICHARD HUNNEWELL	AARON JOHN MILLER	JOHN RUSSELL	JOSIAH WHEELER
BENJAMIN BURTON	JOSEPH KAYRES	RICHARD HUNNEWELL JR.	JAMES MILLS	WILLIAM RUSSELL	THOMAS WHITE
NICHOLAS CAMPBELL	BENJAMIN EDES	THOMAS HUNSTABLE	WILLIAM MOLINEUX	JOHN SAWTELLE	JOHN WHITEHEAD
GEORGE CARLETON	WILLIAM ETHERIDGE	ABRAHAM HUNT	FRANCIS MOORE	GEORGE SAYWARD	DAVID WILLIAMS
THOMAS CHASE	SAMUEL FENNO	DANIEL INGERSOL	THOMAS MOORE	EDMUND SEARS	ISAAC WILLIAMS
NATHANIEL CHILD	SAMUEL FOSTER	DANIEL INGOLDSON	ANTHONY MORSE	ROBERT SESSIONS	JEREMIAH WILLIAMS
BENJAMIN CLARK	THOMAS FRACKER	CHARLES JAMESON	JOSEPH MOUNTFORT	JOSEPH SHED	THOMAS WILLIAMS
JONATHAN CLARK	NATHANIEL FROTHINGHAM JR.	ROBERT JAMESON	ELIPHALET NEWELL	BENJAMIN SIMPSON	NATHANIEL WILLIS
JOHN COCHRAN	JOHN FULTON	JARED JOY	JOSEPH NICHOLLS	PETER SLATER JR.	JOSHUA WYETH
GILBERT COLESWORTHY	JOHN GAMMELL	DAVID KINNISON	SAMUEL NOWELL	SAMUEL SLOPER	THOMAS YOUNG
GERSHAM COLLIER	ELEAZER GAY	ROBERT LASH	JOSEPH PEARSE PALMER	EPHRAIM SMITH	
ADAM COLLSON	THOMAS GERRISH	AMARIAH LEARNED	JONATHAN PARKER	JOSIAH SMITH	
JAMES FOSTER CONDY	SAMUEL GORE	JOSEPH LEE	JOSEPH PAYSON	JOSIAH SNELLING	
DANIEL COOLIDGE	MOSES GRANT	NATHANIEL LEE	SAMUEL PECK	THOMAS SPEAR	
JOSEPH COOLIDGE	NATHANIEL GREENE	AMOS LINCOLN	JOHN PETERS	SAMUEL SPRAGUE	
			WILLIAM PIERCE		

Ships & Museum, we were immensely proud to see Joshua's name on a sign on the wall of the museum giving the names of hundreds of participants in the Boston Tea Party.

On a different trip we toured the Jason Russell house in Arlington, Massachusetts, because I read his mother-in-law was Elizabeth Wyeth. Jason was killed on the first day of the American Revolution. When I told our guide about the connection, she said the actor Kurt Russell was descended from Jason Russell. When I got home, I studied the line from Elizabeth's father, John

Wyeth Sr., to Kurt Russell and discovered Kurt is my eighth cousin 1x removed.

Knowledge of Nicholas Wyeth's burial in the Gamage family tomb in Cambridge's Harvard Square led me to another intriguing discovery. While tracing the tree of Caroline Rodema Scott Wyeth, my great grandmother, I found she descends from Nicholas' granddaughter Deborah Wyeth Gamage. Interestingly, Caroline's husband, William Grate Wyeth, descends from Deborah's first cousin, Ebenezer Wyeth Sr. Heretofore, no one knew my great grandparents were sixth cousins 1x removed.

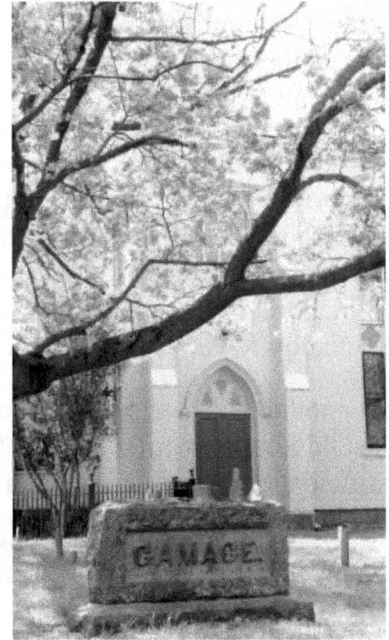

In 1998, we made our first trip out of the United States. We combined vacation with family research in Tricarico, Italy – the ancestral homeland of my mother, Natalie Domenica Soldo. Ten years later, we were blessed to be able to see Saxtead, Suffolk County, England – the ancestral homeland of my father, Richard Caldwell "RC" Wyeth. I sent Jeff brochures and pictures from the places we visited but otherwise did not have much time to collaborate with him on genealogical research. While my daughters were young, I worked full time during the day and Art worked second shift. My evenings were spent driving the girls to softball games, dance lessons, school functions and other events. For ten of those busy years, I took college classes two evenings each week until I earned a Bachelor's Degree in Business and Organizational Communication. Subsequently, I worked as a technical writer until retiring the first time in 2001.

Then Jeff's hints for me to organize his research into a book became more frequent. He greatly enjoyed gathering information but the process of actually writing the book was overwhelming him. When I retired for a second time, I gave in and started helping him in 2010. I agreed to manage the project as we feared the old crash-prone computer where Jeff stored his records could at any time wipe out all his hard work.

It was my turn to be overwhelmed when I uploaded Jeff's GEDcom file of 6,719 families of 17,618 individuals to my computer, on 27 Jul 2012.* (*Please note: this Genealogical Standard Date Format is used throughout this book.)

Often working 70-80 hours a week, my primary task has been verifying data and gathering sources for people in the family tree. I did cut out over 8,000 people who were not descendants of Nicholas. On the other hand, I researched and added parents of spouses bringing the tree up to over 10,000 people. Through the years, Jeff carefully stored some sources in notebooks. They were in hard copy form and had to be tediously scanned and attached to the electronic data. However, most of the facts in the GEDcom were not backed up with the essential source of the information. Not only have I spent more than 12,000 hours searching the indispensable Ancestry.com, I had to track down sources by researching online and in libraries, in cemeteries, in historical societies, as well as at the National Archives in Waltham, Massachusetts and Washington, D.C.

I also attached to the tree digital photographs of places and cemeteries I visited through the years. Some of the pictures appear in part one of this book. Unless otherwise noted, all those types of photographs are my own. Family and individual portraits come from a variety of sources. If I can find the time, many more family photos will appear in a second book or in a blog. Please continue sending family group photos and stories to me at WyethBaker6@gmail.com.

By adding the basis of the facts and adding the parents of spouses, I was able to correct many errors in the original GEDcom data. Nevertheless, it is impossible that there should not be mistakes or omissions in a work of this nature. This is largely due to variations in source data. As I have written this book from scratch, I take responsibility for grammatical, formatting and spelling errors. Nevertheless, changes in software have made the project more difficult. The Family Tree Maker software I used at the start of this book, for the basis of the register reports, was then owned by Ancestry.com. However, when Software MacKiev acquired the line in 2017, they changed register numbered descendant-based reports so data could not be cut and pasted from them. This forced me into typing data in the book by hand from my research housed in Ancestry. I tried using Rootsmagic software, but their register descendant-based reports give a number to married couples without children, causing lots of unnecessary repetition.

Thus, blank pages at the end of the first section of this book are for corrections and additions. Please email, to the above address, any corrections you would like shared to the blog for this book.

In reality, section one of this book is a lengthy introduction to section two.

The first section includes: 1) the Wyeth / Wythe family beginnings in the English countryside, 2) theories for the connection of Declaration of Independence signer George Wythe to Nicholas Wyeth, 3) Nicholas' emigration from Saxtead, England to Cambridge, Massachusetts, 4) Rebecca, the ancestress of almost everyone in this book, and her children who were accused of witchcraft, 5) the heroism and sacrifice of individual family members in conflicts from King Philip's War to the Philippine-American War, 6) Nicholas' famous descendants, 7) Wyeth homes in Cambridge, and 8) my own Wyeth / Baker family story.

Section two of this book is divided into chapters by generation. The first chapter is the generation of Nicholas Wyeth and his children. It tells his story as well as the stories of his first wife, Margaret Clarke, and his second wife, Rebecca Parks Andrews. Subsequent chapters detail families by generation as they move forward from Nicholas.

Suffice it to say, I had little concept of the amount of time and labor necessary to bring this book to fruition. Time and time again, I wanted to throw in the towel. However, the desire for my grandsons, Jack Edward Brown and Dylan Arthur Brown, to know their heritage, has kept me going. At the same time, I have been encouraged to press on by many who believe this work is meaningful. It is my sincere hope that the legacy presented in these pages will be a source of pride and inspiration to families who now, and families who will, trace their lineage to Nicholas Wyeth.

~ Christina "Tina" Wyeth Baker, Howard, Ohio, 2016

WYTHE / WYETH COAT OF ARMS

Azure (blue) - three griffins (mythical winged creatures) - per pale (divided vertically) - passant (walking) - or (gold or yellow)[1]

Compiled from a photograph taken by Mike Dixon of the heraldry in a window at St. Martin at Palace Church, Norwich, Norfolk County, England[2]

"No story really ends. It only links the past and future."

~ From the movie *Enchantment* by John Patrick

SECTION ONE: NICHOLAS WYETH'S FAMILY STORY READS LIKE AN AMERICAN HISTORY BOOK

The Wyeth / Wythe family is American history in action. We came to the New World around the time of the Great Migration, struggled through King Philip's War, suffered cruelly in the Salem Witch Trials, died at the hands of Native Americans in Queen Anne's War, fought in the Seven Years' War, protested taxation without representation in the Boston Tea Party, marched as minutemen at Lexington, Concord, Lincoln and Menotomy and served in General George Washington's Continental Army. We encountered the British again in the War of 1812, clashed with Mexico, and battled for both the North and the South in the Civil War. In the Spanish American War, Philippine-American War, World Wars I and II, in Korea, Vietnam, Iraq and Afghanistan, Wyeth / Wythe families were there as well.

Striving to thrive in times of war and peace, Wyeth / Wythe families helped build America. They were masons, farmers, mechanics, fishermen, carpenters, factory workers, teamsters, blacksmiths, coopers, shoemakers, tanners and more. They were among the ranks of teachers, coaches, bankers, preachers, lawyers, bus drivers, hairdressers, undertakers, shopkeepers, ranchers, salespersons, secretaries, librarians, postmasters, police officers, doctors, nurses, and first responders. Some were pioneers in women's rights, early education, and medical education. Others were well-known explorers, inventors, architects, writers, actors, athletes, musicians, investors, legislators, newspaper publishers, manufacturers, drug company founders and iconic artists.

Wyeth / Wythe stories are wide ranging. George McClelland "Clel" Wyeth stealing chickens in 1906 to feed his ten children in Monongahela, PA is light years away from the 1910 high society party of George Edward Wyeth's debutante daughter, Charlotte Grosvenor Wyeth, on 42nd Street in New York City, NY. Nevertheless, their stories are equally American. They were born of the aspirations of one man, Nicholas Wyeth, when he bravely set his sights on a strange new world over 3,000 miles away from the familiar golden fields of his home in Suffolk County, England.

My father, Richard Caldwell "RC" Wyeth, painted this large mural in the early 1970s. It depicts Nicholas Wyeth and the progression of his descendants across America and into the future. RC and his fourth wife, Naomi, are pictured on the right. The profiles below RC, from left to right, are of the seven of his children who were raised together: Bob, Sid, Jeff, Marc, Kitty, Tina (me), and Laura. The car on the right is my red 1965 Mustang. I wish I still had that classic car.

Remember me in the family tree

My name, my days, my strife;

Then I'll ride upon the wings of time

And live an endless life."

~ Linda Goetsch

THE WYETH AMERICAN HISTORY BEGINS IN THE ENGLISH COUNTRYSIDE

Nicholas Wyeth, like most of the first settlers of Cambridge, Massachusetts, emigrated from Great Britain. But where, specifically, was unknown until 1948 when his fifth great grandson, Marion Sims Wyeth, discovered the location.

Marion was attempting to prove a relationship of Nicholas to Declaration of Independence signer George Wythe. He privately published his findings in a booklet called *Nicholas and George Wythe: An Account of a Search for Their English Antecedents.*

From the response of the Rector of Framlingham and Saxtead to Marion's inquiries, we know Nicholas was baptized 20 Jan 1600 in All Saints Church in Saxtead, Suffolk County, England.[3]

The church is pictured with me, his eighth great granddaughter, Christina Wyeth "Tina" Baker. Supposedly, the church was built prior to 1307 by Thomas de Brotherton, Earl of Norfolk.[4] Most of the church dates to the Perpendicular stage (1377 to 1546) of English Gothic church architecture.[5] The church's well-worn octagonal baptismal font, decorated with plain shields within quatrefoils, dates to the 15th century.[6] Thus, it is the same basin from which Nicholas was sanctified over 400 years ago.

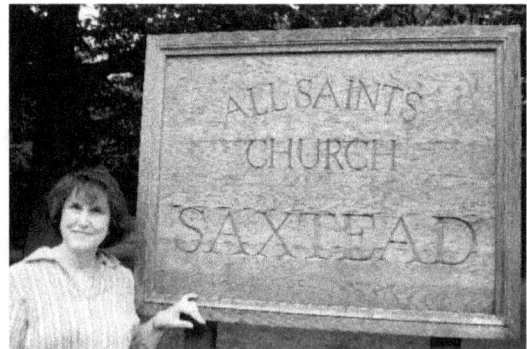

Equally as important as Marion's discovery of Nicholas' baptism place, was his gifting a copy of the research booklet to my brother, Jeffrey Micheal Wyeth. Jeff was only 19 years old when he received Marion's gift. So interested was Jeff in his Wyeth roots, he immediately began searching records and writing letters to descendants of Nicholas Wyeth all over the United States and Canada.

Marion Sims Wyeth Sr. - photo courtesy of the Preservation Foundation of Palm Beach, Palm Beach, Florida.

Jeff literally took to heart what Marion said on page three of the booklet... that he "is issuing this account at the

> You have my hearty approval of your project, and I hope that in due time the book you mention will come to be. I will be happy to help you in any way I can, although as I said, I am handicapped by poor vision.
>
> Sincerely yours,
>
> 20 May 1977
>
> Marion Sims Wyeth

present time in its very incomplete condition for fear that the notes might be destroyed and over 25 years of part-time research be lost to ***some other member of the family who may be interested in carrying on this search.***"

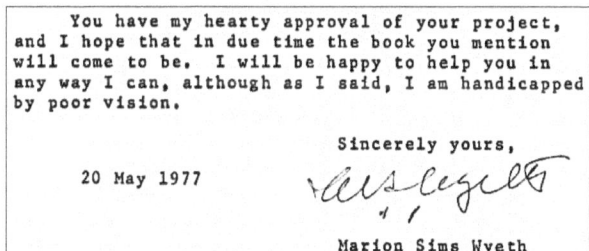

Prior to Marion's breakthrough, much confusion existed about Nicholas' birthplace. On 23 Mar 1847, his third great grandson, Jonas Wyeth 2[d], a Cambridge selectman (city councilman), born 14 Dec 1806, wrote in a set of journals that Nicholas was believed to have emigrated from Wales.[7]

John Herbert Barker (1870-1951), the grandson of Andrew Newell Wyeth Sr., in his 1940 handwritten Wyeth family manuscript,[8] quoted J. Gardner Bartlett who wrote Nicholas Wyeth was from Mellis, Suffolk, England. Nicholas' first wife, Margaret Clarke, was born a few miles from Mellis, in Westhorpe.

John Herbert Barker, *Some notes on the Wyeth family 1595-1940*, courtesy of the New England Historic Genealogical Society (NEHGS), Boston, MA.

Nicholas' testimony to join the First Church of Cambridge and Margaret's birthplace near Mellis must have been the basis of the assumption Bartlett used in *The English Ancestral Homes of the Founders of Cambridge* published by the Cambridge Historical Society.[9]

There are at least three different types of handwriting in the Wyeth journals. It is apparent Major Jonas Wyeth (1762-1828) and his son Jonas Wyeth 2[d] did most of the recording. We are most fortunate the New England Historic Genealogical Society (NEHGS) has archived our family treasures of John Herbert Barker and Jonas Wyeths' handwritten records all these years in Boston.

Jonas Wyeth journal, *Wyeth family records* (Mss A 3058), R. Stanton Avery Special Collections. Courtesy of the New England Historic Genealogical Society (NEHGS), Boston, MA.)

GEORGE WYTHE
Painted by John F. Weir after Trumbull's likeness of Wythe
in the "Signers of the Declaration of Independence."
(Courtesy of Independence Hall, Philadelphia, Pa.)

JOHN ALLAN WYETH, M.D., LL.D.
From a photograph by Bradley, 1914

Page 6 of Marion Sims Wyeth's privately printed notes

Marion Sims Wyeth became fascinated with his family history while studying at Princeton University. In the school's Pyne Library, he saw a copy of Sanderson's *Lives of the Signers* and in it, a profile portrait of George Wythe (pronounced "with"). He was struck by the resemblance of George Wythe to his own family. Like Marion's family, particularly his father, Dr. John Allan Wyeth, George Wythe had a high, bald forehead and prominent Roman nose.

Trying to prove a connection, Marion Sims Wyeth began his research by studying the Massachusetts family of Nicholas Wyeth and his first wife, Margaret Clarke. Marion's breakthrough was finding J. Gardner Bartlett's article in the *Genealogical Bulletin, Vol. I*, indicating that Margaret Clarke was born in Westhorpe, Suffolk, England to Thomas Clarke and Rose Kerridge.[10] Equally helpful were details Marion gathered on Margaret's well-known brother,

Dr. John Clarke. Dr. Clarke co-founded Rhode Island [11] and authored the 1663 Charter that, for the first time ever, made religious freedom an essential part of democracy.[12]

G. Andrew Moriarity wrote a more complete pedigree for Dr. Clarke and his sister Margaret's family showing their mother was baptized in Saxtead, Suffolk, England.[13] After studying documents from Dr. John Clarke's estate as well as other sources showing the proclivity of the Wyeth surname in Suffolk County, Marion took a blind shot and wrote the Rector of Framlingham and Saxtead.

Marion felt he had hit the jackpot for an amateur genealogist when Rev. Martin Bulstrode furnished lists of 32 people with names similar to Wyeth who were baptized, married or buried in Saxtead. Naturally, he was most pleased to receive the baptismal date and

This painting, housed in the Redwood Library, Newport, RI, is titled *Portrait of a Clergyman* by Guilliam de Ville, c. 1659. This public domain work of art is believed to be Dr. John Clarke and is used courtesy of Wikimedia Commons.

7

marriage information for Nicholas Wyth as shown in this trial pedigree Marion prepared.[14]

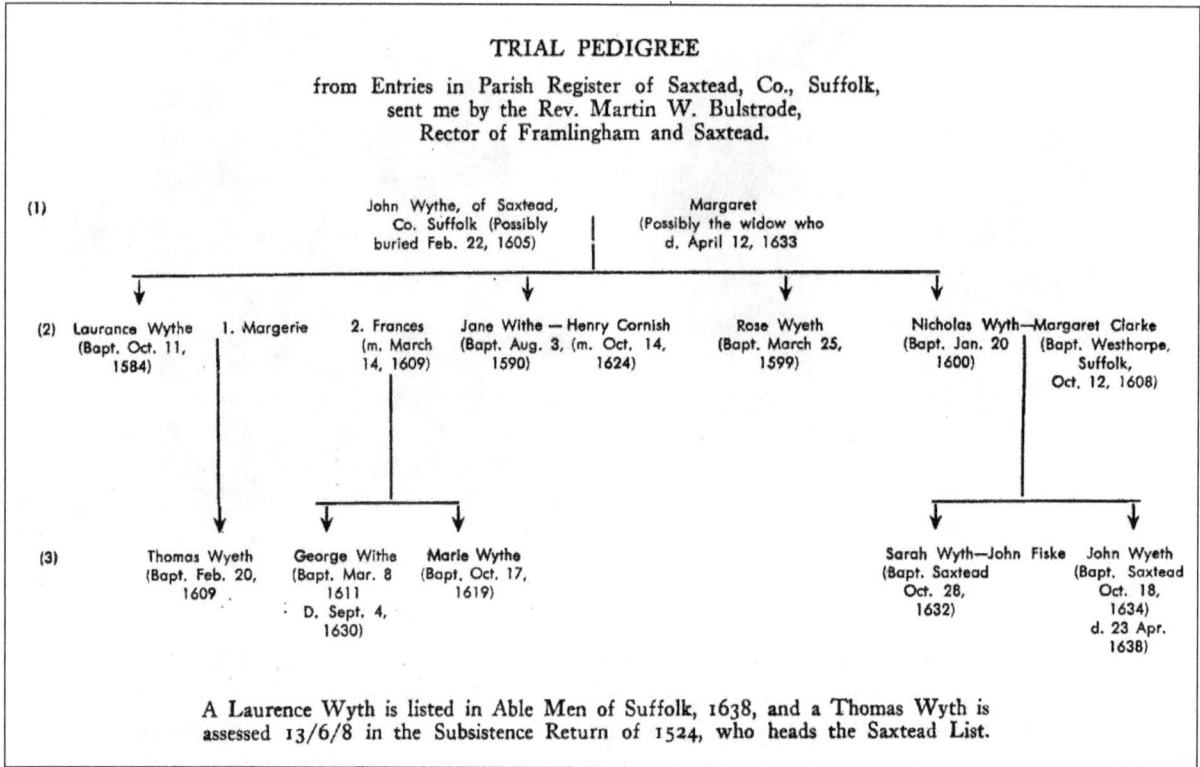

TRIAL PEDIGREE

from Entries in Parish Register of Saxtead, Co., Suffolk,
sent me by the Rev. Martin W. Bulstrode,
Rector of Framlingham and Saxtead.

(1) John Wythe, of Saxtead, Co. Suffolk (Possibly buried Feb. 22, 1605) — Margaret (Possibly the widow who d. April 12, 1633

(2) Laurance Wythe (Bapt. Oct. 11, 1584) 1. Margerie 2. Frances (m. March 14, 1609) Jane Withe — Henry Cornish (Bapt. Aug. 3, 1590) (m. Oct. 14, 1624) Rose Wyeth (Bapt. March 25, 1599) Nicholas Wyth—Margaret Clarke (Bapt. Jan. 20 1600) (Bapt. Westhorpe, Suffolk, Oct. 12, 1608)

(3) Thomas Wyeth (Bapt. Feb. 20, 1609 . George Withe (Bapt. Mar. 8 1611 D. Sept. 4, 1630) Marie Wythe (Bapt. Oct. 17, 1619) Sarah Wyth—John Fiske (Bapt. Saxtead Oct. 28, 1632) John Wyeth (Bapt. Saxtead Oct. 18, 1634) d. 23 Apr. 1638)

A Laurence Wyth is listed in Able Men of Suffolk, 1638, and a Thomas Wyth is assessed 13/6/8 in the Subsistence Return of 1524, who heads the Saxtead List.

Because many people could not read or write in the past, the spelling of surnames depended on the clerk who recorded the name. In Norfolk and Suffolk counties, England, variations in the Wyeth name include Wieth, With, Withe, Wyethe, Wyth, and Wythe. In Nicholas' time, records of Middlesex County, Massachusetts, show Wieth, Withe, Wyth, Wyeth and Wythe, but by the next generation, the name was generally spelled "Wyeth." In Virginia, however, the "Wythe" spelling remained.[15] Still the spellings were frequently interchanged.

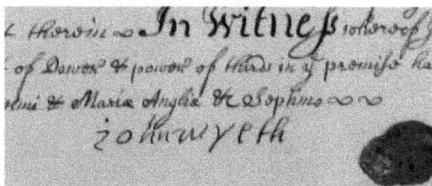

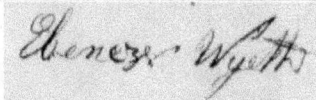

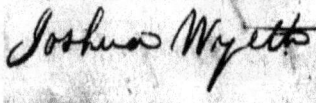

In a 1695 land sale between John and William Wyeth, members of the second generation from Nicholas, John signed his name "Wyeth." Generally, that spelling continued as shown in the early 1800s Revolutionary War pension application signatures of two sons of Ebenezer Wyeth Jr. Interestingly, one of Joshua's grandsons reverted to the "Wythe" spelling. Also shown are the 1830 and 1837 Shaker grave markers of Eunice Bathrick and Joseph Wyeth. Notice that Eunice's marker has the "Wythe" spelling but her husband Joseph's marker has the "Wyeth" spelling.

LOOKING CLOSER AT THE GEORGE WYTHE CONNECTION

According to *Virginia Historical Genealogies* by John Bennett Boddie, George Wythe's great grandfather, Thomas Wythe Sr., came from Norfolk County, England. [16] George Wythe's bookplate of three walking griffins [17] does indeed directly connect him to the Wythe families in the eastern area of England. Burke's *Encyclopaedia of Heraldry* indicates griffins appear on the arms of the eastern counties of Cambridgeshire and Norfolk. [18] On the other hand, lions appear on the Wythe arms of Worcestershire in the West Midlands of England. [19]

"George Wythe's Book Plate"
(Courtesy of the Metropolitan Museum of Art)

Page 10 of Marion Sims Wyeth's notes.

In turn, the heraldry in George Wythe's bookplate connects him to Suffolk County, England as well. One of the earliest mentions of the Wyeth – Wyth – Wythe name in England was Sir Jeffrey Wythe of Norfolk County. His son, Sir Oliver Wythe, through his wife, Winesia de Riveshall, inherited Rushall Manor in Hepworth, Suffolk County, England a few miles south of the Waveney River – the boundary between the East Anglian counties of Norfolk and Suffolk.

When Sir Oliver died in 1367, share in the manor passed to his son, Sir Jeffrey Wythe, of Smallburgh, Norfolk County. Sir Jeffrey asked in his 1373 will to be buried in the churchyard of the brethren of Mount Carmel (the White Friars) of Norwich, Norfolk County, England. [20] Per H.R. Barker in *West Suffolk, Illustrated*, Rushall Manor is now known as Reeves Hall. [21] [22] Since 1999, Reeves Hall has been owned by Peter and Hazel Holloway of Eniti Limited, a tea and coffee logistics company.

The older section of Reeves Hall as it appeared on 31 Mar 2018. Not only did the Holloway's let us take this photo, but they invited us inside to see the manor's ancient wooden beams and fireplace.

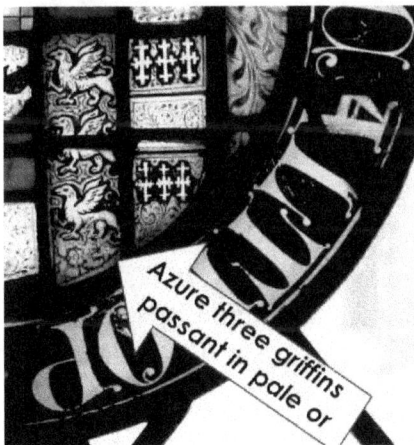

Azure three griffins passant in pale or

The last Wythe to own Reeves Hall/Rushall Manor was Amy Wythe and her husband Sir John Calthorpe. [23] A memorial window at St. Martin at Palace Church, Norwich, Norfolk County, England honors their granddaughter, Elizabeth Calthorpe. The Wythe family heraldry – azure, three griffins, passant in pale, or (gold) – shows in the bottom right quarter of the encircled arms making up the Calthorpe family tree. The window was photographed by Mike Dixon, a professional photographer who specializes in taking pictures of stained glass throughout East Anglia for the Norwich Historic Churches Trust. [24]

**St. Martin at the Palace Church,
Norwich, Norfolk County, England
(photo taken 09 Jul 2014 by Tina Baker).**

This Wythe-Calthorpe pedigree from page 127 of *The Proceedings of the Suffolk Institute of Archaeology* shows an interesting connection of the Calthorpe family to Queen Anne Boleyn.[25]

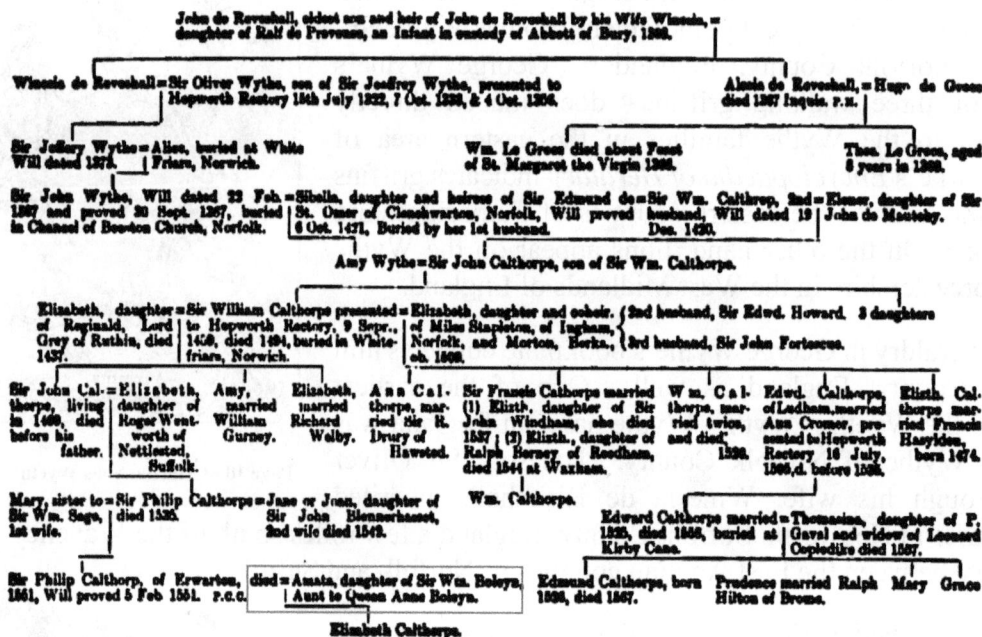

Also linking the Norfolk Wythe arms to Suffolk County is a reference in *A Supplement to the Suffolk Traveller* stating that in 1655 Gentleman James Wythe had an estate in Framsden, Suffolk County worth £300 per annum. He used the same Wythe arms – azure, three griffins, passant, or.[26]

However, records for Wythe families among the gentry of Suffolk County are scarce as compared to Norfolk County. In 1434, John, Nicholas and William Wythe appear on the patent rolls as swearing their allegiance to King Henry VI.[27] They were recorded as members of the upper class of Norfolk entitled to have a coat of arms. During the reign of Henry VIII, in 1512, Thomas Wythe was a member of Parliament from Lynn, Norfolk, England. Thomas was elected again in 1515. However, his name was spelled "Wyth" in that election.[28] Also during the reign of Henry VIII, high-ranking

The motto "nitor in adversum" (struggle against adversity) shows below the griffins in the Wythe / Wyeth arms on china belonging to William Maxwell "Will" Wyeth, the third president of the Wyeth Hardware Co. of St. Joseph, MO. Photo courtesy of his great nephew, Max Wyeth IV.

official, Edmund Wythe, appeared in court over a land dispute in Aylesham, Norfolk, England.[29] John, Roger, Thomas and William Wyth all of Lynn in Norfolk County appear in the *Manuscripts of the House of Lords* published during the period of 1678 to 1693.[30]

Perhaps George Wythe's great grandfather, Thomas, came from one of the Wythe lines of Lynn in Norfolk County. Due to his large landholdings in Elizabeth City County, Virginia, he was a member of the aristocracy and held the title "gentleman." In a time when the ruling class came largely from the gentry, Thomas Sr. was appointed a county court justice.[31] Then on 09 Jun 1680, Thomas Wythe began a term as a member of the Virginia House of Burgesses.[32]

On the other hand, the paper trail shows Nicholas and the Wyeths from Suffolk County were largely of the yeoman class in English society. They were generally freeholders who cultivated their own land. Yeomen were of a lower status than gentlemen. In Rev. Bulstrode's letter to Marion Sims Wyeth, he said the Wyeths had been in the area of Saxtead for some 50 years before Nicholas was born. It appears Nicholas' family must have moved into Suffolk from Norfolk.

English spelling was not consistent or standardized until the 18th century,[33] so the difference in the spelling of George Wythe's and Nicholas Wyeth's surnames is of minor importance to their being related. Quoting from *Suffolk Surnames* written in 1861 by Nathaniel Ingersoll Bowditch, Marion Sims Wyeth noted the names Wyeth and Wythe are listed in a chapter titled "Names from Trees."[34] The two names are variants of "withe" which, according to *Webster's dictionary*, is a flexible slender twig or branch. Another derivation comes from the Old Norse word "vithr" which means wood.[35] Yet another variation of "wythe" is a single thickness of bricks in masonry construction.[36]

Marion made an excellent case relating the Virginia Wythes to the Massachusetts Wyeths. Obviously, in both cases they descended from the same ancient family who were Lords of Rushall. If we were to put the Norfolk and Suffolk branches of the family together circa 1500 when it is likely Nicholas' branch moved to Saxtead, by comparing the generations, members of the 11th generation (my generation) from Nicholas would call George Wythe a seventh cousin 7x removed.

Another possibility that would make the descendants of Nicholas Wyeth more closely related to George Wythe, is that the Richard Withe / Rich Wyeth listed in the town records of 1649 as having land near Cambridge Common is Nicholas' brother and is the same Richard Wyth who was on a 1635 list of early Virginia immigrants.[37] [38] [39] Perhaps Richard was engaged in trade via ship between the Colonies.

The notion Nicholas Wyeth's and George Wythe's ancestors were brothers has long been a legend in the Wyeth / Wythe family. Indeed, as pointed out before, it was the mention of the legend in his father's 1914 autobiography, *With Sabre and Scalpel,* that started Marion Sims Wyeth on his quest. Dr. John Allan Wyeth wrote: "Nicholas Wyeth (or Wythe, as the name appears in some of the earlier records) and a brother came from England to America in 1630 the former, settling at New Town, near Boston, Massachusetts, the latter joining the colonists of Virginia."[40]

View from Mount Auburn, engraving by James Smillie, courtesy of Mount Auburn Cemetery's Historical Collections.

As previously stated, when Marion presented his own book to my brother, Jeff Wyeth, it launched him on his quest to try to track every descendant of Nicholas Wyeth. My first support of Jeff's work was the 1979 photo of the Wyeth monument in Mt. Auburn Cemetery shown in this book's preface.

The stone sits on Mimosa Path in the lush garden cemetery straddling the border between Cambridge and Watertown. Part of the cemetery, established in 1832, is on land Ebenezer Wyeth Jr. bought in 1751 when he married Mary Winship.[41] [42]

This 1847 engraving shows the view of Fresh Pond from the top of Mt. Auburn Hill. Through the trees, to the right of the new Bigelow Chapel, is the Fresh

The Mt. Auburn Cemetery gate.

Pond Hotel and the house Jacob Wyeth Sr. built on his father Ebenezer's land. On the pond, are the icehouses of Ebenezer's grandson and Jacob's son, Nathaniel Jarvis Wyeth (1802-1856).[43] The gate to Mt. Auburn sits opposite of where another one of Ebenezer's grandsons, John Wyeth (1805-1871), built a home circa 1841.[44][45] Not only does some of Mt. Auburn sit on Wyeth land, but nearly 200 members of the Wyeth family are buried there.[46]

Here is an updated photo of Nicholas' monument from a 2018 visit to Mt. Auburn. The top name shown is "Nicholas, 1595-1680, settled in Newe Towne 1630." This monument was erected by the previously mentioned selectman, Jonas Wyeth 2[d]. Jonas father's name is the last one shown. It was from the engraving on this stone that Dr. John Allan Wyeth based the information he wrote in his autobiography.

We cannot definitively say Nicholas Wyeth and Richard Wyth were indeed brothers. As compared to the wealth of records available in Massachusetts, the Virginia records are severely limited. Probate records in Suffolk County, England for the years 1444 – 1700 show a proliferation of Wyeths and Wythes with similar first names.[47] Of course, many people did not leave wills. However, for those who did, it would be impossible to determine how the families match, even if all recorded wills were read.

Wieth	Wythe	Wythe	Wythe
Edward of Sternfield, 1638	Agnes of Pettaugh, 1638	John of Kesgrave, 1578	Richard of Sibton, 1634
Francis of South Cove, 1590	Alice of Coddenham, 1682	John of Stratford, 1573	Robert of Bealings, 1578
John of Hollesley, 1605	Alice of Martlesham, 1583	John of Stutton, 1679	Robert of Framsden, 1590
Robert of Saxtead, 1617	Ann of Ipswich, 1691	John of Tannington, 1680	Robert of Kessingland, 1542
Withe	Edmund of Martlesham, 1583	John of Tunstall, 1581	Robert of Southolt, 1636
George of Cretingham, 1612	Elizabeth of Laxfield, 1670	Lionel of Cretingham, 1625	Robert of Woodbridge, 1630
John of Lowestoft, 1689	Frances of Blakenham, 1671	Lionel of Flowton, 1687	Rose of Framsden, 1629
Lionel of Blakenham, 1635	Francis of Brundish, 1620	Lionel of Ipswich, 1691	Thomas of Dunwich, 1691
Matthew of Ufford, 1579	Humphrey of Harkstead, 1567	Margaret of Wangford, 1553	Thomas of Ellough, 1529
Thomas of Bawdsey, 1636	James of Framsden, 1536	Margaret of Woodbridge, 1642	Thomas of Framsden, 1561
Thomas of Bawdsey, 1637	James of Framsden, 1689	Mary of Bawdsey, 1619	Thomas of Helmingham, 1695
Thomas of Ipswich, 1685	John of Athelington, 1627	Mary of Ispwich, 1690	William of Brandeston, 1625
William of Bedfield, 1632	John of Athelington, 1643	Richard of Bramfield, 1615	William of Framsden, 1607
Wyeth	John of Brantham, 1682	Richard of Eyke, 1695	William of Hasketon, 1692
Alice of Hintlesham, 1639	John of Dunwich, 1691	Richard of Framsden, 1678	
Henry of Hintlesham, 1638	John of Hasketon, 1700	Richard of Halesworth, 1691	
John of Shottisham, 1589	John of Helmingham, 1501	Richard of Pettaugh, 1588	
Robert of Monk Soham, 1622	John of Helmingham, 1538	Richard of Pettaugh, 1638	

Not only would it be impossible to match families, but also the wills are written in old English before spelling was standardized. Sometimes they are written all or partly in Latin. They are often damaged and faint. To study the difficulties of reading these old wills, I have copied the introduction to Robert Wieth's 1617 will. Since he is from Saxtead and shows on Marion Sims Wyeth's lists, he is very likely Nicholas' uncle.

Robert's will was nuncupative, meaning it was delivered orally to witnesses. Had it been written in usual form with a proper format, it might have detailed more information about his heirs. As it is, only the first name of Robert's wife (Margerie) appears in the document as executor of the will.

12

Claire Barker, Secretary of the Suffolk Records Society, kindly provided the will's translation. Rather than scanning the original document to show how difficult it is to read these ancient documents without proper training, I have attempted to imitate the ancient handwriting of the time in the hand drawn example below. For an additional example, see the scribbles on the water-damaged photocopy of John Wyeth's marriage document later in this book.

"Memorandum that the five and twentieth day of June Anno Domini–1617–Robert Wieth of Saxsted in the County of Suffolk yeoman did declare his will nuncupative in the presence of us…"

According to George Wythe biographer, Joyce Blackburn, the oldest records in Virginia for George Wythe's ancestors are from 1676 when his great grandfather, Thomas Wythe Sr., is mentioned in an Elizabeth City County land patent book.[48] The county is now Hampton and NASA Langley sits on this land at the Back River, an inlet to Chesapeake Bay and the Atlantic Ocean.[49] Blackburn confirms it cannot be proved that George Wythe's great grandfather was the first Wythe to come to America.[50] Other historians use 1680 when Thomas Sr. served in the House of Burgesses as the date the progenitor came to America.[51][52] There is a record of one Thomas born in Norfolk County, England in 1568[53], but he would be too old. Two other English records showing a Richard Wythe with a son named Thomas are a possibility.[54][55] Marion Sims Wyeth thought Richard in the Cambridge records was the son of Humphrey Wyeth of Ipswich, but that is not the case.[56] Along with Richard, only Nicholas and his sons are in the Cambridge records. The sons appear late in the book but Richard and Nicholas are likely brothers for they are in the early period. Thus, the door is wide open for Richard Wyth being George Wythe's first New World ancestor.

From the Wythes, George inherited social standing and leadership ability. From his mother, Margaret Walker, he inherited his love of learning and concern for the human condition. Margaret was well educated by her own mother, Anne Keith, the daughter of noted progressive Quaker evangelist and abolitionist, George Keith.[57]

At age 16, George Wythe was apprenticed to study law with an uncle. So neglectful was his tutor, George profited from the experience by developing his own excellent teaching methods. While maintaining a private law practice and a legislative career, in 1761, George began teaching law at the College of William and Mary. His admiring students included Henry Clay, James Monroe, John Marshall and Thomas Jefferson. The author of the Declaration of Independence and our third president was particularly glowing in his praise of Wythe. "To his enlightened and affectionate guidance of my studies… I am indebted for everything." The affection was indeed mutual. In his will, George left his library to Jefferson. Those same books were among the ones Jefferson sold to the government to found the Library of Congress.[58]

Links to George's last will and testament can be found on the Library of Congress website. Parts of this will resulted in shockingly tragic consequences. Details are provided after this hypothetical pedigree based on the assumption Nicholas Wyeth and Richard Wyth were brothers.

Hypothetical Pedigree for George Wythe Prepared from the Theory Nicholas and Richard Wyth were Brothers *Based on the Entries in the Parish Register of Saxtead, Co., Suffolk sent to Marion Sims Wyeth and the* *Statistics of John Bennett Boddie written in Virginia Historical Genealogies*					
John Wythe (possibly buried 22 Feb 1605)			Margaret (possibly widow who d. 12 Apr 1633)		
Laurance Wythe (Bapt. 11 Oct 1584)	Jane Withe (Bapt. 03 Aug 1590)	Richard Wyth – born c. 1596. He possibly traded between Virginia, appearing there in 1635, and Cambridge, appearing there in 1649.		Rose Wyeth (Bapt. 25 Mar 1599)	Nicholas Wyth Bapt. 20 Jan 1600 d. 19 Jul 1680
		Thomas Wythe Sr. – Back River land mentioned in 1676 in Elizabeth City County patent book. m. widow Anne Smith. His 14 Dec 1693 will was probated 19 Mar 1693/94 leaving his grandson Thomas III, land he bought from Mr. Sweeney; Exrs., son Thomas Jr. and grandson Thomas III.			John Wyeth Sr. b. 15 Jul 1655 d. 13 Dec 1706
		Thomas Wythe Jr. – born c. 1670. m. Anne Shephard (widow of Quintillian Gutherick who d. 1689; she m. third to James Wallace). His 10 Mar 1693/94 will benefited his son Thomas III.			Ebenezer Wyeth Sr. b. 24 Jul 1698 d. 05 Apr 1754
		Thomas Wythe III – born c. 1691 (his birth date is confirmed by death of his mother's first husband, Gutherick, in 1689). Delegate to the house of Burgesses in 1718, 1723, and 1726; m. 1720 to Margaret Walker. His 03 Nov 1728 will was probated 15 Oct 1729.			Ebenezer Wyeth Jr. b. 08 Apr 1727 d. 04 Aug 1799
		George Wythe – Lawyer, judge, law professor, slavery opponent, and signer of the Declaration of Independence was born c. 1726 on the Back River plantation in Elizabeth City County (now Hampton) that had been in his family for three generations. When his older brother, Thomas IV, died without heirs in 1755, George inherited the Back River property. In 1747, George married Anne Lewis and in 1755, Elizabeth Taliaferro. He had one unnamed child who was born and died in 1756.[59] George Wythe died 08 Jun 1806 in Richmond of arsenic poisoning apparently administered by his grandnephew and namesake, George Wythe Sweeney.[60] He lived long enough to disinherit him in favor of Sweeney's siblings Anne, Jane, and Charles.[61] George Wythe is buried at St. John's Church in Richmond,[62] the same church in which Patrick Henry made his "Give me Liberty, or give me Death!" speech.[63]			Ebenezer Wyeth III b. 17 Dec 1752 d. 30 Dec 1836

George's will also asked Jefferson to take charge of the schooling of Michael Brown, a 15-year-old, mixed-race youth, Wythe was educating. Though George never practiced the faith of his mother, he did internalize Quaker tenets. From the bench of Virginia's first Chancery court, Wythe was known to adjudicate for the abolishment of slavery.[64] His ideals were so ingrained in the minds of some of his students that they freed their slaves. Chancellor Wythe emancipated Lydia Broadnax and Benjamin before moving his court from Williamsburg to Richmond. Still they remained in his employ in the new capital city. Wythe was so devoted to Lydia, Benjamin and Michael that he made arrangements in his will for them.[65]

Always the teacher, Wythe was known to have trained some of his servants to read and write. Young Michael Brown was particularly gifted. George taught him Latin, Greek and some science. He no doubt expected to teach his grandnephew, George Wythe Sweeney, when he joined the Richmond household. However, by age 17, his namesake was stealing and selling the chancellor's valuable law books to cover gambling debts. Curiously, the chancellor overlooked Sweeney's behavior and added a codicil to his will dividing his bank stock equally between Sweeney and Michael Brown. This set in motion jealous Sweeney's desperate plan to gain access to all of the money by poisoning Michael, the chancellor, and the housekeeper – Lydia Broadnax.[66]

Only Broadnax survived. However, since Virginia race laws prohibited blacks from testifying against whites, she was unable to validate seeing Sweeney put a powder in their morning coffee. Although 14 witnesses did testify about the arsenic and Sweeney's forging his grand uncle's name on checks, Sweeney went free. The only known punishment he suffered, before disappearing into oblivion, was being cut out of his grand uncle's will. Although racked with spasms, diarrhea and continuously vomiting blood and bile, when George Wythe learned of Michael Brown's death, he remade his will to benefit Sweeney's siblings.[67]

50 years after his horrific death, another scandal surfaced about the venerated chancellor. Dr. John Dove, who claimed to have been present during the sickness and death of George Wythe, declared the judge "had a yellow woman by the name of Lydia who lived with him as wife and mistress… By this woman he had a son named Mike." Then in her 1974 psychobiography of Thomas Jefferson, historian Fawn Brodie wrote, without footnote, about Wythe. "For a white man to leave a house and grounds to his mulatto housekeeper, and bank stock to her yellow son, and to ask none other than the President of the United States to be responsible for the boy's education seemed such an obvious advertisement of the boy's paternity that it left many of the citizens of Richmond aghast." She went on to say, "so appalled were Richmond citizens that they rushed to defend Wythe's murderer, who was in turn hastily acquitted, so that Wythe's paternal gesture could be repudiated."[68]

However, Philip D. Morgan, PhD, a prize winning British historian specializing in colonial British America and slavery in the Americas, calls Dove and Brodie's claims pure myth. His scrutiny and conclusions include the following facts.[69]

First Lydia's age made it unlikely she could have mothered Michael Brown. When Wythe freed Broadnax in 1787, she was then more than 45 years of age. She would have been close to age 50 when Brown was born. Ten years after her emancipation, Lydia owned her own home in Richmond. She continued to cook for her former master but did not live in his house. She did not appear to be Wythe's mistress in Richmond. It was more likely she was the wife of the Benjamin mentioned in the chancellor's 1803 will. Apparently, Benjamin died before the codicil was added splitting funds between Sweeney and Brown.

Morgan could find no clear answer for the parents of Michael Brown. No proof existed for Michael being a former slave. Brown was a common family name for free blacks in Richmond. When Wythe heard Michael predeceased him, he reportedly said, "Poor boy." He made no acknowledgment of the boy being his son on his deathbed or in his will.

Of the 14 people who testified to Wythe's poisoning, not one witness said Lydia Broadnax was George's concubine or that Michael Brown was his son. Nor did any newspaper record such hearsay. More was published about Wythe's death than Washington's death seven years earlier.

If Dr. Dove was indeed at George Wythe's deathbed, Dove would have been but 14 years of age. Additionally, a property disagreement between the heirs of the Wythe estate and the doctor's father could have had a bearing on the rumormongering.

Dr. Philip Morgan concluded his findings with these words, "The preponderance of evidence in Wythe's case points against his having an interracial liaison. His attachment to his housekeeper, his benevolence in freeing slaves, and his educational experiment in testing the intelligence of a mulatto boy, have been misinterpreted."[70]

To Fawn Brodie's claims, Richmond's citizens were neither aghast nor appalled by Wythe's behavior. They clearly revered and exalted the scholarly chancellor. His body lay in state in the hall of the House of Delegates. Contemporary notices said "a great concourse of citizens" witnessed his burial in St. John's Church cemetery. Virginia statesman and author, William Wirt, recalled that Wythe "was universally beloved in the society of Richmond."[71]

NICHOLAS WYETH'S EMIGRATION

Now let us turn our attention to Nicholas. As mentioned previously, Nicholas Wyeth's family moved to Saxtead in the 1550s. At that time, the stronghold for Suffolk County was Framlingham Castle. The castle for the duke of the shire sits a few miles from Saxtead. It had been the refuge of Mary Tudor before she became Queen Mary I in 1553.

In 1572, the castle's duke was executed for treason by Mary Tutor's sister, Elizabeth I, and the castle passed back to the Crown to be used as a prison for individuals who refused to attend Anglican religious services.[72]

Documents held in the Suffolk Records office in Ipswich also confirm Nicholas was baptized on Thursday, 20 Jan 1600 at All Saints Church, Saxtead, England.[73] 1595 is the date shown in Jonas Wyeth's early records of the Wyeth family and was the date Jonas used on the cenotaph monument he had erected in Mt. Auburn Cemetery for Nicholas. However, *The Population History of*

England, 1541-1871, indicate baptisms in the 16th and 17th centuries were held on the first Sunday or Holy Day after birth and rarely later than eight days after birth.[74] Thus, it is most likely Nicholas was born mid-January near the end of 1600 (since January is the 11th month of the Julian calendar). Also verifying that Nicholas was born circa 1600, is his oath taken in court at Cambridge on 04 Apr 1671. He said, "I Nicholas Withe aged about 70 years do testifie ye survey..."[75]

Equally unclear is the maiden name of Nicholas' mother. Some have written it was Elizabeth Hauser who married John Wythe on 26 Apr 1570 at Ellough, Suffolk, England.[76] Others take data from Family History Library (FHL) Film 919626 showing Margerye Pyke married John Wyethe on 18 Oct 1573 in Pettistree, Suffolk, England. However, Nicholas' father married in 1583, so these are incorrect.

Early on, my brother Jeff recorded that Margaret Wyard, born circa 1562, married John Wythe on 27 Jan 1583 in Saxtead, Suffolk County, England. He could not recall where he got Margaret's maiden name, which was alternately spelled Ward or Wiard. Perhaps the name came from the will of Nicholas Wiard of Saxtead dated 09 Feb 1620/21. He names his daughter, Margaret, in the will but does not give her last name as "Wyeth."[77]

Here is a photocopy purchased on 11 Jul 2014 at the Suffolk Record Office of John Wyeth's marriage. The top is a transcription by Muriel L. Kilvert taken from page 41 of the parish register of Saxtead All Saints Church, Church of England.[78] It does not show Margaret's name at all.

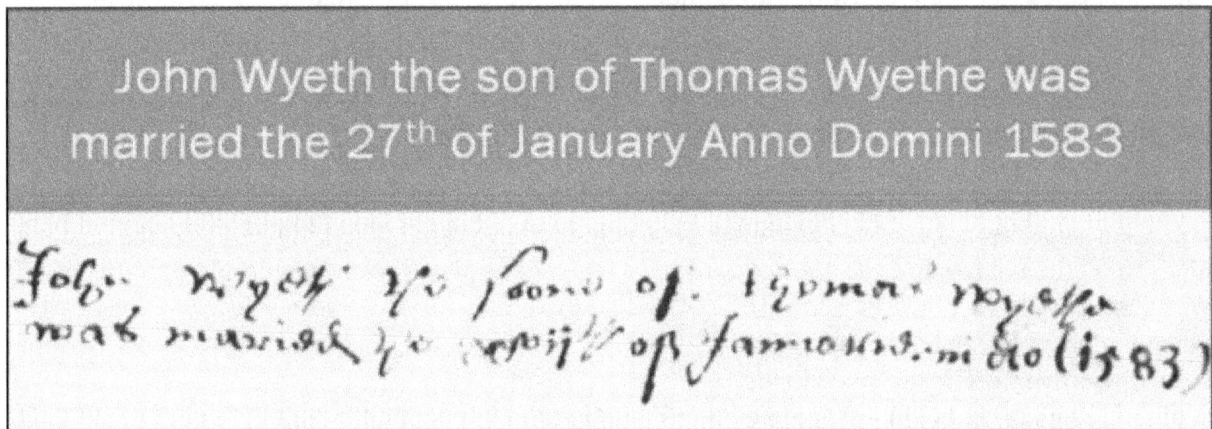

John Wyeth the son of Thomas Wyethe was married the 27th of January Anno Domini 1583

When I visited the Suffolk Record Office in Ipswich, UK, the staff advised there were no other marriage records available to confirm the name of John's wife. We do, however, know her first name from the baptism records of three of her children. The name "Margaret" appears on the registry for Jane, Rose and Nicholas. However, it does not appear on the 1584 Saxtead record of John's oldest child, Lawrence.[79]

It is not unusual that Margaret's name did not appear on Lawrence's baptism record. Mothers' names were frequently omitted. On the other hand, perhaps Margaret was not Lawrence's mother since there is a six years' gap between Lawrence's 1584 baptism and Jane's baptism in 1590. Of course, not all baptisms were recorded at the time.

Although her age works against it, another possibility for Margaret's maiden name is "Cutler." Robert Cutler's will probated in 1611 mentions his mother Dorothy Maddock of Ipswich and three natural sisters, Jilliam Baxter, Margaret Wyeth, and Anne Carey. Executors were brothers-in-law Allen Cary and William Vesey.[80]

FHL microfilm 942.64 I2 V26M includes these baptism dates for children of William Cutler at Saint Mary at the Quay, Ipswich, England, William – 13 Sep 1561, Julian – 04 Mar 1562, John – 21 May 1564, Richard – 24 Jun 1565, Abraham – 02 Jul 1566, Anthony – 07 Dec 1567, and Margaret – 22 Nov 1569.[81] The 1579 will of William Cutler of Ipswich, County Suffolk, merchant mentions his wife, Dorothy, and makes his son John Cutler and brother Robert Cutler executors. The 1589 will of Anthony Cutler of Ipswich, also mentions his mother, Dorothy Maddock; uncle, Renold Barker; and his brother, Richard.[82]

Further binding this family together, is a pedigree in *Suffolk Manorial Families* that gives the parents of William Carey of Woodbridge, County Suffolk as Allen Carey of Halesworth and Anne Cutler sister and devisee of Robert Cutler.[83]

Conclusions to be drawn from these facts are Margaret Cutler who was baptized on 22 Nov 1569 is the daughter of William Cutler and Dorothy Cutler Maddock (Barker is likely Dorothy's maiden name). Obviously, this same Margaret Cutler was the Margaret Wyeth named in Robert Cutler's will. What is not so obvious is could she have married John Wyeth the son of Thomas Wyethe on 27 Jan 1583 at age 13-15? Using a sampling of just nine people in the period of 1600-1649, *The Population History of England* states the average age of females marrying in England was age 26. The book does state canon law tradition ended childhood in the 14th year and marriages at young ages did occur.[84]

Nevertheless, if Margaret Cutler was the mother of Nicholas Wyeth, we would need to consider she was neither the first wife of John nor the mother of Lawrence.

Returning now to the history of Framlingham castle … at Queen Elizabeth's death on 24 Mar 1603, her successor, James I, controlled the castle for ten years. The king restored the castle in 1613 to Thomas Howard, the Earl of Suffolk,[85] when Nicholas Wyeth was in his early teens. It was just out of the duke's control[86] when Nicholas began his voyage from Ipswich[87] down the River Orwell to the port of Harwich to begin sailing the perilous journey of over 3,000 miles on wild and turbulent waters, aboard a tiny ship, to the New World.[88]

As Nicholas gazed for the last time at those golden Suffolk fields of old England, his determination to provide a better life for his family, both spiritually and financially, in New

Port of Harwich, England … photo taken by Tina Baker on 26 Jul 2014

England must have been uppermost in his thoughts. The hazardous, brutal sea crossing was just the first test of his resolve, tenacity, and determination. Emigration experiences are usually stressful and miserable under the best of circumstances, but the challenge of leaving the known for the unknown in the 17th century proved Nicholas had great strength of character.

From a book about Yeoman Nicholas Danforth, who held lands off the same Saxtead road in the same time period as Yeoman Nicholas Wyeth, we learn the occupation of yeoman had a greater meaning in the past. Now the word means a farmer who owns the land he farms. Long ago, the yeoman held a station in the country after that of the gentleman who lived without doing manual labor. Although yeomen worked their land, their rank was immediately before that of the tradesman. Yeomen held real property of a value of at least 40 shillings a year. This qualified them to serve on juries and vote for knights of the shire.[89]

Included in another book about Danforth are the records of Rev. Richard Golty who was rector of Framlingham and Saxtead for much of the 17th century. In 1931 when author John Booth made his study, Golty's volume was in the possession of William Brunger of Framlingham. From the names in the book, Booth prepared a directory of the inhabitants and occupiers in Framlingham and Saxtead between 1628, when the accounts began, and 1650, when Golty was ejected from the church after the execution of King Charles I. When the monarchy was restored in 1660, Golty was restored as well. These records show in Appendix I of *Nicholas Danforth and his Neighbours*.[90] By mistake, notes online at kdreeves.com and geni.com (#6000000003526116779) for Nicholas Wyeth reference page 55 of Robert Hawes's *History of Framlingham, Suffolk County* as the source of these records.

Outedwellers Towardes Saxted. (Page 52)	Outedwellers tht have grounde in Framlingham. (Page 53)	Saxted: Streete. (Page 55)	Bradley Woode. 89 acres. (Page 55)
Robert Button	Anthony Wiard of Solme	Ellin Button	William Button
Nicholas Dampforde	**William Withe** and Stephen Payne of Dinnington	James Button	Henry Legate
William Wiarde		Thomas Kerrich	Edward Olderinge
		Nickholas Withe	John Ruvance
		William With, taylor	**Nicholas Withe**
		Anthony Wyard	
		Humphery Wyard	
		John Wyard	

With the exception of Bradley Woode, not all names are included, from the original, for each category. The names of Button, Wyard and Kerrich are included as they are mentioned in Saxtead's All Saints Church records as marrying into the Wyeth family. In addition, a 1636 will proves William With, the tailor, married Humphery Wyard's daughter, Elizabeth Wyard.[91]

Golty indicated Dampforde (Danforth) lived outside the town, towards Saxtead, and was one of the largest tithe payers in the two parishes. Amazingly, Nicholas Danforth's home still stands on New Street. It is visible from route B1119 which is the lower Saxtead Road going from Framlingham to the Post Mill at Saxtead Green. I did not realize how close New Street Farm is to the 89 acres of land Nicholas Wyeth owned with four other men until I learned the location of Bradley Woode is south of present day Bradley Hall.[92] The information from Booth's book was so helpful to understanding where Nicholas Wyeth's lands were in Saxtead, I was able to prepare a map using Ordnance Survey data.

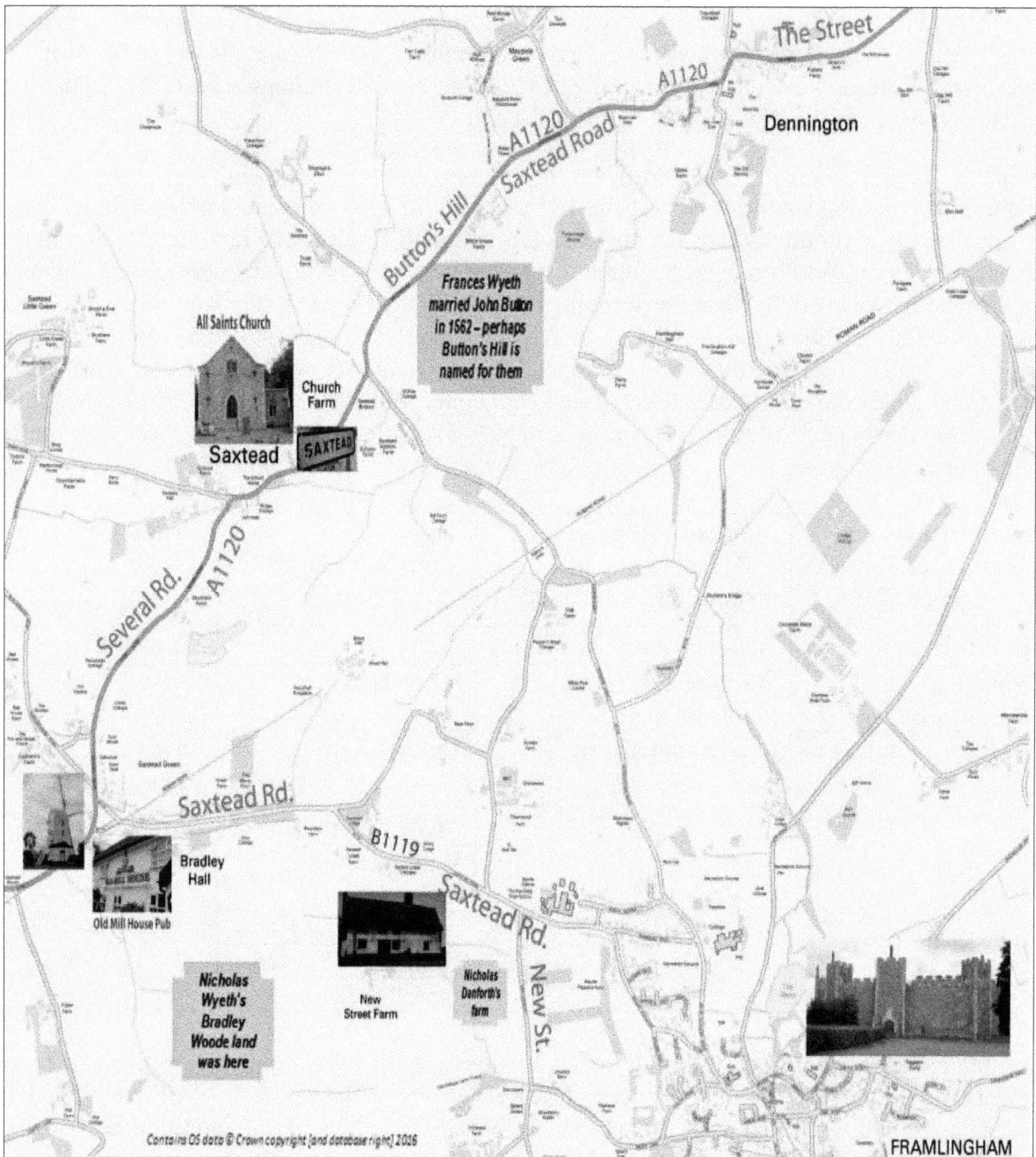

Of particular note is that All Saints Church is on A1120, which is called Several Road in front of the church.[93] The road name then changes to Button's Hill, then Saxtead Road and after it crosses B1116 near Dennington, it becomes "The Street" which, according to the Framlingham Historical Society, is indicative that "The Street" was another name for Saxtead Road. The A1120 title was assigned in the 20th century when B1119 and other nearby roads were merged into it.[94]

The Society also advised that Saxtead Streete may be the generic name for Saxtead Green where the Post Mill is now located. In any case, Nicholas Wyeth's other land must have been west of Bradley Hall.

It was quite a coincidence how we found the location of Nicholas Danforth's home when we were in England in 2014.

St. Michael's Church Framlingham.

On the day we drove to Norwich to see the window with the Wythe family crest in it, we first stopped to visit the Parham Airfield Museum. The World War II airfield was on the grounds of several farms owned by the Kindred family in Parham … the next town southeast of Framlingham. Pete Kindred, who still farms those lands, was our tour guide.

When we told Pete we were in the area mainly to do research on my Saxtead ancestors, Pete asked if my ancestor was Nicholas Danforth? Surprised, I replied,

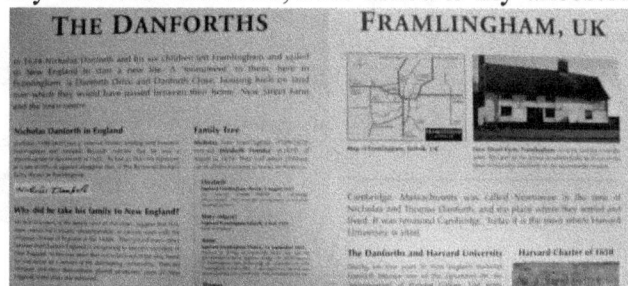

"No, but Nicholas Danforth was my ancestor's friend." Pete then divulged, when he was a child, his grandmother lived in Nicholas Danforth's home on New Street. He did not think the new owners would let us in the home but advised we should stopover to see the display on the Danforth family at Framlingham's St. Michael's Church.

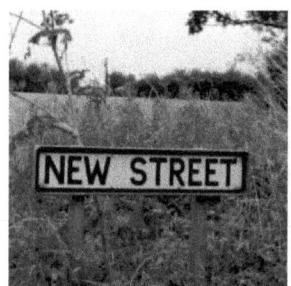

Above are photos of St. Michael's where Nicholas Danforth served as a parish official alongside the pastor, Richard Golty. Danforth's signature on the display comes from Golty's records. The map on the display helped us find New Street on the outskirts of Framlingham going toward Saxtead. We could not get very close to the house during our 2014 visit.

This side-view photo of Nicholas Danforth's New Street Farm was taken on 11 Jul 2014 from Saxtead Road (B1119).

However, on our 02 Apr 2018 re-visit to Parham, Pete Kindred surprised us by extending our tour of the airfield by five miles. He drove us all the way to Framlingham and up the long lane to the back of his grandmother's house. While recalling his childhood days inside New Street Farm, Pete allowed us to take this fabulous photo of the oldest side of Nicholas Danforth's home.

The 2014 photo of Nicholas Danforth's home from B1119 – Saxtead Road was taken as we made our way to the Old Mill House. At the time, we did not realize the Old Mill House is the next property west of Nicholas Wyeth's Bradley Woode land.

We were so late in Norwich doing research, we did not have time to follow Pete Kindred's advice in 2014 for a couple of days. Thus, these pictures are out of order. Our visit to Framlingham started with lunch at the Crown Hotel. The timbers at the staircase are no doubt the same ones under which Nicholas stood almost 400 years ago.

We next went to St. Michael's Church to study the Danforth display. Art struck up a conversation with someone at the church so he sent me alone to tour Framlingham Castle. From the castle, we headed to New Street and then on to the 17th century Old Mill House to make dinner reservations in the pub named for the nearby Saxtead Green Post Mill.

We were extremely fortunate to arrive at Saxtead All Saints while the church was being cleaned or we would not have been admitted. After the gentleman doing the work showed us the bits of medieval glass remaining in the windows, he left us to lock up the church gate on our own. All Saints was joined with Framlingham's St. Michael Church long before Nicholas Wyeth's baptism there. Today the two churches are still affiliated under one rector in the Church of England Diocese of St. Edmundsbury and Ipswich.[95]

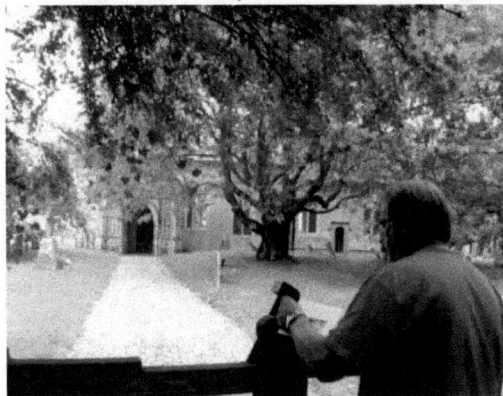

From Golty's records, we know both Nicholas Wyeth and Nicholas Danforth were active in the Anglican Church (Church of England). However, at some point, they became committed Puritans. Danforth, born in 1589, was over ten years older than Wyeth was.

No records exist showing Danforth was persecuted for his Puritan beliefs. Nevertheless, in his mid-40s, just after losing his wife, Danforth left his comfortable home in East Anglia with six motherless children.

22

It is thought Danforth arrived in Boston on 18 Sep 1634 aboard the *Griffin*. From there he settled in Newtowne (Cambridge) where he was a leading citizen until his death in Apr 1638 (which was the second month of the year under the Julian calendar.)[96]

Unlike the Separatists of the radical Puritan wing advocating a total separation from the Church of England, many of whom settled Plymouth in 1620, the Puritans who settled in Boston and Cambridge strove to purify the existing Anglican Church from within. All Puritans opposed the continuation of ostentatious Roman Catholic rituals and holiday celebrations in the Church of England. They wanted to return to the simple faith of the New Testament.[97]

Central to the Puritans' beliefs was reading the Bible to fulfill one's own spiritual needs. Out of necessity, Puritans needed to know how to read, women and girls included, in order to receive salvation. Additionally, they sought to eliminate poverty through reading and by prohibiting vices like drunkenness and gambling. The Puritans' philosophy on education said if people could read, it would enable them to conduct business and earn their own income.[98]

However, the educational and social reforms the Puritans tried to establish in England fizzled when King Charles I made pro-catholic William Laud the Archbishop of Canterbury in 1633. Not only did Laud enforce rules on matters of ritual, but he began persecuting nonconformists by taking their jobs and property and by torturing and imprisoning them as well. This cruelty toward the Puritans caused them to leave England in droves. This Great Migration abated greatly when Laud was arrested in 1640 just prior to the English Civil War.[99]

While William Laud sat in his cell at the Tower of London awaiting his 1645 execution, Nicholas Wyeth was preparing to join the Puritan church in America. To be admitted to Newtowne's First Church, he was required to give a confession to Rev. Thomas Shepard who also had recently arrived from Suffolk County. Having been forced out of the Anglican ministry by William Laud for his Puritan teachings, Shepard had been hiding in Ipswich, Suffolk, England.[100]

The practice of confession was innovated in New England to keep unfit people out of the Puritan church. In Wyeth's testimony, he twice mentions his friend, Nicholas Danforth. Additionally, he gives many clues about his life in old England. Not only are we fortunate to have a first-hand account of the faith of our ancestor, but, moreover, it is one of the few dated confessions.

The handwritten notes dated Jan: 7 1644 are from page 18 of Marion Sims Wyeth's privately published book.[101] As mentioned before, together with J. Gardner Bartlett's article, Marion used the references contained in them to track Nicholas' first wife, Margaret Clarke to Saxtead, Suffolk County, England, through her mother, Rose Kerridge.

In the book *God's Plot,* edited by Michael McGiffert, Nicholas' narrative is translated from Rev. Thomas Shepard's hieroglyphics. Shepard, minister to the first generation of Massachusetts settlers, is considered the founder of the First Church of Cambridge.[102]

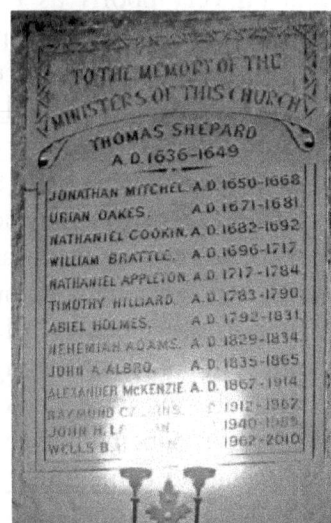

Thomas Shepard's name tops this plaque inside the First Church in Cambridge, Congregational, U.C.C.

"It pleased the Lord acting first out of his free mercy he let me see the evil of not keeping the Sabbath. About sixteen years of age, being a **prentice**, wherein I went to that company that drew to idleness and Lord helped me out of 16 of Ezekiel — when I was in my blood and when no eye pitied. (Ezek. 16:5-6) I saw he was the refuge for pity, for I had profaned the Sabbath much. But I saw through Lord's help I was not in my way, and I was much troubled that I had so spent the Sabbath. And hence I went out to hear the word, and having none at home, I desired to hear them that were most suitable to my condition to stir up my heart. And going to hear one **Mr. Salby** (Robert Selby), I did much affect his ministry, and I did somewhat profit by it, and so I had much love to the word, for I saw that I was lost and that it was the means of help. And preaching out of Canticles showing – my beloved is mine and I his – and he showed they that loved Christ, he loved them as his own. And the Lord kept me and encouraged me hereby much still to go and hear other good men. And every Sabbath day I went four miles to hear him about a year, but I went on very poorly as I have done ever since. And I took every opportunity I could

"Reverend Thomas Shepards Manuscript"
(Courtesy of the New England Historical & Geneological Society)

and could get liberty of my master to go out to hear but yet, though I went on poorly, yet had much love to the word and loved society of them and God's people. And so I lived twelve years, and Lord brought Mr. **Burrows** (Jeremiah Burroughs) some sixteen miles off, and I was then able-bodied then and went often to hear him; and by **Brother (Nicholas) Danforth** went out and having means in the town. But I heard **Mr. Burrows** out of Galatians. He said, as a man sows, so shall he reap; he showed a natural man did (not) sow anything that was good, everything was evil. And I saw I was in my natural condition, yet I went out to hear and went twenty miles off to **Mr. Rogers** (? John Rogers), out of Colossians – if risen, seek things which are above – but though I did hear much, yet I could not see my heart was brought so near as I did desire, for I had been very careless in remembering what I heard and for sixteen years went on so in old England. Hence I came to New England, being persecuted and courted for going from the place where we lived, and hence I used means to come hither where we might enjoy more freedom. And I had much joy in going about this work; though I had lived very foul, yet my heart much convinced me that I should live under means most powerful. And so I was much opposed by my friends, and enemies of God discouraging of me, and the Lord helped me to withstand them that did oppose me, for I could not be content to live where I did, and I went through many difficulties before and when I came to sea yet I went on. **And God took away my son,** some telling me the Lord was displeased for going on, but discouragements of natural friends I regarded not, and I did not care <u>though the Lord took away all I had.</u> <u>Yet I had many things to call me back, my wife all the time going through many afflictions.</u> And then I thought of what others said – the Lord would meet with me – **but I did not look as coming to New England was the cause but did believe if the Lord should bring my child and self hither,** the Lord would recompense me by means. **When we came here, the Lord raised up my wife,** and <u>I did much rejoice to see the place and see the people and hear God's</u> <u>servants.</u> Only <u>troubled me to see death of</u> **Mr. Danforth,** yet I thought God's people were a loving people. So the <u>Lord stirred up some friends here</u> and having friends at <u>Long Island, yet I</u> <u>would not go thither.</u> And yet God's hand hath been much against me since I came hither, <u>and I</u> <u>know not but it hath been for my carelessness in not watching over my child in regard</u> of the sin of the family, which God sit on. <u>Though I have been much drawn away unto new plantations,</u> <u>though I could never see a clear way to go away, for I saw so much of love of God's people here</u> <u>that I thought I should bring much evil on me if I did remove.</u> But for that sin which brake out, <u>it</u> <u>had been good for me if had never come hither to this place.</u> The Lord's hand hath been much out against me and is so still. <u>He gave me a child after my own heart, and God hath taken it from me,</u> and 'tis so just for I have gone <u>on so formally and coldly since I came here.</u> Though I have enjoyed much in public, yet I have been very unfruitful and unchristianlike."

Nicholas was admitted to the church. He was, however, rigorously cross-examined by Thomas Shepard, elder Edmund Frost and several members of the congregation. He was asked more than 20 questions. The last one, in particular, shows Wyeth's nervousness and humility. Question: "Why do you forget things, brother?" Nicholas replied, "I see cause enough in my own heart why Lord should deny me. I know many things in my practice. I have not so meditated on the word."[103]

From Marion Sims Wyeth's pedigree, we know in the testimony that Nicholas is referring to his first wife, Margaret Clarke (baptized 12 Oct 1608 in Westhorpe, Suffolk County, England)[104] and his daughter Sarah Wyeth (baptized 28 Oct 1632;[105] she married John Fiske).

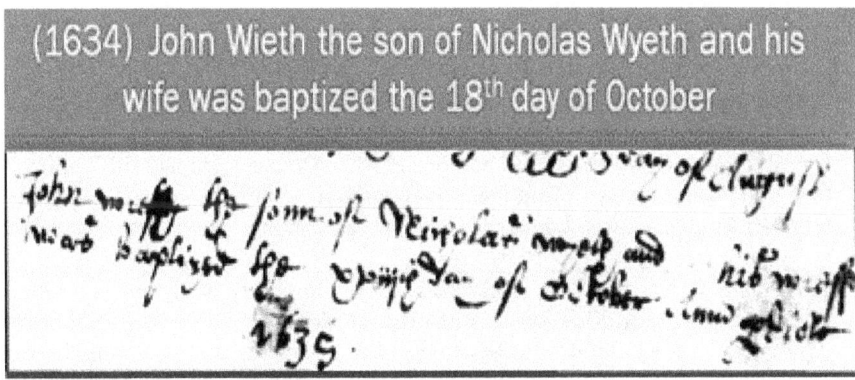

(1634) John Wieth the son of Nicholas Wyeth and his wife was baptized the 18th day of October

The son he mentions is most likely John Wieth, who was baptized 18 Oct 1634 and buried on 23 Apr 1638 in Saxtead.[106]

Here is a photocopy purchased on 11 Jul 2014 at the Suffolk Record Office of John Wyeth's baptism. The top is a transcription by Muriel L. Kilvert taken from page 25 of the parish register of Saxtead All Saints Church, Church of England.

Describing the migration to America as a transition from ignorance to enlightenment, Malcolm Gaskill wrote in *Between two Worlds: How the English Became Americans*, that Nicholas came in 1638.[107] Gaskill interpreted Nicholas' confession on 07 Jan 1644 to join Thomas Shepard's First Church, that he came with his wife and two children, one of whom died at sea. However, in looking closer at each statement Nicholas made, the two mentions about his child's death may not be chronological… thus it is not entirely clear one child died at sea as Gaskill suggested.

Actual Statements in *God's Plot* from Nicholas Wyeth's Confession to Thomas Shepard	Possible Meaning with Additional Information from the Footnotes in *God's Plot* and details from Marion Sims Wyeth's research
About sixteen years of age, being a **prentice**, wherein I went to that company that drew to idleness.	In 1616, as an **apprentice** of *about* 16 years old, he was lazy about hearing God's word.
And hence I went out to hear the word, and having none at home ...going to hear one **Mr. Salby**... every Sabbath day I went four miles to hear him about a year	Then for *about* a year, until he was almost 17, he went four miles every Sabbath day to hear **Robert Selby** rector at Bedfield, Suffolk.
And I took every opportunity I could and could get liberty of my master to go out to hear but yet, though I went on poorly, yet had much love to the word and loved society of them and God's people.	He took every opportunity his (masonry) teacher would allow to go out to hear Puritan lectures and associate with others who believed as he did.
And so I lived twelve years, and Lord brought **Mr. Burrows** some sixteen miles off, and I was then able-bodied then and went often to hear him.	After 12 years (in 1629) when Wyeth was about age 29, he went with **Nicholas Danforth,** a man of means in town, to hear **Jeremiah Burroughs** 16 miles away in Bury St. Edmunds, Suffolk. In the second volume of *Magnalia Christi Americana*, Cotton Mather wrote about Nicholas Danforth, he "procured that famous lecture at Framlingham in Suffolk, where he had a fine manor; which lecture was kept by Mr. Burroughs..." [108] Perhaps Danforth hired Burroughs to speak at the New Street Farm.
And by **Brother [Nicholas] Danforth** went out and having means in the town. But I heard **Mr. Burrows** out of Galatians. He said, as a man sows, so shall he reap; he showed a natural man did not sow anything that was good, everything was evil.	
And I saw I was in my natural condition, yet I went out to hear and went twenty miles off to **Mr. Rogers**	Wyeth realized he was not sowing anything good and went, most likely, to hear **John Rogers** of Dedham, Essex County, who died in 1636.
I had been very careless in remembering what I heard and for sixteen years went on so in old England.	He forgot what he learned in past lectures and went on in old England 16 years to circa 1644 as a member of the Church of England in Saxtead. Records for his children appear there from 1632 to 1638.
Hence I came to New England, being persecuted and courted for going from the place where we lived, and hence I used means to come hither where we might enjoy more freedom.	He was persecuted for going **from** the place he lived, not for his beliefs. He had money enough of his own to go to New England to enjoy more freedom.
I went through many difficulties before and when I came to sea yet I went on. **And God took away my son**, some telling me the *Lord was displeased for going* on,	He had difficulties before he went to sea which must have been the death of his son as it is unlikely people on the ship would have criticized him for leaving old England with his family.
I had many things to call me back, my wife all the time going through many afflictions... **but I did not look as coming to New England was the cause but did believe if the Lord should bring my child and self hither,** the Lord would recompense me by means.	Many things happened to call him back to old England. His wife was ill. However, he did not believe coming to New England was the cause of his trouble and the Lord would help him and his child (Sarah) through.
When we came here, the Lord raised up my wife, and I did much rejoice to see the place and see the people and hear God's servants. Only troubled me to see death of **Mr. Danforth**	When he came to New England, his wife died. He was pleased to see New England and meet the people but was troubled to hear of the death of his friend Nicholas Danforth.
So the Lord stirred up some friends here and having friends at Long Island, yet I would not go thither.	He is backtracking a bit. It sounds like he had thought of first going to Long Island.
And yet God's hand hath been much against me since I came hither, and I know not but it hath been for my carelessness in not watching over my child in regard of the sin of the family, which God sit on.	Perhaps he is referring to not watching over Sarah in regard to taking her to church.

Though I have been much drawn away unto new plantations, though I could never see a clear way to go away, for I saw so much of love of God's people here that I thought I should bring much evil on me if I did remove.	He was drawn to go to other plantations – Long Island? But could not see his way clear to go. He was so much loved there in Cambridge; he thought he would bring even more evil on himself if he left Cambridge for other plantations.
The Lord's hand hath been much out against me and is so still. He gave me a child after my own heart, and God hath taken it from me, and 'tis so just for I have gone on so formally and coldly since I came here. Though I have enjoyed much in public, yet I have been very unfruitful and unchristianlike."	Repeats he would have been better off if he had never left England. God gave him a child and then took the child from him… we don't know if he is referring to John who died in England or another child that had been taken from him since he left England. In any event, he went on formally and coldly since he came, unfruitful and unchristian-like … perhaps meaning he had not been going to church.

Gaskill apparently calculated Wyeth's arrival as 1638 since Danforth died early in 1638.[109] However, because Wyeth clearly was religious, it does not seem feasible he would have waited from 1638 to 1644 – six years to join the church. In addition, he was in old England until approximately age 44 if we add the ages given in the testimony.

Statement	Years	Age	Year
*About** sixteen years of age, being a <u>prentice</u>, wherein I went to that company that drew to idleness	16	16	1616
And every Sabbath day I went four miles to hear him (Mr. <u>Salby</u>) *about* a year (*zero since he used word "about")	*0	16	1616
And so I lived **twelve years**, and Lord brought Mr. Burrows some sixteen miles off	12	28	1628
careless in remembering what I heard and **for sixteen years** went on so in old England	16	44	1644

On the other hand, since he'd went on for 16 years not going to lectures, maybe he was not that interested in joining the church quickly after his arrival in New England.

Another factor to consider about the 1638 arrival date is it was during the decade of 1630 to 1640, known as the Great Migration, when an estimated 200 ships carried over 20,000 English people, most from the East Anglian counties of Norfolk, Suffolk and Essex, to Massachusetts. Given that kind of traffic between England and New England, it is unlikely it would have taken six years for news of the death of Danforth to reach Wyeth in East Anglia.[110]

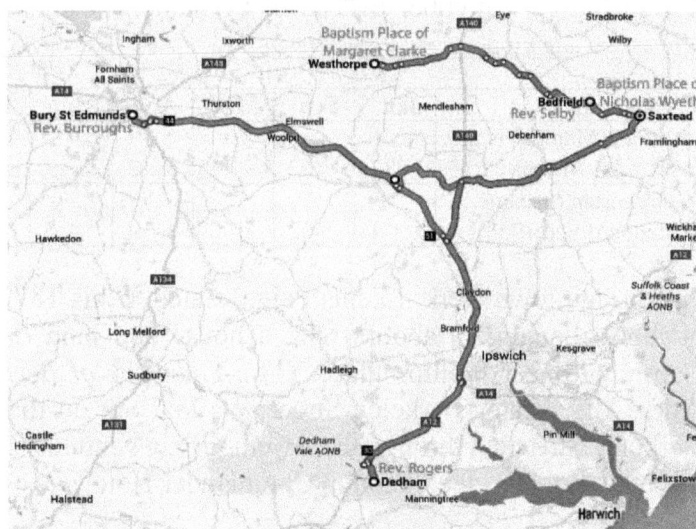

Some suggest Nicholas Wyeth may have first settled in Watertown. That is unlikely since he does not appear on Watertown's land inventory records of 1634, 1635 or 1639.[111]

Google map showing related baptism and confession locations in and around Suffolk County, England.

If Nicholas Wyeth did, however emigrate in 1638, soon after his son died in Saxtead, he arrived in Newtowne (the New Town) just as its name was changed to Cambridge on 02 May 1638.[112]

The town was originally chosen to be the capital of the Massachusetts Bay Colony. Just prior to the Cambridge name change, Harvard, the oldest institution of higher education in the United States, was ordered in 1637 to be at Newtowne.[113]

Some have confused the name Newtowne with Newton. Although Newton was originally part of Cambridge, it was merely known as the large territory on the south side of the Charles River until about 1654 when it was named "Cambridge Village." Then in 1691, by the authority of the General Court, Cambridge Village was renamed "Newtown." The second "w" was dropped and the name became "Newton" in 1766.[114]

According to page 119 of the *Cambridge Proprietors' Records*, on the 20th of 5th month 1645 (a Julian calendar date meaning 20 Jul 1645) Nicholas Wyeth purchased Robert Daniell's home and property.[115] Although this was seven months (per Julian calendar) after his testimony to join the congregation at Thomas Shepard's First Church, it does show he must have been well off financially in old England. He would not otherwise have been able to pay for the passage of himself and his family and be able to buy a home and lands so soon upon his arrival.

> [119] NICHOLAS WYTHE bought of Robert Daniell in the West-end one dwellinge-houfe wth out-houfes & about halfe an Acr of Land Gilbert Crackbone northweft, John Bridge foutheaft Thomas Parifh fouthweft, Comon Northeaft.
>
> Itm Bought of George Willowes Two Acr of Land more or leffe in weft-field Edward Hall Northeaft, the highwaye foutheaft, the fwampe northweft, Comon fouthweft.

Here is a chart for general use to help convert dates from the Julian calendar when the month is designated by a number instead of by name. A great source for more specific conversions is http://www.adamsonancestry.com/calendar.

Calendar	Jan	Feb	Mar	Apr	May	Jun	Jul	Aug	Sep	Oct	Nov	Dec
Julian (Mar 25th is the first day of the year)	11	12	1	2	3	4	5	6	7	8	9	10
Gregorian (became standard Sep 1752)	1	2	3	4	5	6	7	8	9	10	11	12

Cambridge town clerk, Lucius Paige, stated in his 1877 book on the history of Cambridge that Nicholas bought, in about 1645, a house and land on the westerly side of Garden Street in Cambridge near Phillips Place.[116] In *A History of Berkeley Street, Cambridge, Massachusetts*, Alice Allyn states Berkeley Street was laid out on the old Wyeth farm in the 1850s.[117] When Berkeley Street cut through the Wyeth farm, eventually it, instead of Phillips Place, met at Garden Street. Currently, the Sheraton Commander Hotel sits on some of the land of the Wyeth farm.[118]

In addition to farming, which at the time was an absolute necessity, Nicholas also kept busy in other endeavors. Given the emphasis the Puritans had on the importance of education, it appears the first grammar school in Cambridge was quickly established by Elijah Corlett in a house owned in 1642 by Henry Dunster, the President of Harvard. Five years later, on the same land, President Dunster commissioned the first building erected specifically for use as a grammar school in Cambridge. One of the three masons he hired to build the school was Nicholas Wyeth.[119]

The contract introduction from the *Colonial Society of Massachusetts* reads: "Articles of agreement between Henry Dunster and Edward Goffe on the one party and Nicholas Withe and Richard Wilson, Daniel Hudson, masons, on the other party, witness as followeth:

> Impr. That we Nicolas Wite (sic), Richard Wilson and Daniel Hudson, masons, have undertaken to get at Charlestowne Rock one hundred and fifty load of rock stone, and to lay them in convenient place whence they may be fetched with carts, and that between this present third month 1647 [May 1647] and the tenth of the ninth month [10 Nov] next ensuing, for the which stones Henry Dunster and Edward Goffe covenant to pay to us six pence to the load."

Here is a summary of payments for creating the building:[120]

> 12 pence per yard for laying the stones in a wall to form the cellar. For the middle story, 18 pence per yard including building arched doorways and window spaces. For a chimney, 18 pence a yard where they walled with stone and 10 shillings a thousand for the square bricks to build the chimney until it reached the roof and then 16 shillings a thousand for the bricks that appeared out of the roof. Dunster and Goffe were to lay out the bricks, but they were to be cut by the masons. For two gable ends their prize was 18 pence a yard. For tiling the roof, the charge was six shillings per thousand of tile. The masons agreed to perfect the said work by 1st of the 6th month 1648 [01 Aug 1648] provided Dunster and Goffe procured all necessary materials. The payment to the masons could be in goods or merchandise, whether corn or cattle at the going rate.

Unfortunately, this sturdy stone and brick schoolhouse was demolished in 1769.[121] The approximate location of the school shows at #2 on this 1894 map of Cambridge from the Library of Congress.[122] Claverly Hall on Linden at Mt. Auburn, positioned the next street over from the 1648 grammar school on Holyoke, is still standing. #3 is the location of Wyeth Street, which is

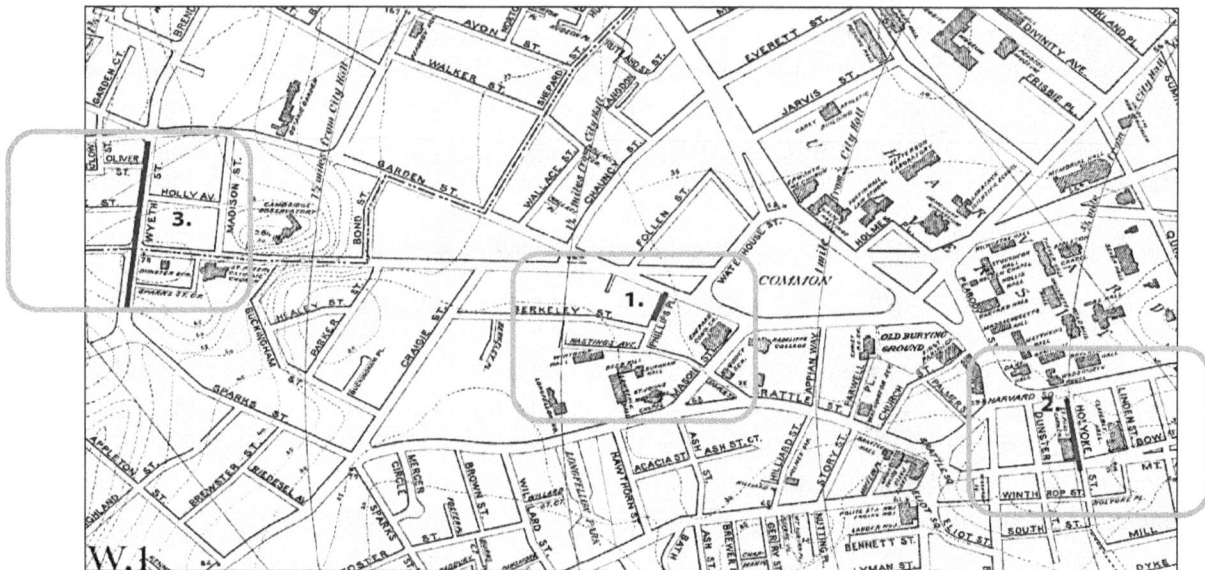

now part of Huron Avenue. In his autobiography, John Allan Wyeth said Wyeth Street was named for Nicholas Wyeth.[123] In 1889, there was a Wyeth Square in Cambridge. It is now Taylor Square. Both Wyeth Street and Wyeth Square bordered Noah Wyeth's property at 107 Garden Street. The

1903 Wyeth Terrace is now part of Fresh Pond Parkway.[124] Given the long history of the Wyeth family in Cambridge and the family's steadfast devotion to the founding of the United States, it is unfortunate the Wyeth name was stripped from Cambridge when Brattle Street and Vassal Lane carry the name of prominent Cambridge Tories who were loyal to British King George III during the War for American Independence.[125] [126] The Wyeth name does, however, carry on at the newly opened apartment and condominium building "The Wyeth Cambridge" at 120 Rindge Avenue.[127]

Garden Street has had several name changes as well. It was originally known as the Way to the Great Swamp and the highway to the Fresh Pond and then as the road to the Brickyards. Parts of it were called Washington Street and Milk-Porridge Lane after the Revolution. Its present name, given in 1848, is for the Harvard Botanic Garden at the corner of Linnaean Street.[128] [129]

So, by 1647, Nicholas and his daughter, Sarah, had been by themselves for at least three years on the highway near the common. As Sarah was baptized on 28 Oct 1632 in Saxtead, she was about 13 when her mother, Margaret Clarke, died. Certainly, Puritan children were expected to help at home, but Sarah's responsibilities as the woman of the house, undoubtedly, left her with little time to enjoy adolescence. Among other things, she would have fetched water, made bread, cooked the meals, poured candles and soap, cut wood, helped her father with gardening, washed clothes in a nearby creek, emptied the chamber pot, churned butter, wove cloth, and looked after livestock.

Apparently, Nicholas and Sarah Wyeth's work was too much for the two of them. They were spread so thin that Nicholas was fined in 1646 for an infraction involving his two oxen and for having an unattended hog on the common four times.[130] Other items in the *Proprietors' Records* ranged from being given liberty to fell timber on the common to build a barn before May Day 1647,[131] to selling land upon the rocks near Alewife Meadow to Thomas Danforth on the 9th of the 8th month 1648 (09 Oct 1648).[132]

Thomas Danforth was the son of Nicholas Wyeth's friend in old England, Nicholas Danforth. Because he was appointed Middlesex County recorder in 1652 and held the position until 1686, Thomas' name appeared often through the years on the records of the Wyeth family. Many years later when Thomas Danforth was appointed to the highest court in Massachusetts, and opposed the way Chief Justice William Stoughton conducted the 1692 Salem Witch Trials,[133] he held an unparalleled role in the lives of Nicholas Wyeth's second wife, Rebecca, and her children Thomas, Daniel and Rebecca Andrews.

REBECCA THE RESILIENT WIFE AND THE WITCHCRAFT TRIALS

It has been said the permanence of a family depends largely upon the love, strength, intelligence and character of its women. Few women fit this description better than Rebecca Parks Andrews Wyeth Fox. Although we know little about our matriarch's background, we do know from the paper trail she left behind that the endurance of the Wyeth family is directly traceable to Rebecca's resilience and determination.

Rebecca was obviously of strong stock. She gave birth to three children with her first husband, Thomas Andrews, and seven or eight children with Nicholas Wyeth. She married for a third time, to Thomas Fox, and outlived him by five years.

30

Rebecca's maiden name and her birth year of 1620 come from *U.S. and International Marriage Records, 1560-1900*, referencing Rebecca Parks' marriage to Thomas Andrews and the 1648 marriage of Rebecca Parks Andrews to Nicholas Wyeth.[134]

Some mistakenly believe Rebecca's maiden name was Craddock because of a petition a Thomas Andrews joined in with a Mrs. Rebecca Craddock. In her book, *Horns A'Plenty,* Agnes McClellan Grousset, refers to this petition and states Thomas Andrews, a leather seller of London wed Damaris Craddock the daughter of Matthew Craddock and Damaris Winne. Grousset further said Thomas went to Massachusetts where Damaris "must have changed her name to Rebecca." Additionally, she wrote that Thomas Andrews' Medford, Massachusetts, estate was sold in Mar 1644 by his heirs to Ed. Collins.[135]

Unfortunately, this particular Rebecca / Damaris did not marry Nicholas Wyeth. Per volume LXIV of *The New England Historical and Genealogical Register,* after the leather seller's death, in about 1654, his widow Damaris Craddock Andrews married Rev. Ralph Cudworth, the Master of Cambridge's Christ College, in Great Britain. The *Register* goes on to clear up the Rebecca Craddock and Thomas Andrews' petition as well. After Damaris Winne Craddock died, Matthew Craddock married Rebecca Jordan. The Mrs. Rebecca Craddock in the petition with Thomas Andrews apparently is Mrs. Rebecca Jordan Craddock. Interestingly, Rebecca Jordan Craddock is not the Rebecca who married Nicholas Wyeth either. In 1641, after Matthew's death in London, England, his widow, Rebecca Jordan Craddock, then married Richard Glover.[136]

Although Matthew Craddock never visited New England, as the governor of the Massachusetts Bay Company, he procured so much land in Medford, Massachusetts, he is considered the town's founder. *The History of the Town of Medford* states the only member of the Craddock family to visit New England was George Craddock. This means neither Damaris Craddock nor her husband, Thomas Andrews, or her stepmother Rebecca Jordan Craddock Glover, ever set foot in New England. Matthew Craddock did have a number of servants in the New World, however. Because of Matthew Craddock's vast land holdings in Middlesex County, his will was recorded by Thomas Danforth in 1642. The will sheds light on Grousset's statement regarding the sale of Medford land to Ed. Collins. Those lands were not held by Thomas Andrews' heirs but by Matthew Craddock's heirs – Rebecca Jordan Craddock Glover and Damaris Craddock Andrews Cudworth.[137]

On page 18 of *Pioneers of Massachusetts*, Charles Pope also mistakenly affiliates Mrs. Rebecca Craddock of old England with Rebecca Andrews of New England who married Nicholas Wyeth. However, Pope does give us other facts about the Thomas and Rebecca Andrews' family of Watertown and Cambridge, Massachusetts. Pope indicates Thomas Andrews of Watertown appeared before the court 27 Sep 1631 and moved to Cambridge about 1645.[138]

The 1631 date coincides with information from Charles Edward Banks in *The Planters of the Commonwealth* and with Laurence Clyde Andrew in *Thomas Andrew, Immigrant.* Banks stated Thomas was in one of the vessels of the Winthrop Fleet. Andrew pinpointed the specific craft of Thomas' journey ... *The Arbella.* She was the Winthrop flagship that left Yarmouth, Isle of Wight on 08 Apr 1630 with three escort vessels. They landed in Salem, Essex, Massachusetts. Both books state that Thomas Andrew(s) soon settled in Watertown.[139] [140]

Some researchers discount the 1631 court date. They assume Thomas and Rebecca were the same age and came from England a few months prior to the 15 Oct 1641 birth of their first child. Of course, husbands are not always close in age to wives. Case in point, Nicholas Wyeth was at least 20 years older than Rebecca. It appears that Thomas Andrews was many years older than Rebecca, as well. Even though Thomas came as a servant to Josiah Plaistow of the Gentleman Class, Thomas soon took his place in society as a man of means. On 27 Jun 1630, he lent money to the town of Salem and on 29 Sep 1630, he was one of 19 men to decide a new settlement location. The location apparently was Watertown since he is considered one of the town's founders.[141]

The *Lands, Grants and Possessions* section of Watertown Records state: "The courts of 1st day of 2nd month of 1634, of 4th day of 1st month 1634/5, and of 9th day of 7th month 1639 ordered records of every man's house and land should be taken, entered in the town book, and a transcript thereof handed into court, and that such record should be sufficient assurance of title."[142]

Thomas Andrews' name shows on page 63 of the original inventory prepared for the courts of 01 Apr 1634.[143] His name, alternately spelled Andrew, Andrews and Andrewes, is sprinkled throughout the records of 1634, 1635 and 1639.

---

[90] (63)

Thomas Andrewes.

1. Foure Acres & halfe of Planting ground being an Home-ftall bounded the Eaft with Thomas Brigan & the South the Weft with John Trane & the North with Cambridge line.
2. Forty Acres of vpland being a great Divident in the 4 Divifion & the 13 Lott.
3. Six Acres of Plowland in the further Plaine & the 82 Lott.
4. Eight Acres of Meddow in the remote Meddowes & the 30 Lott.

Indeed, given on page eight of the *Births, Marriages and Deaths* section of the Watertown records book is the 15 Oct 1641 birth date of Thomas Andrews, "son of Thomas and Rebeckah." The editors indicate the record appeared in 1641 on page 10 of the original book.[144]

Second child, Daniel Andrews, was born in Watertown, but the first record we have of his birth shows on the indenture document of 1659 for his masonry training under his stepfather, Nicholas Wyeth. In the document (which appears later in this book), his mother, Rebecca, verifies his age is 16. Thus, he was born in 1644.

Third child, Rebecca Andrews, was born after the family moved to Cambridge. Here is her birth record dated 18th of the 2nd month, 1646 in the Julian calendar, which is 18 Apr 1646 in our present Gregorian calendar.

Interestingly, neither the index of Watertown Records nor the index of Cambridge carries persons with the name of Cradock or Craddock. There are, however, Parks, Park and Parke names on page 76 of the Watertown index[145] and on page 405 of the index to the *Proprietors' Records of Cambridge*.[146] Unfortunately, we do not know how Rebecca Parks relates to any of them.

We do not know specifically when Nicholas and Rebecca married either. Most researchers say 1648. However, it was probably just prior to when he started building the grammar school in May 1647. Page 254 of the *Founders and Patriots of America Index* provides Jan 1647 as the date Rebecca Parks Andrews married Nicholas Wyeth.[147] Since the marriage date is between Rebecca Andrews' birth in 1646 and Mary Wyth's birth on 18 Jan 1648, it should be an accurate date.

Although some have written Rebecca and Nicholas' first child was born 18 Nov 1648, they were calculating the 11th month with the Gregorian calendar. As shown below, their first child, Mary, was born the 18th of the 11th month 1648. In the Julian calendar, the 11th month is January.

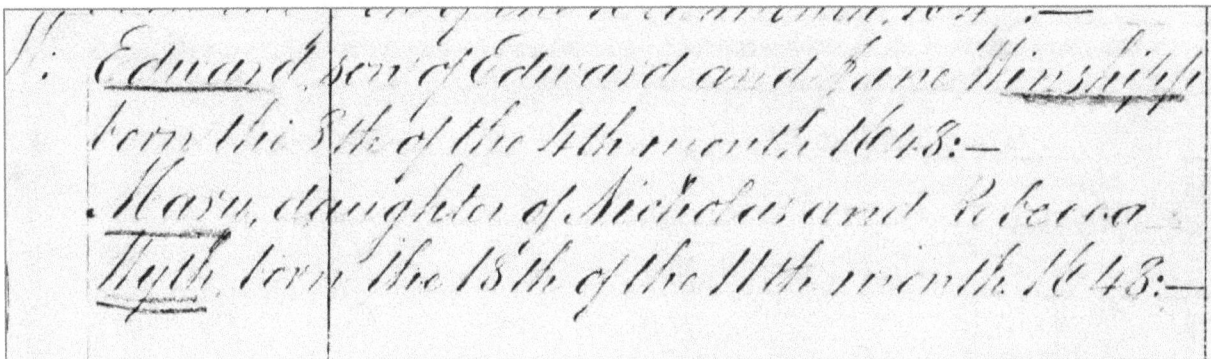

Nicholas was 47 and Rebecca was about 27 years old when they married. 16-year-old Sarah's almost 10 years as an only child ended. Her new step-siblings, Thomas, age five; Daniel, age four; and baby Rebecca at nine months, put new life into the household. To the Andrews' children, Nicholas was the only father they had ever known.

Then in rapid succession, Nicholas and Rebecca brought more babies into the home. The children's birth records from the *Massachusetts, Town and Vital Records* carry the surname spelling of "Withe" except the first-born child, Mary. For Mary, "Wyth" was reflected in the records.[148] There are many reasons why we are fortunate Nicholas settled in Massachusetts. Uppermost are the records. Massachusetts possesses some of the oldest and most extensive records in the United States. The vital records in this collection are remarkably accurate as well. The birth dates for two of the children are too close, but it is unclear whether they have been converted from the Old Style to the New Style calendars. The records of Jonas Wyeth 2[d], shown earlier in this book, are comparable to the dates in the following chart, but he did not include the first Martha.

With Nicholas' testimony to join First Church in mind, likely he thought the Lord was still against him when baby Mary died so soon after birth. Then again to lose a son, his first namesake, Nicholas must have been devastated.

Though steadfast and loving, Rebecca likely faced each birth with fear and trepidation. Birth in those early times was closely shadowed by death. Nevertheless, Rebecca endured. When she blessed Nicholas with two daughters and three sons, her sorrow and grief was surely overwhelmed by happiness and joy.

Nicholas and Rebecca Wyeth's Children from *Mass., Town and Vital Records, 1620-1988*	
1.	Mary Wyth born **18 Jan 1648** and died as an infant.
2.	Mary Withe born **26 Jan 1649** one year after #1.
3.	Nicholas Withe born **20 Sep 1650** in the Julian calendar, eight months after #2 (he died before birth of #4).
4.	Nicholas Withe born **10 Aug 1651** almost one year after #3.
5.	Martha Withe – the record states **11 Jan 1652**, which would be 18 months after #4 in the Julian calendar. (She died before birth of #6.) (In the handwritten notes of Jonas Wyeth 2[d], shown at the beginning of this book, this record is not included.)
6.	Martha Withe born **10 Jul 1653** – only seven months after #5 in the Julian calendar. (Seven months is very little time between children. Maybe #5 and #6 are the same person).
7.	John Withe born **15 Jul 1655** almost two years after #6.
8.	William Withe born **01 Jan 1657** almost two and a half years after #7 in the Julian calendar.

Nicholas and Rebecca's family was complete. Included in the 1658 records of the First Church at Cambridge in New England, was the following written portrait of the family.[149]

So, we see Sarah was married and living in Watertown in 1658. Eventually, Nicholas Jr. also gravitated to Watertown, Middlesex County, Massachusetts. Sarah's husband, John Fiske, was a first cousin 1x removed to the junior Nicholas' first wife, Lydia Fiske. Thomas Andrews Jr., Mary, John and William remained in Cambridge, Middlesex County.

However, Rebecca's other three children moved 20 miles north to Essex County. They settled in Salem and Salem Village (now Danvers) well before the infamous witch trials were conducted there in 1692 and 1693.

In 1672, Martha married Thomas Ives in Salem, Massachusetts. In the same year, Rebecca Andrews' first husband, John Frost, died. She then moved to Salem where she married George Jacobs Jr. The year was pivotal for Daniel Andrews, as well. Although he moved to Salem in 1669,[150] 1672 was the first time his name appeared in Salem's records. He was listed as both a schoolteacher and a mason.[151]

As evidenced by this indenture document dated 13 Oct 1659, Daniel received his bricklayer training from his stepfather.[152] Notice – Nicholas' surname is spelled both "Withe" and "Wythe" on the very same paper. Thomas Andrews Jr., who earlier was taught the masonry trade by Nicholas, is a witness, as is the county recorder, Thomas Danforth. Daniel's mom, Rebecca, verified his age to be 16 in the middle of Mar 1660. In addition, we see Nicholas did not know how to write his name… an all-around very telling and interesting document.

Another noteworthy item is that Daniel Andrews signed his name with an "s" on the end. Records for Salem – and there are a lot of them when he was suspected of witchcraft there in 1692 – drop the "s." Going forward, the name will generally be spelled according to the source.

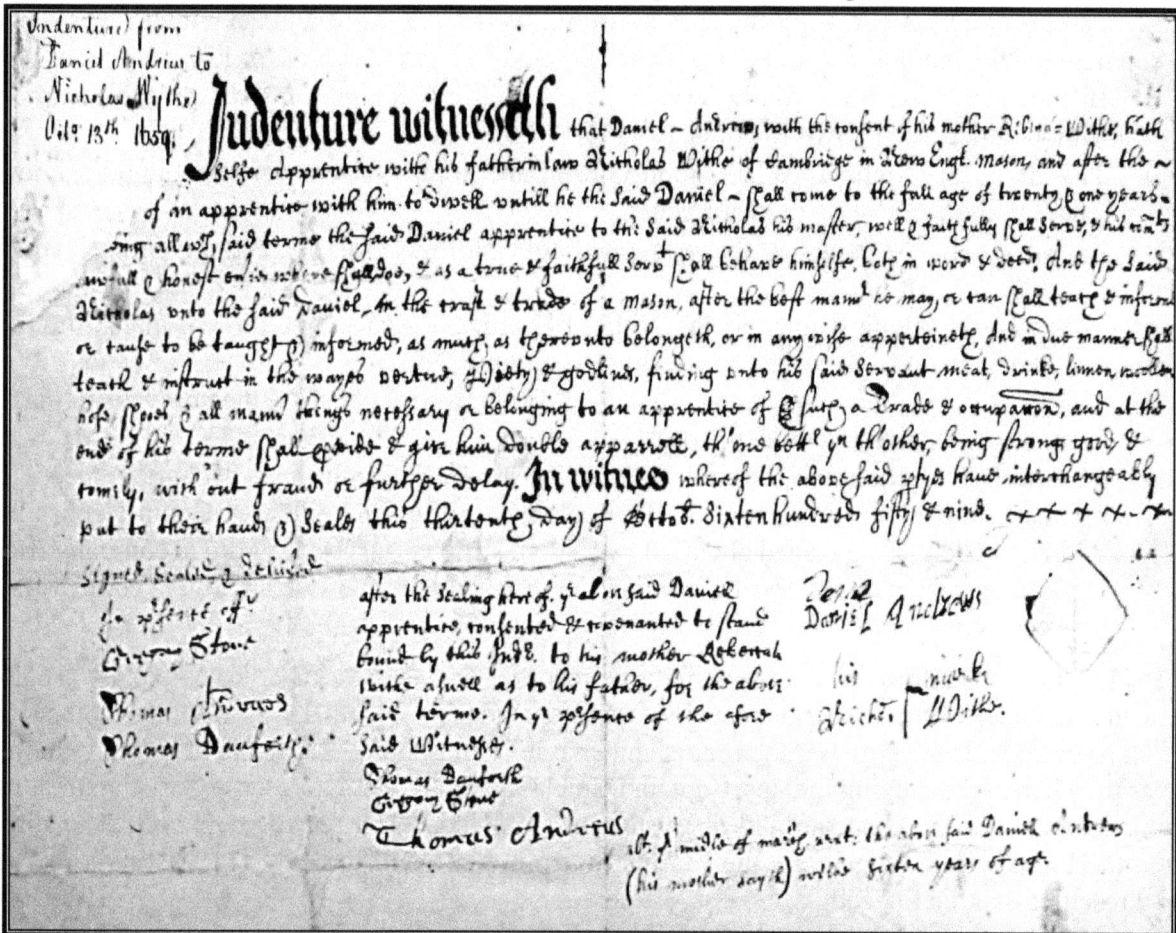

Indenture from Daniel Andrews to Nicholas Wythe. *Nicholas and William Wyeth papers (Mss 73).* R. Stanton Avery Special Collections. Courtesy of the New England Historic Genealogical Society (NEHGS), Boston, MA.

In his book, Marion Sims Wyeth provided other glimpses into the lives of Rebecca and Nicholas Wyeth. Here is a quick look at the references Marion found as well as some records from Harvard College, *the Town of Cambridge,* and Paige's *History of Cambridge.*

- 23 Apr 1651: Nicholas contributed monies to the steward of Harvard College for the education of Joshua Moodey of Newbury who graduated 10 Aug 1653.[153]
- 28 Apr 1652: In a west field owners' meeting, the fencing between Nicholas' land and Marrett, Chesholme and Cutter's land was adjusted.[154]
- 09 Jun 1652: The Church had the General Court divide a large body of lands at Shaw Shine (now Billerica along the Shawsheen River) among Cambridge proprietors. Lot # 70 went to Nicho. Withe – 90 acres. (Town Records, p. 98)[155]
- 12 Mar 1655: Nicholas Withe and Thomas Fox given fence duty. (Town Records, p. 107)
- 09 Mar 1657: Nich: Withe was fined for breaching the towne ordinance by his swine. (Town Records, p. 117)
- 15 Feb 1657: In testimony to the Townsmen, it was determined that Nicholas Withe had the right to build a house in the town 19 years past. The right of which was sold by Nicholas Withe to John Cooper. (Town Records, p. 123)
- 21 Feb 1658: Nicholas Withe, Robert Parker and David Fisk were assigned to survey fences about the west field. (Town Records, p. 128)
- 19 Mar 1660: Nicholas Withe said he would work with Gilbert Crackbone to make and maintain a common fence between their two lands. (Town Records, p. 130)
- 10 Feb 1661: Nicholas Withe was fined six shillings for felling trees on the common without a license. (Town Records, p. 137)
- 09 Mar 1663: Nicholas Withe, John Gibson and John Watson were appointed to view fences in the west field. (Town Records, p. 143)
- 16 Jan 1664: Nicholas Withe was fined four shillings for neglecting fences. (Town Records, p. 153)
- 17 Oct 1664: Along with Nicholas Withe, 142 citizens signed a petition of thanks "to the honored General Court of the Massachusetts Colony."[156]
- 11 Mar 1667: Liberty was granted Nicholas Withe for timber from the common to make fence posts. (Town Records, p. 166)[157]
- 04 Apr 1671: Nicholas testified in favor of Thomas Danforth in a court proceeding between Gookin et al vs. Danforth. In an oath sworn in the Middlesex County Court, he said, "I Nicholas Withe aged about 70 years do testifie ye survey …, I did accompany Ric: Jackson and Thomas Danforth when they set ye bounds of the swamp now in controversy between yem." (This also verifies Nicholas was born circa 1600.)[158]

In 1671, Thomas Danforth was at the same time recorder of deeds for Middlesex County (1652-86) and a member of the Colony's council of assistants (1659-79). In 1675, war broke out with Indian leader, Metacom, who had the English nickname "King Philip." Danforth, together with the Superintendent of the Praying Indians, Captain Daniel Gookin, worked to resettle Christian Indians who were opposed by Metacom and distrusted by Colonists. The resettlement ended horribly when the Indians were taken from their farms — from their food source. The vast majority of those resettled starved to death.[159]

Lucius Paige states that on 03 Dec 1675, John Wyeth Sr., Nicholas' son, was impressed into serving in the war by order of Captain Gookin. The history also says Corporal Jonathan Remington reported to Captain Gookin that John was not mustered in because "John Wyeth is not yet come to his father's, neither can I hear any tidings of him." Furthermore, Paige declared that Captain Gookin was appointed sergeant major of the Middlesex Regiment on 05 May 1676.[160] However, according to George Bodge's critical account of the war, Remington was not corporal to Major Daniel Gookin or to his son, Captain Daniel Gookin Jr. Remington was corporal to Captain Nathaniel Davenport and mustered in at the end of 1675 with 14 others including John Withe.[161] Although no source is provided for it, another claim is that John served at the rank of major.[162]

Many consider King Philip's War as one of the greatest catastrophes of all time due to loss of life as compared with population. Two years after the war ended on 12 Apr 1678, Nicholas died in Cambridge. Here is his will, with name spelled "Wythe" from Marion Sims Wyeth's book.[163]

WILL OF NICHOLAS WYTHE PROVED OCT. 5th 1680

NICH. WYTHE

IN THE NAME OF GOD AMEN. I Nicholas Wythe of Cambridge in the Coun of Middlesex in New England, being weak in body, yet through the Lords favour of sound judgment& memory: do make my last will & Testament in manner following viz. My immortall soul I do freely resigne into the armes & mercyes of God my Maker, Jesus Christ my only Redeemer, & to the holy Spiritt to carry me on & lead me forever my body to be decently interred by my Christian freinds, and for my outward goods I do dispose of them as followeth Inpes . I do give and bequeath to Rebecca my beloved wife my dwelling house in Cambridge,with all other outhousing, with all my lands adjoyning to my house, also all my land lying in the west field excepting two acres lying next the brook by ffrancis Mores land which I give and bequeathe to my son John Wythe, also my land in Watertown lying neer to Cambridge line, during her naturall life or widdowhood, & my will is, that after the decease of my beloved wife or in case she shall marry, all my housing and lands above expressed shall be disposed of by her to my four children viz. Nicholas & John William & Mary, she being at liberty to proportion whatevery ones part shall be. Also I give to my beloved wife two Cows, Also my will is that my beloved wife shall have the use of all my household goods during her naturall life or widdowhood & to be disposed of by her according to her discretion to my four children above mentioned, excepting such goods as I shall dispose of in this my will, also my will is yt my wife shall have the best bed, with all furniture belonging therunto, also her wearing cloathes linnen & woollen also two Cows to dispose of she shall see meet at her death and marriage. Itm I give to my daughter Sarah ffiske the wife of John ffiske as an addition to what I have formerly given her forty five acres of land scittuated in the village, twenty five acres of it I purchased of old Goodman Shepard the other twenty acres I purchased of Thomas Andrew, also one featherbed, one boulster & one Rugg, also six sheep, shee to have possession of all these particulars within a month after the will is proved. Also I give to my son Nicolas Wythe my eldest son: my house & land in Watertowne, which I purchased of Daniel Andrew. Only my will is in case he dye without an heyre & leave a widdow, she shall enjoy her thirds of the land during her naturall life or widdowhood. Also my will is that Nicholas shall have liberty during his life to cutt & carry away four loads of firewood every yeare out of my land, lying on the other side of the River, joyning to the land called the hundred acres. Also my will is that my son shall let my wife have three barrells of cyder yearly during her naturall life

shee providing the barrells; my will is in case Nicholas dye without heyrs the land shall be equally divided among the rest of my children then living. Also my will is that after all debts & charges are payd by my Executrix out of what of my Estate not yet disposed of I give to my two sons John & William, And my will is that my two sons shall keep two Cowes for my wife providing for them both winter and summer & reringe two Cowes to her disposing at her death or marriage & provide her sufficient firewood for her use during her widdowhood, or till her death: Also my will is that they my two sons shall have the care of their sister Mary Wythe, & see that she be comfortably provided for while she lives a single life: but my will is, in case she shall marry they shall give her forty pound as a legacy: To be paid fifteen pound at her marriage & fifteen pounds within a yeare after & fifteen pounds the year following, and my will is that my daughter Mary shall imploy herself so as may be for the comfort of her livelyhood according to her ability. Also I give to my son Ives[SR] as an addition to what I have formerly given him Thirty shillings to be payd in currant pay within a year after my decease. Also I give to his two children which he had by my daughter Martha five pouds a piece to be payd in currant mony when they come of age only my will is that in case either one of them shall dye before they come of age, the whole ten pound to be paid to the other surviving & to be payd by my sons John & William. And my will is that my beloved wife shall be sole Executrix to this my will. Also I do constitute & appoynt & desire my beloved freinds Daniel Andrew of Salem & John Stone of Cambridge, my lawfull overseers to this my will & in case any difference arise between ye legatees it shall be in the powr of them to determine any such difference as shall arise but in case they my overseers agree not it shall be at their liberty to make choyse of a third meet person & such two of them to determine, & in case any of the legatees, make disturbance & not rest satisfyed therin; they shall cutt off from their legacy & to be divided among the rest; Also my desire is that these my overseers will please to assist my beloved wife in her Executorship & to advise her according to their best ability, enterlined before signing & sealing, the words (four loads of firewood) between the seventeenth & eighteenth line.

Nicolas Wythe his mark & seal.

Signd & seald in presence of
  Richard Robbins
  Richard Eccles
    Octob. 5. 80
  Richard Robbins & Ri: Eccles made oath
  in Court to the abovsd will as attest
                                    J R. C.

Thomas Danforth's service as recorder continued to overlap while he served as deputy governor (1679-86.) It is likely he recorded Nicholas' last will and testament dated 05 Oct 1680 into the county records. Perhaps Thomas called on Rebecca after Nicholas died on 19 Jul 1680 to remember the friend he had known since he was a child in old England. Thomas was not yet a teenager when his father, Nicholas Danforth, brought him to New England. He was born in Framlingham, England in 1623.[164] At age six, in their New Street home, Thomas, undoubtedly, overhead his father and Nicholas Wyeth discuss many of the Puritan lectures they had traveled around Suffolk County to hear in 1629.

Nicholas Wyeth made his wife sole executrix, with Daniel Andrew of Salem and John Stone of Cambridge, overseers. Inventory included the dwelling house and orchard with privilege of the Commons (£75), 4 acres in Watertown (£16), 11 acres in the west field (£40), land "in the necke" (£60), 40 acres "ovr the River" (£70), 40 acres "in the village in two pieces" (£30), 50 acres "lying in the village" (£25), a house & land in Watertown (£62.10s.), and "Corne upon the land" (£4.10s.).[165]

Summarizing the will (spelling uncorrected), Nicholas gave:

- to **Rebecca** my beloved wife
  - my dwelling house in Cambridge, with all other out housing, with all my lands adjoining to my house, also all my land in the west field except two acres [given to son **John***]
  - also my land in Watertown lying neer to Cambridge line, during her natural life or widowhood
  - Also I give to my beloved wife two cows,
  - Also my will is that my beloved wife shall have the use of all my houshold goods during her natural life, or widowhood, my wife shall have the best bed, with all furniture belonging thereunto,
  - also her wearing cloathes linen & woolen
- <u>After the decease of my beloved wife or in case she shall marry,</u> all my housing and lands above expressed shall be disposed of by her to my four children. Viz. **Nicholas, John, William & Mary.**
- I give to my daughter **Sarah Fiske**, the wife of **John Fiske** as an addition to what I have formerly given her
  - forty five acres of land situated in the village, 25 acres of it I purchased off old Goodman Shepard the other 20 acres I purchased off Thomas Andrew,
  - also one featherbed, one boulster and one rug, six sheep.
- To my son **Nicholas Wythe**, my eldest son: my house and land in Watertowne, which I purchased off Daniel Andrew.
  - Also Nicholas shall have liberty during his life to cut and carry away four loads of firewood every year out of my land lying on the other side of the river joining the land called the hundred acres.
  - Also Nicholas shall let my wife have three barrells of cider yearly.
  - If Nicholas should die without heirs, the land shall be divided among the rest of my children then living.
- After debts and charges are paid by my Executrix, out of what of my estate not yet disposed of, I give to my two sons **John and William**. (*including two acres in the west field given to son **John Wythe** above)…shall keep two cowes for my wife providing for them both winter and summer & provide her sufficient firewood for her use during her widowhood, or 'till her death.
- Also my two sons shall have the care of their sister **Mary Wythe** and see that she be comfortably provided for while she lives a single life… Mary shall employ herself so as may be for the comfort of her livelyhood according to her ability.

- Also I give to my son [Thomas] **Ives** as an addition to what I have formerly given him 30 shillings to be paid in currant pay… I give to his two children which he had by my daughter **Martha**, 5 pounds apiece to be paid in currant money when they come of age."

Nicholas' remains are buried in the family tomb of his granddaughter, Deborah Wyeth Gamage, in the Old Burying Ground on Massachusetts Avenue. It is across from the Johnston Gate to Harvard Yard. [166] Although the address for First Parish (Unitarian) is 3 Church Street, Massachusetts

Avenue crosses Garden Street in front of the cemetery. Just as the cemetery runs across three streets, there are three churches affiliated with the Old Burying Ground.

First Parish's fifth meetinghouse, pictured above, was built in 1833. Their first house was built in 1632 near the corner of present Dunster and Mt. Auburn Streets. During the church's first 100 years, when it was called the First Church or the Church of Christ, Thomas Shepard (recorder of Nicholas Wyeth's 1644 confession), and his successors, preached Calvinistic doctrine. However, in the next century, members became more liberal in their views. By 1829, the majority of the Parish became Unitarian.[167]

Evidence shows that most of the Wyeth family stayed with the Unitarians. [168] Harrisburg postmaster, John Wyeth, was married in the Unitarian church and his brother, Ebenezer Wyeth III, is buried in the Old Burying Ground of the Unitarian Church in Ashby, Massachusetts. An 1865 diagram held by the Harvard Map Archives shows Andrew Newell Wyeth Sr. held pew 26 and Jonas Wyeth held pew 69 in the First Parish Unitarian Church in Harvard Square.[169] Artist N. C. Wyeth was baptized and married in the Unitarian church.[170]

Looking across Cambridge Common to First Church (Congregational) at dusk.

39

At the split in 1829, the conservative members of the original church left to found the Shepard Congregational Society. Shepard Congregational is now called First Church in Cambridge (Congregational) and is part of the United Church of Christ.[171] Their stone building at 11 Garden Street at Mason is one block north of Christ Church Cambridge (Episcopal).[172]

The rooster meets the sexton.

Benjamin Francis Wyeth was Shepard's sexton from 1851 to his death in 1890.[173] This photo of Benjamin with the rooster that currently adorns their steeple is courtesy of the church and the steeple photo is from Geri Wyeth Watson. The rooster points to the dawning of a new day and to the joy of the Resurrection. It stood from 1721 to 1869 on the spire of the New Brick meetinghouse on Hanover Street, Boston. Cotton Mather preached the first sermon under it in 1721. The Shepard Church installed it in Cambridge on 28 Jun 1873.[174]

The Episcopal Church that frames the Old Burying Ground on the north is pictured below left. The cemetery in Harvard Square is about three blocks from the original Wyeth homestead. A Harvard office building and the Sheraton Commander Hotel now sit on part of Nicholas and John Wyeth Sr.'s original properties.

This photo is looking north from the site on Cambridge Common where tradition states George Washington took control of the Continental Army on 03 Jul 1775. Richard Withe, possibly Nicholas' brother, held land near this same common. Also, as mentioned, Nicholas left a hog unattended several times on the common, near his farm, in 1646.[175]

Before marrying her third husband, Thomas Fox, on 16 Dec 1685, Rebecca disposed of property as Nicholas prescribed in his will. Because John was already living on an estate he purchased on the west side of his father's land, Rebecca left her dwelling place to her youngest son, William.

If Washington did indeed take control of the Continental Army here, as the monument and as legend says, on 03 Jul 1775, Jonas Wyeth Sr. and his family were then living in the area of the present day Sheraton hotel.

Prior to William's death, he, in turn, left the property to trustees for the benefit of his minor children, Deborah Wyeth (Gamage) and Martha Wyeth (Fessenden).

Since William died before John, John's will left instructions for his wife Deborah to purchase William's land. At Deborah's death, the house was assigned to Hannah.[176] Ebenezer Sr., only eight when his father died, purchased his father's property from Hannah and passed it on to his descendants through his son, Jonas Sr. It was eventually inherited by Jonas Wyeth 2^d (1806-1868).

Here is part of Rebecca's 07 Dec 1685 property agreement with original spellings and grammar.[177]

"By & Rebecca Wythe the relict widow & executrix of the last will & testament of Nicholas Wythe late of Cambridge deced, **Nicholas Wythe, John Wythe, William Wythe & Mary Wythe** her children. Witnesseth that whereas the sd. Rebeckah Wythe is intended (God permitting) shortly to enter into a marryed estate & remove her dwelling from the place where shee now is:
They the above named prties do mutually agree that on her removall her son **William Wythe**…shall have & posses her sd dwelling place, barne, orchard, Garden & all that prcell of land adjoyning had of Matthew Bridge, with the four accrs of land which lyeth in Watertown & the privileges of the Commons that belong to the house & shall hold the same during the time that the sd Rebeckah his mother shall be in a marryed estate:
And that **John Wyth** shall in like manner have & enjoy that prcell of land lying in west field in Cambridge conteyning about eleven accrs
…and in case it shall happen that sd **Rebeckah their mother shall again be in a widdow hood** estate they the sd **John Wythe and William Wythe [shall grant and deliver to their mother the above mentioned property** for her natural life and perform duties toward her as required in their father's will.]
…. And the abovenamed **John Wythe & William Wythe** doe covenant & promise that in case their sister **Mary Wythe** shall survive her mother for more than two months & shall continue unmarryed that then she providing her selfe & quitting them of further care & charge for her maintenance they will then pay unto her her legacy of ffourty pounds within the Compass of three years then next following: i. e. by each of them Twenty Nobles a year until sd forty pounds be fully paid & contented….
They the above named **Rebeckah Wythe, Nicholas Wythe, John Wythe, William Wythe and Mary Wythe** do bynd themselves… respectively each to other firmly …

Sealed & delivered in prsence of us	
Tho: Danforth	*Rebecca Wythe* her mark & seale
John Cooper	*Nicholas Wythe* & seale
Walter Hastings	*John Wythe* & seale
ffra. Moore	*William Wythe* & seale
	Mary Wythe her mark & seale

Recorded 25. 10. 85 (25 Dec 1685) by Tho: Danforth R *(Middlesex County Deeds, 9:514-517.)*"

There are two extraordinary things about this document being recorded by the long time Wyeth family friend, Thomas Danforth, on Christmas day 1685. First, it shows the Puritans did not celebrate Christmas. They believed it was a day just like any other day. In fact, Massachusetts did not celebrate it until President Grant made Christmas a Federal holiday in 1870.[178]

Secondly, at the time, Thomas Danforth was doing double duty as the deputy governor for the whole Massachusetts Bay Colony. He had been Recorder for Middlesex County since the inception of the office in 1652 and had been deputy governor since 1679. When King James II tried to consolidate all of New England under the rule of unpopular Sir Edmund Andros in 1686, Danforth was put out of office. However, at the collapse of the Dominion of New England in 1692, Danforth was reinstated as Governor William Phips' secondary and held the position until May 1692 when Phips replaced him with William Stoughton.[179]

Before leaving office, Danforth, the close friend of the Wyeth family from old England, traveled to Salem on 11 Apr 1692 for the preliminary witchcraft examinations of Elizabeth Proctor and Sarah Towne Cloyse.[180] Sarah and her husband, Peter, were Daniel Andrew's Salem Village neighbors and tenants.[181]

The Wyeths are related to the Andrews' family on the maternal side through Nicholas' second wife, Rebecca Parks Andrews Wyeth Fox. Thus, all families in this book, except for the offspring of Sarah Wyeth Fiske (1632-1701), are descendants of Rebecca. As evidenced by the indenture document between Nicholas Wyeth and his step son, Daniel Andrews, Nicholas was more than just a step father to the Andrews' children. He was the only father they'd ever known. Nicholas made Daniel an executor of his will and so did Mary Wyeth. Mary's will also demonstrates how close she was to her half brothers and sister. Then when Rebecca Jacobs was arrested on witchcraft charges, the heart-wrenching letters mother Rebecca (then married to Thomas Fox) wrote on her daughter's behalf show the Andrews and Wyeths were a very loving family.

During the Salem witch hunts, leaders spread the darkness of hate to such a degree that they caused mass hysteria by turning neighbor against neighbor. To help understand this toxic period, the next several pages are a chronological account of how the witchcraft trials affected our ancestors.

This Salem Village (now Danvers) map is adapted from the one William Phineas Upham constructed for his brother's two-volume work – *Salem Witchcraft: With an Account of Salem Village and A History of Opinions on Witchcraft and Kindred Subjects* by Charles Upham.[182] As can be seen, siblings Daniel Andrews and Rebecca Andrews Frost Jacobs were neighbors.

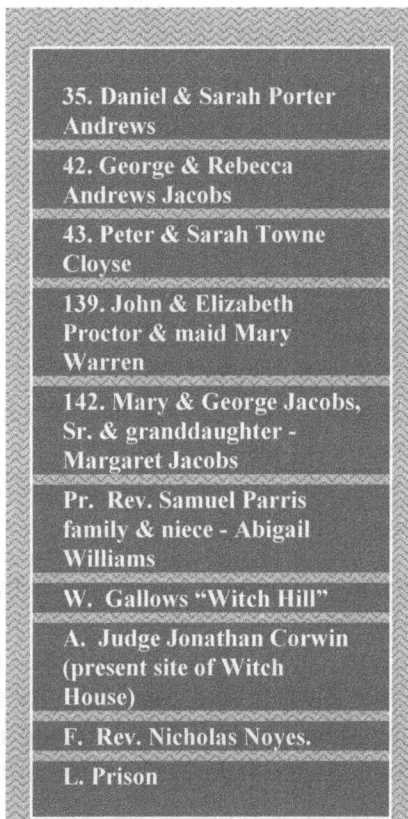

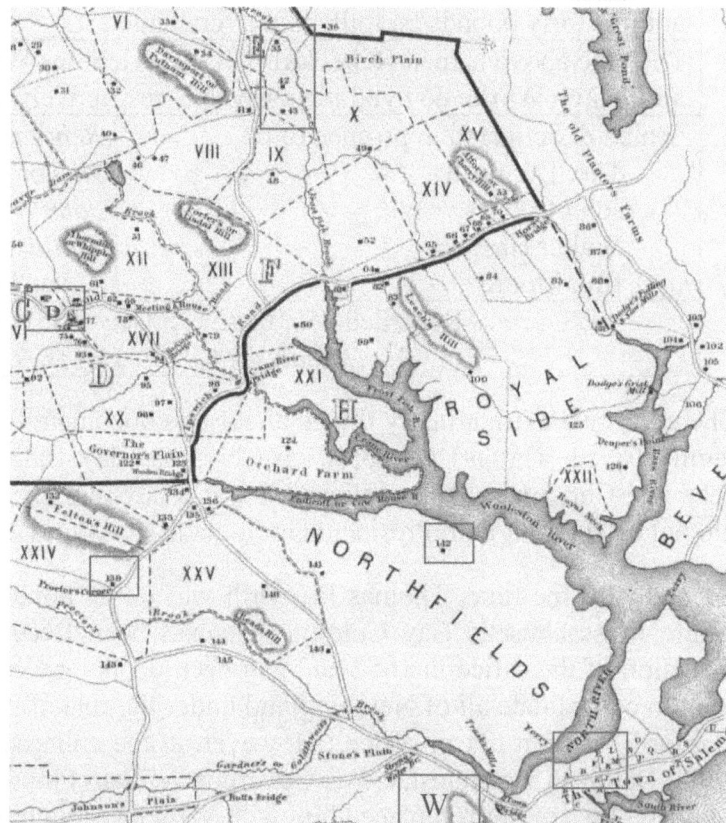

35. Daniel & Sarah Porter Andrews

42. George & Rebecca Andrews Jacobs

43. Peter & Sarah Towne Cloyse

139. John & Elizabeth Proctor & maid Mary Warren

142. Mary & George Jacobs, Sr. & granddaughter - Margaret Jacobs

Pr. Rev. Samuel Parris family & niece - Abigail Williams

W. Gallows "Witch Hill"

A. Judge Jonathan Corwin (present site of Witch House)

F. Rev. Nicholas Noyes.

L. Prison

In her painstakingly researched day-by-day chronicle of the Salem witch trials, Marilynne Roach, indicates Judge Thomas Danforth was but an observer of the proceedings conducted by the local magistrates, John Hathorne and Jonathan Corwin. However, the rapt attention of such an important man at the 11 Apr 1692 examinations was naturally most flattering to the several afflicted young accusers attendant on the court.[183]

Between Thomas Danforth's first Salem appearance in Apr and his next involvement in the trials on 03 Jan 1693, witchcraft hysteria had spun wildly and horrifically out of control.

The bewitchments started in hellfire and brimstone preacher Rev. Samuel Parris' Salem Village Parsonage. There his daughter, Betty, age nine; and his niece, Abigail Williams, age 11; met over the winter of 1691-1692 to practice palmistry, fortune telling and magic with friends, including Ann Putnam Jr., Mary Walcott and Mercy Lewis. As such practices were highly forbidden in Puritan society, the girls may have pretended to be bewitched in order to take blame off themselves. Some modern-day theorists believe they may have been suffering from clinical hysteria or ergot-infected rye grain poisoning that mimics the effects of LSD. Whether it was madness, illness or deliberate fraud, the community was much alarmed when the girls began suffering convulsions, contorting themselves into odd and unnatural positions, making antic gestures and babbling incoherent and unintelligible noises.[184] [185] [186]

When a doctor diagnosed the girls "as under an evil hand," prayer was first applied. Hoping to reveal the children's bewitcher, Tituba and her husband, mixed-race slaves Rev. Parris had brought with him from Barbados, helped bake a witch cake of rye meal and the afflicted girls' urine. After the cake was fed to a dog, the girls' afflictions got worse. Parris and his supporters, chief among them being Thomas Putnam Jr., beleaguered the girls to name scapegoats. Among the first named by the girls was Tituba. Arrest warrants charging her, and two other outcast women of the village, on suspicion of witchcraft, were issued on Monday, 29 Feb 1692.[187] [188]

Charles Wentworth Upham, in his extensive 1867 history of the witchcraft trials, wrote the girls at first had no intention of accusing anyone. However, once they named names and those they accused were brought to court, "then the awful power in their hands was revealed to them." Upham went on to say the notice and sympathy of the public, along with the importance given to those common girls by the magistrates, as they acted their parts, made the girls' power irresistible.[189]

Stirred into a boiling pot was the incompetent doctor who was quick to find evil at hand, overzealous ministers and magistrates puffed up with their own self-importance, a strong belief among the populace in witchcraft fueled by the writings of Rev. Cotton Mather, and a feud between the two most powerful families in Salem Village – the Porters and the Putnams.

From this mixture, individuals critical of the proceedings quickly found themselves accused of witchcraft. Their children were forced into the care of friends and family. Their lands and property confiscated before they were even found guilty. Their crops rotted in the fields while their cattle roamed unattended. Those who confessed lived to accuse other witches. Those who declared their innocence were executed.

By 22 Dec 1692, when Massachusetts Governor William Phips appointed Thomas Danforth to the newly established Superior Court of Judicature, the hysteria had spread widely.[190] Over 200 people all over New England had been accused of witchcraft. 140 to 150 had been arrested. As many as 13 died in prison. 19 were executed on the gallows and one, Giles Corey, was crushed to death. In order to preserve his property for his heirs, Corey refused to enter a plea. Had he declared himself not guilty or guilty, the courts would have had his property confiscated.[191]

Apparently, Thomas Danforth had a change of heart in the months between Apr 1692 and Jan 1693. He told others he disagreed on how the courts had prosecuted individuals accused of witchcraft. Danforth did, however, believe in witchcraft. At an early 1692/3 trial, Danforth admonished one woman to repent after she was found not guilty.[192] Earlier, he and other magistrates jailed Martha Sparks for witchcraft in Boston on 27 Oct 1691 until a new government could deal with her case. The particulars of the Sparks' witchcraft charge have been lost, but an earlier conviction in 1677 showed Martha had been sentenced for beating her own mother bloody.[193]

While visiting Cambridge on 15 Oct 1692, Judge Samuel Sewall saw Thomas Danforth at his home there. Sewall had been one of Danforth's assistants at the Apr examinations in Salem. Of the Oct meeting, Sewall wrote in his diary that though they were observers of the Apr examinations, Danforth had long disagreed with the court's proceedings.[194]

Particularly noteworthy is that on page 101 of Upham's second volume, Upham wrote Danforth personally questioned the accusers and the accused during the Apr examinations. However, a few pages later, Upham conceded the obvious beforehand knowledge of what the witnesses were to say made it apparent Danforth and his assistants, strangers as they were to Salem and the details of the affair, could not have had the knowledge to ask such leading questions.[195]

By going back to the source of what Upham wrote on page 101, it is evident he misread Thomas Hutchinson's words from his 1767 *History of the Province of Massachusets-Bay*. The reason Upham conceded it was not Danforth doing the questioning is because Hutchinson wrote Rev. Parris did the questioning at a court held by Thomas Danforth. Hutchinson proceeded to give specimens of Parris' leading questions that put words into the mouths of the witnesses.[196]

INSTEAD of suspecting and sifting the witnesses, and suffering them to be cross examined, the authority, to say no more, were imprudent in making use of leading questions, and thereby putting words into their mouths or suffering others to do it. Mr. Parris was over officious; most of the examinations, although in the presence of one or more of the magistrates, were taken by him. The following examinations, of several of the accused, may serve as specimens they being generally made in the same manner. "At

MASSACHUSETS-BAY. 27

"At a court held at Salem 11th April 1692, by the honoured Thomas Danforth, Deputy Governor. Q. John ;† who hurt you ? A. Goody Procter first, and then Goody Cloyse. Q. What did she do to you ? A. She brought the book to me. Q. John ! tell the truth, who hurts you ? Have you been hurt ? A. The first, was a gentlewoman I saw. Q. Who next ? A. Goody Cloyse. Q. But who hurt you next ? A. Goody Procter. Q. What did she do to you ? A. She choaked

Another way Upham's work alludes to Danforth's epiphany is by quoting from William Brattle's letter to an unknown cleric. The letter, also written in Oct 1692, stated Thomas Danforth utterly condemned the witch trials.[197]

A portion of the letter, shown below, is from *Narratives of the Witchcraft Cases, 1648–1706*. The book's author, George Lincoln Burr, states Brattle was an affluent Boston merchant, a graduate and a master of arts of Harvard, a noted mathematician and astronomer, as well as, from 1693 to his death in 1713, treasurer of Harvard College.

"….But although the Chief Judge, and some of the other Judges, be very zealous in these proceedings, yet this you may take for a truth, that there are several about the Bay, men for understanding, Judgment, and Piety, inferior to few, (if any,) in N. E. that do utterly condemn the said proceedings, and do freely deliver their Judgment in the case to be this, viz. that these methods will utterly ruin and undo poor N. E. I shall nominate some of these to you, viz. The honorable Simon Bradstreet, Esq. (our late Governor); the honorable Thomas Danforth, Esq. (our late Deputy Governor)…"

Burr indicates the letter did not see print in Brattle's own day, but it likely circulated with discretion to reach the ears of Governor Phips. The letter was donated in the 18th century by the author's grandnephew, Thomas Brattle, Esq., of Cambridge, to the Massachusetts Historical Society.[198]

Also, from Judge Sewall comes the most telling statement of Danforth's conversion. In his *History of Framingham*, author Josiah Temple wrote that Judge Sewall said of Danforth, "He had, as Judge of the Court, a chief hand, under God, in putting an end to the troubles under which the country groaned in 1692." Temple points to Sewall's statement as a clue to the legend Danforth gave land in Framingham to Sarah Towne Cloyse and others whose families were persecuted during the Salem witch trials.[199]

The Framingham History Center states, "It is likely that Danforth invited the family to settle on the far western portion of his land." Today five homes of the early settlers from Salem still stand. The oldest of the five, Peter and Sarah Clayes' house (circa 1693) is on the appropriately named Salem End Road. Once in Framingham, the family changed their name from Cloyse / Cloyce / Cloyes to Clayes, while members of Sarah's sister's family changed their name from Nurse to Nourse.[200] Of course, the name "Framingham" was a variation of Thomas Danforth's hometown in England. At some point, the "L" was dropped from it.

As mentioned before, Peter and Sarah Cloyse were tenants and neighbors of Daniel Andrews. They lived south of Daniel's nearest neighbors – his sister, Rebecca Andrews Frost Jacobs and her husband George Jacobs Jr. George helped farm his brother-in-law's land. On 14 May 1692, shortly after Daniel assumed office as a selectman (city councilman) for the village, he, George and Rebecca were named in the same arrest warrant. Paul Boyer and Stephen Nissenbaum wrote in *Salem Possessed*, that Daniel and George were warned ahead of time and went into hiding. Ultimately, they were saved from the gallows through Daniel's status and connections.[201]

With four young children in her care, Rebecca was not able to flee. However, perhaps it was her brother's influence with Thomas Danforth that her case was the very first one before the court when Magistrate Danforth began arbitrating the witch trials in Jan 1693. Conceivably, Daniel also could have interceded with Danforth to help relocate his Cloyse neighbors to Framingham.

Back home in Cambridge, Daniel's mother, Rebecca Andrews Wyeth Fox, was frantic with concern for her daughter. The younger Rebecca suffered a nervous breakdown in 1680 and then blamed herself for the 1685 death of her toddler who fell in a well. In Nov 1692, the month before Massachusetts Governor William Phips appointed Thomas Danforth as a justice of the newly formed Superior Court of Judicature; the anxious mother wrote fretful letters to both Phips and William Stoughton. Stoughton, with Cotton Mather's help, superseded Danforth as deputy governor in May 1692. In June 1692, Phips formed a special court of oyer and terminer [Anglo-French words meaning to hear and to determine] for the witchcraft trials and commissioned Stoughton as its chief justice.[202]

Here is one letter. It shows a loving and tender mother with extraordinary bravery and strength. Those who endeavored to help individuals accused of witchcraft, risked being accused as well.

"To His Excellency Sir William Phips, Knight, Governor, and the Honorable Council sitting at Boston," in the following terms:— *The Humble Petition of Rebecca Fox, of Cambridge, showeth*, that

Whereas Rebecca Jacobs (daughter of your humble petitioner) has, a long time,—even many months,—now lain in prison for witchcraft, and is well known to be a person crazed, distracted, and broken in mind, your humble petitioner does most humbly and earnestly seek unto Your Excellency and to Your Honors for relief in this case.

"Your petitioner,—who knows well the condition of her poor daughter,—together with several others of good repute and credit, are ready to offer their oaths, that the said Jacobs is a woman crazed, distracted, and broken in her mind; and that she has been so these twelve years and upwards.

"However, for (I think) above this half-year, the said Jacobs has lain in prison, and yet remains there, attended with many sore difficulties.

"Christianity and nature do each of them oblige your petitioner to be very solicitous in this matter; and, although many weighty cases do exercise your thoughts, yet your petitioner can have no rest in her mind till such time as she has offered this her address on behalf of her daughter.

"Some have died already in prison, and others have been dangerously sick; and how soon others, and, among them, my poor child, by the difficulties of this confinement may be sick and die, God only knows.

"She is uncapable of making that shift for herself that others can do; and such are her circumstances, on other accounts, that your petitioner, who is her tender mother, has many great sorrows, and almost overcoming burdens, on her mind upon her account; but, in the midst of all her perplexities and troubles (next to supplicating to a good and merciful God), your petitioner has no way for help but to make this her afflicted condition known unto you. So, not doubting but Your Excellency and Your Honors will readily hear the cries and groans of a poor distressed woman, and grant what help and enlargement you may, your petitioner heartily begs God's gracious presence with you; and subscribes herself, in all humble manner,

> your sorrowful and distressed petitioner,
> *Rebecca Fox.*"[203]

Although my eighth great-grandmother Rebecca's letters to Phips and Stoughton fell on deaf ears, I have no doubt she gave her Cambridge compatriot, former Deputy Governor Danforth, an earful. At the time, she was living with her third husband, Thomas Fox, on Holmes Place across the street from the Old Burying Ground. Although several acres divided them, Rebecca Fox and Thomas Danforth were next-door neighbors. Danforth's home was located at what is now the north corner of Kirkland Street near Oxford Street in Cambridge. Before 1830, when Kirkland was renamed for one of the presidents of Harvard, the street was known as the path from Charlestown to Watertown. Danforth lived on the northern side of the path.[204]

On the following map from page 124 of *An Historic Guide to Cambridge*, published in 1907 by the Hannah Winthrop Chapter of the DAR, Rebecca's home is listed as the Hastings House #66. Her old home, at the Wyeth farms, was above #61 and the Washington Elm.

At his death, Thomas Fox willed his home to his son, Jabez, whose descendants sold it in 1737 to Jonathan Hastings. Thomas Danforth's home is #67 – the Foxcroft House. When Danforth died in 1699, he left the home to his daughter, Elizabeth, wife of Francis Foxcroft.[205]

When the special oyer and terminer court was abolished, and Danforth was appointed to the new court that replaced it, the rejoicing must have been great at the crossroads separating Rebecca Andrews Frost Jacobs' siblings, Mary, John and William Wyeth, on Garden Street (then known as the highway to the Great Swamp) and their mother on Holmes Place. Rebecca Jacobs had been the only child of Cambridge jailed on witchcraft charges in Salem.[206]

It could not have been an accident, nor a coincidence, that Rebecca Andrews Frost Jacobs, the girl Thomas Danforth had seen grow up in the arms of his father's friend from old England, was the first person on the docket for his first court session as the newly appointed Associate Justice of the Massachusetts Superior Court of Judicature.

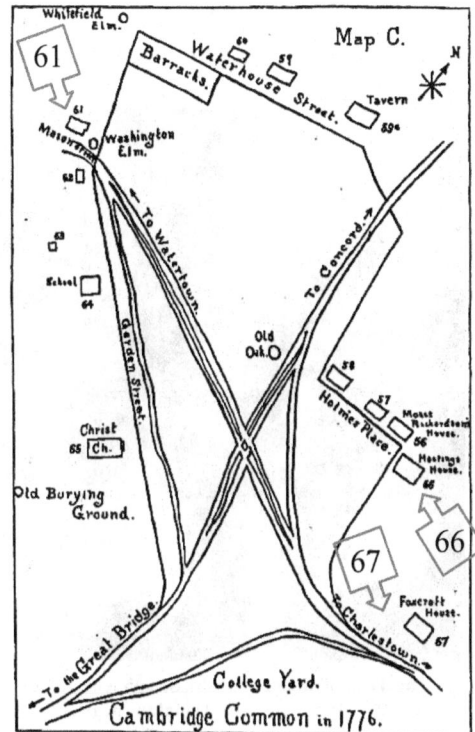

During the Salem witchcraft hysteria, when Rebecca wrote letters on behalf of her daughter, she was living at #66. Thomas Danforth was living at #67 and the Wyeth farms were above #61.

Back in Apr, Danforth did not know Elizabeth Proctor or Sarah Cloyse personally. On the other hand, he knew Daniel Andrews and his sister, Rebecca Jacobs, well. Likely, he even knew they lived in Salem Village. However, they were not implicated in the hysteria until 14 May 1692. Thomas Danforth could do nothing to help them. Just two days later, on 16 May 1692; he was put out of office and replaced by William Stoughton.[207] Danforth's help could only be from behind the scenes.

It was William Stoughton's acceptance of spectral evidence (evidence based on dreams and visions) that had brought Rebecca Jacobs and hundreds like her before the courts. To Thomas Danforth, Rebecca Jacobs was a real person whose life had intersected with his since he was 23 years old. He had likely heard nine-month-old Rebecca cooing at the dinner following the 1647 wedding of her mother to Nicholas Wyeth. Undoubtedly, Rebecca looked older than her 46 years when she came to the bar at 9:00 am on 04 Jan 1693.[208] Still in his mind's eye, he must have seen the child who sat quietly with her seven siblings every Sabbath day in the Wyeth pew at the First Church meetinghouse back home in Cambridge.

This photo of the Danforth home on New Street, near Framlingham on the Saxtead Road in Suffolk County, England was taken 02 Apr 2018.

Perhaps when Rebecca's daughter, Margaret, the second to stand trial on that wintery January day, came to the bar, Danforth's mind wandered back to when he was about Margaret's age. He alone could see the contrast between the delightful memories he had of Margaret's step-grandfather, Nicholas Wyeth, and New Street Farm and Framlingham as contrast to the horror surrounding

47

Margaret's other grandfather, George Jacobs Sr. Although Margaret had retracted her testimony, it was still used to send her grandfather Jacobs to the gallows on 19 Aug 1692.

The Trial of George Jacobs, Sr., 05 Aug 1692, was painted in 1855 by Thomkins Matteson

This painting depicts Margaret accusing her grandfather, George Jacobs Sr., of witchcraft at his trial in Salem Town in early Aug 1692. In reality, Margaret's accusation and recantation took place around their May examinations.[209] Still, Matteson's dramatization of events is vivid.[210] Standing behind the bench on the left is the court of oyer and terminer's chief justice, William Stoughton. In the center of the painting, Margaret points to her grandfather in an attempt to save her own life. Margaret's mother, Rebecca, with arms outstretched, is being held back. A girl and boy in the foreground are having fits, caused allegedly by Jacobs' specter.[211] John Hathorne, the judge hearing the accusation, is holding a paper while pointing to the clerk seated at the table. Judge John Hathorne was an ancestor to *Scarlet Letter* author Nathaniel Hawthorne. The author reportedly changed the spelling of his name to distance himself from the overzealous judge.[212]

As noted, the convictions, from the special court to hear (oyer) and to determine (terminer) witchcraft, that was created by Governor Phips in Jun 1692, relied heavily on spectral evidence.

However, when the governor's wife, Lady Mary Spencer Phips, was accused of witchcraft in Boston on 29 Sep 1692, Phips began to question the credibility of accusers whose only evidence was spectral. With public opinion changing, by mid-October of 1692, Phips ordered a halt, unless absolutely necessary, against starting further court proceedings or any further actions against those already arrested. On 29 Oct 1692, Phips officially ended Salem's special oyer and terminer court. On 07 Dec 1692, the courts of Massachusetts were reorganized into the Massachusetts Superior Court of Judicature and William Stoughton again became chief justice. Then on 16 Dec 1692, due to the crowded jails and numerous petitions, a supplementary act was passed authorizing a special sitting of the new Superior Court of Judicature, beginning on 03 Jan 1693, in Salem. However, going forward, Governor Phips insisted that the judges not accept spectral evidence.[213]

03 Jan 1693 was taken up with formally opening the court, swearing in the grand jury and counseling them that they were to put no weight on spectral evidence.

So, the next day, with the evidence of Goody Jacobs' specter distressing Elizabeth Hubbard declared inadmissible, Rebecca Jacobs' case was declared ignoramus for lack of evidence. Her daughter then approached the bar to face trial on her indictment for two counts of spectral tormenting during her examination on 11 May 1692. Margaret submitted the following document explaining why she retracted her confession of guilt.[214]

"The Humble Declaration of Margaret Jacobs unto the Honored Court now sitting at Salem showeth, that, whereas your poor and humble declarant, being closely confined here in Salem jail for the crime of witchcraft,—which crime, thanks be to the Lord! I am altogether ignorant of, as will appear at the great day of judgment,—may it please the honored Court, I was cried out upon by some of the possessed persons as afflicting them; whereupon I was brought to my examination; which persons at the sight of me fell down, which did very much startle and affright me. The Lord above knows I knew nothing in the least measure how or who afflicted them. They told me, without doubt I did, or else they would not fall down at me; they told me, if I would not confess, I should be put down into the dungeon, and would be hanged, but, if I would confess, I should have my life: the which did so affright me, with my own vile, wicked heart, to save my life, made me make the like confession I did, which confession, may it please the honored Court, is altogether false and untrue. The very first night after I had made confession, I was in such horror of conscience that I could not sleep, for fear the Devil should carry me away for telling such horrid lies. I was, may it please the honored Court, sworn to my confession, as I understand since; but then, at that time, was ignorant of it, not knowing what an oath did mean. The Lord, I hope, in whom I trust, out of the abundance of his mercy, will forgive me my false forswearing myself. **What I said was altogether false against my grandfather and Mr. Burroughs, which I did to save my life,** and to have my liberty: but the Lord, charging it to my conscience, made me in so much horror, that I could not contain myself before I had denied my confession, which I did, though I saw nothing but death before me; choosing rather death with a quiet conscience, than to live in such horror, which I could not suffer. Where, upon my denying my confession, I was committed to close prison, where I have enjoyed more felicity in spirit, a thousand times, than I did before in my enlargement. And now, may it please Your Honors, your declarant having in part given Your Honors a description of my condition, do leave it to Your Honors' pious and judicious discretions to take pity and compassion on my young and tender years, to act and do with me as the Lord above and Your Honors shall see good, having no friend but the Lord to plead my cause for me; not being guilty, in the least measure, of the crime of witchcraft, nor any other sin that deserves death from man. And your poor and humble declarant shall for ever pray, as she is bound in duty, for Your Honors' happiness in this life, and eternal felicity in the world to come. So prays Your Honors' declarant,

Margaret Jacobs."[215]

Many have noted that Margaret Jacobs was one of the bravest persons accused of witchcraft. She chose to die rather than live with a guilt-ridden conscience. Samuel Wardwell was the only other person to recant his confession. He was put to death on 22 Sep 1692.[216]

Margaret was found not guilty. However, both mother and daughter were not released until their jail fees were paid. Outrageously, those found guilty or not guilty had to pay for their jail room and board, chains and cuffs, fees to midwives and doctors for searching for witch marks, court costs and bail bonds, transportation to and from jail, and for every piece of paper including their pardon. The families of the executed were even charged for the salaries of hangmen.[217]

Rebecca remained in Salem jail until the family could afford to pay her fees two months later.[218]

Charles Wentworth Upham reported in his account on Salem witchcraft that Margaret got out of jail before her mother due to the kindness of a noble-hearted fisherman. Philip Gammon… "apparently a stranger, happened to hear of her case, and, touched with compassion, raised the money required, and released her."[219]

However, from the phenomenal research of Marilynne K. Roach, we learn Mr. Gammon was not as compassionate as Upham paints him. Just four months after her Feb jail release, on 05 Jun 1693, Philip Gammon had Margaret arrested for debt and brought from her job in Marblehead to the magistrates at the Ship Tavern in Salem. Although her father, George Jacobs Jr., was back from hiding, he pleaded for more time to repay the £3-12-0 lent Margaret for jail fees.[220]

Patience was not one of Gammon's virtues either. Just a couple of weeks later, on 27 Jun 1693, witnesses testified in court to Margaret Jacob's good intent. Her father reiterated his aim to repay Gammon's generosity, but he was hard pressed for cash owing to the many confiscations of his property by the courts due to witchcraft charges against his daughter, wife and father. The day before the court appearance, George Jr. began farming his father's land which the probate courts insisted was to be shared with his sister and her husband. The probate court refused to recognize George Jacobs Sr.'s second will, which had cut out his daughter and husband because they did not help him through his trials. The probate court also refused to pay Margaret the £10 legacy her grandfather had added to his second will. As far as the land went, George Jr. simply ignored the probate court and began its recovery. Perhaps that enabled him to repay Gammon for there were no more mentions in the records of the outstanding debt.[221]

One cannot help but wonder why Daniel Andrews did not pay his sister and niece's jail fees totaling £12.[222] According to many sources, Daniel was one of the most successful residents of Salem Village. Since he had escaped before he could be jailed on witchcraft charges, he did not suffer the property confiscations that ruined his neighbors.

As mentioned before, one theory for the outbreak of the witchcraft hysteria was bad blood between the Putnam and the Porter families of Salem Village. Through marriage, Daniel Andrews was a Porter. However, before he married Sarah Porter, the daughter of the wealthiest man in the Village, Daniel was already well off. From his apprenticeship with stepfather Nicholas Wyeth, Daniel emerged as a highly skilled craftsman. He owned land in Watertown. As noted, he sold some of his property there to his stepfather. In 1675, Daniel supervised the renovation and enlargement of Judge Jonathan Corwin's town house. Two years later he won the contract to build the town's meeting house. Through his construction business and wise land purchases, by 1695, he was the fourth wealthiest person in the village.[223] He taught school in his home, was a deputy to the General Court and was elected selectman (councilman) of Salem Village five times.[224]

Now a museum, the Witch House at 310 1/2 Essex Street is the only building still standing in Salem that was related to the witch trials. It was owned by trial magistrate Jonathan Corwin and renovated by Daniel Andrews.

In politics and in marriage, Daniel was at odds with the Putnams. The Putnam faction who supported Rev. Samuel Parris, led by Thomas Putnam Jr., was replaced on 16 Oct 1691 by a committee that included Daniel Andrews. The name of Dan: Andrew and other members of the new leadership, noted in the margin of Rev. Parris' church record of 01 Nov 1691, was viewed as an ominous foreshadowing of 1692 events.[225]

Many historians believe Thomas Putnam Jr. and Rev. Samuel Parris orchestrated the witchcraft trials as vengeance against people for whom they held a grudge. Indeed, Thomas Putnam entered 36 complaints against witch suspects... over twice as many as the next prolific accuser, his brother-in-law, Jonathan Walcott, at 17.[226] According to Rebecca Beatrice Brooks' blog *The History of Massachusetts,* Thomas Putnam testified against 43 people during the trials. Of those, 12 were executed, three were found guilty but pardoned, six were found not guilty, 13 were never indicted and two died in jail. The rest either evaded arrest or escaped from prison. Into the last group are Daniel Andrews and George Jacobs Jr. Rebecca Jacobs was found not guilty and George Jacobs Sr. was found guilty and executed.[227] Therefore, Thomas Putnam's fingerprints clearly hover over the horrendous sufferings of Daniel, his sister Rebecca and her father-in-law, her husband and her daughter.

It was on 14 May 1692, Thomas Putnam Jr. and Nathaniel Ingersoll filed a complaint for witchcraft against Daniel, his sister Rebecca, and her husband George Jacobs Jr. Ingersoll was the innkeeper in Salem Village. He also was related to the Putnams through his nephew, Jonathan Walcott.[228] The arrest warrant's second signature was that of the very same Jonathan Corwin whose house Daniel had remodeled several years earlier.[229]

"To the Constables in Salem
You are in theire Majests names hereby required to Apprehend and bring before us on Tuesday next being the seaventeenth day of this Instant moneth of May aboute ten of the Clock in the forenoon at the house of L't Natha[nbar] ll Ingersons of Salem Village, Daniell Andrew of Salem Village Bricklayer. George Jacobs Jun'r of Salem Village husbandman And Rebecka Jacobs the wife of said George Jacobs and Sarah Buckley the wife of W'm Buckley of Salem Village Cord wayner, And Mary withridge the daugter of sayd Buckley. who all stand Charged in behalfe of theire Majesties with high Suspition of Sundry acts of Witchcrafts by them donne or Committed on the Bodys of Ann putnam Marcy Lewis Mary Walcot and Abigail Williams and Others of Salem Village (Lately) whereby hurt hath been donn them. And hereof you are not to faile Dated Salem May the 14th. 1692

John. Hathorne } Assists
Jonathan. Corwin } Assists

[Reverse]

In prosecution of this warant I have apprehended and brought the bodyes of Sarah Buckley and Marye Withredg and Rebekah Jacobs all of Salem velage according to the tener of the within written warrant: and have Likewise made delegant sarch at the house of Daniell Andrew and at the house of Georg Jacobs for them Likewise but cannot find them

[*Jonathan Putnam*, Constable in Salem]"

So, we see, yet another one of Thomas Putnam's relatives deeply involved in bringing the accused to trial, was his cousin, Constable Jonathan Putnam.[230]

Charles Upham's book describes one jaw dropping revelation after another. When the constable and his officers arrived at the Jacobs' wooded home to make the arrests on the May 15th Sabbath day, they found Rebecca alone with her four children.[231] Her husband and brother had escaped overnight. With her eldest daughter, Margaret, already in jail, and her youngest child still nursing, Rebecca was inclined to resist arrest. However, rather deviously, Officer Putnam convinced

Rebecca to go by telling her she would soon be able to return home. As the policemen carted Rebecca off to jail, the children, who could, ran crying after their mother… futilely trying to catch the cart as it moved quickly out of their grasp. With their father and uncle gone, the heartbroken children were forced into the care of neighbors for ten long months while their mother was kept in irons in Salem jail.[232]

When she arrived in Salem jail on the 15th, Rebecca could not even fall into the arms of her daughter, Margaret. For recanting the confession browbeaten out of her four days before, that her grandfather was a wizard, the magistrates, insisting Margaret had relapsed into practicing witchcraft, put her in solitary confinement. It was called close prison because the room was such a small single room, often the prisoner could only stand.

Margaret's grandfather, George Jacobs Sr., had been incredulous at his first examination on 10 May 1692. Tradition indicates Judge Jonathan Corwin's house was the inquisition site. [233] Although he was quite elderly and walked on two sticks, George's mind was sharp and quick. His first words were, "Well, let us hear who are they and what are they." When Abigail Williams testified and threw her usual fits, George expressed his contempt for her and the other accusers with a skeptical laugh. The magistrates, as was their custom, took the girls' words for total truth and reprimanded George. Later George angrily, yet amusingly snapped, "You tax me for a wizard. You may as well tax me for a buzzard. I have done no harm."[234]

The next day at Beadle's tavern on May 11, Margaret added her voice to those falsely implicating her grandfather.[235] On 12 May 1692, George Jacobs Sr. was transferred to Boston jail.[236]

Until the 13th, Margaret reported seeing specters. However, when she learned her grandfather would hang, it overwhelmed her. No longer concerned only for her own self-preservation, and fearing eternal damnation more than the magistrates, she denied her earlier confession.[237]

On May 16, although Rebecca Jacobs was being held in jail, and her husband, George Jr., had departed for parts unknown, Susanna Sheldon reported being threatened by specters of Rebecca and George Jacobs Jr. Unbelievably, when judges questioned Rebecca on Wednesday, 18 May 1692, the afflicted accusers did not even know who she was. Finally, one of them cried, "Don't you know Jacobs, the old witch?" To create a diversion to cover their mistake, the girls immediately fell down and began writhing in unholy contortions on the floor.[238] [239]

On 20 May 1692, Susanna Sheldon switched the identity of the spirit tormenting her from Rebecca to her brother, Daniel Andrews, who fled the country to save his life. Although some historians believe Daniel returned by the 29th of June or the 4th of July to aid his neighbor, Peter Cloyse's sister-in-law, Rebecca Towne Nurse,[240] [241] the two documents with Daniel's name on them are undated. It is likely his statement that he was "ready to testify on oath" for Rebecca Nurse was made 24 Mar 1692.[242] Daniel's signature, among the 39 on an undated petition declaring Rebecca Nurse was innocent, was probably done in May before his arrest.[243]

However, no one could save Rebecca Nurse from the gallows. The 19 Jul 1692 demise of the pious 71-year-old grandmother was said to influence public opinion away from further witch executions.[244] Sadly, the change did not come soon enough to help George Jacobs Sr. During the sitting of the special court of oyer and terminer on 05 Aug 1692, George was found guilty and condemned to hang with former Salem Village minister George Burroughs, John Procter and his wife Elizabeth, John Willard of Salem Village, and Martha Carrier of Andover.[245]

After George's sentencing, the sheriff seized over £89 worth of livestock and goods from his farm. The confiscations included five cows, five pigs, one horse, several chickens, eight loads of hay, 60 bushels of Indian corn, apples enough for 12 barrels of cider, bedding, two brass kettles, and more than a few pieces of pewter and furniture. Also appropriated was 12 shillings in coin, a gold thumb ring, and, because it technically belonged to George, the sheriff took his wife Mary's wedding ring. With difficulty, she eventually got her wedding ring back but had to buy some of her own foodstuffs in order to eat. Fortunately, she had neighbors who helped her through since her relatives could not or would not. As shown, son, George Jacobs Jr. was a fugitive. His wife was in jail. Their other child, Ann, and her husband were of so little help, when George Sr. remade his will on 12 Aug 1692, Ann's bequest was eliminated. Apparently, George had learned of his brave granddaughter's confession withdrawal. For Margaret, he had the scribe squeeze between two paragraphs, a legacy to her of £10 in silver.[246]

Witch Trials Memorial bench for George Jacobs installed in Salem Town in 1992.

On the day before the 19 Aug 1692 execution, Margaret was allowed time to seek forgiveness from Rev. George Burroughs for lying about him, her grandfather and John Willard. Rev. Burroughs kindly absolved her and they prayed together. The next day from atop a ladder, with a rope around his neck, Rev. Burroughs, spoke affectingly of his innocence. Many of those gathered were so moved to tears that officials became concerned the crowd might stop the capital punishment. Once Burroughs' life was choked out, to calm the disruptive people, Cotton Mather reminded them Burroughs was guilty as charged. The hangings went on until all the condemned, except for pregnant Mrs. Proctor, were executed. The bodies were then cut down and dragged by horse to a nearby ditch. There they were so hastily buried, that the ground did not fully cover them.[247]

Some believe 15-year-old George Jacobs III, later removed his grandfather's body from the common pit and reburied it at his home. In the mid-1800s, a single grave of an infirm, toothless old man was found on the grounds of the Jacobs' farm. When a developer removed the grave in the 1950s, various Danvers' historical societies cared for George's bones until the 300th anniversary of the witch trials. The tercentennial committee's funeral for George Jacobs Sr. and his interment in the Nurse Homestead burying ground was poignant and fitting.[248]

The day after her grandfather's execution, Margaret wrote about her change of heart to her father. She referred to her poor, crazy mother and to her uncle D.A. Margaret obviously knew where her father and Uncle Daniel Andrews were hiding.

From the Dungeon in Salem Prison.   "August 20, 1692.

"Honored Father,—After my humble duty remembered to you, hoping in the Lord of your good
health, as, blessed be God! I enjoy, though in abundance of affliction, being close confined here in a
loathsome dungeon: the Lord look down in mercy upon me, not knowing how soon I shall be put to
death, by means of the afflicted persons; my grandfather having suffered already, and all his estate
seized for the king. The reason of my confinement is this: I having, through the magistrates'
threatenings, and my own vile and wretched heart, confessed several things contrary to my
conscience and knowledge, though to the wounding of my own soul; (the Lord pardon me for it!)
but, oh! the terrors of a wounded conscience who can bear? But, blessed be the Lord! he would not
let me go on in my sins, but in mercy, I hope, to my soul, would not suffer me to keep it any longer:
but I was forced to confess the truth of all before the magistrates, who would not believe me; but it
is their pleasure to put me in here, and God knows how soon I shall be put to death. Dear father, let
me beg your prayers to the Lord on my behalf, and send us a joyful and happy meeting in heaven.
My mother, poor woman, is very crazy, and remembers her kind love to you, and to uncle; viz., D.A.
So, leaving you to the protection of the Lord, I rest, your dutiful daughter,   *Margaret Jacobs.*"[249]

Margaret knew not when her death would come, but having confessed her perjury to the
magistrates, she was fearless. She had courageously freed her soul. Her body was, however,
imprisoned in gruesome conditions. In 1686, Englishman John Dunton said in letters from New
England, "a prison is the grave of the living"… "the suburbs of Hell."[250] In the chronicle, *Crime
and Punishment in Early Massachusetts, 1620-1692*, "un-sanitary" is the mildest word author
Edwin Powers uses to describe those colonial institutions. They were dark, unventilated, freezing
in winter and sweltering in summer. The smells of unwashed bodies and human waste were
overwhelming. Salem Jail, where Margaret and her mother were confined, shows as "L" on
Upham's preceding map. The prison's location on the banks of the North river, meant it was a
continuously damp breeding ground for disease due to rats, vermin and contagious diseases. It
was so overcrowded, many of those accused of witchcraft were sent to jails in Boston and
Ipswich.[251][252] For these reasons, Rebecca Fox wrote letters begging for her daughter's release
before she died from the squalor of her imprisonment.

Frances Hill wrote in her powerful narrative, *A Delusion of Satan*, that because the accused witches
were the worst of the worst, they were kept in the dungeons below the jail. As enemies of God
and mankind, they were treated with deliberate cruelty. Doctors and midwifes sexually abused
them by prodding their most private places for witch marks that could be suckled by demons.[253]
The prisoners were restrained by iron cuffs chained to the wall so their apparitions could not torture
the afflicted while their bodies were in jail. They were underfed, kept thirsty to elicit confessions
easier, and were tortured beyond comprehension. John Proctor wrote to Cotton Mather's father,
Increase, to tell of the method used to extract a confession from two young men, one of whom was
his son, William Proctor. The boys were tied neck and heels together until blood ran out their
noses. When testimony was given to show fraud on the part of the accusers, it was ignored. Sarah
Nurse saw Goodwife Bibber, an accuser, pull out pins and stick them into the afflicted children.
When an afflicted person cried out against Samuel Willard, pastor of the Old South Church in
Boston, the accuser was evicted from the court for striking at a person too high in authority.[254]

As previously mentioned, the ultimate strike too high was against Governor William Phips' wife.
When Lady Phips was accused of witchcraft, her husband abolished the lower court of oyer and
terminer that used torture and fraud to send innocents to the gallows. Phips put in motion a new
court where Thomas Danforth, skeptical of spectral evidence, could back up Chief Justice

William Stoughton. Stoughton was so supportive of spectral evidence, to protest its ban, he occasionally refused to come to court. Phips' new court, the Superior Court of Judicature, continues today as the Supreme Judicial Court. It is the oldest appellate court in continuous existence in the Western Hemisphere.[255]

Since Thomas Danforth clearly had a change of heart between his court appearances in Apr 1692 and January 1693, it was ironic that Arthur Miller used Danforth's name as the tyrannical judge in his famous play, *The Crucible*. In reality, Miller's character most resembled Judge William Stoughton. Miller explained in his introduction the fact to fiction changes he found necessary:

> "A NOTE ON THE HISTORICAL ACCURACY OF THIS PLAY
> This play is not history in the sense in which the word is used by the academic historian. Dramatic purposes have sometimes required many characters to be fused into one; the number of girls involved in the "crying-out" has been reduced; Abigail's age has been raised; while there were several judges of almost equal authority, I have symbolized them all in Hathorne and Danforth."[256]

Written in 1953, Miller compared the Salem witchcraft trials to Senator Joseph McCarthy's hunt for Communists in the early 1950s. For the most part, Miller portrayed Rev. Samuel Parris as he was considered in real life by the people of Salem Village. They called him an "instrument of our miseries."[257] Like other leaders in history who spread fear and hatred of groups of people, Miller showed that Parris had a huge ego and was obsessed with his reputation. As a minister and a court prosecutor, Parris helped to convict the majority of those accused of witchcraft. Parris and his followers were so consumed with destroying the devil in the darkness, they ignored Christ's commandment in the light of John 15:12 – "Love each other as I have loved you."

Miller's dark metaphor was a powerful commentary on how irrational fears, created by using dubious tactics and inconclusive evidence, can lead to mass hysteria and paranoia. The 20 people executed during the witch hunt of the late 17th century pales in comparison to the Holocaust of the 20th century. However, the parallels to the irrational hatred and fear of the Jewish people that resulted in the systematic extermination of six million Jews and millions of non-aryans is nevertheless apparent. Now, at the beginning of the 21st century, many in our contemporary society are alarmed to again see leaders creating division by using fear tactics and twisted propaganda to stir hate and unwarranted fear of many different groups of people.

Before her death in 1698, Rebecca Parks Andrews Wyeth Fox and her children walked in one of the darkest periods of American history. Quoting John 3:19, "This is the judgment, that the Light has come into the world, and men loved the darkness rather than the Light, for their deeds were evil." Whatever the causes – superstition, sickness, a lack of compassion, failure of the law, jealous rivalries, child abuse, feuds over land – they combined to create a whirling torrent that turned the world upside down. Those who would not confess deeds they did not commit, were put to death for their honesty. Those who implicated others, lived to dishonestly implicate more.

Eventually, Rev. Joseph Green replaced Rev. Parris. They were as different as day and night... as distinctive as light and shadow. Joseph, grandson of Thomas Fox's second wife, Ellen, was from Cambridge. Whereas Parris' journals were filled with ominous, threatening notes, Green's records were filled with warm, loving thoughts. His leadership style brought much sorely needed healing to the Village. At Green's death at age 40, Deacon Edward Putnam entered in the church record a tribute to him as "the choicest flower and greenest olive-tree in the garden of our Lord here cut down in its prime and flourishing estate."[258]

Another flower cut down too soon, was Mary Wyeth. As soon as Rebecca Jacobs was freed from Salem jail in 1693, her mother's heart was hurt again by the death of her third husband, Thomas Fox, on 25 Apr 1693. As Mary's will indicates, her mother then turned her attentions to nursing Mary. Rebecca Parks Andrews Wyeth Fox died in May 1698.[259] Her daughter, Mary, died shortly thereafter. Mary's words [transcribed by Claire Barker of the Suffolk Records Society] paint a heartwarming picture of a very loving mother who was very much loved.[260] Mary's will also shows her love for her siblings whether half or full.

> "In the Name of God Amen I Mary Wyeth of Cambridge in the county of Middlesex in the Province of the Massachusetts Bay in New England single woman being at present of sound Judgment and Memory though as to my Body very weak and languishing and dayly expecting my dissolution, Do therefore make and ordain, this my last will and testament as followeth.
>
> First and principally I Commit my immortall soule into the hands of God and my Body to the Earth to be decently Buried at the discretion of such persons as are hereafter named, And forasmuch as it hath pleased God in his holy **Providence lately to bereave me of my dear and tender Mother who tooke the care of me in my long and languishing sickness**, I Do therefore earnestly desire and request that my loving and Christian friends, namely Deacon Walter Hasting, John Gove and my brother Daniel Andrew (whom I do Nominate and appoint my executor to this my Will) would take the like Care of me during the little time I have to Continue in this World and of my decent Buriall after my Decease Also what shall appear to be my due from the estate of my Father Wyeth and my Mother Fox my will is it be disposed of to my **five Brothers Thomas Andrew, Daniel Andrew, Nicolas (sic) Wyeth, John Wyeth and William Wyeth** and to **my sisters Sarah Fiske and Rebecca Jacobs** and to my Cousins Thomas Frost and Rebecca Cooledge and that it be disposed to all the persons above named according to the discretion of my executor above mentioned.
>
> In Witness whereof I the above named Mary Wyeth, to this my last will and testament set my hand and seale this twenty sixth day of May Anno Domini: one thousand six hundred and ninety eight Annoque RR Guilielmi Tertii Anglia & Decimo [And in the year of the reign of the King William the third [&] ten = 13 Feb 1698-12 Feb 1699]

Signed Sealed and Published   The Marke
In presence of us   of *Mary Wyeth*
Josiah Torrey
Walter Hastings Jr.
Jonathan Remington

Probated 17 Jun 1698"

Soon after Daniel Andrew probated Mary's will, their brother, Nicholas Wyeth Jr. married Deborah Parker on 30 Jun 1698 in Watertown. Not surprisingly, family friend and son of Nicholas Danforth, the honorable Judge Thomas Danforth, Esquire, performed the ceremony.[261] Interestingly, on 01 Oct 1873 the Danforth line merged with the Wyeth line when Nicholas Danforth's 6th great granddaughter, Jennie Elizabeth Danforth, married Nicholas Wyeth's 5th great grandson, Orrin Judson Wyeth, in Broadway, Union County, Ohio.

This photo of Orrin and Jennie Danforth Wyeth is courtesy of their great niece, Erma Lockwood Hutchman.

Daniel Andrew, along with two of his sons, died of the highly contagious disease of smallpox in the epidemic of 1702-1703.[262] It was rather ironic that the same man, Rev. Cotton Mather, whose writings helped create the fear and suspicion leading to the witchcraft hysteria, also had much to do with finding a cure for smallpox. Before going into the ministry, he first trained as a doctor.[263] The first inoculation in American history was completed in Boston in 1721 by Dr. Zabdiel Boylston based on his and Rev. Mather's research.[264]

Having little, if any, natural resistance to contagious diseases, Native Americans were disproportionately affected during outbreaks of smallpox.[265] Due to their great cultural differences, relationships between the Indians and the Puritans became increasingly inhumane on both sides. As previously mentioned, the war in which John Wyeth Sr. was involved was one of the most savage in American History. By the end of that First Indian war in 1676, over 3,000 Native Americans and over 1,000 Colonists were killed. Practically every home in Massachusetts suffered a loss.[266] However, for the Wyeth family, death at the hands of Indians came almost 27 years after King Philip's war. The youngest son of Nicholas, William, fell prey to angry Native Americans, during Queen Anne's War, in the autumn of 1703.[267] His tragic death at age 46 orphaned his two young daughters, Deborah and Martha Wyeth.

HEROISM AND SACRIFICE

After King Philip's and Queen Anne's Wars, the next major American conflict was also with Native Americans. Nicholas Wyeth's 3rd great grandson Phinehas Stearns (1736-1798); 2nd great grandson, Samuel Cutter (1740-1820); great grandsons, Jonas Wyeth Sr. (1730-1813), Jason Winship Jr. (1730-1775); and William Gamage (1714-1783), valiantly served in the French and Indian War. Although it began in 1753, war was not formally declared until 1756. It ended in 1763. This long conflict started a period of Wyeth and Wythe families being of service to, and sacrificing for, America that continues to this day.[268] [269]

"The Shot Heard 'Round The World" is engraved below this statue of the farmer / minuteman that marks the 19 Apr 1775 North Bridge stand of the Patriots in Concord, MA.

Some 20 years after the French and Indian War, Jonas Wyeth Sr. continued his service to America when he fought as a minuteman in the first battles of the American Revolution on 19 Apr 1775. On the same day, while he sat in Cooper's Tavern in Menotomy, Massachusetts, innocently celebrating the birth of his first son, Jason Winship Jr., and his brother-in-law, Jabez Wyman, were brutally killed by British soldiers.[270] [271]

The battles of Lexington and Concord are hailed as the birthplace of liberty because the opposing forces faced each other in traditional battle order.[272] However, much of the hostility on that first day of armed conflict between the Colonies and England, took place in Lincoln, Menotomy, Cambridge, Somerville, and Charlestown after the British Army attempted to capture the Massachusetts Militia's military supplies which had been in storage in Concord.[273] Before being renamed Arlington in 1867, Menotomy was the 2nd precinct of Cambridge.[274] Somerville was then part of Cambridge as well. In the Cambridge region, more people on both sides of the conflict were killed or wounded than in any other fighting of the day.[275]

57

Burdened by increasing taxes and diminishing liberties, of the over 100 Cambridge area patriots willing to risk everything on 19 Apr 1775 for an abstract ideal called democracy, at least 14 were descendants of Nicholas Wyeth.

In addition to Jonas Wyeth Sr. (1730-1813), other militia men, descended from Nicholas, under the command of Colonel Thomas Gardner and Captain Samuel Thatcher on 19 Apr 1775, included Joshua Gamage, drummer, (1753-1843); Daniel Prentice (1744-1796); Thomas Prentice (1752-1800); Samuel Prentice (1758-1795); Nathaniel Prentice (1743-1817); John Prentice (1748-1806); Ebenezer Wyeth Jr. (1727-1799); Noah Wyeth (1742-1811); Joseph Wyeth (1751-1837); and Jonas Wyeth Jr. (1757-1817).[276]   The Cambridge muster roll says they marched toward Concord early in the morning. They had been alerted hours before that a British column was on the move from Boston to capture and destroy the colonists' military supplies stored there. William Dawes had carried the message as he sped across Cambridge Common in front of the Wyeth home.[277]

The first confrontation of the Revolutionary War occurred on Lexington Green at 5:00 am. The Lexington Militia's captain, John Parker, initially ordered his men to disperse after seeing his troops were vastly outnumbered by the British. However, Thomas Fessenden III (1741-1804) testified he saw a British officer fire the first shot.[278] In the battle that followed, eight of Captain Parker's men were killed and another nine wounded.[279] With a couple of the Redcoats only slightly injured, the British Army easily moved on to attempt the completion of their mission at Concord. There at the North Bridge, at 9:30 am, after the British killed two Acton minutemen, the Patriots returned fire and killed two of their adversaries. The Redcoats, shocked that the Americans held their ground, scattered and retreated to Concord town. There the quarter mile long column of British regulars began their hazardous march back to Boston.[280]

Formed for a surprise attack along the Battle Road near the Lincoln / Lexington town line, Captain Parker rallied his men to avenge those who had fallen at dawn on Lexington Common. Newly arrived from Cambridge, 77 of Captain Thatcher's militia joined 120 Lexington men for the 2:00 pm ambush. Parker's Revenge was part of the long string of attacks by the Americans that inflicted heavy casualties on the British.[281] [282]

Parker's Revenge took place on the Battle Road here at the Lincoln / Lexington town line.

Participating in the running battle against the retreating British soldiers were minutemen from the Menotomy precinct of Cambridge, including Nicholas' descendants Andrew Cutter (1757-1794) and William Winship III (1756-1821), both under Captain Benjamin Locke, and Thomas Hunt (1754-1808) under Captain Samuel Barnard in Watertown.[283] [284] [285]

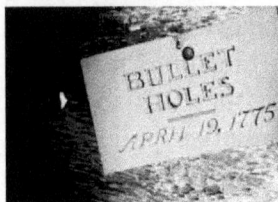

As the road from Concord and Lexington to Boston went directly through Menotomy, there occurred some of the fiercest fighting on the first day of the American Revolution. Civilian, Jason Russell (1716-1775), the husband of Nicholas' great granddaughter, Elizabeth Winship Russell, helped minutemen set up a defense near his home to intercept the British for a skirmish. However, the Redcoats easily overtook the lame 59-year-old Jason as he attempted to run for the safety of his house. On his doorstep, he was shot twice and bayoneted several times. The bullet holes are still visible in the home now owned by the Arlington Historical Society.[286]

Ten minutes away, in Cooper's Tavern, Elizabeth Winship Russell's first cousin, Jason Winship Jr. (1730-1775), made the fatal mistake of toasting the recent birth of his only son while British soldiers were looking to get even for the attacks on their retreating columns. Jason had lost his first wife in childbirth as well as three children who died the day they were born. Although he and his second wife, Mary Piper, had one five-year-old daughter, the joy of having a son at age 44 was certainly a cause for celebration.[287] However, the timing could not have been worse.[288] While Jason sat drinking Flip with his sister Lydia's husband, Jabez Wyman (1736-1775), the incensed Redcoats fired over 100 bullets into the building, smashed through the tavern door and savagely beat and stabbed

This Arlington marker at the corner of Medford St. and Mass. Ave. gives the location of Cooper's tavern.

the two men to death.[289] Grief, rather than joy, was the overriding emotion when baby Jason Winship III, was baptized four days later on 23 Apr 1775.[290]

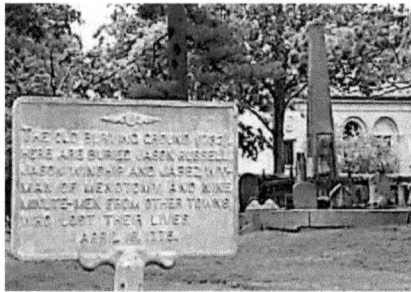

In Arlington's Old Burying Ground, the obelisk behind this sign marks the graves of Jason Russell, Jason Winship Jr. and Jabez Wyman. Also listed on the obelisk are the names of local men who served in the military during the Revolution. The word "Patriot" is etched after the names of the three civilians.

Several of the minutemen who fought on that first day of the war, went on to fight in the Battle of Bunker Hill on 17 Jun 1775. Although many of their names are lost to history, we do know Joshua Gamage (1753-1843) had the added distinction of continuing to serve as a drummer in Colonel

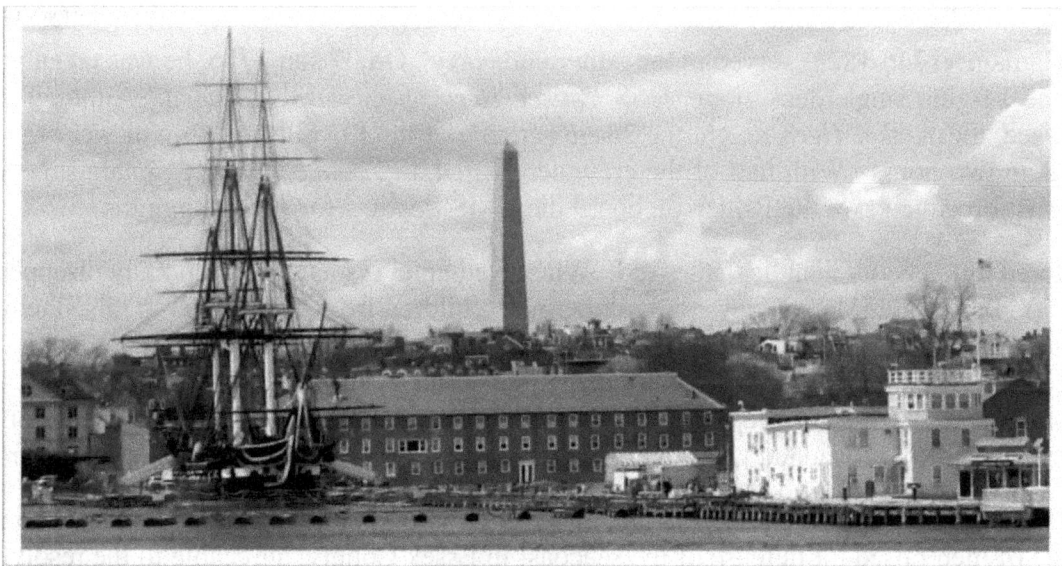
View from Boston Harbor of the USS *Constitution* and the Bunker Hill Monument sitting at the top of Breed's Hill in Charlestown, MA.

Gardner's Regiment during the battle. Joshua was 90 years old when he died from over excitement while attending the Bunker Hill Monument dedication ceremony on 17 Jun 1843.[291] Two of

Joshua's brothers, Daniel and Samuel, fought in the Revolution as well. All the Gamage descendants shown are related to Nicholas Wyeth's granddaughter, Deborah Wyeth Gamage.

Although volume six of *Massachusetts Soldiers and Sailors of the Revolutionary War* gives records for six Daniels, their 1780 description fits Daniel Gamage (1761-1791). He was age 20, light complexion; hair, light; eyes, blue; occupation, laborer or farmer; stature 5 ft. 10 in.[292]

Apparently, Daniel followed his brother Joshua, the drummer, to Fryeburg, Maine. A receipt dated 14 Mar 1781 shows a bounty paid to credit the town of Fryeburg for Daniel enlisting in the Continental Army for a term of three years.[293] However, on 12 Jun 1781, Daniel engaged for a term of three years for the town of Cambridge. Later Cambridge, not Fryeburg, received credit for Daniel's enlistment.[294] On 11 Jul 1781, Daniel signed a receipt acknowledging a bounty paid him for recruiting a black Cambridge man named William Newport to serve alongside him for three years in the Continental Army.[295] Daniel was a private on the West Point, New York, garrison muster rolls for Sep 1781 to Jan 1782 of Captain Sylvanus Smith's Company of Colonel Rufus Putnam's 5th Regiment. At the time of his death in 1791, his last will and testament showed he worked as a mariner.[296]

In that will, Daniel left money to his brother Samuel Gamage (1751-1832) a barrel maker in Hudson, New York. During the Revolution, Samuel was a lieutenant in Captain Gray's Regiment of Artillery and served one year as a lieutenant of Marines on board the frigate *Dean*.[297]

This photo of Lt. Samuel Gamage is from Arabella Gamage Morton's 1906 book.

Arabella Morton's book shows Daniel Gamage, born in Cambridge on 16 Mar 1734 to Joshua and Deborah Wyeth Gamage, also was a soldier in the Revolution. Under Captain John Walton, Daniel was dispatched twice to guard the troops on 27 Jul 1778 and on 04 Sep 1778.[298]

John Gamage (1746-1824) served in the American Navy. On 07 Jun 1776, he was taken prisoner from the 14-gun, single-deck sloop, USS *Yankee Hero* by the HMS *Milford*. Although greatly outclassed, the *Yankee Hero* fought the 28-gun frigate of the Royal Navy ship of war bravely for more than two hours. With half of the crew debilitated, the *Yankee Hero's* captain surrendered. John was forced to serve the British on board the HMS *Renown* for several months.[299] [300]

John fared much better than his father did. When Nathaniel Gamage mysteriously disappeared in 1750, John's mother, Mary Norwood, took her nine children from Cambridge to raise them in her hometown of Sandy Bay (Rockport), Essex, Massachusetts. Nathaniel never returned. Many believed he was seized by a press gang (a method used to secure men for the English Navy). Losing her son, in the same method as she lost her husband, must have been horrifying for Mary. The joy of John's return added years to his mother's life… Mary lived to be almost 100 years old.[301]

Joshua Gamage (1741-1810), another one of Mary Norwood and Nathaniel Gamage's sons, was on a list of men raised for defense of the seacoast in Essex County, agreeable to the resolve of 27 Jun 1775, and stationed at Gloucester under 1st Lt. Joseph Lane. Joshua also served from 19 Jul 1775 to 31 Dec 1775 as a private in Captain Joseph Whipple's Essex County Company.[302]

Several members of the Stearns family served during the Revolution. Particularly noteworthy were Colonel Abijah Stearns (1724-1783) of Lunenburg and Captain Phinehas Stearns (1736-

1798) of Watertown. Abijah was commissioned head of the 8th Worcester Regiment of the Massachusetts Militia on 07 Feb 1776.[303] After the French and Indian War (Seven Years' War), Phinehas participated in the Boston Tea Party. Due to his efforts at Lexington and Concord, he was promoted to captain to lead a company at Dorchester Heights that ended the Siege of Boston.[304]

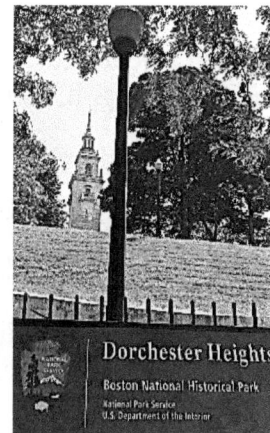

Dorchester Heights
Boston National Historical Park
National Park Service
U.S. Department of the Interior

Captain Joshua Bowman (1747-1780), a graduate of Harvard, served in the Continental Army as a captain of dragoons (horse-mounted infantry). On 29 Mar 1780 with Lt. Gen. Charles Cornwallis' troops within two miles of Charlestown, South Carolina, a combination of several Patriot units went out to repel the British in a skirmish that lasted until sunset. The next day, 30 Mar 1780, a large body of British grenadiers and infantry crossed the Ashley River. While attempting to stop their advance, Captain Bowman was shot from his horse. The Harvard graduate is often confused with another North Carolinian captain of the same name who was wounded at Charleston and killed at Ramsour's Mill on 20 Jun 1780.[305] Sadly, Captain Joshua Bowman's son, Nathaniel, was orphaned at his father's death. Nathaniel was brought up by his Bowman grandparents in Cambridge and was also educated at Harvard.[306]

Another one of Nicholas Wyeth's descendants to achieve officer status in the Revolutionary War was Thomas Hunt (1754-1808). Thomas began his career as a private. He marched in the Watertown Militia on the alarm of 19 Apr 1775 in Capt. Samuel Barnard's Company.[307] [308] [309] Thomas was promoted to sergeant and fought under Watertown's Captain Abner Craft in the Battle of Bunker Hill on 17 Jun 1775.[310] He then served first as a lieutenant and then as a captain in Col. Henry Jackson's Regiment of the Continental Army. He was wounded on 16 Jul 1779 at the Battle of Stony Point, New York, and again on 14 Oct 1781 at the Siege of Yorktown. Thomas stayed in the Army after the Revolution. He was eventually promoted to colonel and served at that rank until his death at Fort Bellefontaine, Missouri.[311]

Daniel Sawin Jr. (1757-1834) also marched as a minuteman on the alarm of 19 Apr 1775 in Captain Samuel Barnard's Watertown Company.[312] On 04 Mar 1776, his company was ordered by General Washington to reinforce the army at the taking of Dorchester Heights. Daniel's brothers, John (1759-1786) and Samuel (1762-1849) were active in the military as well.[313] As will be noted later, Samuel was helpful in obtaining a pension for his cousin's wife, Elizabeth E. Smith Wyeth.

Andrew Cutter (1757-1794) of Cambridge went on from the 19 Apr 1775 Alarm to serve as a private in Captain Benjamin Lock's Co. of Lt. Colonel William Bond's 37th Regiment. He was 18 years old and 5 ft. 9 in. tall when he enlisted on 04 May 1775. Starting with his name on a Prospect Hill return dated 06 Oct 1775, Andrew's military service continued in 1776 and 1777.[314]

Nehemiah Cutter (1753-1828) was a private in Capt. John Minott's Co., Col. Dike's Regiment. His service from 5 Jan 1777 to 01 Mar 1777 was credited to the town of Cambridge.[315]

After his service in the Lexington and Concord Alarm, William Winship III (1756-1821) of Menotomy enlisted on the same day and in the same company as his cousin, Andrew Cutter. He was 18 years old and 5 ft. 8 in. tall. Also, he was on the Prospect Hill return of 06 Oct 1775 with Andrew. Then with his cousin, Daniel Sawin Jr., William marched at the request of General

Washington to fortify Dorchester Heights above Boston on 04 Mar 1776. On 15 Aug 1777, William re-enlisted in Cambridge to serve in Capt. Joseph Fuller's Co., Col. Samuel Bullard's Regiment. At Stillwater, he was credited with over three months service and 240 miles of travel.[316]

Jason Russell Jr. (1742-1825) moved to Mason, New Hampshire many years before his father's death at the hands of British soldiers on his own Menotomy doorstep. Nevertheless, Jason Jr. was a patriot like his father. Jason enlisted in Wilton, New Hampshire and spent the winter of 1777-1778 encamped at Valley Forge.[317]

Also, according to volume 12 of *Mass. Soldiers and Sailors of the Revolutionary War,* several members of the Prentice family were active in the military after their service on 19 Apr 1775.[318]

The same is true for the Wyeths who show in those same Revolutionary War books. Minutemen Ebenezer Wyeth Jr. (1727-1799), Jonas Wyeth Sr. (1730-1813), Jonas Wyeth Jr. (1757-1817), Joseph Wyeth (1751-1837), and Noah Wyeth (1742-1811) are in volume 17. Also, in that volume are Rev. John Wyeth (1743-1811) and Ebenezer Wyeth III (1752-1836). John was credited with £6 cash for serving on an expedition to Canada in Jul 1776.[319] Ebenezer III (labeled Jr.) was ordered by Col. Thatcher to appear in Cambridge on 31 Oct 1778 with three days' provisions, armed and equipped to march to Boston to serve under General Heath until 09 Nov 1778.[320]

Newell Convers "N. C." Wyeth, *The Old Continentals*, 1922, oil on canvas, Permanent Collection of The Hill School, Pottstown, Pennsylvania. Used with their permission. Courtesy of Louis Jeffries, The Hill School Archivist.

Although volume 17 references that service for Ebenezer III and also states Jonas Wyith (sic) was a seaman, it makes no mention of their Continental Army service with brother, Joshua, in Captain Eliphalet Newell's Co. of Colonel Henry Knox's Artillery Regiment of the Massachusetts Line.

For that portion of the three Wyeth brothers' service, The Gilder Lehrman Institute of American History holds an abstract written by Captain Newell in Dec 1775 for service in his company. The document shows Jonas Jr. (1757-1817) received pay for 15 days of service. Ebenezer III (1752-1836) and Joshua Wyeth Sr. (1758-1829) were each paid for 11 days of service.[321]

The rest of the brothers' Continental Army service is detailed in pension applications. Of which, Joshua completed applications both in 1818 and in 1820. Here are abbreviated transcriptions.[322]

"State of Ohio, Champaign County –
Personally appeared before me John Runyan Esquire an associate judge of the court of common pleas

.... Joshua Wyeth and upon his corporal oath made the following declaration (to wit) –
That he, the said Joshua Wyeth, sometime in the latter part of the summer or the beginning of the fall of the **year 1775**, enlisted as a private soldier in the company of **Captain Newell** belonging to the **First Massachusetts Regiment** commanded by **Colonel Henry Knox** in the Massachusetts Line on the Continental Establishment in the Revolutionary War and that he served in said regiment in the capacity of a private soldier for the **term of 12 months.** Then he was permitted by his officers to become a **laborer in the Artificers of the Army** in the Revolutionary War and that he served as a laborer for the artificers as aforesaid for the **further time of 12 months.** When his time of service expired, he was honorably discharged at **Springfield in the state of Massachusetts.** Which said discharge has since been destroyed by fire. And the said Joshua Wyeth further saith that he is near 60 years of age, **has had 21 children** born in lawful wedlock. 17 of whom are yet alive. That he is a resident of the county of Champaign in the state of Ohio and from his reduced circumstances, he greatly needs the assistance of his country for support.

Sworn and subscribed ... the 30th day of April AD 1818."

Records show Joshua received $96 annually beginning 30 Apr 1818 under the act of Congress of 18 Mar 1818. It must have been necessary to reapply under the act of 01 May 1820. The pension again was approved and continued to Sep 1828... the period just before Joshua's death.[323] His 22 Jan 1829 death date is noted on the Pension Roll.[324]

"State of Ohio, Clark County – Supreme Court of the term of July AD 1820 – On this 21st day of July in the year of our Lord 1820, personally appeared in open court, being a court of record, for the said state and county, **Joshua Wyeth aged 61 years, nine months and 14 days**, resident in said county, who being first duly sworn according to law doth on his oath declare that he served in the Revolutionary War as follows –

"I was on board the East India Company ships in the harbor of Boston and **assisted in throwing the tea overboard** on the 18th (sic) December in the year AD 1773, **being then 15 years of age.** That I was a volunteer in the **Battle of Bunker Hill in June AD 1775. I afterwards enlisted into and served in Capt. Eliphalet Newell's Company** in Colonel Knox's Regiment, Massachusetts Line in the Artillery Corps for 12 months in the Continental Service.

I also after that period belonged and served as blacksmith in the corps of artificers under Captain Saxon.

I also further swear that during the time I was in service as aforesaid, **I was in the Battle of Flatbush on Long Island** and in the **skirmish at Harlem Heights** and **at the Battle of the White Plains in 1776**.

> That my original declaration as appears by my certificate was made on the 30th day of April AD 1818 and the number of my pension certificate is 12,007….

> … I am by **occupation a blacksmith** but that **from wounds**, age and debility I am unable to pursue it for a livelihood. My family consists of **a third wife** by the name of Elizabeth and five children living at home, Anna aged 11; William aged 9; Nelson aged 6, Adaline aged 4 and Amanda aged 2 …

> Sworn to and declared on this 21 day of July AD 1820…."

Interestingly, Joshua swore in open court that he assisted in throwing tea overboard on 16 Dec 1773. It certainly was not something he had to say in order to qualify for a pension. His oath makes his presence on the East India Company's ships even more definite than his 1827 Timothy Flint interview in Cincinnati. The year before Flint's interview appeared in the papers, another widely circulated news item called Joshua "a temperate, hardy old veteran" who "often boasts of the 'Boston tea party.'" No evidence exists that the term "Boston Tea Party" was used before Joshua used it in the mid-1820s. So, it is likely the credit of coining the phrase "Boston Tea Party" belongs to Joshua Wyeth.[325]

Through the years, there has been confusion as to the identity of the Wyeth in the family who threw tea overboard. As authors of the *History of Pharmacy and the Pharmaceutical Industry* refer to the founders of the Wyeth pharmaceutical company, John (1834–1907) and Francis Houston Wyeth (1836–1913), they mistakenly state, "Their great uncle ***Noah*** Wyeth (1742–1811) was one of the groups which participated in the now famous Boston Tea Party..."[326]

Instead of Noah's name, Francis Houston Wyeth used Jonas' name in his application to join the Sons of the American Revolution. Francis wrote, "***Jonas*** Wyeth, noted for his wit, was one of the Boston Tea Party and is said to have been the one who replied to Admiral Montague's remark that they would have to pay the fiddler by shouting 'Com down, Squire and we'll settle the bill now.'" This quote was not said by Jonas Wyeth, but by Lendall Pitts as per Esther Forbes' book *Paul Revere and the World He Lived In*. The book also shows it was Joshua Wyeth who made a teapot of Boston harbor – not Jonas.[327]

The definitive proof that Joshua was the only Wyeth in the Tea Party comes from a "list of the tea party, furnished in 1835, by an aged Bostonian, well acquainted with the subject." The list is in Francis S. Drake's 1884 book *Tea Leaves: Being a Collection of Letters and Documents*.[328]

Jonas was, however, a tremendous patriot and served devotedly in both the Navy and the Continental Army. He started his service by marching on the Lexington and Concord Alarm. This fact is further confirmed by his wife's application for a pension. Here is Elizabeth E. Smith Wyeth's (1771-1853) letter to the Secretary of the Commonwealth asking him for an examination of the rolls and documents in his office in order to prove Jonas' service.[329]

> "I, Elizabeth Wyeth, of Cambridge in the county of Middlesex and Commonwealth of Massachusetts, 73 years of age do testify and say that my husband, Jonas Wyeth, was in the service of the Revolution, that he was at **Lexington & Concord** under the command of Capt. Samuel Thatcher, and according to the best of my recollections, he was **in the service at Ticonderoga** and was also in the **Continental service in the state of New York**; and was also at **Norwich in the state of Connecticut**, at which place he was attended with sickness and that he was afterwards in the **Naval Privateer service and was captured and**

> put aboard the British prison ship called *Chatham* where he remained in a distressful situation **until he with the other American prisoners were exchanged for the British prisoners**.
>
> That at the time of the Revolution, my husband bore the name of Jonas Wyeth 2nd, and according to the best of my recollection of his statement, he must have been in the service for more than one year. And I request the Secretary of this Commonwealth to examine the rolls and documents in his office for proof of my said husband's service, *Elizabeth Wyeth*
>
> Middlesex, Cambridge – March 17th 1845
> Subscribed and acknowledged before me, *Elijah Clark*, Justice of the Peace"

To assist her, Elizabeth's brother-in-law, Jacob Wyeth Sr. (1764-1857) gave this testimony on the same day in 1845.[330]

> "I, Jacob Wyeth, of Cambridge in the county of Middlesex and Commonwealth of Massachusetts, in the 81st year of my age do testify and say that I have always resided in this town. That I well recollect the Revolutionary War. I was not in the service myself, but **I have three brothers who were in the service, viz: Ebenezer, Jonas, Joshua.** And my deceased brother Jonas Wyeth has a widow living in the neighborhood. And my said brother Jonas Wyeth was at the time of the Revolution, was called Jonas Wyeth, <u>Second</u>, and I well recollect that he was in the **Lexington and Concord engagement.** I **think he was in the company of Lieut. David Bradley**, and I recollect that he enlisted in the service in **December 1775 or January or February 1776** for one year. And it is my impression he was in the Company of Lieut. Bradley in that service at which time **he was in the service in the state of New York**. And was sick the last part of this service. A year or two after his return from this year's service, he engaged in a Naval Privateer service, and I think he was at one time captured by a British cruiser & was held a prisoner for some time. It is also my full impression he was in the **Penobscot expedition**, and was under **Captain Manley in one of his Naval services.** *Jacob Wyeth*
>
> Middlesex, Cambridge – March 17th 1845. Then personally appeared Jacob Wyeth and made oath to the truth of the above affidavit by him subscribed. He being a <u>credible witness</u>, before me
> *Elijah Clark*, Justice of the Peace"

As it turns out, Jacob did a remarkable job thinking back to his boyhood. Except for the name of Jonas' superior, Capt. Eliphalet Newell, Jacob's affidavit was very accurate. He was only 11 years old when his older brothers entered the Continental Army. Like Jacob, his younger brothers, Gad (1768–1843) and John (1770–1858), were too young for service in the Revolution.

Of course, Jacob did not have the benefit of his older brothers' input in 1845. Jonas died in 1817, Joshua in 1829 and Ebenezer in 1836. Neither did Jacob, nor anyone working on Jonas' widow's claim, have access to the abstract for pay written by Captain Newell for service in his company in Dec 1775. As mentioned before, Newell's document proves Jonas was paid for 15 days of service

This notation in Ebenezer's pension file says an account book was procured from Capt. Newell's widow proving Ebenezer's 12 month's service in the Massachusetts Line.

that month while Joshua and Ebenezer were each paid for 11 days of service.[331] Newell's pay record and Jacob and Elizabeth's statements about Jonas' New York service, makes it highly likely Jonas' service mirrored the service Joshua and Ebenezer mentioned in their pension applications. Both Joshua and Ebenezer wrote they fought in the New York battles on Long Island and at White Plains while serving for over a year in Captain Newell's Company of Colonel Henry Knox's Regiment of Artillery.[332] [333] Ebenezer's service started in Nov 1775.[334] His file also shows Captain Newell's account book was procured from the widow of Capt. Newell… noting "Ebenezer Wyeth is credited for 12 months service and stayed with the Mass. line for that term."[335]

Additionally, as mentioned previously, volume 17 of The Secretary of the Commonwealth's *Massachusetts Soldiers and Sailors of the Revolutionary War* book, does not include the three brothers' yearlong service in the Continental Army. Even though the secretary was mistakenly looking on the rolls of David Bradley, it appears they did not carry the rolls of Captain Newell either. This is how the records office responded to Elizabeth's request.[336]

> "Commonwealth of Massachusetts. – Secretary's office, Boston; June 2^d 1845. I hereby Certify, that from an examination of the Books and Documents, relating to Military Services in the War of the Revolution, which remain in this Department, it appears that the name of **Jonas Wyeth junr** is borne as a private upon a **muster roll of Capt Samuel Thatcher** Compr in Col. Gardner's regt. Which marched on the **alarm April 19, 1775 – 3 days** – as Jonas Wyeth, upon a pay abstract **of Capt John Walton**, Col. Saml Thatcher, for service at Cambridge from **Sept 2 to 3 1778 – 1 day** – upon a pay roll of the same **for service from Sept 4 to 11 – 7 days**; – upon a order signed by Capt John Walton, notifying Jonas Wyeth jun that he was detached to join Capt Frost the next day to be marched to Boston for such service as should be directed by the Council, – order dated at Cambridge, **Sept 23^d 1778**; – *upon another order from Capt Walton, dated Oct 30, he is notified as Jonas 3rd to march to Boston and serve under Gen'l Heath, until the 9th of Nov following*; – the name of **Jonas Wyeth is also borne upon an index, as a seaman on board the** *Hague*, **Capt John Manley** – the commencement and end of the service of this vessel, is stated upon the index, **to be from June 1, 1782 to May 10, 1783** – there are no rolls of it in this office. The name of said Wyeth, **Wyeth junr or 3^d is not found upon any rolls of David Bradley**, who was a Lieut. in 1775, and a Capt. at a later period; and the preceding is all the evidence of service in the case, shown by any of the records …
>
> *Secretary of the Commonwealth"*

Interestingly, in this certification, Jonas "is notified as Jonas 3rd to march to Boston and serve under Gen'l Heath until the 9th of Nov following." This matches the aforementioned Ebenezer III being ordered to march to Boston to serve under General Heath until 09 Nov 1778. This shows two Wyeths served together again near the end of 1778.

Unfortunately, for Elizabeth, the secretary saying "Wyeth junr or 3^d" opened a can of worms. In her letter of 24 Jun 1845[337] transferring documents to the commissioner of pensions, Elizabeth briefly touched on the manner her husband's name was distinguished from his uncle Jonas Sr.

> "On this 24th day of June … 1845, personally appeared before the court of Probate in and for the county of Middlesex and state aforesaid, Elizabeth Wyeth being 73 years of age, who being first duly sworn according to law doth on her oath make the following declaration in order to obtain the benefits of the provision made by the Act of Congress passed 07 Jul 1838 entitled an act granting half pay and pensions to certain widows. Also, the act of 03 Mar 1843 and 17 Jun 1844 continuing pensions to certain widows.
>
> That she is the widow of Jonas Wyeth of Cambridge who was in the Lexington and Concord Alarm and was immediately after stationed at Cambridge for 3 or 4 days. From the 12th of Apr 1775 in the company of Capt Samuel Thatcher and in the last part of the year 1775 or the first of 1776, he enlisted for a year's service and was in the service in the state of New York and returned by the way of Norwich in the state of Connecticut

> where he remained sick for some time. That after his return to Cambridge, he was in the guard service at Cambridge in 1778 in Capt. John Walton's company at several different times at an amount to one month or more and that he was also in the service on guard in Boston… and in 1780 or 1781, he engaged in the Naval service and was on board the ship *Hague* under Capt Manley and continued in the service until near the close of the War. That all his services rendered his country would amount to near two years.
>
> And when in Cambridge in the time of the Revolution, he bore the name of Jonas Wyeth Junior or 2^d, all this she verily believes. – She further declares that she was married to the said Jonas Wyeth on the 8th day of April in the year 1792. That the ceremony was performed by the Rev. Abiel Holmes, pastor of a church and society in Cambridge aforesaid. That her husband, the said Jonas Wyeth, died in said Cambridge on the 3rd day of Oct 1817. That she was not married to him prior to his leaving the service but the marriage took place previous to the 1st day of Jan 1794 "viz" at the time above stated… *Elizabeth Wyeth*
>
> Subscribed and sworn to by said Elizabeth Wyeth at her dwelling house in Cambridge, she being unable by reason of age and infirmity to attend court …."

For ten years, his widow and her attorneys were put through the wringer trying to prove Elizabeth's husband was *the* Jonas, out of all the Jonas Wyeths in Cambridge, who served under Captain Manley. An index record on 19 Jul 1845 shows Elizabeth's 07 Aug 1838 certificate was suspended for authenticity that he was the specific Jonas in service on board *The Hague*. On 26 Aug 1845, the commissioner of pensions wrote for more proof of Jonas' identity. Of the documents sent to the commissioner, the following letter proved most helpful.[338] Its author, Samuel Sawin (1762-1849), was Jonas Jr.'s first cousin… the son of his aunt Susannah Wyeth Sawin (1734-1794).

> "I, Samuel Sawin of Livermore … "rendered service in the Revolution from said town of Watertown – my place of residence was near that part of the town of Cambridge where there resided a family by the name of Wyeth one of the sons bore the name of Jonas and was called Jonas Wyeth Junr or 2^d. I was well acquainted with him, I well recollect he was engaged in the Lexington & Concord Fight the 19th of April 1775 – **that he took a fine gun, a Queen's arm from one of the British soldiers** which I well recollect seeing. I well recollect that the said Jonas Wyeth Jr joined the Army a little before they left Cambridge and went with them to New York and according to my best recollection was gone seven or eight months; After his return I went to sea with him. We started for Turk Island after a cargo of salt. We were taken on the *Papage* and carried to Baggaduce now Custine and imprisioned on board the ship *Chatham* until we were exchanged. After this he went to sea but whether in a national vessel or a privateen I do not recollect….
>
> *Samuel Sawin … 01 Nov 1845*"

Over 20 documents were forwarded as proof to the pension board. They are summarized later in Appendix 2.

The first letter of proof was from Lydia Convers Francis Wyeth (1776–1840), wife of Captain Job Wyeth, stating she knew Jonas Jr. since she was placed in the home of Ebenezer and Mary Wyeth at age nine. Also, Elizabeth Jarvis Wyeth (1768–1858), wife of Jacob, wrote of her knowledge of the Wyeths. She was a daughter of Nathaniel Jarvis, for whom her son, the Oregon explorer, was named. Even Salem witchcraft author, Charles Upham, and the famous educator, Horace Mann, then a member of the United States House of Representatives, tried to help.[339] In exasperation, after ten years of document submissions, and almost two years after Elizabeth's death on 12 Sep 1853, her attorney wrote the following letter to the pension commissioner.[340]

This portrait of Lydia, attributed to Mr. Witfield, hangs in the dining room of her great grandson, Newell Convers "N.C." Wyeth. Credit: Wyeth Family Archives, Chadds Ford, PA.

> "Washington, D.C. on June 12th 1855 – Honorable Judge Waldo, Com. Pensions
>
> My dear sir, In the case of the Widow of Jonas Wyeth of Mass claiming a Rev. Pension for the services of her said husband in the Rev. War under act of 1838 evidence like as follows, has been furnished the case, which I desire reviewed with reference to allowing the case.
>
> 1st the declaration of the widow jointly with the declaration of his brother, to be sent to the Hon Secy of the state of Mass. upon a requisition for proof of his Rev. Services from records there, his land service is not only stated but also his sea service declared for by them… of his sea service they (the secy) "declare" he served on board the same ship, the *Hague* and under the same Capt Manly as the records of Mass show he did serve! How could this be, were it not for the records of Mass are a sealed book to all, prior to the sworn application, now on file in the case.
>
> Then the testimony of one witness in the case is that he previously went to sea with him to Turks Island after a load of salt… and narrates circumstances of the voyage as that they were captured and imprisoned by the British also that he heard of his being in our Naval ship service of war after that.
>
> Then there are more than 20 witnesses in the case – all respectable gray haired old people, men and women who have lived to a great age in the same county and neighborhood and testify that they knew him for full half a century – "knew him as merchant Jonas" – that he was ever respected, regarded, believed by all to have so served, as above, in the Rev. War – that there was another Jonas Wyeth of the family, but he was his uncle … also there was still another Jonas W – but he was equally, too young… the record evidence in this case so complete, what shall we do with the joint testimony of these veteran witnesses in the case, who have lived youth out till the blossoms of age; with him, and the other Jonases and testify what he do know and have a right to know, in the case – that he was the man – But all is submitted, respectfully.   I am sir most obediently yours,   *S. B. True*"

Most of the letters referred to Jonas Wyeth Sr. (1730-1813), as an elderly man too old to serve in the Revolutionary War. Even Jonas Wyeth 2d (1806-1868), son of Major Jonas Wyeth (1762-1828), wrote a letter stating he had not heard of his aged grandfather nor of his father's war service.

However, Jonas Wyeth Sr. was 45 years old when he and his older brother, Ebenezer Wyeth Jr. (1727-1799), marched as minutemen on 19 Apr 1775. Jacob Wyeth's letter of 26 Jun 1852 authenticated his father Ebenezer's service of that day.[341]

As mentioned before, volume 17 of the records of the Secretary of the Commonwealth, also states Noah Wyeth (1742-1811), Jonas Wyeth Jr. (1757-1817), and Joseph Wyeth (1751-1837) served on that first day of conflict.[342] Those three men were Jonas Wyeth Sr.'s youngest brother, his nephew, and his first cousin 1x removed.

To illustrate William J. Long's 1923 book, *America, A History of Our Country*, N. C. Wyeth painted Washington's first salute to his newly formed American army, on 03 Jul 1775, under the elm tree on Cambridge Common. The site is now considered the birthplace of the U.S. Army. So knowledgeable was N.C. of his heritage, he probably knew Jonas Wyeth Sr. then lived a stone's throw away on the farm Nicholas Wyeth purchased in 1645.

Jonas Wyeth Jr. portrayed by Tucker Ahlers of the Minute Man National Park.

Although Jonas Sr.'s son, later known as Major Jonas, was 13 at the beginning of the war, he may have served at age 16 on 30 Oct 1778.[343] While the confusion over the three Jonases was understandable, it was disgraceful that it took ten years (1845-1855) to sort out. When Elizabeth's attorney, S. B. True, received her approved pension certificate on 14 Aug 1855, it was almost two years after her death on 12 Sep 1853. It showed an allowance of $42.64 per annum commencing in arrears to 04 Mar 1836.[344] Curiously, the actual ledgers appear as if Elizabeth had received a pension payment for the service of her husband, Jonas Wyeth Jr., all along just like all the other ladies on the lists.[345]

In any event, no one followed up on the statement in Elizabeth Jarvis Wyeth's 04 Feb 1850 letter. She said, "… it was formally stated that Ebenezer Wyeth, Jonas Wyeth and Joshua Wyeth, were all of them in the service of the Revolution, and that Ebenezer Wyeth received a pension under the first law for the soldiers of the Revolution, and resided in the town of Ashby, Massachusetts."[346] If the pension commissioner would have studied Ebenezer's file, Jacob's misstatement of commanding officer, Bradley, could have been easily corrected to Newell.

While living near the MA / NH state line in Ashby, Ebenezer Wyeth III started receiving a pension of $48 per year on 01 May 1818. It stopped in Mar 1820 because of property he held.[347] He then submitted this statement of his service in the Revolution.[348]

"Oath to Samuel Dana Judge of Middlesex County Court at Cambridge on 20th of July 1820. File #34,576 under act of 18 Mar 1818 and 01 May 1820

… the said Wyeth declares that he will be 68 years old next December – his occupation is now a toll gate tender at only $4.25 per month but while he was able to work as a farmer, he is very unable to labor. He has a breach [hernia] which is a very bad one unfits him for any business a considerable part of the time. He otherwise has all the infirmities of old age upon him, that he has a wife who is 58 years old next Feb who enjoys a tolerable degree of health as well as people in general of her age. That he has three children one girl of 19 years of age who is incompetent to take care of herself on account of ill health and probably never will be any better or able to take care of herself, one girl of 18 years old in August next who enjoys pretty good health and one boy 14 years old who is pretty well, ….

….. and the said Wyeth on oath further declares that he served in the Revolutionary army on the Continental estate – for the term of one year AD 1776 – under Capt. **Eliphalet Newell** of Charlestown in Col. Henry Knox's Reg. of Artillery. 'I then marched from Cambridge to New York in the Massachusetts Line, I was in the **battle at Long Island** and at **the battle of White Plains**. I was a while in the **hospital at North Castle** at which place my term for which I enlisted expired and from thence returned home by receiving a pass from an officer of the same whose name was Howard.'"

Apparently, a veteran had to be destitute to receive a pension. Rather than as a reward for serving in the military, pensions seemed a form of welfare. Ebenezer was forced to sell his land, worth $300, in order to reinstate his allowance. When the land sold, his income restarted in Mar 1824 and continued to his 30 Dec 1836 death. Ebenezer's case was reopened with these statements.[349]

"I, Oliver Cook of Boston… on the 1st day of March 1815… loaned to Ebenezer Wyeth, then of Westford in the County of Middlesex, and now of Ashby in the same county, who has since been a pensioner of the United States, and whose name has been struck from the roll on account of his property, the sum of

$300, for which I took his promissory note and a mortgage on a parcel of real estate situated in said Ashby, as collateral security for payment thereof. Then he became indebted to me for another $50 and then previous to 05 Sep 1818, the said Wyeth became further indebted to me for groceries consumed in his family in the sum of about $100 and on the said 5th day of Sep 1822, the said Wyeth, not having paid either of the aforesaid notes or interest thereon, or any part thereof; agreed to give me a deed ... of the said parcel of land mortgaged as aforesaid, he having no other property within my knowledge to secure to me the payment of said debt, and I allowed him $600 for said real estate, being a little less than the sum, he then owed me on said notes and account... I consider said sum of $600 a high price for said real estate... but necessary to secure a precarious debt. *Oliver Cook*" ... notarized 10 Dec 1823

One of the great things about the second pension application of Ebenezer Wyeth III, is it clears up the mystery of who married Naomi Russell Cooke. Lucius Paige wrote that Ebenezer Wyeth IV married Naomi and sold his father's estate to Jonathan Hastings. Then the fourth Ebenezer disappeared from the records.[350] In fact, it was Ebenezer III who married Naomi as his second wife. Ebenezer III sold his father's (Ebenezer Jr.) Cambridge estate. After moving to Westford, Massachusetts, the third Ebenezer's oldest son, Ebenezer IV, died unmarried in 1813.[351]

"On the 10th day of Dec 1823, personally appeared in open court, being a court of record for the county of Middlesex, Ebenezer Wyeth resident in Ashby in said county aged 70 years who being first duly sworn according to law, doth, on his oath, make the following declaration in order to obtain the provision made by the acts of Congress, of the 18 Mar 1818, and the 01 May 1820, that he, the said Ebenezer Wyeth enlisted for the term of one year in the month of **November in the year AD 1775**, in the state of Massachusetts in the Company commanded by **Captain Eliphalet Newell** in the regiment **commanded by Colonel Henry Knox** in the line of the state of Massachusetts on the Continental establishment; that he continued to serve in the said corps **until January in the AD 1777**, when he was **discharged from the said service, in Bedford in the state of New York**; that his name has been placed on the Pension list, and dropt therefrom on account of his property; that he is a **husbandman by occupation**, but on account of a breach [hernia] and the infirmities of age, wholly unable to labor; that he has no family, except his **wife, Naomi**, aged 58 years. *Ebenezer Wyeth*"

From Ebenezer's 20 Jul 1820 Massachusetts statement and from Joshua's 21 Jul 1820 statement in Ohio, we learn the brothers fought in the Battle of Long Island and at the Battle of White Plains. It is likely Jonas was with them and all three also fought at the Harlem Heights Skirmish mentioned in Joshua's affidavit. For the Americans, Harlem Heights was the one bright spot of the New York campaign. Before and after that skirmish, General Washington's troops suffered humiliating defeats at the hands of the British.[352]

In a video on *George Washington's Mt. Vernon* website, Joseph Ellis, author of *Revolutionary Summer,* calls the New York Campaign of 1776 the

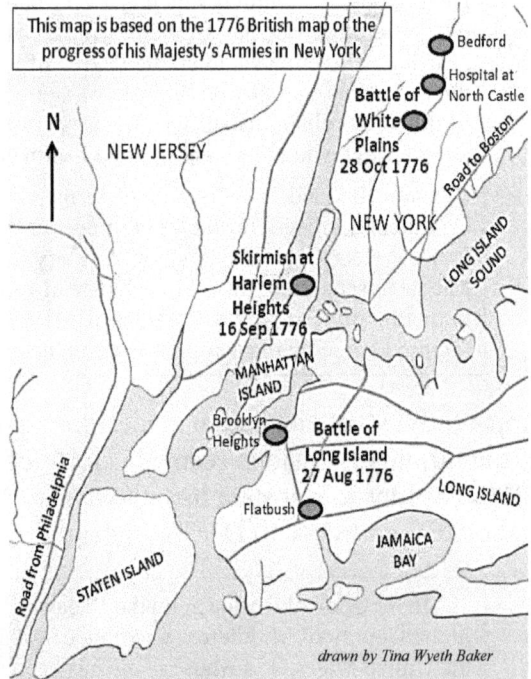

This map is based on the 1776 British map of the progress of his Majesty's Armies in New York

drawn by Tina Wyeth Baker

Just as Washington moved south from Cambridge to NY, so did the Wyeth brothers. These are the locations mentioned in Ebenezer's and/or Joshua's pension affidavits. Ebenezer's discharge in January 1777, was in Bedford after being in the hospital at North Castle, New York. Joshua served another year and was discharged in Springfield, MA.

70

most difficult time in Washington's military career. The General nearly lost everything and was severely depressed. He wrote in letters, "I want to die rather than suffer the humiliation of a defeat." However, Ellis says Washington learned from the disastrous period and developed the strategy that would eventually win the war. When the General found he could not fight the British tactically, he concluded that prolonging the war would weaken the British economy and diminish their will to fight.[353]

In addition to his foresight, Washington's charismatic leadership contributed greatly to American victory. With the same problems, a lesser leader could not have triumphed. Washington was faced with a vacillating loyalty among the general population, an uncooperative Congress, and a poorly paid, inadequately outfitted army who deserted in the thousands. Still because of his incomparable character, enough soldiers so trusted and so loved the General, they stayed with him and supported his ideas.[354]

Three such soldiers who remained loyal to George Washington and his ideals were the Wyeth brothers. Not only did Ebenezer, age 22; Jonas, age 18; and Joshua, age 17, serve out their original one-year term, but rendered additional service after their enlistment period ended in Jan 1777.

It was of the young men who remained in the service that Thomas Paine wrote in Dec 1776, "These are the times that try men's souls. The summer soldier and the sunshine patriot will, in this crisis, shrink from the service of their country; but he that stands it now, deserves the love and thanks of man and woman."[355]

Near the end of their enlistment, the Wyeth brothers would have worn the blue uniform coats of the Massachusetts Regiment of Artillery.[356] [357] Perhaps Joshua continued to wear the uniform after he enlisted for another year's service as a blacksmith in the Corps of Artificers under Captain Saxon.[358] Artificers were skilled craftsmen who kept military equipment in good working order so the troops could operate effectively.[359]

drawn by Tina Wyeth Baker

Between the Battles of Long Island and White Plains, the Continental Army began wearing actual uniforms. Their coats were blue trimmed in red.

When Ebenezer was in the hospital in North Castle, near Bedford, Westchester County, New York, his term of enlistment expired.[360] He returned to Cambridge and continued to provide military service as needed in Massachusetts. Most notable of which, was the previously mentioned 1778 service with his brother, Jonas, under General Heath.

Jonas was ailing, as well, at the end of his year of service in Colonel Henry Knox's Regiment. In support of his sister-in-law's pension claim, Jacob Wyeth wrote a second letter on 26 Jun 1852 detailing his brother Jonas' service and convalescence at his uncle's home in Norwich, Connecticut, after serving in New York. The mention of Joshua and Ebenezer III being at Lexington and Concord is interesting. However, no official record supports Jacob's claim.[361]

71

"I, Jacob Wyeth, of Cambridge in the county of Middlesex and Commonwealth of Massachusetts, 87 years of my age … On oath do testify and say that I am one of the family of Ebenezer and Mary Wyeth of said Cambridge. That I well recollect the Revolutionary War. That my said father, with his oldest son and my two other brothers by the name of Jonas and Joshua were in the service of the Lexington and Concord alarm on the 19th of April 1775 and I think they belonged to Capt. Thatcher's company of Cambridge, and my said brother Jonas was … in the service at New York in 1776 and was under a Capt. Bradley of Charleston; that **he had a fever in the service near New York**, and on his way home stopped at his uncle Mannings in Norwich in the state of Connecticut and **my father the aforesaid Ebenezer Wyeth went to Norwich and brought home his son Jonas**, aforesaid. I recollect that after the said Jonas recovered his health, he was as before ready to engage in most any service and did engage in privateer services … and **was in the Naval services** and it is my impression that he was under Capt. Manley some of the time… My father Ebenezer Wyeth had a brother by the name of Jonas Wyeth, and he also had a son by the name of Jonas … I never heard that Jonas Wyeth, son of my uncle Jonas Wyeth ever went in the service, but **my brother Jonas was of that character by which he was always ready to engage in any dangerous engagements**….

Jacob Wyeth"

Before he died in 1817, Jonas Jr. witnessed that his brave nature was inherited by his son, Jonas Wyeth 3d (1794–1867). On 10 Sep 1814, Jonas 3d began his military service in the Cambridge Light Infantry during the War of 1812. His first cousin, Stephen Wyeth (1791–1883), son of Ebenezer III, had been drafted into the same organization the month before.[362]

This second war with Great Britain began on 18 Jun 1812. At stake was Britain impeding trade between France and the United States and British support of Indian attacks on America's frontier. Additionally, as they did with Nathaniel Gamage (1712–1750), England continued to forcibly impress Americans as sailors for the Royal Navy.[363]

Stephen's grave in Bartlett Cemetery, Killingly, CT, was unmarked until 2014 when Donna Lopez, Cambridge City Clerk, helped me furnish proof of his service to the Veterans Admin.

Many historians believe the United States wanted to acquire Canada during the war. The Treaty of Ghent ended hostilities on 17 Feb 1815 but resolved only a few of the underlying causes of the war. However, the arbitration clauses in the treaty did lay the groundwork, which today sustains the Canada / United States border… the longest unfortified border in the world.[364]

Lt. Thomas Cheney (1751-1835), grandson of Martha Wyeth Fessenden, served with distinction in two wars against Great Britain. Records show on 05 Oct 1775 he was a sergeant in Capt. Edward Payson Williams' Company, 36th Regiment and on 22 Dec 1775 he was in camp at Cambridge with John Greaton's Regiment.[365] His experience in the Revolution enabled him to serve in the War of 1812 at South Boston, from 13 Sep 1814 to 07 Nov 1814, at the higher rank of lieutenant.[366]

John Hampden Palmer (1780-1813) is another descendant of Martha Wyeth Fessenden who served in the War of 1812. John enlisted on 05 May 1813 as a private in the 31st U.S. Infantry. He died in the service two months later in Windsor, Vermont at the age of 33.[367]

Undoubtedly, many other descendants of Nicholas Wyeth served in the War of 1812. Concentrating on the Gamage Family, we see the amazing number of grandsons and great grandsons of Nathaniel Gamage (1712-1750) who served in that war. Perhaps Nathaniel's 1750 kidnapping and impressing into the Royal Navy had some bearing on his descendants' service.

Daniel Gamage (1764-1838), Joshua Gamage III (1789–1862), Thomas Gamage (1794–1877), and William Gamage (1796–1862) were in the Maine Militia of Lt. Col. Robert Day's Regiment, Capt. John Sprowl's Detachment. They saw service on Jun 20-22, Jun 30-Jul 1, and Sep 10-15, 1814. Nathaniel Gamage (1793-1823), son of Dr. William Gamage, was in Lt. G. King's Company of Lt. Col. P. Osgood's Boston Regiment, from 01 Jul to 20 Jul 1814. Stephen Gamage (1787–1834) served Gloucester, Essex County, Massachusetts in Captain Benjamin Haskell's Detached Company under General Hovey from 01 Jun 1814 to 18 Sep 1814.[368]

Also serving in Gloucester were John Blatchford III (1790-1873), Nehemiah Grover III (1776–1854), Samuel Gott Gamage (1774–1857) and Ebenezer Gamage (1773–1838). They were in Lt. Col. James Appleton's Regiment, from 19 Sep 1814 to 12 Oct 1814. The first of those dates saw the company locked in a sea battle with British barges.[369]

Although there were many conflicts in the United States after the War of 1812, service records for descendants of Nicholas Wyeth during those years are scarce. We know of two men who fought in the Mexican–American War in 1847. Their details will be provided later. But during the Civil War of Secession, that began when rebels fired on the United States Army at Fort Sumter in Charleston Harbor, South Carolina on 12 Apr 1861, descendants of Nicholas Wyeth were heavily involved. The overwhelming majority of them supported the Union cause.

According to Civil War authority, Professor Gary W. Gallagher, the North fought to force the Confederate states to rejoin the Union because they understood how easily the country could lose what it had gained only 87 years before. Furthermore, Gallagher said the South's decision to leave the Union had little to do with states' rights. Instead it was almost entirely predicated on the question of slavery.[370] It must be said though, due to the basis of the founding of the Republican Party in the North, some argue the cause of many Republicans was not entirely noble as slavery impeded the Party's stress on free market capitalism.[371]

Efforts to abolish slavery in America pre-dated the Declaration of Independence. John Adams called it a "foul contagion in the human character" and "an evil of colossal magnitude." Benjamin Franklin thought that slavery was "an atrocious debasement of human nature" and "a source of serious evils." He and Benjamin Rush founded the Pennsylvania Society for Promoting the Abolition of Slavery in 1774. John Jay founded a similar society in New York. After the Revolutionary War, Marquis de Lafayette said, "I would never have drawn my sword in the cause of America, could I have conceived that thereby I was founding a land of slavery."

George Washington and Thomas Jefferson owned slaves, but they spoke against slavery. In 1786, Washington wrote of slavery, "there is not a man living who wishes more sincerely than I do, to see a plan adopted for the abolition of it." That same year, Jefferson wrote, "What a stupendous, what an incomprehensible machine is man! who can endure toil, famine, stripes, imprisonment, and death itself, in vindication of his own liberty, and the next moment be deaf to all those motives whose power supported him through his trial, and inflict on his fellow-men a bondage, one hour of which is fraught with more misery than ages of that which he rose in rebellion to oppose."

From the Declaration of Independence, Jefferson edited out words to appease South Carolina and Georgia delegates who would not concede slavery went so far as to violate the "most sacred rights of life and liberty." Nevertheless, the fundamental principle of Jefferson's document "that all men are created equal" remained as an evident criticism of the institution of slavery.[372]

When delegates met in 1787 to write the United States Constitution, James Madison noted, "The real difference of interests lay not between large and small states but between the Northern and Southern states. The institution of slavery and its consequences formed a line of discrimination." To promote unification among the delegates for the Constitution's ratification, concessions were made to the pro-slavery interests. The compromises written into the Constitution included tolerating slavery where it currently existed and not endorsing or advancing it further.[373]

However, after the invention of the cotton gin in 1793, and as more states were added to the Union, the compromises in the Constitution exploded into the deadliest war in American history.

Of the 36 men who carried the name Wyeth or Wythe at their military enlistment, records show nine of them died in the Civil War. They are James Madison Wyeth (1820–1863) and John Milton Wyeth (1840–1862) of Illinois; Jonathan Wheeler Wyeth (1843–1863) of Ohio; Milton Lewis Wyeth, M.D. (1825–1862), Otis Wyeth (1848–1864), Zachariah Taylor Wyeth (1848–1865), and Allen Willie Wythe (1839–1863) of Indiana; and twins Richard Harvey Wyeth (1844–1864) and William Henry Wyeth (1844–1864) from Massachusetts.

Most all Americans of the time were affected by the Civil War, however, none more significantly than the soldiers who fought in it and the women on the home front who supported them.

Wyeth and Wythe women met endless challenges as they moved west from Massachusetts to practically every state in the Union and to the frozen Canadian prairie. On farms, wives worked alongside their husbands while they cared for and educated the children, grew, preserved and cooked food, wove cloth, spun yarn, and sewed, washed and mended clothes.

Because maiden names are sometimes difficult to find, the stories of the women who built our families, and the names of their children buried across America in unmarked graves, are often difficult to find as well. However, when recorded history is lost to us, we can assume these women's stories parallel the stories we do have. All of humankind share far more in common than what divides us.

Here are stories of a few Wyeth women's Civil War sacrifices.

Not only did Dr. Milton Lewis Wyeth serve Indiana in the Civil War, but he and his first cousin, Willis B. Wyeth fought in the Mexican–American War, as well. The two men enrolled on 12 Jun 1847 in Jeffersonville, Indiana in the 4th Indiana Regiment, Co. H.[374] [375] When Milton came home in 1848, he married Mary Eliza Davis (1828–1906). They had two sons, James who died in 1854 and Willie who died two years after his father died aboard a hospital ship on the Mississippi River on 04 May 1862. Mary lost her whole family in ten short years. She never remarried.

Mary's sister-in-law, Dorcas Tankersley Wyeth (1818–1911), also suffered devastating losses to her family. Dorcas' husband, Sgt. Francis Martin Wyeth served under his brother, 1st Lieutenant

Dr. Milton Lewis Wyeth, in Co. G of the 43rd Indiana Infantry. Not only did Dorcas send her husband, Francis, off to fight in the Civil War, but she sent three sons as well. James Erasmus served almost the full length of the war. But from Dorcas, the war took John Milton on 24 Jun 1862 and it took Otis, not yet 16 years old, on 29 Aug 1864. Francis, ill, broken and disabled, returned home in 1862 (the year both his brother, Milton, and his son, John, died). His health fragile ever after, Francis left Dorcas a widow in 1877.

Sisters were not immune from the consequences of the war either. Mary Elizabeth Wyeth (1842–1929) was a 24-year-old schoolteacher when she assumed the care of her orphaned sisters and brother in Cambridge, Massachusetts. The family first lost brother-in-law, Alphonse D. Titus, on 21 Jan 1863 when he died during the Civil War of a brain concussion at Potomac Creek, Virginia. Later that year mother Lucy Harvey died of dropsy. In 1864, twin brothers Richard Harvey and William Henry were killed in the mud and the blood of two different Civil War battles. In 1866, the stress so overwhelmed Mary's father, Noah, he died of heart failure.

Although the hardships of my great, great grandmother, Rebecca Grate Wyeth (1833–1919), were not as tragic, she was left with tremendous responsibilities to shoulder alone when the War took her husband from their Meigs County, Ohio, farm for the summer of 1864. Perhaps my great grandfather, six-year-old William, could feed the chickens and gather their eggs, but the care of three-year-old Peter and one-year-old Harman undoubtedly restricted Rebecca's work in the fields. Thankfully, her husband, Francis John Higginson Wyeth, returned before the harvest.

Francis was a month shy of his 33rd birthday when he enlisted as a "Hundred Days Man" on 04 May 1864 in Gallipolis, Ohio, the seat of the county south of Meigs. On 03 Sep 1864, he mustered out in Gallipolis as well. The nickname "Hundred Days Men" was given to several Union Army volunteer regiments raised in 1864 for 100 days of service during the height of the Civil War. The lightly trained troops freed regular army personnel from routine duty, enabling the regulars to spend more time on the front lines.[376]

Francis' granddaughter, Donna Hampton McKinney, inherited this certificate for Francis' service. She passed it on to her daughter, Betty McKinney Jurski.

It reads, in part, "The President's Thanks and Certificate of Honorable Service – To Private Francis J. Wyeth, 140th Reg't Ohio National Guard. Whereas the President of the United States has made the following Executive Order, returning Thanks to the Ohio Volunteers for One Hundred Days." It is signed "By the President: Abraham Lincoln."

Of the sacrifices, both great and small, made during the terrible War Between

the States, none compares with the wretched legacy of the inhumane and horrific treatment of captured prisoners.

Captured in 1863 during the Second Battle of Winchester, my great, great grandfather Captain David S. Caldwell (from whom my father, Richard Caldwell Wyeth, took his middle name) was confined to Libby Prison in Richmond, Virginia with 1,100 other officers.[377] Prisoners were restricted to the upper two floors of the converted three-story warehouse in six poorly furnished rooms, each measuring about 105 by 45 feet. There were no bunks and few benches. Wooden bars covered small windows that were otherwise open to the elements. Although the windows admitted little light, they did let in the sweltering summer heat and the frigid drafts of winter.[378]

On the lower floor, Libby served as a processing center for all Union prisoners. Union enlisted men were often sent to nearby Belle Isle Prison Camp in the middle of the James River. With no barracks for protection, the enlisted soldiers faired far worse than the Union officers quartered in Libby Prison. The Camp housed prisoners in 3,000 tents with no blankets. However, by 1863 with some 10,000 soldiers held on the island, many slept outside on the ground. During the winter months, as many as 25 men died each day. Those who survived were sent to a prison where "they would have new and better facilities" in Andersonville, Georgia.[379]

Facts of Belle Isle are confirmed by the diary of prisoner, Zelotes A. Musgrave.[380]

1 Nov 1863: Took the cars at Petersburg for Richmond Va. We arrived in Richmond Va. at 12 noon. 430 of us prisoners marched on to Belle Island [near Richmond Va.] which is in the James River.
2 Nov 1863: We are laying on Belle Island with no tents or blankets.
3 Nov 1863: On Belle Island near Richmond Va. One forth rations issued to us today.
4 Nov 1863: Same place, I am sick today.
5 Nov 1863: Belle Island. Plenty of body lice here.
6 Nov 1863: Belle Island. Laying out on the ground.
7 Nov 1863: Belle Island. Still laying out on the ground.

Soon after his imprisonment at Libby, Captain Caldwell became so unwell from a lack of food that he could scarcely hold his head up and spread the blankets he had brought with him upon the floor to "endeavor to seek some repose." Of the occasion, he had this to say about Libby prison inspector, Dick Turner.

Four Libby prison escapees, Col. Abel Streight, Major Bedan McDonald, Lt. Wm. Williams, and Captain David S. Caldwell – photo courtesy of Matthew L. Burr, Firelands Historical Society.

"… casting his eyes about in quest of evil, soon discovered me lying upon the floor in the embrace of that balmy restorer of exhausted nature, sweet sleep. This was too enviable a position to be long tolerated, and doubtless incited by his envious nature, and a desire to torture, he bounded across the floor, his eyes flashing fire the meanwhile, presenting more the appearance of a demon from the pit of perdition, than an intelligent human being. He approached me, as I have been told by my comrades, (of course being asleep, I can in this recital, only give their testimony), and reached across me, seizing the blankets up which I was lying, gave them a sudden jerk, turning me topsy turvy, and bringing my face in an unpleasant and violent contact with the floor, which you will readily imagine was not the most salubrious antidote for the head-ache… I beheld Dick Turner near my side with my two blankets under his arm … I remember one thing very distinctly, that he seemed to get in a great hurry about that time, and soon was down stairs, having stolen both my blankets, which I never saw afterward."[381]

Firsthand knowledge of incarceration conditions in a Union prison come from Confederate soldier, John Allan Wyeth (1845-1922). Captured by a squadron of Ohio cavalry near Chattanooga on 05 Oct 1863, John was imprisoned at Camp Morton in Indianapolis, Indiana.[382] Just a few days before his capture, John's gray army fought in the Battle of Chickamauga. Battling there in the ranks of the blue army was John's 2nd cousin, Jonathan Wheeler Wyeth (1843–1863).

"...barracks had been erected as cattle sheds and stables: they were about 20 feet wide, in height 10 feet to the eaves, 15 feet to the middle of the roof, and 80 feet long. The sides were of weather-boards 10 to 12 inches wide, set on end and presumably touching one another, and covered with strips when first put up. When they served as shelter for us, however, the planks had shrunk, and many of the strips had disappeared, leaving wide cracks, through which the winds whistled and the rain and snow beat in upon us. I have often seen my top blanket white with snow when we were hustled out for morning roll-call. The roof was of shingles and did not leak. Along the comb an open space about a foot wide extended the entire length of the shed. The earth served as floor, and the entrance was through a large barn door at each end. Along each side of this shelter, extending seven feet towards the center, were constructed four tiers of bunks, the lowest about one foot from the ground, the second three feet above this, the third three feet higher, while the fourth tier was on a level with the eaves.

John Allan Wyeth, Co. I, 4th Alabama Cavalry, from a photo taken in 1861.

Upon these long shelves, not partitioned off, the prisoners slept, or lay down, heads to the wall, feet towards the center or passageway. About two feet of space was allotted to each man, making about 320 men housed in each shed. As we had no straw for bedding, and as each man was allowed only one blanket, there was little comfort to be had in our bunks until our miseries were forgotten in sleep. The scarcity of blankets forced us to huddle together in cold weather, usually three in a group, with one blanket between us and the planks, and the other two to cover us with."[383]

Interestingly, John Allan Wyeth's second cousin 1x removed, John Wesley Wythe (1844–1919), had been a guard at Camp Morton earlier in 1863. Due to exposure, John Wesley developed heart disease and bronchitis. He was medically discharged from the Union Army on 13 Apr 1863.[384]

Several other members of the Wyeth / Wythe family died in, or were confined to, Confederate facilities. William Henry Wyeth (1844–1864) was incarcerated in the Confederate States Military Prison, Florence, SC. James Madison Wyeth (1820–1863) died in the Rutherford, TN Military Hospital. Zachariah Taylor Wyeth (1848–1865) died in General Hospital 4 / the Confederate Hospital at Wilmington, NC. Allen Willie Wythe (1839–1863) died in the Regimental Hospital in Spotsylvania County, Virginia near Fredericksburg.

In the following charts are the Civil War stories of as many Wyeth / Wythe family members as I could find. Some records are more detailed than others depending on the source of the records. They include the *United States Civil War Pension Index: General Index to Pension Files*, *Illinois Civil War Muster and Descriptive Rolls*, the National Park Service's *Civil War Soldier details database*, *Indiana Digital Archives*, and *Fold3* military records. The most detailed records were those I accessed on visits to the National Archives in Washington, D.C.

In the pension files are some rare gems. For instance, Dr. Alexander Reed Wyeth's appointment as assistant surgeon, with the rank of first lieutenant is amazing.

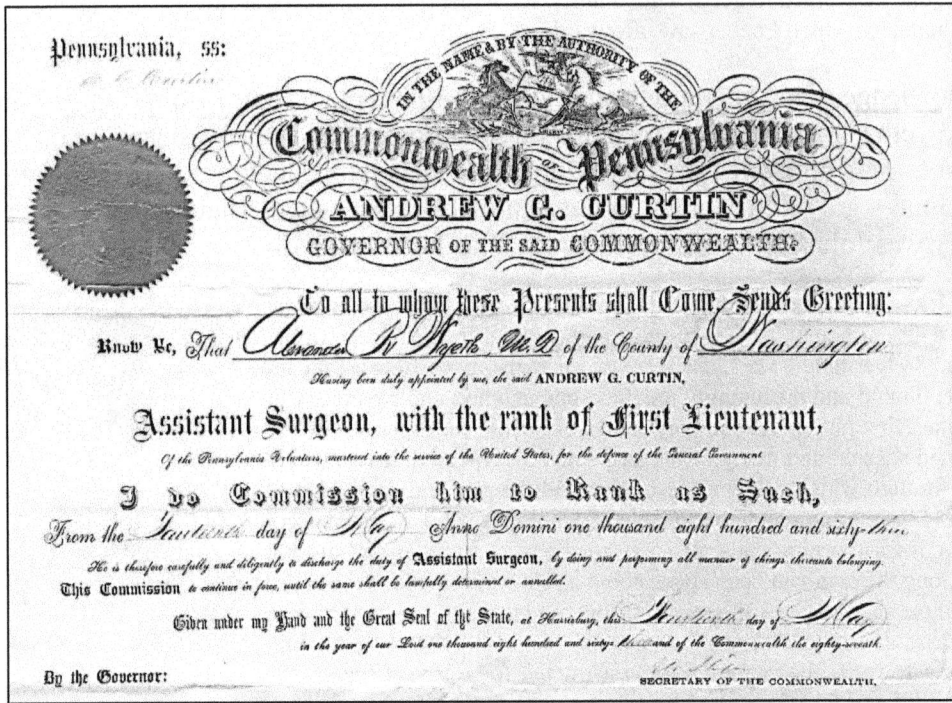

This letter to the commissioner of pensions from George Washington Wyeth (1835–1916) gives an account of his ancestors as he knew them. Dated Chico, CA – 12 Oct 1903, it reads as follows:

"… This is a short record of the Wyeth family. Nicholas Wyeth Born in Manchester, England 1592 came to the collones (sic) in 1636. Was born to him by a second marriage a son John and to John Wyeth was born a son Ebenezer and to Ebenezer was born a son Ebenezer 2 and to him was born a son whose name was Josnay who was my Grand Father and a Revolutionary Soldier and was with Washington at Valley Forge and was also one of the Tea Party at Boston. Ebenezer … was my great Grand Father and one of his Brothers was a signer of the Declaration of Independence. My Wife died in Leavenworth 1889 May 25th. I have lived single since that time. Excuse me for occupying your valuable time. Yours Respectfully, George W. Wyeth"

George Washington Wyeth's family line was unparalleled in military service to America. His grandfather was Boston Tea Party participant Joshua Wyeth who also fought at the Battle of Bunker Hill and in the Continental Army in New York. He may have been at Valley Forge, as George said, when Joshua served in the artificers corps. George, himself, served in both the Army and the Navy during the Civil War. His son, Guy Angus Wyeth, was killed in Lanpay, Philippines on 02 May 1900 during the Philippine-American War.[385]

Name	Reg't	Company	Service
Abiel Augustus Wyeth (1843-1895)	1st 62nd	MA Infantry, Co. F MA Infantry, Co. A	From 28 Jul 1862 to 25 May 1864 he served the 1st. Described as a clerk, 5 ft. 7 in., hazel eyes, brown hair, fair complexion, he re-enlisted in the service on 06 Apr 1865 in the 62nd in Boston, MA. Augustus mustered out as a corporal in Readville, MA on 05 May 1865.[386]
Alexander Reed Wyeth, M.D. (1813-1876)	22nd 208th	PA Volunteer Cavalry, Co. I, C & D PA Volunteer Infantry, Co. F & S	He mustered in on 31 Aug 1861 to serve as quarter-master sergeant with a cavalry organized near Pittsburgh. In Washington, D.C., they were assigned to the 1st PA Cavalry, Co. I. Just after the 1st PA combined forces to become the Ringgold Battalion, on 01 Sep 1862, Alex became their acting assistant surgeon at the rate of $100 per month. While marching to Romney, (West) Virginia on 12 Dec 1862, Dr. Wyeth suffered a severe rupture of his pelvis causing an inguinal hernia when he was thrown forward in his saddle. Still he continued in the Army. On 14 May 1863, he was commissioned assistant surgeon, with the rank of 1st lieutenant of the PA volunteers / Ringgold Battalion. In Mar 1864, Ringgold's was organized as the 22nd.[387] A few months later, Alex joined the 208th on 12 Sep 1864 and continued with them until 03 Mar 1865 when he received a medical discharge due to the hernia and to a more recent compound fracture of his left leg. While visiting his daughter, in Independence, TX, Dr. Wyeth died at the age of 63 of complications directly traceable to his war injuries.[388]
Augustus Greenleaf "A.G." Wyeth (1841-1914)	76th	OH Infantry, Co. B	He enlisted as a private on 01 Oct 1861 at Camp Sherman, Newark, OH.[389] Discharged on disability 01 Apr 1863 at Gayoso Army Hospital, Memphis, TN.[390][391]
Benjamin Franklin Wyeth Sr. (1845-1909)	12th	MA Militia Infantry, Co. Unattached	He mustered in at Readville, MA on 16 May 1864 and was stationed at Long's Point on the tip of Cape Cod. Benjamin mustered out 15 Aug 1864.[392][393]
Charles Alonzo Wyeth (1836-1915)	11th 3rd	IN Infantry, Co. D IN Light Artillery, Independent	He enrolled in the 11th at Terre Haute, IN on 18 Apr 1861 and mustered out at Indianapolis on 04 Aug 1861. 20 days later he re-enlisted at Terre Haute as a private on 24 Aug 1861 in the 3rd Battery. Charles was discharged for disability on 05 Feb 1863.[394]
Charles Sheafer Wyeth (1843-1923)	48th	PA Infantry Militia, Co. D	Charles enlisted as a sergeant on 01 Jul 1863 in Lebanon County, PA due to the emergency created by the South's invasion of Pennsylvania. After helping in the mining region of Scranton, he mustered out on 26 Aug 1863.[395]
Francis John Higginson Wyeth (1831-1911)	140th	OH Infantry (National Guard), Co. H	He was a farmer, age 33, when he enlisted as a private on 02 May 1864 in the command of Capt. Waldo Strong. On 03 Sep 1864, he mustered out at Gallipolis, OH. In his pension application for $10/mo., due to lumbago, his description was 5 ft. 8 in., fair complexion, sandy hair, and blue eyes.[396]
Francis Martin Wyeth (1814-1877)	43rd	IN Infantry, Co. G	Enrolled in Terre Haute at age 47 as a sergeant on 01 Oct 1861 in the company of which his brother, Dr. Milton Lewis Wyeth, was lieutenant. Francis, discharged for disability in 1862,[397] not only lost his brother in the war, but two of his sons, John Milton and Otis Wyeth, as well.

George Nelson Wyeth (1842-1912)	149th	IN Infantry, Co. K	He enlisted on 14 Feb 1865 in Terre Haute, IN and was discharged after the close of the Civil War on 27 Sep 1865 in Nashville, TN. When he entered the Danville, IL home for disabled soldiers at age 60, he had been employed as a blacksmith and was described as 5 ft., light complexion, blue eyes, gray hair, and protestant.[398]
George W. P. Wyeth (1844-1914)	6th 13th	NH Infantry, Co. K Veterans Reserve Corps, Co. K	George enlisted in New Ipswich, NH as a private on 20 Nov 1861. He was given a disability discharge from the Infantry at David's Island, NY on 26 Mar 1863 due to being shot in the arm during the 2nd Battle of Bull Run on 29 Aug 1862. The wound was still open and bone was seeping out of it on 01 Jul 1863 when he registered for the draft in Ashby, MA. Although his pension application said the injury bothered him the rest of his life, George went on to serve in the Veterans Reserve starting 03 Sep 1864. When discharged as a corporal on 01 Sep 1865, he was described as 5 ft. 8 in., light complexion, hazel blue eyes, and light brown hair. Farming and later a paper mill machinist were his occupations.[399]
George Washington Wyeth (1835-1916)	56th Navy	IL Infantry, Co. F Co. U.S.	He enlisted as a private on 12 Sep 1861 in Michigan City, IN and was discharged due to a double hernia on 01 Feb 1862 at Camp Douglas, IL. Starting on 25 Aug 1864 in Cincinnati, OH, he served in the Mississippi Flotilla on the gunboat USS *Tyler*. He was discharged in Mound City, IL on 12 Jun 1865.[400] At age 65, when he entered the home for disabled soldiers in Leavenworth, KS, he was a cooper (barrel maker) described as 5 ft. 9 in., light complexion, blue eyes, gray hair, and protestant.[401]
Henry Elisha Wyeth (1836-1904)	31st	IN Infantry, Co. C	Henry enrolled on 20 Sep 1861 in Terre Haute, IN. He was wounded on 06 Apr 1862 at Shiloh, TN.[402] His promotions included corporal, 01 May 1862 and sergeant, 01 Sep 1862. On 01 Jan 1864 in Bridgeport, AL, Henry enrolled again in the 31st. He was made commissary sergeant, Field & Staff, 16 Sep 1864 and promoted to 2nd lieutenant on 01 Aug 1865. He was honorably discharged on 08 Dec 1865 and mustered out at Victoria, TX. [403] [404]
James Erasmus Wyeth (1842-1924)	12th 7th	IL Infantry, Co. E IL Cavalry, Co. A	He enlisted in Paris, IL on 18 Apr 1861 to serve the infantry for three months as a private. On 10 Aug 1861, he enlisted in the cavalry and mustered in at Camp Butler, IL on 15 Sep 1861. He was promoted to sergeant and mustered out in Springfield, IL on 15 Oct 1864. He was described as a farmer, 5 ft. 10 in., brown hair, blue eyes, and fair complexion.[405]
James Madison Wyeth (1820-1863) **Supreme Sacrifice**	75th	IL Infantry, Co. I	Farmer James enrolled as a private on 07 Aug 1862 in Fulton, IL. He was discharged for disability on 26 Feb 1863 at Camp Sill, Murfreesboro, TN by order of Maj. Gen. Rosecrans. A few days later he died on 05 Mar 1863, at the age of 42, in the Rutherford, TN Military Hospital. Through over exertion and exposure from ministering to sick and wounded after the Battle of Stones River, while in the hands of the enemy, James had contracted chronic diarrhea resulting in dropsy.[406]

John Allan Wyeth (1845-1922)	4th	Alabama Cavalry (Russell's), Co. I Morgan's Raiders	After attending La Grange Military Academy in Colbert County, AL for two years, John enlisted as a private in the Confederate Army on 01 Dec 1862 in Guntersville, AL at age 17. In the summer of 1863, he was a raider under Brigadier General John Hunt Morgan. Later he served in Russell's Reg't at the Battle of Chickamauga. Captured on 05 Oct 1863, he was taken by train to Camp Morton, near Indianapolis. Severely ill, he returned to Dixie through a prisoner exchange on 01 Mar 1865.[407] However, from of the kind care of Morton's physician, John decided to become a doctor after the War.[408]
John Bound Wyeth (1842-1926)	12th	MA Infantry (Militia), Unattached Co.	Employed as a clerk, he enlisted in Cambridge, MA on 16 May 1864 as a private and mustered out in Boston, MA on 15 Aug 1864. John was described as having a dark complexion, 5 ft. 6 1/4 in., brown eyes and hair.[409]
John Jasper Wyeth (1841-1906)	44th	MA Infantry (Militia), Co. E	John's Company formed on 29 Aug 1862 at Boston's Boylston Street Mall for the train trip to camp in Readville, MA. In his journal he wrote, "We enlisted in those dark days of '62, at the call of President Lincoln, for nine months' troops. No promises were held out to us that we would not be put to as severe tests of courage, or have a chance to achieve as great deeds of heroism, as any who had preceded us. I doubt if there was one who asked or thought of where he was going, as he signed the roll at Mercantile Hall. We soon learned, to our sorrow, that a bullet could maim and kill, as well at Rawls's Mills, as at Antietam, as well in a short, as a long campaign." Again in Readville, he mustered out as a private on 18 Jun 1863.[410]
John Milton Wyeth (1840-1862) **Supreme Sacrifice**	7th	IL Cavalry, Co. A	John enlisted as a private in Paris, IL for a three-year term. On 15 Sep 1861 he mustered in with his brother, James Erasmus, at Camp Butler, IL. John was described as a farmer, 5 ft. 8 in., black hair, gray eyes, and dark complexion.[411] Less than a year later, he died at age 22 of typhoid fever on 24 Jun 1862 in the U.S. Army General Hospital, No. 3 Evansville, IN.[412] [413]
John Westlake Wyeth (1842-1905)	9th	PA Cavalry (92nd Volunteers) Co. E & L	Private Wyeth was a telegraph operator when he enlisted in Harrisburg, PA on 05 Sep 1861. He was promoted to sergeant and then to 2nd lieutenant of Co. L on 30 May 1864.[414] He mustered out 18 Jul 1865 in Harrisburg.[415]
Jonathan Wheeler Wyeth (1843-1863) **Supreme Sacrifice**	124th	OH Infantry, Co. A	Jonathan enlisted on 04 Aug 1862 in Cleveland, OH. He was reported missing on 06 Oct 1863 after the Battle of Chickamauga (fought in southeastern Tennessee and northwestern Georgia.)[416] Apparently, he made his way from the battle to Annapolis, MD[417] where he died from typhoid fever in General Hospital Div. 1 on 02 Dec 1863 at the age of 20. He is buried in a Soldier's grave at Sec. K, site 891 in the Annapolis National Cemetery.[418]
Louis Weiss Wyeth (1812-1889)	49th	AL Infantry, Co. E	Although opposed to secession, due to illness, he served only a short time in the Confederate Army.[419] [420]
Marquis de Lafayette Wyeth (1839-1864)	19th 56th 137th	OH Infantry, Co. I IL Infantry, Co. H PA Infantry, Co. B	Lafayette enlisted as a private in the 19th Ohio for three months on 27 Apr 1861.[421] After mustering out on 30 Aug 1861 in Columbus, OH, he went to IL. There he joined the Mechanics Fusiliers of the 56th as a sergeant. They

Marquis de Lafayette Wyeth (Cont'd)			were organized at Shawneetown, IL and mustered in 27 Feb 1862. Before his term of enlistment was up, Lafayette moved back to his home state to enlist as a private in the 137th in Conneautville, PA on 06 Aug 1862. He mustered out on 01 Jun 1863 at Harrisburg, PA.[422] Sadly, the next year, he was killed in a sawmill boiler explosion while working in Crossingville, PA.[423]
Matthew Wing Wyeth (1826-1909)	128th	IN Infantry, Co. E	He enlisted as a private in Valparaiso, IN on 16 Dec 1863 and was honorably discharged on 24 May 1865 in Beaufort, NC. His pension forms described him as 5 ft. 10 in., light complexion, blue eyes, and brown hair.[424]
Milton Lewis Wyeth, M.D. (1825-1862) **Supreme Sacrifice**	43rd	IN Infantry, Co. G	Milton served as a 1st lieutenant medical doctor. He contracted typhoid dysentery at Fort Pillow, located 40 miles north of Memphis, TN. He died on the steamer USS *De Soto* on 04 May 1862 near Missouri Island #10 on the Mississippi River while being transported to a military hospital in Cairo, IL.[425]
Norman DeAngelis Wyeth (1844-1886)	68th 109th 143rd	IL Infantry, Co. C IN Infantry, Co. A IL Infantry, Co. A	When Norman joined Captain St. John's Co. on 30 May 1862 in Charleston, IL, he was described as 5 ft. 6 in., light complexion, gray eyes, and dark hair. He mustered out on 20 Jul 1862. He served one week in the 109th. Then for 100 days of service, he enlisted again at Charleston, IL from 28 Apr 1864 to 26 Sep 1864 – mustering out in Mattoon, IL.[426] Just prior to leaving the service, he had been treated for the effects of drinking unsafe water in Helena, AK.[427]
Otis Wyeth (1848-1864) **Supreme Sacrifice**	11th	IN Cavalry, Co. D	Otis enlisted as a private on 09 Dec 1863 in Terre Haute, Vigo, IN.[428] His tombstone in Mewhinney Cemetery, Riley Township, Vigo County, IN says he died in the service of his country on 29 Aug 1864 at the extremely young age of 15 years, 8 months and 21 days.[429]
Richard Harvey Wyeth (1844-1864) **Supreme Sacrifice**	1st 3rd	MA Cavalry, Co. A MA Cavalry, Co. D	When he enlisted in Co. A., on 10 Sep 1861 in Boston, MA, his occupation was as a farmer. He was described as 5 ft., 11 in., having a dark complexion, hazel eyes and dark brown hair. After being discharged on a Writ of Habeas Corpus on 01 Apr 1863 in Maryland, he enlisted in Co. D on 25 Feb 1864 in Brookline, MA. He first was reported as a POW after the 19 Sep 1864 Battle of Winchester, VA.[430] However, the memorial tombstone he shares with his twin brother, William, in Cambridge Cemetery sadly confirms his death in that battle.
Samuel Kellogg Wyeth (1831-1907)	143rd	Illinois Infantry, Co. H	His name was spelled "Wyett" in the enlistment records at Hillsboro, IL on 11 Jun 1864. Samuel mustered out on 26 Sep 1864 at Mattoon, IL.[431]
Walter Herbert Wyeth (1836-1910)	11th	MI Cavalry, Co. M	He enlisted on 13 Jan 1864 in Hastings, MI and mustered out in Detroit, MI on 04 Sep 1865. Walter contracted typhoid fever in Jun 1864 at Louisa, KY. The illness gradually resulted in total deafness and death. On 12 Jun 1910, while walking on RR tracks, Walter did not hear an approaching locomotive and was killed instantly.[432]
Warren Augustus Wyeth (1843-1874?)	23rd	MA Infantry, Co. H	His enlistment was credited to Lunenburg, MA on 15 Oct 1861.[433] After mustering out in Newbern, VA on 28 Sep 1864,[434][435] Warren, a nail maker, also served the militia of Westford, MA.[436] Warren disappeared and his wife

Warren Augustus Wyeth (Cont'd)			divorced him for abandonment in 1878 – two years after their only child died at age four.[437]
William Edward Wyeth (1840–1915)	10th	MI Infantry	William mustered in as a private on 16 Mar 1865 in Stockbridge, MI. He mustered out 15 May 1865 at Hart's Island, New York Harbor, NY.[438]
William H. Wyeth (1840-1912)	1st	NY Light Artillery, Co. H	He was a farmer, described as 5 ft. 8 in., light hair, blue eyes, and light complexion, when he enrolled in Watertown, NY as a private on 02 Oct 1861. On 09 Oct 1864 he mustered out near Petersburg, VA. The hernia William got from moving a cannon under heavy fire at the Battle of Fair Oaks, VA on 30 Jun 1862, along with gunshot deafness, plagued him the rest of his life.[439]
William Henry Wyeth (1844-1864) **Supreme Sacrifice**	1st	MA Cavalry, Co. A & B	He enlisted in Co. A in Boston, MA on 21 Aug 1862. Like his twin, Richard, William also was a farmer. The pair apparently were not identical for William was 6 ft. tall, light complexion, gray eyes, and brown hair. On 17 Jun 1863, he was MIA at Aldie, VA. He was confined by the enemy and paroled a few days later. On 04 Jan 1864, he enlisted in Co. B at Warrenton, VA. Captured on 26 Jun 1864 in Petersburg, VA, he was confined in the Confederate States Military Prison, Florence, SC. [440] According to his memorial tombstone in Cambridge Cemetery, he was killed at the battle of Lee's Mills, VA.
Zachariah Taylor Wyeth (1848-1865) **Supreme Sacrifice**	37th	IN Infantry, Co. D	Taylor enrolled as a substitute on 06 Oct 1864 in Indianapolis, IN for Private William A. Moore.[441] Taylor died in General Hospital 4 / The Confederate Hospital at Wilmington, NC on 27 Mar 1865. The cause of death was not stated in the records.[442]
Allen Willie Wythe (1839-1863) **Supreme Sacrifice**	14th	IN Infantry, Co. F	Allen mustered in on 07 Jun 1861 in Terre Haute, IN. He died on 04 Apr 1863 at the age of 23 of typhoid fever in the Regimental Hospital in Spotsylvania County, VA near Fredericksburg.[443] [444] His gravestone verifies this.
Edwin Ruthven Wythe Sr. (1837-1888)	14th	IN Infantry, Co. F	Edwin enrolled 07 Jun 1861 in Terre Haute, IN. His Infantry fought at the battle of Gettysburg in Jul 1863. After almost three years' service, he was discharged for disability at Falmouth, Virginia on 06 May 1864.[445]
John Wesley Wythe (1844-1919)	71st	IN Volunteers, Co. B, (later known as the 6th Cavalry Unit)	He enrolled as a private 02 Aug 1862 at Terre Haute for a three-year term. At age 18, he was 5 ft. 9 in., gray eyes, dark hair and complexion. After the Battle of Richmond, KY, to the end of the year, John was at home in Vigo County on sick furlough due to measles. Before he had fully recovered, he was ordered to join the regiment then at Indianapolis guarding rebel prisoners in Camp Morton. Not fully recuperated, he took cold which was followed by severe coughing and splitting of blood. After a few more months service, John was discharged on 13 Apr 1863 in Indianapolis for disability due to heart disease and bronchitis. He suffered greatly the rest of his life. On 01 May 1915, he signed his name "Wyeth" but spelled his children's names "Wythe" on the same form. He stated the name could be spelled either way.[446]

As shown in the above, John Jasper Wyeth (1841–1906) kept a journal of his experiences as a private in Company E of the 44th Massachusetts Infantry (Militia). John, with a bit of humor, gives an excellent firsthand account of the harsh life of a soldier. The following shows under the date 02 Nov 1862 at Rawls's Mill, North Carolina.

> "The writer, not wishing to be wounded, persistently held his gun ready to ward off all shot, consequently one of the numerous well-aimed shots struck the gun instead of his leg, fracturing the rifle badly; the bullet, after going through the stock of the gun, entered his pantaloons, scraping a little skin from his leg, and finally found its way to his boot."[447]

When the surgeon refused to report John as wounded or missing, he reported back to his company hoping for some sleep. He found his blanket and tried to turn in, but it was of no use. There was more work at hand. It would be many more hours before John and his regiment were able to obtain some much-needed rest.

John Jasper Wyeth, private, Co. E, 44th MA Infantry. Photo courtesy of MA Soldiers, Sailors and Marines in the MA Commandery of MOLLUSGAR Dept. of MA 1866-1947 (Sargent).

> "We were detailed as baggage guard, which duty we did bravely!! Everytime the line halted we would lie down, and were asleep as soon as we struck the mud!! Finally we made a grand start, forded the stream again, and, after being frightened to death by a stampede of horses up the road, we found a cornfield, and, after forming line several times for practice with the rest of the regiment, spread ourselves on the ground and hugged each other and our wet rubber blankets to get warm.
>
> November 3. – At four o'clock this morning 'all was wrong.' We were aroused from the most miserable attempt at sleep our boys ever dreamed of trying. It was a mercy to awaken us; only we were so stiff, sore, cold, and hungry, that it was most impossible to get up at all. We were covered with dirt and frost. Our guns were in fearful condition, and we were ordered to clean them and be ready for the road in half an hour. That was good; no chance to eat anything or clean up ourselves; but such is the luck of war."[448]

Many other descendants of Nicholas Wyeth fought in the War Between the States. However, they are harder to track than those who carry the names Wyeth or Wythe.

Probably the most well-known of Nicholas' descendants in the War of Secession was General Henry Jackson Hunt (1819–1889). He was the Chief of Artillery in the Army of the Potomac. Hunt's contemporaries considered him the greatest artillery tactician and strategist of the Civil War. Even today, he is featured prominently in Civil War sagas such as the "what if" history *Gettysburg: A Novel of the Civil War* by Newt Gingrich and William R. Forstchen.

Hunt was a master of the science of gunnery and rewrote the manual on the organization and use of artillery in early modern armies. Although Hunt recognized the necessity of the power of massed artillery batteries to repel infantry, he urged his cannon crews to fire slowly and deliberately at an average of one shot per minute. He believed quicker firing impaired accuracy and depleted ammunition faster than could be replenished. He once admonished a gunner of a fast-firing cannon, "Young man, are you aware that every round you fire costs $2.67?"

His courage and tactics greatly added to the success of the Army at the battles of Malvern Hill, Antietam, Fredericksburg, and Gettysburg. When his expertise was not used to best advantage, it too affected the Army's success. Maj. Gen. Joseph Hooker angrily took Hunt's command from him in May 1863. The lack of coordination of the artillery forces that resulted were well-known factors contributing to the Union defeat in the Battle of Chancellorsville.

Maj. Gen. George G. Meade had greater respect for Hunt than Hooker did. Meade gave him enormous latitude at the Battle of Gettysburg. Hunt's handling of the artillery was prominent in the repulse of Pickett's Charge on Jul 3. Hunt directed his cannons to cease fire slowly to create the illusion that they were being destroyed one by one. This method of cannon fire fooled the Confederates into thinking Hunt's batteries were destroyed. It triggered their disastrous assault. In addition, Hunt's concealed placement of Lt. Col. Freeman McGilvery's batteries north of Little Round Top, contributed significantly to the Confederate infantry losing that hill.[449] [450]

Commanders of the Army of the Potomac, Gouverneur K. Warren, William H. French, George G. Meade, Henry J. Hunt, Andrew A. Humphreys and George Sykes in September 1863. Photo courtesy of Library of Congress Prints and Photographs Division.

Other descendants of Nicholas Wyeth who served in the Civil War include Wallace Mewhinney (1845-1875), Elliott Dudley Hewson (1831-1920), Charles Leigh Hadley (1842-1918), and Charles Augustus Read (1833-1869). Nehemiah Grover enrolled in the 78th Regiment, Ohio Infantry but there were many men with that name in Ohio, it is difficult to pinpoint which one was in the War. Also, there were many young men with the name "Gamage" in both the Union and Confederate Armies. Undoubtedly, some descended from Deborah Wyeth Gamage, but it would be almost impossible to determine how they fit.

Although he was not a soldier, Francis Wyeth (1806-1893) served the Union effort. At the outbreak of the Civil War, he was placed in charge of the quartermaster's department at Camp Curtin near Harrisburg, Pennsylvania until the central government assumed control over the military organizations of the state. On 20 Jul 1862, Pennsylvania's governor chose him as a commissioner to visit the hospitals of the Army of the Potomac in the interest of the volunteer soldiers of the state. From those visits, Francis made valuable suggestions that were quickly instituted. He served again as hospital commissioner in 1863 before retiring to private life.[451]

Francis' sons also helped with the war effort. To protect St. Joseph property from bushwhacking marauders, Francis Wyeth's oldest son, William Maxwell Wyeth (1832-1901), joined the Missouri Enrolled Militia.[452] Two other sons, John Wyeth (1834-1907) and Francis Houston Wyeth (1836–1913), supplied drugs to the war effort. The Wyeth Brothers innovation of mixing medicinal compounds in large batches in advance enabled them to sell commonly prescribed drugs at a lower price than competitors. Their main success, however, came from a government contract during the Civil War to deliver medicines and beef extract to the Union Army.[453]

A side note to John and Francis Houston Wyeth's government contract is that in Aug 1864, Dr. William Hammond, the U.S. Surgeon General, was dismissed by President Lincoln from holding any office of trust in the Government. One of the charges brought against Hammond in his court martial was that he favored the Wyeth Brothers of Philadelphia over other suppliers.[454] [455]

As shown in the preceding charts, hospital commissioner Francis Wyeth's brother, Judge Louis Weiss Wyeth (1812–1889) fought for a short time in the Confederacy. Louis appears to be the only one of Nicholas Wyeth's descendants who owned slaves. There are a Richardson Wyeth and a John / James Wyeth in the Slave Schedules. However, other schedules show "Wyatt" and "Wyett" as their correct last names. In the 1850 U.S. Federal Census Slave Schedule for District 22, Marshall County, Alabama, Louis owned a female, age 50; a male, age 23; and a female, age 12.[456] In the 1860 Schedule, he owned a female, age 33; and two children, a female, age 8; and a male, age 2.[457]

Judge Wyeth's son, Dr. John Allan Wyeth, explained in his book *With Sabre and Scalpel: The Autobiography of a Soldier and Surgeon* about his father's slave ownership.

> "As there were no white domestic servants in the South and no freed negroes in Alabama, since the law required that all emancipated slaves should be transported to a free state or exported to Liberia, my parents, both of whom favored emancipation, bought for house service two families of negroes, each consisting of the father and the mother and their children, some twelve or fifteen in all… When 'Mack,' our majordomo, was taken seriously ill, a room was given him, not in his own comfortable house, but in our residence, where we thought he could be more carefully watched. His wife, a woman of fine character, was a second mother to us as children… When in later unhappy years the war came on and I was about to mount my horse and ride away to take my place in the ranks, and said good-by to my mother and my father, I knew that back in the kitchen this devoted black woman was waiting for me to come to have her blessing; and there with her arms around 'the boy she had brought up' – for I was not yet 18 years old – I had the only 'crying-spell' of the parting scene."[458]

Dr. Wyeth was born on 26 May 1845 in Missionary Station (Guntersville), Marshall, Alabama. His father, Louis Weiss Wyeth, a Harrisburg, Pennsylvania lawyer, settled in Marshall County just after President Andrew Jackson forced the Cherokee from their Alabama lands to Oklahoma through the New Echota Treaty of 1835.[459] Having spent his entire childhood in the Deep South, John's autobiography provides a southern viewpoint for the cause of the Civil War.

John's maternal grandfather, for whom he was named, was a well-known advocate to the cause of abolition. John Allan not only organized the first Society for the Emancipation of Slavery in Alabama, but also published an anti-slavery newspaper. Dr. Wyeth stated, "Slavery was already doomed, and a bloody war was not necessary for its extinction."[460]

However, Dr. John Allan Wyeth's statement that "slavery was already doomed," seems to be contradicted by his blame of pro-slavery politicians and northern abolitionists for the Civil War.

Unlike many northerners and historians, Dr. Wyeth did not believe the introduction of the cotton gin increased the demand for slave labor. His analysis was that increases in bales of cotton produced were inconsistent with the increased price of slaves – from $50-$100 per person in early colonial days to $1000-$1500 by 1860. Dr. Wyeth pointed to three main factors for the War. First, was the success of pro-slavery politicians expanding slavery to Missouri in 1820 to counteract the influence of northern abolitionists. Second, was the repeal of the Missouri Compromise in 1854 and the passage of the Kansas-Nebraska Bill, which allowed each territory to decide the issue of slavery by popular vote. Third, John blamed the resulting Kansas conflict as "… the battleground between the contending forces of slavery and anti-slavery." He believed, it "…. spread a cyclone of insanity which swept over North and South alike in its maddening progress."[461]

Dr. Wyeth wrote that John Brown, and radical abolitionists who backed him, emerged from the ensuing turmoil. Wyeth said Brown "… sought to incite a widespread slave insurrection and the consequent massacre of thousands of helpless women and children. This wicked deed, known as the 'Harper's Ferry Raid,' made secession possible and brought on the Civil War."[462]

Perhaps in time, slavery would have ended in America as Dr. Wyeth thought. Nevertheless, so much damage was done that we are still trying to overcome it yet today. Many believe a starting point for healing is for more people to acknowledge that African Americans' American history is different from the American history of those descended from white Europeans. One example we can point to in our family's history is that Nicholas Wyeth made his own decision to sail to the Colonies. Although his ship was tiny and crowded, he was not kidnapped from his homeland by his own people, chained to the floor and lying in his own waste for the hazardous ocean voyage.

Black history also differs greatly when looking at the family as a unit. Separation through sale was a constant threat to slave families. Because of the high value placed on the labor of men, they were the most likely to be parted from their families.[463]

H. L. Stephens is the artist of *The Parting – Buy us too*, circa 1863, courtesy of the Library of Congress.

In 1965, Daniel Patrick Moynihan, an employee of the Office of Policy Planning in the Labor Department during President Lyndon Johnson's Administration, released a report called, "The Negro Family: The Case for National Action." The report, based on the work of sociologist E. Franklin Frazer, traced problems African Americans encountered in 1965 back to slavery. The report garnered both disagreement of and support for Frazer and Moynihan's findings.[464]

Moynihan's report claimed that stripping fathers from slave families had developed a fatherless, mother-centered pattern within those families. Men, he said, did not learn roles of providing and protecting. Those failings were passed down through generations.[465]

On the heels of the passage of the Civil Rights Act of 1964, Moynihan's commentary explained that equal opportunities for African Americans would not occur for generations to come unless a new and special effort is made. He cited two reasons. "First, the racist virus in the American blood stream still afflicts us: Negroes will encounter serious personal prejudice for at least another generation. Second, three centuries of sometimes unimaginable mistreatment have taken their toll on the Negro people."[466]

87

In the generation since the 1965 report, Barack Obama, an African American was elected president in 2008 and re-elected in 2012. The majority of his total vote nationwide came from white voters.[467] Undoubtedly, Moynihan would not have anticipated such an outcome. In the president's 2014 State of the Union address, he said, "What I believe unites the people of this nation, regardless of race or region or party, young or old, rich or poor, is the simple, profound belief in opportunity for all – the notion that if you work hard and take responsibility, you can get ahead." He implored Congress to help all hard-working Americans.[468]

Additionally, President Obama encouraged Americans not to leave Democracy totally in the hands of politicians. He declared, "Change will not come if we wait for some other time. We are the ones we've been waiting for. We are the change that we seek."

In 2016, presidential candidate, Bernie Sanders advocated for more people coming into the political process by running for office. Sanders declared, "Democracy is not a spectator sport. People fought and died for ordinary people to determine the future of our country."

Many descendants of Nicholas Wyeth fought and died for America's democratic ideals. A quote on the memorial stone of two Wyeth brothers who died in the Civil War expresses gratitude for all those who made noble sacrifices for the freedom of ordinary people... "The flag they died for thank God floats o'er their graves." No stronger words than Abraham Lincoln's describe this extraordinary heroism ...

In Memory of Twin Brothers
William H. Wyeth–Killed at Lee's Mills, VA
Richard H. Wyeth–Killed at the
Battle of Winchester, VA
"The flag they died for thank God floats o'er their graves"
Cambridge Cemetery, Cambridge, MA.

> "... from these honored dead we take increased devotion to that cause for which they gave the last full measure of devotion. That we here highly resolve that these dead shall not have died in vain. That this nation, under God, shall have a new birth of freedom and that government of the people, by the people, for the people shall not perish from the earth."

Unfortunately, heroism and sacrifice did not end with the Civil War. Of Nicholas Wyeth's decendants, Albert Wyeth was shot on 21 Jun 1869 at age 22 in Cuba's Ten-Year War. Harrison Everett Fillebrown (1871-1906), Dr. Marlborough Churchill Wyeth (1855–1924), Huston Wyeth (1863-1925), Ernest Norman Wyeth (1865–1932), Paul Chamberlain Wyeth (1854-1930) and George Henry Wyeth (1874-1949) were in the service in the period of the Spanish-American War. Norman Augustus Wyeth (1880-1911) and Guy Angus Wyeth (1874-1900) served in the Philippine-American War. Guy, shot in the hip in Lanpay, died of his wounds. This quote from an unknown soldier's grave defines the heroic sacrifice of too many Americans, "Freedom is a light for which many men have died in darkness."

God willing, I will write another book to tell the stories of the veterans of that war to end all wars. We know, of course, it did not end all wars. When I wrote this concluding paragraph to this section on *Heroism and Sacrifice*, it was 07 Dec 2016 – the solemn 75th anniversary of the bombing of Pearl Harbor. That attack plunged the United States into World War II and launched the greatest generation. You know them best... they were your grandfathers and grandmothers, your fathers and mothers, your uncles and aunts. Please send me their stories for another book. I am going to take the advice of Lin-Manuel Miranda, "Tomorrow is not promised, but make plans anyway."

FAMOUS FAMILIES

Celebrated artist, James Browning "Jamie" Wyeth, a five-year veteran of the Delaware Air National Guard, paints portraits of pigs and presidents with equal skill.[469] Walking in the legendary footsteps of his father, Andrew, and grandfather, N. C., Jamie is undoubtedly now the most famous Wyeth-named descendant.

On a 2015 visit to the Brandywine River Museum in Chadds Ford, Pennsylvania, my siblings Jeff, Kitty and Marc Wyeth helped me demonstrate the size of Jamie Wyeth's *Portrait of Pig*, oil on canvas, painted in 1970. Jamie's biography from the sign to Jeff's left appears in quotes in the text box on this page.

The portrait of John F. Kennedy shown on the foreword page of this book was acquired by the Boston Museum of Fine Arts in 2014.[470] In 1967, Jamie painted JFK in the space pictured below. It is located just outside the room that was his father's studio.

We learned another interesting fact regarding Jamie while taking tours from the museum. It concerns the cubes, cones and spheres on these shelves in N. C.'s studio. For a whole year, Jamie's aunt Carolyn Bockius Wyeth made him draw them, and nothing else, over and over until he was absolutely bored to tears.

> **"Jamie Wyeth**
>
> Over a period of five decades Wyeth has created a body of work that clearly speaks to his evolution as an artist. Familiar subjects — whether they be people, animals, landscapes or found objects — are often transformed by the artist's hand and dexterous imagination.
>
> The youngest child of Andrew and Betsy Wyeth, Jamie Wyeth (born in 1946) demonstrated precocious drawing ability and was given formal art training as a child by his aunt, Carolyn Wyeth. By his early 20s he had achieved attention for his portraits, including that of John F. Kennedy. Those early oil portraits are characterized by precise detail and a dark, earth-tone palette, and his exuberant landscapes in watercolor at times recall those of his father, with whom he shared a studio space until 1968.
>
> Wyeth continued the family legacy of painting the Brandywine region and mid-coast Maine and found inspiration in the people and landscapes of these two distinctive locales. While embracing the longstanding realist tradition, the artist has developed a singular approach. Throughout his career, Wyeth has experimented in his use of drawing and painting mediums. He freely mixes media and applies them to a variety of painting surfaces, creating complex effects of surface and texture."

It is to Jamie whom many Wyeths want to know how they relate. Following is a chart to help answer the question we often hear when someone learns our surname… "So how are you related to the Wyeth artists?" I used this chart in Hawaii when a tour guide at Doris Duke's Shangri La asked me how the estate's architect, Marion Sims Wyeth, was related to the Wyeth artists.

To use the chart, replace the name in block one with your common ancestor. Then replace the names down the column to you and replace the names across the top row to Jamie.

	1	2	3	4	5	6	7	8
1	Ebenezer Sr. Common Ancestor	Noah Wyeth Son or Daughter	Captain Job Grandson or Daughter	Andrew Newell Sr. Great Grandson or Daughter	Andrew Newell Jr. 2nd Great Grandson or Daughter	Newell Convers "NC" 3rd Great Grandson or Daughter	Andrew Newell "Andy" 4th Great Grandson or Daughter	James Browning "Jamie" 5th Great Grandson or Daughter
2	Ebenezer Jr. Son or Daughter	Siblings (Brother or Sister)	Nephew or Niece	Grand Nephew or Niece	Great Grand Nephew or Niece	2nd Great Grand Nephew or Niece	3rd Great Grand Nephew or Niece	4th Great Grand Nephew or Niece
3	Ebenezer III Grandson or Daughter	Nephew or Niece	First Cousin	First Cousin Once Removed	First Cousin Twice Removed	First Cousin Three Times Removed	First Cousin Four Times Removed	First Cousin Five Times Removed
4	Stephen Great Grandson or Daughter	Grand Nephew or Niece	First Cousin Once Removed	Second Cousin	Second Cousin Once Removed	Second Cousin Twice Removed	Second Cousin Three Times Removed	Second Cousin Four Times Removed
5	Francis John 2nd Great Grandson or Daughter	Great Grand Nephew or Niece	First Cousin Twice Removed	Second Cousin Once Removed	Third Cousin	Third Cousin Once Removed	Third Cousin Twice Removed	Third Cousin Three Times Removed
6	William 3rd Great Grandson or Daughter	2nd Great Grand Nephew or Niece	First Cousin Three Times Removed	Second Cousin Twice Removed	Third Cousin Once Removed	Fourth Cousin	Fourth Cousin Once Removed	Fourth Cousin Twice Removed
7	Florin 4th Great Grandson or Daughter	3rd Great Grand Nephew or Niece	First Cousin Four Times Removed	Second Cousin Three Times Removed	Third Cousin Twice Removed	Fourth Cousin Once Removed	Fifth Cousin	Fifth Cousin Once Removed
8	Richard Caldwell Fifth Great Grandson or Daughter	4th Great Grand Nephew or Niece	First Cousin Five Times Removed	Second Cousin Four Times Removed	Third Cousin Three Times Removed	Fourth Cousin Twice Removed	Fifth Cousin Once Removed	Sixth Cousin
9	Tina Wyeth Baker Sixth Great Grandson or Daughter	5th Great Grand Nephew or Niece	First Cousin Six Times Removed	Second Cousin Five Times Removed	Third Cousin Four Times Removed	Fourth Cousin Three Times Removed	Fifth Cousin Twice Removed	Sixth Cousin Once Removed

In the late 1960s, 40 years before Jamie's father won the Presidential Medal of Freedom and 20 years before the sensational Helga paintings brought him to the covers of both *Time* and *Newsweek*, Andrew Wyeth was chiefly known as the creator of *Christina's World*.[471]

Since my given name is "Christina," my father thought perhaps if I would write to our famous and distinguished cousin, he would write back. Indeed, Andrew Wyeth did respond to my letter with suggestions to help my father in his own painting pursuits. The letter from Andrew has been

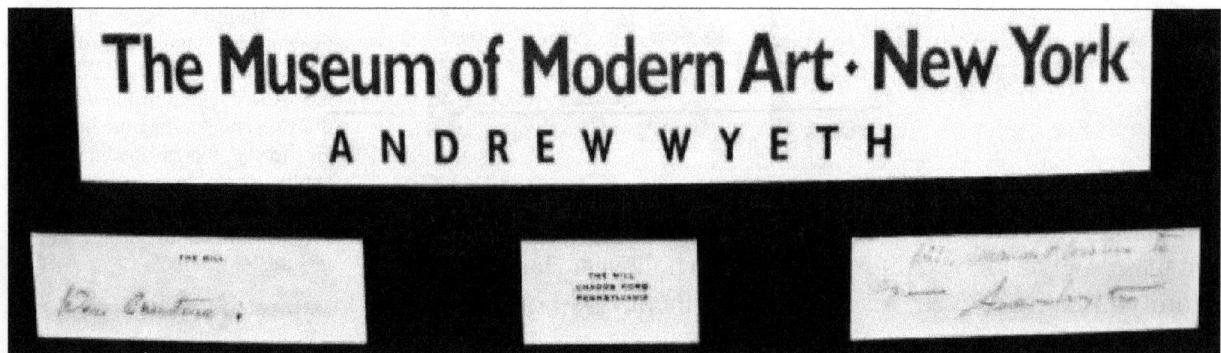

framed for a long time below a *Christina's World* print I purchased at MOMA. I am not sure of the letter's date. I think it is probably 1967. It is one of my most prized possessions.

This photo of Andrew Wyeth standing outside his father's studio is courtesy of my brother, Marc Wyeth.

Alternatively, through the centuries, many Wyeths / Wythes have taken pride in being related to other family members who have distinguished the surnames.

Nathaniel Jarvis Wyeth did not have children, but many Wyeths, including Andrew's father, N. C., proudly talked of their collateral connection to the renowned Oregon explorer. In 1925, referring to his painting of Oregon Trail historian, Francis Parkman, N. C. Wyeth said, "The Oregon Trail has always been deep in my blood. I feel very much stirred to interpret my dreams into pictures."[472]

The portrait on the wall of the dining room in N. C.'s Chadds Ford home is of N. C.'s great uncle, John Bound Wyeth, who accompanied Nathaniel Jarvis Wyeth westward.

Courtesy of Marvel June Wyeth Cardella Ucen, we have a letter in which N. C. Wyeth mentions John Bound Wyeth. It was sent to June's uncle, Charles Eugene "Charlie" Wyeth. June was one of my brother's earliest correspondents. She sent Jeff many letters outlining her ancestors from the son of Ebenezer Jr., Gad Wyeth, to her father, Frank Wallace Wyeth. Charlie and Frank's grandfather, Silas Jabez Wyeth, was born in New York while his ancestors were making the trek west from Cambridge. Gad and some of his family settled in Ohio, but Silas went on to Iowa where Charlie, Frank and June, were born. Charlie Wyeth eventually landed in California, as did June's son, Richard Cardella … who found a bit of fame on his own. Richard starred in the 1977 horror film *The Crater Lake Monster*.

N. C. Wyeth's letter to Charlie is postmarked Chadds Ford, PA – 14 Apr 1933. Although it is addressed minimally to "Master Charlie Wyeth of Modesto, California," it maximally addresses the vast knowledge N. C. had of his Wyeth roots as well as the pride he had in his family name.

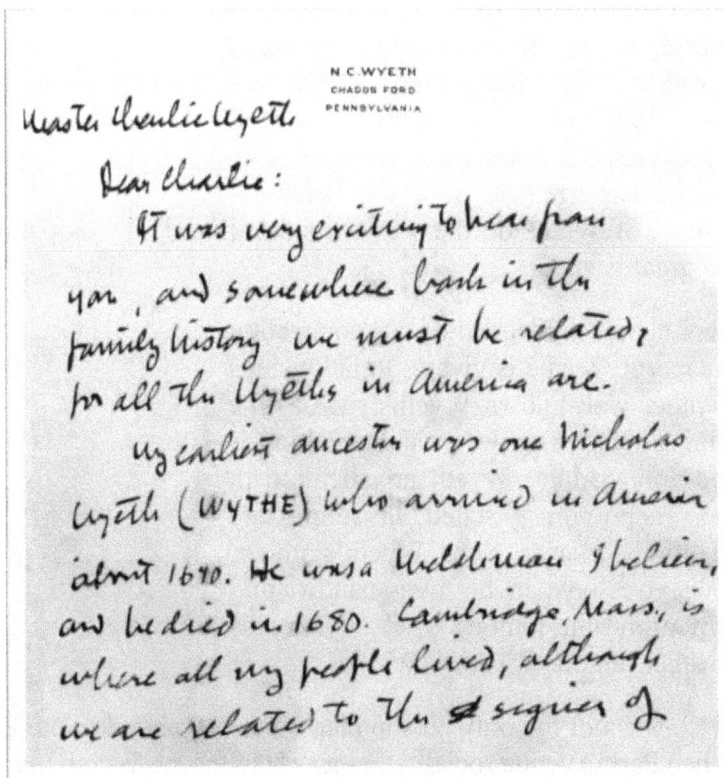

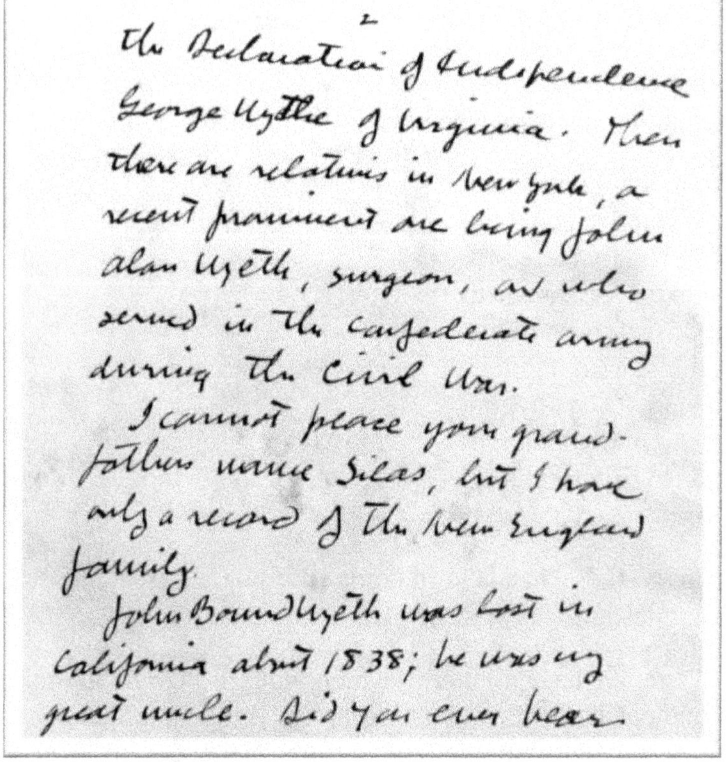

[Handwritten letter, page 2:]

the Declaration of Independence
George Wythe of Virginia. Then
there are relations in New York, a
recent prominent one being John
Alan Wyeth, surgeon, and who
served in the Confederate army
during the Civil War.

I cannot place your grandfather's name Silas, but I have
only a record of the New England
family.

John Bound Wyeth was lost in
California about 1838; he was my
great uncle. Did you ever hear

N. C. starts the letter stating all Wyeths in America are related. True indeed. Up to the time of his father's birth, all we know who spelled their name *Wyeth*, did descend from Nicholas Wyeth. It is largely true yet today. Exceptions include John H. Wyeth who married E. Rodeheaver. John's family came from England in the 1840s. Perhaps he was the perfumer who advertised Cream of Lilies of London in Doggett's 1846 directory of New York City.[473] Their children were Harry Bissell, John Hamilton, Frank Burford and George Austin Wyeth. Also, not from Nicholas, are the Knox County, Ohio offspring of William R. Wythe, born in Ireland about 1815, as well as descendants of a Philadelphia Wythe family who settled there in about 1830.

N. C. mentions in his letter that Nicholas was a Welshman. In 1933, N. C. was, of course, basing his information on Jonas Wyeth's 1850s family tree. It was not until 1948 that Marion Sims Wyeth discovered Nicholas came from Saxtead on the eastern side of Great Britain – instead of Wales on the western side of the great island.

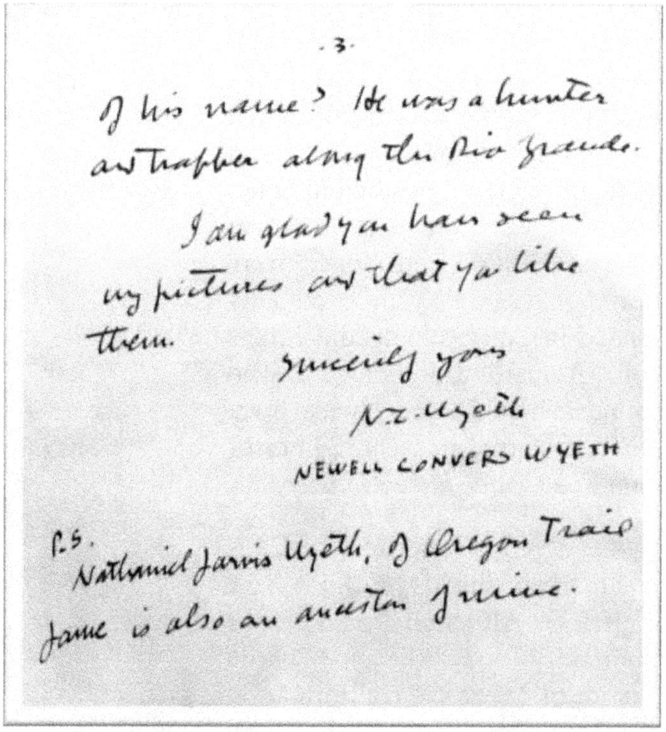

Here again, the legend of our connection to George Wythe is given. Relationships to other well-known Wyeths such as the aforesaid brave explorers Nathaniel Jarvis and John Bound Wyeth are mentioned, too. As previously stated, Dr. John Allan Wyeth is Marion Sims Wyeth's father. Thus, we have in his own handwriting how proud the famous N. C. Wyeth was of other famous Wyeths / Wythes.

[Handwritten letter, page 3:]

of his name? He was a hunter
and trapper along the Rio Grande.

I am glad you have seen
my pictures and that you like
them.
            sincerely yours
            N. C. Wyeth
            NEWELL CONVERS WYETH

P.S.
Nathaniel Jarvis Wyeth, of Oregon Trail
fame is also an ancestor of mine.

N. C. was not the only person pleased to be related to the famed surgeon, Dr. John Allan Wyeth. When Park Avenue socialite Frances Hawthorne Wyeth married Edward Kenneth Hadden in 1915, her father, George Edward Wyeth, was still alive. Curiously, her father's name did not appear in the notice of her nuptials. Frances' stepfather walked her to the altar. However, a wedding guest, her distant cousin, Dr. John Allan Wyeth, was proudly mentioned in the *New York Times* article.[474]

Dr. John Allan Wyeth founded the New York Polyclinic (the first post-graduate medical school in the United States). He is considered the father of graduate medical and surgical education. In his 1914 autobiography, *With Sabre and Scalpel: The Autobiography of a Soldier and Surgeon*, Dr. Wyeth also proudly shared the legend handed down in the family that George Wythe, Signer of the Declaration of Independence, and Nicholas Wyeth, his fourth great-grandfather, were of the same British family.[475]

Although, he was well known for writing about the U.S. Capitol Building, Samuel Douglass Wyeth's 1881 obituary referred to his relationship to the Philadelphia Walnut Street druggist, John Wyeth.[476] The obituary, however, confused his nephew, the founder of Philadelphia-based John Wyeth and Brother, Inc. with Samuel's brother, John Wyeth Jr., a druggist who lived in Harrisburg, Pennsylvania.

Speaking of confusion, some people believed that John Wyeth, the Walnut Street druggist, also developed the much-advertised Wyeth's Sage and Sulphur Compound. Actually, John's first cousin, Louis Wyeth, developed the hair dye / restorer for the Wyeth Chemical Company, Inc. of Rochester, New York. When Louis' son, John Louis Wyeth, took over the company circa 1905, he started an ad campaign claiming he would grow hair on the head of John D. Rockefeller or forfeit $1,000.[477] [478] In 1926, American Home Products (AHP) purchased Wyeth's Sage and Sulphur, then of New York City.[479] When AHP acquired the Philadelphia-based John Wyeth and Brother, Inc. from Harvard University in 1931, the first cousins' companies did then indeed come under the same umbrella of ownership.[480]

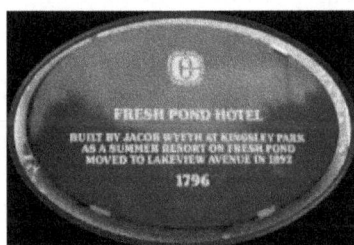

A Wyeth compound of another sort, Cambridge's Fresh Pond Hotel was one of the most celebrated vacation destinations around Boston in the 18th century. Jacob Wyeth Sr., father of Oregon explorer, Nathaniel Jarvis, owned and operated the hotel until his 1816 retirement. Jacob then leased it to his nephew, Jonas Wyeth 3d, who managed it until circa 1840.[481] The resort was built on land Jacob purchased from his father, Ebenezer Wyeth Jr.

Among many other interesting family connections to Ebenezer Wyeth Jr. are Governor John Hancock, the LARGE signer of the Declaration of Independence, was his 2nd cousin, and Major General Artemas Ward, George Washington's second in command of the Continental Army, was Ebenezer's 2nd cousin 1x removed.[482]

While the Declaration of Independence was discussed in July 1776, John Hancock sat at the head table in the Assembly room of Philadelphia's Independence Hall (then called the Pennsylvania State House). George Wythe, together with his former pupil, Thomas Jefferson, sat with the rest of the Virginia delegation at the tables closest to my camera. That is Jefferson's cane on the right hand table.

93

Ebenezer Wyeth Jr.'s son, Joshua Wyeth Sr., participated in the Boston Tea Party at age 15. Over 50 years later, Timothy Flint's 1827 Cincinnati interview with Joshua was the earliest widely-published, first-person account of the event.[483] [484] Excerpts from Joshua's report follow.

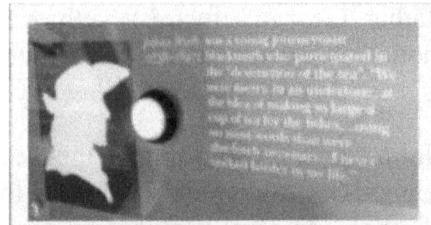

Some of Joshua Wyeth's story about the Boston Tea Party can be heard by pushing a button on a diorama in Boston's South Meeting House.

"We were dressed to resemble Indians, as much as possible. We had smeared our faces with grease and soot, or lampblack. We should not have known each other, except by our voices, and we surely resembled devils from the bottomless pit, rather than men.... "Some of our number jumped into the hold, and passed the chests to the tackle. As they were hoisted on deck, others knocked them open with axes, and others raised them to the railing, and discharged their contents overboard.... "I never labored harder in my life; and we were so expeditious that, although it was late in the evening when we began, we had discharged the whole three cargoes before morning dawn.... "Proclamations and rewards to procure detection were all to no purpose. We pretended to be as zealous to find out the perpetrators as the rest. We often talked with the Tories about it. We were all so close and loyal that the whole affair remained in Egyptian darkness. "We used sometimes afterwards to meet and talk the affair over, never failing to end by drinking, 'The hearty boys of America forever.'"

Another one of Ebenezer Wyeth Jr.'s sons, John, a Harrisburg newspaper owner, was made the postmaster of the Pennsylvania capital under President George Washington. However, believing it conflicted with the newspaper business, the position was removed by Thomas Jefferson's postmaster general on 27 Jan 1802.[485] Later, John Wyeth made a remarkable contribution to popular music when he published an introduction to the grounds of music in his shape-note *Repository of Sacred Music*.[486] [487]

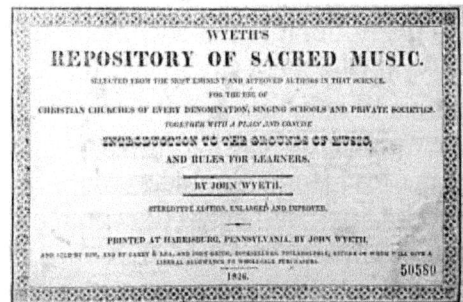

Prolific Shaker music composer, Eunice Bathrick Wyeth, wrote over 600 hymns from 1791 to her death in 1830.[488] Her hymn, *The Humble Heart*, is still sung 200 years later.[489]

Three of Postmaster John Wyeth's grandsons, all sons of Francis Wyeth, became some of the most well-known businessmen of their time. The aforementioned Philadelphia Walnut Street druggists, John, and his brother, Francis Houston Wyeth, built the humble drugstore and research lab they founded in 1860 into the pharmaceutical giant, Wyeth. In 2009, Pfizer purchased Wyeth (AHP) for a $68 billion cash-and-stock deal.[490]

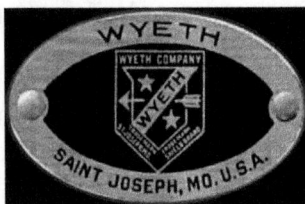

While John and Francis developed their manufacturing facilities in the east, their brother, William Maxwell Wyeth, established a hardware industry at the departure point to the Wild West. His St. Joseph, Missouri, company grew swiftly to meet the supply demands of wagon trains needing everything, from hatchets to dishes, for their journey to resettlement. In 1872, William began manufacturing horse harnesses and saddles.[491] Saddles displaying the Wyeth logo, like the emblem pictured (a gift from my sixth cousin William Maxwell "Max" Wyeth IV), are highly prized by collectors.

Actors Bing Russell and his son, Kurt, are descended from Elizabeth Wyeth and Deacon John Winship through their daughter Elizabeth's marriage to Jason Russell Sr. Neil Oliver "Bing" Russell appeared in over 100 movies and TV shows during his 40-year career as a character actor. Many of his performances were in westerns. Although uncredited, Bing was in one of the greatest westerns of all time, *Rio Bravo* with John Wayne and Dean Martin.[492]

Kurt Russell is one of the few child actors to emerge successfully as an adult star. In 1963, he performed with Elvis Presley in *It Happened at the World's Fair*. In 2015, he starred in Quentin Tarantino's movie, *the Hateful Eight*. Through the years, he played in a wide variety of vehicles from *Overboard* with his long-time partner, Goldie Hawn, to his critically acclaimed role as Wyatt Earp in *Tombstone*. While Kurt played the title part to perfection in the 1979 TV biopic, *Elvis*, his real-life father, Bing Russell, played Elvis' real-life father, Vernon Presley.[493]

The Russells are a charming and close-knit family. Kurt actively promotes sister Jody Philbrick's Bridges for Brain Injury program. His youngest sibling, Jami Way, is director of sales for Kurt's GoGi Wines. Oldest sister, Jill, is mom to baseball athlete, Matthew Neil Franco. Although Kurt and Bing both played minor league baseball, Matt had a long career in the majors. First drafted in 1987 by the Chicago Cubs, he played the positions of first and third baseman and pinch hitter. Matt ended his baseball career on 27 Sep 2003 with the Atlanta Braves.[494]

Another famous baseball player in the family, Eddie Taubensee, descends from Orrin and Jennie Danforth Wyeth. Eddie played catcher for three different ballclubs during his ten-year career in the majors. He started with the Cleveland Indians in 1991 and ended there in 2001. He was traded to the Houston Astros and then to the Cincinnati Reds where he became one of the Reds' best hitters in 1999.[495]

The exploits of New York Lawn Tennis star George Lorraine Wyeth filled newspaper sports' sections from 1895 to 1910. On 03 Aug 1906, he won the state of Ohio Tennis Championship in Cleveland.[496]

This photo of George Lorraine Wyeth, circa 1890, is courtesy of Deb Wyeth Wilkie, his granddaughter.

Starting his career by winning 14 Gold Medals in the 1981 Michigan Regional Cerebral Palsy Games, Duncan Orn Wyeth has won numerous discus and cycling events. After participating in the 1988 Paralympic Games in Seoul, South Korea, Duncan moved to administration and was honored with the Rick Knas Lifetime Achievement Award in 2004.[497]

Frederick William Cox, a descendant of Joshua Wyeth, was a pre-med student at the University of Pittsburgh when he was drafted in 1961 by both the NFL for the Cleveland Browns and by the AFL for the New York Titans. Although Fred did not play for either team, he had a dazzling career from 1963 to 1977 with the Minnesota Vikings. He is the Vikings all-time leader in scoring (1,365 points) and field goals (282). Fred is one of 11 men who played in all four of the 1970s Vikings' Super Bowls. Amazingly multi-talented, Dr. Fred practiced chiropractics, is a pilot, and invented the Nerf football.[498]

Public domain photo of Fred Cox from *Boy's Life* Dec. 1975

In 1860, Elizabeth Palmer Peabody, who descended from William Wyeth through his daughter, Martha Wyeth Fessenden, founded the first public Kindergarten in the U.S. Elizabeth, a leader in the transcendentalist movement believed firmly in the inherent goodness of both man and nature. Overshadowed by other intellectuals in her circle, like her brothers-in-law, Horace Mann and Nathaniel Hawthorne, Elizabeth is nevertheless considered one of the most important women of her time for her work in education and social reform.[499] [500] Her selflessness was shadowed by her niece, Rose Hawthorne, a Dominican sister now being considered for sainthood by the Vatican.[501]

Pete Souza's photo of President Barack Obama greeting White House Press Secretary Josh Earnest's son, Walker, and his wife, Natalie Wyeth Earnest, in the Outer Oval Office, 1/21/2016.

We turn now to the musical talent of Howard Pyle Wyeth, a rock drummer and jazz pianist, best known for his work with Bob Dylan.[502] Howard's father, Nathaniel Convers "Nat" Wyeth, son of the aforementioned artist N. C. Wyeth, helped invent the plastic soda bottle. Political fame for the family comes through the inventor's granddaughter, Natalie Pyle Wyeth. She was appointed as the U.S. Department of the Treasury's Public Affairs Assistant Secretary on 16 May 2013.[503] Not only were her great grandfather, grandfather and uncle Howard well known but Natalie is married to Josh Earnest, President Barack Obama's Press Secretary.[504] [505]

While we are talking about the President, it is an appropriate time to mention architect Nathan Corwith Wyeth who designed the entire West Wing of the White House as well as scores of other structures in the Capital city. Additionally, in 1909, it was Nathan's idea to make the President's Office oval to mirror the Blue Room.[506] Unfortunately, the Oval Office Nathan created for President Taft was damaged by fire in 1929. Although it kept the oval feature, the President's office of today was built when the West Wing was enlarged in 1934.[507]

White House, President's Office, 1909 - Courtesy Harris & Ewing, Inc. gift to the Library of Congress.

We end this section with another prominent architect – Marion Sims Wyeth. He has already been mentioned several times in this book for his excellent genealogical skills. However, for his incredible architectural skills, he was legendary. While Marion is primarily associated with the design of opulent gilded-age mansions, his work includes hospitals, churches, the Governor's Mansion in Tallahassee, and High Point monument in New Jersey. However, his most notable creation is Shangri La, built for Doris Duke's Islamic art collection in Honolulu, Hawaii.[508] Also, celebrated among his designs is Palm Beach's Mar-a-Lago. He was hired by cereal heiress Marjorie Merriweather Post to do the lush external design while Joseph Urban did the interior design.[509] [510] Now, in 2019, the estate is often called the Florida White House.

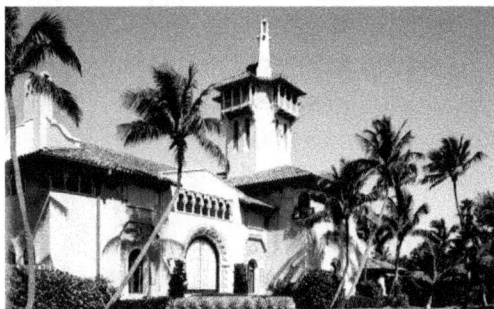

Mar-a-Lago image courtesy of the Federal Historic American Buildings Survey in Florida gift to the Library of Congress.

AT HOME IN CAMBRIDGE WITH A DASH OF NOTORIETY

Although there are several Wyeth / Wythe homes and buildings still standing in Cambridge, here are pictures of two that no longer exist. The first is a tracing I did from a photo in NEHGS Mss A 3058 manuscript file.[511] The old house with three ladies

in the yard is probably the home first owned by Nicholas Wyeth in 1645 since it matches the shape of the Wyeth home on Garden and Phillips Place on the 1854 H. F. Walling map. The Sheraton Commander now sits at that corner. Jonas Wyeth 2^d (1806-1868) was the last Wyeth to reside there at 18 Garden Street, but he later moved to other houses he built on Wyeth land.[512] In 1849, he paid taxes on seven properties.[513]

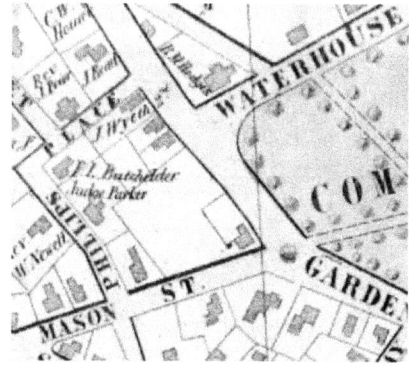

Harvard University's Wyeth Hall, the law school dormitory at 1595 Massachusetts Avenue, Cambridge, was taken down in 2008 to make way for The Wasserstein Hall, Caspersen Student Center, and Clinical Wing law school complex.[514] Photos of the Wyeth Hall building comes to us via the kind permission of Nor'East Architectural Antiques and the Harvard Archives.[515] [516] The building was originally owned by Sargent College before Sargent was moved in 1958 from Cambridge to the Charles River Campus of Boston University.[517]

Harvard's Wyeth Hall Dormitory – photo courtesy of Donna Eldredge, Nor'East Architectural Antiques.

Wyeth Hall - UAV 605 Box 88 (GS 45). Courtesy of the Harvard University Archives.

After Harvard purchased and remodeled the building, they named it for their 1884 alumnus Stuart Wyeth (1862-1929) who willed them $5,800,000 and the pharmaceutical company his father, John Wyeth (1834-1907) and Uncle Francis Houston Wyeth (1836-1913), founded in Philadelphia.[518] Wyeth's gift to the University built the Biological Laboratories, the Museum of Comparative Zoology, Harvard Observatory, the Peabody Museum, and the School of Dental Medicine. Beginning in Sep 1958, Wyeth Hall was the first dorm open to women at the University when 73 female students of the graduate schools of Public Administration, Law, Design, Education, and Divinity, called the building home.[519]

A First Lady was one of the most famous ladies to call Wyeth Hall home. Michelle Lavaughn Robinson lived in room 503 some seven years before she became Mrs. Barack Obama.[520]

Other fame for Wyeth Hall was its "appearance" as Wyeth House in the movie *Legally Blonde*. However, due to Harvard's unwillingness to have their campus shown in films, Wyeth Hall's "stunt" double in the movie was in actuality a relabeled, dressed-up University of Southern California building.[521]

Wyeth Hall. UAV 605 Box 88 (GS 44), Harvard University Archives

Just as Wyeth Hall came and went at Harvard, so did Stuart Wyeth's 1929 bequest. Only two years after Harvard acquired the John Wyeth and Brother pharmaceutical company, they sold it to AHP for $2.9 million on the strength of the 1930 purchase of Anacin – the popular headache pain medicine.

Although Stuart was a bachelor and John's only son, Francis had a son, Maxwell, and two grandsons. Maxwell Wyeth held a degree in pharmacy and had been active in the family business until he fell out with first cousin, Stuart. Stuart was trained as an attorney and was known for having more interest in traveling than in the company. Maxwell resigned in 1913, the same year his father died. He did, however, maintain a presence on the board of directors until 1929.[522]

This yellow Wyeth-Wesselhoeft house at 26-28 Garden Street was originally in the Greek Revival style, but was greatly remodeled in 1897.

As the crow flies, one block west of the Harvard Law School are three houses Jonas Wyeth 2[d] (1806-1868) built on land which was originally owned by Nicholas and his son, John. The yellow house, at 26-28 Garden Street in Cambridge, was built in 1841 and the red cottage at 10 Concord Avenue was built in 1837. Concord Avenue, almost 200 years younger than Garden Street, was laid out from the town common in 1803.[523]

This red Federal cottage, the Wyeth-Murdock house, was built by Jonas 2[d] in 1837 at 10 Concord Avenue.

The 1782 home of Noah Wyeth Sr. at 107 Garden Street (not shown) sits on or near Nicholas' west-field land on what was called in 1645 the "highway to the Great Swamp" and the "highway to the Fresh Pond."[524] [525] The heirs of his son, Captain Job Wyeth (1776–1840), built this white house at 99 Garden Street in 1841.[526] Nearby Taylor Square used to be called Wyeth Square.[527]

Captain Job's family home photo is courtesy of Geri Wyeth Watson.

This gray house at 22 Garden Street was built or substantially renovated in 1837 as well. The basement contains the frame of a possibly much earlier structure indicating it could have been

This gray house at 22 Garden is known as the Wyeth-Webster house.

the location of John Wyeth Sr.'s 17th century home.[528] It is known as the Wyeth-Webster house because Jonas Wyeth 2[d] leased the house to Harvard Professor Dr. John White Webster before White murdered Dr. George Parkman in 1849. Although Parkman was killed at the Harvard Medical School on North Grove Street in Cambridge, large crowds thronged outside this Garden Street home during Webster's highly publicized trial. Webster's motive was his desperation over a debt he owed Parkman. He was hanged in Boston on 30 Aug 1850.[529] [530]

Jonas Wyeth 2[d] was the subject of much notoriety himself. Beginning in 1838, while the family lived in Philadelphia, Jonas became convinced his wife, Mary Torrey Hancock (1812-1904), was having an affair with Horatio Hastings, a second cousin on the maternal side of his family. Jonas and Mary separated in 1842, shortly after their son Edwin was born.[531]

When his brother, Augustus Wyeth (1801-1831) died unmarried, Jonas Wyeth 2[d] inherited much of the Cambridge land that had been in the Wyeth family for almost 200 years. The land fell in line from Ebenezer Wyeth Sr. (1698-1754), to Jonas Wyeth Sr. (1730-1813), to Jonas Wyeth (1762-1828) who styled himself "Major Jonas." As the beneficiary of those lands, together with the stint as a merchant in Philadelphia, Jonas 2[d] was quite a wealthy man.

In those days, the intention to divorce had to be published several times in the newspaper. So, beginning in 1844, Jonas published a notice that he would no longer pay his wife's debts.[532]

Four years later, the divorce case came to trial in the Supreme Court at Cambridge. Another indication of Jonas' wealth was his attorney …THE Daniel Webster.[533] The divorce trial details were sensationalized in newspapers all over the country.[534] *The New York Herald* published actual testimony of two employees who lived in the Wyeth household in 1838. Horace Keay saw Mrs. Wyeth and Hastings frolicking in the hay during harvest. Hannah Maria Wheeler surprised Mrs. Wyeth and Hastings as they were both lying down on a bed. Hastings had his coat, vest and boots off.[535] Even with such testimony, Webster's vast skill as a courtroom lawyer did not procure the divorce Jonas desired. After Mary testified, claims of her adultery were dismissed.[536] On 15 Feb 1849, Boston newspapers published the divorce was refused.[537]

Undeterred, Jonas Wyeth 2[d], having learned divorce practices were looser in Iowa, went to that state's capital. He did not move there – for the 1850 census showed Jonas living in Cambridge with his three children Augusta, Lucy and Edwin. Mary Torrey was boarding in a separate house next door. On 28 Jun 1851, two Burlington, Iowa, attorneys detailed to the District Court of Des Moines County Jonas' reasons for desiring a divorce. One of whom, James Grimes, would later be the state's governor from 1854 to 1858.[538]

Jonas' petition stated he furnished Mary with a comfortable life, complete with many luxuries and that he was kind and affectionate to her. He said Mary told him she did not return the affection and only married him for the sake of his money. Jonas declared Mary's bad temper, stubbornness and lack of decorum set poor examples for their children. Also, unbecoming for a mother was her conduct with other men, particularly, Horatio Hastings. Although she deserted him in Dec 1842, Jonas did not desire for her to return because of Mary's bad influence on their children. Furthermore, Jonas' petition asked the court to make Mary Torrey Wyeth, late Hancock, a party to the suit as defendant, that a subpoena be issued against her, requiring her to appear at the next term of the court to answer the allegations.[539]

Per Jonas' wish, on 10 Sep 1851, a subpoena was issued for Mary to appear at the next term of court. However, on the same date, E. H. Ives, Des Moines County Sheriff, wrote on the return, "The herein named Mary Torrey Wyeth not found in my bailiwick." This does not necessarily mean Mary did not receive notice of the impending divorce. A similar return appeared on the notice to Jonas when he was sued for divorce a few years later by Sarah Elizabeth Benson Johnson. In the latter case, there was a separate notice stating he was served in Massachusetts.[540] As in Massachusetts, the intention to divorce had to appear in the state's newspapers. It is unlikely the following newspaper notice from the 02 Oct 1851 *Burlington Hawk Eye* of Burlington, Iowa, or the other five notices the paper published, reached the eyes or ears of Mary Torrey Hancock Wyeth 1,300+ miles away in Cambridge.[541] Perhaps distance is why Jonas chose Iowa.

"STATE OF IOWA, Des Moines County, ss. District Court of Des Moines County
Jonas Wyeth vs. Mary Torrey Wyeth late Mary Torrey Hancock.
The state of Iowa, to Mary Torrey Wyeth late Mary Torrey Hancock. You are hereby notified that there is now on file in the office of the clerk of the District Court in Des Moines County, Iowa, a petition of Jonas Wyeth, praying to be divorced from the bonds of matrimony, and unless you appear and answer thereto on or before the second day of the next term of the said court to be begun and held at Burlington on the 27th day of October next (1851)the said court will decree a dissolution of the marriage contract now existing between you and the said Jonas Wyeth, as prayed for in his said petition.   GRIMES & STARR, attys for Plaif. O. C. Wightman, Clerk."

In the 31 Oct 1851 Des Moines County, Iowa, District Court hearing, notice was made of Mary's failure to plead, appear or answer Jonas' allegations. Due to her default, the court ruled Jonas to be the injured party and rendered the statements in his petition for divorce true. Furthermore, the ruling stated it was "adjudged by the Court here, that the bonds of matrimony heretofore existing between said Jonas Wyeth and Mary Torrey be forever and unconditionally dissolved, and that said Jonas Wyeth be restored to all the rights and privileges of an unmarried man, and that the plaintiff have custody of his children, to wit, Lucy Coolidge Wyeth, Josephine Augusta Wyeth, and Edwin Augustus Wyeth."[542]

Apparently, Jonas Wyeth 2[d] did not divorce Mary so he could immediately take another wife. In fact, he waited over two and a half years to remarry. Jonas' wedding on 02 May 1854 in Scott County, Iowa to Mrs. Sarah Elizabeth Benson Johnson was solemnized by Erastus Ripley.[543] However, wedded bliss for Jonas and Sarah was short lived. From the depositions Sarah and her brother, Arthur Benson, gave for her divorce, we learn much about the Wyeth-Johnson marriage.

Firstly, Sarah's maiden name was obviously Benson. Secondly, both depositions state she was the widow of M. A. Johnson and was a resident of Brooklyn, New York in 1854.[544] We learn her brother Arthur also lived in Brooklyn. After the wedding in Iowa, Sarah and Jonas stayed for a few weeks at Arthur's home. On 31 May 1854, Jonas and Sarah each took their daughters aboard the Packet ship *George Hurburt* and moved to Europe. Although they were planning to stay for several years, Jonas and three of the daughters returned to the United States after only six months in Europe. Because Jonas' daughter, 19-year-old Augusta, was ill, Sarah stayed behind with her in the Isle of Wight. Jonas left Sarah's two daughters with their uncle in Brooklyn and returned to Cambridge with his daughter, Lucy.[545]

About a month later, Sarah and Augusta returned from Europe. Jonas asked Arthur to meet him at a hotel in New York City. Of the interview, Arthur remembered Jonas advised him, "He could not live with my sister any longer on account of her violent temper and extravagance." The next day Jonas went to Arthur's house in Brooklyn where the differences were worked out and adjusted to the satisfaction of all parties. Arthur reported Jonas and Sarah occupied the same room and bed that night. However, a few days later, Jonas wrote Arthur that he had changed his mind with respect to living with Sarah.[546] The letter, attached to Arthur's deposition, follows.[547]

"Cambridge, June 23, 55

My dear Sir

Yours of the 20th was not received till Saturday afternoon. Two facts which Sarah made known to me the morning I left Brooklyn satisfied me that the decision made previously on my part was necessary for the peace and safety of my children and was the only course that could be taken after my experiences of the past year and in this view I cannot see that any good result can be reached by coming to New York with your Father – my mind with respect to living with Sarah is made up and cannot be changed. In coming to this conclusion, I have passed through distress and agony which I hope falls early to the lot of humanity.

Any proposition which is reasonable and is within my compass, I will receive favorably.

It is my wish that Augusta should come on when your Father returns.

Your constant and uniform kindness to myself and children I shall always fully appreciate.

Yours truly, *Jonas Wyeth*"

100

Jonas wanted his daughter, Augusta, to return to Cambridge with Sarah and Arthur's father, John Benson. John moved the family from Bucksport, Maine, to Cambridge, Massachusetts, when Sarah was about ten years old.[548] While researching the Benson family, it came to notice that Arthur was the President of Brooklyn Gas Light. He developed the Brooklyn suburb of Bensonhurst which today is known to us as the home of Lenny's pizza. In the 1977 movie *Saturday Night Fever*, it was there Tony Manero told the pizza girl "Two. Two. Give me two."[549] In 1869, Benson was one of only nine individual investors in the Brooklyn Bridge.[550] It stands to reason why Arthur, in his 18 Nov 1887 last will and testament, could afford to forgive all Sarah's debt, as well as give his sister an additional $2,000.[551]

The timing of Jonas' letter points to another possible factor in his change of heart for leaving Sarah to go back to Mary. Just before the letter, and about the time of his return from Europe, was the death of his mother, Susan Stearns Wyeth on 28 Mar 1855. From *A History of Berkeley Street, Cambridge, Massachusetts*, author Alice C. Allyn points out "Mr. Wyeth divorced his first wife and married again, but his mother, on her death bed, confessed she had been the cause of all the trouble and had told falsehoods about his wife."[552]

As previously mentioned, Allyn also stated in her history that the whole of Berkeley Street was built on the old Wyeth farms, originally owned by Nicholas and his son, John.[553] This further verifies Jonas 2^d inherited those lands, which had been in the family for 200 years. In 1852, Jonas Wyeth 2^d built house #5 on Berkeley Street as a home for the Lyman sisters. They ran a school for young ladies in the long room, added in 1853, at the back of the house.[554] [555]

Page 34 of the 01 Jun 1855 Massachusetts state census gives their names as Mary, Catherine and Charlotte Lyman. Jonas, living with his sister, Emely Wyeth Read, shows on page 25 of the same census. Mary Torrey Hancock Wyeth and daughters Augusta and Lucy were five miles away in Brighton, Massachusetts. As he does not reside with either parent, perhaps Edwin Augustus Wyeth was away at school or travelling abroad.

Unquestionably, Alice Allyn was familiar with the gray house pictured here because her mother owned it from 1861 until her death in 1897. She said Professor George La Piana lived next door at #3 Berkeley Street.[556] With that information, and the Cambridge property database, I figured out the #5 house must have been split at some point from house #7 into two properties. Currently, the part of the house with the Victorian front is #7 Berkeley Street, whereas the still attached former schoolroom at the back is #5 Berkeley Street.[557]

In any event, Jonas and Mary reunited in Jul 1856, and moved into the house. On Friday, 08 Aug 1856, Iowa state agent, William Hall, illegally attempted to abduct Jonas from his home on Berkeley Street to carry him back to Iowa to face bigamy charges.[558]

It seems the bigamy charges stemmed from Arthur Benson's inability to negotiate a compromise with his sister in reply to Jonas' statement from 23 Jun 1855, "... Any proposition which is reasonable and is within my compass, I will receive favorably." Arthur knew Jonas was worth $100,000 from papers he left with Arthur before he and Sarah left for Europe to start their honeymoon.[559] Undoubtedly, Sarah's demand for $50,000 in alimony, half of Jonas' fortune, was likely deemed by Jonas as not reasonable or within his financial range.

Unable to form an agreement with Jonas, Sarah moved to Davenport, Iowa, in May 1856, to begin the six months' residency requirement for a divorce. Although the divorce could not be filed until Nov 1856, within days of her arrival, showing her intense bitterness, Sarah gave her story to a Scott County grand jury. On 20 May 1856, that jury issued a bill of indictment for bigamy against Jonas Wyeth. The next day a capias warrant was issued ordering his arrest for a court appearance in Scott County, Iowa, on the 5th Monday in Sep 1856. However, on 07 Jun 1856, Deputy James Lindsey certified that the named defendant was not found in his jurisdiction.[560]

Nevertheless, an arrest warrant was carried to Cambridge by William Hall, an agent of Iowa governor Grimes. On the day Hall served the warrant, Jonas' counsel obtained a writ of habeas corpus from the Massachusetts Supreme Judicial Court and made representations to the state's governor. He advised his attorney general to investigate the case and report back in one month.[561]

On 31 Jul 1856, the attorney general agreed Jonas did not intentionally run from Iowa justice and recommended the orders, to have Wyeth carried out of Massachusetts, be rescinded. Defying explanation, William Hall, himself a Harvard-educated lawyer, ignored the attorney general's recommendation and a week later endeavored to covertly seize Jonas at his Berkeley Street home. The tables were turned on Hall the next day when he was arrested on 09 Aug 1856 for attempting to abduct Jonas against his will and contrary to the law.[562]

Back in Davenport, at the completion of her six months of Iowa residency, Sarah filed a petition for divorce on 12 Nov 1856. In it, Sarah stated that although she is Jonas' lawful wife, Jonas had been living in an open and notorious state of adultery with Mary Torrey Wyeth in Cambridge since Jul 1856. On the other hand, Sarah said Jonas' previous divorce was a fraud since he was not a resident of Iowa, had listed an invalid cause, and Mary was not served with notice in Cambridge. Sarah charged Jonas with pretending he was a single man when he married her.[563] Given that Sarah, the daughter of John Benson, moved to Cambridge in 1825 when she was ten years old, she surely knew Jonas was married to Mary Torrey Hancock. Cambridge was then a very small town. Jonas and Mary's 1848 divorce proceedings and 1849 dismissal filled the newspapers.

Sarah must have been referring to Jonas telling her relatives he did not have a valid divorce while she was still in Europe caring for his sick daughter. She went on to say, he not only abandoned her, but, although he is quite wealthy, he refused to support her. Thus, she asked for alimony suitable to her station in life of $50,000.

Sarah's divorce was then filed on 29 Nov 1856 in Davenport, Scott, Iowa. Sheriff Richardson of Cambridge delivered the divorce notice to Jonas on 02 Dec 1856.[564] Apparently, Jonas' Iowa divorce to Mary was declared invalid because the state decided to change their divorce practices. It is unclear when the state determined Jonas was not really divorced for not meeting Iowa's residency requirements. In *A Treatise on Extradition,* Jonas was quoted as believing his divorce was valid even though he was only in Iowa for one day and two nights.[565]

102

Sarah's brother's deposition was six months later on 19 May 1857 in Brooklyn, Kings, New York. In addition to what has been mentioned already, Arthur Benson said Jonas told him since he was divorced in Iowa, it would be better to be married there.[566] This, too, seems to contradict Sarah's statement of Jonas pretending to be single when he married her.

The divorce of Sarah and Jonas was finalized in 1857 because Jonas refused to return to Iowa to fight it. It is unclear if Sarah received any alimony from Jonas. She was restored, however, to her previous married name of Johnson.[567]

Efforts to get Jonas back to Iowa on bigamy charges went all the way to President James Buchanan. The *Lowell Daily Citizen and News* reported on Tuesday, 16 Jun 1857, "U.S. Attorney General Black has given an opinion that the President has no power to cause the state of Massachusetts to surrender Jonas Wyeth to the authorities of Iowa where he is charged with bigamy."[568]

President Buchanan's refusal of Governor Grimes' appeal to require Jonas to be returned to Iowa had far-reaching consequences. It opened a national commentary on Jonas' case in newspapers all over the United States. The 04 Jul 1857 *Anti-slavery Bugle* asked why would the President not require Jonas to return to Iowa but would call out the Army and the Navy to have a fugitive slave returned across state lines? They quoted the *Cincinnati Gazette's* question as to why this distinction is made between two requirements of the Constitution. The *Anti-slavery Bugle* gave two sections of the U.S. Constitution side by side to help with the comparison.[569]

> 1. "A person charged in any state with treason, felony or other crime, shall flee from justice and be found in another state, shall, on demand of the Executive authority of the state from which he fled, be delivered up, to be removed to the state having jurisdiction of the crime."

> 2. "No person held to service or labor in one state under the laws thereof, escaping into another shall in consequence of any Law or Regulation therein, be discharged from such service or labor, but shall be delivered up on claim of the party to whom such service or labor may be due."

On 09 Feb 1858, William Hall was found guilty of the charge of attempting to kidnap Jonas Wyeth from his Berkeley Street home.[570] However, on 03 Mar 1858, the decision was overturned as the writ of habeas corpus was improperly obtained.[571] Finally, since President Buchanan would not force Jonas to return to Iowa to face bigamy charges, on 11 Jun 1858, the state of Iowa filed a motion to dismiss the indictment.[572]

At long last, Jonas Wyeth 2^d and Mary Torrey Hancock Wyeth were shown living together in their new house on Raymond Street in the 1860 Cambridge census. One of their neighbors was artist N. C. Wyeth's Swiss grandfather, Denys Zirngiebel.

Mary outlived Jonas 2^d by 31 years. At the age of 92, her ashes were laid to rest by his side in Mt. Auburn Cemetery. Their Wyeth name died when son Edwin Augustus Wyeth adopted a daughter who never married. Jonas and Mary's genes, however, live on through their daughters. One of their descendants, Wendy Burden, recently published *Dead End Gene Pool: A Memoir* about an interesting ancestor on her father's side… Cornelius Vanderbilt. Although less well known, Jonas Wyeth 2^d, an ancestor from Wendy's mother Leslie Hamilton's side, may be equally as interesting.

The monument Jonas 2[d] (1806-1868) installed for his ancestors is on the front of his stone with Mary Hancock. The last names on the monument were his father Major Jonas Wyeth (1762-1828) and his grandfather Jonas Wyeth Sr. (1730-1813) who was the second son of Ebenezer Wyeth Sr. (1698-1754). Ebenezer Sr. was a cordwainer who made new shoes from new leather.[573]

The first son of Ebenezer Sr., the shoemaker, was Ebenezer Wyeth Jr. (1727-1799). To make things even more confusing, Ebenezer Jr. had a son who went by the name Jonas Wyeth Jr. (1757-1817). This Jonas Jr. was the father of Jonas Wyeth 3[d] (1794-1867).

Three years before the shoemaker died, his eldest child, Ebenezer Jr. married Mary Winship (1731-1798). At his 1751 marriage, Ebenezer Jr. purchased a vast acreage that ran all the way from Fresh Pond to Watertown.[574] The 16-acre homestead contained a farmhouse (pictured below), a cider mill, a barn and a 13-acre orchard.[575] The home originally sat at the corner of Fresh Pond Lane and the County Road to Watertown (Mt. Auburn Street). In 1915, it was moved to its present location at 36 Larch Road.[576] Some confuse this home with the overgrown one at 17 Fresh Pond Parkway.[577]

Ebenezer Jr. and Mary Winship Wyeth raised their 11 children in this farmhouse. They also raised Lydia Convers Francis here after her mother died when she was only nine years old. Lydia married the Wyeths' nephew, Captain Job Wyeth. This home is one of the few remaining houses in Cambridge built before the American Revolution.

On 23 Feb 1754, Ebenezer Sr. wrote his will making his two eldest sons' co-executors. He instructed all estate equity, both real and personal, be divided between his executors. He willed they pay equal shares to their sisters and 12-year-old brother, Noah Wyeth.[578] As Ebenezer Jr. purchased his own land prior to his father's death, it must have been determined the Wyeth farms near Cambridge Common would go to his second son, Jonas Wyeth Sr. (1730-1813).

Fast-forwarding now to the last year of the 18th century when Ebenezer Jr. died intestate. In the division of the estate by the probate court, his oldest son, Ebenezer Wyeth III (1752-1836), paid the other heirs for five acres of land and for the house where he and his siblings had grown up.[579] Ebenezer III sold the house in 1801 to the Hastings' family, who built a mansion next to it. For a time, they used the farmhouse as a service wing. In 1808, the mansion and farmhouse were in turn sold to the Gray family who also altered the Wyeth house considerably.[580]

Additionally, the probate court deducted a $616.68 note from fifth son Jacob Wyeth's (1764-1857) inheritance.[581] The note was to reimburse the estate for land Jacob purchased from his father, Ebenezer Jr., in 1796 to build a hotel.[582]

The Fresh Pond Hotel Jacob built on the land was such a popular resort and was so astutely managed by Jacob; it made him very wealthy. When he retired 20 years later, he leased the hotel to his nephew, Jonas Wyeth 3^d (1794-1867), who also was quite well off when he retired in about 1840.[583]

Jacob Wyeth Sr. resided in a home he built near the hotel until his death at nearly 93 years of age. In 1892, the hotel was moved from its original location at Fresh Pond to 234 Lakeview Avenue. The four-story building, as shown above, is now home to six condominiums.[584] It was added to the National Historic Register in 1982.[585] Jacob's home was moved to 479 Concord Avenue circa 1893. It now is a homeless solutions organization facility of Heading Home, Inc.[586]

Also added to the National Historic Register in 1982, was another home belonging to Jacob Wyeth. This two and a half stories, wood farmhouse was built in 1820 and leased to Ebenezer Smith, a tenant farmer who may have been uncle to Jacob's sister-in-law, Elizabeth E. Smith. Originally located at the intersection of Fresh Pond Parkway and Huron Avenue, it was moved to its present site at 152 Vassal Lane in 1893.[587]

Close to Vassal Lane is the 1839 home Jonas Wyeth 3^d (1794-1867) built from the proceeds of managing his Uncle Jacob's Fresh Pond Hotel. Jonas' home at 17 Fresh Pond Parkway was so terribly overgrown with trees and vines, as shown in my 2015 photo, I have used Christopher Hail's 24 Mar 1986 photo taken for his fantastic Harvard / Radcliffe Online Historical Reference Shelf.[588] This home stayed in the Wyeth family until 1909, when Jonas' son, James Hicks Wyeth (1830-1924), sold it to Charles

Eliot, President of Harvard. Eliot had the house enlarged to its current size.[589]

The Fresh Pond Hotel was integral, as well, to the success of Jacob's son, Oregon pioneer, Nathaniel Jarvis "Nat" Wyeth (1802-1856). Nat was born at the hotel. His work there as a boy was so uninteresting to him, he determined to strike out on his own. Having collected ice from Fresh Pond for the hotel's use for many years, he found a ready business just outside his door.[590]

In 1825, Nathaniel made the first of many inventions to improve ice harvesting and storage. The horse-drawn plow he designed was so much more efficient than pickaxe and chisel methods, Frederick Tudor, known as the Ice King, offered Nat $500 a year to manage his business.[591] Tudor's investment was well founded. On 27 Jan 1828, Tudor wrote in his journal of Nathaniel, "Wyeth was out on the pond without hat or coat. He is equal to any difficulty which to common minds seems insurmountable."[592]

It did not take the vigorous, ingenious Nathaniel long to determine he would never become rich as Tudor's employee. By the early 1830s, Nat became convinced he could make his fortune by establishing a salmon fishery and fur trade industry over 3,000 miles away on the banks of Oregon's Columbia River. As Captain Wyeth, he led two expeditions across country to the American Northwest in 1832 and in 1834. He devised a half wagon / half boat vehicle, dubbed the *Natwyethum*, for the land and river crossing part of the journey. Supplies needed to set up a trading station were sent separately via the brig, *Sultana*, which sailed from Boston around Cape Horn. Unfortunately, when the brig wrecked in the South Pacific, it spelled doom for the first expedition.[593]

The second trip was also unsuccessful due to Captain Wyeth's inability to compete against the unscrupulous methods of the firmly entrenched Hudson Bay Company (HBC).[594]

Swindled, sick and dejected, Nat wrote his wife on 22 Sep 1835, "We have lost by drowning and disease and warfare 17 persons to date and 14 now sick." To others, he wrote of his inability to send a full shipload of salmon to Boston.[595] Once back in Cambridge in Nov 1836, Nat was determined to cut his losses. He quickly sold both Fort Hall, established in present-day Idaho, and Fort William, located near present-day Portland, Oregon, to the HBC.[596]

Although the venture was not financially rewarding, it did succeed scientifically because botanist Thomas Nuttall, who quit his Harvard professorship to accompany the Captain, gathered and identified 113 species of western plants on the journey. Nuttall named a sunflower genus "Wyethia" in Nat's honor. Additionally, the Fort Hall site Nat and his men built, turned out to be the most important trading post in the Snake River Valley through the 1860s. More than 270,000 emigrants reached it while moving west on the Oregon Trail.[597] In the *History of the Northwest Coast*, author Hubert Howe Bancroft, wrote although "…Wyeth's Oregon adventures were a failure, his influence on Oregon occupation and settlement was second to none. The flag of the United States was planted by him simultaneously in the heart of the continent at Fort Hall and on the seaboard of the Pacific."[598]

Once back on the ice fields, it did not take the hardworking Wyeth long to get out from under his debt. Having access to both his and his father's portion of the pond, Nat started his own ice business. His crusade to bring the railroad to Fresh Pond in 1841 brought huge dividends by increasing the efficiency of ice transportation to the ships in Charlestown. Then the unintended consequence of the trains' sparks setting the wooden icehouses on fire, led to Nat's early entry into the brick-making business. He built new icehouses out of brick from his own facility.[599]

This humble brick house at 336 Rindge Avenue (pictured left) was built circa 1848 for the superintendent of Nat's brick making yard. It is one of the few reminders of the once-thriving, 19th century, Cambridge brick industry that sealed Nathaniel Jarvis Wyeth's fortune. The house has retained many of its Greek Revival features. In 1982, it was added to the National Historic Register.[600]

Yet another Greek Revival Cambridge house added to the National Historic Register in 1982 is John Wyeth's (1805-1871) 1841 home. John was the son of Jonas Wyeth Jr. (1757-1817) and grandson of Ebenezer Wyeth Jr. (1727-1799). John's residence was a public temperance house that originally stood on Brattle Street across from the gate to Mt. Auburn Cemetery.[601] This is not surprising since maps in

Harvard's archive show some of the cemetery was built on Ebenezer's land. Circa 1922, the house (pictured above right) was moved to its current site at 56 Aberdeen Avenue.[602]

One of the newer Wyeth homes in Cambridge is this two-and-a-half story at 9 Rutland Street. The house was built in 1892 for funeral undertaker and director Benjamin Franklin Wyeth Sr. (1845-1909).[603] Benjamin's son, Henry Dunton Wyeth, inherited both his father's business and his home. Henry died on 17 Oct 1975 and is thought to be the last one of Nicholas Wyeth's descendants to carry the Wyeth name in Cambridge.[604]

This photo of the Wyeth home at 9 Rutland Street is courtesy of Trish Marti.

Although the Wyeth-named descendants may have all moved away from Cambridge, Trish Marti and her husband, James J. Gray, are current Cambridge residents. Together with their three children, they live in this charming Greek Revival home, built in 1844, at 84 Kirkland Street.[605] Trish is the eighth great granddaughter of Deborah Wyeth Gamage (1690-1773). Deborah rests with her grandfather, Nicholas Wyeth, in Gamage tomb in the Old Burying Ground at Harvard Square. The cemetery is just a few blocks walk across Harvard Yard from the Gray family's lilac home.

Trish and James were inspired to paint their house to match the lovely lilac bushes in their yard.

Of the few remaining houses in the Harvard Square area built in the

early 19th century, the Augustus Wyeth (1801-1831) house at 69 Dunster Street is very typical of the period. This two-story Federal-style home was built in 1829 by Oliver Hastings, a local builder. The fan shaped window above the door and the low-pitched roof are quite distinctive characteristics of the house. [606] Sadly, Augustus only enjoyed the house (pictured left) for a very short time. At his death, he left it to his sister, Emely Wyeth Read.[607]

Another Federal-period house near Harvard University is the 1824 home of my third great grandfather, Stephen Wyeth (1791-1883), at 5-9 Hilliard Place. A talented carpenter, Stephen built the two-story, gable roof, wooden frame residence himself. Christopher Hail's *Cambridge Buildings and Architects* database indicates Stephen purchased the land from the heirs of Thomas Brattle under deed book 247, page 428 in 1823.[608] When it was built, the home had a view of the Charles River. Unfortunately, after just five years in the house, Stephen lost it to a creditor in 1829.[609] Sadly, on 17 Jul 1831, Stephen suffered an even more devastating loss. His wife, Sarah Ann Wright, died due to complications from the 29 Jun 1831 birth of her seventh child, Francis John Higginson Wyeth.[610]

A decade later, Stephen's finances got the better of him and he filed bankruptcy on 21 Mar 1842 while living in Erving, Franklin, Massachusetts.[611] In 1847, the home he built in Cambridge was changed to a double house.[612] In 2016, that two-family residence was valued at $2,401,200.[613] So, when Stephen migrated west with his son Francis, he not only set the stage for the Wyeth name to continue through his great grandson Florin Wyeth's five sons, but he also made it possible for his descendants to buy an equivalent-sized Ohio house for under $200,000.

AN EXAMPLE OF ONE, MORE OR LESS, AVERAGE WYETH FAMILY

Like Stephen, financial prosperity eluded my Grandpa Florin Royal Wyeth. A tenant farmer most of his life, Grandpa's dream of owning his own farm was crushed by the Great Depression.

Cash poor, but rich in faith and love, Florin and Marselle Allen Wyeth founded a remarkable heritage in the state of Ohio. Through five sons and 29 grandchildren, Grandpa was the only one of Stephen's descendants to carry on the Wyeth name.

Grandpa Florin was one of the greatest men I have ever known. He was so proud of his ancestry and would often enthrall his grandchildren with fascinating anecdotes from our family tree. Sometimes he would read from Grandma Marselle's *Genealogy of the Wyeth Family of America*. Her research, etched on 16 blue ditto stencils, was mimeographed into five booklets ... one for each of her sons. After crediting John Herbert Barker with the early research on the Wyeth family, Grandma supplemented his material with her own descendants. The birth of granddaughter Alice Bernice Wyeth (pictured above) in 1947 was the last date Grandma recorded.

Grandpa, circa 1953, with some of his grandchildren. Back: Dottie Wyeth holding Donny, Herbie, Harmon, Bob, and Laura – Front: Alice, Grandpa Florin holding Tina (me), and June Wyeth.

108

Although Marselle died in 1952, the year before I was born, thanks to her booklet, I knew at a very young age that Governor John Hancock was my distant cousin. I knew my eighth great grandfather, Nicholas Wyeth, bought a home in 1645 on the westerly side of Garden Street in Cambridge, Massachusetts. I knew he had a son, William Wyeth, who was killed by Native Americans. Apparently, Jeff and I inherited our genealogy genes from Grandma Marselle.

Marselle and Florin, circa 1940, with some of their grandchildren. Back: Grandma Marselle holding Bob; Steve, Francis, Helen, Florin and Grandpa Florin – Front: Scottie, Harmon, Marselle "Bunnie", Ruth and Carole Wyeth.

From Grandpa's stories about Marselle, I felt like I knew her. Apparently, silly slapstick humor appealed to Grandma. One of Grandpa's most vivid stories was of Grandma laughing so hard at a fellow who tripped over a dog that a stream of water flowed out from under her long skirts.

After every night's narratives, Grandpa would look up to heaven and say, "I look forward to the day I am with her again." He loved her immensely. She was his strength.

Marselle, the second of eight children of Malcolm Allen and Laura Belle Caldwell, drew strength from her very close knit, religious family. Her grandfather, Rev. Captain David S. Caldwell, was a United Brethren minister who so admired Abraham Lincoln's policies that at age 41, he left his Seneca County, Ohio church to enlist as a private in the 123rd Ohio Volunteer Infantry. Before the week was out, on 22 Aug 1862, David was promoted to 1st lieutenant. Within five months, the hard working, intelligent man achieved the rank of Captain. As previously mentioned, in Jun 1863, Captain Caldwell was captured at the 2nd Battle of Winchester and imprisoned in Richmond, Virginia's Libby prison. In one of the most famous and successful POW breaks of the Civil War, Captain Caldwell escaped through a narrow, rat-filled tunnel in Feb 1864. From a combination of wits and guts and help from a couple of slave families, of the 109 escapees, Marselle's grandfather was among the 59 who succeeded in reaching the advancing Union front over 50 miles away in Williamsburg. After the War Between the States ended, Rev. Caldwell returned to minister in Upper Sandusky, Ohio.[614]

In addition to his ministry, Captain D. S. Caldwell was an excellent writer. In 1864 the United Brethren Printing Establishment of Dayton, Ohio published a narrative he wrote about his Civil War experiences called *Incidents of War and Southern Prison Life*. My cousin, Helen Wyeth Hampson, republished the book and copies are available from her son, James Edward Bright.

The determination Marselle inherited from her family was the glue that kept the Wyeth family together. In their 49 years of marriage, Florin and Marselle moved numerous times around the state of Ohio and across the state line into Pennsylvania. Grandpa frequently got angry with employers and simply walked off many jobs. Marselle always took Florin's part in his work battles. One time she went after one of Grandpa's bosses with a broom. Every time he quit, Grandma patiently packed up the house and the boys and followed Florin to his next job.

Whereas Marselle drew stamina and endurance from her caring, supportive family, Florin's family experience was converse. His father, William, died the month after he turned eight years old. When his mother, Caroline Rodema Scott, remarried, her husband did not like children. Florin was sent to live with her parents, John Scott and Sarah Jane Smith, while his little sister, Mae Vantonia Wyeth, was sent to live with their father's parents, Francis John Higginson Wyeth and Rebecca Grate.

The parents of Blanche Tullis and Florin Wyeth were 6th cousins once removed. Blanche was descended from Nicholas' son, William, and Florin from Nicholas' son, John. Interestingly, Blanche's great granddaughter, Trish Marti and her family, may be the only descendants of Nicholas now living in Cambridge, MA.

Even though his mother abandoned him, Grandpa seemed to harbor no bitterness about his upbringing. He loved his family a great deal. He was particularly close to his first cousin, Blanche Butcher Tullis, who also was brought up by their Scott grandparents. Although the adversity of his childhood gave him toughness and strength of character, it, nevertheless, may have empacted his ability to adapt at work.

Both Grandma and Grandpa had a strong faith in God. They were active in the Methodist Church in every town of their many residences. Grandpa read the Bible every day. By the end of his life, he had read it from cover to cover at least five times. Marselle's daughter-in-law, Velma South Wyeth told her daughter, Ruth Marselle Wyeth Fannin, that before Grandma died, her last words were, "Lord, I am coming."

They tried diligently to pass their faith on to their five boys, William Allen, Royal Francis, Scott Harmon, Harold Harrison and Richard Caldwell "RC" Wyeth. Although their youngest, my father, RC, may have been the most unruly of their children, it brings tears to my eyes to recall him singing, around the house, "The Old Rugged Cross" and "There's a Church in the Wildwood."

Harold, Marselle, Royal, William, Florin and Scott Wyeth, circa 1915.

I do not recall him going, as an adult, to the Methodist Church. My mother, Natalie Soldo, was a first generation Italian-American so we were raised in the Roman Catholic Church. Dad was good about making sure we got to Mass every Sunday. Occasionally, he would attend one of our baptisms or confirmations.

110

Although he did not practice his faith by going to church, I do believe my father was deeply spiritual. This statement may seem incongruous with the fact that he was a serial philanderer. He was indeed full of contradictions.

Perhaps the incongruities grew out of the first six years of my father's life when his mother tied up his long blond hair in ribbons to match the frilly frocks he wore. After having had four boys in ten years, Marselle desperately wanted a daughter. When her fifth child, another boy, was born on 17 May 1917, my grandmother was naturally disappointed. Marselle finally did have a girl in 1926; but, sadly, baby Sarah Belle Wyeth lived only a few hours.

My dad was married five times and had numerous girlfriends in between and during his marriages. I was named "Christina" for one of his sweethearts. For several months at the end of my parents' marriage, we lived upstairs with Mom, while he lived in the basement with a lady friend.

Dad living close by in the basement was actually a good thing. It meant we were more likely to have food in the house. When he was living away from home with one of his female companions, we'd often not see him for weeks at a time. Food supplies ran so low that frequently we supplemented them with mushrooms and berries from the vast woods behind our house. My half-brother, Bob Wyeth, who had children of his own,

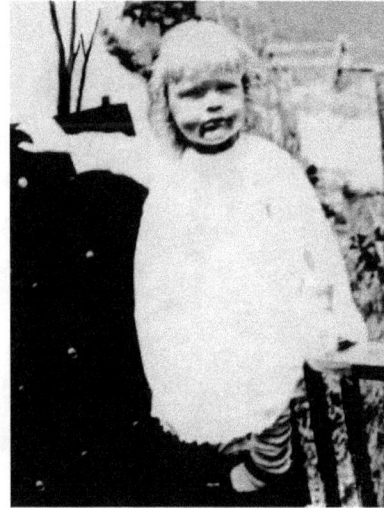

Marselle's "little girl," Richard Caldwell (RC) Wyeth, 1918.

sometimes stopped by to share meals out of his lunch box. In the fall, Mom sent us off to gather black walnuts. She would then pick out their nutmeats until her hands were as black and cracked as the walnut shells. Only Cornhusker's Lotion could sooth them. Since Mom did not drive, my brother Sid, age six, and I, age nine, carried the precious cargo a mile and a half away to the nearest store to trade it for ham hocks and Navy beans. As an adult, bean soup was one dish Sid did not like to eat.

RC was an extremely talented carpenter. He built our house, complete with beautiful hard wood floors and hand-made furniture, out of one cottonwood log. The home sat at the bottom of Roley Hill on Rt. 13 between Jacksontown and Thornville, Ohio. For some unknown reason, my father never got around to adding a bathroom. Just like emptying the chamber pot was a daily chore for Sarah Wyeth in 1645, we had the same daily chore in 1964.

Fortunately, we did have running water … most of the time. Occasionally, when our well's electric pump would stop working, Sid and I were called into action to fetch drinking water in a large galvanized metal wash tub from the Big Spring a half mile away. It was, however, a wonder we got any water to the house since it sloshed back and forth violently as we walked.

Of course, with water in such short supply, showers had to wait until a warm summer downpour. We'd put on our swim suits, grab a bar of soap and a wash cloth and joyfully take a rain bath.

Laura Belle, age 13; RC holding Tina, age 3; Natalie holding Sid, age 6 months; and Bob Wyeth, age 16; in 1956.

Every day was a fun-filled adventure. My mother was obsessive about keeping the house clean so we were rarely allowed to remain inside.

On the days we did stay indoors, we'd play house with the baby bed Grandpa Florin made for me and the wooden table and chairs Dad made. I still have the baby bed but the table and chairs rotted in my grandpa Soldo's grape arbor. Yet, I can describe them as though they were now in front of me. The set was white with black trim. Dad painted the seats of the three-legged chairs to look like they were upholstered with black cushions. Around the edge of each cushion, he carefully and lovingly painted a border of white tacks.

My father's artistic talent was most apparent in his landscape, train and boat paintings. One of my most treasured possessions is a canvas depicting the scenery of the Grand Tetons. He gave it to me as a wedding gift. His childhood nickname was "Dick" but he signed his paintings "RC," which is why I use it in this book.

Although RC left school after graduating from the 8th grade of the Elk Rural school district in Vinton County, Ohio, he was highly intelligent. He said high school had been out of reach. It was too far from home to ride a valuable horse and leave it standing in the hot sun all day.

Another one of my dad's nicknames was "Whispers." A bi-product of his intellect was his excellent story-telling skills. His tales were made more fascinating because he told them in such a quiet voice that we had to be right next to him to hear. Our favorite

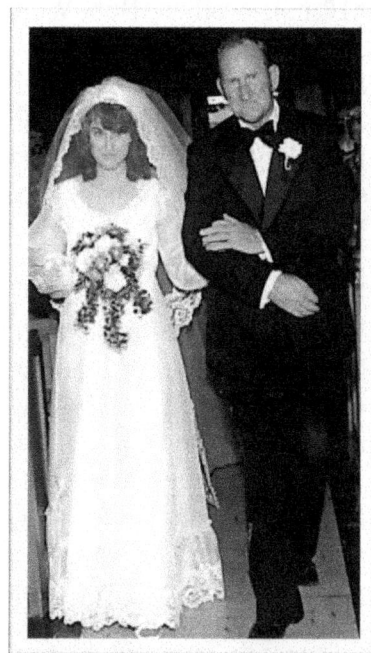

Tina and RC Wyeth, Our Lady of Mt. Carmel Church – 1974.

stories were of his Navy days aboard the escort class aircraft carrier, USS *Kadashan Bay*, as it sped toward Japan near the end of World War II. His stories were both amusing and profound.

This 1945 photo of RC Wyeth was scanned from the collection of his son, Robert Calvin "Bob" Wyeth.

In the amusing category was the time he fell asleep in the back of a fighter plane. We never could understand why he took off his uniform before the unauthorized nap. But it still is a funny mental picture to see him gathering his dungarees and "Dixie Cup" hat before jumping on to the flight deck just as the plane taxied for take off.

My father was 27 years old when he started boot camp training at the Naval Station in Great Lakes, Illinois on 11 Nov 1944. He told us under normal circumstances, a man his age with two children, would not have been drafted. However, in the months before the Japanese surrendered on 02 Sep 1945, circumstances were so dire, older men with children were drafted in record numbers. Not only did the ranks swell with older men, but younger men as well. Two years before my father was inducted, draft age had been lowered from age 21 to age 18. Since voting age remained at age 21, until the 26th Amendment to the Constitution was signed in 1971, those young men could not even vote. Many had never been away from home. Their fear and uncertainty about the future was palpable.

My dad was a father figure to many of the boys who shared the seamen's close sleeping quarters. He described sleeping in bunks stacked three or four deep and so near to the sailor above, he could not sleep on his side. For me, the most chilling part of my father's story was he could hear the young boys crying themselves to sleep.

While he was away, my father's first wife moved in with another man. As she had a problem with alcohol due to the death of her first baby, the care of five-year-old Robert Calvin "Bob" Wyeth and two-year-old Laura Belle Wyeth, fell to Grandpa Florin and Grandma Marselle Wyeth. They encouraged my dad to start divorce proceedings before his Navy discharge on 17 Nov 1945. He told me he was one of the first men in Fairfield County, Ohio to be awarded custody of his children.

The Wyeth siblings who were raised together as one family... back (left to right) – Bob, Sid, Jeff, and Marc; front – Kitty, Laura Belle, and Tina.

Bob and Laura never saw their own mother again. My mom, Natalie Soldo, was the woman who raised them. Bob, much like Grandpa Florin Wyeth, was not bitter about his abandonment. Laura, on the other hand, was. Still they both cherished the care my mother took of them. Shortly after Bob graduated from high school, mom decided she could no longer let her Catholic faith stand in the way of a divorce from my father.

Their first separation was in 1959. I was six; Sid, three; Jeff, two; and baby Marc Anthony Wyeth was one when we moved to East Palestine, Ohio to live with our Italian grandparents, Rocco Soldo and Maria Carmela Dell'Aquila.

113

Soon after I settled into first grade and got comfortable with the Ursuline nuns, Mom found out she was pregnant for the fifth time. So, back we went to Licking County. Of all the moves in my life, that was the most difficult for me. The other first graders had already formed their friendships. Recess was not fun. I was always ready for playground breaks to be over so I could return to the comfort of the classroom.

As far as friendship, a once in a lifetime friend was born a few months after we returned to the house on Route 13. Through all the ups and downs of our lives, my sister Kathleen Ann "Kitty" Wyeth, and I have never grown apart.

When Kitty was four, Mom finally divorced Dad. My dad, in tears, on the day we left for East Palestine is a still vivid vision in my memory. It unnerved me to see that strong 6'3" man break down.

My father's nephew, Steve Wyeth, drove us to Grandpa and Grandma Soldo's home. Mom, Kitty and Marc sat in the cab, while Sid, Jeff and I were stuffed, with as many of our possessions that would fit, in the back of the pickup truck. Before freeways and before sun-block, the three back passengers emerged red, wind-blown and exhausted from the four-hour trip. However, Grandma's food feast that greeted us relieved all manner of ills.

Love in the Soldo family was expressed more in action than in word. Even though the house was filled with noisy arguments typical of many large Italian households, all knew love because of my grandparents' emphasis on education, cleanliness and eating well. The house overflowed with the aroma of Grandma's cooking using vegetables from one of Grandpa's three immense gardens. No one could come into the Soldo home and go away hungry.

Domenichella (Minnie) Natalina "Natalie" Soldo – circa 1947.

Our arrival was in the summer of 1964. I was 11 years old and in love with Paul McCartney. In rural Licking County, the nearest movie house was ten miles away in Newark. In East Palestine, the cinema was just ten blocks away. Not only could I see John, Paul, George and Ringo bigger than life on the silver screen for only 25 cents, but I could walk to the theatre as well.

My mother also liked the Beatles. The lyrics of many of their songs so struck her fancy, she scribbled them down in shorthand from the Mop Top's Saturday morning cartoons. She also greatly appreciated Dean Martin and passed her admiration of his comedic, acting, and vocal talents on to me.

Mom had a delightful singing voice, too. She was beautiful, hardworking, and capable. 15 years of living away from her family under sometimes unbearable conditions, took a toll on her spirit. Poor diet spoiled her figure and well water destroyed her gorgeous smile. Once she obtained dentures and had the comfort of being back in the town of her birth, with supportive friends and family, Mom's confidence got a boost.

Mom's Soldo family roots are deep in Tricarico, an ancient municipality in the Basilicata region of southern Italy. The town is perched high atop three mountains which is implied in the Greek

114

translation of Tricarico – treis akros (three summits). The medieval town is well preserved and still surrounded by walls and gates originally built to keep out invaders. Regardless of the walls, gates, and mountaintop view of hundreds of miles in all directions, Tricarico was, nevertheless, invaded by Greeks, Turks, Arabs, Normans and others throughout the centuries. The town is still dominated by the round tower the Normans built in 1048.

In 1492, Italian Christopher Columbus became the first emigrant to America. But not until the early 20th century did Italians arrive on American shores in large numbers. Between 1900 and 1910, over 2,000,000 people braved an often rough and tortuous ocean voyage to escape Italy's low wages, high taxes and overcrowding.

One such individual was 5' tall Rocco Soldo who sailed on the SS *Indiana* from Naples, Italy, on 21 Nov 1910 to Ellis Island in New York Harbor. He was bound for East Palestine to join his brother, Innocenzo, at the McGraw Tire and Rubber Company. Although tiny in height, my grandfather, Rocco, had boundless energy. He worked and studied hard. When another brother, Domenico, came from Italy in 1914, the three Soldos took English classes together. On 02 May 1916, at the Court of Common Pleas in Lisbon, Ohio, my grandpa became a full-fledged U.S. citizen.

With his new roots firmly planted in American soil, Rocco's next dream was to marry and raise a family in East Palestine. He returned to Tricarico to find a bride.

Before Natalie Soldo and RC Wyeth were born, Rocco Soldo (first row – 2nd left) and Florin Wyeth (first row – 2nd right) worked at the McGraw Tire and Rubber Co. At the time, my grandfathers had no idea someday they'd be family. It is amazing they were sitting so close to one another in this 1914 photo since almost 400 people fill the entire photo.

There on the steps of the post office, Rocco first saw 22-year-old Maria Carmela Dell'Aquila, the dark-haired beauty, who would become his mate for life. Maria was a dressmaker who operated a boutique from the home she shared with her parents and three sisters. According to the custom of the time, the marriage was arranged between Rocco and Maria's father, Pancrazio. The ceremony took place on Sunday, 06 Feb 1921. At summer's end of the same year, Maria left Tricarico and never again set foot on the soil of her Italian homeland.

By 1938, my grandmother gave birth to a total of eight children. My mother, Maria's fifth child, was born on 25 Dec 1928, making for a very happy Christmas or in Italian a "Buon Natale." In honor of the event, their daughter was given the name Domenichella (shortened to Domenica and Americanized to Minnie) Natalina or, as she preferred for her first name, "Natalie." Unlike her husband, Maria never officially studied English. Her whole life revolved around raising her children and later her grandchildren. Family success was everything to her and Grandpa. They were so proud that all eight of their children graduated from high school.

Like many immigrants seeking a better life for their family in America, the Soldo family was subjected to contempt and told to go home. My mother recounted her adolescence in East Palestine when people called them horrible names, accused them of being in the Mafia, said they were dirty carriers of impetigo, and told them they were taking Americans' jobs. My grandfather hated the Mafia. To him, they were lazy bums who preyed on hard-working Italians. Mom said her family and their home were far cleaner than any of those who criticized her. Indeed, it was. Grandma and her daughters were immaculate housekeepers. Five to six hours every day, excluding Sunday, were devoted to housework.

To reduce the effect of bigotry, the Soldo family assimilated as quickly as they could into American society. Mom and her seven siblings rarely spoke the Italian language except to Grandma. Financially, things were rough. Grandpa Rocco, like Grandpa Florin, was hit hard by the depression. A mason by trade, the bank repossessed the three-story brick house his brothers helped him build. Rocco ever after detested banks, but he greatly cherished his American citizenship. On every patriotic American holiday, he went outside, bent down and kissed the ground. "I looova dis a country."

The family practiced the religion brought from the old country. A devout Roman Catholic, Mom's hands guided each of her five children in their first *Sign of the Cross*. After divorcing my father, a second marriage was questionable. Canon law did not allow remarriage after divorce. However, because my mother and father did not marry in an actual Catholic church, Mom obtained a dispensation – a relaxation from the Canon law – that allowed her to marry again.

Like many women of her time, Mom believed she needed a man to take care of her. She would only let a couple of us kids sit with her during Mass. She did not want a potential suitor to know she had five children. Having so many children also made it difficult for her to work outside of the home. We lived on the charity of her parents. For Christmas, our gifts came from Catholic Social Services. I do not know if welfare was available then, but we did not get any. Finally, after two years of fighting for it, Mom got my dad to pay $50 a month for child support.

On the year I turned 13, she somehow scraped together enough money to move us from my grandparents' home to a nearby house converted into three apartments. At about the same time, Mom started dating the man who would become her second husband. He was a strange man who alternated between snuggling too close to me or trying to hit me with his wallet chain. Granted I was a mouthy teenager who balked when he turned the channel from the *Monkees* or *Get Smart*. Neither could I hold my tongue when awakened by smells of spaghetti cooking after we'd been put to bed hungry. For my sassiness, he locked me out in the cold, literally and figuratively. At 2:00 am in frigid February, our upstairs' neighbor called my father after finding me shivering at the apartment building's unheated entryway. I returned to Licking County to live with my dad.

Two months later, my mother married my stepfather. Just prior, he sent me a note announcing the big day "…roses are red, violets are blue, we are getting married without you."

By summertime of that year, 1967, my father started proceedings to obtain custody of Sid, Jeff, Marc and Kitty. My mother and stepfather came down for the hearing in Newark. Only three bits of the experience remain in my memory. My stepfather had a folding cup he used to get water from the drinking fountain and unlike *Perry Mason*, the lawyers remained seated during questioning. Of my testimony, I only remember saying my stepfather swore a lot. Mom's attorney asked "Doesn't your father swear?" I replied, "No, he doesn't." He truly never did.

116

To this day, I am heartbroken for my mother. Her life with my stepfather was little better than her life with my dad. I feel sorry for my stepfather, too. His personality may have been altered by a high voltage shock he received at work long before he met my mother.

Although I did not see my mother again until I was 17, she monitored my brothers, sister and me via the mail. She was a prolific letter writer. Every school semester she asked to see our grades. I dutifully wrote her Sid's, Jeff's, Marc's, Kitty's and mine for each subject. Her interest in my education helped me to get better grades. I did not want to disappoint her. I got all A's and B's throughout high school with the exception of a "D" in driver's education because I had no access to a car in which to practice. Undoubtedly, I did not report that grade to Mom. Art, who taught driver's education when I met him, considers my one poor grade quite amusing.

A solitary life is certainly advantageous for quiet study and decent grades. Having few friends and working six days a week, kept me out of trouble. I got a scholarship for good grades, a Pell grant, and a small student aid loan because of Dad's low salary. Together with my waitress income, I paid all of the tuition at Columbus Technical Institute myself. Dad drove me to the big city to enroll. When I emerged from the registration building into the bright sunshine, I found him sitting patiently on a bench, sketching the four buildings that then made up the campus.

After graduation, I grew tired of the hour-long commute from Licking County to Columbus. On the $2.20 minimum wage of the time, from my full-time life insurance company clerking job, I relocated to an apartment near The Ohio State University campus. My dad, afraid I would get in with the wrong crowd, was panicky about me moving so far away.

Curiously, at the time, I had taken an interest in learning tennis. Since the OSU courts were not far from my apartment, I strolled over to hit balls against the practice wall. There in the shadow of the Horseshoe, I met the love of my life… Arthur Allen Baker. Art's white shorts showed off his tan legs. His smile and friendliness made such an impression on me, I forgot all my dad's warnings about strangers and accepted Art's offer to buy me a Pepsi. My father liked Art. However, because he was a college boy, Dad told me Art was a playboy. My father's usual good discernment of character was for once lacking as Art and I have been married for over 44 years.

Our contentment comes from our common background. His father's alcoholism and death, when Art was only 14 years old, kept his family struggling. My father did not drink alcohol at all, but our family struggled for other reasons. Both Art and I were encouraged by the pride our parents had in us. We both had not only the desire for a better life, but the ambition to work hard to get it. We knew an education was our ticket out of poverty. Art paid for his own education, too. His OSU degree was courtesy of the GI bill from spending 1967 to 1971 in the USAF.

My father was proud of all his children. However, when his fourth wife died in 1974, Dad was adrift. He could not show the four children still under his roof the same attention he did me. Each left, one by one, before Dad's fifth marriage. Jeff was the first to leave. He went to live with our mother in Alliance, Ohio. Sid did not want to change high schools, so he moved in with neighbors in Buckeye Lake. Marc moved in with our half-brother, Bob, in Cardington, Ohio. After completing 8th grade, Kathleen Ann "Kitty" Wyeth came to live with Art and me in Columbus.

Although Kitty is just seven years younger than I am, through the years many believed I was her mother. Maybe it is from the bossy persona I developed from being the oldest of five and so often put in the position of caretaker. As a teenager, from my waitress earnings, I bought my siblings' school clothes and encouraged them to get an education. When Marc wanted to quit high school, I would not let him. After helping Kitty obtain grants to attend Nelsonville's Hocking College, I got some curious looks at the parents' meetings when she enrolled.

There was never any doubt Traci Michelle Baker and Tricia Elise Baker were going to college. When they were babies, Art and I began investing monthly in mutual funds. The money grew large enough to pay tuition for their OSU degrees with a little left over for their weddings. As I did not want to be the only one in the family without a bachelor's degree, when Tricia started grade school, I started taking classes at Westerville's Otterbein College after work. The girls and I often did our homework together. All three of us were very persistent. I graduated magna cum laude in 1992 while my industrious daughters consistently made honor roll grades.

In the front, left to right, are Jack and Eric Brown, Art Baker, and Ian Kerns – in the back are Tina Wyeth Baker, Tricia Baker Brown holding Dylan Brown, and Traci Baker Kerns.

Art and I agree that our daughters are our outstanding contributions to this world. They both married fine, hard-working young men. Eric Brown and Ian Kerns are also OSU graduates. Education is important to the two adorable little guys in this photo, too. At ages nine and six, Jack Edward Brown and Dylan Arthur Brown are already discussing colleges they want to attend.

Education is empowering because it builds self-confidence. After retiring from proposal writing, I was drawn to helping others lift themselves into prosperity. To that end, volunteering at the Dominican Sisters' adult literacy mission in Columbus is a perfect opportunity. Helping others to read for the first time, get their GED, learn English as a Second Language or become an American citizen, are quite gratifying experiences. Most who come to the literacy center are motivated by the basic human need to improve their lives and to provide better for their families.

To improve himself and to provide better for his family are the reasons Nicholas Wyeth came to America. Those same reasons punctuate the stories of his descendants. It is impossible to write each family chronicle with as much personal knowledge as I wrote my own. However, through research, windows have been opened to glimpse the joys, the successes, the struggles, and the tragedies recorded in the stories on the following pages. The sturdy roots Nicholas and his descendants planted continue to grow and continue to nourish the rich, still flowering branches of the Wyeth and Wythe family tree.

[1] Henry Gough and James Parker, *A Glossary of Terms Used in Heraldry* (Oxford, England: James Parker and Company, 1894). <www.heraldsnet.org/saitou/parker/index.htm> code by Karl Wilcox, Jim Trigg and "Saitou."

[2] Mike Dixon, *Norfolk Stained Glass, St. Martin at Palace Norwich,* email of uncompressed photo and permission to use photo received 3/22/2014. http://www.norfolkstainedglass.co.uk/St_Martin_at_Palace/home.shtm (accessed 2/2/2014).

[3] Marion Sims Wyeth, *Nicholas and George Wythe: an account of a search for their English antecedents* (Palm Beach, FL: Unk., 1958), 14.

[4] William White, *History, Gazetteer, and Directory of Suffolk* (Sheffield, England: Robert Leader, 1855), 395. <https://books.google.com/books?id=KO8NAAAAQAAJ&pg>

[5] William Caveler, *The ecclesiastical and architectural topography of England* (London: John Henry and James Parker, 1855), 211. <https://books.google.com/books?id=Gw8HAAAAQAAJ&pg>

[6] D. P. Mortlock, *The Guide to Suffolk Churches* (Cambridge, UK: Lutterworth Press, 2009), 410.

[7] Wyeth, Jonas. *Wyeth family records (Mss A 3058).* R. Stanton Avery Special Collections, New England Historic Genealogical Society. (https://www.americanancestors.org/terms-and-conditions.aspx states publishing of documents is allowed that are "unique elements that are part of a unique family history or genealogy." Terms and Conditions accessed 2/26/2019. Timothy Salls, Manager of Manuscript Collections, approved use of documents in an email dated 6 May 2019.)

[8] John Herbert Barker, *Some notes on the Wyeth family 1595-1940 - Giving eight generations of the Descendants of Nicholas Wyeth who came to America about 1645* (Cambridge, MA: Handwritten genealogy, 1940), 1.

[9] J. Gardner Bartlett, *The English Ancestral Homes of the Founders of Cambridge* (Cambridge, MA: Cambridge Historical Society, Apr, 1919), 94-95. <http://www.cambridgehistory.org/content/english-ancestral-homes-founders-cambridge>

[10] J. Gardner Bartlett, "Marriages from Sources not in the Line of a Direct Search," *The Genealogical Bulletin, Volume 1, No. 23* (Boston, MA: The Research Publication Company, 16 Jul 1904), 171. <https://books.google.com/books?id=bGVbAAAAMAAJ&pg=PA170&dq>

[11] "Guilliam de Ville, c. 1659, Painting believed to be John Clarke (Baptist minister), housed in the Redwood Library in Newport, RI (no longer under copyright)," *Wikipedia*, https://en.wikipedia.org/wiki/John_Clarke_(Baptist_minister) (accessed 01/23/2016).

[12] James Wermuth, "The Forgotten Patriot." *The Boston Globe.* 28 Apr 2011. (Boston.com) <http://archive.boston.com/bostonglobe/editorial_opinion/oped/articles/2011/04/28/the_forgotten_patriot/>

[13] G. Andrews Moriarity, Jr., "Genealogical Research in England," *New England Historical and Genealogical Register, Vol. LXXV* (Boston: New England Historic and Genealogical Society (NEHGS), 1921), 279. <https://books.google.com/books?id=88sUAAAAYAAJ&pg>

[14] Marion Sims Wyeth, 24.

[15] Marion Sims Wyeth, 4.

[16] John Bennett Boddie, *Virginia Historical Genealogies* (Baltimore, MD: Reprinted for Clearfield by Genealogical Publishing Co., 2008), 122. <https://books.google.com/books?id=AyhusD7Hc2MC&pg=PA122&dq>

[17] "George Wythe Coat of Arms," *Wikipedia*, https://commons.wikimedia.org/wiki/File:Coat_of_Arms_of_George_Wythe.svg (accessed 01/23/2016).

[18] John Burke and John Bernard Burke, *Encyclopaedia of heraldry, or General armory of England, Scotland, and Ireland, comprising a registry of all armorial bearings from the earliest to the present time, including the late grants by the College of Arms* (London: Bohn, 1844), Withe, Wyth, Wythe. <https://books.google.com/books?id=Y11BAAAAYAAJ>

[19] "Wythe [Worcestershire]," *Coats of Arms*, http://www.heraldry.ws/html/wythe-worcestershire.html (accessed 01/23/2016).

[20] Walter Arthur Copinger, *The Manors of Suffolk: The hundreds of Babergh and Blackbourn* (London: T. Fisher Unwin, 1905), 306-307. <https://books.google.com/books?id=6TtOAAAAYAAJ&pg>

[21] H. R. Barker, *West Suffolk, Illustrated* (Bury St. Edmund's: F.G. Pawsry and Co., Ltd., 1907), 198. <https://books.google.com/books?id=0h4vAAAAMAAJ&pg>

[22] "Reeves Hall, Hepworth," *British Listed Buildings*, <http://www.britishlistedbuildings.co.uk/en-284272-reeves-hall-hepworth-suffolk#.VahW1PlViko (accessed 7/15/2015).

[23] Augustine Page and John Kirby, *A Supplement to the Suffolk Traveller, or, Topographical and Genealogical Collections: Concerning that County* (Ipswich, England: Joshua Page, 1844), 779-781. <https://books.google.com/books?id=TP8HAAAAQAAJ&pg>

[24] Mike Dixon, *www.norfolkstained glass.co.uk*, http://www.norfolkstainedglass.co.uk/aboutus/aboutus.shtm (accessed 1/20/2014).

[25] Suffolk Institute of Archaeology, *The Proceedings of the Suffolk Institute of Archaeology, Volume 10* (Ipswich, England: Ancient House Press, 1900), 127.

[26] Augustine Page and John Kirby, 517-518.

[27] H.C. Maxwell Lyte, *Calendar of the Patent rolls preserved in the Public record office.* (London: H.M. Stationery Office by Eyre and Spottiswoode, 1891-1916), 405. <https://books.google.com/books?id=lJs9AAAAMAAJ&pg>

[28] Hamon Le Strange, *Norfolk Official Lists from the Earliest Period to the Present Day.* (Norwich: Agas H. Goose, 1890), 211. <https://books.google.com/books?id=scDRAAAAMAAJ&pg>

[29] R. J. Harper, John Caley and W. Minchin, *Ducatus Lancastriae Calendar to Pleadings, Depositions, etc.* (London: Record Commission, 1823-1834), 20. <https://books.google.com/books?id=n0JNAAAAcAAJ&pg>

[30] Royal Commission on Historical Manuscripts, *Manuscripts of the House of Lords, 1678-1688* (London: H.M. Stationery Office by Eyre and Spottiswoode, 1887), 290. <https://books.google.com/books?id=zKUKAAAAYAAJ&pg>

[31] Joyce Blackburn, *George Wythe of Williamsburg* (New York: Harper & Row, 1975), 2.

[32] John Bennett Boddie, 122.

[33] Dennis Freeborn, *From Old English to Standard English: A Course Book in Language Variation* (Ottawa, Ontario: University of Ottawa Press, 1998), 322.

[34] Nathaniel Ingersoll Bowditch, *Suffolk Surnames* (London: Trübner and Company, 1861), 255, 258. <https://books.google.com/books?id=y-U8AQAAIAAJ&printsec>

[35] Mary Marshall Duffee, "Your Last Name," *The Evening Journal* (Wilmington, Delaware), 8 Feb 1928, 8.

[36] English, *Oxford Living Dictionaries*, https://en.oxforddictionaries.com/definition/wythe (accessed 9/15/2018).

[37] Cambridge (Mass.), *The Records of the Town of Cambridge (formerly New-towne) Massachusetts: 1630-1703.* (Cambridge, MA: The Council, 1901), 83 (Richard Withe in 1649), 350 (Rich Wyeth). <https://books.google.com/books?id=p7N4AAAAMAAJ&pg=PP1&dq>

[38] Southworth Lancaster, "Fire in Cambridge - read 24 Apr 1956 " *The Proceedings of the Cambridge Historical Society, Volume 36,* 1955-1956, 76. <http://cambridgehistory.org/wp-content/uploads/2017/08/Proceedings-Volume-36-1955-1956.pdf>

[39] George Cabel Greer, *Early Virginia Immigrants 1623-166.* (Richmond, VA: W. C. Hill Printing Co., 1912), 374.

[40] John Allan Wyeth, *With Sabre and Scalpel: The Autobiography of a Soldier and Surgeon* (New York: Harper & Brothers, 1914), 528.

[41] Roger Gilman, *The Wyeth Background* (Cambridge, MA: Cambridge Historical Society, 1942), 30. <http://cambridgehistory.org/wp-content/uploads/2017/08/Proceedings-Volume-28-1942.pdf>

[42] Susan E. Maycock, Charles M. Sullivan, *Building Old Cambridge* (Cambridge, MA: MIT Press, 2016), 238.

[43] Jill Sinclair, *Fresh Pond: The History of a Cambridge Landscape* (Cambridge, MA: The MIT Press, 2009), 24.

[44] Lucius R. Paige, *History of Cambridge, Massachusetts, 1630-1877: with a genealogical register* (Boston: H.O. Houghton, 1877), 706. <https://books.google.com/books?id=Yc00AQAAMAAJ&pg>

[45] John Ford, *The Cambridge Directory: Containing a General Directory of Citizens and a General Directory of Citizens* (Cambridge, MA: Chronicle Office, 1848), 59. <https://books.google.com/books?id=EqQtAAAAYAAJ&pg=PA59&dq>

[46] Mount Auburn Cemetery, *webCemeteries app* (accessed 2/4/2019). [73 people counted with Wyeth name and over 100 other relatives.]

[47] M. E. Grimwade, *Index of the Probate Records of the Court of the Archdeacon of Suffolk, 1444-1700* (Keele, Staffordshire: The British Record Society, 1980), 547, 551, 563, 565-566.

[48] Joyce Blackburn, 1.

[49] "Langley Research Center," *NASA Cultural Resources*, https://crgis.ndc.nasa.gov/historic/Langley_Research_Center (accessed 2/19/2016).

[50] Joyce Blackburn, 1.

[51] Frederick Wallace Pyne, *Descendants of the Signers of the Dec. of Independence, Volume 6,* VA (Rockport, ME: Picton Press, 1997), 5.

[52] John Bennett Boddie, 122.

[53] "Region Fiche," *Country: England, County: Norfolk* (as of Jul 1984), 19, 721.

[54] Ancestry.com, Northamptonshire Record Office; Northampton, England, *Norfolk, England, Church of England Baptism, Marriages, and Burials, 1535-1812* (Provo, UT: Ancestry.com Operations, Inc., 2016).

[55] Ancestry.com, *England, Select Births and Christenings, 1538-1975* (Provo, UT: Ancestry.com Operations, Inc., 2014).

[56] "Humphrey Wyeth (1600-1635)," *Ancestry.com*, http://www.ancestry.com/genealogy/records/humphrey-wyeth_20458468 (accessed 2/24/2016).

[57] Joyce Blackburn, 7-8.

[58] William Clarkin, 6, 41, 218.

[59] Frederick Wallace Pyne, 6.

[60] W. Edwin Hemphill, *Examinations of George Wythe Swinney for Forgery and Murder: A Documentary Essay,* The William and Mary Quarterly, Vol. XII, No. 4 (Williamsburg, VA: Omohundro Institute of Early American History and Culture, Oct., 1955), 574. <http://lawlibrary.wm.edu/wythepedia/images/f/f3/HemphillExaminationsOfGeorgeWytheSwinneyOctober1955.pdf>

[61] Steve Henkel, "Murder in the Family," *The American Genealogist, Vol. 78, No. 2* (New Haven, CT: D. L. Jacobus, Apr 2003), 89, 94.

[62] Patricia Law Hatcher, *Graves of Revolutionary Patriots, Vol. 4, S – Z* (Dallas, TX: Pioneer Heritage Press, 1988), 221.

[63] "George Wythe Founding Father," *Red Oak School District Social Studies*, http://www.redoakschooldistrict.com/vnews/display.v/ART/4e5673f8946c4?template=m (accessed 2/22/2016).

[64] "George Wythe," *Wikipedia*, https://en.wikipedia.org/wiki/George_Wythe (accessed 2/24/2016).

[65] William Clarkin, 198-199, 207-209.

[66] Joyce Blackburn, 132-136.

[67] Joyce Blackburn, 137-138.

[68] Philip D. Morgan, "Interracial Sex in the Chesapeake," *Sally Hemings and Thomas Jefferson: History, Memory and Civic Culture*, ed. J.E. Lewis and P.S. Onuf (Charlottesville, VA: University Press of Virginia, 1999), 57-58. <https://books.google.com/books?id=jaoC2BtS4OIC&pg>

[69] Philip D. Morgan, 57-59, 78.

[70] Philip D. Morgan, 60.

[71] Philip D. Morgan, 58.

[72] "Framlingham Castle," *CastlesFortsBattles.co.uk,* www.castlesfortsbattles.co.uk/framlingham_castle.html (accessed 2/9/2016).

[73] All Saints Church Registers, Saxtead, UK, 1546 to 1742, Suffolk Record Office, Ipswich, UK, transcribed by Muriel L. Kilvert, 12.

[74] E. A. Wrigley, R. S. Schofield, *The Population History of England 1541-1871* (Cambridge, UK: Press Syndicate of the University of Cambridge, 1989), 96. <https://books.google.com/books?id=pV9SZS4WpjkC&pg>

[75] Marion Sims Wyeth, 27, referencing: oath in Gookin et al vs Danforth "Middlesex County, MA: Court Records, 1643-1674."

[76] Agnes M. Grousset, *Horns A'Plenty* (Baltimore, MD: Gateway Press, Inc., 1980), 3.

[77] Marion E. Allen, Suffolk Records Society, *Wills of the Archdeaconry of Suffolk, 1620-1624* (Woodbridge, UK: Boydell Press, 1989), 207.

[78] All Saints Church Registers, Saxtead, UK, 1546 to 1742, Suffolk Record Office, Ipswich, UK, transcribed by Muriel L. Kilvert, 41.

[79] "Region Fiche," *Country: England, County: Suffolk* (as of Jul 1984), 16530-16532.

[80] F. Apthorp Foster, Editor, *The New England Historical and Genealogical register,* Volume LXIV (Boston: The New England Historic and Genealogical Society (NEHGS), 1910), 137. <http://books.google.com/books?id=2ihAAAAAYAAJ&pg=PA85&dq>

[81] "England Births and Christenings, 1538-1975," *index, FamilySearch* (https://familysearch.org/pal:/MM9.1.1/V5G4-3HF), Margt. Cutler, 22 Nov 1569; citing Saint Mary At The Quay, Ipswich, Suffolk, England, reference ; FHL microfilm 942.64 I2 V26M.

[82] Nahum S. Cutler, *A Cutler memorial and genealogical history* (Greenfield, MA: E. A. Hall & Co., 1889), 592, 594.

[83] Joseph James Muskett, Editor, *Suffolk Manorial Families, Volume II* (Exeter, UK: William Pollard & Co., Ltd., 1908), 224. <https://books.google.com/books?id=1U1fv9pQA1UC&pg>

[84] E. A. Wrigley, R. S. Schofield, 255-256; 216 (Canon Law).

[85] "Framlingham Castle," *CastlesFortsBattles.co.uk,* www.castlesfortsbattles.co.uk/framlingham_castle.html (accessed 2/24/2016).

[86] David Ross, "British Express," *Passionate about British Heritage,* www.britainexpress.com/counties/suffolk/Framlingham_Castle.htm (accessed 7/28/2015).

[87] James Marston, "Do you know Suffolk's county town?," *Ipswich Star* (Ipswich, UK), 29 Jan 2007. <https://www.ipswichstar.co.uk/news/do-you-know-suffolk-s-county-town-1-113090>

[88] J. Gardner Bartlett, *The English Ancestral Homes of the Founders of Cambridge,* 93.

[89] John Booth, *The Home of Nicholas Danforth in Framlingham, Suffolk, England in 1635* (Framingham, MA: Framingham Historical and Natural History Society, 1954), 15.

[90] John Booth, *Nicholas Danforth and his Neighbours, Framlingham and Saxtead in the 17th Century with Introductory Paper, Nicholas Danforth the Puritan Layman by John M. Merriam* (Framingham, MA: Lakeview Press, 1935), 13-18, 52-53, 55.

[91] Marion E. Allen and Nesta R. Evans, *Wills from the Archdeaconry of Suffolk: 1629-1636* (Boston: NEHGS, 1986), 1632.

[92] Magnus Alexander, "Research Department Report Series no. 106-2007," *Framlingham Castle, Suffolk, The Landscape Context Desk-Top Assessment,* http://services.english-heritage.org.uk/ResearchReportsPdfs/106_2007WEB.pdf (accessed 2/28/2016).

[93] "All Saints, Saxtead," *The Suffolk Churches Site,* www.suffolkchurches.co.uk/saxtead.html (accessed 12/20/16).

[94] Ross Clark, "The long and winding road," *The Telegraph* (London, UK), 12 Apr 2003. <http://www.telegraph.co.uk/motoring/2721693/The-long-and-winding-road.html>

[95] "Saxtead, All Saints, Saxtead," *The Church of England,* www.achurchnearyou.com/saxtead-all-saints/ (accessed 1/4/2017).

[96] John Booth and John M. Merriam, 5-10.

[97] Heyrman, Christine Leigh, "Puritanism and Predestination." *Divining America, TeacherServe©,* National Humanities Center, http://nationalhumanitiescenter.org/tserve/eighteen/ekeyinfo/puritan.htm (accessed 3/3/2016).

[98] R. Sós. "The Puritans Leave England for America," *The Historic Present* (17 Sep 2008). <thehistoricpresent.wordpress.com>

[99] "William Laud," *Wikipedia,* https://en.wikipedia.org/wiki/William_Laud (accessed 1/26/2016).

[100] John Booth and John M. Merriam, 8-9.

[101] Marion Sims Wyeth, 18.

[102] Thomas Shepard; Michael MacGiffert, *God's plot: Puritan spirituality in Thomas Shepard's Cambridge* (Amherst, MA: Univ. of Massachusetts Press, 1994), 201-203.

[103] Thomas Shepard; Michael MacGiffert, 205.

[104] G. Andrews Moriarity, 279.

[105] All Saints Church Registers, Saxtead, UK, 1546 to 1742, Suffolk Record Office, Ipswich, UK, transcribed by Muriel L. Kilvert, 24.

[106] All Saints Church Registers, Saxtead, UK, 1546 to 1742, Suffolk Record Office, Ipswich, UK, transcribed by Muriel L. Kilvert, 25 and 67.

[107] Malcolm Gaskill, *Between Two Worlds: How the English Became Americans* (New York: Basic Books, 2014), 167. <https://books.google.com/books?id=Db3CAwAAQBAJ&pg>

[108] Cotton Mather, *Magnalia Christi Americana* (Hartford, CT: Silas Andrus & Son, 1858), 59.

[109] John Joseph May, *Danforth Genealogy* (Boston: Charles H. Pope, 1902), 5. <https://books.google.com/books?id=nWUNAwAAQBAJ>

[110] Carl L. Bankston III, *History of immigration, 1620-1783,* http://immigrationtounitedstates.org/548-history-of-immigration-1620-1783.html (accessed 2/25/2016).

[111] Watertown (Mass.) Historical Society, *Watertown Records: The First and Second Books of Town Proceedings with the Lands, Grants and Possessions also the Proprietors' Book and the First Book and Supplement of Births, Deaths, and Marriages* (Watertown, MA: Press of Fred G. Barker, 1894), 81. <https://books.google.com/books?id=tvcPAAAAYAAJ&pg=RA2-PA8&dq>

[112] Lucius R. Paige, 43.

[113] "About Harvard/Harvard at a Glance: History," *Harvard University,* http://www.harvard.edu/about-harvard/harvard-glance/history (accessed 3/12/2016).

[114] Samuel Francis Smith, *History of Newton, Massachusetts* (Boston: The American Logotype Company, 1880), 37, 80. <https://books.google.com/books?id=sxOAuf1PSC8C&printsec>

[115] Cambridge, Mass. Proprietors, Printed by Order of the City council under the direction of the city clerk, *The Register Book of the Lands and Houses in the "New Towne" and the Town of Cambridge with the Records of the Proprietors of the Common Lands being the records generally called "The Proprietors' Records"* (Cambridge: University Press - John Wilson and Son, 1896), 119. <https://books.google.com/books?id=Q2EDAAAAYAAJ&q>

[116] Lucius R. Paige, 702.

[117] Alice C. Allyn, *A History of Berkeley Street, Cambridge Massachusetts* (Cambridge: Cambridge Historical Society, 1931), 58. <http://cambridgehistory.org/wp-content/uploads/2017/08/Proceedings-Volume-21-1930-1931.pdf>

[118] Charles M. Sullivan, *Memorandum to the Historical Commission,* 22 Feb 1995, 3.

[119] Colonial Society of Massachusetts, *Publications of the Colonial Society of Massachusetts Transactions 1913-1914* (Cambridge, MA: University Press - John Wilson and Son, 1915), 135.

[120] Colonial Society of Massachusetts, 135-137.

[121] Lucius R. Paige, 373.

[122] Cambridge (Mass.) City Engineer, *Map of the city of Cambridge* (Cambridge, MA: City Engineer, 1894). <https://www.loc.gov/resource/g3764c.ct006024>

[123] John Allan Wyeth, *With Sabre and Scalpel,* 528.

[124] Christopher Hail, "Harvard/Radcliffe Online Historical Reference Shelf," *Cambridge Buildings and Architects,* https://wayback.archive-it.org/5488/20170330145521/http://hul.harvard.edu/lib/archives/refshelf/cba/ (accessed 1/31/2019.

[125] "William Brattle," *Wikipedia,* https://en.wikipedia.org/wiki/William_Brattle (accessed 2/5/2019).

[126] Susan E. Maycock, Charles M. Sullivan, 22.

[127] "The Wyeth Cambridge," *Facebook,* https://www.facebook.com/TheWyethCambridge (accessed 7/1/2016).

[128] Lucius R. Paige, 12, 14.

[129] Susan E. Maycock, Charles M. Sullivan, 251.

[130] Cambridge (Mass.), 55.

[131] Cambridge (Mass.), 57.

[132] Cambridge (Mass.), Proprietors, 135.

[133] John Joseph May, 18.

[134] Yates Publishing, *U. S. and International Marriage Records, 1560-1900* (Provo, UT: Ancestry.com Operations, Inc., 2004), Source number: 16033.000 (Andrews) 15857.000 (Wyeth).

[135] Agnes M. Grousset, 4, 227.

[136] F. Apthorp Foster, 86.

[137] Charles Brooks, William Whitmore, James Usher, *The History of the Town of Medford, Middlesex County, Mass.* (Boston: Rand, Avery, 1886), 54-56. <https://books.google.com/books?id=ASwWAAAAYAAJ&pg>

[138] Charles Pope, *The pioneers of Massachusetts: a descriptive list, drawn from records of the colonies, towns, and churches, and other contemporaneous documents* (Baltimore: Genealogical Pub. Co., 1991), 18. <https://books.google.com/books?id=k___uh7sQAkC&>

[139] Charles Edward Banks, *The Planters of the Commonwealth* (Boston: Riverside Press for Houghton Mifflin Company, 1930), 65-66.

[140] Laurence Clyde Andrew, *Thomas Andrew, Immigrant* (Portland, ME: Casco Printing Co., 1972), 3.

[141] Laurence Clyde Andrew, 3-5.

[142] Watertown (Mass.) Historical Society, Lands, Grants and Possessions section, 15.

[143] Watertown (Mass.) Historical Society, Lands, Grants and Possessions section, 50.

[144] Watertown (Mass.) Historical Society, Birth, Deaths, and Marriages section, 8.

[145] Watertown (Mass.) Historical Society, 76.

[146] Cambridge, Mass. Proprietors, 405.

[147] National Society of Daughters of Founders and Patriots of America, *Founders and Patriots of America Index* (Baltimore, MD: Genealogical Publications, 1975), 254. <https://books.google.com/books?id=7dGPyld17G4C&printsec>

[148] Ancestry.com, *Massachusetts, Town and Vital Records, 1620-1988* [database on-line] (Provo, UT: Ancestry.com Operations, Inc., 2011), 778 (Withe), 790 (Wyth). Original data: Town and City Clerks of Massachusetts, Holbrook Research Institute (Jay and Delene Holbrook).

[149] Stephen Paschall Sharples, *First Church (Cambridge, Mass.) Records of the Church of Christ at Cambridge, in New England: 1632-1830* (Boston: Eben Putnam, 1906), 11-12. <https://books.google.com/books?id=RoLJh2dqZcgC&printsec>

[150] Paul S. Boyer and Stephen Nissenbaum, *Salem Possessed* (Cambridge, MA: Harvard University Press, 1974), 120.

[151] Lucius R. Paige, Mary Isabella Gozzaldi, *History of Cambridge, Massachusetts, 1630-1877: with a genealogical register–Supplement and Index* (Cambridge, MA: The Cambridge Historical Society, 1930), 14.

[152] Nicholas and William Wyeth, *Nicholas and William Wyeth papers (Mss 73)*, R. Stanton Avery Special Collections, New England Historic Genealogical Society (NEHGS). (Timothy Salls, Manager of Manuscript Collections, approved use of documents in an email dated 6 May 2019.)

[153] Marion Sims Wyeth, 26-27.

[154] Cambridge, Mass. Proprietors, 334, 336.

[155] Cambridge (Mass.), 98, 107, 117, 123, 128, 130, 137, 143, 153.

[156] Lucius R. Paige, 75.

[157] Cambridge (Mass.), 166.

[158] Marion Sims Wyeth, 27, referencing: oath in Gookin et al vs Danforth "Middlesex County, MA: Court Records, 1643-1674."

[159] "Yale Indian Papers Project – Danforth, Thomas, 1623-1699 and Gookin, Daniel, 1612-1687", *Yale University*, http://yipp.yale.edu/bio/bibliography/danforth-thomas-1623-1699 and http://yipp.yale.edu/bio/bibliography/gookin-daniel-1612-1687 (accessed 3/30/2016).

[160] Lucius R. Paige, 398-399.

[161] George Madison Bodge, *Soldiers in King Philip's War* (Boston: The Rockwell and Churchill Press, 1906), 168-172, 474. <https://books.google.com/books?id=ewMOAAAAIAAJ&pg>

[162] Frederick Adams Virkus, *The abridged compendium of American genealogy, v.3.* (Chicago: F. A. Virkus & Co., 1928),184. <https://babel.hathitrust.org/cgi/pt?id=wu.89062959150;view=1up;seq=11>

[163] Marion Sims Wyeth, 32-33.

[164] Yale Indian Papers Project – Danforth, Thomas *Yale University,*

[165] Alicia Crane Williams, Lead Genealogist, *Early Families of New England* (AmericanAncestors.org, NEHGS, 2013), 2. <http://www.americanancestors.org/databases/early-new-england-families-1641-1700/image/?volumeId=13908&pageName=1&rId=250755076>

[166] Richard B. Anderson, Ed.D., *Harvard Square Old Burying Ground Map and Index* (Cambridge, MA: Cambridge Historical Commission, 2000), 16. <https://www.cambridgema.gov/historic/aboutchc/faqpage> <file:///C:/Users/tbake/Downloads/OBG_nameindex.pdf>

[167] "Our Historic Roots," *The First Parish in Cambridge, Unitarian Universalist*, http://firstparishcambridge.org/welcome/our-historic-roots (accessed 3/25/2016).

[168] John Allan Wyeth, *With Sabre and Scalpel*, 529.

[169] Harvard University Maps Archive, *First Parish Cambridge Pew Diagram*, G3764.c2:2F5 1865. P6.

[170] Andrew Wyeth, "My Father, N. C. Wyeth (1882-1945)," *the digital library of Unitarian Universalism,* http://www.harvardsquarelibrary.org/biographies/n-c-wyeth/ (accessed 9/25/2017).

[171] "History," *First Church in Cambridge,* http://www.firstchurchcambridge.org/about-us/first-church-history (accessed 3/25/2016).

[172] "History," *Christ Church Cambridge,* http://cccambridge.org/about/history (accessed 3/25/2016).

[173] Shepard Congregational Society (Cambridge, Mass.), *The Manual of The first Church in Cambridge (Congregational)* (Boston: Samuel Usher, 1900), 19. <https://books.google.com/books?id=ZN2M_zs8EBEC&pg=PA35&dq>

[174] Lois Lilley Howe, *The History of Garden Street* (Cambridge, MA: Cambridge Historical Society, 1953), 45.

[175] Cambridge (Mass.), *The Records of the Town of Cambridge (formerly New-towne) Massachusetts: 1630-1703* (Cambridge, MA: The Council, 1901), 83 (Richard Withe), 350 (Rich Wyeth) 55 (Brother Withe - Hog) 57 (Brother Withe – Barn). <https://books.google.com/books?id=p7N4AAAAMAAJ&pg=PP1&dq>

[176] Lucius R. Paige, 703.

[177] Marion Sims Wyeth, 28-29.

[178] R. Sós. "Christmas in Puritan New England, Or Not," *The Historic Present* (blog), 19 Dec 2013. <thehistoricpresent.wordpress.com>

[179] John Joseph May, 18.

[180] Marilynne K. Roach, *The Salem Witch Trials–Day-by-Day Chronicle of a Community Under Siege* (NY: Cooper Square Press, 2002), 69.

[181] Paul S. Boyer and Stephen Nissenbaum, 182.

[182] Charles Wentworth Upham, *Salem Witchcraft: with an Account of Salem Village, and a History of Opinions on Witchcraft and Kindred Subjects, Volume 1* (New York: Frederick Ungar Publishing Co. 1867) xv – xxvii. <http://www.gutenberg.org/files/17845/17845-h/salem1-htm.html#MAP_AND_ILLUSTRATIONS> *Index to Map: SWP No. d1e533* <http://salem.lib.virginia.edu/texts/tei/Uph1Wit?div_id=d1e533> and <http://salem.lib.virginia.edu/maps/mapframe2.html> <https://books.google.com/books?id=7ywLAAAAYAAJ&pg>

[183] Marilynne K. Roach, 70.

[184] Charles Wentworth Upham, *Salem Witchcraft: with an Account of Salem Village, and a History of Opinions on Witchcraft and Kindred Subjects, Volume 2* (Boston: Wiggin and Lunt, 1867), 3-6. <https://books.google.com/books?id=qiwLAAAAYAAJ&pg>

[185] Marilynne K. Roach, 18-19.

[186] Frances Hill, *A Delusion of Satan* (New York: Da Capo Press, 2002), 20-23.

[187] Rebecca Beatrice Brooks, "Tituba: The Slave of Salem," *History of Massachusetts* (blog), 02 Jan 2013. <http://historyofmassachusetts.org/tituba-the-slave-of-salem>

[188] Marilynne K. Roach, 21.

[189] Charles Wentworth Upham, Volume 2, 388-389.

[190] Marilynne K. Roach, 352.

[191] Rebecca Beatrice Brooks, "The Salem Witch Trials Victims: Who Were They?," *History of Massachusetts* (blog), 19 Aug 2015. <http://historyofmassachusetts.org/salem-witch-trials-victims>

[192] Robert Calef, *More Wonders of the Invisible World* (London: Hillar & Collyer, 1700), 141. <https://archive.org/details/morewondersofinv1700cale>

[193] Marilynne K. Roach, xliv, 329.

[194] Marilynne K. Roach, 318.

[195] Charles Wentworth Upham, Volume 2, 101-104.

[196] Thomas Hutchinson, *The History of the Province of Massachusets-Bay, from the Charter of King William and Queen Mary, in 1691, until the year 1750* (Boston: Thomas & John Fleet, 1767) 26-27. <https://archive.org/stream/historyofprovinc02hutc#page/26/mode/1up>

[197] Charles Wentworth Upham, Volume 2, 450, 455.

[198] George Lincoln Burr, *Narratives of the New England Witchcraft Cases* (Mineola, New York: Dover Publications, 2002), 184. <https://books.google.com/books?id=uJooAwAAQBAJ&printsec> <http://www.berkano.hu/downloads/narratives.pdf>

[199] Josiah Howard Temple, *History of Framingham, Massachusetts, Early Known as Danforth's Farms* (Framingham, MA: Pub. By the town of Framingham, 1887), 94, 124-125 <https://books.google.com/books?id=Q4AlAQAAMAAJ&pg>

[200] "Sarah Towne Clayes (Cloyes)," *Framingham History Center*, http://www.framinghamhistory.org/wp-content/uploads/2015/04/Sarah-Towne-Clayes-Cloyes.pdf (accessed 5/16/2016).

[201] Paul S. Boyer and Stephen Nissenbaum, 132, 182.

[202] Charles Wentworth Upham, Volume 2, 250-251.

[203] Charles Wentworth Upham, Volume 2, 188-190.

[204] Massachusetts Daughters of the American Revolution, Hannah Winthrop Chapter, Cambridge, *An Historic Guide to Cambridge* (Cambridge, MA: N. S. D. A. R., 1907), 158-163. <https://books.google.com/books?id=ogwNrgEACAAJ&printsec>

[205] Massachusetts Daughters of the American Revolution, Hannah Winthrop Chapter, Cambridge, 124, 158-159, 161-162.

[206] Lucius R. Paige, 352-354.

[207] Marilynne K. Roach, 126-129.

[208] Marilynne K. Roach, 361.

[209] Marilynne K. Roach, 318.

[210] Tompkins Harrison Matteson, "The Trial of George Jacobs 5 Aug 1692," (1855), *Rulers and Leaders Free Area*, <http://rulersandleaders.com/historic_paintings/hp_trial_georgejacobs.htm>

[211] "George Jacobs (Salem witch trials)," *Wikipedia*, https://en.wikipedia.org/wiki/George_Jacobs_(Salem_witch_trials)#Victuallers (accessed 4/28/2016).

[212] Rebecca Beatrice Brooks, "The Life of Nathaniel Hawthorne," *History of Massachusetts* (blog), 15 Sep 2011. <http://historyofmassachusetts.org/nathaniel-hawthorne>

[213] Marilynne K. Roach, 155, 602, 304, 315, 326, 343, 348

[214] Marilynne K. Roach, 360-362

[215] Charles Wentworth Upham, Volume 2, 316-317.

[216] Frances Hill, 186-7, 229.

[217] Charles Wentworth Upham, Volume 2, 384.

[218] Marilynne K. Roach, 362.

[219] Charles Wentworth Upham, Volume 2, 354.

[220] Marilynne K. Roach, 406.

[221] Marilynne K. Roach, 408.

[222] Frances Hill, 203.

[223] Paul S. Boyer and Stephen Nissenbaum, 120-122.

[224] George Lincoln Burr, 366.

[225] Charles Wentworth Upham, Volume 1, 319-320.

[226] Marilynne K. Roach, 620-62.

[227] Rebecca Beatrice Brooks, "Thomas Putnam: Ringleader of the Salem Witch Hunt?," *History of Massachusetts* (blog), 19 Nov 2013. <http://historyofmassachusetts.org/thomas-putnam-ringleader-of-the-salem-witch-hunt/>

[228] Frances Hill, 104.

[229] Paul Boyer and Stephen Nissenbaum / revised, corrected, and augmented by Benjamin C. Ray and Tara S. Wood, *The Salem Witchcraft Papers*, used with permission of Benjamin Ray (The Rector and Visitors of the University of Virginia, 2002), SWP No. 81.1. <http://salem.lib.virginia.edu/texts/tei/swp?div_id=n81>

[230] Frances Hill, xii.

[231] Marilynne K. Roach, 128.

[232] Charles Wentworth Upham, *Volume 2*, 187-188.

[233] Charles Wentworth Upham, *Volume 2*, 117-118.

[234] Charles Wentworth Upham, *Volume 2*, 167.

[235] Marilynne K. Roach, 35, 120-121.

[236] Marilynne K. Roach, 123.

[237] Marilynne K. Roach, 125-126.

[238] George Lincoln Burr, 371.

[239] Marilynne K. Roach, 128, 132.

[240] Charles Wentworth Upham, Volume 2, 348.

[241] Marilynne K. Roach, 137, 184.

[242] M. Burns, "Statement of Daniel Andrew, Peter Cloyce, Israel & Elizabeth Porter for Rebecca Nurse," *A Guide to the On-line Primary Sources of the Salem Witchcraft Trials*, http://www.17thc.us/primarysources/document.php?id=31 (accessed 8/27/16).

[243] M. Burns, "Petition of Israel Porter et al. for Rebecca Nurse."

[244] Rebecca Beatrice Brooks, "The Trial of Rebecca Nurse," *History of Massachusetts* (blog), 5 Nov 2012. <http://historyofmassachusetts.org/the-trial-of-rebecca-nurse/>

[245] George Lincoln Burr, 360.

[246] Marilynne K. Roach, 237.

[247] William Conant Church, Editor, *The Galaxy, Volume 19* (New York: Sheldon & Company, 1875), 373-374. <https://books.google.com/books?id=C0OgAAAAMAAJ&pg>

[248] Marilynne K. Roach, 245, 587.

[249] Charles Wentworth Upham, Volume 2, 318.

[250] John Dunton, *The Publications of the Prince Society: John Dunton's Letters from New-England* (Boston: T. R. Marvin & Son, 1867), 119. <https://books.google.com/books?id=bLe8nPFIhbcC&pg>

[251] Frances Hill, 95.

[252] Edwin Powers, *Crime and Punishment in Early Massachusetts, 1620-1692: A Documentary History* (Boston: Beacon Press, 1966), 216.

[253] Frances Hill, 95.

[254] William Conant Church, 365, 372-373.

[255] Massachusetts Court System, *About the Supreme Judicial Court,* http://www.mass.gov/courts/court-info/sjc/about (accessed 6/1/2016).

[256] Arthur Miller, *The Crucible a Play in Four Acts* (New York: Viking Press, 1953), 2. <http://asbamericanlit.edublogs.org/files/2011/10/21078735-The-Crucible-Arthur-Miller-2hmdzot.pdf>

[257] Marilynne K. Roach, 561.

[258] Charles Wentworth Upham, Volume 1, 507-508, 512.

[259] William Henry Egle, *Pennsylvania Genealogies* (Harrisburg, PA: L. S. Hart, printer, 1886), 756. <https://books.google.com/books?id=d7_akH9VO_cC&pg>

[260] Ancestry.com, *Massachusetts, Wills and Probate Records, 1635-1991* [database on-line] (Provo, UT: Ancestry.com Operations, Inc., 2015). Will transcribed by Claire Barker, Secretary, Suffolk Records Society, Westhorpe Lodge, Westhorpe, Stowmarket, Suffolk, IP14 4TA.

[261] Historical Society of Watertown (Mass.), *Watertown Records* (Watertown, MA: Fred G. Barker, 1900), 4. <https://books.google.com/books?id=e_cLAAAAYAAJ&pg>

[262] *Epidemics in U.S. – 1633-1952* (sources: South Bend, IN Area Genealogical Society, Apr 1996, Encyclopedia of Plague and Pestilence, edited by George C. Kohn, published by Facts On File, Inc., 1995 and The Family Education Network.) <http://www.rootsweb.ancestry.com/~wijuneau/Epidemics.htm>

[263] Frances Hill, 213.

[264] "First Inoculation in America, 1721," *Celebrate Boston*, www.celebrateboston.com/first/inoculation.htm (accessed 6/1/2016).

[265] Ancestry.com, *Massachusetts, Town and Vital Records, 1620-1988* [database on-line] (Provo, UT: Ancestry.com Operations, Inc., 2011), Original data: *Vital Records of Salem, Massachusetts to the end of the year 1849, Volume V-Deaths*, pages 47-48.

[266] "King Philip's War," *History of the USA*, http://www.usahistory.info/NewEngland/King-Philips-War.html (accessed 6/6/2016).

[267] William Henry Egle, *Pennsylvania Genealogies*, 681.

[268] Lucius Paige, 404-405.

[269] Arabella Morton, 19.

[270] Frank Warren Coburn, *The battle of April 19, 1775: in Lexington, Concord, Lincoln, Arlington, Cambridge, Somerville, and Charlestown, Massachusetts* (Boston: F. L. Coburn and Company, 1912), 142-143, 40-41 (muster rolls) <https://archive.org/details/battleofapril19100cobu> <https://archive.org/stream/battleofapril19100cobu#page/142/mode/2up/search/jabez+wyman>

[271] Doris Birmingham, Editor, *Jason Russell House Tour Guide Manual*, (Arlington, MA: Arlington Historical Society, 2016-2017), 16. <https://arlingtonhistorical.org/wp-content/uploads/2017/07/JRHManualBody20164.pdf>

[272] Duane Hamilton Hurd, *History of Middlesex County, Massachusetts* (Philadelphia: JW Lewis & Co., 1890), 180. <https://books.google.com/books?id=m74TAAAAYAAJ&pg>

[273] Lucius Paige, 411-412.

[274] Benjamin and William Cutter, *History of the Town of Arlington, Massachusetts: Formerly the Second Precinct in Cambridge or District of Menotomy, afterward the town of West Cambridge, 1635-1879* (Boston: David Clapp & Son, 1880), 160. <https://books.google.com/books?id=ZPePzTEEhsYC&pg=PA16&dq>

[275] Lucius Paige, 408, 411-412.

[276] Frank Warren Coburn, 40-41 (muster rolls), 104-105. <https://babel.hathitrust.org/cgi/pt?id=yale.39002004528155;view=1up;seq=257>

[277] "The Midnight Ride of Paul Revere," *The History Junkie*, http://thehistoryjunkie.com/paul-revere-facts/ (accessed 4/27/2015).

[278] Frank Warren Coburn, 64. <https://babel.hathitrust.org/cgi/pt?id=yale.39002004528155;view=1up;seq=92>

[279] Frank Warren Coburn, 70.

[280] Frank Warren Coburn, 99 and 85.

[281] National Park Service, U. S. Dept. of the Interior, Minute Man National Historical Park brochure and Parker's Revenge lecture given by Rick Lawson, Park Ranger.

[282] Frank Warren Coburn, 104-105.

[283] Duane Hamilton Hurd, 180.

[284] Benjamin and William Cutter, 328.

[285] Frank Warren Coburn, 75 (muster rolls). <https://babel.hathitrust.org/cgi/pt?id=yale.39002004528155;view=1up;seq=293>

[286] Doris Birmingham, 15.

[287] Benjamin and William Cutter, 327.

[288] Lucius Paige, 698.

[289] Doris Birmingham, 16.

[290] William and Benjamin Cutter, 327.

[291] Arabella Morton, *Descendants of John Gamage of Ipswich, Mass.* (Worcester, MA: Press of Charles R. Stobbs, 1906), 24. <https://books.google.com/books?id=QidMAAAAMAAJ&pg>

[292] Secretary of the Commonwealth, *Massachusetts Soldiers and Sailors of the Revolutionary War, Volume 6* (Boston: Wright & Potter Printing Co., State Printers, 1903), 243. Ancestry.com. [database on-line]. Provo, UT, USA: Ancestry.com Operations Inc., 2004.

[293] Secretary of the Commonwealth, 243.

[294] Maine Historical Society, *Documentary History of the State of Maine, Volume 20* (Portland, ME: Lefavor-Tower Company, 1914), 44-45. <https://books.google.com/books?id=mk1IAAAAYAAJ&pg=PA45&dq>

[295] Secretary of the Commonwealth, *Massachusetts Soldiers and Sailors of the Revolutionary War, Volume 11* (Boston: Wright & Potter Printing Co., State Printers, 1903), 383. <https://books.google.com/books?id=mJtDAQAAMAAJ&pg=PA383&dq>

[296] Daniel Gamage, Massachusetts. Probate Court (Suffolk County); *Suffolk County (Massachusetts) Probate Records, Volumes 91-92* (Suffolk, Massachusetts: Probate Court, 1792-1793), 316-319 (157 – case number 19951).

[297] Secretary of the Commonwealth, 23.

[298] Arabella Morton, 19.

[299] "HMS Milford (1759)," *Wikipedia*, https://en.wikipedia.org/wiki/HMS_Milford_(1759) (accessed 9/27/2016).

[300] Thomas Nicholas, *Annals and antiquities of the counties and county families of Wales, Volume 2* (London: Longmans, Green, Read, and Co., 1872), 569. <https://books.google.com/books?id=Y1IBAAAAQAAJ&pg>

[301] Arabella Morton, 19.

[302] Secretary of the Commonwealth, *Massachusetts Soldiers and Sailors of the Revolutionary War, Volume 6*, 245.

[303] Secretary of the Commonwealth, *Massachusetts Soldiers and Sailors of the Revolutionary War*, Volume 14, 871.

[304] "Phineas Stearns," *Boston Tea Party Ships and Museum*, https://www.bostonteapartyship.com/phineas-stearns (accessed 6/2/2017).

[305] "Revolutionary War Raids & Skirmishes in 1780," *American Revolutionary War*, http://www.myrevolutionarywar.com/battles/1780-skirmish (accessed 9/29/16).

[306] Clifford Kenyon Shipton, *Sibley's Harvard Graduates, Volume 16* (Boston: Massachusetts Historical Society, 1968) 327. <https://dcms.lds.org/delivery/DeliveryManagerServlet?dps_pid=IE7613052>

[307] Secretary of the Commonwealth, *Massachusetts Soldiers and Sailors of the Revolutionary War, Volume 8*, 541.

[308] Frank Warren Coburn, 47-48.

[309] Watertown (Mass.), *Watertown's military history*. Authorized by a vote of the inhabitants of the town of Watertown, Massachusetts. Published under the direction of a committee representing the Sons of the American revolution, and Isaac B. Patten post 81, Grand Army of the Republic (Boston: David Clapp & Son, 1907), 78. <https://books.google.com/books?id=WUyQkyv5eDgC&pg>

[310] SAR Committee and Isaac B. Patten, 81.

[311] "Thomas Hunt (Soldier)," *Wikipedia*, https://en.wikipedia.org/wiki/Thomas_Hunt_(soldier) (accessed 9/29/2016).

[312] Frank Warren Coburn, 47-48.

[313] Secretary of the Commonwealth, *Massachusetts Soldiers and Sailors of the Revolutionary War, Volume 13*, 850.

[314] Secretary of the Commonwealth, *Massachusetts Soldiers and Sailors of the Revolutionary War, Volume 4*, 329.

[315] Secretary of the Commonwealth, *Massachusetts Soldiers and Sailors of the Revolutionary War, Volume 4*, 334.

[316] Secretary of the Commonwealth, *Massachusetts Soldiers and Sailors of the Revolutionary War, Volume 17*, 627.

[317] Georgiana I. Sluman, *The Russell Family*, a story found in the Mason, New Hampshire Historical Room, about 1985, page 1.

[318] Secretary of the Commonwealth, *Massachusetts Soldiers and Sailors of the Revolutionary War, Volume 12*, 738-743

[319] Secretary of the Commonwealth, *Massachusetts Soldiers and Sailors of the Revolutionary War, Volume 17*, 972-974.

[320] Secretary of the Commonwealth, *Massachusetts Soldiers and Sailors of the Revolutionary War, Volume 17*, 972.

[321] Eliphalet Newell, *Abstract of pay for Captain Newell's Company in Henry Knox's regiment* (Jan 1776), Gilder Lehrman Collection #: GLC02437.09497 <http://www.gilderlehrman.org/collections/ddef21d4-9296-4fd7-ab16-428856309333>

[322] Ancestry.com, *U.S., Revolutionary War Pension and Bounty-Land Warrant Application Files, 1800-1900* [database on-line] (Provo, UT: Ancestry.com Operations, Inc., 2010). Original data: Application, 1819, Joshua Wyeth, Survivor's Pension Application File, No. S40734 (Private, Continental Army, First Mass. Regiment); "Revolutionary War Pension and Bounty-Land Warrant Application Files," NARA microfilm publication M804, Dept. of Veterans Affairs, Record Group 15, Roll No. 2654; National Archives, Washington, D.C., image 165.

[323] Ancestry.com, Survivor's Pension Application File, No. S40734, Joshua Wyeth, Revolutionary War, RG 15; NA–Washington, image 169.

[324] Ancestry.com. U.S., *The Pension Roll of 1835* [database on-line]. Provo, UT: Ancestry.com Operations, Inc., 2014. Original data: United States Senate. The Pension Roll of 1835. 1968 Reprint, with index. Baltimore: Genealogical Publishing Company, 1992, Vol. 4, 174.

[325] Benjamin L. Carp, *Defiance of the Patriots* (New Haven, CT: Yale University Press, 2010), 223. <https://books.google.com/books?id=upd6d3UDfTgC&pg>

[326] Patrice Boussel, Henri Bonnemain, Frank J. Bové ; first part ... translated into English by James Desmond, second part ... original text in English by Frank J. Bové, *History of Pharmacy and the Pharmaceutical Industry* (Paris: Asklepios Press, 1982), 273. <http://www.herbmuseum.ca/content/history-wyeth-pharmaceuticals>

[327] Esther Forbes, *Paul Revere and the World He Lived In* (Boston: Houghton-Mifflin, 1969), 198-99, 449.

[328] Francis S. Drake, *Tea Leaves: Being a Collection of Letters and Documents* (Boston: A. O. Crane, 1884), xciii. <https://books.google.com/books?id=ezgZAAAAYAAJ&printsec>

[329] Ancestry.com, *U.S., Revolutionary War Pension and Bounty-Land Warrant Application Files, 1800-1900* [database on-line] (Provo, UT: Ancestry.com Operations, Inc., 2010), image 116. Original data: Application, 1855, Elizabeth Wyeth, Widow's Pension Application, No. W14205; service of Jonas Wyeth (Navy, Mass., Revolutionary War); "Revolutionary War Pension and Bounty-Land Warrant Application Files," NARA microfilm publication M804, Dept. of Veterans Affairs, Record Group 15, Roll No. 2654; National Archives, Washington, D.C.

[330] Ancestry.com, Widow's Pension Application, No. W14205, Elizabeth Wyeth, Revolutionary War, RG 15; NA–Washington, image 105.

[331] Eliphalet Newell, Gilder Lehrman Collection #: GLC02437.09497.

[332] Ancestry.com, Survivor's Pension Application File, No. S40734, Joshua Wyeth, Revolutionary War, RG 15; NA–Washington, image 169.

[333] Ancestry.com, *U.S., Revolutionary War Pension and Bounty-Land Warrant Application Files, 1800-1900* [database on-line] (Provo, UT: Ancestry.com Operations, Inc., 2010). Original data: Application, 1819, Ebenezer Wyeth, Survivor's Pension Application File, No. S34,576 (Private, Continental Army, First Mass. Regiment); "Revolutionary War Pension and Bounty-Land Warrant Application Files," NARA microfilm publication M804, Dept. of Veterans Affairs, Record Group 15, Roll No. 2654; National Archives, Washington, D.C., image 56.

[334] Ancestry.com, Survivor's Pension Application File, No. S34,576, Ebenezer Wyeth, Rev. War, RG 15; NA–Washington, image 69.

[335] Ancestry.com, Survivor's Pension Application File, No. S34,576, Ebenezer Wyeth, Rev. War, RG 15; NA–Washington, image 53.

[336] Ancestry.com, Widow's Pension Application, No. W14205, Elizabeth Wyeth, Rev. War, RG 15; NA–Washington, image 102.

[337] Ancestry.com, Widow's Pension Application, No. W14205, Elizabeth Wyeth, Rev. War, RG 15; NA–Washington, image 79-80.

[338] Ancestry.com, Widow's Pension Application, No. W14205, Elizabeth Wyeth, Rev. War, RG 15; NA–Washington, image 149, 118.

[339] Ancestry.com, Widow's Pension App., No. W14205, Elizabeth Wyeth, Rev. War, RG 15; NA–Washington, image 96, 82, 127, 155, 157.

[340] Ancestry.com, Widow's Pension Application, No. W14205, Elizabeth Wyeth, Revolutionary War, RG 15; NA–Washington, image 144.

[341] Ancestry.com, Widow's Pension Application, No. W14205, Elizabeth Wyeth, Revolutionary War, RG 15; NA–Washington, image 90.

[342] Secretary of the Commonwealth, *Massachusetts Soldiers and Sailors of the Revolutionary War, Volume* 17, 972-974.

[343] Secretary of the Commonwealth, *Massachusetts Soldiers and Sailors of the Revolutionary War, Volume* 17, 973.

[344] Ancestry.com, Widow's Pension Application, No. W14205, Elizabeth Wyeth, Revolutionary War, RG 15; NA–Washington, image 99.

[345] Ancestry.com, U.S., *Revolutionary War Pensioners, 1801-1815, 1818-1872* [database on-line] (Provo, UT: Ancestry.com Operations, Inc., 2007), images 136 and 159. Original data: "Ledgers of Payments, 1818-1872, to U.S. Pensioners Under Acts of 1818 Through 1858, From Records of the Office of the Third Auditor of the Treasury, 1818-1872," Citing Pension Payment Roll of Veterans of the Revolutionary War and the Regular Army and Navy for Elizabeth Wyeth; service of Jonas Wyeth (Navy, Massachusetts, Revolutionary War); NARA microfilm publication T718, Department of Veterans Affairs, Record Group 217, roll No. 19 (136) and 17 (159); National Archives, Washington, D.C.

[346] Ancestry.com, Widow's Pension Application, No. W14205, Elizabeth Wyeth, Revolutionary War, RG 15; NA–Washington, image 127.

[347] Ancestry.com, Series T718: 1818 - 1872 04: Revolutionary War, 1833-1848, Image 90.

[348] Ancestry.com, Survivor's Pension Application File, No. S34,576, Ebenezer Wyeth, Rev. War, RG 15; NA–Washington, Image 56 and 57.

[349] Ancestry.com, Survivor's Pension Application File, No. S34,576, Ebenezer Wyeth, Rev. War, RG 15; NA–Washington, Image 60 and 69.

[350] Lucius Paige, 705.

[351] The Essex Institute, *Vital Records of Westford, Massachusetts to the end of the year 1849* (Salem, MA: Newcomb & Gauss, 1915), 325.

[352] Duane W. Krohnke, "dwkcommentaries," *The American Revolutionary War's Campaign for New York and New Jersey, March 1776–January 1777,* https://dwkcommentaries.com/2012/08/13/the-american-revolutionary-wars-campaign-for-new-york-and-new-jersey-march-1776-january-1777/ (accessed 10/13/2016).

[353] Joe Ellis, "Video from Mount Vernon on Vimeo, Washington's challenges, mistakes, and lessons learned during the NY Campaign of 1776," *George Washington's Mount Vernon,* www.mountvernon.org/digital-encyclopedia/article/battle-of-long-island/ (accessed 10/13/2016).

[354] Richard C. Stazesky, "George Washington, Genius in Leadership," *Washington Papers,* 22 Feb 2000. <gwpapers.virginia.edu/history/articles/george-washington-genius-in-leadership/>

[355] Thomas Paine, *The American Crisis* (London: R. Carlile, 1819), 11. <https://books.google.com/books?id=jUVHAQAAMAAJ>

[356] "The Battle of White Plains," *BritishBattles.com,* www.britishbattles.com/white-plains.htm (accessed 10/13/2016).

[357] "Massachusetts Regiment of Artillery, 1775-1776 "Knox's Artillery"," *Uniforms of the American Revolution,* http://www.srcalifornia.com/uniforms/p13.htm (accessed 10/14/2016).

[358] Ancestry.com, Survivor's Pension Application File, No. S40734, Joshua Wyeth, Revolutionary War, RG 15; NA–Washington, image 169.

[359] johndeeben, "Family Tree Friday: Artificers in the Revolutionary War," *The National Archives Narations,* 15 Oct 2010. <https://narations.blogs.archives.gov/2010/10/15/family-tree-friday-artificers-in-the-revolutionary-war/>

[360] Ancestry.com, Survivor's Pension Application File, No. S34,576, Ebenezer Wyeth, Rev. War, RG 15; NA–Washington, Image 57 and 69.

[361] Ancestry.com, Widow's Pension Application, No. W14205, Elizabeth Wyeth, Rev. War, RG 15; NA–Washington, image 90.

[362] Lucius Paige, 431.

[363] David and Jeanne Heldler, "War of 1812, United Kingdom-United States History," *Encyclopaedia Britannica,* 2016. <https://www.britannica.com/event/War-of-1812>

[364] David and Jeanne Heldler.

[365] Secretary of the Commonwealth, *Massachusetts Soldiers and Sailors of the Revolutionary War, Volume* 3, 392.

[366] Gardner W. Pearson, *Records of the Massachusetts Volunteer Militia* (Baltimore, MD: Clearfield Company, 1993 / 1913), 42. <http://interactive.ancestry.com/1873/32501_1220702381_0128-00031>

[367] Deaths, *Boston Daily Advertiser* (Boston, MA), 16 Jul 1813, 3.

[368] Gardner W. Pearson, 193, 84, 13.

369 Gardner W. Pearson, 10, 12.

370 Ted Strong, "Civil War expert: North fought to preserve Union," *The Daily Progress* (Charlottesville, VA) 21 Feb 2011. <http://www.dailyprogress.com/news/civil-war-expert-north-fought-to-preserve-union/article_17c3e625-48cd-506b-b1f9-91606bf4d927.html>

371 "History of the United States Republican Party," *Wikipedia*, https://en.wikipedia.org/wiki/History_of_the_United_States_Republican_Party (assessed 4/2/2019).

372 Matthew Spalding, Ph.D., "How to Understand Slavery and the American Founding," *The Heritage Foundation White Paper #138*, 26 Aug 2002. <www.heritage.org/research/reports/2002/08/how-to-understand-slavery-and-americas>

373 Matthew Spalding, Ph.D.

374 "Indiana Digital Archives -Willis B. Wyeth, Ref. # MEX3342," *Indiana Archives and Records Administration*, https://secure.in.gov/apps/iara/search/Home/Detail?rId=771265 (accessed 25 Oct 2016).

375 "Indiana Digital Archives - Milton L. Wyeth, MEX4628," *Indiana Archives and Records Administration*, https://secure.in.gov/apps/iara/search/ (accessed 10/25/2016).

376 Tom Emery, "'Hundred-days' men left checkered Civil War legacy," *Dispatch-Argus QCOnline.com* (Moline, IL), 29 Sep 2012. <http://www.qconline.com/life/hundred-days-men-left-checkered-civil-war-legacy/article_dcfafd2d-2517-563d-9c85-ff7c3cdcfe15.html>

377 D. S. Caldwell, *Incidents of War and Southern Prison Life* (Dayton, OH: United Brethen Printing Establishment, 1864), 23.

378 Angela M. Zombek, "Libby Prison," *Encyclopedia Virginia*, 23 Jan 2014.<http://www.encyclopediavirginia.org/Libby_Prison#start_entry>

379 Brenda Smelser Hay, "Belle Isle Civil War Prison," *CensusDiggins.com*, 2002-2008. <http://www.censusdiggins.com/prison_bellisle.html>

380 Zelotes A. Musgrave, *Diary of Zelotes A. Musgrave (1862-1865)*, Copied by William Frank Musgrave (1914) and Daniel L. Musgrave (1993). <http://ohio45.homestead.com/musgrave.html>

381 D. S. Caldwell, 7-8.

382 John A. Wyeth, "Cold Cheer in Camp Morton," *Century Monthly Magazine*, Apr 1891, 844. <https://babel.hathitrust.org/cgi/pt?id=coo.31924079633362>

383 John A. Wyeth, "Cold Cheer in Camp Morton," 846.

384 Soldier's Pension Application File, 30 Aug 1883, service of John W. Wythe (Co. B, 71st Indiana Cavalry (later known as the 6th Cavalry Unit) Civil War); Soldier's Application No. 494,130; National Archives catalog title: Civil War and Later Pension Files; Records of the Department of Veterans Affairs; Record Group 15; National Archives, Washington, D.C.

385 Ancestry.com, *U.S. National Cemetery Interment Control Forms, 1928-1962 for Guy Angus Wyeth* [database on-line] (Provo, UT: Ancestry.com Operations, Inc., 2012).

386 Widow's Pension Application File, 01 Nov 1895, Alice S. Wyeth, widow's pension application no. 622,670; service of Abiel Wyeth (Co. F, 1st Mass. Infantry and Co. A, 62nd Mass. Infantry, Civil War); National Archives catalog title: Civil War and Later Pension Files; Records of the Department of Veterans Affairs; Record Group 15; National Archives, Washington, D.C..

387 Georgeann Malowney Knoles, "George T. Work," *Irishgenealogy.com*, assessed 24 Oct 2016. <www.irishgenealogy.com/us/pa/default.htm>

388 Soldier's Pension Application File, 26 Oct 1870, service of Alexander R. Wyeth (Co. F&S, 6th PA Cavalry, Civil War); soldier's pension application no. 160,817; Widow's Pension Application, 09 Feb 1877, Elizabeth Wyeth; widow's pension application no. 229,955; NA catalog title: Civil War and Later Pension Files; Records of the Dept. of Veterans Affairs; Record Group 15; National Archives, Washington, D.C.

389 "Camp Sherman," *Ohio Civil War Central*, http://www.ohiocivilwarcentral.com/entry.php?rec=17 (accessed 9 Feb 2018).

390 Historical Data Systems, comp, Augustus G. Wyeth, *U.S., Civil War Soldier Records and Profiles, 1861-1865* [database on-line] (Provo, UT: Ancestry.com Operations Inc., 2009).

391 "A. G. Wyeth dies Suddenly at Granville Street Home Upon Return from Drive," *Newark Advocate* (Newark, OH), 20 Jun 1914, 1.

392 Soldier's Pension Application File, 21 Jan 1908, service of Benjamin F. Wyeth (Co. unattached, 12th Massachusetts Infantry, Civil War), soldier's pension application no. 1,370,330; Widow's Pension Application, 28 Aug 1909, Caroline E. Wyeth, widow's pension application no. 926,344; NA catalog title: Civil War and Later Pension Files; Dept. of Veterans Affairs Records; RG 15; National Archives, Washington, D.C.

393 "Unattached Companies Massachusetts Volunteer Militia," *Wikipedia*, https://en.wikipedia.org/wiki/Unattached_Companies_Massachusetts_Volunteer_Militia (accessed 11/27/2017).

394 "Indiana Digital Archives – Charles A. Wyeth, Ref. # CIV211194 and # CIV211195," *Indiana Archives and Records Administration*, https://secure.in.gov/apps/iara/search/ (accessed 10/25/2016).

395 Ancestry.com, *Pennsylvania, Civil War Muster Rolls, 1860-1869* [database on-line], (Provo, UT: Ancestry.com Operations, Inc., 2015).

396 Soldier's Pension App. File, 06 Sep 1890, service of Francis J. Wyeth (Co. H, OH 140th Infantry, Civil War); soldier's pension application no. 896,857; Widow's Pension Application, 11 Nov 1911, Rebecca Wyeth; widow's pension application no. 974,856; ; NA catalog title: Civil War and Later Pension Files; Dept. of Veterans Affairs Records; RG 15; National Archives, Washington, D.C.

397 "Indiana Digital Archives – Francis M. Wyeth, Ref. # CIV211197," *Indiana Archives and Records Administration*, https://secure.in.gov/apps/iara/search/ (accessed 10/25/2016).

398 Ancestry.com. *U.S. National Homes for Disabled Volunteer Soldiers, 1866-1938* [database on-line]. Provo, UT: Ancestry.com Operations Inc., 2007, Image 284 (George N. Wyeth.)

399 Soldier's Pension Application File, 3 Jun 1863, service of George W. P. Wyeth (Co. K, NH 6th Infantry and Co. K, 13th Veterans Reserve Corps, Co. K Civil War); soldier's pension app. no. 24,713; Widow's Pension Application, 1 Sep 1926, Sarah Wyeth; application no. 1,032,906; NA catalog title: Civil War and Later Pension Files; Dept. of Veterans Affairs Records; RG 15; National Archives, Washington, D.C.

400 Soldier's Pension Application File, 7 Aug 1890, service of George W. Wyeth (Navy and Co. F, Illinois 56th Infantry, Civil War); Navy pension certificate no. 27,895, soldier's application no. 842,320; National Archives catalog title: Civil War and Later Pension Files; Records of the Department of Veterans Affairs; Record Group 15; National Archives, Washington, D.C.

401 Ancestry.com. *U.S. National Homes for Disabled Volunteer Soldiers, 1866-1938* [database on-line]. Provo, UT: Ancestry.com Operations Inc., 2007, Image 715 (George W. Wyeth.)

402 "Complete List of Killed and Wounded of the 31st and 11th Regiments," *The Terre Haute Star* (Terre Haute, Indiana),16 Apr 1862, 2.

403 "Indiana Digital Archives – Henry E. Wyeth, Ref. # CIV211199 and # CIV211200," *Indiana Archives and Records Administration*, https://secure.in.gov/apps/iara/search/ (accessed 10/25/2016).

[404] Soldier's Pension Application File, 07 Oct 1887, service of Henry E. Wyeth (Co. C, 31st Indiana Infantry, Civil War), soldier's pension application no. 625,054; Widow's Pension Application, 12 Sep 1904, Hannah Wyeth, application no. 813,387; NARA catalog title: Civil War and Later Pension Files; Records of Dept. of Veterans Affairs; Record Group 15; National Archives, Washington, D.C.

[405] "Illinois Civil War Muster and Descriptive Rolls Detail Report, Illinois State Archives, Wyeth, Erasmus J.," *Office of the Illinois Secretary of State*, http://www.ilsos.gov/isaveterans/civilMusterSearch.do?key=283697 (accessed 10/26/2016).

[406] "Approved pension applications of widows and other dependents of Civil War veterans who served between 1861 and 1910," digital images, *Fold3* (http://www.fold3.com: accessed 21 Nov 2016), 75th Illinois Infantry; Pages: 2, 5, 7, and 9; veteran: James M. Wyeth; Company: I; Widow: Almira Thompson Wyeth, pension application no. 7,841; citing NARA catalog title: *Case Files of Approved Pension Applications of Widows and Other Veterans of the Army and Navy Who Served Mainly in the Civil War and the War With Spain, compiled 1861 - 1934, NARA Catalog Id: 300020, Record Group: 15, roll: WC118320-WC118350.*

[407] Roderick Davis, "John Allan Wyeth," *Encyclopedia of Alabama*, 05 Sep 2013. <http://www.encyclopediaofalabama.org/article/h-3522>

[408] Dr. John A. Wyeth, *With Sabre and Scalpel*, 287.

[409] Soldier's Pension Application File, 30 Apr 1907, service of John B. Wyeth (Co. N/A, MA 12th Unattached Company, Militia Infantry, Civil War); soldier's pension application no. 1,363,684; Widow's Pension Application, 01 Sep 1926, Emma E. Wyeth; application no. 1,552,850; NA catalog title: Civil War and Later Pension Files; Dept. of Veterans Affairs Records; RG 15; National Archives, Washington, D.C.

[410] John J. Wyeth, *Leaves from a Diary Written While Serving in Co. E, 44 Mass., Dep't of No. Carolina, from September 1862 to June 1863* (Boston: L.F. Lawrence & Company, 1878), 5. <https://books.google.com/books?id=jYgvAAAAYAAJ&printsec>

[411] "Illinois Civil War Muster and Descriptive Rolls Detail Report, Illinois State Archives, Wyeth, John M.," *Office of the Illinois Secretary of State*, http://www.ilsos.gov/isaveterans/civilMusterSearch.do?key=283700 (accessed 10/26/2016).

[412] Ancestry.com. *U.S., Registers of Deaths of Volunteers, 1861-1865* (Provo, UT: Ancestry.com Operations, Inc., 2012), Image 42.

[413] Alice J. Gayley, Valerie Little-Vaughn, "Civil War Hospitals," *Pennsylvania in the Civil War*, http://www.pa-roots.com/pacw/hospitals/hospitallist.htm (accessed 10 Nov 2016).

[414] Soldier's Pension Application File, 19 Dec 1904, service of John W. Wyeth (Co. E&L, 9th Pennsylvania Cavalry, Civil War), soldier's pension application no. 1,329,061; Widow's Pension Application, 27 Apr 1908, Frances A. Wyeth, app. no. 840,659; NARA catalog title: Civil War and Later Pension Files; Records of Dept. of Veterans Affairs; Record Group 15; National Archives, Washington, D.C.

[415] "The Civil War Soldiers and Sailors Database - Wyeth, John W.," *National Park Service*, https://www.nps.gov/civilwar/soldiers-and-sailors-database.htm (accessed 10/26/2016).

[416] "From the 124th Ohio," *The Daily Cleveland Herald* (Cleveland, Ohio), 6 Oct 1863, 3.

[417] Roster Commission, *Official roster of the soldiers of the State of Ohio in the War of the Rebellion, 1861-1865*, Vols. 1-12 (Akron, OH: The Werner Company, 1893), 768. [Ancestry.com database on-line] image 2418.

[418] "The Civil War Soldiers and Sailors Database - Wyeth, Jonathan," *National Park Service*, https://www.nps.gov/civilwar/soldiers-and-sailors-database.htm (accessed 10/26/2016) and U.S. National Cemetery Interment Control Forms, image 45 from Ancestry.com.

[419] *Find A Grave*, database and images (https://www.findagrave.com : accessed 14 April 2018), memorial page for Louis W Wyeth (20 Jun 1812–7 Jun 1889), Find A Grave Memorial no. 63347379 citing Guntersville City Cemetery, Guntersville, Marshall County, Alabama; Maintained by Johnny Tidmore (contributor 47270806); Larry A. McCoy, photographs.

[420] John Allan Wyeth, *With Sabre and Scalpel*, 530.

[421] Roster Commission, *Official roster of the soldiers of the State of Ohio in the War of the Rebellion, 1861-1865, Vols. 1-12* (Akron, OH: The Werner Company, 1893), 404. [Ancestry.com database on-line] image 209.

[422] "The Civil War Soldiers and Sailors Database - Wythe (Wyeth), Lafayette," *National Park Service*, https://www.nps.gov/civilwar/search-soldiers.htm?submitted=1&firstName=lafayette&lastName=wythe&warSideCode=U&battleUnitName= (accessed 10/26/2016).

[423] "Terrible Boiler Explosion – Three men killed," *The Elk County Advocate* (Ridgway, PA), 27 Aug 1864, 2.

[424] Soldier's Pension Application File, 25 Aug 1871, service of Matthew W. Wyeth (Co. E, 128th Indiana Infantry, Civil War), soldier's pension application no. 168,330; Widow's Pension Application, 06 Aug 1909, Fanny Wyeth, widow's pension application no. 925,070; NARA catalog title: Civil War and Later Pension Files; Records of Dept. of Veterans Affairs; Record Group 15; National Archives, Washington, D.C.

[425] "Approved pension applications of widows and other dependents of Civil War veterans who served between 1861 and 1910," digital images, *Fold3* (http://www.fold3.com : accessed 20 Oct 2016), 43rd Indiana Infantry; Pages: 2 and 4; veteran: Milton Lewis Wyeth; Company: G; Widow: Mary Eliza Davis Wyeth, pension application no. 6,816; citing NARA catalog title: *Case Files of Approved Pension Applications of Widows and Other Veterans of the Army and Navy Who Served Mainly in the Civil War and the War With Spain, compiled 1861 - 1934, NARA Catalog Id: 300020, Record Group: 15, roll: WC30831.*

[426] "Illinois Civil War Muster and Descriptive Rolls Detail Report, Illinois State Archives, Wyeth, Norman D.," *Office of the Illinois Secretary of State*, http://www.ilsos.gov/isaveterans/civilMusterSearch.do?key=283701 (accessed 10/26/2016).

[427] Widow's Pension Application File, 14 Sep 1888, Amelia Wyeth, widow's pension application no. 380,667; service of Norman D. Wyeth (Co. A, 143rd Illinois Infantry, Civil War); National Archives catalog title: Civil War and Later Pension Files; Records of the Department of Veterans Affairs; Record Group 15; National Archives, Washington, D.C.

[428] Ancestry.com, "Otis Wyeth," *Indiana, Civil War Soldier Database Index, 1861-1865* (Provo, UT: Ancestry.com Operations, Inc. , 2015). <https://secure.in.gov/apps/icpr/search/Home/Detail?rId=1199463>

[429] *Find A Grave*, database and images (https://www.findagrave.com : accessed 14 April 2018), memorial page for Otis R Wyeth (8 Dec 1848–29 Aug 1864), Find A Grave Memorial no. 18997532, citing Mewhinney Cemetery, Riley, Vigo County, Indiana, USA; Maintained by Gary Totten (contributor 47138664); originally created by Wabash Valley Genealogy Society.

[430] "Compiled Service Records of Volunteer Union Soldiers Who Served in Organizations from the State of Massachusetts," digital images, *Fold3* (http://www.fold3.com : accessed 21 Nov 2016), 1st Cavalry / Pages: 1-16, 3rd Cavalry / Pages: 1-24, veteran: Richard H. Wyeth; Company: D; citing NARA catalog title: *Carded Records Showing Military Service of Soldiers Who Fought in Volunteer Organizations During the American Civil War, compiled 1890 - 1912, documenting the period 1861 - 1866, NARA Catalog Id: 300398, Record Group: 94, roll: RG94-CMSR-MA-1CAV-Bx0078 and RG94-CMSR-MA-3CAV-Bx0236.*

[431] Illinois Military and Naval Dept; Reece, Jasper N; Elliott, Isaac Hughes, *Report of the adjutant general of the state of Illinois, Volume 7* (Springfield, IL: Phillips Bros., 1900), 203. <http://www.archive.org/stream/reportofadjutant07illi1#page/193/mode/1up>

[432] Soldier's Pension Application File, 17 Nov 1879, service of Walter H. Wyeth (Co. M, 11th Michigan Cavalry, Civil War), soldier's pension application no. 323,729; Widow's Pension Application, 08 Jul 1906, Frances E. Wyeth, widow's pension application no. 945,418; NARA catalog title: Civil War and Later Pension Files; Records of the Dept. of Veterans Affairs; Record Group 15; National Archives, Washington, D.C.

[433] "The Civil War Soldiers and Sailors Database - Wyeth, Warren," *National Park Service*, http://www.nps.gov/civilwar/search-soldiers-detail.htm?soldierId=AF1450E1-DC7A-DF11-BF36-B8AC6F5D926A (accessed 10/26/2016).

[434] James A. Emmerton, *A Record of the Twenty-Third Regiment Mass. Vol. Infantry in the War of the Rebellion, 1861-1865: With Alphabetical Roster, Companys Rolls, Portraits, Maps, Etc.* (Salem, MA: Salem Press, 1886), 334.

[435] Historical Data Systems, *U.S., American Civil War Regiments, 1861-1866* (Provo, UT: Ancestry.com Operations Inc., 1999).

[436] Ancestry.com, *Massachusetts Vital and Town Records,* Online publication (Provo, UT: Operations, Inc., 2011). Original data - Town and City Clerks of Massachusetts. Provo, UT: Holbrook Research Institute (Jay and Delene Holbrook).

[437] "Supreme Judicial Court – (Middlesex County) – Nov. 9 Before Judge Endicott," *Boston Post* (Boston, MA), 11 Nov 1878, 3.

[438] Historical Data Systems of Kingston, MA., *U.S., Civil War Soldier Records and Profiles, 1861-1865*, Online publication, (Provo, UT: Ancestry.com Operations Inc., 2009).

[439] Soldier's Pension Application File, 08 May 1882, service of William H. Wyeth (Co. H, 1st New York Light Artillery, Civil War); soldier's pension application no. 448,961; National Archives catalog title: Civil War and Later Pension Files; Records of the Department of Veterans Affairs; Record Group 15; National Archives, Washington, D.C.

[440] "Compiled Service Records of Volunteer Union Soldiers Who Served in Organizations from the State of Massachusetts," digital images, *Fold3* (http://www.fold3.com : accessed 21 Nov 2016), 1st Cavalry, Pages: 1-25, veteran: William H. Wyeth; Company: A, B; citing NARA catalog title: *Carded Records Showing Military Service of Soldiers Who Fought in Volunteer Organizations During the American Civil War, compiled 1890 - 1912, documenting the period 1861 - 1866, NARA Catalog Id: 300398, Record Group: 94, roll: RG94-CMSR-MA-1CAV-Bx0082_MISC.*

[441] "Indiana Digital Archives - Taylor Wyeth," *Indiana Archives and Records Administration,* https://secure.in.gov/apps/iara/search/Home/Detail?rId=1199464 (accessed 21 Nov 2016).

[442] Adjutant General's Office. *Registers of Deaths of Volunteers, compiled 1861–1865,* ARC ID: 656639. Record Group 94 Indiana S-Z, National Archives Washington, D.C., 182-183.

[443] Adjutant General's Office. *Registers of Deaths of Volunteers, compiled 1861–1865,* 152-153.

[444] "Indiana Digital Archives - Allen Wyeth," *Indiana Archives and Records Administration,* https://secure.in.gov/apps/iara/search/Home/Detail?rId=1084303 (accessed 21 Nov 2016).

[445] "Indiana Digital Archives - Edwin Wyeth," *Indiana Archives and Records Administration,* https://secure.in.gov/apps/iara/search/Home/Detail?rId=1084306 (accessed 22 Nov 2016.)

[446] Soldier's Pension Application File, John W. Wyeth / Wythe, no. 494,130; Civil War, RG 15; NA–Washington.

[447] John J. Wyeth, 18-19.

[448] John J. Wyeth, 19.

[449] "Henry Jackson Hunt," *Wikipedia,* https://en.wikipedia.org/wiki/Henry_Jackson_Hunt (accessed 11/27/2016).

[450] Culpeper, Va. Generals of the Army of the Potomac: Gouverneur K. Warren, William H. French, George G. Meade, Henry J. Hunt, Andrew A. Humphreys, George Sykes, September, 1863. Call #LC-B817- 7329. *Library of Congress Prints and Photographs Division,* https://www.loc.gov/item/cwp2003000220/PP/ (accessed 11/27/2016).

[451] "Francis Wyeth Dead," *The Harrisburg Patriot* (Harrisburg, Pennsylvania), 3 Jul 1893. 2.

[452] Bartlett Boder, "William Wyeth and His Times," *Museum Graphic,* St. Joseph Museum (Saint Joseph, MO), Summer 1956, 6-7.

[453] "John Wyeth," *NNDB Tracking the entire world,* http://www.nndb.com/people/515/000206894/ (accessed 11/28/2016).

[454] "The Court Martial of Surgeon General Hammond," *Pittsburgh Daily Post* (Pittsburgh, Pennsylvania), 24 Aug 1864, 2.

[455] "Trial and Sentence of Surgeon General Hammond," *The Ashland Union* (Ashland, Ohio), 31 Aug 1864, 2.

[456] Ancestry.com. *1850 U.S. Federal Census - Slave Schedules,* AL, Marshall, District 22 (Provo, UT: Ancestry.com Ops. Inc, 2004), 2.

[457] Ancestry.com. *1860 U.S. Federal Census - Slave Schedules,* AL, Marshall, Western Div. (Provo, UT: Ancestry.com Ops. Inc, 2010), 6.

[458] John Allan Wyeth, *With Sabre and Scalpel,* 53-54.

[459] John Allan Wyeth, *With Sabre and Scalpel,* 3.

[460] John Allan Wyeth, *With Sabre and Scalpel,* 45, 74, 77.

[461] John Allan Wyeth, *With Sabre and Scalpel,* 79, 81-82.

[462] John Allan Wyeth, *With Sabre and Scalpel,* 82.

[463] H. L. Stephens, "The Parting – Buy us too," Circa 1863. *Library of Congress Prints and Photographs Division,* https://www.loc.gov/item/93503990/ (accessed 12/6/2016).

[464] Heather Andrea Williams, "Slavery Affected African American Families," *Freedom's story, Teacherserve©, National Humanities Center,* http://nationalhumanitiescenter.org/tserve/freedom/1609-1865/essays/aafamilies.htm (accessed 11/26/16).

[465] Heather Andrea Williams, (accessed 11/26/16).

[466] Daniel Patrick Moynihan, "The Negro Family: The Case for National Action," *United States Department of Labor, Office of the Assistant Secretary for Administration and Management,* March 1965. <https://www.dol.gov/oasam/programs/history/webid-meynihan.htm>

[467] Chris Cillizza; Jon Cohen, "President Obama and the white vote? No problem," *The Washington Post* (Washington, D.C.) 08 Nov 2012. <https://www.washingtonpost.com/news/the-fix/wp/2012/11/08/president-obama-and-the-white-vote-no-problem/?utm_term=.73b8a75cfe1c>

[468] Barack Obama, "President Barack Obama's State of the Union Address," *The White House, Office of the Press Secretary,* 28 Jan 2014. <https://obamawhitehouse.archives.gov/the-press-office/2014/01/28/president-barack-obamas-state-union-address>

[469] "Jamie Wyeth," *Wikipedia,* https://en.wikipedia.org/wiki/Jamie_Wyeth (accessed 12/7/2016).

[470] Sarah Cascone, "JFK Portrait by Jamie Wyeth Lands at MFA Boston," *artnet news,* 08 Jul 2014. <https://news.artnet.com/art-world/jfk-portrait-by-jamie-wyeth-lands-at-mfa-boston-57402>

[471] Newsweek Staff, "Transition: Andrew Wyeth, 91, Artist," *Newsweek,* 16 Jan 2009. <http://www.newsweek.com/transition-andrew-wyeth-91-artist-78451>

[472] "Francis Parkman," *Brandywine River Museum: N. C. Wyeth Catalogue Raisonne',*

http://brandywine.doetech.net/Detlobjps.cfm?ParentListID=135094&ObjectID=1532125&rec_num=5 (accessed 7/26/15).

[473] C.R. Rode, *1846 and 1847 Doggett's New York City Directory* (New York: John W. Doggett, Jr., 1847), 435. <https://books.google.com/books?id=XSVEAQAAMAAJ&pg>

[474] "Throng At Wedding of Frances Wyeth," *New York Times* (New York, NY), 17 Feb 1915, 11.

[475] John Allan Wyeth, *With Sabre and Scalpel*, 528.

[476] "The Man in the Dome: The Checkered Career of Samuel Douglass Wyeth," *St. Louis Globe-Democrat* (St. Louis, MO), 28 Jan 1881, 7.

[477] "Agency Makes an Assignment," *Democrat and Chronicle* (Rochester, New York) 14 Oct 1905, 12. (Newspapers.com)

[478] "Wyeth Chemical Bankruptcy," *American Druggist and Pharmaceutical Record* (New York, NY), 25 Dec 1905, 358. <https://books.google.com/books?id=7NEAAAAYAAJ&pg>

[479] "New Issue 225,000 Shares Capital Stock, American Home Products Corporation," *Daily Eagle* (Brooklyn, NY), 09 Feb 1926, 18.

[480] "American Home Products - Company Profile, Information, Business Description, History, Background Information," *Reference for Business*, www.referenceforbusiness.com/history2/64/American-Home-Products.html#ixzz4DEaz5KpG (accessed 1/1/2017).

[481] The Cambridge Historical Society, *Publications I Proceedings 19 Jun 1905–24 Apr 1906* (Cambridge, MA: University Press, 1906), 34. <https://books.google.com/books?id=csY4AQAAMAAJ&pg>

[482] "Revolutionary War Commander Artemas Ward Dies October 28, 1800," *Mass Moments,* http://massmoments.org/moment.cfm?mid=311 (accessed 3/25/2016).

[483] "Account by Joshua Wyeth," *Boston Tea Party Historical Society*, http://www.boston-tea-party.org/account-Joshua-Wyeth.html (accessed 3/26/2016).

[484] Jeff Suess, "Honoring America's original patriots," *Cincinnat!com* (Cincinnati, OH), http://www.cincinnati.com/story/news/history/2014/04/13/honoring-americas-original-patriots/7666783/ (accessed 3/26/2016).

[485] William Henry Egle, *Notes and queries historical, biographical, and genealogical, relating chiefly to interior Pennsylvania, Volume II* (Harrisburg, PA: Harrisburg Publishing Company, 1896), 87. <https://books.google.com/books?id=d8IxAQAAMAAJ&pg>

[486] Russell Sanjek, *American Popular Music and its Business: The First Four Hundred Years, Volume II, From 1790 to 1909* (New York: Oxford University Press, 1988), 191. <https://books.google.com/books?id=7UbS22L6neQC&pg>

[487] "John Wyeth," *Center for Church Music Songs & Hymns*, http://www.songsandhymns.org/people/detail/john-wyeth (accessed 3/25/2016).

[488] Suzanne Ruth Thurman, "O *Sisters Ain't you Happy?*": Gender, Family, and Community Among the Harvard and Shirley Shakers, 1781-1918 (Syracuse, NY: Syracuse University Press, 2002), 64. <https://books.google.com/books?id=zqgOwvtKlKUC&pg>

[489] PineTree Productions, "Shaker Music," *AmericanMusicPreservation.com*, 2016. <http://www.americanmusicpreservation.com/TheHumbleHeart.htm>

[490] Dan Flanagan, "John Wyeth & Brother: A Family Legacy in the History of Pharmacy." *The Bulletin* (Philadelphia, PA), Summer 2014, 7. <https://usciencesblogs.typepad.com/bulletin_102_1/john-wyeth-brother-a-family-legacy-in-the-history-of-pharmacy.html>

[491] Walter Williams, *A History of Northwest Missouri, Volume 3* (Chicago: Lewis Publishing Company, 1915), 1608. <https://books.google.com/books?id=M2UUAAAAYAAJ&pg>

[492] "Bing Russell, Father of Kurt Russell," *Find-a-Death.com,* http://www.findadeath.com/forum/showthread.php?20681-Bing-Russell-Father-of-Kurt-Russell (accessed 3/26/2016).

[493] "Kurt Russell Biography," *IMDb,* http://www.imdb.com/name/nm0000621/bio?ref_=nm_ov_bio_sm (accessed 3/25/2016).

[494] "Matt Franco," *Baseball-Reference.com,* http://www.baseball-reference.com/bullpen/Matt_Franco (accessed 3/25/2016).

[495] "Eddie Taubensee," *Wikipedia,* https://en.wikipedia.org/wiki/Eddie_Taubensee (accessed 12/28/2018).

[496] "Sports of the Amateur," *Brooklyn Life* (Brooklyn, NY), 3 Oct 1908, 20.

[497] Kenneth Stern, "Duncan Wyeth," *My Child at CerebralPalsy.org,* 2016. <http://www.cerebralpalsy.org/inspiration/athletes/duncan-wyeth>

[498] Tom Speicher, "Where are They Now: Fred Cox," *Minnesota Vikings,* 23 Jun 2011. http://www.vikings.com/news/article-1/Where-Are-They-Now-Fred-Cox/28a2116f-76f0-4e7f-b1ee-5cf12634e915

[499] Maggie MacLean, "Elizabeth Peabody Founder of the First Public Kindergarten," *Civil War Women,* 7/16/2012. <www.civilwarwomenblog.com/elizabeth-peabody/>

[500] "About Us," *The Elizabeth Peabody House,* 2016. <teph.org/about-us/>

[501] "Servant of God, Rose Hawthorne," *Dominican Sisters of Hawthorne,* www.hawthorne-dominicans.org/rose-hawthorne.html#canonizationprocess (accessed 5/27/2017).

[502] "Howard Wyeth, 51, A Rock Drummer," *The New York Times* (New York, NY), 29 Mar 1996, D000019. <http://www.nytimes.com/1996/03/29/nyregion/howard-wyeth-51-a-rock-drummer.html>

[503] "About Natalie Wyeth Earnest," *U.S. Department of the Treasury,* https://www.treasury.gov/about/organizational-structure/Pages/natalie-e.aspx (accessed 3/25/2016).

[504] "Natalie Wyeth Earnest – White House Press Secretary Josh Earnest's wife," *Daily Entertainment News,* http://dailyentertainmentnews.com/breaking-news/natalie-wyeth-earnest-white-house-press-secretary-josh-earnests-wife/ (accessed 3/25/2016).

[505] Pete Souza, "January 2016: Photo of the Day," *The White House President Barack Obama,* 21 Jan 2016. (Government-produced materials on this site are not copyright protected.) <https://obamawhitehouse.archives.gov/photos-and-video/photogallery/january-2016-photo-day>

[506] Harris & Ewing, photographer, "White House. President's Office" [between 1905 and 1945] photograph, From *Library of Congress Prints and Photographs Division*, Harris & Ewing LC-H25- 3880-BM [P&P], LC-DIG-hec-14832, no known restrictions on use, www.loc.gov/pictures/item/hec2009001530/ (accessed 5/30/2016).

[507] "About the White House." *The Oval Office,* http://whitehousegiftsandapparel.com/ovaloffice.html (accessed 3/25/2016).

[508] "People in the Collections / Duke, Doris, 1912-1993," *Duke University Libraries,* http://library.duke.edu/rubenstein/collections/people/dorisduke/ (accessed 3/28/2016).

[509] Jack Boucher, photographer, "7. April 1967 East (Front) Elevation from Southeast - Mar-a-Lago, 1100 South Ocean Boulevard, Palm Beach, Palm Beach County, FL" photograph, From *Library of Congress Prints and Photographs Division*, under the digital ID hhh.fl0181. Image courtesy of federal HABS—Historic American Buildings Survey in Florida project, no known restrictions on images made by the U.S. Government, http://www.loc.gov/pictures/item/fl0181.photos.053242p/ (accessed 3/25/2016).

[510] David Rogers, "Marion Sims Wyeth leaves legacy of varied architectural styles, says architect Dragisic," *Palm Beach Daily News* (Palm

Beach, FL), 23 Dec 2010. <http://www.palmbeachdailynews.com/news/entertainment/arts-theater/marion-sims-wyeth-leaves-legacy-of-varied-architec/nMCPm/#sthash.y4sl2tn2.dpuf>

[511] Jonas Wyeth, *Wyeth family records (Mss A 3058),* R. Stanton Avery Special Collections, New England Historic Genealogical Society.

[512] Christopher Hail, *Garden Street.*

[513] Charles M. Sullivan, 3.

[514] "Wasserstein Hall," *CPCI.ca Project of the Month*, 02 Jul 2016. <http://www.cpci.ca/en/about_us/project_month/october_2012/>

[515] Donna Eldredge, "Harvard Law School Wyeth Hall Dormitory," *Nor'East Architectural Antiques*, (2014). Photo courtesy of the Co-Owner of Nor'East Architectural Antiques, llc., 16 Exeter Rd., South Hampton, NH. <http://www.noreast1.com/harvard1.html>

[516] Wyeth Hall, UAV 605 - Box 88 (GS 44 and GS 45), Harvard University Archives.

[517] "Our History: Education Gets Physical," *BU College of Health & Rehabilitation Sciences: Sargent College,* http://www.bu.edu/sargent/about-us/our-history/ (accessed 7/2/16).

[518] "Harvard Gets $5,800,000," *The New York Times* (New York, NY), 24 Apr 1931, 24.

[519] "Wyeth Hall First University Dorm Open to Women," *The Harvard Crimson* (Cambridge, MA), 29 Sep 1958. <http://www.thecrimson.com/article/1958/9/29/wyeth-hall-first-university-dorm-open/>

[520] Clennon L. King, "Student directories reveal Michelle Obama's Cambridge address." *Somerville Times* (Somerville, MA), 19 May 2013. <http://www.thesomervilletimes.com/archives/38316>

[521] "Universities earn big bucks as Harvard's stunt double." *The Harvard Law Record,* (Cambridge, MA), 11 Dec 2002. <http://hlrecord.org/2002/12/universities-earn-big-bucks-as-harvards-stunt-double/>

[522] Dan Flanagan, 7-8.

[523] Charles M. Sullivan, 3-6.

[524] Lucius R. Paige, 12, 14.

[525] Roger Gilman, 30.

[526] Lucius R. Paige, 704.

[527] Christopher Hail, *Taylor Square.*

[528] Charles M. Sullivan, 4, 7.

[529] Abby Y. Fung, "Cambridge Residents Oppose Expanding Sheraton Parking," *The Harvard Crimson* (Cambridge, MA), 20 Oct 1995. <http://www.thecrimson.com/article/1995/10/20/cambridge-residents-oppose-expanding-sheraton-parking>

[530] "People & Events: John White Webster (1793-1850)," *Murder at Harvard,* http://www.pbs.org/wgbh/amex/murder/peopleevents/p_webster.html (accessed 6/26/2016).

[531] "Divorce Case in Cambridge," *Emancipator and Republican* (Boston, MA), 08 Dec 1848, 3.

[532] "Caution," *The Daily Atlas* (Boston, MA), 31 Jul 1844, 1.

[533] "Divorce Case in High Life," *Baton-Rouge Gazette* (Baton Rouge, LA), 23 Dec 1848, 2. <http://chroniclingamerica.loc.gov/lccn/sn82003383/1848-12-23/ed-1/seq-2/>

[534] "Divorce Case in Cambridge," *Emancipator and Republican* (Boston, MA), 08 Dec 1848, 3.

[535] "Interesting Divorce Case at Cambridge," *The New York herald* (New York, NY), 11 Dec 1848, 4. <http://chroniclingamerica.loc.gov/lccn/sn83030313/1848-12-11/ed-1/seq-4/#>

[536] "Wyeth Divorce Records," *File #211*, Scott County, Iowa District Court records.

[537] "Divorce Refused," *Emancipator and Republican* (Boston, MA), 15 Feb 1849, 2.

[538] "James Wilson Grimes," *National Governors Association*, 2015. <http://www.nga.org/cms/home/governors/past-governors-bios/page_iowa/col2-content/main-content-list/title_grimes_james.default.html>

[539] "Wyeth Divorce Records," *File #211*, Scott County, Iowa District Court records.

[540] "Wyeth Divorce Records," *File #211*, Scott County, Iowa District Court records.

[541] "State of Iowa, Des Moines County, ss. District Court of Des Moines County Jonas Wyeth vs. Mary Torrey Wyeth, late Mary Torrey Hancock," *Burlington Hawk Eye* (Burlington, IA), 02 Oct 1851, 3.

[542] "Wyeth Divorce Records," *File #211*, Scott County, Iowa District Court records.

[543] Scott County, Iowa Marriage Certificates and License Returns.

[544] "Wyeth Divorce Records," *File #211*, Scott County, Iowa District Court records.

[545] Arthur W. Benson, "Brooklyn, NY Deposition to Lawrence Marcellus,"*File #211*, Scott County, Iowa District Court records, 19 May 1857.

[546] Arthur W. Benson.

[547] Jonas Wyeth 2d, "letter to Arthur Benson," *File #211*, Scott County, Iowa District Court records, 23 Jun 1855.

[548] Thomas W. Baldwin, compiler, *Vital Records of Cambridge, Massachusetts, to the year 1850* (Boston: Wright & Potter, 1914), 467.

[549] "Saturday Night Fever (1977) Quotes," *IMDb*, www.imdb.com/title/tt0076666/quotes (accessed 12/27/2017).

[550] "The Benson Family: Putting 'Benson' in Bensonhurst," *Wandering NYC*, 12 Dec 2010. <https://wanderingbrooklyn.wordpress.com/2010/12/12/the-benson-family-putting-the-benson-in-bensonhurst>

[551] Arthur W. Benson, "Last Will and Testament,*" New York Wills, Volume 0142-0144*, 1889-1890.

[552] Alice C. Allyn, 63-64.

[553] Alice C. Allyn, 58.

[554] Alice C. Allyn, 63.

[555] "Property Database for 5 Berkeley St.," *Cambridgema.gov*, http://www.cambridgema.gov/propertydatabase/18471 (accessed 7/5/2016).

[556] Alice C. Allyn, 60, 63-64

[557] "Property Database for 5 Berkeley St.," *Cambridgema.gov.*

[558] "Attempted Abduction of a Citizen of Cambridge," *The Cambridge Chronicle* (Cambridge, MA), 09 Aug 1856, 2.

[559] Arthur W. Benson, "Brooklyn, New York Deposition to Lawrence Marcellus."

[560] Scott County District Court, *Criminal Case Number 1* (Scott County, IA), May 1856 to Jun 1858.

[561] "Attempted Abduction of a Citizen of Cambridge," 2.

[562] "Attempted Abduction of a Citizen of Cambridge," 2.

131

563 Sarah Benson Johnson Wyeth, "Divorce Petition," *File #211*, Scott County, Iowa District Court records.

564 Sarah Benson Johnson Wyeth, "Divorce Petition," *File #211*, Scott County, Iowa District Court records.

565 John Bassett Moore, *A Treatise on Extradition and Interstate Rendition* (Boston: The Boston Book Company, 1891), 911. <https://books.google.com/books?id=fzk-AAAAIAAJ&pg=PA911&dq>

566 Arthur W. Benson, "Brooklyn, New York, Deposition to Lawrence Marcellus."

567 "Wyeth Divorce Records," *File #211*, Scott County, Iowa District Court records.

568 "United States Attorney General Black has given an opinion that the President has no power to cause the state of Massachusetts to surrender Joseph (Jonas) Wyeth to the authorities of Iowa, where he is charged with bigamy" *Lowell Daily Citizen and News,* (Lowell, MA) 16 Jun 1857, 2. 19th Century U.S. Newspapers. Web. 24 Jul 2016.

569 "An Important Case," *Anti-slavery Bugle* (Salem, OH), 4 Jul 1857, 1.

570 Horace Gray, Jr., *Reports of Cases Argued and Determined in the Supreme Judicial Court of Massachusetts, Volume 9 (*Boston: Little, Brown and Company, 1864), 264. <https://books.google.com/books?id=6K5LAAAAYAAJ&pg>

571 "Middlesex Law Decisions." *Lowell Daily Citizen and News* (Lowell, MA) 3 Mar 1858, 2. 19th Century U.S. Newspapers. Web. 7/24/16.

572 Scott County District Court, *Criminal Case Number 1.*

573 Benjamin and William Cutter, 331.

574 Henry Bond, Horatio Gates Jones, *Genealogies of the Families and Descendants of the Early Settlers of Watertown, Massachusetts, Including Waltham and Weston: To which is Appended the Early History of the Town* (Boston: Little Brown and Company, 1855), 992.

575 Susan E. Maycock, Charles M. Sullivan, 239-240.

576 Roland Gray, "The William Gray House in Cambridge," *Cambridge Historical Society Publications XIV, Proceedings for the Year 1919* (Cambridge, MA: Cambridge Historical Society, 1926), 104-106. <https://books.google.com/books?id=558yAQAAMAAJ&pg>

577 Roger Gilman, 30.

578 Ancestry.com, *Massachusetts, Wills and Probate Records, 1635-1991* [database on-line] (Provo, UT: Ancestry.com Operations, Inc., 2015), 484-490. Original data: Massachusetts County, District and Probate Courts, Ebenezer Wyeth, case number: 25805.

579 Ancestry.com, *Massachusetts, Wills and Probate Records, 1635-1991,* Ebenezer Wyeth, case number: 25805.

580 Roland Gray, 104.

581 Ancestry.com, *Massachusetts, Wills and Probate Records, 1635-1991,* Ebenezer Wyeth, case number: 25805.

582 Chauncey Depew Steele, Jr., *A History of Inns and Hotels in Cambridge* (Cambridge, MA: Cambridge Historical Society, 1957), 34. <http://cambridgehistory.org/wp-content/uploads/2017/02/CHS-Index-to-Proceedings.pdf>

583 Jill Sinclair, 22-23.

584 Chauncey Depew Steele, Jr., 34.

585 "The Fresh Pond Hotel," *Wikipedia,* https://en.wikipedia.org/wiki/Fresh_Pond_Hotel (accessed 6/7/2016).

586 "The Changing Face of Homelessness," *Heading Home,* http://www.headinghomeinc.org/ (accessed 6/17/2016).

587 "The Wyeth-Smith House," *Wikipedia,* https://en.wikipedia.org/wiki/Wyeth-Smith_House (accessed 6/25/2016).

588 Christopher Hail, *Fresh Pond Parkway.*

589 "President Eliot Buys a House," *Cambridge Tribune,* Volume XXXI, Number 46 (Cambridge, MA), 16 Jan 1909, 1. <http://cambridge.dlconsulting.com/cgi-bin/cambridge?a=d&d=Tribune19090116-01.2.11&srpos=2&e=-------en-20--1--txt-txIN-eliot+wyeth>

590 Jill Sinclair, 36.

591 Jill Sinclair, 33, 36.

592 Samuel Atkins Eliot, *All Aboard the "Natwyethum"!* (Cambridge, MA: Cambridge Historical Society, 1942), 38.

593 Samuel Atkins Eliot, 39, 41, 46 49.

594 Samuel Atkins Eliot, 52-53.

595 Nathaniel Jarvis Wyeth, *The Correspondence and Journals of Captain Nathaniel J. Wyeth, 1831-6* (Eugene, OR: University Press, 1899), 153-154. <https://books.google.com/books?id=5CIwAAAAYAAJ&printsec>

596 "Nathaniel Jarvis Wyeth," *Wikipedia,* https://en.wikipedia.org/wiki/Nathaniel_Jarvis_Wyeth (accessed 2/16/2016).

597 "Nathaniel Jarvis Wyeth," *Wikipedia.*

598 Hubert Howe Bancroft, *History of the northwest coast. Vol. II. 1884-86* (San Francisco: A. L. Bancroft & Company, 1884), 598. <https://books.google.com/books?id=Ndg1AAAAIAAJ&pg>

599 Jill Sinclair, 40, 43, 46.

600 "Wyeth Brickyard Superintendent," *Wikipedia,* en.wikipedia.org/wiki/Wyeth_Brickyard_Superintendent's_House (accessed 6/25/2016).

601 John Ford, 59.

602 "The John Wyeth House," *Wikipedia,* https://en.wikipedia.org/wiki/John_Wyeth_House (accessed 6/25/2016).

603 Christopher Hail, *Rutland Street.*

604 Susan E. Maycock, Charles M. Sullivan, 280.

605 Christopher Hail, *Kirkland Street.*

606 R. Rettig, "National Register Criteria Statement," *Cambridge Historical Commission* (1969, 1980).

607 Ancestry.com, *Massachusetts, Wills and Probate Records, 1635-1991* [database on-line] (Provo, UT: Ancestry.com Operations, Inc., 2015), 476-483. Original data: Massachusetts County, District and Probate Courts, Will Number 25801.

608 Christopher Hail, *Hilliard Place.*

609 Susan E. Maycock, Charles M. Sullivan, 185.

610 Thomas W. Baldwin, compiler, *Vital Records of Cambridge, Massachusetts, to the year 1850,* 787.

611 "Docket 00904 - Wyeth, Stephen," *Record Group 21: Records of District Courts of the United States, 1685 – 2009* (Series: Bankruptcy Act of 1841 Case Files, 1842 - 1844), National Archives Identifier: 4659096. <https://research.archives.gov/id/4659096>

612 Christopher Hail, *Hilliard Place.*

613 "Property Database for 5-9 Hilliard Pl.," *Cambridgema.gov,* http://www.cambridgema.gov/propertydatabase/13084 (accessed 7/5/2016).

614 Leggett, Conaway & Co., *The History of Wyandot County, Ohio containing a history of the county; its townships, towns, churches, schools, etc.* (Chicago: Leggett, Conaway & Co., 1884), 699. <https://books.google.com/books?id=vltFAQAAMAAJ&pg>

BLANK PAGES FOR ADDITIONS AND CORRECTIONS

As mentioned in the preface, it is impossible that there should not be mistakes or omissions in a work of this nature. These blank pages are for corrections and additions.

Section Two: Descendants of Nicholas Wyeth by Generation

Tips for Understanding Section Two of this Book

The next seven chapters of this book use the register numbering system developed by the New England Historic and Genealogical Society (NEHGS) in 1870. This descendant-ordered format starts with Nicholas Wyeth as the primary individual and moves forward in time to his descendants.

Unfortunately, to avoid an unwieldy tree, not all of Nicholas' known descendants could be included. For that reason, please note, in many cases, when the names of descendants' spouses are provided, the couple probably did have children.

Also, to hopefully make the book more readable and to avoid confusion, most sources from Ancestry.com are only listed in the bibliography. If every census, birth, marriage, death, grave, will and military record from Ancestry.com were in the endnotes, that would add at least 300 pages to this book.

The following explanation of this descendant-based design is adapted from Kimberly Powell's article, "Numbering your Family Tree" at ThoughtCo.com.[1]

- The key to reading a register report is understanding its numbering system. The progenitor, or primary individual, is given the number 1.
  ### 1. NICHOLAS^1 WYETH
- Using lower-case Roman numerals (i, ii, iii, iv, etc.), his children are then numbered in sequential order by birth.
- Children with known lines of descent, in most cases, are included again later in the report. In addition to the Roman numerals, they are also assigned an Arabic number (1, 2, 3, 4, etc.).
  ### 18. vii. EBENEZER WYETH SR.
- Except for the primary individual, every person assigned an Arabic number in the register numbering system appears first as a child. The number they are assigned as a child indicates his/her position in the adult descent line.
- If only a Roman numeral appears next to a child, then there are no descendants included in the report for that individual, and it is the last time that child will appear in the register report.
- Superscript numbers listed immediately following a person's first name indicate the number of generations that person is removed from the progenitor.
  ### 18. EBENEZER^3 WYETH SR. (John^2, Nicholas^1).

When reading the dates in these reports, please keep in mind that documentation back up is often very limited. Although a Federal Population Census of the United States has been taken every ten years since 1790, prior to 1850, only the name of the head of the household was provided. Then in 1921, much of the 1890 Federal Population Census was destroyed by fire, smoke and water damage in the basement of the Department of Commerce. On 20 Feb 1933, the cornerstone for the National Archives Building was laid. Ironically, the next day, government ineptitude in another branch authorized the destruction of the rest of the 1890 census.[2] The loss of the 1890 data is a huge hole in genealogical research. Additionally, information from recent censuses are not available after 1940 because of a 72-year restriction on access to the Census.

For the Colonial period, church records are the best source of marriages, baptisms/births, and deaths. Some states mandated civil registration of births and deaths in the mid-19th century. However, the majority did not require such recordkeeping until the beginning of the 20th century. Even then, death records are only as accurate as the knowledge of the person who provided the information.[3]

In early records, spelling of surnames depended on the clerk who recorded the name. Variations in Nicholas' surname include Wieth, With, Withe, Wyeth, Wyethe, Wyth, and Wythe. By the second generation, most of the Massachusetts' family used the "Wyeth" spelling. Other surnames shown frequently in the following chapters refer to the same family. For example, Park, Parks and Parkes; Clark and Clarke; Andrew and Andrews; Torry and Torrey; Winshipp and Winship; and Woodward and Woodard were often interchanged. Sometimes names were spelled differently within the same document. Not only were names differentiated, but English spelling, in general, was not consistent or standardized until the 18th century.[4]

Names, dates and places in more recent records are inconsistent as well. Here is one example of varying data... the 1850 Federal Census gives the name "Martin Wyath" for Francis Martin Wyeth and "Darcus Wyath" for his wife. In the 1860 census, he is called "Francis Martin Wyeth" and she is "Dorcas Wyeth." In the 1870 census, he is called "Martin Wyeth" and she is "Tebitha Wyeth." Thankfully, in this particular case, the name on her cemetery marker confirms the spelling of her preferred name, "Dorcas Wyeth." In the tree following, I combined her names to "Dorcas Tabitha Tankersley Wyeth." Interestingly, Tabitha may not be her middle name but instead a variation of her first name. Acts 9:36 refers to "a disciple named Tabitha (in Greek her name is Dorcas)."

Unfortunately, often, there are no records to definitively confirm data. Sometimes I have used the residence of the bride as the location of a couple's marriage. Just as it is now, most marriages in days gone by were in the bride's home or the bride's family church. Similarly, many names, dates and places in this book are based on my best judgment at the time.

If you have questions about the statistics in this book or would like to provide pictures or stories, please write to me at WyethBaker6@gmail.com. I will put updates in a blog devoted to this book at https://wyeth-wythe.blogspot.com. Also, if I can find the time, many more family photos you have given to me personally will appear in a second volume book. Please continue sending family group photos and stories to the email address above. As they depict many people in one photo, for size, family group photos will have priority in future books. Family stories you send will be given preferential treatment as well.

Pablo Picasso once said a painting is not finished until it is sold. In a sense, a compiled family tree is a work of art. But it is never finished. The family tree is always in progress. Lines are redrawn with every new marriage, birth and death. Even facts that were once thought to be set in stone, change as new records become available.

FIRST GENERATION – THE GREAT PURITAN MIGRATION

1. **NICHOLAS**[1] **WYETH** was baptized during the reign of Queen Elizabeth I on 20 Jan 1600 at All Saints Church, Saxtead, Suffolk, England.[5] Nicholas Wyeth and Margaret Clarke were married about 1630 in Suffolk County, England. **MARGARET CLARKE**, daughter of Thomas Clark and Rose Kerridge, was baptized 12 Oct 1608 in Westhorpe, Suffolk, England.[6] She died about 1643, at about age 35, most likely in Cambridge, Middlesex, Massachusetts. In Jan 1647, Nicholas married the widow **REBECCA PARKS ANDREWS**, in Cambridge.[7] Nicholas died on 19 Jul 1680, at about age 80, in Cambridge.[8] Rebecca died there in May 1698 at about age 78.

Nicholas Wyeth and Margaret Clarke had the following children:

2. i. **SARAH**[2] **WYETH** was baptized 28 Oct 1632 at All Saints Church, Saxtead, Suffolk, England.[9] She married John Fiske, 11 Dec 1651, Watertown, Middlesex, Massachusetts and died there about 1701.

   ii. **JOHN WYETH** was baptized on 18 Oct 1634 in All Saints Church, Saxtead. According to the records of Saxtead Parish, he was buried there on 23 Apr 1638 at age three.[10]

   iii. **NATHANIEL WYETH** was baptized on 11 Dec 1636 in All Saints Church, Saxtead. According to the parish register of Saxtead, he was an infant when he was buried there on the church grounds on 21 May 1637.[11]

Although they look much older, most of the graves at All Saints, Saxtead are from the late 1800s to early 1900s. Unfortunately, published transcriptions of the cemetery fail to show John and Nathaniel's actual burial locations.

Notes for Nicholas Wyeth:

Nycholas, as his name was spelled on page 12 of the Parish Registry of Saxtead's All Saints Church, is "the son of John Wyth and Margaret his wife." For the year preceding his 20 Jan 1600 baptism, this is written: "The Regester booke of Saxtead made in the tenthe day July in the fortieth and one yeare of the raigne of the Sovraigne Ladye Elizabeth in A.D. 1599."

At the time of Nicholas' christening in the first year of the 17th century, English baptisms generally took place within eight days after birth.[12] Thus, he must have been born mid-January 1600 (the 11th Julian-calendar month). Also proving that Nicholas was born late in the year 1600, is his oath taken while testifying for Thomas Danforth in a Middlesex County court proceeding on 04 Apr 1671. He said, "I Nicholas Withe aged about 70 years do testifie ye survey..."[13]

We do not know for sure what his mother's maiden name was. Her marriage to John did not give a surname in the record. It merely said, "John Wyeth the son of Thomas Wyethe was married the 27th of January Anno Domini 1583."[14] As mentioned previously, two strong possibilities for Margaret's last name are Cutler or Wyard.

Nicholas married Margaret Clarke circa 1630 and they came to New England eight to 13 years later. This time frame is based on several factors. Many researchers have published 1638 as the emigration date. 1638 is indeed a possibility since their son, John, was buried in Saxtead that year. However, once in Massachusetts, Nicholas gave a confession to join the church in Cambridge on 07 Jan 1644. The timeline in the testimony alludes to being in old England until about 1643 and to Margaret's death soon after they arrived in New England.

In 1647, Nicholas married Rebecca Parks Andrews, the young widow of Thomas Andrews. She brought three children to the marriage – Thomas Andrews Jr., age five; Daniel Andrews, age four; and baby Rebecca Andrews, just nine months. Nicholas was the only father they ever knew.

Nicholas also stated in his confession that he was apprenticed to a mason in old England when he was age 16. In turn, he taught the brick mason trade to his stepsons, Thomas and Daniel Andrews, and to his son, John Wyeth Sr. Nicholas was quite successful in his work as he was able to buy lands and homes in both Cambridge and Watertown, Massachusetts.

On 11 Feb 1666, while talking with the selectmen of Cambridge about building fences on some of his property, Nicholas complained, "that he is injured by not having his full due granted him on the south side the river neere Boston line, by reason that part of the townes grant was layd into the property of Richard Parkes." To satisfy Nicholas, the town granted him wooded land within the Swamp on the west side of the Winottime river.[15] (Anne Crockett of the Cambridge Public Library advises the Winottime is now known as Alewife Brook. It ran from the Mystic River to Fresh Pond. Thus, the granted land would have been in current day Arlington.)

Interestingly, Alewife fish were so thick in the Winottime during mating season, that one could cross the river by walking on them. They spilled the river bank and became easy pickins "land fish." Alewifes were plentiful enough that Native Americans advised settlers to plant corn with fish for fertilization in a practice called "fishing the corn."[16]

This section of the Cambridge town records is particularly noteworthy. It shows how extensive Nicholas' lands were, as well it makes mention of a Richard Parkes, who very well could be his second wife's kinsman. There appears to have been more than one Richard Parke(s) in the Cambridge / Watertown area. Nicholas' great-grandson, Ebenezer Wyeth Jr., married Mary Winship a descendant of Richard Parke whose 12 Jul 1665 will benefitted three children, Thomas, Isabel and Elizabeth.[17] Although that Richard was not Rebecca's father, he, or the Richard Parkes, living near Nicholas in 1666, probably were her kin.

Nicholas died on 19 Jul 1680 and was buried not far from his home. He rests in the Old Burying Ground at Harvard Square in his granddaughter Deborah Wyeth Gamage's family tomb. No stone marks his specific grave. However, a ceremonial monument was installed by his third great grandson, Jonas Wyeth 2[d] (1806-1868), on Mimosa Path in Cambridge's Mt. Auburn Cemetery. According to Jonas' personal records, on 12 Sep 1845, the remains of his father (Major Jonas Wyeth), two sisters, brother, grandmother and grandfather (Jonas Wyeth Sr.) were "removed from the family tomb in old Cambridge to the Mt. Auburn Cemetery and deposited in the north corner of lot number 1161." It is likely Jonas placed the memorial monument shortly afterwards.

Notes for Margaret Clarke:

Margaret's father, Thomas Clarke, was born 01 Nov and baptized 03 Nov 1570, Westhorpe, Suffolk County, England.[18] It is rare for birthdates to be provided during that time period, so Thomas' data serves as another confirmation of how quickly baptisms took place then. A birth date is not given for Margaret's mother. Rose Kerridge / Kerrich was baptized at Saxtead, 08 Apr 1572.[19] She married Thomas there 18 May 1600.[20] Both Thomas and Rose are buried at St. Margaret's Church in Westhorpe.

Margaret, Thomas and Rose's second daughter with the same name, was baptized at Westhorpe in 1608.[21] She is often confused with her older sister who was born 01 Feb 1601.[22] Since all the Clarke siblings were baptized in Westhorpe, that is likely where Margaret and Nicholas married. Their nuptials were not listed in the records of All Saints, Saxtead.

Margaret's younger brother, Dr. John Clarke, was a well-educated physician, writer and Baptist minister. According to Louis F. Asher, in *John Clarke (1609-1676): Pioneer in American Medicine, Democratic Ideals, and Champion of Religious Liberty*, Dr. Clarke authored the charter for religious tolerance separating church and state in the Rhode Island Colony. As a result, Rhode Island became a religious refuge for people of many faiths. It is believed that Dr. Clarke influenced Thomas Jefferson and James Madison's writings on religious freedom.[23]

Asher confirms that Dr. Clarke was born in the country parish of Westhorpe, Suffolk County, England (like his older sister, Margaret) on 03 Oct 1609. He was baptized in the local parish on 08 Oct 1609. He was the third son and sixth child of a family of eight. Dr. Clarke's ancestors were of "prosperous yeoman" stock who originally lived in Finningham, the adjacent parish to Westhorpe on the northeast. Clarke's grandfather John, "established himself at Westhorpe after his marriage to Katherine Cooke of that parish." Dr. John Clarke came to New England in 1637.[24]

As mentioned before, Margaret and Nicholas may have followed Dr. Clarke a year later, but it is more likely they came to the Massachusetts Bay Colony in 1643. Perhaps Nicholas came with Richard Withe (who very likely was his brother.) According to Cambridge town records, both Nicholas and Richard owned land near the town common in the mid-17th century.[25] [26] For them to own land so close to one another, there surely must have been a relationship between Richard and Nicholas. Richard appears to be of the same generation as Nicholas so he could not have been Nicholas' child and all of Nicholas' children, including his daughter with Margaret Clarke, were listed in the records of First Church.[27]

Margaret apparently did not die on the voyage to America as some believe. Nicholas said in his 07 Jan 1644 testimony to join the First Church in Cambridge, "*When* we came here, the Lord raised up my wife." Thus, Margaret died in America at around 35 years of age. John Clarke outlived his sister by many years. In John's 1676 will, he left legacies to Margaret's family… the children of Sarah Wyeth Fiske.

As stated, after settling in Cambridge, Nicholas married a second time in Jan 1647 to the widow Rebecca Parks Andrews.[28] **REBECCA PARKS** was born circa 1620 in England. She died in Cambridge in May 1698 at the age of about 78.

Records for Nicholas Wyeth and Rebecca Parks include the following children:

        i.   MARY[2] WYETH, born 18 Jan 1648, Cambridge; died there an infant.

       ii.   MARY WYETH, born 26 Jan 1649, Cambridge; died there in Jun of 1698 at the age of 49.

      iii.   NICHOLAS WYETH, born 20 Sep 1650, in Cambridge; died there an infant.

3.   iv.   NICHOLAS WYETH JR., born 10 Aug 1651, Cambridge; married (1) LYDIA FISKE, 06 Sep 1681, Cambridge; married (2) DEBORAH PARKER, 30 Jun 1698, Watertown, Middlesex, Massachusetts. He died about 1723 in Watertown.

       v.   MARTHA WYETH, born 11 Jan 1652, Cambridge; she was still an infant when she died in Cambridge.

4.   vi.   MARTHA WYETH, born 10 Jul 1653, Cambridge; married THOMAS IVES SR., 01 Apr 1671, Salem, Essex, Massachusetts. She died circa 1676 in Salem.

5.   vii.   JOHN WYETH SR., born 15 Jul 1655, Cambridge; married DEBORAH JACKSON WARD, 02 Jan 1682, Cambridge; died there, 13 Dec 1706.

6.   viii.   WILLIAM WYETH, born 01 Jan 1657, Cambridge; married RUTH SHEPARD there 16 Oct 1683. He died about 01 Oct 1703 … probably near present day Wells or Saco, Maine.

Notes for Rebecca Parks:

U.S. and International Marriage Records, 1560-1900, from Rebecca's marriage in 1641 to Thomas Andrews, indicate her maiden name was "Parks." Some erroneously believe Rebecca Parks Andrews' maiden name was Craddock because of a petition Thomas Andrews, the husband of Damaris Craddock, joined in with a Mrs. Rebecca Craddock in 1648. That Mrs. Rebecca Craddock was the widow of Matthew Craddock and was stepmother to Damaris Craddock. When that Thomas Andrews died in England, Damaris married Rev. Cudworth.

In reality, Rebecca's first husband, Thomas Andrews, arrived in Salem, Essex, Massachusetts with the Winthrop fleet.[29] He settled in Watertown, Middlesex, Massachusetts.[30] It was there Thomas Andrews Jr. and Daniel Andrews were born. The youngest child, Rebecca Andrews, was born on 18 Apr 1646, after the family moved to Cambridge. Following Rebecca's marriage to Nicholas Wyeth, the three Andrews' children were baptized by Rev. Thomas Shepard at the First Church in Cambridge.

Rebecca and Nicholas' children were baptized there as well. There is some confusion about whether they had seven or eight children. Massachusetts vital records exist for two children named Mary, two named Nicholas, two named Martha, one named John and one named William. All dates except for the first Martha are spaced far enough apart to be accurate.

A few years after Nicholas died in 1680, Rebecca became the fourth wife of Thomas Fox, of Cambridge, on 16 Dec 1685. He had one son, Jabez Fox, with his first wife. Rebecca moved into Thomas' home. The very same house would later be occupied by General Artemas Ward of Shrewsbury, Massachusetts, while he commanded the forces at Bunker Hill. In 1809, Oliver Wendell Holmes was born in the Fox house.

In the same year of the Fox marriage, 1685, Rebecca's daughter, Rebecca Andrews Frost Jacobs, blamed herself for the accidental death of one of her children. It worsened her already tenuous mental condition.

The younger Rebecca's mental illness led to her being accused of witchcraft during the Salem Village madness of 1692. By the end of the hysteria, two of Rebecca Parks Andrews Wyeth Fox's children, Daniel and Rebecca; her granddaughter, Margaret Jacobs; her son-in-law, George Jacobs Jr. and his father, George Jacobs Sr.; were accused of witchcraft.

As shown before and in the second note below, Rebecca Parks Andrews Wyeth Fox wrote heart-wrenching letters from Cambridge to the governor and head magistrate asking for the release of her mentally unstable daughter. Her desperate pleadings fell on deaf ears. Margaret and her mother languished in jail until 04 Jan 1693 when they were found not guilty by a new court who would not accept spectral evidence (proof based upon dreams and visions). They were not released from Salem Dungeon for a few more months until they could afford to pay for their jail room and board, chains and fetters, court costs and bail bonds, and for every piece of paper including their pardon.[31]

Salem Witch Trials Memorial, Salem town, MA

To the Hon'ble: William Stoughton Esq'r Chief Judge of Their Maj'ties Special Court of Oyer & Terminer Holden at Salem &c The Humble Petition of Rebecca Fox Sheweth

That Whereas Rebeccah Jacobs (daughter to the Humble Petitioner) has long lyen in Prison for Witchcraft, & she at some times has uttered hard words of her self as tho she had killed her Child, which words are much accounted of as is famed. These may acquaint your Hon'r that the s'd Rebeccah Jacobs is a Woman broken & distracted in her mind, & that she has been so at times above these 12 Years, & this I am ready to take my oath to, & I can bring several Others that will do the same & therefore Your Humble Petitioner thought her self bound in Conscience for your Hon'r's information to declare the same to Your Hon'r & Prays that due regard may be had thereto, that so there may not be stresse laid on the Confession of a Distracted Woman to the Prejudice of her life; So not doubting of your Hon'r's Integrity in this Matter Your Petitioner prays to God Almighty, that Wisedome may not be witholden from your Hon'r. who is Wise, & subscribes her Self Hon'ble S'r

Your Hon'r's Dutiful Servat and Humbl Petition'r *Rebecca Fox*[32]

About the time of her daughter's release, Rebecca was again left a widow when Thomas Fox died on 25 Apr 1693. Two years later, on 03 May 1695, Rebecca and two of her sons transferred land in Cambridge to one John Russell. Courtesy of the Massachusetts Historical Society, here is the deed's signature block showing Rebecca's mark and John and William Wyeth's signatures.

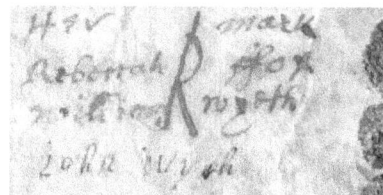
Her mark Rebeccah R ffox - William Wyeth - John Wyeth

After Thomas' death, Rebecca turned her attentions to the care of her daughter, Mary Wyeth, who had suffered ill health for many years. Mary's will, shown earlier in this book, dated 26 May 1698, expressed her bereavement over the loss "of my dear and tender Mother who took the care of me in my long and languishing sickness…" Mary asked her brother, Daniel Andrew, to be her executor and to take care of Mary in her few remaining days on earth, as her mother had before she passed away. *Pennsylvania: Genealogies* by William Egle states Rebecca died in May 1698.[33] Indeed it does appear from reading Mary's will that her loving mother had just left her.

"Yesterday was the birthplace of today.

Today is the birthplace of forever."

~ Marvin Gaye

SECOND GENERATION – KING PHILIP'S WAR & THE WITCH TRIALS

2. **SARAH² WYETH** (Nicholas¹) was born circa Oct 1632 in Saxtead, Suffolk, England and baptized there on 28 Oct 1632 in All Saints Church.[34] According to the handwritten records of Watertown, Middlesex, Massachusetts, Sarah Wyeth and John Fiske were married there on 11 Dec 1651. **JOHN FISKE**, son of Nathaniel Fiske and Dorothy Symonds, was born 1619 in Weybread, Suffolk, England. He died on 28 Oct 1684 at the age of 65 in Watertown. Sarah died there circa 1701 at about the age of 69.

This photograph, taken 02 Apr 2018, shows the width of All Saints Church, Saxtead.

John Fiske and Sarah Wyeth had the following children:

- i.   SARAH³ FISKE, born 01 Feb 1652, Watertown; died after Aug of 1677. Her death date is based on the fact that the first payments from her great uncle John Clarke's estate started in Aug 1677. (Sarah Fiske is sometimes confused with her cousin who married Abraham Gale.)
- ii. JOHN FISKE was born on 07 Nov 1653 in Watertown. He was just three months old when he died there on 14 Feb 1654.
- 7. iii. JOHN FISKE, born 20 Nov 1655, Watertown; married (1) ABIGAIL PARKE, 09 Dec 1679, Watertown; married (2) HANNAH RICHARDS, 19 Jan 1699 Watertown; died there, 06 Jan 1718.
- iv. MARGARET FISKE was born on 28 Nov 1658 in Watertown. The only document that can be used to determine her death date is the legacy she received from the will of her great uncle John Clarke in 1684. Thus, she died after 1684.
- 8. v. MARY FISKE, born 05 Jul 1661, Watertown; married JOSEPH MASON, 05 Feb 1684, Watertown; died there, 06 Jan 1723.
- 9. vi. WILLIAM FISKE, born 23 Feb 1663, Watertown; married HANNAH SMITH, 25 Oct 1693, Watertown; died there before 29 Mar 1742.
- 10. vii. MARTHA FISKE, born 15 Dec 1666, Watertown; married GEORGE ADAMS, 28 Feb 1683, Lexington, Middlesex, Massachusetts; died there, 07 May 1747.
- 11. viii. ELIZABETH FISKE, born 11 May 1669, Watertown; married SIMON MELLEN, 27 Dec 1688, Sherborn, Middlesex, Massachusetts; death date is unknown.
- ix. NATHANIEL FISKE, born on 11 Sep 1672, Watertown; death date is unknown.
- 12. x. ABIGAIL FISKE, born 08 Oct 1675, Watertown; married DEACON JONATHAN SANDERSON, 14 Jul 1699, Watertown; died 29 Apr 1759, Waltham, Middlesex, Massachusetts.

Notes for Sarah Wyeth:

Sarah's birth date is based on her baptism in All Saints Church, Saxtead. Records of the First Church in Cambridge state she came to Cambridge at the age of 13. Her age when she arrived in New England further supports the theory that her father, Nicholas, arrived shortly before his confession to Thomas Shepard on 07 Jan 1644.

After Sarah's marriage to John Fiske, she spent the rest of her life in Watertown.

Curiously, in the will of her uncle, Dr. John Clarke, Sarah was not identified by name. From a book called *John Clarke and his Legacies* by Sydney James, we find Dr. Clarke wrote his will in Newport, Rhode Island ... the town he had founded many years before. The document, held at the Newport Historical Society, shows Dr. Clarke put a blank for the first name of his sister Margaret's daughter. However, receipts for payments beginning in Aug 1677 and ending in Jan 1700/01 include nine single shares to children of John and Sarah Fiske of Watertown, Massachusetts. Although she was unnamed in the will, Sarah was to receive a double share.[35]

Genealogies of the families and descendants of the early settlers of Watertown, Massachusetts confirm legacies were indeed paid to four Fiske children. When Sarah, Margaret, Mary and Martha turned 18, each received a single share. The book also states Sarah Wyeth Fiske died shortly after a deed she and her sons signed on 21 Jul 1701.[36]

3. **NICHOLAS[2] WYETH JR.** (Nicholas[1]) was born on 10 Aug 1651 in Cambridge, Middlesex, Massachusetts. He died about 1723 in Watertown.

Nicholas Wyeth Jr. married (1) Lydia Fiske on 06 Sep 1681 in Cambridge. **LYDIA FISKE,** daughter of David Fiske and Lydia Cooper, was born on 29 Apr 1647 in Lexington, Middlesex, Massachusetts. She died on 10 Mar 1698 at the age of 50 in Watertown. Nicholas and Lydia did not have any children.

Nicholas Wyeth Jr. married (2) Deborah Parker on 30 Jun 1698 in Watertown. The service was performed by family friend, Thomas Danforth, Esq. **DEBORAH PARKER,** daughter of Edmund Parker and Elizabeth Howe, was born on 06 Jan 1655 in Lancaster, Worcester, Massachusetts. She died in Jan of 1740 at the age of 85 in Waltham, Middlesex, Massachusetts. Her death date comes from page 72 of *Waltham, Past and Present*. In the book, author Charles Alexander Nelson describes the 05 Jan 1740 vote of the selectmen (councilmen) of Waltham to provide rum for the funeral of the poor widow Wyeth. (Waltham was part of Watertown until 1738.)[37]

Nicholas Wyeth Jr. and Deborah Parker had the following child:

> i. MERCY[3] WYETH was born on 05 Jul 1699 in Watertown. She died there a few days later on 27 Jul 1699.

Notes for Nicholas Wyeth Jr.:

He was granted by the will of his father, Nicholas Wyeth Sr., the house and land in Watertown, which was originally purchased from Daniel Andrews. He was also given the liberty to cut and carry away four loads of firewood every year from his father's land.

Nicholas worked as a tanner, but something must have happened to affect his work or he grew too old to work. In Watertown records of 1716, he and second wife, Deborah, were listed as paupers. His death date comes from the fact that 1723 was the first year his wife appears in the records of Watertown as a "helpless widow."

4. **MARTHA**^{2} **WYETH** (Nicholas^1) was born on 10 Jul 1653 in Cambridge, Middlesex, Massachusetts. Martha Wyeth and Thomas Ives Sr. were married on 01 Apr 1671 in Salem, Essex, Massachusetts. **THOMAS IVES SR.** was born about 1648 in England. Martha died about 1676 in Salem. Administration of Thomas' will was granted to his second wife, Elizabeth Metcalf Ives White, on 05 Aug 1695 in Salem. Therefore, it is apparent he died before that date.

Thomas Ives and Martha Wyeth had the following children:

	i.	ELIZABETH^3 IVES was born on 08 Feb 1672 in Salem, Essex, Massachusetts. She died there on 21 Jul 1673 at the age of one.
13.	ii.	THOMAS IVES JR., born 31 Mar 1674, Salem; married ELIZABETH MATTHEWS, 21 Aug 1710, Marblehead, Essex, Massachusetts; death date is unknown.
	iii.	DEBORAH IVES was born on 08 Dec 1675 in Salem; death date is unknown.

Notes for Martha Wyeth:

There are several records for Martha's marriage to Thomas Ives in Salem. 01 Apr 1671 from *New England Marriages* appears to be the correct record of five. 01 Feb 1672 is from *Massachusetts Marriages*; 16 May 1672 and 01 Jul 1672 are from *Essex County Quarterly Court* records; and 1671, with no date attached, is from *U.S. and International Marriage Records*.

Martha's death date naturally comes before her husband's marriage in 1679 to Elizabeth Metcalf. Also, Martha was deceased when her father wrote his will in 1680. Nicholas left legacies to Martha's surviving children, Thomas and Deborah. According to a book on the *Driver Family* by Harriet Cooke, Martha's children were baptized in Mar of 1683, with their half brothers, Joseph and John Ives, in the First Church of Salem, Massachusetts.[38]

Gamage family records confuse Martha with her sister, Mary. It was Mary, not Martha, who was the spinster who remembered William Wyeth, the father of Deborah Wyeth Gamage, in her last will and testament.

5. **JOHN**^{2} **WYETH SR.** (Nicholas^1) was born on 15 Jul 1655 in Cambridge, Middlesex, Massachusetts. John Wyeth Sr. and Deborah Jackson Ward were married there on 02 Jan 1682.[39] **DEBORAH JACKSON WARD**, daughter of John "the turner" Ward and Hannah Jackson, was born on 19 Jul 1662 in Cambridge. John Wyeth Sr. died there on 13 Dec 1706 at the age of 51. Deborah died in Cambridge before 1725.

John Wyeth Sr. and Deborah Jackson Ward had the following children:

| | i. | ELIZABETH^3 WYETH, born 06 Oct 1684, Cambridge; died there before 1701. |
| 14. | ii. | DEBORAH WYETH, born 20 Nov 1686, Cambridge; married DEACON SAMUEL BOWMAN in 1714; she died about 1783, Cambridge. |

iii. JOHN WYETH, born 21 Dec 1688, Cambridge; died there on 22 Dec 1688.

15. iv. JONATHAN WYETH, born 03 Mar 1690, Cambridge; married HEPZIBAH CHAMPNEY, circa 1714, Cambridge; died there, 24 Sep 1743.

16. v. HANNAH WYETH, born about 1693, Cambridge; married (1) NATHANIEL PRENTICE, 1712, Cambridge; married (2) JASON WINSHIP SR., 05 Mar 1723, probably in Cambridge; died 12 Dec 1756, Menotomy (Arlington), Middlesex, Massachusetts.

17. vi. THANKFUL WYETH, born about 1696, Cambridge; married WILLIAM WINSHIP, 06 Dec 1716, Cambridge; died before 1739, Menotomy.

18. vii. EBENEZER WYETH SR., born about 1698, Cambridge; married SUSANNAH HANCOCK, about 1726, Cambridge; died there, 05 Apr 1754.

19. viii. ELIZABETH WYETH, born 22 May 1701, Cambridge; married DEACON JOHN WINSHIP, 02 Oct 1718, Cambridge; died 08 Oct 1759, Menotomy.

20. ix. JOHN WYETH JR., born 27 Dec 1705, Cambridge; married ELIZABETH HANCOCK, 20 Dec 1733, Cambridge; died there, 23 Oct 1756.

Notes for John Wyeth Sr.:

According to Lucius Paige's *The History of Cambridge*, on 26 Nov 1675, John Wyeth was impressed to serve in King Philip's War by order of Captain Daniel Gookin.[40] There seems to be some confusion about his service in that First Indian War (sometimes called Metacomet's War).[41] Paige indicates John was to serve under Captain Gookin, but, according to Corporal Jonathan Remington, Wyeth did not muster.

Metacomet, the Wampanoag chief who adopted the English name Philip. This picture is courtesy of the Library of Congress Prints and Photographs Division.

However, other records show that John Withe (sic) was impressed on 03 Dec 1675 to serve in Captain Nathaniel Davenport's Company. Furthermore, according to George Bodge's critical account of the war, Captain Gookin was not appointed sergeant major of the Middlesex Regiment until 05 May 1676. Also, Remington was not corporal to Major Daniel Gookin or to his son, Captain Daniel Gookin Jr. Remington was corporal to Captain Nathaniel Davenport and was impressed in Cambridge at the end of 1675 with 14 others, including John Withe.[42] Yet another record states that John served in King Phillip's war at the rank of major.[43]

Around the time of his 1682 marriage, John purchased an estate to the west of his mother's farm near Cambridge Common.[44] At Nicholas' death in 1680, John had inherited some land from his father. Then before his mother married Thomas Fox in 1685, she distributed more lands to John. No doubt some of those lands were sold in 1695 to brother William as shown in the deed for land sale document on the next page.[45]

John Wyeth was mentioned often in the *Records of the Town of Cambridge*.[46] Here are a few references:

- 21 May 1688: John was chosen town constable for two years. (P. 288)
- 09 Nov 1691: He was chosen as a driver to view fences in the west field. (P. 296) (The

west field started near 107 Garden Street, where Noah Wyeth Sr. had his home and went west to Fresh Pond meadow. At the time, Garden Street was called both the "highway to the Great Swamp" and the "highway to the Fresh Pond.")[47]

- 25 Jul 1692: John was fined for a defect in his fence. (P. 297)
- 20 Mar 1693: At a meeting of selectmen, John was assigned to check the fences in the west field. (P. 300)
- 14 Mar 1697: John Withe was chosen hog constable for the Common. (P. 321)
- 14 Mar 1698: John was to inspect the yoaking and ringing of swine on Cambridge Common. (P. 319)
- 10 Mar 1700: John had hog checking duty. (P. 336)
- 11 Mar 1700: John had hayward's duty on the west field. (P. 329) (Hayward is an officer in charge of hedges and fences around a town common or field in order to confine cattle.)

1695 deed for land sale by John Wyeth to his brother, William. *Nicholas and William Wyeth papers* (Mss 73). R. Stanton Avery Special Collections. Courtesy of the New England Historic Genealogical Society (NEHGS), Boston, MA.

John's last will and testament, numbered 25806, was dated 29 Nov 1706. In summary, it states he is a mason and that his estate shall be…

> "… under the management of Deborah my beloved wife while bringing up my beloved children while in their minority. As they come of age, my wife shall deliver some of the estate to each of them as she can spare.
>
> I give to my son Jonathan a double part of the remainder of my estate. And the rest of my children viz: Deborah, Hannah, Thankful, Ebenezer, Elizabeth and John to have equal shares. Jonathan is to have the house and lands adjoining and to pay the value of the difference to the rest of my children.

The housing and land appertaining to the children of my brother: William Wyeth, Deceased may possibly be upon sale before a distribution of my estate can be made. My will is that if this is to happen, my executrix shall make a sale of my land at the farms to purchase said lands or any part of them for the use of my children..."

Notes for Deborah Jackson Ward:

Deborah was born in the part of Cambridge that soon after became known as Cambridge Village, then Newtown in 1691 and finally Newton in 1766. The house Deborah grew up in was constructed for use as a garrison. In 1676 it was used as such during King Philip's War.[48] Her father was called John "the turner" because of his occupation–he was skilled in turning wood on a lathe. He was also active politically. Per Andrew Henshaw Ward in the *Ward Family*, John Ward was a selectman (city councilman) for nine years and served an additional nine years as representative to the General Court.[49]

It is through Deborah that the Wyeth / Wythe family connects to Artemas Ward, the major general who was second in command to George Washington in the American Revolution. Deborah's grandfather and Artemas' great grandfather, William Ward, founded both Sudbury and Marlborough, Massachusetts.[50]

On 25 Nov 1696, Deborah Ward Wyeth was listed on the same page as Thomas Danforth as a full member of the First Church under the direction of Rev. William Brattle, Pastor.[51]

A record of Deborah's death cannot be found, however, on page 331 of the *History of the Town of Arlington*, there is information about her children signing a quitclaim to Joseph Winship's heirs on 17 Feb 1725 because "Joseph Winship Sr. married the widow of John Wyeth."[52] The probate records for Joseph Winship also confirm the marriage to John Wyeth's widow. Such a marriage would have taken place after the death of Joseph's first wife in 1710 and his marriage to Sarah Stearns in 1714. So, perhaps Deborah died circa 1714.

6. **WILLIAM**[2] **WYETH** (Nicholas[1]) was born on 01 Jan 1657 in Cambridge, Middlesex, Massachusetts. William Wyeth and Ruth Shepard were married there on 16 Oct 1683. **RUTH SHEPARD**, daughter of Thomas Shepard and Hannah Ensign, was born in 1662. Although some records give Watertown for Ruth's birthplace, she likely was born in Malden as that is where her parents married and her mother died. Ruth's father, born aboard the *Abigail* on his way to America in 1635, died in Milton, Norfolk, Massachusetts. Ruth died in Cambridge before 1702.[53] According to a record from the time period, William was "killed by the Indians about 01 Oct 1703."[54] [55] His death likely occurred along the coast of Maine during the first major campaign of Queen Anne's War.[56]

William Wyeth and Ruth Shepard had the following children:

      i. RUTH[3] WYETH, born 29 Nov 1685, Cambridge; died there before 1702.

      ii. WILLIAM WYETH, born 31 Jan 1687/8, Cambridge; died there before 1702.

21.   iii. DEBORAH WYETH, born 1690, Cambridge; married JOSHUA GAMAGE SR., 22 Jun 1710, Cambridge; died there, 1773.

22.   iv. MARTHA WYETH, born circa 1696, Cambridge; married WILLIAM FESSENDEN, 12 Oct 1716, Cambridge; died there, 27 Jan 1726.

Notes for William Wyeth:

When his mother remarried, she gave William her home and property. John had recently purchased his own estate on the westerly side of his parents' farm. Oldest brother, Nicholas Jr., was given land in Watertown in his father's will. As well, the will entrusted John and William to care for their maiden sister, Mary.

The Records of the *Town of Cambridge* show on –

- 18 Mar 1689: William was chosen to view fences in the west field. (P. 289)
- 10 Nov 1690: William was viewer and driver checking fences in the west field. (P. 292)
- 20 Mar 1693: At a meeting of selectmen, William was chosen to inspect the yoking and ringing of swine on Cambridge Common. (P. 300)
- 09 Mar 1695: William Withe was chosen hog constable. (P. 315)[57]

According to the following land record, apparently, William was not taught the mason trade by his father. His social status of husbandman (a free tenant farmer or small landowner) was a rung below the level of yeoman. In the document, witnessed by Cambridge's town clerk, Andrew Bordman, on 22 Mar 1701, William sold land in Watertown to Joseph Coolidge.[58] Deacon Joseph Coolidge (1666-1737), a Cambridge tailor, was married to Rebecca Frost, the daughter of William's half-sister, Rebecca Andrews Frost Jacobs.

On 19 Aug 1702, William conveyed his estate to trustees for the benefit of his only surviving descendants, Deborah, age 12, and Martha, age five.[59] The original copy of the conveyance is held at the Middlesex South Registry of Deeds in Cambridge. The document, written in tiny letters on page 481 of book 13, shows the trustees were the aforementioned Andrew Bordman and Joseph Coolidge.

It is rather curious why William would pass his estate to trustees a full year before his death. Perhaps there are clues in the almost indecipherable conveyance document. The legible dates on the document are 19 Aug 1702, the date William signed it, and 08 Nov 1703, when it was received and entered in the records of Charlestown.

Conceivably William transmitted his property in preparation for an expedition to the frontier of present-day Maine. In the *History of Cambridge*, Lucius Paige states William was killed by Indians on about 01 Oct 1703.[60] At age 46, William very well could have been a member of the militia that fought in the Northeast Coast Campaign of 10 Aug 1703 to 06 Oct 1703.[61] He could have been among the settlers of Maine (which then was part of Massachusetts), but that is less likely given his daughters were still in Cambridge.

The Northeast Coast Campaign was the first major campaign of Queen Anne's War in New England. Like the preceding King Philip's War (1675–1678) and King William's War (1688–1699), Queen Anne's War (1703–1713) was fought for control of the North American Continent.[62] Struggling to thwart English settlements above the Kennebec River in southern Maine, 500 troops of French-Canadian forces and Indians of the Wabanaki Confederacy burned and destroyed over 50 miles of New England's north country. The five principal Indian nations making up the Wabanaki confederation were the Abenaki, Maliseet, Mi'kmaq, Passamaquoddy, and Penobscot.[63]

22 Mar 1701 Watertown land sale deed between William Wyeth (husbandman) and Joseph Coolidge (tailor).
Nicholas and William Wyeth papers (Mss 73). R. Stanton Avery Special Collections. Courtesy of the New England Historic Genealogical Society (NEHGS), Boston, MA. Used as a unique element that is part of a unique family history.

In what is commonly called the "Six Terrible Days", the French and Indian forces killed or captured more than 130 settlers at Wells, Cape Porpoise, Saco, Scarborough, Spurwink, Purpooduck (now in Cape Elizabeth), and Casco (now Portland).[64] At the fort in Casco, the besieged colonists unflinchingly defended themselves for almost a week as everything around them was destroyed. Finally, they were relieved by the arrival of a British war ship. Still the desolation of the Maine seaboard was almost complete. All that was left standing were a few isolated garrisons.[65]

Emboldened by their success, the French and Indian attacks became more savage. The inhumanity toward the killed and captured defied description. Although the French were equally brutal, the English came to look upon Indians and wolves with the same repugnance. The story of Mrs. Hannah Bradley particularly demonstrates their reasoning. Thoughtless of danger, she and a soldier left the gates of their garrison open. A small party of Indians rushed in, killed the soldier and took Hannah captive. She was obliged to travel on foot in deep snow, with little food, carrying a burden that would have been heavy for a strong man to bear. To heighten her misery, a child was born to her during the long march to Canada. With a mother's devotion, Mrs. Bradley sought to save the baby's life at great risk to her own. It, however, was impossible to do so. "Her captors seemed to take a fiendish delight in torturing the hapless little waif of the wilderness, and at length put it to death by throwing hot embers into its mouth to stop its crying."[66] [67]

White Captives Driven to Canada by Indians. Picture is courtesy of the New York Public Library, Art and Picture Collection.

In the Autumn of 1703, the governor of the Massachusetts Bay Colony ordered troops of militia to Maine to man the garrisons and fight the attackers. It could be that William Wyeth was among their number.[68]

As William did not leave a last will and testament, probate case number 25830 shows Joseph Coolidge and Andrew Bordman served as administrators of William's estate. Their bond was taken on 19 Nov 1703. With the land already transferred, the inventory submitted by Coolidge and Bordman on 10 Mar 1703/4 included minor items like napkins and towels, curtains and valances and an iron pot and hooks.

A few years later, William's homestead came up for sale at about the time his brother, John Wyeth Sr., wrote his will on 29 Nov 1706. Although he was close to death himself, John asked his executrix to purchase the old homestead from Deborah and Martha's trustees in order to keep the house and lands in the Wyeth family.

In the year 2016, the house Jonas Wyeth 2[d] (1806-1868) built / renovated in 1837 at 22 Garden Street is on the land John Wyeth Sr. bought in 1680 from Thomas Oakes.[69] In 1832, Jonas resided at 18 Garden Street which today is in the middle of Berkeley Street, northwest of the Sheraton Commander at 16 Garden Street. Apparently, 18 Garden Street was the house William owned.[70]

Although the Andrews' children were Nicholas' step children, he was the only father they ever knew because their own father died when they were quite young. As the three children are descended from Nicholas Wyeth's wife, Thomas Jr. and Daniel are indeed distant uncles and Rebecca Andrews Frost Jacobs is a distant aunt to the descendants of Rebecca Parks Andrews Wyeth Fox. Here is an abbreviated family tree for the Andrews' family. It is based on data from David L. Greene's article in the April 1982 issue of *The American Genealogist*.[71]

THOMAS ANDREWS was born in 1614 in Essex County, England. On 08 Apr 1630, he left Yarmouth, Isle of Wight, in *The Arbella*, the flagship of the first four vessels of the Winthrop Fleet that landed in Salem, Essex, Massachusetts on 12 Jun 1630.[72] [73] Thomas settled in Watertown, Middlesex, Massachusetts.[74] There he married **REBECCA PARKS** circa 1641. She was born circa 1620 in England. He died about 1647 in Cambridge, Middlesex, Massachusetts. Rebecca then married Nicholas Wyeth and after his death, she married Thomas Fox. Rebecca died in May 1698 in Cambridge.

Thomas Andrews and Rebecca Parks Andrews had the following children:

i. **THOMAS ANDREWS JR.** was born on 15 Oct 1641 in Watertown, Middlesex, Massachusetts. His stepfather, Nicholas Wyeth, taught him the masonry trade. Thomas married **MARTHA ECCLES** on 30 Oct 1673, probably in Cambridge. She was born in 1642 in Cambridge. She died there in 1685. He died about 1700 in Cambridge. Per the *History of Cambridge*, he apparently died just before his daughter, Rebecca, married on 21 Nov 1700 because he conveyed his estate to her.[75]

Rebecca Andrews, daughter of Thomas Andrews Jr. and Martha Eccles was born in Cambridge in 1674. She married Deacon Samuel Bowman. He was born on 14 Aug 1679 in Watertown, Middlesex, Massachusetts. He died in 1746 in Cambridge. Rebecca and Samuel Bowman had seven children: Andrew, Samuel Jr., Martha, Mary, Rebecca, Hannah, and Andrew II. After Rebecca's death on 18 Nov 1713, Deacon Bowman married Deborah Wyeth daughter of John Wyeth Sr. and Deborah Jackson Ward.

ii. **DANIEL ANDREWS** was born in Mar 1644 in Watertown. On 13 Oct 1659, he signed an indenture to have his stepfather, Nicholas Wyeth, teach him masonry. He married **SARAH PORTER**, daughter of John Porter and Mary Endicott in 1677 in Salem, Essex, Massachusetts. Sarah was baptized there on 03 Jun 1649. In 1678, Daniel was the overseer of Nicholas Wyeth's will. Daniel Andrews was a teacher and a mason in Salem and Salem Village. Daniel died 03 Dec 1702 in Salem Village, Essex, Massachusetts. Sarah died there in 1731. (In 1752, Salem Village was renamed Danvers for Danvers Osborn.)

Per Daniel Andrews' will, written 04 Sep 1702, he and Sarah Porter had eight children. They were: Sarah, Daniel, Thomas, Samuel, Elizabeth, Daniel Jr., Israel and Mehitabel Andrews. Father Daniel and two of his sons, Samuel and Thomas, died from smallpox within days of each other.

iii. **REBECCA ANDREWS** was born on 18 Apr 1646 in Cambridge. She married (1) **JOHN FROST**, son of Elder Edmund Frost and Thomasine Clench, on 26 Jun 1666 in Cambridge. He was born about 1632 in England. John died before 30 Sep 1672 in Cambridge. She married (2) **GEORGE JACOBS JR.**, son of George Jacobs Sr. and Mary Jacobs, in 1674 in Salem, Essex, Massachusetts. He was born about 1649 in Salem. Rebecca Jacobs was named in her husband George's will of 1717. She died after 05 Mar 1717/18 when her husband's will was probated in Salem.

John Frost and Rebecca Andrews had three children: John, Rebecca (who married Joseph Coolidge (1666-1737), and Thomas Frost. Deborah and Martha Wyeth went to live with their Coolidge cousins when their father, Rebecca Frost Coolidge's uncle, William Wyeth, was killed by Native Americans in 1703. George Jacobs Jr. and Rebecca Andrews' children included Margaret, George III, John, Jonathan, Mary, and Joseph Jacobs.

After Rebecca Andrews Frost married George Jacobs Jr. she settled next door to her brother, Daniel, in Salem Village, Essex, Massachusetts. Sister Martha Wyeth Ives lived nearby, as well.

Daniel's activity in politics, and the fact that he married into the Porter family, put him into the center of the storm in the Salem Village madness of 1692. By the end of the hysteria, Daniel, his sister Rebecca; her daughter, Margaret Jacobs; her husband, George Jacobs Jr. and his father, George Jacobs Sr.; were accused of witchcraft. As mentioned before, many scholars of the period point to politics between two of Salem Village's wealthiest families – the Porters and the Putnams – as the driving force behind the witchcraft accusations.

In 1685, the Jacobs' child, Mary, not yet age two, fell in a well and drowned. It was said Mary's death caused or contributed to Rebecca Andrews Jacobs' mental breakdown. Her youngest child, Joseph, born in Sep 1689, is believed to be the nursing baby torn from his mother's arms when she was arrested for witchcraft.[76]

The Mother, Myra Albert Wiggins, photographer. 1901 image courtesy of the Library of Congress, Prints and Photographs Division.

On 14 May 1692, Thomas Putnam and Nathaniel Ingersoll filed a witchcraft complaint against Daniel, his sister, Rebecca Andrews Jacobs, and her husband George Jacobs Jr. The next day, when Constable Jonathan Putnam and his officers arrived at their homes to make the arrest, they found Daniel and George had escaped.[77] [78]

This 1992 monument was built in Danvers (Salem Village) near the site of Rev. Parris' meetinghouse. The quote of George Jacobs Sr. "Well ! burn me, or hang me, I will stand in the truth of Christ" shows on the tablet far left rear.

Rebecca was alone with her four children.[79] As the policemen carted her off to jail, the children, who could, ran crying after their mother. With their father and uncle gone, the children were forced into the care of neighbors for ten long months while their mother was kept in irons in Salem jail.[80]

Rebecca Jacobs' father-in-law, George Jacobs Sr. and her 16-year-old daughter, Margaret, had been arrested for witchcraft four days earlier. George Sr. was found guilty partly through Margaret's accusations. Margaret bravely recanted. Saying she would rather die than live a lie She was allowed to apologize to her grandfather before his execution on 19 Aug 1692.

At the time of George's trial, guilt was determined largely on evidence based upon dreams and visions. In this drawing by Howard Pyle (N.C. Wyeth's teacher) from *Harper's Magazine*, the accuser is pointing out a flock of yellow birds that only she can see.[81] The courts and the church ministers sided with the afflicted. Many were sent to the gallows merely on the basis of this type of spectral evidence.

Rebecca and Margaret's trial on 04 Jan 1693 was the first one held after spectral evidence was rendered inadmissible. The mother and daughter were found not guilty. However, they were not released from Salem Dungeon for a few more months until they could afford to pay for their court costs, jail room and board, the irons around their wrists, and for every piece of paper including their pardon.[82]

In time, George Jacobs Jr. and Daniel Andrews returned home. Salem historian Jim McAllister noted they had escaped almost certain death by fleeing to Europe.[83]

"There is a Flock of Yellow Birds around her Head" – 1892 drawing by Howard Pyle is courtesy of the New York Public Library, Art and Picture Collection.

On 21 Jul 1697, acting as attorneys for the village, Daniel with three other representatives of the village signed a petition to remove Rev. Samuel Parris as minister of Salem Village. They explained they could not tolerate Parris as their minister let alone pay him. The witchcraft lunacy had started in Rev. Parris' home in Jan 1692. Because his niece and daughter had fits of screaming, throwing things, making strange sounds, and contorting themselves, a doctor said they were bewitched. The document for his removal charged Rev. Parris with starting the hysteria and with directing the young afflicted girls to accuse many innocent men, women and children of witchcraft. The complaint stated that by spreading fear, hatred and lies, Parris had begun the "sorest afflictions" ever to befall the village or the country.[84] Daniel Andrews and the representatives were ultimately successful in removing Parris.

When Margaret Jacobs married John Foster on 30 Nov 1699, she refused to be married in the local Salem town parish by Rev. Nicholas Noyes.[85] Noyes, the Salem minister, together with Rev. Samuel Parris, the minister of Salem Village, had treated her family horrifically during the witchcraft trials. Noyes, in attendance on the day her grandfather stood at the scaffold, had refused to pray with the condemned.[86]

On 25 May 1709, George Jacobs Jr. and others signed a petition asking for restoration of witchcraft suspects' reputations and reimbursement of their estates.[87] In 1711, the names of most of the condemned were cleared. The Jacobs' family finally collected some compensation for their losses from the Massachusetts legislature in Jan and Feb of 1712.[88]

THIRD GENERATION – THE FRENCH AND INDIAN WAR

7. **JOHN**[3] **FISKE** (Sarah[2] Wyeth, Nicholas[1]) was born on 20 Nov 1655 in Watertown, Middlesex, Massachusetts. He married (1) **ABIGAIL PARKE,** daughter of Thomas Parke and Abigail Dix, on 09 Dec 1679 in Watertown. She was born on 03 Mar 1658 in Cambridge, Middlesex, Massachusetts. She died before 1699 in Watertown. John Fiske married (2) **HANNAH RICHARDS** on 19 Jan 1699 in Watertown. She likely was born 24 Oct 1677 in Dedham, Norfolk, Massachusetts. She died on 21 Jul 1714 in Watertown.[89] He died there on 06 Jan 1718.

John Fiske and Abigail Parke had the following children:

23.   i. ABIGAIL[4] FISKE, born 12 Jun 1684, Watertown; married JOHN STEARNS, 24 Feb 1701 in Watertown; died there after 1735.
         ii. ELIZABETH FISKE was born on 20 Jan 1685 in Watertown. She married BENJAMIN WHITNEY, son of Joseph Whitney and Martha Beach, on 01 Mar 1709 in Watertown. He was born on 31 Jan 1684 in Watertown. He died there on 19 Oct 1736. Elizabeth's death date is unknown.
         iii. JOHN FISKE, born 15 May 1687, Watertown; married ELIZABETH CHINERY in 1727, Watertown. He died there on 06 Jun 1718. (Their son, DANIEL FISKE, born 06 Sep 1735 in Watertown; married, SARAH KENDALL, 07 Apr 1763; died 16 Jan 1788 in Wendell, Franklin, Massachusetts.)
         iv. JONATHAN FISKE was baptized 08 Dec 1689 in Watertown. He married LYDIA BEMIS, daughter of John Bemis and Mary Harrington, on 10 Apr 1716 in Newton, Middlesex, Massachusetts. Jonathan died there on 22 May 1777.
         v. HEPZIBAH FISKE was born on 13 Jan 1693 in Watertown. She married GEORGE PERKINS HARRINGTON, son of Thomas Harrington and Rebecca Bemis, on 05 Dec 1715 in Watertown. He was born there on 31 Aug 1695. George died on 25 Mar 1736 in Watertown and she died there the next day.
         vi. DAVID FISKE was baptized 13 Apr 1697 in Watertown. He died on 25 Mar 1748 in Windham, Windham County, Connecticut.

The children of John Fiske and Hannah Richards included:

         i. HANNAH[4] FISKE was baptized 08 Oct 1704 in Watertown; death unknown.

8. **MARY**[3] **FISKE** (Sarah[2] Wyeth, Nicholas[1]) was born on 05 Jul 1661 in Watertown, Middlesex, Massachusetts. She married **JOSEPH MASON SR.**, son of Captain Hugh Mason and Esther Wells, on 05 Feb 1684 in Watertown. He was born on 10 Aug 1646 in Watertown. He died there on 22 Jul 1702. She died on 06 Jan 1723 in Watertown.

Joseph Mason Sr. and Mary Fiske had the following children:

         i. HESTER[4] MASON, born 08 Jul 1686, Watertown; died there, 07 Mar 1754.
         ii. JOSEPH MASON JR., born 02 Oct 1688, Watertown; died there, 06 Jul 1755.

9. **WILLIAM**[3] **FISKE** (Sarah[2] Wyeth, Nicholas[1]) was born on 23 Feb 1663 in Watertown, Middlesex, Massachusetts. He married **HANNAH SMITH**, daughter of John Smith and Mary

Beers, on 25 Oct 1693 in Watertown. She was born on 27 Dec 1672 in Watertown. She died there on 07 Dec 1728.[90] He died in 1742 in Watertown. His will was proved on 29 Mar 1742 in Middlesex County, Massachusetts.

William Fiske and Hannah Smith had the following children:

      i.   William[4] FISKE, born on 24 Aug 1694 in Watertown; died there on 13 Dec 1702 at age eight.

      ii.   HANNAH FISKE, born 13 Oct 1696, Watertown; died there about 1700.

      iii.   MARY FISKE, born 16 Jan 1698 in Watertown; died there on 24 Dec 1702.

      iv.   THOMAS FISKE, born 12 Sep 1701, Watertown; died there on 28 Sep 1778.

      v.   WILLIAM FISKE was born on 13 Mar 1703 in Watertown. He died on 28 Mar 1760 in Waltham, Middlesex, Massachusetts. (Waltham split off from Watertown in 1738.)

      vi.   JOHN FISKE, born 24 Aug 1706, Watertown; married SARAH CHILD there, 13 Jun 1734; death unknown.

24.   vii.   SAMUEL FISKE was born on 04 Jan 1709, Watertown; married ANNE BEMIS there on 26 Feb 1735, Watertown; died on 22 Mar 1761 in Waltham.

10.   **MARTHA**[3] **FISKE** (Sarah[2] Wyeth, Nicholas[1]) was born on 15 Dec 1666 in Watertown, Middlesex, Massachusetts. She married **GEORGE ADAMS,** son of George Adams Sr. and Frances Taylor, on 28 Feb 1683 in Lexington, Middlesex, Massachusetts. He was born on 19 Jun 1648 in Watertown. He died on 17 Feb 1733 in Lexington. Martha Fiske died there on 07 May 1747.

The children of George Adams and Martha Fiske include:

      i.   GEORGE[4] ADAMS III was born on 28 Apr 1685 in Lexington, Middlesex, Massachusetts. He died in 1767 in Waltham, Middlesex, Massachusetts.

      ii.   MARTHA ADAMS, born 10 Jan 1687, Lexington; died after 1757.

      iii.   JOHN ADAMS, born 02 Sep 1688, Lexington; died there, 18 May 1774.

      iv.   BENJAMIN ADAMS was born on 20 Dec 1701 in Lexington. He died on 26 Dec 1784 in Waltham.

11.   **ELIZABETH**[3] **FISKE** (Sarah[2] Wyeth, Nicholas[1]) was born on 11 May 1669 in Watertown, Middlesex, Massachusetts. Elizabeth Fiske married **SIMON MELLEN**, son of Simon L. Mellen and his wife Mary, on 27 Dec 1688 in Sherborn, Middlesex, Massachusetts. He was born on 25 Sep 1665 in Winnisimmet (Chelsea), Suffolk, Massachusetts. Simon died on 30 Aug 1717 in Framingham, Middlesex, Massachusetts. Her death date is unknown.

Simon Mellen and Elizabeth Fiske had the following children:

      i.   SIMON[4] MELLEN JR., born 16 May 1690, Sherborn; death unknown.

      ii.   MARY MELLEN, born on 04 Jun 1694 in Sherborn; died 30 Apr 1711, Framingham.

      iii.   JAMES MELLEN, born on 08 Mar 1698 in Framingham; married his cousin, ABIGAIL SANDERSON, the daughter of his aunt Abigail Fiske, 29 Sep 1720, Watertown; death unknown.

12. **ABIGAIL**[3] **FISKE** (Sarah[2] Wyeth, Nicholas[1]) was born on 08 Oct 1675 in Watertown, Middlesex, Massachusetts. She married **DEACON JONATHAN SANDERSON**, son of Jonathan Sanderson and Abiah Bartlett, on 14 Jul 1699 in Watertown. He was a twin, born on 28 Oct 1673 in Cambridge, Middlesex, Massachusetts. He died on 04 Oct 1743 in Waltham, Middlesex, Massachusetts. Abigail Fiske died there on 29 Apr 1759.

Deacon Jonathan Sanderson and Abigail Fiske had the following children:

    i.   JONATHAN[4] SANDERSON, born 25 Jul 1700, Watertown; married GRACE BARNARD, 1736; a weaver and farmer, he died 02 Aug 1790, Waltham.

    ii.   ABIGAIL SANDERSON was born on 23 Oct 1702 in Watertown; she married her cousin, JAMES MELLEN, 29 Sep 1720; death unknown.

    iii.   MARGARET SANDERSON, born 09 Sep 1704, Watertown; married BENJAMIN WHITNEY there, 24 Feb 1731; death unknown.

    iv.   EUNICE SANDERSON, born 01 Jul 1707, Watertown; married ISAAC PEIRCE there, 1725; died 14 Sep 1803, Waltham.

    v.   THOMAS SANDERSON, born 18 Jun 1710, Watertown; married ANNA DIX there, 1737; died circa 1764, Waltham.

    vi.   NATHANIEL SANDERSON, born 30 May 1713, Watertown; died 07 Sep 1774, Petersham, Worcester, Massachusetts.

    vii.   DAVID SANDERSON, born 25 Jun 1715, Watertown; died 1805, Petersham.

13. **THOMAS**[3] **IVES JR.** (Martha[2] Wyeth, Nicholas[1]) was born on 31 Mar 1674 in Salem, Essex, Massachusetts. He married **ELIZABETH MATTHEWS** on 21 Aug 1710 in Marblehead, Essex, Massachusetts. She was born about 1680.[91] Deaths unknown.

Thomas Ives Jr. and Elizabeth Matthews had the following children:

    i.   THOMAS[4] IVES III was baptized 20 May 1711 in the First Church of Marblehead, Essex, Massachusetts. His death is unknown.

    ii.   SAMUEL IVES was born circa Aug 1713 in Marblehead. He married HANNAH HODGES, daughter of Gamaliel Hodges and Sarah Williams, on 21 Nov 1737 in Salem, Essex, Massachusetts. She was born on 30 Nov 1718 in Salem. He died circa 1756. Hannah died in Salem on 05 Jul 1803.

14. **DEBORAH**[3] **WYETH** (John[2], Nicholas[1]) was born on 20 Nov 1686 in Cambridge, Middlesex, Massachusetts. When she married **DEACON SAMUEL BOWMAN** son of Francis Bowman and Martha Sherman, in 1714, she became the stepmother of several children of her half first cousin, Rebecca Andrews Bowman. Deacon Bowman was born on 14 Aug 1679 in Watertown, Middlesex, Massachusetts. He died in 1746 in Cambridge. Deborah appears to have lived to an extremely old age. The estate of her husband was not completely distributed until 1783.[92]

The children of Deacon Samuel Bowman and Deborah Wyeth included:

25.   i.   MARTHA[4] BOWMAN, born 10 Feb 1714, Cambridge; married NEHEMIAH CUTTER there, 17 Jul 1739; died 01 Jul 1790, Menotomy (Arlington), Middlesex, Massachusetts.

26.   ii.   DEBORAH BOWMAN was born on 30 May 1716 in Cambridge. She married NATHANIEL KIDDER, son of Samuel Kidder and Sarah Griggs, on 17 Sep 1741 in Cambridge. He was born on 20 Nov 1702 in Cambridge. He died there on 28 Mar 1789. She died two days later on 31 Mar 1789 in Cambridge.

27.   iii. NOAH BOWMAN was born on 23 Oct 1718 in Cambridge. His marriage to HANNAH WINSHIP, daughter of Ephraim Winship Sr. and Hannah Cutter, was published in Cambridge on 14 Jul 1744. She was born on 18 Aug 1718 and baptized six days later in Lexington, Middlesex, Massachusetts. His will was proved 02 Oct 1782 in Cambridge. Because she was included in Noah's will, she died after Oct 1782.

      iv.   ELIZABETH BOWMAN, baptized 07 May 1721, Cambridge; died there on 11 Oct 1739.

      v.   EUNICE BOWMAN, baptized 04 Nov 1722, Cambridge; death unknown.

28.   vi.   ABIGAIL BOWMAN was baptized 15 Mar 1724 in Cambridge. She married WILLIAM WINSHIP JR., son of William Winship and Thankful Wyeth, on 30 Dec 1755 in Cambridge. He was baptized 01 Jul 1722 in Cambridge. Abigail and William both died, due to old age, in the Almshouse in Menotomy (Arlington), Middlesex, Massachusetts. She at age 85 on 22 Jun 1809, and he at age 88 on 04 Feb 1811.[93]

      vii. SUSANNAH BOWMAN, baptized 10 Jul 1726, Cambridge; death unknown.

15.   **JONATHAN[3] WYETH** (John[2], Nicholas[1]) was born on 03 Mar 1690 in Cambridge, Middlesex, Massachusetts. He married **HEPZIBAH CHAMPNEY**, daughter of Daniel Champney and Hepzibah Corlett Minot, circa 1714 in Cambridge. She was born on 23 Jun 1687 in Cambridge. He died there on 24 Sep 1743.

Jonathan Wyeth and Hepzibah Champney had the following children:

      i.   JONATHAN[4] WYETH II was born on 12 Oct 1714 in Cambridge, Middlesex, Massachusetts. He died there sometime before 27 Jul 1716.

29.   ii.   JONATHAN WYETH JR. was born on 27 Jul 1716 in Cambridge. He married SARAH WILSON on 14 Nov 1750 in Menotomy (Arlington), Middlesex, Massachusetts. He died on 26 Apr 1767 in Cambridge.

      iii. SARAH WYETH, baptized 17 Aug 1718, Cambridge; died there unmarried on 23 Sep 1743.

30.   iv.   DEBORAH WYETH was baptized 29 Apr 1720 in Cambridge; married DANIEL PRENTICE SR., 29 Dec 1743 in Cambridge; died 11 Jul 1811 in the Shaker settlement at Harvard, Worcester, Massachusetts.

      v.   NOAH WYETH, baptized 28 Oct 1722, Cambridge; died there before 1743.

Notes for Jonathan Wyeth:

As Jonathan, the oldest son, was 16 at his father's death, John Wyeth Sr., left him a double share of the estate. Like his father, Jonathan also was a brick mason. The family lived in Cambridge on the County Road to Watertown (now Mt. Auburn Street).[94] The land stayed in the family for a couple more generations until some of it was sold to John Vassall.[95]

Jonathan died the day after his daughter, Sarah, and two months before his son, Noah. His estate was divided among his wife, son Jonathan, and daughter Deborah.

These two monuments are in the Old Burying Ground in Harvard Square, Cambridge.

The smaller stone reads, "Here lies the body of Sarah Wyeth, Daughter of Mr. Jonathan & Mrs. Hepzibah Wyeth; who died Sept. the 23rd 1743, in the 26th year of her age."

The larger marker reads, "Here lies buried the body of Jonathan Wyeth; who departed this life Sep the 24th, Anno Domni 1743, in the 53rd year of his age."

16. **HANNAH[3] WYETH** (John[2], Nicholas[1]) was born about 1693 in Cambridge, Middlesex, Massachusetts.[96] In 1712, she married (1) **NATHANIEL PRENTICE**, son of Solomon Prentice and Hepzibah Dunton, in Cambridge. He was born there on 18 Oct 1689. Nathaniel died on 24 Oct 1722 in Cambridge. His will was probated 23 Nov 1722. Hannah Wyeth married (2) **JASON WINSHIP SR.**, son of Edward Winship Jr. and Rebeckah Barsham, on 05 Mar 1723. Jason was baptized on 29 Oct 1699, probably in Cambridge. Hannah died on 12 Dec 1756 in Menotomy (Arlington), Middlesex, Massachusetts. Jason drowned on the night of 25/26 Dec 1762 after going from a neighbor's house, near Menotomy Pond, to his home. He missed his way and fell through the ice.

Nathaniel Prentice and Hannah Wyeth had the following children:

31. i. JONAS[4] PRENTICE was born on 25 Apr 1713 and baptized the next day in Cambridge, Middlesex, Massachusetts. He married MERCY PIERCE on 22 Apr 1736 in Charlestown, Suffolk, Massachusetts. His Cambridge farm was occupied by soldiers during the Revolution. Jonas Prentice died of dysentery on 14 Nov 1775 in Cambridge.

     ii. NATHANIEL PRENTICE was born on 19 May 1715 and baptized on 22 May 1715 in Cambridge. He worked as a tailor. He married ABIGAIL WARE, daughter of Joseph Ware and Hannah Wood, on 02 Sep 1742 in Sherborn, Middlesex, Massachusetts. She was born there on 07 Jan 1722. They both died in Sherborn. She died on 01 Mar 1788 and he died on 23 Jan 1796.

32. iii. HANNAH PRENTICE was born on 16 Dec 1716 in Cambridge. She married THOMAS FESSENDEN JR. on 19 Jun 1735 in Lexington, Middlesex, Massachusetts. She died there on 22 Oct 1768 … just three months after her husband's death.

     iv. TABITHA PRENTICE was born on 30 Aug 1718 in Cambridge. She married ELIEZER RUSSELL, son of Jonathan Russell and Elizabeth Pattin, on 10 Jan 1739 in Lexington. He was born there on 05 May 1717. He died about 1742 in Cambridge and she died after 1752.

33. v. SOLOMON PRENTICE was born on 31 Jan 1720 in Cambridge. He was a beekeeper and a farmer. He married HANNAH FILLEBROWN on 02 Nov 1744 in Cambridge. Solomon died 10 Sep 1799 in Watertown, Middlesex, Massachusetts.

Jason Winship Sr. and Hannah Wyeth had the following children:

i. LYDIA[4] WINSHIP was born on 05 Dec 1724 and baptized on 13 Dec 1724 in Cambridge. She married JABEZ WYMAN JR., son of Jabez Wyman Sr. and Mary Smith, on 13 Jan 1767 in Menotomy (Arlington), Middlesex, Massachusetts. He was baptized on 26 Dec 1736 in Woburn 2nd precinct (Burlington), Middlesex, Massachusetts. Jabez was a laborer employed by Rev. Samuel Cooke when he was killed at Cooper's Tavern in Menotomy on the first day of the American Revolution, while innocently celebrating the birth of his brother-in-law's son, Jason Winship III.[97] On that fateful day, 19 Apr 1775, during the rejoicing over her nephew, Lydia lost both her brother, Jason, and her husband in a vicious British attack on two unarmed civilians. According to Middlesex County deed book, volume 77, page 513, Lydia transferred land to her cousin, William Winship III on 04 Jun 1777. Her death date is unknown.

34. ii. PRUDENCE WINSHIP, was born on 04 Sep 1726 in Cambridge; married (1) MICHAEL GEOGHEGAN on 08 May 1743 in Boston, Suffolk, Massachusetts; married (2) CHRISTOPHER THORNTON on 10 Aug 1749 in Boston; married (3) THOMAS PEIRCE on 09 Jun 1768 in Charlestown, Suffolk, Massachusetts.

iii. NATHAN WINSHIP was baptized on 23 Feb 1728 in Cambridge; he died on 27 Sep 1766 in Menotomy.

35. iv. JASON WINSHIP JR., born circa 1730, Cambridge; served in the French and Indian War; married (1) RUTH CARTER on 26 Apr 1764 in Woburn, Middlesex, Massachusetts. Both she and her first child died in childbirth on 30 Jan 1765 in Menotomy. Jason married (2) MARY PIPER on 16 Jan 1768 in Cambridge. While innocently celebrating the birth of his only son, Jason was killed on 19 Apr 1775 by British Troops at Cooper's Tavern in Menotomy on the first day of the Revolutionary War.[98]

Notes for Hannah Wyeth:

Although three years apart in age, Hannah and her sister, Thankful, were baptized together on 18 Apr 1697 in Cambridge. Hannah and Thankful, along with their younger sister, Elizabeth, married three Winship brothers. Hannah, the oldest of the Wyeth sisters, married Jason, the youngest of the Winship brothers.

Hannah's first husband, Nathaniel Prentice, is buried in Cambridge's Old Burying Ground at Harvard Square. Nathaniel was Hannah's next-door neighbor on the highway to the Great Swamp (Garden Street). They resided across from the Cambridge Common. She married her second husband, Jason Winship Sr., five months after Nathaniel's death in a speedy purpose of marriage.[99] On 09 Sep 1739, Hannah joined the Menotomy church at its organization.

Apparently, both Jason and Jason Jr. served in the French and Indian War (Seven Years' War). Later Jason Jr., Hannah's youngest child, and her daughter Lydia's husband, Jabez Wyman, were savagely killed by the British at Cooper's Tavern on the first day of the American Revolution while celebrating the birth of Jason Winship III.[100]

17. **THANKFUL³ WYETH** (John², Nicholas¹) was born about 1696 in Cambridge.[101] She married **WILLIAM WINSHIP**, son of Edward Winship Jr. and Rebeckah Barsham, on 06 Dec 1716 in Cambridge, Middlesex, Massachusetts. He was born in 1691 in Cambridge. She died before 1739 in Menotomy (Arlington), Middlesex, Massachusetts.[102] He died there on 26 Jan 1774.

William Winship and Thankful Wyeth had the following children:

      i.   JOANNA⁴ WINSHIP, baptized on 16 Jan 1718 in Cambridge. She died unmarried on 09 Apr 1795 in the Menotomy Almshouse.[103]

      ii. DEBORAH WINSHIP was baptized on 27 Dec 1719 in Cambridge. She married MOSES HARRINGTON, son of John Harrington and Elizabeth Cutter, on 23 Jun 1760 in Menotomy. He was born on 06 Jan 1710 and was baptized on 14 Jun 1710 in Lexington, Middlesex, Massachusetts. He died there on 11 Jan 1787. She died on 21 Oct 1790 in Menotomy.[104]

36.   iii. WILLIAM WINSHIP JR. was baptized 01 Jul 1722 in Cambridge. He married (1) MARY JOHNSON on 14 Jul 1748 in Menotomy. She was born about 1725 in Charlestown, Suffolk, Massachusetts. She died on 18 Jun 1749 in Menotomy. William married (2) ABIGAIL BOWMAN, daughter of Deacon Samuel Bowman and Deborah Wyeth, on 30 Dec 1755 in Cambridge. She was baptized 15 Mar 1724 in Cambridge. William and Abigail both died, due to old age, in the Almshouse in Menotomy (Arlington), Middlesex, Massachusetts. She died at age 85 on 22 Jun 1809 and he died at age 88 on 04 Feb 1811.[105]

      iv. AARON WINSHIP, baptized 16 Feb 1724, Cambridge; death date unknown.

37.   v.   ABIGAIL WINSHIP, baptized 30 Oct 1726, Cambridge; married JOSEPH COOK SR. on 22 May 1746, Cambridge. Abigail died before 1756.

      vi. REBECCA WINSHIP, baptized 13 Mar 1728, Cambridge; died young.

     vii. TABITHA WINSHIP was baptized 26 Jul 1730 in Cambridge. She died unmarried on 15 Mar 1813 in the Menotomy Almshouse.

    viii. BENONI WINSHIP was baptized 30 Mar 1735 in Cambridge. Benoni probably was unmarried when he died on 22 May 1805 in the Menotomy Almshouse.

Notes for the family of Thankful Wyeth:

Sisters Thankful and Hannah were baptized together on 18 Apr 1697 in Cambridge. The three sisters, Thankful, Hannah and Elizabeth, married three Winship brothers. According to Lucius Paige, after Thankful's death, some catastrophe befell her family. Thankful's children, Joanna, Tabitha, William, and Benoni Winship and her grandsons, William and Aaron, all became paupers and most of them died in the almshouse at Menotomy (Arlington), Massachusetts.[106] Several of them were over the age of 80 and probably no longer had relatives to care for them.

18. **EBENEZER³ WYETH SR.** (John², Nicholas¹) was baptized on 24 Jul 1698 in Cambridge, Middlesex, Massachusetts. He married **SUSANNAH HANCOCK**, daughter of Ebenezer Hancock and Susanna Clark Hill, about 1726 in Cambridge. Susannah was baptized there on 06 Jul 1707. According to the handwritten notes of their grandson, Major Jonas Wyeth, Ebenezer Wyeth Sr. died 05 Apr 1754, Cambridge and Susannah died there, 27 Jul 1759.[107]

Ebenezer Wyeth Sr. and Susannah Hancock had the following children:

38. i. EBENEZER[4] WYETH JR., born 08 Apr 1727, Cambridge; married MARY WINSHIP, 05 Nov 1751, Charlestown, Suffolk, Massachusetts; died 04 Aug 1799, Cambridge.

39. ii. JONAS WYETH SR., born 19 Feb 1730, Cambridge; married HEPZIBAH TIDD, 18 Mar 1753, Cambridge; died there, 17 Feb 1813.

40. iii. SUSANNAH WYETH, born 02 Mar 1734, Cambridge; married DANIEL SAWIN SR., 27 May 1755, Cambridge; died 23 Mar 1794, Watertown, Middlesex, Massachusetts.

41. iv. MARY E. WYETH, born 30 Sep 1739, Cambridge; married MANSFIELD TAPLEY JR., 01 Oct 1760, Cambridge; died 05 Jan 1825, Charlestown, Suffolk, Massachusetts.

42. v. NOAH WYETH SR., born 07 Jul 1742, Cambridge; married ELIZABETH "BETTY" FITCH, 30 Mar 1763, Lexington, Middlesex, Massachusetts; died 10 Sep 1811, Cambridge.

43. vi. SARAH WYETH, born 02 Apr 1746, Cambridge; married (1) TORRY HANCOCK SR., 05 Jul 1774, Cambridge; married (2) DEACON JAMES MUNROE, 23 Jul 1783, Cambridge; died there on 31 Mar 1815.

Ebenezer Wyeth Sr. and Susannah Hancock notes:

According to the records of Cambridge's First Church, William Brattle baptized Ebenezer there on 24 Jul 1698. Ebenezer next appears in the church records on 08 May 1726 when he and Susannah were admitted to Full Communion with the church.[108] This 1726 date could also be the year of their marriage. During his lifetime, Ebenezer earned his living as a cordwainer, which is a shoemaker who makes new shoes from new leather. The cordwainer trade can be contrasted with cobblers who are in the business of repairing shoes.

From page one of Major Jonas Wyeth's handwritten notes. *Wyeth family records* (Mss A 3058). R. Stanton Avery Special Collections, Courtesy of the New England Historic Genealogical Society and AmericanAncestors.org.

Susannah's baptism in Cambridge on 06 Jul 1707 was performed by William Brattle as well.[109] In 1719, when Susannah was 12 years old, her grandfather, Nathaniel Hancock, left her a legacy in his will. Elizabeth Hancock, wife to her husband's brother, John Wyeth Jr., was Susannah's first cousin. Governor John Hancock, the LARGE signer of the Declaration of Independence, was Susannah's second cousin 1x removed. All three cousins descended from Nathaniel Hancock.

The New England Historical and Genealogical Register for the year 1863, by John Ward Dean, talks about the estates of Ebenezer and his nephew, Jonathan. Apparently, before moving to the old homestead on the highway to the Great Swamp (Garden Street), Ebenezer lived about a quarter of a mile south of it, near the Charles River, on an estate once owned by Samuel Bull. The street is now called Ash Street but was then known as "the highway to the brick wharf." Ebenezer sold that land on 27 Nov 1741 to John Vassal Sr. for £260.[110]

According Lucius Paige's *History of Cambridge*, Ebenezer Wyeth Sr. lived on the old homestead on the westerly side of Garden Street near the town common. He purchased it from his sister, Hannah.[111] In the years before houses were numbered, we do not have the address of the house. Likely it was William Wyeth's farm that his brother, John Wyeth Sr., instructed his executrix, in his 29 Nov 1706 will, to purchase from William's estate.

The date of transfer from Hannah to Ebenezer is uncertain. It was probably after the 24 Oct 1722 death of Hannah's first husband, Nathaniel Prentice. Nathaniel was the next-door neighbor to the Wyeths so it would make sense for her to have Nicholas' old homestead.[112] When Hannah married Jason Winship Sr., they followed their siblings Elizabeth Wyeth and John Winship to Menotomy (which was renamed Arlington in 1867). *The History of the Town of Arlington* shows Hannah was admitted to the precinct church when it was first organized on 09 Sep 1739.[113]

Regardless of when the old homestead was transferred to Ebenezer Sr., in his last will and testament, dated 23 Feb 1754, he passed all of his estate on to his sons Ebenezer Wyeth Jr. and Jonas Wyeth Sr. He included particular items for his wife, and his underage children, Susannah, Mary, Noah and Sarah, as well. Noah eventually inherited Nicholas' west-field land at Garden Street and Wyeth Street (Huron Avenue). Specifically, Ebenezer Sr. said, "My will is that my beloved sons Ebenezer and Jonas Wyeth be executors to this my Last Will and Testament. Unto whom I give all my estate equally to be divided between them both real and personal whatsoever and where to ever it may be found and my will is that they pay to their brother and sisters their equal proportion."

The will was signed in the presence of Jacob Hill; Ebenezer's brother, John Wyeth Jr.; and his nephew, Jonathan Wyeth. On 30 Apr 1754, Susannah Hancock Wyeth wrote the courts that she was "…contented with what my late husband Ebenezer Wyeth has given me in his Last Will and am willing to quit my right of dower…"

In other probate documents, Ebenezer, the son, is shown to be a husbandman; son, Jonas, a brick maker; and brother, John Wyeth Jr., a brick mason. Of his children, only Ebenezer and Jonas were married when their father died in 1754. At his marriage in 1751, Ebenezer, Jr. purchased a vast acreage on the Watertown county road near Fresh Pond. For that reason, Jonas (1731-1813) received the homestead near the common. It remained in Jonas' family for over 100 years more.

19. **ELIZABETH³ WYETH** (John², Nicholas¹) was born on 22 May 1701 and was baptized on 25 May 1701 in Cambridge, Middlesex, Massachusetts. Elizabeth Wyeth and Deacon John Winship were married on 02 Oct 1718 in Cambridge. **DEACON JOHN WINSHIP** son of Edward Winship Jr. and Rebeckah Barsham, was born in 1693 in Lexington, Middlesex, Massachusetts. She died on 08 Oct 1759 in Menotomy, Middlesex, Massachusetts. He died shortly after his wife on 07 Nov 1759 at the age of 66 in Menotomy. Elizabeth and John rest together in the Old Burying Ground in Arlington.

Here lyes buried ye body Mrs. Elizabeth Winshipp wife to Deacon John Winshipp who departed this life [8 Oct 1759 aged 58]

Deacon John Winship and Elizabeth Wyeth had the following children:

           i.   JOSIAH[4] WINSHIP I, born 01 Oct 1719, Cambridge; died there before 1738.

44.   ii.   ELIZABETH WINSHIP, born 24 Mar 1721, Cambridge; married JASON RUSSELL, 28 Jan 1740, Cambridge; died 11 Aug 1786, Menotomy (Arlington), Middlesex, Massachusetts.

        iii. JOHN WINSHIP II was baptized 08 Dec 1723 in Cambridge; he died there before 1728.

        iv. RUTH WINSHIP, born 14 Jun 1726 in Cambridge; died there before 1731.

         v. JOHN WINSHIP III was born on 24 Aug 1728 in Cambridge. He died on 20 Jul 1740 at the age of 11 in Menotomy.

45.   vi. RUTH WINSHIP, baptized 24 Oct 1731, Cambridge; married EBENEZER SHED JR., 24 Mar 1760, Cambridge; died there in 1777.

       vii. NOAH WINSHIP, born about 1734 in Cambridge; died on 18 Oct 1759 in Menotomy.

46.   viii. REV. JOSIAH WINSHIP, born 21 May 1738, Cambridge; married (1) JUDITH GOSS, 07 Jul 1766, Bolton, Worcester, Massachusetts; married (2) ELIZABETH FORD, 27 Mar 1780, Wilmington, Middlesex, Massachusetts; died 29 Sep 1824, Woolwich, Sagadahoc, Maine.

        ix. JOHN WINSHIP IV, born 03 May 1742, Menotomy; married JUDITH CARTER, 05 Dec 1763, Wolburn, Middlesex, Massachusetts; died 01 Aug 1819, Mason, Hillsborough, New Hampshire.

47.   x. THANKFUL WINSHIP, born 14 Mar 1745, Menotomy; married ROBERT STINSON, 16 Apr 1780, Woolwich, Lincoln, Maine; died 25 Jan 1832, Georgetown, Sagadahoc, Maine.

Notes for Elizabeth Wyeth Winship:

As mentioned previously, she and two of her sisters, Hannah and Thankful, married three Winship brothers. Per the *History of Cambridge*, Elizabeth and her husband, John Winship, moved to Menotomy (Arlington) very early in its history. He was elected as one of the first deacons in the church there on 17 Nov 1739. In 1742, Deacon Winship also served the town as a selectman (city councilman).[114]

The home of Elizabeth Wyeth's daughter, Elizabeth Winship Russell, has been preserved by the Arlington Historical Society to appear like it was when Elizabeth Wyeth Winship's son-in-law, Jason Russell, was shot and bayoneted on his own doorstep by British soldiers retreating from Lexington and Concord on 19 Apr 1775.[115] Across town, while they innocently drank Flip in Cooper's Tavern, sister Hannah's son, Jason Winship Jr., and Hannah's son-in-law, Jabez Wyman, were also brutally killed by British troops.[116]

20. **JOHN[3] WYETH JR.** (John[2], Nicholas[1]) was born on 27 Dec 1705 in Cambridge, Middlesex, Massachusetts. John Wyeth Jr. and Elizabeth Hancock were married on 20 Dec 1733 in Cambridge. **ELIZABETH HANCOCK**, daughter of Nathaniel Hancock Jr. and Prudence Russell, was born on 16 Nov 1704 in Cambridge. John died there on 23 Oct 1756 at the age of 50. She died there on 23 Feb 1793 at the age of 88.

John Wyeth Jr. and Elizabeth Hancock had the following children:

     i. JOHN[4] WYETH III was baptized 29 Dec 1734 in Cambridge; died young.

    ii. ELIZABETH WYETH was baptized 04 Jul 1736 in Cambridge. She died there from smallpox at a very young age.

   iii. MARTHA WYETH was baptized 23 Jul 1738 in Cambridge. She was an infant when she died there.

   iv. ELIZABETH WYETH, baptized 30 Nov 1740 in Cambridge. She never married and died of consumption on 17 Sep 1804 at the age of 63 in Cambridge.

    v. (REV.) JOHN WYETH was born 01 Mar 1743 in Cambridge. He graduated there in 1760 from Harvard College. John died of consumption on 02 Feb 1811 at the age of 67 at the home of his cousin, Noah Wyeth Sr., in Cambridge.

   vi. PRUDENCE WYETH was baptized 28 Apr 1745 in Cambridge. Since she is one of the three children mentioned in her father's 1756 will, she died after that year in Cambridge.

  vii. JONATHAN WYETH was baptized 13 Nov 1748 in Cambridge. He died there less than one month before his father. The stone near his father's reads: "Here lies the body of Jonathan Wyeth son of John and Mrs. Elizabeth Wyeth, aged 8 years. Died 29 Sep 1756."

Notes for John Wyeth Jr. and (Rev.) John Wyeth:

Following in the footsteps of John Sr., his father, and Nicholas, his grandfather, John Wyeth Jr. also was a brick mason. He served in that capacity as one of the four "college servants of Harvard."[117] He was active in the affairs of Cambridge. On 21 Sep 1741 he provided a home and care for Ruth Maddocks, the youngest child of John Maddocks. From 1750 to his death, John Jr. served the community as a selectman. In 1753, he was on the First Church committee to build a new meetinghouse.[118]

Here lies buried the body of John Wyeth, who departed this life
Oct 23ᵈ 1756

In his will, file #25808, dated 11 Oct 1756, John Jr. left his estate to his wife, Elizabeth, until his only surviving son turned age 21. The three children mentioned in the will were John, Elizabeth, and Prudence. Son Jonathan died a few days before his father. Both rest in the Old Burying Ground at Harvard Square. John Jr.'s line of descent ended when his daughter, Prudence, died young and neither Elizabeth nor Rev. John ever married.

Rev. John Wyeth paints quite a colorful character. He lived at home on Garden Street until his senior year at Harvard College. For his M.A. he prepared the affirmative of *A Dei Justitia, in Hominibus puniendis, sit amabilis?* Five years after his 1760 graduation, he accepted a position to be the minister of the Third Congregational Parish of Gloucester in the village of Annisquam, Massachusetts.[119] He was paid £93 per year for his services. However, soon after his 05 Feb 1766 ordination, some members of the parish so opposed John's efforts, they expressed their dissatisfaction by committing violent acts against him. On one occasion, musket-balls were fired into his house.[120]

A lighter account of the parishioners' misdeeds also appears in the *History of the Town of Gloucester*. Tradition has it that when Rev. John went to saddle his horse for a trip to preach in a neighboring town, there was no black horse like his in the pasture. With the help of some friendly parishioners, the missing horse was eventually found. Although, it was indeed in the correct field, John's horse had been changed from black to white via a coat of whitewash paint.[121]

Needless to say, John was dismissed from Annisquam's Third Parish. He took his leave on 17 May 1768 and had to sue for unpaid wages. Thereafter, he preached for a time in towns near Cambridge including Malden and Sherborn as well as in the Connecticut valley and in Mason, New Hampshire.[122] However, in 1773 he left the ministry and went to practice law back home in Cambridge. Unfortunately, he was not very proficient as a lawyer and had to supplement his income by farming.[123]

Annisquam Village Church, established 1728, built 1830.

In 1775, John served on the Cambridge committee which offered General Washington land for the Continental Army's use in the town.[124] Although John was drafted at age 33 to serve in the army in Jul 1776, he apparently had the means to hire John Badger to serve in his place. Wyeth paid all but 13 shillings and 4 pennies to Badger. The remainder due Badger was paid from monies raised by the town of Cambridge. Wyeth apparently did personally go on an expedition to Canada the same month for he was credited with £6 cash.[125]

Two years later, John moved to Chelmsford, Massachusetts to practice law but was equally unsuccessful there. By 1780, he returned to Cambridge and was popular enough in the town to be elected selectman (city councilman). The unpleasantries of his early career must have affected his personality. He was also well known in the town for being tightfisted and bad tempered ... so much so, young boys called him "Janny." They threw stones at his house and harassed him with songs like: "Janny Wyeth was a lawyer and a very good lawyer too. He never had but one case and that he could not get through."[126]

Bachelor John and spinster Elizabeth, lived together near North Avenue and Avon Street. After his sister died, John moved to a cousin's home. At his death, from consumption, he was living in Cambridge with another one of his cousins, Noah Wyeth Sr., on the northern part of Garden Street. A statement in his will attests to his peculiarity: "My body I commend to the dust, and order that no one shall see my dead body but only as shall lay it out immediately after death.[127]

21. **DEBORAH³ WYETH** (William², Nicholas¹) was born about 1690 in Cambridge. Deborah Wyeth and Joshua Gamage were married on 22 Jun 1710 in Cambridge. **JOSHUA GAMAGE**, son of John Deol Gamage and Mary Knight, was born either in 1680 or on 06 Feb 1675 in Ipswich, Essex, Massachusetts. He died in Attleboro, Bristol, Massachusetts about 1738 as his son, Nathaniel, was appointed administrator of his estate on 20 Jun 1738.[128] At his brother John's death in 1753, only Joshua's children were mentioned in John's will. Deborah died circa 1773 at the age of 83 in Cambridge.[129]

Joshua Gamage and Deborah Wyeth had the following children:

        i. MARY⁴ GAMAGE was born on 06 Apr 1711 in Cambridge, Middlesex, Massachusetts. She died there in infancy.[130]

48.   ii. NATHANIEL GAMAGE, baptized 01 Mar 1712, Cambridge; married MARY NORWOOD, 23 May 1734, Gloucester, Essex, Massachusetts; died after 1750 (disappeared, probably unwillingly impressed by the Royal Navy).[131]

49.   iii. WILLIAM GAMAGE, born 21 Feb 1714, Cambridge; married ABIGAIL COOK, 01 Aug 1746, Boston, Suffolk, Massachusetts; served in the French and Indian War; died about 21 Dec 1783, Cambridge.

        iv. RUTH GAMAGE, baptized 19 Jul 1719, Cambridge; died there at a young age.

50.   v. SARAH GAMAGE, born 01 Sep 1721, Cambridge; married STEPHEN PALMER, 17 Jan 1750, Cambridge; died there, 15 Mar 1794.

51.   vi. JOHN GAMAGE, born 14 Feb 1724, Cambridge; married AGNES DICK, circa 1749, New York; died 09 May 1772, Shrewsbury, Monmouth, New Jersey.

52.   vii. MARTHA GAMAGE, baptized 17 Apr 1726, Cambridge; married (1) DANIEL PARKHURST, 06 Nov 1746, Waltham, Middlesex, Massachusetts; married (2) JOHN HAGAR, 11 Oct 1770, Weston, Middlesex, Massachusetts; died after 1773.

        viii. REBECCA GAMAGE, baptized 21 Dec 1729, Cambridge; married JACOB BULL, 25 Mar 1756, Cambridge; died 15 Sep 1802, Boston.

        ix. ELIZABETH GAMAGE was baptized on 02 Apr 1732 in Cambridge. She died at a young age in Attleboro, Bristol, Massachusetts.

        x. DANIEL GAMAGE was baptized on 16 Mar 1734 in Cambridge. He served for three years as a soldier in the Revolution under Capt. John Walton; died after 04 Sep 1778.

Notes for Deborah Wyeth and Joshua Gamage:

As will be shown in her sister's notes, Deborah and Martha apparently went to live with their first cousin, Rebecca Frost Coolidge, after their father was killed by Native Americans. At age 13, Deborah was, no doubt, a big help in caring for four-year-old Rebecca and three-year-old Joseph Coolidge Jr. as well as two other little ones who arrived after the Wyeth sisters moved into Joseph Coolidge's home.

Following her 1710 marriage to Joshua Gamage, Deborah put her child-care training to good use while raising their ten children. From the book *Prominent Families of the United States of America*, we learn Joshua was a weaver by trade. He settled in Cambridge, about 1708; and was admitted to the membership of First Church in 1727.[132]

It may well be that Joshua's father, John, came from Bristol or Taunton, England. A Thomas Gamage, from that part of England, settled in Boston after several years of servitude in Barbados. Apparently, Thomas was a convicted rebel from Cromwell's second army or from Monmouth's Rebellion. It would be natural that after his sentence was served, he would settle near his brother in Massachusetts. It is also noteworthy to find two of Joshua's sisters married in Boston... further linking the Ipswich and Boston Gamage families.[133] [134]

The home where Deborah and Joshua lived was likely constructed at their marriage. It is pictured in *An Historic Guide to Cambridge* by the Hannah Winthrop Chapter of the Massachusetts Daughters of the American Revolution (DAR). The house was on Holmes Place... due east of the Old Burying Ground at First Parish. It was built next door to the house Deborah's grandmother, Rebecca, lived in with her third husband, Thomas Fox.[135]

Joshua Gamage built the house, to the right of the round roofed building, before 1717 for his wife, Deborah Wyeth. This drawing comes from page 156 of *An Historic Guide to Cambridge* issued in 1907 by the Massachusetts Daughters of the American Revolution, Hannah Winthrop Chapter, Cambridge.

In 1737, the Gamages sold the house to Edmund Goffe and moved to Attleboro, Bristol County, Massachusetts. However, according to author Arabella Morton, Joshua was laid to rest in Gamage Tomb in Cambridge's Old Burying Ground.[136] Perhaps Deborah returned to Cambridge after Joshua's death and Nathaniel's disappearance to live with her son, William. When Deborah died at age 83, she joined her husband; as well as her grandfather, Nicholas; in the Old Burying Ground across Harvard Square from the Holmes Place house they had built 63 years before.

22. **MARTHA³ WYETH** (William², Nicholas¹) was baptized on 14 Mar 1696 in Cambridge, Middlesex, Massachusetts. Martha Wyeth and William Fessenden were married there on 12 Oct 1716. **WILLIAM FESSENDEN**, son of Nicholas Fessenden and Margaret Cheney, was born in 1694 in Cambridge. Martha died there on 27 Jan 1726. William died in Cambridge on 26 May 1756.

William Fessenden and Martha Wyeth had the following children:[137]

53.   i.   RUTH[4] FESSENDEN, born 28 Jun 1717, Cambridge, Middlesex, Massachusetts (there also is a record of her birth in Lexington); married JOHN HUNT, 02 Nov 1738, Boston, Suffolk, Massachusetts; died 01 Jan 1801, Watertown Middlesex, Massachusetts.

ii.   (REV.) WILLIAM FESSENDEN, born 07 Dec 1718, Cambridge; graduated Harvard College 1737; married MARY PALMER, 31 Mar 1740, Cambridge; died 17 Jun 1758, Cambridge. (There are also records of his birth in Lexington and his marriage and death in Boston.)

54.   iii.   MARTHA FESSENDEN, born 29 Feb 1719/20, Cambridge; married JOHN CHENEY there on 23 Sep 1738; died 1781, Roxbury, Suffolk, Massachusetts.

iv.   MARGARET FESSENDEN, born 08 Nov 1721 in Cambridge; died there at ten months old on 17 Sep 1722.

v.   BENJAMIN FESSENDEN, born 14 Jan 1722/3, Cambridge; died there on 21 Sep 1723 at nine months old.

vi.   BENJAMIN FESSENDEN II, born 23 Oct 1724, Cambridge; died there at three weeks old on 21 Nov 1724.

vii.   NICHOLAS FESSENDEN, born 22 Nov 1725, Cambridge; died young.[138]

Notes for Martha Wyeth and William Fessenden:

Her father's death at the hands of Native Americans, left Martha orphaned when she was just seven years old. The portion of case number 25830 that survives shows Joseph Coolidge and Andrew Bordman as administrators of William's estate. Lucius Paige's *History of Cambridge* indicates Andrew lived at Harvard Square and Dunster whereas Deacon Joseph Coolidge and his wife, Rebecca Frost, purchased a large estate in 1696 extending from Holyoke to Bow streets.[139]

Paige's work, together with Mary Wyeth's will, probated 17 Jun 1698, give us clues on why Coolidge was administrator of William Wyeth's estate. In Mary Wyeth's will she refers to Thomas Frost and Rebecca Coolidge as cousins. They were the children of Mary and William's half-sister, Rebecca Andrews Frost Jacobs. Thus, they were actually nephew and niece to Mary and William.[140]

It stands to reason that Joseph and Rebecca Frost Coolidge were also guardians of Martha and her 13-year-old sister, Deborah. At the time of William Wyeth's death, Mr. and Mrs. Coolidge had only two toddlers to fill their large home. They must have welcomed Martha and Deborah with open arms.

If we base her age on her baptism date, Martha was about 20 years old when she married William Fessenden on 12 Oct 1716. Martha's marriage was about two weeks after she and her sister, Deborah Gamage, owned the Covenant on 30 Sep 1716 at First Church.[141] William Fessenden was a farmer and a tanner, whose family arrived in Cambridge about 1638. The Fessenden estate, on the westerly side of Eliot Street, south of Mt. Auburn Street, was but a five-minute walk from the Coolidge home. According to the *History of Cambridge*, that house remained in the Fessenden family for over 100 years.[142]

After giving birth to seven children in ten years, Martha died shortly after the birth of her youngest child. William remarried two years later. With Ruth just eight years old, William, six, and Martha, five, at their mother's death, undoubtedly Martha Wyeth's foster mother, Rebecca Frost Coolidge helped with the three surviving children.

Throughout this book there are many instances showing births coupled with deaths. Martha's death at age 30 was surely linked to childbirth. Of her seven children, only three lived to share in the estate of their father, William Fessenden.

Birth was often shadowed by death when America was young. Mortality rates were high due to contagious diseases and infections caused by unsanitary medical methods. Although many babies and children died, as well as their mothers, death was rarely accepted in those early times without sadness. To most, the anguish and sorrow from death was just as intense then as it is now.

The words of Thomas Shepard illustrate how profoundly he was affected by the childbirth death of his wife.[143] Shepard was the Puritan minister who took Nicholas Wyeth's confession in 1644. And because a picture is worth a thousand words, the poignant memorial of Rebecca Frost Coolidge's 5th great granddaughter visually demonstrates the emotion of a baby's death.[144] Undoubtedly, these two sketches will exemplify the agony behind most of the death statistics in this book.

Mary Wigglesworth (29 Jan 1883 - 19 Dec 1884) descends from Rebecca Frost Coolidge who raised Martha and Deborah Wyeth. Photo courtesy of Kristin Jones from Find A Grave Memorial #40308880.

"April the second, 1646, as He [the Lord] gave me another son, John, so He took away my most dear, precious, meek and loving wife in childbed after three weeks lying in, having left behind her two hopeful branches, my dear children Samuel and John… Thus God hath visited and scourged me for my sins and sought to wean me from this world, but I have ever found it a difficult thing to profit even but a little by the sorest and sharpest of afflictions." ~ Thomas Shepard

23. **ABIGAIL**[4] **FISKE** (John[3], Sarah[2] Wyeth, Nicholas[1]) was born on 12 Jun 1684 in Watertown, Middlesex, Massachusetts. She married **JOHN STEARNS**, son of Samuel Stearns and Hannah Manning, on 24 Feb 1701 in Watertown. He was born on 25 Jun 1677 in Watertown. John died there in 1729. Abigail finished administering her husband's estate in 1735.[145]

The children of John Stearns and Abigail Fiske included:

        i. JOHN[5] STEARNS, born 18 Nov 1702, Watertown; died in 1775, Westminster, Worcester, Massachusetts.

55.   ii. JOSIAH STEARNS, born 14 Oct 1704, Watertown; married (1) SUSANNA BALL there, 31 Dec 1729; married (2) DOROTHY PRENTICE, in 1741 in Watertown; married (3) MARY BOWMAN, 23 Apr 1752, Watertown; died there on 11 Apr 1756.

      iii. ABIGAIL STEARNS, born 03 Jun 1708, Watertown; married (COLONEL) BENJAMIN BELLOWS, 07 Oct 1735, Lunenburg, Worcester, Massachusetts; died 09 Nov 1757, Walpole, Cheshire, New Hampshire.

      iv. (REV.) DAVID STEARNS, born 24 Dec 1709, Watertown; graduated Harvard College 1728; ordained, 18 Apr 1733, Lunenburg; died there, 09 Mar 1761.

       v. JAMES STEARNS, born 10 Jan 1713, Watertown; died there, 15 Jan 1713.

      vi. HANNAH STEARNS, born 20 Dec 1713, Watertown; married DEACON SAMUEL JOHNSON, 06 Jan 1746; died on 04 Aug 1779, Lunenburg.

     vii. BENJAMIN STEARNS, born in Watertown circa 1714; died 22 Nov 1761, Lunenburg.

    viii. PETER STEARNS born circa 1715 in Watertown; died there on 04 May 1738.

      ix. WILLIAM STEARNS, born 11 Mar 1717, Watertown; married ELIZABETH JOHNSON, 22 Jan 1746, Lunenburg; died there, 10 Jul 1792.

       x. LYDIA STEARNS, born 07 Oct 1719, Watertown; married JOSHUA GOODRIDGE, 25 Jun 1739, Lunenburg; died there, 07 Mar 1805.

      xi. JAMES STEARNS, born 09 Jul 1721 in Watertown; died young.

     xii. (COLONEL) ABIJAH STEARNS, born 19 Dec 1724, Watertown; married SARAH HEYWOOD, 12 Nov 1751, Lunenburg; commissioned head of the 8th Worcester Regiment of the Massachusetts Militia on 07 Feb 1776; died on 06 Nov 1783 in Lunenburg.

24. **SAMUEL**[4] **FISKE** (William[3], Sarah[2] Wyeth, Nicholas[1]) was born on 04 Jan 1709 in Watertown, Middlesex, Massachusetts. Samuel Fiske married **ANNE BEMIS**, daughter of John Bemis Jr. and Anna Livermore, on 26 Feb 1735 in Watertown. She was born there on 29 Apr 1714. Samuel died in Waltham, Middlesex, Massachusetts on 22 Mar 1761. Anne died there on 07 Jan 1793.

The children of Samuel Fiske and Anne Bemis included:

56.   i. SAMUEL[5] FISKE JR., born 02 Nov 1741, Waltham; married ABIGAIL WHITE, 29 Oct 1761, Waltham; died 30 Apr 1792, Watertown.

     ii. WILLIAM FISKE, born 28 Dec 1753, Waltham; died there, 13 Aug 1803.

25. **MARTHA**⁴ **BOWMAN** (Deborah³ Wyeth, John², Nicholas¹) was born on 10 Feb 1714 in Cambridge, Middlesex, Massachusetts. Martha Bowman married **NEHEMIAH CUTTER**, son of Gershom Cutter Jr. and Mehitable Abbott, on 17 Jul 1739 in Cambridge. He was baptized on 14 Apr 1717 in Medford, Middlesex, Massachusetts. Martha and Nehemiah both died in Menotomy (Arlington), Middlesex, Massachusetts. Her gravestone, in the north-western part of the Arlington Burying Ground, is inscribed, "In memory of Mrs. Martha Cutter the wife of Mr. Nehemiah Cutter, died 01 Jul 1790, aged 75 years." His stone reads, "In memory of Mr. Nehemiah Cutter who died on 12 Sep 1798, aged 81 Years."

Nehemiah Cutter and Martha Bowman had the following children: [146] [147]

       i. SAMUEL⁵ CUTTER was born on 17 May 1740 in Menotomy (Arlington), Middlesex, Massachusetts. Samuel married HANNAH HARTWELL there on 01 Dec 1760. Samuel, a tanner, served as a private in the French and Indian War in 1762. He lived the last part of his life on the Neck at Charlestown, Middlesex, Massachusetts where he died circa 1820.

      ii. MARTHA CUTTER, born 01 Nov 1742, Menotomy; married HENRY LUCKIS, son of Oliver Luckis and Elizabeth Starkey, on 12 Feb 1767 in Cambridge. He was born on 11 Feb 1742 in Boston, Suffolk, Massachusetts. Martha died of "grief" on 07 Jun 1772 in Menotomy.

     iii. ELIZABETH CUTTER was born on 14 Feb 1744 in Menotomy. Her funeral was held there on 04 Aug 1775.

     iv. JOSEPH CUTTER, born 21 Sep 1745, Menotomy; died there, 23 Dec 1749.

57.   v. (LT.) WILLIAM CUTTER, born 14 Apr 1748 in Menotomy; married RUTH HARRINGTON on 11 May 1780 in Weston, Middlesex, Massachusetts; died 09 Oct 1788 in Menotomy.

     vi. SARAH CUTTER, born 14 Feb 1750 in Menotomy; married JAMES FOSTER of Boston on 26 Jan 1773; death unknown.

    vii. JOSEPH CUTTER, born 23 Dec 1751, Menotomy. His funeral was held there on 18 Aug 1775.

58. viii. NEHEMIAH CUTTER, born 03 Jun 1753 in Menotomy; married DEBORAH HILL on 30 Oct 1781 in Cambridge; he died on 03 May 1828 in West Cambridge (Arlington), Middlesex, Massachusetts.

     ix. MEHITABEL CUTTER, born 28 Apr 1755, Menotomy; married THOMAS HOPKINS, 30 Dec 1778, Cambridge; married (2) JAMES PERKINS, 24 Jun 1792, Boston, Suffolk, Massachusetts; death unknown.

     x. ANDREW CUTTER, born on 09 Feb 1757 in Menotomy; married REBECCA CUTTER, daughter of Gershom Cutter and Rebecca Crosby, on 15 Jul 1779. He died on 08 Jan 1794 in Menotomy.

26. **DEBORAH**⁴ **BOWMAN** (Deborah³ Wyeth, John², Nicholas¹) was born on 30 May 1716 in Cambridge, Middlesex, Massachusetts. Deborah Bowman married **NATHANIEL KIDDER**, son of Samuel Kidder and Sarah Griggs, on 17 Sep 1741 in Cambridge. He was born there on 20 Nov 1702. Nathaniel, a farmer, died on 28 Mar 1789 and Deborah died three days later on 31 Mar 1789 in Cambridge. They were buried together in one grave in the Old Burying Ground in Harvard Square. [148]

Nathaniel Kidder and Deborah Bowman had the following children:

    i.   EUNICE[5] KIDDER, born 16 Aug 1742, Cambridge; married JOHN RANSHON SIGOURNEY, son of Andrew Sigourney and Mary Ranshon, 1764, Boston, Suffolk, Massachusetts. He was born there on 29 May 1740. In May 1802, Eunice and John died in Boston within days of each other.

    ii. NATHANIEL KIDDER was born on 10 Apr 1747 in Cambridge. He died in 1828 in New Market, Rockingham, New Hampshire.

    iii. SAMUEL KIDDER, born on 26 Sep 1753, Cambridge; died there on 08 Apr 1832.

27. **NOAH[4] BOWMAN** (Deborah[3] Wyeth, John[2], Nicholas[1]) was born on 23 Oct 1718 in Cambridge, Middlesex, Massachusetts. His marriage to **HANNAH WINSHIP**, daughter of Ephraim Winship Sr. and Hannah Cutter, was published 14 Jul 1744 in Cambridge. Hannah was born on 18 Aug 1718 in Lexington, Middlesex, Massachusetts. She was named in Noah's will that was proved in Cambridge on 02 Oct 1782.

Noah Bowman and Hannah Winship had the following children:

    i.   HANNAH[5] BOWMAN, born on 25 Feb 1745, Cambridge; married NICHOLAS PIKE, the son of James Pike and Sarah Gilman. He was born on 06 Oct 1743 in Somersworth, Strafford, New Hampshire. He graduated Harvard 1766, A.A.S; well known for his works on arithmetic. She died on 07 Jul 1778 in Newburyport, Essex, Massachusetts. He died there on 09 Dec 1819.[149]

59.   ii. CAPTAIN JOSHUA BOWMAN, born 17 Feb 1747, Cambridge. He graduated from Harvard in 1766 with his sister Hannah's husband, Nicholas Pike. Joshua married ABIGAIL FOWLE on 09 Apr 1767 in Watertown, Middlesex, Massachusetts. While serving as a captain of Dragoons in the Continental Army, he died on 30 Mar 1780 in Charleston County, South Carolina after being shot from his horse in battle.[150]

    iii. ELIZABETH BOWMAN, born 10 Apr 1748, Cambridge; died there on 15 Jan 1749.[151]

    iv. (DR.) ANDREW BOWMAN, born 02 Mar 1754, Cambridge. He studied medicine with Dr. Kittredge of Andover and settled in New Market, New Hampshire. Just short of age 23, he died on 09 Feb 1777 in Cambridge and is buried there in the Old Burying Ground.[152]

    v. SUZANNA BOWMAN, born 12 May 1758, Cambridge; died there on 28 Nov 1778 at the age of 20.

28. **ABIGAIL[4] BOWMAN** (Deborah[3] Wyeth, John[2], Nicholas[1]) was baptized on 15 Mar 1724 in Cambridge, Middlesex, Massachusetts. On 30 Dec 1755 in Cambridge, Abigail became the second wife of her first cousin, **WILLIAM WINSHIP JR.**, son of William Winship and Thankful Wyeth. He was baptized on 01 Jul 1722 in Cambridge. Due to old age, both Abigail and William died in the Menotomy (Arlington), Middlesex, Massachusetts Almshouse. Abigail was at least age 85 when she died on 22 Jun 1809 and William was almost age 89 at his death on 04 Feb 1811.[153]

William Winship Jr. and Abigail Bowman had the following children:

    i.   WILLIAM⁵ WINSHIP III, born on 31 Oct 1756 in Menotomy; fought as a minuteman at Lexington and Concord and in other battles of the Revolution; died 30 Jun 1821 in the Menotomy almshouse.

    ii. SUSANNA WINSHIP, baptized 09 Jul 1758, Menotomy; married JABEZ THORNE, 14 Sep 1809, Boston; after his death, she resided in Cambridge on the west side of North Ave.; buried in Cambridge on 03 Dec 1841.

    iii. LUCY WINSHIP, born 29 Aug 1760, Menotomy; died there on 01 Aug 1772.

    iv. AARON WINSHIP, born 08 Apr 1763, Menotomy; may have been the pauper called "vagrant" who died in Menotomy in 1808.

    v. CALEB WINSHIP, born 26 Feb 1765, Menotomy; died 15 Sep 1805 in Boston, Suffolk, Massachusetts.

    vi. SAMUEL WINSHIP, born 25 Feb 1768, Menotomy; death unknown.

    vii. MARY WINSHIP, was born 07 Dec 1771 in Menotomy. She never married and lived on the West Side of North Avenue in Cambridge with her sister Mrs. Susanna Thorne. She was buried on 17 Sep 1847 in Cambridge.

29.   **JONATHAN⁴ WYETH JR.** (Jonathan³, John², Nicholas¹) was born on 27 Jul 1716 in Cambridge, Middlesex, Massachusetts. Jonathan Wyeth Jr., a brick mason by trade, married Sarah Wilson on 14 Nov 1750 in Menotomy (Arlington), Middlesex, Massachusetts. **SARAH WILSON**, daughter of Andrew Wilson and Sarah Sherman, was born on 01 Nov 1722 in Cambridge. At Jonathan's death on 26 Apr 1767, he was laid in the Old Burying Ground at Harvard Square, Cambridge. Sarah died in Apr 1785 in Cambridge.

"Here lyes Buried the Body of Mr. Jonathan Wyeth who departed this Life April ye 26ᵗʰ 1767 in the 52ⁿᵈ year of his age."

Jonathan Wyeth Jr. and Sarah Wilson had two sets of twins:

60.   i.   JOSEPH⁵ WYETH (twin), baptized in Cambridge, 26 Jul 1751; married EUNICE BATHRICK, 17 Jan 1775, Boston; died 29 Oct 1837, Shakers' Square House, Harvard, Worcester, Massachusetts.

    ii. JONATHAN WYETH (twin), baptized 26 Jul 1751, Cambridge. He apparently had trouble managing his own affairs. A guardian was appointed for him in 1791. He died unmarried on 16 May 1796 at the age of 44 in Cambridge.

    iii. SARAH WYETH (twin), baptized 22 Feb 1761, Cambridge; married EBENEZER SMITH JR., son of Ebenezer Smith and Ann Bissell, 29 Apr 1779, Boston, Suffolk, Massachusetts. Sarah is buried in the Old Burying Ground in Cambridge, "Here lies the Body of Mrs. Sarah Smith wife of Mr. Ebenezer Smith who departed this life Augst. the 1ˢᵗ 1780, in ye 20ᵗʰ year of her age." Her daughter Sally Smith was named in Jonathan Wyeth's 1796 probate papers. Sally was apparently an infant at her mother's death.

    iv. HEPZIBAH WYETH (twin), baptized 22 Feb 1761, Cambridge; married SAMUEL BROOKS; died before 1796. Her three children (Hepzibah, Sarah and Samuel) are named in brother Jonathan's probate papers. However, nothing else is known about the Brooks family.

30. **DEBORAH**[4] **WYETH** (*Jonathan*[3], *John*[2], *Nicholas*[1]) was baptized 29 Apr 1720 in Cambridge, Middlesex, Massachusetts. Deborah Wyeth married yeoman **DANIEL PRENTICE SR.**, son of Solomon Prentice and Lydia Prentice, on 29 Dec 1743 in Cambridge. He was born there 17 May 1717. On 11 Mar 1777, Daniel's four-and-a-half-acre estate near the Botanic Gardens in Cambridge was distributed to his heirs Deborah, Daniel, Samuel, Hepzibah, and Beulah. [154] Deborah then moved to Harvard, Worcester, Massachusetts where she was an original member of the Harvard Shaker Community. She died there at the Shaker Square House on 11 Jul 1811 at age 91. [155] [156]

Jack E. Boucher's public domain photograph from the Library of Congress of a staircase in the Shaker Church Family Square House, Harvard, MA.

Daniel Prentice Sr. and Deborah Wyeth had the following children:[157]

      i.   DANIEL[5] PRENTICE, baptized 30 Dec 1744, Cambridge. He built houses for a living. In 1775, he served as a private in the Revolutionary War. After his father's death, he moved with his mother to the Shaker religious community in Harvard, Worcester County, Massachusetts.[158] Apparently, Daniel became disenchanted with the celibate Shaker life and returned to Cambridge circa 1796.

     ii.   SARAH PRENTICE, baptized 14 Sep 1746, Cambridge; died young.

   iii.   SARAH PRENTICE, baptized 06 Nov 1748, Cambridge; died young.

   iv.   JONATHAN PRENTICE, baptized 19 Aug 1750, Cambridge; death unknown.

    v.   MARY PRENTICE, baptized 15 Oct 1752, Cambridge; died young.

   vi.   HEPZIBAH PRENTICE, baptized 14 Mar 1755, Cambridge; married there THOMAS GODDARD, son of Thomas Goddard Sr. and Hannah Gove, on 11 Dec 1777. Thomas, baptized in Charlestown, Suffolk, Massachusetts on 12 Jul 1747, died 17 Mar 1830, Cambridge. She died there, 17 Aug 1836.

  vii.   SAMUEL PRENTICE, baptized 21 May 1758, Cambridge; served as a private in the Revolutionary War; married MARY "POLLY" TODD, 13 Jun 1782; died Cambridge, 25 Jul 1795. She died there, 27 Apr 1832 at about the age of 82.

61.   viii.   BEULAH PRENTICE, born circa 1761 in Cambridge; married TIMOTHY TUFTS JR. there, 09 May 1784; died 30 Oct 1795, Charlestown.

Notes for Daniel Prentice Sr. and Deborah Wyeth:

According to Charles J. F. Binney's Prentice family history, Dr. Nathaniel S. Prentice said his mother took him and his siblings to Deborah's house for safety during the battle of Lexington. Dr. Prentice recalled, while there, "Daniel Prentice Sr. came in, took down his gun, powder-horn, etc., picked his gun flint, and started off to harass the retreating British troops." Of Deborah's sons, Daniel and Samuel and perhaps Jonathan were on the Alarm list for that first battle of the Revolutionary War.[159]

The Prentice home near the Botanic Gardens was just a bit northwest of the original Wyeth property near Cambridge Common on Garden Street. In fact, Garden Street was named for the Botanic Gardens.[160]

After her husband's death in 1776, widow Prentice gave more than £160 to the Shaker Church. Her gift, one of the largest single amounts ever given by an individual, most likely came from the inheritance she received from her husband.[161]

Deborah's grave is marked with a cast-iron "lollipop" marker in the Harvard Shakers Burying Ground.

31. **JONAS[4] PRENTICE** (Hannah[3] Wyeth, John[2], Nicholas[1]) was born on 25 Apr 1713 and baptized on 26 Apr 1713 in Cambridge, Middlesex, Massachusetts. He married **MERCY PIERCE**, daughter of John Pierce and Eliza Shepherd, on 22 Apr 1736 in Charlestown, Suffolk, Massachusetts. She was born on 22 Jun 1714 in Charlestown. He died of dysentery on 14 Nov 1775 in Cambridge. Mercy died there on 24 Feb 1789.

The children of Jonas Prentice and Mercy Pierce included:

    i.   NATHANIEL[5] PRENTICE, born 14 Oct 1743, Cambridge; served under Capt. Samuel Thatcher on 19 Apr 1775; died in Cambridge on 18 Jun 1817.

    ii.   THOMAS PRENTICE was baptized on 19 Jan 1752, Cambridge; fought near Lexington / Lincoln in Parker's Revenge; died 06 Nov 1800, Cambridge.

    iii.   JOHN PRENTICE, baptized 28 Aug 1748, Cambridge; fought along side his brothers as a minuteman on 19 Apr 1775; died 02 Jan 1806, Cambridge.

32. **HANNAH[4] PRENTICE** (Hannah[3] Wyeth, John[2], Nicholas[1]) was born on 16 Dec 1716 in Cambridge, Middlesex, Massachusetts. She married **THOMAS FESSENDEN JR.**, son of Thomas Fessenden Sr. and Abigail Poulter, on 19 Jun 1735 in Lexington, Middlesex, Massachusetts. He was born on 09 Dec 1709 in Cambridge. He died at age 58 on 22 Jul 1768 in Lexington. Hannah died on 22 Oct 1768.

Thomas Fessenden Jr. and Hannah Prentice had the following children:

    i.   THOMAS[5] FESSENDEN III was born on 10 Jul 1741 in Lexington, Middlesex, Massachusetts. He gave a deposition on 23 Apr 1775 about witnessing that the British fired first on Lexington Green on the morning of 19 Apr 1775. He was almost 64 at his death on 25 Feb 1804 in Lexington.

  62. ii.   NATHAN FESSENDEN, born 10 Apr 1749, Lexington; married SARAH WINSHIP on 17 Oct 1771 in Lexington; died there on 24 Apr 1797.

Deposition of Thomas Fessenden III on 23 Apr 1775:

"I, Thomas Fessenden, of lawful age, testify and declare, that, being in a pasture near the meeting house, at said Lexington, on Wednesday last, at about half an hour before sunrise, I saw a number of regular troops pass speedily by said meeting house, on their way towards a company of militia of said Lexington, who were assembled to the number of about one hundred in a company, at the distance of eighteen or twenty rods from said meeting house; and after they had passed by said meeting house, I saw three officers, on horseback, advance to the front of said regulars, when one of them, being within six rods of the said militia, cried out, 'Disperse, you rebels, immediately,' on which he brandished his sword over his head three times; meanwhile the second officer, who was about two rods behind him, fired a pistol, pointed at said militia, and the regulars kept huzzaing till he had finished brandishing his sword, and when he had thus finished brandishing his sword, he pointed it down towards said militia, and immediately on which the said regulars fired a volley at the militia, and then I ran off as fast as I could, while they continued firing, till I got out of their reach. I further testify, that as soon as ever the officer cried 'Disperse, you rebels,' the said company of militia dispersed every way, as fast as they could, and, while they were dispersing, the regulars kept firing at them incessantly. And further saith not.

Thomas Fessenden." [162]

33. **SOLOMON**[4] **PRENTICE** (Hannah[3] Wyeth, John[2], Nicholas[1]) was born on 31 Jan 1720 in Cambridge, Middlesex, Massachusetts. He was a farmer and kept bees. He married **HANNAH FILLEBROWN**, daughter of Isaac Fillebrown and Hannah Pierce, on 02 Nov 1744 in Cambridge. Hannah Fillebrown was baptized on 06 Feb 1725/26 in Cambridge. Solomon died on 10 Sep 1799 in Watertown, Middlesex, Massachusetts. His 21 Sep 1793 will was probated 02 Oct 1799 in favor of his wife and only descendant still living, granddaughter Hannah Prentice Sanderson, who was on born 10 Jun 1775 in Watertown. Hannah Fillebrown Prentice died on 26 Aug 1805 at the poorhouse in Cambridge.

Solomon Prentice and Hannah Fillebrown had the following children:

    i.   SOLOMON[5] PRENTICE, born 11 Aug 1745, Cambridge; died there on 08 Sep 1765.

    ii.   HANNAH PRENTICE was born 27 Jul 1748 in Cambridge. She married ISAAC SANDERSON circa 1774. He died 17 Sep 1775 in Watertown. Hannah died there a few days later on 30 Sep 1775.

    iii.   ISAAC PRENTICE, born 11 Dec 1750, Cambridge; died prior to 1793.

    iv.   SARAH PRENTICE, born 18 Jul 1761, Cambridge; died prior to 1793.

34. **PRUDENCE**[4] **WINSHIP** (Hannah[3] Wyeth, John[2], Nicholas[1]) was born on 04 Sep 1726 and baptized on 11 Sep 1726 in Cambridge, Middlesex, Massachusetts. She married (1) **MICHAEL GEOGHEGAN** on 08 Mar 1743 in Boston, Suffolk, Massachusetts. He apparently was born about 1715 in Ireland. She next married (2) **CHRISTOPHER THORNTON** on 10 Aug 1749 in Boston and married (3) **THOMAS PEIRCE** on 09 Jun 1768 in Charlestown, Suffolk, Massachusetts. Her death date is unknown.

Michael Geoghegan and Prudence Winship had the following child:

    i.   PRUDENCE[5] GEOGHEGAN was born in 1745 in Boston. She married EDWARD GOODWIN on 03 Dec 1771 in Boston. The names of their children are not known. He was born on 13 Sep 1735 in Charlestown. She died of liver cancer on 08 Aug 1794 in Charlestown. He died there on 02 Nov 1810.

35. **JASON**[4] **WINSHIP JR.** (Hannah[3] Wyeth, John[2], Nicholas[1]) was baptized on 28 Jun 1730 in Cambridge, Middlesex, Massachusetts. Jason served in the French and Indian War. He married (1) **RUTH CARTER**, daughter of Joseph Carter and Sarah Perry, on 26 Apr 1764 in Woburn, Middlesex, Massachusetts. She was born on 21 May 1738 in Woburn. She and her only child died in childbirth on 30 Jan 1765 in Menotomy (Arlington), Middlesex, Massachusetts. He married (2) **MARY PIPER**, daughter of Josiah Piper and Sarah Conant, on 16 Jan 1768 in Cambridge. She was born on 26 Jul 1739 in Acton, Middlesex,

Massachusetts. On their return from battle at Lexington and Concord on 19 Apr 1775, British troops smashed their way into Cooper's Tavern in Menotomy and killed Jason while he sat drinking Flip to innocently celebrate the birth of his first son. [163] It would be understandable that he would be happy about the birth of his son. He lost his first wife and child during childbirth and his second wife, Mary, gave birth to two stillborn children. Thus, Jason had but two of five children survive. After much hardship and loss, Mary Piper Winship died circa 1809. [164]

The children of Jason Winship Jr. and Mary Piper who survived their birth are:

    i.   PRUDENCE PEIRCE[5] WINSHIP, named for her aunt Prudence Winship Peirce, was born on 09 Apr 1770 in Menotomy. She married NOAH STEARNS, son of Benjamin Stearns and Hannah Seager, on 05 Jun 1806 in Lexington, Middlesex, Massachusetts. He was baptized there on 21 Sep 1766. Prudence died 10 Sep 1820 in Lexington.

    ii.   JASON WINSHIP III was born at the end of Mar 1775 in Menotomy. Jason never knew his father. Just a few days after he was born, Jason's father was at Cooper's tavern in Menotomy, with his uncle Jabez Wyman, celebrating his birth. Several British Army soldiers broke into the tavern on the first day of the American Revolution and viciously slaughtered Jabez and Jason Jr. Baby Jason's baptism on 23 Apr 1775 was only four days after his father's horrible death. [165] Jason Winship III died circa 1820; place unknown.

36. **WILLIAM[4] WINSHIP JR.** (Thankful[3] Wyeth, John[2], Nicholas[1]) was baptized 01 Jul 1722 in Cambridge, Middlesex, Massachusetts. He married (1) **MARY JOHNSON** on 14 Jul 1748 in Menotomy (Arlington), Middlesex, Massachusetts. She was born about 1725 in Charlestown, Suffolk, Massachusetts. She died from childbirth complications on 18 Jun 1749 in Menotomy. A few days later, on 27 Aug 1749, William joined the Menotomy church. He married (2) **ABIGAIL BOWMAN**, daughter of Deacon Samuel Bowman and Deborah Wyeth, on 30 Dec 1755 in Cambridge. She was baptized 15 Mar 1724 in Cambridge. Both died in the Menotomy Almshouse. Abigail died at about age 85 on 22 Jun 1809 and William died on 04 Feb 1811 at the age of 88 years and seven months. Apparently, they had no family who could help and had to seek charity due to their age. [166]

William Winship Jr. and Mary Johnson had the following child:

    i.   MARY[5] WINSHIP, born 11 Jun 1749, Menotomy; died there on 13 Sep 1749 at three months old.

William Winship Jr. next married Abigail Bowman, his first cousin, so their children show under her #28.

37. **ABIGAIL[4] WINSHIP** (Thankful[3] Wyeth, John[2], Nicholas[1]) was baptized 30 Oct 1726 in Cambridge, Middlesex, Massachusetts. She married **JOSEPH COOK SR.**, son of Samuel Cook and Joanna Prentice, there on 22 May 1746. Joseph was born on 12 Jan 1727 in Cambridge. After Abigail's death circa 1756, Joseph married Margery Dickson in May 1756 and moved around the state quite a bit. At one point, he lived in Bowdoinham and moved from there to Medford, Middlesex, Massachusetts to stay with his second wife's

relatives. He was last warned to leave Medford on 08 Nov 1766 because the selectmen wanted to be sure he didn't go on the welfare rolls of the town.[167] He must have moved back to Medford, because according to the One World Tree, he died there on 17 Mar 1777.

Joseph Cook Sr. and Abigail Winship had the following children:

> i. JOSEPH[5] COOK JR., baptized 23 Aug 1747, Cambridge; he died circa 1818.
> ii. ELIZABETH COOK, baptized 14 Oct 1750, Cambridge; according to Medford's vital records, she was buried there on 18 Feb 1784 in Medford.
> iii. WILLIAM COOK, baptized 20 May 1753, Cambridge; died on 25 Apr 1761, Medford. Their records mistakenly give Margery as his mother's name.

38. **EBENEZER[4] WYETH JR.** (Ebenezer[3] Sr., John[2], Nicholas[1]) was born on 08 Apr 1727 in Cambridge, Middlesex, Massachusetts. Rev. Mr. Hull Abbot married Ebenezer to **MARY WINSHIP**, daughter of Joseph Winship and Anna Whitmore, on 05 Nov 1751 in Charlestown, Suffolk, Massachusetts. Although she was living in Charlestown before their marriage, Mary was born on 18 Apr 1731 in Cambridge and died there on 09 Sep 1798 at age 67. Ebenezer died in Cambridge on 04 Aug 1799 at the age of 72. One source mistakenly says Ebenezer was buried in Cambridge, New York.[168] His burial place is most likely in the Old Buying Ground in Harvard Square, Cambridge, Massachusetts.

Ebenezer Wyeth Jr. and Mary Winship had the following children:

> 63.   i. EBENEZER[5] WYETH III, born on 17 Dec 1752 in Watertown, Middlesex, Massachusetts; married (1) ELIZABETH WINSHIP, the widow of Joseph Green, 03 May 1777, Cambridge; married (2) NAOMI RUSSELL, the widow of Abraham Cooke, circa Mar 1800 (intention filed 01 Mar 1800), Cambridge; died 30 Dec 1836, Ashby, Middlesex, Massachusetts.
>   ii. MARY "POLLY" WYETH, born 17 Sep 1755, Cambridge; died there unmarried on 07 Oct 1790 at the age of 35.
> 64.   iii. JONAS WYETH JR., born 17 May 1757, Cambridge; married ELIZABETH E. SMITH, 08 Apr 1792, Cambridge; died there on 03 Oct 1817.
> 65.   iv. JOSHUA WYETH SR., born 06 Oct 1758, Cambridge; married (1) PAULINE JONES, about 1774, Boston, Suffolk, Massachusetts; married (2) MARY ELIZABETH BREWER, 27 Apr 1780, Waltham, Middlesex, Massachusetts; married (3) ELIZABETH RICHARDSON, 07 Jan 1808, Watertown; died 22 Jan 1829, Cincinnati, Hamilton, Ohio.
>   v. WILLIAM WYETH, born 22 May 1760, Cambridge; died there, 08 Jun 1775.
> 66.   vi. SUSANNAH WYETH, born 14 May 1762, Cambridge; married WILLIAM WATSON SR., 06 Dec 1779, Cambridge; died there, 29 Dec 1789.
> 67.   vii. JACOB WYETH SR., born 29 Apr 1764, Cambridge; married ELIZABETH JARVIS, 08 Nov 1796, Cambridge; died there on 14 Jan 1857.
>   viii. ANNA WYETH was born on 22 Feb 1766 in Cambridge. She married BENJAMIN CUTTER, son of Ammi Cutter and Esther Pierce, on 06 Mar 1785 in Cambridge. He was born there on 07 Nov 1761. They both died in Charlestown, Suffolk, Massachusetts on the estate that her grandfather, Joseph Winship, had purchased in 1742 from the heirs of Henry Dunster, the

President of Harvard College. Benjamin died on 07 Mar 1824 and Anna died on 15 Apr 1842. In consideration of Benjamin and Anna assuming the care of grandmother Anna Whitmore Winship, who lived past the age of 100, the estate was given to Benjamin by Joseph Winship's heirs sometime after 1784. When Anna Wyeth Cutter died, the estate was divided among her surviving brothers, Jacob, Gad and John and the children of her siblings who predeceased her.[169]

68.   ix.   GAD WYETH SR., born 27 Jul 1768, Cambridge; married MARY "POLLY" KENDALL, 01 Dec 1793, Cambridge; died 01 Nov 1843, McKean Township, Licking, Ohio.

69.   x.   JOHN WYETH, born 31 Mar 1770, Cambridge; married (1) LOUISA WEISS, 06 Jun 1793, Philadelphia, Philadelphia County, Pennsylvania; married (2) LYDIA ALLEN, 02 May 1826, Philadelphia; died there on 23 Jan 1858.

       xi.   ELIZABETH WYETH, born 12 Feb 1772, Cambridge; died there unmarried on 23 Feb 1793 at the age of 21.

Notes for Ebenezer Wyeth Jr. and Mary Winship:

At his 1751 marriage, Ebenezer Jr. purchased a vast acreage that ran all the way from present day Mt. Auburn Street near the Watertown border to the Fresh Pond in present day Belmont, Massachusetts.[170] In 1915, the farmhouse where Ebenezer Jr. and Mary raised their 11 children was moved to its present location at 36 Larch Road, Cambridge. At its purchase, the estate was in Watertown sitting at the corner of Fresh Pond Lane and the county road to Watertown, now called Mt. Auburn Street.[171]

Because Mary and Ebenezer wanted to continue attending First Church in Cambridge, they joined in a petition requesting their Watertown property be annexed to Cambridge. On 19 Apr 1754, the governor of Massachusetts consented to changing the dividing line between the towns of Cambridge and Watertown.

After the change, the border began at the Charles River and ran to "the line between the lands of Simon Coolidge, Moses Stone, Christopher Grant, and the

Ebenezer and Mary Wyeth's farmhouse was altered considerably when it was used as a service wing by the Hastings family. It is one of the few houses still standing in Cambridge that was built before the Revolution.

Thatchers (on the one side), and the lands of Colonel Brinley and Ebenezer Wyeth, to the Fresh Pond, so called (on the other)."[172]

For this reason, Mary gave birth to Ebenezer Wyeth III in Watertown in 1752 and without moving from her home, gave birth to the rest of her children in Cambridge starting in 1755.

20 years later, Ebenezer Jr., and his sons who were old enough, actively helped establish American independence.

After son Joshua Wyeth's involvement in the Boston Tea Party, at age 15, on 16 Dec 1773, Ebenezer Jr., age 48, and his son, Jonas Wyeth Jr., age 17, fought as minutemen on the first day of the Revolution. They marched very early in the morning on the alarm carried hours before by Paul Revere, Dr. Samuel Prescott and other riders, including William Dawes. Dawes rode across Cambridge Common in front of the Wyeth farm that Nicholas Wyeth purchased in 1645.[173]

Father and son entered the battle at Lincoln, Massachusetts on 19 Apr 1775 with Ebenezer's two brothers, Jonas Sr. and Noah; their cousin, Joseph Wyeth; and 72 other farmers in Captain Samuel Thatcher's company of militia. Together with Captain John Parker's Lexington Militia, they skirmished with the British columns retreating from Concord near the boundary line of Lexington and Lincoln.[174] The battle there came to be known as Parker's Revenge.

Hours earlier on Lexington Green, Captain Parker said, "Stand your ground! Don't fire unless fired upon! But, if they want to have a war, let it begin here." Although both sides had orders not to shoot, a fight broke out. Eight militia were killed and nine wounded. Two British soldiers were slightly injured.[175]

It is believed Ebenezer Jr. joined his son Joshua at the Battle of Bunker Hill on 17 Jun 1775.[176] Joshua's pension application states that after the June battle, he enlisted for 12 months in the Continental Service of Captain Eliphalet Newell's Company, Colonel Henry Knox's Artillery Corps Regiment, Massachusetts Line. The captain's records prove similar service in his company by brothers Ebenezer III and Jonas Wyeth Jr., too.[177] Many other records for Wyeth men appear in volume 17 of the *Massachusetts Soldiers and Sailors of the Revolutionary War.*

In 1785, with half of the children of Ebenezer Jr. and Mary still living at home, the family took in nine-year-old Lydia Convers Francis to live at the farmhouse.[178] In 1804, Lydia married her benefactors' nephew, Captain Job Wyeth.

On and off between 1781 and 1790, farmer and brick-maker Ebenezer Wyeth Jr. served for a total of seven years as a Cambridge selectman (city councilman).[179][180] The first Federal Census of the Population of the United States, in 1790, confirmed Cambridge as his residence.

When Mary died of putrid fever (diphtheria) on 09 Sep 1798, Ebenezer struggled on without her for 11 months. He died without a will on 04 Aug 1799.

Mary's mother, Anna Whitmore Winship, outlived both of them. She died just after turning 100 on 02 Feb 1806.[181] Her namesake, Anna Wyeth Cutter, cared for her in her later years. Apparently, longevity in this branch of the Wyeth family comes from Anna Whitmore.

Also, from Anna Whitmore Winship, her descendants have a link to British Royalty through Whitmore's mother, Anna Pierce, daughter of Richard Pierce and Sarah Cotton. Whitmore's 2nd great grandparents were Massachusetts governor Simon Bradstreet and his wife, Anne Dudley, the first published poet in Massachusetts.[182] Anne's father, Thomas Dudley, was the chief founder of Newtowne, (Cambridge, Massachusetts) and signed Harvard College's new charter during his 1650 term as governor of the Massachusetts Bay Colony. Dudley's mother, Susanna Thorne, was descended from the Plantagenet King Henry II.[183] Increase Mather was Anna

Whitmore Winship's distant uncle and his son, Cotton Mather, her distant cousin.[184]

Inside the now closed Bacon Gate between Harvard's Lamont Library and Massachusetts Avenue is a small garden that memorializes Thomas Dudley, a founder of both Harvard and the city of Cambridge.

Without a last will and testament, an administrator distributed Ebenezer Wyeth Jr.'s estate. The inventory provided to the probate court on 25 Sep 1799, shows a personal estate of $638.94. The real estate of $3,980 and notes and receipts totaling $1,251.90 are itemized as follows:

About 17 acres of land with mansion house and other buildings	$2,260.00	
About 13 acres of land adjoining Watertown	910.00	
About 2.5 acres salt marsh	220.00	
About 12 acres in Watertown	540.00	
A pew in the meeting house	50.00	$3,980.00
Joshua Wyeth Rec. dated 21 May 1791	50.00	
Joshua Wyeth Rec. dated 19 Feb 1793	125.66	
Jonas Wyeth Jr. Note 17 Nov 1795	50.00	
Jonas Wyeth Jr. Note 16 Jun 1797	20.00	
Jacob Wyeth's Note and Rec.	816.68	
Amount charged to Susanna Watson (deceased)	43.78	
Amount charged to Anna Cutter	108.28	
Amount charged to John Wyeth	37.50	$1,251.90

The administrator divided the property among Ebenezer III, Jonas Jr. and Gad. The three brothers then paid shares to their siblings less the value that each had already received in their father's lifetime. It apparently was a fair allocation of the estate for the brothers and Anna remained friendly afterwards … as evidenced by letters and visits detailed in Benjamin and William Richard Cutter's *History of the Town of Arlington*.[185]

39. **JONAS**[4] **WYETH SR.** (Ebenezer[3] Sr., John[2], Nicholas[1]) was born on 19 Feb 1730 in Cambridge, Middlesex, Massachusetts. He married **HEPZIBAH TIDD,** daughter of Daniel Tidd and Hepzibah Reed, on 18 Mar 1753 in Cambridge. According to the handwritten records of their son, Major Jonas Wyeth, Hepzibah was born on 22 Aug 1730 in Lexington, Middlesex, Massachusetts.[186] She died on 24 May 1801 in Cambridge. Jonas Sr. died there two days short of his 83rd birthday on 17 Feb 1813. The cause of death was old age.

Jonas Wyeth Sr. and Hepzibah Tidd had the following children:

70.   i. LUCY[5] WYETH, born 07 Feb 1754, Cambridge; married THOMAS COOLIDGE, Apr 1773; died 16 Oct 1850, Livermore, Androscoggin, Maine.

71. ii. (MAJOR) JONAS WYETH, born 13 Apr 1762, Cambridge; married (1) HEPHZIBAH HASTINGS, the widow of John Sawin, 14 Nov 1787, Cambridge; married (2) SUSAN STEARNS, 29 Nov 1800, Waltham, Middlesex, Massachusetts; died 08 Jul 1828, Cambridge.

72. iii. TAPLEY WYETH M.D., born 11 May 1765, Cambridge; married SARAH FISKE, 26 Mar 1795, Sherborn, Middlesex, Massachusetts; died there, 17 Sep 1813.

Notes for Jonas Wyeth Sr.:

In his will, Jonas' father, Ebenezer Wyeth Sr., gave him the 17th century homestead near Cambridge Common. It remained in Jonas' family for over 100 years more. His father's 1754 probate documents listed Jonas as a brick maker.

Shortly after his father's death, Jonas served as a private in the French and Indian War. 20 years later, Jonas Sr. marched on the alarm carried by William Dawes across the Common in front of Jonas' home on 19 Apr 1775. Brothers, Jonas Sr., Ebenezer Jr. and Noah; a nephew, Jonas Jr.; and a cousin, Joseph Wyeth were members of Captain Samuel Thatcher's Company of Colonel Gardner's Regiment. They fought in Parker's Revenge at the Lincoln and Lexington town line.[187]

"General George Washington having taken command of the Army of the United Colonies at Cambridge inspects the troops near this spot on the 4th day of July 1775." This relief hangs inside the Sheraton Commander Hotel which sets on some of the land where Jonas Wyeth Sr. lived in 1775.

Given that Jonas Wyeth Sr. had a nephew, a son, a grandson and a grandnephew named for him, there has been a lot of confusion on which Jonas was which. As discussed before, the mix-up was particularly great for Elizabeth E. Smith Wyeth as she tried to prove the military service of her husband Jonas Wyeth Jr. Also, as previously mentioned, instead of Joshua Wyeth, one of the Jonas Wyeths was incorrectly credited with participation in the Boston Tea Party.

Jonas Sr. served as a Cambridge selectman (city councilman) in 1777 and 1778. When he signed his will on 07 Aug 1807, he called himself a yeoman. In the will, Jonas Sr. bequeathed his real estate and his Quarto Bible to his son Jonas. Because of all the property son Jonas ended up owning in Cambridge, he apparently was bestowed the honorary title of "major" and became known as Major Jonas Wyeth. Jonas Wyeth Sr. left Major Jonas' sons, Jonas 2d and Augustus, $100 each out of his securities. Since his wife Hepzibah predeceased him, Jonas Sr. directed that all his household furniture, the residue of his securities and money on hand, at his decease, be equally divided between his children Dr. Tapley Wyeth and Lucy Wyeth, the wife of Thomas Coolidge. The will was probated 07 May 1813.

His name is the first Jonas on this monument. According to the records of Mt. Auburn Cemetery for Mimosa Path, lot 1161, Cambridge, the remains of Jonas, his wife Hepzibah, son Major Jonas and daughter-in-law Susan Stearns Wyeth were buried there on 12 Sep 1845. Son Augustus Wyeth's remains were transferred on 14 Sep 1845. Jonas Wyeth 2d wrote in the family records that the remains were originally in the family tomb in old Cambridge.[188]

40. **SUSANNAH**[4] **WYETH** (Ebenezer[3] Sr., John[2], Nicholas[1]) was born on 02 Mar 1734 in Cambridge, Middlesex, Massachusetts. She married **DANIEL SAWIN SR.**, son of John Sawin and Elizabeth Coolidge, on 27 May 1755 in Cambridge. He was born on 26 Oct 1727 in Watertown, Middlesex, Massachusetts. The inscription on Susannah's grave in the Old Burying Ground in Watertown reads, "Sacred to the Memory of Mrs. Susannah Sawin, Wife of Mr. Daniel Sawin who died 23 Mar 1794 Æt. 59. Daniel died on 11 Feb 1800 in Watertown and rests near his wife.[189]

Daniel Sawin and Susannah Wyeth had the following children:

   i. MARY[5] (MOLLY) SAWIN was born on 21 Mar 1756 in Watertown. She married WILLIAM COX, son of Matthew Cox and Elizabeth Russell, on 25 Nov 1779 in Cambridge. He was born on 08 Apr 1750 in Cambridge. He died on 27 Jul 1833 in Orange County, Vermont. She died there on 17 May 1848 and is buried in West Fairlee Cemetery.[190]

   ii. DANIEL SAWIN JR. was born on 01 May 1757 in Watertown. He marched as a minuteman on the alarm of 19 Apr 1775 as a member of Captain Samuel Barnard's Watertown Company. They entered the first battle of the American Revolution in Menotomy.[191] General Washington ordered Daniel's company to reinforce the Continental Army at the taking of Dorchester Heights in Mar 1776. On 02 Sep 1799, Daniel married LUCY DICKSON in Watertown. They both rest in Watertown's Old Burying Place. The inscription on his grave reads: "Sacred to the Memory of Mr. Daniel Sawin, son of Mr. Daniel Sawin; who died March 24, 1834; Æt. 77. Friends nor physicians could not save, My mortal body from the grave; Nor can the grave confine me here, When Christ shall call me to appear."[192]

73.   iii. JOHN SAWIN was born on 07 Feb 1759 in Watertown. During the War for Independence, he served as a corporal in Captain Joseph Fuller's Company, Colonel Samuel Bullard's Regiment. He engaged in the service on 20 Aug 1777 and left at Stillwater, Maine on 29 Nov 1777.[193] John married HEPHZIBAH HASTINGS, daughter of Samuel Hastings and Lydia Tidd, on 17 Apr 1781 in Watertown. She was born on 03 Jul 1762 in Lexington, Middlesex, Massachusetts. After John died 22 Mar 1786 of consumption, at age 27, in Cambridge, Hepzibah married Major Jonas Wyeth.

   iv. LUCY SAWIN, born 10 Jul 1760, Watertown; married there (1) JOSEPH PALMER on 21 May 1784. Joseph was born about 1760 in Cambridge. After his death circa 1789, Lucy married (2) LEVI MILLS on 06 Jun 1790 in Newburyport, Essex, Massachusetts. He was born in 1756 in Westminster, Worcester, Massachusetts. Levi died on 24 Nov 1817 in Newburyport. Lucy died there on 17 Apr 1846.

   v. SAMUEL SAWIN was born 08 May 1762, Watertown. When he enlisted for six months on 04 Jul 1780, in the 4th Division Massachusetts Artillery, he was described as age 18; height, 5 ft. 11 in.; light complexion. He arrived at Springfield, Massachusetts on 05 Jul 1780 and was discharged, 04 Jan 1781. His name was on the Watertown Selectmen's Return.[194] He married (1) MARTHA MASON, daughter of Nehemiah Mason and Rebecca Fillebrown, on

18 Apr 1792 in Watertown. She was born on 05 Jan 1768 in Watertown. He married (2) SARAH WEBB, daughter of Henry Webb and Annie Riggs, on 17 May 1820 in Portland, Cumberland, Maine. She was born there in 1783. Samuel died 12 Jan 1849, Cambridge. Annie died there on 15 Nov 1869.

   vi. ABIJAH SAWIN, born 16 Jan 1764, Watertown; died in 1827, Livermore, Androscoggin, Maine.

  vii. JOSEPH SAWIN was born on 08 May 1766 in Watertown. He married (1) SALLY KENDALL, daughter of Jabez Kendall and Mary Pool, in 1793 in Cambridge. She was born there about 1774 and died there on 18 Aug 1802. He married (2) MARTHA MONROE on 24 May 1807 in Boston, Suffolk, Massachusetts. Joseph died on 23 Oct 1838 in Newton Lower Falls, Middlesex, Massachusetts.

 viii. BENJAMIN SAWIN, born 25 May 1768, Watertown; died 05 Mar 1841, Wayland, Middlesex, Massachusetts at the age of 73.

   ix. SUSANNA SAWIN, born 22 Sep 1770, Watertown; worked for many years as a housekeeper for her siblings. She died unmarried on 22 Aug 1848 in the Watertown Almshouse.[195]

    x. ELIZABETH "BETSEY" SAWIN was born on 04 Dec 1772 in Watertown. She married (CAPTAIN) SETH BIRD on 17 Jul 1796 in Watertown. He was born in Massachusetts about 1773 to Benjamin Bird and Mary Prentice. Betsey died in 1826 in Portland, Cumberland, Maine. Seth died there on 23 Jun 1852.

   xi. JOSHUA SAWIN was born on 08 Apr 1775 in Watertown. He married ABIGAIL KENDALL, daughter of Jabez Kendall and Mary Pool, on 21 Feb 1804 in Cambridge. She was born about 1781 in Cambridge. She died there in 1836. He died on 10 Nov 1846 in Cambridge.

  xii. SARAH SAWIN, born 04 Oct 1777, Watertown; died there, 01 Nov 1778.

Remarks about the Sawin family from Thomas E. and John Sawin's 1866 book:

Daniel Sawin and Susannah Wyeth raised their 12 children in a parsonage house Daniel's grandfather built across from the burying ground in Watertown. Daniel was a farmer and a brick mason. A practicing Baptist, his faith was said to account for the tradition of him being considered eccentric. Oddly, he was known to be fearful of fire, yet he refused to leave his fireplace and was found dying in front of it the next morning. He was 72 at his death.[196]

The family's fifth child, Samuel Sawin, also followed the Baptist tradition. After Continental Army service and many years of labor as a farmers' man, he settled in Livermore, Maine, upon land "left by his father." There he and his first wife, Martha Mason, reared seven children. When Martha died, Samuel married Sarah Webb—a woman over 20 years his junior. Together they too had seven children. While living in Maine, Samuel wrote a letter on 01 Nov 1845 to help Elizabeth E. Smith Wyeth appeal for a widow's pension based on the Revolutionary War service of her husband, Jonas Wyeth Jr. (1757-1817). In his old age, Samuel returned to Massachusetts to live with his son Daniel in Cambridge. Another one of Samuel's 14 children, Nathaniel, served as an active witness in the murder trial of Dr. John White Webster, the infamous resident of the #22 Garden Street house owned by Jonas Wyeth 2[d] (1806-1868).[197]

The lives of the Sawins and their Wyeth cousins are remarkably intertwined.

Before his marriage, Susannah's third child, John Sawin, served as a blacksmith apprentice to Newton Baxter, near Watertown bridge. Then in partnership with his cousin and fellow blacksmith, Joshua Wyeth, he built carriages for one year. Finally settled in Cambridge, John bought one acre with its half-house for £100 borrowed off the town. There he erected a shop from a Prospect Hill barrack abandoned by General John Burgoyne's soldiers. At John Sawin's premature death, his wife Hephzibah Hastings Sawin married John's first cousin Major Jonas Wyeth (1762-1828), the father of Jonas Wyeth 2^d (1806-1868).[198]

Joshua Wyeth also was in a partnership of sorts with his cousin Mary Sawin's husband, William Cox. Together Joshua and William dressed as Indians to steep tea in Boston Harbor on 16 Dec 1773.[199] Over a half century later, Joshua unwittingly named that event the "Boston Tea Party."[200]

One of Joshua Wyeth's brothers, Gad, had an even closer relationship to some of the descendants of their aunt Susannah Wyeth Sawin. Three Sawins were his brothers-in-law. In 1793, Gad Wyeth Sr. married Mary "Polly" Kendall and the seventh Sawin child, Joseph, married Mary's sister, Sally Kendall. Mary and Sally along with Abigail, Eunice and Lydia were the five daughters of Mary Pool and Jabez Kendall Jr. Jabez, who owned a successful wheelwright shop in Cambridge, had no sons. It appears he took the Sawins under his wing. The youngest Sawin boy, Joshua Sawin, was Jabez's employee.[201]

Jabez Kendall built a large house in Wendell, Massachusetts about 1800 for his daughter Mary, with whom he intended to live. But when he died in Cambridge on 20 Oct 1803, he left the house to her as Mrs. Gad Wyeth.[202]

Middlesex County probate records show Abigail Kendall was under age at the time of her father's death, so Jacob Wyeth (1764-1857), the owner of the Fresh Pond Hotel, became her guardian. The next year, Abigail married her father's shop assistant, Joshua Sawin. A few years later, the youngest Kendall daughter, Lydia, married John and Hephzibah Hastings Sawin's son, John Sawin Jr. (the stepson of Major Jonas Wyeth (1762-1828)).[203]

Of the Kendall daughters, only Eunice did not marry a descendant of Nicholas Wyeth. She lived with her sister Mary "Polly" Kendall Wyeth in Wendell. When Eunice Kendall died unmarried on 23 Dec 1821, her probated will showed yet another link to the Wyeth family. She had made a loan to her nephew, Joseph Sawin Wyeth (1796-1872). Perhaps it was to help him make the move to the Black River country of Jefferson County, New York.

After burying Eunice in the Wendell Center Cemetery in Franklin County, Massachusetts,[204] Mary and Gad moved on to Jefferson County, New York and ultimately to Licking County, Ohio. However, they left yet another Kendall-Wyeth connection behind in Wendell. Circa 1772, Jabez Kendall's sister, Sarah, moved 90 miles from Cambridge to Wendell.[205] Interestingly, this could explain why Jabez had the desire to build a home there in 1800. Also interesting is the fact that the man Sarah Kendall married on 07 Apr 1763, Daniel Fiske, is the great grandson of Sarah Wyeth Fiske (1632-1701).[206]

41. **MARY E.**^{4} **WYETH** (Ebenezer^3 Sr., John^2, Nicholas^1) was born on 30 Sep 1739 in Cambridge, Middlesex, Massachusetts. She married **MANSFIELD TAPLEY JR.,** son of Mansfield Tapley Sr. and Mary Johnson, on 01 Oct 1760 in Cambridge. He was born on 05 Feb 1731 in Charlestown, Suffolk, Massachusetts. Because Mansfield was an infant

when his parents died, he was raised by widow Sarah Kidder in Cambridge. Sarah may have been the mother-in-law of Deborah Bowman Kidder (1716-1789). Mansfield died on 02 Feb 1781 in Cambridge.[207] Mary died on 05 Jan 1825 in Charlestown.[208]

The children of Mansfield Tapley Jr. and Mary E. Wyeth included:

   i.   MARY[5] "POLLY" TAPLEY, born 06 Mar 1769, Cambridge; married JOSEPH MILLAR there on 03 Dec 1788; died circa 1812, Charlestown.
   ii. ISAAC TAPLEY, born 22 Feb 1771, Cambridge; married NANCY WAYNE, 16 Jan 1794, Boston, Suffolk, Massachusetts; death unknown.
   iii. SARAH TAPLEY, born 04 Jan 1773, Cambridge; died there, 15 Sep 1777.
74. iv. JOHN TAPLEY, born 07 Apr 1774, Cambridge; married LYDIA TUFTS, 03 Nov 1795, Cambridge; died 26 Dec 1847, Charlestown.

42. **NOAH[4] WYETH SR.** (Ebenezer[3] Sr., John[2], Nicholas[1]) was born on 07 Jul 1742 in Cambridge, Middlesex, Massachusetts. He married **ELIZABETH "BETTY" FITCH,** daughter of Benjamin Fitch and Miriam Gray, on 30 Mar 1763 in Lexington, Middlesex, Massachusetts. She was baptized on 14 Jun 1739 in Bedford, Middlesex, Massachusetts. He died of consumption at the age of 69 on 10 Sep 1811 in Cambridge. According to the records of First Church, she died on 05 May 1823 in Cambridge. However, the church listed her as Hepzibah Wyeth.[209]

Noah Wyeth Sr. and Elizabeth "Betty" Fitch had the following children:

75.   i.   (CAPTAIN) NOAH[5] WYETH, born 24 Jun 1763, Cambridge; married HANNAH KIMBLE THOMAS, 25 Dec 1795, New York City, New York County, New York; mariner lost at sea; estate probated 29 Jan 1806.
76.   ii. ELIZABETH WYETH, born 04 Mar 1765, Cambridge; married (1) ANDREW S. NEWELL, 14 Feb 1785, First Church, Cambridge; married (2) SIMEON FAWCETT, 22 Apr 1802, New York City; died there, 13 Apr 1829.
      iii. LYDIA WYETH, born 03 Feb 1766, Cambridge; married NATHANIEL WOODWARD of Watertown, Middlesex, Massachusetts, 26 Sep 1804, Cambridge; died 22 Oct 1843, Watertown.
77.   iv. RHODA WYETH, born 18 May 1768, Cambridge; married ARTEMAS MANNING, 23 Oct 1794, Mason, Hillsborough, New Hampshire; died 17 Feb 1866, Lempster, Sullivan, New Hampshire.
      v.   DORCAS WYETH, born 21 Nov 1770, Cambridge; married SAMUEL HILL JR., 29 Oct 1789, Williamsburg, Hampshire, Massachusetts; died on 19 Jan 1807 in Mason, Hillsborough, New Hampshire.
      vi. ISAAC WYETH, born 10 Feb 1773, Cambridge; died there, 06 Sep 1779.
78.   vii. (CAPTAIN) JOB WYETH, born 14 Jun 1776, Cambridge; married LYDIA CONVERS FRANCIS, 31 Jan 1804, Cambridge; died there, 05 Jun 1840.
79.   viii. JONATHAN WYETH, born 1787, Cambridge (probably informally adopted); married (1) DEBORAH SARGENT, 04 Aug 1811, Malden, Middlesex, Massachusetts; married (2) LUCY STILES circa 1827, Norwich, Windsor, Vermont; [210] married (3) HARRIET THAYER, 03 Jul 1853, Moretown, Washington, Vermont; died 13 Feb 1863, Cambridge.

Notes on the family of Noah Wyeth Sr.:

Noah was a brick maker in Cambridge.[211] His marriage record to Betty Fitch is also recorded as 12 Mar 1763 in Cambridge but that date may have been the banns because the Cambridge records show he and Betty were definitely married in Lexington. Undoubtedly, they were married in 1762 at the end of the double year 1762/1763 since their first child was born on 24 Jun 1763.

Along with his older brothers, Ebenezer Jr. and Jonas, nephew Jonas Jr., and cousin Joseph Wyeth, Noah Wyeth Sr. marched on 19 Apr 1775 as a minuteman on the alarm announcing British troops were advancing to Concord to confiscate the Patriots' supply of ammunition and powder. In that first battle of the Revolutionary War, Noah served as a private in Captain Samuel Thatcher's Company of Colonel Gardner's Regiment of militia. On 27 Sep 1776, Noah was drafted to go to Horse Neck, New York; but, apparently, he paid a fine and Job Littlefield went in his place. He did, however, see other service in the war including guarding prisoners of war at their transfer to Rutland, Massachusetts on 27 Jul 1778.[212]

The family lived on the northwest end of Garden Street at Huron Avenue.[213] Their 1782 home, behind a high privacy fence at 107 Garden Street, is now an apartment building. It apparently sits on Nicholas Wyeth's west-field land on what was called, in 1645, the "highway to the Great Swamp" and the "highway to the Fresh Pond."[214][215] Adjacent Taylor Square used to be called Wyeth Square and the cross street, Huron Avenue, was Wyeth Street.[216]

When he wrote his will in 1807, Noah called himself a yeoman (farmer). Indeed, he must have been for there is a record of his barn burning to the ground on 13 Jul 1791 as a result of a lightning strike. Just the day before, Noah had collected all of his hay into the barn. So, unfortunately, in addition to the barn, the fire consumed 12 tons of English hay.[217] Just a few months before Noah's own death, his cousin Rev. John Wyeth died at Noah's house on 02 Feb 1811.[218]

In his will, written 19 Aug 1807, Noah left his wife Betty all the furniture and the income from his real estate so long as she did not remarry. He left son Job his clock, which Job could not dispose of without Betty's permission. After Betty's death or remarriage, Job was then to pay his sisters, Elizabeth, Lydia and Rhoda, $50 each. $50 was to go to the children of Noah Wyeth deceased. Also, $50 was to go to all of the children of Dorcas in care of her husband, Samuel Hill. The Hill children were Sarah (d. 1873), Dorcas (d. 1793), Samuel III (d.?), Isaac (d. 1830), Lydia (d. 1800), Noah Wyeth (d. 1803), Lydia (d. 1803), Rebecca (d. 1893), and Louisa Hill (d.?). Likely only three of Dorcas' nine children were living at the time of their grandfather Noah's death. The will was presented for probate by Job Wyeth, Gentleman, on 12 Nov 1811.

In no part of Noah Wyeth's will is Jonathan Wyeth mentioned. However, Jonathan apparently fits in this family in some manner because he named his first child Lydia Woodward Wyeth after Noah's daughter, Lydia Wyeth Woodward (sometimes spelled Woodard). The family was used to naming children after in-laws. Case in point, Captain Job's son, Andrew Newell Wyeth Sr., was named for Job's sister Elizabeth's first husband. The name Andrew Newell Wyeth carried through several generations to the 1917 birth of the son of Newell Convers "N. C." Wyeth.

Another link of Jonathan to this family is through his first wife, Deborah Sargent. After their marriage in 1811, they relocated to Vermont. The wife of Noah and Betty Wyeth's grandson, Mary Fillebrown (Mrs. Abiel Wyeth), also married a Sargent from Vermont.

According to his death record, Jonathan was born in Cambridge, so he definitely was a descendant (perhaps adopted) of Nicholas. He is of the age to be a grandchild to Ebenezer Wyeth Jr. and Mary Winship. However, Ebenezer and Mary's descendants were well covered in their daughter Anna Wyeth Cutter's estate distribution and Jonathan was not named in it. He does not seem to fit with descendants of any other Wyeths of the period.

The best guess is Jonathan was adopted by Noah and Betty Wyeth. In the 1800 census, Noah had three boys under age 16 living with him. At that point, Isaac was dead and his brothers were well over 16. Noah's grandsons from his daughters lived out of state in 1800. Thus, Noah obviously had other children living with him and perhaps helping on the farm. They were not legally adopted since such formalities did not occur until 1850.

Jonathan could even have been the son of Lydia Wyeth before she married Nathaniel Woodward in Watertown. As Jonathan lived in Watertown when he married Deborah Sargent in nearby Malden, his residence, as well, links him to the Woodwards. Also, there is a history of taking in children to raise in the Wyeth family. For instance, Lydia Convers Francis was raised by Ebenezer Wyeth Jr. and Mary Winship before she married Captain Job Wyeth.[219]

43. **SARAH[4] WYETH** (Ebenezer[3] Sr., John[2], Nicholas[1]) was born on 02 Apr 1746 in Cambridge, Middlesex, Massachusetts. She married there (1) **TORRY HANCOCK SR.**, son of Solomon Hancock and Mary Torry, on 05 Jul 1774. He was born on 15 Nov 1745 in Cambridge, where he made his living as a bricklayer. When he died of smallpox, this was inscribed on his grave in Cambridge's Old Burying Ground at Harvard Square, "In memory of Mr. Torry Hancock who died 17 Jul 1778 in the 33 year of his age. Now I am gone I can't return, For you once more to see, But it is true that all of you Will soon come after me." Sarah Wyeth Hancock married (2) **DEACON JAMES MUNROE**, son of William Munroe and Rebecca Locke, on 23 Jul 1783 in Cambridge. James was a blacksmith and a deacon in the First Church in Cambridge. The couple lived on Brattle Street near the church. He was born on 12 Dec 1735 in Lexington, Middlesex, Massachusetts and died 14 Sep 1804 in Cambridge.[220] Sarah died from palsy on 31 Mar 1815 in Cambridge.

Torry Hancock Sr. and Sarah Wyeth had the following children:

> i.   JOHN[5] HANCOCK, baptized 22 Oct 1775, Cambridge; died there on 29 Sep 1796 at the age of 22.
> ii.   SOLOMON HANCOCK, born 09 Jul 1776 Cambridge; died there, 06 May 1862.
> iii. SAMUEL HANCOCK, baptized 10 Aug 1777, Cambridge; died there, 01 Sep 1860.
> 80.   iv.   TORREY HANCOCK JR., the record of his baptism at First Church Cambridge reads: "son of widow Sarah whose husband died of smallpox a few months ago, bp. 15 Nov 1778". Torrey married (1) OLIVE ORCUTT, 28 Feb 1805, Cambridge; married (2) ISABELLA RICE, 05 Jun 1811, Wayland, Middlesex, Massachusetts. He died in 1852. Probate Record 33434, dated 18 May 1852, shows his last residence was Cambridge.

Deacon James Munroe and Sarah Wyeth had the following children:

  i.   NATHANIEL⁵ MUNROE, born 07 Mar 1784, Cambridge; died there, 08 Jun 1854.
81. ii. SARAH TAPLEY MUNROE, baptized 21 Aug 1785, Cambridge; married (LT.) PETER COOLIDGE, 28 Jun 1813, Cambridge; died 04 Jan 1823, Framingham, Middlesex, Massachusetts.
  iii. SUSANNAH MUNROE, born 08 Aug 1786, Cambridge; died there unmarried on 13 Apr 1863.
  iv. MARY "POLLY" MUNROE, born 19 Dec 1788, Cambridge; died there unmarried on 16 Sep 1863.

44. **ELIZABETH⁴ WINSHIP** (Elizabeth³ Wyeth, John², Nicholas¹) was born on 24 Mar 1721 in Cambridge, Middlesex, Massachusetts. She married **JASON RUSSELL**, son of Hubbard Russell and Elizabeth Dickson, on 28 Jan 1740 in Cambridge. He was born on 25 Jan 1716 in Cambridge. He was killed by the British Army on 19 Apr 1775 in Menotomy (Arlington), Middlesex, Massachusetts while protecting his home on the first day of the American Revolution. Elizabeth died on 11 Aug 1786 in Menotomy.

The children of Jason Russell and Elizabeth Winship included:

82. i.   JASON⁵ RUSSELL JR., born 07 Mar 1742, Menotomy; married (1) ELIZABETH LOCKE, 28 Oct 1762, Cambridge; served in the Revolution at Bunker Hill and Valley Forge; married (2) LYDIA LORING, 08 Sep 1799, Mason, Hillsborough, New Hampshire; died there, 25 Sep 1825.
  ii. ELIZABETH RUSSELL, born 27 Dec 1743, Menotomy; died there, 29 Mar 1751 at the age of seven.
  iii. JOHN RUSSELL, born 04 Aug 1746, Menotomy; married RUHAMAH FROST there, 31 Aug 1769; died 15 Dec 1832, Mason.[221]
  iv. HUBBARD RUSSELL, born 25 Mar 1749, Menotomy; married SARAH WARREN, 26 May 1774, Cambridge; a Loyalist during the War,[222] Hubbard died 06 Nov 1836, Mason.
  v.   MARY RUSSELL, born circa 1750, Menotomy; died there on 11 Apr 1762 at about 12 years old.
  vi. THOMAS RUSSELL, born 22 Jul 1751 in Menotomy; died on 07 Jun 1809 in West Cambridge (Arlington), Massachusetts.
  vii. NOAH RUSSELL, born 15 Jul 1753 in Menotomy; died there on 13 Oct 1754.
  viii. ELIZABETH RUSSELL, born 03 Jul 1756, Menotomy; married (DEACON) JOTHAM WEBBER, 12 Mar 1778, Cambridge; died 06 Mar 1838, Mason.
  ix. NOAH RUSSELL, born on 08 Mar 1763 in Menotomy; died on 06 Nov 1824 in West Cambridge.

Notes for Elizabeth Winship and Jason Russell:

In 1740, Jason built a sturdy home for his 19-year old bride, Elizabeth. It originally had two rooms, one above the other, with the chimney and staircase on the right-hand side. He constructed the house of solid oak timbers from trees that grew on the Menotomy property.[223]

35 years later, British troops, retreating from the battles at Lexington and Concord, were expected to pass by the Russell home on their return to Boston. For Elizabeth's and youngest child Noah's protection, Jason took them to a neighbor's house that sat atop a nearby hill. Although Jason was 59 and lame, he refused safety for himself, saying "An Englishman's house is his castle" and he returned to defend it.[224]

Near his home, Jason, joined by minutemen from several towns around Menotomy, took part in some of the fiercest fighting on that first day of the American Revolution. Attacked by a British flank guard, Jason and some of the militia fled for cover in Jason's home. Old and slow Jason was in the rear. At his front door, he was shot twice and bayoneted 11 times. The British stumbled over him into the house, killing everyone in sight. Eight Americans made it to the basement and survived by pointing their guns up the stairs. When Elizabeth returned, she found her husband and all of the dead placed side by side in the kitchen. She said the blood in that room was almost ankle deep. The house itself was riddled with bullet holes, many of them still visible yet today.[225]

Jason and Elizabeth Russell's home is now owned by the Arlington Historical Society.

On the same day her husband was killed, Elizabeth's first cousin, Jason Winship Jr., and her first cousin, Lydia Winship's husband, Jabez Wyman, were slaughtered nearby by the British at Cooper's Tavern while celebrating the birth of Jason Winship III. Together with minutemen killed in Menotomy, they were buried together in a mass grave in the town's Old Burying Ground. The inscription on their grave reads, "Erected by the Inhabitants of West Cambridge, A.D. 1848, over the common grave of Jason Russell, Jason Winship, Jabez Wyman and nine others, who were slain in this town by the British Troops on their retreat from the Battles of Lexington and Concord, April 19th, 1775. Being among the first to lay down their lives in the struggle for American Independence."[226]

45. **RUTH⁴ WINSHIP** (Elizabeth³ Wyeth, John², Nicholas¹) was baptized on 24 Oct 1731 in Cambridge, Middlesex, Massachusetts. On 24 Mar 1760, she married **EBENEZER SHED JR.**, son of Ebenezer Shed Sr. and Abigail Ireland, in Cambridge. He was born on 08 Apr 1726 in Charlestown, Suffolk, Massachusetts. Ruth died circa 1777 – many years before her husband's death on 13 Dec 1811 in Cambridge.

Ebenezer Shed Jr. and Ruth Winship had the following children:

   i.   JOHN⁵ SHED, born 09 Dec 1763 in Charlestown; died in 1815 in Boston, Suffolk, Massachusetts. His will was probated 25 Apr 1815.
   ii. ELIZABETH SHED was born on 26 Nov 1770 in Charlestown. She died there unmarried about 1809.
   iii. MARY SHED, born 31 Jul 1772, Charlestown; married WINSLOW DALRYMPLE, 1794; died 16 Apr 1835, probably at her son William Shepard Dalrymple's home in Homer, Cortland, New York.

Notes for Ebenezer Shed Jr. and Ruth Winship:

Ebenezer and Ruth were married after his military service in the French and Indian War. At the start of the Revolutionary War, they lived in Charlestown where the British created £419 of damage to the Shed property, crops, fences and farm goods as they retreated from Lexington on 19 Apr 1775. In the burning of Charlestown, during the battle of Bunker Hill, on 17 Jun 1775, the Shed family suffered additional losses of almost £184.[227]

46. **REV. JOSIAH**[4] **WINSHIP** (Elizabeth[3] Wyeth, John[2], Nicholas[1]), per the records of Harvard College, was born on 21 May 1738 in Cambridge, Middlesex, Massachusetts. He graduated from Harvard University in 1762 and was ordained a minister at Woolwich, Lincoln (Sagadahoc), Maine on 12 Jun 1765. He married (1) **JUDITH GOSS**, daughter of Thomas Goss and Abigail Wade, on 07 Jul 1766 in Bolton, Worcester, Massachusetts. She was born there on 24 Jan 1745. She died on 26 May 1768 in Woolwich. He married (2) **ELIZABETH FORD**, daughter of Cadwallader Ford and Mary Jenkins, on 27 Mar 1780 in Wilmington, Middlesex, Massachusetts. She was born in Wilmington on 20 Mar 1740 and died on 11 Sep 1809 in Woolwich. Josiah died there on 29 Sep 1824.

(Rev.) Josiah Winship and Judith Goss had the following child:

> i. MARY[5] WINSHIP, born 20 May 1767, Woolwich; married (CAPTAIN) SAMUEL REED, son of Jonathan Reed and Keziah Converse, in 1785 in Woolwich; Mary died there, 30 Apr 1825.

(Rev.) Josiah Winship and Elizabeth Ford had the following child:

> ii. JOSIAH[5] WINSHIP JR., born 06 Jun 1781, Woolwich; and died there a few days later on 28 Jun 1781.

47. **THANKFUL**[4] **WINSHIP** (Elizabeth[3] Wyeth, John[2], Nicholas[1]) was born on 14 Mar 1745 in Menotomy (Arlington), Middlesex, Massachusetts. Thankful married Deacon Robert Stinson on 16 Apr 1780 in Woolwich, Lincoln (Sagadahoc), Maine. **ROBERT STINSON**, son of Elder Thomas Stinson and Catherine Carr, was born 17 Aug 1736 in Georgetown, Sagadahoc, Maine. He died on 06 Nov 1808 at the age of 72 in Woolwich. Thankful was almost 87 at her death on 25 Jan 1832 in Georgetown.

Robert Stinson and Thankful Winship had the following children:

> i. JOHN[5] WINSHIP STINSON was born on 19 Sep 1781 in Woolwich, Lincoln (Sagadahoc), Maine; died 30 Mar 1832 in Woolwich.
> ii. THANKFULL STINSON, born 04 May 1785, Woolwich; married ISAAC SMITH there, 31 Jan 1805. She died 13 Sep 1826 in Belfast, Waldo, Maine. Isaac died on 21 Aug 1871 at age 90. Thankfull and Isaac are buried in the old section of Grove Cemetery, Belfast.
> iii. FANNY STINSON, born 05 Aug 1788, Woolwich; died there, 25 Aug 1845.
> iv. INDIANA STINSON was born on 15 Oct 1790 in Woolwich and died there a few weeks later on 11 Nov 1790.

48. **NATHANIEL**[4] **GAMAGE** (Deborah[3] Wyeth, William[2], Nicholas[1]) was baptized on 01 Mar 1712/1713 in Cambridge, Middlesex, Massachusetts. He married **MARY NORWOOD**, daughter of Joshua Norwood and Elizabeth Andrews, on 23 May 1734 in Gloucester, Essex, Massachusetts. Mary was born at Gap Head in the Sandy Bay (Rockport) area of Gloucester, Essex, Massachusetts on 15 Apr 1717. Circa 1750, Nathaniel mysteriously disappeared. He apparently was seized by a press gang and forcibly taken to serve in the English Navy.[228] Of three death records for Mary, it appears most likely she died on 04 Mar 1821 at age 103 in Bristol, Lincoln, Maine.

Nathaniel Gamage and Mary Norwood had the following children:

      i. MARY[5] GAMAGE, baptized 23 Feb 1735, Cambridge; death unknown.[229]

      ii. HANNAH GAMAGE, born 09 Aug 1736, Attleboro, Bristol, Massachusetts; married JOHN GOTT, 23 Jan 1754, Gloucester, Essex, Massachusetts; died there, 18 Sep 1762.

83.   iii. BETTY GAMAGE, born 11 May 1738, Attleboro; married NEHEMIAH GROVER JR., 21 Feb 1755, Fifth Parish, Sandy Bay (Rockport) area of Gloucester; died after 1800, Gloucester.

      iv. NATHANIEL GAMAGE JR., born 01 Mar 1740, Attleboro; married SARAH PLATTS, 27 Nov 1759, Gloucester (banns 22 Sep 1759); death unknown.

84.   v. JOSHUA GAMAGE, baptized 03 Jan 1741/1742, Cambridge;[230] married ELINOR FOSTER, 27 Dec 1764, Fifth Parish, Sandy Bay (Rockport) area of Gloucester; death unknown, but likely after 1810 in Bristol, Lincoln, Maine.

      vi. RUTH GAMAGE, baptized 25 Dec 1743, Cambridge;[231] married (1) SAMUEL TARR, 09 Sep 1760, Gloucester; married (2) JOHN TURNER, 21 Jan 1772, Fifth Parish at Sandy Bay; death unknown.

85.   vii. JOHN GAMAGE, baptized 12 Jan 1746, Cambridge;[232] married ANNA GOTT, 15 Aug 1765, Fifth Parish at Sandy Bay; died 23 Apr 1824, Sandy Bay.

      viii. REBECCA GAMAGE, baptized 23 Oct 1748, Cambridge;[233] married SOLOMON NORWOOD, 02 Nov 1766, Gloucester; died there, circa 1788.

86.   ix. SARAH GAMAGE, baptized 15 Sep 1751, Third Parish of Gloucester at Annisquam, Essex, Massachusetts; married WILLIAM GOTT V, 27 Apr 1769, Fifth Parish at Sandy Bay; died 17 Apr 1810, Starks, Somerset, Maine.[234]

Notes on the family of Nathaniel Gamage and Mary Norwood:

When Mary Norwood was born, Gloucester's boundaries originally included the colony of Sandy Bay on Cape Ann. Mary's grandfather, Francis Norwood, and her father, Joshua, were some of the earliest settlers of the area. Joshua owned land near present day Halibut State Park as well as near Straitsmouth Island at Gap Head.[235]

For a time, Joshua Norwood lived in Attleboro. On their way south, the Norwoods stopped in Cambridge where Mary had found employment as a servant.[236] As shown by the baptism of their first child, for the first year of their marriage, Mary

Sunset 06 Aug 2018 at the Lobster Pool Restaurant by Halibut Park. Minus the motor boat, Mary Norwood would have seen this same sunset 280 years ago.

and Nathaniel Gamage made their home in Cambridge with his parents, Joshua and Deborah Wyeth Gamage. It appears they then moved south of Boston to Attleboro circa 1736 with his parents. The whole family was in Attleboro in 1738 when Nathaniel was made administrator of his father Joshua Gamage's Attleboro estate.[237] Mary's father, Joshua Norwood, was also in Attleboro as he was mentioned in Gamage probate documents.

After the estate was settled in 1740, Nathaniel and Mary moved back to Cambridge. In 1743/44 they tried to settle in Watertown, but were cautioned against it.[238] Then in 1750, Nathaniel went to England to settle an estate and mysteriously vanished.[239] The family could find no reason for his disappearance other than Nathaniel Sr. was forcibly recruited into the British Navy.[240] Abducting men for military service in Great Britain started in the mid-17th century. It continued into the 19th century and was one of the causes of the War of 1812.

Based on the baptism date of youngest child, Sarah, Mary returned to Sandy Bay in about 1751. She was described as a "small but very active woman, intelligent and quick witted. She had bright, black eyes and dark hair that never turned gray." Mary supported her family as a midwife and as church sexton of Sandy Bay's Fifth Parish.[241] For her services, the church paid her 9 shillings and 4 pence ($1.55) a year.[242] The church split off from the First Parish of Gloucester on 13 Feb 1755.[243] Not until 1840 would the Sandy Bay area of Gloucester be set off in the separate town of Rockport.[244]

Soon after 1795, Mary moved with her son Joshua to Bristol, Lincoln, Maine.[245] There are three death records for her death there. The most likely date is 04 Mar 1821 at age 103. Another record says she was 97 years of age and another indicates she was 105. The Norwoods were noted for their longevity. Indications are Mary may have held the record for living the longest in the Norwood family.[246]

49. **WILLIAM*4* GAMAGE** (Deborah*3* Wyeth, William*2*, Nicholas*1*) born 21 Feb 1714, Cambridge, Middlesex, Massachusetts. Per the records of First Church, he was baptized on 27 Feb 1714. His intention to marry **ABIGAIL COOK**, daughter of Stephen Cook and Hannah Fuller, was published on 16 Jun 1746 and they married on 01 Aug 1746 in Boston, Suffolk, Massachusetts. She was born on 02 Aug 1721 in Watertown, Middlesex, Massachusetts and it was there the couple settled. William served as an Ensign in 1763 in a Middlesex Regiment at the end of the French and Indian War (Seven Years' War). In 1765 he was promoted to lieutenant.[247] He died on 21 Dec 1783, presumably in Cambridge. Abigail married Dr. Ephraim Ware, 13 Oct 1785 in Cambridge. She died on 21 Dec 1803 at her son John's house in New York City.

The children of William Gamage and Abigail Cook included the following:

      i. WILLIAM*5* GAMAGE M.D. was born on 24 Feb 1748 in Watertown. He graduated from Harvard in 1767 and went on to use his medical expertise to great extent during the War for Independence. He married LUCY WATSON on 21 Oct 1784 in Cambridge. Their son, Nathaniel (1793-1823), served in the military during the War of 1812 in Lt. G. King's Company of Lt. Col. P. Osgood's Boston Regiment.[248] On 01 Jan 1821, at age 72, while on his way to see a patient, Dr. Gamage was killed by a sleigh without bells on it near his home on Garden Street at the corner of Appian Way in Cambridge.[249]

    ii. SAMUEL GAMAGE, born 25 Aug 1751, Watertown. During the American Revolution, he served as a lieutenant in Captain Gray's regiment of artillery and served one year as a lieutenant of Marines on board the frigate *Dean*. He died on 04 Aug 1832 in Hudson, Columbia, New York.[250]

    iii. JOSHUA GAMAGE was born on 17 Jan 1753 in Cambridge. He settled in Fryeburg, Maine while serving the army during the American Revolution. He married HANNAH GORDON on 23 Apr 1826, Fryeburg. Having been a drummer in Col. Gardner's Regiment at Bunker Hill, he died on 24 Jun 1843, at the age of 90, due to the excitement of attending the dedicatory services of the Bunker Hill Monument in Charlestown, Suffolk, Massachusetts.[251]

    iv. DANIEL GAMAGE, born in Mar 1755, Cambridge; died young.

    v. ABIGAIL GAMAGE, born 28 May 1759 and baptized 03 Jun 1759 in Cambridge, was the second child of the same name. Her sister was born in 1750 and probably died as an infant. Abigail did marry as she was called "Mrs. Abigail Byles of New York City" when her brother Daniel mentioned her in his 1791 will.[252]

    vi. DANIEL GAMAGE was born 04 May 1761 in Cambridge. His service as a soldier in the Revolution included Sep 1781 to Jan 1782 at West Point. He was reported on fatigue duty in Oct and Nov 1781. The last record of his military career showed him sick in a garrison hospital. He called himself a mariner when he wrote his will on 20 Aug 1791. It was probated on 07 May 1792 in Boston, Suffolk, Massachusetts.

    vii. JOHN GAMAGE, M.D., born in Mar 1765 in Cambridge; died on 11 Oct 1816 at the age of 51 in New Utrecht on Long Island, New York (which today is Bensonhurst, Brooklyn, New York).

50. **SARAH**[4] **GAMAGE** (Deborah[3] Wyeth, William[2], Nicholas[1]) was born on 01 Sep 1721 and baptized on 10 Sep 1721 in Cambridge, Middlesex, Massachusetts. She married **STEPHEN PALMER JR.**, son of Stephen Palmer Sr. and Sarah Grant, on 17 Jan 1750 in Cambridge. He was baptized on 12 Oct 1718 in Cambridge. She died on 15 Mar 1794 in Cambridge. He died there on 30 Mar 1806.

The children of Stephen Palmer Jr. and Sarah Gamage included:

    i. STEPHEN[5] PALMER III, born 09 Jan 1753, Cambridge; a year after moving from Cambridge, Stephen drowned 01 Sep 1781, Fryeburg, Oxford, Maine.

51. **JOHN**[4] **GAMAGE** (Deborah[3] Wyeth, William[2], Nicholas[1]) was born on 14 Feb 1724 in Cambridge. He married **AGNES DICK** about 1749 in New York. He died intestate on 09 May 1772 in Shrewsbury, Monmouth, New Jersey.

John Gamage and Agnes Dick had the following child:

    i. WILLIAM DICK[5] GAMAGE, born circa 1750; died at sea on 02 Apr 1793 near Bengal, India.

52. **MARTHA**^{4} **GAMAGE** (Deborah^3 Wyeth, William^2, Nicholas^1) was baptized 17 Apr 1726 in Cambridge, Middlesex, Massachusetts.[253] She married (1) **DANIEL PARKHURST**, son of George Parkhurst and Tabitha Whitney, on 06 Nov 1746 in Waltham, Middlesex, Massachusetts. He was born on 11 Feb 1726/7 in Weston, Middlesex, Massachusetts.[254] He died in 1769 in Weston. She married (2) **JOHN HAGAR** on 11 Oct 1770 in Weston.[255] Martha was mentioned in the sale of her mother's real estate on 18 Jun 1773. She died after that date – probably in Weston.[256]

Daniel Parkhurst and Martha Gamage had the following children:

    i. MARTHA^5 PARKHURST was born on 28 Dec 1747 in Weston.[257] Find-a-Grave #139134784 gives her death in Richmond, Berkshire, Massachusetts prior to 1782 when her husband, ISRAEL LEADBETTER, remarried.

    ii. RUTH PARKHURST, born 29 Jan 1749, Weston; died there on 10 Apr 1769.

    iii. CATHERINE PARKHURST, born 15 Dec 1752; baptized on 07 Jan 1753, Weston;[258] married REUBEN WILLARD, 03 Jan 1775, Harvard, Worcester, Massachusetts; died 17 Aug 1838, Channahon, Will, Illinois.

    iv. (MAJOR) DANIEL PARKHURST, born 08 May 1755, Cambridge; died 17 Jul 1810 at the age of 55 in Hubbardston, Worcester, Massachusetts.

    v. GEORGE PARKHURST, baptized 25 Jun 1758, Cambridge; death unknown.

53. **RUTH**^{4} **FESSENDEN** (Martha^3 Wyeth, William^2, Nicholas^1) was born on 28 Jun 1717 in Cambridge, Middlesex, Massachusetts. (There is a record of her birth in Lexington, too.) She married **JOHN HUNT**, son of Samuel Hunt and Mary Langdon, on 02 Nov 1738 in Boston, Suffolk, Massachusetts. He was born on 19 Nov 1716 in Boston and died on 19 Jan 1777 in Watertown, Middlesex, Massachusetts. Ruth died there in Jan of 1801.

John Hunt and Ruth Fessenden had the following children:

    i. MARY "POLLY"^{5} HUNT, born 21 Jan 1740, Watertown; married RICHARD PERKINS, 18 Jun 1781, Boston; died 19 Apr 1806, Bridgewater, Plymouth, Massachusetts.

    ii. KATHERINE HUNT, born 03 May 1742, Watertown; died young.

    iii. KATHERINE HUNT, born 10 May 1744, Watertown; died young.

    iv. SAMUEL HUNT, born 25 Oct 1745, Watertown; died on 08 Oct 1816 at the age of 71 in Lexington, Fayette, Kentucky.

    v. JOHN HUNT JR., born 16 Jan 1747 in Watertown; died 18 Dec 1824.

    vi. RUTH HUNT, born on 21 Aug 1748 in Watertown; died on 30 Nov 1778 at the age of 30 in Pomfret, Windham, Connecticut.

    vii. WILLIAM HUNT, born 12 Jan 1750, Watertown; graduated Harvard, 1768; married JANE BETHUNE on 15 Nov 1787 in Boston; died 10 Nov 1804 at the age of 54 in Boston. William and Jane were the grandparents of Mary Bethune Craig, the wife of General Henry Jackson Hunt (1819-1889) who was the grandson of Colonel Thomas Hunt.

    viii. KATHERINE "KATE" HUNT, born 01 Oct 1751, Watertown; died unmarried on 26 Feb 1814 in Boston.

87.   ix. (COLONEL) THOMAS HUNT, born on 17 Sep 1754 in Watertown; married

EUNICE WELLINGTON on 16 Aug 1788 in Watertown; died on 16 Aug 1808, Fort Bellefontaine, Missouri.

88.   x.   ELIZABETH "BETSY" HUNT, born 01 Oct 1755, Watertown; married JOSEPH PEARSE PALMER, 02 Nov 1772, Sanborn's Tavern, Hampton, Rockingham, New Hampshire;[259] died at her daughter Mary Palmer Tyler's home on 08 Jan 1838 in Brattleboro, Windham, Vermont.

        xi.   SARAH "SALLY" HUNT, born 17 Oct 1756, Watertown; died there unmarried, circa 1805.

      xii.   EPHRAIM HUNT, born on 05 Nov 1758 in Watertown. He died 02 Nov 1805 in Albany, Albany County, New York.

Notes for the family of John Hunt and Ruth Fessenden:

While a student at Harvard, John observed a group of girls having fun rolling down a hill. Because the exposed stockings and undergarments of one were so nice, he believed she would be a good housekeeper and resolved to make her his wife. Perhaps embarrassed, Ruth, nevertheless agreed to the match. They settled in Watertown where John established himself as a merchant and later a distillery owner.

The family became quite wealthy and gave their sons a fine education. Some graduated from Harvard.[260] However, a sign of the times, the Hunt daughters could barely read or write. Father John Hunt believed it sufficient for women to be able to "make a shirt and a pudding." That adage became quite a problem when Elbridge Gerry became enamored with Katherine. The romance soon faded since she could not read or respond to his love letters. Elbridge went on to marry someone else and afterward became a key person in the framing of the United States Constitution. Kate remained unmarried until the end of her days.[261]

The lack of education did not extend to John and Ruth's granddaughter Elizabeth "Eliza" Palmer and her three daughters… one founded the first English Kindergarten; one a writer, married Horace Mann; another, an artist, married Nathaniel Hawthorne.[262] Eliza's mother, Elizabeth "Betsy" Hunt, had been schooled by Joseph Pearse Palmer before they married. Although Joseph was Harvard educated, he came from a family where the education of women was valued.[263]

54. **MARTHA[4] FESSENDEN** (Martha[3] Wyeth, William[2], Nicholas[1]) was born on 29 Feb 1719/20 in Cambridge, Middlesex, Massachusetts. She married **JOHN CHENEY**, son of Benjamin Cheney and Mary Harbert, 23 Sep 1738 in Cambridge. John was born there in 1715 and died 1758 in Roxbury, Suffolk, Massachusetts. Martha's will was probated in Roxbury on 18 Mar 1781.[264]

The children of John Cheney and Martha Fessenden included:

        i.   MARY[5] CHENEY, baptized 18 Mar 1744, Cambridge; married BENJAMIN COTTERELL, 26 Nov 1765, Roxbury; death unknown.

       ii.   (LT.) THOMAS CHENEY, born 20 May 1751, Roxbury; served in the Revolution and the War of 1812; died 20 May 1835 at the age of 84 in Southbridge, Worcester, Massachusetts.

      iii.   LUCY CHENEY, born 09 Jan 1755, Roxbury; death unknown.

"History does not move you more than when

it's in the iron of your own blood."

~ J.R. Thompkins

55. **JOSIAH**[5] **STEARNS SR.** (Abigail[4] Fiske, John[3] Fiske, Sarah[2] Wyeth, Nicholas[1]) was born on 14 Oct 1704 in Watertown, Middlesex, Massachusetts. He married (1) **SUSANNA BALL**, daughter of James Ball Sr. and Elizabeth Fiske, on 31 Dec 1729 in Watertown. She was born there on 16 Mar 1708 and died there about 1740. He married (2) **DOROTHY PRENTICE**, daughter of John Prentice and Prudence Foster, in 1741, in Watertown. She was born circa 1717 in Lancaster, Worcester, Massachusetts and died circa 1750 in Watertown. He married (3) **MARY BOWMAN**, daughter of Deacon Samuel Bowman and Rebecca Andrews (granddaughter of Thomas Andrews Sr. and Rebecca Parks), on 23 Apr 1752 in Watertown. She was born on 14 Aug 1706 in Cambridge, Middlesex, Massachusetts. He died on 11 Apr 1756 at the age of 51 in Watertown. Widow Mary Bowman Stearns and son Phinehas Stearns were administrators of his will #21279.

The children of Josiah Stearns Sr. and Susanna Ball included:

    i.   JOSIAH[6] STEARNS JR., born 11 Jul 1730, Watertown; died on 21 Jan 1802 in Wilmington, Windham, Vermont.

    ii. SUSANNA STEARNS, born 14 Sep 1731 in Watertown; died young.

    iii. JOHN STEARNS was born on 08 May 1733 in Watertown. He died on 16 Oct 1804 in Bethel, Oxford, Maine.

    iv. (CAPTAIN) PHINEHAS STEARNS was born on 05 Feb 1736 in Watertown. He served in the French and Indian War, was in the Boston Tea Party, was promoted to captain during the Battle of Lexington and Concord and commanded militia during the siege of Boston.[265] He married three times. With his first wife, MARY WELLINGTON, he had several children including Susan Stearns who married Major Jonas Wyeth. Captain Stearns died on 27 Mar 1798 at the age of 62 in Watertown.

89.   v. (DEACON) JONAS STEARNS, born 27 Feb 1738, Watertown; married SUBMIT DAVIS, 14 May 1758, Lunenburg, Worcester, Massachusetts; died 13 Sep 1782, Chesterfield, Cheshire, New Hampshire.

56. **SAMUEL**[5] **FISKE JR.** (Samuel[4], William[3], Sarah[2] Wyeth, Nicholas[1]) was born on 02 Nov 1741 in Waltham, Middlesex, Massachusetts. He married **ABIGAIL WHITE**, daughter of Andrew White and Jane Dix, on 29 Oct 1761 in Waltham. She was born in 1738 in Watertown. He died there on 30 Apr 1792. She died about 1829 in Waltham.

The children of Samuel Fiske Jr. and Abigail White included:

90.   i.   FRANCIS[6] FISKE, born 24 Aug 1772, Waltham, Middlesex, Massachusetts; married SARAH LIVERMORE, 21 Oct 1798, Waltham; died 15 Feb 1856, Saugus, Essex, Massachusetts.

57. **(LT.) WILLIAM**[5] **CUTTER** (Martha[4] Bowman, Deborah[3] Wyeth, John[2], Nicholas[1]) was born on 14 Apr 1748 in Menotomy (Arlington), Middlesex, Massachusetts. He married **RUTH HARRINGTON** on 11 May 1780 in Cambridge, Middlesex, Massachusetts. He died on 09 Oct 1788 in Menotomy. His children are mentioned in his will #5645-5738. (He

apparently was called Lieutenant due to his wealth. There was another Lieutenant Cutter in Captain Walton's Company, born 1759 and died 1846.)

(Lt.) William Cutter and Ruth Harrington had the following children:

    i. WILLIAM[6] CUTTER, baptized 03 Jun 1781 in Menotomy; death unknown.
    ii. HENRY CUTTER, born about 1783 in Menotomy; death unknown.
    iii. RUTH CUTTER, born about 1785 in Menotomy; death unknown.

58. **NEHEMIAH[5] CUTTER** (Martha[4] Bowman, Deborah[3] Wyeth, John[2], Nicholas[1]) was born on 03 Jun 1753 in Menotomy (Arlington), Middlesex, Massachusetts. Nehemiah Cutter and Deborah Hill were married on 30 Oct 1781 in Cambridge, Middlesex, Massachusetts. **DEBORAH HILL**, daughter of Zechariah Hill and Rebecca Cutter, was born on 16 Jul 1756 in Menotomy. Nehemiah's military service from 05 Jan 1777 to 01 Mar 1777, as a private in Captain John Minott's Company, Col. Dike's Regiment, was credited to the town of Cambridge. Deborah died in 1824 in West Cambridge (Arlington), Middlesex, Massachusetts. Nehemiah died there, 03 May 1828 at age 74.

The children of Nehemiah Cutter and Deborah Hill included:

91.   i. ELIJAH[6] CUTTER, born 17 Mar 1788, Menotomy (Arlington), Middlesex, Massachusetts; married ABIGAIL HILL, 04 Jan 1818, West Cambridge (Arlington), Middlesex, Massachusetts; died 17 May 1885, Arlington, Middlesex, Massachusetts. It is interesting to note that Elijah lived in Arlington through all of its name changes.

59. **(CAPTAIN) JOSHUA[5] BOWMAN** (Noah[4] Bowman, Deborah[3] Wyeth, John[2], Nicholas[1]) was born on 17 Feb 1747 in Cambridge, Middlesex, Massachusetts. He married **ABIGAIL FOWLE**, daughter of Edmund Fowle and Abigail Whitney, on 09 Apr 1767 in Watertown, Middlesex, Massachusetts. She was born on 11 Nov 1745 in Watertown. Her death apparently was before her husband's because after Joshua died on 30 Mar 1780 while fighting in the American Revolution, their son was brought up by his grandparents, Noah Bowman and Hannah Winship.[266]

Captain Joshua Bowman and Abigail Fowle had the following child:

92.   i. NATHANIEL[6] BOWMAN, born on 18 Mar 1768, Cambridge. Like his father, Nathaniel also graduated from Harvard.[267] He married SARAH "SALLY" JOHNSON, 13 Oct 1789, Andover, Essex, Massachusetts. Nathaniel died on 08 Jun 1797 in Gorham, Cumberland, Maine when part of a steeple fell on him at the raising of a meetinghouse.

Notes on Captain Joshua Bowman:

Joshua and his sister Hannah's husband, Nicholas Pike, graduated from Harvard in 1766. Joshua served as a captain of Dragoons in the Continental Army.[268] On 29 Mar 1780 with Lt. Gen. Charles Cornwallis' troops approaching Gibbes Plantation in Charleston County, South

Carolina, several Patriot units were put together to stop the British advance. After a series of attacks and counterattacks, the advancing guard of the enemy came within two miles of Charlestown. To repel them, a party of 200 men went out to skirmish the force until sunset. The next day, 30 Mar 1780, a large body of British grenadiers and infantry crossed the Ashley River. While attempting to stop the British, Captain Bowman was shot from his horse. At the same time, a major and two privates were wounded. The British loss was reported to be from 12 to 16 killed. The Harvard graduate is often confused with another North Carolinian captain of the same name who was killed at Ramsour's Mill on 20 Jun 1780.[269]

60. **JOSEPH**[5] **WYETH** (Jonathan[4] Jr., Jonathan[3], John[2], Nicholas[1]) was of the first of two sets of twins born to Jonathan and Sarah Wilson Wyeth in Cambridge, Middlesex, Massachusetts. Sarah was pregnant only two times but gave birth to four children… Joseph and Jonathan in Jul 1751 and ten years later, to Sarah and Hepzibah. The births were so rare their details were published in the Boston newspapers in 1761.[270] Joseph and his twin, Jonathan, were baptized together on 26 Jul 1751 at First Church in Cambridge. Joseph married **EUNICE BATHRICK**, daughter of John Bathrick Jr. and Mary Hastings on 17 Jan 1775. The marriage was published on 30 Dec 1774 in Boston. Eunice Bathrick was born on 26 Feb 1755 in Cambridge. She died on 16 Jan 1830 at the age of 74 and Joseph died 13 Oct 1837 at the age of 86 in the Shakers' Square House, Harvard, Worcester, Massachusetts.

Joseph Wyeth and Eunice Bathrick had the following children:

93.   i.   JONATHAN[6] WYETH SR., born about 1775, Cambridge; married (1) ELIZABETH "BETSY" WARREN, 03 Dec 1799, Littleton, Middlesex, Massachusetts; married (2) EMMA KEMP, 02 Jun 1829, Townsend, Middlesex, Massachusetts; died 27 Feb 1847, Townsend.

94.   ii.   ABIGAIL EMELINE WYETH, born about 1776, Cambridge; married JOHN ROBBINS, 02 Oct 1798, Groton, Middlesex, Massachusetts; died 13 May 1824, Charlestown, Suffolk, Massachusetts.

           iii.   ELIZABETH WYETH, born about 1777 in Cambridge; died in 1795 in Harvard, Worcester, Massachusetts.

95.   iv.   EUNICE PAMELA WYETH, born about 1781, Cambridge; married STEPHEN TEMPLE, 15 Mar 1807, Littleton; died 27 Sep 1839, Poor House, Groton.

Notes for Joseph Wyeth and Eunice Bathrick:

Joseph fought as a minuteman alongside his Wyeth cousins in Colonel Gardner's Regiment just after the battles of Lexington and Concord. He entered at Lincoln, Massachusetts on 19 Apr 1775 to skirmish in Parker's Revenge against the British as they made their way back to Boston. Additionally, he served many times in Captain John Walton's Company as well as a stint with General Heath in Nov 1778.

After meeting Ann Lee, the founder of the United Believers in Christ's Second Appearing, Eunice Bathrick Wyeth became a devoted follower. The sect is better known by the irreverent name "Shakers," a term given to them by non-believers who observed their practice of whirling and trembling to "shake off" the sins of the world in their jubilant dance-filled meetings. The basic tenets of Shakerism were celibacy, communal life, and confession of sin. They also believed in separation from the world, equality of the races and genders, and pacifism.[271]

Eunice convinced Joseph to buy land from fellow Shaker Solomon Cooper of Groton. In 1785, after purchasing 12 acres in Groton for $168, Joseph Wyeth moved his family, along with Eunice's parents, John and Mary Bathrick, from Cambridge to be closer to the Shakers.[272] Census statistics from 1790 to 1810 back up their Groton residence. Joseph's aunt, Deborah Wyeth Prentice, who apparently joined the Shakers in 1781, may have also influenced the relocation.[273]

Eunice lived in the Square House in Harvard, Worcester, Massachusetts in 1791 until she was forced to leave the house in 1793 when Joseph was having difficulty caring for their crippled daughter, Elizabeth, on his own. During her time in the Square House and at her own home, Eunice, proved to be a prolific writer of Shaker songs and hymns. Many of the over 600 pieces she composed were well known among the Shakers and appeared in a variety of manuscript collections.

For his part, Joseph embraced a celibate life but was in and out of the church until his final commitment in 1824. In 1829, the year before Eunice's death, Joseph sold his 20-acre estate and 14 acres of forest to the Shaker Church family trustees for $200.[274]

Jack E. Boucher's public domain photograph of the south (front) elevation of the Shaker Church Family Square House, Shaker Road, Harvard, Worcester County, MA. Photo is courtesy of the Library of Congress.

Both Eunice and Joseph died in the Harvard Shaker Square House and are buried nearby in the community's cemetery.[275]

202

61. **BEULAH⁵ PRENTICE** (Deborah⁴ Wyeth, Jonathan³, John², Nicholas¹) was born circa 1761 in Cambridge, Middlesex, Massachusetts. She married **TIMOTHY TUFTS JR.**, son of Timothy Tufts and Anna Adams, there on 09 May 1784. He was born on 17 Jun 1762 in Charlestown, Suffolk, Massachusetts. She was about 34 when she died of the postpartum infection, puerperal fever, after the birth of her sixth child, on 30 Oct 1795 in Charlestown. Timothy Tufts Jr. died on 03 Oct 1802 in Cambridge.

The children of Timothy Tufts Jr. and Beulah Prentice included:

    i. MARY⁶ PRENTICE TUFTS was born on 03 Mar 1785 in Lynnfield, Essex, Massachusetts; died on 02 Nov 1853 in Cambridge.

    ii. TIMOTHY TUFTS III, baptized 24 Sep 1786, Cambridge; died in Mar 1839 in Charlestown.

    iii. ARTEMAS TUFTS, baptized 31 Aug 1788, Lynnfield; died in May 1854 in Gallatin, Sumner, Tennessee.

    iv. WILLIAM TUFTS, baptized 01 May 1791, Lynnfield; died 06 Aug 1793.

    v. ANNA TUFTS, baptized 10 Nov 1793, Cambridge; died a few months later on 08 Sep 1794.

    vi. WILLIAM TUFTS, baptized 13 Sep 1795, Cambridge; died there, 13 May 1796.

62. **NATHAN⁵ FESSENDEN** (Hannah⁴ Prentice, Hannah³ Wyeth, John², Nicholas¹) was born on 10 Apr 1749 in Lexington, Middlesex, Massachusetts. He married **SARAH WINSHIP**, daughter of Isaac Winship and Hannah Durant, on 17 Oct 1771 in Lexington. She was born there on 13 May 1753. He died on 24 Apr 1797 in Lexington. She also died in Lexington, in 1809.

The children of Nathan Fessenden and Sarah Winship included:

96.   i. NATHAN⁶ FESSENDEN JR., born 25 Apr 1772, Lexington; married JANE GOODRICH, 21 Jun 1801, Roxbury, Suffolk, Massachusetts; died 24 Jan 1866, Lexington.

63. **EBENEZER⁵ WYETH III** (Ebenezer⁴ Jr., Ebenezer³ Sr., John², Nicholas¹) was born on 17 Dec 1752 in Watertown, Middlesex, Massachusetts. He married (1) **ELIZABETH WINSHIP**, the widow of Joseph Green, on 03 May 1777 in Cambridge. Elizabeth, the daughter of (Captain) Joseph Winship and Elizabeth Lathrop, was born on 29 Jul 1756 in Norwich, New London, Connecticut. She died on 25 Jan 1799, probably near the Town of Union, Tioga (Broome), New York. He married (2) **NAOMI RUSSELL**, the widow of Abraham Cooke, circa Mar 1800 (intention filed 01 Mar 1800) in Cambridge. Naomi, daughter of Patten Russell and Mary Dickson, was born on 25 Jan 1759 in Menotomy (Arlington), Middlesex, Massachusetts. He died on 30 Dec 1836 in Ashby, Middlesex, Massachusetts. Naomi died on 28 Jul 1842, of consumption, in Chelsea, Suffolk, Massachusetts.

Ebenezer Wyeth III and Elizabeth Winship had the following children:

    i. EBENEZER⁶ WYETH IV, baptized 17 May 1778, Cambridge; died unmarried 14 Dec 1813 at age 35 in Westford, Middlesex, Massachusetts.[276]

97.   ii.   WILLIAM W. WYETH, baptized 23 Jan 1780, Cambridge; married ZERUAH WAIT, 19 Jul 1807, Chester, Hampden, Massachusetts; died on 22 Aug 1810, Chester.

        iii.   JOSEPH WYETH was baptized on 29 Jul 1781 in Cambridge. He apparently died before his half-brother, Joseph, was born in 1806. The elder Joseph may have been the crew member who died on 09 May 1803 while serving under master William Waters on the brig *Fame of Philadelphia* bound for Curacao. Maritime records describe him as from Massachusetts, age 22, 5'6", light complexion, brown hair, and blue eyes.[277]

98.   iv.   ELIZABETH WYETH, born Mar 1783, Menotomy (Arlington), Middlesex, Massachusetts; married SOLOMON PRENTICE JR., 15 Apr 1803 in Menotomy; died 20 Feb 1808, West Cambridge (Arlington), Middlesex, Massachusetts.

99.   v.   MARY WYETH, born 1785, Connecticut; married SAMUEL BELLOWS, 27 Mar 1809, West Cambridge (Arlington); died 19 Mar 1860, Cambridge.

        vi.   ABBEY WYETH, born about 1789, New York; married WILLIAM KLINE, 27 May 1830. Her cousin (Charles) Augustus Wyeth witnessed the wedding in the Silver Spring Presbyterian Church, Silver Spring Township, Cumberland, Pennsylvania.[278] She died 09 Apr 1840, Harrisburg, Dauphin, Pennsylvania. Her death notice in the *National Gazette*, confirmed her father's name.[279] William died 22 Apr 1869 at the age of 71 in Harrisburg.

Mary Wyeth Bellows' monument on Asclepia Path, Lot 2187, Mt. Auburn Cemetery, Cambridge, MA.

100.   vii.   STEPHEN WYETH, born circa 1791, probably in Union, Tioga (Broome), New York; married SARAH ANN WRIGHT, 10 Dec 1815, Cambridge; died at age 92 on 05 Apr 1883 in Foster, Providence, Rhode Island (or a few miles away in Killingly, Windham, Connecticut.)

Ebenezer Wyeth III and Naomi Russell had the following children:

101.   i.   LUCY[6] WYETH, born 17 Aug 1802, Littleton; married CALVIN HODGMAN, 25 May 1828, Watertown; died in Jun 1845, Edwardsville, Madison, Illinois.[280]

102.   ii.   CATHERINE W. WYETH, born 17 Oct 1803, Littleton; married JALEL GATHLEED BAKER, 23 May 1824, Watertown; died 22 Mar 1883, Waltham, Middlesex, Massachusetts.

103.   iii.   JOSEPH RUSSELL WYETH, born 03 Jul 1806, Littleton; married EMELINE JONES, 22 Apr 1834, Boston; died 25 Mar 1870, Chelsea.

Notes for Ebenezer Wyeth III:

Ebenezer III was born in Watertown, whereas the rest of his siblings were born in Cambridge. The family did not move, the town line moved. Shortly after Ebenezer's birth, his father and several neighbors petitioned to have the Watertown border changed so they could continue to attend church in Cambridge.[281] On 24 Dec 1752, like his father, grandfather and great grandfather, Ebenezer III was baptized in the First Church of Cambridge.

Ebenezer's birth put him at the prime age to fight in the American Revolutionary War. With brothers Joshua and Jonas, Ebenezer enlisted in the Massachusetts Line of the Continental Establishment in Nov 1775.[282] While serving for over a year in Captain Eliphalet Newell's Company of Colonel Henry Knox's Regiment of Artillery, the three brothers fought in New York battles on Long Island and at White Plains.[283] Ebenezer was discharged from military service while hospitalized in Bedford, Winchester, New York in Jan 1777.[284]

According to the statement of brother Jacob Wyeth for the widow's pension of Elizabeth E. Smith Wyeth, on his way home from New York to Cambridge, Jonas stopped off to stay with family in Connecticut. Perhaps Ebenezer did so as well. He may have collected his newly widowed cousin, Elizabeth Winship Green, in Norwich and took her home to Cambridge where they married in May 1777. Just seven years earlier, Elizabeth, at age 14, had been summoned to appear before a Norwich court justice to answer for the heinous crime of walking upon the street with friends on the Sabbath day.[285]

Per the DAR Historian General's Office, starting in 1939, for a $10 donation each, names of Revolutionary War ancestors, regardless of where they served, were added to the brass plaques in the Washington Memorial Bell Tower at Valley Forge. The Wyeth names on the insert appear at the bottom of the right wall. The service for Noah should be minuteman and Ebenezer Jr. (III) should be PVT.

Ebenezer again served in the military in Nov 1778 for three days under General Heath in Boston. Also, in 1778, Ebenezer Owned the Covenant so his children could be baptized, like he had been, in Cambridge's First Church. His first four children apparently were baptized there before Ebenezer moved the family west. With records in other states being scarce at the time, the best guess is Mary was born in Connecticut, as she indicated in the 1850 census report, and Abbey and Stephen were born on the frontier of New York.

Records of the first United States census of 1790 show Ebenezer lived in the vast New York county of Montgomery. Brother Joshua was south of him just across the Pennsylvania border. Soon the south-central New York counties of Chemung, Broome and Tioga were formed from Montgomery. Probably without moving, in Nov 1791, Ebenezer resided in the Town of Union, Tioga, New York where he signed a document authorizing a road.[286] It appears he was still living in New York when his wife Elizabeth died in Jan 1799. However, he was back in Cambridge eight months later to see his father's estate settled after his Aug death.

As Ebenezer Wyeth Jr. did not have a will, a probate administrator divided the property among Ebenezer III, Jonas Jr., and Gad. The three brothers then paid shares to their siblings Joshua, Jacob, Anna, and John, less the value that each had already received during their father's lifetime. Ebenezer and Gad had not received any money or land from their father prior to his death, so no deductions were taken from their share of the estate. It apparently was a fair allocation of the estate for the brothers and Anna remained friendly afterwards … as evidenced by letters and visits detailed in Benjamin and William Richard Cutter's *History of the Town of Arlington*.[287]

From his share, Ebenezer III paid the other heirs for five acres of land and for the house where he and his siblings had grown up.[288] Ebenezer III sold the house in 1801 to Jonathan Hastings who was the son of a Harvard College steward. The Hastings family built a mansion next door and used the farmhouse as a service wing. In 1808, the mansion and farmhouse were, in turn, sold to the Gray family. This 1854 *Walling* map gives an amazing view of how large the lands were that the sons of Ebenezer Jr. inherited at his 1799 death.[289]

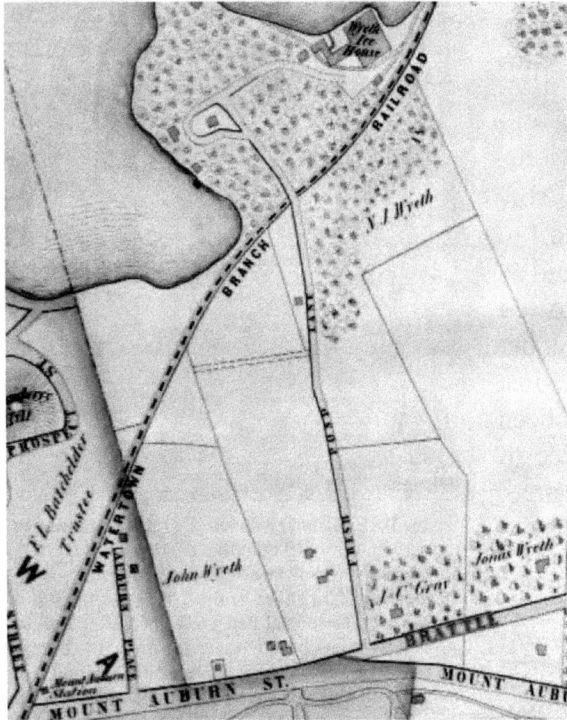

H. F. Walling's 1854 map of the City of Cambridge is from the Harvard Map Collection. At the top of the map, on the southern shore of Fresh Pond, is Nathaniel Jarvis Wyeth's ice house. At the bottom is John Wyeth's property across from the gate to Mt. Auburn cemetery and at the corner of Fresh Pond Lane and Brattle is the Gray property that Ebenezer Wyeth III received in the distribution of his father's estate. The shaded area on the left is the Watertown border, which at Ebenezer III's birth, was farther east.

After considerable alteration, the Wyeth house and the Gray family mansion were moved to the Larches in Cambridge, where they stand yet today.[290] The photo below of the Wyeth house was taken at Thanksgiving time in 2017.

After the sale in Cambridge, Ebenezer apparently moved to Westford, Middlesex, Massachusetts for he was listed in their 1810 census. Also, Ebenezer's oldest son, Ebenezer Wyeth IV died unmarried in Westford in 1813.[291]

Much confusion exists about Ebenezer IV. Lucius Paige wrote in the *History of Cambridge* that the fourth Ebenezer married Naomi.[292] In fact, it was Ebenezer III who married Naomi and by 1818, the couple were living in Ashby, Middlesex County, in northern Massachusetts near the New Hampshire border. It was in Ashby that Ebenezer gave his service record when he applied for a Revolutionary War pension. In the application he mentioned Naomi by name and talked about their one son age 14 and two girls – 19 and 18. He said his 19-year-old daughter was not well.

Ebenezer Wyeth III started receiving a pension of $48 per year on 01 May 1818.

When Congress amended the 1818 pension law to include a financial need requirement, his pension stopped in Mar 1820 because of property he held.[293] The young government struggled to keep payments up to veterans. It would seem a veteran had to be destitute to receive a pension. Rather than as a reward for serving in the military, pensions became a form of welfare. Ebenezer was forced to sell his land, worth $300, in order to reinstate his allowance. When the land sold, his income restarted in Mar 1824 and continued to his 30 Dec 1836 death.[294]

The second statement of his service, sworn to reinstate the pension, contains the reference to his wife, Naomi. It is transcribed from the pension file of Ebenezer Wyeth III in the following oath.

On the 10th day of Dec 1823, personally appeared in open court, being a court of record for the county of Middlesex, Ebenezer Wyeth resident in Ashby in said county aged 70 years who being first duly sworn according to law, doth, on his oath, make the following declaration in order to obtain the provision made by the acts of Congress, of the 18 Mar 1818, and the 01 May 1820, that he, the said Ebenezer Wyeth enlisted for the term of one year in the month of **November in the year AD 1775**, in the state of Massachusetts in the Company commanded by **Captain Eliphalet Newell** in the regiment **commanded by Colonel Henry Knox** in the line of the state of Massachusetts on the Continental establishment; that he continued to serve in the said corps **until January in the AD 1777**, when he was **discharged from the said service, in Bedford in the state of New York**; that his name has been placed on the Pension list, and dropt therefrom on account of his property; that he is a **husbandman by occupation**, but on account of a breach [hernia] and the infirmities of age, wholly unable to labor; that he has no family, except his **wife, Naomi**, aged 58 years.   *Ebenezer Wyeth*

"Mr. Ebenezer Wyeth, died Dec. 30, 1836, age 85, Patriot Soldier, Rest in Peace, Here thy toils and battles cease, Farewell sorrow pain & care, Burdens weary, age must bare."

Ebenezer Wyeth III continued to live in Ashby near the MA / NH border as evidenced by the 1820 and 1830 census reports of the town. At his death in Ashby, he was buried in the Unitarian Church cemetery near the town's common. Naomi went to live with her son Joseph in Chelsea and is buried nearby in the Rumney Marsh Burial Ground, Revere, Suffolk, Massachusetts.

64. **JONAS⁵ WYETH JR.** (Ebenezer⁴ Jr., Ebenezer³ Sr., John², Nicholas¹) was born on 17 May 1757 in Cambridge, Middlesex, Massachusetts. During the War for Independence, Jonas served as a minuteman and in the Continental Army and Navy. According to documents in his widow's pension file, certified by Cambridge Town Clerk Lucius Paige, Jonas wed **ELIZABETH E. SMITH**, daughter of Joseph Smith and Abigail Nutting, on 08 Apr 1792 in Cambridge's First Church. The marriage was solemnized by Reverend Abiel Holmes, the father of Oliver Wendell Holmes. Elizabeth was baptized on 11 Aug 1771 in Cambridge. Her father's brother, Ebenezer Smith Jr., was married to Sarah Wyeth (1761-1780) – Jonas' second cousin. Jonas died on 03 Oct 1817 in Cambridge. Elizabeth died there on 12 Sep 1853. MA death records say she died on 16 Sep 1853 but those are incorrect as Mt. Auburn Cemetery records state her burial in their lot 1800, grave 2 on Yarrow Path, occurred on 15 Sep 1853. Mt. Auburn's records show Jonas' remains were moved there in 1842.

Jonas Wyeth Jr. and Elizabeth E. Smith had the following children:

       i.   ELIZABETH⁶ E. WYETH, born 22 Jul 1792, Cambridge; died unmarried on 08 Aug 1889, just 17 days after her 97th birthday. In 1888, she had been named the oldest resident of Cambridge.[295][296]

104.   ii.   JONAS WYETH 3^D, born 03 Sep 1794, Cambridge; married ELIZABETH NUTTING FLAGG, 08 Feb 1820, Cambridge; died there, 14 Jun 1867.

105.   iii. NANCY WYETH, born 09 Sep 1796, Cambridge; married RICHARD CLARK HASTINGS, 05 Jun 1823, Cambridge; died 20 Aug 1873, Boston.

106.   iv. SUSAN WYETH, born 06 May 1798, Cambridge; married OREN WILLARD, 11 Mar 1828, Cambridge; died 13 May 1896, Leominster, Massachusetts.

107.   v.   HARRIET WYETH, born 30 Sep 1800, Cambridge; married REUBEN WINSLOW, 20 Jun 1824, Cambridge; died 13 Apr 1879, Boston.

vi.   MARY WYETH, born on 02 Dec 1802, Cambridge. Soon after their mother's death in 1853, the single sisters, Mary and Elizabeth, purchased land near Fresh Pond and Mt. Auburn Street from their married siblings. On 28 Nov 1868 they sold property to Alexander McDonald. On the same day, McDonald sold the land to Mt. Auburn Cemetery.[297] [298] Mary died 21 May 1885 in Medford, Middlesex, Massachusetts. She is buried in Mt. Auburn Cemetery as shown in the photo below.

108.   vii.   JOHN WYETH, born 17 Jan 1805,[299] Cambridge; married MARY ANN NEWMAN, 12 Nov 1839, Roxbury, Suffolk, Massachusetts; died 25 Sep 1871, Boston.

viii.   FRANCIS WYETH was born on 14 May 1807 in Cambridge. He is listed in the book, *America On Stone,* for his work as a Boston Lithographer in 1832-33.[300] After many overseas trips in his later years, he died unmarried on 27 May 1862 in Cambridge.

ix.   SARAH WYETH, born 29 Oct 1809, Cambridge; died there, 19 Aug 1817.

x.   JOSEPH WYETH, born 20 Jan 1813, Cambridge; died in Mar 1845 in Point Petre, Guadeloupe, Lesser Antilles.[301] [302]

Per Mt. Auburn's plot map, James Wyeth and Elizabeth Wyeth are buried far left here. James Wyeth is the veteran Jonas Wyeth Jr. who was re-interred there in 1842. Only the footstone for Elizabeth, buried there on 15 Sep 1853, is legible. It says "Our Mother". Their daughter Mary Wyeth, the second grave, is marked 2 Dec 1802 – 21 May 1885. Next is their son Francis Wyeth, 27 May 1862. Marion E. Wyeth, 26 Aug 1865, the daughter of John and Mary Newman Wyeth, is the next grave. Then Jonas and Elizabeth's son, John, and his wife, Mary A. Newman are last on the right. Six unmarked graves are in the plot including Civil War veteran, John Jasper Wyeth. At Thanksgiving time in 2017, I submitted paperwork to Mt. Auburn to get VA markers for the two veterans.

Notes for Jonas Wyeth Jr. and Elizabeth E. Smith:

The first day of the American Revolution, 19 Apr 1775, is now known as Patriot's Day. Jonas Wyeth Jr. was unquestionably a tremendous patriot. He fought as a minuteman in Captain Samuel Thatcher's Co. along with his father, his uncles Jonas and Noah Wyeth, and his second cousin Joseph Wyeth. Although it is commonly known as the Battle of Lexington and Concord, Thatcher's men skirmished with the British on their return from Concord in an engagement called Parker's Revenge. According to his first cousin, Samuel Sawin (1762-1849), Jonas fought bravely and well. He even captured a Queen's Arm (British flintlock musket).[303] [304]

Jonas went on to serve a year in the Continental Army and a year in the Continental Navy. Although volume 17 of the *Massachusetts Soldiers and Sailors of the Revolutionary War* says Jonas "Wyith" (sic) was a seaman,[305] it makes no mention of his service with brothers Ebenezer III and Joshua in Captain Eliphalet Newell's Co. of Colonel Henry Knox's Continental Artillery

Regiment of the First Massachusetts Line. For that portion of the three Wyeth brothers' service, The Gilder Lehrman Institute of American History holds an original abstract for pay written by Captain Newell for service in his company for the month of Dec 1775. The document shows Jonas received pay for 15 days of service and his brothers were each paid for 11 days of service.[306]

After the war, in the division of his father's Cambridge estate in 1799, Jonas received the southwesterly portion of it at Belmont and Mt. Auburn streets.[307] That evidently is where he was living during the 1800 and 1810 census reports for his brothers are nearby. After his death, Elizabeth's name appeared in the 1830, 1840 and 1850 census reports on the same page as Jonas' brother, Jacob, whose Fresh Pond Resort was north of Jonas' land.

In a family noted for longevity, Jonas' death at age 60 was apparently due to continued illness he sustained from his time in the service. He made his living as a tanner and, as evidenced by her letters to the Pension Board, Elizabeth struggled after his death. Undoubtedly, her son, Jonas Wyeth 3[d], helped when he began managing the Fresh Pond Resort for his uncle Jacob. Still, Elizabeth needed a supplemental income. So she could apply for a pension based on Jonas' military service, Elizabeth wrote the following letter to the secretary of the commonwealth.[308]

> "I, Elizabeth Wyeth, of Cambridge … 73 years of age do testify and say that my husband, Jonas Wyeth, was in the service of the Revolution, that he was in at **Lexington & Concord** under the command of Capt. Samuel Thatcher, and according to the best of my recollections, he was **in the service at Ticonderoga** and was also in the **Continental service in the state of New York**; and was also at **Norwich in the state of Connecticut**, at which place he was attended with sickness and that he was afterwards in the **Naval Privateer service and was captured and put aboard the British prison ship called _Chatham_** where he remained in a distressful situation **until he with the other American prisoners were exchanged for the British prisoners**. That at the time of the Revolution, my husband bore the name of Jonas Wyeth 2nd, and according to the best of my recollection of his statement, he must have been in the service for more than one year. And I request the Secretary of this Commonwealth to examine the rolls and documents in his office for proof of my said husband's service, _Elizabeth Wyeth_ … March 17th 1845 …"

To assist her, Elizabeth's brother-in-law gave this testimony on the same day in 1845.[309]

> "I, Jacob Wyeth, of Cambridge … in the 81st year of my age do testify and say that I have always resided in this town. That I well recollect the Revolutionary War. I was not in the services myself, but **I have three brothers who were in the service, viz: Ebenezer, Jonas, Joshua.** And my deceased brother Jonas Wyeth has a widow living in the neighborhood. And my said brother Jonas Wyeth was at the time of the Revolution, was called Jonas Wyeth, <u>Second</u>, and I well recollect that he was in the **Lexington and Concord engagement**. **I think he was in the company of Lieut. David Bradley**, and I recollect that he enlisted in the service **in December 1775 or January or February 1776** for one year. And it is my impression he was in the Company of Lieut. Bradley in that service at which time **he was in the service in the state of New York**. And was sick the last part of this service. A year or two after his return from this year's service, he engaged in a Naval Privateer service, and I think he was at one time captured by a British cruiser & was held a prisoner for some time. It is also my full impression he was in the **Penobscot expedition**, and was under **Captain Manley in one of his Naval services**. _Jacob Wyeth …_"

As it turns out, Jacob did a remarkable job thinking back to his boyhood. Except for the name of Jonas' superior, Capt. Eliphalet Newell, Jacob's affidavit was very accurate. He was only 11 years old when his older brothers entered the Continental Army. Like Jacob, his younger brothers, Gad and John, were too young for service in the Revolution.

Of course, Jacob did not have the benefit of his older brothers' input in 1845. Jonas died in 1817,

Joshua in 1829 and Ebenezer in 1836. Neither did Jacob, nor for that matter anyone working on Elizabeth's pension claim, have access to the abstract for pay written by Captain Newell for service in his company in December 1775.[310] Newell's pay record and Jacob and Elizabeth's statements about Jonas' New York service, makes it highly likely Jonas' service mirrored the service Joshua and Ebenezer mentioned in their pension applications. Both Joshua and Ebenezer wrote they fought in the New York battles on Long Island and at White Plains while serving for over a year in Captain Newell's Company of Colonel Henry Knox's Regiment of Artillery.[311] [312]

Additionally, as mentioned previously, volume 17 of the Secretary of the Commonwealth's *Massachusetts Soldiers and Sailors of the Revolutionary War*, does not include the three brothers' yearlong service in the Continental Army. Even though the secretary was mistakenly looking at the rolls of David Bradley, it appears they did not carry the rolls of Captain Newell. Here is part of how the Secretary's office responded to Elizabeth's request.[313]

> … it appears that the name of **Jonas Wyeth junr** is borne as a private upon a **muster roll of Capt Samuel Thatcher** Company in Col. Gardner's regt. Which marched on the **alarm April 19, 1775** – 3 days – as Jonas Wyeth, upon a pay abstract **of Capt John Walton**, Col. Saml Thatcher, for service at Cambridge from **Sept 2 to 3 1778** … *upon another order from Capt Walton, dated Oct 30, he is notified as Jonas 3rd to march to Boston and serve under Gen'l Heath, until the 9th of Nov following*; – the name of **Jonas Wyeth is also borne upon an index, as a seaman on board the *Hague*, Capt John Manley** …
>
> *Secretary of the Commonwealth*

Interestingly, in this certification, Jonas "is notified as Jonas 3^d to march to Boston and serve under Gen'l Heath until the 9th of Nov. following." This matches the aforementioned Ebenezer III being ordered to march to Boston to serve under General Heath until 09 Nov 1778 and shows the two Wyeths served together again near the end of 1778.

Unfortunately, for Elizabeth, the secretary saying "Wyeth junr or 3^d" opened a can of worms. In her letter of 24 Jun 1845 transferring documents to the commissioner of pensions,[314] Elizabeth briefly touched on the manner her husband's name was distinquished from his uncle, Jonas Sr. For ten years, his widow and her attorneys were put through the wringer trying to prove Elizabeth's husband, who served under Captain Manley, was *the* Jonas, out of all the Jonas Wyeths in Cambridge. An index record on 19 Jul 1845 shows Elizabeth's 07 Aug 1838 pension certificate was suspended for authenticity that he was the specific Jonas in service on board *The Hague*. On 26 Aug 1845, the commissioner of pensions wrote for more proof of Jonas' identity.

After ten years of document submissions, and almost two years after Elizabeth's death on 12 Sep 1853, her attorney, S. B. True, finally received her approved pension certificate on 14 Aug 1855. It showed an allowance of $42.64 per annum commencing in arrears to the 4th day of Mar 1836.[315] Curiously, the actual ledgers appear as if Elizabeth received a pension payment every period just like all the other ladies on the lists.[316] For more information, please see Appendix 2 of this book.

All things considered, it took a long time to obtain a monument for Jonas and his grandson John Jasper Wyeth's unmarked graves on Yarrow Path in Mt. Auburn Cemetery. Founded in 1831 on the principle of "commemorating the dead in a landscape of beauty and tranquility," Mt. Auburn, later inspired a public parks movement in the United States.[317] Its 175 acres, some of it on Wyeth land,[318] are indeed the most stunning and well-kept grounds I have ever seen. In evidence, on my every visit there, is the army of workers and volunteers dedicated to the cemetery's standard.

Understandably, Mt. Auburn's emphasis must be on new burials and maintaining its immaculate terrain. They are a very busy organization. It took them almost one year to submit the forms to the V.A. that I dropped off at their office on 21 Nov 2017. For every four emails of follow up on the Wyeth monuments, I usually got only one response back. Much of the delay was due to the cemetery requiring an advance payment of $500 to install the monuments. Being retired, on a fixed income, it was not an option for me to pay the fee out of my own pocket. Thankfully, when I turned to the Massachusetts Society of the Sons of the American Revolution for help, their State Secretary, Robert Bossart, Commander, Col. Henry Knox Regimental Color Guard, arranged the payment for Jonas Wyeth's marker. A friend in The Friends of Mt. Auburn took care of the fee for John Jasper Wyeth's stone.

As I worked on getting this monument for my 5th great uncle's grave, Thomas Paine's words helped me persist. He wrote in 1776, "These are the times that try men's souls. The summer soldier and the sunshine patriot will, in this crisis, shrink from the service of their country; but he that stands it now, deserves the love and thanks of man and woman." Jonas' love and thanks for serving in the Army and

✝
JONAS WYETH JR
KNOX'S REGT
MASS LINE
CONTINENTAL NAVY
REVOLUTIONARY WAR
MAY 17 1757   OCT 3 1817

This V.A. stone will mark the grave of Jonas Wyeth Jr. in the Spring of 2019. Photo courtesy of Mt. Auburn Cemetery.

Navy was overdue by over 200 years, but will be corrected when the ground softens in the Spring.

65. JOSHUA[5] WYETH SR. (Ebenezer[4] Jr., Ebenezer[3] Sr., John[2], Nicholas[1]) was born on 06 Oct 1758 in Cambridge, Middlesex, Massachusetts. He helped steep the tea in the Atlantic, fought in the Battle of Bunker Hill; and served two years in the Continental Army during the Revolutionary War. Per International Marriage Records, he married (1) PAULINE JONES about 1774 in Boston. He married (2) MARY ELIZABETH BREWER on 27 Apr 1780 in Waltham, Middlesex, Massachusetts. The daughter of (Captain) Moses Brewer and Elizabeth Davis, Mary was born on 16 Jan 1761 in Sherborn, Middlesex, Massachusetts. [319] Mary died in 1805 in Towanda, Luzerne (Bradford), Pennsylvania. Joshua married (3) ELIZABETH RICHARDSON in Watertown, Middlesex, Massachusetts on 07 Jan 1808. Joshua died of bilious fever on 22 Jan 1829 at the age of 70 in Cincinnati,

Robert Reid's 1904 mural of the Boston Tea Party is courtesy of the Library of Congress.

Hamilton, Ohio. His obituary incorrectly states his age as 77. [320] On 17 Dec 1836, Cincinnati records show Elizabeth as administratrix of Joshua's estate.

The children of Joshua Wyeth Sr. and Mary Elizabeth Brewer included:

      i. SUSANNA "SUKEY"[6] WYETH, born about 1781, probably Boston, Suffolk, Massachusetts; married a MR. LEONARD, about 1799, Towanda, Luzerne (Bradford), Pennsylvania; died 1826, Lebanon, Warren, Ohio.

109.   ii. ELISHA WYETH was born on 11 Mar 1782, probably Boston; married NANCY SALISBURY, circa 1804, Towanda; died 01 Oct 1854, Riley Township, Vigo, Indiana.

110.   iii.   JOSHUA WYETH JR., born 17 Jan 1784, probably Boston; married (1) GRACE JACKSON, 07 Feb 1805, Hanover Township, Luzerne, Pennsylvania;[321] married (2) HANNAH POND, 30 Aug 1810, Orwell Township, Luzerne (Bradford), Pennsylvania; died 23 Oct 1870, Riley Township, Vigo, Indiana.

111.   iv.   GEORGE MORRIS WYETH SR., born 09 Oct 1785, probably Boston; married ELIZA H. COOKE, 27 Jul 1809, Erie, Erie County, Pennsylvania; died 04 Jun 1844, Scott County, Illinois.

        v.   HARRIETT WYETH, born 1786, probably Boston; married JOHN BATES; died after 1843, Covington, Kenton, Kentucky.

112.   vi.   MARY "POLLY" WYETH was born circa 1789 in Cambridge, Middlesex, Massachusetts; married (1) DANIEL GILBERT, 09 Jul 1809, Towanda; married (2) OLIVER WILLIAMS DODGE, about 1837, Bradford County; died 09 Dec 1881, Franklin Township, Bradford, Pennsylvania.[322]

        vii.   PRENTICE WYETH, born circa 1791, probably in Harvard, Worcester, Massachusetts; died 29 Aug 1810, Cincinnati, Hamilton, Ohio.[323]

113.   viii.   FRANCIS B. WYETH, born 1796, Towanda; married (1) MARGARET CARNEY, 1817, probably in Allegheny County, Pennsylvania; (2) ELIZABETH FELTER PATMORE, 04 Jul 1835, Hamilton County, Ohio; (3) ELIZABETH KENT, 27 Jul 1861, Morgan County, Indiana; (4) CAROLINE H. BAILEY BRUNER, 30 Nov 1862, Clay County, Indiana; (5) MARY BELL BUNTIN, 05 May 1865, Monroe County, Indiana; (6) ELIZABETH DOVER CHANDLER, 21 Oct 1867, Monroe County; (7) PRISCILLA CREAMER WILLIAMS, 09 Feb 1875, Morgan County; Francis died about 1882.

114.   ix.   ELIZA JANE WYETH, born 07 Jul 1797, Towanda; married PETER KING, 07 Sep 1813, Bardstown, Nelson, Kentucky; died 29 Jun 1882, Green Township, Morgan, Indiana.

        x.   NANCY WYETH, born in 1798 in Towanda; died well before 1842.[324] Craft's *History of Bradford County*, indicates she married and moved to Kentucky. On 15 Jan 1818 a Mary Wythe married JAMES W. SHARP in Champaign County, Ohio. Those particular Ohio county records are typewritten so there may have been a transcription error. Surely the record is for Nancy because her father was living in Champaign County in 1818 when he applied for his Revolutionary War pension. Nancy's sister, Mary "Polly", had remained in Towanda on the farm her husband, Daniel Gilbert, purchased from Polly's father, Joshua Wyeth Sr., before Joshua moved to Ohio.[325]

115.   xi.   HENRY WYETH, born 15 Aug 1800, Towanda; married EMILINE WEST there 01 Dec 1823; died 28 Feb 1886, Spring Township, Crawford, Pennsylvania.

116.   xii.   FRANCES "FANNY" WYETH, born circa 1802, Towanda; married JAMES BAILEY, 17 Jul 1822, Harmony Township, Clark, Ohio; died there about 1871.

        xiii.   HANNAH WYETH, born circa 1805 in Towanda; death unknown. However, she appears to have been alive when her aunt Anna Wyeth Cutter's estate was distributed in 1842.[326]

The children of Joshua Wyeth Sr. and Elizabeth Richardson included:

117.   i.   ANNA ELIZABETH[6] WYETH, born Mar 1808, Cincinnati, Hamilton, Ohio;

212

married JOHN HEWSON, about 1830, probably in Cincinnati; died about 1839.

ii. WILLIAM P. WYETH, born in 1811, Cincinnati; died after the 1842 distribution of his aunt Anna Wyeth Cutter's estate.[327]

118. iii. ENOCH NELSON WYETH, born Jun 1813, Cincinnati; married (1) ELIZABETH FOWLER, 26 May 1836, Cincinnati; married (2) LUCINDA M. PRATHER, 20 Sep 1840, Terre Haute, Vigo, Indiana; died there, 16 Jul 1896.

iv. ADELINE WYETH, born 1817, in Champaign County (or in Cincinnati, Hamilton), Ohio. In 1818 her father applied for his pension in Champaign County. On 16 Apr 1827, Joshua wrote his sister Anna and gave Adeline's age as 10. Adeline died after 1842 as one document for Anna Wyeth Cutter's estate states Adeline was then living in Cincinnati.[328]

119. v. OLIVE AMANDA WYETH, born 1818, Champaign County, Ohio; married EDWIN WALLACE HARRISON SR., 08 Jan 1837, Cincinnati; died in Apr 1878, Riley Township, Vigo, Indiana.

vi. CHARLES WYETH was probably born about 1821 in Springfield, Clark, Ohio (the place of Joshua's 1820 pension application). Charles died in Cincinnati. In 1827, Joshua said in a letter to his sister Anna that one of the six children of his third marriage had died. Although he did not give the child's name, based on others in the family, Joshua was undoubtedly referring to Charles.[329]

Notes for Joshua Wyeth Sr.:

Perhaps the highest praise for Joshua Wyeth Sr. comes from being included in Ray Raphael's 2009 book *Founders: The People Who Brought You a Nation*. Raphael states we not only should credit our nation's birth to Washington, Franklin, Jefferson, Hamilton, Adams, and Madison, but to the entire generation of American patriots who pushed for independence, fought a war, and set the United States on its course.

Detailed on Raphael's pages is Joshua Wyeth's courage for throwing tea into Boston Harbor on 16 Dec 1773. The destruction of tea was a protest in reaction to the duty Parliament added to it. The tax was intended not only to help the British government raise funds following the French and Indian War, but also to bail out the struggling East India Company and to reassert Parliament's control over the Colonies. Many years later, Joshua would playfully be the first person to call the group who destroyed the tea a "Tea Party."[330] However, at the time, the protest was a serious act of rebellion. He and the others in the secret society, Sons of Liberty, saw themselves as patriots, but had they been caught, they would have been executed as traitors.[331]

Joshua's 1827 interview with Rev. Timothy Flint was the first widely published account of the protest against Great Britain. In the article, Joshua stated he was but 15 years of age when he dressed as an Indian and threw tea into Boston Harbor. At the time, Joshua was a newly trained Boston blacksmith. Due to the fact he was a young man and not known in town, at the South Meeting House in Boston, leaders proposed he and other similarly unknown men should smear their faces with soot or lamp-black to make them totally unrecognizable. As he talked with Flint, Joshua said they resembled "devils from the bottomless pit."

In his Revolutionary War Military Pension affidavit, Joshua stated that after volunteering at the Battle of Bunker Hill, he served as a private in the 1st Massachusetts Regiment under Captain

213

Eliphalet Newell as well as a blacksmith in the corps of artificers under Captain Faxon. He fought at the Battle at Flatbush on Long Island, in the skirmish at Harlem Heights and in the 1776 Battle of White Plains, New York. Following the war, Joshua returned to Massachusetts. He likely resided in Waltham after marrying Mary Elizabeth Brewer there.

Joshua next lived in Boston where he was burnt out on 20 Apr 1787 by the great Boston fire.[332] It is probable most of his older children were born in Boston. Three years later, during the 1790 census, he lived near the Shakers in the town of Harvard, Worcester County, Massachusetts. According to the *History of the Towandas* by Clement Ferdinand Heverly, Joshua soon afterward moved to the Lake Region of central New York where his eldest brother, Ebenezer, was then residing. Finding the area not well suited to his family, in 1792, Joshua purchased land from John Heath on Towanda Creek in Pennsylvania and moved his family there in 1794.[333]

In 1800 he apparently was still on the Heath land, for the census of that year showed him in Wysox Township near Towanda, Luzerne (now Bradford County), Pennsylvania. Five years later, after giving birth to at least 15 children in 25 years, his second wife, Mary Elizabeth Brewer Wyeth, died at age 44.

She was buried on the 250-acre farm Joshua purchased from John Heath in an area called "the Flats." The location later became known as the George Bowman place. Railroad tracks now pass over her grave.[334]

In 2017, Jeff Wyeth took this photo near the burial place of Mary Brewer Wyeth in Towanda, PA.

Joshua returned again to Massachusetts in 1808 to marry third wife, Elizabeth Richardson, in Watertown. Later that year, he sold his Towanda land to the young man who would soon be his son-in-law, Daniel Gilbert. Joshua Wyeth Sr. apparently moved to Cincinnati since his son, Prentice, died there in 1810.[335] Then on 19 Sep 1813, Joshua wrote to his sister, Anna Wyeth Cutter that he had just built a house on Cincinnati's Main Street.

On 30 Apr 1818, while living in Champaign County, Ohio, he applied for a Revolutionary War pension and stated he had 21 children born in lawful wedlock… with 17 of them yet alive. When Congress amended the 1818 pension law to include a financial need requirement, Joshua reapplied on 21 Jul 1820 while living in Springfield, Clark, Ohio. In that second document he stated he was married to his third wife, Elizabeth, and had 21 children by two of his wives.[336]

He apparently had one more child with Elizabeth Richardson between 1820 and 1826. In a 28 Sep 1826 article for *The Long-Island Star*, Joshua said he had 22 children with 13 still living.[337] Confirmation comes from letters to Anna Wyeth Cutter dated Cincinnati 16 Apr 1827 and 09 Sep 1827 published in *The History of the Town of Arlington, Massachusetts*. In one letter, Joshua told his sister one of the seven children by his third wife was deceased.

Of Cincinnati, he spoke very highly ... the country was superior "to the land of Canaan of old, spoken of in Moses's law!" His house and lot cost about $1000. Fruit, vegetables and meat were in abundance and the sale of them brought him a good living. He told Anna he followed the market and together with his pension and earnings, he lived very comfortably. He also related, "The canal from Cincinnati to Lake Erie is expected to be finished by the next summer."[338]

By reviewing his letters and pension applications, together with the *History of the Towandas* and Anna Wyeth Cutter's 1842 will, the names of 19 children can be determined.[339] [340] It appears in each of these name combinations, documents refer to the same person: Susannah/Sukey, Francis/Frank, Harry/Henry, Mary/Polly and Eliza/Elizabeth. According to a 1975 article written by Dorothy Clark for the *Terre Haute Tribune*, four of Joshua's sons came to Vigo County and one returned to Cincinnati. Clark believed Joshua Jr., Elisha and Frank now lie quietly in the old Mewhinney Cemetery unless their burial places were strip-mined.[341]

Besides details pertaining to his children, the 1820 pension application revealed Joshua could no longer work as a blacksmith due to wounds, age, and debility. It is also interesting to note, that he spelled his name "Wyeth" on both of his pension applications. In a few generations, some of his descendants reverted to the old English spelling of the name – "Wythe." Another interesting note is Joshua swore in open court that he assisted in throwing tea overboard on 16 Dec 1773. It certainly was not something he had to say in order to qualify for the pension. His oath to the Supreme Court of Ohio makes his presence on the East India Company's ships even more definite than his 1827 Timothy Flint interview.

At the time of the interview for Flint's *Western Review,* Joshua was firmly settled in Cincinnati, Hamilton, Ohio. The interview was then covered by numerous outlets. Here are some excerpts:[342]

"I labored, as a journeyman blacksmith, with Western & Gridley, blacksmiths by trade, and Baptists by profession. Western, at the time, was neutral, but afterwards became a Tory...

...We were met together one evening, talking over the tyranny of the British government, such as the heavy duties, shutting up the port of Boston, the murdering of Mr. Gray's family, sending people to England for trial, and sundry other acts of oppression. Our indignation was increased by having heard of the arrival of the tea ships at this time.

...We had observed that very few persons remained on board the three ships, and we finally concluded that we could take possession of them and discharge the tea into the harbor without danger or opposition. ... to prevent ourselves from being discovered, to wear ragged clothes and disfigure ourselves... We dressed to resemble Indians as much as possible. ... We placed a sentry at the end of the wharf, another in the middle, and one on the bow of each ship as we took possession. ... The leader of our company ordered the captain and crew to open the hatchways, and hand us the hoisting tackle and ropes. ... Some of our numbers then jumped into the hold, and passed the chests to the tackle.

As they were hoisted on deck, others knocked them open with axes, and others raised them to the railings and discharged their contents overboard. All that were not needed for discharging the tea from this ship, went on board the others and warped them into the wharf, where the same ceremonies were repeated...

While we were unloading, the people collected in great numbers about the wharf to see what was going on. They crowded about us so as to be much in our way. We paid no attention to them, nor did they say anything to us. They evidently wished us success. Our sentries were not armed, and could not stop any who insisted on passing. ... stationing the sentries, was to communicate information, in case we were likely to be detected by the civil or military power. They were particularly charged to give us notice, in case any known Tory came down to the wharf.

...We were merry, in an undertone, at the idea of **making so large a cup of tea for the fishes** but were as still as the nature of the cause would admit. No more words were used than absolutely necessary. Our most intimate friends among the spectators had not the least knowledge of us. I never labored harder in my life; and we were so expeditious, that, although it was late in the evening when we began, we had discharged the whole three cargoes before morning dawn."

Joshua died about a year and a half after Flint's interview. In *The History of the Town of Arlington, Massachusetts*, he was said to have died in Feb 1832, however, Joshua's pension records and his obituary in the *Daily Cincinnati Gazette* say he died at his home on Longworth Street in Cincinnati on 22 Jan 1829.[343] Illogically, Bradford County, Pennsylvania history said he was buried in Columbus, Ohio, which is over 100 miles north of Cincinnati.[344]

Finding out where Joshua was buried and getting approval from the U.S. Department of Veterans Affairs (V.A.) for a memorial tombstone, would take me almost four years' time to accomplish.

After having no success with the National Cemetery in Dayton, I turned to Cincinnati's Spring Grove Cemetery to see if they would accept a memorial marker honoring Joshua. Spring Grove's Tracey Brumley was the first person to show any enthusiasm for the project.

Then when Christopher Smith, reference librarian in the Genealogy and Local History Department at the Public Library of Cincinnati and Hamilton County, advised me Joshua was likely buried a few steps from his home in the Old 12th Street Burying Grounds, I had concrete information to provide to the V.A.

Still, the V.A. was not convinced a marker was not already erected at Joshua's grave. At that point, I turned to Michael Gunn of the Cincinnati Chapter of the Sons of the American Revolution. Michael suggested I send the V.A. the introduction to an 1895 book written by Samuel F. Cary about the state of Revolutionary Soldiers' graves in Cincinnati.

Postmaster General Cary's paragraphs are particularly poignant and may have been the turning point in getting the V.A. to furnish a monument for Joshua.[345]

> "The vandalism of our Christian civilization has long since blotted out the old grave yards of Cincinnati, scattered the bones of the departed and broken down the memorial stones planted at their graves by the hand of affection. It is safe to say that not a single grave of a Revolutionary soldier can now be identified in Cincinnati. The tenants in these cities of the dead have been evicted, a small number of them have been removed to the Wesleyan and Spring Grove cemeteries."

On 22 Jan 2014, the 185th anniversary of Joshua's death, Spring Grove Cemetery placed his government-issued monument in garden LN – Veterans' section 131E – space 354.[346] Following the lead of Joshua's brothers, Unitarians Ebenezer and John, I requested the V.A. have the Unitarian flaming chalice emblem adorn the stone.

To further honor her 4th great grandfather, Gary and Diana Wythe Totten had "Boston Tea Party, 1773" engraved on the marker.

The Cincinnati Chapter of the Sons of the American Revolution also included Joshua's name in the 25 added to a monument honoring all Revolutionary War veterans memorialized or buried at Spring Grove Cemetery. To dedicate the monuments, SAR hosted two superb ceremonies in the cemetery on 19 Apr 2014. The first was to recognize the 25 veterans and the second was to dedicate Joshua's V.A. monument.

In honor of the occasion, Jeff Suess wrote an article for the *Cincinnati Enquirer* called "Honoring America's original patriots" ... sub-heading, "Boston Tea Party veteran among those who fought in Revolutionary War, buried here, forgotten." Following is a portion of the article.[347]

"History has not been kind to the graves of the soldiers of the American Revolution. Untold veterans who fought for this country's independence lie in unmarked graves. Some have been lost entirely.

The Cincinnati Chapter of the Sons of the American Revolution [SAR] is helping to rectify that on Saturday, April 19, by adding 25 names to a memorial for Revolutionary War veterans buried in Spring Grove Cemetery....

Some were buried in Spring Grove but were not identified as Revolutionary War veterans. Others buried elsewhere were supposed to be relocated to Spring Grove when their burial grounds were appropriated for other uses, but there are no records that they were moved. Their graves have been lost.

One of those lost graves was for Joshua Wyeth, a participant in the Boston Tea Party and a volunteer at the Battle of Bunker Hill.

On Saturday, in honor of Patriots Day commemorating the Battles of Lexington and Concord and the 'Shot Heard 'Round the World' on April 19, 1775, the SAR is hosting two ceremonies at Spring Grove Cemetery.

The Revolutionary War veterans' monument will be rededicated with the additional names, along with the dedication of a grave marker for Wyeth.

Wyeth was in Boston Tea Party and fought at Bunker Hill.

It began with the Wyeth family.

Three years ago, Tina Wyeth Baker of Howard, Ohio, was helping with the family genealogy but found no grave for Joshua Wyeth, the brother of her fourth great grandfather.

Baker then compiled Wyeth's story from books, newspapers and government records.... Baker's research found that Wyeth died on Jan. 22, 1829, with a funeral at his home on Longworth Street (an east-west street between Fifth and Sixth that was wiped out by Interstate 75). There is no record of his burial.

So, Baker sought help from Christopher Smith, reference librarian in the Genealogy and Local History Department at the Public Library of Cincinnati and Hamilton County.

Smith determined that Wyeth was probably buried at the Episcopal and Presbyterian burying grounds on 12th Street in Over-the-Rhine, though there are no known burial records of the site.

In 1855, the city bought the grounds to convert them into Washington Park. Notices were placed in newspapers calling for families to pay to move their loved ones to the Wesleyan or Spring Grove cemeteries, but many, like Wyeth, had no family nearby.

'Most of the people buried in Washington Park were not moved,' Smith said. 'They put two to three feet of extra dirt over the cemetery, and the stones were laid down on the ground and covered with earth. They found over 100 burial sites during the renovation of Washington Park in 2010. But a great number of them were covered over and forgotten.'

Smith believes Wyeth's grave is probably still under the south portion of the park. 'He (Wyeth) was there,' Smith said. 'We have no firm belief he was ever moved. There is no record that he was.'

Armed with this knowledge, Baker was able to get approval from the U.S. Department of Veterans Affairs for a memorial tombstone for Wyeth, placed in Spring Grove, where his remains should have been reburied.

'There are many monuments to honor the leaders of our drive for independence ...' Baker wrote, "but for the ones who did the grunt work, they are lucky if a stone in a cemetery still marks their contribution.

At the very least, all veterans deserve a memorial marker for their grave.'

217

On Saturday, 25 more of those patriots will be remembered. 'The hearty boys of America forever."

On Patriots' Day 2014, over 30 descendants of Ebenezer III, Joshua, Gad and Joseph Wyeth attended the SAR ceremony honoring the Revolutionary War veterans buried in or memorialized at Spring Grove Cemetery. From L to R: Sid, Harmon, Marc and Allison Wyeth, Judith Bernet Evans, Tina Baker, Pam Henderson, Sue Hill, Brad, Kitty, Teresa and Jeff Wyeth, Chuck Walker, Elizabeth Slemons Pack, Jordan Slemons, Chris Pack, Diana Wythe Totten, Tom, Mike and Sherry Slemons, Karen Kent, James Bright, Kim and Julia Kinsel, Helen Wyeth Hampson, Kat Kinsel and Dorothy Wyeth Burrows. Not present for the picture, but in attendance, were Dawn Meyer Slemons, Grayson Rees Slemons, Cheryl Wyeth Cook, Geraldine Wyeth Watson, Lily Bright, Gary Totten, Art Baker and Andrew, Rene', and Marselle Wyeth Margraff.

Diana Wythe Totten along with U. S. Army Col. Donald McGraw and Hamilton County Assistant Police Chief James Schaffer, president and past president of Cincinnati SAR, and many other officials of SAR and DAR, spoke at the dedication of Joshua's monument at the Patriots' Day ceremony in 2014. I spoke as well... ending my remarks about Joshua with, "The marker was installed in these beautiful gardens ... 185 years after the death of a man who did much to help shape our country ... and give us the freedom that now shapes our lives."

66. SUSANNAH[5] WYETH (Ebenezer[4] Jr., Ebenezer[3] Sr., John[2], Nicholas[1]) was born on 14 May 1762 in Cambridge, Middlesex, Massachusetts. Susannah married William Watson Sr. on 06 Dec 1779 in Cambridge. WILLIAM WATSON SR., son of Isaac Watson and Elizabeth Whittemore, was born on 24 May 1755 in Cambridge.[348] Susannah died on 29 Dec 1789 at the age of 27 in Cambridge. William remarried. He was almost 56 when he died on 09 Feb 1811 in Cambridge. He had outlived all of his children from his first marriage. Susannah and all five of their children died between the ages of 19 to 27.

William Watson Sr. and Susannah Wyeth had the following children:

120.   i. SUSANNA WYETH "SUKEY"[6] WATSON, born 06 Dec 1780, Cambridge; married ARTENATUS MOORE, 07 Feb 1802, Cambridge; died there on 24 May 1807 at age 26 of consumption.
        ii. NANCY WATSON, born 23 Oct 1782, Cambridge; died there on 24 Dec 1803.
       iii. PRISCILLA WATSON, born 09 Apr 1784, Cambridge; died there, 05 Nov 1803.
        iv. WILLIAM WATSON JR. was born on 13 Jun 1785 in Cambridge. He died there on 04 Nov 1805, at the age of 20.
         v. MARY "POLLY" WATSON, born 12 Dec 1788, Cambridge; died there on 22 Jul 1812, at the age of 23.

218

67. **JACOB**⁵ **WYETH SR.** (Ebenezer[4] Jr., Ebenezer[3] Sr., John[2], Nicholas[1]) was born 29 Apr 1764 in Cambridge, Middlesex, Massachusetts. He graduated from Harvard in the class of 1792.[349] Jacob Wyeth Sr. and Elizabeth Jarvis were married on 08 Nov 1796 in Cambridge. Although her grave in Mt. Auburn Cemetery says she was born in 1770, **ELIZABETH JARVIS**, daughter of (Captain) Nathaniel Jarvis and Elizabeth Taintor, was baptized in Cambridge on 21 Feb 1768.[350] Both Jacob and Elizabeth died in Cambridge. He on 14 Jan 1857 at the age of 92 and she on 20 Jan 1858 at the age of 90. They are buried in lot 1672 on Pine Avenue in Mt. Auburn Cemetery, Cambridge.

Jacob Wyeth Sr. and Elizabeth Jarvis had the following children:

121. i. (DR.) JACOB[6] WYETH, born 10 Feb 1797[351] (or 08 Jan 1800)[352] Cambridge, Middlesex, Massachusetts; graduated Harvard College, 1820; married MARY CATHERINE BRADY, 11 Jun 1834, Sinsinawa Mound, Grant, Wisconsin;[353] died 24 Aug 1841, Sainte Genevieve County, Missouri.[354]

122. ii. LEONARD JARVIS WYETH SR., born circa 1797, Cambridge; married CAROLINE ARCHER, 02 Oct 1821, Baltimore County, Maryland; died 01 Feb 1855, Manhattan, New York County, New York.

123. iii. CHARLES WYETH, born 11 Nov 1798, Cambridge;[355] married (1) ELIZABETH NORRIS, 27 Jun 1827, Baltimore City, Maryland;[356] married (2) CAROLINE COGSWELL KNEELAND, widow of Francis Bartlett there, on 16 Jul 1859;[357] died 27 Jan 1891, Baltimore City.

iv. (CAPTAIN) NATHANIEL JARVIS "NAT" WYETH, born 29 Jan 1802, Cambridge; married ELIZABETH JARVIS STONE, 29 Jan 1824, Cambridge. She was the daughter of Phineas Stone and Nat's aunt, Mary Jarvis. Elizabeth was born in 1799 in Littleton, Middlesex, Massachusetts.[358] Nat died on 31 Aug 1856 and Elizabeth on 29 Aug 1865 in Cambridge. They are buried in Fountain Avenue lot 3031, behind Elizabeth's niece and namesake, Elizabeth Wyeth Perry Keen, in Mt. Auburn Cemetery, Cambridge.

Notes for Jacob Wyeth Sr.:

Jacob worked in his father's brick-making business until his early 20s.[359] At that point, he decided to obtain a liberal education. After just six months of preparatory study, he was admitted to the freshman class of Harvard College. Even though he was so imperfectly prepared, his undergraduate degree at age 28 was with distinction.[360] According to Harvard records, Jacob went on to earn a Master's degree three years later in 1795.

Before his marriage in 1796, Jacob traveled to Germany to transact business for Andrew Craigie of Cambridge. While there, Jacob purchased some European goods that he sold upon his return home for a great profit. Encouraged by that success, Jacob went into partnership with his brother-in-law, Phineas Stone, husband of his wife Elizabeth's sister, Mary Jarvis. The pair fared poorly as country traders in Littleton, Massachusetts. Although Jacob returned to Cambridge flat broke, he was, nevertheless, bursting with great ideas for a new venture.[361]

On 20 Sep 1796, Jacob purchased from his father, Ebenezer Wyeth Jr., eight acres of land on a bluff overlooking Fresh Pond in northwest Cambridge.[362] Jacob hired architects John Walton and Joseph Moore to build a Federal-style, three-story wood frame hotel on the land. To finance the project, the architects took out a mortgage on the property. The Fresh Pond Hotel officially opened to guests in the summer of 1797. The resort was so popular, within 18 months, Jacob repaid Walton and Moore.[363] It is safe to say the acreage was paid off at Ebenezer's death in 1799. Probate records show the deduction of a $616.68 note for land from Jacob's inheritance.[364]

Several factors contributed to the hotel's success. One was the building of a rail line that brought people seeking to escape the summer heat of Boston directly to Fresh Pond. A second factor was the nearby tourist destination – Mt. Auburn Cemetery. Third was Jacob's skillful management. He offered fishing, fowling, sailing, rowing, bowling, and an orchestra for dancing. He brought in such exceptional chefs, superior wines and top-quality spirits; the hotel soon became famous for fine dining.[365]

The Fresh Pond resort as it appeared circa 1845 in a lithograph advertisement issued by Lyman Willard. From left to right are boat houses with sail boats and row boats for rent, steps leading up to the hotel, the Jacob Wyeth home, stables for the horses who pulled the winter sleighs, and cages for the ducks used in the sport of fowling. This photo was purchased from the Wyeth Family Collection of the Cambridge Historical Commission and is used with the permission of Kathleen L. (Kit) Rawlins, Assistant Director.

Jacob managed the Fresh Pond Hotel so astutely, that when he retired after 20 years, he was very wealthy. He then leased the hotel to his nephew, Jonas Wyeth 3ᵈ (1794-1867).[366] Eventually, Jacob sold the hotel to Lyman Willard, brother-in-law of Jacob's niece and Jonas' sister, Susan Wyeth Willard (1798-1896).[367]

In 1816, Jacob had a home built near the hotel. He lived there until his death in 1857 at nearly 93 years of age.

In 1885, Jacob's house became a convent for the Sisters of St. Joseph. In the sisters' hands, the hotel was completely repurposed into a Catholic girls' school. Fresh Pond was converted to a reservoir and the area around the old resort became known as Kingsley Park. As the city of Cambridge sought to keep the reservoir's water pure, in 1889 they took the former hotel and grounds from the sisters via eminent domain. The next year, the city paid the sisters almost twice what they had paid five years before for the former resort.[368] Jacob's home / the sisters' convent was moved to 479 Concord Avenue in 1893.[369] It currently serves as a homeless shelter.[370] The hotel was moved from its original location to 234 Lakeview Avenue. The four-story building is now home to six condominiums.[371] It was added to the National Historic Register in 1982.[372]

Notes for Captain Nathaniel Jarvis Wyeth:

Oregon pioneer Nathaniel Jarvis "Nat" Wyeth was born at the hotel his father Jacob Wyeth Sr. built on land near Fresh Pond. Nat's work there as a boy was so uninteresting to him, he determined to strike out on his own. Having collected ice from the pond for the hotel's use for many years, he found a ready business just outside his door.[373]

Shortly after his marriage to his maternal first cousin, Nathaniel made the first of many inventions to improve ice harvesting and storage. The horse-drawn plow he designed was so much more efficient than pickaxe and chisel methods, Frederick Tudor, known as the Ice King, offered Nat $500 a year to manage his business.[374] Tudor's investment was well founded. On 27 Jan 1828, Tudor wrote of Nat in his journal, "Wyeth was out on the pond without hat or coat. He is equal to any difficulty which to common minds seems insurmountable."[375]

Public domain photo from "Nathaniel J. Wyeth and The Struggle For Oregon" by John Allan Wyeth M.D., *Harper's New Monthly Magazine*, Nov. 1892.

It did not take the vigorous, ingenious Nathaniel long to determine he would never become rich as Tudor's employee. By the early 1830s, Nat became convinced he could make his fortune by establishing a salmon fishery and fur trade industry over 3,000 miles away on the banks of Oregon's Columbia River. More than 25 years after Lewis and Clark landed at the river's mouth, Captain Wyeth led two expeditions across country to the American Northwest in 1832 and in 1834. He devised a half wagon / half boat vehicle, dubbed the *Natwyethum*, for land and river crossings.

Although they trained as best they could for the journey, the hardships of the trip were too great for several of the men. Many turned back on the western side of the Grand Tetons, including Nat's brother, Dr. Jacob Wyeth, and his second cousin, John Bound Wyeth.[376]

What spelled doom for the first expedition was the wreck in the South Pacific of the brig, *Sultana*. Supplies needed to set up a trading station had been sent separately via the brig from Boston around Cape Horn. The loss of the supplies was too critical to overcome.[377]

The second trip was also unsuccessful due to Captain Wyeth's inability to compete against the unscrupulous methods of the firmly entrenched Hudson Bay Company (HBC).[378] This passage from Nat's journal for that expedition is particularly poignant. It not only speaks to Nathaniel's suffering but to his indomitable spirit.

> "11 Jan 1835 …the cracking of the falling trees and the howling of the blast was more grand than comfortable. It makes two individuals feel their insignificance in the creation to be seated under a blanket with a fire in front and 3 ½ feet of snow about them and more coming and no telling when it will stop. Tonight tis calm and nearly full moon. It seems to shine with as much indifference as the storms blow... The thoughts that have run through my brain while I have been lying here in the snow would fill a volume and of such matter as was never put into one, my infancy, my youth, and its friends and faults, my manhood's troubled stream, its vagaries [wandering journeys; whimsical, wild ideas], its aloes mixed with the gall of bitterness and its results viz under a blanket hundreds, perhaps thousands, of miles from a friend, the blast howling about, and smothered in snow, poor, in debt, doing nothing to get out of it, despised for a visionary, nearly naked…"[379]

Swindled, sick and dejected, Nat wrote his wife on 22 Sep 1835, "We have lost by drowning and disease and warfare 17 persons to date and 14 now sick." To others, he wrote of his inability to send a full shipload of salmon to Boston.[380] Once back in Cambridge in Nov 1836, Nat was determined to cut his losses. He quickly sold both Fort Hall, established in present-day Idaho, and Fort William, located near present-day Portland, Oregon, to the HBC.[381]

Although the venture was not financially rewarding, it did succeed scientifically because botanist Thomas Nuttall, who quit his Harvard professorship to accompany the Captain, gathered and identified 113 species of western plants on the journey. Nuttall named sunflower genus "Wyethia" in Nat's honor.

Additionally, the Fort Hall site Nat and his men built, turned out to be the most important trading post in the Snake River Valley through the 1860s. More than 270,000 emigrants reached it while moving west on what would become known as the Oregon Trail.[382]

Even though the establishment of the Oregon Trail was not Captain Wyeth's goal, he goes down in history for leading the first westbound land expedition of Americans to travel along the trail from

The Wyeth State Park, named for Nathaniel Jarvis Wyeth, is off I-84 near Cascade Locks, Oregon in the Columbia River Gorge National Scenic Area. This photo is from a 1999 Baker family vacation. Art did a great job pulling off the road after I exclaimed, "Look! There's my name."

the Atlantic to the Pacific. In the *History of the Northwest Coast*, author Hubert Howe Bancroft, wrote although "…Wyeth's Oregon adventures were a failure, his influence on Oregon occupation and settlement was second to none. The flag of the United States was planted by him simultaneously in the heart of the continent at Fort Hall and on the seaboard of the Pacific."[383]

Once back on the ice fields, it did not take the hardworking Wyeth long to get out from under his debt. Having access to both his and his father's portion of the pond, Nat started his own ice business.

His crusade to bring the railroad to Fresh Pond in 1841 brought huge dividends by increasing the efficiency of ice transportation to the ships in Charlestown. Then the unintended consequence of the trains' sparks setting the wooden icehouses on fire, led to Nat's entry into the brick-making business. He built new icehouses out of brick from his own facility.[384]

Nat and Elizabeth did not have children. Undoubtedly, Nat's inventions were his babies.

The ice cutter he invented in 1825, had reduced the cost of harvesting ice from 30 cents to 10 cents per ton. After the Oregon expeditions, he improved the ice cutter even further. In 1844, Nat used it to free the Cunard steamship *Britannia*, then frozen into Boston harbor. Within three days, Nat cut a 200-foot channel, seven miles long, to free the ship to the open sea.[385]

Following are some of Nathaniel's inventions that qualified for a patent.[386]

When Issued	Inventions or Discoveries
18 Mar 1829	Ice, manner of cutting
1 Dec 1837	Ice, preparing for shipping
1 Dec 1840	Ice, cutting
1 Dec 1840	Ice, machinery for reducing blocks to uniform thickness
1 Dec 1840	Sleds, for transporting ice in blocks
1 Dec 1840	Ice machinery for raising blocks of, from the water-side and placing in sleds
10 Dec 1840	Ice, machinery for raising blocks of, depositing them in storehouse
10 Dec 1841	Carriages, railroad, machinery for elevating and depositing ice in
10 Dec 1841	Ice, machinery for raising blocks of
10 Dec 1841	Carriage, railroad, discharging blocks of ice there from to platforms
25 Oct 1843	Ice, cars and receiving platforms for removing blocks of
25 Oct 1843	Ice cutters and markers
28 Mar 1844	Composition for making brick

Nathaniel's inventing was not stilled until his death in 1856. The expeditions to Oregon were understandably hard on his health. He died at the comparatively young age of 54. Both his father, then at age 92, and mother, at age 88, were still living.

Captain Wyeth's grave in Mt. Auburn is inscribed, "He believed in himself." He and his wife, Elizabeth, are buried near the Perry sisters, Mary Jarvis Fish and Elizabeth Wyeth Keen. He was so close to these two nieces on his wife's side, he asked them to fulfill the wishes of his 29 Apr 1856 will should his wife not be able to do so.

Additionally, Mary Jarvis Perry Fish was entrusted with the manuscript that became, in 1899, *The Correspondence and Journals of Captain Nathaniel J. Wyeth, 1831-6*. The book's editor, F. G. Young, remarked when Mrs. Fish sent the manuscript to Oregon, "it took its third trip westward across the continent, but this time it was not 'to be painfully borne by wearisome marches through almost unbroken solitudes for weary months,' but now after 63 years to be 'swiftly carried in a few days, to find no longer at the journey's end the wilderness of nature, but the homes of an enlightened and progressive people.'"[387]

68. GAD[5] WYETH SR. (Ebenezer[4] Jr., Ebenezer[3] Sr., John[2], Nicholas[1]) was born on 27 Jul 1768 in Cambridge, Middlesex, Massachusetts. He married Mary Kendall on 01 Dec 1793 in Cambridge. **MARY "POLLY" KENDALL**, daughter of Jabez Kendall and Mary Pool, was born on 03 Dec 1770. Her parents were married in Cambridge so it is likely the city of her birth. Both Gad and Polly died in McKean Township, Licking County, Ohio … he on 01 Nov 1843 and she on 13 Jul 1855. Their graves say he was 76 and she 85 at their deaths. They rest in the cemetery across from the church their grandson, David Goddard Wyeth, built at the corner of Liberty Church Road and Dutch Lane near Johnstown, Ohio.[388]

Following are the children of Gad Wyeth Sr. and Mary "Polly" Kendall:[389] [390]

124.   i.   JONAS PARKER[6] WYETH, born 27 Oct 1794, Cambridge; married MARGARET PHILES, 25 Jul 1825, New York; died 13 May 1855, Humboldt, Coles, Illinois.

125.   ii.   GAD WYETH JR., born 04 Jul 1795, Wendell, Franklin, Massachusetts; married ELIZABETH ELLEN CHASE, 18 May 1823, Jefferson County, New York; died 01 Aug 1858, Wilna, Jefferson, New York.

126.   iii.   JOSEPH SAWIN WYETH, born 08 Nov 1796, Wendell; married (1) SARAH "SALLY" HORR, 11 Oct 1819, Denmark, Lewis, New York;[391] married (2) CYNTHA GOULDING, circa 1851, Pamelia, Jefferson, New York; he died 02 Apr 1872, Denmark, Lewis, New York.

127.   iv.   MARY WYETH born on 15 Sep 1799 [392] in Wendell; married SILAS D. STILES, 10 Feb 1825,[393] Pownal, Bennington, Vermont; died on 11 Mar 1852, Milford, Jefferson, Wisconsin.

128.   v.   NATHAN S. WYETH, born 16 May 1801, Wendell; married HANNAH PUTNAM KELLOGG,[394] on 15 Nov 1823 in Wendell (intention 11 Nov 1823); died 11 Aug 1864, while visiting one of his sons in Tuscola, Douglas, Illinois.[395]

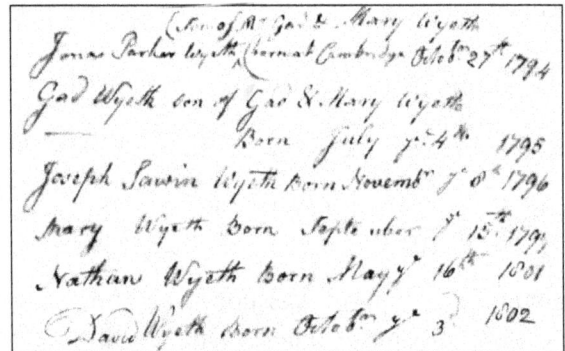

These six birth dates are from "ye" original records of Wendell in the Holbrook collection, now owned by Ancestry.com. They have been photoshopped to make them a bit more legible.

129.   vi.   DAVID G. WYETH, born 03 Oct 1802, Wendell; married SALLY KELLOGG, 02 Jan 1826,[396] Wendell; died 19 Feb 1881, Liberty Township, Licking, Ohio.

Notes for Gad Wyeth Sr. and Mary "Polly" Kendall:

Gad was just four days old when he was baptized at the First Church in Cambridge on 31 Jul 1768.[397] He and Polly were married there as well. They likely met through Gad's first cousin, Joshua Sawin, who worked in Jabez Kendall's wheelwright shop in Cambridge. Mary "Polly" Kendall was the oldest of the five Kendall daughters. Joshua Sawin also married one of the Kendall sisters – Abigail. Two more of Gad's cousins, married into the Kendall family. Joseph Sawin, married Sally Kendall and John Sawin Jr. married Lydia Kendall.[398]

Jabez built a large house in Wendell, Franklin, Massachusetts, near his sister Sarah, the wife of Daniel Fiske (1735-1763), who also was a descendant of Nicholas Wyeth.[399] In 1800, Mary and Gad resided there. Jabez also intended to move to Wendell, but when he died in Cambridge on 20 Oct 1803, he left the house to his daughter "Mrs. Gad Wyeth."[400]

Of the Kendall daughters, only Eunice did not marry a descendant of Nicholas Wyeth. She lived with her sister Mary in Wendell. When Eunice died unmarried on 23 Dec 1821, her probated will showed yet another link to the Wyeth family. She had made a loan to Gad and Mary's son, Joseph Sawin Wyeth, who was then living in the Black River country (Le Ray) of Jefferson County, New York.[401] Eunice is buried in the Wendell Center Cemetery in Franklin County, Massachusetts.[402]

On 19 Jun 1825, Gad dated a newsy letter at Wendell to his sister Anna Wyeth Cutter. His youngest son David was still at home. Four of his children were living away from him in a town where a revival of religion was in progress and two of them had become converts. After a winter marriage to Silas D. Stiles, his only daughter moved 300 miles from him to Sackets Harbor, Jefferson County, New York. He told Anna he had about 20 head of cattle, two horses and many sheep. The stage ran three times a week by his house, and he was one of its proprietors.[403]

According to the 1830 Census of the United States, Gad and Mary still lived in Wendell. Their sons David and Nathan were neighbors. Gad Wyeth Jr. and Jonas Parker Wyeth joined Joseph Sawin Wyeth in Jefferson County, New York. In the same period, Mary Wyeth Stiles' family moved from New York to the Wisconsin Territory.

At almost 70 years of age, Gad moved to be closer to his sons, Jonas Parker and Nathan S. Wyeth, both of whom had relocated to Licking County, Ohio in 1837. With their son David and his large family, Gad and Mary travelled from Wendell by stage coach over the mountains to Albany, New York to board a boat on the Erie Canal bound for Buffalo. Once in Buffalo, they boarded a scow across Lake Erie to Cleveland, Ohio. Finally, they arrived in Newark, Licking County, Ohio, on 12 Jun 1838 via an Ohio and Erie Canal packet boat. Coincidentally, the date was the first birthday of the youngest member of the group, grandson David Goddard Wyeth.[404]

Liberty Chapel, dedicated in 1867, is still active today. Chuck Walker is a current member of this church. Chuck, Gad's 3rd great grandson, lives at Sycamore Hill Farm on some of the original Wyeth land near the cemetery.

Although Gad and Mary are not named in Ohio census reports, they lived in McKean Township when the estate of Gad's sister, Anna Wyeth Cutter, was probated in 1842. In fact, their son David lived in McKean until after the 1850 census was taken.

Wyeth lands owned by David's sons, Stillman, Augustus, David Goddard, and Gad Kellogg Wyeth were in both Liberty and McKean Townships. Liberty Church Road, that runs between the cemetery where Gad and Mary rest and the church their grandson built, forms the border. All of the Wyeth brothers were significant contributors to Liberty Chapel.[405]

69. **JOHN[5] WYETH** (Ebenezer[4] Jr., Ebenezer[3] Sr., John[2], Nicholas[1]) was born on 31 Mar 1770 in Cambridge, Middlesex, Massachusetts. John married (1) Louisa Weiss on 06 Jun 1793 in the Moravian Church, Philadelphia, Philadelphia County, Pennsylvania. **LOUISA WEISS**, daughter of Wilhelm Ludwig "Lewis" Weiss and Joanna Maria Pfluger, was born on 29 Apr 1775 in Philadelphia. She died 31 May 1822, of consumption, at the age of 47 in Harrisburg, Dauphin, Pennsylvania.[406] On 02 May 1826, according to the records of the Philadelphia First Unitarian Church, John Wyeth married (2) Lydia Allen in a Unitarian ceremony at the home of Lydia's mother on Wood Street in Philadelphia. **LYDIA ALLEN**, daughter of Thomas Allen and Jane Miller, was born about 1802 in Pennsylvania. John died on 23 Jan 1858 at the age of 87 in Philadelphia. Lydia died there on 01 Nov 1862. They are buried together in Philadelphia's Laurel Hill Cemetery whereas Louisa rests next to her infant children in Harrisburg Cemetery.[407]

Laurel Hill Cemetery records show John's grave is the grassy area to the left of this grave. Although the name on this stone is worn off, this is Lydia Allen Wyeth's grave since the words "November" and "1862" are legible.

From the records of John Churchill Wyeth Jr., the known children of John Wyeth and Louisa Weiss are as follows.[408] Per William Henry Egle's genealogies, they were all born in Harrisburg after John was appointed postmaster there in 1793.[409]

     i. CHARLES[6] WYETH, born 29 Apr 1795 and died a few months later on 29 Aug 1795, Harrisburg. Per the archives of Harrisburg Cemetery, he is buried there in section L, lot 35, space 2 next to his mother who is in the first space.

130.   ii. LOUISA WYETH, born 06 Aug 1796; married SAMUEL DOUGLAS, 22 Apr 1817, Zion German Lutheran Church, Harrisburg; died 10 Nov 1875. Documentation for her will, probated on 21 Mar 1876, gave her residence as Chambersburg, Franklin, Pennsylvania.

131.   iii. JOHN WYETH JR., born 06 Jun 1798; married ELMIRA JANE "MYRA JANE" CANFIELD, 18 Mar 1828, Carlisle, Cumberland, Pennsylvania; died 11 May 1876, Chambersburg.

132.   iv. MARY WYETH, born 25 Sep 1800; married REV. DANIEL MCKINLEY JR., 31 May 1827, Harrisburg; died 15 Jan 1892 at her daughter Louisa's home in Chambersburg.[410]

    v. SARAH ANN "SALLY" WYETH, born 13 Sep 1802; died in Harrisburg less than a month later on 10 Oct 1802.

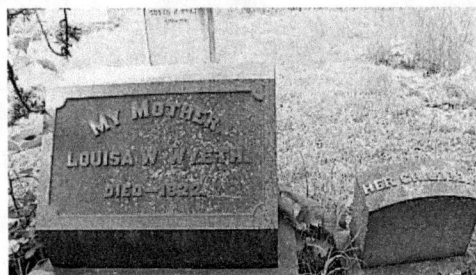

Erected by Francis for his mother Louisa Weiss Wyeth and her children, Charles, Sarah, Lewis, unnamed infant boy, Elisa and Elizabeth.

    vi. LEWIS WYETH, born 30 Aug 1804; died in infancy, 02 Oct 1804 in Harrisburg; buried section L, lot 35, space 2.

133.   vii. FRANCIS WYETH, born 05 Apr 1806; married (1) SUSAN HOUSTON MAXWELL, 12 May 1829, Mercersburg, Franklin, Pennsylvania; married (2) SARAH CAMPBELL CARSON, 13 Mar 1845, First Presbyterian Church, Harrisburg; died 02 Jul 1893, Harrisburg, Dauphin, Pennsylvania.

134. viii. (REV.) CHARLES AUGUSTUS WYETH, born 11 Nov 1808;[411] married ADELINE "ADDIE" SHEAFER, 12 May 1842, Harrisburg; died 02 Aug 1889, Warren, Warren County, Pennsylvania.[412]

ix. INFANT BOY WYETH, born 30 Mar 1811; died the same day in Harrisburg.

135. x. LOUIS WEISS WYETH, born 20 Jun 1812; married EUPHEMIA ALLAN, 09 Apr 1839, Huntsville, Madison, Alabama; died 07 Jul 1889, Guntersville, Marshall, Alabama.

xi. ELISA REBECCA WYETH, born 01 Jan 1815, as per the Zion German Lutheran Church records, which gives this spelling of her name when she was baptized in 1816. She died on 22 Apr 1816 at the age of 16 months in Harrisburg and is buried there with her infant siblings in section L, lot 35, space 2.

136. xii. SAMUEL DOUGLASS WYETH, born 16 May 1817; married CAROLINE "CARRIE" CHURCHILL WARDWELL, 11 Sep 1844, Smithfield, Providence, Rhode Island; died 15 Jan 1881, Washington, D.C.[413]

xiii. ELIZABETH WYETH was born on 21 Dec 1821. Six months later, her mother Louisa Weiss, died of consumption. Elizabeth must have caught the terribly contagious disease from her mother because she also died of it. Elizabeth was not quite two years old when she died on 06 Sep 1823 in Harrisburg.

Notes on the postmaster, newspaper publisher and printer John Wyeth:

In his excellent histories of Pennsylvania, William Henry Egle wrote about John Wyeth on several different occasions.

Egle states John first worked as a printer's apprentice to the *American Recorder* about 20 miles from Cambridge in Charlestown, Massachusetts. Then at age 18, John made a long journey from Cambridge to take a foreman's position on a newspaper in Santo Domingo.[414] However, when the 1791 slave insurrection and rebellion in neighboring Haiti spilled over the border into the Dominican Republic, John barely managed to escape with his life. He had to dress and work as a sailor to avoid detection when ships were searched before leaving the port.[415]

In due course, John landed in Philadelphia where he continued for a time working in the printing business. Anxious to strike out on his own, in 1792, together with John W. Allen, he purchased a Harrisburg, Pennsylvania, newspaper and published it successfully under the name *Oracle of Dauphin and Harrisburgh Advertiser*.[416] During John's tenure, the paper reported on all the important events of the period including the French Revolution, the death of George Washington in 1799, as well as the inauguration of five of his successors, the Louisiana Purchase in 1803, the dual of Aaron Burr and Alexander Hamilton in 1804, the Napoleonic Wars, and the admission of ten states to the union.

In the *History of Dauphin County*, author Luther Reily Kelker shows John Wyeth followed his business partner as the third postmaster of Harrisburg in Oct 1793 during the administration of George Washington.[417] William Egle wrote Wyeth was removed by President John Adams, but in another volume Egle corrected himself. The position was, in fact, removed by Thomas Jefferson's postmaster general on 27 Jan 1802.

As publisher of the *Oracle of Dauphin*, ex-postmaster John Wyeth made the following statement on the subject in the 01 Mar 1802 issue of his paper.[418]

> The public are informed that the Post Office which has been held for a number of years past by the Editor of this paper is now transferred into the hands of Mr. Wright. Mr. Jefferson's Postmaster General, Gideon Granger, having in the plenitude of his sagacity, discovered that a "printer of a newspaper is more susceptible to perjury and mal-conduct in transacting the duties required in that department," than any other profession, notwithstanding a difference of opinion hitherto held by predecessors as experienced and nearly as respectable as citizen Gideon. But whether this disgraceful stigma fixed on all newspaper printers by the Postmaster General, arises from his intimacy with Duane and other printers belonging to his sect must remain a secret in the breast of the exalted man. Be this as it will, the ex-postmaster is happy to inform his customers and friends that he has another office at present not at the disposal of Mr. Granger, in which he will be happy to receive their commands.
>
> *The Editor*

Additionally, Egle wrote John kept a book store and published books and pamphlets along with publishing the *Oracle* until 1827 when he turned the paper over to his son, Francis Wyeth. Wyeth's bookstore was well stocked with books of all kinds. He took a particular interest in music and kept supplies of tune books and sheet music on hand at all times.[419]

Later, John Wyeth made a remarkable contribution to popular music when he published an introduction to the grounds of music in his shape-note *Repository of Sacred Music.*[420] [421]

In a magazine article for music teachers entitled *John Wyeth – Early American Tunebook Publisher*, author Ross W. Ellison boldly stated: "John Wyeth has earned a niche in the history of American music not because he was a musician, but rather because he was a shrewd enough publisher to recognize the cultural and musical forces at work in Pennsylvania, weigh their relative importance, and capitalize on them by printing numerous and influential tunebooks which proved to be extremely popular and extremely profitable."[422]

Ellison also wrote that the first tunebook to come from Wyeth's press was Joseph Doll's *Der Leichte Unterricht in der Vocal Musik*. It was first advertised for sale in the Oracle of Dauphin on 13 Oct 1810.[423]

John Wyeth as depicted on page 554 of William Egle's 1888 *History of the counties of Dauphin and Lebanon in the Commonwealth of Pennsylvania.*

In that same year, John compiled *Wyeth's Repository of Sacred Music*. It sold so well, Wyeth published a second part in 1813. Ellison said part two contained a number of the folk-hymns which were widely performed at camp meetings and revivals of the early 19th century. Furthermore, Ellison believed Wyeth's music compilations were the source of many of the tunes which appeared in later shape-note collections of folk-hymns... which are religious words set to a traditional, secular folk-tune.[424]

Irving Lowens wrote shape-notes were not developed by Wyeth, but by William Little circa 1798 and published in 1803 in a book called *The Easy Instructor*.[425] However, Little's claim was challenged by Andrew Law of Connecticut who had taught singing-schools and sold tunebooks in Philadelphia. Law claimed he printed tunebooks in a similar manner as early as 1783. Regardless, Wyeth claimed no originality in the works he published.[426]

Patent medicines also sold well in John Wyeth's bookshop. Brands included Hamilton's Worm-Destroying Lozenges, Genuine Persian Lotion, Restorative Powder for the Teeth and Gums, and Asiatic Razor Strops. Ellison thought perhaps his grandsons, John and Francis Houston Wyeth, had their grandfather's medicinal success in mind when they founded Wyeth Laboratories, the great pharmaceutical house in Philadelphia.[427]

Unfortunately, drugs had not yet been invented to treat consumption, the wasting disease more commonly known today as pulmonary tuberculosis. After giving birth to 13 children in 26 years, Louisa succumbed to the deadly and very contagious infection at the young age of 47. John found the strength to carry on through his religious convictions.

Louisa and John had married in one of the oldest Protestant denominations in the world, the Moravian Church.[428] Louisa's father, the German born, Wilhelm Ludwig "Lewis" Weiss served as the denomination's attorney in Philadelphia. Louisa's sister, Rebecca, married George Kline of Carlisle, Pennsylvania. He also was a newspaper publisher.[429] Their son, William Kline, married John's niece, Abbey Wyeth, the daughter of Ebenezer Wyeth III.[430]

In Harrisburg, John and Louisa attended the Salem Reformed Church and the Zion German Lutheran Church, as evidenced by the baptisms of some of their children. The Reformed Church, like John's church back in Cambridge, would eventually merge with the Evangelicals and the majority of Congregational Christian Churches to form the United Church of Christ.[431] John had grown up in the Congregationalist tradition listening to the Calvinistic doctrine that was central to the Puritan beliefs of his ancestors. However, in the beginning of the 19th century, many members of the Cambridge church became more liberal in their views and turned toward Unitarianism.[432]

Like several members of his own Cambridge family,[433] John also made the shift away from fundamentalist theology to the Unitarian church. In 1826, John chose the newly ordained Unitarian minister, Rev. William Henry Furness, to perform the ceremony when he married his second wife, Lydia Allen, in Philadelphia.[434] [435]

Lydia may have been related to John's early *Oracle of Dauphin* partner. Soon after their marriage, John retired to Philadelphia. There he continued to be constantly busy. He believed strongly in education and saw to the higher education of his children.

The 1850 census shows John living with Lydia's brother, Dr. George W. Allen and sister, Jane Allen, in the Spring Garden Ward of Philadelphia, Pennsylvania. It must have been a lively household as John's youngest son, Samuel Douglass Wyeth, his daughter-in-law, Caroline Wardwell Wyeth and three of John's grandchildren, George Wardwell, Rebecca Churchill and Frances Jane Wyeth, all under the age of five, filled the house. John was noted for his likeable and cheerful personality and he undoubtedly enjoyed time with the young children.

When John died on 23 Jan 1858 in Philadelphia, he was approaching 88 years of age. According to his obituary, he was universally respected for his integrity and uprightness. He had a reputation for courage and honesty worthy of emulation.[436]

He left his heirs a considerable fortune for the time period. Surviving children, Louisa Douglas, Mary McKinley, John Wyeth Jr., Francis Wyeth, Rev. Charles Augustus Wyeth, and Louis Weiss Wyeth, were all bequeathed property in John's will. To his last son, he stated, "I have already paid and advanced to my son Samuel Douglass Wyeth his full share of my estate, and therefore have not given or devised to him any part thereof except a portion of the residue as here in after mentioned." To his "beloved wife, Lydia Wyeth," John left an income from interest on property valuations.[437]

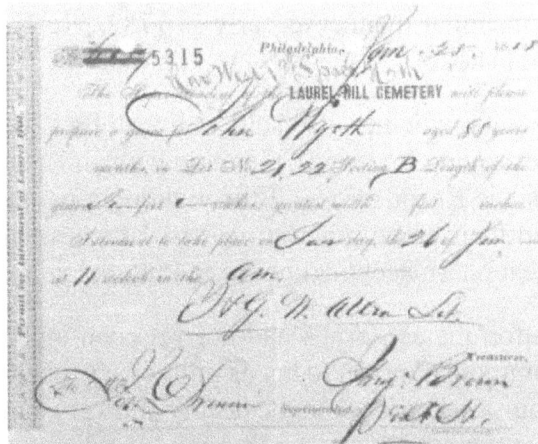

This 25 Jan 1858 Allen family plot grave preparation request for John Wyeth is courtesy of Laurel Hill Cemetery.

One of the investments specifically mentioned in the will was the 1822 Shakespeare House situated on Locust Street and Raspberry Alley in Harrisburg that he left to his two daughters. It contained a ballroom, a theatre and a social center. Under vintage photos at www.pennlive.com, there is a picture, from the Historical Society of Dauphin County, of the building after it was converted into the Bijou Theatre. Although the structure was torn down in 1907, Wyeth Street in midtown Harrisburg, near the banks of the Susquehanna River, still honors John Wyeth in the year 2018.

70. **LUCY[5] WYETH** (Jonas[4] Sr., Ebenezer[3] Sr., John[2], Nicholas[1]) was born on 07 Feb 1754 in Cambridge, Middlesex, Massachusetts. She married **THOMAS COOLIDGE** in Apr 1773.[438] Thomas, the son of David Coolidge and Mary Mixer, was born 05 Mar 1748 in Watertown, Middlesex, Massachusetts. Thomas died on 07 Jan 1835 in Livermore, Androscoggin, Maine, at age 86.[439] Lucy died there on 16 Oct 1850 at the age of 96.[440]

The photo of this portrait of Lucy Wyeth Coolidge, painted by an itinerant artist circa 1845, is courtesy of Muriel Bowerman, President of the Livermore/Livermore Falls Historical Society with help from Lucy's 4th great granddaughter, Jane Winslow Coolidge.

The nine children of Thomas Coolidge and Lucy Wyeth included:

    i. JONAS[6] COOLIDGE born on 14 Feb 1774 in Watertown; died on 11 May 1860 in Boston, Suffolk, Massachusetts.

    ii. CORNELIUS COOLIDGE, born on 30 Sep 1776 in Watertown; died 04 Sep 1843 in Dexter, Penobscot, Maine.

    iii. THOMAS COOLIDGE JR., born on 14 Feb 1778 in Watertown; married PHEBE PAUL, 1810; died on 23 Jun 1846 in Livermore.

    iv. ELISHA COOLIDGE, born 30 May 1784, Watertown; died on 08 Nov 1862 in Solon, Somerset, Maine.

Notes for Thomas Coolidge and Lucy Wyeth:

Thomas was a descendant of John Coolidge the seventh great grandfather of President Calvin Coolidge. Interestingly, John Coolidge is also the ancestor of Deacon Joseph Coolidge who married the daughter of Rebecca Andrews Frost Jacobs and raised Deborah Wyeth Gamage (1690-1773) and Martha Wyeth Fessenden (1696-1726).

Thomas and Lucy moved to Livermore in 1790. There the family grew grafted apples that they transported to Portland, Maine for shipping to England.[441] Although unrecognizable from its early days, their house, now covered in bright blue siding, still stands in 2018 at 360 Sanders Road, Livermore, Maine.[442] Lucy and Thomas are buried a few fields away, in Alden Cemetery, at the corner of Bowles and Sanders Roads.[443]

71. (MAJOR) JONAS⁵ WYETH (Jonas⁴ Sr., Ebenezer³ Sr., John², Nicholas¹) was born on 13 Apr 1762 in Cambridge, Middlesex, Massachusetts. According to his own handwritten records now archived at the New England Historic Genealogical Society (NEHGS) in Boston, he was married twice.[444] He married (1) Hephzibah Hastings, the widow of Joseph Sawin, on 14 Nov 1787 in Cambridge. **HEPHZIBAH HASTINGS**, daughter of Samuel Hastings and Lydia Tidd, was born on 03 Jul 1762 in Lexington, Middlesex, Massachusetts. She died on 17 May 1790 in Lexington. Major Jonas Wyeth married (2) Susan Stearns on 29 Nov 1800 in Waltham, Middlesex, Massachusetts. **SUSAN STEARNS**, daughter of (Captain) Phinehas Stearns and Mary Wellington, was born on 08 Aug 1774 in Waltham, Middlesex, Massachusetts. Phinehas also is descended from Nicholas Wyeth through his daughter Sarah Wyeth Fiske. Major Jonas died in Cambridge on 08 Jul 1828. Susan died on 25 Mar 1855 in Cambridge.

The dates for Major Jonas Wyeth's seven children come from his journal of family records held by NEHGS. With his first wife, Hephzibah Hastings Sawin, Jonas had the following children:

> i. LYDIA⁶ HASTINGS WYETH, born 16 Aug 1788 and baptized 24 Aug 1788, Cambridge, Middlesex, Massachusetts;[445] died on 17 Feb 1789 at the age of six months in Cambridge.
>
> ii. HENRY HASTINGS WYETH, born 27 Feb 1790 and baptized 07 Mar 1790, Cambridge;[446] died 18 May 1790, at two months and 21 days, probably at the home of his Lexington grandparents.

Major Jonas Wyeth and Susan Stearns had the following children:

> i. AUGUSTUS⁶ WYETH, born on 15 Dec 1801, Cambridge; died there, 15 Jul 1831 at age 29 years and seven months.
>
> ii. LYDIA WYETH, born on 25 Jul 1804 in Cambridge. On 29 Jul 1804 she was baptized at First Church, in private, due to being dangerously ill from cancer. She died on 13 Sep 1804 at the age of seven weeks and two days.[447]
>
> 137. iii. JONAS WYETH 2ᵈ, born 14 Dec 1806, Cambridge; married (1) MARY TORREY HANCOCK, 01 Jan 1833, Cambridge; married (2) SARAH ELIZABETH BENSON, widow of Malthus Augustus Johnson, 02 May 1854, Scott County, Iowa; died 03 Jun 1868, Cambridge.
>
> 138. iv. EMELY WYETH, born 12 Sep 1809, Cambridge; married JAMES BARNARD READ, 09 Nov 1828, Cambridge; died 19 Sep 1864, Boston.
>
> v. SUSANNA STEARNS WYETH, born 03 Oct 1816, Cambridge; died there, 31 Aug 1817 at the age of nine months and 29 days of dysentery.

Notes on Major Jonas Wyeth's family:

Lucius Paige in the History of Cambridge, said Jonas was generally known as Major Wyeth.[448] Indeed, the 1820 census for Cambridge lists him as such. It is not clear why he held the title "major" since Jonas had very limited military experience, if any. (Alyssa Pacy, Archivist at the Cambridge Public Library could find no records for the designation. She thought perhaps the title was honorary due to Jonas' wealth or that he served in the militia between wars.)

With all the Jonas Wyeths in Cambridge, it is difficult to distinguish who was called on 30 Oct 1778 to appear the following day at Cambridge with three days provisions, armed and equipped to march to Boston to serve under General Heath until 09 Nov 1778.[449] As shown in the pension application for Elizabeth E. Smith Wyeth, that 1778 service was credited to her husband, Jonas Wyeth Jr. (1757-1817). When Major Jonas' son, Jonas Wyeth 2d, wrote a letter to the commissioner of pensions to help Elizabeth E. Smith Wyeth, he stated his father was too young for service during the Revolutionary War.[450] Major Jonas was, in fact, only 16 in 1778.

By contrast, Major Jonas Wyeth was too old to serve in the War of 1812. The Jonas drafted for service in Captain Samuel Child's Cambridge Light Infantry, camped at South Boston for 51 days starting on 10 Sep 1814, was Jonas Wyeth 3d (son of Elizabeth E. Smith Wyeth). Elizabeth Nutting Flagg wife of Jonas Wyeth 3d (1794-1867), applied for a pension based on the 1814 service.[451]

Major Jonas was a Cambridge selectman (councilman) during the years 1819-1821. Having inherited the Garden Street homestead that had been passed down for over 150 years from Nicholas to his father Jonas Wyeth Sr., the major apparently was very wealthy and quite a large landowner in the area. Referred to also as Jonas Wyeth Esquire, the honor signifies he was of superior rank, ability, or power in a specified class. According to *Random House Kernerman Webster's College Dictionary*, that signification is the secondary definition of the word "major."

Although well off financially, his life was not without hardship. He lost four children while they were still infants. He buried one, his first son, in the same grave with his young wife who had died the day before. He wrote in his journal "Hephzibah Wyeth, wife to Jonas Wyeth Jun dyed May 17th 1790. Aged 27 years 10 months and 13 days – and had been married two years, six months and three days – Henry Wyeth son of said Jonas and Heph. dyed 18 May 1790. Aged two months and 21 days." The sorrow of those words diverges starkly with the entry on the journal's previous page where Jonas had proudly written he was 25 years and seven months and Hephzibah 25 years and four months at their wedding.[452]

It was over ten years more when Major Jonas Wyeth wrote he was in the 39th year of his age and Susan was in her 27th year when they married. This long gap probably had some bearing on why he did not believe he had the ability to raise Hephzibah's children from her first marriage, Sarah "Sally" Sawin and John Sawin Jr. Hephzibah's daughter was brought up by her Hastings' grandfather and her five-year-old orphan son was sent out to be a farm hand.[453]

Jonas' next journal entry said "My honored mother Heph. Wyeth wife of Jonas Wyeth first – dyed May 24th 1801 in the 71st year of her age."

He went on to give the births of his five children with his second wife, Susan, and the deaths of their babies Lydia and Susanna Stearns Wyeth. This journal entry, undoubtedly written by Jonas 2ᵈ about his father, appeared next after baby Susanna's death record.

Major Jonas wrote his will on 03 Jun 1828. The date was about a month before his death. It was recorded as case #25816 in the

This 1828 notation by Jonas Wyeth 2ᵈ of Major Jonas Wyeth's death comes from the *Wyeth family records* (Mss A 3058), R. Stanton Avery Special Collections. Courtesy of the New England Historic Genealogical Society (NEHGS).

Middlesex County Court House in Cambridge. Curiously, the will also appeared in the records of Chittenden, Vermont and Strafford, New Hampshire. Here are a few excerpts from the will:

Item – I give bequeath and devise to my son Augustus Wyeth all my real estate situated in Cambridge, West Cambridge and Brighton in said county also all and every part of my said dwelling house subject to the rights therein above given to my said wife, also all my farming utensils and all my livestock, also the two beds, bedding and bedsteads which are in the kitchen chamber and entry chamber and the use of the cooking furniture in common with my said wife so far as shall be necessary… I also give, bequeath and devise unto my said son Augustus Wyeth all my wearing apparel and all my property real and personal which I have herein given to my said wife during the term she shall remain my widow excepting therefrom said plate, but on condition of his paying my son, Jonas, $2,000 out of the same, in one year…

Item – I give and bequeath the use of my library equally to my said wife and to my said two sons Augustus and Jonas during her life and at her decease, I give and bequeath said library to my said two sons equally.

Item – I give and bequeath unto my daughter, Emely Wyeth, for her sole and separate use and control, without the interference, in any way whatever, of any person to whom she shall, at any time hereafter be married, the income or interest of $1,500 to be paid to her, and to her only, semi-annually from the time of my death, by my said executor, … but if said Emely shall marry, then I hereby order my said executor, during the time she shall be a married woman, not to pay any part of said income, or interest, of said $1,500, as aforesaid to said Emely, or her husband… But if said Emely shall marry, and while she continues to be a married woman, shall in the opinion of my said executor, be poor and necessitous, then, if said executor, in the exercise of his direction shall think it expedient and necessary for her support, to pay the whole, or part of said last mentioned income, or interest, of said $1,500 then I so far qualify what is above written in the item, as to authorize and empower said executor, in the exercise of his discretion, to pay her during the period of such poverty and necessity, the whole, or any part, of said last mentioned income or interest…

Item – … I give and bequeath unto my two sons, Augustus Wyeth and Jonas Wyeth, to be equally divided between them, all the residue and remainder of the money, or monies, which, at the time of my decease, shall be, in any way, due and owing to me, on my book accounts, promissory notes, bonds, mortgages, other securities …

Lastly – I do hereby nominate, constitute and appoint my said son, Augustus Wyeth, to be the sole executor of this my last will and testament…"

The will was signed, sealed, published and declared by the said Jonas Wyeth Esquire and witnessed by Job Wyeth, Torrey Hancock and Abraham Hilliard.[454]

Unfortunately, the executor, Augustus Wyeth, only lived three years after his father's death. His house at 69 Dunster Street is one of the few remaining houses in the Harvard Square area built in the early 19th century. At his death, Augustus left the house to Emely Wyeth and most of his and his father's estates to Jonas Wyeth 2^d.

Susan never remarried. She remained Major Jonas' widow for almost 27 years. On her death bed, Susan apologized to her son, Jonas Wyeth 2^d and his wife, Mary Torrey Hancock, for falsehoods she had told before their marriage separation.[455]

Susan was buried alongside her husband in Mt. Auburn Cemetery, Mimosa Path, lot 1161. Before the entry in the family journal for his mother's death, Jonas Wyeth 2^d wrote, "12 Sep 1845 = the remains of Hepsibah Wyeth (Tidd), of Lydia Wyeth, of Jonas Wyeth son of Ebenezer Wyeth (the first Jonas mentioned in these records), of Susanna Wyeth, of Jonas Wyeth the second in these records, and of Augustus Wyeth, were removed from the family tomb in old Cambridge to the Mt. Auburn Cemetery and deposited in the north corner of lot number 1161."[456] Major Jonas Wyeth's name is the last one listed on the monument erected by Jonas Wyeth 2^d to honor his ancestors back to Nicholas Wyeth.

The remains of Jonas Sr. and Major Jonas were moved to Mt. Auburn in 1845. The remains of Nicholas, John and Ebenezer (top three names on this stone) still rest at the Old Burying Ground in Harvard Square.

72. **TAPLEY⁵ WYETH M.D.** (Jonas⁴ Sr., Ebenezer³ Sr., John², Nicholas¹) was born on 11 May 1765 in Cambridge, Middlesex, Massachusetts.[457] He graduated there from Harvard College in 1786. Dr. Tapley Wyeth and Sarah "Sally" Fiske were married on 26 Mar 1795 in Sherborn, Middlesex, Massachusetts. **SARAH "SALLY" FISKE**, daughter of John Fiske and Sarah Hill, was born there on 08 Jul 1772. Tapley died in his adopted town on 17 Sep 1813 at the age of 48. Sally spent a long time as a widow. She died on 18 Mar 1853 at the age of 80 in Sherborn.[458]

Dr. Tapley Wyeth and Sarah "Sally" Fiske had the following children:

> i. ELIZABETH "ELIZA" FISKE⁶ WYETH, born 21 Jan 1799, Sherborn, Middlesex, Massachusetts; died there, unmarried, on 17 May 1823 at the age of 24.
> ii. LUCY COOLIDGE WYETH, born on 16 May 1801 in Sherborn; died there, unmarried, on 20 Nov 1881, at the age of 80.

Family notes for Dr. Tapley Wyeth and Sarah "Sally" Fiske:

On the official website of the Town of Sherborn, Dr. Tapley Wyeth is referred to as one of their most prominent late 18th and early 19th century citizens.[459]

He apparently moved to the town shortly after his 1786 graduation from Harvard College. The central part of his house, which still stands at 46 North Main Street, was built circa 1790-1798 specifically for Dr. Wyeth.[460] Additionally, Dr. Wyeth's early arrival in the town is confirmed by his listings in the 1800 and 1810 Sherborn census reports.

Also shown on the Sherborn website is the notation of author Francis Bardwell that "The name Tapley brands him of Essex County, for the family of Tapley is as much of Essex County as are Choate and Peabodys." [461] Indeed, he was likely named for his uncle Mansfield Tapley Jr. whose family was originally from Salem, Essex, Massachusetts. But, of course, Tapley Wyeth grew up in Cambridge on land his second great grandfather, Nicholas Wyeth, had purchased on 20 Jul 1645 near the town common.

Tapley Wyeth's house still stands in the same Sherborn location where it was built over two centuries ago.

Betsy Johnson, curator of Sherborn's Historical Society, kindly sent documentation about the smallpox hospital Dr. Wyeth set up in 1792. [462] He was on the forefront of the work to eradicate the deadly disease through inoculation. Tapley, as well, served the government of Sherborn for six years as a selectman (city councilman). Then in the year of his death, he represented Sherborn in the General Court. [463]

Tapley's obituary described him as "an eminent physician, and highly useful and respectable member of society, a member of the Massachusetts Medical Society, and of the Legislature of this Commonwealth." [464]

Eliza died ten years after her father. She apparently had her own monument before her name was added to this marker showing Tapley, Sarah, Eliza and Lucy all on one stone. The new owners of the Main Street house recently discovered her original stone in their basement. [465]

Daughter, Lucy Coolidge Wyeth, was named for her aunt who settled in Livermore, Maine. Lucy, a dressmaker, never married. [466] She lived to be almost as old as her mother, Sarah. "Sally" was aged 80 years, eight months and 10 days at her death. All four family members are buried in the Plain Burial Ground at 112 North Main Street, Sherborn.

73. **JOHN^5 SAWIN** (Susannah^4 Wyeth, Ebenezer^3 Sr., John^2, Nicholas^1) was born on 07 Feb 1759 in Watertown, Middlesex, Massachusetts. During the Revolution, he was a corporal in Capt. Joseph Fuller's Company, Colonel Samuel Bullard's Regiment. He engaged in the service on 20 Aug 1777 and was discharged at Stillwater, Maine on 29 Nov 1777. [467] Then John served an apprenticeship with blacksmith Newton Baxter near Watertown bridge. He followed his training in a one year carriage-making partnership with his cousin, Joshua Wyeth Sr. On 17 Apr 1781, John married **HEPHZIBAH HASTINGS** in Watertown and they settled in Cambridge where he set up shop in barracks built on Prospect Hill for British Lieutenant General John Burgoyne's soldiers. On 23 Feb 1786, John and Hephzibah were admitted to First Church as full members and their children, Sally and John, were both baptized. The ceremonies took place at their Cambridge home due to John being deathly ill from consumption. John was just 27 years old when he died on 22 Mar 1786. The next year,

on 14 Nov 1787, Hephzibah married John's first cousin, Major Jonas Wyeth.[468] Hephzibah, too, was only 27 when she died on 17 May 1790. Jonas buried her in the same grave with their infant son who died just one day after his mother.[469]

John Sawin and Hephzibah Hastings had the following children:

    i. SARAH "SALLY"[6] SAWIN was born on 04 Sep 1782 in Cambridge, Middlesex, Massachusetts. She married (COLONEL) JOSHUA RUSSELL, son of Jesse Russell and Elizabeth Whipple, in 1812. He was born on 09 Jun 1766 in Woburn, Middlesex, Massachusetts. Sally died 03 Jul 1822, Lexington.[470]

    ii. JOHN SAWIN JR., born 11 May 1785 in Cambridge; married LYDIA KENDALL, daughter of Jabez Kendall and Mary Pool, on 19 Oct 1806 in Cambridge. Lydia was born on 10 Apr 1787 in Cambridge. He died on 25 Sep 1865 in Wendell, Franklin, Massachusetts. She died on 05 Nov 1872 in Belchertown, Hampshire, Massachusetts.[471]

74. **JOHN[5] TAPLEY** (Mary E.[4] Wyeth, Ebenezer[3] Sr., John[2], Nicholas[1]) was born on 07 Apr 1774 in Cambridge, Middlesex, Massachusetts. John, employed as a blacksmith, then living in Waltham, married **LYDIA TUFTS**, daughter of Samuel Tufts and Martha Adams, on 03 Nov 1795 in Cambridge. She was born on 24 May 1778 in Charlestown, Suffolk, Massachusetts and, like Charles Tufts (1781–1876), of Tufts University fame, Lydia is descended from Peter Tufts (1617–1700). Both John Tapley and his wife Lydia died in Charlestown ... he on 27 Dec 1847 and she on 15 Jul 1860.

The children of John Tapley and Lydia Tufts included:

    i. JOHN MANSFIELD[6] TAPLEY, born 24 Apr 1798, Newburyport, Essex, Massachusetts; died in Charlestown on 12 May 1843 of consumption.

    ii. SAMUEL TUFTS TAPLEY, born 26 Jul 1810, Charlestown; died 08 Feb 1872 at the age of 61 in Lexington, Middlesex, Massachusetts.

75. **(CAPTAIN) NOAH[5] WYETH** (Noah[4] Sr., Ebenezer[3] Sr., John[2], Nicholas[1]) was born on 24 Jun 1763 in Cambridge, Middlesex, Massachusetts. Captain Noah Wyeth and Hannah Kimble Thomas were married on Christmas day 1795 in New York City, New York County, New York. **HANNAH KEMBLE THOMAS**, daughter of Alexander Thomas and Mary Kemble, was baptized on 08 Oct 1775 in Andover, Essex, Massachusetts. She grew up in Boston. After mariner Wyeth was lost at sea, and because he died without a will, Hannah was made administratrix of his estate in New York City on 29 Jan 1806.

Captain Noah Wyeth and Hannah Kimble Thomas had the following children:

    i. ISAAC[6] WYETH, born 25 Apr 1797, New York City; died there, 01 Sep 1817.[472]

    ii. ANDREW WYETH, born 11 Aug 1798, New York City; died there, 07 Sep 1835.[473]

    iii. ALEXANDER THOMAS WYETH was born on 14 Aug 1800 in New York City. Following in his father's footsteps, he was a mariner with New York Seaman's Protection Certificates issued in 1820 and 1823. At some point, he moved to Newburyport, Essex, Massachusetts which was his residence while not at sea. On 27 Jan 1832, near Havana, Cuba, he fell to his death from the main-top-gallant-yard of the New York port ship *Huntsville*.[474]

139. iv. MARY KEMBLE THOMAS WYETH, born 12 Aug 1801, New York City; married JOHN SPENCER HADLEY, 03 Jun 1820, Dutch Reformed Church, New York City;[475] died there at her home at 47 West 52nd St. on 23 Mar 1880.

140. v. NOAH WYETH III was born 28 Aug 1804, New York City; he also was a mariner with Seamen's Protection Certificates issued to him in 1815 and 1824. He married MARY KEMBLE JOHNSON, circa 1843, New York City. He died 18 Feb 1870 on Staten Island at Sailor's Snug Harbor, New Brighton, New York.[476]

Notes about Captain Noah Wyeth:

For five years at the end of the 18th century, advertisements for Captain Wyeth's sailing ship, *Pallas*, filled the pages of New York newspapers. The first one preserved is from 02 Dec 1795. In the old writing of the day the ad apparently talks about selling rugs that were damaged during shipping from Leith, Scotland aboard the *Pallas*. "… and at 10:00, under the inspection of the ardens of the port, for account of the Underwriters, 2 bales carpetting, imported and damaged on board the brig *Pallas*, Noah Wyeth, master, on passage from Leith."[477]

Then on 28 Jan 1796, papers advertised space for cargo and passengers on the *Pallas*. One read, "For Amsterdam, the launch brig *Pallas,* Noah Wyeth, Commander, will sail in a few days, having great part of her cargo engaged. For the remainder, or passage, apply to the master on board, Moore's wharf, or Waning and Edwards."[478]

After returning from Amsterdam, on 17 Aug 1796, the captain had some stock collected on the trip for sale. A handwritten notice, found recently on an eBay auction, states, "At Jones's wharf from on board the brig *Pallas*, Noah Wyeth, master 17 butts Holland proof Brandy... for terms, apply to Thomas Buchanan, No. 41 Wall-Street."

In an ad from the *New-York Gazette* dated 16 Mar 1797, the *Pallas* is no longer listed as a "brig." Instead it is called a "snow."

Lance Woodworth photograph of the Brig *Niagara* full sail near South Bass Island, Ohio on Lake Erie in June 2009.

Webster's 1913 dictionary describes a snow as a square-rigged vessel, differing from a brig only in that she has a trysail mast close behind the mainmast, on which a large trysail is hoisted.[479] Apparently, brigs were a little slower due to the way the aft sail was attached.

One of the few remaining brigs afloat is the USS *Niagara* which served as the relief flagship for Oliver Hazard Perry in the Battle of Lake Erie during the War of 1812. This beautiful photo of it, originally posted to Flickr, is courtesy of Lance Woodworth and creativecommons.org.[480]

With his modified ship, on 16 Mar 1797, Captain Wyeth was bound for Dublin, Ireland. "The snow *Pallas*, Noah Wyeth, master, burthen 190 tons will sail with all dispatch, having part of her cargo engaged. She is a strong good vessel. For freight or passage, having good accommodations, apply to the Captain on board, at Hallet's wharf..."[481]

Two more records for 1797 exist for Captain Noah along with the 1800 census when he lived near the Bowery neighborhood in Manhattan Ward No. 7.[482] In the census, in addition to his wife, he had three boys, his sons, under the age of ten. There also was one girl. As she was aged between 10 through 15, she was too old to be a daughter. She may have been a household servant.

In the year 1801, when his fourth child and only daughter, Mary, was born, page 319 of the *New-York Directory* shows this listing: "Wyeth, Noah, shipsmaster, Bowery."

Sometime before Nov of 1801, Noah apparently changed commands. Shipping news of the *Commercial Advertiser* on 29 Jan 1802, under the heading "From French papers, Nov. 15-16" states the brig *Happy Couple,* commanded by Wyeth is at St. Malo, France whereas the *Pallas* commanded by Alford is at Bordeaux.[483]

A few months earlier, the armed brig *Happy Couple*, returned to New York on 02 Sep 1801 from Genoa and Leghorn, Italy. She was laden, not only with a cargo of nutmeg, soap, sweet oil, vermicelli, Moroccan leather, parmesan cheese and fine bandana handkerchiefs, but with intelligence for the government.[484] [485] On 12 Jul 1801, while guiding his ship through the waters of the Barbary Coast, Captain Wyeth witnessed British Admiral James Saumarez's victory in the battle for the Gut of Gibraltar, during the French Revolutionary Wars. There a small Royal Naval force fought a more superior squadron of ships from the Spanish and French Fleets. On the morning after the attacks, Captain Wyeth saw two Spanish ships blow up. They were supposedly two deckers, each having 1,040 men on board. Captain Wyeth's story to the *New-York Gazette* was so important, it was carried in dispatches to Washington, D.C. as well.[486]

The captain's next charge appears to be the ship *Alknomack*. On her way to Jamaica, she was boarded on 26 Sep 1803 by a well-armed French privateer warship carrying between 60 and 70 men. However, after detaining Wyeth's vessel for an hour, the privateer allowed the *Alknomack* to proceed on to Falmouth.[487] Loaded with 35 puncheons of rum, the ship arrived in her home port of New York on 03 Dec 1803.[488]

Shortly before, or just after, the birth of his fifth child in 1804, Captain Wyeth must have died at sea. His 30-year-old widow was left to care for four boys and one girl ranging in age from eight years old to just a few months old.

Starting with a salute to U.S. independence, Noah's probate record reads, "The People of the State of New York, by the Grace of God, Free and Independent: To Hannah Wyett (sic) the widow of Noah Wyett (sic) late of the City of New York Mariner deceased … lately died intestate … appoint you, the said Hannah administratrix … at the city of New-York, the 29th day of January in the year of our Lord 1806 and of our independence the 30th." [489]

Hannah's death date is unknown. Records show, however, that at least two of her sons, Alexander Thomas and Noah, followed in their mariner father's footsteps. The family's grief must have been beyond belief when Alexander Thomas Wyeth also died at sea.

76. **ELIZABETH**[5] **WYETH** (Noah[4] Sr., Ebenezer[3] Sr., John[2], Nicholas[1]) was born on 04 Mar 1765 in Cambridge, Middlesex, Massachusetts. Elizabeth Wyeth married (1) Andrew S. Newell on 14 Feb 1785 in First Church, Cambridge. **ANDREW S. NEWELL**, son of David Newell and Mary Gardner, was baptized on 10 Feb 1751 in Charlestown, Suffolk, Massachusetts. Andrew died on 31 Aug 1798 in New York City.[490] Elizabeth married (2) Simeon Fawcett (Fawsit) on 22 Apr 1802 in New York City.[491] **SIMEON FAWCETT** was born about 1765 in London, England. He died on 25 Dec 1811 in New York City. Elizabeth died there on 13 Apr 1829.[492]

The children of Andrew S. Newell and Elizabeth Wyeth included:[493]

        i. CATHERINE[6] NEWELL was born on 14 Jun 1786 in Charlestown; married (1) JACOB WARNER circa 1802; married (2) NICHOLAS STRIPPEL, 20 Apr 1821, New York City; died 12 Mar 1869, Fishkill, Dutchess, New York.

141.   ii. MARY FROTHINGHAM NEWELL, born 22 Aug 1787, Charlestown; married ANTHONY TIEMANN, 28 Apr 1804, New York City; died 27 Dec 1864, New York City.

       iii. ELIZABETH NEWELL, born 12 Jun 1789, Charlestown; NATHANIEL CONKLIN, 12 May 1804; died 07 Mar 1824, in New York City.

       iv. ABIGAIL NEWELL, born 12 Feb 1793, New York City; married CORNELIUS CONKLIN, 06 Sep 1811; died 15 Feb 1886, Brooklyn, Kings, New York.

Simeon Fawcett and Elizabeth Wyeth had the following children:[494]

       i. CATHARINE ELIZABETH[6] FAWCETT, born 20 Jan 1805, New York City; married GEORGE ARMSTRONG, circa 1834, New York City; died 18 Oct 1871, Fishkill, Duchess, New York. It is unusual to have two children living at the same time with the same name; however, her name is confirmed in the 1842 death record of her son, Charles H. Armstrong.

       ii. CHARLES NEWELL FAWCETT, born on 17 Aug 1806, New York City; died there on 22 Aug 1812.

Notes on the family of Elizabeth Wyeth:

Elizabeth was Andrew S. Newell's third wife. She and Andrew only had daughters… two of whom were named for Andrew's wives, Mary Frothingham and Abigail Bridges.

During the Revolutionary War, Andrew served as a cook on the brig *Massachusetts*.[495] In private life, he was a cooper. Many of Andrew's relatives served in the Revolution. Most notably, his first cousin once removed, Eliphalet Newell Jr. (1735-1803), was Ebenezer, Jonas, and Joshua Wyeth's captain.

Andrew's male line ended when he and his only sons, by his second marriage, died from yellow fever within days of each other.[496][497] Andrew's name does, however, carry on famously through his second great grandnephew, Chadds Ford artist, Andrew Newell Wyeth (1917-2009).

While settling her husband Andrew's estate, Elizabeth gave notice of her address as 10 Crane

Street, corner of Front Street.[498] She apparently was still living there in her second marriage, for Simeon Fawcett's funeral was held at that residence.[499] Old Manhattan maps show Crane's Wharf (Crane Street) on the East River close to Beekman Street on the southern part of the island. Thus, Elizabeth lived a few streets east of her Bowery brother, Captain Noah. Crane's Wharf is gone, but present day it would be between the Brooklyn Bridge and the South Street Seaport Museum.

When Elizabeth married Simeon Fawcett in New York City, the newspaper report listed his London, England birthplace.[500] Like Andrew S. Newell, Simeon also was a barrel maker. At Simeon's death, three different New York City newspapers spelled his name "Simon Fawsit" in death notices. But at Elizabeth's death, notices spelled her name "Fawcett." Her funeral was held in Manhattan at the house of Anthony Tiemann, Bloomingdale Road, on 15 Apr 1829.[501]

77. **RHODA[5] WYETH** (Noah[4] Sr., Ebenezer[3] Sr., John[2], Nicholas[1]) was born on 18 May 1768 in Cambridge, Middlesex, Massachusetts. Rhoda Wyeth married **ARTEMAS MANNING**, son of John Manning and Prudence Houghton, on 23 Oct 1794 in Mason, Hillsborough, New Hampshire. He was born on 13 Aug 1766 in Lancaster, Worcester, Massachusetts. He died on 08 May 1838 at the age of 71 in Washington, Sullivan, New Hampshire. She died on 17 Feb 1866 at the age of 97 in Lempster, Sullivan, New Hampshire.

The children of Artemas Manning and Rhoda Wyeth included:

    i. ARTEMAS[6] MANNING II, born 19 Jul 1795, Mason; died there, 13 Sep 1796.

    ii. SALLY MANNING, born 21 Feb 1797, Mason; married MOSES LOWELL, 27 Mar 1823, Washington, Sullivan, New Hampshire; died there, 04 May 1835.

    iii. ARTEMAS MANNING III, born 24 Nov 1798, Mason; died there, 08 Aug 1800.

    iv. HORATIO MANNING, born 25 Jun 1800, Mason; died there on 10 Jul 1810.

    v. RHODA MANNING, born 30 Sep 1802, Mason; married (1) JOSHUA FARNUM, 09 Jan 1820, Stoddard, Cheshire, New Hampshire; married (2) JAMES REED, 24 Feb 1828, Dunstable, Hillsborough, New Hampshire; died 02 Mar 1841, Boston, Suffolk, Massachusetts.

    vi. PRUDENCE MANNING, born on 25 Aug 1804 in Mason; married (1) LIEUMAN THOMPSON, 14 May 1829, Washington, Sullivan, New Hampshire; married (2) RALPH SPENCER, 29 Nov 1843, Stoddard, Cheshire, New Hampshire; died on 05 Oct 1878, Lempster, Sullivan, New Hampshire.

    vii. BETSEY MANNING, born 06 Jun 1808, Mason; married (1) EZRA LOWELL WRIGHT, 07 Jul 1826, Washington, Sullivan, New Hampshire; married (2) ZOPHAR WRIGHT, 04 Sep 1877, Nelson, Cheshire, New Hampshire; died there, 12 Apr 1879.

Notes for Artemas Manning and Rhoda Wyeth:

At the age of 20, Artemas enlisted as a soldier to fight insurgents in Shays' Rebellion of 1787. He moved to Mason in 1816 and then to Washington, Sullivan, New Hampshire. Although he was a tanner by trade, at one point he taught singing-schools, but eventually settled to farming. He was active as a captain in the militia and was twice elected selectman (city councilman) of Mason in 1801 and 1802.[502]

After her husband's death, Rhoda continued to live in Washington. According to the town's 1850 census, Rhoda lived with her granddaughter, Sylvania Lowell Farnum (daughter of Sally Manning); her grandson, Herman Farnum (son of Rhoda Manning); and her great grandson, Edgar Farnum. In the 1860 census, Rhoda Wyeth Manning was still in Sullivan County but she had moved to Lempster, New Hampshire to live with her daughter, Prudence Manning Thompson Spencer, and her grandchildren, Altamont Thompson and Horatio Thompson. Rhoda Wyeth Manning was only three months shy of her 98th birthday when she was laid to rest near her husband in lot 283 of the Old Cemetery in Washington, New Hampshire.

78. (**CAPTAIN**) **JOB**[5] **WYETH**, (Noah[4] Sr., Ebenezer[3] Sr., John[2], Nicholas[1]) was born on 14 Jun 1776 in Cambridge, Middlesex, Massachusetts. Job Wyeth married Lydia Convers Francis on 31 Jan 1804 in Cambridge. **LYDIA CONVERS FRANCIS**, daughter of Benjamin Francis and Sarah Hall, was born 10 Apr 1778 in Medford, Middlesex, Massachusetts. Job died on 05 Jun 1840 at the age of 63 in Cambridge. She died there as well at the age of 71 on 04 Jan 1850, from paralytic shock.

The children of Captain Job Wyeth and Lydia Convers Francis were:

This painting of Captain Job, attributed to Mr. Witfield, hangs in the dining room of N.C. Wyeth's home (viewed via Brandywine River Museum tour). Credit: Wyeth Family Archives, Chadds Ford, PA.

142. i. NOAH L.[6] WYETH, born 13 Apr 1805, Cambridge; married LUCY HARVEY, 01 Dec 1836, Nashua, Hillsborough, New Hampshire; died 31 Aug 1866 in Boston.

ii. ELIZA WYETH (twin), born 06 Mar 1807, Cambridge; baptized 15 Mar 1807 at First Church in Cambridge. She probably is the unnamed child of Job and Lydia who died on 14 Oct 1807 at age seven months. The name "Eliza" is mistakenly given both for a child baptized on 15 Mar 1807 and a child who earlier died on 08 Mar 1807.[503]

iii. ELIZABETH WYETH (twin), born 06 Mar 1807, Cambridge; died there two days later.[504] [505] (Some give this twin's name as Francis Wyeth. But, that is probably a confusion with the son of Jonas Wyeth Jr., born 14 May 1807).

143. iv. ABIEL WYETH, born 23 Apr 1809, Cambridge; married MARY FILLEBROWN, 29 Dec 1831, Cambridge; died there, 11 Aug 1841.

144. v. BENJAMIN FRANCIS WYETH, born 31 Mar 1812, Cambridge; married ZOA ANN DUNTON, 07 Apr 1836, Cambridge; died there, 06 Jul 1890.

vi. JOHN BOUND WYETH was born on 22 Jun 1815 in Cambridge. Deathly ill, John aborted an expedition with his cousin, Nathaniel Jarvis Wyeth (1802-1856), before reaching Oregon. John returned to Cambridge on 02 Jan 1833. However, wanderlust had become part of his nature. After publishing his memoirs of the western trek, he left Cambridge a second time. John told his baby brother, Andrew Newell Wyeth, that he would not return until he made a million dollars.[506] It is uncertain when or where he died. His great grandnephew, John Herbert Barker (1870-1951), wrote John Bound was last heard from in 1839. Many believe John died in New Mexico or California.

145.   vii.   ANDREW NEWELL WYETH SR., born 29 Apr 1817, Cambridge; married AMELIA HEPZIBAH BIGELOW STIMSON, 04 May 1843, Cambridge; died there, 13 Apr 1900.

Notes for Lydia Convers Francis, Captain Job and John Bound Wyeth:

Lydia's name comes from her father's first wife, Lydia Convers. A few years after her mother, Sarah Hall Francis, died in 1784, nine-year-old Lydia moved five miles south of her Medford home to live with Ebenezer Wyeth Jr. and Mary Winship on the shores of Fresh Pond in Cambridge. Here is part of the 01 Sep 1845 letter Lydia wrote on behalf of Elizabeth E. Smith Wyeth (1771-1853) to the commissioner of pensions to help him understand the difference between Jonas Wyeth Jr. (1757-1817) and Jonas Wyeth Sr. (1730-1813).[507]

Because the Wyeths were a close-knit family, Lydia and Job grew up together. Job's father, Noah Wyeth Sr., fought alongside his brothers Ebenezer Jr. and Jonas Sr. in the first battle of the American Revolution. Since Ebenezer Wyeth Jr. purchased his Fresh Pond land before his father's death, Jonas Wyeth Sr. inherited the old homestead on Garden Street, near the common in Cambridge. The home was originally purchased by Nicholas Wyeth from Robert Daniel on 20 Jul 1645. Job lived with his father on Nicholas' original Wyeth property in the west-field at 107 Garden Street. At one time, nearby Taylor Square at Huron Avenue, as well as part of Huron Avenue, was named for the Wyeth family.[508]

During the War of 1812, Job captained his own privately-financed warship. Many years later, the beautifully detailed mermaid figurehead from the ship was handed down to Job's grandson, N. C. Wyeth. The renowned artist gave it as a gift to his friend and teacher, Howard Pyle.[509]

As a privateer, Captain Job Wyeth, had a government license to attack and pillage British vessels for profit. Privateering ships greatly enhanced the success of the American Navy who had a mere 16 major vessels at the beginning of the War of 1812. By contrast, the Royal Navy held over 1,500 war ships. Unlike the illegal activity of pirates, at war's end, the privateer's activity ceased.[510] This certainly was the case for Job. In the 1820 census he was back in Cambridge listed as "Capt. Job Weyth" (sic) with 11 other persons at his home.

Counted among the males under the age of five in the 1820 census was John Bound Wyeth, who was named for his aunt Sarah Francis Bound's family. 13 years later, John wrote a pamphlet called *Oregon; or a Short History of a Long Journey from the Atlantic Ocean to the Region of the Pacific by Land* about his trip west with his cousin, Captain Nathaniel Jarvis Wyeth (1802-1856).

John's story of the expedition began in Boston on 11 Mar 1832 aboard a vessel loaded with 20 men. They were headed for Baltimore to pick up four more men. From there, the band travelled by rail to the Allegheny mountains. In Brownsville, a distrustful Pennsylvania Dutch innkeeper refused them lodging because they were Yankees. The disagreement between Captain Wyeth and the tavern keeper was so heated, each seized a rifle. Needless to say, all slept with one eye open. The next morning, the group began marching on foot in search of steamboat passage to the thriving cities of Pittsburgh and Cincinnati.[511]

This painting of John Bound Wyeth, by an unknown artist, hangs in the dining room of N. C. Wyeth's home, now a museum, in Chadds Ford, PA. Credit: Wyeth Family Archives.

On 18 Apr 1832, John, and most of Nat's party, arrived in St. Louis. From there to the Rocky Mountains, food ran low and danger from snakes, Native Americans and wild animals ran high. Many of the men, including John Bound and Captain Wyeth's brother, Dr. Jacob Wyeth, were so sick, they voted to leave the expedition at Pierre's Hole on the western side of the Grand Tetons in present day Idaho. The hardships of the trip had become too great them.[512]

So, on 28 Jul 1832, after the band had marched four days beyond the ridge of the Rocky Mountains, John Bound Wyeth turned back. Ragged and starving, he reached New Orleans via steamboat while horrific cholera and yellow fever epidemics ravaged the city. With death, disease and filth all around him, John barely managed to survive. By digging graves, he accumulated enough money to purchase a ticket back to Massachusetts by boat. When he arrived home on 02 Jan 1833, John wasted no time converting his notes of the discouraging 10-month expedition into a saleable publication.[513] 11 months later, on 06 Nov 1833, Nathaniel Jarvis Wyeth returned to Cambridge and quickly wrote friends to discredit his cousin's story. Captain Wyeth plainly stated, "John Wyeth's book is one of little lies told for gain."[514]

With John Bound gone to seek his fortune, the other children married, and Captain Job recently deceased, Lydia and Andrew Newell Wyeth were alone in the 1840 Cambridge census. The man who would shortly be Andrew's father-in-law, Royal Stimson, lived next door.

79. **JONATHAN⁵ WYETH** (Noah⁴ Sr., Ebenezer³ Sr., John², Nicholas¹) was born in Cambridge in 1787. Since his name does not appear in Noah's will, he apparently is not Noah's biological child. However, for reasons shown later, Jonathan appears to fit Noah's family. Jonathan married (1) Deborah Sargent on 04 Aug 1811 at the First Church of Malden, Middlesex, Massachusetts. **DEBORAH SARGENT**, daughter of Jacob Sargent and Lydia Paine, was born on 16 Aug 1786 in Fitzwilliam, Cheshire, New Hampshire. She died on 20 Jul 1826 at the age of 39.[515] Some records say she died in Malden, but that is unlikely. Census reports of the time show the family lived in Vermont. Jonathan married (2) Lucy Stiles circa 1827 in Norwich, Windsor, Vermont. **LUCY STILES**, daughter of Peleg Stearns Stiles and Rebecca

Wyman, was born 06 Mar 1792 in Norwich.[516] The couple later divorced. Lucy died on 04 Sep 1874 at the age of 82 in Stoneham, Middlesex, Massachusetts. Jonathan Wyeth married (3) **HARRIET THAYER** on 03 Jul 1853 in Moretown, Washington, Vermont. He and Harriet did not have children and according to his Cambridge death record of 13 Feb 1863, he was divorced at his death, so Harriet must have been Jonathan's second divorce.

Jonathan Wyeth and Deborah Sargent had the following children:

146.   i. LYDIA WOODWARD[6] (WOODARD) WYETH, born 28 Apr 1812, Watertown, Middlesex, Massachusetts; married ALPHA SAWYER, 10 May 1835, Boston, Suffolk, Massachusetts; died 1857; buried in Forest Hills Cemetery, Jamaica Plain, Suffolk, Massachusetts.

147.   ii. NAHUM SARGENT WYETH, born 12 Jul 1818, Moretown, Washington, Vermont; married ELVIRA PERSES PHILLIPS, 29 Nov 1843, Boston; died there, 03 Nov 1882.

148.   iii. HOLLIS NYE WYETH, born 23 Jul 1822, Fayston, Washington, Vermont; married (1) MARY JANE STILES, 22 Jun 1846, Middlesex, Washington, Vermont; married (2) FRANCENA LOVINA LOUISA HOOK, 06 Jul 1870, Stoneham; died 11 May 1896, Watertown.

        iv. LOUISA M. WYETH, born in 1826 in Vermont; died on 10 Mar 1849 at the age of 23 in Boston; buried with her sister Lydia in Forest Hills Cemetery.

Jonathan Wyeth and Lucy Stiles had the following children:

149.   i. MARTHA ANN[6] WYETH, born 03 Mar 1828, Moretown; married HENRY CAUD BLISS, 08 Apr 1852, Boston; died 23 Nov 1908, Stoneham; buried with her mother in Sleepy Hollow Cemetery, Concord, Massachusetts.

        ii. SARAH JANE WYETH, born 19 Nov 1829, Middlesex Village, Washington, Vermont; married GEORGE F. SHAW, 01 Dec 1850, Dorchester, Suffolk, Massachusetts; died 14 Apr 1912, Stoneham.

Notes on Jonathan Wyeth:

Although Jonathan does not appear in the will of Noah Wyeth, written 19 Aug 1807, Jonathan apparently fits in Noah and Betty Wyeth's family in some manner.

The most apparent detail connecting Jonathan to Noah Sr. is that Jonathan named his first child "Lydia Woodward (Woodard) Wyeth" after Noah's daughter, Lydia Wyeth, the wife of Nathaniel Woodward (in some records spelled Woodard), of Watertown. The family was used to naming children after in-laws. Case in point, Captain Job's son, Andrew Newell Wyeth, was named for his sister Elizabeth's first husband. The name Andrew Newell Wyeth was carried through several generations to the 1917 birth of the youngest son of Newell Convers "N. C." Wyeth.

Secondly, Jonathan's Watertown residence links him to the Woodwards. Besides Jonathan, the only Wyeths residing in Watertown in those early years of the 19th century, were Lydia Wyeth and her husband Nathaniel Woodward. Because Jonathan lived in Watertown, the banns for his 04 Aug 1811 marriage to Deborah Sargent in nearby Malden were published in Watertown on 14

Jul 1811. Perhaps the Woodwards had taken Jonathan into their home. There is a history of Wyeths taking in children to raise. For instance, Lydia Convers Francis was raised by Ebenezer Jr. and Mary Winship Wyeth before she married their nephew, Captain Job Wyeth.[517]

Another linking of Jonathan to this family is through his first wife, Deborah Sargent. After their marriage in 1811, they relocated to Vermont. The wife of Noah and Betty Wyeth's grandson, Mary Fillebrown (Mrs. Abiel Wyeth), also married a Sargent from Vermont.

There is no birth record for Jonathan, but his death certificate shows he was born in 1787 in Cambridge. Apparently, his son Hollis could not provide the names of Jonathan's parents. They are marked as unknown in the handwritten document. The death record does indicate that Jonathan earned his living as a cabinet maker, he was divorced, and was age 76 when he died of lung congestion in Cambridge.[518]

Since Jonathan was born in Cambridge, his Wyeth name definitely links him to the descendants of Nicholas. He is of the age to be a grandchild to Ebenezer Wyeth Jr. and Mary Winship. However, their descendants were well covered in their daughter Anna Wyeth Cutter's estate distribution and Jonathan was not named in it. Nor does he seem to fit with descendants of any other Wyeths of the period, except Noah.

The best guess is Jonathan was adopted by Noah and Betty Wyeth. In the 1800 census, Noah had three boys under age 16 living with him. At that point, Noah's son Isaac was dead and Isaac's brothers were well over age 16. Noah's grandsons from his daughters lived out of state in 1800. Thus, it is likely Noah had other children living with him and perhaps helping on the farm. They were not legally adopted since such formalities did not occur until 1850. Jonathan could even have been the son of Lydia Wyeth before she married Nathaniel Woodward in Watertown.

Jonathan is buried in lot 486, grave one, Lindenwood Cemetery, Stoneham, MA. The name on the other side of this stone is Hollis Wyeth, Jonathan's son.

80. **TORREY[5] HANCOCK JR.**, (Sarah[4] Wyeth, Ebenezer[3] Sr., John[2], Nicholas[1]) a posthumous child, was born a few months after his father's death. He was baptized on 15 Nov 1778 in the First Church of Cambridge. Torrey Hancock Jr. married (1) Olive Orcutt on 28 Feb 1805 in Cambridge. **OLIVE ORCUTT** was born at the start of the American Revolution. Her parents appear to be Luke Orcutt and Anna Worlin. She died on 10 Oct 1809 in Cambridge. Torrey married (2) Isabella Rice on 05 Jun 1811 in Wayland, Middlesex, Massachusetts. **ISABELLA RICE** was born on 12 Aug 1789 in Wayland to Edmund Rice and Abigail Cutting. She died on 29 May 1838 in Cambridge. Torrey's probate record 33434, dated 18 May 1852, shows Cambridge was his last residence.

Torrey Hancock Jr. and Olive Orcutt had the following children:

       i. ANNA ELIZABETH[6] HANCOCK, born 08 Jun 1807, Cambridge; married JOHN DOLBEER, 19 Jul 1831, Cambridge; died 02 Jun 1874, Detroit, Wayne, Michigan.

ii. SARAH HANCOCK, born 16 Sep 1809, Cambridge; married JOSIAH WELLINGTON COOK, 11 Oct 1829, Cambridge; died there, 30 Aug 1887.

Torrey Hancock Jr. and Isabella Rice had the following children:

150.   i. MARY TORREY[6] HANCOCK, born 10 Jun 1812, Cambridge; married her second cousin JONAS WYETH 2[d], 01 Jan 1833, Cambridge; died 16 Nov 1904, Marblehead, Essex, Massachusetts.

ii. ISABELLA HANCOCK, born 26 Jul 1815, Cambridge; married SHEPHARD LAUGHTON, 11 Aug 1846, Cambridge; death unknown.

iii. ABIGAIL LOUISA HANCOCK, born 16 Sep 1817, Cambridge; died there unmarried on 29 Nov 1843 at the age of 26.

iv. JOHN TORREY HANCOCK, born 26 Apr 1820, Cambridge; died 17 Aug 1900, Orion, Olmsted, Minnesota.

v. HORACE AUGUSTUS HANCOCK, born 22 Nov 1823, Cambridge; died 07 Jun 1912 at the age of 88 in Concord, Merrimack, New Hampshire.

vi. CHARLES EDWARD HANCOCK, born 10 Nov 1827, Cambridge; died there, 27 Apr 1910, age 82.

81. **SARAH TAPLEY[5] MUNROE** (Sarah[4] Wyeth, Ebenezer[3] Sr., John[2], Nicholas[1]) was baptized on 21 Aug 1785 in Cambridge. She married (Lt.) Peter Coolidge on 28 Jun 1813 in Cambridge. **PETER COOLIDGE**, son of David Coolidge and Dorothy Stearns, was born on 02 Jul 1787 in Framingham, Middlesex, Massachusetts. Sarah died there on 04 Jan 1823. Peter died in Framingham on 02 Nov 1850.

The children of Peter Coolidge and Sarah Tapley Munroe included:

i. JOSIAH ADAMS[6] COOLIDGE, born 30 Oct 1816, Framingham; died 06 Oct 1865, Lexington, Middlesex, Massachusetts.

82. **JASON[5] RUSSELL JR.** (Elizabeth[4] Winship, Elizabeth[3] Wyeth, John[2], Nicholas[1]) was born on 07 Mar 1742 in Menotomy (Arlington), Middlesex, Massachusetts. He married **ELIZABETH LOCKE**, daughter of Samuel Locke and Deborah Butterfield, on 28 Oct 1762, in Menotomy. Elizabeth was born on 06 May 1745 in Menotomy. Jason fought at the Battle of Bunker Hill during the Revolutionary War and spent the winter of 1777-1778 camped at Valley Forge, Pennsylvania. Records show he had little contact with his Loyalist brother, Hubbard Russell, due to their political differences. For the most part, Hubbard kept his views quiet for fear of having his property confiscated.[519] Elizabeth died on 24 May 1799 in Mason, Hillsborough, New Hampshire. Jason married (2) **LYDIA LORING**, the widow of William Chambers, on 08 Sep 1799 in Mason. Lydia, the daughter of Joseph Loring and Keziah Gove, was born 27 Aug 1745 in Lexington, Middlesex, Massachusetts. Jason died on 25 Sep 1825 in Mason. The last record for Lydia concerned the administration of Jason's estate.

The children of Jason Russell Jr. and Elizabeth Locke included the following:

151.   i. JASON[6] RUSSELL III, born 02 Jun 1763, in Menotomy; married REBECCA LAUGHTON, 08 Nov 1786, Norridgewock, Somerset, Maine; died 08 Oct 1840, Brighton, Somerset, Maine.

83. **Betty⁵ Gamage** (Nathaniel⁴, Deborah³ Wyeth, William², Nicholas¹) was born on 11 May 1738 in Attleboro, Bristol, Massachusetts. Betty Gamage and Nehemiah Grover Jr. were married on 21 Feb 1755 in the Fifth Parish of Gloucester at Sandy Bay (Rockport), Essex, Massachusetts. **Nehemiah Grover Jr.**, son of Nehemiah Grover Sr. and Abigail Harris, was born on 08 Jun 1730 in Gloucester. Nehemiah defended the seacoast during the Revolutionary War with his brother-in-law Joshua Gamage in Captain Joseph Whipple's Essex County Company. Betty and Nehemiah both died in the town of their birth. She about 1800 and he on 28 Feb 1808.[520]

Gloucester's boundaries originally included the area of Sandy Bay. Since the Grovers lived at Sandy Bay on Cape Ann in Gloucester, now the principal part of Rockport, it is likely all their children were born there. A week before the marriage of Nehemiah Grover Jr. and Betty Gamage, Sandy Bay's Fifth Parish split off on 13 Feb 1755 from the First Parish of Gloucester.[521] All of the Grover children, as follows, were baptized at the Fifth Parish in Sandy Bay.[522]

	i.	Betty⁶ Grover, born 15 Feb 1756; baptized 07 Mar 1756; married Benjamin Row, 17 Apr 1779, Gloucester; death unknown.
	ii.	Mary Grover, born 14 Jan 1758; married in Gloucester (1) Isaac Jacobs, 18 Feb 1780; (2) Edward Higgins, 06 Jan 1793; died circa 1796.
	iii.	Eliezer Grover, born 1760; died Gloucester on 15 May 1833.
	iv.	Nehemiah Grover III, baptized 06 Mar 1763; died young.
152.	v.	Anna Grover, baptized 07 Sep 1766; married (1) John Blatchford, 04 Mar 1784, Gloucester; married her sister's widower (2) Edward Higgins, 31 Aug 1797, Gloucester; died 03 Mar 1841, Rockport.
153.	vi.	Hannah Grover, baptized on 04 Dec 1768; married Francis Noble, 01 Aug 1790, Gloucester; died 06 Sep 1843, Rockport.
154.	vii.	Elizabeth Grover, baptized 28 Apr 1771; married William Gott VI, 14 Dec 1790, Fifth Parish, Sandy Bay. She died after 1850.
	viii.	Sarah Grover, baptized 03 Oct 1773; death unknown.
155.	ix.	Nehemiah Grover III, baptized 22 Sep 1776; married Esther Rowe, 22 Oct 1798, Gloucester; served there during the War of 1812.[523] After the war, he relocated to Cheshire Township, Gallia, Ohio and died there in 1854.
	x.	Esther Grover, born 16 Jun 1779; married Daniel Norwood circa 1801; died 23 Feb 1873, Salem, Essex, Massachusetts.

84. **Joshua⁵ Gamage** (Nathaniel⁴, Deborah³ Wyeth, William², Nicholas¹) was baptized on 03 Jan 1741 in Cambridge, Middlesex, Massachusetts.[524] Joshua Gamage and Elinor Foster were married on 27 Dec 1764 in the Fifth Parish of Gloucester at Sandy Bay (Rockport), Essex, Massachusetts. **Elinor Foster**, daughter of Nathan Foster and Miriam Norwood, was born about 1748 in Essex County. Joshua served in the Revolution. He was on a list of men raised for the defense of the seacoast in Essex County agreeable to the resolve of 27 Jun 1775 and stationed at Gloucester under 1st Lt. Joseph Lane. Joshua also served from 19 Jul 1775 to 31 Dec 1775 as a private in Captain Joseph Whipple's Essex County Company.[525] The boundaries of Gloucester originally included the town of Rockport, in an area dubbed "Sandy Bay." It was formally called Rockport on 27 Feb 1840.[526] Death dates for the Gamages are unknown. But they likely died just after 1810 in Bristol, Lincoln, Maine.

Joshua Gamage and Elinor Foster had the following children:

       i. DANIEL[6] GAMAGE, born 1764, Gloucester; served in the War of 1812 in the Maine Militia of Lt. Col. Robert Day's Regiment, Capt. John Sprowl's Co. Daniel's will was probated Lincoln County, Maine on 08 May 1838.

156.   ii. JOSHUA GAMAGE JR., baptized 02 Feb 1766, Fifth Parish of Gloucester at Sandy Bay (Rockport), Essex, Massachusetts; married SARAH WEBSTER, 15 Nov 1787, Fifth Parish; died 18 Apr 1838, Bristol, Lincoln, Maine.

     iii. ELINOR GAMAGE, baptized 29 Nov 1767, Fifth Parish; intention for her marriage to ANDREW PARSONS was published there on 01 Dec 1785; Elinor died 11 Sep 1855, Montville, Waldo, Maine.

     iv. RUTH GAMAGE, baptized 11 Mar 1770, Fifth Parish; married JOHN POOL on 21 Mar 1787, Gloucester; they settled near the Damariscotta River shore in Maine.[527] She died on 14 May 1847 in Edgecomb, Lincoln, Maine.

     v. NATHANIEL GAMAGE, baptized 01 Dec 1771 at the Fifth Parish; died 16 Jan 1840 in Maine.[528]

     vi. JENY GAMAGE, baptized 06 Mar 1774, Fifth Parish; death unknown.

     vii. WILLIAM GAMAGE, baptized 19 Nov 1775, Fifth Parish; died an infant.

    viii. WILLIAM GAMAGE, born 1776, baptized 31 May 1778, Fifth Parish; married ELIZABETH "BETSEY" BEAL, 16 Jan 1801, Georgetown, Sagadahoc, Maine; died 31 Oct 1863, Anson, Somerset, Maine.

     ix. JEMIMA GAMAGE, baptized 02 Jul 1780, Fifth Parish; married in Bristol (1) JOHN MCFARLAND, 11 May 1797; married (2) EBENEZER CLEVELAND POOL, 04 Dec 1805; died in Bristol on 12 Jan 1870 at age 89 years, seven months.

     x. SAMUEL GAMAGE, baptized 22 May 1783, Fifth Parish of Gloucester at Sandy Bay (Rockport); death unknown.

     xi. STEPHEN GAMAGE was born in 1787 in Gloucester.[529] He served there during the War of 1812 in Captain Benjamin Haskell's Detached Company under General Hovey. Stephen died 20 Aug 1834 in Gloucester.[530]

     xii. JANE GAMAGE was born circa 1789 in Gloucester; death unknown.[531]

85. **JOHN[5] GAMAGE** (Nathaniel[4], Deborah[3] Wyeth, William[2], Nicholas[1]) was baptized on 12 Jan 1746 in the First Church, Cambridge, Middlesex, Massachusetts.[532] John Gamage and **ANNA GOTT** were married on 15 Aug 1765 in the Fifth Parish of Gloucester at Sandy Bay (Rockport), Essex, Massachusetts. Anna, daughter of William Gott IV and Elizabeth Wanson, was born on 02 Sep 1740 in Gloucester. On 07 Jun 1776, during the Revolutionary War, John was taken prisoner from the 14-gun, single-deck sloop, USS *Yankee Hero* by the HMS *Milford* and forced to serve aboard the HMS *Renown*.[533] [534] On 18 Jan 1777, John was on a list of prisoners brought in the first cartel from Rhode Island.[535] Anna died on 09 Apr 1823 in Sandy Bay (Rockport) and John died there just over a year later on 23 Apr 1824. They are buried in the old cemetery across from Front Beach in Rockport.

John Gammage, Anna Gott their son, John and his wife Dolly York appear on this monument in the Old First Parish grounds in Rockport.

The children of John Gamage and Anna Gott included:

    i. JOHN[6] GAMAGE JR., born 14 Jan 1771, Sandy Bay; married DOLLY YORK there on 14 Oct 1794; died 07 Nov 1856, Rockport, Essex, Massachusetts.

    ii. EBENEZER GAMAGE, born 31 Oct 1773 in Gloucester; married NANCY TARR there on 09 Dec 1801. Ebenezer served in defense of the Essex County seacoast, with his cousin Nehemiah Grover III (1776–1854), and his brother Samuel Gott Gamage. He was in Captain Charles Tarr's Company, Lt. Col. J. Appleton's Regiment, from 19 Sep 1814 to 12 Oct 1814. The first of those dates saw the company locked in a sea battle with British barges.[536] Ebenezer died in the town of his birth on 27 Dec 1838.

    iii. SAMUEL GOTT GAMAGE, born 17 Jun 1774, Gloucester; married NANCY E. KRUTTSFORD, 21 Dec 1806, Gloucester. Samuel's will, written in Rockport 25 Dec 1851, was probated 03 Feb 1857 in Salem, Essex, Massachusetts. In it, he willed $10 each to sons Samuel G. Gamage and Charles Gamage. He devised the rest of his estate to be divided equally among his only daughter, Nancy E. Gamage Mills, and his youngest son, George W. Gamage After his wife's death, Samuel had resided with his daughter.

86. **SARAH[5] GAMAGE** (Nathaniel[4], Deborah[3] Wyeth, William[2], Nicholas[1]) was baptized on 15 Sep 1751 in the Third Parish of Gloucester at Annisquam, Essex, Massachusetts (where in 1765, Rev. John Wyeth would be installed as pastor and have his horse whitewashed). Sarah Gamage and William Gott V were married on 27 Apr 1769 in the Fifth Parish of Gloucester at Sandy Bay (Rockport), Essex, Massachusetts. **WILLIAM GOTT V,** son of William Gott IV and Elizabeth Wanson, was born on 06 Dec 1747 in Gloucester. He died circa 1800 in Madison, Somerset, Maine and she died 17 Apr 1810 in Starks, Somerset, Maine.[537]

Details for the children born in Massachusetts to William Gott V and Sarah Gamage:

    i. SARAH[6] GOTT, baptized 25 Feb 1770 at Fifth Parish, Sandy Bay. Her baptism shows on the next line below the 18 Feb 1770 baptism of her half-brother, William Gott VI.[538]

    ii. WILLIAM GOTT JR., baptized 29 Sep 1771, Fifth Parish, Sandy Bay; settled in Maine near his mother, Sarah. He married (1) DEBORAH BYRANT, 26 Dec 1790, Turner, Androscoggin, Maine. Before taking her own life, Deborah killed one of her children with an axe. William married (2) RHODA KNAPP in 1795 in Leeds, Androscoggin, Maine. Depending on the source, they had 8 to 14 children. William died 10 Jan 1859 in Wayne, Kennebec, Maine.[539] (William Gott Jr. is often confused with his illegitimate half-brother, William Gott VI who married Elizabeth Grover and remained in Gloucester.)[540]

    iii. HONOR GOTT, baptized 20 Feb 1774, Fifth Parish, Sandy Bay; death unknown.

Notes for William Gott V and Sarah Gamage:

In addition to the three children born in Massachusetts, William and Sarah Gamage Gott had five children born in Maine. According to author, William Sawtelle, their names are Elijah, John, Jemima, Anne, and Rebecca.[541]

Sawtelle mistakenly states that the William, who married Elizabeth Grover, is Sarah Gamage Gott's son. However, that William Gott died before 1840 because Elizabeth Grover Gott is alone in the 1840 census of Gloucester. The William who remained in Massachusetts apparently is the one baptized on 18 Feb 1770. Per the records of the Fifth Parish in Sandy Bay, William baptized on 18 Feb 1770 was born out of wedlock to William Gott V and Martha "Patty" Sheldon. In 1771, Fifth Parish records show a baptism for a son named William legitimately born to William Gott V and Sarah Gott (Gamage). Sarah's son lived for 87 years and is buried a few miles from her.

More proof the man herein called William Gott VI married Elizabeth Grover is that they named two of their girls Martha and Patty. After giving birth to William Gott VI, Martha "Patty" Sheldon married Ebenezer Rowe. Their daughter Esther Rowe (1780-1850) married Nehemiah Grover III (1776-1854) and resettled in Gallia County, Ohio. They thus carried the genes of Nicholas' son, William Wyeth, and Nicholas' granddaughter, Deborah Wyeth Gamage, to Ohio.

After William Gott V was wounded in the Revolutionary War, a report of his death reached his wife Sarah in Starks, Maine. William Gott V was known to be a "seer gifted with second sight." He saw in a vision the marriage of Sarah Gamage with a Mr. Gray of Starks. Upon his discharge from the army, William Gott V made his way home to find that his wife had indeed married just as he had dreamed. The story goes that Sarah Gamage Gott Gray and the children were so unhappy to see the man returned from the dead, they drove him away. William Gott V settled nearby in Madison, Maine. However, at his death, he was buried in Starks and now rests for eternity near his former wife, Sarah Gamage.[542]

87. **(COLONEL) THOMAS[5] HUNT** (Ruth[4] Fessenden, Martha[3] Wyeth, William[2], Nicholas[1]) was born on 17 Sep 1754 in Watertown, Middlesex, Massachusetts. There he married **EUNICE WELLINGTON**, daughter of Samuel Wellington and Abigail Sanderson, on 16 Aug 1788. She was baptized on 11 Dec 1768 in Watertown.[543] Thomas and Eunice both died at Fort Bellefontaine, Missouri. He died on 16 Aug 1808 and she on 19 Jan 1809.[544]

(Colonel) Thomas Hunt and Eunice Wellington had the following children (most of the dates shown are from the Massachusetts Society of the Cincinnati):[545]

      i. HENRY JACKSON[6] HUNT was born circa 1789 in Watertown; in 1811 he married ANNE MACKINTOSH, daughter of Angus Mackintosh, the Earl of Moy, and Mary Archange Baudry, in Detroit, Wayne, Michigan. Henry died in office on 16 Oct 1826 while serving as the second mayor of Detroit.[546] Anne died 30 years later, on 14 Dec 1856, in Detroit.

      ii. RUTH FESSENDEN HUNT, born 07 Jul 1790 in Watertown; married DR. ABRAHAM EDWARDS, son of Aaron Edwards and Desire Miner, 1805, Fort Wayne, Allen, Indiana; Ruth died 29 Dec 1867, Kalamazoo, Michigan.

      iii. GEORGE HUNT, born 28 Sep 1791, Watertown; married ELOISE L. KEENEY, circa 1810 in Detroit; died in 1874 near Bridgeport, Fairfield, Connecticut.[547] He was the second Hunt child with the same name.[548]

      iv. (CAPTAIN) THOMAS HUNT JR., born 30 Jan 1793, Watertown; died in 1838 in Detroit.[549]

      v. ABIGAIL HUNT, born on 23 Jan 1797 in Watertown; married (1) JOSIAH

SNELLING, 14 Aug 1812, Detroit; married (2) JONATHAN CHAPLIN, 24 May 1841, Maumee, Lucas, Ohio; died 06 Sep 1888 in Newport, Campbell, Kentucky. She is buried in Spring Grove Cemetery, Cincinnati.

    vi. (GENERAL) JOHN ELLIOT HUNT was born on 11 Apr 1798 in the fort at Fort Wayne. Orphaned at age 10, he went to live with his eldest brother in Detroit. With no schools then existing in Michigan, in 1812, Henry sent John to Sandwich, Canada for one year of instruction. By 1816, John had settled in northwest Ohio's Maumee River Valley. There he spent many years in public service including being postmaster in Toledo. On 26 May 1822, he married MARY SOPHIA SPENCER. In 1837, John was elected by the legislature as major-general of the 18th division, Ohio Militia. He died on 22 Jul 1877 in Toledo, Lucas, Ohio and is buried there in Forest cemetery.[550]

157.   vii. (LT.) SAMUEL WELLINGTON HUNT, born 05 Nov 1799, at the fort in Fort Wayne, Indiana.[551] He was appointed to the U.S. Military Academy at West Point in 1814 but dropped out to marry JULIA HERRICK of Plattsburgh, Clinton, New York. He died 11 Sep 1829 at the Jefferson Barracks Military Post near St. Louis, Missouri.[552]

    viii. WILLIAM BROWN HUNT, born 16 Nov 1800 in Detroit, while his father commanded the post there; died in Detroit in 1851.[553]

    ix. CHARLES COTESWORTH PINCKNEY HUNT, born 29 Mar 1802, Detroit; died 21 Apr 1892, Chicago, Cooke, Illinois.

    x. MARY LEBARON HUNT, born 06 Nov 1803 in Fort Mackinac, Michigan while her father commanded the post there; married twice in Detroit: (1) JOSEPH GLEASON, 1819; (2) TUNIS WENDELL, circa 1825; died in Detroit at the home of her daughter, Alice Hunt Wendell Curtis, on 06 Sep 1872.[554]

    xi. ELIZA MITCHELL HUNT, born 18 Dec 1804, Detroit; married JAMES SOULARD, 20 Mar 1820, St. Louis, Missouri; died 11 Aug 1894, Galena, Jo Daviess, Illinois.[555]

Notes for Colonel Thomas Hunt:

Thomas Hunt started his military career as a sergeant in Captain Craft's Company of minutemen at the alarm which led to the first battles of the American Revolution at Lexington and Concord on 19 Apr 1775.

The next month, Thomas was commissioned an ensign and served in the Siege of Boston and fought at the Battle of Bunker Hill. By 20 Oct 1776, he attained the rank of brigade major. Then on 01 Feb 1777 he was commissioned as a captain-lieutenant in the regiment commanded by Colonel Henry Jackson. Two years later, Thomas was promoted to captain on 01 Mar 1779.

He was twice wounded – at the Battle of Stony Point on 16 Jul 1779 and at the Siege of Yorktown on 14 Oct 1781. Still, he continued to serve the Continental Army until his regiment was disbanded on 20 Jun 1784.

On 04 Mar 1791, he was commissioned a captain in the United States Army. He was one of the few survivors of St. Clair's Defeat later that year. Two years after, Thomas was promoted to major on 18 Feb 1793 and fought in the 1794 Battle of Fallen Timbers.

His final promotion, to colonel, came on 11 Apr 1803. He remained in that position until his death at Fort Bellefontaine, Missouri. The fort was the first U.S. military outpost west of the Mississippi River. Colonel Hunt and his wife, Eunice, were originally buried there but were later moved to Jefferson Barracks National Cemetery near St. Louis.[556][557]

In Dec after Thomas' death, Eunice filed a request for relief from the U. S. government, she having been left a widow "with a numerous family of infant children." Although it was accompanied by another entreaty signed by Meriwether Lewis, Congress did not wish to establish a precedent since Colonel Hunt had not died in battle. They gave Eunice leave to withdraw her petition. She died the next month. The cause of death given as "literally of a broken heart."[558]

Alvah Bradish's portrait of Colonel Thomas Hunt was handed down through Gen. John Elliott and Mary Sophia Spencer Hunt to their grandson Sheldon Spencer Smith. It is courtesy of Dan Keenan, Smith's step grandson.

In *The John Hunt Memoirs, Early Years of the Maumee Basin*, edited by Richard J. Wright, Thomas and Eunice's son, General John Elliott Hunt, explains how the children were parceled out to live with friends and relatives. He and Mary first lived with their brother-in-law and sister, Dr. Abraham and Ruth Fessenden Edwards, in Fort Wayne, but then joined their brother Thomas who was staying in Detroit with their oldest brother, Henry. George Hunt was raised by Colonel John Johnston, an Indian agent in Fort Wayne. The rest of the 11 children were left in charge of family and friends in Watertown and Boston.[559]

John Elliott Hunt's memoir paints many fascinating scenes of life on the frontier in the early 19th century. One of his most vivid stories concerns the negotiations of commissioner and Michigan Territorial Governor, General Lewis Cass, when he purchased vast acreage in northern Ohio, southern Michigan and part of Indiana from Native American tribes of the area. The resulting Treaty of the Maumee Rapids was signed near Fort Meigs at present day Perrysburg, Ohio. Lewis and John were brothers-in-law. In 1806, Lewis

Drawing of John E. Hunt from Horace S. Knapp's 1872 *History of the Maumee Valley*.

married Elizabeth Spencer and in 1822, John Elliott Hunt married Elizabeth's sister, Mary Sophia Spencer.[560] The sisters were daughters of Joseph Spencer and Deborah Selden. In 1848, Cass ran as the Democratic candidate for the U.S. presidency.[561]

As a witness to the opening of the grand council, some seven weeks before the treaty was signed, John Elliott Hunt related a story showing the particular bravery of the commissioner. Cass Lewis began by stating that their great father, the President, had sent him to buy land. In reply, Mash-ke-mau, a noted Ottawa warrior and friend of the British, said, "that he saw distinctly what their father the President wanted. It was to cheat them again as they had been cheated from the beginning by the whites…" After Mash-ke-mau sat down, General Cass conceded agreement by stating, "That the first white man that cheated them was their French father. That the second white man that cheated them the most was their British father."[562]

Immediately, Mash-ke-mau got up and advanced toward General Cass with his tommy hawk raised and tapping the general on the breast, said "Cass, you lie, you lie." He frothed at the mouth and acted like a mad bull. John Elliott Hunt wrote, "I expected every moment that he would kill the general." However, Cass kept perfectly cool and told the interpreter, "take that squaw away and put a pretty coat upon her." Hunt went on to write, "nothing could be more insulting to a warrior than this." Mash-ke-mau raved more than ever. General Cass then told the interpreter to tell the warrior, "no one but an old woman would act as he did in a grand council. He better behave himself and act like a man." [563]

Apparently, Mash-ke-mau settled down. On 29 Sep 1817, the day for the signing of the treaty arrived. The Native Americans arrived at the council house dressed in their fanciest clothes. They were advanced by tribes moving in excited war dances. John Elliott Hunt wrote, "leading them all was a white headed, half bent down with age, old woman. This old woman was the mother of Ottusson and grandniece of the celebrated chief Pontiac. The veneration [of this woman] by all these Indian tribes was so great that not a man would touch the pen to sign the treaty until this old woman signed it." [564]

This photo of Lewis C. Hunt, Col. 67th Ohio, is courtesy of the Library of Congress.

John Elliott Hunt named one of his sons for his brother-in-law. Colonel Lewis Cass Hunt of the Ohio 67th is often confused with his first cousin of the same name, Brigadier General Lewis Cass Hunt (son of Lt. Samuel Wellington Hunt). [565] At the rank of captain, John Elliott Hunt's son Lewis, pictured here, commanded the Sixth Offensive of the Siege of Petersburg, Virginia on 31 Oct 1864. [566] Lewis died in Toledo, Maumee, Ohio, 30 Apr 1868. He is buried there in Forest Hill Cemetery with his father General John Elliott Hunt. [567]

88. **ELIZABETH "BETSY"**[5] **HUNT** (Ruth[4] Fessenden, Martha[3] Wyeth, William[2], Nicholas[1]) was born on 01 Oct 1755 in Watertown, Middlesex, Massachusetts. She married **JOSEPH PEARSE PALMER**, son of Brigadier General Joseph Palmer and Mary Cranch, on 02 Nov 1772 at Sandborn's Tavern in Hampton, Rockingham, New Hampshire. [568] He was born on 31 Jul 1750 in Boston, Suffolk, Massachusetts. He graduated from Harvard in 1771. Joseph died from a fall from a bridge on 25 Jun 1797 at the age of 46 in Woodstock, Windsor, Vermont. [569] He suffered from depression and his last letter home was full of regrets. The letter together with the nature of the accident suggested an act of despair. [570] Betsy died on 08 Jan 1838 at the age of 82 at her daughter Mary's house in Brattleboro, Windham, Vermont.

Joseph Pearse Palmer and Elizabeth "Betsy" Hunt had the following children: [571]

    i. JOSEPH[6] PALMER, born Aug 1773, "Friendship Hall," Braintree (Quincy), Norfolk, Massachusetts; when the Palmer family was financially crushed by the devaluation of the dollar after the Revolutionary War, Joseph was sent to sea, at age 11, as a cabin boy on a ship; he died at sea circa 1799. [572]

    ii. MARY HUNT PALMER, born 01 Mar 1775, Watertown; married ROYALL TYLER, 11 May 1794, Framingham, Middlesex, Massachusetts; died 07 Jul 1866, Brattleboro, Windham, Vermont. [573]

158.   iii. ELIZABETH "ELIZA" PALMER, born 28 Feb 1778, [574] Watertown; married (DR.)

NATHANIEL PEABODY, 03 Nov 1802, Andover, Essex, Massachusetts; died 11 Jan 1853, West Newton, Middlesex, Massachusetts.[575]

iv. JOHN HAMPDEN PALMER was born on 22 Feb 1780 in Watertown. During the War of 1812, he enlisted on 05 May 1813 for one year as a private in Lt. Levi Power's Company, Capt. Rufus Newcut's Regiment of the 31st U.S. Infantry of Vermont volunteers. He died while serving the infantry on 06 Jul 1813 in Windsor, Windsor County, Vermont.[576] [577]

v. EDWARD PALMER was born on 03 Sep 1782 in Boston. On 02 Jul 1797, just one week after his father's death, Edward, at age 14, drowned in the Connecticut River in Brattleboro. He is buried there in Prospect Hill Cemetery with the young man who died trying to save him.[578]

vi. AMELIA PALMER CRANCH was born on 03 Aug 1784 at "Friendship Hall," Braintree (Quincy), Norfolk, Massachusetts. In 1791, at age seven, Amelia went alone all the way from Framingham to West Point, New York, to live with her aunt Elizabeth Palmer Cranch.[579] The family adopted her a few years later and they eventually settled in Salem. There she married ABEL WINSLOW CURTIS on 25 Nov 1812. Amelia died 28 Jul 1854 and is buried in Lakeview Cemetery, New Canaan, Connecticut.

vii. SOPHIA PEARSE PALMER, born 02 Sep 1786, Boston; married THOMAS PICKMAN, 21 Dec 1815, Salem, Essex, Massachusetts; died there on 22 Dec 1862. It is believed that Royall Tyler fathered Sophia when Joseph Pearse Palmer was absent on business for a considerable time.[580] [581]

viii. GEORGE PALMER, born 04 Sep 1788, Boston; married ALICE SHEPHERD WINSHIP, 1813, Boston; died there, 25 Jul 1855.

ix. CATHERINE HUNT PALMER, born 01 Mar 1791, Framingham; married HENRY PUTNAM, 13 Sep 1807, Jamaica Plain, Suffolk, Massachusetts.[582] She died 08 Jan 1869 in New York City while living with her daughter Elizabeth Putnam and son-in-law Isaac T. Smith. Her funeral was held at their home at 259 West 23rd St.[583] Catherine is believed to have been fathered by Royall Tyler when Joseph Pearse Palmer was away for several months.[584]

Notes on the family of Joseph Pearse Palmer and Elizabeth "Betsy" Hunt:

All of the birth dates and most of the birth places above come directly from Elizabeth "Betsy" Hunt Palmer through her daughter, Mary. Both mother and daughter were keen to pass on family history to their grandchildren. Their narratives are given in *Grandmother Tyler's Book – the Recollections of Mary Palmer Tyler, 1775-1866*. Not only did Mary Hunt Palmer Tyler write about her own family, but she wrote one of the earliest childcare manuals published by an American woman. In 1811, she anonymously published *The Maternal Physician* through her husband Royall Tyler's publishing contacts.[585]

As *Grandmother Tyler's Book* includes remembrances of both mother and daughter, it starts prior to John Hunt's 1734 Harvard graduation. Betsy related that her father fell in love with Ruth Fessenden when he saw her and some friends amusing themselves by rolling down a hill. In later life, John... "boasted that he was then determined to have that exquisitely neat maiden for his wife because her stockings, shoes and all her underclothes were so exquisitely neat and nice." John was implying that Ruth's clean underclothes suggested she would be a good housekeeper. Betsy further noted "It was a maxim of my father's that it was sufficient for a woman to know enough to make a shirt and a pudding."[586]

Harvard-educated Joseph Pearse Palmer was the exception to men like John Hunt Sr. and others of the Colonial period. Joseph posed this first question to Betsy on the day they met –"What books have you read?" When she stuttered a reply about the only thing she had read, Joseph said, "But your reading should be more extensive. I have a large library at college which shall be at your service." Thereafter 19-year-old Joseph gave 14-year-old Betsy wide-ranging weekly lessons in writing, arithmetic and a host of other subjects.[587]

The women in Joseph Pearse Palmer's life were not hindered by prejudices against educating women. In fact, his aunt Mary Smith, the wife of his uncle Richard Cranch, was First Lady Abigail Smith Adams' sister. Although entirely educated at home, Abigail Adams was so intelligent and such an important advisor to her husband, John Adams, that many consider her to be one of the founders of the United States. Interestingly, Abigail credited her brother-in-law, Richard Cranch, with introducing her to great literature.[588]

Another one of the founders that the Palmers knew well was John Hancock. However, their relationship with him was most unhappy. Joseph Pearse Palmer's father, commissioned Brigadier General of the Suffolk County Militia in 1776, firmly supported the Revolutionary cause. In doing so, General Palmer incurred tremendous debt by using his own funds in the war effort. At the War's end, the General's liability necessitated borrowing money from Hancock. Then adding insult to injury, the peace brought devaluation of the over-issued, highly-inflated Continental money. John Hancock, then Massachusetts governor, publicly gave notice he would accept the depreciated money at a rate of $25 for $1. On the strength of that offer, General Palmer sold land to cover his debt to Hancock. However, when the General tendered the money, the Governor refused it. The money had fallen further. Angry words were exchanged. The argument ended with Hancock swearing an oath to Palmer, "I'll be the ruin of your family."[589]

Unfortunately, the oath became true. Both father and son lost their businesses and their estates, including Friendship Hall, the Palmer home in the Germantown section of Braintree (Quincy), Norfolk, Massachusetts.

Joseph Pearse Palmer spent many months at a time away from home trying to earn a living while his wife, Betsy, took in boarders. One of whom was Royall Tyler. Tyler, a Harvard-educated lawyer and playwright, was fresh off a romantic relationship with John and Abigail Adams' daughter, Nabby.[590] The soon to be President of the United States did not think highly of Royall – as evidenced by this 04 Feb 1783 letter John Adams penned from Paris to his wife, Abigail:

> My dearest Friend
>
> Your two Letters concerning Mr. T. [Tyler] are never out of my Mind. He is of a very numerous Family and Connection in Boston who have long had great Influence in that Town … But I don't like the Trait in his Character, his Gaiety. He is but a Prodigal Son, and though a Penitent, has no Right to **your Daughter**, who deserves a Character without a Spot. That Frivolity of Mind, which breaks out into Such Errors in Youth, never gets out of the Man but Shews itself in some mean Shape or other through Life. You seem to me to have favoured this affair much too far, and I wish it off…[591]

Indeed, the youthful errors of Royall Tyler were many. Before his romance with Nabby, he had an illegitimate son, Royal Morse, born in 1779 to a Harvard cleaning woman.[592] He and his landlady, Elizabeth "Betsy" Hunt Palmer, flirted so openly that Mary Smith Cranch wrote to her sister Abigail Smith Adams about it.[593] Betsy's indiscretions were rooted in desperation. With the Palmer fortune in ruins courtesy of John Hancock and her husband away, Betsy became financially dependent on her wealthy lodger Tyler for necessities like groceries.[594]

Although the Palmer, Tyler and Cranch families never openly acknowledged Sophia and Catherine's paternity, it was, nevertheless, known. For instance, when she learned of Sophia's early birth, Mary Smith Cranch wrote this letter on 24 Sep 1786 to Abigail Adams, Braintree:

> My dear sister
>
> ... We live in an age of discovery. One of our acquaintance has discover'd that a full grown, fine child may be produc'd in less than five months as well as in nine, provided the mother should meet with a small fright a few hours before its Birth. You may laugh: but it is true. The Ladys Husband is so well satisfied of it that he does not seem to have the least suspicion of its being otherways, but how can it be? for he left this part of the country the beginning of September last, and did not return till the Sixth of April, and his wife brought him this fine Girl the first day of the present Month... Now the only difficulty Seems to be, whether it is the product of a year, or twenty weeks. She affirms it is the Latter, but the learned in the obstretick Art Say that it is not possible. The child is perfect large and Strong. I have seen it my sister: it was better than a week old tis true, but a finer Baby I never Saw. It was the largest she ever had her Mother says... I was ask'd to walk up, by, and was follow'd by her Husband. The Lady was seting by the side of the Bed suckling her Infant and not far from her—with one sliper off... He did not rise from his seat, perhaps he could not. I spoke to him and he answer'd me, but hobble'd off as quick as he could without saying any thing more to me. There appear'd the most perfect harmony between all three. She was making a cap and observ'd that She had nothing ready to put her child in as she did not expect to want them so Soon. I made no reply—I could not... Your own mind will furnish you with sufficient matter for Sorrow and joy, and many other sensations, or I am mistaken....[595]

As his aunt Mary Smith Cranch described, Joseph Pearse Palmer did not express dissatisfaction with Royall nor with Betsy.

After his daughter Mary Hunt Palmer's surreptitious marriage to Royall, Joseph loved Royall even more so as a son. The Tyler's secret nuptials had to be exposed earlier than planned because of Mary's pregnancy.[596]

Mary's pride in her husband Royall's accomplishments is apparent throughout her book. She was particularly thrilled with the success of his play, *The Contrast*. It was the first comedy by an American author staged by a professional company. Another one of Mary's proudest days was when Royall was chosen as a side judge for the Vermont Supreme Court.[597]

Public domain photo of Mary Hunt Palmer Tyler shared to ancestry.com by npschutz.

Judge Tyler's charm was lost, however, on one person in Mary Hunt Palmer Tyler's immediate family... her sister, Elizabeth "Eliza" Palmer Peabody. In 1833 Eliza wrote an unkind article about Royall entitled "Seduction" for the *Christian Examiner*. Then in 1851's *The House of the Seven Gables*, Eliza's son-in-law, Nathaniel Hawthorne, based the character of evil Judge Jaffrey Pyncheon on Royall Tyler.[598]

SIXTH GENERATION – THE WAR OF 1812

89. **DEACON JONAS**[6] **STEARNS** (Josiah[5], Abigail[4] Fiske, John[3], Sarah[2] Wyeth, Nicholas[1]) was born on 27 Feb 1738 in Watertown, Middlesex, Massachusetts. Jonas Stearns and Submit Davis were married on 14 May 1758 in Lunenburg, Worcester, Massachusetts. **SUBMIT DAVIS** was born in Lunenburg on 17 May 1741 to Samuel Davis and Sarah Boynton. In addition to being a deacon in the Congregational church, Jonas was a cabinet maker. He died on 13 Sep 1782 in Chesterfield, Cheshire, New Hampshire. Submit died on 24 Feb 1815 in Marlboro, Windham, Vermont.[599]

Jonas Stearns and Submit Davis had the following children:[600]

   i. SAMUEL[7] STEARNS, born 08 Sep 1759, Lunenburg, Worcester, Massachusetts; served in Ashley's Regiment of Militia during the Revolution; he married three times and had 14 children; Samuel died 15 Jan 1844 at the age of 84 in Chesterfield, Cheshire, New Hampshire.

   ii. JONAS STEARNS, born 09 Sep 1761, Shirley, Middlesex, Massachusetts; died 19 Oct 1773 at the age of 12 in Chesterfield.

   iii. SUSANNA STEARNS, born on 06 May 1764 in Chesterfield; married GUY HILLS, 30 May 1794; died before 1834 in Pittstown, Rensselaer, New York (as noted in Guy's pension application).

159. iv. AMOS STEARNS, born 10 Jul 1766, Chesterfield; married LUCY FLETCHER there, 19 Aug 1790; died 16 May 1829, Newfane, Windham, Vermont.

   v. ABIJAH STEARNS, born 22 Jan 1769, Chesterfield; married LYDIA DAVIS there, 31 Dec 1792; in 1809 became insane and was accused of murder;[601] believed to have drowned in Lake Champlain, Vermont about 1815.[602]

   vi. SUBMIT STEARNS, born on 02 Sep 1771 in Chesterfield; married JEREMIAH DAY, 14 Jul 1793, Addison County, Vermont; died in May 1843 in Bastard Township, Leeds and Grenville United Counties, Ontario, Canada.

   vii. MARY SARAH STEARNS, born 07 Jan 1774 in Chesterfield; married EDMOND LAWRENCE, 1795; died 10 Mar 1850, Day, Saratoga County, New York.

   viii. RELIEF STEARNS, born 29 Jan 1777, Chesterfield; married JUDAH HIGLEY there, 11 Feb 1800; they had eight children; she died on 16 Nov 1849 at the age of 72 in Marlboro Windham, Vermont.

   ix. POLLY STEARNS, born 22 Sep 1780, Chesterfield; married DANIEL MILLER circa 1800; died circa 1855, Yorkville, Kalamazoo, Michigan.

   x. JONAS BOARDMAN STEARNS, born 25 Jan 1783 in Chesterfield; married POLLY PAGE there, 29 Jul 1804; died 06 Feb 1846 at the age of 63 in Somerset, Windham, Vermont.

90. **FRANCIS**[6] **FISKE** (Samuel[5] Jr., Samuel[4], William[3], Sarah[2] Wyeth, Nicholas[1]) was born on 24 Aug 1772 in Waltham, Middlesex, Massachusetts. Francis Fiske and Sarah Livermore were married there on 21 Oct 1798. **SARAH LIVERMORE,** daughter of Abijah Livermore and Mary Dix, was born on 01 Jun 1781 in Waltham. Francis, a farmer, died on 15 Feb 1856 at the age of 83 in Saugus, Essex, Massachusetts. Sarah died there at the age of 84 on 29 Mar 1866.

The children of Francis Fiske and Sarah Livermore included:

> i. ABIJAH LIVERMORE[7] FISKE, born 11 Dec 1803, Waltham; married RUTH COATS RHODES on 03 Apr 1825 in Saugus, Essex, Massachusetts; served in the Civil War; died 13 Nov 1871, Saugus.
>
> 160. ii. FRANCIS FISKE JR., born 30 Jun 1824, Bedford, Middlesex, Massachusetts; married SARAH E. HOUGHTON, died 16 Dec 1889, Saugus.

91. **ELIJAH[6] CUTTER** (Nehemiah[5], Martha[4] Bowman, Deborah[3] Wyeth, John[2], Nicholas[1]) was born on 17 Mar 1788 in Menotomy (Arlington), Middlesex, Massachusetts. He married Abigail Hill on 04 Jan 1818 in West Cambridge (Arlington). **ABIGAIL HILL**, daughter of Nathaniel Hill and Abigail Simonds, was born on 31 Jan 1798 in Menotomy. Elijah Cutter died on 17 May 1885 at the age of 97 in Arlington. She died there on 20 Dec 1894 at the age of 96. The Cutters apparently did not move from the town of their birth. Originally, Menotomy was part of Cambridge, Massachusetts. It was incorporated on 27 Feb 1807 as West Cambridge. In 1867, the name "Arlington" was chosen in honor of those buried in Arlington National Cemetery.[603]

The children of Elijah Cutter and Abigail Hill included:

> 161. i. CYNTHIA[7] CUTTER, born 23 Feb 1821, West Cambridge (Arlington), Middlesex, Massachusetts; married BENJAMIN FRANKLIN RUSSELL there on 21 May 1843; died 11 Apr 1917, Arlington, Middlesex, Massachusetts.

92. **(DR.) NATHANIEL[6] BOWMAN** (Joshua[5], Noah[4], Deborah[3] Wyeth, John[2], Nicholas[1]) was born on 18 Mar 1768 in Cambridge. After his father was killed in the Revolutionary War, Nathaniel was raised by his grandparents. At grandfather Noah's death in 1786, Nathaniel was the only person besides his grandmother named in the will. Later that year, he graduated from Harvard College and began the study of medicine with Dr. Kittredge, of Andover, Essex, Massachusetts. There Nathaniel Bowman married Sarah "Sally" Johnson on 13 Oct 1789. **SARAH "SALLY" JOHNSON**, daughter of Samuel Johnson and Elizabeth Gage, was born on 15 Apr 1768 in Andover. Dr. Bowman died on 08 Jun 1797 at the age of 29 when part of a steeple fell on him at the raising of a meetinghouse in Gorham, Cumberland, Maine. Sally died on 08 May 1858 at the age of 90 in Bath, Sagadahoc, Maine.[604]

The children of Dr. Nathaniel Bowman and Sarah "Sally" Johnson included:

> 162. i. (COLONEL) SAMUEL GARDNER[7] BOWMAN, born 09 Oct 1790, Gorham; married MARCIA STOCKBRIDGE, 19 May 1816, Hanover, Plymouth, Massachusetts; died 29 Mar 1841, Bath, Lincoln (Sagadahoc), Maine. (Sagadahoc County website shows it was formed from Lincoln in 1854.)
>
> ii. SARAH BOWMAN, born 19 Nov 1792, Bath; married SAMUEL WINTER, 15 Mar 1821, Bath; died on 08 Apr 1828 at the age of 35 in Bath.
>
> iii. JOSHUA BOWMAN, born 24 Oct 1795, Gorham; died 02 Sep 1823 at the age of 27 in Bath.

93. **JONATHAN⁶ WYETH SR.** (Joseph⁵, Jonathan⁴ Jr., Jonathan³, John², Nicholas¹) was born about 1775 in Cambridge, Middlesex, Massachusetts. Jonathan Wyeth Sr. married (1) **ELIZABETH "BETSY" WARREN** on 03 Dec 1799, by Samson Tuttle, Esq., in Littleton, Middlesex, Massachusetts. Betsy, daughter of Ephraim Warren and Sarah Kezer, was born on 18 Sep 1778 in Shirley, Middlesex, Massachusetts. Jonathan married (2) **EMMA KEMP** on 02 Jun 1829 in Townsend, Middlesex, Massachusetts (intention filed in Apr 1829). Emma daughter of Simeon Kemp and Tryphena Parker, was born on 03 May 1802 in Mason, Hillsborough, New Hampshire. Jonathan, called a laborer at his death in Townsend on 27 Feb 1847 of lung fever, was age 72. Emma died there on 14 May 1874.

As per the handwritten vital records of Townsend, 1726-1891, Jonathan Wyeth Sr. and Elizabeth "Betsy" Warren had the following children: [605]

163.　 i. JOSEPH⁷ WYETH, born 06 Mar 1800, Groton, Middlesex, Massachusetts; married ELVIRA WHEELER, 14 Dec 1836, Cuyahoga County, Ohio; Elvira filed probate papers on 19 Feb 1845 so he died there late 1844 or early 1845. [606] [607]

164.　 ii. JONATHAN WYETH JR., born 20 Jan 1802, Groton; married ESTHER BAILEY on 23 Feb 1825 in Townsend; died 05 Feb 1876, Lunenburg, Worcester, Massachusetts.

　　 iii. WILLIAM D. WYETH, born 09 Nov 1804, Harvard, Worcester, Massachusetts; death unknown.

　　 iv. ELIZA PHILLIPA WYETH, born 17 Oct 1806, Ashby, Middlesex, Massachusetts; married BENJAMIN WINCHESTER NUTTING, 22 May 1861, Groton; died 26 Jul 1895, Ayer, Middlesex, Massachusetts.

　　 v. GARDNER WYETH, born 09 Aug 1810 in Townsend; death unknown.

165.　 vi. WALTER WYETH, born 07 Apr 1812, Townsend (one birth records calls him "Walker"); married SUSAN P. ADAMS, 06 Jan 1842, Townsend; died there of consumption on 19 Mar 1855.

　　 vii. AARON WYETH, born 03 May 1813 in Townsend; death unknown.

Jonathan Wyeth Sr. and Emma Kemp had the following children:

　　 i. CHARLES H.⁷ WYETH, born about 1830, Mason; married (1) ELIZABETH H. CHANDLER, 02 Jul 1854, Townsend, Middlesex, Massachusetts; married (2) HANNAH FOLSOM WHITTLE, widow of Charles Farnsworth, 25 Jul 1874, Mason; married (3) MARY BOYCE, widow of John Morse, 01 Dec 1886, Hollis, Hillsborough, New Hampshire. Charles died on 10 Jun 1897 in Goffstown, Hillsborough, New Hampshire.

166.　 ii. HIRAM WYETH, born 10 Jan 1832, Mason; married ABIGAIL BURGESS, 30 May 1854, Townsend; died there on 07 Oct 1897.

167.　 iii. ALONZO WYETH, born 16 May 1834, Mason; married SARAH ALTHENA LAWRENCE, 06 Jun 1854, Fitchburg, Worcester, Massachusetts; died 12 Jan 1920, Townsend.

168.　 iv. EMELINE WYETH, born 22 Nov 1836, Mason; married WARREN NEWTON, 28 Nov 1854, Westborough, Worcester, Massachusetts; died 02 May 1902, Westborough.

169.	v.	ORIN T. WYETH, born 19 Dec 1839, Mason; married (1) ANNA ISABELLA TARBELL, 05 Nov 1867, Townsend; married (2) FLORA ETTA SARTELLE, 05 Jun 1873, Townsend; died 15 Jun 1920 at the State Infirmary, Tewksbury, Middlesex, Massachusetts.

94.	**ABIGAIL EMELINE⁶ WYETH** (Joseph⁵, Jonathan⁴ Jr., Jonathan³, John², Nicholas¹) was born about 1776 in Cambridge, Middlesex, Massachusetts. In 1785 her father purchased 12 acres in Groton for $168 and moved his family from Cambridge to be nearer to the Shaker religious sect. Abigail was a Shaker for a short time before her marriage to **JOHN ROBBINS JR.** on 02 Oct 1798 in Groton, Middlesex, Massachusetts. John died there about 1806. Abigail died on 13 May 1824 in Charlestown, Suffolk, Massachusetts.

John Robbins Jr. and Abigail Emeline Wyeth had the following children:

	i.	NATHANIEL⁷ ROBBINS was born on 07 May 1798 in Groton. He died from paralysis in Feb 1870 in Peabody, Essex, Massachusetts.
170.	ii.	ABIGAIL EMELINE ROBBINS, born 12 Aug 1799, Groton; married HOSEA DANA WINCHESTER, 09 Sep 1835, Boston; died there, 15 Dec 1837.
	iii.	SARAH ROBBINS, born 11 Sep 1803, Groton; death unknown.
	iv.	THOMAS ROBBINS, born 12 Nov 1804, Groton; death unknown.

95.	**EUNICE PAMELA⁶ WYETH** (Joseph⁵, Jonathan⁴ Jr., Jonathan³, John², Nicholas¹) was born circa 1781 in Cambridge, Middlesex, Massachusetts before the family moved to Groton, Middlesex, Massachusetts. She was married, by Samson Tuttle, Justice of Peace, to **STEPHEN TEMPLE**, son of Joseph Temple and his wife Lucy, on 15 Mar 1807 in Littleton, Middlesex, Massachusetts. The intention for marriage was filed on 17 Jan 1807 in Groton and Charlestown. Stephen was born on 17 Dec 1782 in Buckland, Franklin, Massachusetts. He earned a living dressing Moroccan leather.⁶⁰⁸ Stephen died on 30 Mar 1824 in Groton. She died on 27 Sep 1839 at the age of 58 in Groton's Poor House.

Stephen Temple and Eunice Pamela Wyeth had the following children, most were likely born in Groton:

	i.	JAMES⁷ TEMPLE was born on 15 May 1808; death unknown.
	ii.	SAMUEL S. TEMPLE was born on 11 Sep 1809; death unknown.
171.	iii.	ALEXANDER THAYER TEMPLE, born 15 May 1811, Boston, Suffolk, Massachusetts; married SOPHIA LEGG, 20 Jun 1841, Hopkinton, Middlesex, Massachusetts; died 17 Feb 1905, Upton, Worcester, Massachusetts.
	iv.	STEPHEN TEMPLE JR. was born on 13 Jun 1813 in Charlestown, Suffolk, Massachusetts. He served in the second Seminole War in Florida. He married MARY CHENEY, daughter of Timothy Cheney and Priscilla Plimpton, on 17 Feb 1841 in Dover, Norfolk, Massachusetts. She was born on 23 Feb 1817 in Medfield, Norfolk, Massachusetts. He was employed by the U.S. government as a blacksmith for many years at the arsenal at Augusta, Maine. He died in Augusta on 30 Mar 1853. Mary died on 18 Sep 1891 in Westborough, Worcester, Massachusetts.
	v.	BENJAMIN TEMPLE was born on 11 Apr 1816; death unknown.

96. **NATHAN**[6] **FESSENDEN JR.,** (Nathan[5], Hannah[4] Prentice, Hannah[3] Wyeth, John[2], Nicholas[1]) born 25 Apr 1772, Lexington, Middlesex, Massachusetts. He married **JANE GOODRICH,** 21 Jun 1801, Roxbury, Suffolk, Massachusetts. Jane Goodrich was born to Philip Goodridge and Sybil Ritter, 05 Aug 1778, Lunenburg, Worcester, Massachusetts. Jane died in Lexington on 10 Feb 1849. Nathan died there, 24 Jan 1866.

The children of Nathan Fessenden Jr. and Jane Goodrich included the following:

172.   i. CHARLES FRANKLIN[7] FESSENDEN, born 05 Nov 1812, Lexington, Middlesex, Massachusetts; married (1) MARTHA ELIZABETH NEWTON, 30 Jan 1840, Fitchburg, Worcester, Massachusetts; married (2) SARAH COWDIN NEWTON (Martha's sister) on 11 May 1852 in Fitchburg; he died there on 28 Dec 1884 at age 72.

97. **WILLIAM W.**[6] **WYETH** (Ebenezer[5], Ebenezer[4] Jr., Ebenezer[3], John[2], Nicholas[1]) was baptized 23 Jan 1780, Cambridge, Middlesex, Massachusetts. He married **ZERUAH WAIT**, daughter of Jonathan Wait and Margaret Smith, on 19 Jul 1807 in Chester, Hampden, Massachusetts. Zeruah was born on 28 Feb 1786 (birth record says 31st) in Chester. William died there on 22 Aug 1810. Zeruah died on 06 Jan 1862 at the age of 75 in Aurora, Portage, Ohio. Her marker in

The Graves of Mary Ann, Zeruah and Caroline Wyeth in the Aurora Plainview (Mennonite) Cemetery in Portage County, Ohio

the Aurora Mennonite Cemetery mistakenly says she was 79 years old at her death.

William W. Wyeth and Zeruah Wait had the following children:

     i. CAROLINE CORNELIA[7] WYETH (twin), born on 04 Nov 1807, Chester; died unmarried 25 Nov 1877 at the age of 70 in Aurora, Portage, Ohio.

     ii. CATHARINE MARGARET WYETH (twin), born on 04 Nov 1807, Chester; died there on 19 Mar 1812, at the age of four.

173.   iii. ELIZA WYETH, born 14 Feb 1809, Chester; married JOHN C. JUDSON, 14 Apr 1835, Aurora; died there, 17 Aug 1891.

     iv. MARY ANN WYETH was born on 16 Dec 1810 in Chester; died unmarried on 02 Aug 1851 at the age of 40 in Aurora.

98. **ELIZABETH**[6] **WYETH** (Ebenezer[5], Ebenezer[4] Jr., Ebenezer[3], John[2], Nicholas[1]) was born in Mar 1783 in Menotomy (Arlington), Middlesex, Massachusetts. Apparently, she did not live with her father and his new wife, Naomi, during the 1800 census. Elizabeth was probably then living in Charlestown as that is where she was when the intention of her marriage to Solomon Prentice Jr. was published on 27 Mar 1803. They married 15 Apr 1803 in Menotomy. **SOLOMON PRENTICE JR.**, son of Solomon Prentice and Rebecca

Frost, was born on 22 Mar 1776 in Menotomy (Arlington). Elizabeth was not yet 25 at her death on 20 Feb 1808 in West Cambridge (Arlington), Middlesex, Massachusetts. Solomon died there on 06 Oct 1821.

Stone in Arlington's Old Burying Ground reads "In Memory of Mrs. Elizabeth Prentice wife of Mr. Solomon Prentice who died Feb 20 1808 aged 24 years and 11 months."

Solomon Prentice Jr. and Elizabeth Wyeth had the following children:

    i. JAMES[7] PRENTICE, born 21 Dec 1803, Menotomy; died there in 1814 at age 11.

    ii. ELIZABETH PRENTICE, born 23 Jan 1806, in Menotomy; died 09 Mar 1818 at the age of 12 in West Cambridge (Arlington), Middlesex, Massachusetts.

    iii. MARY PRENTICE, born on 11 Jan 1808, West Cambridge; died there, 13 Oct 1809 at age one.

99. **MARY[6] WYETH** (Ebenezer[5], Ebenezer[4] Jr., Ebenezer[3], John[2], Nicholas[1]) was born about 1785. Proof of her parentage comes from her death certificate. Although it says she was born in Cambridge, it is more likely she was born in Connecticut as she indicated in the 1850 census. Perhaps she was living with her sister Elizabeth when she was baptized as an adult on 22 Dec 1805 in Menotomy (Arlington), Middlesex, Massachusetts. Elizabeth passed away in West Cambridge (Arlington) the month before Mary Wyeth married Samuel Bellows there on 27 Mar 1809.[609] The intention to marry was filed on 04 Mar 1809 in Cambridge because the groom lived there. **SAMUEL BELLOWS,** son of Ebenezer Bellows and Lydia Morse, was born on 10 Aug 1787 in Southborough, Worcester, Massachusetts. He died 15 Dec 1821 in Watertown, Middlesex, Massachusetts. Mary died on 19 Mar 1860 in Cambridge. She is buried there in lot 2187 on Asclepias Path in Mt. Auburn Cemetery.

These monuments on Asclepia Path are from left to right – Abby and Mary (their dates are on the back of their markers), William Wyeth and his wife, Mary Ann Bates Bellows, and Samuel Morse Bellows. Mother Mary Wyeth Bellows made the original purchase on 28 Feb 1854. Also, buried there in unmarked graves are, Mary Wyeth Bellows Hunt and three of William's children –Willie, Samuel and Daniel Bates Bellows. It appears Mary Wyeth's husband, Samuel Bellows, was not reburied there.

Samuel Bellows and Mary Wyeth had the following children:

    i. MARY WYETH[7] BELLOWS, born 14 Sep 1809, Cambridge, Middlesex, Massachusetts; married JAMES L. HUNT, son of Luther Ball Hunt and Sally Gove, on 09 Mar 1846, Boston, Suffolk, Massachusetts; died 18 Aug 1870, Royalston, Worcester, Massachusetts.

174.   ii. SAMUEL MORSE BELLOWS was born on 20 Nov 1811 in Cambridge. He married (1) MARY POTTER PEABODY, on 01 May 1836 in Lowell, Middlesex, Massachusetts. He married (2) HARRIET N. TURNER TODD in about 1844. Samuel died on 09 Nov 1887 in Dorchester, Suffolk, Massachusetts.

175.   iii. WILLIAM WYETH BELLOWS, born 17 Oct 1814, Watertown, Middlesex,

Massachusetts; married MARY ANN BATES, circa 1845, Maine; died 30 Aug 1904, Boston.

    iv. CATHERINE ABBOT "ABBY" BELLOWS was born on 07 Sep 1815 in Watertown. She died unmarried on 11 Jun 1860 in Boston.

100. **STEPHEN**[6] **WYETH** (Ebenezer[5], Ebenezer[4] Jr., Ebenezer[3], John[2], Nicholas[1]) was born about 1791 in the Town of Union, Tioga (Broome), New York. He served in the Cambridge Light Infantry during the War of 1812. Stephen married **SARAH ANN WRIGHT**, daughter of Ezekiel Wright and Sarah Melvin Jewett, on 10 Dec 1815 in Cambridge. Sarah Ann Wright was born on 06 Mar 1793 in Littleton, Middlesex, Massachusetts. She died in Cambridge at the age of 38, soon after the birth of her seventh child Francis, on 17 Jul 1831. Circa 1855 Stephen and Francis moved to Meigs County, Ohio. In his 80s, Stephen returned to New England to live with his daughter Sophia. He died there at age 92 on 05 Apr 1883 in Foster, Providence, Rhode Island (or in Killingly, Windham, Connecticut). He was buried in Bartlett Cemetery #One, Route 101, Killingly.

Although heavily retouched due to discoloration and age, this glass Daguerreotype of Stephen Wyeth quite resembles the original taken circa 1855. It is courtesy of his 3rd great grandson, Scott Allen Wyeth, from the collection of Mae Vantonia Wyeth Edmundson (1887-1965).

Stephen Wyeth and Sarah Ann Wright had the following children:

          i. LUTHER[7] WYETH, born about 1816; sailor, lost at sea before 1846.

176.   ii. EMELINE ELIZABETH WYTHE, born 1817, Cambridge; married WILLIAM RAWSON JONES, 15 Aug 1838, Cambridge; died 07 Jun 1894, Worcester, Worcester County, Massachusetts.

177.   iii. SOPHIA BRADFORD WYETH, born 24 Apr 1821, Cambridge; married (1) PALMER CLEVELAND CHANDLER, 30 Sep 1844, Pomfret, Windham, Connecticut; married (2) REV. DAVID OLNEY HOPKINS, 05 Dec 1862, Pomfret; died 19 Mar 1883, Foster, Rhode Island. (Her death was also registered in Killingly.)

      iv. SARAH WYETH, born 23 Mar 1823, Cambridge; died there after the 1840 census was taken.

       v. LUCY ANN WYETH, born 03 Oct 1825, Cambridge; died there, 30 May 1833.

      vi. WILLIAM WALLACE WYETH, born 03 Aug 1828, Cambridge; sailor, lost at sea before 1846.

178.   vii. FRANCIS JOHN HIGGINSON WYETH, born 29 Jun 1831, Cambridge; married REBECCA GRATE, 13 Aug 1857 in Salem Township, Meigs, Ohio; died there, 25 Oct 1911.

Notes for Stephen Wyeth:

The first Federal Population Census of the United States, in 1790, shows Stephen's father, Ebenezer, living in Chemung Township, Montgomery County, New York. In addition to Ebenezer, there was one male over age 16 (Ebenezer IV) and two under 16 (William and Joseph). Since birth records did not exist for that early time in the settlement of the New York frontier, the

1790 census, along with the 1870 census, contradict accounts stating Stephen was born in Massachusetts or Pennsylvania.

In 1791, Tioga County including, Chemung Township, was split off from Montgomery County. Then in 1806, Tioga County was divided, with Union then becoming part of Broome County. Chemung Township, west of Union, eventually became Chemung County, New York.[610]

Although Ebenezer Wyeth III was back in Massachusetts when Broome separated from Tioga, he definitely was still in New York in 1791. Evidence is a list attached to the 07 Nov 1791 report from the commissioners of highways. Ebenezer's name appears as an inhabitant of district No. 4. That district ran east along the Susquehanna river and included the village of Union all the way to the Pennsylvania state line as well as a large area of territory both north and south of the Susquehanna.[611] The highway documents corroborate Stephen's 1791 birth in the village of Union, Tioga (Broome), New York.

It appears the family still lived in New York when Stephen's mother, Elizabeth Winship, died in Jan 1799. After her death, the family returned to Cambridge to settle the estate of Stephen's grandfather, Ebenezer Wyeth Jr.

Stephen's name was first recorded in Cambridge town records when he was drafted into the military in Aug 1814. Stephen and his first cousin, Jonas Wyeth 3d (1794-1867), were in camp at South Boston with the Cambridge Light Infantry for 51 days commencing on 10 Sep 1814.[612]

Cambridge town records also show his 1815 marriage to Sarah Ann Wright. The couple apparently met sometime during the years 1803 to 1806 when the Wyeths lived in Littleton, Massachusetts. It was there that Stephen's stepmother, Naomi Russell, gave birth to Lucy (Hodgman), Catherine (Baker) and Joseph Wyeth. The Cambridge census reports from 1820 to 1840 do not list children's names. However, by studying the ages in the reports, they do confirm all seven of Stephen and Sarah's children.

In 1823, Stephen purchased land overlooking the Charles River near Harvard College from the heirs of Thomas Brattle. On 02 Feb 1824, both Stephen and Sarah signed a mortgage instrument.[613] The home still stands at 5-9 Hilliard Place in an area originally settled by tradesmen. Stephen, a talented carpenter, built the two-story residence himself. Unfortunately, after just five years in the house, Stephen lost it to a creditor in 1829.[614] Then on 17 Jul 1831, Stephen suffered a more precious loss when Sarah died due to complications from the birth of Francis John Higginson Wyeth.[615]

Sadly, many years later when Francis filled out his marriage application, he wrote "unknown" in the blank for his mother's name. Because he was not even three weeks old when his mother died, it is understandable. Francis' death certificate claims his mother's name was Lucy Baker. But that may be a confusion of the married names of his aunts Lucy Hodgman and Catherine Baker. The family of Francis' older sister, Emeline Elizabeth Wythe Jones, gave Sophia Wright as the mother's name on Emeline's death certificate. They probably confused Sarah Wright with her daughter, Sophia Bradford Wyeth Hopkins.

Since a census or marriage record of Stephen with a Lucy Baker cannot be found, apparently Stephen remained a widower after Sarah's death in 1831 until his own death over 50 years later. That is evidence of how much he loved Sarah and how lost he was without her.

By 1842, Stephen had left all the remembrances of Sarah behind in Cambridge. He moved west to Erving's Grant, Franklin, Massachusetts. While living there, his name appeared in two sets of records for 1842. One was for inheriting $75 from the estate of his aunt Anna Wyeth Cutter. He did not collect the money, however, until after the property sold on 26 Oct 1843.[616] His aunt's estate originally belonged to Stephen's great grandmother, Anna Whitmore Winship.

The second record was a declaration of bankruptcy. The following notice appeared on the front page of the 30 Jun 1842 *Boston Post*: "Upon the petition of Stephen Wyeth, of Erving, in the County of Franklin, in said District of Massachusetts, who has been declared a Bankrupt ... Ordered, that a hearing will be had on the said petition at the United States Court Room, in Boston, in said District, on the First Tuesday of October next, at ten o'clock in the forenoon..."[617]

The court required Stephen to furnish an inventory of his property. The following document, from Stephen's file held by the National Archives in Waltham, Massachusetts, equates his property to a value of $79.25.

Hopefully, Stephen was allowed to hold onto his $30 worth of carpentry tools in order to earn an income. He had already lost his home. The 1855 Massachusetts census shows Stephen boarding in Erving with the family of James Tufts Trask. The Trask family hailed from Littleton where Stephen spent his formative years.

Shortly after the Erving census, Stephen and son Francis emigrated to Meigs County, Ohio. They likely sailed from Boston to Baltimore, then traveled by covered wagon across the National Road to Wheeling, (West) Virginia. From there they took a boat down the Ohio River to Pomeroy – the county seat of Meigs County. By 15 Dec 1857, the *Meigs County Telegraph* newspaper stated 1856 taxes were overdue on 40 acres of Francis Wyeth's Salem Township property in Meigs County, Ohio.[618]

The 1860 census of Salem Township shows Stephen "With," a farmer, age 60, born in Massachusetts. He was the head of the household with John (Francis), Rebecca (Grate) and William Wyeth, age two, living with him. In the 1870 census, Stephen Wyeth was listed as a retired carpenter, age 80, born in New York. He still lived in Salem Township but was boarding with the Bunte family. Francis lived nearby with his wife and four children.

Soon after, Stephen grew tired of Ohio and returned to New England. At that point, trains were readily available. The 1875 Rhode Island census shows him residing in the town of Foster, Providence, Rhode Island with his daughter, Sophia, and her husband Rev. David Olney Hopkins.

Stephen surely must have been a hardy fellow. The 1880 Federal Population Census of Foster lists Stephen, age 89, working on David's farm. But three years later, Stephen's strength and zest for living gave out when his daughter Sophia died on 19 Mar 1883, at age 62, of heart and lung disease. Sophia's death so profoundly affected Stephen that he died just two weeks later of apoplexy (a stroke).

Sophia Bradford Wyeth Hopkin's death was certified in both Foster and Killingly, but Stephen's death was registered only in Killingly. It seems unlikely Stephen would have moved to Killingly, Connecticut at the advanced age of 90+. It is more likely both daughter and father died in Foster, Rhode Island, but their deaths were registered in Connecticut because they are buried in that state. Bartlett cemetery is only three miles west of Foster – just across the Rhode Island state line.

Buried near Stephen and Sophia in Bartlett cemetery is Asa Carroll. After Sophia's death, David Olney Hopkins married Carroll's widow, Thankful Simmons. Thankful's descendant, Lynn LaBerge, as well as Marilyn Labbe of the Killingly Historical Society, were of enormous help in finding the death records and locations of the Wyeth graves. It took from 2009 to 2014 to finally get Stephen's V.A. marker installed. Most of the delay was due to the unkindness of the man who held Bartlett's plot map. Once Kraig Griffin of Everlasting Memorials came into possession of the plot map, things moved quickly.

Seated are David Hopkins; his third wife, Thankful is holding their baby, Mercy Hopkins; and David's mother Mercy Shippee Hopkins is in the dark scarf. David's Carroll step-children are surrounding. Photo courtesy of Lynn LaBerge, Killingly Historical Society.

On my last visit to the Killingly Historical Society in 2014, I was absolutely amazed when Lynn gave me this photo. It was taken in Foster about seven years after Stephen's death. Stephen Wyeth had lived in this house with his daughter, Sophia, and son-in-law David Olney Hopkins.

101. **LUCY[6] WYETH** (Ebenezer[5], Ebenezer[4] Jr., Ebenezer[3], John[2], Nicholas[1]) was born on 17 Aug 1802 in Littleton, Middlesex, Massachusetts. She married Calvin Hodgman on 25 May 1828 in Watertown, Middlesex, Massachusetts. **CALVIN HODGMAN**, son of Jonas Hodgman and Orpa Wright, was born on 14 Feb 1804 in Ashby, Middlesex, Massachusetts. Lucy died in Jun 1845 in Edwardsville, Madison, Illinois.[619] Calvin remarried on 26 Sep 1845 to Roana Peirce. Calvin died on 20 Apr 1857 in Ridgely, Madison, Illinois.[620]

The children of Calvin Hodgman and Lucy Wyeth included:

179.   i.   (CAPTAIN) AMOS[7] HODGMAN, born 21 Jun 1829, Ashby; married MARTHA ANN DENTON, 01 Jan 1850, Madison County, Illinois; died on 16 Oct 1863 near Oxford, Lafayette, Mississippi of wounds received in a Civil War battle at Wyatt, Mississippi. Hodgeman County, Kansas, was named in Captain Hodgman's honor.[621]

102. **CATHERINE W.[6] WYETH** (Ebenezer[5], Ebenezer[4] Jr., Ebenezer[3], John[2], Nicholas[1]) was born on 17 Oct 1803 in Littleton, Middlesex, Massachusetts. Catherine W. Wyeth and Jalel Gathleed Baker were married on 23 May 1824 in Watertown, Middlesex, Massachusetts. **CAPTAIN JALEL GATHLEED BAKER**, son of Amos Baker and Amy Prescott, was born on 13 Oct 1789 in Lincoln, Middlesex, Massachusetts. He was a farmer and caretaker of the Watertown poorhouse. He died on 24 Jan 1873 in Waltham, Middlesex, Massachusetts. Jalel wrote his will on 10 Dec 1872 for the benefit of his wife, adopted daughter and several Baker and Wyeth nieces and nephews. Catherine died on 22 Mar 1883 in Waltham.

Jalel Gathleed Baker and Catherine W. Wyeth adopted the following child:

i.   ELIZA[7] BAKER, born about 1853, Brighton, Middlesex, Massachusetts. She married HOWARD L. STONE. He was born 21 Aug 1850 in Fayette, Kennebec, Maine to Kendall Stone and Emily Willoughby. Eliza died 17 May 1877, Waltham. Howard's death date is unknown.

103. **JOSEPH RUSSELL[6] WYETH** (Ebenezer[5], Ebenezer[4] Jr., Ebenezer[3], John[2], Nicholas[1]) was born on 03 Jul 1806 in Littleton, Middlesex, Massachusetts. Joseph Russell Wyeth and Emeline Jones were married on 22 Apr 1834 in Boston, Suffolk, Massachusetts. **EMELINE JONES** was born there on 31 Jul 1810. Since one of her children held the middle name "Henry," it is quite likely that her parents were Henry Jones and Sally Fyars.[622] Joseph died on 25 Mar 1870 at the age of 63 of heart problems, in Chelsea, Suffolk, Massachusetts. She died there on 19 Jan 1882.

Joseph Russell Wyeth and Emeline Jones had the following children:

180.   i.   GEORGE EBENEZER[7] WYETH, born 22 Feb 1835, Boston; married RUTH JANE EATON, 30 Dec 1858, Chelsea; died there of heart problems on 30 Jun 1919.

181.   ii.   REBECCA AURELIA WYETH, born 16 May 1836, Boston; married (CAPTAIN) EDWARD BOYLSTON WALKER RESTIEAUX, 18 Feb 1857, Chelsea; died there on 19 May 1915 of heart problems.

182.   iii.   JOSEPH HENRY WYETH, born 08 Jan 1838, Chelsea; married (1) MARY ANN CHEEVER, 05 Oct 1862, Charlestown, Suffolk, Massachusetts; married (2)

CAROLINE "CARRIE" OLDBURY, 27 Sep 1885, Reading Middlesex, Massachusetts; died 29 Jul 1920, Boston, of chronic arteriosclerosis.

183.   iv.   CATHARINE BAKER WYETH, born 16 Sep 1839, Chelsea; married STILLMAN HIGGINS LIBBY, 01 Mar 1860, Chelsea; died 07 Mar 1902, Somerville, Middlesex, Massachusetts.

       v.   MARY A. G. WYETH, born 03 Aug 1841, Chelsea; taught school; married ALFRED INSKIPP WAGSTAFF, 22 Aug 1883, Chelsea; died of pneumonia on 08 Mar 1892, Newton, Middlesex, Massachusetts; buried Woodlawn Cemetery, Everett, Massachusetts.

     vi.   EMELINE "EMMA" JONES WYETH, born 15 Jan 1844, Chelsea; married CURTIS CUTTING TEWKSBURY, 29 Aug 1865, Chelsea; died there of lung disease on 17 Oct 1866, at age 22.

   vii.   ELIPHALET J. WYETH, born 24 Nov 1845, Chelsea; died there, while teething, on 04 Apr 1847, at age one. He probably was named for Eliphalet Jones who might be Henry Jones' brother. Both Henry and Eliphalet Jones are buried in Copp's Hill Burying Ground, Boston, but Henry's grave is not marked.[623]

  viii.   LUCY J. WYETH was born on 20 Feb 1847 in Chelsea. She died there unmarried on 01 Dec 1868 at the age of 21.

    ix.   LILLIAN WYETH, born 18 Sep 1848, Chelsea; died unmarried of nervous exhaustion on 15 May 1896 at the age of 47 in Somerville; buried Woodlawn Cemetery.

Notes for Joseph Russell Wyeth:

Joseph's middle name comes from the combinations of the death records of his son and grandson. Both had the first name "Joseph" but records show the son's middle name was "Henry" and the grandson's name was "Russell." Thus, the Russell name was carried on from the three men's maternal ancestor, Naomi Russell Wyeth.

Boston directories and newspapers show that in 1830 Joseph was in a grocery partnership with Oliver Cook and in 1831 with Henry Andrews. Then, just before his marriage, he began a partnership with George Partridge.

Perhaps Joseph got his start in that business with Henry Jones who was a Boston grocer living close to the Charles Street Baptist Church where Joseph married Emeline. Daniel Sharp, D.D. performed the ceremony.[624]

Before Joseph moved to Chelsea, circa 1839, he was in another Boston grocery partnership with Stephen Bass. In 1842, Stephen Bass helped Joseph provide surety to Joseph's half-brother, Stephen Wyeth, when Stephen declared bankruptcy in Erving, Massachusetts.

Once in Chelsea, Joseph changed occupations to become a trader. Since he had $20,000 of real estate in 1850, Joseph was well off. In the 1860 Chelsea census, Joseph was listed as a broker.

At his death in 1870, records showed he was an assessor for the government and a trader. His obituary called him a prominent citizen and said, "the Assistant U.S. Assessor of the Third District died suddenly at his 11 Essex Street home in Chelsea on Friday, 25 Mar 1870."[625]

104. **JONAS**[6] **WYETH 3**[D] (Jonas[5] Jr., Ebenezer[4] Jr., Ebenezer[3], John[2], Nicholas[1]) was born on 03 Sep 1794 in Cambridge, Middlesex, Massachusetts. Jonas Wyeth 3[d] and Elizabeth Nutting "Betsey" Flagg were married on 08 Feb 1820 in Cambridge. **ELIZABETH NUTTING FLAGG**, daughter of Timothy Flagg and Sarah Hicks, was born on 19 Jan 1797 in Cambridge. Jonas died on 14 Jun 1867 at the age of 72 in Cambridge. Betsey died there on 17 May 1895 at the age of 98. They are buried in Mt. Auburn Cemetery, Cambridge, on Lupine Path in lot 771 with several of their children and grandchildren.

Back (L to R): Annie, Mary Ann, and Sarah Wyeth and Maria Wyeth Angus; middle: Sidney, Ada, Jonas 3[d], and Elizabeth Nutting Flagg Wyeth; front left: Maria Warland and James Hicks Wyeth II.

Jonas Wyeth 3[d] and Betsey Flagg had the following children:

      i. JAMES HICKS[7] WYETH I, born 11 Jun 1820, Cambridge. He died in Watertown, Middlesex, Massachusetts on 28 Mar 1829 at the age of eight.[626]

      ii. SARAH ELIZABETH WYETH was born on 21 May 1822 in Cambridge. She died there unmarried on 10 Aug 1889.

      iii. MARY ANN WYETH was born on 09 May 1824 in Cambridge. She died there unmarried on 18 Oct 1907.

184.   iv. MARIA WYETH, born 18 Sep 1826, Watertown; married WILLIAM ANGUS, 02 Sep 1858, Cambridge (same day as her sister);[627] died of anemia, 10 Mar 1868, Montréal, Québec, Canada.

      v. CAROLINE E. WYETH, born 29 Jul 1828, Watertown; died there, 30 Sep 1843 at the age of 15 from dropsy on brain.

185.   vi. JAMES HICKS WYETH, born 24 Jul 1830, Watertown; married MARIA CARTER WARLAND, 05 Jun 1860, Cambridge; died there on 19 May 1924.

186.   vii. HARRIETT L. WYETH, born 18 Jun 1833, Cambridge; married WILLIAM PRATT MCLAREN, 02 Sep 1858, Cambridge (same day as her sister);[628] died 14 Mar 1928, Seattle, King, Washington.

   viii. MARTHA WYETH, born 30 Jun 1835, Cambridge; died there at one month old.

Notes for Jonas Wyeth 3[d] and Elizabeth Nutting Flagg:

Just after celebrating his 20th birthday, Jonas volunteered in Boston as a member of the Cambridge Light Infantry for the period of 10 Sep 1814 to 30 Oct 1814. The Infantry had been called out by the Massachusetts governor to suppress a threatened invasion by the British during the War of 1812-14. He served with his first cousin, Stephen Wyeth. In the records of Lt. Colonel Joseph Valentine's Regiment, Captain Samuel Child's Company, Jonas was listed as "Jonas Wythe 3[d]".[629]

Shortly after his military service, Jonas took over the management of the Fresh Pond hotel from his uncle Jacob Wyeth Sr. and first cousin Nathaniel Jarvis Wyeth. Under Jonas' care, the hotel continued to flourish. It had a reputation of being the place to go for Boston social events. To keep up with the styles of the day, Jonas remodeled the hotel in 1838 into a more contemporary Greek-revival style with trim and gables.[630]

Upon Jonas' retirement in 1840, Lyman Willard, brother-in-law of Jonas' sister, Susan Wyeth Willard (1798-1896), took ownership and continued the success of the hotel for the next decade.

Fresh Pond Hotel, as it appeared circa 1888, while it was owned by the Sisters of St. Joseph and serving as Mount St. Joseph Academy. Jacob Wyeth's house, in the rear, served as the sisters' convent. This photo was purchased from the Wyeth Family Collection of the Cambridge Historical Commission. Used with the permission of Kathleen L. (Kit) Rawlins, Assistant Director. https://www.cambridgema.gov/historic.

After Lyman built his own hotel at 38 Brattle Street in downtown Cambridge, the Fresh Pond Hotel passed through many hands.[631] Eventually, it was purchased by the Sisters of St. Joseph and turned into a Catholic boarding school for young ladies. After the city of Cambridge purchased the land from the sisters, it was rechristened. Today it is known as Kingsley Park. The hotel was moved in 1892 from its original location at Fresh Pond to 234 Lakeview Avenue.[632] The four-story building is now home to six condominiums.[633]

Wyeth-Eliot house
credit: Christopher Hail, photographer, Harvard and Cambridge Buildings and Architects, courtesy of the Harvard University Archives.

From the proceeds of managing his Uncle Jacob's Fresh Pond Hotel, Jonas purchased a farm from Seth Hastings. The estate then extended from Mt. Auburn Street to Fresh Pond.[634] In 1839, Jonas built a house on the property where he resided until his death. The house faces Brattle Street and was addressed as such at the time. Since the driveway now faces Fresh Pond Parkway, the home's street address changed to 17 Fresh Pond Parkway. The house stayed in the Wyeth family until 1909 when Jonas' son, James Hicks Wyeth, sold it to Charles Eliot, President of Harvard. Eliot had the house enlarged to its current size.[635]

Jonas was devoted to civic affairs. He served frequently as an overseer of the poor. In 1844 he acted as a Cambridge selectman and in 1851 as a member of the Common Council.[636]

Betsey, too, championed the poor. When she died, at age 98, in the Brattle Street house, her obituary said, "She possessed a large and kindly heart and was a ready sympathizer with the needy and unfortunate." She was granddaughter of the patriot, John Hicks, who was killed by British troops in Cambridge, 19 Apr 1775. Her obituary also mentioned that since she was born just before George Washington left office on 04 Mar 1797, she had lived under all 24 presidents … to the second presidency of Grover Cleveland. She was at the time of her death, with one exception, the oldest inhabitant of Cambridge.[637] According to the records of the Wyeth Funeral Home of Cambridge, her funeral cost $92.[638]

105. **NANCY**^{6} **WYETH** (Jonas^5 Jr., Ebenezer^4 Jr., Ebenezer^3, John^2, Nicholas^1) was born on 09 Sep 1796 in Cambridge, Middlesex, Massachusetts. Nancy Wyeth and Richard Clark Hastings married there on 05 Jun 1823. **RICHARD CLARK HASTINGS**, the son of Benjamin Hastings and Rebecca Clark, was born on 19 Sep 1793 in Watertown, Middlesex, Massachusetts. He died on 22 Apr 1860 at the age of 66 in Belmont, Middlesex, Massachusetts. Nancy died on 20 Aug 1873 at the age of 76 in Boston, Suffolk, Massachusetts. They are buried in Mt. Auburn Cemetery on Linden Path.

Richard Clark Hastings and Nancy Wyeth had eight children.[639] They included:

> i. GEORGE CLARK^7 HASTINGS, born 02 Mar 1824 in Watertown. According to California voter registers, he mined gold at Mokelumne Hill which was one of the richest gold mining towns in California. George died unmarried on 21 Mar 1880 at the age of 56 in San Andreas, Calaveras, California and was buried in the Gold Hill House County Hospital Cemetery.
> ii. ANN SUSAN HASTINGS, born 17 Mar 1826, Boston; died 11 Apr 1848, Cambridge, aged 22.
> iii. ANDREW JACKSON HASTINGS, born 30 Dec 1834, Boston; died there, 12 Aug 1836 at age one.
> iv. JOANNA FRANCES HASTINGS, born 22 Jan 1838, Boston; she died there, of pneumonia, on 17 Apr 1893.
> v. HARRIET WYETH HASTINGS, born 06 Nov 1843, Belmont; married FREDERICK PAUL RIPLEY, 17 Apr 1868, Cambridge; died 29 Jan 1932, Worcester, Worcester County, Massachusetts.

106. **SUSAN**^{6} **WYETH** (Jonas^5 Jr., Ebenezer^4 Jr., Ebenezer^3, John^2, Nicholas^1) was born on 06 May 1798 in Cambridge, Middlesex, Massachusetts. Susan Wyeth and Oren Willard were married on 11 Mar 1828 in Cambridge. **OREN WILLARD**, son of Simon Willard and Anna Nancy Cotting, was born on 16 Jun 1802 in Ashburnham, Worcester, Massachusetts. Orin's brother, Lyman Willard, ran the Fresh Pond Hotel when Jonas Wyeth 3^d retired. Orin died on 29 Jan 1879 at the age of 76 in Leominster, Worcester, Massachusetts. Susan died there on 13 May 1896 at the age of 98.

Oren Willard and Susan Wyeth had the following children:

> 187. i. FRANCIS OREN^7 WILLARD, born 13 Jan 1829, Ashby, Middlesex, Massachusetts; married ELIZABETH LEE CAMPBELL, 08 Jul 1850, Newton, Middlesex, Massachusetts; died 06 Apr 1906, Leominster.
> 188. ii. GEORGE OTIS WILLARD, born 10 Mar 1831, Ashby; married LUCY F. CAMPBELL, 17 Nov 1869, Fitchburg, Worcester, Massachusetts; died 11 Mar 1893 at the age of 62 in Boston, Suffolk, Massachusetts.
> 189. iii. SUSAN LOUISA WILLARD, born 21 Jan 1833, Ashby; married WILLIAM HENRY GROUT, 30 Apr 1855, Leominster; died 08 Oct 1892, Fitchburg.
>   iv. HANNAH AUGUSTA WILLARD, born 05 Feb 1835, Leominster; married (DR.) WASHINGTON AYER, 12 Sep 1867, San Francisco, San Francisco County, California; died 19 Aug 1916, Oakland, Alameda, California.

v. SARAH ELIZABETH WILLARD, born 30 Jan 1837, Lowell, Middlesex, Massachusetts; married ALPHEUS DEAN, 21 Nov 1858, Leominster, died 19 Nov 1929, Galesburg, Knox, Illinois.

190.   vi. MARY ANN WILLARD, born 28 May 1839, Ashburnham; married CROSBY ALPHEUS PERRY, 21 Sep 1858, Ashburnham; died 12 Jan 1916, Leominster.

vii. ELLEN MARIA WILLARD, born 30 May 1841, Ashburnham. She died there a week before her fifth birthday on 23 May 1846.

107. **HARRIET**^{6} **WYETH** (Jonas^5 Jr., Ebenezer^4 Jr., Ebenezer^3, John^2, Nicholas^1) was born on 30 Sep 1800 in Cambridge, Middlesex, Massachusetts. Harriet Wyeth and Reuben Winslow were married on 20 Jun 1824 in Cambridge. **REUBEN WINSLOW**, son of Isaac Winslow and Elizabeth Snow, was born on 26 Aug 1800 in Brewster, Barnstable, Massachusetts. Reuben died on 28 Apr 1862 in Roxbury, Suffolk, Massachusetts. Harriet died on 12 Apr 1879 in Boston, Suffolk, Massachusetts.

Reuben Winslow and Harriet Wyeth had the following children:

   i. JOSEPH WARREN^7 WINSLOW, born on 28 May 1825 in Roxbury; died 19 Dec 1898, Boston.
   ii. HARRIET WINSLOW, born 11 Feb 1827 in Roxbury; married LEWELLYN DANA DAVENPORT, 27 Jan 1853; died in Brookline, Norfolk, Massachusetts on 04 Jul 1920.
   iii. SARAH LOUISA WINSLOW, born in 1829 in Roxbury; married GEORGE KITTREDGE GOODWIN, 18 Nov 1847, Roxbury, died 15 Jan 1891, Boston.
   iv. REBECCA WINSLOW, born 28 May 1831 in Roxbury; married GEORGE WARREN (ONION), 18 Aug 1853 in Roxbury; died 14 May 1884, Boston.
   v. ELIZABETH WINSLOW, born 21 Sep 1836, Roxbury; died there, 07 Jun 1850.

108. **JOHN**^{6} **WYETH** (Jonas^5 Jr., Ebenezer^4 Jr., Ebenezer^3, John^2, Nicholas^1) was born 17 Feb 1805 in Cambridge, Middlesex, Massachusetts.[640] John Wyeth and Mary Ann Newman were married on 12 Nov 1839 in Roxbury, Suffolk, Massachusetts. **MARY ANN NEWMAN**, daughter of William Jasper Newman and Sarah "Sally" Babcock, was born on 12 Nov 1815 in Roxbury. John died on 25 Sep 1871 at the age of 66 of Bright's disease at his home at 58 Eustis St., in Boston, Suffolk, Massachusetts. (His home address was originally Roxbury, but the town was annexed to Boston in 1868.) Mary Ann died on 08 Feb 1887 in Sharon, Norfolk, Massachusetts.

John Wyeth and Mary Ann Newman had the following children:

191.   i. JOHN JASPER^7 WYETH, born 25 Dec 1841, Cambridge; enlisted in the Union Army, 29 Aug 1862; married MARGARET ELIZA HIXON, 12 Nov 1867, Sharon, Norfolk, Massachusetts; died 11 Mar 1906, Quincy, Norfolk, Massachusetts.
   ii. MARION ELIZA WYETH, born 08 Apr 1844, Cambridge; died there at age 21. The date on her grave in Mt. Auburn Cemetery, lot 1800, Yarrow Path gives her death date as 26 Aug 1865.

iii. SARAH ELIZABETH "LIZZIE" WYETH, born on 06 Dec 1846 in Cambridge; died there, unmarried, on 01 Nov 1933, at the age of 86. She was buried near her sister in Mt. Auburn Cemetery on 03 Nov 1933. Her grave is not marked.

Sarah Elizabeth "Lizzie" Wyeth earned her living as a bookkeeper. Her photo is courtesy of her great grand nephew, Keith Lyon Wyeth.

Notes for John Wyeth:

John, a merchant trading in the West Indies and in other foreign markets, built a large house in 1841 nearly opposite the Mt. Auburn Cemetery gate.[641] The next year, he advertised, "Auburn House... a Temperance Refreshment House." It was open daily, except Sundays, for ladies and gentlemen visiting Mt. Auburn. They sold soda, mead (an alcoholic beverage created by fermenting honey with water), ice creams and fruits of the season.[642]

John Wyeth's 2.5 story wood frame house was moved to its present location at 56 Aberdeen in 1922-23; it is one of the oldest Greek Revival houses in Northwest Cambridge.

The 1848 Cambridge Directory shows the facility continued to serve as a public temperance house catering to individuals during the movement that swept the United States from the 1820s to the beginning of the Civil War.[643] Moderation, not abstinence, was the goal of the many temperance societies established at that time. Alcohol was blamed for crime, illness, poverty, and domestic abuse. Temperance houses were symbols of middle-class respectability in the towns where they were located.[644]

In the 1850 and 1860 census reports, John was a farmer. Land records show John sold his Cambridge property in 1866. In the 1870 census, John was retired and living in the Roxbury neighborhood of Boston with Mary Ann and their whole family, including daughter-in-law, Margaret, and grandson, John Hixon Wyeth.

109. ELISHA[6] WYETH (Joshua[5], Ebenezer[4] Jr., Ebenezer[3], John[2], Nicholas[1]) was born on 11 Mar 1782 in Massachusetts. Elisha Wyeth and Nancy Salisbury were married circa 1804 in Towanda, Luzerne (Bradford) County, Pennsylvania. NANCY SALISBURY, daughter of Henry Salisbury and Catherine Head, was born on 06 Jan 1786 in Kinderhook, Columbia, New York. Nancy died on 01 Apr 1854 in Riley Township, Vigo, Indiana. Elisha died there on 01 Oct 1854. Mewhinney cemetery records show he was age 72 years, 6 months and 20 days.[645]

Elisha Wyeth and Nancy Salisbury had the following children:

192. i. LOUISA[7] WYETH, born 13 Oct 1804, Luzerne (Bradford) County, Pennsylvania; married (1) REUBEN SAILORS, 18 May 1821, Brookville, Franklin, Indiana; married (2) ISAAC WASHINGTON MCCARTY, 21 Feb 1841, Van Buren County, Iowa; married (3) JOHN MILTON CORDER, 19 Aug 1878, Wayne County, Iowa; died 05 Oct 1890, Jefferson Township, Wayne, Iowa.

193.   ii.   AMY WYETH, born circa 1808, Towanda, Luzerne (Bradford) County, Pennsylvania; married AVENENT T. LEWIS, 27 Apr 1823, Brookville; died in Dec 1870 and interred 24 Dec 1870 in Woodlawn Cemetery, Vigo County, Indiana.[646]

194.   iii. JAMES SALISBURY WYETH, born 19 Jul 1810, Towanda; married (1) MARTHA MEWHINNEY, 29 May 1834, Vigo County, Indiana; married (2) SARAH ANN JENKS, 11 Dec 1862, Terre Haute, Vigo, Indiana; died there, 02 Apr 1882.

195.   iv.   FRANCIS MARTIN WYETH, born 13 Sep 1814, Towanda; married DORCAS TABITHA TANKERSLEY, 07 Jul 1836, Riley Township, Vigo, Indiana; died 29 Mar 1877, Terre Haute.

196.   v.   ELIZA WYETH, born 09 May 1817, Brookville; married JOHN M. HARPER, 02 Apr 1837, Riley; died 20 Feb 1888, Lost Creek Township, Vigo, Indiana.

197.   vi.   SARAH MARIA WYETH, born circa 1822, Brookville; married WILLIAM BENJAMIN MEWHINNEY, 26 Dec 1841, Vigo County; died there circa 1857.

198.   vii. MILTON LEWIS WYETH M.D., born in Mar 1825, Brookville; married MARY ELIZA DAVIS, 31 Dec 1848, Vigo County; died 04 May 1862, on the steamer USS *De Soto* by Island #10 on the Mississippi River in Missouri while on active duty in the Civil War.[647]

Notes for Elisha Wyeth and Nancy Salisbury:

Elisha was likely born in Boston. When he was five years old, the family lived south of the town's common in an area now occupied by the Tufts-New England Medical Center on Washington Street. At sunset on 20 Apr 1787 a fire broke out in William Patten's malt house. Although it was some distance from the Wyeth home, a hard-blowing northeasterly wind carried flakes of fire to such height and distance it devastated the very dry, wooden houses on several streets in the area. The destruction was similar to the great Boston fire of 1760. The fire wreaked havoc for about three hours. It burned 56 dwelling houses, 13 stores, eight barns, and the Hollis Street Church. No lives were lost, but 86 families were left homeless.[648] Joshua Wyeth's family was one of more than two dozen burnt out on the east side of Orange Street.[649]

With their home totally destroyed, Joshua took his five children to their grandparents' home in Cambridge for a time. It was there Elisha's sister, Mary "Polly" Wyeth Gilbert Dodge, was born.[650] By 1790, they moved to Harvard, Worcester, Massachusetts, as shown in the first Federal Population Census of the United States. Soon afterward, the family moved to the Lake Region of central New York where Elisha's uncle, Ebenezer Wyeth III, was then residing. Finding the area not well suited to his family, in 1792, Joshua purchased land from John Heath on Towanda Creek in Pennsylvania and moved the family there in 1794.[651]

At age 19, while living in Towanda, Elisha took a great rafting trip adventure with his father down the Susquehanna River to visit his uncle John Wyeth. On 09 Apr 1801, from Harrisburg, Joshua wrote his sister, Anna Wyeth Cutter, that the two came with rails (poles) and raft. He said the raft was stove twice, but they got off safely. At the time, John was publishing the *Oracle of Dauphin* newspaper and serving as Harrisburg's postmaster under President Thomas Jefferson. Joshua told Anna that he and Elisha were well treated during the visit.[652]

Three years later, circa 1804, Elisha married Nancy Salisbury in Luzerne County, in an area that is now Bradford County, Pennsylvania. Although created on 21 Feb 1810 from parts of Lycoming and Luzerne counties, it was not named Bradford until 1812.[653] Nancy hailed from Kinderhook, New York, where she had gone to school with future U.S. President Martin Van Buren.[654]

While in the Towanda area, Elisha was active in civic affairs. On 25 May 1809, Elisha Wyeth, as Constable of Towanday Township, offered a reward in the Wilkes-Barre newspaper for the apprehension of one John E. Kent for passing a counterfeit $20 bill on the New York State Bank.[655] In addition to his policing duties, Elisha served as treasurer in 1811 and as secretary in 1812 of the Towanda Union Lodge No. 108 of Free & Accepted Masons (F. & A. M.).[656] This was a tradition Elisha's son, James, would later carry on in Vigo County, Indiana.

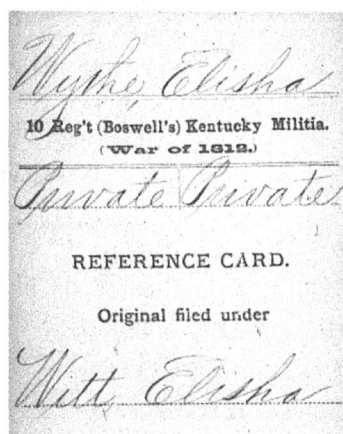

Shortly after Bradford County was named, Elisha and all his siblings, except Mary, followed their father west. Most spent time near Joshua in Cincinnati, Ohio. They arrived in the area when the War of 1812 still was underway. On 07 Apr 1813, the Kentucky Volunteer Light Infantry, commanded by Colonel William E. Boswell marched from Cincinnati to Fort Meigs (near present day Toledo, Ohio).[657] There is one record of an Elisha Wythe / Elisha Witt being a member of Boswell's Regiment of militia.[658] Here is the confusing index file card.

The 1820 and 1830 census reports show Elisha and his brother, Joshua Wyeth Jr., living near Brookville, Franklin County, Indiana. Soon after, on 28 Oct 1835, Elisha purchased public lands in the far western part of the state. The certificate was acknowledged in the Vincennes, Indiana, land office for President Andrew Jackson. Joshua Jr. also made the move west and together the brothers became some of the earliest settlers of Riley Township, Vigo County, Indiana.[659]

In the 1850 census for Riley Township, Elisha's name appears to be spelled "Chastin." But careful perusal reveals the first letter to be an "E." This misspelling on the census apparently caused some researchers to give him a middle name. He was listed as a cabinetmaker with $2,000 in real estate. Two of his sons and his brother, Francis B. Wyeth, lived nearby.

Elisha's will, dated 12 Apr 1847, was probated on 06 Oct 1854. Elisha left one dollar to each of his children, except for his youngest child, Milton Lewis Wyeth. Elisha wrote that all his older children had already received their fair share of property. Perhaps it was Elisha's intention to fund Milton's medical education that he started in 1852 at Starling Medical College in Columbus, Ohio.[660]

110. **JOSHUA[6] WYETH JR.** (Joshua[5], Ebenezer[4] Jr., Ebenezer[3], John[2], Nicholas[1]) was born 17 Jan 1784 in Massachusetts. He married (1) **GRACE JACKSON** about 07 Feb 1805 in Hanover Township, Luzerne, Pennsylvania.[661] Joshua married (2) **HANNAH POND**, 30 Aug 1810, Orwell, Luzerne (Bradford), Pennsylvania.[662] Hannah Pond, daughter of Enoch Pond and Peggy Smith, was born on 28 Nov 1791 in Wrentham, Norfolk, Massachusetts.[663] She died on 26 Jan 1849 at the age of 57 in Riley Township, Vigo, Indiana. He died there on 23 Oct 1870 at the age of 86.

Joshua Wyeth Jr. and Hannah Pond had the following children: [664]

199.	i.	CHARLES PRENTICE[7] WYTHE, born 18 Dec 1811, Towanda, Luzerne (Bradford), Pennsylvania; married NANCY RECTOR, 15 Sep 1836, Riley Township, Vigo, Indiana; died there, 02 Aug 1869.
200.	ii.	ELIZA BREWER WYETH, born 30 Jul 1813, Towanda; married WILLIAM LAFORGE, 30 Sep 1830, Brookville, Franklin, Indiana; died 14 Sep 1834, Brookville.
201.	iii.	EMILY WYETH, born 29 Sep 1815, Cincinnati, Hamilton, Ohio; married BENJAMIN MEWHINNEY, 03 Nov 1830, Brookville; died 09 Mar 1876, Riley Township.[665]
202.	iv.	MARY WYETH, born 31 Jan 1818, Cincinnati; married DANIEL H. COLLINS, 18 Jan 1838, Riley Township; died there, 22 Jan 1849.
203.	v.	CLARISSA WYETH, born 31 Jan 1820, Cincinnati; married JOHN MEWHINNEY, 15 Dec 1839, Riley Township; died there, 14 May 1876.
204.	vi.	SEVELAN WYETH, born 15 Apr 1822, Brookville; married MARY JANE MARSHALL, 29 Mar 1849, Riley Township; died there, 03 Jul 1885.
205.	vii.	WILLIS B. WYETH, born 27 Oct 1824, Brookville; married SARAH ELLEN CAHILL, 05 Jan 1859, Clay County, Indiana; died 09 Sep 1876, Riley Township.
	viii.	SOPHRONIA WYETH was born on 27 Jan 1826 in Brookville; she died there on 14 Feb 1826 at the age of two weeks.
	ix.	GEORGE NELSON WYETH was born on 17 Oct 1832 in Brookville; he died there on 04 Dec 1832 at the age of two months.

Notes for Joshua Wyeth Jr.:

As with the other older children of Mary Elizabeth Brewer and Joshua Wyeth Sr., Joshua Jr. was likely born in Boston before the great fire of 1787. Most of the dates above come from the family Bible held by Sevelan Wyeth. Sevelan's great granddaughter, Ethel Ross "Rossie" Wyeth Canion, provided that information.

In a letter dated 15 Sep 1806, while he was in Woodstock, Vermont, on business, Joshua Wyeth Sr. reported to his sister, Anna Wyeth Cutter, about many of his children. Of Joshua Jr., he said that he was not married yet.[666] This makes it curious if the Grace Jackson marriage was correctly reported by editor Horace E. Hayden. Also, referring to Joshua Jr., in a letter dated Cincinnati, 09 Sep 1827, his father wrote to his sister, "My children of the first crop have gone from me, from Dan to Beersheba." He did not know where some of them were residing. Two exceptions were he knew his sons, Elisha and Joshua, now lived 40 miles from him.[667] Amazingly, a Google map search from John Street, Cincinnati (where Joshua Sr. then lived) to Brookville, Indiana (where Elisha and Joshua Jr. then lived) is 40 miles.

From Brookville near the eastern border of Indiana, Joshua Wyeth Jr. followed Elisha to the western border of Indiana near the Wabash River. Along with Martin Bratt, John Rector, Benjamin and Thomas Mewhinney, the Wyeth brothers were some of the earliest settlers of Riley Township, Vigo County, Indiana.[668] Of course, Wyeth children married their neighbors. So, in turn, many Bratt, Rector, and Mewhinney descendants are also descendants of Nicholas Wyeth.

The move across Indiana occurred circa 1834. For the 1840 census of Riley Township, Vigo County, Joshua's name appears directly above the names of Thomas and Benjamin Mewhinney. In the 1850 census, the first Federal Census that included spouses' and children's names, since Hannah died the year before, Joshua had sons Willis and Sevelan lodging with him along with his daughter-in-law, Mary Jane Marshall. By the 1870 Riley Township census, Joshua's living arrangements were reversed. 87-year-old Joshua Jr. resided with Sevelan and Mary Jane. Willis occupied the house next door. Joshua outlived his wife Hannah Pond by more than 20 years. He did not remarry but spent his days helping his sons farm the land he purchased almost four decades earlier.

111. **GEORGE MORRIS⁶ WYETH SR.** (Joshua⁵, Ebenezer⁴ Jr., Ebenezer³, John², Nicholas¹) was born 09 Oct 1785 in Massachusetts. George Morris Wyeth Sr. and Eliza H. Cooke were married on 27 Jul 1809 in Erie, Erie County, Pennsylvania.[669] **ELIZA H. COOKE**, daughter of Peyton Cooke and Isabella Fulton, was born in Washington County, Pennsylvania on 01 Apr 1790.[670] George died on 04 Jun 1844 in Scott County, Illinois. His will was written on 25 May 1844 and probated on 27 Jun 1844 in the Court of Probate, Justice of the Peace, Morgan County, Illinois. It states the names of his six lawful children as shown below. Eliza died on 18 Oct 1848 at her daughter Mary Isabella Metcalf's home in Waverly, Morgan, Illinois.

George Morris Wyeth Sr. and Eliza H. Cooke had the following children:

       i. PEYTON COOKE⁷ WYETH was born circa 1811 in Williamsport (Monongahela), Washington, Pennsylvania. He married his cousin, DEBORAH P. "DORA" COOKE, daughter of Robert Fulton Cooke and Elizabeth White, circa 1843. She was born on 22 Aug 1819 in Clermont County, Ohio. Deborah died on 20 Feb 1851 of consumption, at the age of 31, in Storrs Township, Hamilton, Ohio. She was originally buried with her parents in the downtown Cincinnati Presbyterian cemetery, but was moved 03 Oct 1857 to Spring Grove Cemetery, Cincinnati.[671] Peyton's death was published on 08 Aug 1862 in Barbados.[672] He died there on 15 Jul 1862 and was buried at St. Michael but on 14 Jan 1865 his remains were moved to lot 15567, section 84, Green-Wood Cemetery, Brooklyn.[673] Unfortunately, his stone there is unreadable.

206.   ii. (DR.) ALEXANDER REED WYETH, born 08 Jan 1813, Williamsport (Monongahela); married (1) HARRIETT PAMELA BEEBE, 07 Mar 1837, Morgan County, Illinois; married (2) ELIZABETH M. WINTER, 23 Oct 1843, Donegal Township, Washington, Pennsylvania; served as an assistant surgeon with the rank of 1ˢᵗ Lieut. in Pennsylvania's Ringgold Battalion during the Civil War;[674] died 24 Mar 1876, Independence, Washington, Texas.

207.   iii. ANNE ELIZA J. WYETH, born 1817, Williamsport (Monongahela); married ANDREW LEEDS PENNOYER, 03 Dec 1838, Morgan County, Illinois; died 30 Apr 1881,[675] Roseville, Ellison Township, Warren, Illinois.

208.   iv. ISABELLA MARY WYETH, born 03 Jul 1820, Williamsport (Monongahela); married DR. JOHN MILTON METCALF, 08 Apr 1838, Morgan County, Illinois; died one month short of age 95 on 07 Jun 1915 in Oakland, Alameda, California.[676]

209.   v.   DR. GEORGE MORRIS WYETH JR. was born on 30 Sep 1822, Williamsport (Monongahela); married MARY ETHEL CHAMBERLAIN, 10 May 1853, St. Louis, Missouri; died 15 Oct 1899, Jacksonville, Duval, Florida.[677]

          vi.   FULTON WYETH, born 03 Jan 1828, Williamsport (Monongahela); died there on 23 Oct 1828 of croup at age nine months and 20 days.[678]

         vii.   HARRIETTE LOUISA "HALLIE" WYETH was born circa 1834 in Washington County, Pennsylvania. After her parents' deaths, she attended a Sabbath school called Monticello Female Seminary in Godfrey, Madison, Illinois. She later was a teacher at the Benton School in St. Louis.[679] According to census reports, after she moved to live with her brother, Peyton Cooke Wyeth, she taught music in Brooklyn. She was the sole beneficiary of Peyton's will. Hallie died in May 1875 in Brooklyn, Kings, New York. She is buried there with her brother and nephew, both named Peyton, in Green-Wood Cemetery.

Notes on George Morris Wyeth Sr. and his son, the artist, Peyton Cooke Wyeth:

His stone in the Old Manchester Cemetery, Scott County, Illinois, shows George M. Wyeth, age 60 – calculated to have been born in 1784. However, that would conflict with his brother Joshua's birth in Jan of 1784.[680] As with the other older children of Mary Elizabeth Brewer and Joshua Wyeth Sr., George also was likely born in Boston before its 1787 fire. His middle name comes from the fact he called himself George Wyeth Sr. in his will and the pension papers of his grandson, Paul Chamberlain Wyeth, confirm the Morris name of George Wyeth Jr.

George trained in the publishing business with his uncle John Wyeth in Harrisburg.[681] His father proudly wrote to sister Anna Wyeth Cutter that George would complete his apprenticeship on 06 Oct 1806.[682] A year later, George founded *The Mirror*, the first newspaper in Erie, Pennsylvania. Unfortunately, editor Wyeth was not firm enough to refuse contributions from irresponsible writers. To avoid libel prosecution, for publishing another author's unscrupulous story, George skipped town on 13 May 1811.[683]

Lesson learned, George moved south to the Pittsburgh area, settling in Williamsport, Washington County, Pennsylvania. He continued in the publishing business. In Dec 1811, George started publishing *The Monongahela Expositor* and the *Williamsport Weekly Chronicle*.[684]

Like his tutor, uncle John Wyeth, George served as a postmaster. According to the official post office guide, he became postmaster of Parkinson's Ferry in 1813.[685] Department of the Interior documents, dated 30 Sep 1823, show George Wythe, postmaster Parkinson's Ferry, paid a salary of $46.22, was born in Massachusetts.[686] In 1828, George Wyeth was still on the postmaster list in Parkinson's Ferry. The office was shown as being 226 miles from Washington and 213 miles from the state capital (Harrisburg).[687] George soon after relinquished his duties. The 1830 postal tables show Jesse Martin, postmaster, Parkinson's Ferry.[688]

The town had not been called Parkinson's Ferry since 25 Jul 1796 when Joseph Parkinson advertised that he had laid out a new town called Williamsport on his Parkinson's Ferry plantation. However, the post office retained the name Parkinson's Ferry until Williamsport was incorporated as a borough on 08 Apr 1833.[689] To differentiate it from another similarly named town in the state, Williamsport was designated Monongahela on 01 Apr 1837.[690]

George may have been drawn to Washington County by his wife. Eliza grew up there and her mother, Isabella Fulton Cooke, resided in the county. Isabella's brother, the well-known inventor, Robert Fulton, recognized his siblings in his 13 Dec 1814 will. The following is paraphrased from the will, probated in New York City: "... out of the profits of my Steam boats or any other of my property... I leave to my wife and children ... surplus of my estate, if any, I leave to my brother Abraham Smith Fulton $3,000, to my sister Elizabeth Scott, I leave $1,000 and the farm on which she now lives ... to my sister Isabelle Cook, I leave $2,000 and to each child of my deceased sister Mary Morris I leave $500."

Robert Fulton originally purchased Elizabeth Fulton Scott's farm in Washington County for his mother, Mary Smith Fulton. In an article, from *The Pittsburgh Press,* dated 03 Oct 1909, the steamboat inventor's many links to the area are given.[691] Of particular note is a letter provided by W. P. Bryson that Robert Fulton wrote to his sister, Isabella Fulton Cooke, about her son-in-law, George. It reads as follows:

"New York, March 20th, 1814

Dear Sister – I have your letter by Mr. Wyth (sic). I have been much pleased with him and I have made him a present of all my right and title to certain lands of potatoe garden—Located by your husband, which lands were secured to me for a debt to Francis and John West of Phila. Now amounting to $1,250. This lands (sic) I hope will be of use to Mr. Wyeth and his family and through him of some use to you in the evening of life, and while I make this gift to one of the family I hope it will not excite any ungenerous feelings in any of your other children for whom it is my intention to do what will be at least an equivalent, as to my respect and affection for you and other branches of my family they have never abated. My acts are the best proff (sic) of this fact but mere letters of ceremony cannot be frequent because I realy (sic) have not time. I hope to be with you in the course of the Summer and am Affectionately your Brother,

Robert Fulton"

W. P. (Wilfred Peyton "Fred") Bryson (1862-1947), great grandson of George Morris Wyeth Sr., said the letter was sent to Isabella when "George Wyeth was a temporary resident of Parkinson's Ferry, now Monongahela, on the river of the same name." Fred told *The Pittsburgh Press*, "A daughter of Mrs. Isabella Cook married George Wyeth, a nephew of the signer of the Declaration of Independence and an ancestor of the well-known Wyeth family of Philadelphia." Fred confirmed George's son, Dr. Alexander Reed Wyeth, was a Union soldier in the Civil War.

Fred also confirmed the confusion surrounding the Wyeth roots. Fred's great grandfather was not an ancestor to the Philadelphia Wyeths. Philadelphia drug company founders John and Francis Houston Wyeth were the grandsons of George Morris' uncle John Wyeth of Harrisburg, his printing business instructor. Thus, they were George Morris' first cousins once removed. Also, he could not have been signer George Wythe's nephew. Wythe's only brother, Thomas, did not have any heirs.[692]

Some researchers believe George Morris Wyeth Sr. is the ancestor of Monongahela resident, Francis Stephen Wyeth (1823-1888). A lot of confusion existed with their names, too. George Morris Wyeth's name was thought to be George William Wyeth and Francis Stephen Wyeth was thought to be Francis John Wyeth.

A little clarity came after purchasing the Daughters of the American Revolution (DAR) documentation of Francis Stephen Wyeth's granddaughter, Genevieve Wyeth Tuttle. To link her name with early Wyeths of Washington County, Genevieve, born in Monongahela in 1904, used a reference to Parkinson's Ferry postmaster Geo. Wythe from the historical magazine of *Monongahela's Old Home Coming Week: Sept. 6-13, 1908*.[693]

Genevieve did not say she was descended from George, but from Francis Wyeth and Margaret Carney who were married in 1817. She quoted Bible records from her father, James Alexander Wyeth (1855-1936), to make the link to Francis and Margaret through their son, Francis Stephen Wyeth.[694] The Carney / Kearney family were some of the earliest settlers of Monongahela.[695] Although she did not realize it, the senior Francis Wyeth that Genevieve referred to is Francis B. Wyeth, the brother of George Morris Wyeth Sr. Apparently, while visiting his brother George, Francis B. Wyeth met and married Margaret Carney. It is from Francis B. Wyeth, that the Wyeths, Finns, and Shaffers of Monongahela and Pittsburgh hail. See more on this later under Francis B. Wyeth.

Concurrent with his post office duties, George was a merchant in Williamsport. His store was on Main Street, a couple of blocks from the Monongahela River.[696] According to ads in Washington County's *Washington Review and Examiner*, George sold books and general products. Additionally, he held a license to sell foreign merchandise.[697]

One of the frequently advertised items at Wyeth's Williamsport store were books written by Rev. Samuel Ralston answering Rev. Alexander Campbell's views on Christian Baptism.[698] [699]

Alexander Campbell, the leader of a movement to restore the New Testament church, was a friend of the Wyeth family. The Churches of Christ trace their history to his leadership. The site of the Washington County Brush Run Church, where Campbell was ordained in 1812, is near Avella, Pennsylvania.[700] It was about ten miles from Claysville, Donegal Township, Pennsylvania, where the Wyeths lived just prior to and during the 1830 census.

Another indication of the closeness of Alexander Campbell to the Wyeth family is a letter he wrote to Peyton Cooke Wyeth on 01 Apr 1834. Peyton, age 23, was in England at the time. In the note, Campbell estimated the membership size, organization, and growth rate of the Restoration Movement in the U.S.[701] Being an Evangelist for the Church of Christ, my brother, Jeff Wyeth, takes particular pride in this connection of Alexander Campbell to the Wyeth family.

George Morris Wyeth Sr. was a proponent of religious education. While living in Claysville, he was active in the 1830 reorganization of the Washington County Sabbath School Union.[702] Politics interested him as well. Two years before, from his home in Nottingham Township, George served on committees for the 1828 election of Andrew Jackson.[703]

Deed records for Washington County show that in 1837, Eliza and George Wyeth, merchant, of Donegal sold their land to a James Warrell.[704] The next year, George purchased public lands in Morgan County, Illinois. He was living in Manchester of that county when his aunt Anna Wyeth Cutter's estate was divided on 15 Apr 1842.[705] Also, George's will was probated in Morgan County. However, he and Eliza and son Alex's wife and child, Harriett Pamela Beebe and Peyton Beebe Wyeth, were buried in Scott County, Illinois in the Old Manchester Cemetery. This part of Scott County was split off of Morgan.[706]

George and Eliza's oldest son, Peyton Cooke Wyeth, was an artist of some renown. He studied painting in Rome and worked several places in the United States… spending much time in Cincinnati and New York. He twice exhibited at New York City's National Academy in 1846 and in 1858.[707] His group portrait of the sons of Charles Lewis Shrewsbury, painted circa 1850, still hangs in the Shrewsbury home in Madison, Indiana.[708] By using the 1850 census of the town, the boys can be identified as Culver (seated) and (L to R) Samuel, Lewis, William and John.

Shewsbury boys painted by Peyton C. Wyeth courtesy of John Staicer, President & Executive Director, Historic Madison Foundation, Inc.

112. **MARY "POLLY"[6] WYETH** (Joshua[5], Ebenezer[4] Jr., Ebenezer[3], John[2], Nicholas[1]) was born in 1789 in Cambridge, Middlesex, Massachusetts. [709] Mary "Polly" Wyeth married (1) Daniel Gilbert on 09 Jul 1809 in Towanda, Luzerne (Bradford), Pennsylvania.[710] **DANIEL GILBERT**, son of Samuel Gilbert and Mary Dodge, was born on 18 Dec 1783 in Lyme, New London, Connecticut. He died on 13 Apr 1835 in Towanda.[711] Polly married (2) Major Oliver Williams Dodge about 1837 in Bradford County. **OLIVER WILLIAMS DODGE**, son of Oliver Dodge and Abigail Harris, was born on 03 Oct 1775 in Colchester, New London, Connecticut. He died on 01 Feb 1845 at the age of 69 in Franklin Township, Bradford, Pennsylvania. Polly died there, at her son Nelson's home, on 09 Dec 1881 at the age of 92 and was carried to her final resting place, Cole's burial ground, on 14 Dec 1881.[712]

The children of Daniel Gilbert and Mary "Polly" Wyeth included:

210.   i. NELSON[7] GILBERT, born 24 Dec 1811, Towanda, Bradford, Pennsylvania; married there (1) JANE HOLLENBACK circa 1837; married (2) CATHERINE MOYER, circa 1862, Franklin Township, Bradford, Pennsylvania; died 26 Feb 1891, Franklin Township.[713]
       ii. SAMUEL GILBERT, born 11 Apr 1821, Towanda; married twice; died 06 Feb 1906, Franklin Township.
      iii. ELIZABETH GILBERT, born 06 Jun 1825, Towanda; married JOHN HENRY HAYNES after 01 Aug 1850, Bradford County; died 28 Apr 1916, Clinton County, Pennsylvania at age 90.
       iv. JOHN W. GILBERT, born in Mar 1834, Towanda; married once; died 1901, Nebraska City, Otoe County, Nebraska at age 67.

Notes on Daniel Gilbert and Mary "Polly" Wyeth:

When Mary "Polly" Wyeth's mother, died in 1805, at age 44, Mary Elizabeth Brewer Wyeth was buried on the flat area of the family farm.[714] According to David Craft's *History of Bradford County, Pennsylvania*, Joshua Wythe (Craft uses this spelling) returned to New England to marry again. Joshua then moved west, selected a home, and sent for his children. Craft stated, "… all of whom went to him except his daughter Mary (now Mrs. Mary Dodge), who, as she said to us, 'had made other arrangements, and stayed behind.' She consummated those arrangements shortly afterwards, being married in 1808 [other records say 1809]."[715]

Daniel Gilbert bought 250 acres of land from Joshua Wyeth Sr. and built a house on it the same year he married Joshua's daughter. The farm was situated about two miles above the mouth of Towanda Creek, on what was known as the George Bowman place. Craft goes on to say that Daniel "… subsequently exchanged this farm for the Greenwood place, and that again for the Mintz place, known as the dry saw-mill, being the next farm above the Wythe farm."[716] Daniel then moved to the Edsall Carr place in 1827 – where he died eight years later. At his death, Polly married Major Dodge. In 1861, after the Major's death, Mrs. Dodge moved to her son Nelson's home in Franklin Township.[717] Her obituary called her a devoted and faithful member of the Methodist Episcopal Church.[718]

Daniel and Mary are buried at the Cole's Farm Cemetery, Towanda Township, Bradford County, Pennsylvania.[719] Although it contains errors in the spelling of Mary's maiden name and her death year, a wonderful transcription of the Gilbert graves appears on the site *Tri-Counties Genealogy & History* by Joyce M. Tice.

113. **FRANCIS B.[6] WYETH** (Joshua[5], Ebenezer[4] Jr., Ebenezer[3], John[2], Nicholas[1]) was born in 1796 in Towanda, Luzerne (Bradford), Pennsylvania. Many of his six marriages ended in divorce. He married (1) **MARGARET CARNEY** in 1817.[720] She was born circa 1795 in Virginia and died 19 Feb 1877 near Pittsburgh, Allegheny, Pennsylvania.[721] Francis married (2) **ELIZABETH FELTER PATMORE** on 04 Jul 1835 in Hamilton County, Ohio. Elizabeth Felter was born there circa 1804. She died on 06 Nov 1860 in Riley Township, Vigo, Indiana. He married (3) **ELIZABETH KENT**, 27 Jul 1861, Morgan County, Indiana. Francis then married (4) **CAROLINE H. BAILEY BRUNER** on 30 Nov 1862 in Clay County, Indiana. Caroline Bailey was born on 27 Jun 1814 in Virginia. After their divorce, Caroline died 03 Feb 1884 in Perry Township, Clay County. Francis married (5) **MARY BELL BUNTIN** on 05 May 1865 in Monroe County, Indiana. Mary Bell, born about 1830 in Indiana, divorced Francis 14 Nov 1865 in Bloomington, Monroe, Indiana.[722] Francis married (6) **ELIZABETH DOVER CHANDLER** on 21 Oct 1867 in Benton Township, Monroe, Indiana. Elizabeth Dover was born 11 Nov 1806 in Kentucky. They divorced in 1873 in Bloomington.[723] She died 26 Nov 1882 in Monroe County, Indiana. Francis married (7) **PRISCILLA CREAMER WILLIAMS** on 26 Feb 1875 in Morgan County, Indiana. Priscilla Creamer was born circa 1804 in Kentucky. Their death dates are unknown. The last record for Francis is the 1880 census of Benton Township when he was a widower, age 85, living with his daughter, Minerva Culver.

Francis B. Wyeth and Margaret Carney had the following children:

211.   i.   FIDALIA ANNA[7] WYETH was born circa 1817 in McKeesport, Allegheny, Pennsylvania; baptized at age nine on 14 Nov 1826, Pittsburgh, Allegheny, Pennsylvania;[724] married SIMON SHAFFER, 27 Jun 1836, St. Paul's Cathedral, Pittsburgh;[725] died 04 Jan 1890, Chartiers, Washington, Pennsylvania.[726]

212.   ii.   MARGARET WYETH, born 11 Jun 1818, Washington Township, Warren, Ohio; married JOHN FINN, 28 Jun 1838, Pittsburgh;[727] died there, 29 Jan 1905.

213.   iii.   FRANCIS STEPHEN "FRANK" WYETH, born circa 1820, Washington Township, Warren, Ohio; married MARY HILLMAN, 15 Oct 1846,[728] Allegheny County; died 28 Jan 1888 Monongahela, Washington, Pennsylvania.[729]

Francis B. Wyeth and Elizabeth Felter Patmore had the following children:

214.   i.   HENRY ELISHA[7] WYETH, born 23 Apr 1836, Cincinnati, Hamilton, Ohio; wounded in the Civil War; married HANNAH BRATT, 08 Sep 1868, Terre Haute, Vigo, Indiana; died 30 Jul 1904, Terre Haute.

215.   ii.   MINERVA WYETH, born Jan 1838, Cincinnati; married (1) LAWRENCE H. W. CULVER, 26 Apr 1860, Riley Township; married (2) EDWARD R. POTTER, 15 Aug 1886, Monroe County, Indiana; married (3) JAMES B. CAMPBELL, 31 May 1890, Brown County, Indiana; married (4) FREDERICK R. DRABENSTOTT, 01 Nov 1911, Brown County; died 17 Jul 1919, Monroe County.

           iii.   MELISSA WYETH, born circa 1841, Riley Township; death unknown.

           iv.   SUSAN TABITHA WYETH, born 06 Jun 1842, Riley Township; married JAY M. PRINGLE there on 11 May 1863; died, age 22, 10 Apr 1865, Green Township, Morgan, Indiana; buried there in the Old Mt. Olive Methodist Cemetery.

           v.   MARY JANE WYETH, born 04 Mar 1847, Riley; married (1) JOHN D. WALKER, 16 Jun 1864, Vigo County; married (2) GEORGE H. BARKER, 26 Oct 1893, Clay County, Indiana; died 07 Aug 1912 Terre Haute; buried there in Highland Lawn Cemetery.[730] According to the 1880 census of Van Buren, Clay, Indiana, Mary's children included Josephine Walker (m. Albert T. Jackson), Eugenie Walker (m. Richard Doyle) and Grace Walker (m. William Baxter Jr.)

           vi.   ZACHARIAH TAYLOR WYETH was born circa 1848 in Riley Township. Taylor, the name he preferred, enrolled as a private in Indianapolis on 06 Oct 1864 to fight in the Civil War. He served as a substitute for one William A. Moore in the 37th Indiana Volunteer Infantry, Company D.[731] Taylor, shown in military records as just 18 years old, died of disease in the Confederate General Hospital #4 at Wilmington, New Hanover, North Carolina on 27 Mar 1865.[732]

Notes for Francis B. Wyeth:

Many researchers believe Francis' middle name is "Brewer." That is highly likely since Brewer is his mother's maiden name. The census reports of 1830, 1850, and several marriage and land records show "B." as Francis' middle initial. Every Federal Population Census, from 1850 to 1880, gave his occupation as "blacksmith" … a skill he learned from his father. On 19 Sep 1813 from Cincinnati, Joshua Wyeth Sr. proudly wrote his sister, Anna Wyeth Cutter, that his son Francis was a "pretty good [black]smith" and son Harry was "coming on."[733]

Since Federal Census reports prior to 1850 do not provide occupational or family information, it is very difficult to document Francis' first marriage and his children born between 1817 and 1826. The starting points are the will of George Morris Wyeth Sr. (1785-1844) and the 1938 DAR application of Francis Stephen "Frank" Wyeth's granddaughter, Genevieve Wyeth Tuttle (1904-1971). George's will proves Fidalia, Margaret, and Francis Stephen Wyeth are not his children. The DAR record, though valuable, was short on details. As a result, facts from many early source records are presented below to help paint the fullest picture possible of this family.

The first census for Francis B. Wyeth was enumerated on 07 Aug 1820 in Washington Township, Warren County, Ohio. Washington Township, near Fort Ancient, is a few miles east of Lebanon,

Ohio and 40 miles north of the Ohio River in Cincinnati (where Joshua Wyeth Sr. was then living). Age ranges on the report were males –16 thru 25: one (Francis B.); females – under 10: two (Fidalia and Margaret); and females –16 thru 25: one (Margaret Carney). Margaret Wyeth Finn's obituary in 1905 says she was born in Marietta, Washington County, Ohio.[734] It is more likely that she was born when the family lived here in Washington Township, Warren County, Ohio.

On 09 Sep 1827, Francis' father again wrote to Anna Wyeth Cutter from Cincinnati. He said his daughter Susanna had died about a year before near Lebanon, Ohio. He thought she left nine children "to mourn her absence." Of his children, Francis, George, Polly and Henry, Joshua said they resided near the Susquehanna River in Pennsylvania, where he had formerly lived.[735] As the Susquehanna runs through Bradford County, Joshua's letter confirms the 1830 Federal Census records when Francis B. Wyeth lived there near his sister, Mary "Polly" Wyeth Gilbert.

The name "Francis B. Wythe" tops page 11 of that 1830 census of Columbia Township, Bradford, Pennsylvania. Age ranges on the report were males – 10 thru 14: one (Francis Stephen Wyeth) males – 30 thru 39: one (Francis B. Wyeth); females – under 5: one (unknown); females – 10 thru 14: one (Margaret Wyeth); females – 15 thru 19: one (Fidalia Anna Wyeth); and females – 40 thru 49: one (Margaret Carney).

Apparently, while moving from southern Ohio to northern Pennsylvania, Francis stopped in Pittsburgh to have his children baptized. In those pioneer times, Pittsburgh was home to the solitary Catholic church in western Pennsylvania.[736] Only Fidalia Anna Wyeth's record survives. At the time, proper names on Roman Catholic baptism records were written in Latin. Thus, the 14 Nov 1826 St. Patrick Parish, Strip District, record reads, "Baptized Fidelia Anna, daughter of Francisci and Margaretha Wythe, age nine years, sponsor: Carolo (Charles) Kenny."[737] At the time, Francis' brother, George Morris Wyeth Sr. was still postmaster in nearby Monongahela. Margaret Carney had family there, too. Census reports in later years show Edward Carney lived near Francis Stephen Wyeth in Monongahela, Carroll Township, Washington County, Pennsylvania. Edward, it seems, was Margaret Carney Wyeth's brother.[738]

Apparently, Margaret Carney was born to Irish Catholics in Berkeley County, (West) Virginia. The Carney / Kearney family moved to the Monongahela area in 1816.[739] Although Genevieve Wyeth Tuttle's DAR app says Margaret's father was Timothy Carney, more records point to James Carney being her parent.[740] Perhaps James and Timothy were one and the same.

In any event, Genevieve using Timothy Carney's name as her Revolutionary War ancestor to gain admission to DAR is telling. It confirms that she did not know she descended from Joshua Wyeth Sr. Joshua's service would have been much easier to prove. Apparently, the family Bible records did not go far enough back for her to make that connection. Also, her father, James Alexander Wyeth (1855-1936), did not know or did not tell Genevieve about the relationship to Joshua. Obviously, since Genevieve's grandfather, Francis Stephen Wyeth, named one son Joshua Wyeth (1860-1911), Francis Stephen Wyeth knew his grandfather's name.

In documents that accompanied her paperwork to DAR, Genevieve referred to a connection to "Geo. Wythe," one of Monongahela's early postmasters.[741] As shown, this postmaster was Francis B. Wyeth's brother, George Morris Wyeth Sr. Evidently, Genevieve did not know how the postmaster was related to her for she only used his name as proof of the Wyeth family being in early Monongahela. Undoubtedly, she, like many of her Washington County relatives, thought she descended from George Wythe (1726-1806) who signed the Declaration of Independence. Of course, that cannot be since the signer left no descendants when he died in Richmond, Virginia, from poison administered to him by his heir and nephew, George Wythe Sweeney.

The absence of documentation connecting the brothers, Francis and George, created a mystery for generations of descendants of the Monongahela, Washington County, Pennsylvania Wyeths.

With marriage records of early Pennsylvania being non-existent, the best guess is that Francis B. Wyeth, while visiting his brother, postmaster George, met and married Margaret Carney circa 1816. From Monongahela, the couple relocated to Washington Township, near Lebanon, Ohio to be close to Francis' oldest sister Sukey. There, children Margaret and Francis Stephen were born before Francis B. moved the family to Bradford County, Pennsylvania to live near his sister Polly Wyeth Gilbert. Then circa 1834, Francis B. decided to return to Ohio to reside near his half-brother, Enoch Nelson Wyeth, in Hamilton County. Perhaps Margaret refused to accompany her husband and went instead, with her children, to the Carney family home in Monongahela. George Morris Wyeth Sr. was no longer postmaster there, but he was still in the same county.

Lacking concrete proof of their heritage, here are some assumptions made by the descendants of Francis Stephen Wyeth, Margaret Wyeth Finn, and Fidalia Anna Wyeth Shaffer.

> From Francis Stephen Wyeth's descendants in *The Schroeder-Wyeth Newsletter* of 04 Nov 1976: "Our early Wyeth ancestors migrated to Virginia from England in the autumn of 1676. The Wyeth family was among those brave pioneers who left the relative security of the East for a new and unknown life in the Oregon Territory. Nothing is known, at this time, of their life there, but after a few years it was determined that some of them would return east. A wagon train was formed, and their steps were retraced across the Oregon Trail... Among the members of that wagon train were George William Wyeth and his wife Mary Hillman. Conflicting records show that George's son, John Francis Wyeth, was also a member of that train, while others say that he and his brothers and sisters were all born in Monongahela, Pa."[742]

> In Alph L. Millbach's 11 Oct 1912 application to join the Sons of the American Revolution (SAR) through Timothy Carney, Alph stated he was the grandson of John Finn and Margaret Wyeth and the great-grandson of Francis Wyeth and Margaret Carney. He added, "I am also a direct descendent of George Wyeth (sic), signer of the Declaration of Independence, but am unable to trace same as family records have not been kept, so base my claim on Timothy Carney..."

> From Fidalia Anna Wyeth Shaffer's descendants, the following appeared in the 14 Jun 1969 *Daily Republican* newspaper of Monongahela: "George Wyeth's (sic)... most singular claim to fame came as a signer of the Declaration of Independence. Wyeth's act of affixing his signature to one of the United States' most famous historical documents takes on special significance during Monongahela's current bicentennial celebration. For among those residents celebrating the City's 200th anniversary are many of his direct descendants... Mrs. John (Elsie Manning) Magaruh of Hoon Street and Margaret Massey Falter of 308 Wall Street – both of Monongahela – are Wyeth's great - great - great granddaughters."[743]

Julie Rowan Wolford is descended from Fidalia Anna Wyeth Shaffer. Julie's research has been invaluable in determining the ancestry of the Monongahela Wyeth family. Julie's important first find, a deed dated 28 Jul 1860, links Simon Shaffer and his wife Fidalia to Francis Stephen Wyeth and his wife Mary Hillman.[744] However, the most helpful of Julie's research was the discovery of

Fidalia's baptism record. It is the essential authentication of Francis B. Wyeth's parentage of the Monongahela / Pittsburgh area Wyeths.

When Julie's source documents are combined with Alph L. Millbach's SAR application and a Federal Population Census enumerated 08 Apr 1930, we have a good picture of Francis B. Wyeth and Margaret Carney's family. The 1930 census shows Alph's sister, Ida Millbach, living with two cousins, Catherine Wyeth and Pauline Wyeth Carlin, at 318 Fram Street, Pittsburgh. Catherine and Pauline are Genevieve Wyeth Tuttle's sisters.

It is unclear how Margaret Carney and Francis B. Wyeth separated circa 1830. With Margaret being Catholic, it is doubtful they divorced. However, the death certificate of one Martha Ellen Murray Smith, with ties to Monongahela via the 1860 Federal Census of Carroll Township, Washington, Pennsylvania, indicates her parents were Margaret Carney and Daniel Murray. Julie found an 1875 newspaper article that links Margaret Carney Wyeth Murray to her descendants Mrs. (Fidalia Wyeth) Shaffer and Mrs. (Anna Burgan) Pelkey. The article definitely confirms Margaret Carney did indeed marry Daniel Murray after she separated from Francis.[745]

Perhaps Margaret Carney remarried because she thought Francis B. Wyeth was deceased. At that time in history, it would have been very easy to disappear and be presumed dead. Since Pennsylvania marriage records were rare before 1885, we cannot be sure of the date of Margaret Carney's remarriage. On the other hand, Ohio officials began recording marriage dates as soon as each county was established.[746] Thus we know that after his return to Ohio, Francis B. Wyeth married Elizabeth Felter Patmore on Independence Day, 1835.[747]

Hamilton County, Ohio, Justice of the Peace Henry Jones spelled Elizabeth's name "Potuare" in the 1835 marriage record. But, by looking back at Elizabeth's first marriage on 19 Aug 1824, we learn her married name was "Patmore" and her maiden name "Felton" … a variation of Felter.

Elizabeth Felter and Mathias Felter Patmore were married in Hamilton County, Ohio, as well. It appears they were first cousins. Her father was probably William Felter and her mother Susanna Trapp. Mathias' father, Abraham, and his mother, Elsie Felter, along with several of her siblings were early settlers of Montgomery, Sycamore Township, Hamilton, Ohio.[748] Mathias died on 27 Sep 1832 in Montgomery. He is buried there in the pioneer section of the Hopewell Cemetery.

Montgomery was likely the location of Elizabeth Felter Patmore and Francis B. Wyeth's marriage. The town is about 20 miles south of Francis' 1820 census residence. The marriage also could have taken place in Cincinnati. Within five years of this Ohio marriage, Francis again followed siblings to another locale. This time, according to the 1840 census of Riley Township, Vigo, Indiana, his neighbors were brothers Joshua Wyeth Jr. and Elisha Wyeth.

After 20 years in Riley Township, Elizabeth Felter was buried there in the Mewhinney Cemetery. Within five years, the Civil War would take the lives of her sons Jacob Patmore and Taylor Wyeth.

Soon after son Henry Elisha Wyeth was wounded on 06 Apr 1862 at the Battle of Pittsburg Landing (Shiloh) in Tennessee, Francis B. Wyeth married his fourth wife.[749] 48-year-old Caroline H. Bailey was on her third marriage. She first married Bayless Triplett and then Mason Bruner. After divorcing Francis, she married John Corbin.

In Jul of the summer of 1865, two months after marrying Mary Bell Buntin, Francis purchased land in Monroe County, Indiana.[750] However, by winter, his marriage to Mary was kaput. Francis stated in the Indiana, Monroe County Court of Common Pleas divorce papers, that shortly after he commenced living with Mary and her large family in May, "so far as he was able, that he always treated her kind and affectionate (sic)." His statement for the Dec 1865 court term requested a divorce from Mary for three reasons.

> 1."… said deft a short time after said marriage commenced a series of cruel and abusive conduct to your petitioner and continued her cruel and abusive conduct until your petitioner was compelled to leave his home." 2. "… has further refused to permit or let your petitioner have sexual intercourse with her." 3. "… has begun and kept up a constant strain of abuse and cruel treatment in many ways… not providing for his general comfort… and by permitting her children who lives (sic) about the house to treat him cruelly and abusively."[751]

Having recovered from his injuries, Henry Elisha Wyeth was eventually promoted to 2nd lieutenant of his regiment. After four horrendous years at war, on 08 Dec 1865, Henry came home to Riley to farm his father's land.[752] Soon after, Francis put the land in Henry's name.[753]

Some of the same justifications from the 1865 divorce are included in Francis B. Wyeth and Elizabeth Dover Chandler's divorce documents. Due to Francis' abandonment, their divorce was eventually granted to Elizabeth, as plaintiff, after the Indiana, Monroe County Court of Common Pleas term of Dec 1872.[754] However, Francis originally filed for divorce in the Aug 1871 term of the Monroe County Court of Common Pleas. As plaintiff, Francis stated they had no children together and through his attorney provided these reasons for Elizabeth's abandonment:

> 1."… he has done everything in his power to make their home pleasant and agreeable to deft yielding to her whimsical desires..." 2. "… said deft without any justification whatever and disregarding the solemnity of the marriage vow, has … shown herself to be a very disagreeable companion … refusing the plff the right of sexual intercourse with her… at the same time declaring herself impotent and doing everything in her power to make home … unpleasant… threatening continually to abandon him and has positively refused to live with plff again as his lawful and wedded wife." 3. "… since his marriage, aforesaid deft has frequently been guilty of the most unnatural practices to wit: cohabiting with her son Zephania Chandler, said son being of mature age."[755]

After finalizing the divorce in 1873, Francis moved north from Monroe County to Morgan County, Indiana. There he married 71-year-old Priscilla Creamer Williams in early 1875. She was the widow of Burgin Pettit and Jacob Waugh. She had also married William Reynolds and Harvey Williams. Although Pettit family trees indicate she died in 1887, Francis was listed seven years before as a widower in the 1880 census. At the time, he lived with his daughter, Minerva, and son-in-law, Lawrence H. W. Culver near Bloomington, Monroe, Indiana.

The 1907 plot map of Riley Township, Vigo, Indiana, shows that Francis B. Wyeth's land there was in the name of Henry Elisha Wyeth's daughter, Florence Marie Wyeth.[756] Calls to Florence's granddaughter, Vickie Sutton Bays, a resident of Terre Haute, to see if she knows the date of Francis' death, have thus far been unsuccessful.

114. **ELIZA JANE[6] WYETH** (Joshua[5], Ebenezer[4] Jr., Ebenezer[3], John[2], Nicholas[1]) was born on 07 Jul 1797 in Towanda, Luzerne (Bradford), Pennsylvania. Eliza Jane Wyeth and Peter King were married on 07 Sep 1813 in Bardstown, Nelson, Kentucky. **PETER KING**, son of

Cornelius King and Sarah Barnes, was born on 26 Jan 1795 in Bardstown. He served in the U.S. military during the War of 1812. He died on 14 Dec 1847 at the age of 52 in Green Township, Morgan, Indiana. Eliza Jane died there on 29 Jun 1882 at the age of 84 years, 11 months and 22 days old. They rest together in the Williams Bradford Cemetery in Green Township near Martinsville, Morgan, Indiana.

The children of Peter King and Eliza Jane Wyeth included:

216.   i.   ELIZABETH[7] KING, born 25 Jul 1815, Bardstown, Nelson, Kentucky; married SAMUEL SCOTT JR., 23 Oct 1831, Green Township; died there, 08 Jun 1866.

217.   ii.   RANSOM CORNELIUS KING, born 1816, Lawrence County, Indiana; married SECELIA "CELIA" FARRAN, 23 Apr 1835, Morgan County, Indiana; 13 Aug 1862, joined the 87th Illinois Infantry, Co. D., discharged for disability on 29 Jun 1863 at Mound City, Pulaski, Illinois; died before 1870, Wayne County, Illinois; buried Brown Cemetery, Mount Erie, Wayne County, Illinois.

218.   iii.   SARAH KING, born 24 Jan 1818, Lawrence County; married JAMES MADISON CARRELL, 29 Dec 1841, Green Township; died there, 29 May 1846.

        iv.   WILLIAM KING, born circa 1819, Lawrence County, Indiana; death unknown.

        v.   FRANCILLO KING, born 07 Jun 1822, Morgan County, Indiana; died 05 Feb 1896, Union Township, Cumberland, Illinois; buried there in Bell Cemetery.

219.   vi.   SERELDA KING, born 1824, Morgan County; married (1) BARTHOLOMEW CARRELL, 15 Sep 1842, Morgan County, Indiana; married (2) SILAS GOODWIN, 04 Jun 1857, Crawford County, Illinois; died there in 1875.

        vii.   ANN KING, born circa 1828, Morgan County, Indiana; death unknown.

        viii.   JOSHUA W. KING, 1829, Green Township, Morgan, Indiana; married LUCY JANE HARPER, 13 Jun 1850, Morgan County; died there, 06 Feb 1860.

        ix.   ROBERT KING, born 19 May 1834, Green Township; married ADALINE GLEESON there, 09 Mar 1856; died 15 Mar 1908, Pleasant Grove, Coles, Illinois.

220.   x.   ADALINE KING, born 09 Dec 1838, Green Township; married AARON ST. JOHN there, 24 Dec 1854; died 29 Aug 1888, Green Township.

        xi.   ELVIRA S. KING, born 14 Feb 1841, Morgan County; married ZACHARIAH LANGLEY DAVEE there on 28 Aug 1859; died on 27 Oct 1882, Cumberland County, Illinois; buried there in Bell Cemetery near her brother Francillo.

115. **HENRY[6] WYETH** (Joshua[5], Ebenezer[4] Jr., Ebenezer[3], John[2], Nicholas[1]) was born on 15 Aug 1800 in Towanda, Luzerne (Bradford), Pennsylvania. Although he was a farmer, "Harry" learned the blacksmith trade from his father. On 19 Sep 1813 from Cincinnati, Joshua Wyeth Sr. proudly wrote his sister, Anna Wyeth Cutter, that his son Francis was a "pretty good smith" and son Harry was "coming on."[757] Henry Wyeth and Emiline West married on 01 Dec 1823 in Towanda. **EMILINE WEST**, daughter of Elijah West and Polly Salisbury, was born there on 17 Dec 1807.[758] She died on 17 Jul 1878 at the age of 70 in Spring Township, Crawford, Pennsylvania. He died there,

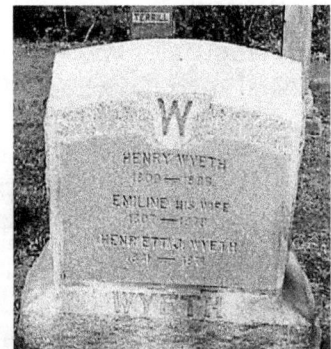

Monument of Henry, Emiline and Henrietta Wyeth - 14 May 2016 - photo courtesy of Jeff Wyeth.

at his daughter Mary's home, on 28 Feb 1886 at the age of 85.[759] Emiline and Henry are buried in East Spring Cemetery, Springboro, Crawford, Pennsylvania.

Birthdates for the following children of Henry Wyeth and Emiline West were provided by their great, great granddaughter Sue Hummel Hill:

221.   i.   MATTHEW WING[7] WYETH, born 10 Oct 1826, Cabot Hollow, Columbia Township, Bradford, Pennsylvania; married FANNY MICHAEL, 27 Jan 1850, Springboro;[760] enlisted 16 Dec 1863 in Co. E of the Indiana 128th Infantry Regiment; died 30 Jul 1909, Wheeler, Porter, Indiana.

        ii. CHRISTOPHER WYETH, born circa 1827, Bradford County, Pennsylvania; died after 1850, probably in Miami Township, Montgomery, Ohio.

222.   iii. MARY ELIZABETH WYETH, born 22 May 1829, Beaver Township, Crawford, Pennsylvania; married JOHN H. PERKINS circa 1856, Crawford County; died 25 Feb 1891, Spring Township.[761]

        iv. EUNICE EVELYN WYETH, born 12 Feb 1831, Beaver Township; married HENRY FISHER; died 12 Apr 1923, Canton, Stark, Ohio.[762]

223.   v.   OLIVE ELLEN WYETH, born 12 Feb 1833, Spring Township; married (1) JOHN W. HICKERNELL, 01 Feb 1852, Spring Township; married (2) a man with the last name of TERRILL; married (3) LEVI CHURCH circa 1885; died 25 Nov 1913, Crawford County Infirmary, Saegertown, Crawford, Pennsylvania.

224.   vi. GEORGE WASHINGTON WYETH, born 02 Feb 1835, Spring Township; enlisted in the 56th Illinois Infantry, Co. F on 12 Sep 1861 and was discharged due to a double hernia. On 25 Aug 1864, George joined the U.S. Navy and served as a landsman in the Mississippi Flotilla on the gunboat USS *Tyler*. He was discharged in Mound City, Illinois on 12 Jun 1865.[763] He married MARY ELIZABETH ANIE THOMAS, 13 Feb 1866, Riley Township, Vigo, Indiana.[764] George died on 19 Mar 1916 at the Soldiers' Home, Los Angeles, California.

        vii. BETSY A. WYETH, born 29 Jun 1837, Spring Township; married ANDERSON GARWOOD there, 1864; died 30 Apr 1922, of tuberculosis, Harborcreek Township, Erie, Pennsylvania.

        viii. MARQUIS DE LAFAYETTE WYETH was born on 13 Aug 1839 in Spring Township. Lafayette enlisted as a private for three months service in Co. I, 19th Ohio Infantry on 27 Apr 1861 in Columbus, Franklin, Ohio.[765] After mustering out there on 30 Aug 1861, he continued his service in the 19th at Camp Dennison, Hamilton County, Ohio. From there he joined the Mechanics Fusiliers of Co. H, 56th Illinois Infantry on 27 Feb 1862, serving as a sergeant. Before his term of enlistment was up, Lafayette moved back to his home state to enlist as a private in Co. B of the 137th Regiment, Pennsylvania Infantry in Conneautville on 06 Aug 1862. He mustered out on 01 Jun 1863 in Harrisburg.[766] Sadly, the next year, he was killed on 25 Aug 1864 in a sawmill boiler explosion while working in Crossingville, Crawford, Pennsylvania.[767]

        ix. HENRIETTA J. WYETH, born 11 Oct 1841, Spring Township; died there unmarried in 1871 at the age of 30; buried with her parents in Springboro.

225.   x.   ALMIRA ROSANNA WYETH, born 10 Jun 1847, Spring Township; married (1) HENRY MOSES, 27 Jul 1865, Spring Township; married (2) WILLIAM FRANKLIN

CUMMINGS, circa 1915; died 24 Apr 1931, Erie, Erie County, Pennsylvania.
xi. EMMELINE WYETH, born 01 May 1850, Spring Township; death unknown.

116. FRANCES "FANNY"^{6} WYETH (Joshua^5, Ebenezer^4 Jr., Ebenezer^3, John^2, Nicholas^1) was born in 1802 in Towanda, Luzerne (Bradford), Pennsylvania. Frances "Fanny" Wyeth and James Riley Bailey were married on 17 Jul 1822 in Harmony Township, Clark, Ohio. **JAMES RILEY BAILEY**, son of Capt. Timothy Bailey and Zerviah Blodgett, was born on 06 Oct 1783 in Lisbon, Grafton, New Hampshire. For his service in the War of 1812, he received Bounty Land near Lisbon, Clark County, Ohio. Fanny and James lived their last years at the home of their daughter, Elvira Bailey Canady, near Plattsburg, Harmony Township, Clark, Ohio. He died there circa 1861 and Fanny died circa 1871.

James Riley Bailey and Frances "Fanny" Wyeth had the following children:

226.   i. ELVIRA^7 BAILEY, born Jun 1827, Harmony Township; married MATTHEW CANADY there, 02 Jan 1848; died 17 May 1923, Plattsburg.

        ii. PHILMA BAILEY, born in 1832 in Harmony Township; death unknown.

227.   iii. MARTHA REBECCA BAILEY, born 07 Mar 1837, Harmony Township; married WILLIAM W. CANADY, 07 Aug 1855, Springfield, Clark, Ohio; died 25 Jun 1909, Goshen Township, Auglaize, Ohio.

        iv. ATHALIA A. BAILEY (SMITH), born circa 1838, Harmony; death unknown.

228.   v. WILLIAM HENRY BAILEY, born 22 Apr 1840, Harmony Township; private 20th Illinois Infantry, Co. I; married MARY ANN BAKER, 06 Mar 1866, Clark County; died 07 Dec 1914, Fairfield Township, Madison County, Ohio.

117. ANNA ELIZABETH^6 WYETH (Joshua^5, Ebenezer^4 Jr., Ebenezer^3, John^2, Nicholas^1) was born in Mar 1809 in Cincinnati, Hamilton, Ohio. From there, on 19 Sep 1813, her father wrote to his sister back home that daughter Fanny was 12, Anna five and a half, William two and a fourth, and another child (Enoch), three months.[768] Anna married **JOHN HEWSON** who was born in 1796 in New York. As John remarried and started having children by 1841, Anna apparently died circa 1839. John Hewson died circa 1887.

The children of John Hewson and Anna Elizabeth Wyeth included:

229.   i. ELLIOTT DUDLEY^7 HEWSON, born 02 May 1831, Cincinnati; enlisted there on 15 Aug 1862, in the 83rd Ohio Infantry, Co. H, discharged 24 Jul 1865, Galveston, Texas; married ELLEN BARTLETT, 04 Aug 1853, Cincinnati; died 17 Aug 1920, Indianapolis.

118. ENOCH NELSON^6 WYETH (Joshua^5, Ebenezer^4 Jr., Ebenezer^3, John^2, Nicholas^1) was born in Jun 1813 in Cincinnati, Hamilton, Ohio.[769] S. W. Lynd performed the ceremony when Nelson married (1) Elizabeth Fowler on 26 May 1836 in Cincinnati. **ELIZABETH FOWLER** was born about 1815 in Ohio and died before Sep 1840. Enoch Nelson Wyeth married (2) Lucinda M. Prather on 20 Sep 1840 in Terre Haute, Vigo, Indiana. **LUCINDA M. PRATHER** was born to Henry Prather and Mary Prayer on 30 Nov 1820 in Kentucky. Enoch died on 16 Jul 1896 in Terre Haute.[770] Lucinda died there on 12 Oct 1900. Her birth was calculated on her death certificate age of 79 years, 10 months, 12 days.

Enoch Nelson Wyeth and Elizabeth Fowler had the following child:

230.   i.   CHARLES ALONZO[7] WYETH, born 14 Oct 1836, Cincinnati, Hamilton, Ohio;[771] served during the Civil War in both the Indiana 11th and the Indiana 3rd Battery Light Artillery; married (1) TRESSA MEWHINNEY, 21 Mar 1864, Riley Township, Vigo, Indiana; married and divorced twice (2) THERESA P. FLOYD, 25 Dec 1889, Denver, Arapahoe, Colorado and 02 Dec 1896, Golden, Jefferson Colorado; married (3) RACHEL AMANDA SCHOENLEBER, 27 Jul 1906, Minneapolis, Hennepin, Minnesota; died 30 Mar 1915, Minnesota Soldiers Home, Minneapolis, Hennepin, Minnesota.[772]

Enoch Nelson Wyeth and Lucinda M. Prather had the following children:

231.   i.   GEORGE NELSON[7] WYETH, born 21 Jan 1842, Terre Haute, Vigo, Indiana; married MARY DEMARIS "POLLY" KESTER, 24 Sep 1863, Linton Township, Vigo, Indiana; enlisted on 14 Feb 1865 in the 149th Indiana Infantry, Co. K; died 28 Dec 1912 in Union Hospital, Terre Haute.

        ii. ALBERT WYETH was born about 1851 in Terre Haute; died on 12 Jun 1851, Terre Haute; buried there in Woodlawn Cemetery next to his mother.

232.   iii. JAMES THOMAS WYETH, born 03 Jul 1859, Crab Orchard, Lincoln, Kentucky; married MARGARET JENNIE DOAN, 12 Nov 1889, Terre Haute; died 09 May 1947, Detroit, Wayne, Michigan. (His marriage record says his parents were Daniel Wyeth and Rebecca Gudge. However, it appears he may have been adopted by Enoch and Lucinda. James and Margaret are buried in Vigo County's Hull Cemetery near George Nelson Wyeth who named a son Daniel.

119. **OLIVE AMANDA**[6] **WYETH** (Joshua[5], Ebenezer[4] Jr., Ebenezer[3], John[2], Nicholas[1]) was born in 1818 in Champaign County, Ohio.[773] This is where the family lived when Joshua Wyeth Sr. applied for his Revolutionary War pension.[774] Some researchers say she was born in Cincinnati, Ohio on 19 Sep 1818. However, that date belongs to Nancy Rector Wythe. Olive Amanda Wyeth and **EDWIN WALLACE HARRISON SR.** were married by Rev. William Burke on 08 Jan 1837 in Cincinnati. The son of Ebenezer Harrison and Martha Enyart, Edwin was born in Jan 1816 in Cincinnati.[775] Amanda died on 11 Apr 1878 in Riley Township, Vigo, Indiana. He died there on 15 Sep 1879. Edwin and Amanda are buried in Woodlawn Cemetery, Terre Haute, Vigo, Indiana.

The children of Edwin Wallace Harrison Sr. and Olive Amanda Wyeth included:

233.   i.   EDWIN WALLACE[7] HARRISON JR., born Dec 1840, Cincinnati, Hamilton, Ohio; married ELEANOR "ELLA" CANNON, 18 Jun 1863, Cincinnati; died 25 Dec 1884, Newton, Jasper, Illinois.[776]

        ii. ELIZABETH HARRISON, born about 1842, Cincinnati; death unknown.

       iii. CLINTON RICHARDSON HARRISON, born about 1844, Cincinnati; enlisted in Co. F, Ohio 83rd Infantry Regiment on 09 Aug 1862, mustered out 17 Oct 1864 in Hempstead, Waller, Texas; death unknown.

       iv. CLARA OLIVE HARRISON, born about 1858 in Cincinnati; death unknown.

120. **SUSANNA WYETH "SUKEY"[6] WATSON** (Susannah[5] Wyeth, Ebenezer[4] Jr., Ebenezer[3], John[2], Nicholas[1]) was born on 06 Dec 1780 in Cambridge, Middlesex, Massachusetts. Susanna Wyeth "Sukey" Watson and **ARTENATUS MOORE** were married on 07 Feb 1802 in Cambridge. Artenatus Moore, a baker, son of Josiah Moore and Mary Hastings was born circa 1777 in Cambridge. Sukey died there of consumption on 24 May 1807 at the age of 26. After his remarriage, Artenatus died in Cambridge, of the same disease, on 15 Oct 1814 at the age of 37.

Artenatus Moore and Susanna Wyeth "Sukey" Watson had the following children:

      i. SUSANNA WYETH[7] MOORE, born 06 Dec 1802, Cambridge; baptized there on 16 Jan 1803; died, unmarried, on 21 May 1875 in Cambridge.

      ii. MARY HASTINGS MOORE, born 07 Sep 1804, Cambridge; baptized there on 23 Sep 1804; died unmarried on 13 Feb 1865, Cambridge.

      iii. NANCY PRISCILLA WATSON MOORE, born 04 May 1806, Cambridge; died there on 01 Mar 1807 at the age of ten months.

121. **(DR.) JACOB[6] WYETH** (Jacob[5] Sr., Ebenezer[4] Jr., Ebenezer[3], John[2], Nicholas[1]) was born 08 Jan 1800 (or 10 Feb 1797) in Cambridge, Middlesex, Massachusetts.[777] He earned a M.D. from Harvard College in 1825.[778] Dr. Jacob Wyeth married **MARY CATHERINE BRADY** on 11 Jun 1834 in Sinsinawa Mound, Grant, Wisconsin.[779] Mary was born 21 Dec 1815 in St. Louis, Missouri to Thomas Brady and Harriet Jones.[780] Dr. Jacob Wyeth died 24 Aug 1841 in Ste. Genevieve, Ste. Genevieve County, Missouri.[781] Mary died 27 Jul 1864 in Chicago.

Dr. Jacob Wyeth and Mary Catherine Brady had the following children:

   234.   i. CHARLES JONES[7] WYETH, born circa 1835, Galena, Jo Daviess County, Illinois;[782] married JULIA ELIZABETH MCREYNOLDS, 04 Apr 1865, Detroit, Wayne, Michigan;[783] died 12 Apr 1873, Cairo, Alexander, Illinois.[784]

         ii. HARRIET ELIZABETH WYETH, born circa 1841; died on 15 Oct 1841 in Sainte Genevieve County, Missouri.[785]

Notes for Dr. Jacob Wyeth and Mary Catherine Brady:

Not only does the date used by most historians for Jacob's birth, 10 Feb 1797 seem illogical because it is only three months after his parents married, but 1797 is the same year his brother Leonard Jarvis Wyeth Sr. was born.[786][787] There are no references to the brothers being twins. *The History of Jo Daviess County, Illinois* says Jacob was born 08 Jan 1800.[788] That date realistically fits into the range of birth dates for his brothers.

Regardless of the date of his birth, Jacob grew up on the shores of Fresh Pond at his father's hotel there. The enterprise was so successful, Jacob Wyeth Sr. ably financed an excellent education for his namesake. Jacob Wyeth Jr. graduated from Harvard College in 1820.[789] Before his 1825 medical degree from the college, Jacob earned a Master of Arts there in 1823.[790]

When Dr. Wyeth's brother, Nathaniel Jarvis Wyeth, was determined to establish a salmon fishery and fur trade industry over 3,000 miles away on the banks of Oregon's Columbia River, Jacob signed on to be the company's physician. However, four months later, Dr. Wyeth became so ill from drinking tainted water, that he, his cousin, John Bound Wyeth, and many others, left the expedition in Idaho's Grand Teton Basin on 28 Jul 1832 after battling Black Hawk Indians.[791]

The next year, Jacob settled in Galena, Jo Daviess, Illinois where he opened a medical practice, a drug store and helped found the Galena Library. He was described as "...the soul of principle and integrity... There was not a mean or unmanly flaw in his composition.[792] His 1834 marriage to Mary Catherine Brady, celebrated by Rev. Father Charles Fitzmaurice, was but a few miles north of Galena across the Illinois / Wisconsin state line in Sinsinawa Mound, Wisconsin.[793]

Mary was baptized in the Roman Catholic faith on 16 Mar 1820 in St. Louis, Missouri.[794] Her father, Thomas Brady, was active in church, business and political affairs of the city. Within four years of arriving from Ireland, he was elected a commissioner to receive subscriptions to the first bank in St. Louis. He owned stores in St. Louis, Ste. Genevieve and St. Charles, Missouri. The Missouri Hotel he built in 1816 was the social center of early St. Louis.[795]

After Brady's death in 1821, Mary's mother, Harriet Jones, married Missouri Congressman John Scott. It was at the congressman's home in Ste. Genevieve that Dr. Jacob Wyeth died of consumption at age 42.[796] Just two months after her husband's death, Mary's infant daughter also died at the home of Mary's step-father. Mary returned to Galena where, according to the 1850 census, she and son Charles lived next door to her sister Eliza Joanna Brady and brother-in-law George W. Campbell. In 1860, Mary and Charles resided in the Campbells' Galena home.

George W. Campbell's niece, Mary E. Campbell, was married to Galena banker and pig iron dealer, Nathan Corwith. In Nathan's honor, Charles Jones Wyeth named his youngest son Nathan Corwith Wyeth. In his will, Charles designated Nathan Corwith to protect his fortune for his two sons. Corwith failed miserably by comingling trust funds with his own money.[797] Apparently, when Charles moved to Chicago, circa 1863, to seek that later destroyed fortune, his mother went with him. Cook County records show Mary Catherine Brady Wyeth died there in 1864 at age 48.

122. **LEONARD JARVIS "L.J."[6] WYETH SR.** (Jacob[5] Sr., Ebenezer[4] Jr., Ebenezer[3], John[2], Nicholas[1]) was born in 1797 in Cambridge, Middlesex, Massachusetts.[798] Leonard Jarvis Wyeth Sr. and Caroline Archer were married in Baltimore, Maryland's First Independent Christ's Church (Unitarian), on 02 Oct 1821.[799] **CAROLINE ARCHER**, daughter of George Archer and Judith Hathorne, was baptized on 18 Nov 1798 in Salem, Essex, Massachusetts. Leonard died on 01 Feb 1855 in Manhattan, New York. Caroline died there on 16 Jan 1882 at the Everett House Hotel.[800] They rest in a private family mausoleum in Brooklyn's Green-wood Cemetery.

Leonard Jarvis Wyeth Sr. and Caroline Archer had the following children:

> i. ELIZABETH JARVIS[7] WYETH I, baptized 09 Mar 1823, First Independent Christ's Church (Unitarian), Baltimore;[801] died 01 Aug 1831, New York City.
>
> 235. ii. SARAH ARCHER WYETH, born circa 1824, Baltimore; married CHARLES P.

CARPENDER, 09 May 1849, New York City; died there, 13 Apr 1861.

        iii.   MARY FRANCES WYETH, born circa 1828, Brooklyn; died unmarried on 12 Jan 1878 in Newport, Rhode Island.[802]

236.   iv.   ELIZABETH JARVIS WYETH, born 16 Aug 1832, New York City; married ANDERSON CARROLL DANA there on 18 May 1859; died there, 23 Mar 1915.

237.   v.   LEONARD JARVIS WYETH JR., born 29 Oct 1833, New York City; graduated Harvard College, 1854; married CHARLOTTE PRIME, 27 Dec 1858, New York City; died there on 05 May 1909, at his home, at 1142 Madison Avenue.[803]

238.   vi.   EMILY WYETH, born 06 Oct 1835, New York City; married FREDERICK GEORGE SWAN, 21 Feb 1861, New York City; died there, 16 Mar 1910.

        vii.   CAROLINE A. WYETH, born circa 1836, New York City; died there before 1850.

Notes for Leonard Jarvis "L.J." Wyeth Sr. and Caroline Archer:

Leonard became known as "L.J." to distinguish himself from the uncle for whom he was named. Leonard Jarvis, a prosperous wholesale dry goods businessman, hired brothers L.J. and Charles to work for him in Baltimore, Maryland. After a few years, the brothers bought their uncle's business.[804] However, L.J. was soon drawn to New York City. There he imported and sold fancy dry goods at 126 Pearl Street.[805] Later L.J. entered into a British lace goods importing partnership with offices in New York City and in Nottingham, England.[806] He also served on the board of directors of the American Exchange Bank, 18 Wall St.[807] and the Williamsburgh Fire Insurance Co., 62 Wall St.[808]

This photo of Leonard Jarvis Wyeth Sr. is courtesy of his 3rd great grandson, Leonard Jarvis "Trip" Wyeth VI.

His obituary said, "Died …This morning, 01 Feb 1855, after a severe and prolonged illness, Leonard Jarvis Wyeth in the 58th year of his age."[809] The given age also confirms L.J.'s 1797 birth.[810] Leonard, along with his first child, Elizabeth; last child, Caroline; his son-in-law, Charles P. Carpender and two Carpender grandchildren, were first buried in New York City's Marble Cemetery on 2nd Avenue.[811] On 31 Dec 1855 they were reinterred in the Wyeth mausoleum at lot 9201, section 8 of Brooklyn's Green-Wood Cemetery.[812]

In his will, probated in Manhattan, Leonard generously included $600 a year to his 90-year-old father, Jacob Wyeth Sr., and 86-year-old mother, Elizabeth Jarvis. He left such substantial incomes to his wife and children, that Caroline and her daughter, Mary Frances Wyeth, purchased an expensive summer residence in 1870 for $19,000 on Ayrault Street in Newport, Rhode Island.[813] By comparison, Victorian-era homes in that area now rent for over $22,000 per month during the summer season.[814]

Salemite Caroline Archer's own family was prosperous as well, and through her mother, Judith Hathorne, she had other interesting connections to the Wyeth family. Judge John Hathorne, who oversaw the Salem witchcraft trials of L.J.'s half 3rd great aunt, Rebecca Andrews Jacobs and her family, was Caroline's second great grandfather. Author Nathaniel Hawthorne, married to L.J.'s distant cousin, Sophia Amelia Peabody, was Caroline's first cousin.[815]

When Caroline's father, sea captain George Archer, died, she, her mother, and sister, Sarah

Archer, followed Sarah's husband, Robert Hawkins Osgood, to Baltimore, Maryland. There Robert, a thriving wholesale clothing merchant, rubbed shoulders with the Wyeth brothers and no doubt sparked Caroline and Leonard's marriage. When mother Judith died in 1827, Caroline and L.J. followed the Osgoods to New York City.[816] The Osgoods eventually settled on Staten Island.[817] There the Wyeths joined them in a rented home during NYC's sweltering summers.[818]

Likewise, Caroline Archer and Mary Frances Wyeth were lured to Rhode Island to escape NYC's summer heat. However, they eventually remained in Newport year-round. After Mary's death there, 80-year-old Caroline decided to return to Manhattan. In the process, she gifted one of her servants a treasure so spectacularly generous that newspapers across America, from Vermont to Montana, reported on it. This is from the 09 Dec 1878 *Cincinnati Daily Gazette*:

> "Mrs. Caroline A. Wyeth, a wealthy and benevolent lady owning a cottage at Newport, has broken up her establishment and returned to New York, where she will reside in the future. To her coachman, who has been a faithful servant, she has given her horses, her carriage, and a sleigh, and told him to get a living with them. The gift is estimated at being worth in the neighborhood of $2,000."[819]

Caroline was equally considerate to her family in her last will and testament subscribed on 22 Mar 1879. To be as fair as possible, she divided her estate three ways for her surviving children, Elizabeth J. Dana, Emily Wyeth Swan and Leonard Jarvis Wyeth Jr. Additionally, her two daughters shared her silver-plate and wardrobe. To her son, she bequeathed all her household linens, blankets, books, and portraits of her deceased husband and grandchild, Charles P. Carpender Jr. She gave a $1,000 railroad bond to each of her grandchildren, namely, Caroline Archer Dana, Charlotte H., Leonard J., and George Edward Wyeth, and Frances Wyeth Swan.

123. **CHARLES**[6] **WYETH** (Jacob[5] Sr., Ebenezer[4] Jr., Ebenezer[3], John[2], Nicholas[1]) was born on 11 Nov 1798 in Cambridge, Middlesex, Massachusetts.[820] Charles Wyeth married (1) **ELIZABETH NORRIS**, 27 Jun 1827 in Baltimore City, Maryland. Elizabeth, daughter of William Norris and Rebecca Smith, was born there on 09 Jan 1806.[821] At age 38, she died in Baltimore on 16 May 1843 and was buried there in Green Mount Cemetery.[822][823] Charles married (2) **CAROLINE COGSWELL KNEELAND**, widow of Francis Bartlett, on 16 Jul 1859 in Baltimore's First Independent Christ's Church (Unitarian).[824] Caroline, daughter of Benjamin Kneeland and Eve Cogswell, was born in Westford, Middlesex, Massachusetts on 14 Mar 1815. Charles died in Baltimore on 27 Jan 1891.[825] Caroline was buried near him at Green Mount Cemetery, Baltimore on 22 Jan 1895.[826]

Although, Elizabeth, Charles, Caroline, Rebecca, Helen, William and Henry are buried there, there are no monuments in the Green Mount Wyeth lot. The large white tombstone in the center of the next lot behind is that of Charles' uncle, Leonard Jarvis.

Charles Wyeth and Elizabeth Norris had the following children:[827]

239.   i. CHARLES JARVIS[7] WYETH, born 05 May 1828, Baltimore; married MARGARET JOHNSON there, 17 Jul 1849;[828] died 18 Nov 1874, Manhattan.

240.   ii. NATHANIEL JARVIS "NATHAN" WYETH, born 08 Sep 1830, Baltimore; earned a Harvard Law LL.B. degree, 1852, Cambridge; married ANN CAROLINE FROST there, 03 Oct 1854; died 22 Mar 1916, Staten Island, Richmond, New York.

      iii. REBECCA ANN WYETH, baptized 21 May 1834, St. Peter's Protestant Episcopal Church, Baltimore; buried Green Mount Cemetery on 10 Nov 1843.[829]

      iv. HELEN WYETH, born 10 Oct 1834, Baltimore; died there, 26 Apr 1890.[830]

241.   v. WILLIAM NORRIS WYETH SR., born 29 Sep 1837, Baltimore; married ELEANOR J. MAYNARD there on 24 Feb 1863,[831] died 15 Apr 1890, Baltimore.[832]

242.   vi. HENRY CLARENCE WYETH, born 28 Oct 1839, Baltimore; married ANNIE COLLINS HILL there, 23 Nov 1865;[833] died 26 Aug 1880, Maryland.[834]

Notes for Charles Wyeth:

For the period, the 28 Jan 1891 tribute to Charles in the *Baltimore Sun* was quite detailed. The first part of it confirmed much of the family data above. The second aspect was his life's work:

> "...Charles Wyeth came to Baltimore when he was a young man and entered the wholesale dry goods house of his uncle, Leonard Jarvis. After a few years he and his brother, L.J. Wyeth bought the business. L.J. Wyeth went to New York, and the firm was dissolved. A few years later the firm of Wyeth & Norris was established, and a very large importing business in silks and dry goods resulted. At the dissolution of this firm Mr. Wyeth associated himself with Mr. N.F. Blacklock and established a large wholesale business under the name of Wyeth and Blacklock. About this time Mr. Wyeth was a large owner of real estate in San Francisco. The great fire in 1851 burned considerable of his property. Mr. Wyeth went out to California after the fire and remained for several years. When he returned to Baltimore, he invested his capital in real estate and devoted the latter portion of his life to looking after his property. He was a popular man in business and social circles, and was known to all the older merchants in Baltimore. He was a trustee in the First Independent Christ's Church [Unitarian] ..."[835]

Additionally, in 1846, Charles helped found the Equitable Life Insurance Co. of Baltimore[836] and, according to an 1853 ad in the *Baltimore Sun*, Charles laid out Wyeth Street.[837] His namesake street still exists in Baltimore, although it was apparently renumbered. Google maps show the first house starts near Hamburg St. at 646 Wyeth St. and goes three blocks to 502 Wyeth St. at Washington Blvd. The stadium where the Baltimore Ravens play is about a 13-minute walk southeast along West Hamburg St.

At age 86, Charles Wyeth testified before the Pension Board on 03 Apr 1885 about an Augusta Clary who lived in one of his rental homes on Wyeth Street. Mrs. Clary's husband died in the Civil War in 1864 and she needed to prove she had not remarried in order to qualify for a widow's pension. Charles' fascinating and honest answers did not help her case.

Charles Wyeth's signature on the Clary deposition is quite distinct for an 86-year-old.

> "... my name is Charles Wyeth. *What is your occupation?* ... retired merchant... I am 86 years of age... *When were you born?* 11 Nov 1798 at Cambridge, Mass. *Are you personally acquainted with the claimant... Augusta Clary ...?* A woman lived in my house No. 18 Wyeth St., Baltimore, Md. from about Jan 1879 to Sep 1884 with Charles Cameron... as his wife... some three years ago she told me that she was not legally married to Charles Cameron... they owed me $251 for rent... When I ordered him and his so called wife, Augusta Cameron, out of the house in Sept. 1884 for non payment of rent, Cameron offered me a faction of the furniture which was in the house in payment of the rent, which I declined..."[838]

Charles lived a couple miles north of Wyeth St. at 1304 McCulloh St. At his death, his widow and her daughter, Sarah Bartlett Roche, stayed in the home. Both Caroline and Sarah died before the 1900 census was taken. So, at the start of the new century, Charles Wyeth's home was occupied by his stepdaughter's husband, George W. Roche and George's second wife.

Apparently, unconcerned with the McCulloh property, Charles' only surviving child, Nathaniel Jarvis "Nathan" Wyeth, an attorney who lived on Staten Island sued his stepmother, Caroline Cogswell Kneeland Bartlett, in 1893 for control of some of the Wyeth St. property.[839]

Not only did Charles Wyeth outlive all of his children, except the son he named for his daring Oregon-explorer brother, but he was the only one of his siblings to inherit their parents' longevity genes. Charles and his father, Jacob Wyeth Sr., both were almost 93 at their deaths. Charles' mother, Elizabeth Jarvis, was age 89. Due to weakened health from the harshness of their rigorous expedition, Dr. Jacob Wyeth died at age 44 and Captain Nathaniel Jarvis Wyeth at age 54. Leonard Jarvis Wyeth Sr., who together with Charles, helped finance their brothers' western journey, died at only 57. For Charles, the joy of growing old must have competed with the sadness of losing so many of his loved ones.

124. **JONAS PARKER**[6] **WYETH** (Gad[5] Sr., Ebenezer[4] Jr., Ebenezer[3], John[2], Nicholas[1]) was born on 27 Oct 1794 in Cambridge, Middlesex, Massachusetts. Jonas and Margaret Philes were married on 25 Jul 1825, probably in New York. **MARGARET PHILES** (or Files) was born there circa 1802. Jonas Parker Wyeth died on 13 May 1855 at age 60 in Humboldt, Coles, Illinois.[840] Per Margaret's tombstone in Riverside Cemetery, Three Rivers, St. Joseph, Michigan, she died there on 24 Aug 1870 at age 68.

Jonas Parker Wyeth and Margaret Philes had the following child:

243.   i. JOSEPH BENJAMIN[7] WYETH, born 20 Jun 1820, Le Ray, Jefferson, New York;[841] married CHARLOTTE MARY HORTON, 07 Apr 1842, Granville, Licking, Ohio;[842] died 17 Apr 1884, Judsonia, White, Arkansas.

125. **GAD**[6] **WYETH JR.** (Gad[5] Sr., Ebenezer[4] Jr., Ebenezer[3], John[2], Nicholas[1]) was born on 04 Jul 1795 in Wendell, Franklin, Massachusetts. Gad Wyeth Jr. and Elizabeth Ellen Chase were married on 18 May 1823[843] near the Black River in Adams, Jefferson, New York.[844] **ELIZABETH ELLEN CHASE** was born on 06 Feb 1807 in New York. She died on 16 Feb 1854 in North Wilna, Jefferson, New York. He died there on 01 Aug 1858. They are buried nearby in the Lake School Road Cemetery on the grounds of Fort Drum.[845]

Sheila Baum and James Allen Wyeth furnished a century-old family record containing most of the following dates for the children of Gad Wyeth Jr. and Elizabeth Ellen Chase:[846]

244.   i. SILAS JABEZ[7] WYETH, born 29 Jan 1825,[847] Adams, Jefferson, New York; married HARRIET M. NUTTING, 21 Jan 1851, Wilna, Jefferson, New York; they later divorced; he died 21 Sep 1898, Garden Township, Boone, Iowa.

245.   ii. NELSON WYETH, born 06 Nov 1826, Adams, married SARAH POTTER, 06 Feb 1853, Champion, Jefferson, New York; died 14 Oct 1899, Rutland, Jefferson, New York.

297

iii. BETSEY ANN WYETH, born 27 Aug 1828, Adams; died 29 Aug 1857, Wilna.

246. iv. RACHEL WYETH, born 06 Nov 1830, Adams; married (1) THADDEUS OLDS, 14 Feb 1849, Wilna; married (2) DAVID PEELER, 19 Sep 1878, Rutland, Jefferson, New York; died 15 Apr 1897, Great Bend, Jefferson, New York.

247. v. PARKER WYETH, born 27 Jan 1833, Adams; married (1) ABBY JANE COON, 25 Aug 1852, Theresa, Jefferson, New York; married (2) SARAH ANGELINE "SILA" COON there, 07 May 1858; died 26 Mar 1864, North Wilna.

248. vi. MARY M. WYETH, born 05 Jan 1835 Adams; married CHARLES HIRAM TOWNSEND, 29 Nov 1854, Wilna; died 02 Nov 1861, North Wilna.

249. vii. LORINDA B. WYETH, born 15 Feb 1837, Adams; married JOHN NEWSAM, 02 Jul 1859, Wilna; died circa 1921, Grundy County, Illinois.

250. viii. ABIE WYETH, born 15 Jan 1839, Wilna; married GEORGE NEWSAM JR., 29 Nov 1858, Wilna; died 20 Oct 1919, Seward Township, Kendall, Illinois.

251. ix. WILLIAM H. WYETH, born 15 Oct 1840, Wilna; served in the Civil War; married MARY ANN BARNUM, 13 Dec 1864, Antwerp, Jefferson, New York; died 07 Oct 1912, Watertown, Jefferson, New York.[848]

252. x. JOSEPH WYETH, born 06 Apr 1843, Wilna; married MARIA NEWSAM, 18 Jan 1868, Lisbon, Kendall, Illinois; died 08 Sep 1933, Aurora, Kane, Illinois.

xi. ABIGAIL A. WYETH, born 06 Mar 1845, Wilna; married CHARLES J. DRAKE, 1874, Jefferson County, New York; died there, 1923.

253. xii. CHARLES E. WYETH, born 25 Mar 1847, Wilna; married (1) MARTHA ESTHER VERNON, 04 Jul 1867, Kendall County, Illinois; married (2) HANNAH "ANNA" HARROP, 08 Sep 1898, in Minooka, Seward Township, Kendall, Illinois; died 14 Jul 1926, Aurora, Kane, Illinois.[849]

126. **JOSEPH SAWIN[6] WYETH** (Gad[5] Sr., Ebenezer[4] Jr., Ebenezer[3], John[2], Nicholas[1]) was born on 08 Nov 1796 in Wendell, Franklin, Massachusetts. Joseph married (1) **SARAH "SALLY" HORR** on 11 Oct 1819[850] in Denmark, Lewis, New York. Sally was born on 05 Aug 1794 in Middleboro, Plymouth, Massachusetts. When Sally's parents, Deacon Luther Horr and Elisabeth Hoar, retired, they gave her their home in Denmark.[851] Sally died there on 03 May 1849. Just after the 1850 census enumeration of Pamelia, Jefferson, New York, Joseph married (2) **CYNTHA GOULDING** there. Cyntha, daughter of Curtis Goulding and Rachel Russell, was born circa 1806 in Madison County, New York. Per her tombstone in Denmark's Hillside Cemetery, Cyntha died in her 65th year on 21 Mar 1871. Joseph died on 02 Apr 1872. He, like both of his wives, passed in Denmark. All three rest at Hillside.

Joseph Sawin Wyeth and Sarah "Sally" Horr had the following children:

254. i. JAMES MADISON[7] WYETH, born 02 Oct 1820, LeRay, Jefferson, New York; married ALMIRA THOMPSON, 30 Mar 1847, Lowville, Lewis, New York; enlisted in the 75th Illinois Infantry, Fulton, Whiteside, Illinois, 07 Aug 1862; died on 05 Mar 1863 in Murfreesboro, Rutherford, Tennessee from disease contracted while nursing sick and wounded after the Battle of Stones River.[852]

255. ii. MARY KENDALL WYETH, born 22 Jun 1822, LeRay; married GEORGE HENDEE circa 1849, Jefferson County, New York; died 28 Oct 1898, Omaha, Douglas, Nebraska.

iii. ELIZABETH H. WYETH, born 09 Jul 1824, LeRay; married JOHN H. BROWN in 1848, Lewis County; died there in 1901.

256. iv. WILLIAM HOAR WYETH, born 22 May 1826, LeRay; married (1) SUSAN ELIZABETH ANDERSON, 25 Feb 1851, Denmark, Lewis, New York; married (2) JENNIE L. "JANE" TALLMAGE, 22 May 1878; married (3) FREDERICA MELLNITZ, 1880, Lewis County; died 08 May 1900, Denmark, New York.

257. v. MONROE CLAY WYTHE, born 27 Jul 1832, LeRay; married (1) EMMA ELVIRA KNIGHT, 20 Oct 1856, Fulton, Whiteside, Illinois; married (2) CAROLINE NYE FREEMAN WING, 13 Oct 1880, Georgetown, Clear Creek, Colorado; died 23 Mar 1891, Rand, Jackson, Colorado.[853]

127. **MARY[6] WYETH** (Gad[5] Sr., Ebenezer[4] Jr., Ebenezer[3], John[2], Nicholas[1]) was born on 15 Sep 1799 in Wendell, Franklin, Massachusetts. Mary Wyeth and Silas D. Stiles were married on 10 Feb 1825 in Pownal, Bennington, Vermont. **SILAS D. STILES**, son of Benjamin Stiles and Elizabeth Cutler, was born on 31 Oct 1788 in Wendell. On 19 Jun 1825, Mary's father, Gad Wyeth Sr., dated a newsy letter at Wendell to his sister Anna Wyeth Cutter. He said his only daughter moved 300 miles from him to Sackets Harbor, Jefferson, New York.[854] Silas Stiles died on 10 Feb 1848, in Milford, Jefferson, Wisconsin.[855] Mary died there on 11 Mar 1852.

Silas D. Stiles and Mary Wyeth had the following children:

i. HANNAH K.[7] STILES, born 28 May 1826, Sackets Harbor; died on 13 Feb 1844, at age 17, in Milford, Jefferson, Wisconsin.
ii. PARKER W. STILES, born 21 Mar 1828, Sackets Harbor; drowned 10 May 1831.
iii. MARY H. STILES, born 04 Sep 1829, Sackets Harbor; death unknown.
iv. ELIJAH H. STILES, born 13 May 1831, Sackets Harbor; death unknown.
v. WILLIAM P. STILES, born on 08 Mar 1833, Sackets Harbor; death unknown.
vi. GEORGE F. STILES, born 18 Mar 1838, Milford. According to the *New York Times* of 26 May 1857, he shot himself on 24 Apr 1857, at age 19, in Milford. Spiritualism said to be the cause of his suicide.

128. **NATHAN S.[6] WYETH** (Gad[5] Sr., Ebenezer[4] Jr., Ebenezer[3], John[2], Nicholas[1]) was born on 16 May 1801 in Wendell, Franklin, Massachusetts. The marriage intention of Nathan S. Wyeth and **HANNAH PUTNAM KELLOGG** was filed on 11 Nov 1823 in Wendell. According to *Wendell Massachusetts, Town and Vital Records*, they were married four days later by Rev. David Goddard. Hannah, daughter of Samuel Kellogg and Susannah Felton, was born on 06 Dec 1800 in New Salem, Franklin, Massachusetts. Nathan died on 11 Aug 1864, at his son Leonard's home in Tuscola, Douglas, Illinois.[856] Hannah died 06 Feb 1866 in Seven Hickory Township, Coles, Illinois. They are buried in Greasy Point Cemetery (Union), Rardin, Illinois.

This 1880 photograph of the home Nathan built in Wendell, circa 1830, is courtesy of Nathan's third great grandson, George Bullock Wyeth.

Nathan S. Wyeth and Hannah Putnam Kellogg had the following children:

     i. NANCY ELIZABETH[7] WYETH, born 07 Nov 1825, Wendell; died 20 Jan 1830 at age six; buried in the Wyeth plot on Jennison Road, Wendell.[857]

258.   ii. LEONARD JACKSON WYETH, born 13 Jan 1827, Wendell; married MELINDA NORTHWAY, 1847,[858] Liberty Township, Licking, Ohio; died 24 Jan 1898, Tuscola, Douglas, Illinois.

259.   iii. JOSEPH SAWIN WYETH, born 15 Apr 1828, Wendell; married JOANNA HUNT, 28 Apr 1850, McKean Township, Licking County, Ohio; died 14 Jun 1898, Garrett Township, Douglas, Illinois.

260.   iv. ALBERT ROBERT WYETH, born 22 Dec 1829, Wendell; married ANGELINE CARRIS, circa 1852, Charleston, Coles, Illinois; died there on 15 Sep 1911.

261.   v. SAMUEL KELLOGG WYETH, born 20 Nov 1831, Wendell; married LAMIRA CATHERINE COMBS, 21 Oct 1857, Charleston; served in the 143rd Illinois Infantry Regiment; died Charleston, 11 Apr 1907.

262.   vi. THOMAS EVANS WYETH, born 21 Jun 1833, Wendell; married (1) NANCY B. COMBS, 27 Dec 1855, Charleston; married (2) JULIA ANN PRICE, 12 May 1875, Douglas County; died 12 Apr 1905 in Seven Hickory Township.

263.   vii. ELLEN ROXANNA WYETH, born 28 Jan 1835, Wendell; married OLIVER CROMWELL HACKETT, 14 Mar 1854, Coles County, Illinois; died 05 Mar 1875, Tuscola, Douglas, Illinois.

264.   viii. MARY KENDALL WYETH, born 28 Dec 1838, Liberty Township, Licking, Ohio; married JOHN STITH COFER, 21 Oct 1857, Charleston;[859] died 05 Dec 1924, Hackensack, Cass, Minnesota.

     ix. DELILAH JANE WYETH, born 07 Jun 1841, Liberty Township; died there on 05 Aug 1842 at age one year, two months.

129. **DAVID G.[6] WYETH** (Gad[5] Sr., Ebenezer[4] Jr., Ebenezer[3], John[2], Nicholas[1]) was born 03 Oct 1802 in Wendell, Franklin, Massachusetts and named for the town's church minister. David G. Wyeth and Sally Kellogg were married on 02 Jan 1826 in Wendell.[860] **SALLY KELLOGG**, daughter of Samuel Kellogg and Susannah Felton, was born in New Salem, Franklin, Massachusetts on 16 Aug 1802. Sally's sister Hannah Putnam Kellogg was married to David's brother, Nathan. David and Sally relocated to McKean Township, Licking, Ohio in 1838. In 1850 they crossed the border to Liberty Township. David died there on 19 Feb 1881 at age 78. Sally was almost 90 when she died on 30 Apr 1892 at Libbie Wright Wyeth's home in Liberty Township. David and Sally are buried there in Liberty Cemetery, Dutch Lane and Liberty Church Roads.

David G. and Sally Kellogg Wyeth's photos are courtesy of their great, great grandson, Charles Arthur "Chuck" Walker. The back of the photos tell of their trip to Licking County on the Erie Canal and state that Sally died at her son Stillman's home.

David G. Wyeth and Sally Kellogg had the following children:

265.   i.   PARKER JUDSON[7] WYETH, born 28 Nov 1826, Wendell, Franklin, Massachusetts; married AMY NASH, 19 Sep 1850,[861] Fredonia, Licking, Ohio; died 10 Sep 1908, Broadway, Union, Ohio.

266.   ii.   HENRY MARBLE WYETH, born 13 Dec 1827, Wendell; married RACHEL MARGERY AVERY, 07 Sep 1854, Liberty Township, Licking, Ohio;[862] died 03 Aug 1911, Salt Lake City, Salt Lake County, Utah.

267.   iii.   STILLMAN SAMUEL WYETH, born 12 Nov 1829, Wendell; married ELIZABETH "LIBBIE" WRIGHT, 01 Dec 1853, McKean Township, Licking, Ohio; died 01 Apr 1891, Liberty Township.

268.   iv.   LUCY SNOW WYETH, born 13 Dec 1830, Wendell; married BENJAMIN FRANKLIN RUNNELS, 25 Jan 1853, McKean Township; died 30 Dec 1878, Hawthorn, Montgomery, Iowa.

269.   v.   GAD KELLOGG WYETH, born 20 Mar 1832, Wendell; married (1) AMANDA CATHERINE SMITH, 07 Apr 1859, Richland County, Ohio; married (2) LORETTA SUSAN "RETTA" WOOD, 07 Aug 1862, Liberty; died there, 17 Sep 1871.

270.   vi.   (REV.) WALTER NEWTON WYETH, born 17 May 1833, Wendell; married (1) ISABELLA EMELINE WAIT, 09 May 1859, Portsmouth, Scioto, Ohio; married (2) CLIMENA MUNSON, 29 May 1866, Marietta, Washington, Ohio; married (3) EMILY WATERMAN M.D., 18 Oct 1888, Philadelphia; died there, 20 Oct 1899.

        vii.   WILLIAM MASON WYETH, born 22 Aug 1834, Wendell; died there, 26 Oct 1836 at age two; buried Wyeth plot on Jennison Road, Wendell.[863]

271.   viii.   DAVID GODDARD WYETH, born 12 Jun 1837, Wendell; married JENNIE NAOMI WRIGHT, 03 Apr 1862, McKean; died 25 May 1912, 585 Hudson Ave., Newark, Ohio.[864]

272.   ix.   EUNICE KENDALL WYETH, born 09 Jan 1839, McKean Township; married (REV.) CHARLES BRYON LEWIS, 13 Mar 1864, Liberty Township;[865] died 18 Nov 1927, Bloomfield, Essex, New Jersey.

        x.   WILLIAM MASON WYETH II, born 19 Jun 1840, McKean Township; died there a few days later on 26 Jun 1840.

This photo of David & Jennie Wyeth at the Liberty Church he built is courtesy of Richard L. Hoffman.

273.   xi.   AUGUSTUS GREENLEAF "A.G." WYETH, born 12 Oct 1841, McKean Township; married (1) EMMA PEARL STRAUGHAN, 30 May 1876, Fort Wayne, Allen, Indiana; married (2) Emma's sister, ALICE F. STRAUGHAN, the widow of Charles Howey, 07 Jul 1909, Mansfield, Richland, Ohio; died 19 Jun 1914, 201 Granville St., Newark, Ohio.

130. LOUISA[6] WYETH (John[5], Ebenezer[4] Jr., Ebenezer[3], John[2], Nicholas[1]) was born on 06 Aug 1796 in Harrisburg, Dauphin, Pennsylvania.[866] Louisa Wyeth and Samuel Douglas were married on 22 Apr 1817 in Harrisburg's Zion German Lutheran Church. SAMUEL DOUGLAS, son of Henry Douglas and Jane Blair, was born on 10 May 1781 in Newtown-Limavady, Londonderry, Northern Ireland.[867] He served in the War of 1812, became a lawyer and rose in 1830 to the rank of attorney general for the state of Pennsylvania. He died just after his term ended on 08 Jul 1833, at age 52, in Harrisburg. Louisa died on 10

Nov 1875 in Chambersburg, Franklin, Pennsylvania. They are buried in Harrisburg Cemetery, section L-34, with their oldest son and three of their daughters, two of whom were infants.

In addition to the infants, Mary McKinley and Jane Blair Douglas, Samuel Douglas and Louisa Wyeth had the following children:

Mary J., J. Wyeth, Mary McKinley and Jane Blair Douglas is engraved on the back of this monument while their parents, Samuel and Louisa, are on the other side.

   i. JOHN WYETH[7] DOUGLAS, born about 1824, Harrisburg; died unmarried 10 (24 per grave) May 1895 at the Union Protestant Infirmary, Baltimore, Maryland, buried in Harrisburg Cemetery.[868]

  ii. JOSEPH DOUGLAS, born about 1825 in Harrisburg; married ELIZABETH BANTON circa 1855; had several children; death unknown.

 iii. LOUISA W. DOUGLAS, born in Mar 1828, Harrisburg; died unmarried 10 Oct 1910, Pikesville, Baltimore, Maryland.[869]

 iv. MARY J. DOUGLAS, born about 1832 in Harrisburg; died there, 02 Apr 1854, buried in Harrisburg Cemetery.

131. **JOHN[6] WYETH JR.** (John[5], Ebenezer[4] Jr., Ebenezer[3], John[2], Nicholas[1]) was born, according to his tombstone, on 06 Jun 1798 in Harrisburg, Dauphin, Pennsylvania. John Wyeth Jr. and **ELMIRA JANE "MYRA JANE" CANFIELD** were married on 18 Mar 1828 in Carlisle, Cumberland, Pennsylvania. Myra Jane Canfield, daughter of Elijah Walker Canfield and Betsey Baldwin, was born on 18 Feb 1811 in Connecticut.[870] Well educated, John Wyeth Jr. earned his living as both a druggist and a lawyer. On 07 Mar 1833, Pennsylvania's Chief Justice Ellis Lewis appointed John Jr. the deputy attorney general for Cumberland County, Pennsylvania. In his younger days, Ellis Lewis had forfeited on an indenture to John Wyeth Sr. at the *Oracle of Dauphin* printing offices.[871] John Wyeth Jr. died at age 77 on 11 May 1876 in Chambersburg, Franklin, Pennsylvania. Myra Jane died there on 16 Aug 1878 at age 67.

John Wyeth Jr. and Myra Jane Canfield had the following children:

274.   i. GERTRUDE[7] WYETH, born 30 May 1833, Carlisle; married WILLIAM FINDLAY SHUNK, 08 Apr 1852, Harrisburg; died there, 11 Dec 1912.

      ii. MARY WYETH, born in 03 May 1838, Harrisburg; died 15 Mar 1927, Susquehanna, Dauphin, Pennsylvania.

275. iii. LOUIS WYETH, born 29 Nov 1840, Harrisburg;[872] married FLORENCE ABIGAIL "ABBY" ROGERS, 19 Jun 1876, Washington, D.C.; died 14 Mar 1923, Pueblo, Pueblo County, Colorado.[873]

     iv. JOHN WESTLAKE WYETH, born 09 Oct 1842, Harrisburg. Served in Co. E and L of the Pennsylvania 9th Cavalry; promoted to 2nd lieutenant on 30 May 1864; mustered out 18 Jul 1865. Married FRANCES ANN "FANNIE" McCULLOUGH, 17 Oct 1878, Chambersburg.[874] Frances, daughter of John Williamson McCullough and Mary Louisa Duncan, was born about 1833 in New York. On 18 Jan 1905, when he applied for a pension, he was 5'8", 155 lbs., with gray eyes and light hair and complexion. He died later that year on 29 Nov 1905 in Front Royal, Warren, Virginia.[875] She died on Easter day, 11 Apr 1909 in Atlantic City, New Jersey.

   v. LUCY DOUGLAS WYETH, born 02 Dec 1845, Harrisburg; died unmarried 06 Nov 1870 at age 24 in Chambersburg.

   vi. ALBERT WYETH was born about 1848 in Harrisburg. While innocently sailing aboard the schooner *Grapeshot* at Falmouth, Jamaica, for benefit of his health, he was forced to land in Santiago, Cuba during the Cuban's Ten-Year War against Spanish rule. Without even the pretense of a trial, Spanish troops executed Albert on 21 Jun 1869. Diplomatic correspondence published in 1870 insisted upon monetary compensation being paid by the Spanish government to Albert's family for his unjustifiable homicide.[876]

   vii. EDWARD WYETH, born 29 Nov 1849 in Harrisburg; died young.

132. **MARY⁶ WYETH** (John⁵, Ebenezer⁴ Jr., Ebenezer³, John², Nicholas¹) was born on 25 Sep 1800 in Harrisburg, Dauphin, Pennsylvania. Mary Wyeth and Daniel McKinley Jr., D.D. were married on 31 May 1827, by Rev. William Radcliff DeWitt, in Harrisburg. **DANIEL MCKINLEY JR.**, son of Daniel McKinley Sr. and Sarah Smith, was born in Oct 1801 in Carlisle, Cumberland, Pennsylvania. Rev. McKinley died on 07 Dec 1855 at age 54 years and two months in Chambersburg, Franklin, Pennsylvania. Mary died there on 15 Jan 1892 at age 91.[877]

Daniel McKinley Jr. and Mary Wyeth had the following children:

276.   i. LOUISA WEISS⁷ MCKINLEY, born 20 Nov 1828, Harrisburg; married JAMES FERGUSON KENNEDY on 06 Jul 1852 in Carlisle; died on 11 Oct 1906 in Chambersburg.

      ii. ESTHER MARY MCKINLEY was born about 1831 in Carlisle; died there on 03 Oct 1838.

133. **FRANCIS⁶ WYETH** (John⁵, Ebenezer⁴ Jr., Ebenezer³, John², Nicholas¹) was born on 05 Apr 1806 in Harrisburg, Dauphin, Pennsylvania. In 1827, Francis graduated from Jefferson College, Canonsburg, Pennsylvania. Francis, having learned the printing trade from his father, John Wyeth, edited the old *Oracle of Dauphin* under its new name, *The Harrisburg Argus,* when he was married by Rev. David Elliott to (1) **SUSAN HOUSTON MAXWELL** on 12 May 1829 in Mercersburg, Franklin, Pennsylvania. Susan, daughter of William Maxwell and Anne Huston, was born 30 Sep 1811 in Mercersburg and baptized there in Jan 1812, according to the records of the Presbyterian Church of The Upper West Conococheague. She died on 24 Dec 1841, at age 29, in Harrisburg.[878] Francis married (2) **SARAH CAMPBELL CARSON** on 13 Mar 1845 in Harrisburg. Sarah, daughter of Charles Smith Carson and Mary Ann Campbell, was born there on 15 Sep 1821.[879] Francis died in Harrisburg on 02 Jul 1893 at age 87.[880] Sarah died there on 18 Sep 1902 at age 81.[881]

This photo of Susan Houston Maxwell Wyeth is courtesy of the Wyeth-Tootle Mansion Museum, St. Joseph, Missouri.

The birth dates for Francis and Susan Houston Maxwell Wyeth's children are from the family Bible held in the care of William Maxwell "Max" Wyeth IV. The Bible also notes the brothers William, John, and Francis had whooping cough in Oct 1836.

        i.   WILLIAM MAXWELL[7] WYETH I, born 17 Apr 1830 in Harrisburg, Dauphin, Pennsylvania; died there, 20 May 1830.

277.   ii. WILLIAM MAXWELL WYETH, born 17 Feb 1832, Harrisburg; married ELIZABETH MORRIS "ELIZA" RENICK, 28 Sep 1858, Chillicothe, Ross, Ohio; in 1859, founded the Wyeth Hardware & Manufacturing Company of St. Joseph, Buchanan, Missouri; died there, 08 Mar 1901.

278.   iii. JOHN WYETH, born 04 May 1834, Harrisburg; married SARAH BELL "SADIE" STEWART, 1862, Chambersburg, Franklin, Pennsylvania; in 1860, founded the prominent drug firm, John Wyeth & Brother, Inc. of Philadelphia; died there, of pneumonia, at his home at 1511 Locust Street on 30 Mar 1907.

279.   iv. FRANCIS HOUSTON "FRANK" WYETH, born 14 Jul 1836, Harrisburg; married HENRIETTA BRAXTON HORNER on 20 Feb 1862 at Holy Trinity Church, Philadelphia; junior partner of John Wyeth & Brother, Inc. of Philadelphia; died there at his home, 1912 Rittenhouse Square, on 12 Jun 1913.[882]

        v.   GEORGE HUSTON WYETH, born 17 Jul 1838, Harrisburg; died there at age three on Christmas morning 1841. His mother had died the day before at 8:00 pm.

Francis Wyeth and Sarah Campbell Carson had the following children:

        i.   CHARLES CARSON[7] WYETH, born 15 May 1848, Harrisburg, Dauphin, Pennsylvania; died there at age three on 31 Jul 1851; buried near his parents in lot 43, space 3, Harrisburg Cemetery.

280.   ii. PARKER CAMPBELL WYETH, born 15 Jun 1854,[883] Harrisburg; married ELLEN ASHTON HORNER, 11 Sep 1890, Warrenton, Fauquier, Virginia; founded Rossi Saddlery Co. in St. Joseph, Buchanan, Missouri; died there, 02 Dec 1928.

Francis Wyeth - photograph courtesy of his third great grandson, William Maxwell "Max" Wyeth IV.

Notes for Francis Wyeth:

Shortly after his first marriage, Francis sold his father's newspaper and went into the business of selling books until 1859. For more than 40 years he served as a trustee of his alma mater, the Harrisburg Academy, 15 of which he held the office of President. He was also an elder of the Pine Street Presbyterian Church in Harrisburg.

During the Civil War, Francis was placed in charge of the quartermaster's department at Harrisburg's Camp Curtin until the government took it over. Then on 20 Jul 1862 Pennsylvania's Governor Curtin appointed him the Dauphin County hospital commissioner to visit the hospitals of the Army of the Potomac in the interest of the volunteer soldiers of the state. Among his many implemented recommendations was bringing the injured home to local hospitals to more readily receive the loving care of their families.[884]

134. CHARLES AUGUSTUS[6] WYETH (John[5], Ebenezer[4] Jr., Ebenezer[3], John[2], Nicholas[1]) was born on 11 Nov 1808 in Harrisburg. Charles married **ADELINE "ADDIE" SHEAFER** there on 12 May 1842. Addie, daughter of Michael Sheafer and Susanna Cloud, was born on 18 Sep 1824 in Lancaster County, Pennsylvania. Due to Augustus being struck by several paralytic strokes, he and Addie moved to their daughter Annie's home in Warren, Warren County, Pennsylvania in 1884. They both died there. Addie was age 62 at her death on 25 Dec 1886.[885] Augustus was age 80 when he died on 02 Aug 1889.[886]

Rev. Charles A. Wyeth, from Simon Woelfly's 1907 paper on the Swatara Institute.

The children Charles and Adeline Sheafer Wyeth included:

281.
 i. CHARLES SHEAFER[7] WYETH, born 01 Mar 1843, Harrisburg; married FRANCES MARIE BURNHAM, 17 Jun 1875, Concord, Ottawa, Kansas; died 26 Dec 1923, Milton, Umatilla, Oregon.
 ii. MARY LOUISA WYETH, born in 1846, Harrisburg; died there, 13 Oct 1884.[887]
 iii. ANNIE FRANCES WYETH, born in 1848, Harrisburg; married DR. JOHN W. CURWEN, 06 Sep 1881, Harrisburg; died 04 Sep 1899, Warren.
 iv. DOUGLAS R. WYETH, born 12 Dec 1851, Tremont, Schuylkill, Pennsylvania; a bookkeeper and a champion chess player;[888] died unmarried 14 Feb 1935, Philadelphia, Philadelphia County, Pennsylvania.

Notes on Rev. Charles Augustus Wyeth and Adeline "Addie" Sheafer:

There is some confusion about the details of Addie's birth. Her obituary says she was 62 at death. That helps to confirm her birthdate; however, the notice says she was born in Wiconisco. Since the well-known Civil War veteran, Major Henry Jackson Sheafer, is Addie's younger brother, details from his biography also apply to Addie. Author William Egle wrote that Henry was born 21 May 1826 in Lancaster County. When he was about six years of age, his father removed to what was then called "Bear Gap," now Wiconisco, in the upper end of Dauphin County.[889]

Turning to Augustus, we find that he first followed in his father's footsteps by being appointed postmaster of Tremont, Schuylkill, Pennsylvania on 19 Dec 1850. However, he soon found he was more suited to teach, to preach and to write. During the years 1861 to 1866, he served as the second principal of Swatara Collegiate Institute in Lebanon County, Pennsylvania. According to a former student of the Institute, Simon Woelfly, the Wyeths had six children including two daughters who apparently died as infants. They are Susan H. Wyeth who died on 20 Jul 1845 and Emma C. Wyeth who died on 25 Oct 1856.[890]

In the spring of 1868, Rev. Charles A. Wyeth returned to Harrisburg to serve as the temporary minister of the Seventh Street Presbyterian Church. After his unanimous election as the church's regular pastor on 05 Mar 1870, he was duly installed on 26 Jun 1870, serving until 12 Jun 1883, when his health failed and he moved to Warren. His name and memory are held in such high esteem that a memorial window was placed in his honor in the church's new building, Covenant Presbyterian Church, erected in 1894 at the corner of Fifth and Peffer Streets.[891]

> When chilling death shall o'er me creep,
> May I, dear Saviour, fall asleep
> Upon Thy gentle breast.
> For there secure from all alarm,
> Protected by Thy mighty arm,
> Alone is perfect rest.
> ~ Rev. Charles A. Wyeth

135. **LOUIS WEISS[6] WYETH** (John[5], Ebenezer[4] Jr., Ebenezer[3], John[2], Nicholas[1]) was born on 20 Jun 1812 in Harrisburg, Dauphin, Pennsylvania. After graduating from the Harrisburg Academy, Louis began the study of law at age 18. Although admitted to the bar in his home state, he relocated to Marshall County, Alabama in 1836 and was elected a county judge there at age 25.[892] Judge Louis Weiss Wyeth and Euphemia Allan were married on 09 Apr 1839 in Huntsville, Madison, Alabama. **EUPHEMIA ALLAN**, daughter of Rev. John Allan and Nancy Hodge, was born on 16 Jul 1817 in Gallatin, Sumner, Tennessee. Although strongly opposed to succession, he served in the Civil War for a short time in Co. E of the 49th Alabama Infantry Regiment.[893] Louis died on 07 Jul 1889 in Guntersville, Marshall, Alabama. Euphemia died there on 27 Dec 1895.[894]

From page 74 of the
1896 *National
Cyclopaedia of American
Biography.*

Judge Louis Weiss Wyeth and Euphemia Allan had the following children:

     i. MARY A.[7] WYETH, born 08 Jan 1840, Alabama; married HUGH CARLISLE, 18 Dec 1861, Guntersville, Marshall, Alabama; died 28 Apr 1922, New York City.

     ii. JOHN ALLAN WYETH I, born 28 Apr 1841, Huntsville, Madison, Alabama; died there a few months later on 20 Nov 1841.[895]

282.   iii. LOUISA WEISS WYETH, born 09 Apr 1843, Guntersville; married CAPTAIN WILLIAM HOUSTON TODD, 23 Nov 1871, Guntersville; died there, 21 Jul 1927.

283.   iv. (DR.) JOHN ALLAN WYETH, born 26 May 1845, Guntersville; served the CSA, Co. I, 4th Regiment, Alabama Cavalry (Russell's), taken prisoner 04 Oct 1863 and confined at Camp Morton, Indiana; severely ill, he returned to the South through a prisoner exchange on 01 Mar 1865;[896] received medical degrees in 1869 from the University of Louisville School of Medicine and in 1873 from New York's Bellevue Hospital Medical College; founded the first post-graduate medical school in the U.S. in 1881;[897] married (1) FLORENCE NIGHTINGALE SIMS, 10 Apr 1886, Manhattan, New York City, New York; married (2) MARGUERITE CHALIFOUX, 15 Nov 1918, Manhattan; died there at his office at 242 Lexington Ave., 28 May 1922.[898]

Notes on Louis Weiss Wyeth and Euphemia Allan:

In a newspaper interview for the celebration of his and Euphemia's 50th wedding anniversary, Judge Wyeth indicated he was called from the bustling Pennsylvania capital of his birth to the wilderness of Marshall County, Alabama for a milder climate.[899] At age 21, he had been admitted to the bar in Carlisle, Pennsylvania and began practicing law in his hometown in 1833.[900] Sickly and frail as a child, Louis saw the opportunity for fairer weather when Cherokee lands were opened for settlement in northern Alabama through the New Echota Treaty signed on 29 Dec 1835.[901] Although the Cherokee National Council did not approve the treaty, it was the basis President Andrew Jackson used to forcibly remove the Cherokee to Oklahoma on the Trail of Tears.[902]

Louis, undoubtedly ignorant of the blight of the Native Americans, set his sights on the new county of Marshall that had been created from a part of the Cherokee land on 09 Jan 1836.[903] Journeying by stage from Harrisburg to Pittsburgh, by steamboat down the Ohio to Louisville,

Kentucky, by stage to Huntsville, Alabama, and on foot for the remainder of the way (for as yet there were only trails in the Cherokee purchase), he arrived in Guntersville on 29 Apr 1836. So impressed were the men of the backwoods, they made 25-year-old Louis a county judge just one year after his arrival. Later he became Marshall's leading law practitioner.[904]

Determined to bring the railroad to grow the county, in 1847, while in the legislature, he secured the charter and became president of the Tennessee & Coosa Railroad. In 1848, he founded Marshall County's seat, Guntersville. To the town, he donated lands for churches and a cemetery, and had built, at his private expense, a brick courthouse and jail.[905] The courthouse was one of the few buildings in the county to survive the Civil War and it remains the core of the 1895 and 1935 enlargements.[906]

This 1888 public domain photograph of the Guntersville, Marshall County, courthouse Louis financed in 1848 comes from the www.alabamapioneers.com website.

The judge opposed secession in 1861, but when the convention voted to join the Confederacy, he gave himself to the cause. Although beyond the legal military age, he volunteered and served at the front until a serious illness left him unfit for duty. However, in an effort to repel Sherman's 1864 invasion of Georgia, he again volunteered in the state troops.[907]

Even though they owned slaves, Louis and Euphemia morally opposed slavery as well. With strong Presbyterian religious convictions, they would have preferred to hire domestic servants. Of course, Louis, had been born and bred in the North and Euphemia's father, Rev. John Allan, not only organized the first slavery emancipation society in Alabama, but also published an anti-slavery newspaper. Unfortunately, there were no white domestic servants or freed blacks to hire in Alabama.[908] By that time the Alabama Supreme Court had ruled a master did not even have the right to emancipate slaves by last will or other legal instruments. Additionally, Alabama law required all emancipated slaves be transported to Liberia or to a free U.S. state.[909] Indicating their devotion to the Wyeths, their slaves refused to leave when freed by advancing Union troops.[910]

After the war, Louis tirelessly worked to feed those left hungry and desperate by the Civil War in his adopted state. In a letter dated 02 Apr 1866 to the Alabama governor, Wyeth detailed plans to seek aid in cities such as Nashville, Louisville, and Cincinnati to help 3,000 starving citizens in Marshall County.[911] Newspapers advanced the judge's quest. Here is part of one such notice in the Louisville *Courier-Journal* – "Give freely of your abundant store ... Send the missionary back to his now unhappy home burdened with munificent gifts that shall gladden the hearts – nay, preserve the liver – of thousands who are ready to welcome death as their friend."[912]

In 1874, Louis was elected judge of the Fifth Judicial Circuit and served eight years, declining re-election. A couple of years into that service, with flooding in the area closing roads and limiting steamboat transportation, it appeared there would be a delay in opening the circuit court on time. Undaunted, the 63-year-old got a canoe and paddled 30 miles from Guntersville to Huntsville, Alabama. He arrived Sunday night and opened the court, as scheduled, on Monday morning.[913] In 1883, Louis was offered the Chief Justiceship of the Supreme Court of Alabama but turned it down. He was a director in the Wyeth City Land Co., from which the town of Wyeth City, Alabama was named for him.[914] Unfortunately, a few years after Louis' death, much of Wyeth City was flattened by a tornado.[915] However, today it is incorporated into Guntersville proper. There the Guntersville Museum & Cultural Center displays their gratitude for the judge's contributions with a Wyeth Room dedicated to members of the Wyeth family.[916]

For several weeks after his death, praises filled Alabama newspapers. One tribute, in particular, seems to sum up the remarkable judge best – "Beloved of all Classes."[917]

136.   **SAMUEL DOUGLASS**[6] **WYETH** (John[5], Ebenezer[4] Jr., Ebenezer[3], John[2], Nicholas[1]) was born on 16 May 1817 in Harrisburg, Dauphin, Pennsylvania. He learned the printing trade from his father and became a journalist in Philadelphia. Samuel married Caroline Churchill Wardwell on 11 Sep 1844 in Smithfield, Providence, Rhode Island. [918] **CAROLINE "CARRIE" CHURCHILL WARDWELL**, daughter of George Smith Wardwell and Rebecca Jenks Churchill, was born on 23 Jun 1824 in Rhode Island. When Carrie left him in 1862, after his stereotype printing business failed, Samuel settled in Washington, D.C. There he set up a souvenir shop in the Capitol dome and wrote pamphlets on the capital city, including 1865's *The Federal City*. He died there on 15 Jan 1881 at age 63. His obituary said he was a highly cultured gentleman possessed of a keen intellect, albeit somewhat eccentric. After their split, Carrie never saw her husband again.[919] She died on 07 May 1908 in East Orange, Essex, New Jersey and was buried in nearby Montclair's Rosedale Cemetery in Wardwell lot 14. Samuel was buried in the Falling Spring Presbyterian Church Cemetery, Chambersburg, Pennsylvania.

According to the 1900 census, Samuel Douglass Wyeth and Caroline Churchill Wardwell had seven children. All but Marlborough are buried in Rosedale Cemetery. They are:

284.   i.   GEORGE WARDWELL[7] WYETH, born 04 Jan 1846, Philadelphia, Philadelphia County, Pennsylvania; married (1) FRANCES IDA BARBE, 21 Sep 1875, Philadelphia; married (2) ANNA R. GINTER, about 22 Sep 1917, Baltimore, Maryland; died 10 Oct 1929, Brooklyn, Kings County, New York.[920]

       ii.   REBECCA CHURCHILL WYETH, born 28 Oct 1847, Philadelphia; married (1) Henry Spalding on 17 Nov 1875 in Montclair, Essex, New Jersey. HENRY SPALDING died four days after the wedding on 21 Nov 1875, at age 43, in Washington, D.C.[921] His will was written the day of his marriage. He was born 19 Feb 1832 in Rhode Island to Brigham Spalding and Lucretia Loveridge. Rebecca married (2) Allen Wardwell, 31 Jan 1891 at St. Andrew's Episcopal Church, 2067 5th Avenue at 127th Street in the Harlem neighborhood of Manhattan. ALLEN WARDWELL, son of William Taylor Wardwell and Mary Harvey, was born in Jun 1837 in Michigan. His daughter with his first wife, Margaret Louise Wilkeson Wardwell (1868-1928), married Maxwell Wyeth (1866-1936). Rebecca died on 09 Jul 1900 at age 52 in Brooklyn, Kings, New York.[922] Allen died on 29 Apr 1910 at age 72 in New York City.

       iii.   FRANCES JANE HOWE "FANNIE" WYETH, born 30 Oct 1849, Philadelphia;[923] a school teacher; died unmarried 16 Sep 1891 in New York City.[924]

       iv.   ANNIE WARDWELL WYETH, born 21 Jan 1852, Camden, Camden County, New Jersey; died 23 Jan 1933 in Montclair, Essex, New Jersey.[925]

285.   v.   JOHN DOUGLAS WYETH, born 17 Sep 1853, Camden; married FANNIE JOHNSON OSBORN, 27 Feb 1894, New York City; died 23 Sep 1924, East Orange.[926]

286.   vi.   MARLBOROUGH CHURCHILL WYETH M.D., born 16 Sep 1855, Woonsocket,

Providence, Rhode Island; married LUCIA ORA HORTON, 03 Apr 1888, Augusta, Richmond, Georgia; died 14 May 1924, New York City.

vii. WILLIAM LORRAINE WYETH, was born 12 May 1858 in Camden. On 24 Jan 1889 he appeared at the Tombs Court in Manhattan charged with larceny.[927] He was then living in the city at 37 W. 124th St. His relative, William T. Wardwell, who was Prohibition

Mother Caroline rests between her two children who died in 1891. Fannie is on her right and William is on her left in Rosedale Cemetery, 408 Orange Road, Orange, New Jersey.

candidate for Mayor of New York, signed his bail bond.[928] Cleared, William moved to Kansas City, Missouri. He died there unmarried on 01 Sep 1891.[929]

Photo courtesy of NEHGS Mss A 3058 file presumed to be Jonas Wyeth 2d.

137. **JONAS[6] WYETH 2[D]** (Major Jonas[5], Jonas[4] Sr., Ebenezer[3], John[2], Nicholas[1]) was born on 14 Dec 1806 on an estate in Cambridge, Middlesex, Massachusetts owned by the Wyeth family, near the town common, for upwards of a century and a half.[930] Jonas Wyeth 2d married (1) his second cousin, **MARY TORREY HANCOCK**, on 01 Jan 1833 in Cambridge. Mary daughter of Torrey Hancock and Isabella Rice, was born on 10 Jun 1812 in Cambridge. Represented by the famous attorney, Daniel Webster, Jonas attempted to divorce Mary in Cambridge in 1848.[931] Unable to do so, Jonas went west to divorce Mary on 31 Oct 1851 in Des Moines County, Iowa.[932] Jonas Wyeth 2d married (2) **SARAH ELIZABETH BENSON**, the widow of Malthus Augustus Johnson on 02 May 1854. Their wedding was solemnized by Erastus Ripley in Scott County, Iowa.[933] Sarah daughter of John Benson and Sarah Buck, was born 22 Sep 1815 in Bucksport, Hancock, Maine. After their marriage was dissolved in 1857, when Jonas refused to return to Iowa for a bigamy trial because his 1851 divorce there from Mary had been invalidated, Sarah assumed her previous married name.[934] Jonas returned to Mary. The 1860 census showed Mary and Jonas living in their newly built home on Raymond Street. Artist, N. C. Wyeth's mother, Henriette "Hattie" Zirngiebel, then a two-year-old toddler, lived nearby.[935] Jonas died there of peritonitis on 03 Jun 1868. Sarah died at her novelist daughter Virginia Wales Johnson's home in Florence, Italy on 26 Nov 1891. Mary died 16 Nov 1904, at age 92, in Marblehead, Essex, Massachusetts.

Jonas Wyeth 2d and Mary Torrey Hancock had the following children:

287. i. LUCY COOLIDGE[7] WYETH, born 25 Oct 1833, Cambridge, Middlesex, Massachusetts; married JONATHAN WHEELER BEMIS M.D., 16 Nov 1859, Cambridge; died there on 09 May 1899.

288. ii. JOSEPHINE AUGUSTA WYETH, born 27 May 1835, Cambridge;[936] married WILLIAM BRACKETT STEARNS there, 15 Dec 1858; died 25 Feb 1899, Marblehead, of liver cancer at age 63.

289. iii. EDWIN AUGUSTUS WYETH, born 21 Nov 1840, Philadelphia; married ELIZABETH JANE TILTON, the widow of Charles Erving Davis, on 25 May 1870, Boston; died there, 05 Mar 1917.

138. **EMELY**[6] **WYETH**, (Major Jonas[5], Jonas[4] Sr., Ebenezer[3] Sr., John[2], Nicholas[1]) per her father's handwritten records, was born on 12 Sep 1809 in Cambridge, Middlesex, Massachusetts. Emely Wyeth and **JAMES BARNARD READ** were married there on 09 Nov 1828.[937] James Barnard Read, son of James Read and Mary Stebbins Brown, was born on 26 Aug 1802 in Tobago, West Indies. Emely died on 19 Sep 1864 at age 55 in Boston.[938] He died on 24 Sep 1883 at age 81 in Wilton, Hillsborough, New Hampshire. They are buried in Mt. Auburn Cemetery, Cambridge. Her name is spelled "Emily" on her stone.

James Barnard Read and Emely Wyeth had the following children:

1st Lt. Read photo attached to VT roster courtesy of Ed Italo.

    i. CHARLES AUGUSTUS[7] READ, based on his age at death, he was born 30 May 1833, Cambridge; baptized there 29 Dec 1833; mustered in 4th Reg. Vermont Infantry during the Civil War in Cavendish, Vermont on 21 Sep 1861, promoted to 1st Lt. of Co. F on 17 Jul 1862, mustered out 02 Jan 1863;[939] married MARY A. MARSON, 21 Oct 1868, Boston; died there, 19 Oct 1869.

    ii. GEORGE JAMES READ, baptized with brother Charles on 29 Dec 1833, Cambridge; death unknown.

    iii. EDWIN BARNARD READ, baptized 05 Jul 1835, Cambridge; died there on 21 Oct 1838; buried on Yarrow Path in Mt. Auburn Cemetery near his brother Charles and his parents who are on Saffron Path.

    iv. EMILY BARNARD READ, born 21 May 1838, Cambridge; married CHARLES CARROLL PEARSON, 11 Dec 1866, Boston; died 05 Sep 1919, Arlington, Middlesex, Massachusetts; buried Concord, Merrimack, New Hampshire.

139. **MARY KEMBLE THOMAS**[6] **WYETH** (Captain Noah[5], Noah[4] Sr., Ebenezer[3] Sr., John[2], Nicholas[1]) was born on 12 Aug 1801 in New York City, New York County, New York.[940] Mary Kemble Thomas Wyeth and John Spencer Hadley were married there on 03 Jun 1820 in the Dutch Reformed Church. **JOHN SPENCER HADLEY**, son of Isaac Hadley and Ann Sumacher, was born on 23 Jul 1796 in Yonkers, Westchester, New York.[941] He and many members of his family were successful in the crockery, china, and glass business. John died in New York City on 30 Apr 1864 at age 67.[942] Per the 1880 census mortality schedules, Mary died there at 47 West 52nd St. on 23 Mar 1880 of pneumonia at age 78.

John Spencer Hadley and Mary Kemble Thomas Wyeth were living in New York City for the 1820 census of the year they married. Thus, all the following children were born in Manhattan:

    i. ELISABETH JANE "ELIZA"[7] HADLEY, born 1821; married JOHN AUGUSTUS RISLEY,[943] in New York City on 31 Jan 1843; died there at 126 East 78th St. on 15 Jan 1900 at age 79.

    ii. CORNELIA HADLEY, born 27 Apr 1827; married LUCIEN B. TERRY, 14 Jan 1854, New York City; death unknown.[944]

290.   iii. WASHINGTON HADLEY, born 18 Jul 1829, married (1) MARY ELIZABETH DAVIS, 08 Jun 1854, New York City; married (2) ANNE WOOD, 1865; died 11 Jun 1913, New York City; buried in the Green-Wood Cemetery Catacombs in Brooklyn with his parents, wives and youngest son, John A. Hadley.

291.   iv. EMILY LOUISE HADLEY, born 01 Oct 1832;[945] married CHARLES H. WHITFIELD,

02 Jun 1854, New York City; died there at 27 W. 84th on 24 Sep 1913.[946]

     v. MARTHA TIEMANN HADLEY, born 17 Dec 1838, married CHARLES HENRY LOWERRE, 12 Nov 1862;[947] died 20 Nov 1914, 17 W. 76th St., New York City.[948]

292.   vi. HENRY CLAY HADLEY, born 02 Aug 1840;[949] married FRANCES "FANNIE" ELTON, 06 Jun 1866 in the Madison Square Church, New York City; died 03 May 1905, Brooklyn;[950] buried there in the Green-Wood Cemetery Catacombs.

293.   vii. CHARLES LEIGH HADLEY, born 29 Nov 1842; he served in Co. B of the 7th New York Regiment during the Civil War; married SARAH ANN MARTIN, 09 Dec 1871, New York City; died there on 18 Nov 1918.[951]

140. **NOAH⁶ WYETH III** (Captain Noah⁵, Noah⁴ Sr., Ebenezer³ Sr., John², Nicholas¹) was born on 28 Aug 1804 in New York City, New York County, New York. Like his father, he was a mariner. Seamen's Protection Certificates were issued to him at ages 11 and 21. Noah Wyeth III and Mary Kemble Johnson were married in New York City circa 1843. **MARY KEMBLE JOHNSON** was baptized there in Sep 1808 at Christ Episcopal Church on Broadway and 71st Streets.[952] According to the 1870 mortality schedule for Castleton, Richmond, New York, Noah died of paralysis there. Specifically, his *New York Herald* obituary states he died 18 Feb 1870 on Staten Island at Sailor's Snug Harbor, New Brighton (Richmond County) and was interred in Green-Wood Cemetery in Brooklyn.[953] Notice of her death on 19 Feb 1875 stated, "Mrs. Mary K. Johnson, widow of Noah Wyeth, aged 66 years." The funeral was held at her late residence, 102 Ludlow St., near Delancy on the Lower East Side of Manhattan.[954]

The children of Noah Wyeth III and Mary Kemble Johnson included:

     i. HANNAH ELIZABETH⁷ WYETH, born 20 Mar 1845, New York City; baptized there 02 Aug 1846; died young.[955]

     ii. MARY LUCRETIA WYETH, born circa 1849, New York City; married SOLOMON LEVI there on 29 Jul 1874. Marriage record #4875 states Solomon, age 24, was a merchant in and a resident of Baltimore. Mary, also age 24, was a resident of New York City. The license was signed there in the presence of Mary K. D. Johnson Wyeth. Mary Lucretia died 22 Nov 1882, New York City.[956]

141. **MARY FROTHINGHAM⁶ NEWELL** (Elizabeth⁵ Wyeth, Noah⁴ Sr., Ebenezer³ Sr., John², Nicholas¹) was born on 22 Aug 1787 in Charlestown, Suffolk, Massachusetts.[957] Mary Frothingham Newell and Anthony Tiemann were married on 28 Apr 1804 in New York City. He was born Johann Anton Tiemann, on 11 Nov 1778 in Karlshofen, Hesse, Germany to Johann Daniel Tiemann and Anna Gertrude Stubecke. Once in America, he shortened his name to **ANTHONY TIEMANN**. The funeral of Mary's mother, Elizabeth Wyeth Newell, was held in Manhattan on 13 Apr 1829 at the house of Anthony Tiemann, Bloomingdale Road, which was then part of Broadway.[958] Anthony died on 23 Dec 1862 at age 84 in New York City. Mary died there on 27 Dec 1864 at age 77.[959]

Per *Horns A'Plenty,* by Agnes McClellan Grousset (Anthony Tiemann and Mary Frothingham Newell's descendant), the Tiemann children were all born in New York City. They included:[960]

     i. DANIEL FAWCETT⁷ TIEMANN, born 09 Jan 1805; married MARTHA CLOWES, 30

Aug 1826, New York City; served as mayor of New York City, 1858-1860; owned Manhattanville Paint & Color Works, a company started by his father in 1804; died 29 Jun 1899, New York City.[961]

294.   ii. ELIZABETH ANNA GERTRUDE TIEMANN, born 14 Sep 1808; married ALBERT HORN, 27 Dec 1825; died 28 Aug 1897, Mt. Vernon, Westchester, New York.

295.   iii. JULIA TIEMANN, born 03 Mar 1811; married JOHN STEPHENSON, 09 Jan 1833, New York City; died 27 Feb 1891, New Rochelle, Westchester, New York.

        iv. NICHOLAS STRIPPEL TIEMANN, born 21 Jul 1813; married MARY ROTHGANGLE, 28 Jul 1835, Rochester, Monroe, New York; died 11 Oct 1891, Bronx, New York City, New York.

296.   v.   JULIUS WILLIAM TIEMANN, born 15 Aug 1817; married (1) JANE WAUGH STEPHENSON, 27 Aug 1838, New York City; married (2) MARIE ANTOINETTE MEGIE, 28 Mar 1860, Boonton, Morris, New Jersey; died 14 Feb 1903, New York City.

        vi. ANDREW NEWELL TIEMANN, born 03 Jul 1819; died 15 Sep 1820, New York City at age one.

142. **NOAH L.^{6} WYETH** (Captain Job^5, Noah^4 Sr., Ebenezer^3 Sr., John^2, Nicholas^1) was born on 13 Apr 1805 in Cambridge. He was baptized there with his mother, Lydia Convers Francis, at First Church on 25 Jul 1805.[962] Noah married Lucy Harvey on 01 Dec 1836 in Nashua, Hillsborough, New Hampshire. **LUCY HARVEY**, daughter of Silas Harvey and Dorothy Cushman, was born on 26 Oct 1811 in Waterford, Caledonia, Vermont. Noah, a baker by trade, patented a dough kneading machine in Hingham, Plymouth, Massachusetts on 12 May 1834.[963] Lucy died of dropsy on 02 Oct 1863 in Lunenburg, Worcester, Massachusetts. Noah died of heart disease on 31 Aug 1866 at 20 Lawrence Street, Boston.

Noah L. Wyeth and Lucy Harvey had the following children:

297.   i.   EMELINE FRANCES^7 WYETH, born 13 Sep 1838,[964] Nashua, Hillsborough, New Hampshire; married (1) ALPHONSE D. TITUS, 24 Oct 1860, Boston, Suffolk, Massachusetts; married (2) OTIS HARRINGTON BOWLER, 24 Jul 1867, Charlestown, Suffolk, Massachusetts; died 22 Nov 1900, Pasadena, California.

        ii. NATHANIEL FRANCIS WYETH, born 18 Jul 1840, Nashua; drowned there in a well on 20 May 1843.[965]

298.   iii. MARY ELIZABETH WYETH, born 11 Mar 1842, Nashua; married WILLIAM A. CARPENTER III, 26 Dec 1877, Somerville, Middlesex, Massachusetts; died 19 Mar 1929, Potsdam, St. Lawrence, New York.

        iv. RICHARD HARVEY WYETH, twin of William, was born 17 Jan 1844 in Nashua. When he enlisted in the 1st Mass. Cavalry, Co. A, on 10 Sep 1861 in Boston, Richard was described as 5 ft., 11 inches, having hazel eyes, dark brown hair and a

In Cambridge Cemetery, the graves of Noah L. Wyeth, Lucy Harvey, Alphonse and Lucy Titus, Emeline Frances Titus Bowler, Otis Bowler, Annie Caroline, Lucy Catherine and Noah Lyman Wyeth, surround the memorial for twins, Richard and William.

dark complexion. At first it was thought he deserted, but he was, in fact, discharged on 01 Apr 1863 by a Writ of Habeas Corpus due to being a minor at enlistment. Richard reenlisted on 25 Feb 1864 in Co. D of the 3rd Cavalry in Brookline, Massachusetts. The town records show he died later that year while being held a prisoner. Sadly, a memorial marker in Cambridge Cemetery and a War Dept. notation dated Washington, 13 Apr 1878, confirms he died in action on 19 Sep 1864 in (the 3rd Battle of) Winchester, Virginia.[966]

v. WILLIAM HENRY WYETH (twin), born 17 Jan 1844 in Nashua, was only 18 when his father consented on 15 Aug 1862 in Lunenburg, Worcester, Massachusetts for him to join Co. A of the 1st Mass. Cavalry. Enlistment records show he and his twin were not identical. William had a light complexion, gray eyes, brown hair and was 6 ft. tall. Captured on 17 Jun 1863 at the Battle of Aldie, Virginia, he was paroled a few days later. On 04 Jan 1864, William re-enlisted in Co. B of the same cavalry at Warrenton, Fauquier, Virginia. As a veteran volunteer, he received $110, a larger than usual bounty.[967] His memorial tombstone in Cambridge Cemetery says he was killed at the Battle of Lee's Mills, Virginia. The 1st Mass. Cavalry fought there on 30 Jul 1864 at the start of nine months of trench warfare led by U.S. Grant in the Richmond–Petersburg Campaign.[968] However, a War Dept. record dated Washington, 25 Feb 1890, states, "this soldier was captured at Petersburg, Va., 26 Jun 1864 and confined at Florence, South Carolina on 02 Oct 1864. Investigation fails to elicit further information."[969]

vi. ANNIE CAROLINE WYETH, born 01 Dec 1846 in Cambridge; was unmarried when she took her own life on 19 Apr 1891 at age 44 in Cambridge. Her residence at the time was Taunton, Middlesex, Massachusetts.

vii. LUCY CATHERINE WYETH, born on 13 Sep 1849 in Boston; retired after a lifetime of teaching in Cambridge; died on 31 Jul 1920 in Potsdam.

viii. NOAH LYMAN WYETH, born 12 Aug 1855, Somerville; died there, 29 Jan 1878.

143. **ABIEL⁶ WYETH** (Captain Job⁵, Noah⁴ Sr., Ebenezer³ Sr., John², Nicholas¹) was born on 23 Apr 1809 in Cambridge. Abiel Wyeth and Mary Fillebrown were married there on 29 Dec 1831. **MARY FILLEBROWN**, daughter of Edward Fillebrown and Elizabeth Barrett, was born in 1808 in Cambridge. Abiel died there on 11 Aug 1841 at age 32. Mary then married Solomon Sargent of Rockingham, Vermont. She died in Cambridge on 07 Jul 1866.

Abiel Wyeth and Mary Fillebrown had the following children:

i. EDWARD FRANCIS⁷ WYETH, born 27 Nov 1832, Cambridge; married FRANCES "FANNIE" WILBUR, 27 Apr 1867, New York City, New York. New York marriage record #2211 states Edward, a hotel keeper, age 34 and Fanny, age 21, both are residents of New York City. Frances "Fannie" Wilbur was born about 1846 in Boston, Suffolk, Massachusetts. Her death is unknown but Edward died 17 Nov 1895 in Boston.

ii. CHARLES WYETH, born 14 Apr 1837, Cambridge; died there, 01 Apr 1861.[970] He is buried with his parents and brother in lot 3040 on Evergreen Path in Mt. Auburn Cemetery, Cambridge.

144. **BENJAMIN FRANCIS[6] WYETH** (Captain Job[5], Noah[4] Sr., Ebenezer[3] Sr., John[2], Nicholas[1]) was born on 31 Mar 1812 in Cambridge, Middlesex, Massachusetts. Benjamin Francis Wyeth and Zoa Ann Dunton were married there on 07 Apr 1836. **ZOA ANN DUNTON**, daughter of Rhodes Dunton and Millie Walker, was born on 08 Jan 1814 in Ashby, Middlesex, Massachusetts. In 1850, after serving as a RR depot master, Benjamin established the Wyeth undertaking business in Cambridge. In 1851, he began serving as the sexton of the Shepard Congregational Society. The Shepard Society, now called First Church in Cambridge (Congregational), is part of the United Church of Christ.[971] Benjamin was also an overseer of the poor. Zoa died on 30 May 1875 in Cambridge. Benjamin died there on 06 Jul 1890 at age 78.

Zoa and Benjamin Wyeth, circa 1865. Photograph courtesy of the Cambridge Historical Commission.

Benjamin Francis Wyeth and Zoa Ann Dunton had the following children:

299.　　i.　LYDIA FRANCES[7] WYETH, born 13 Jan 1837, Cambridge; married LEVI H. WEST there, 08 Feb 1865; died 20 Apr 1920, Cambridge.[972]

　　　　ii.　ZOA ANN WYETH, born 05 Aug 1838, Cambridge; died there unmarried on 03 Jul 1926 at age 87.

　　　　iii.　JOHN BOUND WYETH I, born 04 Sep 1839, Cambridge; died there, 06 Jul 1840.

300.　　iv.　JOHN BOUND WYETH, born 18 Feb 1842, Cambridge; served in the 12th Mass. Infantry during the Civil War; married EMMA REBECCA EINWECHTER, 06 Jan 1881, Philadelphia, Philadelphia County, Pennsylvania; died 22 Jul 1926, Haddon Heights, Camden, New Jersey.[973]

301.　　v.　ABIEL AUGUSTUS WYETH, born 21 Nov 1843, Cambridge; he served in both the 1st and the 62nd Mass. Infantry; married ALICE SNOW HODGES, 13 Sep 1876, Chelsea, Suffolk, Massachusetts; died 18 Oct 1895, Cambridge.

302.　　vi.　BENJAMIN FRANKLIN WYETH SR., born 27 Dec 1845, Cambridge; enlisted with his brother, John, in the 12th Mass. Infantry on 16 May 1864; he married CAROLINE ELIZABETH BIRD on 12 Oct 1876 in Watertown, Middlesex, Massachusetts; died 07 Aug 1909, Cambridge.

　　　　vii.　HENRY ALONZO WYETH, born 01 Jul 1847, Cambridge; married MARY ELLA GRAFTON there on 27 Sep 1870. They both died in Cambridge. He at age 57 on 10 Sep 1904 and she at age 79 on 30 Nov 1926.

　　　　viii.　ALICE AMELIA WYETH I (twin), born 24 Apr 1852, Cambridge; died an infant there on 22 Oct 1852.

　　　　ix.　AGNES MARIA WYETH born 24 Apr 1852, Cambridge; married there ALBERT FRANCIS "FRANK" PUTNEY, son of Albert Putney and Nancy Higgins, on 03 Jul 1890. He was born on 20 Feb 1857 in Cambridge. Agnes died there on 18 Jan 1891. His death date is unknown.

　　　　x.　ALICE AMELIA WYETH, born 17 Jan 1857, Cambridge; secretary to Charles W. Eliot, the president of Harvard College; retired as keeper of Harvard's official records; died unmarried on 29 Apr 1958, at age 101, in Cambridge's home for aged people.

Alice Amelia Wyeth - photo from the HUP Collection, courtesy Harvard University Archives.

145. **ANDREW NEWELL[6] WYETH SR.** (Captain Job[5], Noah[4] Sr., Ebenezer[3] Sr., John[2], Nicholas[1]) was born on 29 Apr 1817 in Cambridge, Middlesex, Massachusetts. Whereas his brother Benjamin stayed with the Congregationists at the split of the Cambridge church and eventually became their sexton, Andrew joined the Unitarians in 1831. Rev. William Newell, Cambridge's first avowedly Unitarian minister, married Andrew Newell Wyeth Sr. and Amelia Hepzibah Bigelow Stimson there on 04 May 1843. **AMELIA HEPZIBAH BIGELOW STIMSON**, daughter of Royal Stimson and Leaffa Relief Walker, was born in Cambridge on 05 Apr 1818. Amelia died on 22 Feb 1891 at age 72 in Cambridge. Andrew died there of heart failure on Good Friday, 13 Apr 1900, at age 82.[974] He was buried near Amelia in Cambridge Cemetery on Easter Monday, 16 Apr 1900.[975]

Andrew Newell Wyeth Sr. and Amelia Hepzibah Bigelow Stimson had the following children:

303.   i.   AMELIA ANNIE[7] WYETH, born 04 Jan 1846, Cambridge; married JOHN BARKER, 08 Apr 1869, Cambridge; died there, 06 Oct 1903.

          ii. SUSAN ELIZABETH WYETH, born 28 Dec 1847, Cambridge; retired in 1917 from teaching after 48 years – 30 years of which as principal of Cambridge's Dunster School.[976] She died on 26 Sep 1934 at the age of 86 in Milford, Hillsborough, New Hampshire and is buried near her parents in Cambridge.

304.   iii. ANDREW NEWELL WYETH JR., born 02 Feb 1853, Cambridge; married HENRIETTE "HATTIE" ZIRNGIEBEL on 21 Dec 1881 in Needham, Norfolk, Massachusetts; died there, 29 Jul 1929.

          iv. HARRIET CONVERS WYETH, born 21 Jul 1855, Cambridge; died there unmarried on 01 Mar 1923, buried with Susan in Cambridge Cemetery.

Because they also provide a sketch of early Cambridge, notes for Andrew Newell Wyeth Sr. are quoted verbatim from "An Octogenarian" in the 01 May 1897 *Cambridge Chronicle*:

"Mr. Andrew N. Wyeth, of 23 Wyeth Street, entered the ranks of Cambridge octogenarians on Thursday, when the 80th anniversary of his birth was very quietly marked by an informal family gathering of about 25 at his pleasant home that evening. A representative of the *Chronicle* of which Mr. Wyeth has been a steady reader since the paper was started by John Ford in 1846, called upon him Thursday morning and enjoyed a half hour's chat with him. Mr. Wyeth does not look the man of his years, being of a hale appearance and remarkably active for the time of life which he has now reached. He has lived a busy, successful life, and is a true son of Cambridge, where he was born and has always lived. His birthplace is within a stone's throw of his present residence which is located on a part of what was then a large farm owned by his father, and since cut up into streets and building lots.

As a boy, Mr. Wyeth attended school in Cambridge, one of his teachers being a Mr. Worcester, brother of the Worcester of dictionary fame. At the age of sixteen he began work in Cambridgeport as an apprentice in the making of chaise furnishings, which business he learned. But the development of the Fitchburg railroad soon claimed his attention, and he found himself in 1843 looking after the construction of a branch road from Charlestown to Fresh Pond which was constructed for carrying ice. Later he was appointed the first station agent at Porter's Station when the Harvard branch of the Fitchburg Road was road was opened running from this city to Somerville and connecting with trains for Boston. In 1868, Porter's Hotel was built and the cattle market was opened and it now fell to the lot of Mr. Wyeth to have charge of all the cattle trains at that point. He was succeeded at the station by Mr. John Murray. Mr. Wyeth's next move in railroading was to go to the large Fitchburg freight yard in Charlestown, where he had charge until 1881. At that time, he retired from the exacting duties to which his energies had been so long applied, and for seven years, until 1888, he assisted cashier Milton L. Walton, at the North Avenue Savings Bank.

Mr. Wyeth was married in 1843 to Amelia B. Stimson, who lived on Concord Ave. Mrs. Wyeth died in 1891. Four children are living. They are Miss Susan E. Wyeth a teacher in the Dunster School, Miss Hattie Wyeth who lives at home, Mrs. John Barker, and Mr. Andrew N. Wyeth Jr.

When Mr. Wyeth was a boy, his father's farm covered the large tract of land which now is thickly built up with houses, and he can see two very different pictures as he thinks of the former day and this. He can easily remember the days when Cambridge was a quiet town, and his collection of old town documents reveal many interesting facts. By the town treasurer's statement of 1833-34, the total expenses of the town for that year were $16,382.89, not quite the "budget" which the Cambridge city council of 1897 is just through discussing. Another piece of antiquity is a time table of the old "Harvard Branch Railroad," printed at the *Chronicle Press*.

Mr. Wyeth is a brother of the late sexton Wyeth, who served the Shepard Memorial church for so many years and an uncle of the well-known Old Cambridge undertakers, Henry A. and Benjamin F. Wyeth. Since 1831, he has constantly attended the First Parish church, where he remembers the able preaching of Rev. Dr. Holmes, father of Oliver Wendell Holmes, and that of Rev. Dr. Newell. Mr. Wyeth's good health and keen interest in affairs betoken what all hope for him, many years in the period of life which he has now begun."[977]

146. **LYDIA WOODWARD**[6] **WYETH** (Jonathan[5], Noah[4] Sr., Ebenezer[3] Sr., John[2], Nicholas[1]) was born on 28 Apr 1812 in Watertown, Middlesex, Massachusetts. Lydia Woodward / Woodard Wyeth and Alpha Sawyer were married on 10 May 1835 in Boston, Suffolk, Massachusetts. Born there in 1811, **ALPHA SAWYER** was the son of Paul Sawyer and Keziah Hunnewell. Lydia died in 1857 at age 45. He died on 08 Apr 1883 in Boston. They are buried with daughter Mary Jane in Forest Hills Cemetery, Jamaica Plain, Massachusetts.

Alpha Sawyer and Lydia Woodward Wyeth adopted the following child:

> i. MARY JANE[7] WYETH, born circa 1848 in Boston (probably to Hollis Nye Wyeth and Mary Jane Stiles); died 16 Jun 1851. Quoting deaths shown in *The Boston Daily Atlas* of 19 Jun 1851, "At West Newton, 16th inst, Mary Jane Wyeth, adopted daughter of Alpha and Lydia Sawyer, two years, seven months."[978]

147. **NAHUM SARGENT**[6] **WYETH** (Jonathan[5], Noah[4] Sr., Ebenezer[3] Sr., John[2], Nicholas[1]) was born on 12 Jul 1818 in Moretown, Washington, Vermont. Nahum Sargent Wyeth and Elvira Perses Phillips were married on 29 Nov 1843 in Boston. **ELVIRA PERSES PHILLIPS**, daughter of Joseph D. Phillips and his wife Sarah, was born on 05 Aug 1824 in Decatur, Otsego, New York. Nahum, a baker, had such difficulties with his business that he filed bankruptcy on 08 Dec 1873.[979] Elvira died on 31 Aug 1879 at age 55 in Boston. Nathum died there on 03 Nov 1882 at age 64. He willed his daughter and siblings, Martha, Sarah and Hollis, $1 each and left the rest to the Odd Fellows of Boston.

Nahum Sargent Wyeth and Elvira Perses Phillips had the following children:

> i. GEORGE R.[7] WYETH, born about 02 Jun 1845 in Boston; died there of bowel disease at age three months on 02 Sep 1845.

305. ii. MARY H. WYETH, born 17 Oct 1846, Boston; married ELI A. LITHGOW there on 23 May 1877; died 29 Jan 1901, New Haven County, Connecticut.

iii. NAHUM F. WYETH, born 08 Oct 1851, Boston; died there an infant 27 Oct 1851.

148. **HOLLIS NYE[6] WYETH** (Jonathan[5], Noah[4] Sr., Ebenezer[3] Sr., John[2], Nicholas[1]) was born on 23 Jul 1822 in Fayston, Washington, Vermont. On 14 Dec 1843, he became a charter member of the Columbian Lodge, No. 29 of the Odd Fellows in Stoneham, Middlesex, Massachusetts.[980] Nicknamed "Shoe Town," Hollis owned a shoe making factory there for the better part of his life. A century later, a retrospective article in the Stoneham newspaper indicated his shop, stable and home were all in one in the Central Square across from Stoneham Common.[981] Hollis Nye Wyeth married (1) **MARY JANE STILES** on 22 Jun 1846 in Middlesex, Washington, Vermont. Mary Jane, daughter of Peleg Stearns Stiles and Sarah Buck McElroy, was born on 22 Jul 1825 in Moretown, Washington, Vermont.[982] She was half-sister to Hollis' stepmother, Lucy Stiles. Mary Jane died from heart disease, at age 23, on 15 Nov 1848 in Stoneham. Hollis married (2) **FRANCENA LOVINA LOUISA HOOK** on 06 Jul 1870 in Stoneham. Lovina, daughter of Eldred Kelley Hook and Louisa Blood Lovejoy, was born on 19 Jul 1837 in West Cambridge (Arlington), Middlesex, Massachusetts. Lovina died on 09 Mar 1880 in Moretown, Washington, Vermont. Hollis died on 11 May 1896 at age 73 at his daughter Ella's house in Watertown, Middlesex, Massachusetts.[983] He is buried with both of his wives in Lindenwood Cemetery, lot 486, Stoneham.

Hollis' name and his wives Mary Stiles and Lovina Hook are on one side of this monument. The name of Hollis' father, Jonathan, is engraved on the other side.

According to Mary Stiles Guild's genealogy,[984] Hollis Nye Wyeth and Mary Jane Stiles had two children – so Mary Jane Wyeth, adopted by Hollis' sister, is probably their child along with:

306. i. ELLA CAROLINE[7] WYETH, born 13 Aug 1847, Stoneham; raised by her aunt Nancy Stiles Chamberlin in Middlesex, Washington, Vermont; married JAMES DAVID EVANS, 01 Jan 1864, Moretown; died 05 Feb 1918, Watertown.

149. **MARTHA ANN[6] WYETH** (Jonathan[5], Noah[4] Sr., Ebenezer[3] Sr., John[2], Nicholas[1]) was born on 03 Mar 1828 in Moretown, Washington, Vermont. Martha Ann Wyeth and **HENRY CAUD BLISS** were married on 08 Apr 1852 in Boston, Suffolk, Massachusetts. Henry, son of James Bliss and Anna Walbridge, was born on 02 Jan 1817 in Stanstead, Quebec, Canada. He died on 19 Nov 1884 in Melrose, Middlesex, Massachusetts. In his will, he left everything to Martha except a watch for his son. Martha died 23 Nov 1908 at age 80 at 26 Gould Street, Stoneham, Middlesex, Massachusetts. They are buried in Sleepy Hollow Cemetery, Concord, Massachusetts.

Henry Caud Bliss and Martha Ann Wyeth had the following children:

i. CHARLES S.[7] BLISS, born 15 Oct 1857, Nottingham, Rockingham, New Hampshire; died there an infant, of inflammation, on 13 Apr 1858.

307.   ii. WILLIAM IRVING BLISS, born 23 Jul 1859, Nottingham; married MAMIE FRANCES KIMBALL, 04 Jan 1881, Steubenville, Jefferson, Ohio; died 20 Jun 1923, Cleveland, Cuyahoga, Ohio.

150. **MARY TORREY^6 HANCOCK** (Torrey^5 Hancock, Sarah^4 Wyeth, Ebenezer^3 Sr., John^2, Nicholas^1) was born on 10 Jun 1812 in Cambridge. She married her second cousin, **JONAS WYETH 2^D**, there on 01 Jan 1833. Jonas Wyeth 2^d, son of Major Jonas Wyeth and Susan Stearns, was born on 14 Dec 1806 in Cambridge. Their children were Lucy Coolidge Wyeth Bemis, Josephine Augusta Wyeth Stearns and Edwin Augustus Wyeth. To avoid listing their data twice, the children's information appears under Jonas #137. Mary and Jonas separated 08 Dec 1848.[985] They were divorced on 31 Oct 1851 in Des Moines County, Iowa, but the divorce was later invalidated.[986] Mary and Jonas reunited after the death of Jonas' mother, who confessed on her death bed to causing strife in her son's marriage.[987] Jonas died 03 Jun 1868 at age 61 in Cambridge. At the impressive age of 92, Mary died at her Front Street home in Marblehead, Essex, Massachusetts on 16 Nov 1904.

151. **JASON^6 RUSSELL III** (Jason^5 Jr., Elizabeth^4 Winship, Elizabeth^3 Wyeth, John^2, Nicholas^1) was born on 02 Jun 1763 in Menotomy (Arlington), Middlesex, Massachusetts. Jason Russell III and **REBECCA LAUGHTON** married 08 Nov 1786 in Norridgewock, Somerset, Maine. Rebecca was born to John Laughton and Jane Lampson on 07 Feb 1769 in Groton, Middlesex, Massachusetts. Jason died on 08 Oct 1840 in Brighton, Somerset, Maine. Rebecca died there on 20 Feb 1848.

The children of Jason Russell III and Rebecca Laughton included:

308.   i. WILLIAM^7 RUSSELL, born 06 Sep 1796, Madison, Somerset, Maine; married ACHSA KELLEY there in Jan 1820; died 13 May 1864 in Athens, Somerset, Maine.

152. **ANNA^6 GROVER** (Betty^5, Nathaniel^4 Gamage, Deborah^3 Wyeth, William^2, Nicholas^1) was baptized 07 Sep 1766 in the Fifth Parish of Gloucester at Sandy Bay (Rockport), Essex, Massachusetts.[988] It is now the First Congregational Church of Rockport, United Church of Christ. Anna Grover married (1) **JOHN BLATCHFORD** there on 04 Mar 1784. John, son of John Blatchford Sr. and Rachel Clark, was born in 1762 in Sandy Bay. Like Anna's grandfather, Nathaniel, John was impressed into the service of the British Navy. Author Charles Bushnell related the story of John's sufferings in an 1865 book. Blatchford died in 1794 in Port Au Prince, Haiti, French West Indies.[989] Anna married (2) **EDWARD HIGGINS** (the widower of her sister, Mary) on 31 Aug 1797 in Gloucester. Edward was born there about 1760 to Edward "Ned" Higgins and Sarah Hilton. After Edward died circa 1805 in Gloucester, Anna earned a living first as a weaver and then as a nurse. According to town records, Anna died 03 Mar 1841 in Rockport (town formally named so in 1840).

Founded in 1755 as the Fifth Parish of Gloucester, the church was built in 1804-05 as the Sandy Bay Meetinghouse. Fishermen nicknamed it the "Old Sloop" because its tall steeple and white facade resembled a ship's sail.

John Blatchford and Anna Grover had the following children:[990]

<blockquote>
i. NANCY[7] BLATCHFORD, born in 1784 in the Sandy Bay area of Gloucester (Rockport), Essex, Massachusetts; death unknown.

309.   ii. RACHEL BLATCHFORD, born circa 1786, Sandy Bay; married FRANCIS HILTON, there on 17 Dec 1805; death circa 1866.

iii. WILLIAM BLATCHFORD, born circa 1789, Sandy Bay; died there, 20 Jan 1864.

iv. CAPTAIN JOHN BLATCHFORD III, born 21 Mar 1790, Sandy Bay; married there by Rev. David Jewett to MARGARET OAKES MARSHALL on 24 Sep 1809 at the Fifth Parish (then known as the "Old Sloop"[991]). They had 12 children. He was a mariner who had served as a private in Captain David Elwell's Co., Lt. Col. James Appleton's Regiment, from 19 Sep 1814 to 12 Oct 1814.[992] John died 25 May 1873 in Rockport.
</blockquote>

John and Margaret Blatchford's stone in Beech Grove cemetery, Rockport.

153. **HANNAH[6] GROVER** (Betty[5], Nathaniel[4] Gamage, Deborah[3] Wyeth, William[2], Nicholas[1]) was baptized on 04 Dec 1768 at the Fifth Parish in Gloucester at Sandy Bay (Rockport), Essex, Massachusetts.[993] Hannah Grover and Francis Noble married there on 01 Aug 1790. **FRANCIS NOBLE** was born in May 1763 in Gloucester. He died there on 05 Jun 1825. Hannah died on 06 Sep 1843 at age 76 in Rockport (town formally named so in 1840).

The children of Francis Noble and Hannah Grover included:

<blockquote>
i. HANNAH[7] NOBLE, born 06 Dec 1792, Sandy Bay; married JOHN VOSS CLEAVELAND there, 13 Jun 1812; died 10 Apr 1872, Quincy, Adams, Illinois.
</blockquote>

154. **ELIZABETH[6] GROVER** (Betty[5], Nathaniel[4] Gamage, Deborah[3] Wyeth, William[2], Nicholas[1]) was baptized 28 Apr 1771 in the Fifth Parish of Gloucester at Sandy Bay (Rockport), Essex, Massachusetts.[994] Elizabeth Grover and William Gott VI were married there on 14 Dec 1790. There were two William Gotts born about the same time to William Gott V. Elizabeth's husband, **WILLIAM GOTT VI**, was born out of wedlock to Martha "Patty" Sheldon.[995] He was baptized on 18 Feb 1770 in Sandy Bay. William Gott V had just married Sarah Gamage before Martha Sheldon gave birth. Elizabeth's husband died before 1840 as he was not with her in the 1840 or 1850 Gloucester census reports. Elizabeth died circa 1851. The legitimate William Gott Jr., baptized, 29 Sep 1771 in Sandy Bay, relocated to Starks, Maine. That William died at age 87 (see Sarah Gamage #86).

The names of William Gott VI and Elizabeth Grover's children, as shown below, come from William Otis Sawtelle's book, *Daniel Gott, Mount Desert Pioneer*. Additionally, Gloucester records confirm all were born or baptized there and Gloucester's birth records show Elizabeth Grover is the mother's name. As the *Mount Desert* author confuses the man he labels William Gott VI with the man who would generally be known as William Gott Jr., apparently Sawtelle did not know both Williams were sons of William Gott V.[996] Another indication that the husband of Elizabeth Grover is William Gott VI, is two of their children were named for his mother, Ebenezer Rowe's wife, Martha "Patty" Sheldon.

William Gott VI and Elizabeth Grover had the following children:

    i. MARTHA[7] GOTT, born 01 Jun 1791; death unknown.

    ii. WILLIAM GOTT VII, born 30 May 1793; death unknown.

    iii. JOHN GOTT, baptized 07 Dec 1794; death unknown.

    iv. PATTY GOTT, baptized 07 Dec 1794; death unknown.

    v. SARAH GOTT, born 09 Jul 1797; death unknown.

    vi. BETSEY GOTT, born 06 Feb 1800; married (1) WILLIAM SADLER, 28 Aug 1817, Edgecomb, Lincoln, Maine; married (2) SAMUEL ELWELL SMITH, 01 Feb 1867, Beverly, Essex, Massachusetts; died Gloucester, 09 Nov 1879.

    vii. JAMES GOTT, born 30 Aug 1802; death unknown.

    viii. MARY GOTT, born 25 May 1805; death unknown.

    ix. HANNAH T. GOTT, born 09 Jun 1807; married SAMUEL ELWELL SMITH, 19 Jun 1829, Gloucester; died there, 14 Mar 1860.

    x. NATHAN E. GOTT, born 04 Mar 1810; died 08 Dec 1856, Gloucester.

    xi. JANE GOTT, born 02 Oct 1814; death unknown.

155. **NEHEMIAH[6] GROVER III** (Betty[5], Nathaniel[4] Gamage, Deborah[3] Wyeth, William[2], Nicholas[1]) was baptized on 22 Sep 1776 in the Fifth Parish of Gloucester at Sandy Bay (Rockport), Essex, Massachusetts.[997] He married **ESTHER ROWE** there on 22 Oct 1798. Esther, daughter of Ebenezer Rowe and Martha "Patty" Sheldon, was baptized on 05 Sep 1780 in Sandy Bay. Nehemiah served Gloucester during the War of 1812 in Captain Charles Tarr's Co., Lt. Col. J. Appleton's Regiment, from 19 Sep 1814 to 12 Oct 1814. The first of those dates saw the company locked in a sea battle with British barges.[998] After the war, the Grovers relocated to Cheshire Township, Gallia, Ohio. Esther died there in 1850 and Nehemiah died circa Jan 1854.

Nehemiah Grover III and Esther Rowe had the following children:

310.   i. NEHEMIAH[7] GROVER IV, born 1799 in the Sandy Bay area of Gloucester (Rockport), Essex, Massachusetts; married ELECTA WHITLOCK, 26 Sep 1818, Cheshire Township; died 10 Oct 1862, Springfield Township, Gallia, Ohio.

311.   ii. JOHN GROVER, born 25 Dec 1800,[999] Sandy Bay; married (1) MARY BRYANT, 02 Nov 1824, Gloucester; married (2) JANE CUTLER, 15 Jun 1837, Darke County, Ohio; died 06 Oct 1863, Wabash County, Indiana.

312.   iii. EBENEZER ROWE GROVER, born 14 May 1801, Sandy Bay; married NANCY SCOTT in 1836 in Ohio; died 18 Jul 1874, Cheshire Township.

313.   iv. MARY ESTHER GROVER, born about 1805, Sandy Bay; married (1) ELISHA KENT, 23 Oct 1828, Gallia County, Ohio; married (2) GEORGE ROBERT SMITH, 03 Nov 1833, Salem Township, Meigs, Ohio; died there, 01 Apr 1842.

314.   v. EPHRIAM R. GROVER, born Jun 1807, Sandy Bay; married (1) MARY CLARK, 22 Nov 1832, Gallia County; married (2) SUSANNAH BRADBURY, 14 Nov 1841, Meigs County; married (3) AMELIA MCCOY, 07 Oct 1858, Gallia County; died 22 Jun 1872, Cheshire Township.

    vi. ELIJAH GROVER, born about 1810, Sandy Bay; died 1855, Gallia County.

315.   vii. ELISHA GROVER, born circa 1817, Sandy Bay; married HARRIET J. PETTINGILL, 26 Dec 1850, Gallia County; died there in Jan 1864.

316.   viii. WILLIAM HOSKINS GROVER, born 02 Apr 1818, Sandy Bay; married (1) ELIZABETH CATHERINE WEEKS, 16 Mar 1837, Meigs County, Ohio; married (2) SARAH WILLIAMS, the widow of Charles Higley, 23 Jan 1868, Rutland Township, Meigs County; died 18 Jan 1892, Kyger, Gallia, Ohio.

156. **JOSHUA[6] GAMAGE JR.** (Joshua[5], Nathaniel[4], Deborah[3] Wyeth, William[2], Nicholas[1]) was baptized 02 Feb 1766 in the Fifth Parish of Gloucester at Sandy Bay (Rockport), Essex, Massachusetts. Joshua Gamage Jr. and **SARAH WEBSTER** were married on 15 Nov 1787 at the Fifth Parish. Sarah, the daughter of Thomas Webster and Deborah Lane, was baptized on 11 May 1766 in the Third Parish of Gloucester at Annisquam. Joshua moved with his father to Bristol, Lincoln, Maine circa 1795.[1000] He died there on 18 Apr 1838. Sarah died in Bristol on 04 Sep 1853.

Joshua Gamage Jr. and Sarah Webster had the following children:

    i. JOSHUA[7] GAMAGE III, born about 1789 and baptized 26 Jul 1791 in the Sandy Bay area of Gloucester (Rockport), Essex, Massachusetts. Brothers Joshua, Thomas and William and brother-in-law, Moses Rogers, served in Capt. John Sprowl's detachment of the Maine Militia during the War of 1812.[1001] Joshua Gamage, fisherman, died on 13 Nov 1862, Swampscott, Essex, Massachusetts.

317.   ii. SARAH "SALLY" GAMAGE, born about 1790 and baptized 26 Jul 1791, Sandy Bay; married MOSES BEAUJEAN ROGERS on 03 Jan 1811 in Bristol, Lincoln, Maine; died 03 Nov 1856, Gloucester.

    iii. THOMAS GAMAGE, born 20 Jan 1794, Gloucester; served in the Maine Militia during the War of 1812;[1002] died on 27 Sep 1877 in Bristol.

    iv. JEMIMA GAMAGE, born circa 1795 in Bristol; death unknown.

    v. WILLIAM GAMAGE, born in Apr 1796, Bristol; served the Maine Militia during the War of 1812;[1003] died 14 Dec 1862, Bristol.

    vi. SAMUEL GAMAGE, born circa 1798, Bristol; died there, 28 Aug 1887.

    vii. JANE GAMAGE, born circa 1799, Bristol; married HENRY TIBBETS, 30 Dec 1819, Bristol; died there, 23 Sep 1872.

318.   viii. HANNAH GAMAGE, born 17 Dec 1801, Bristol; married GEORGE MCFARLAND, 12 Oct 1818, Bristol; died there, 28 May 1872.

319.   ix. MARTHA GAMAGE, born 30 Apr 1803, Bristol; married THOMAS THOMPSON, 17 Nov 1825, Bristol; died there, 11 Jun 1862.

    x. WEBSTER GAMAGE, born 1807, Bristol; died there, 04 Jun 1880.

157. **(LT.) SAMUEL WELLINGTON[6] HUNT** (Thomas[5], Ruth[4] Fessenden, Martha[3] Wyeth, William[2], Nicholas[1]) was born 05 Nov 1799 in Fort Wayne, Indiana.[1004] He was appointed to the U.S. Military Academy at West Point in 1814, but dropped out in 1818 to marry **JULIA HERRICK** of Plattsburgh, Clinton, New York.[1005] Julia was born there in 1799 to Dr. Elijah Herrick and Lucinda Prentice. Julia died from childbirth complications in Mar 1827 at the Jefferson Barracks Military Post near St. Louis, Missouri.[1006] The toxic camp was so teaming with disease, Samuel died there two years later on 11 Sep 1829.[1007]

Samuel was born in the fort at Fort Wayne.

(Lt.) Samuel Wellington Hunt and Julia Herrick had the following children:

320.   i. (GENERAL) HENRY JACKSON[7] HUNT, born 14 Sep 1819, Detroit, Wayne, Michigan; married (1) EMILY CAROLINE DERUSSY, 18 Dec 1851, Old Point Comfort, Hampton, Virginia; married (2) MARY BETHUNE CRAIG, 27 Dec 1860, Washington, D.C.; he died there, 11 Feb 1889 at the Soldiers' Home.

    ii. GEORGE HUNT, born 1821, Fort Bellefontaine, St. Louis, Missouri; died 1827, Jefferson Barracks.

    iii. (BRIGADIER GENERAL) LEWIS CASS HUNT, born 23 Feb 1824, Fort Howard, Green Bay, Wisconsin; educated at Kenyon College, Gambier, Knox, Ohio and West Point Military Academy, Orange County, New York; married ABBY PEARCE CASEY 28 Nov 1860, Fort Steilacoom, Pierce, Washington. He spent his life in the military… last commanding the 14th Regiment of Infantry in 1881.[1008] He is often confused with his first cousin of the same name who was a captain in the Ohio 67th.[1009] Most Internet sites mistakenly depict him by using his mutton-chopped cousin's photo.[1010] Brigadier General Hunt had a full beard. He died 06 Sep 1886, Fort Union, Mora, New Mexico.

This photo of Brigadier General Lewis C. Hunt comes from U.S., Civil War Soldier Records and Profiles on Ancestry.com.

    iv. JULIA HERRICK HUNT, born 01 Mar 1826, Howard, Chippewa, Wisconsin; married RICHARD J. TOMKINS, 01 May 1843, Jo Daviess County, Illinois; died 03 Mar 1915, Mt. Carroll, Carroll County, Illinois.[1011]

158. **ELIZABETH "ELIZA"[6] PALMER** (Elizabeth[5] Hunt, Ruth[4] Fessenden, Martha[3] Wyeth, William[2], Nicholas[1]) was born 28 Feb 1778 in Watertown, Middlesex, Massachusetts. She married **(DR.) NATHANIEL PEABODY**, son of Isaac Peabody and Mary Potter, 03 Nov 1802 in Andover, Essex, Massachusetts. He was born on 30 Mar 1774 in Topsfield, Essex, Massachusetts and grew up in New Boston, New Hampshire. Nathaniel graduated from Dartmouth College in 1800. Eliza died on 11 Jan 1853 in West Newton, Middlesex, Massachusetts.[1012] He died 01 Jan 1855 at the home of his oldest child while she was teaching in Eagleswood, Raritan Bay Union near Perth Amboy, Middlesex, New Jersey.[1013]

Dr. Nathaniel Peabody and Elizabeth "Eliza" Palmer had the following children:[1014]

    i. ELIZABETH PALMER[7] PEABODY, born 16 May 1804, Billerica, Essex, Massachusetts; died unmarried 03 Jan 1894 at her home at 6 Gordon St., Jamaica Plain, Suffolk, Massachusetts.

321.   ii. MARY TYLER PEABODY, born 16 Nov 1806, Cambridge; married HORACE MANN, 01 May 1843, Boston; died 11 Feb 1887, Jamaica Plain.

322.   iii. SOPHIA AMELIA PEABODY, born 21 Sep 1809, Salem, Essex, Massachusetts; married NATHANIEL HAWTHORNE, 09 Jul 1842, Boston; died 26 Feb 1871, London, England.

    iv. NATHANIEL CRANCH PEABODY, born 11 Dec 1811, Salem; married SARAH HIBBARD there 14 Mar 1835; died 23 Jun 1881, Concord, Middlesex, Massachusetts.

v. GEORGE FRANCIS PEABODY, born 10 Oct 1813, Salem; died there unmarried on 29 Nov 1839 at age 26.

iv. (DR.) WELLINGTON PEABODY, born 16 Dec 1815, Salem; died unmarried at age 21, while trying to cure yellow fever, on 29 Sep 1837 in New Orleans, Louisiana.

v. CATHARINE PUTNAM PEABODY, born 26 Apr 1819, Salem; was an infant when she died there on 14 Jun 1819.

Notes on the family of Dr. Nathaniel Peabody and Elizabeth "Eliza" Palmer:

The influence of Eliza Palmer Peabody, a writer and a teacher, on her ground-breaking daughters cannot be overstated. Eliza wrote women may "shine in the domestic sphere." Yet, she continued, "God has giv'n to both men and women the same immortal mind."[1015]

Under their mother's guidance, all three daughters were trailblazers nearly a century before women gained the right to vote. Mary, a teacher and a writer, married the politician, educational reformer and founder of Ohio's Antioch College, Horace Mann. Sophia, a painter and illustrator, married Nathaniel Hawthorne whose books the *Scarlet Letter* and the *House of the Seven Gables* are American classics.

The Peabody's oldest child, Elizabeth Palmer Peabody, did not marry. She is considered one of the most important women of her time for her work in education and as the founder of the first English-speaking public Kindergarten in the United States.

Elizabeth, an activist in the antislavery and women's suffrage movements, also worked tirelessly promoting the rights of Native Americans.[1016] As a writer and intellectual, Elizabeth earned the respect of not only her brothers-in-law, Mann and Hawthorne, but of Emerson, Thoreau and Longfellow.

Public Domain photo of Elizabeth Palmer Peabody.

After her death at age 89, to honor her, friends founded The Elizabeth Peabody House to help families in the Boston (now Somerville) area to reach their full potential through early childhood education, youth development and enrichment, and family services.[1017]

"All of us have special ones who have loved us into being."

~ Fred Rogers

SEVENTH GENERATION – THE WAR BETWEEN THE STATES

159. **AMOS⁷ STEARNS** (Jonas⁶, Josiah⁵, Abigail⁴ Fiske, John³, Sarah² Wyeth, Nicholas¹) was born on 10 Jul 1766 in Chesterfield, Cheshire, New Hampshire. Amos Stearns and Lucy Fletcher were married on 19 Aug 1790 in Chesterfield. **LUCY FLETCHER**, daughter of Timothy Fletcher and Sarah Brewer, was born on 19 Aug 1765 in Acton, Middlesex, Massachusetts. She died on 11 Dec 1809 in Marlboro, Windham, Vermont. He died on 16 May 1829 in Newfane, Windham, Vermont.

The children of Amos Stearns and Lucy Fletcher included the following:

        i. NANCY⁸ STEARNS, born 14 Dec 1791, Chesterfield; married JOHN BURROWS there on 19 Aug 1807; death unknown.

323.   ii. LUCY STEARNS, born 21 Apr 1802, Chesterfield; married (1) ELI BRUCE there, circa 1823; married (2) JAMES BALL, 03 Dec 1826, Marlboro; died there, 03 Mar 1891.

160. **FRANCIS⁷ FISKE JR.** (Francis⁶, Samuel⁵ Jr., Samuel⁴, William³, Sarah² Wyeth, Nicholas¹) was born on 30 Jun 1824 in Bedford, Middlesex, Massachusetts. He married **SARAH E. HOUGHTON**, daughter of Thomas Houghton and Sarah Wells, circa 1851. She was born on 07 Aug 1832 in Saugus, Essex, Massachusetts. He died on 16 Dec 1889 in Saugus. She died there, 01 Mar 1912.

The children of Francis Fiske Jr. and Sarah E. Houghton included:

        i. HENRY FREEMAN⁸ FISKE, born 10 Jan 1861, Saugus; died there in 1921.
       ii. FREDERICK M. FISKE, born 10 Jun 1863, Saugus; died there, 28 May 1886.

161. **CYNTHIA⁷ CUTTER** (Elijah⁶, Nehemiah⁵, Martha⁴ Bowman, Deborah³ Wyeth, John², Nicholas¹) was born on 23 Feb 1821 in West Cambridge (Arlington), Middlesex, Massachusetts. She married **BENJAMIN FRANKLIN RUSSELL** there on 21 May 1843. Ben, son of Jeremiah Russell and Esther Hall, was born on 29 Dec 1818 in West Cambridge. He died on 19 Apr 1881 in Arlington. She died there on 11 Apr 1917.

The children of Benjamin Franklin Russell and Cynthia Cutter included the following child:

324.   i. LUCIUS KIMBALL⁸ RUSSELL, born 04 Mar 1861, Arlington; married GRACE ROSS CARPENTER, daughter of William A. Carpenter III and Mary Elizabeth Wyeth (Lucius and Grace were 5th cousins) on 26 Apr 1905 in Arlington; Lucius died 03 Nov 1935, Potsdam, St Lawrence, New York.[1018]

162. **(COLONEL) SAMUEL GARDNER⁷ BOWMAN** (Nathaniel⁶, Joshua⁵, Noah⁴, Deborah³ Wyeth, John², Nicholas¹) was born on 09 Oct 1790 in Gorham, Cumberland, Maine. Samuel Gardner Bowman and Marcia Stockbridge married on 19 May 1816 in Hanover, Plymouth, Massachusetts. **MARCIA STOCKBRIDGE**, daughter of William Stockbridge and Ruth Bailey, was born on 07 Apr 1795 in Hanover. He died on 29 Mar 1841 in Bath, Sagadahoc, Maine. Marcia died 19 May 1862 in Bath.

The children of Colonel Samuel Gardner Bowman and Marcia Stockbridge included:

    i. NATHANIEL[8] BOWMAN, born 27 Jul 1817, Bath, Sagadahoc, Maine; died 07 Oct 1847, St. Francisville, West Feliciana, Louisiana.[1019]

    ii. RUTH ELIZABETH BOWMAN, born on 17 Sep 1820 in Bath; married (REAR ADMIRAL) JOSEPH FOSTER GREEN, 26 Jun 1840, Bath; died 10 Jan 1900, Brookline, Norfolk, Massachusetts.

163. **JOSEPH[7] WYETH** (Jonathan[6], Joseph[5], Jonathan[4] Jr., Jonathan[3], John[2], Nicholas[1]) was born on 06 Mar 1800 in Groton, Middlesex, Massachusetts. The records of nearby Shirley give that date of birth and say he died in Ohio.[1020] Joseph married **ELVIRA WHEELER** in Cuyahoga County, Ohio on 14 Dec 1836. Elvira was born 27 Jun 1812 in Ellisburg, Jefferson, New York. This is confirmed by the fact her parents, Jonathan Wheeler and Sibbel Carkins, were living there for the 1820 census. As per his great grandson, Charles Leon Wyeth, Joseph died circa 1844 in Parma Township, Cuyahoga, Ohio.[1021] Since Elvira filed papers on 19 Feb 1845 to administer Joseph's estate, Joseph's death was definitely between Dec 1844 and Feb 1845.[1022] Elvira next married Hiram Beebe on 21 May 1848. She died on 11 Jan 1888 in Parma Township.

Probate papers for Joseph Wyeth, late of Parma, were filed 19 Feb 1845 in Cuyahoga County, Ohio. They are signed by Elvira Wyeth and her father Jonathan Wheeler.

Joseph's probate papers only listed three children.* It is highly likely that Fales was a posthumous child, born in 1845 after his father's death, since the 1850 census said he was age five on 13 Aug 1850. According to Charles Leon Wyeth, Joseph and Elvira Wheeler Wyeth had five children:

325.   i. WALTER HERBERT[8] WYETH,* born 01 Aug 1836, Cuyahoga County, Ohio; married FRANCIES ELIZA WARREN, 07 Oct 1860, Hastings, Barry, Michigan; enlisted in the 11th Regiment of the Michigan Calvary on 13 Jan 1864 and mustered out at Detroit, Michigan on 04 Sep 1865; died in a train accident on 12 Jun 1910, Riverdale, Gratiot, Michigan. The accident was the direct result of deafness caused by the typhoid fever he contracted in the Civil War.[1023]

326.   ii. WILLIAM EDWARD WYETH, born 07 Mar 1840, Parma Township, Cuyahoga, Ohio;[1024] married NANCY ELIZABETH RIGGS, 1860, Bath, Clinton, Michigan; served the 10th Michigan Infantry for three months in 1865; died 27 Aug 1915, Michigan Soldiers' Home Hospital, Grand Rapids, Kent, Michigan.

327.   iii. JOSEPH J. WYETH,* born 25 Sep 1841, Parma Township; married (1) JANE E. "JENNIE" BENJAMIN, 22 Aug 1865, Niles, Berrien, Michigan; married (2) CARRIE F. COOMBS MCCARTY, 17 Jan 1912, Alhambra, Los Angeles, California; died 19 Mar 1923, Los Angeles, California.

iv.   JONATHAN WHEELER WYETH* was born about 1843 in Parma Township and named for both of his grandfathers. He mustered in the 124th Ohio Infantry Regiment, Co. A, on 04 Aug 1862 in Cleveland. *The Daily Cleveland Herald* reported on 06 Oct 1863 that he was missing after the 20 Sep 1863 Battle of Chickamauga, Georgia. [1025] From there he made his way north to Annapolis, Maryland where he died of typhoid fever on 02 Dec 1863, at age 20. He is buried in a Soldier's grave at Sec. K, site 891 in the Annapolis National Cemetery.[1026]

Elvira Wheeler Wyeth Beebe circa 1865. Photo courtesy of Bill Wheeler.

328.   v.   FALES EDWIN WYETH was born in Cleveland about 04 Feb 1845 as he was five in the 1850 census and 23 when he married (1) DELPHEM ELVIRA TURNER on 25 Dec 1867 in Laketon, Berrien, Michigan.[1027] He married (2) CHARLOTTE "LOTTIE" M. CHURCH, 03 Feb 1873, Charlotte, Eaton, Michigan; married (3) HATTIE AUGUSTA BURROUGHS, 17 Jul 1888, Lansing, Ingham, Michigan; died 01 Feb 1899, Sumner, Gratiot, Michigan.

164. **JONATHAN⁷ WYETH JR.** (Jonathan⁶, Joseph⁵, Jonathan⁴ Jr., Jonathan³, John², Nicholas¹) was born on 20 Jan 1802 in Groton, Middlesex, Massachusetts. Jonathan Wyeth Jr. and **ESTHER BAILEY** were married on 23 Feb 1825 in Townsend, Middlesex, Massachusetts. Esther, daughter of Jonathan Bailey and Sarah Holt, was born on 12 Sep 1805 in Townsend. He died on 05 Feb 1876 at age 74 in Lunenburg, Worcester, Massachusetts. She died on 15 Feb 1901 at age 95 in Fitchburg, Worcester, Massachusetts.

The children of Jonathan Wyeth Jr. and Esther Bailey included the following:

329.   i.   LUCY BAILEY⁸ WYETH, born 09 Jun 1825, Townsend; married JAMES A. PARKER, 10 Nov 1843, Pepperell, Middlesex, Massachusetts; died 27 Dec 1913, Lancaster, Worcester, Massachusetts.
       ii.   SARAH H. WYETH, born 28 Feb 1828, Townsend; died 04 Mar 1908, Pepperell.
       iii.   ESTHER WYETH, born 18 Sep 1832, Townsend; died 23 Jul 1847, Groton.
330.   iv.   HARRIET ANN "HATTIE" WYETH, born 30 May 1838, Brookline, Hillsborough, New Hampshire; married GEORGE ALBERT LANCEY, 18 May 1859, Lunenburg; died 07 May 1881, Shirley, Middlesex, Massachusetts.
331.   v.   ESTHER AUGUSTA WYETH, born 19 Jul 1841, Townsend; married (1) ADOLPHUS M. HARRIS, 01 Feb 1859, Lunenburg; (2) married THOMAS GOULD FILLEBROWN, 15 Jun 1866, Westford, Middlesex, Massachusetts; died 30 Dec 1925, Attleboro, Bristol, Massachusetts.
332.   vi.   WARREN AUGUSTUS WYETH, born 1843, Townsend; served the 23rd MA Regiment and the Westford Militia; married HANNAH PRESCOTT, 19 Apr 1865, Nashua, Hillsborough, New Hampshire; disappeared 1874; death unknown.
333.   vii.   ADELINE DELANIA "ADDIE" WYETH, born 29 Jul 1846, Dunstable, Middlesex, Massachusetts; married GEORGE W. BERRY, 1868; died 15 Oct 1924, Buffalo, Erie, New York.
334.   viii.   WILLIAM JONATHAN WYETH, born 06 Oct 1848, Groton; married CLARA EVA MARSHALL, 14 Sep 1886, Fitchburg; died there, 27 Jan 1917.

165. **WALTER[7] WYETH** (Jonathan[6], Joseph[5], Jonathan[4] Jr., Jonathan[3], John[2], Nicholas[1]) was born on 07 Apr 1812 in Townsend, Middlesex, Massachusetts. In some records his name was misspelled Walker and Seth. He earned his living as a cooper. Walter Wyeth married **SUSAN P. ADAMS** in Townsend on 06 Jan 1842. Susan, daughter of Pharis Adams and his wife Susannah, was born on 19 Oct 1819 in Townsend. Walter died on 19 Mar 1855 at age 42 in Townsend. Susan died there at age 37 on 11 Dec 1856 of consumption.

The children of Walter Wyeth and Susan P. Adams included two unnamed daughters who died in Townsend on 27 Dec 1843 and 16 Aug 1854:

335.   i.   GEORGE W. P.[8] WYETH, born 23 Apr 1844, Townsend; discharged for disability from the 6th Regiment NH infantry due to being shot in the arm during the 2nd Battle of Bull Run on 29 Aug 1862 (the wound was open and bone still seeping out of it); he reenlisted in the Veterans Reserve Corps; discharged a corporal on 01 Sep 1865 from the 13th Regiment MA infantry; married SARAH JANE LEIGHTON, 21 Aug 1872, Saccarappa (Westbrook), Cumberland, Maine; died 12 Aug 1914, at 1207 Brighton Ave., Portland, Cumberland, Maine. [1028]

       ii. RALPH H. WYETH, born 11 Jan 1848, Townsend; died there, 09 Sep 1851.

       iii. SUSAN ELISA "CLARE" WYETH, born 17 Feb 1851, Townsend; death unknown.

166. **HIRAM[7] WYETH** (Jonathan[6], Joseph[5], Jonathan[4] Jr., Jonathan[3], John[2], Nicholas[1]) was born on 10 Jan 1832 in Mason, Hillsborough, New Hampshire. He earned his living as a cooper. Hiram married **ABIGAIL BURGESS** in Townsend, Middlesex, Massachusetts on 30 May 1854. Abigail, daughter of Daniel Burgess and Abigail Dix, was born on 06 Nov 1834 in Brookline, Hillsborough, New Hampshire. Hiram died of consumption on 07 Oct 1897 in Townsend. She died on 18 Jul 1900 in Nashua, Hillsborough, New Hampshire.

Hiram Wyeth and Abigail Burgess had the following children:

336.   i.   ELLIS HIRAM[8] WYETH, born 11 Mar 1855, Brookline; married (1) HARRIET ANN "HATTIE" ARKWELL, 17 Sep 1876, Townsend; married (2) MELENDA DEMARIS SMITH, 28 Nov 1922, Worcester, Worcester County, Massachusetts; died 26 Jul 1943, Los Angeles, California.

337.   ii. WARREN N. WYETH, born 09 Nov 1857, Townsend; married (1) ELLEN AURLINE SWAN, 01 Jan 1883, Worcester; married (2) MARY MCKIM, 01 Oct 1925, Townsend; died there, 12 Oct 1940.

338.   iii. WILLARD BENJAMIN WYETH, born 09 May 1861, Townsend; married MARGARET "MAGGIE" MCLENNAN, 24 Dec 1884, South Hadley, Middlesex, Massachusetts; died 25 Mar 1942, Hudson, Hillsborough, New Hampshire.

339.   iv. ABBY JANE WYETH, born 22 Nov 1863, Townsend; married WILLIAM BUSH, 15 Mar 1893, Townsend; died there, 22 May 1936.

340.   v.   ELMER JOSEPH WYETH, born 22 Dec 1865, Townsend; married JENNIE ETHEL CARRUTH, 30 May 1897, Townsend; died there, 14 Sep 1929. [1029]

       vi. GEORGE DANA WYETH, born 31 Mar 1868, Townsend; married (1) MARY OLIVE GORHAM, 18 Feb 1888, Somerville, Middlesex, Massachusetts; married (2) ADDIE ELFLEDA WOODS, 18 Jan 1899, Nashua; married (3) JENNIE ETHEL CARRUTH, his sister-in-law, 21 Apr 1933, Townsend; died there, 13 Feb 1950.

341.   vii. MARY ALICE ANN WYETH, born 10 Apr 1870, Townsend; married (1) WALTER E. BLOOD, 09 May 1892, Fitchburg, Worcester, Massachusetts; married (2) LEVI HOPKINS, 16 Sep 1919, Townsend; died 18 Apr 1961, Fitchburg.

342.   viii. MARTHA EMMA WYETH, born 29 Mar 1873, Townsend; married (1) WALTER ERWIN WILDER, 06 Feb 1895, Salisbury, Addison, Vermont; married (2) ARTHUR ORMAND SAWYER, 19 May 1945, Bangor, Penobscot, Maine; died in 26 Jul 1957, Malden, Middlesex, Massachusetts.

167. **ALONZO**[7] **WYETH** (Jonathan[6], Joseph[5], Jonathan[4] Jr., Jonathan[3], John[2], Nicholas[1]) was born in 16 May 1834 in Mason, Hillsborough, New Hampshire. Alonzo Wyeth , a farmer, and Sarah Althena Lawrence were married on 06 Jun 1854 in Fitchburg, Worcester, Massachusetts. **SARAH ALTHENA LAWRENCE**, daughter of Daniel Lawrence and Sarah Blood, was born on 20 Nov 1830 in Mason. She died on 05 Oct 1908 in Townsend, Middlesex, Massachusetts. Alonzo died there, 12 Jan 1920.

Alonzo Wyeth and Sarah Althena Lawrence had the following children:

        i. WILLIE A.[8] WYETH, born circa 1854, Mason; married ALMEDA FURBISH, 15 Oct 1879, Worcester; died of consumption on 20 Jul 1884, Townsend.

        ii. EMMA SARAH WYETH, born 12 Mar 1856, Mason; married GEORGE LILLIS WHITCOMB, 26 Mar 1876, Townsend; died there, 12 Feb 1951.

        iii. CYNTHIA A. WYETH, born 02 Mar 1858, Townsend; died there on 16 Dec 1858.

343.   iv. ELZORA OLIVIA WYETH, born "Alzora" on 01 Aug 1860, Townsend; married HENRY WYMAN, 24 Dec 1884, Worcester; died there, 05 Jun 1910.

        v. EUNICE ADALINE "ADDIE" WYETH, born 17 Sep 1862, Townsend; a housekeeper, married her employer, DARIUS OSCAR EVANS, 23 Sep 1909, Townsend; died 1951, Chester, Hampden, Massachusetts.

344.   vi. MILES ULYSSES SIMPSON GRANT WYETH, born 23 Jul 1868, Townsend; married (1) EMMA ZANIRA WOOD, 02 Aug 1890, Townsend; married (2) MATTIE A. WALKER, 04 May 1937, Sarasota County, Florida; died 17 Jul 1957, Tampa, Hillsborough, Florida.

168. **EMELINE**[7] **WYETH** (Jonathan[6], Joseph[5], Jonathan[4] Jr., Jonathan[3], John[2], Nicholas[1]) was born on 22 Nov 1836 in Mason, Hillsborough, New Hampshire. Emeline Wyeth and Warren Newton were married on 28 Nov 1854 in Westborough, Worcester, Massachusetts. **WARREN NEWTON** was born to Shubael Newton and Abigail Pike on 29 Aug 1825 in Framingham, Middlesex, Massachusetts. He died on 05 Oct 1894 in Westborough. She died there on 02 May 1902.

Warren Newton and Emeline Wyeth had the following children:

        i. ELDORA AUGUSTA[8] NEWTON was born on 08 Apr 1858 in Westborough, married NATHANIEL PIERCE there, 12 Aug 1885; died 27 Sep 1935, Townsend.

        ii. LOTTIE MARIA NEWTON, born 08 Aug 1861, Westborough; died there unmarried on 28 May 1903.

        iii. ELBRIDGE EUGENE NEWTON, born 10 Dec 1866, Westborough; died there on 19 Nov 1868.

169. **ORIN T.**[7] **WYETH** (Jonathan[6], Joseph[5], Jonathan[4] Jr., Jonathan[3], John[2], Nicholas[1]) was born on 19 Dec 1839 in Mason, Hillsborough, New Hampshire. Orin T. Wyeth married (1) **ANNA ISABELLA TARBELL**, on 07 Nov 1867 in Townsend, Middlesex, Massachusetts. Anna, daughter of John Tarbell and Sophronia Elliott, was born circa 1852 in Alton, Belknap, New Hampshire. They were divorced in Mason in 1869. Anna died 09 Jan 1917 in Townsend. Orin married (2) **FLORA ETTA SARTELLE** on 05 Jun 1873 in Townsend. Flora, daughter of Nathaniel Prentice Sartelle and Elizabeth Knight, was born on 08 Jun 1851 in Shirley, Middlesex, Massachusetts. They were divorced in Sep 1885 in New Hampshire. Flora married several times but kept the last name of William Newton. Oren died on 15 Jun 1920 in the State Infirmary, Tewksbury, Middlesex, Massachusetts. Flora died in Nov 1949 at age 98 in Ayer, Middlesex, Massachusetts.[1030]

This photo of Oren T. Wyeth is courtesy of his great granddaughter, Marian Gertrude Wyeth, of Cape Cod.

Orin T. Wyeth and Flora Etta Sartelle had the following children:

      i.   ALBERT NATHANIEL[8] WYETH was born in Lancaster, Worcester, Massachusetts in 1871; married ANNIE MARIA SMITH, 11 Feb 1908, Newport, Sullivan, New Hampshire; died 03 Jan 1937, Littleton, Middlesex, Massachusetts.

345.   ii.   GEORGE HENRY WYETH, born 04 Dec 1874, Townsend; joined the Army in Boston on 18 Dec 1890 and left it 02 Jul 1892 on disability, Angel Island, California; married (1) JANE FRANCES "JENNIE" SULLIVAN, 16 Dec 1892, Lunenburg, Worcester, Massachusetts; married (2) EMMA ADELIMA FAUBERT on 13 Nov 1901 in Shirley; George died 17 May 1949, Fitchburg, Worcester, Massachusetts.

     iii.   MABEL LUELLA WYETH was born in Harvard, Worcester, Massachusetts on 03 Nov 1877; died 24 Feb 1885 at age seven in Shirley.

     iv.   JOSEPH L. WYETH was born in Groton, Middlesex, Massachusetts in Mar 1881; died 28 Sep 1881 in Shirley.

170. **ABIGAIL EMELINE**[7] **ROBBINS** (Abigail Emeline[6] Wyeth, Joseph[5], Jonathan[4] Jr., Jonathan[3], John[2], Nicholas[1]) was born on 12 Aug 1799 in Groton, Middlesex, Massachusetts. Abigail married **HOSEA DANA WINCHESTER** on 09 Sep 1835 in Boston, Suffolk, Massachusetts. He was born 16 Apr 1796 in Wales, Hampden, Massachusetts and died 25 Sep 1866 in Belleville, Essex, New Jersey. She died on 15 Dec 1837 in Boston.

Hosea Dana Winchester and Abigail Emeline Robbins had the following children:

      i.   HOSEA DANA[8] WINCHESTER JR., born about 1836 in Boston; died there, an infant, on 16 Aug 1836.

     ii.   EMELINE ROBBINS WINCHESTER, born about 1837, Boston; married GEORGE ADAMS, 16 Apr 1856, Belleville; died in 1916, Little Falls, Passaic, New Jersey. She was living with her daughter Myra Adams, who was a secretary and a magazine editor in New York. She had two other daughters who married and died young – Gertrude Corby and Elsie Francisco Sutphen.

171. **ALEXANDER THAYER**[7] **TEMPLE** (Eunice Pamela[6] Wyeth, Joseph[5], Jonathan[4] Jr., Jonathan[3], John[2], Nicholas[1]) was born on 15 May 1811 in Boston, Suffolk, Massachusetts. He married **SOPHIA LEGG**, daughter of Elijah Legg and Lydia Warren, on 20 Jun 1841 in Hopkinton, Middlesex, Massachusetts. She was born on 03 Jul 1813 in Milford, Worcester, Massachusetts. She died on 28 May 1893 in Upton, Worcester, Massachusetts. He died there on 17 Feb 1905.

The children of Alexander Thayer Temple and Sophia Legg included:

346.　　i.　STEPHEN ELIJAH[8] TEMPLE, born 29 Aug 1842, Upton; married IDA M. PHILLIPS 09 Oct 1874, Boston; worked as a head waiter for 30 years in Boston hotels, including the Parker House; died 27 Aug 1902, Upton.

172. **CHARLES FRANKLIN**[7] **FESSENDEN** (Nathan[6] Jr., Nathan[5], Hannah[4] Prentice, Hannah[3] Wyeth, John[2], Nicholas[1]) was born on 05 Nov 1812 in Lexington, Middlesex, Massachusetts. Charles married (1) **MARTHA ELIZABETH NEWTON** on 30 Jan 1840 in Fitchburg, Worcester, Massachusetts. Martha was born there on 07 Jan 1819. She died on 19 Feb 1851 in Fitchburg. Charles married (2) Martha's sister, **SARAH COWDIN NEWTON**, on 11 May 1852 in Fitchburg. Martha and Sarah were the daughters of Martin Newton and Susan Chamberlin. Sarah was born 08 Apr 1821 in Fitchburg. Charles died there on 28 Dec 1884 and Sarah on 11 Aug 1903.

The children of Charles Franklin Fessenden and Martha Elizabeth Newton included:

i.　CHARLES NEWTON[8] FESSENDEN, born 15 May 1848, Fitchburg; graduated Harvard 1872; assistant secretary of the Chicago Board of Education; died 23 Dec 1914 at age 66 in Chicago.

173. **ELIZA**[7] **WYETH** (William[6], Ebenezer[5], Ebenezer[4] Jr., Ebenezer[3], John[2], Nicholas[1]) was born on 14 Feb 1809 in Chester, Hampden, Massachusetts. The ceremony was performed by John Seward when Eliza married **JOHN C. JUDSON** on 14 Apr 1835 in Aurora, Portage, Ohio. John was born in 1806 in Aurora. He died there on 18 Apr 1875 and she died there on 17 Aug 1891.

Large stone left – John Judson, Eliza Wyeth and Mary Jane Judson; around tree – Dr. Judson and Amanda; back – Mary Ann, Zeruah Wait and Caroline Wyeth in the Aurora Plainview (Mennonite) Cemetery.

John C. Judson and Eliza Wyeth had the following children:

i.　AMANDA MARIE[8] JUDSON, born 17 Jan 1840, Aurora; died there, 01 Sep 1881, at age 41, of congestive chills. Was a nurse in New York City.

ii.　ELIZABETH ELIZA JUDSON M.D was born in 1842 in Aurora. She graduated from Oberlin College and the Philadelphia Medical College. Dr. Judson died 01 Feb 1880 at West New Brighton, Staten Island, New York while working to provide medical care to neglected and abandoned infants and to poor pregnant women at the country branch of The Nursery and Child's Hospital.[1031]

iii.　MARY JANE JUDSON, born 24 Dec 1846, Aurora; worked at Christian Women's Board of Missions, Indianapolis; struck by a street car there, died 17 Oct 1931.

174. **SAMUEL MORSE[7] BELLOWS** (Mary[6] Wyeth, Ebenezer[5], Ebenezer[4] Jr., Ebenezer[3], John[2], Nicholas[1]) was born 20 Nov 1811 in Cambridge, Middlesex, Massachusetts. While working as the publisher of the *Lowell Advertiser,* he was active in the Lowell Young Men's Anti-Slavery Society.[1032] Samuel married (1) **MARY POTTER PEABODY** on 01 May 1836 in Lowell. Mary, daughter of Moses Peabody and Elizabeth Cochran, was born 16 Jan 1813 in New Boston, Hillsborough, New Hampshire. Mary, the niece of Nathaniel Peabody and Eliza Palmer, died in child birth in Boston, Suffolk, Massachusetts on 31 Jul 1839. Struggling greatly after Mary's death, Samuel turned to clerking in Lowell's post office and filed bankruptcy in 1842.[1033] He married (2) **HARRIET N. TURNER TODD**, daughter of Lucy Moulton Turner Todd, about 1844. Harriet, was born on 06 Mar 1812 in Newburyport, Essex, Massachusetts. Samuel died 09 Nov 1887 at his daughter Mary's home in Dorchester, Suffolk, Massachusetts.[1034] Harriet died 24 Sep 1891 in Boston.

Samuel Morse Bellows and Mary Potter Peabody had the following child:

> i. WILLIAM H.[8] BELLOWS, born 31 Jul 1839, Boston; died at age 10 on 13 Aug 1849 of scarlatina in Lowell.

Samuel Morse Bellows and Harriet N. Turner Todd had the following children:

> i. LUCY FRANCES "ABBYE"[8] BELLOWS, born 16 Apr 1846 in Lowell; died 25 Feb 1941, Boston. She never married.
> ii. MARY AUGUSTA BELLOWS, born 13 Dec 1848, Lowell; married HENRY JOHN EDWARD CAREW there on 21 Feb 1872; died 03 May 1928, Boston.

175. **WILLIAM WYETH[7] BELLOWS** (Mary[6] Wyeth, Ebenezer[5] III, Ebenezer[4] Jr., Ebenezer[3] Sr., John[2], Nicholas[1]) was born on 17 Oct 1814 in Watertown, Middlesex, Massachusetts. A merchant, he married **MARY ANN BATES**, daughter of Henry Bates and Mary Rogers Bickford. She was born on 04 Sep 1819 in Cooper, Washington, Maine and died at age 76 on 24 Aug 1898 in Boston. He died there on 30 Aug 1904 at age 89. They are buried near his mother in lot 2187 Mt. Auburn Cemetery on Asclepias Path.

William Wyeth Bellows and Mary Ann Bates had the following children:

> i. DANIEL BATES[8] BELLOWS, born 13 Feb 1847, Calais, Washington, Maine; he was a hotel clerk; died unmarried 31 May 1911, Laconia, Belknap, New Hampshire.
> 347. ii. MARY JAMES H. BELLOWS, born 16 Sep 1848, Calais; married CHARLES ALBERT ROYCE, 20 Jun 1872, Boston; died there, 13 Jan 1899.
> iii. WILLIE W. BELLOWS, born 11 Mar 1854, Boston; died there, 05 Feb 1856.
> iv. SAMUEL W. BELLOWS, born 14 Jan 1856, Boston; died there, 19 Feb 1858.
> v. CHARLES HENRY BELLOWS, born 13 Sep 1858, Boston; died 03 Oct 1914, Baltimore, Maryland.

176. **EMELINE ELIZABETH**[7] **WYTHE** (Stephen[6], Ebenezer[5], Ebenezer[4] Jr., Ebenezer[3], John[2], Nicholas[1]) was born in 1817 in Cambridge, Middlesex, Massachusetts. Emeline Elizabeth Wythe and William Rawson Jones were married on 15 Aug 1838 in Cambridge. **WILLIAM RAWSON JONES** was born 09 Apr 1810 in Winchendon, Worcester, Massachusetts to Abel Jones and Hannah Knight. He died on 08 Apr 1865 in Columbus, Muscogee, Georgia. She died on 07 Jun 1894 in Worcester, Worcester County, Massachusetts. Her "Wythe" surname appears there on her grave in Hope Cemetery.

William Rawson Jones and Emeline Elizabeth Wythe had the following children:

348.　　i.　JOHN PAUL[8] JONES, born 30 May 1839, Columbus; married FRANCES A. PERKINS, 06 Jun 1869, Worcester; died there, 30 Aug 1918.

　　　　ii.　LUCY E. JONES, born 17 Jun 1841, Columbus; died on 17 Dec 1854 at age 13 Fall River, Bristol, Massachusetts.

349.　　iii.　HARRIETT E. "HATTIE" JONES, born in Jul 1844, Columbus; married woolen mill owner, SAMUEL WHITE SCOTT, 21 Jul 1875, Uxbridge, Worcester, Massachusetts; died 20 Aug 1904, Old Orchard Beach, York, Maine.

350.　　iv.　MARY FLORENCE JONES was born in Oct 1847, Columbus; married THEODORE M. REMINGTON, 21 Feb 1866, Worcester; died there, 03 Mar 1931.

177. **SOPHIA BRADFORD**[7] **WYETH** (Stephen[6], Ebenezer[5], Ebenezer[4] Jr., Ebenezer[3], John[2], Nicholas[1]) was born on 24 Apr 1821 in Cambridge, Middlesex, Massachusetts. Sophia Bradford Wyeth married (1) **PALMER CLEVELAND CHANDLER** on 30 Sep 1844 in Pomfret, Windham, Connecticut. Palmer, son of Charles Chandler and Hannah Cleveland, was born on 07 Jan 1816 in Pomfret and died there on 08 Jun 1854 at age 38. Sophia married (2) **REV. DAVID OLNEY HOPKINS**, 05 Dec 1862 in Pomfret. David, son of George W. Hopkins and Mercy Shippee, was born on 27 Jan 1823 in Scituate, Providence, Rhode Island. Sophia died 19 Mar 1883 in Foster, Providence, Rhode Island. Her death was also registered across the state line in Killingly, Windham, Connecticut where she was buried in Bartlett Cemetery in an unmarked grave. David died 15 Sep 1912 at age 89 in Foster and is buried nearby in the Turner-Cooke Lot.

Beloved Child of Stephen Wyeth
SOPHIA BRADFORD HOPKINS
24 APR 1821 - 19 MAR 1883
Rest in Peace

The above proof is for the stone we bought for my 3rd great aunt's grave in Bartlett Cemetery in 2014.

Palmer Cleveland Chandler and Sophia Bradford Wyeth had one child:

　　　　i.　MARY EMMA[8] CHANDLER, born 09 Jan 1853, Pomfret; died 05 Jun 1870 at age 17 Foster and was buried near her father in Pomfret Street Cemetery.

178. **FRANCIS JOHN HIGGINSON**[7] **WYETH** (Stephen[6], Ebenezer[5], Ebenezer[4] Jr., Ebenezer[3], John[2], Nicholas[1]) was born on 29 Jun 1831 in Cambridge, Middlesex, Massachusetts. Francis John Higginson Wyeth and Rebecca Grate were married on 13 Aug 1857 in Salem Township, Meigs, Ohio. **REBECCA GRATE**, daughter of Peter Grate and Vilinda Barton, was born on 19 Sep 1833 in Middleton Township, Columbiana, Ohio. Francis, a farmer, served in the military during the Civil War. He died on 25 Oct 1911 at age 80 in Salem Township. Rebecca died there on 23 Feb 1919 at age 85.

Francis John Higginson Wyeth and Rebecca Grate had the following children:

351.   i.   WILLIAM GRATE[8] WYETH, born 15 Jun 1858, Salem Township, Meigs, Ohio; married CAROLINE RODEMA SCOTT, 01 Jun 1879, Salem Township; died there, at age 30, 23 Apr 1889 due to a chill he caught while harvesting Nebraska corn.

        ii.   PETER GEORGE WYETH, born 20 Feb 1861, Salem Township; died 16 Nov 1939, at age 78, in Gallipolis, Gallia, Ohio.

        iii.   HARMAN EBENEZER WYETH, born 09 Jan 1863, Salem Township; married MAGGIE D. REYNOLDS, 21 Nov 1892, Gallia County; died 17 Nov 1936, Langsville, Meigs, Ohio, at age 73, of pulmonary tuberculosis.

352.   iv.   SARAH ANN WYETH, born 07 Jan 1870, Salem Township; married WILLIAM ALONZO HAMPTON there on 21 Dec 1907; died 25 Jul 1965, Fremont, Sandusky, Ohio at age 95.

Francis John Higginson, Rebecca Grate, William Grate, Peter George, Harman Ebenezer and Maggie Reynolds Wyeth – all six of them rest together in Meigs County's Coy Hill Cemetery. Photos courtesy of siblings Helen Wyeth Hampson and Scott Allen Wyeth.

Notes for the family of Francis John Higginson Wyeth:

After his birth record, the first time Francis appeared in record books was the 01 Jun 1855 census of Townsend, Massachusetts. There he was listed as Frank Wyeth, a pail maker. The next record for him concerned land he purchased in 1856, valued at $495, in Salem Township, Meigs, Ohio.[1035]

In 1857, when he applied to marry, Francis said he did not know his mother's name. Since Sarah Ann Wright died a few days after Francis' birth, it was logical. Apparently, Stephen, who moved with his son, provided the information. Francis named his only daughter Sarah Ann Wyeth.

He was named for Dr. Francis John Higginson, a Cambridge abolitionist who attended Harvard with Francis' cousin, Dr. Jacob Wyeth. Over 30 years before the Civil War ended slavery, Dr. Higginson, wrote a book on its horrors and atrocities. Here is one of the doctor's observations.

> "Ask the meanest Irish laborer, who heaves the weary spade, upon our railroads or canals, what brought him from his native land. He will tell you, – hope. And did he want to come? Oh No! It was tearing the very fibers of his heart to leave the loved home of his childhood... He is glad, now, for success is before him, he is in freedom and plenty. But what has the slave to do with all these? Hope – it is not for him; freedom – it is not his birthright; success – he knows not what it means." [1036]

Inspired, not only by his own name, but also by the *Battle Hymn of the Republic*, "As He died to make men holy, let us die to make men free," Francis John Higginson Wyeth joined the effort to end slavery. At age 33, he responded to President Lincoln's call for lightly trained troops to handle routine assignments so regular army personnel could spend more time on the front lines. Francis volunteered as a "Hundred Days Man" on 02 May 1864 in Gallipolis, Ohio, in Co. H of the 140th Infantry Regiment (Ohio National Guard).

Eight months before he enlisted, Confederate General John Hunt Morgan brought the South's rebellion to Francis' door step. On 19 Jul 1863, the first of two Civil War battles fought in Ohio, ended in Salisbury Township, at present day Laurel Cliff and Hiland Roads, just ten miles east of the Wyeth home. Seeking to spread doubt that the South would still prevail and to spread fear in villages throughout Ohio, Hunt's 2,000 marauders suffered a devastating blow in Meigs County. With numbers vastly reduced, Morgan's Raiders escaped north to Columbiana County, Ohio. The site of their surrender, the northernmost point ever reached from the south by Confederate forces, was but a few miles from Rebecca Grate Wyeth's childhood home. [1037]

Rebecca hailed from a prominent Columbiana County family. Her uncle, William Grate, laid out the town of East Palestine there.[1038] Peter Grate moved the family to Salem Township in 1839 and remained there until his death. Most of his lands were divided equally between his heirs. At the time of probate, the Wyeths lived in Alberta, Meigs, Ohio. The town is gone but undoubtedly the location is the same as described in Francis Wyeth's will – between Danville and Rutland in section 7, township 8, range 13 of the Ohio Company's purchase.

Harmon Wyeth,
ALBERTA.
Meigs Co.   OHIO.

Another town no longer on the Meigs map is Hanesville. Harman E. Wyeth, a very busy man, was postmaster there until the RFD route went to Langsville. Harman farmed, ran a photo studio and taught school. Here, his great grandnephew and namesake, Harmon Harold Wyeth, holds the bell Harman used to summon his students to class.

This photo of Sarah Ann Wyeth, taken by her brother in Alberta, is courtesy of Scott Allen Wyeth.

Second son, Peter G. Wyeth never married. Extremely close to his parents, he had a difficult time functioning without them. At his father's death, Peter acted out so violently that he was committed to the Athens State Hospital on 27 Jun 1912. Discharged as improved on 15 Nov 1912, he was again declared a danger to the community during his mother's final illness and re-admitted to the hospital on 21 Feb 1919. Once released, Peter lived out the rest of his life on the 75-acre farm he inherited from his father.

Francis J. H. Wyeth also remembered his grandchildren, Mae Vantonia and Florin Royal Wyeth, with a small inheritance of $35 each. It is through Florin, Francis and Rebecca's one and only grandson, that the Wyeth name carried through to the author of this book, Christina Wyeth Baker.

179. (CAPTAIN) AMOS[7] HODGMAN (Lucy[6] Wyeth, Ebenezer[5], Ebenezer[4] Jr., Ebenezer[3], John[2], Nicholas[1]) was born on 21 Jun 1829 in Ashby, Middlesex, Massachusetts. Amos Hodgman and Martha Ann Denton were married on 01 Jan 1850 in Edwardsville, Madison, Illinois. MARTHA ANN DENTON, daughter of Samuel H. Denton and Mary S. Tindall, was born on 04 Oct 1824 in Edwardsville. Amos, captain of Co. H, 7th Kansas Cavalry, died of battle wounds on 16 Oct 1863 near Oxford, Lafayette, Mississippi. Hodgeman County, Kansas was named for him.[1039] Martha died on 28 May 1867 at age 42 in Bethalto, Madison, Illinois.

Captain Amos Hodgman and Martha Ann Denton had the following child:

      i. S. CATHARINE B.[8] HODGMAN, born 13 Feb 1853, Edwardsville; died 23 Nov 1863 at age 10 in Bethalto.

180. **GEORGE EBENEZER[7] WYETH** (*Joseph Russell[6], Ebenezer[5], Ebenezer[4] Jr., Ebenezer[3], John[2], Nicholas[1]*) was born 22 Feb 1835 in Boston, Suffolk, Massachusetts. George Ebenezer Wyeth, a hatter, and Ruth Jane Eaton were married in Chelsea, Suffolk, Massachusetts on 30 Dec 1858. **RUTH JANE EATON**, daughter of Ezra Oliver Eaton and Mary Jane Cazneau, was born on 09 Jan 1839 in Chelsea. She died there on 26 Oct 1902 at age 63. He died in Chelsea of heart problems on 30 Jun 1919 at age 84.

George Ebenezer Wyeth and Ruth Jane Eaton had the following children:

- i. GEORGE EZRA[8] WYETH, born 18 Oct 1859, Chelsea; died there at two months of dropsy of the brain on 10 Dec 1859.
- 353. ii. EDWARD CAZNEAU WYETH, born 22 Jan 1862, Chelsea; married LOUISE HANNAY PHEMISTER, 17 Jan 1887, Chelsea; died 18 Jan 1922, Brookline, Norfolk, Massachusetts.
- iii. ALICE GERTRUDE WYETH, born 16 Aug 1866, Chelsea; married JOHN ADAMS WALKER there at the Universalist Church, 04 Jun 1895; was active in women's rights as Director of Women's Public Safety in Chelsea; died there in 1942.
- 354. iv. WILLIAM HENRY WYETH SR., born 23 Feb 1869, Chelsea; married there to GEORGIE BELCHER MITCHELL, 27 Nov 1891; an alderman in Chelsea, William died 05 Mar 1915, Essex, Essex County, Massachusetts.
- 355. v. OLIVER EATON WYETH, born 04 Sep 1875, Chelsea; married JENNETTE CHESTER BLACK, 19 Sep 1900, Wakefield, Middlesex, Massachusetts; died 22 Feb 1935, Chelsea.

181. **REBECCA AURELIA[7] WYETH** (*Joseph Russell[6], Ebenezer[5], Ebenezer[4] Jr., Ebenezer[3], John[2], Nicholas[1]*) was born on 16 May 1836 in Boston. Rebecca Aurelia Wyeth and Edward Boylston Walker Restieaux, a druggist, were married on 18 Feb 1857 in Chelsea, Suffolk, Massachusetts. **(CAPTAIN) EDWARD BOYLSTON WALKER RESTIEAUX**, the son of Robert Restieaux and Susanna Walker, was born on 24 Sep 1832 in Chelsea. He died of typhoid fever there on 19 Mar 1878. Rebecca died of arteriosclerosis in Chelsea on 19 May 1915.

Edward Boylston Walker Restieaux and Rebecca Aurelia Wyeth had the following children:

- i. JOSEPH EDWARD WYETH[8] RESTIEAUX, born 09 Feb 1858, Chelsea; U. S. Navy Yard employee; died 26 Apr 1915, Somerville, Middlesex, Massachusetts of an overdose of chloral hydrate and whiskey.[1040]
- ii. SUSANNA B. RESTIEAUX, born 25 Jul 1859, Chelsea; died unmarried on 31 Dec 1924, Worcester, Worcester County, Massachusetts at age 65.

182. **JOSEPH HENRY[7] WYETH** (*Joseph Russell[6], Ebenezer[5], Ebenezer[4] Jr., Ebenezer[3], John[2], Nicholas[1]*) was born 08 Jan 1838 in Boston, Suffolk, Massachusetts. Joseph Henry Wyeth and (1) Mary Ann Cheever were married on 05 Oct 1862 in Charlestown, Suffolk, Massachusetts. **MARY ANN CHEEVER**, daughter of Joseph Cheever and Deborah Laighton, was born on 13 Mar 1842 in Portsmouth, Rockingham, New Hampshire. Joseph had a series of business reversals and filed bankruptcy on 29 May 1868. He wrote off some extravagant purchases such as $211.15 of tobacco, cigars and pipes.[1041] Joseph, a jeweler, had other legal troubles due to his financial situation.[1042] After divorcing Mary, Joseph married (2)

CAROLINE "CARRIE" OLDBURY on 27 Sep 1885 in Reading Middlesex, Massachusetts. Carrie was born in Jul 1855 in Birmingham, England to Edward Oldbury and Caroline Hinton. Joseph's first wife, Mary, died on 05 Apr 1909 in Somerville, Middlesex, Massachusetts. Carrie died on 13 Apr 1909 in Hyde Park, Suffolk, Massachusetts. Joseph died 29 Jul 1920 in Boston of chronic arteriosclerosis.

Joseph Henry Wyeth and Mary Ann Cheever had the following children:

       i. EDGAR ALAN[8] WYETH, born 01 May 1863, Chelsea, Suffolk, Massachusetts; died unmarried, 25 May 1919, Worcester, Worcester County, Massachusetts.

      ii. WILFRED CHEEVER WYETH, born 05 Sep 1865, Chelsea; a bookkeeper; died unmarried, 02 Nov 1924, Somerville.

356.   iii. STILLMAN LIBBY "LAIGHTON" WYETH, born 16 Apr 1868, Boston; married FRANKIE LUCINDA TIER, 18 Sep 1895, Waltham, Addison, Vermont; died 03 Mar 1909, Danvers, Essex, Massachusetts.

     iv. JOSEPH RUSSELL WYETH, born 05 Nov 1869, Boston; a dental supply jobber; married HENRIETTA HENDRICKSON, 11 Aug 1896, Saco, York, Maine; died 06 Sep 1931 from stomach cancer, Asheville, Buncombe, North Carolina.

183. **CATHARINE BAKER[7] WYETH** (Joseph Russell[6], Ebenezer[5], Ebenezer[4] Jr., Ebenezer[3], John[2], Nicholas[1]) was born on 16 Sep 1839 in Chelsea, Suffolk, Massachusetts. Catharine Baker Wyeth and **STILLMAN HIGGINS LIBBY** were married on 01 Mar 1860 in the Universalist Church of Chelsea. Stillman, son of John Adams Libby and Abigail Sawyer, was born on 03 Apr 1826 in Lymington, York, Maine. Catherine died on 07 Mar 1902 in Somerville, Middlesex, Massachusetts. Stillman died there on 10 Aug 1906.

Stillman Higgins Libby and Catharine Baker Wyeth had the following children:

       i. EMMA WARREN[8] LIBBY, born 22 Mar 1867, Chelsea; died at age two on 13 Oct 1869 in Somerville.

      ii. ANIBEL LIBBY, born 26 Jul 1872, Somerville; died there, 16 Sep 1872.

     iii. ELMER (ELMA) ROSWELL LIBBY, born on 26 Oct 1875, Somerville; died 28 Jul 1917, Boston. He never married.

184. **MARIA[7] WYETH** (Jonas[6] 3d, Jonas[5] Jr., Ebenezer[4] Jr., Ebenezer[3], John[2], Nicholas[1]) was born on 18 Sep 1826 in Watertown, Middlesex, Massachusetts. Maria Wyeth and William Angus were married in Cambridge on 02 Sep 1858. **WILLIAM ANGUS** was born to William Angus Sr. and Jane McKim on 24 Jun 1834 in Parkhead, Lanarkshire, Scotland. Maria died of anemia on 10 Mar 1868 in Montréal, Québec, Canada. He died there on 12 May 1916.

Maria's grave is number five in Mt. Auburn Cemetery, Lot 771 on Lupine Path.

William Angus and Maria Wyeth had the following children:

357.   i. GRACE WYETH[8] ANGUS, born 05 Dec 1865, Montréal; married WILLIAM RUFUS GREGG, 05 Aug 1890, Montréal; died in Nov 1948.

      ii. GEORGE ROBB ANGUS, born 06 Feb 1868, Montréal; married H. LOUISE GILL, 17 Jul 1899, Newton, Middlesex, Massachusetts; died there, 23 Jan 1949.

185. **JAMES HICKS^7 WYETH** (Jonas^6 3^d, Jonas^5 Jr., Ebenezer^4 Jr., Ebenezer^3, John^2, Nicholas^1) was born on 24 Jul 1830 in Watertown, Middlesex, Massachusetts. James Hicks Wyeth and Maria Carter Warland were married on 05 Jun 1860 in Cambridge. **MARIA CARTER WARLAND** was born in Jul 1835 in Claremont, Sullivan, New Hampshire to John Henry Warland and Mary Ann Phelps. He owned the James H. Wyeth and Company grocery store at 6 Brattle Street in Cambridge for many years. [1043] Maria died on 01 Oct 1877 in Cambridge. After selling his parents' home at 17 Fresh Pond Parkway to the president of Harvard, Charles Eliot, James retired to Pomona Park, Putnam, Florida to grow oranges. He was living there for the 1920 census with his daughter Elizabeth, but returned to Cambridge where he died on 19 May 1924 at age 93. He is buried in Mt. Auburn Cemetery, lot 771 on Lupine Path with his wife and seven of their nine children, five of whom died as infants.

James Hicks Wyeth as depicted in Samuel Atkins Eliot's 1913 *History of Cambridge, Massachusetts*, page 266.

James Hicks Wyeth and Maria Carter Warland had the following children:

      i. JAMES DINANT^8 WYETH, born 02 Oct 1861, Cambridge; died unmarried on 23 May 1912, West Palm Beach, Palm Beach, Florida.

      ii. ELIZABETH FLAGG WYETH, born 27 Jun 1863, Cambridge; died there unmarried on 19 Apr 1938.

      iii. SIDNEY E. WYETH, born 16 Dec 1864 in Cambridge; died there, 17 Jul 1865.

      iv. ADA MARIA WYETH, born 13 Mar 1868, Cambridge; died there, 23 Sep 1868.

      v. EDWARD A. WYETH, born 30 Dec 1871; Cambridge; died there, 20 Jul 1872.

      vi. MABEL F. WYETH, born 30 Mar 1873, Cambridge; died there, 14 Sep 1874.

      vii. ANNIE L. WYETH, born 17 Oct 1874, Cambridge; died there, 27 Sep 1892.

358.   viii. WALTER FRANCIS WYETH SR., born 21 Apr 1876, Cambridge; graduated Harvard, 1899; married JOSEPHINE HALL SHAILER, 26 Oct 1905, Brookline, Norfolk, Massachusetts; died 04 Dec 1931, Stow, Middlesex, Massachusetts.

      ix. WILLIAM W. WYETH, born 30 Sep 1877, Cambridge; died there, 13 Oct 1877.

186. **HARRIETT L.^{7} WYETH** (Jonas^6 3^d, Jonas^5 Jr., Ebenezer^4 Jr., Ebenezer^3, John^2, Nicholas^1) was born on 18 Jun 1833 in Cambridge, Middlesex, Massachusetts. Harriett L. Wyeth and William Pratt McLaren were married on 02 Sep 1858 in Cambridge (in a double wedding with her sister, Maria). [1044] **WILLIAM PRATT MCLAREN** was born on 19 Jun 1834 in Glasgow, Lanarkshire, Scotland to John McLaren and Catherine Pratt. William died on 02 Mar 1904 at age 69 in Milwaukee, Milwaukee County, Wisconsin. Harriett died at age 94 on 14 Mar 1928 in Seattle, King, Washington.

William Pratt McLaren and Harriett L. Wyeth had the following children:

      i. ELLEN "NELLIE"^{8} MCLAREN, born 23 Oct 1859, Montréal, Québec, Canada; died at age 12 on 26 Mar 1872 in Milwaukee.

      ii. WILLIAM MCLAREN, born 05 Oct 1862 in Montreal; died there, 25 Jun 1863.

      iii. ARTHUR WYETH MCLAREN, born 29 Dec 1863, Montreal; died at age eight on 16 Sep 1872 in Milwaukee.

      iv. MARY MCLAREN, born 1865, Milwaukee; died 24 Oct 1960, Seattle, age 95.

v. MARIA MCLAREN, born 26 May 1868, Milwaukee; married STANTON ALLEN there on 04 Aug 1892; died 25 Mar 1952, Seattle.

vi. GEORGE SAUNDERS MCLAREN, born 07 Nov 1871, Milwaukee; married VIRGINIA CARAWAY on 30 Apr 1901 in Philadelphia, Pennsylvania; died on 03 Aug 1911 at age 39 in Seattle.

359. vii. WILLIAM PRATT MCLAREN JR., born 15 Nov 1876, Milwaukee; married BLANCHE ELIZABETH ARNOLD there on 10 Oct 1902; died 18 Aug 1955, Lake Grove on Lake Oswego, Clackamas, Oregon.

187. **FRANCIS OREN**[7] **WILLARD** (Susan[6] Wyeth, Jonas[5] Jr., Ebenezer[4] Jr., Ebenezer[3], John[2], Nicholas[1]) was born on 13 Jan 1829 in Ashby, Middlesex, Massachusetts. He married **ELIZABETH LEE CAMPBELL**, daughter of John D. Campbell and Mary Ann Gillam Warren, on 08 Jul 1850 in Newton, Middlesex, Massachusetts. Elizabeth was born on 20 Sep 1827 in Boston, Suffolk, Massachusetts. Francis was a piano manufacturer in Leominster, Worcester, Massachusetts. He died there on 06 Apr 1906. She died 31 Oct 1915 in Boston.

The children of Francis Oren Willard and Elizabeth Lee Campbell included:

i. GEORGE SUMMER[8] WILLARD, born 27 Aug 1857, Ashburnham, Worcester, Massachusetts; died 01 Mar 1942, Reading, Middlesex, Massachusetts.

360. ii. CARRIE LOUISA WILLARD, born 24 Mar 1860, Leominster; married WILBUR FRANKLIN WOODBURY, 05 Jan 1893, Leominster; died there, 15 Apr 1926.

361. iii. EDGAR LINCOLN WILLARD, born 28 Jan 1864, Leominster; married (1) LUELLA E. OSBORNE there, 24 Oct 1891; married (2) ESTELLA LITCHFIELD, 12 Apr 1899, Marshfield, Plymouth, Massachusetts; died 16 Dec 1932, North Scituate, Plymouth, Massachusetts.

iv. IDA LUCY WILLARD, born 27 May 1867, Leominster; married CHARLES HENRY PREBLE, 05 Jan 1897, Leominster; died 04 Nov 1946, Springfield, Hampden, Massachusetts.

188. **GEORGE OTIS**[7] **WILLARD** (Susan[6] Wyeth, Jonas[5] Jr., Ebenezer[4] Jr., Ebenezer[3], John[2], Nicholas[1]) was born on 10 Mar 1831 in Ashby, Middlesex, Massachusetts. George married **LUCY FARROLL CAMPBELL** on 17 Nov 1869 in Fitchburg, Worcester, Massachusetts. Sister to Elizabeth Lee Campbell, Lucy was born on 22 Feb 1843 in Watertown, Middlesex, Massachusetts to John D. Campbell and Mary Ann Gillam Warren. A gold miner, George died on 11 Mar 1893 of morphine poisoning in Boston. Lucy died on 09 Jun 1929 in Weymouth, Norfolk, Massachusetts.

George Otis Willard and Lucy Farroll Campbell had the following children:

i. MARY WYETH PERRY[8] WILLARD, born 31 Mar 1868 in Leominster to Crosby Alpheus Perry and Mary Ann Willard (she was adopted by her uncle George Willard and his wife Lucy Campbell); Mary, a long time Cambridge realtor and candidate for assessor in 1920, died unmarried, 10 Apr 1956, Cambridge.[1045]

ii. LULU C. WILLARD, born 18 Apr 1871, Fitchburg; died there, 28 Apr 1871.

iii. EMMA CARRIE WILLARD, born 07 Jul 1874, Leominster; married DANIEL BUTLER NYE, Sep 1901, Yokohama, Japan;[1046] died 10 Apr 1949, Weymouth.

189. **SUSAN LOUISA**[7] **WILLARD** (Susan[6] Wyeth, Jonas[5] Jr., Ebenezer[4] Jr., Ebenezer[3], John[2], Nicholas[1]) was born on 21 Jan 1833 in Ashby, Middlesex, Massachusetts. She married **WILLIAM HENRY GROUT** on 30 Apr 1855 in Leominster, Worcester, Massachusetts. He was born on 02 Jan 1835 in Highgate, Franklin, Vermont. She died on 08 Oct 1892 in Fitchburg, Worcester, Massachusetts. He died there on 02 Jul 1902.

The children of William Henry Grout and Susan Louisa Willard included:

      i. HERBERT HENRY[8] GROUT, born 26 Mar 1858, Ashburnham, Worcester, Massachusetts; died 17 May 1889, Fitchburg.

      ii. ALICE LOUISA GROUT, born 25 Aug 1867, Fitchburg; married FREDERICK A. WATSON there, 14 Dec 1896; died 23 Feb 1949, Boston.

190. **MARY ANN**[7] **WILLARD** (Susan[6] Wyeth, Jonas[5] Jr., Ebenezer[4] Jr., Ebenezer[3], John[2], Nicholas[1]) was born on 28 May 1839 in Ashburnham, Worcester, Massachusetts. Her marriage intention was filed there to **CROSBY ALPHEUS PERRY**, a peddler, on 21 Sep 1858. He was born on 01 Mar 1838 in Concord, Essex, Vermont to Micah Perry and Susannah Woodbury. Once he became a doctor, they divorced. Mary Ann struggled so much then that she let her brother adopt her baby. Although she raised her other children, the children took George Otis Willard's name. Mary Ann died 12 Jan 1916 in Leominster. Crosby died 19 Jan 1926 in North Adams, Berkshire, Massachusetts.

Crosby Alpheus Perry and Mary Ann Willard had the following children:

362.   i. SUSAN ANNETTE[8] WILLARD, born 13 Apr 1861, Ashburnham, married HENRY BRIGGS there, 27 Sep 1881; died 05 Jun 1940, San Bernardino, California.

      ii. CHARLES CHESTER WILLARD, born 11 Aug 1865, Leominster; death unknown.

      iii. MARY WYETH PERRY WILLARD, born Mary Beth Perry, was adopted by her uncle George Otis Willard and aunt Lucy Farroll Campbell (see # 188).

191. **JOHN JASPER**[7] **WYETH** (John[6], Jonas[5] Jr., Ebenezer[4] Jr., Ebenezer[3], John[2], Nicholas[1]) was born on 25 Dec 1841 in Cambridge, Middlesex, Massachusetts. John, with a bit of humor, gave an excellent firsthand account of the harsh life of a Civil War soldier in a journal published in 1878 called *Leaves from a Diary Written While Serving in Co. E, 44 Mass., Dep't of No. Carolina, from September 1862 to June 1863.*[1047] John married **MARGARET ELIZA HIXON** in Sharon, Norfolk, Massachusetts on 12 Nov 1867. She was born there on 03 Jan 1842 to Albert Hixon and Elizabeth Billings. Margaret died on 16 Jul 1904 in St. Louis, Missouri. John died in Quincy, Norfolk, Massachusetts on 11 Mar 1906. They are buried on Yarrow Path in lot 1800, Mt. Auburn Cemetery, Cambridge.

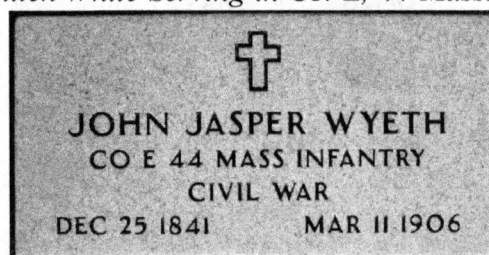

JOHN JASPER WYETH
CO E 44 MASS INFANTRY
CIVIL WAR
DEC 25 1841   MAR 11 1906

It took almost a year to find a donor to finance John's stone installation. Once Mt. Auburn sent the marker application to the V.A., it was quickly approved, but won't be put in place until the ground softens in Spring 2019. Photo courtesy of Mt. Auburn Cemetery.

John and Margaret Eliza Hixon Wyeth's children were:

363.   i. JOHN HIXON[8] WYETH SR., born 22 Oct 1869, Boston; married MARY FAYE MCKERNAN there, 06 Jun 1906; died 05 May 1942, Amesbury, Massachusetts.

364.   ii.   MARION ELLIS WYETH, born 16 Nov 1871 in Sharon; married WALDEMAR ROBERT WRIGHT there on 20 Oct 1898; died 18 Oct 1923, St. Louis, Missouri.

192. **LOUISA**[7] **WYETH** (Elisha[6], Joshua[5], Ebenezer[4] Jr., Ebenezer[3], John[2], Nicholas[1]) was born 13 Oct 1804, Luzerne (Bradford) County, Pennsylvania. Louisa married (1) **REUBEN SAILORS** on 18 May 1821 in Brookville, Franklin, Indiana. He was born on 09 Feb 1801 in Little River, Abbeville District, South Carolina. They divorced in 1834. Reuben died on 13 Sep 1870 in Ashland, Wabash, Indiana. Louisa married (2) **DR. ISAAC WASHINGTON MCCARTY**, 21 Feb 1841, Van Buren County, Iowa. The son of Benjamin McCarty and Sarah Connor, Isaac was born on 13 Mar 1803 in Hawkins Barr, Grainger, Tennessee. The first sheriff of Wayne County, Iowa, he died there on 14 Feb 1873 in Lineville, Jefferson Township. Louisa next married (3) **JOHN MILTON CORDER** in Wayne County, Iowa on 19 Aug 1878. John was born 13 Aug 1798 in Tazewell County, Virginia and died 13 Nov 1883 in Jefferson Township. Louisa died there on 05 Oct 1890.

Reuben Sailors and Louisa Wyeth had the following child:

365.   i.   FRANCES ALVIRA[8] SAILORS, born 19 Aug 1822, Rush County, Indiana; married WILLIAM HOWARD there, 15 Dec 1842; died 09 Jul 1905, La Fontaine, Indiana.

Isaac Washington McCarty and Louisa Wyeth had the following children:

366.   i.   CATHERINE[8] MCCARTY, born 25 Sep 1842, Farmington, Van Buren, Iowa; married JAMES ALEXANDER BELVEL, 1860, Lineville; died there, 05 Aug 1926.
367.   ii.   ISAAC DARROW MCCARTY, born 15 Mar 1845, Van Buren County; during the Civil War he entered the Iowa Cavalry on 29 Feb 1864; married (1) REBECCA JORDAN, circa 1865; married (2) LYDIA RITCHERSON, 13 Oct 1898, Doniphan County, Kansas; died 23 Apr 1914, Marshalltown, Marshall, Iowa.

193. **AMY**[7] **WYETH** (Elisha[6], Joshua[5], Ebenezer[4] Jr., Ebenezer[3], John[2], Nicholas[1]) was born about 1808 in Towanda, Luzerne (Bradford), Pennsylvania. Amy Wyeth and **AVENENT T. LEWIS** were married on 27 Apr 1823 in Brookville, Franklin, Indiana. Avenent was born in 1801 in Kentucky to Thomas Powers Lewis and Elizabeth Thompson. Amy died in 1870 and Avenent in 1877, both just before Christmas, in Vigo County, Indiana.

The children of Avenent T. Lewis and Amy Wyeth included:

         i.   WILLIAM F.[8] LEWIS, born 21 May 1824, Franklin County, Indiana; married BASHELON ELLEN DUBRE, 11 Jan 1850, Riley Township, Vigo, Indiana; died 21 Aug 1886 in Buena Vista, Richland, Wisconsin.
368.   ii.   NANCY ELIZABETH LEWIS, born in 1826, Franklin County, married (1) JOHN COLLINS, 30 Nov 1845, Vigo County, married (2) WILLIAM BENJAMIN MEWHINNEY there, 28 Jan 1858; died 10 Mar 1895, Terre Haute, Vigo, Indiana.
         iii. MORTON E. LEWIS, born 27 Dec 1840, Riley; served Co. D, Indiana 115th; married three times; died 25 Oct 1922, Brazil, Clay, Indiana.
369.   iv.   ALCESTA AMY LEWIS, born circa 1843, Riley; married HARRISON BALLEW, 24 Dec 1862, Terre Haute; died 19 Mar 1912, Aberdeen, Brown, South Dakota.[1048]

370.   v. HOMER E. LEWIS, born 15 Jun 1848, Riley; married ALICE L. THOMPSON there, 16 Dec 1869; died 02 Nov 1928, Danville, Vermilion, Illinois.

194. **JAMES SALISBURY[7] WYETH** (Elisha[6], Joshua[5], Ebenezer[4] Jr., Ebenezer[3], John[2], Nicholas[1]) was born on 19 Jul 1810 in Towanda, Luzerne (Bradford), Pennsylvania. James married (1) **MARTHA MEWHINNEY** on 29 May 1834 in Terre Haute, Vigo, Indiana. Martha was born circa 1814 in Ohio to James Mewhinney and Elizabeth McKee. James Salisbury Wyeth, a machinist by trade, was elected a councilman, on 30 May 1852, for the town of Terre Haute. [1049] Martha died on 19 Aug 1856 in the town while James was the Worshipful Master of the Terre Haute Lodge of Free & Accepted Masons (F. & A. M.), 1855-1859.[1050] James married (2) **SARAH ANN JENKS** on 11 Dec 1862 in Terre Haute. Sarah was born in New York circa 1821. James died on 02 Apr 1882 at age 71 in Terre Haute. Sarah died there on 19 Jan 1899.

James Salisbury Wyeth, as he appeared shortly after heading the Terre Haute Lodge No. 19 F. &A. M. Used with permission of the Grand Lodge of Indiana.

Children of James Salisbury Wyeth and Martha Mewhinney included:

        i. ANN MARIA[8] WYETH, born circa 1838, Terre Haute; married there to OBEDIAH C. FUQUA, 25 May 1864; died at age 31 of congestion; buried on 01 Jul 1869 in Terre Haute's Woodlawn Cemetery.
        ii. ALBERT WYETH, born about 1852, Terre Haute; died after the 1860 census.

195. **FRANCIS MARTIN[7] WYETH** (Elisha[6], Joshua[5], Ebenezer[4] Jr., Ebenezer[3], John[2], Nicholas[1]) was born on 13 Sep 1814 in Towanda, Bradford, Pennsylvania. Francis married **DORCAS TABITHA TANKERSLEY** on 07 Jul 1836 in Riley Township, Vigo, Indiana. Dorcas, daughter of Charles Tankersley and Dorcas Skeen, was born on 03 Mar 1818 in Jefferson County, Tennessee. Francis served as a sergeant in Co. G of the 43rd Indiana Infantry in the Civil War. Discharged for disability in 1862 and devastated by the loss of two sons in the War, Francis died at age 62 on 29 Mar 1877 in Terre Haute. Dorcas died at her son Charles' home in Fowler, Otero, Colorado on 05 Apr 1911 at age 93.

Francis Martin Wyeth and Dorcas Tabitha Tankersley had the following children:

371.   i. MARY ETTA[8] WYETH, born 06 Jul 1837, Riley Township; married (1) JOHN H. EASTER, 16 Sep 1852, Clay County, Indiana; married (2) JOHN C. CARPENTER, 01 May 1877, Sullivan County, Indiana; died 29 Jan 1932, Terre Haute.
        ii. JOHN MILTON WYETH was born on 08 Mar 1840 in Riley Township. On 15 Sep 1861, he enlisted at Paris, Illinois in Co. A of the 7th Illinois Cavalry. Less than a year later, he died of typhoid fever on 24 Jun 1862, at age 22, in the U.S. Army General Hospital, No. 3, Evansville, Vanderburgh, Illinois. The inscription on his grave in Mewhinney Cemetery, Riley Township, states he "died in the service of his country."
372.   iii. JAMES ERASMUS WYETH, born 17 Jul 1842, Riley Township; beginning 18 Apr 1861 served in both the 12th Illinois Infantry and the 7th Illinois Cavalry Regiments; was promoted to sergeant and mustered out in Springfield,

Sangamon, Illinois on 15 Oct 1864; married LOUISA JANE ROBERTS, 21 Jul 1866, Terre Haute; died there on 30 Mar 1924.

373.   iv.   MARIA ABIGAIL "BABE MARION" WYETH, born circa 1846, Riley Township; married JAMES MCGRIFF, 14 Apr 1866, Lost Creek Township, Vigo, Indiana; died there in 1874.

        v.   OTIS WYETH, born 08 Dec 1848, Riley Township; enlisted as a private in Co. D, 11th Regiment Indiana Cavalry on 09 Dec 1863, Terre Haute. His tombstone in Mewhinney Cemetery says he died in the service of his country on 29 Aug 1864 at the extremely young age of 15 years, 8 months and 21 days.

        vi.   NANCY E. WYETH, born circa 1851, Riley Township; married FRANCIS M. HAYDEN, 04 May 1871, Terre Haute; died there on 12 Dec 1875.

374.   vii.   CHARLES LEWIS WYETH, born 01 Oct 1852, Riley Township; married (1) MARY ELIZABETH "LIBBIE" SHRIMP, 29 Oct 1872, Danville, Vermilion, Illinois; married (2) ANNA BEATRICE ESLER, 02 Apr 1895, Joliet, Will, Illinois; died on 19 Mar 1925, Watsonville, Santa Cruz, California.

196. **ELIZA^7 WYETH** (Elisha^6, Joshua^5, Ebenezer^4 Jr., Ebenezer^3, John^2, Nicholas^1) was born on 09 May 1817 in Brookville, Franklin, Indiana. Eliza Wyeth and John M. Harper were married on 02 Apr 1837 in Riley Township, Vigo, Indiana. **JOHN M. HARPER** was born on 19 Jul 1816 in Hamilton County, Ohio. She died on 20 Feb 1888 at age 70 in Lost Creek Township, Vigo County, Indiana. He died there two days later on 22 Feb 1888 at age 71. They were buried together in the same tomb in Riley's Oak Hill Cemetery.

John M. Harper and Eliza Wyeth had the following children:

375.   i.   WILLIAM SALISBURY^8 HARPER, born 21 May 1838, Riley Township; served three years in Co. G of the 43rd Indiana Infantry, discharged as a sergeant on 16 Oct 1864; married LAURA EMELINE LAWRENCE, 25 Nov 1865, Clay County, Indiana; died 24 Mar 1911, Davenport, Lincoln, Washington.

        ii.   AMY A. HARPER, born about 1840 in Riley Township; died there circa 1880.

        iii.   CATHARINE HARPER, born circa 1842, Riley Township; married NATHANIEL BEENER, 05 Aug 1866, Vigo County; died there circa 1879.

376.   iv.   MARIA HARPER, born 09 May 1844, Riley Township; married WILLIAM H. TURNER, 26 Dec 1867, Vigo County; died 22 Jul 1929, Riley Township.

        v.   MARY C. HARPER, born about 1849, Vigo County; died there before 1860.

        vi.   SARAH E. HARPER, born 19 Jul 1854, Vigo County; married MICAGA A. HYDE, 09 Dec 1875, Vigo County; according to her death certificate, she was murdered there at age 64 on 18 Jan 1919 in Lost Creek Township.

        vii.   INDIANA HARPER, born circa 1855, Vigo County; married FRANKLIN T. BUTT there on 31 Aug 1876; died before 1888, Posey, Clay, Indiana.

        viii.   EMALINE "LINNA" HARPER, born in 1867, Vigo County; died there circa 1869.

197. **SARAH MARIA^7 WYETH** (Elisha^6, Joshua^5, Ebenezer^4 Jr., Ebenezer^3, John^2, Nicholas^1) was born circa 1822 in Brookville, Franklin, Indiana. Sarah Maria married **WILLIAM BENJAMIN MEWHINNEY**, on 26 Dec 1841 in Riley Township, Vigo, Indiana. William, son of Thomas Mewhinney and Mary Miller, was born on 03 Mar 1819 in Ohio. Sarah died circa 1857 in Vigo County. He next married his wife's niece, Nancy Elizabeth Lewis

Collins (#368). William died in Terre Haute Vigo, Indiana, 23 Aug 1868.

William Benjamin Mewhinney and Sarah Maria Wyeth had the following children:

377.   i.   JAMES MANFORD[8] MEWHINNEY, born 1842, Riley Township; 02 Oct 1867 married MINERVA "MINNIE" ADAMS, Terre Haute; died in Aug 1886, Kansas City, Wyandotte, Kansas where he was employed as a cooper (barrel maker).

          ii. WALLACE MEWHINNEY, born circa 1845, Riley Township; enlisted on 04 Mar 1863 in Co. B of the 6th Indiana Cavalry, mustered out as a sergeant on 15 Sep 1865 in Murfreesboro, Tennessee; in 1871, he was foreman of a 45-hand cooper shop in Wyandotte, Kansas;[1051] died 25 Nov 1875, Denver, Colorado.[1052]

378.   iii. TRESSA MEWHINNEY,[1053] born Jan 1848, Riley Township; married (1) CHARLES ALONZO WYETH there, 21 Mar 1864; married (2) GEORGE O. DRAKE, circa 1890; died 28 Jan 1897, Deadwood, Lawrence, South Dakota.[1054]

         iv. FLORA BAYMILLER MEWHINNEY, born 27 Jul 1857, Terre Haute; married JOHN LEE GORDON, 29 Nov 1877, Clay County, Indiana; they had three children; Flora died 13 Jul 1939, Chicago, Cook, Illinois.

198. **MILTON LEWIS[7] WYETH** M.D. (Elisha[6], Joshua[5], Ebenezer[4] Jr., Ebenezer[3], John[2], Nicholas[1]) was born in Mar 1825 in Brookville, Franklin, Indiana. He served in the Mexican-American War. Milton married **MARY ELIZA DAVIS** on 31 Dec 1848 in Vigo County, Indiana. Mary, daughter of Louis H. Davis and Mary Dickinson, was born on 18 Jun 1828 in Mason, Warren, Ohio. While on active duty in the Civil War, Dr. Wyeth died on the Mississippi River on 04 May 1862 in the steamer *De Soto*. An active member of the Universalist Church, Mary, died on 02 Sep 1906 in Terre Haute, Vigo, Indiana and was buried with her husband and two sons in the New Harmony Cemetery, Prairieton Township, Vigo, Indiana.

Dr. Wyeth died soon after the Bombardment and Capture of the Mississippi River's Island #10 on 07 Apr 1862. This Currier & Ives lithograph is in the public domain.

Dr. Milton Lewis Wyeth and Mary Eliza Davis had the following children:

         i.   WILLIAM WORTH "WILLIE"[8] WYETH, born 14 Oct 1849, Riley Township, Vigo, Indiana. Some think he was in the Civil War, but that was William Wyett. Willie died at age 15 on 03 Nov 1864 in Terre Haute.

         ii. JAMES COURTNEY WYETH, born 11 May 1851 in Vigo County; he died there on 08 Jan 1854 at age two.

Notes for Dr. Milton Lewis Wyeth and Mary Eliza Davis:

Responding to President Polk's call for expanding U.S. territory through armed conflict, Milton and his first cousin, Willis B. Wyeth, enlisted to serve in the Mexican-American War. They joined Co. H of the 4th Indiana Regiment on 12 Jun 1847 in Jeffersonville, Indiana. The 03 Feb 1848 Treaty of Guadalupe Hidalgo ended the war and established the Rio Grande River as the U.S.-Mexican border. Mexico accepted the U.S. annexation of Texas and agreed to sell, to the

U.S., territory that includes Arizona, California, Colorado, Nevada, New Mexico and Utah.[1055] Still a nationalist, after returning to Indiana, on 07 Jul 1848, Milton was commissioned 1st Lieutenant in an independent militia called the Riley Guards.

After his marriage, Milton decided to pursue a career in medicine. In 1852, he moved to Columbus, Ohio to enroll in the Starling Medical College.[1056] The college, one of six predecessors to The Ohio State University College of Medicine, was named for Mr. Lyne Starling. Starling donated the land at State and Sixth Streets, Columbus (the present site of Grant Medical Center) as well as the money to build both the college and St. Francis Hospital. The resulting organization was the first to combine patient care and clinical teaching in the same U.S. facility.[1057]

Built in 1847, St. Francis Hospital comprised two-thirds of the building with Starling Medical College housed in the remainder. This post card is in the public domain.

Medical degree in hand, Milton likely made the 300-mile journey from central Ohio to his home on the western border of Indiana via the Terre Haute and Richmond Rail Road. In addition to practicing medicine in Vigo County, Dr. Wyeth was appointed postmaster of the town of Prairieton on 07 Feb 1856. He was also engaged in commercial trade there. Then for a short time, starting in 1859, he farmed in Stratton, Edgar, Illinois.[1058]

When the Civil War broke out, Milton responded to his country's call for a second time. First, he enlisted in Jul, 1861 in the 31st Indiana Volunteer Infantry. Then on 20 Sep 1861, Dr. Wyeth volunteered his services as a physician. He helped to organize Co. G, of the Indiana 43rd Regular Volunteers and was elected first lieutenant. Less than a year later, Milton contracted typhoid dysentery at Fort Pillow on the Mississippi River near Henning, Tennessee. Sadly, he died on the steamer USS *De Soto* on 04 May 1862 near Missouri Island #10 on the Mississippi River while being transported to a Cairo, Illinois hospital.[1059] He was only 37 years old.

Widowed for life at age 33 and childless by age 36, Mary Eliza's heart wrenching grief can only be imagined at the death of her precious 15-year-old Willie just five months before the Civil War ended. In her misery, undoubtedly, Mary Eliza empathized with Mary Todd Lincoln. On the day President Lincoln was assassinated, he told his wife, "We must both be more cheerful in the future. Between the war and the loss of our darling Willie we have been very miserable."

Mary Todd Lincoln descended into severe depression and never found the strength to be cheerful again. The First Lady's story leaves us to wonder how Mary Eliza Davis Wyeth had the strength and fortitude to cope with the tragedies of her life, alone, for 42 years to her death at age 78.

199. **CHARLES PRENTICE**[7] **WYTHE** (Joshua[6] Jr., Joshua[5], Ebenezer[4] Jr., Ebenezer[3], John[2], Nicholas[1]) was born on 18 Dec 1811 in Towanda, Luzerne (Bradford), Pennsylvania. Charles Prentice Wythe and **NANCY RECTOR** were married on 15 Sep 1836 in Riley Township, Vigo, Indiana. Nancy, daughter of John Preston Rector and Catherine Price, was born on 19 Sep 1818 in Riley Township. He died in Riley Township on 02 Aug 1869. She died there on 06 May 1881.

Charles Prentice Wythe and Nancy Rector had the following children:

379.   i.   EDWIN RUTHVEN[8] WYTHE SR., born 20 Oct 1837, Riley Township; named for a Scottish warrior; enlisted in Co. F, 14th Indiana Infantry on 07 Jun 1861, his regiment fought in the battle of Gettysburg, discharged for disability 06 May 1864; married NANCY JENNIE HANA, 22 Oct 1867, Terre Haute, Vigo, Indiana; died there at his home at 527 S. 15th St. on 12 Dec 1888 as a result of a skull fracture sustained at the Gainey & Hover's saloon, Terre Haute.[1060]

        ii.   ALLEN WILLIE WYTHE, born 23 Oct 1839 in Riley Township. He mustered in the 14th with his brother in Terre Haute. He died during the Civil War on 04 Apr 1863, at the age of 23, of typhoid fever in the Regimental Hospital in Spotsylvania County, Virginia near Fredericksburg.[1061]

380.   iii.   JOHN WESLEY WYTHE, born 02 Jan 1844, Riley Township; served in the Indiana 6th Cavalry Unit. Although he had not fully recovered from the measles, he was ordered to guard rebel prisoners in Camp Morton, Indiana. His health deteriorated further and he was discharged on disability on 13 Apr 1863. He signed his name "Wyeth" when he applied for a military pension. He stated the name could be spelled either way. John married LUCY ANNETTA CAMPBELL 28 Apr 1872, Riley Township; died 15 Dec 1919, Terre Haute.

381.   iv.   HANNAH POND WYTHE, born 23 Dec 1846, Riley Township; married AUSTIN MILLER COLLINS there, 10 Feb 1870; died 18 Apr 1878, Riley Township.

382.   v.   CATHARINE PRICE WYTHE, born Riley Township, 1850; married WILLIAM PERRY BENNETT, 25 Jan 1870, Riley Township; died 04 Apr 1889, Terre Haute.

383.   vi.   JULIA ANN WYTHE, born 1852, Riley Township; married GEORGE A. HABERMEIER, 27 Nov 1874, Terre Haute; died there circa 1894.

This photo of Hannah Pond Wythe Collins is from her great granddaughter Naoda Little. Hannah's funeral march was over a mile long.

384.   vii.   CLARISSA ELIZABETH "CLARA" WYTHE, born 1854, Riley Township; married ROBERT SLAVENS BROWN there, 02 Dec 1875; died 01 Oct 1892, Vigo County.

200. **ELIZA BREWER[7] WYETH** (Joshua[6] Jr., Joshua[5], Ebenezer[4] Jr., Ebenezer[3], John[2], Nicholas[1]) was born on 30 Jul 1813 in Towanda, Bradford, Pennsylvania. Eliza Brewer Wyeth and William LaForge were married on 30 Sep 1830 in Brookville, Franklin, Indiana. **WILLIAM LAFORGE**, son of John L. LaForge and Mary Smith, was born on 25 Jul 1811 in Brookville. Eliza died there in childbirth on 14 Sep 1834 at age 21. He died on 10 Mar 1903 at age 91 in the Grant County Infirmary, Gas City, Indiana.

William LaForge and Eliza Brewer Wyeth had the following children:

385.   i.   ALEXANDER[8] LAFORGE, born 21 Aug 1831, Brookville; married MELEZINE EMILEY JENNINGS, 27 Dec 1855, Burnet County, Texas; 1862 served in Captain John Barton's Co. of the 3rd Frontier District Texas State Troops,[1062] in Dec 1863 his group was mustered into the Confederate States of America;[1063] died 01 Jul 1923, Marble Falls, Burnet, Texas at age 91.

386. ii. EMILY LAFORGE, born 12 Jan 1834, Brookville; married EDWARD JONES, 16 Nov 1851, Rush County, Indiana; died 13 Sep 1881, Grant County, Indiana.

201. **EMILY[7] WYETH** (Joshua[6] Jr., Joshua[5], Ebenezer[4] Jr., Ebenezer[3], John[2], Nicholas[1]) was born on 29 Sep 1815 in Cincinnati, Hamilton, Ohio. [1064] Emily Wyeth and Benjamin Mewhinney were married on 03 Nov 1830 in Brookville, Franklin, Indiana. **BENJAMIN MEWHINNEY**, son of John Mewhinney and Margaret Burns, was born in Nov 1809 in Hamilton, Butler, Ohio. She died at age 60 on 09 Mar 1876 in Riley Township, Vigo, Indiana. He died there in 1893. [1065]

Benjamin Mewhinney and Emily Wyeth had the following children:

387. i. MARTHA[8] MEWHINNEY, born 24 Aug 1831, Brookville; married JEREMIAH MILLER, 03 Mar 1855, Riley Township; died 19 Jun 1869, Vigo County.
388. ii. JOHNSON MEWHINNEY, born 22 Mar 1834, Riley Township; married RACHEL MCGILL there, 28 Jul 1855; died 30 May 1913, Hickman, Fulton, Kentucky.
389. iii. MARY ANN MEWHINNEY, born 18 May 1836, Riley; married THOMAS M. COLLINS there, 24 Oct 1851; died 04 Jan 1926, Perry, Clay, Indiana.
390. iv. CLARISSA MEWHINNEY, born 21 Oct 1838, Riley Township; married GEORGE W. LIGHT, 21 Jan 1855, Riley Township; died there, 06 Mar 1928.
391. v. HOWARD MEWHINNEY, born 15 Apr 1846, Riley Township; married MARTHA LYONS, 23 Sep 1868, Riley Township; died 06 Apr 1906, Terre Haute.

202. **MARY[7] WYETH** (Joshua[6] Jr., Joshua[5], Ebenezer[4] Jr., Ebenezer[3], John[2], Nicholas[1]) was born on 31 Jan 1818 in Cincinnati, Hamilton, Ohio. Mary Ann Wyeth and **DANIEL H. COLLINS** were married on 18 Jan 1838 in Riley Township, Vigo, Indiana. Daniel was born on 29 Jun 1816 in Columbus, Franklin, Ohio. She died on 22 Jan 1849 at age 30 in Riley Township. He died on 22 Aug 1883 in Big Creek, Neosho, Kansas.

Daniel H. Collins and Mary Wyeth had the following child:

i. JOHN W.[8] COLLINS, born circa 1837, Riley Township; enlisted as a corporal in Co. F, Indiana 17th Infantry, 12 Jun 1861; promoted to full Captain, 08 Dec 1864; [1066] mustered out 08 Aug 1865, Macon, Georgia; married ANGELINE MODESITT, 28 Oct 1869, Riley Township; died 12 Aug 1873, Kansas Township, Edgar, Illinois.

203. **CLARISSA[7] WYETH** (Joshua[6] Jr., Joshua[5], Ebenezer[4] Jr., Ebenezer[3], John[2], Nicholas[1]) was born on 31 Jan 1820 in Cincinnati, Hamilton, Ohio. Clarissa Wyeth and John Mewhinney were married on 15 Dec 1839 in Riley Township, Vigo, Indiana. **JOHN MEWHINNEY**, son of Thomas Mewhinney and Mary Miller, was born on 13 Aug 1820 in Warren County, Ohio. John disappeared between baby Bennie's death in 1853 and Hannah's birth in 1854. Without funds to support their five children, Clarissa was desperate. Although his whereabouts were unknown, she sued John in 1861 for a share of his father's estate. [1067] Clarissa, who was blind at the time, lived with her sister Emily in Riley Township. Beat down by life, Clarissa died there on 14 May 1876 at age 56.

John Mewhinney and Clarissa Wyeth had the following children:

392.   i.   MELVINA[8] MEWHINNEY, born 19 Jul 1841, Lost Creek Township, Vigo, Indiana; married JOHN MCKEE there, 24 Dec 1857; died after 1885.

393.   ii. CATHERINE MEWHINNEY, born 24 Feb 1843, Lost Creek Township; married JAMES B. MILLER, 22 Feb 1865, Riley Township; died circa 1905.

       iii. ROBERT BRUCE MEWHINNEY, born 07 Dec 1844, Lost Creek Township; mustered into Co. B of the 71st Indiana Infantry on 18 Aug 1862; late in 1862, the bulk of the regiment was captured by General John Hunt Morgan's troops; they were paroled and sent back to Indianapolis to reorganize. Robert mustered out on 17 Jun 1865. He died on 28 Jan 1867 at age 22 in Riley Township.[1068]

394.   iv. ALBERT B. MEWHINNEY, born 25 Jan 1847, Lost Creek Township; married EMELINE BELT DAWSON, 10 Mar 1870, Riley Township; died 04 Jan 1918, Indianapolis, Marion, Indiana.[1069]

       v. BENNIE MEWHINNEY, born 24 Jan 1851, Lost Creek Township; died there on 27 Jul 1853 at age two.

       vi. HANNAH MEWHINNEY, born 01 Jan 1854, Riley Township; married ELIJAH O. RECTOR, 21 Dec 1871, Riley Township; died there, 25 Feb 1923.

204. **SEVELAN[7] WYETH** (Joshua[6] Jr., Joshua[5], Ebenezer[4] Jr., Ebenezer[3], John[2], Nicholas[1]) was born on 15 Apr 1822 in Brookville, Franklin, Indiana. Due to an 1860 census transcription error, he has been called Loveland by mistake. After a steel mill eye injury, Sevelan turned to farming.[1070] He married **MARY JANE MARSHALL** on 29 Mar 1849 in Riley Township, Vigo, Indiana. She was born to William Marshall and Rachel Parker on 28 Apr 1827 in Ripley, Brown County, Ohio. Mary Jane died on 07 Aug 1881 at the age of 54 in Riley Township. Sevelan died there on 03 Jul 1885 at age 63.

These photos of Sevelan and Mary Jane are courtesy of their great granddaughter, Ethel Ross "Rossie" Wyeth Canion.

Sevelan Wyeth and Mary Jane Marshall had the following children: [1071]

395.   i.   WILLIAM JASPER[8] WYETH, born 09 Jul 1850, Riley Township; married (1) MARY ELIZABETH BRATT there, 13 Jan 1876; married (2) MARSELLA JOSEPHINE HULTS, 29 Apr 1880, Riley Township; died 16 Jan 1911, Terre Haute, Vigo, Indiana.

       ii. EMILY ELLEN WYETH, born 27 Sep 1851, Riley Township; died there on 07 Aug 1853 at age one.

396.   iii. ALBERT LANGE WYETH, born 23 Dec 1852, Riley Township; married MARIA J. WHALLON, 19 Dec 1880, Clay County, Indiana; died 07 Jul 1923 after being crushed by a raging bull near Jasonville, Greene, Indiana.

       iv. JOSHUA NEWTON WYETH, born 23 Oct 1855, Riley Township; died there on 25 Jun 1878 at age 22.

v. FREMONT WYETH, born 03 Apr 1857, Riley Township; died there on 13 Apr 1860 at age three.

397.　vi. SARAH ALICE WYETH, born 30 Jun 1859, Riley Township; married GEORGE WASHINGTON MCHENRY there, 16 Feb 1877; died 09 Apr 1943, Jasonville.

398.　vii. JACKSON WYETH, born 30 Sep 1860, Riley Township; married ALMA JOSEPHINE COLLINS there, 02 Sep 1885; died 31 Jul 1946, Terre Haute.[1072]

399.　viii. HANNAH WYETH, born 05 Dec 1863, Riley Township; married AUSTIN MILLER COLLINS, 22 Oct 1881, Terre Haute; died there, 31 Jul 1949.

Alma Collins, Jackson Wyeth and their son-in-law, Ezra Hutchens, at the old homestead in Riley Twp. Courtesy of Ethel "Rossie" Canion.

205. **WILLIS B.**[7] **WYETH** (Joshua[6] Jr., Joshua[5], Ebenezer[4] Jr., Ebenezer[3], John[2], Nicholas[1]) was born on 27 Oct 1824 in Brookville, Franklin, Indiana. Willis enrolled on 12 Jun 1847 in Jeffersonville, Indiana in the 4th Indiana Regiment, Co. H and fought in the Mexican–American War.[1073] Willis B. Wyeth and Sarah Ellen Cahill were married on 05 Jan 1859 in Clay County, Indiana. **SARAH ELLEN CAHILL** was born on 15 May 1831 in Clay County to Solomon Cahill and Martha Parker. Sarah died on 08 Dec 1870 at age 39 in Riley Township, Vigo, Indiana. Willis died there on 09 Sep 1876 at age 51.

The following children were named in the 23 Jan 1871 will of Willis B. Wyeth:

400.　i. SOPHRONA ELIZA[8] WYETH, born 07 Oct 1859, Riley Township; married GEORGE MELVIN SLAVENS, 16 Jul 1881, Riley Township; died 13 Dec 1921, Puxico, Stoddard, Missouri.

401.　ii. MARTHA "MATTIE" WYETH, born 27 Jan 1864, Riley Township; married MORGAN E. GREEN, 10 Dec 1882, Clay County; died 25 Jul 1938, Civray Township, Sullivan, Indiana.

　　iii. ELLSWORTH WYETH, born in Jan 1866, Riley Township; died after 1900, probably in Mississippi. A stir arose in 1892 when newspapers confused him with infamous Dalton Gang member Ellsworth Wyatt who was arrested near Terre Haute when Ellsworth Wyeth and brother Willie were in business there.

　　iv. WILLIS "WILLIE" WYETH, born 09 Nov 1868, Riley Township; died unmarried 31 Dec 1940 in Puxico of influenza.

402.　v. EMILY ELLEN WYETH, born 14 Apr 1870, Riley Township; married JOHN WESLEY COREY SR., 03 Feb 1889, Clay County; died 07 Mar 1947, Terre Haute, Vigo, Indiana.

206. **(DR.) ALEXANDER REED**[7] **WYETH** (George Morris[6], Joshua[5], Ebenezer[4] Jr., Ebenezer[3], John[2], Nicholas[1]) was born on 08 Jan 1813 in Williamsport (Monongahela), Washington, Pennsylvania. He married (1) **HARRIETT PAMELA BEEBE**, 07 Mar 1837, Morgan County, Illinois. Harriett, daughter of Francis Beebe and Susannah Welch, was born on 22 May 1815 in Williamsport. She died at age 26 on 06 Dec 1841 in Scott County, Illinois. He married (2) **ELIZABETH MARGARET WINTER** on 23 Oct 1843 in Donegal Township,

Washington, Pennsylvania. Elizabeth, daughter of David Winter and Elizabeth McCoy, was born about 1819 in Donegal.[1074] Alexander served as an assistant surgeon at the rank of 1st Lieutenant during the Civil War. Dr. Wyeth died on 24 Mar 1876, due to complications from his war injuries, while visiting his daughter in Independence, Washington, Texas.[1075] Elizabeth died at age 68 in Donegal on 16 Oct 1887. On 21 Oct 1887, her will came to probate in Washington County.

Dr. Alexander Reed Wyeth and Harriett Pamela Beebe had the following children:

i. PEYTON BEEBE[8] WYETH, born 14 Aug 1838, Winchester Township, Scott, Illinois; died there one month later on 14 Sep 1838.

403. ii. HARRIETTE LOUISA MARIA WYETH, born 20 May 1840, Winchester Township; married (1) WILLIAM BRYSON JR., 04 Aug 1859, Pleasant Hill Female Seminary, West Middleton, Washington, Pennsylvania; married (2) LUCILIOUS ASBURY ROBERTSON circa 1878, Waxahachie, Ellis, Texas; died 15 Jan 1885, Midlothian, Ellis, Texas.[1076]

Notes for Dr. Alexander Reed "Alex" Wyeth and his family:

In 1837, Alex followed his soon to be father-in-law, Francis Beebe, to Illinois. The next year his own father, George Morris Wyeth Sr., purchased public lands there in Morgan County and followed the already happily-settled newlyweds to the Prairie State. Through the kindness of Lillian Neisz, a Fulton family researcher, we have transcriptions of some of the family's letters. Here is part of one that Harriett Pamela Beebe wrote to her husband while he was staying in Madisonville, Mississippi, circa 1839:

> "Manchester, Morgan Co., Ills. December 23th
> My dear husband and only earthly comforter...
>
> I received your very kind letter of Nov 28 on Dec 20th with pleasure. I was glad to hear you were well for I very much feared some accident had happened to you until I got the newspaper... your father took the letter out and Judge Marks was so good as to bring it to me. I cannot describe my feelings when I read it. It was a feast... It had a healing influence upon a broken heart. Your mother wishes me to appear to be happy when I write to you but you would not believe me if I did. You know by this time what it is to feel lost even in society. I feel desolate indeed and nothing but your society can make me happy.
>
> I have been at home most of the time since you left and have had many trials. Mama has been blind ever since you left. *(Harriett then talks of the health of her siblings, Aurora, Leighton and Miles.)* I shall soon go to your father's to stay a while as they treat me as if I was their own child. *(She then mentions Alexander's siblings, Peyton Cooke Wyeth, Anne Pennoyer, Isabella Metcalf and some problems with collecting money on accounts apparently due Alex.)* I have taken most of the medicine you left me. I don't disobey you often. I am writing now by candlelight... My fingers are very cold ... I will close by subscribing myself your affectionate wife,
>
> *H. P. Wyeth* - I wish I could send a kiss ... write often."

In the letter, Harriett alludes to her illness. It most likely was consumption (now known as tuberculosis). Death by consumption was one of the most common killers of young adults in 19th century America. It was not until the disease took the life of President Andrew Jackson in 1845 that scientists, looking for a cure, first learned the disease was contagious.[1077] Heartbroken, Alex buried his beautiful young wife with their infant son Peyton in Scott County's Old Manchester

Cemetery and headed home to Pennsylvania.[1078]

With three-year-old Louisa in tow, he returned to the lands his great uncle, Robert Fulton, purchased in 1785 for Alexander's great grandmother, Mary Smith Fulton. Fulton gave the lands to his mother while he was still painting miniatures in Philadelphia... over 20 years before his *Clermont* launched the first long-term, financially prosperous steamboat business in the world. [1079] It is likely that Alex was a beneficiary of his great uncle's success as well. Alex quickly became a pillar of the community and just as quickly, according to family tradition, fell madly in love with Elizabeth Margaret Winter. She was a beautiful red head with a terrible temper. [1080]

Following in his father's literary footsteps, Alex also was a gifted writer. In 1848, Cropper & Son of Cincinnati published his book, *The Laws of Life, or Self Culture: Applied to the Restoration and Preservation of Health, and Prolongation of Life, with an Appendix to Ladies.*

Undoubtedly, antidotes from Dr. Wyeth's *Laws of Life* are present in this 1859 letter he wrote to Louisa from St. Louis. Lillian's transcription comes from a document provided by Louisa's granddaughter, Margaret Wyeth Hawkins. It hints at the temperament of Louisa's step-mother.

> "Sabbath morning, May 15
>
> As I told you, my dear child, in my last letter I would shortly write to you again, I now take my pen to perform one of the great pleasures of my life, communing with the loved ones at home. Yes, daughter, the loved ones. For let what will come, I can't but love Elizabeth, and I must say that I could not this morning resist the desire to write to her yet once more. And in closing I forgot to tell her where to direct, if she should think proper to write to me again – which is Box 2045, St. Louis... and now my darling child, I will turn my attention entirely to you for the present.
>
> You have asked my consent to your marriage with Mr. Bryson and I have given it to you because first, I look on him as a gentleman and second, because I think that his age and experience will be a warranty for your enjoying a comfortable and as far as possible happy life. Mr. B is a young man of good education and of unblemished character, and one whose circumstances will enable him to provide in unison with your own efforts a comfortable support in life; but my dear child, you must not enter the married state with the delusive idea that your path of life will all be strewed with flowers. No dear, it will not all be sunshine but you must expect that many shadows will fall over your pathway... I fear that you will have to learn a great deal of self-control. You have been a petted and spoiled child. ... be governed in everything you say or do by the golden rule of doing as you would wish to be done by.
>
> Never let your angry passions gain mastery over your reason and judgment... Let not the sun go down on your wrath... Don't, my dear child, now because you are engaged, allow any liberties to be taken and remember, dear daughter. Pa doesn't say this because he lacks confidence in either Mr. or you, but because you are both human. If you allow one step, it excites passion and passion dethrones reason.
>
> And now, my child, permit me to make some remarks on the subject of your bridal wardrobe... First let your dress be such as becomes the Christian... plain though of good material... not gaudy... waste no money on nonsensical jewelry such as ear rings... I would further suggest that you make but a small wedding party, the more particularly as it is the gift of Mary Winter (Mary Jane Bryson Winter was Elizabeth's sister-in-law as well as the groom's sister) for you know how parsimonious they are.
>
> Circumstances have occurred since I last wrote you... I can't be there in time for your wedding... Therefore I desire that you go on with it just as you have agreed... Be very kind to Elizabeth and if she will be at all friendly, strive to make her happy as you can... May God bless you, my child...
>
> *Alex R. Wyeth*"

The 1860 census of Hopewell Township, Washington County, Pennsylvania, describes Alex as a farmer and a physician. He was an inventor as well. Dr. Wyeth specified a new method of tanning animal skins and hides under patent No. 31,640 on 05 Mar 1861.

On the day before the patent's issue, the end of Abraham Lincoln's first inaugural address showed how much he misjudged the South's intentions. "The mystic chords of memory… will yet swell the chorus of the Union, by the better angels of our nature." However, all doubt of the South's plan to divide the nation was erased when their Confederate forces fired on Fort Sumter on 12 Apr 1861. Then at Bull Run on 21 Jul 1861, the Union again underestimated the resolve of the South. The 90-day volunteers summoned to fight for the Federal cause were so ill prepared, their retreat from the battle turned into a rout. Losses in that first battle of the Civil War convinced the Federals to recruit and prepare regiments for a long and costly war.

By the end of the summer of 1861, Alex was among those recruits devoted to saving the Union. He served almost to the end of the war in the Ringgold Battalion / 22nd and the 208th Pennsylvania Volunteers, organized at Harrisburg. Surprisingly, Alex did not start his military service as a physician but as a quartermaster sergeant. On 01 Sep 1862, he turned to the medical field, earning $100 per month as an acting assistant surgeon. Though suffering from a hernia injury, hemorrhoids and constant neuralgia from a healed leg fracture, Dr. Wyeth soldiered on. Commissioned assistant surgeon, at the rank of first lieutenant, on 14 May 1863, he spent most of the summer of 1863, as a contract physician in a field hospital at Murfreesboro, Tennessee. He enlisted in the 208th on 12 Sep 1864. When his injuries got the best of him, special orders from the headquarters of the Army of the Potomac led to a disability discharge on 03 Mar 1865.

From his home near Acheson, Washington County, Pennsylvania, on 13 Mar 1871, Alex gave this description of himself in pension application #160,817: complexion, dark; 5 ft. 4 ½ in; weight 120. [1081] He defined how the 12 Dec 1862 severe rupture of the left side of his pelvis caused an inguinal hernia protrusion the size of a walnut. Not only did his war injury bar him from doctoring on horseback, but it caused his death at age 63.

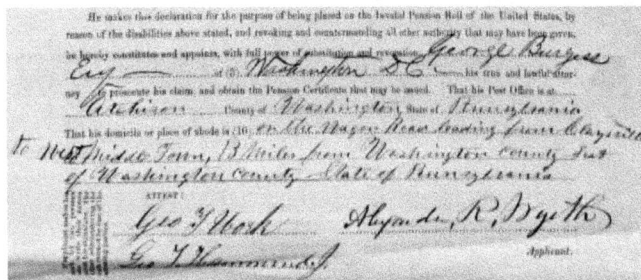

Dr. Wyeth says his abode is on the wagon road leading from Claysville to West Middletown in Washington County, PA.

Elizabeth Margaret Winter Wyeth too was in Acheson when she applied for a widow's pension on 20 Sep 1877. She said her husband's only child, Mrs. Louisa M. Bryson, age 37, then lived in Millican, Brazos, Texas. By the time Elizabeth wrote her will on 02 Aug 1887, her step-daughter was dead. Elizabeth left no inheritance to her step-grandchildren. She directed that she be plainly and decently interred in the Zion Church burying ground near her present residence with a tombstone erected, not to exceed $50 or $60. The rest of her estate went to her nephews and nieces, all descendants of David B. and Mary Jane Bryson Winter.

207. **ANNE ELIZA J.**[7] **WYETH** (George Morris[6], Joshua[5], Ebenezer[4] Jr., Ebenezer[3], John[2], Nicholas[1]) was born in 1817 in Williamsport (Monongahela), Washington, Pennsylvania. Anne Eliza J. Wyeth and Rev. Andrew Leeds Pennoyer were married on 03 Dec 1838 in Morgan County, Illinois. **ANDREW LEEDS PENNOYER** was born 27 Oct 1807 in Fairfield

County, Connecticut to Leeds and Sarah Pennoyer. He died 23 Dec 1880 in Roseville, Warren, Illinois. She died there on 30 Apr 1881 due to complications from diabetes. They are buried in the Roseville Cemetery.[1082] [1083]

Andrew Leeds Pennoyer and Anne Eliza J. Wyeth had the following children:

404.   i.   SARA E.[8] PENNOYER, born 12 Jun 1842, Morgan County, Illinois; married FRANKLIN H. SPENCER, 02 Oct 1857, Hancock County, Illinois; died 12 Mar 1896, Newton, Harvey, Kansas.

       ii.   ANNABELL PENNOYER, born circa Sep 1844, Morgan County; died there on 09 Nov 1844; buried in the Old Manchester Cemetery, Scott County, Illinois, near her Wyeth grandparents and first cousin Peyton Beebe Wyeth.[1084]

     iii.   FLORENCE PENNOYER, born 1848, Morgan County; deaf from measles; died 27 Dec 1880, Roseville, Warren, Illinois; buried there with her parents in the town of Roseville cemetery.

208. **ISABELLA MARY[7] WYETH** (George Morris[6], Joshua[5], Ebenezer[4] Jr., Ebenezer[3], John[2], Nicholas[1]) was born 03 Jul 1820 in Williamsport (Monongahela), Washington, Pennsylvania. Isabella Mary Wyeth and John Milton Metcalf M.D. were married on 08 Apr 1838 in Morgan County, Illinois. **JOHN MILTON METCALF** was born on 26 Nov 1814 in Hopkins County, Kentucky to William Metcalf Jr. and Elizabeth Jones. They had seven children, including Fredrika and Richard who died young. Dr. Metcalf died on 12 Dec 1858 aboard a ship in the Gulf of Mexico.[1085] Isabella died one month short of age 95 on 07 Jun 1915 in Oakland, Alameda, California.[1086]

The children of John Milton Metcalf and Isabella Mary Wyeth included:

405.   i.   JULIA ELIZABETH[8] METCALF, born 15 Jun 1840, Winchester, Scott, Illinois; married SILAS CHRISTAL BURNETT, 07 Apr 1856, Jacksonville, Morgan, Illinois; died 04 Feb 1922, Sayre, Beckham, Oklahoma.

406.   ii.   EDWIN THEODORE METCALF M.D., born 27 Jul 1843, Macoupin County, Illinois; enlisted 09 Aug 1862 as a sergeant in Co. G of the Illinois 101st Infantry Regiment, mustered out 01 Mar 1863; married CHARITY "CHATTIE" BURNETT, 11 Sep 1864, Waverly, Morgan, Illinois; died 27 Nov 1930, Colony, Anderson, Kansas.

407.   iii.   GEORGE DICKSON METCALF, born 30 Sep 1847, Macoupin County; graduated from Yale University, 1870; married MARY FIELD BROCKWAY, 22 Jan 1873, Oakland; died 28 Apr 1923, Berkeley, Alameda, California.

     iv.   HARRIETT "HALLIE" METCALF, born 14 Apr 1849, Waverly; married PETER CASSERLY, 22 Dec 1866, Springfield, Sangamon, Illinois; died there, 17 Sep 1934 at age 85.

      v.   JOHN WILLIAM METCALF, born in Dec 1856, Waverly; music teacher; died unmarried, 19 Jul 1926, Piedmont, Alameda, California.

209. **(DR.) GEORGE MORRIS[7] WYETH JR.** (George Morris[6], Joshua[5], Ebenezer[4] Jr., Ebenezer[3], John[2], Nicholas[1]) was born on 30 Sep 1822, Williamsport (Monongahela), Washington, Pennsylvania. George Morris Wyeth Jr. and **MARY ETHEL CHAMBERLAIN** were married

on 10 May 1853 in St. Louis, Missouri. Mary Ethel daughter of Benjamin Brown Chamberlain and Jane Elizabeth Targee, was born on 01 Dec 1832 in Salem, Essex, Massachusetts. A renowned writer, Mary used the pen names Ethel Grey and Mrs. M.E.C. Wyeth.[1087] She died on 26 May 1887 in Jacksonville, Duval, Florida at age 54. He died there on 15 Oct 1899 at age 77.[1088] They are buried there in Evergreen Cemetery, lot A-117.[1089]

Dr. George Morris Wyeth Jr. and Mary Ethel Chamberlain had the following children:

    i. PAUL CHAMBERLAIN[8] WYETH, born 03 Feb 1854, St. Louis, Missouri; married FRANCES MARIE PANISI, 22 Aug 1881, Cincinnati, Hamilton, Ohio; they did not have children. Just after the Spanish American War, Paul enlisted in Havana, Cuba in the U.S. Army on 01 Feb 1899. He received a disability discharge on 18 Aug 1899 at Columbia Barracks Hospital, Cuba. Enlistment papers described him as dark with brown hair and 5' 10 ½". On 20 Aug 1921, a Bureau of Pensions' official painted quite a different picture of Paul: "This claimant appears to be an educated man and I suspect he is the 'black sheep' of a good family. He claims to have studied medicine and he had down pat the technical description of his disabilities... I am rating him fair. He has been a chronic drinker though he says he never was a steady drinker..." Paul died of heart disease on 28 Aug 1930, City Hospital, Indianapolis, Indiana.

408.   ii. ETHEL WYETH, born 23 Sep 1857, Godfrey, Madison, Illinois; married (1) GEORGE BOARDMAN MACLELLAN, 23 Sep 1879, Chicago; married (2) JAMES A. CONOVER, 19 Mar 1890, Jacksonville; between her weddings, she edited the *Florida Times-Union* news and was the only staff member to survive the yellow fever epidemic of 1888;[1090] died 24 May 1930, Santa Barbara, California.

409.   iii. IRENE WYETH, born circa 1863, Godfrey; married JAMES ANDERSON GIBSON, 25 Apr 1887, Jacksonville; died there, 08 Apr 1900;[1091] she is buried in lot A-142, Evergreen Cemetery.[1092]

    iv. GEORGE PEYTON WYETH, born on 04 Dec 1866, Godfrey; married MARY JANE "JENNIE" MADDEN on 05 Apr 1893, Chicago; distraught after being terminated from his insurance manager's position, due to heavy losses in the Great Baltimore Fire of 1904, Peyton committed suicide with cyanide of potassium, 03 Jun 1904, Brooklyn, Kings County, New York.[1093] He is buried there in Green-Wood Cemetery near his aunt Harriette Louisa "Hallie" Wyeth whose attendance at Godfrey's Monticello seminary in 1850 drew the Wyeths to the town of Peyton's birth.

    v. MARY VIRGINIA "BIRDIE" WYETH, born on 01 Aug 1879 in St. Louis; married FRANK WILLIS BRADLEY, 06 Jun 1900, Chicago; died 18 Nov 1951, at her niece Mabel Gibson Holt's home in Berkeley, Alameda, California.[1094]

Scattered throughout Green-Wood Cemetery are descendants of Noah Wyeth Sr. of Cambridge as well as descendants from three of his nephews – Joshua, Jacob, and John. Of Joshua's line, the graves of George Peyton, his niece Ethel Conover Drew, his aunt Harriette and uncle Peyton Wyeth, are on a hill overlooking the Green-Wood Chapel.

210. **NELSON**[7] **GILBERT** (Mary Polly[6] Wyeth, Joshua[5], Ebenezer[4] Jr., Ebenezer[3], John[2], Nicholas[1]) was born on 24 Dec 1811 in Towanda, Bradford, Pennsylvania. Nelson married (1) **JANE HOLLENBACK** circa 1837 in Bradford County. She was born about 1816 in New York. Jane died from measles in Apr 1860 at age 44 in Bradford County. Nelson married (2) **CATHERINE MOYER** circa 1862 in Franklin Township, Bradford, Pennsylvania. Catherine daughter of Phillip Moyer and Martha Ann Evans, was born 10 Aug 1828 in Luzerne County, Pennsylvania. Nelson died on 26 Feb 1891 in Franklin Township and Catherine died in 1899.

Nelson Gilbert and Jane Hollenback had the following children:

       i. MARY ELIZABETH[8] GILBERT, born about 1838, Towanda; death unknown.

      ii. OLIVER T. GILBERT, born in 1845, Towanda; enlisted 23 Sep 1863 as a substitute in the 49th Pennsylvania Infantry, Co. G; killed in action at Sailor's Creek, Virginia, 06 Apr 1865, while under the command of Gen. Philip H. Sheridan. The battle was part of the Appomattox Campaign. It took place on the fourth day of Gen. Robert E. Lee's retreat from Petersburg... just three days before the Civil War ended with Lee's surrender in Appomattox Courthouse.[1095]

    iii. DELPHINE IRENE GILBERT, born Jul 1848, Towanda; married JOHN F. MILLER, 28 Mar 1866 at the First United Methodist Church of Towanda; died 1904.

    iv. PERRY N. GILBERT, born 28 Dec 1850, Towanda; married MARY H. DODGE, 1875, Bradford County; died there, 10 Dec 1918 in Standing Stone Township.

     v. HELEN MAE GILBERT, born circa 1852, Franklin Township; married JOHN W. WILKINSON there, 22 Dec 1871; died 26 Sep 1916, Osawatomie, Miami, Kansas.

    vi. ELIJAH B. GILBERT, born 07 Mar 1856, Franklin Township; married (1) CYNTHIA JANE LINDLEY there, circa 1879; married (2) CLARA AUGUSTA THORNTON, 1889, Bradford County; died on 11 Dec 1905 after being scalded at work at the Greenwood Tannery, Monroeton, Bradford, Pennsylvania.

410.   vii. ROSETTA GILBERT, born 18 Oct 1859, Franklin Township; married MERTON MELVERN McKEE, 1880, Franklin Township; died there, 30 Aug 1915.

Nelson Gilbert and Catherine Moyer had the following children:

411.   i. GEORGE MILTON[8] GILBERT, born 10 Aug 1862, Franklin Township; married ADELAIDE O'NEILL, 1885; died 27 Feb 1927, Elmira, Chemung, New York.

     ii. IDA GILBERT, born 07 Mar 1865, Franklin Township; died there, unmarried, on 31 Jan 1918 at age 53.

211. **FIDALIA ANNA**[7] **WYETH** (Francis B.[6], Joshua[5], Ebenezer[4] Jr., Ebenezer[3], John[2], Nicholas[1]) was born about 1817 in McKeesport, Allegheny, Pennsylvania. Fidalia married Simon Shaffer, 27 Jun 1836, St. Paul's Cathedral, Pittsburgh, Allegheny, Pennsylvania.[1096] **SIMON SHAFFER**, the son of Henry Shaffer and Mary Chambers, was born circa 1818 in McKeesport. Fidalia died on 04 Jan 1890 at the home of her son-in-law, Thomas Maloney, in Chartiers, Washington, Pennsylvania.[1097] Simon died on 28 Sep 1894 at his daughter Susan Massey's home in Monongahela, Washington, Pennsylvania. Fidalia and Simon rest in the St. Mary's Cemetery section of Monongahela Cemetery.

Simon Shaffer and Fidalia Anna Wyeth had the following children:

412.   i.   MARY ANN^8 SHAFFER, born 1839, Mifflin Township, Allegheny, Pennsylvania; married JOHN PETER BURGAN circa 1856, Monongahela; died there circa 1896.

        ii. ELIZA J. SHAFFER, probably born in Mifflin Township in 1842; death unknown.

413.   iii. SUSAN SHAFFER, born 18 Feb 1846, Monongahela; married JESSE MASSEY there, 23 Jul 1861; died on 04 Sep 1933 at the Washington County home.

      iv. SARAH B. SHAFFER, born 1848, Monongahela; buried St. Mary's, 29 Sep 1864.

414.   v. KATHERINE SHAFFER, born 31 May 1854, Monongahela, married (1) JAMES M. CRAVEN, 31 Aug 1868, Washington County; married (2) ISAAC M. BROWN about 1918, North Charleroi, Washington, Pennsylvania; died on 29 Dec 1947 at age 93 in the Washington Hospital, Washington County.

      vi. JOHN SHAFFER, born 1857, Monongahela; died at age eight from a mule accident suffered at a coal mine on 15 Aug 1865, buried St. Mary's Cemetery, 05 Sep 1865.[1098]

    vii. HARRIET AGNES SHAFFER, born 26 Aug 1859, Monongahela; married river boat Captain FINLEY POLLOCK there in 1877; had nine children; died 09 Feb 1923, Monongahela from breast cancer at age 63.

   viii. MARTHA D. "MATTIE" SHAFFER, born 07 Jun 1864, Monongahela; married (1) THOMAS MALONEY, 18 Oct 1882, Elizabeth, Allegheny, Pennsylvania; married (2) THOMAS HENRY SPRAGUE, 27 Nov 1909, Greensburg, Westmoreland, Pennsylvania; died 09 Apr 1931, Donora, Washington, Pennsylvania.

Notes for Simon Shaffer and Fidalia Anna Wyeth:

Fidalia's first name appeared differently in many records, but used here is the spelling from her tombstone. One source gives her first name as "Phedelia." Her baptism record from St. Patrick Parish, Strip District, Pittsburgh, written in Latin, used a slightly different spelling for both her first and last name. It said, "Baptized 14 Nov 1826, Fidelia Anna, daughter of Francisci and Margaretha Wythe, age nine years, sponsor: Carolo (Charles) Kenny.[1099] Confirming that Charles Kenny was Fidalia's godfather is the $15 legacy he left her in his 20 Aug 1839 will.[1100] The original Kenny property is currently the site of Kennywood Amusement Park in West Mifflin, Allegheny County, Pennsylvania, a few miles north of McKeesport.[1101]

The census report of 1830 shows the residence of Henry Shaffer in Mifflin Township, Allegheny, Pennsylvania. The township, incorporated in 1788, is now West Mifflin.[1102] It is confused with the borough of Mifflin in Juniata County, Pennsylvania. The 1840 census of Mifflin Township for Simon showed one girl under age five, she most likely was first daughter, Mary Ann Shaffer.

212. MARGARET^7 WYETH (Francis B.^{6}, Joshua^5, Ebenezer^4 Jr., Ebenezer^3, John^2, Nicholas^1) was born on 11 Jun 1818 in Washington Township, Warren County, Ohio. Her obituary gives Marietta, Washington County, Ohio as her birthplace. However, at the time, her father lived over 200 miles southwest of Marietta near Cincinnati. Margaret Wyeth and John Finn were married on 28 Jun 1838 in St. Paul's Cathedral, Pittsburgh, Allegheny, Pennsylvania.[1103] They had four children. JOHN FINN was born in Jan 1806 in Ireland. John died in the 17 Sep 1862 Allegheny Butler Street Arsenal explosion in the Central Lawrenceville area of Pittsburgh.[1104] Margaret died on 29 Jan 1905 in Pittsburgh.

The children of John Finn and Margaret Wyeth included the following:

        i.   MARY[8] FINN, probably born in Pittsburgh circa 1841; death unknown.

415.   ii. SARAH FINN, born 09 Aug 1846, Pittsburgh; married JOHN B. MILLBACH, 25 Jul 1865, Pittsburgh; died there, 25 Apr 1923.

213. **FRANCIS STEPHEN "FRANK"[7] WYETH** (Francis B.[6], Joshua[5], Ebenezer[4] Jr., Ebenezer[3], John[2], Nicholas[1]) was born circa 1820 in Washington Township, Warren County, Ohio. His sister's obituary claims Marietta, Washington County, Ohio as their birth place, but their father lived just north of Cincinnati during the 1820 U.S. Census. Frank married **MARY HILLMAN**, 15 Oct 1846 in Allegheny County, Pennsylvania.[1105] Mary was born in Allegheny County, circa 1827, to Benjamin Hillman and Mary Shaffer. Francis died on 28 Jan 1888 in Monongahela, Washington, Pennsylvania.[1106] Mary died there at her home on Waverly Place on 22 Nov 1894.[1107]

According to *The Schroeder-Wyeth Newsletter*, written by Frank and Mary's descendants, Edna Schroeder Evans and Lynda Evans Levin, all of Francis Stephen "Frank" Wyeth and Mary Hillman's children, were born in Monongahela.[1108] They include the following:

        i.   ROBERT[8] WYETH, born about 1847; died young.

416.   ii. CLARA JOSEPHINE WYETH, born 31 Aug 1848; married CYRUS KITCHEL BAXTER, 27 Jun 1866, Monongahela; died 31 Aug 1913, Tarentum, Allegheny.

       iii. FRANCIS ALVIN "BUB" WYETH, born 1849; died, unmarried, at the family home on Waverly in Monongahela of typhoid fever on 09 Oct 1882.[1109]

417.   iv. SARAH ANN "SALLIE" WYETH, born in Mar 1850; married JOHN CUNNINGHAM, circa 1872, Monongahela; on 02 Aug 1884 at her residence on Spring Street in Pittsburgh.[1110]

       v. MARTHA WYETH, born 1852; married PAUL GROSSMAN; death unknown.

418.   vi. JAMES ALEXANDER WYETH, born 20 Nov 1855; married MARTHA V. CURDIE, 17 Apr 1894, Monongahela; died there, 18 May 1936.

       vii. BENJAMIN E. WYETH, born in Feb 1857; a jeweler, married CAROLINE CADY, 1883, Monongahela; confined to the Allegheny County Workhouse on 17 May 1895 for selling illegal liquor; arrested again for the same charge on 22 Jan 1896, escaped from jail the next day.[1111] Caroline divorced him on 26 Oct 1905 in Monongahela on grounds of desertion.[1112] He had moved to Steubenville, Jefferson, Ohio to start a bicycle shop. Ben died 11 Feb 1924 in the Jefferson County Infirmary, Wintersville, Ohio.[1113]

       viii. JOSHUA "JOCK" WYETH, born in Feb 1860, was a hard-working, hard-drinking young man who never married. He seemed to have nine lives but they ended when he was killed in a drunken brawl in Forward Township, Alleghany, Pennsylvania on 07 Oct 1911.[1114] Prior to his murder, which occurred just across the Monongahela River from his home town, accounts of his scrapes filled *The Daily Republican* newspaper. Here are three examples: On 11 Apr 1887, a John Gillingham got into a fuss with the Wyeths at the ferry and drew a revolver. One of several shots fired hit Jock in the head. On 06 Jul 1896, Jock and his brother Clel Wyeth got into such a heated argument, that Mrs. Clel

Wyeth had Jock arrested for assault and battery. On 24 Jun 1901, Jock, employed at the mines at Hazel Kirk near Monongahela, was so seriously hurt when he fell down a mine shaft, that he was transported to a Pittsburgh hospital on the train.[1115]

419.   ix.   GEORGE McCLELLAND "CLEL" WYETH, born 12 Dec 1861; married ELLA ELIZABETH "LIZZIE" HARTMAN, 10 Mar 1885, Monongahela. When Lizzie died at age 33 from typhoid fever, Clel was desperate to provide for his 11 children, who ranged in age from one to 17 years old. Efforts to feed his brood with stolen chickens resulted in an arrest on 06 Aug 1906.[1116] George died 29 Jan 1922 in Washington, Washington County, Pennsylvania.

420.   x.   MARY ROSE WYETH, born 04 Apr 1864; married BERNARD BINGHAM BALZER, 24 Nov 1887, Monongahela; died 03 Dec 1931, Columbus, Franklin, Ohio.

421.   xi.   MARGARET MAE "MAGGIE" WYETH, born 21 Aug 1866; married DR. HARRY NEGLEY TEETERS, 24 May 1892, Allegheny County, Pennsylvania; died 11 Nov 1943 at her daughter's house in Takoma Park, Montgomery, Maryland.

214. **HENRY ELISHA[7] WYETH** (Francis B.[6], Joshua[5], Ebenezer[4] Jr., Ebenezer[3], John[2], Nicholas[1]) was born on 23 Apr 1836 in Cincinnati, Hamilton, Ohio. He served in Co. C of the 31st Indiana Infantry Regiment from his 20 Sep 1861 enrollment in Terre Haute, Vigo, Indiana to his 08 Dec 1865 honorable discharge in Victoria County, Texas.[1117] Henry was wounded on 06 Apr 1862 in the battle of Pittsburg Landing.[1118] The battle was more commonly known as the Battle of Shiloh and was the bloodiest battle in American history up to that time. Henry Elisha Wyeth and **HANNAH BRATT** were married on 08 Sep 1868 in Terre Haute. Hannah, daughter of Martin Bratt and Mary Moreton Pearson, was born on 29 Oct 1843 in Riley Township, Vigo, Indiana. The Wyeths lived in Riley in 1880 as shown in the census that Henry personally enumerated for his township. Henry died of paralytic stroke on 30 Jul 1904 in Terre Haute while Hannah and Florence were visiting the 1904 St. Louis World's Fair. A telegram was forwarded to them there and they immediately returned by first train, arriving two days after Henry's death.[1119] Hannah passed away on 09 Apr 1923 at her home at 1509 South 6th Street, Terre Haute.

Henry Elisha Wyeth and Hannah Bratt had the following child:

422.   i.   FLORENCE MARIE[8] WYETH, born 07 Sep 1879, Terre Haute, Vigo, Indiana; married CHARLES STACY BATT, 10 Jan 1907, Terre Haute; died 01 Aug 1948, St. Anthony's Hospital, Terre Haute.

215. **MINERVA[7] WYETH** (Francis B.[6], Joshua[5], Ebenezer[4] Jr., Ebenezer[3], John[2], Nicholas[1]) was born in Jan 1838 in Cincinnati, Hamilton, Ohio. Minerva married (1) **LAWRENCE H. W. CULVER** on 26 Apr 1860 in Riley Township, Vigo, Indiana. A newspaper article on 23 Apr 1884 said Lawrence died ten days after a branch fell on him while he was cutting down trees on his property in Benton Township, Monroe, Indiana.[1120] Minerva married (2) **EDWARD R. POTTER** there on 15 Aug 1886. She married (3) **DR. JAMES B. CAMPBELL**, her son's father-in-law, 31 May 1890 in Brown County, Indiana. After James' death on 08 Feb 1900 in Brown County, she married (4) **FREDERICK R. DRABENSTOTT** there on 01 Nov 1911. Minerva died in Monroe County on 17 Jul 1919. Frederick died on 22 Nov

1924 in Mexico, Miami, Indiana.

Lawrence H. W. Culver and Minerva Wyeth had the following children:

423.   i.   WILLIAM CURTIS[8] CULVER, born 21 Mar 1861, Benton Township, Monroe, Indiana; married ANNA M. CAMPBELL, 04 Nov 1882, Monroe County; died 08 Mar 1916, Kokomo, Howard, Indiana of heart disease.

424.   ii. ONA BELLE CULVER, born 14 Mar 1879, Benton Township; married JOHN CAMPBELLE MOSER, 22 Mar 1905, Brown County; died 09 Apr 1911, Jackson, Brown, Indiana of consumption at age 32.

216. **ELIZABETH[7] KING** (Eliza Jane[6] Wyeth, Joshua[5], Ebenezer[4] Jr., Ebenezer[3], John[2], Nicholas[1]) was born on 25 Jul 1815 in Bardstown, Nelson, Kentucky. She married **SAMUEL SCOTT JR.** on 23 Oct 1831 in Green Township, Morgan, Indiana. Samuel, the son of Samuel Scott Sr. and Mary Myers, was born on 04 Dec 1805 in Tennessee. He died on 22 Aug 1849 in Clay Township, Morgan, Indiana. She died in Green Township on 08 Jun 1866.

The children of Samuel Scott Jr. and Elizabeth King included:

    i.   FRANCIS MARION[8] SCOTT, born 03 Dec 1832, Morgan County; married LUCINDA SARVER there, 30 Oct 1853; served two years in Co. B of the 123rd Illinois Infantry, fought at Chickamauga in 1863; died on 25 Jan 1894, Westville, Chariton, Missouri.

    ii. NELSON WYTHE SCOTT, born 12 Jul 1846, Morgan County; married HANNAH ROSE TRAUB there, 22 Oct 1876; died there, 20 Aug 1907 of typhoid fever.

    iii. ELLEN SCOTT, born 05 Apr 1848, Morgan County; married JESSE BLANA there in 1867; died 08 Mar 1906, Washington Township, Morgan, Indiana.

217. **RANSOM CORNELIUS[7] KING** (Eliza Jane[6] Wyeth, Joshua[5], Ebenezer[4] Jr., Ebenezer[3], John[2], Nicholas[1]) was born in 1816 in Lawrence County, Indiana. Ransom married **SECELIA "CELIA" FARRAN**, 23 Apr 1835, Morgan County, Indiana. Celia daughter of Michael Farran and Sarah Fowler, was born circa 1816 in Dearborn County, Indiana. Ransom joined the 87th Illinois Infantry, Co. D on 13 Aug 1862. He was discharged for disability on 29 Jun 1863 at Mound City, Pulaski, Illinois. He died before 1870 in Wayne County, Illinois and is buried there in Brown Cemetery, Mount Erie, Wayne, Illinois. Celia died near there circa 1875.

The children of Ransom Cornelius King and Secelia "Celia" Farran included:

    i.   SARAH ELIZABETH[8] KING, born 06 Mar 1836, Green Township, Morgan, Indiana; married ADAM CAUBLE, 31 Jan 1856, Washington County, Indiana, died there, 27 Aug 1895.

    ii. MARTHA KING, born 25 Nov 1837, Green; married WILLIAM J. FRAZIER on 22 Aug 1858, Fairfield, Wayne, Illinois; died there, 26 Apr 1866.

    iii. HARRIET KING, born Mar 1840, Green; married STEPHEN DEMPSEY, 1878, Wayne County; died 24 Aug 1914, Johnson County, Arkansas.

425.   iv. CORDELIA ELLET KING, born 15 Oct 1842, Green; married WILLIAM STEPHEN

WILLIAMS, 1860, Wayne County; died 05 Jan 1910, Johnson County.

> v. THOMAS HENRY BURTON KING, born 21 Oct 1843, Green Township; joined the 87th Illinois Infantry, Co. D with his father on 13 Aug 1862, mustered out in Helena, Arkansas, 16 Jun 1865; married MARY ANNA WALKER in 1867 in Wayne County; died there, 04 May 1905.
>
> vi. MARIETTA KING, born 12 Jan 1855, Gibson County, Indiana; married JOHN MARVEL there, 1872; died 04 May 1930, Fairfield, Wayne, Illinois.

218. SARAH⁷ KING (Eliza Jane⁶ Wyeth, Joshua⁵, Ebenezer⁴ Jr., Ebenezer³, John², Nicholas¹) was born on 24 Jan 1818 in Lawrence County, Indiana. Sarah King and James Madison Carrell were married on 29 Dec 1841 in Green Township, Morgan, Indiana. **JAMES MADISON CARRELL** was born on 19 Jul 1813 in Kentucky to Adam Columbus Carrell and Sarah Swinford. Sarah King Carrell died on 29 May 1846 near Martinsville, Morgan, Indiana. James died on 29 Sep 1880 in Greenup, Cumberland, Illinois.

James Madison Carrell and Sarah King had the following children:

> i. DAYTON HOWARD⁸ CARRELL, born 14 Nov 1842, Green Township; served the 123rd Illinois Infantry, Co. B, promoted to full corporal, mustered out 01 Jul 1863; married RUTH HARDEN, 1864, Cumberland County; died on 08 Mar 1916, Marionville, Lawrence, Missouri.
>
> 426. ii. PARRIS GORMON CARRELL, born 18 Feb 1845, Green Township; married (1) FRANCES ANN GREEN there, 1867; married (2) MARY JANE HEDDINS, circa 1871, Green Township; died 09 Dec 1880, Greenup, Cumberland, Illinois.

219. SERELDA⁷ KING (Eliza Jane⁶ Wyeth, Joshua⁵, Ebenezer⁴ Jr., Ebenezer³, John², Nicholas¹) was born in 1824 in Morgan County, Indiana. Serelda married (1) **BARTHOLOMEW CARRELL** on 15 Sep 1842 in Morgan County. Bartholomew, son of William Carrell and Sally Doane, was born about 1823 in Morgan County. He died in Oct 1856 in Prairieton, Vigo, Indiana. Serelda married (2) **SILAS GOODWIN**, 04 Jun 1857, Crawford County, Illinois. Silas was born in 1813 in Indiana to William Goodwin and Ruth McConnell. He died in 1868 in Crawford County. Serelda died there in 1875.

Bartholomew Carrell and Serelda King had the following children:

> i. PETER SANFORD⁸ CARRELL, born 26 Nov 1845, Martinsville, Morgan, Indiana; served in the 54th Illinois Infantry, Co. E from 29 Mar 1864 to 15 Oct 1865; married several times; died 23 Sep 1922, Charleston, Coles, Illinois.
>
> ii. HENRY MANFORD CARRELL, born 28 Jun 1848, Martinsville; served in the 54th Illinois Infantry, Co. E during the Civil War; married twice, (1) SARAH A. JENKINS; (2) AMANDA JANE SHANKS; died 10 Dec 1933, Casey, Clark, Illinois.
>
> iii. MILTON WYETH CARRELL, born 21 Dec 1853, Cumberland County, Illinois; married twice, (1) MILLIE JENKINS; (2) ELIZABETH MATTHEWS; died 01 Dec 1909, York Township, Clark, Illinois.
>
> 427. iv. MARY ELIZABETH CARRELL, born 12 Jan 1857, Prairieton; married (1) SYLVESTER MCDERMOTT, 31 Jul 1880, Coles County, Illinois; married (2) JOHN HUBBARD FISHER, circa 1881; died 30 Mar 1921, West Union.[1121]

Silas Goodwin and Serelda King had the following children:

   i. ELVIRA⁸ GOODWIN, born 1859, Crawford County; died 1896, Cumberland.
   ii. RANSOM GOODWIN, born 12 Feb 1862, Crawford; married (1) CORDELIA COX; (2) MARY STUART; died 14 Aug 1937, Rockville, Parke, Indiana.
   iii. ADELINE GOODWIN, born 1867, Crawford County; married CHARLES DENNY, 1883, Cumberland County; died 16 Aug 1945, Houston, Harris, Texas.

220. **ADALINE⁷ KING** (Eliza Jane⁶ Wyeth, Joshua⁵, Ebenezer⁴ Jr., Ebenezer³, John², Nicholas¹) was born on 09 Dec 1838 in Morgan County, Indiana. Adaline King and Aaron St. John were married on 24 Dec 1854 at the home of her mother Eliza Jane Wyeth King near Martinsville, Morgan, Indiana. **AARON ST. JOHN**, son of John St. John and Rhoda Wood, was born on 16 Oct 1821 in Warren County, Ohio. Adaline died on 29 Aug 1888 in Green Township, Morgan, Indiana. Aaron died there on 17 Nov 1896.

The children of Aaron St. John and Adaline King included:

	i.	MINERVA JANE⁸ ST. JOHN, born 20 Nov 1855, Green Township; married CHRISTOPHER RINKER there, 19 Nov 1874; died there, 08 Jan 1897.
428.	ii.	MANFORD E. ST. JOHN, born 20 Mar 1857, Green Township; married MARTHA WILLIAMS there, 05 Oct 1882; died 08 Nov 1934, Banta, Morgan, Indiana.
	iii.	MARGARET "MAGGIE" ST. JOHN, born 08 Jan 1866, Green Township; died there, 25 Jan 1873 at age seven.
429.	iv.	OSCAR ST. JOHN, born 22 Sep 1867, Green Township; married LUCY BAILEY, 30 Jul 1891, Morgan County; died 22 Jun 1928, Indianapolis, Marion, Indiana.
	v.	MARY ETTA ST. JOHN, born 23 Jun 1869, Green Township; married GEORGE WESLEY BARLOW, 17 Oct 1890, Morgan County; died on 21 Jan 1940 in Indianapolis, Marion, Indiana.

221. **MATTHEW WING⁷ WYETH** (Henry⁶, Joshua⁵, Ebenezer⁴ Jr., Ebenezer³, John², Nicholas¹) born 10 Oct 1826, Cabot Hollow, Columbia Township, Bradford, Pennsylvania. Matthew Wing Wyeth and **FANNY MICHAEL** (divorced from Jacob Doring) were married on 27 Jan 1850 in Springboro, Crawford, Pennsylvania.[1122] Fanny, daughter of John Michael and Mary Ann Hickernell, was born on 17 Oct 1823 in Frankford, Cumberland, Pennsylvania. Matthew enlisted 16 Dec 1863 in Co. E of the 128ᵗʰ Infantry in Valparaiso, Porter, Indiana. He was discharged on 24 May 1865 in Beaufort, North Carolina. Matthew, a carpenter, died 30 Jul 1909 in Wheeler, Porter, Indiana. Fanny died there on 07 Aug 1912.

Matthew Wing Wyeth and Fanny Michael had the following children:

430.	i.	MARY MATILDA⁸ WYETH, born 11 Sep 1851, Spring Township, Crawford, Pennsylvania; married WALTER CHARLES BAKER, 11 Jan 1876, Stark County, Indiana; died 24 Dec 1895, Center Township, Porter, Indiana.
	ii.	AMANDA WYETH, born 1854, Spring Township; married BENJAMIN E. LOUKS, 03 Sep 1876, Lake County, Indiana; died 28 Apr 1894, Wheeler.
431.	iii.	FANNY LOVINA WYETH, born 16 May 1858, Winfield, Lake, Indiana; married CHARLES E. WALSH, 23 Nov 1873, Lake County; died 28 May 1925, Wheeler.

222. **MARY ELIZABETH**[7] **WYETH** (Henry[6], Joshua[5], Ebenezer[4] Jr., Ebenezer[3], John[2], Nicholas[1]) was born on 22 May 1829 in Beaver Township, Crawford, Pennsylvania. She married **JOHN H. PERKINS** circa 1856 in Crawford County. He was born there in Dec 1821. She died 25 Feb 1891 in Spring Township, Crawford, Pennsylvania.[1123] As she was a charter member of Wide Awake Division, No. 261, Sons of Temperance, in memory of their dear sister, the chapter was draped in mourning for 30 days.[1124] John died 21 Feb 1904 in Saegertown, Crawford, Pennsylvania.[1125]

The children of John H. Perkins and Mary Elizabeth Wyeth included:

    i. OLIVE E.[8] PERKINS, born 04 Oct 1856, Spring Township; married HARRY ELLERY STONE there in 1879; died 17 Dec 1919, Ashtabula County, Ohio.
    ii. AUGUSTA MAY PERKINS, born 13 Aug 1857, Spring Township; married ALONZO RENIFF (twin) there, 1875; died 27 Jan 1947, Summit Township, Erie, Pennsylvania.

432.   iii. ESTELLA D. PERKINS, born 21 Jul 1860, Spring Township; married LAVERNE SPERRY there, 1880; died 22 Apr 1921, Cranesville, Erie, Pennsylvania.

433.   iv. ELIZA A. PERKINS, born 11 Jun 1862, Spring Township; married ALPHONSO MELVIN RENIFF (twin) there in 1881; died 23 Mar 1939, Springboro.

    v. CLAYTON EUGENE PERKINS, born 02 Jun 1873, Spring Township; enlisted in the 3rd Cavalry in Buffalo, New York, 18 Jun 1896, description: fair, blue eyes, dark brown hair, 5'10", discharged 17 Jun 1899, Ft. Myer, Virginia; married (1) FLORENCE A. HILLS, 13 Feb

Estella Perkins Sperry's wedding photo comes through the research of her great, great granddaughter, Carissa Sperry-Douglass.

1900, Springboro, Crawford, Pennsylvania; married (2) EMILY A. HARYETT, 05 Aug 1919, San Francisco, California; developed real estate and the Signal Hill oil district ; served as commander of the East Oakland Camp of the United Spanish War Veterans; died 12 May 1947, Oakland, Alameda, California.[1126]

223. **OLIVE ELLEN**[7] **WYETH** (Henry[6], Joshua[5], Ebenezer[4] Jr., Ebenezer[3], John[2], Nicholas[1]) was born on 12 Feb 1833 in Spring Township, Crawford, Pennsylvania. Olive married (1) **JOHN W. HICKERNELL**, 01 Feb 1852, Spring Township. John was born to Abraham Hickernell Jr. and Sarah Himebaugh on 09 Jun 1829 in Spring Township. He died on 07 Nov 1855 at age 26 in Spring Township. Olive married a man named **TERRILL** and lastly married **LEVI CHURCH** circa 1885. She died at age 80 on 25 Nov 1913 at the Crawford County Infirmary, Saegertown, Crawford, Pennsylvania.

John W. Hickernell and Olive Ellen Wyeth had the following children:

434.   i. JOHN PRENTICE[8] HICKERNELL, born 28 Nov 1853, Spring Township; married FRANCES ALICE SLATER there, 12 Jul 1871; died of consumption on 20 Dec 1893, Hickernell, Crawford, Pennsylvania (town named for John and Royal).

435.   ii. ROYAL HICKERNELL, born May 1855, Spring Township; married JENNIE DEARBORN there, circa 1883; died 13 Dec 1894, near Rundell, Crawford, Pennsylvania, when a felled tree crushed him at age 39.[1127]

224. GEORGE WASHINGTON[7] WYETH (Henry[6], Joshua[5], Ebenezer[4] Jr., Ebenezer[3], John[2], Nicholas[1]) was born 02 Feb 1835 in Spring Township, Crawford, Pennsylvania. He enlisted in the 56th Illinois Infantry, Co. F on 12 Sep 1861 in Michigan City, Indiana and was discharged, due to a double hernia, on 01 Feb 1862 at Camp Douglas near Chicago, Illinois. Between his enlistments, he lived in Riley Township, Vigo, Indiana with one of his uncles. On 25 Aug 1864, in Cincinnati, Ohio, George joined the U.S. Navy and served as a landsman in the Mississippi Flotilla on the gunboat USS *Tyler*. He was discharged in Mound City, Illinois on 12 Jun 1865.[1128] He married **MARY ELIZABETH ANIE THOMAS** on 13 Feb 1866 in Riley Township.[1129] Mary was born in Kentucky on 05 Mar 1851 to William Thomas and Nancy Grisham. She died on 25 May 1889 in Leavenworth, Leavenworth County, Kansas. George died of mitral insufficiency on 19 Mar 1916 at the Pacific Branch Soldiers' Home, Los Angeles, California. He is buried there in the Los Angeles National Cemetery section 29, row G, site 17.

George Washington Wyeth and Mary Elizabeth Anie Thomas had the following children:

436. i. OTIS REDMOND[8] WYETH (twin), born 15 May 1869, Terre Haute; married ANNA CHAPLIN HOSKINS, 15 Oct 1891, Jackson, Jackson County, Missouri; a railway worker, Otis died on duty on 02 May 1897, Liberal, Seward, Kansas.

ii. CHARLES E. WYETH (twin), born 15 May 1869, Terre Haute; died young.

iii. GUY ANGUS WYETH, born on 12 Jan 1874 in Terre Haute; worked as a cooper, described as dark, 5'7 ½" with brown eyes and dark hair when he enlisted in the 23rd Infantry in Fort Worth, Texas on 14 Mar 1894. In a second tour of duty, Guy was shot in the hip during battle and died 02 May 1900, at age 26, in Lanpay, Philippines. Only his name and the number 320G marks his grave in Fort Leavenworth National Cemetery, Kansas.

iv. THOMAS VANCE WYETH, born 18 Aug 1881, Garnett, Anderson, Kansas; grew up with his sister in the Soldiers' Orphans Home, Atchison County, Kansas; an engineer, he was found robbed and murdered, 24 Jan 1918, near Weed, Siskiyou, California.[1130]

437. v. GRACE AGNES WYETH, born 11 Feb 1884, Kansas City, Wyandotte, Kansas; 1903 editor of *Fairplay Flume*, Park County, Colorado; married (1) DAVIS H. TOBEY, 18 Jun 1904, Littleton, Douglas, Colorado; married (2) CLYDE VALENTINE HUMMEL SR., 07 Aug 1907, Ouray, Ouray County, Colorado; died 03 Mar 1928, Chico, Butte, California.

This photo of Grace Wyeth, editor of *Fairplay Flume*, is courtesy of Sue Hummel Hill, Grace's granddaughter.

225. ALMIRA ROSANNA[7] WYETH (Henry[6], Joshua[5], Ebenezer[4] Jr., Ebenezer[3], John[2], Nicholas[1]) was born on 10 Jun 1847 in Spring Township, Crawford, Pennsylvania. Almira married (1) **HENRY MOSES**, there in 1865. Henry, son of Thomas Moses and Rhoda Brown Sturdevant, was born on 29 Apr 1842 in Crawford County. He died on 19 Apr 1910 in Erie, Erie County, Pennsylvania. She married (2) **WILLIAM FRANKLIN CUMMINGS**, circa 1915. William, son of William N. Cummings and Laura Kibble, was born 07 May 1851 in Erie County, New York. William died on 14 Mar 1931 in the town of Erie. Almira died there on 24 Apr 1931.

Henry Moses and Almira Rosanna Wyeth had the following children:

438.   i.   ETTIE LENA[8] MOSES, born 13 Apr 1868, Spring Township; married HENRY GRANT IKELER, 29 Dec 1888, Hillsdale, Hillsdale County, Michigan; died 21 May 1942, Erie, Erie County, Pennsylvania.

          ii.   LEWIS H. MOSES, born 18 Feb 1882, Spring Township; married GENEVIEVE E. ACHERSON, 23 Aug 1906, Meadville, Crawford, Pennsylvania; killed 26 Jan 1912, Winnipeg, Manitoba, Canada in a mill accident; funeral in Erie.[1131]

226. **ELVIRA[7] BAILEY** (Frances "Fanny"[6] Wyeth, Joshua[5], Ebenezer[4] Jr., Ebenezer[3], John[2], Nicholas[1]) was born in Jun 1827 near Plattsburg, Harmony Township, Clark, Ohio. Elvira Bailey and Matthew Canady were married there in Lisbon on 02 Jan 1848. **MATTHEW CANADY**, a shoemaker, was born about 1821 in Clark County, Ohio. After serving the 17th Ohio Light Artillery as a corporal, he was discharged, due to illness, on 15 Aug 1863 in Camp Chase, Columbus, Ohio. Transported by train to his home in Plattsburg 30 miles west, Matthew died there three months later on 22 Nov 1863. His family received a pension for his service. The daughters fell off of it at age 18. However, on 23 Feb 1892, their doctor wrote asking for daughter Almina, who suffered brain damage due to a fever when she was a toddler, to be restored to the pension after her release from the Dayton Asylum…"Mrs. Canady is a deserving and dependent widow and worthy of your kind consideration." Elvira died 60 years after her husband on 17 May 1923 at age 96 in Plattsburg.[1132]

Matthew Canady and Elvira Bailey had the following children:

439.   i.   FRANCES E.[8] CANADY, born 13 Apr 1851, Plattsburg; married JONATHAN M. LINSON there, 24 Dec 1873; died 11 Jul 1923, South Solon, Madison, Ohio.

          ii.   REGINA CANADY, born 29 Jun 1854, Plattsburg; guardian of Almina and her mother (who became an invalid at age 91 from a broken hip); Regina died unmarried on 25 Aug 1929 in Marion Township, Franklin County, Ohio.

         iii.   ELLA CANADY, born circa 1858, Plattsburg; died young.

         iv.   ALMINA CANADY, born 25 Jan 1862, Plattsburg; confined to an asylum for two years; died in 1923; buried near her mother in the Plattsburg Cemetery.

227. **MARTHA REBECCA[7] BAILEY** (Frances "Fanny"[6] Wyeth, Joshua[5], Ebenezer[4] Jr., Ebenezer[3], John[2], Nicholas[1]) was born on 07 Mar 1837 in Lisbon, Harmony Township, Clark, Ohio. In 1850, she lived with Matthew Canady and Elvira Bailey. Martha married **WILLIAM W. CANADY**, in Springfield, Clark, Ohio on 07 Aug 1855. William, son of Samuel H. Canady and Lovina Pharis, was born in Clark County about 1832. Matthew Canady apparently was his half-brother. William, a private in Co. B of the 45th Ohio Infantry, died on 25 Jan 1865 of chronic diarrhea in Huntsville, Madison, Alabama. Martha drew a pension for William's service until the certificate burned in a house fire in 1876. On 23 May 1902, Martha filed a claim to reinstate the pension but it was rejected on 08 Jul 1902 on the grounds her pension was terminated 25 May 1876 due to her remarriage to Joseph H. Brown on said date. The pension board referenced the baptism record of their child, Lilly May Brown, and a statement, signed by both parties, that they were married. Martha denied the signature on the statement was hers. Apparently, Brown submitted the documents in 1876 to get minor Cora Ella Canady's pension reinstated. Martha did admit to living with Brown to the date

of his death in 1894, as his wife. Thus, a common law marriage was fully established. However, on 17 Dec 1904, the chief of the pension law division reconsidered and restored William's pension to Martha. **JOSEPH H. BROWN** was born in Bellefontaine, Logan, Ohio circa 1838. He died on 11 Oct 1894 in Findlay, Hancock, Ohio.[1133] Martha died of tuberculosis on 25 Jun 1909 in Goshen Township, Auglaize, Ohio.[1134]

William W. Canady and Martha Rebecca Bailey had the following children[1135] (note: all of Martha's children were born in New Hampshire, Goshen Township, Auglaize, Ohio):

        i. LEONARD S.[8] CANADY, born 06 Jun 1856; died unmarried 05 Apr 1903 of heart disease in the Toledo State Hospital, Lucas County, Ohio.[1136]

        ii. SOPHRONIA ADALINE "ADDA" CANADY, born 22 Oct 1857; married ZACHARIAH CLOVER, 31 Dec 1874, Auglaize County; died 28 Jul 1925, Allen County, Ohio.

        iii. DAVID WILSON CANADY, born 29 Nov 1859; died unmarried on 10 Feb 1943, New Hampshire, Auglaize, Ohio.

440.   iv. CORA ELLA CANADY, born 03 Dec 1861; married JOHN JACKSON DOWNING, 09 Oct 1879, New Hampshire, Auglaize, Ohio; died there, 29 Jul 1936.

Joseph H. Brown and Martha Rebecca Bailey had the following child:

        i. LILLY MAY[8] BROWN, born 26 Sep 1876; married WILLIAM MONEY, circa 1923; died 07 Sep 1942, Lima, Allen, Ohio.[1137]

228. **WILLIAM HENRY[7] BAILEY** (Frances "Fanny"[6] Wyeth, Joshua[5], Ebenezer[4] Jr., Ebenezer[3], John[2], Nicholas[1]) was on born 22 Apr 1840 in Harmony Township, Clark, Ohio. He was a private in the 20th Illinois Infantry, Co. I from 1861 to 1864. William and **MARY ANN BAKER** were married on 06 Mar 1866 in Clark County. Mary Ann, the daughter of Emanuel Baker and Mary Christina Axline, was born 19 Feb 1844 in Union County, Ohio. She died on 28 Jan 1911 in Fairfield Township, Madison, Ohio. William died there, 07 Dec 1914. They are buried in Oak Grove Cemetery, Georgesville, Ohio.

William Henry Bailey and Mary Ann Baker had the following children:

        i. CORA ETTA[8] BAILEY, born 17 Dec 1867, South Vienna, Clark, Ohio; an unmarried school teacher, she died 04 May 1953 in the University Hospital, Columbus, Franklin, Ohio.[1138]

441.   ii. VIOLA V. BAILEY, born 08 Nov 1869, South Vienna; married JOHN LEONARD JEWETT, 27 Mar 1901, Fairfield; died 21 Feb 1949, Catawba, Clark, Ohio.

        iii. MARY FRANCES BAILEY, born 23 Apr 1873, South Vienna; died unmarried on 09 Feb 1952 in Berger Hospital, Circleville, Pickaway, Ohio.[1139]

        iv. JAMES EDWARD BAILEY, born 10 Mar 1875, South Vienna; died unmarried on 30 Jan 1965 in the Central Ohio Psychiatric Hospital, Columbus.[1140]

        v. WILLIAM ARTHUR BAILEY, born 27 Aug 1877, South Vienna; owned and farmed a 174 ½ acre farm near Chillicothe, died there unmarried on 06 Jul 1936 in Franklin Township, Ross, Ohio.[1141]

442.   vi. DAISY GERTRUDE BAILEY, born 03 Dec 1880, Fairfield Township; married AUGUST CLYDE ANDRIX there, 14 Jun 1904; died 13 Aug 1964, Circleville.

229. **ELLIOTT DUDLEY**[7] **HEWSON** (Anna Elizabeth[6] Wyeth, Joshua[5], Ebenezer[4] Jr., Ebenezer[3], John[2], Nicholas[1]) was born on 02 May 1831 in Cincinnati, Hamilton, Ohio. He married **ELLEN BARTLETT** there on 04 Aug 1853. In Cincinnati, on 15 Aug 1862, he enlisted in Co. H of the 83rd Ohio Infantry. Elliott was discharged on 24 Jul 1865 in Galveston, Texas. Ellen died on 04 Apr 1896 in Indianapolis, Marion, Indiana. He died there on 17 Aug 1920.

The children, all born in Hamilton County, of Elliott Hewson and Ellen Bartlett included:

       i. MARY[8] HEWSON, born circa 1860; married WILLIE D. HUTTON, 23 Feb 1877, Indianapolis; death unknown.

443.   ii. EDWIN CLINTON HEWSON, born 21 Jan 1867; married ALICE BROWNING, 29 Dec 1886, Indianapolis; died 28 Aug 1962, Greenfield, Hancock, Indiana.

      iii. JOHN E. HEWSON, born 07 Mar 1869; married LIZZIE WEISHAAR, 30 Oct 1889, Beech Grove, Marion, Indiana; a Methodist evangelist for 47 years, while confined in the Indianapolis Methodist Hospital, he and Lizzie celebrated 50 years of marriage before his death there on 13 Jan 1940.[1142]

230. **CHARLES ALONZO**[7] **WYETH** (Enoch Nelson[6], Joshua[5], Ebenezer[4] Jr., Ebenezer[3], John[2], Nicholas[1]) was born on 14 Oct 1836 in Cincinnati, Hamilton, Ohio.[1143] A blacksmith, he served as a private in both Co. D of the Indiana 11th Infantry and the 3rd Battery of the Indiana Light Artillery. Charles mustered out on disability 15 Mar 1863 in Indianapolis, Marion, Indiana. He married (1) his first cousin once removed, **TRESSA MEWHINNEY**, on 21 Mar 1864 in Riley Township, Vigo, Indiana. Tressa was born there in Jan 1848 to William Benjamin Mewhinney and Sarah Maria Wyeth. They divorced 20 Jun 1882, Denver, Arapahoe, Colorado.[1144] She married George O. Drake and died 28 Jan 1897 in Deadwood, Lawrence, South Dakota. Charles married (2) **THERESA P. FLOYD** (ex-wife of John O. Knuckey) on 25 Dec 1889 in Denver.[1145] Theresa was born in Jan 1844 in Lawrence County, Tennessee to Merritt Floyd and Mariah Gardner. Charles and Theresa Floyd divorced on 11 Nov 1895, but they remarried on 01 Dec 1896 in Golden, Jefferson Colorado. They divorced a second time on 09 Oct 1902.[1146] Charles married (3) **RACHEL AMANDA SCHOENLEBER** on 27 Jul 1906 in Minneapolis, Hennepin, Minnesota. Rachel was born on 13 Jul 1887 in Stuttgart, Germany to Chris Schoenleber and Frederika Hyde. While still in Denver, Charles invented the highly successful glue called Rocky Mountain Cement. He died on 30 Mar 1915 in the Minnesota Soldiers' Home, Minneapolis.[1147] Rachel, who never remarried, failed with the glue business. She died 05 Mar 1963 in Minneapolis.[1148]

Charles Alonzo Wyeth and Tressa Mewhinney had the following children:

      i. WILLIAM BENJAMIN "WILLIE"[8] WYETH, born circa 1865, Riley Township; death unknown.

444.   ii. FLORA MEWHINNEY WYETH, born 08 Jun 1870, Wyandotte, Wyandotte County, Kansas; married (1) WILLIAM MORGAN, 27 May 1888, Denver; married (2) CHARLES C. SMITH, 20 Nov 1890, Denver; married (3) JOHN A. WANGSNESS, 13 Sep 1893 at her step-father's home in Deadwood; died 18 Apr 1939, Everett, Snohomish, Washington.

      iii. CHARLES AUSTIN WYETH, born 31 Jan 1874, Kansas City, Wyandotte, Kansas. After his 1892 graduation in Denver, he studied jewelry making with

Longbean and Co. in Colorado Springs. After two years there, Charles relocated to the Black Hills region of South Dakota. While living with his mother, and her husband George O. Drake, in Deadwood, he worked for a local jeweler. Next, he accepted a contract with the Homestake Gold Mining Co. in Lead, Lawrence, South Dakota and started a jewelry store of his own. In 1910, Charles moved to Polson, Lake, Montana. There

Before it closed in 2002, the Homestake Mine was the largest and deepest gold mine in North America. This circa 1900 photo is courtesy of the Library of Congress.

he developed his jewelry manufacturing concern into the largest in the state. He married (1) CHRISTINE H. JOHNSON in 1901 in Lead;[1149] and on 21 Aug 1942 married (2) ROSAMOND LAWRENCE (divorcee of Thomas J. Bays) in Seattle, King, Washington. He was an instructor there in the WPA School of Mines. Charles Austin Wyeth died 27 Oct 1943, Centralia, Lewis, Washington.

    iv. JOSEPHINE WYETH (Drake), born circa 1878, Missouri; death unknown.

Charles Alonzo Wyeth and Theresa P. Floyd had the following child:

    i. BERTHA MAYBELLE[8] WYETH, born circa 1885, Denver; an attractive blond beauty pageant contestant, Maybelle married GUSTAV ARTHUR YEAGER, 26 May 1915, Littleton, Arapahoe, Colorado;[1150] death unknown.

Charles Alonzo Wyeth and Rachel Amanda Schoenleber had the following children:

445.   i. RICHARD CHARLES[8] WYETH, born 17 Apr 1908, Lead; married CORRINE AMANDA CARLSON on 09 Apr 1943 in Mason City, Cerro Gordo, Iowa; died 20 May 1966, Minneapolis.[1151]

446. ii. CLIFFORD AUSTIN WYETH, born 06 Mar 1910, Minneapolis; married AUDREY DELORES PYGMAN there on 25 Dec 1941; died 14 Apr 1998 in Robbinsdale, Hennepin, Minnesota. [1152]

   iii. EVELYN MARGARET WYETH, born 18 Jun 1911, Minneapolis; married (1) JAMES ORMEL "POPS" ELDRIDGE there on 25 Jul 1930; married (2) JOSEPH EDWARD SHEPPARD, 18 Apr 1977, Sioux Falls, Minnehaha, South Dakota; died 25 Sep 1988, Minneapolis.[1153]

447. iv. ETHEL MABLE WYETH, born 08 Dec 1912, Minneapolis; she married CHESTER EDWARD KUBICEK (YOKUBICEK), 18 Oct 1937, Mitchell, Davison, South Dakota; died 22 Sep 2001, Sioux Falls.[1154]

This photo of Richard, Rachel, Evelyn, Clifford and Charles, circa 1911, is courtesy of Richard's daughter, Donna Wyeth Thibodeau.

Notes for Charles Alonzo Wyeth:

There are three marriage records for Charles and his first wife, Tressa Mewhinney. The first seems only to be an application dated 15 Apr 1863, Coles County, Illinois. The second record was certified in Vigo County, Indiana on 21 Mar 1864 by L. Nebeker, minister. The third record, from their divorce report of 20 Jun 1882, gives 26 Mar 1865 in Gary, Indiana. The Denver, Colorado divorce report not only clears up the fact that Charles was indeed married to two women with similar first names, but it also lists the names and ages of Charles and Tressa's four children.

The 1880 Denver census shows all six members of Charles and Tressa's family nestled in a home on Holladay St. A series of newspaper articles and reports detail how the idyllic scene shattered.

Source	Story (names are spelled as shown in source documents)
"Hotel Arrivals," *Denver Republican* (Denver, CO), 01 Feb 1882, 7.	Mrs. Theresa Floyd from Golden is staying at the Red Lion Hotel, Denver. *(She was using her maiden name. She was really Mrs. John O. Knuckey.)*
"An Abandoned Family." *Rocky Mountain News* (Denver, CO), 31 May 1882, 5.	"… wife of Charles A. Wyeth (Tressa Mewhinney), an applier of stove polish, living at **707 Holladay street** has been added to the list of mysterious disappearances … she kissed her four small children and went away…"
"Mrs. Wyeth Found," *Denver Republican* (Denver, CO), 03 Jun 1882, 8.	"… to be more explicit, she (Mewhinney) merely was discovered by the police … took refuge with friends… her husband having introduced a mistress into the family and upon being charged with this threatened suicide. He made two bluffs by firing a pistol off in the woodshed, and then his wife left him…"
"Wyeth, Wife and Woman," *Rocky Mountain News* (Denver, CO), 04 Jun 1882, 7.	"… man who attempted recently to cast bad repute upon his wife (Mewhinney) by charging her with having abandoned her family, was yesterday arrested … charging him with adultery with a woman known as Francis Floyd… Mrs. Wyeth having begun an action for divorce, resolved to have her husband and his paramour arrested for adultery. Wyeth was lodged in jail and Constable Newman left last night for Golden, where he expects to find Mrs. Floyd …."
"Lewd Love. A Precious Pair of People, of Doubtful Age. Being Charged on the Crime of Adultery," *Rocky Mountain News* (Denver, CO), 6 Jun 1882, 8.	"… wife (Mewhinney) had simply gone to a friend's house *(George Drake's?)* … her husband had brought a woman to her house that she did not like the looks of. He claimed that the name of the woman was Mrs. Floyd and that she was the wife of a partner of his in the mountains. Mrs. Wyeth subsequently discovered a diary which revealed Mr. Wyeth's true relations with Mrs. Floyd … All parties were in court yesterday. Mrs. Wyeth is a good looking, thin faced blonde… she appears to have a temper of considerable acidity … Wyeth is a dark-complexioned man with a retreating forehead … Mrs. Floyd is a woman whose youth and beauty appears to have long since departed… she is a dark, dried up specimen of a woman… The defense will probably try to show that Wyeth had been simply employing Mrs. Floyd as an assistant polish peddler and that the prosecution must show a continuous state of cohabitation between the parties to prove adultery. They also attempted to show yesterday, in their cross examination, that Mrs. Wyeth had been anxious to get rid of her husband, and… anxious to secure the affections of another man." *(? George O. Drake, 2nd husband, at **665 Holladay** and she at **707 Holladay St.**)*[1155]
"Justices' Courts," *Denver Republican* (Denver, CO), 06 Jun 1882, 8.	"… the testimony at the time yesterday was unfit for publication. One piece of testimony was the most unique ever had in court. It consisted of a diary kept by Wyeth, in which each one of his criminal acts was jotted down in most shameful and obscene words…"
Colorado Statewide Divorce Index, *FamilySearch* image 1107 – Docket: 5296, 20 Jun 1882.	Divorce Record Report – plaintiff: Wyeth (Mewhinney), Tresse – defendant: Wyeth, Charles A.; document, in error, says their marriage was 26 Mar 1865 in Gary, Indiana; lists names and ages of all four of their children.
"Denver Divorces." *Rocky Mountain News* (Denver, CO), 22 Dec 1884, 4.	"Those brought by the wives are as follows: Theresa (Floyd) Knuckey vs. John O. Knuckey."
Las Animas County, Colorado State Census, 01 Jun 1885.	John O. Knuckey is alone with his and Floyd's five children living with him and his brother (or boarder).
Pueblo County, Colorado State Census, 01 Jun 1885.	C. A. is living with T.P. (Floyd) Wyeth shown as his wife born in Tennessee; no children.

Arapahoe County, Colorado State Census, 01 Jun 1885.[1156]	George O. Drake (age 36), boarder of Theressa (Mewhinney) Wyeth (age 37), Flora Wyeth (age 15), C. A. Wyeth (age 11), Josephine Wyeth (age 7)
Colorado Statewide Divorce Index, *FamilySearch* image 1604 – Docket: 8418, 15 Nov 1887.	Divorce Record Report – plaintiff: Drake, Charles O. – defendant: Drake, Emma H., children: Alice age 14 and Charles age 10
Colorado Statewide Divorce Index, *FamilySearch* image 4326 – Docket: 11845, 22 Nov 1889.	Divorce Record Report – plaintiff: Knucky, Theresa P. (Floyd) – defendant: John O. Knucky, no were children listed, however they had five.
Colorado Marriage Index, *Ancestry* image 1024, 25 Dec 1889.	Report No. 8485 shows the first marriage of Theresa P. (Floyd) Knuckey and Charles A. Wyeth in Denver.
"He was Innocent, the Pardons Board Rights a Great Wrong," *Denver Post* (Denver, CO), 10 Jul 1895, 6.	Summary: The conviction of Henry Lee for assaulting Augusta Landslinger was overturned on the emotional testimony of Floyd who said Augusta had a bad reputation and she and her sister, Mrs. Young, broke up Floyd's marriage.
"A Strong Denial. Mrs. Young Questioned the Story of Mrs. Wyeth. Mr. Wyeth Writes," *Denver Post* (Denver, CO), 12 Jul 1895, 4.	"I must emphatically pronounce the statements made by my wife before the pardons board on Wednesday as false in every particular. The woman (T. P. Floyd) is a defamer and a slanderer of the worst type ... will be proven in my suit for divorce ... on the 20th of July."
"Love and Religion. Charles Wyeth gets them Tangled." *Rocky Mountain News* (Denver, CO), 15 Jul 1894, 6.	Summary: Charles Wyeth, of Rocky Mountain Cement, is well-to-do, active in the Odd Fellows and Masons, with a daughter, age nine. Both he and Floyd were arrested when she flew into a jealous rage over notice Charles was paying to Miss Landslinger and her sister, Mrs. Young, a Salvation Army worker.
"Riches Proved too much, Wife of the Discoverer of Rocky Mountain Cement wants Divorce, *"Denver Post* (Denver, CO), 02 Oct 1895.	"Mrs. Wyeth (Floyd) wants the court to compel Mr. Wyeth to support her... so successful has he been with this 'warranted to mend anything' discovery that he now enjoys the munificent income of $50 every month... and also a pension for bravery in the war of the rebellion ... The two have lived together 12 years. But the bliss of those score of years has been marred... She says that he has threatened to kill her and he says that she tried to kill him with a hatchet."
Colorado Statewide Divorce Index, *FamilySearch* image 1105 – Docket: 2784, 11 Nov 1895.	Divorce Record Report – plaintiff: Wyeth, T. P. – defendant: Wyeth, Charles A.; their child's name "Bertha May Wyeth" is given
Colorado Marriage Index, *Ancestry* image 2173, 01 Dec 1896.	2nd marriage of Theresa P. Wyeth and Charles Alonzo Wyeth in Golden, Jefferson, Colorado – Report No. 1464
"News in Brief," *Colorado Transcript* (Golden, CO), 09 Dec 1896, 7.	"Charles A. Wyeth and Teresa Wyeth were united in marriage last Wednesday ... This is the second time this couple has been married; they having been divorced in November 1895."
"John and his Bessie may go to Golden," *Rocky Mountain News* (Denver, CO), 13 Dec 1898, 8.	"Mrs. C. A. Wyeth of 2420 Larimer St. yesterday served written notice upon the county clerk, not to issue a marriage license to her son, John O. Knuckey (Jr.) ... He is only 19... I don't want my son to be the husband of that girl."
Federal Census of Denver, Arapahoe, Colorado, 1900.	Charles and Theresa are living with six children; although the census gives the surname "Wyeth" to all of them, all, but May, are Floyd's Knuckey children.
"Major Vail Too Gallant, Wyeth Claims the Officer Caused his Wife to Leave Him," *Denver Post* (Denver, CO), 05 Sep 1901, 2.	"Charles A. Wyeth, manufacturer of cement for mending china, who has been living at 2057 Lawrence St., is trying to find his wife. He is inclined to hold Major O. B. Vail of the Volunteers of America responsible... Vail left the city for Omaha last night... Mrs. Wyeth (Floyd) is supposed to have left town the same day. 'My wife sold all our furniture,' said the husband, 'and told her friends she was going to Galveston to engage in army work there.'"
Colorado Statewide Divorce Index, *FamilySearch* image 1105 – Docket: 854, 09 Oct 1902.	Divorce Record Report (2nd divorce for couple) – plaintiff: Wyeth (Floyd), T. P. – defendant: Wyeth, Charles A.; Phillips County, Colorado.
"Pseudo Reformer with a Checkered Career is Denounced by Volunteers," *Rocky Mountain News* (Denver, CO), 02 Dec 1905, 6.	Summary: After the Volunteers of America discharged Owens B. Vail and Mrs. Wyeth (Floyd) from their society, Vail organized the Christian Volunteer Warriors. Vail, an ex-con counterfeiter, travelled the country under the guise of collecting money for the poor. He also collected and discarded wives. An early victim being Mrs. Wyeth (Floyd) of Denver.
"Vail's Life Laid Bare," *Rocky Mountain News* (Denver, CO), 03 Dec 1905, 16.	"He (Vail) is a bad man and no one but himself gets any benefit from what he collects for charity. He swipes it all and spends a good deal of it for drink... he has victimized women for years past. About six years ago he ran away with Mrs. Major Wyeth (Floyd) from Denver. After he had spent all the money she had, he deserted her. He had trouble in Minneapolis, where they went..."

369

Clearly, Charles chased Theresa Floyd to Minnesota. Why they did not marry for a third time is a mystery. Perhaps his love for 21-year-old Rachel Schoenleber was too much of a distraction. Charles so much wanted to be with Rachel that he claimed on their marriage license to be only 48 years old. In fact, he was 69 and she was 48 years his junior. He was, however, vigorous and healthy until just days before his death. When he feted an early birthday with his youngest son, Clifford, in Mar 1915, several newspapers described the over seven decades age difference.[1157] A few days later, they reported sons Clifford, age five, and Richard, age seven, spread the National flag over the Civil War veteran's casket.[1158] Rachel struggled greatly for 48 years on her own.

231. **GEORGE NELSON[7] WYETH** (Enoch Nelson[6], Joshua[5], Ebenezer[4] Jr., Ebenezer[3], John[2], Nicholas[1]) was born on 21 Jan 1842 in Terre Haute, Vigo, Indiana. George married **MARY DEMARIS "POLLY" KESTER** on 24 Sep 1863 in Linton Township, Vigo, Indiana. Polly, daughter of Ephraim Kester and Margaret Stark, was born there on 29 Jun 1839. George enlisted on 14 Feb 1865 in Terre Haute in the 149th Indiana Infantry, Co. K and was discharged after the close of the Civil War on 27 Sep 1865 in Nashville, Tennessee. Polly died on 12 May 1897 in Terre Haute. When George entered the Danville, Illinois home for disabled soldiers at age 60, he had been employed as a blacksmith and was described as 5 ft. even, light complexion, blue eyes, gray hair, and protestant.[1159] He died in Terre Haute's Union Hospital on 28 Dec 1912.

The children of George Nelson Wyeth and Mary Demaris "Polly" Kester included:

Photo of Carrie Olive Wyeth Ball courtesy of her great granddaughter, Suzy Broyles.

448.   i. CARRIE OLIVE[8] WYETH, born 27 Sep 1866, Linton Township; married EDWARD HALSEY BALL, 01 Nov 1883, Clark County, Illinois; died 19 Mar 1949, Terre Haute.

ii. AUDRA WYETH, born 17 Feb 1868, Linton Township; died there, 01 Jun 1868.

iii. ARMENTA DEMARIS "MINNIE" WYETH, born 09 Apr 1869, Linton; married MARTIN WERKER there, 27 Jul 1904; died 27 Sep 1949, St. Anthony's Hospital, Terre Haute.

iv. WILLARD EPHRAIM WYETH, born 06 Dec 1872, Linton Township; married JESSIE RANDOLPH there, 05 Feb 1896; died 12 Nov 1936, Ann Arbor, Washtenaw, Michigan.

449.   v. EDWARD ORBIN WYETH, born 14 Apr 1876, Linton; married ALINA "LENA" ACHILLES,[1160] 1907, Salem, Marion, Oregon; died 29 Apr 1956, Goble, Columbia, Oregon.

450.   vi. MAGDELENA WYETH, born 23 Feb 1879, Linton Township; married ROBERT L. ARMSTRONG, 24 Dec 1905, Terre Haute; died 30 Apr 1959, Kansas City, Jackson, Missouri.

vii. DANIEL S. WYETH, born 21 Jan 1882, Honey Creek Township, Vigo, Indiana; died there on 12 Jun 1883; buried at the Old Kester Place, Linton Township.

232. **JAMES THOMAS[7] WYETH** (Enoch Nelson[6], Joshua[5], Ebenezer[4] Jr., Ebenezer[3], John[2], Nicholas[1]) was born on 03 Jul 1859 in Crab Orchard, Lincoln, Kentucky. James Thomas Wyeth and **MARGARET JENNIE DOAN**, were married 12 Nov 1889 in Terre Haute, Vigo, Indiana. Margaret, daughter of Ebenezer Doan and Mary Rigney, was born 14 Mar 1866 in Orange County, Indiana. She died on 18 Jan 1923 in Terre Haute. James died 09 May

1947 in Detroit, Wayne, Michigan. His marriage record says his parents were Daniel Wyeth and Rebecca Gudge. However, he may have been adopted by Enoch and Lucinda Prather Wyeth. There are no records for Daniel and Rebecca in Kentucky or in Indiana. However, Lucinda is from Kentucky. James and Margaret are buried in Vigo County's Hull Cemetery near George Nelson Wyeth who named a son, Daniel.

James Thomas Wyeth and Margaret Jennie Doan had the following children:

> i. MARY ELIZABETH[8] WYETH, born 17 Feb 1894, Terre Haute; married WILLIAM HENRY MOSEL there, 14 Jan 1913; died 02 Mar 1945, Detroit.
> ii. LOUIS EDWARD WYETH, born 10 Sep 1895, Terre Haute; married LOUISE SCHWAB there, 09 Feb 1916; died 01 Aug 1949, Detroit.
> iii. HELEN DOANE WYETH, born 23 Oct 1901, Terre Haute; married (1) JOHN ALBIN BUSWELL there, 01 Aug 1920; married (2) WILLIAM CARPENTER, 10 Feb 1934, Detroit; died 26 Jan 1985, Tawas City, Iosco, Michigan.

233. **EDWIN WALLACE[7] HARRISON JR.** (Olive Amanda[6] Wyeth, Joshua[5], Ebenezer[4] Jr., Ebenezer[3], John[2], Nicholas[1]) was born in Dec 1840 in Cincinnati, Hamilton, Ohio. Edwin Wallace Harrison Jr. and Eleanor "Ella" Cannon were married on 18 Jun 1863 in Cincinnati. [1161] **ELEANOR "ELLA" CANNON**, daughter of H. P. Cannon and Eleanor Hinckley, was born on 14 Jul 1838 in Cincinnati. He died of typhoid pneumonia on 25 Dec 1884 in Newton, Jasper, Illinois. Edwin was buried on 27 Dec 1884 in Cincinnati's Spring Grove Cemetery, section 53, lot 87, space 6. Ella died in Newton of dropsy on 01 Apr 1904. She was buried in space 10 near Edwin on 03 Apr 1904.[1162]

Edwin Wallace Harrison Jr. and Eleanor "Ella" Cannon had the following children:

> i. WILLIAM ROBERT[8] HARRISON, born 08 Apr 1857, Cincinnati; married IDA LANE, 30 Jul 1882, Hillsdale, Vermillion, Indiana; died 05 Nov 1902, Helt Township, Vermillion, Indiana.
>
> 451. ii. EDWIN DUDLEY HARRISON, born 03 May 1864, Cincinnati; married (1) OLIVE ADKINS, 09 Jan 1889, Newton; married (2) NETTIE WHEELER, 09 Jan 1900, Newton; died 05 Jan 1937, Lacomb, Linn, Oregon.
>
> iii. CLARA OLIVE HARRISON (twin), born 31 Dec 1866, Cincinnati; died there at 190 Everett St. of congestion of the lungs on 04 Jun 1868 at age 17 months, four days; buried near her parents in space 2, Spring Grove Cemetery.[1163]
>
> iii. CLARENCE ORMAN HARRISON (twin), born 31 Dec 1866, Cincinnati; married LEAH MCCORMACK, 04 Sep 1895, Jasper County, Illinois; died 27 Apr 1938, Joliet, Will, Illinois.
>
> iv. LEWIS NELSON HARRISON, born 23 Mar 1882, Newton; married (1) NANCY CAROLYN BURFORD there, 18 Mar 1904; married (2) IRENE ELIZABETH FARRELL, 13 Feb 1941, Linn County, Oregon; died there, 23 Jul 1949.

234. **CHARLES JONES[7] WYETH** (Dr. Jacob[6], Jacob[5] Sr., Ebenezer[4] Jr., Ebenezer[3], John[2], Nicholas[1]) was born circa 1835 in Galena, Jo Daviess County, Illinois. In 1854, he graduated from Phillips Exeter Academy, Exeter, New Hampshire. The spelling of his middle name comes from their records.[1164] Charles Jones Wyeth and **JULIA ELIZABETH**

MCREYNOLDS were married on 04 Apr 1865 in Detroit, Wayne, Michigan. [1165]   Julia, daughter of John McReynolds and Elizabeth Hill, was born there on 24 Nov 1841. In route to New Orleans, Louisiana, Charles died from consumption in the St. Charles Hotel in Cairo, Alexander, Illinois on 12 Apr 1873. [1166] Julia remarried eight years later. After her death on 08 Feb 1923 in New York City, Julia was buried with her second husband, Brig. General Orlando B. Willcox, in Arlington National Cemetery. [1167]

Charles Jones Wyeth and Julia Elizabeth McReynolds had the following children:

   i.   CHARLES MCREYNOLDS[8] WYETH, born in Chicago, Cook, Illinois on 04 Feb 1866; died there, 04 Oct 1866, at age nine months of cholera infantum. [1168]

   ii. (DR.) LEONARD JARVIS WYETH, born 15 Oct 1867, Chicago; in 1900 he took a degree in allopathic medicine from Columbian Medical University (now George Washington University School of Medicine), Washington, D.C.; [1169] 1901 began practice of medicine in Colorado; enlisted in the Army Sanitary Corps (dedicated to prevention and control of disease using sanitary methods) on 18 Aug 1918, Camp Lewis, Washington; discharged 18 May 1919, Camp Lewis, due to mental distress. On 13 Sep 1919, Leonard married HELEN V. "NELLIE" STEWART in Seattle, King, Washington. Nellie, daughter of William Stewart and Mary Sherrard, was the wealthy widow of Orion O. Denny, a Seattle pioneer. To honor her first husband, she gave lands near Seattle that now form the O. O. Denny Park. [1170] Nellie became despondent after her divorce from Leonard at the end of 1920. She killed herself on 09 Mar 1922 in Los Angeles. [1171] Leonard continued to suffer from emotional problems as well. After having a nervous breakdown, he was admitted to the Pacific Branch of the National Home for Disabled Volunteer Soldiers and Sailors in Sawtelle, Los Angeles, California in 1927. He was age 59 at the time and described as 5' 10 1/4" tall, fair, blue eyes, light hair. He died there, 11 Aug 1945 at age 77. [1172] His ashes are buried in Mt. Auburn Cemetery, Cambridge near his great grandfather, Jacob Wyeth Sr.

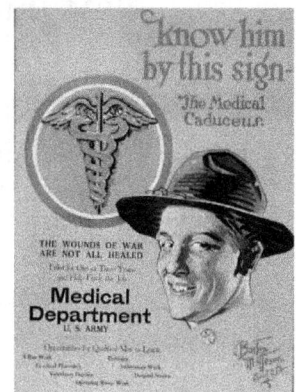

Great War U.S. Army Medical Department recruiting poster, courtesy of the Library of Congress.

452.   iii. NATHAN CORWITH WYETH, born 20 Apr 1870, Chicago; in 1899, he graduated from École nationale supérieure des Beaux-Arts, Paris, France with an Architect Diplômé par le Gouvernement. Nathan married DOROTHY ELLIS LAWSON, 20 Sep 1911, Cleftstone Manor Cottage, Bar Harbor, Hancock, Maine. During a career spent largely in Washington, D.C., his architectural work includes helping craft the Cannon House Office and the Russell Senate Office Buildings, designing the Tidal Basin Inlet Bridge, the USS *Maine* Mast Memorial, the D.C. Armory and the White House's original Oval Office. Commissioned a Major in the U. S. Army Hospital Division in 1918, he designed temporary hospitals for construction in France during World War I. Nathan died 30 Aug 1963, Washington, D.C. at age 93. [1173]

Notes for Charles Jones Wyeth and Julia Elizabeth McReynolds:

As president of the Wyeth & Vandervoort Malting Company on Michigan Avenue, Chicago, Charles Jones Wyeth was quite a successful businessman. Like his father Dr. Jacob Wyeth, Charles suffered from tuberculosis. Knowing he would not live to see his sons grown, he created a trust for them and designated Nathan Corwith trustee. Charles so admired the Galena banker and pig iron dealer, that he named his youngest son, Nathan Corwith Wyeth, in his honor. The two were distantly related through the marriage of Charles' aunt Eliza Joanna Brady to George W. Campbell. Corwith failed the trust miserably by comingling the Wyeth trust funds with his personal accounts to the tune of almost $100,000.[1174]

When Julia married Brig. General Orlando B. Willcox, recipient of the Medal of Honor, she was cut out of the trust in 1881. Nevertheless, she fought for her sons' inheritance. Some of the money apparently was recovered via sale of land that Corwith purchased using Wyeth funds. At Julia's death in 1923, she was buried with the general in Arlington National Cemetery. Her side of their monument is still awaiting a descendant interested in having Julia's name engraved on it.

235. **SARAH ARCHER**[7] **WYETH** (Leonard Jarvis[6], Jacob[5] Sr., Ebenezer[4] Jr., Ebenezer[3], John[2], Nicholas[1]) was born about 1824 in Baltimore, Maryland. Sarah Archer Wyeth and **CHARLES P. CARPENDER** were married on 09 May 1849 in New York City, New York. Charles the son of William Carpender and Lucy Weston Grant was born circa 1810 in Oneida County, New York. He died on 23 Oct 1855 in New York City and was originally interred there in Marble Cemetery with his two children.[1175] They were moved 31 Dec 1855 to Green-Wood Cemetery in Brooklyn where they rest in the Wyeth mausoleum. Sarah was buried with them after her death in New York City on 13 Apr 1861.[1176]

Charles P. Carpender and Sarah Archer Wyeth had the following children:

> i. CHARLES P.[8] CARPENDER JR. , born about 1851 in New York City; died there at 40 East 26 St. on 24 Feb 1855 at age four.
> i. UNNAMED CHILD, born and died Christmastime 1853 in New York City.

236. **ELIZABETH JARVIS**[7] **WYETH** (Leonard Jarvis[6], Jacob[5] Sr., Ebenezer[4] Jr., Ebenezer[3], John[2], Nicholas[1]) was born on 16 Aug 1832 in New York City, New York County, New York. Elizabeth Jarvis Wyeth and **ANDERSON CARROLL DANA** were married there on 18 May 1859. Anderson, son of Anderson Green Dana and Eliza Fuller, was born on 13 Jan 1822 in Salisbury, Addison, Vermont. He died on 03 May 1907 in New York City. She died there on 23 Mar 1915.

Anderson Carroll Dana and Elizabeth Jarvis Wyeth had the following child:

> i. CAROLYN ARCHER[8] DANA, born 06 Jan 1871, New York City; died unmarried there on 15 Dec 1940 at her home overlooking Central Park, 907 5th Ave.[1177]

237. **LEONARD JARVIS**[7] **WYETH JR.** (Leonard Jarvis[6], Jacob[5] Sr., Ebenezer[4] Jr., Ebenezer[3], John[2], Nicholas[1]) was born on 29 Oct 1833 in New York City, New York County, New York. He graduated from Harvard College, 1854. Leonard married **CHARLOTTE PRIME**, 27 Dec 1858 in New York City. Charlotte Prime was born on 12 Nov 1838 to Edward

Prime and Charlotte Wilkins Hoffman in New York City. Leonard died there at his home at 1142 Madison Avenue on 05 May 1909. [1178] Charlotte died on 06 Oct 1923 at her daughter's home, 183 West 58th, New York City. [1179] Leonard and Charlotte both rest in the Wyeth mausoleum in Brooklyn's Green-Wood Cemetery, lot 9201.

Leonard Jarvis Wyeth Jr. - photo from the HUP Collection, courtesy Harvard University Archives.

The children of Leonard Jarvis Wyeth Jr. and Charlotte Prime were:

453.   i.   CHARLOTTE HOFFMAN "DAISY" [8] WYETH, born 05 Nov 1859, Riverdale, Bronx County, New York; married LEWIS LIVINGSTON DELAFIELD JR., 25 Apr 1885, New York City; died there, 24 Apr 1947.

454.   ii. LEONARD JARVIS WYETH III, born 03 Jul 1861, Westchester County, New York; married (1) LOUISE ALLEY HOPKINS, 01 Oct 1889, Church of the Intercession, Washington Heights, Orange, New York; married (2) EVA REITMAYER, 05 Dec 1900, Jersey City, Hudson, New Jersey; died 19 Feb 1908, 61 E. 86th St., New York City.

455.   iii. GEORGE EDWARD WYETH, born 05 May 1863, New York City; married (1) CHARLOTTE GROSVENOR GOODRIDGE, 12 Nov 1890, Springhurst, Riverdale-on-Hudson, New York; married (2) ELIZABETH MAE GRESS, 04 Jun 1914, Lancaster, Butler, Pennsylvania; died 17 Oct 1921, New York City.

238. **EMILY**[7] **WYETH** (Leonard Jarvis[6], Jacob[5] Sr., Ebenezer[4] Jr., Ebenezer[3], John[2], Nicholas[1]) was born 06 Oct 1835 in New York City, New York County, New York. Emily Wyeth and **FREDERICK GEORGE SWAN** were married there on 21 Feb 1861. Frederick, son of Benjamin Swan and Mary Saidler, was born on 22 Feb 1831 in New York City. Frederick died there on 30 Nov 1899. Emily died on 16 Mar 1910 in New York City.

Frederick George Swan and Emily Wyeth had the following child:

456.   i.   FRANCES WYETH[8] SWAN, born 26 Nov 1863, New York City; married BENJAMIN SUMNER WELLES JR. there, 27 Oct 1886; died 25 Feb 1911, Kerhonkson, Ulster, New York. [1180]

239. **CHARLES JARVIS**[7] **WYETH** (Charles[6], Jacob[5] Sr., Ebenezer[4] Jr., Ebenezer[3], John[2], Nicholas[1]) was born on 05 May 1828 in Baltimore, Maryland. He married **MARGARET JOHNSON** there on 17 Jul 1849. [1181] Margaret, daughter of Arthur Livingston Johnson and Margaret Smith, was born in Baltimore about 1829. Charles, an awning maker, fell two stories while making a repair on a building at 47 Broadway in Manhattan. [1182] He died in a hospital there on 18 Nov 1874. Charles was buried in the Wyeth plot in Green Mount Cemetery, Baltimore on 21 Nov 1874. Margaret died 18 Mar 1885 in Brooklyn, Kings, New York. [1183] She is buried there in Green-Wood Cemetery in lot 5499.

Charles Jarvis Wyeth and Margaret Johnson had the following children:

457.   i.   ELIZABETH NORRIS[8] WYETH, born about 1852, Baltimore; married

CHARLES EDWARD BINGHAM, circa 1875; after his death in 1876, Elizabeth adopted Theodore Clinton Bingham; Elizabeth died 22 Feb 1913, Brooklyn. She is buried near her mother in Green-Wood Cemetery, lot 5499, grave 2132.

    ii. MARGARET WYETH, born 1853, Baltimore; died there, 01 Jan 1857.

   iii. CLINTON R. WYETH, born Mar 1856, Baltimore; died unmarried on 17 Feb 1924 in New York City. Buried in Green-Wood Cemetery, lot 5499.

458.   iv. CHARLES L. WYETH, born Jan 1862, Baltimore; married THERESA WALSH, 09 Feb 1890, Brooklyn; a RR conductor, he died 26 Nov 1932 of acute cardiac arrest, Morrisania Hospital, Bronx, New York.[1184]

459.   v. NATHANIEL DOUGLASS WYETH, born Sep 1866, Brooklyn; married LILLIAN IRENE MURPHY there, 30 Oct 1892; died 22 Feb 1944, Little Falls, Passaic, New Jersey from complications of a broken hip.[1185]

460.   vi. CARRIE ELLA WYETH, born 11 Feb 1870, Brooklyn; married FREDERICK WOLF, 14 Jun 1891, New York City, death unknown after 1925.

240. **NATHANIEL JARVIS "NATHAN"[7] WYETH** (Charles[6], Jacob[5] Sr., Ebenezer[4] Jr., Ebenezer[3], John[2], Nicholas[1]) was born on 08 Sep 1830 in Baltimore, Maryland. He graduated in 1852 with a LL.B. degree from Harvard Law School in Cambridge, Middlesex, Massachusetts. Nathan married **ANN CAROLINE FROST** there on 03 Oct 1854. Ann, daughter of William Frost and Susan Hills, was born 23 Jun 1830 in New Orleans, Louisiana. While practicing law in New York City, Nathan's uncle "L.J." Wyeth got him interested in Staten Island.[1186] Ann died there on 20 Dec 1914 at the beautiful Italianate villa called "Florence Home" that Nathan had built on Richmond Hill, Richmond County, New York. He died there on 22 Mar 1916.

Nathaniel Jarvis Wyeth - photo from the HUP Collection, courtesy Harvard University Archives.

Nathan Wyeth and Ann Caroline Frost had the following children:

    i. ANNIE FLORENCE[8] WYETH, born 14 Aug 1855, Cambridge; died 12 Nov 1864 in "Florence Home," 190 Meisner Ave., Richmond Hill, New York.

461.   ii. CHARLES NATHANIEL WYETH, born 12 Oct 1858, Richmond Hill; studied Civil Engineering at the Columbia College School of Mines, New York City; married MARY RUTH ADNEY there, 18 Apr 1900; died 20 May 1922, Manhattan State Hospital on Ward's Island, New York.[1187]

462.   iii. LAURA ADAMS WYETH, born 06 May 1862, Richmond Hill; married TJARK HOUTMAN about 1884; died 19 Dec 1898, New York City.

   iv. HELEN ELIZABETH WYETH, born 22 Feb 1865, Richmond Hill; Cambridge Art School graduate; died unmarried, 25 Dec 1953, Somerville, Massachusetts.

Nathaniel named his Staten Island home for his oldest daughter. It is located at the top of Lighthouse (Richmond) Hill.

   v. LUCILLE HILLS WYETH, born 15 Oct 1867, Richmond Hill; died unmarried on 04 Dec 1938 in Cambridge. She and sister Helen share a monument there in Mt. Auburn Cemetery, Hibiscus Path, Lot 1469.

241. **WILLIAM NORRIS**[7] **WYETH SR.** (Charles[6], Jacob[5] Sr., Ebenezer[4] Jr., Ebenezer[3], John[2], Nicholas[1]) was born 29 Sep 1837 in Baltimore, Maryland.[1188] William married **ELEANOR J. MAYNARD** there on 24 Feb 1863.[1189] Eleanor, daughter of James Maynard and Naomi Gemeny, was born 15 Jan 1845 in Baltimore, Maryland.[1190] William, the senior partner of Wyeth & Brother, an iron and steel business in Baltimore, died there on 15 Apr 1890.[1191] Eleanor died on 17 Mar 1898 at her home, 10 East Madison St., Baltimore.[1192]

William Norris Wyeth Sr. and Eleanor J. Maynard had the following children:

463.   i.   WILLIAM NORRIS[8] WYETH JR., born 31 May 1865, Baltimore;[1193] married (1) THERESA JUDSON, 01 Jun 1892, New York City; married (2) ANNA KOHLER, 17 Jul 1915, New York City; died there, 04 Apr 1938.

   ii.   CHARLES MAYNARD WYETH, born 30 Mar 1871, Baltimore; graduate of the University of Maryland; served in the Maryland National Guard; American Horseshoe Company purchasing agent, Phillisburg, Pennsylvania; married ELEANOR PACKER ALLIS, 1925, Easton, Northhampton, Pennsylvania; died on 05 Feb 1944 in Easton Hospital, Wilson, Northhampton, Pennsylvania.[1194]

   iii.   ELEANOR MAYNARD WYETH, born 22 Dec 1873, Baltimore; married CHARLES GOODWIN JR. there, 22 Feb 1898, at home, at 10 Madison St., so her gravely ill mother could be present; Eleanor Goodwin died on 20 Mar 1937 in Baltimore, buried there in Loudon Park Cemetery.[1195]

   iv.   NATHANIEL JARVIS "NAT" WYETH, born 26 Nov 1882, Baltimore; graduated from Princeton University, 1907; married NORMA LOUISE KEMP, 15 Mar 1924, McDaniel, Talbot, Maryland;[1196] a risk examiner for the Federal Housing Administration, Nat died on 17 Aug 1962, Easton, Talbot, Maryland; buried there in Spring Hill Cemetery with Louise.

Nat Wyeth photo courtesy of the Kemp Family of Talbot County, MD.

242. **HENRY CLARENCE**[7] **WYETH** (Charles[6], Jacob[5] Sr., Ebenezer[4] Jr., Ebenezer[3], John[2], Nicholas[1]) was born 28 Oct 1839, Baltimore.[1197] Henry married **ANNIE COLLINS HILL** there on 23 Nov 1865.[1198] Annie, daughter of Clement Hill and Sarah Parker, was born 04 Apr 1848 in Washington, D.C. Henry, the junior partner of Wyeth & Brother, retired from the iron and steel business in Mar 1878.[1199] At the 1880 Federal Census, Henry was confined to a psychiatric hospital in Catonsville, Maryland. A few years earlier, in 1873, while under his watch, Henry's only son, Harry, then six and a half years old, was seriously injured in a carriage accident.[1200] Henry suffered emotionally from blaming himself. Henry died at age 41 and was buried in the Wyeth plot at Green Mount Cemetery, Baltimore on 27 Aug 1880.[1201] Annie died on 05 Jan 1894 in Washington, D.C. She is buried there with her son and her second husband, Francis V. Robinson, in the Congressional Cemetery.

Henry Clarence Wyeth and Annie Collins Hill had the following child:

   i.   HARRY HILL[8] WYETH, born 09 Aug 1866, Baltimore; clerk in the War Department in Washington, D.C. from 1883 to his death at his mother's home, 1824 G. St., NW, Washington, D.C. on 21 Nov 1892 at age 26.

243. **JOSEPH BENJAMIN[7] WYETH** (Jonas Parker[6], Gad[5], Ebenezer[4] Jr., Ebenezer[3], John[2], Nicholas[1]) was born on 20 Jun 1820 in Le Ray, Jefferson, New York.[1202] Joseph Benjamin Wyeth married **CHARLOTTE MARY HORTON**, 07 Apr 1842, Granville, Licking, Ohio.[1203] Charlotte, daughter of Thomas Horton and Mary Carter, was born on 09 Jul 1820 in Benson, Rutland, Vermont. Joseph died on 17 Apr 1884 in Judsonia, White, Arkansas. Charlotte died there on 04 Mar 1899.

Joseph Benjamin Wyeth and Charlotte Mary Horton had the following children:

464.   i. NORMAN DEANGELIS[8] WYETH, born 1844, near Fredonia, McKean Township, Licking, Ohio; served in the 68th, 109th and 143rd Illinois Infantry during the Civil War; married (1) PRECIOUS LORETTA BRIGGS, 17 Aug 1865, Charleston, Coles, Illinois; married (2) AMELIA LOUISE WILIVIER, 02 Feb 1871, Waterloo, Black Hawk, Iowa;[1204] died 09 Nov 1886, Sullivan, Sullivan County, Indiana.
        ii. JACKSON DELANO WYETH, born 28 Jun 1847, near Fredonia; died there, 13 Aug 1847; likely buried near his brother Horatio.
       iii. HORATIO HORTON WYETH, born 31 Aug 1849, near Fredonia; died there, 15 Oct 1849 at age six weeks, two days; buried in the Old Fredonia Cemetery.
465.   iv. JOSEPH JEROME WYETH, born 30 Aug 1851, near Fredonia; married CLARA BETTY BEANE, 12 May 1875, Stevens Creek, White, Arkansas; died 04 Mar 1903, Judsonia, White, Arkansas.

244. **SILAS JABEZ[7] WYETH** (Gad[6] Jr., Gad[5], Ebenezer[4] Jr., Ebenezer[3], John[2], Nicholas[1]) was born on 29 Jan 1825[1205] in Adams, Jefferson, New York. He married **HARRIET M. NUTTING** on 21 Jan 1851[1206] in Wilna, Jefferson, New York. They later divorced. Harriet, daughter of Stephen Nutting and Betsy Campbell, was born on 01 Apr 1833 in Wilna. Silas died 21 Sep 1898 in Garden Township, Boone, Iowa. She died on 05 Nov 1915 in Madrid, Boone, Iowa.

Per Marvel June Wyeth Ucen the children of Silas Jabez Wyeth and Harriet M. Nutting were:

466.   i. GEORGE EUGENE[8] WYETH, born 18 Jul 1858, North Wilna, Jefferson, New York; married (1) HULDAH ADELINE REDMOND, 23 Dec 1877, Madrid, Boone, Iowa; married (2) ALICE L. RUSTIN, 14 Jun 1896, Madrid; died 22 Nov 1934, Modesto, Stanislaus, California.
        ii. MARY JANE WYETH, born 31 Jul 1863, Carthage, Jefferson, New York; died there, 03 Sep 1863.

245. **NELSON[7] WYETH** (Gad[6] Jr., Gad[5], Ebenezer[4] Jr., Ebenezer[3], John[2], Nicholas[1]) was born on 06 Nov 1826 in Adams, Jefferson, New York. Nelson Wyeth and **SARAH POTTER** were married on 06 Feb 1853 in Champion, Jefferson, New York. Sarah was born on 23 Jan 1820 in Floyd, Oneida, New York to Henry Potter and Sylvia Brockway. He died 14 Oct 1899, Rutland, Jefferson, New York. She died in 1908 in Champion.

Nelson Wyeth and Sarah Potter had the following child:

467.   i. MARY A.[8] WYETH, born in Champion in Nov 1853; married CLINTON CROSS, 20 Feb 1873, Rutland;[1207] died there in 1939.

246. **RACHEL[7] WYETH** (Gad[6] Jr., Gad[5], Ebenezer[4] Jr., Ebenezer[3], John[2], Nicholas[1]) was born on 06 Nov 1830 in Adams, Jefferson, New York. Rachel Wyeth married (1) **THADDEUS OLDS** on 14 Feb 1849 in Wilna, Jefferson, New York.[1208] Thaddeus, son of John Olds and Orphana Fowler, was born on 15 Nov 1822 in Tolland, Hampden, Massachusetts. He died on 14 Apr 1870 in Wilna. Rachel married (2) **DAVID PEELER** on 19 Sep 1878 in Wilna.[1209] David was born in Lewis County, New York, circa 1818. According to the *Watertown Daily Times*, Rachel fell lifeless to the floor while sweeping at home in Great Bend, Jefferson, New York on 15 Apr 1897.[1210] She is buried near her first husband in the Lake School Road Cemetery, on Fort Drum, Jefferson County, New York.

Thaddeus Olds and Rachel Wyeth had the following children:

           i. ANN JENNIE[8] OLDS, born Jan 1850, Wilna; married JOHN S. FORD, 26 Mar 1868, Methodist Church, Natural Bridge, Jefferson, New York;[1211] died 30 Jun 1898, Black River, Jefferson, New York.[1212]

468.   ii. THADDEUS W. OLDS, born 30 Nov 1853, Wilna; married MARILLA HUBBARD, there, 11 Nov 1873; died 30 Jan 1934, Granby, Oswego, New York.[1213]

        iii. WILLIAM WALLACE OLDS, born 06 Jul 1856, Wilna; married ALICE MURPHY 15 Jan 1878, Wilna; died on 03 Feb 1945, West Carthage, Jefferson, New York.

247. **PARKER[7] WYETH** (Gad[6] Jr., Gad[5], Ebenezer[4] Jr., Ebenezer[3], John[2], Nicholas[1]) was born on 27 Jan 1833 in Adams, Jefferson, New York.[1214] Parker Wyeth and (1) **ABBY JANE COON** were married on 25 Aug 1852 in Theresa, Jefferson, New York. Abby, was born on 13 Feb 1835 in Jefferson County. She died in Theresa on 07 May 1857.[1215] One year later, Parker married (2) **SARAH ANGELINE "SILA" COON**. Sarah, born in 1829 in Jefferson County, and Abby Jane were the daughters of Joseph G. Coon and Harriett H. Coon (daughter of Elias Coon). Parker died on 26 Mar 1864 in North Wilna, Jefferson, New York. He is buried near his sister Rachel and their parents in the Lake School Road Cemetery (also known as Derby-Hubbard or Lake District Cemetery) at Fort Drum, New York. Sila next married Edward Rourke. She died on 10 Jun 1891 in Antwerp, Jefferson, New York.[1216]

Parker Wyeth and Abby Jane Coon had the following child:

469.   i. ORVILLE[8] WYETH, born 08 Nov 1853, Theresa; married MALONA "MAY" BROWN on 29 Dec 1885 in Rose, Wayne, New York; died 22 Aug 1932, Watertown, Jefferson, New York.[1217] Buried in Woods Mill Cemetery.

Parker Wyeth and Sarah Angeline "Sila" (also called Sally) Coon had the following child:

470.   i. FLORETIA[8] WYETH, born 11 Jan 1860, North Wilna; married OREN HAMILTON WHITE there, 03 Jun 1875;[1218] died 28 Mar 1879, North Wilna at age 19 due to complications from her son Raymond's birth on 24 Feb 1879.[1219] Floretia is buried near her brother in the Woods Mill Cemetery on the Fort Drum Military Reservation. At the start of World War II, several Jefferson County towns, including Woods Mill and North Wilna, were taken by eminent domain for use by the U.S. Army. Woods Mill Cemetery is just inside an artillery firing practice area. Floretia's marker was hit and damaged in 1968.[1220]

248. **MARY M.**[7] **WYETH** (Gad[6] Jr., Gad[5], Ebenezer[4] Jr., Ebenezer[3], John[2], Nicholas[1]) was born on 05 Jan 1835 in Adams, Jefferson, New York. Mary married **CHARLES HIRAM TOWNSEND** on 29 Nov 1854 in Wilna, Jefferson, New York. Charles, son of Daniel Townsend and Adeline Pardee, was born on 27 Nov 1829 in Antwerp, Jefferson, New York. She died on 02 Nov 1861 in North Wilna. He died on 21 Jun 1897 in Castorland, Lewis, New York.[1221] Both rest in the Lake School Road Cemetery, Fort Drum.

Charles Hiram Townsend and Mary M. Wyeth had the following children:

471.   i. ORVILLE CHARLES[8] TOWNSEND, born 16 Aug 1858, Lebanon Township, Clinton, Michigan; married KATHERINE L. SPERRY, 01 Dec 1880, Saint Johns, Clinton, Michigan; died 09 Dec 1927, Alma, Gratiot, Michigan.

       ii. EDWARD HENRY TOWNSEND, born 29 Jun 1860, Lebanon Township; died there on 16 Dec 1860 at six months old.

249. **LORINDA B.**[7] **WYETH** (Gad[6] Jr., Gad[5], Ebenezer[4] Jr., Ebenezer[3], John[2], Nicholas[1]) was born on 15 Feb 1837 in Adams, Jefferson, New York. Lorinda married **JOHN NEWSAM**, 02 Jul 1859 in Wilna, Jefferson, New York. John, son of George Newsam Sr. and his wife Mary, was born 04 Oct 1826 in Jefferson County, New York. An Illinois directory showed several Newsam and Wyeth siblings moved there circa 1868. Specifically given were John's birth date and other statistics showing he was a Republican, Congregationalist and owned 80 acres of land valued at $5,000 in Seward Township, Kendall, Illinois.[1222] John died there on 06 Jun 1889. Lorinda worked as a weaver in Minooka, Grundy, Illinois after John's death. She died circa 1921. Both are buried in Aux Sable Cemetery in Minooka.

The children of John Newsam and Lorinda B. Wyeth included:

        i. WILLIAM JACKSON "JACK"[8] NEWSAM, born 22 Aug 1861, Jefferson County; died unmarried on 23 May 1945, Phoenix, Maricopa, Arizona.

250. **ABIE**[7] **WYETH** (Gad[6] Jr., Gad[5], Ebenezer[4] Jr., Ebenezer[3], John[2], Nicholas[1]) born on 15 Jan 1839 in Wilna, Jefferson, New York. Abie married **GEORGE NEWSAM JR.**, 29 Nov 1858, Wilna. George, son of George Newsam Sr. and his wife Mary, was born 07 Sep 1827 in Jefferson County, New York. He died on 23 Jan 1908 in Minooka, Seward Township, Kendall, Illinois. Abie died there on 20 Oct 1919. Minooka, a suburb of Chicago, is a village in Grundy, Kendall, and Will counties, Illinois. Abie and George are buried there in Aux Sable Cemetery.

George Newsam Jr. and Abie Wyeth had the following children:

        i. GEORGE CLIFTON[8] NEWSAM, born 14 Sep 1867, Seward Township; married (1) LIZZIE HARROP, 15 Nov 1892, Will County, Illinois; married (2) HAZEL HURST, 31 Jan 1920, Brown County, South Dakota; died 02 Mar 1951, Harrison County, Missouri.

       ii. CHARLES NEWSAM, born 16 Apr 1874, Seward Township; died there, unmarried in 1948.

251. **WILLIAM H.**[7] **WYETH** (Gad[6] Jr., Gad[5], Ebenezer[4] Jr., Ebenezer[3], John[2], Nicholas[1]) was born on 15 Oct 1840 in Wilna, Jefferson, New York. William began three years of service in Co. H of the 1st New York Light Artillery on 02 Oct 1861. While moving a cannon under heavy fire, during the Battle of Fair Oaks, Virginia on 30 Jun 1862, William suffered a hernia. That injury, along with gunshot deafness, plagued him the rest of his life. William married **MARY ANN BARNUM** on 13 Dec 1864 in Antwerp, Jefferson, New York. [1223] Mary was born to Samuel and Renet Barnum on 08 Nov 1834 in Antwerp. Mary died there on 20 Mar 1906. William died in Watertown, Jefferson, New York on 07 Oct 1912.

William H. Wyeth and Mary Ann Barnum had the following children:

       i. MARTHA ABI "MATTIE"[8] WYETH, born 05 Feb 1867, Antwerp; married (1) DR. ROBERT JOSEPH FLINT there, 02 Oct 1900; married (2) MAURICE EDWIN HOBBS, 02 Sep 1912, South Berwick, York, Maine; died there, 17 Dec 1940. [1224]

      ii. MAY ATHALIA WYETH, born 12 Nov 1872 at Woods Mill near Wilna; married FORD MORRIS HOUSE, 05 Apr 1910, Antwerp; died 22 May 1954, Watertown.

252. **JOSEPH**[7] **WYETH** (Gad[6] Jr., Gad[5], Ebenezer[4] Jr., Ebenezer[3], John[2], Nicholas[1]) was born on 06 Apr 1843 in Wilna, Jefferson, New York. Joseph married **MARIA NEWSAM** on 18 Jan 1868 in Lisbon, Kendall, Illinois. Maria, daughter of Thomas Newsam and Hannah Hampson, was born on 21 Apr 1843 in Jefferson County, New York. She died in childbirth on 21 Sep 1884 at age 41 years and five months in Minooka, Seward Township, Kendall, Illinois. He died on 08 Sep 1933 at age 90 in Aurora, Kane, Illinois.

Joseph Wyeth and Maria Newsam had the following children:

       i. MABEL ESTHER[8] WYETH, born 18 Aug 1870, Seward Township; married HARRY C. BANKS there on 18 Jun 1905 in Minooka; died 07 Feb 1927, Aurora.

472.   ii. LULU MARIA WYETH, born 18 Sep 1884, Minooka; [1225] married WARREN BROWNELL, 22 Jan 1916, Aurora; died there, 02 Jul 1971.

253. **CHARLES E.**[7] **WYETH** (Gad[6] Jr., Gad[5], Ebenezer[4] Jr., Ebenezer[3], John[2], Nicholas[1]) was born on 25 Mar 1847 in Wilna, Jefferson, New York. Charles married (1) **MARTHA ESTHER VERNON** on 04 Jul 1867 in Kendall County, Illinois. Martha, daughter of Varnan Vernon and Katherine Hall, was born on 25 Apr 1847 in Newark, Essex, New Jersey. She died in childbirth on 19 Jul 1896 at age 49 in Whitewillow, Kendall, Illinois. Charles married (2) **HANNAH "ANNA" HARROP** on 08 Sep 1898 in Minooka, Seward Township, Kendall, Illinois. Anna, daughter of Thomas Harrop and Anna Lunn, was born on 01 Apr 1853 in England. Charles died on 14 Jul 1926 in Aurora, Kane, Illinois. [1226] Anna died on 31 Dec 1946 in Aurora. [1227]

According to their great grandson, Milton Dirst, the children of Charles E. Wyeth and Martha Esther Vernon included:

473.   i. ESTHER BEATRICE[8] WYETH, born in Nov 1870, Seward Township; married (1) JAMES SWANSON, 27 Dec 1888, Lisbon, Kendall, Illinois; married (2) HARM J. BRAUER circa 1931; died 06 Dec 1945, Aurora.

474.　ii.　MAUDE EVELYN WYETH, born 31 Oct 1874, Whitewillow; married ARTHUR COOP, 18 Dec 1895, Grundy County, Illinois; died 06 Dec 1949, Aurora.[1228]

iii.　MYRTLE MAY WYETH, born 25 May 1880, Whitewillow; died unmarried on 23 Oct 1902 in Lisbon.

475.　iv.　FLORENCE OLIVIA WYETH, born 29 May 1886, Whitewillow; married CARL JOBST HOPKINS, 09 Mar 1910, Aurora; died there, 08 May 1977.

v.　INFANT SON WYETH, born and died on 19 Jul 1896, Whitewillow.

254. **JAMES MADISON[7] WYETH** (Joseph Sawin[6], Gad[5], Ebenezer[4] Jr., Ebenezer[3], John[2], Nicholas[1]) was born on 02 Oct 1820 in LeRay, Jefferson, New York. James Madison Wyeth and **ALMIRA THOMPSON** were married on 30 Mar 1847, Lowville, Lewis, New York. Almira was born on 03 Jul 1824 in Carthage, Jefferson, New York. James, a farmer, enlisted in the 75th Illinois Infantry in Fulton, Whiteside, Illinois on 07 Aug 1862. He was discharged for disability on 26 Feb 1863 at Camp Sill, Murfreesboro, Tennessee by order of Major General Rosecrans. A few days later James died on 05 Mar 1863 in the Rutherford Military Hospital in Murfreesboro, Rutherford, Tennessee. Through over exertion and exposure from ministering to sick and wounded after the Civil War Battle of Stones River in middle Tennessee, while in the hands of the enemy, James had contracted chronic diarrhea resulting in dropsy.[1229] Almira died on 31 Jan 1913 in Santa Ana, Orange, California.

James Madison Wyeth and Almira Thompson had the following children:[1230]

476.　i.　SARAH CELESTIA[8] WYETH, born 25 Feb 1848, Denmark, Lewis, New York; married JOHN MCCREA, 26 Jun 1883, Fulton; died 20 Jan 1933, Vancouver, Clark, Washington.

477.　ii.　HARRIETT JOSEPHINE "HATTIE" WYETH, born 12 Sep 1850, Denmark; married LAURENTINE DEVILLO POPE, 26 Oct 1875, Fulton; died 12 Dec 1939, Marion, Linn, Iowa.

iii.　ANNA MEDORA WYETH, born 17 Mar 1857, Ustick Township, Whiteside, Illinois; married ELIJAH EATON LOWRY, 17 Sep 1890, Fulton; died 09 Feb 1938, Santa Ana, Orange, California.

255. **MARY KENDALL[7] WYETH** (Joseph Sawin[6], Gad[5], Ebenezer[4] Jr., Ebenezer[3], John[2], Nicholas[1]) was born on 22 Jun 1822 in LeRay, Jefferson, New York. Circa 1849, she married **GEORGE HENDEE** who was born about 1822 in Vermont. She died on 28 Oct 1898 in Omaha, Douglas, Nebraska. He died circa 1912 in Albion, Boone, Nebraska.

George Hendee and Mary Kendall Wyeth had the following children:

i.　SUSAN ANNETTE[8] HENDEE, born Sep 1850, Jefferson County, married (1) AUGUSTUS BOOTH, 08 Sep 1870, Fulton, Whiteside, Illinois; married (2) JOHN ALEXANDER SOUTHARD, 08 Nov 1893, Omaha; died 02 Sep 1926, Santa Clara County, California.

478.　ii.　HORATIO K. HENDEE, born 13 Dec 1853, Jefferson County; married JESSIE MARIA PATTERSON, 1887; died 13 Dec 1925, Roundup, Musselshell, Montana.

479.　iii.　RUTH PRENTICE HENDEE, born 16 Oct 1860, Fulton; married ALVIN GARTEN, 16 Nov 1887, Albion; died 17 Sep 1947, Los Angeles, California.

256. **WILLIAM HOAR[7] WYETH** (Joseph Sawin[6], Gad[5] Sr., Ebenezer[4] Jr., Ebenezer[3], John[2], Nicholas[1]) was born on 22 May 1826 in LeRay, Jefferson, New York. He married (1) **SUSAN ELIZABETH ANDERSON**, daughter of Nicholas Anderson and Sybil Buell, on 25 Feb 1851 in Denmark, Lewis, New York. Susan was born on 25 Dec 1828 in Denmark and died there on 07 Dec 1877. He married (2) **JENNIE L. "JANE" TALLMAGE**, 22 May 1878. Jane died on 27 Jan 1879 in Lewis County. In 1880, William married (3) **FREDERICA MELLNITZ**, daughter of Frederick Mellnitz and Christiana Richter. She was born on 08 Apr 1837 in Schlewerothe, Germany. Counted among the substantial businessmen and farmers of Lewis County, his Fairlawn Stock Farm had a beautiful view of the Black River Valley.[1231] William died there on 08 May 1900. Frederica died 06 Sep 1913 in Crogen, Lewis, New York.

According to their grandson, Donald Elwyn Wyeth, William Hoar Wyeth and Susan Elizabeth Anderson had the following children: [1232]

480. i. ELLA ELIZABETH[8] WYETH, born 28 Feb 1854, Denmark; married WILLIAM WALDO ARTHUR, 28 Sep 1881, Lowville, Lewis, New York; died 22 Apr 1907, Thousand Island Park, Jefferson, New York.

481. ii. WILLIAM BUELL WYETH, born Mar 1860, Denmark; married MINNIE EVA KOSTER, 07 Dec 1892, Lyons Falls, Lewis, New York; died 14 Jul 1930, Melrose, Middlesex, Massachusetts.

iii. CLAY MONROE WYETH, born 05 Oct 1865, Denmark; died there, 20 Sep 1892.

482. iv. MADISON JAMES WYETH (twin), born 05 Oct 1865, Denmark; married MARY ELIZABETH "MAMIE" ROSS, 29 Sep 1904, Copenhagan, Lewis, New York; died 07 Feb 1957, Herkimer, Herkimer County, New York.

v. FRANKLIN LINCOLN "FRANK" WYETH, born 08 Dec 1869, Lowville; married (1) LILLIE LANPHEAR, 04 Jan 1900; married (2) EURETTA LANPHEAR EDWARDS, 14 Oct 1944, Bethlehem, Albany, New York; salesman for Buckley Shirts; died 14 Sep 1961, Carthage, Jefferson, New York.

257. **MONROE CLAY[7] WYTHE** (Joseph Sawin[6], Gad[5], Ebenezer[4] Jr., Ebenezer[3], John[2], Nicholas[1]) was born on 27 Jul 1832 in LeRay, Jefferson, New York. Though named for him, his nephew, Clay Monroe Wyeth, reversed his first and middle names and spelled his last name differently. Monroe Clay Wythe married (1) **EMMA ELVIRA KNIGHT** on 20 Oct 1856, Fulton, Whiteside, Illinois. Emma was born on 24 Jan 1839 in Charleston, Coles, Illinois to Wesley Knight and Louisa Wilbur Cowles. They divorced circa 1866. Emma married Luther Puffer in 1868 and died on 04 Jan 1895 in Fulton. Monroe Clay Wythe, a gold and silver miner, married (2) **CAROLINE NYE FREEMAN WING**, 13 Oct 1880, Georgetown, Clear Creek, Colorado. His only surviving child, Frank Austin Wythe, and Caroline's only child,

Monroe Clay Wythe courtesy of Steven Stuart on Ancestry.com.

William G. Harrington, witnessed the marriage. Caroline, widow of Giles Harrington, was born on 08 Oct 1838 in Sandwich, Barnstable, Massachusetts to Clifton Wing and Ann Spooner. Monroe died 23 Mar 1891 in Rand, Jackson, Colorado.[1233] Caroline died

04 Dec 1921 in Leadville, Lake, Colorado.[1234]

Monroe Clay Wythe and Emma Elvira Knight had the following children:

483. i. FRANK AUSTIN[8] WYTHE, born 04 Jul 1859, Fulton; married (1) NELLIE DALEY there, 17 Dec 1885; married (2) FRANCES ELIZABETH DAVIS (Joseph Banks' widow), 26 Nov 1919, Oak Park, Cook, Illinois; died 21 Aug 1947, Fulton.
      ii. EVA WYETH, born in 1864 in Fulton; died an infant.

258. **LEONARD JACKSON[7] WYETH** (Nathan[6], Gad[5], Ebenezer[4] Jr., Ebenezer[3], John[2], Nicholas[1]) was born on 13 Jan 1827 in Wendell, Franklin, Massachusetts. Leonard Jackson Wyeth and **MELINDA NORTHWAY** were married in 1847, in Liberty Township, Licking, Ohio. Melinda was born on 06 Apr 1826 to Samuel Hiram Northway and Charlotte Seagers in Sherman, Chautauqua, New York. In 1851, Leonard moved west to Coles County, Illinois. Then circa 1860, he moved to Tuscola, Douglas, Illinois and opened a dry-goods store. Leonard was not only one of the earliest settlers of that county, he was also one of its wealthiest. He was the president of First National Bank and the largest land owner in Douglas County. After being struck by illness, by the end of 1897, Leonard divided most of his amassed fortune of over $365,000 between his daughter, Emma Wyeth Callaway, and daughter-in-law, Elizabeth Atwell Wyeth.[1235] Leonard died on 24 Jan 1898 in Tuscola. Melinda died there on 19 Feb 1909.

The children of Leonard Jackson Wyeth and Melinda Northway included:

      i. WALTER LEONARD[8] WYETH, born 02 Feb 1850, Liberty Township; died young.
      ii. CLARA WYETH, born circa 1851, Liberty Township; died young, Tuscola.[1236]
484. iii. EMMA CAROLINE WYETH, born 02 Feb 1857, Coles County, Illinois; married GEORGE CALLAWAY M.D., 19 Feb 1879, Tuscola; died there, 03 May 1921.
      iv. MARY E. WYETH, born about 1859 in Tuscola; died there, circa 1886.[1237]
485. v. CLARENCE LEONARD WYETH, born 27 Jul 1860, Tuscola; married ELIZABETH M. ATWELL,[1238] 28 Jun 1882, Atwood, Piatt, Illinois; died 07 Sep 1897, Garrett Township, Douglas, Illinois.

259. **JOSEPH SAWIN[7] WYETH** (Nathan[6], Gad[5], Ebenezer[4] Jr., Ebenezer[3], John[2], Nicholas[1]) was born on 15 Apr 1828 in Wendell, Franklin, Massachusetts. Joseph Sawin Wyeth and **JOANNA HUNT** were married on 28 Apr 1850 at the Hunt's home in McKean Township, Licking, Ohio.[1239] Joanna was born on 28 Nov 1827, to Elijah Hunt and Rhoda Hillyer, in Newark, Licking, Ohio. Soon after their wedding, Joanna and Joseph moved with his brother Leonard to Coles County, Illinois and settled on farms four miles south of Hindsboro, Douglas, Illinois. In about 1860, the brothers moved to Tuscola, Douglas, Illinois to engage in a mercantile business. Leonard remained there when Joseph relocated to a 337-acre farm in Garrett Township, Douglas, Illinois in 1864.[1240] Joseph died on the farm on 14 Jun 1898. Joanna died there on 09 Feb 1917.

Joseph Sawin Wyeth from page 188 of the 1900 *Historical and Biographical Record of Douglas County, Illinois* by John Gresham.

The children of Joseph Sawin Wyeth and Joanna Hunt include:

486.   i. RHODA ELLEN "NELLIE"[8] WYETH, born 18 Jan 1851, Coles County; married WILLIAM BYRANT BRINTON, 29 Oct 1873, Tuscola; died 03 Apr 1932, Chandler, Maricopa, Arizona.[1241]

This photograph of Rhoda Wyeth, William, Bradford, and Catherine Bell Brinton is courtesy of the Brinton Museum, Big Horn, Wyoming.

487.   ii. FRANK LEE WYETH, born 09 Oct 1857, Coles County; married ANNITA HELTON, 29 Nov 1881, Douglas County; died 21 Oct 1943, North Salem, Hendricks, Indiana.

488.   iii. HARRY LESLIE WYETH, born 08 Oct 1859, Coles County; married SARAH JANE ROMINE, 16 Sep 1885, Douglas County; died 08 May 1936, Garrett.

   iv. SUSAN ELIZABETH "SUE" WYETH, born 16 Aug 1861, Garrett; married JOSEPH R. GREGORY there, 30 Jun 1882; died 31 May 1943, Atwood, Piatt, Illinois.

489.   v. LUELLA CORNELIA WYETH, born 09 Feb 1864, Garrett; married WILLIAM RICE ROMINE, 14 Jul 1887, Douglas County; died 18 Jun 1945, Tuscola.

490.   vi. DAISY FAY WYETH, born 22 Feb 1868, Garrett; married JOHN MCNEIL BURK JR., 29 Mar 1891, Douglas County; died 07 Jul 1942, Garrett.

260. **ALBERT ROBERT[7] WYETH** (Nathan[6], Gad[5], Ebenezer[4] Jr., Ebenezer[3], John[2], Nicholas[1]) was born on 22 Dec 1829 in Wendell, Franklin, Massachusetts. Albert Robert Wyeth and **ANGELINE CARRIS** were married circa 1852 in Charleston, Coles, Illinois. Angeline, daughter of John Smith Carris and Hila Ann Tupper was born on 20 Oct 1829 in Orange County, New York. She died on 29 Jun 1910 in Charleston. He died there on 15 Sep 1911.

Albert Robert Wyeth and Angeline Carris had the following children:

491.   i. GEORGE ELLIS[8] WYETH, born 02 Sep 1853, Morgan Township, Coles, Illinois; married INA MAY BILLS, 17 May 1881, Douglas County, Illinois; died 23 May 1925, Charleston.

   ii. MARION S. WYETH, born 05 Oct 1858 in Morgan Township; he died there on 13 Mar 1864.

492.   iii. CORA ANN WYETH, born 20 Aug 1869, Seven Hickory Township, Coles, Illinois; married THOMAS BAXTER NORFOLK, 21 Mar 1888, Kenosha County, Wisconsin; died 22 May 1948, Charleston Township, Coles, Illinois.

261. **SAMUEL KELLOGG[7] WYETH** (Nathan[6], Gad[5], Ebenezer[4] Jr., Ebenezer[3], John[2], Nicholas[1]) was born on 20 Nov 1831 (but his grave says 1832) in Wendell, Franklin, Massachusetts.[1242] He served in Co. H of the 143rd Illinois Infantry Regiment. His last name was spelled "Wyett" in the enlistment records at Hillsboro, Illinois on 11 Jun 1864. Samuel mustered out on 26 Sep 1864 at Mattoon, Illinois.[1243] In a double wedding with his sister, Mary Kendall Cofer, Samuel married **LAMIRA CATHERINE COMBS** on 21 Oct 1857 in Charleston, Coles, Illinois.[1244] Lamira was born to William Combs and Margaret Myers on 29 Aug 1838 in Clark County, Indiana. Samuel lived in Seven Hickory Township, Coles, Illinois where

he owned and farmed 1,540 acres of land there and in Douglas County, Illinois.[1245] Samuel died on 11 Apr 1907 in Charleston. Lamira died there on 09 Jan 1911.

Samuel Kellogg Wyeth and Lamira Catherine Combs had the following children[1246] (based on the 1860 census, apparently, all, except William, were born in Seven Hickory Township):

493.   i.   WILLIAM MADISON[8] WYETH, born 09 Oct 1859, Arcola, Douglas, Illinois; married MARY ALICE MOYER, 24 Dec 1890, Tuscola, Douglas, Illinois; died 28 Mar 1920, Jacksonville, Morgan, Illinois.

494.   ii. JAMES FRANKLIN WYETH, born 09 Mar 1861; married MAUDE RAVENSCRAFT 04 Nov 1891, Oakland, Coles, Illinois; died there, 20 Dec 1897.[1247][1248][1249]

495.   iii. THOMAS BENTON WYETH, born 10 Jan 1863; married EFFIE ETTA BREEDEN, 11 Feb 1891, Douglas County; died 19 Jan 1906, Charleston.

496.   iv. MARY JANE WYETH, born 18 Dec 1865; married ABRAHAM LEWIS HARDIN, 06 Oct 1886, Charleston; died there, 25 Feb 1946.

       v.   JOHN OSCAR WYETH, born about 1869; died in Seven Hickory Township at age three.

       vi. MINNIE WYETH, born circa 1873; died in Seven Hickory Township at age one.

262. **THOMAS EVANS[7] WYETH** (Nathan[6], Gad[5], Ebenezer[4] Jr., Ebenezer[3], John[2], Nicholas[1]) was born 21 Jun 1833 in Wendell, Franklin, Massachusetts. He married (1) **NANCY B. COMBS** on 27 Dec 1855 in Charleston, Coles, Illinois. Nancy was born on 10 Jul 1834 to William Combs and Margaret Myers in Clark County, Indiana. Her sister Lamira married Samuel Kellogg Wyeth. Nancy died on 22 Sep 1873 in Seven Hickory Township, Coles, Illinois. Thomas married (2) **JULIA ANN PRICE** on 12 May 1875 in Douglas County, Illinois. Julia, daughter of Jordan Price and Clarinda Terrell was born on 21 Aug 1846 in Fredericksburg, Virginia. Thomas, one of the wealthiest land owners in Coles and Douglas Counties, left an estate of over $100,000 at his death on 12 Apr 1905 in Seven Hickory Township.[1250] Julia died in Charleston on 08 Jan 1927.

Thomas Evans Wyeth and Nancy B. Combs had the following children:

497.   i.   MARGARET E. "MAGGIE"[8] WYETH, born 09 Dec 1860, Charleston; married STEPHEN A. DOUGLAS HARRY there, 05 Aug 1884; died 11 Jul 1901, Grant, Vermilion, Illinois.

498.   ii. ALPHARETTA "ALLIE" WYETH, born 01 Feb 1863, Charleston; married EMRY BRADFORD, 16 Feb 1887 there; died 08 Jul 1939, Hindsboro, Douglas, Illinois.

499.   iii. CHARLES EDWIN WYETH, born 10 Jan 1867, Hindsboro; married SARAH L. "SADIE" McGAHEY, 30 Nov 1892, Charleston; died 19 Nov 1928, Oakland, Coles, Illinois.

The children of Thomas Evans Wyeth and Julia Ann Price included:

500.   i.   PERCY ETHELBERT[8] WYETH, born 29 May 1878, Seven Hickory Township; married GRACE KNIGHTS, 25 Jan 1906, DuPage County, Illinois; died 27 May 1926, Charleston.

263. **ELLEN ROXANNA**[7] **WYETH** (Nathan[6], Gad[5], Ebenezer[4] Jr., Ebenezer[3], John[2], Nicholas[1]) was born on 28 Jan 1835 in Wendell, Franklin, Massachusetts. Ellen married **OLIVER CROMWELL HACKETT** on 14 Mar 1854 in Coles County, Illinois. Oliver was born on 29 Mar 1822 in Scott County, Kentucky to John Hackett and Elizabeth Murphy. Ellen died on 05 Mar 1875 in Tuscola, Douglas, Illinois. Oliver died there on 08 Apr 1905. Their death dates appear on their tombstones in Tuscola Township Cemetery.

Oliver Hackett and Ellen Roxanna Wyeth had the following children (all born in Tuscola):

      i. MERRILL J.[8] HACKETT, born circa 1855; married NORA TERRY in 1888; died 05 Mar 1930, Andover, Allegany, New York.

      ii. JENNIE MARY HACKETT, born 07 Oct 1856; married NATHANIEL GRATTON ERVIN, 29 Dec 1887, Tuscola; died there, 29 Mar 1923.

      iii. ISABELLA D. HACKETT, born 28 Oct 1858; married ALLEN PHILLIP BARRETT, 24 Dec 1905, Tuscola; died there on 15 Sep 1933.

      iv. ELLA KATHERINE HACKETT, born 01 May 1862; died unmarried on 31 Jul 1945, Los Angeles, California.

501.   v. EMALINE HACKETT, born 12 Feb 1863; married OSCAR SYLVESTER WILDER, 18 Oct 1883, Tuscola; died 24 Mar 1934, Bloomington, McLean, Illinois.

      vi. LEONARD OLIVER HACKETT, born 12 Mar 1865; married JESSIE ELLARS, 22 Nov 1900, Tuscola; died there, 14 Dec 1942.

      vii. LYNN MALINDA HACKETT, born 17 Feb 1867; married CHARLES STALKER, 13 May 1906, Tuscola; died 20 Mar 1947, Crawfordsville, Montgomery, Indiana.

502.   viii. WALTER CLAY HACKETT, born 01 Oct 1869; married LUTA PEARL JONES, 28 Sep 1893, Tuscola; died 02 May 1931, Jacksonville, Morgan, Illinois.

503.   ix. FREDERICK WILLIAM HACKETT, born 21 May 1870; married JESSIE TRUE, 17 Mar 1895, Kankakee County, Illinois; died 12 Sep 1954, Santa Clara, California.

      x. WENDEL PHILLIPS HACKETT, born 04 Mar 1873; died 13 Mar 1874, Tuscola.

      xi. EDITH HACKETT, born Jan 1875; married ROBERT EVERETT ALEXANDER, 03 Oct 1899, Tuscola; died 02 Jun 1939, Los Angeles, California.

264. **MARY KENDALL**[7] **WYETH** (Nathan[6], Gad[5], Ebenezer[4] Jr., Ebenezer[3], John[2], Nicholas[1]) was born on 28 Dec 1838 in Liberty Township, Licking, Ohio. On 21 Oct 1857, Mary married **JOHN STITH COFER** on the Wyeth Homestead on Greasy Point near Charleston, Coles, Illinois.[1251] John, son of Col. John Cofer and Mary Eleanor Macgill, was born on 24 Jun 1833 in Hardin County, Kentucky. He took his own life at his farm near Arcola, Douglas, Illinois on 10 Feb 1886.[1252] Mary died on 05 Dec 1924 at her daughter Ida's home in Hackensack, Cass, Minnesota.

John Stith Cofer and Mary Kendall Wyeth had the following children:

504.   i. ALBERT JUSTIN[8] COFER, born 16 Nov 1859, Charleston; married ANNA JONES, 31 Jan 1885, Arcola; died 21 Aug 1946, St. Paul, Ramsey, Minnesota.

      ii. IDA BELLE COFER, born 12 Dec 1860, Arcola; married WILLIAM EDWARD JOSEPH CARNAHAN, 14 Jan 1886, Tuscola, Douglas, Illinois; died 12 Aug 1925, Longville, Cass, Minnesota.

iii. HARRY PATRICK COFER, born 18 Oct 1863, Arcola; married HELEN SHERIDAN, 24 Oct 1894, Flora, Clay, Illinois; died 08 Apr 1943, Sumner, Lawrence, Illinois.

505. iv. ELLA MARY COFER, born 01 Jul 1868, Arcola; married HOWARD T. BROWN there, 24 Apr 1889; died 09 May 1956, Butte County, California.

v. EDWARD MORTON COFER, born 05 Aug 1870, Arcola; died there, 11 Feb 1871.

vi. LINDA WYETH COFER, born 07 Aug 1873, Arcola; married WILLIAM C. GAMBLE there, 08 Dec 1897; died 28 Dec 1946, Jacksonville, Morgan, Illinois.

vii. EDITH HENRIETTA COFER, born 18 Aug 1875 in Arcola; married WILLIAM W. HOMAN there, 25 Apr 1901; death unknown.

506. viii. JOHN LEONARD COFER, born 26 Sep 1877, Arcola; married HALLIE PEARL HENDERSON there, 06 Dec 1900; died 06 Mar 1946, Wright County, Minnesota.

ix. CORA ALICE COFER, born 01 Mar 1880 in Arcola; married MERLE ECKMAN there, 27 Oct 1902; died 03 Jun 1963, Chattanooga, Hamilton, Tennessee.[1253]

265. **PARKER JUDSON[7] WYETH** (David[6], Gad[5], Ebenezer[4] Jr., Ebenezer[3], John[2], Nicholas[1]) was born on 28 Nov 1826 in Wendell, Franklin, Massachusetts. He married **AMY NASH** on 19 Sep 1850 in Fredonia, Licking, Ohio. Daughter of Vinson Nash and Parthena Chipman, Amy was born in Jericho Corners, Chittenden, Vermont on 05 Nov 1826. Parker died on 10 Sep 1908 at age 81 in Broadway, Union, Ohio. Amy died there at her daughter Sarah Baldwin's home on 19 Mar 1923 at age 96.

This photo, courtesy of Erma Lockwood Hutchman, shows back: Mary, Henry, Lucy, Orrin; seated: Parker, Amy Nash, Sarah, Laura and David Wyeth.

Parker and Amy Nash Wyeth's children were:

507. i. ORRIN JUDSON[8] WYETH, born 27 Jun 1851, Liberty Township, Licking, Ohio; married JENNIE ELIZABETH DANFORTH on 01 Oct 1873 in Broadway. (She descends from Nicholas Danforth – Nicholas Wyeth's friend from Framlingham, England). Orrin died 28 Feb 1907, Broadway.

508. ii. MARY ELIZABETH WYETH, born 12 Jul 1853, Sharon Township, Franklin, Ohio; married ONESIMUS ATHERTON SHEARER, 25 Dec 1870, Magnetic Springs, Delaware, Ohio; died 01 Jun 1940, Warrensburg, Delaware, Ohio.

509. iii. LUCY PHILENA WYETH, born 06 Oct 1855, Liberty Township; married PHILANDER H. SMITH, 13 Jan 1876, Broadway; died 16 Jul 1938, Richwood, Union, Ohio.[1254]

510. iv. SARAH PARTHENA WYETH, born 22 Sep 1858, Sharon Township; married FRANK LESLIE BALDWIN, 19 Oct 1882, Broadway; died 14 Sep 1935, Peoria, Union, Ohio.[1255]

511. v. DAVID VINSON WYETH, born 23 Jun 1861, Scioto Township, Delaware, Ohio; married ADA YEARSLEY, 01 Oct 1885, Broadway; died there, 16 Aug 1926.[1256]

512.   vi.   HENRY STILLMAN WYETH, born 25 Jul 1865, Scioto Township; married NONA LEE OVERHOLSER, 16 Oct 1889, Broadway; died there, 21 May 1905.

513.   vii. LAURA ANN WYETH, born 23 Jan 1868, Scioto Township; married (1) ELMER FREEMAN, 22 Sep 1887, Broadway; married (2) WILLIAM FOGLE, 12 Jul 1912, Marysville, Union, Ohio; died there, 19 Feb 1953.

        viii. JAMES WYETH, born 1870 in Scioto Township; died there, an infant.[1257]

Notes on Parker Judson Wyeth and Amy Nash:

In 1901, Parker described for the *Marysville Tribune* why his grandfather, Gad Wyeth, came from New England to Ohio in 1838. Together with the short summers, and long, cold winters, the Revolution had left many people penniless. With snow in the Bay State often seven or more feet deep, at age 11, Parker hitched oxen to an upside-down sleigh and dragged it over the roads. The thick crust on top of the snow made raising livestock difficult. Of course, Ohio land could not be farmed year-round either. At age 15, Parker completed training to teach algebra and philosophy after the harvest season. But with teaching incomes so low, Parker moved into the lumber business and built the first steam-powered sawmill in Licking County. Drawn west to Ohio's fast-growing capital city, in 1853, Parker bought land near present day Minerva Park. From there, he cut and hauled wood to the Ohio Penitentiary and was active in building the first road into Columbus. Still a teacher, he oversaw and largely financed three Sunday school classes at a time.

Vehemently opposed to slavery, Parker said that by 1860, "We seemed to be in fine shape to succeed in church, Sunday school, farming and milling, but about this time the avaricious notions of the slave holding power in America got so terribly blind in their greed for gain that another war was brought on and much bloodshed. I am glad that I helped to put down the slave power and helped to raise the power which is God-like, though it cost me about $2,000... I am satisfied that the Union lives, and is a strong power for good in this world." Disappointed after being sent home after two weeks of military service, due to his large family, Parker helped nine local families of women and children sow, grow and harvest their crops during the Civil War.[1258]

Adversity continued after the War. An 1894 accident permanently crippled Amy. On 04 Jul 1898, a sky rocket blinded son Henry. In 1905, Parker and Amy's Union County home burned to the ground. At their funerals, their grandson, Rev. Jesse Jeremiah Wyeth, spoke of their sustaining faith. For Amy, strains of the *Beautiful Isle of Somewhere* sang her to her reward.[1259]

266. **HENRY MARBLE[7] WYETH** (David[6], Gad[5], Ebenezer[4] Jr., Ebenezer[3], John[2], Nicholas[1]) was born 13 Dec 1827 in Wendell, Franklin, Massachusetts. Henry married **RACHEL MARGERY AVERY** on 07 Sep 1854[1260] in Liberty Township, Licking, Ohio.[1261] Rachel, daughter of Erastus Avery and Jerusha Bump, was born on 01 Apr 1833 in Woodhull, Steuben, New York.[1262] While living in Iowa, Henry invented a force pump.[1263] Although he continued in manufacturing, in 1875, Henry served as president of Newark, Ohio's Wool Growers Bank with his brother Augustus as cashier.[1264] Rachel and Henry died a few weeks apart in Salt Lake City, Salt Lake County, Utah. She died on 28 Jun 1911 and he on 03 Aug 1911.[1265]

These photos of Henry Wyeth and Rachel Avery are courtesy of their great, great granddaughter Vickilyn Warburton Lallatin.

The children of Henry Marble Wyeth and Rachel Margery Avery were:

Minnie Wyeth photo courtesy of Vickilyn Warburton Lallatin.

- i. PARKER SCOTT[8] WYETH, born 10 Jul 1856 in Prairie Township, Davis, Iowa; died there on 03 Dec 1861 at age five years, four months and 23 days; buried Pulaski North Cemetery, Prairie Township.[1266]
- ii. HENRY CLAY WYETH, born 09 Jan 1859, Prairie Township; died there on 07 Dec 1861 at age two.

514. iii. MINNIE WYETH, born 15 Dec 1866, Licking County; married JOSEPH ALMA MCKENZIE, 16 Aug 1888, Salt Lake City; died there, 05 Nov 1946.

267. **STILLMAN SAMUEL[7] WYETH** (David[6], Gad[5], Ebenezer[4] Jr., Ebenezer[3], John[2], Nicholas[1]) was born on 12 Nov 1829 in Wendell, Franklin, Massachusetts. He married **ELIZABETH "LIBBIE" WRIGHT** on 01 Dec 1853 at her parents' home in McKean Township, Licking, Ohio. Libbie, daughter of Jacob Wright and Sarah Conard, was born on 10 Apr 1834 in McKean Township. Libbie's sister, Jennie Wright, married Stillman's brother, David. Stillman, a farmer, died on 01 Apr 1891 in Liberty Township, Licking, Ohio. Libbie died on 30 Oct 1912 (her tombstone date is wrong) in Newark, Licking, Ohio.[1267]

This 1855 Ambrotype positive photograph of Stillman Samuel Wyeth is courtesy of Chuck and Jane Walker.

The children of Stillman and Libbie Wright Wyeth were:[1268]

515. i. NEWTON[8] WYETH, born 28 Oct 1854, Liberty Township; married ADELAIDE WHIPPLE HEALD, 24 Jun 1884, Canton, Fulton, Illinois; died 02 Mar 1940, Chicago, Cook, Illinois.

516. ii. CLINTON EARL WYETH, born 06 Apr 1856, Liberty Township; married LAMERTE KEENAN, 19 Apr 1894, Newark; died 25 Jun 1939, Buckeye Lake, Licking, Ohio.

Back: Newton, Adelaide Heald, Clinton, Jennie Jackson and LaMerte Keenan Wyeth. Front: Oscar McConoughey, Charles, Elizabeth Wright Wyeth (mother), Arthur, Jennie Wyeth McConoughey and Lydia Butte Wyeth. Photo courtesy of Chuck and Jane Walker.

517.   iii.   JENNIE MATILDA WYETH, born 03 Jan 1859, Liberty Township; married (1) OSCAR MCCONOUGHEY there, 03 Jan 1883; married (2) WILLIAM PRATT, 03 Jan 1921, Champaign County, Illinois;[1269] died there in Tolono, 23 Oct 1925.[1270]

          iv.   MORTON WYETH, born 26 Apr 1864, Liberty Township; died there unmarried at age 23 on 02 Feb 1888 of meningitis.

518.   v.   ARTHUR WYETH, born 16 Feb 1866, Liberty Township; married (1) ALLIE DEE BUTTE there, 24 Oct 1888; married (2) JENNIE MAE JACKSON, 30 Dec 1897, Liberty Township; died 10 Dec 1932, Columbus, Franklin, Ohio.

519.   vi.   DR. CHARLES LEWIS "CHARLEY" WYETH, born 15 Oct 1871, Liberty Township; married LYDIA BUTTE there, 28 May 1896; died 13 Dec 1938, Newark.

268. **LUCY SNOW**[7] **WYETH** (David[6], Gad[5], Ebenezer[4] Jr., Ebenezer[3], John[2], Nicholas[1]) was born on 13 Dec 1830 in Wendell, Franklin, Massachusetts. Lucy married **BENJAMIN FRANKLIN RUNNELS** on 25 Jan 1853 in McKean Township, Licking, Ohio.[1271] Benjamin was born there on 06 Apr 1823 to Stephen Runnels and Jane Brown. Lucy died 30 Dec 1878 in Hawthorn, Montgomery, Iowa. Ben died there on 20 Apr 1914 at age 91.[1272]

Ben Runnels and his daughter Janie's photo is courtesy of Vickilyn Warburton Lallatin.

Including Irving, Marion and Ryland, all of whom died young, Ben and Lucy's children were:

          i.   WALTER[8] RUNNELS, born 12 Apr 1856, McKean; died in Indianapolis, Indiana on 11 Feb 1933; buried with his parents in Clarinda Cemetery, Page, Iowa.

         ii.   FREMONT RUNNELS, born 12 Feb 1858, McKean; died 24 Jul 1858 on the prairie, one day before the end of the family's six-week migration west.[1273]

520.   iii.   SARAH JANE "JANIE" RUNNELS, born 16 Nov 1861, Clarinda; married GUSTAF "ED" ANDERSON, 25 Dec 1883, Hawthorn; died 09 Apr 1937, Red Oak, Iowa.

269. **GAD KELLOGG**[7] **WYETH** (David[6], Gad[5], Ebenezer[4] Jr., Ebenezer[3], John[2], Nicholas[1]) was born on 20 Mar 1832 in Wendell, Franklin, Massachusetts. He married (1) **AMANDA CATHERINE SMITH** on 07 Apr 1859[1274] in Richland County, Ohio. Amanda was born there on 01 Jun 1834 to Jedediah Smith and Catharine Southerland. She died on 22 Jul 1861 in Liberty Township, Licking, Ohio. Gad married (2) **LORETTA SUSAN "RETTA" WOOD** there on 07 Aug 1862. Retta, daughter of Riley Wood and Sarah Butterfield, was born on 27 Jul 1837 in Liberty Township. Gad died there on 17 Sep 1871. Retta died on 18 Apr 1890 in Columbus, Franklin, Ohio.[1275]

Retta Wood Wyeth photo courtesy of Vickilyn Warburton Lallatin.

Gad Kellogg Wyeth and Loretta Susan Wood had the following child:

521.   i.   BURTON RILEY[8] WYETH, born 04 Feb 1865, Liberty Township; married (1) MINNIE ALICE MOCK, 15 Sep 1892, Columbus; married (2) MARY SCOTT LARIMER, 06 Apr 1909, Louisville, Jefferson, Kentucky; died 13 Nov 1939, Pittsburgh, Allegheny, Pennsylvania.

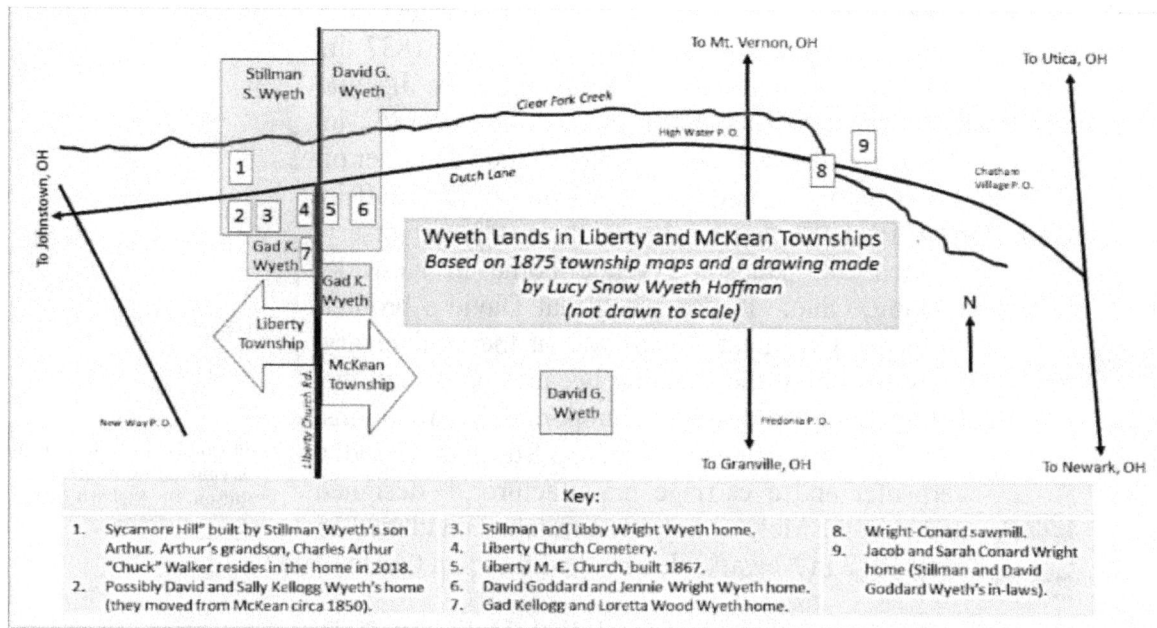

Wyeth Lands in Liberty and McKean Townships
Based on 1875 township maps and a drawing made by Lucy Snow Wyeth Hoffman (not drawn to scale)

Key:

1. Sycamore Hill" built by Stillman Wyeth's son Arthur. Arthur's grandson, Charles Arthur "Chuck" Walker resides in the home in 2018.
2. Possibly David and Sally Kellogg Wyeth's home (they moved from McKean circa 1850).
3. Stillman and Libby Wright Wyeth home.
4. Liberty Church Cemetery.
5. Liberty M. E. Church, built 1867.
6. David Goddard and Jennie Wright Wyeth home.
7. Gad Kellogg and Loretta Wood Wyeth home.
8. Wright-Conard sawmill.
9. Jacob and Sarah Conard Wright home (Stillman and David Goddard Wyeth's in-laws).

270. **(Rev.) Walter Newton^7 Wyeth** (David^6, Gad^5, Ebenezer^4 Jr., Ebenezer^3, John^2, Nicholas^1) was born on 17 May 1833 in Wendell, Franklin, Massachusetts. He studied at Denison University in Granville, Ohio, but took his degree from New York's Madison University (now Colgate).[1276] Walter married (1) **Isabella Emeline Wait**, on 09 May 1859 in Portsmouth, Scioto, Ohio. Isabella, daughter of John Heaton Wait and Malvina Sikes, was born there on 31 Jul 1840. She died on 04 May 1863 in Sunbury, Delaware, Ohio. Walter married (2) **Climena Munson** on 29 May 1866 in Marietta, Washington, Ohio. Climena, daughter of Jasper Munson and Harriet Hubbard, was born on 18 Jul 1830 in Granville, Licking, Ohio. She died on 10 Sep 1871 in Lock, Knox, Ohio. Walter married (3) **Emily Waterman M.D.** on 18 Oct 1888 in Philadelphia, Pennsylvania. Emily, daughter of Richard Waterman and Pamelia Hosford, was born 11 Mar 1850 in Eugene, Vermillion, Indiana. Walter was a prominent Baptist minister and a prolific writer. Walter died on 20 Oct 1899 in Philadelphia. Emily died in Silverman, Fountain, Indiana on 15 Apr 1928. They are buried in West Laurel Hill Cemetery, Bala Cynwyd, Pennsylvania.

Walter Newton Wyeth and Isabella Emeline Wait had the following children:

522.   i. May^8 Wyeth was born on 13 May 1860, Portsmouth; married Frank F. Moore, 05 Jun 1883, Johnson County, Indiana; died 04 May 1950, Riverside, California.

  ii. Frances "Fannie" Wyeth, born 25 Apr 1862, Sunbury; married (1) Robert Gard, 17 Sep 1889, Frankfurt, Clinton, Indiana; married (2) Hobart Scattergood, 27 Jul 1910, New York City; died 30 Jun 1956, Mansfield, Richland, Ohio.

The photos of Walter Newton Wyeth's daughters, May and Fannie, are courtesy of Vickilyn Warburton Lallatin.

391

271. **DAVID GODDARD**[7] **WYETH** (David[6], Gad[5], Ebenezer[4] Jr., Ebenezer[3], John[2], Nicholas[1]) was born on 12 Jun 1837 in Wendell, Franklin, Massachusetts. David married **JENNIE NAOMI WRIGHT**, sister to Libbie Wright, on 03 Apr 1862 in Chatham, McKean Township, Licking, Ohio. Jennie daughter of Jacob Wright and Sarah Conard, was born on 26 Jul 1840 in Chatham. On 03 Apr 1912, they celebrated their 50th anniversary at their 585 Hudson Avenue home in Newark, Licking, Ohio. It was noted that David's brother Augustus Greenleaf Wyeth was at the anniversary party but not at the wedding because he was in the Union Army in 1862.[1277] Supported by donations from brothers, Augustus, Gad and Stillman, David, a carpenter and a carriage manufacturer,[1278] designed and built the McKean Liberty Church. David died 25 May 1912 in Newark. Jennie died there on 04 Dec 1922.

David Goddard Wyeth's photo is courtesy of his great grandson, Dr. Richard Laird Hoffman.

Together with an unnamed daughter, born and died 24 Jan 1863, David Goddard Wyeth and Jennie Naomi Wright had the following children:[1279]

523.   i.   NELLIE[8] WYETH, born 22 Aug 1865, McKean Township; married FRANK HENRY KEENAN (father of LaMerte Keenan), 25 Jan 1893, Newark, Licking, Ohio; died there, 18 Jul 1940.

524.   ii.   WRIGHT DAVID WYETH, born 21 Apr 1871, McKean; married FLAVIA ANNA HARTSHORN, 25 Dec 1906, Newark; founded Wyeth-Scott building supply company there, 1906; died 21 Jun 1956, 585 Hudson Ave., Newark.[1280]

525.   iii.   BESSIE WRIGHT WYETH, born 02 Aug 1876, McKean; married CHALMERS HUTCHISON, 30 Jun 1898, Newark; died 05 Mar 1971, Fort Worth, Tarrant, Texas.

        iv.   LUCY SNOW WYETH, born 12 Feb 1879, McKean; married SIMON BURGET STONEROOK, 24 Feb 1930, San Diego, California; died 19 Aug 1956, Fort Worth.

Wright David Wyeth photo courtesy of Vickilyn Warburton Lallatin.

Jennie Wright and her daughters Nellie, Bessie and Lucy. Photo courtesy of Vickilyn Warburton Lallatin.

Siblings Lucy Snow, Wright David and Bessie Wright Wyeth. Photo courtesy of Richard Laird Hoffman, PhD.

272. **EUNICE KENDALL**[7] **WYETH** (David[6], Gad[5], Ebenezer[4] Jr., Ebenezer[3], John[2], Nicholas[1]) was born on 09 Jan 1839 in McKean Township, Licking, Ohio. She was educated at Oberlin College and taught school while living with her brother, Parker Judson Wyeth, near Columbus, Ohio.[1281] Eunice and **(REV.) CHARLES BRYON LEWIS** were married on 13 Mar 1864 in Liberty Township, Licking, Ohio by her brother Rev. Walter Newton Wyeth.[1282] Charles was born on 18 Oct 1839 in Delaware, Ohio. He died on 03 Feb 1892 in Newark, Licking, Ohio.[1283] She died on 18 Nov 1927 at age 88 at her daughter Rose's home in Bloomfield, Essex, New Jersey. They rest in Cedar Hill Cemetery, Newark.

This photo of 88-year-old Eunice Kendall Wyeth Lewis is courtesy of Chuck Walker. His grandfather, Arthur Wyeth, wrote on the frame that "Aunt Eunice was the first of the family born in Ohio."

The children of Charles and Eunice Kendall Wyeth Lewis were:

526.   i. HARRY AUGUSTUS LEWIS, born on 02 Feb 1866, West Jefferson, Madison, Ohio; married MARY AUGUSTA MOSES, 01 Feb 1885, Petersburg, Rensselaer, New York; died there, 19 Oct 1926.

527.   ii. SYLVANUS DANFORTH LEWIS, born 20 Jan 1870, Franklin Furnace, Scioto, Ohio; married LAURA OLRICH, 27 Mar 1902, Syracuse, Onondaga, New York; died 26 Aug 1939, Port Chester, Westchester, New York.

528.   iii. LORA LEWIS, born 20 Mar 1875, Portsmouth, Scioto, Ohio; married JOHN WALKER FAIRING, 09 Jan 1901, Syracuse; died 24 May 1956, Gainesville, Alachua, Florida.[1284]

    iv. ROSE WYETH LEWIS, born 30 Oct 1877, Blackinton, Berkshire, Massachusetts; a school principal in Bloomfield; died there unmarried on 07 Dec 1962.

These photos of Rev. Charles Bryon Lewis and Eunice Kendall Wyeth and their daughters Rose Wyeth Lewis and Lora Lewis Fairing are from the collection of Eunice's niece, Minnie Wyeth McKenzie. They are courtesy of Minnie's great granddaughter, Vickilyn Warburton Lallatin.

273. **AUGUSTUS GREENLEAF "A.G."** [7] **WYETH** (David[6], Gad[5], Ebenezer[4] Jr., Ebenezer[3], John[2], Nicholas[1]) was born on 12 Oct 1841 in a log cabin near High Water in McKean Township, Licking, Ohio. Augustus enlisted as a private in Co. B of the 76th Ohio Infantry Regiment on 01 Oct 1861 at Camp Sherman, Newark, Licking, Ohio. He mustered out on disability on 01 Apr 1863 from Gayoso Army Hospital in Memphis, Tennessee. After attending Oberlin College, he married (1) **EMMA PEARL STRAUGHAN**, on 30 May 1876 in Fort Wayne, Allen, Indiana.[1285] Emma, daughter of Jesse Rittenhouse Straughan and Caroline Chambers, was born on 07 Oct 1846 in McConnelsville, Morgan, Ohio. She died on 26 Mar 1900 in Fort Wayne. Augustus then married (2) Emma's sister, **ALICE F. STRAUGHAN**, the widow of Charles Howey on 07 Jul 1909 in Mansfield, Richland, Ohio. She was born in Delaware, Ohio on 07 Jun 1860. He manufactured sleigh runners and oil tank wagons in Newark. There, at the time of his death, on 19 Jun 1914, A.G. was serving as the first president of the Park National Bank.[1286] Augustus died at his Newark home, 201 Granville Street.[1287] Alice died on 22 Nov 1927 in San Diego, California.

This $5 note issued by the Park National Bank in the Series of 1902, Ben Harrison pictured, was signed by A. G. Wyeth. Photo courtesy of the bank's current director, C. Daniel DeLawder.

Augustus and Emma Straughan Wyeth's children were:

529. i. RALPH STRAUGHAN[8] WYETH, born 05 Oct 1877, Newark, Licking, Ohio; married ALICE LOUISE MCCUNE, 29 Mar 1906, Newark; died there at his home at 362 Granville St., on 23 Oct 1952.[1288] The Ralph S. Wyeth Scholarship, established in 1965, still helps Licking County students attend college.[1289] [1290]

ii. LEE HOWEY WYETH, born 20 Aug 1882, Newark; he died in the hospital there on 13 Apr 1907 after an operation for a blood-poisoned pimple. Sadly, he was only 24, engaged, and soon to be married to Miss Mary Neal of Newark.[1291]

The two tall men with white beards, stationed far back row middle, are brothers A.G Wyeth, holding his cane and top hat, and David Goddard Wyeth, wearing a straw hat. Although this photo, from the 18 Aug 1897 Wyeth-Wright Reunion, is not labeled, a few others can be picked out. Libbie Wright is the older lady in front of the two men. Wright David Wyeth is sitting near his mother, third row right. Lydia Butte and Arthur Wyeth are far back left. Undoubtedly, that is 15-year-old Lee Wyeth looking jaunty in a straw hat in the third row middle. Photo courtesy of Chuck and Jane Walker.

274. GERTRUDE⁷ WYETH (John⁶ Jr., John⁵, Ebenezer⁴ Jr., Ebenezer³, John², Nicholas¹) was born on 30 May 1833 in Carlisle, Cumberland, Pennsylvania. She married **WILLIAM FINDLAY SHUNK**, son of Pennsylvania Governor Francis Rawn Shunk and Jane Findlay, on 08 Apr 1852 in Harrisburg, Dauphin, Pennsylvania. He was born there on 06 Sep 1830. William, chief engineer New York City's Metropolitan Elevated Railroad, died at the family home, Katahmont, in Lucknow, near Harrisburg on 22 Jun 1907. Gertrude died at 502 North Second St., Harrisburg on 11 Dec 1912.[1292]

Mary Wyeth is buried with her sister and William Shunk's family in the Harrisburg Cemetery. Photo courtesy of Jeff Wyeth.

The children of William and Gertrude Wyeth Shunk included:

    i. ELEANOR FINDLAY⁸ SHUNK, born 19 Apr 1854, Harrisburg; died 07 Jan 1935 at Katahmont.

    ii. MARY DOUGLAS SHUNK, born Jan 1856, Doylestown, Bucks, Pennsylvania; died 29 May 1905 at Katahmont in Lucknow.[1293]

    iii. GERTRUDE WYETH SHUNK, born circa Apr 1859, Harrisburg; married JAMES PARKER V, 01 Jun 1882, Harrisburg;[1294] she died there, 15 Jan 1885 of childbirth complications from the 04 Jan 1885 birth of son James Parker VI.[1295]

    iv. NANCY IRWIN SHUNK, born 18 Feb 1861, Georgetown, D.C.; a contralto vocalist; died 31 Jul 1926 in the family home, Katahmont, in Lucknow.

    v. COL. FRANCIS RAWN SHUNK, born 25 Nov 1862, Harrisburg; graduated head of his class from the West Point Military Academy, 1887; retired from the U.S. Army Corps of Engineers, 1920; died unmarried on 04 Jan 1925 in Tucson, Pima, Arizona.[1296]

530.   vi. ELIZABETH BROWN "LILLIE" SHUNK, born 02 Aug 1865, Harrisburg; married JOHN ALEXANDER HARMAN there, 21 Sep 1887; took her own life on 06 May 1917, Hotel Southern, Madison Avenue and East 62ⁿᵈ St., New York, NY.[1297]

275. LOUIS⁷ WYETH (John⁶ Jr., John⁵, Ebenezer⁴ Jr., Ebenezer³, John², Nicholas¹) was born on 29 Nov 1840 in Harrisburg.[1298] Starting on 11 Sep 1862, due to a physical disability, Louis was only able to serve two weeks with the Pennsylvania 1ˢᵗ Infantry, Co. E.[1299] He married **FLORENCE ABIGAIL "ABBY" ROGERS** on 19 Jun 1876 in Washington, D.C.[1300] Abby was born on 09 Feb 1856 in Pavilion, Genesee, New York, to Matthew Rogers and Elizabeth Buckingham Simmons. Louis, *Chambersburg Herald* news publisher, turned druggist, developed the much-advertised Wyeth's Sage

Photos of Louis and Abby Rogers Wyeth and their family are courtesy of their grandchild, Patricia King Harms.

and Sulphur Compound hair dye / restorer for the Wyeth Chemical Company, Inc. of Rochester, New York.[1301] He died 14 Mar 1923 in Pueblo, Pueblo County, Colorado.[1302] Abby was one century old at her death on 02 Mar 1956 in Cheyenne, Laramie, Wyoming.

From a tree compiled by Patricia King Harms, Louis Wyeth and Florence Abigail "Abby" Rogers had the following children:

531.　i.　MYRA ELIZABETH[8] WYETH, born 11 Jun 1877, Bethany, Genesee, New York;[1303] married LYMAN R. LATHAM, 01 Oct 1895, Neligh, Antelope, Nebraska; died 12 Mar 1941, while visiting her mother, in Cheyenne.

532.　ii.　JOHN LOUIS WYETH, born Chambersburg, Franklin, Pennsylvania, 09 Aug 1881. At the time of his first marriage, while heading the Wyeth Chemical Co., he started an ad campaign claiming Wyeth's Sage and Sulphur would grow hair on John D. Rockefeller's head.[1304] Louis married (1) LILLIAN MAUDE PERRY, 03 Aug 1905, Rochester, Monroe, New York; married (2) MARY VALKO DURNELL, 12 Jul 1922, Pueblo. A noted Native American artifacts archaeologist and museum curator, he died 22 Sep 1971, Pueblo.

533.　iii.　MARY FLORENCE "DOROTHY" WYETH, born 26 Apr 1887, Pavilion; married JOHN KING, 28 Oct 1908, Alliance, Box Butte, Nebraska; died 03 Apr 1963, Bremerton, Kitsap, Washington.[1305]

534.　iv.　ALBERT DOUGLAS "BERT" WYETH, born 04 Feb 1893, Rochester; served the 318th Wyoming Engineers during WWI; married (1) MARY ELIZABETH WHITFIELD, 10 Aug 1921 Sunrise, Platte, Wyoming; [1306] married (2) LAURABELLE BOEHME, 08 Aug 1941, Sidney, Cheyenne, Nebraska;[1307] died 07 Oct 1965, Hightstown, Mercer, New Jersey.[1308]

By comparing to other family photos, these appear to be back: Dorothy, Myra, Louis, Abby Rogers and Lillian Perry - front: Albert and John Louis Wyeth.

276. **LOUISA WEISS[7] MCKINLEY** (Mary[6] Wyeth, John[5], Ebenezer[4] Jr., Ebenezer[3], John[2], Nicholas[1]) was born on 20 Nov 1828 in Harrisburg, Dauphin, Pennsylvania. Louisa married **JAMES FERGUSON KENNEDY** on 06 Jul 1852 in Carlisle, Cumberland, Pennsylvania. James was born to Stewart Kennedy and Ann Ferguson on 27 Sep 1824 in Greenwich, Warren, New Jersey. A doctor, but when he went blind in 1857, James became a preacher. He died on 06 Oct 1901 in Chambersburg, Franklin, Pennsylvania. Louisa died there, 11 Oct 1906.

James Ferguson Kennedy and Louisa Weiss McKinley had the following children:

　i.　DANIEL MCKINLEY[8] KENNEDY, born 08 Apr 1853, Dickinson, Cumberland, Pennsylvania; published the *Chambersburg Herald* with his cousin, Louis Wyeth; married SUSAN MARY SHIELDS, 25 Dec 1879; Mount Pleasant, Westmoreland, Pennsylvania; caught scarlet fever from his only child, Stewart Shields, died from it 23 Oct 1887, Pittsburgh, Allegheny, Pennsylvania.[1309]

　ii.　DR. JAMES STEWART KENNEDY, born 27 Oct 1856, Dickinson; married CORA BELLE HITESHEW, 11 Jun 1889, Chambersburg; a surgeon there, joined the U.S. Army during the Spanish-American War, 1898; rose to the rank of major; he and Cora had two children, Louise and Francis; Dr. Kennedy died 07 Oct 1916, Walter Reed Army Hospital, Washington, D.C.[1310]

277. **WILLIAM MAXWELL**[7] **WYETH** (Francis[6], John[5], Ebenezer[4] Jr., Ebenezer[3], John[2], Nicholas[1]) was born on 17 Feb 1832 in Harrisburg, Dauphin, Pennsylvania. He married **ELIZABETH MORRIS "ELIZA" RENICK** on 28 Sep 1858 in Chillicothe, Ross, Ohio. Eliza was born to Thomas S. Renick and Elizabeth Morris on 25 Aug 1836 in Bainbridge, Ross, Ohio. In 1859, William founded the hugely successful Wyeth Hardware & Mfg. Co. of St. Joseph, Buchanan, Missouri. To help protect his neighbors and his property from bushwhacking marauders, he joined the Missouri Enrolled Militia to serve in the home guard during the Civil War.[1311] William died on 08 Mar 1901 in St. Joseph. Eliza died on 13 Nov 1920 at the home of the granddaughter she adopted, Berenice Smith Bull, in Greenwich, Fairfield, Connecticut.[1312]

Photos of William and Eliza Renick Wyeth are courtesy of their great, great grandson, William "Max" Wyeth IV.

William Maxwell Wyeth and Elizabeth Morris "Eliza" Renick had the following children:[1313]

535.   i.   SUE MAUD[8] WYETH, born 13 Feb 1861, St. Joseph; married (1) DUDLEY SMITH on 11 Oct 1882, St. Joseph; married (2) CHARLES WYNDHAM on 12 Nov 1892, Westminster, London, England;[1314] died 17 Apr 1897, St. Joseph.

536.   ii. HUSTON WYETH, born 08 Jul 1863, St. Joseph; married LEILA BALLINGER there, 04 Apr 1883; died 25 Jan 1925, Miami, Dade, Florida.[1315]

William's 43-room palace at 1100 Charles Steet, St. Joseph, is now a museum. He modeled the 1879 home on those he'd seen during his extensive European travels.

278. **JOHN**[7] **WYETH** (Francis[6], John[5], Ebenezer[4] Jr., Ebenezer[3], John[2], Nicholas[1]) was born on 04 May 1834 in Harrisburg, Dauphin, Pennsylvania.[1316] After graduating from the Philadelphia College of Pharmacy in 1854, John founded the drug firm, John Wyeth & Brother, Inc. of Philadelphia in 1860. As a major supplier to the Civil War, the firm grew quickly. In 1862, John married **SARAH BELL "SADIE" STEWART** in Chambersburg, Franklin, Pennsylvania. Sadie, daughter of John H. Stewart and Mary Clara Scott, was born on 15 May 1839 in Waynesboro, Franklin, Pennsylvania. A fire that destroyed most of the Wyeth facilities in 1889, forced the firm into concentrating full time on mass-produced medicines using rotary compressed tablet machines invented at their firm. Sadie enjoyed travelling in Europe and when John accompanied her, it was obvious business remained topmost on his mind. On display, during a 2015 exhibition at John's alma mater, was a typed transcript of a handwritten note

John Wyeth's portrait by Roy F. Spreter is courtesy of Pfizer, Inc.

John wrote on 15 Feb 1893, from the Grand Hotel in Nice, France, to his chief accountant, Mr. Yeakel. After reviewing the company's 1892 balance sheet John declared, "The profits are not as great as I anticipated." He then proceeded to offer detailed advice regarding products, inventory and accounting. John died on 30 Mar 1907 of pneumonia, at his home at 1511 Locust Street, Philadelphia, Pennsylvania. Sadie died of dementia, at age 81, on 21 Dec 1920 at the Ritz Carlton Hotel, 46th and Madison Ave., New York City.[1317]

John Wyeth and Sarah Bell "Sadie" Stewart had the following children:

Stuart Wyeth - photo from the HUP Collection, courtesy Harvard University Archives.

i. STUART[8] WYETH, born 17 Oct 1862, Philadelphia; graduated from Harvard in 1884; died 30 Dec 1929 of a heart attack, Philadelphia; buried there in Laurel Hill Cemetery with his parents. His next of kin, his uncle Frank's son, Maxwell Wyeth, signed his death record. Stuart and Maxwell had not been compatible at their fathers' drug firm. Stuart willed John Wyeth & Bro. to his alma mater. Harvard sold the firm to American Home Products (AHP) in 1932 for $2.9 million. In 2002, AHP changed its name to "Wyeth" and sold the company to Pfizer, Inc. for $68 billion in 2009.[1318]

ii. HOUSTON MAXWELL WYETH, born 03 Sep 1864, Philadelphia; buried Laurel Hill Cemetery with two listings. One matches Philadelphia records for Houston's death from cholera at age 11 months on 03 Aug 1865 and the other shows an 1866 death date.

279. **FRANCIS HOUSTON "FRANK"[7] WYETH** (Francis[6], John[5], Ebenezer[4] Jr., Ebenezer[3], John[2], Nicholas[1]) was born on 14 Jul 1836 in Harrisburg, Dauphin, Pennsylvania.[1319] Frank married **HENRIETTA BRAXTON HORNER** on 20 Feb 1862 in Holy Trinity Church, Philadelphia, Pennsylvania. The daughter of Richard Brent Horner and Mary Blair Little, Henrietta was born on 09 Oct 1837 at Mountain View Farm near Marshall, Fauquier County, Virginia.[1320] After Fort Sumter was attacked, not even a personal appeal to Abraham Lincoln allowed the couple to travel across the Potomac to wed in Virginia.[1321] Frank, vice president of the wholesale drug company, John Wyeth & Brother, Inc. of Philadelphia, died at his home there at 1912 Rittenhouse Square on 12 Jun 1913. Henrietta died on 30 Apr 1915 in Philadelphia.

This photo of Frank Houston Wyeth is courtesy of Pfizer, Inc.

The children of Frank Houston and Henrietta Horner Wyeth were:

i. RICHARD HORNER[8] WYETH was born on 18 Sep 1863 in Philadelphia; he married ELEANOR ELIZABETH GILMORE, 20 Oct 1891, Manhattan, New York; a journalist, he died 27 Oct 1903, Philadelphia. Richard's wife is a curiosity. The couples' marriage record claims her maiden name is Regnault and her married name Gilmore and that she was born in Savannah to Claire Regnault and Harriet Thompson.[1322] On many census reports and ships' registries, she also said she was born in Georgia and her mother claimed to have been born in England. In reality, she was Ella Gilmore, daughter of Edward Gilmore, a Philadelphia hotel keeper, and Harriet Virginia Thompson. All three of whom were born in Philadelphia. Ella's first husband was a New York artist by the name of Walter Menijay Dunk. For most of their married life, Ella and Richard lived in France and England.[1323] After Richard's death, at age 40, Ella's third marriage was to a French diamond dealer who lived near her in Philadelphia. She died in France in 1950.[1324]

537. ii. MAXWELL WYETH, born in Philadelphia, 15 Jun 1866; married (1) MARGARET LOUISE WILKESON WARDWELL, 19 Sep 1889, South Orange, Essex, New Jersey; married (2) LOUISE C. SCHAUFELE, 06 May 1933, Manhattan; served in World War I, awarded the Navy Cross for distinguished service as Commanding Officer of the USS *Emerald*;[1325] died 11 Sep 1936, Shell, Big Horn, Wyoming.[1326]

This photo of Maxwell and Louise Schaufele Wyeth at their Trapper Creek Lodge in Shell, Wyoming is courtesy of Max's great grandson, Joseph Robert Wyeth.

John Wyeth & Brother

Incorporated

Manufacturing Chemists,

Cor. Washington Avenue and Eleventh Street.

Philadelphia October 10th, 1906.

Mess. Wm. H. Wyeth & Son,

Riverdale, Michigan.

Gentlemen :

We are just in receipt of your favor of 4th inst. inquiring as to the history of the Wyeth family. We know of no member of the Wyeth family throughout the country, who do not owe their origin to the same source. The family came over about 1630 and settled in Cambridge, Mass., from which source I have no doubt all the various branches of the family now existing owe their origin.

I found in visiting Mount Auburn, Cambridge, a monument with the following inscription -

WYETH

Nicholas................1595 - 1680
Settled Newtown 1630

John....................1655 - 1706
Ebenezer................1698 - 1754
Jonas...................1730 - 1815
Jonas...................1762 - 1828

Our Grandfather came from Cambridge and settled in Harrisburg, Pa. He had several brothers, one of whom went to Ohio and settled in Cincinnati, I think. I should be very glad, indeed, should you ever visit Philadelphia, to have you call and see us.

Very truly yours,

F.H.Wyeth

Notes about Frank Houston Wyeth's letter to Walter Herbert and Arthur Walter Wyeth: This letter comes to us courtesy of Juanita Vogt Wyeth. Her husband, Charles Leon Wyeth, was Arthur's son.

Even though the letter is addressed to "Wm. H. Wyeth & son," we know it means Walter H. because Walter's pension file puts him in Riverdale at this period. As a result of contracting typhoid fever during the Civil War, Walter was totally deaf by this 10 Oct 1906 date.

We also know the letter was signed by Frank Houston Wyeth because the signature of "F. H. Wyeth" matches Frank's signature when he applied for membership in S.A.R.

In this letter, Frank confirms many facts written in this book. First, all members of the Wyeth family owe their origin to Nicholas Wyeth. He quotes the inscription from the Mt. Auburn monument shown earlier in this book. Lastly, he refers to his grandfather John's brother, Joshua Wyeth, settling in Cincinnati.

We can only imagine the joy poor deaf Walter must have felt when he read his cousin's invitation to visit.

280. **PARKER CAMPBELL**[7] **WYETH** (Francis[6], John[5], Ebenezer[4] Jr., Ebenezer[3], John[2], Nicholas[1]) was born 15 Jun 1854, in Harrisburg, Dauphin, Pennsylvania. [1327] Parker Campbell Wyeth married **ELLEN ASHTON HORNER** on 11 Sep 1890 in Warrenton, Fauquier, Virginia. Ellen, daughter of Robert Little Horner and Ellen Ashton, was born there on 06 Aug 1869. [1328] Parker, founder of the Rossi Saddlery Co. of St. Joseph, Buchanan, Missouri, died there on 02 Dec 1928. Ellen died on 29 Dec 1954 in St. Joseph. They are buried there in Mt. Mora Cemetery.

Parker Campbell Wyeth, courtesy of Jeff Wyeth. Source unknown.

The children of Parker Campbell Wyeth and Ellen Ashton Horner were:

538.   i.   SARA CAMPBELL[8] WYETH, born 04 Apr 1892, St. Joseph; married WILLIAM HARRIS FLOYD III there, 10 Oct 1916; died 11 Feb 1963, Arlington, Virginia.

       ii.   ELLEN ASHTON WYETH, born 08 Mar 1894, St. Joseph; died there unmarried on 09 Nov 1980.

       iii.   ROBERT HORNER WYETH, born 10 Apr 1897, St. Joseph; died there the day after Christmas in 1897.

539.   iv.   FRANCIS HOUSTON "FANNY" WYETH, born 20 Jan 1900, St. Joseph; married (1) HELEN FRANCES GAFFNEY, 30 May 1922, Portsmouth, Rockingham, New Hampshire; married (2) ANN ELIZABETH SEAMAN, 1957, Newtown, Bucks, Pennsylvania; died 13 Oct 1965, Newtown.

540.   v.   HENRIETTA BRAXTON WYETH, born 08 Aug 1906, St. Joseph; married ROBERT JAMES BROWN SR., 12 Oct 1929, St. Joseph; died there, 04 Jun 1986.

281. **CHARLES SHEAFER**[7] **WYETH** (Charles Augustus[6], John[5], Ebenezer[4] Jr., Ebenezer[3], John[2], Nicholas[1]) was born on 01 Mar 1843 in Harrisburg, Dauphin, Pennsylvania. He served there as a sergeant in the 48th Infantry Militia, Co. D during the summer of 1863. While serving as a judge in Ottawa County, Kansas, Charles married **FRANCES MARIE BURNHAM** there on 17 Jun 1875. Frances was born to Nathan Burnham and Rebecca Foster on 17 May 1845 in West Jefferson, Madison, Ohio. Charles died on 26 Dec 1923 at age 80 in Milton, Umatilla, Oregon. She died there on 23 Jan 1939 at age 93.

Charles Sheafer Wyeth and Frances Marie Burnham had the following children:

       i.   ADELINE BURNHAM[8] WYETH, born 29 May 1876, Minneapolis, Ottawa, Kansas; died unmarried on 11 Oct 1972 in Walla Walla, Washington.

       ii.   BURNHAM NATHAN FRANCIS "BURNIE" WYETH, born on 18 Mar 1877, West Jefferson; died 19 Apr 1890 at age 13 in Minneapolis.

       iii.   REBA F. WYETH, born 20 Dec 1883, Minneapolis; she was not quite two years old at her death there on 08 Dec 1885.

282. **LOUISA WEISS**[7] **WYETH** (Louis Weiss[6], John[5], Ebenezer[4] Jr., Ebenezer[3], John[2], Nicholas[1]) was born on 09 Apr 1843 in Guntersville, Marshall, Alabama. Louisa married **CAPTAIN WILLIAM HOUSTON TODD** there on 23 Nov 1871. Todd, a Lieut. in the Confederate Army and later a Tennessee River steamboat captain was born circa 1843 in Alabama. He died 31 May 1910 in Guntersville. Having outlived all her children she died there, 21 Jul 1927.

Captain William Houston Todd and Louisa Weiss Wyeth had the following children:

      i.   LOUIS WYETH[8] TODD, born 10 Oct 1872, Guntersville; married IDA MOORE THOMASON there, 29 Feb 1908; died on 24 Feb 1912 in Guntersville of consumption.

      ii. MARY CARLISLE TODD, born on Easter morning, 05 Apr 1874, Guntersville; married DR. THURSTON GILMAN LUSK there, 23 Nov 1898; died 11 Mar 1901, New York City.

541.   iii. JOHN ALLAN TODD, born 12 Jul 1879, Guntersville; married MARGARET ELIZABETH STAPLES, 31 Oct 1903, Jackson County, Alabama; died 16 Dec 1917, Huntsville, Madison, Alabama.

283. (DR.) JOHN ALLAN[7] WYETH (Louis Weiss[6], John[5], Ebenezer[4] Jr., Ebenezer[3], John[2], Nicholas[1]) was born on 26 May 1845 in Missionary Station (Guntersville), Marshall, Alabama. He served in the CSA military during the Civil War. John married (1) FLORENCE NIGHTINGALE SIMS on 10 Apr 1886 in Manhattan, New York. Florence, daughter of Dr. James Marion Sims and Eliza Theresa Jones, was born on 22 Aug 1855 in New York City. She died there on 24 Sep 1915. He married (2) MARGUERITE CHALIFOUX on 15 Nov 1918 in Manhattan. Marguerite, daughter of Joseph Oliver Chalifoux and Annie F. Duffy, was born on 01 Nov 1895 in Lynn, Essex, Massachusetts. John died in Manhattan on 28 May 1922 of angina brought on by acute indigestion.[1329] Marguerite then married Henry Staton Sr. She died on 31 Mar 1973 in Volusia County, Florida.

Statue of John Allan Wyeth on the grounds of the Alabama State Capitol is courtesy of the George F. Landegger Collection of Alabama photos in Carol M. Highsmith's America, Library of Congress.

The children of John Allan and Florence Nightingale Sims Wyeth were:

542.   i.   FLORENCE SIMS[8] WYETH, born 26 Jan 1887, Manhattan, New York City, New York; married ALAN DATER MCLEAN there, 30 Sep 1913; died 10 Oct 1942, Manhattan.

543.   ii. MARION SIMS WYETH, born 18 Feb 1889, Manhattan; graduated Princeton University in 1910; married ELEANOR NOYES ORR, on 25 Nov 1915 in Chicago, Cook, Illinois; served in the U. S. Army in World War I; died 04 Feb 1982, West Palm Beach, Palm Beach County, Florida.

John playing the banjo for his daughter, Florence Sims (in the bassinet), his wife and her nieces Fannie Marion, Alice Maud, and France Gregory. This 1887 photo, gift of Alice Wyeth Barkhausen, is courtesy of Julie Patton, Director, Guntersville Museum, 1215 Rayburn Ave., Guntersville.

      iii. JOHN ALLAN WYETH JR., born in Manhattan on 24 Oct 1894;[1330] graduated Princeton University, 1915; served the U. S. Army in World War I and the U. S. Coast Guard in World War II; died unmarried on 11 May 1981, at age 86, at the Princeton Medical Center, Princeton, Mercer, New Jersey;[1331] buried in Blawenburg Cemetery, Somerset County, New Jersey.[1332]

Notes on Dr. John Allan Wyeth Sr. and John Allan Wyeth Jr.:

Dr. Wyeth's book, *With Sabre and Scalpel: The Autobiography of a Soldier and Surgeon*, can be purchased on Amazon or read for free on Google Books. In it are his recollections of life in the old South with a view of slavery and the abolition crusaders. John details his Confederate service, the horrors of war and the misery of a Union prison. He talks of the desolation of the South after the war and his admiration of Nathan Bedford Forrest who started the KKK. John discusses the bios he wrote on Nathaniel Jarvis Wyeth, Abel Streight (see his photo on page 76) and others. He points to the inferior medical education of the time which led him to work as a quarryman and a river boat pilot to earn money for his medical education, as well as to found the Polyclinic to train others in the medical profession. He also wrote about surgical procedures, poetry, travels in Europe, and Wyeth genealogy in the book. Dr. Wyeth's life was so full, it overflowed.

John's common school education ended on 01 Feb 1861 when he matriculated as a cadet at La Grange Military College in present day Colbert County, Alabama. The college closed one year later because 176 of its 179 cadets joined the Confederate military. John, age 17, volunteered with Quirk's Scouts, the advance guard of John Hunt Morgan's Raiders. Toughened by months of skirmishes and raids in Tennessee and Kentucky, in Apr 1863, John transferred to the regular Confederate army, Co. I of Russell's 4th Alabama Cavalry Regiment. Though battle-hardened, nothing prepared him for the incomprehensible losses at Chickamauga.[1333] Of it he wrote:

> "The one object in all this nightmare of horror which touched me most deeply of all was the calm and beautiful expression on the smooth and beardless face of a slender lad who had been shot through the brain... Some comrade had stopped long enough to straighten him out and fold his hands across his breast. Here he was to be laid in a trench with other dead comrades, two or three deep, with just enough earth over them to keep off the hogs and buzzards. I could not help thinking that he, too, must have a mother who, like my own, was praying that her boy might come back to her; and this one could never come. I have asked myself the question a thousand times as I look back on my own life, why cannot men with hearts in them and with heads on them settle their foolish differences in some other way than by shooting holes through one another?"

Shortly after that battle, on 04 Oct 1863, John was captured and taken by train to Camp Morton, near Indianapolis, Indiana. Severely ill with pneumonia and measles he struggled through two bitter northern winters. Considered unable to fight, he returned home through a prisoner exchange on 01 Mar 1865. While helping to rebuild his family's burned-out home, encouraged by the example of the kind Camp Morton physician, Dr. Charles Kipp, who kept him alive, John determined to become a doctor himself.[1334]

1869 degree in hand from the University of Louisville School of Medicine, when John lost his first patient, to diabetes, he became disheartened with his medical training. He took down his shingle and worked to earn income so he could study at New York's Bellevue Hospital Medical College. After graduating there in 1873, John still believed medical education needed vast improvement. This led him to found the Polyclinic Medical School and Hospital in 1881. It was the first post-graduate medical school in the U.S.[1335]

Not only were the Mayo brothers trained at the Polyclinic, but hospital patients including Rudolf Valentino and Marilyn Monroe were newsworthy. Another notable patient was Dr. Wyeth himself. He married his nurse, Marguerite Chalifoux, there while being treated for a broken leg. But the hospital façade's motto said it all, "For the Sick Without Regard to Race or Class."[1336] [1337]

Since John Allan Wyeth Jr. never married, here is a biography of him in his own hand. It is from John's response to my brother Jeff's 27 Feb and 18 Dec 1978 requests for facts on John's branch of the Wyeth family. The letters to Jeff were return addressed in care of John's niece, Jane Marion McLean. John lived the last few years of his life at Jane's home on Beden's Brook Road, Skillman, New Jersey.

In addition to his Princeton education, John studied painting with Duncan Grant, a member of the Bloomsbury Group and with Jean Marchand at the Académie Moderne in Paris for six years in the 1930s. He also was a gifted pianist and a teacher, as shown below in a second letter offering Jeff some grammatical advice.

06 Jan 1979: "I am a Princeton graduate, 1915 class, Princeton Graduate School MA, 4 years, began painting at age of 38 & have been painting from 1932 till now. Have just had a big retrospective show in Princeton, my first (age 84). Veteran of World War I (Somme & Argonne) and World War II, Coast Guard, final year of W. W. II."

16 Jan 1979: "… a note on the military service of my brother (Marion Sims Wyeth) and me (John Allan Wyeth Jr.) in the A.E.F., he in London, I in the Somme and in the Argonne in 1918… En passant, as an old English teacher (H. D. Evans Ranch School, Mesa, Arizona & St. Paul's School, Concord, NH) – let me offer one correction – by "distinguished" letter you surely mean "direct." Thank you for being so direct, for it caught me up sharp…"

Missing from the short, handwritten autobiography of John Allan Wyeth Jr. is notice of his book of poetry *This Man's Army: A War in Fifty-Odd Sonnets.* The first versions of the book, published just before the Great Depression, add "Benedict" as another middle name for John.

Marion Sims Wyeth and John Allan Wyeth Jr., U. S. Army, World War I – photograph courtesy of Marion's granddaughter, France Griggs Sloat.

SQUILLY
HOSPITAL

Fever, and crowds—and light that cuts your eyes—
Men waiting in a long slow-shuffling line
with silent private faces, white and bleak.
Long rows of lumpy stretchers on the floor.
My helmet drops—a head jerks up and cries
wide-eyed and settles in a quivering whine.
The air is rank with touching human reek.
A troop of Germans clatters through the door.
They cross our line and something in me dies.
Sullen, detached, obtuse—men into swine—
and hurt unhappy things that walk apart.
Their rancid bodies trail a languid streak
so curious that hate breaks down before
the dull and cruel laughter in my heart.

The above poem, from page 54 of *This Man's Army*, shows how vividly the sonnets paint scenes from John's World War I service in the U.S. Army.[1338] Fluent in French, beginning on 11 Dec 1917, 2nd Lt. John Allan Wyeth Jr. served as a division translator on the Western Front in the 33rd Division Headquarters of the American Expeditionary Force (A.E.F.). Before his discharge on 23 Oct 1919, John served with the Army of Occupation in Germany.

In 2008, Dana Gioia and B. J. Omanson published a new edition of John's journey through World War I. They state John poems are as fresh and as compelling today as they were 100 years ago.[1339]

284. **GEORGE WARDWELL[7] WYETH** (Samuel Douglass[6], John[5], Ebenezer[4] Jr., Ebenezer[3], John[2], Nicholas[1]) was born on 04 Jan 1846 in Philadelphia, Philadelphia County, Pennsylvania. George married (1) **FRANCES IDA BARBE** on 21 Sep 1875 in Philadelphia. Frances was born there on 22 Sep 1846 to Francis Louis Barbe and Louisa Hoffman. Frances died 13 Apr 1917, from arteriosclerosis and epilepsy, at her sister Marguerite Hoffman's home in Philadelphia. Frances was buried at Arlington Cemetery in Drexel Hill, Pennsylvania. George married (2) **ANNA R. GINTER** shortly after they applied for a license on 20 Sep 1917 in Baltimore, Maryland.[1340] Anna was born there circa 1859 to Francis Ginter and Sarah Scott. Anna died on the way to Manhattan's 5th Ave. Hospital on 11 Mar 1928.[1341] George, a public accountant, died on 10 Oct 1929 in Brooklyn, Kings, New York. Anna and George are buried in Rosedale Cemetery, 408 Orange Road, Montclair, New Jersey.

George Wardwell Wyeth and Frances Ida Barbe had the following children:

544.   i. GEORGE LORRAINE[8] WYETH, born 07 Sep 1876, Montclair, Essex, New Jersey; championship tennis player; married HELENA KATE LIVINGSTON, 11 Sep 1909, Elizabeth, Union, New Jersey;[1342] he died on 02 Mar 1948, Cedar Grove, Essex, New Jersey.

    ii. GRACE WYETH, born 26 Sep 1885, New York City; died 19 May 1968 of arteriosclerosis in Ridley Park, Delaware, Pennsylvania.[1343]

These photos of George and Helena Livingston Wyeth are courtesy of their granddaughter Deb Wyeth Wilkie.

285. **JOHN DOUGLAS[7] WYETH** (Samuel Douglass[6], John[5], Ebenezer[4] Jr., Ebenezer[3], John[2], Nicholas[1]) was born on 17 Sep 1853 in Camden, Camden County, New Jersey. John married **FANNIE JOHNSON OSBORN** on 27 Feb 1894 in New York City, New York.[1344] Fannie, daughter of Lewis Alexander Osborn and Fanny Jane Johnson, was born 07 Mar 1871 in Woodside, Essex, New Jersey. John, an insurance agent, died on 23 Sep 1924 in East Orange, Essex, New Jersey. Fannie died there on 07 Dec 1931.

John Douglas Wyeth and Fannie Johnson Osborn had the following children:

545.   i. HAZEL MABEL[8] WYETH, born 16 Nov 1894, New York City; married ARTHUR FRANKLIN WILLIAMS, 17 Nov 1917, Newark, Essex, New Jersey; died 24 Sep 1975, Newton, Middlesex, Massachusetts.

546.   ii. CAROL WYETH, born 16 Apr 1898, Newark; married HERBERT HUMMEL HOCK, circa 1922; died 17 Mar 1967, Phillipsburg, Warren, New Jersey.

iii. JOHN OSBORN WYETH, born 04 Feb 1902, Newark; died there, 04 Aug 1902.

iv. JOHN WARDWELL WYETH, born 22 May 1903, Newark. In the 09 Jan 1920 census, he lived with sisters Helen and Gertrude Wyeth at 182 Roseville Ave., Newark. The sisters were both born in 1892 in Newark, but no details can be found on them. A few days later, on the 15th, John was shown living at the New Jersey State Hospital, Parsippany, Morris, New Jersey. He died there on 20 Nov 1958 and is buried, near his parents and Carol and Herbert Hock, in Rosedale Cemetery, 408 Orange Road, Montclair, New Jersey. [1345]

Baby John is in the back left, John D., Fannie O., and J. Wardwell Wyeth are in the front.

286. **MARLBOROUGH CHURCHILL[7] WYETH M.D.** (Samuel Douglass[6], John[5], Ebenezer[4] Jr., Ebenezer[3], John[2], Nicholas[1]) was born on 16 Sep 1855 in Woonsocket, Providence, Rhode Island. In 1878, he graduated from the Columbia University College of Physicians and Surgeons and entered the U.S. Army. By 1886, Asst. Surgeon Wyeth achieved the rank of captain. M. C. married **LUCIA ORA HORTON** on 03 Apr 1888 at St. Paul's Church in Augusta, Richmond, Georgia. Lucia was born on 25 Apr 1858 in Greene County, Georgia. Lucia, age two, first appeared with her parents, James William Horton and Georgia America Hart, in the 1860 census. Dr. Wyeth retired 01 May 1908 at the rank of Lt. Colonel to practice medicine in Manhattan. However, at the advent of World War I, he was called to active duty in St. Louis with the Army's medical supply depot. Afterwards, devoting himself to genealogy research, M. C. wrote Charles Leon Wyeth in 1923, "I probably have the completest list of the Wyeths with one exception & that belongs to a very cranky old lady who -

Dr. Marlborough C. Wyeth, Major, Hdqs. Div. of Cuba, 1898 – photo courtesy of John Churchill Wyeth Jr.

!!!!!" At his death in Manhattan on 14 May 1924, the War Dept. stated, that in addition to the Great War, Wyeth served in the Spanish War and in the Philippines. [1346] Ora died on 12 Oct 1940 in Memphis, Shelby, Tennessee. They are buried in Arlington National Cemetery.

Dr. Marlborough Churchill Wyeth and Lucia Ora Horton had the following children:

547.   i. JOHN CHURCHILL[8] WYETH SR., born 16 Feb 1890, Fort McDowell, Cochise, Arizona; married FRANCES LOUISE HUSTER, 16 Feb 1917, New York City;[1347] died 26 Oct 1950, Santa Barbara, Santa Barbara County, California.

548.   ii. DOROTHY LUCIA WYETH, born 22 May 1894, Hot Springs, Garland, Arkansas; married WALTER CLIFT CHANDLER, 10 Oct 1925, St. Thomas Church, New York City; he was a U.S. Congressman for five years starting on 03 Jan 1935 and then Mayor of Memphis; she died 16 Nov 1949, Tucson, Pima, Arizona.

287. **LUCY COOLIDGE**[7] **WYETH** (Jonas[6] 2[d], Major Jonas[5], Jonas[4] Sr., Ebenezer[3] Sr., John[2], Nicholas[1]) was born on 25 Oct 1833 in Cambridge, Middlesex, Massachusetts. Lucy married **JONATHAN WHEELER BEMIS M.D.** on 16 Nov 1859 in Cambridge. Jonathan, son of Seth Bemis and Sarah Wheeler, was born on 17 Sep 1810 in Watertown, Middlesex, Massachusetts. Jonathan died 06 Jan 1895 in Cambridge. Lucy died there on 09 May 1899. They are buried in Mt. Auburn Cemetery, Cambridge.

Jonathan Wheeler Bemis and Lucy Coolidge Wyeth had the following children:

            i. FREDERICK GEORGE[8] BEMIS, born 10 May 1861, Charleston, Suffolk, Massachusetts; graduated from Harvard 1883; died 18 Nov 1890, Colorado Springs, El Paso, Colorado.

549.   ii. JOHN WHEELER BEMIS, born 21 Sep 1863, Charlestown; graduated from Harvard 1885; married LESLIE LEPINGTON FISHER, 01 Jun 1893, Weston, Middlesex, Massachusetts; died there, 25 Nov 1902.

550.   iii. ANNA GLITAN BEMIS, born 25 Mar 1867, Charlestown; married her cousin HARRIS BRACKETT STEARNS, 12 Apr 1893, Cambridge; died 28 Aug 1949, Nahant, Essex, Massachusetts.

551.   iv. LUCY E. BEMIS, born 15 Jul 1869, Charlestown; married ROBERT WATSON POMEROY SR., 24 Jun 1895, Cambridge; died 18 Apr 1958, New York City.

288. **JOSEPHINE AUGUSTA**[7] **WYETH** (Jonas[6] 2[d], Major Jonas[5], Jonas[4] Sr., Ebenezer[3] Sr., John[2], Nicholas[1]) was born on 27 May 1835 in Cambridge, Middlesex, Massachusetts.[1348] Josephine married **WILLIAM BRACKETT STEARNS** on 15 Dec 1858 in Cambridge. William, son of Joshua Brackett Stearns and Louisa Hutchings King, was born on 24 Sep 1825 in Charlestown, Suffolk, Massachusetts. He died on 02 Sep 1883 in Marblehead, Essex, Massachusetts. She died there on 25 Feb 1899 of liver cancer.

William Brackett Stearns and Josephine Augusta Wyeth had the following children:

552.   i. HARRIS BRACKETT[8] STEARNS, born 16 Sep 1859, Charlestown; married his cousin ANNA GLITAN BEMIS, 12 Apr 1893, Cambridge; died 31 Jul 1933, Ipswich, Essex, Massachusetts.

            ii. LUCY BEMIS STEARNS, born 02 Jun 1861, Charlestown; died unmarried, 06 Nov 1952, Framingham, Middlesex, Massachusetts.

            iii. WILLIAM BRACKETT STEARNS JR., born 31 Jan 1870, Charlestown; married on 12 Aug 1908 in Temple, Hillsborough, New Hampshire to LESLIE LEPINGTON FISHER after the death of her first husband, his cousin, John Wheeler Bemis; William died 31 Jan 1947, Milton, Norfolk, Massachusetts.

            iv. EDWIN WYETH STEARNS, born 11 Jan 1880, Boston; died 25 Nov 1888 in Barre, Worcester, Massachusetts of scrofula due to heart failure.

289. **EDWIN AUGUSTUS**[7] **WYETH** (Jonas[6] 2[d], Major Jonas[5], Jonas[4] Sr., Ebenezer[3] Sr., John[2], Nicholas[1]) was born on 21 Nov 1840 in Philadelphia, Pennsylvania. Edwin married **ELIZABETH JANE TILTON**, the widow of Charles Erving Davis, on 25 May 1870 in Boston, Suffolk, Massachusetts. Elizabeth, daughter of Stephen Tilton and Harriet N. Rundlett, was born 14 Oct 1833 (tombstone says in error 1843) in Tilton, Belknap, New Hampshire. She

died on 10 Jan 1908 in Brookline, Norfolk, Massachusetts. He died on 05 Mar 1917 in Boston. They are buried in Mt. Auburn.

Edwin Augustus Wyeth and Elizabeth Jane Tilton had the following child:

> i. HELEN SHERWOOD[8] WYETH (adopted), born 11 Feb 1871, Rochester, Monroe, New York; died 26 Feb 1943; Brookline.

290. **WASHINGTON[7] HADLEY** (Mary Kemble Thomas[6] Wyeth, Captain Noah[5], Noah[4] Sr., Ebenezer[3] Sr., John[2], Nicholas[1]) was born on 18 Jul 1829 in New York City, New York.[1349] Washington married (1) **MARY ELIZABETH DAVIS** there on 08 Jun 1854. Mary was born on 10 Jun 1831 in Preston, New London, Connecticut to Henry Davis and Mary Pollard. She died 20 Jun 1863 in New York City. Washington married (2) **ANNE WOOD** in 1865. Anne was born in 1842 in New Jersey to Alexander Wood and Mary Braddock. Anne died 01 Sep 1912 in New York City. Washington died there on 11 Jun 1913. Washington, with his parents, wives and youngest son, John A. Hadley, are all buried in the Green-Wood Cemetery Catacombs, Brooklyn, New York.

Washington Hadley and Mary Elizabeth Davis had the following child:

> i. HARRY D.[8] HADLEY, born 31 Jul 1857, New York City; death unknown.

Washington Hadley and Anne Wood had one child:

> i. JOHN A. HADLEY, born circa 1865, New York City; died there, 01 Mar 1890.

291. **EMILY LOUISE[7] HADLEY** (Mary Kemble Thomas[6] Wyeth, Captain Noah[5], Noah[4] Sr., Ebenezer[3] Sr., John[2], Nicholas[1]) was born on 01 Oct 1832 in New York City, New York. She married **CHARLES H. WHITFIELD** there on 02 Jun 1854. Charles, son of George Whitfield and Barbara Buckmaster, was born about 1830 in New York City. Charles died at the family's summer home in Belmar, Monmouth, New Jersey on 17 Jun 1898.[1350] Emily died on 24 Sep 1913 at her home at 27 W. 84th in Manhattan, New York City.[1351]

The children of Charles H. Whitfield and Emily Louise Hadley include: [1352]

> i. CHARLES H.[8] WHITFIELD JR. was born 10 May 1858, Manhattan, New York City, New York;[1353] death unknown.
> ii. ALFRED L. WHITFIELD, born 15 Sep 1861, Manhattan; died there, 21 Jan 1919.
> iii. GEORGE BUCKMASTER WHITFIELD, born 25 Mar 1869, Manhattan; married MARIE EMMA BOOTH, 14 Jan 1902, Philadelphia, Pennsylvania; died 21 Aug 1921, St. Petersburg, Pinellas, Florida.[1354]

292. **HENRY CLAY[7] HADLEY** (Mary Kemble Thomas[6] Wyeth, Captain Noah[5], Noah[4] Sr., Ebenezer[3] Sr., John[2], Nicholas[1]) was born on 02 Aug 1840 in Manhattan, New York City, New York.[1355] Henry and **FRANCES "FANNIE" ELTON** were married on 06 Jun 1866 in Madison Square Church, New York City. Fannie, daughter of Robert Henry Elton and Hannah Perkins, was born on 22 Sep 1843 in Manhattan. He died on 03 May 1905 in Brooklyn, Kings, New York.[1356] She died on 24 Jul 1920 at her daughter Belle's home in Brooklyn.[1357] Henry and Fannie are buried there in the Green-Wood Cemetery Catacombs.

Henry Clay Hadley and Frances "Fannie" Elton had the following children: [1358]

       i.   ADELE W.[8] HADLEY, born 09 Aug 1867, Manhattan; died there, 24 May 1874.

553.   ii. HENRY CLARENCE HADLEY, born 18 Aug 1871, Manhattan; married ANNA HAAKE, 07 Oct 1899; death unknown.

554.   iii. ISABEL ALLENDORF "BELLE" HADLEY, born 15 Mar 1876, Manhattan; married JOHN ALBERT DERTHICK, 24 Nov 1896, Brooklyn; her only child, John Albert Derthick Jr., a soldier, died 22 Oct 1918 in WWI, Rouen, France; she died 10 Apr 1966, Brooklyn.

293. **CHARLES LEIGH**[7] **HADLEY** (Mary Kemble Thomas[6] Wyeth, Captain Noah[5], Noah[4] Sr., Ebenezer[3] Sr., John[2], Nicholas[1]) was born on 29 Nov 1842 in Manhattan, New York City, New York. During the Civil War, he served in Co. B of the 7th New York Regiment. Charles married **SARAH ANN MARTIN** on 09 Dec 1871 in the Calvary Church, New York City. Sarah, daughter of William Augustus Martin and Sarah Bogart Greenwood, was born on 28 Dec 1848 in Manhattan. She died there on 01 Jul 1915. He died in Manhattan on 18 Nov 1918. [1359]

Charles Leigh Hadley and Sarah Ann Martin had the following children:

       i.   EDITH MAY[8] HADLEY, born 02 May 1873, Manhattan; died there, 02 Dec 1953.

555.   ii. MARY KEMBLE HADLEY, born 05 Jan 1877, Manhattan; married JOHN CRANNELL MINOR JR. there, 02 Jun 1903, died 18 Nov 1952, New Canaan, Fairfield, Connecticut.

294. **ELIZABETH ANNA GERTRUDE**[7] **TIEMANN** (Mary Frothingham[6] Newell, Elizabeth[5] Wyeth, Noah[4] Sr., Ebenezer[3] Sr., John[2], Nicholas[1]) was born on 14 Sep 1808 in Manhattan, New York City, New York. Elizabeth married **ALBERT HORN** there on 27 Dec 1825. Albert, the son of Joseph Horn and Abigail Wilson, was born on 06 May 1799 in Manhattan. Albert, a sash and blind factory owner, died 30 Apr 1886, Manhattan. Elizabeth died on 28 Aug 1897 in Mt. Vernon, Westchester, New York. [1360]

The children of Albert Horn and Elizabeth Anna Gertrude Tiemann included:

556.   i. ALBERT[8] HORN JR., born 31 Jul 1832, Manhattan; married MARTHA SCHOLEY CROWTHER there, 22 Aug 1855; died 26 Dec 1919, Bath, Steuben, New York.

557.   ii. DANIEL TIEMANN HORN, born 18 Mar 1839, Manhattan; married FRANCES OLIVIA CAPRON, 25 Sep 1866, Morristown, New Jersey; died 15 Dec 1883, Plainfield, Union, New Jersey.

558.   iii. JOSEPHINE MARTINDALE HORN, born 18 Mar 1841, Manhattan; married GEORGE BRINTON BURNETT there, 07 Nov 1860; died 28 Jun 1892, Manhattan.

295. **JULIA**[7] **TIEMANN** (Mary Frothingham[6] Newell, Elizabeth[5] Wyeth, Noah[4] Sr., Ebenezer[3] Sr., John[2], Nicholas[1]) was born on 03 Mar 1811 in Manhattan, New York City, New York. Julia married **JOHN STEPHENSON** there on 09 Jan 1833. John, the son of James Stephenson and Grace Stuart, was born on 04 Jul 1809 in Armagh, Ireland. Julia died on 27 Feb 1891 in Clifford, New Rochelle, Westchester, New York. John died there on 31 Jul 1893. They are both buried in Beechwood Cemetery in New Rochelle. [1361]

The children of John Stephenson and Julia Ann Tiemann included:

559.   i. STUART AUGUSTUS[8] STEPHENSON SR., born 28 Jan 1851, Manhattan; married CLAUDINE WELLING, 19 Mar 1873, New Rochelle, Westchester, New York; died 14 Oct 1925, Bethel, Fairfield, Connecticut.

296. **JULIUS WILLIAM**[7] **TIEMANN** (Mary Frothingham[6] Newell, Elizabeth[5] Wyeth, Noah[4] Sr., Ebenezer[3] Sr., John[2], Nicholas[1]) was born on 15 Aug 1817 in Manhattan, New York City, New York.[1362] Julius, a paint and color maker, married (1) **JANE WAUGH STEPHENSON** there on 27 Aug 1838. Jane, the daughter of James Stephenson and Grace Stuart, was born on 05 Sep 1815 in Manhattan. She died there on 31 Oct 1853. Julius married (2) **MARIE ANTOINETTE MEGIE** on 28 Mar 1860 in Boonton, Morris, New Jersey. Marie was born on 01 Aug 1841 in Succasunna, Morris, New Jersey to Daniel Elston Megie and Margaret Livingston Miller. She died on 10 Jun 1902 in Manhattan. He died there on 14 Feb 1903.

The children of Julius William Tiemann and Jane Waugh Stephenson included:

     i. JULIUS HENRY "HARRY"[8] TIEMANN, born 19 Sep 1840, Manhattan; 1862-1863, served the 159th New York Infantry; married MARGARET AUGUSTA MEGIE (his step-mother's sister), 19 Oct 1867, Boonton; died 08 Jun 1906, Brooklyn.

560.   ii. WILLIAM FRANCIS "FRANK" TIEMANN, born 29 Mar 1844, Manhattan; 05 Sep 1862, enlisted 159th New York Infantry, wounded in 1863, captured 19 Sep 1864 in Opequon, confined to Libby Prison until exchanged Feb 1865, assistant provost marshal, 21 May 1865, Augusta, Georgia;[1363] married (1) CATHERINE MALCOLM BALL, 07 Nov 1867, Brooklyn; married there (2) FRANCES THROCKMORTON, 27 Apr 1886; died 02 May 1926, East Orange, New Jersey.

The children of Julius William Tiemann and Marie Antoinette Megie included:

     i. JOHN ELSTON[8] TIEMANN, born 24 Jun 1861, Manhattan; he was not quite two months old when he died there on 19 Aug 1861 at 93 W. 43rd St.
     ii. HERMANN NEWELL TIEMANN SR., born 02 Feb 1863, Manhattan; married BELLE LOUISE MINOR, 22 Jun 1892, Watertown, New London, Connecticut; died 20 Feb 1957 Wallingford, New Haven, Connecticut.

297. **EMELINE FRANCES**[7] **WYETH** (Noah L.[6], Captain Job[5], Noah[4] Sr., Ebenezer[3] Sr., John[2], Nicholas[1]) was born 13 Sep 1838 in Nashua, Hillsborough, New Hampshire. Emeline married (1) **ALPHONSE D. TITUS** on 24 Oct 1860 in Boston. Alphonse, son of Lenox Titus and Achsah Dimmick, was born 14 Dec 1836 in Wolcott, Lamoille, Vermont. He died on 21 Jan 1863 in the regimental hospital at Potomac Creek, Virginia, of a brain concussion he had suffered while serving in Co. B of the 1st Mass. Cavalry. After the Civil War, Emeline married (2) **OTIS HARRINGTON BOWLER** on 24 Jul 1867 in Charlestown, Suffolk, Massachusetts. Otis, son of Nathan Bowler and Eliza Carr, was born in 1837 in Palermo, Waldo, Maine. Otis died on 21 Oct 1874 in Newton, Middlesex, Massachusetts. Emeline died on 22 Nov 1900 in Pasadena, California. Her ashes rest in Cambridge Cemetery with her husbands', daughter's, and parents', behind a memorial for her brothers, Richard and William, who were killed in the Civil War.

Alphonse D. Titus and Emeline Frances Wyeth had the following child:

      i.   LUCY ELIZABETH^8 TITUS, born 28 Jul 1861, Boston; died unmarried on 22 Jan 1888, Newton, Middlesex, Massachusetts.[1364]

298. **MARY ELIZABETH^7 WYETH** (Noah L.^{6}, Captain Job^5, Noah^4 Sr., Ebenezer^3 Sr., John^2, Nicholas^1) was born on 11 Mar 1842 in Nashua, Hillsborough, New Hampshire. At her father's death in 1866, Mary dutifully assumed the care of her siblings who were then 19, 16, and 11. She was a school teacher and in 1876, she was paid $700 for the year. Interestingly, only one woman on the list of teachers in the *Cambridge Chronicle* was paid $1,000, whereas no man was paid less than $2500. [1365] Mary married **WILLIAM A. CARPENTER III** on 26 Dec 1877 in Somerville, Middlesex, Massachusetts. William, son of William A. Carpenter Jr. and Sophronia Seaver, was born on 20 Oct 1820 in Chelsea, Orange, Vermont. He died on 04 Aug 1900 in Boston. She died on 19 Mar 1929 in Potsdam, St. Lawrence, New York. Together with Grace and Lucius, they are buried on Fountain Avenue in Mt. Auburn Cemetery, lot 3684, Cambridge.

William A. Carpenter III and Mary Elizabeth Wyeth had the following child:

561.   i.   GRACE ROSS^8 CARPENTER, born 13 May 1880, Boston; married her 5th cousin, LUCIUS KIMBALL RUSSELL, in Arlington, Middlesex, Massachusetts on 26 Apr 1905; died on 17 Jul 1980, at age 100, in Arcadia, Los Angeles, California.

299. **LYDIA FRANCES^7 WYETH** (Benjamin Francis^6, Captain Job^5, Noah^4 Sr., Ebenezer^3 Sr., John^2, Nicholas^1) was born on 13 Jan 1837 in Cambridge, Middlesex, Massachusetts. Lydia married **LEVI H. WEST** there on 08 Feb 1865. [1366] Levi, son of Samuel West and Rebecca Whitney, was born on 22 Jul 1820 in Lisbon, Androscoggin, Maine. Levi, a master mechanic, died on 11 Jan 1890 in Cambridge. Lydia died there on 20 Apr 1920.

Levi H. West and Lydia Frances Wyeth had the following child:

      i.   EMMA FRANCES^8 WEST, born 02 Feb 1871, Cambridge; a teacher, Emma died there unmarried on 17 Jul 1941; buried in Mt. Auburn Cemetery.

300. **JOHN BOUND^7 WYETH** (Benjamin Francis^6, Captain Job^5, Noah^4 Sr., Ebenezer^3 Sr., John^2, Nicholas^1) was born in Cambridge, Middlesex, Massachusetts on 18 Feb 1842. During the Civil War, he enlisted as a 90-day man on 16 May 1864 in the 12th Unattached Co. of the Massachusetts Infantry. In Philadelphia, Pennsylvania, on 06 Jan 1881, John Bound Wyeth married **EMMA REBECCA EINWECHTER**. Emma, was born in May 1850 in Philadelphia to Henry Einwechter and Elizabeth Lycett Rees. John was a partner in the steel business with Emma's brother, Harry Einwechter. John died on 22 Jul 1926 in Haddon Heights, Camden, New Jersey. Emma died there on 17 Dec 1927.[1367]

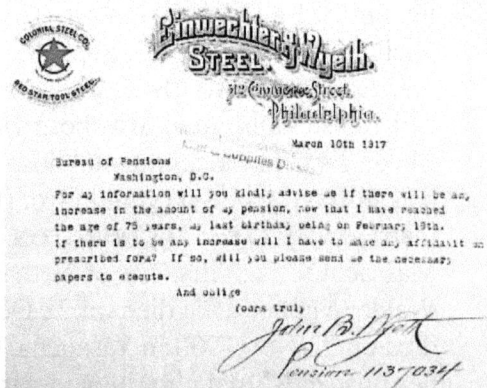

A letter in John Bound Wyeth's pension file from the National Archives, Washington, D.C.

John Bound Wyeth and Emma Rebecca Einwechter had the following children:

562.   i.   FRANK EINWECHTER⁸ WYETH, born 15 Sep 1882, Philadelphia; married (1) MAY ADELE MERRICK there, 14 Jun 1905; married (2) MABEL A. THAW, 1917, Philadelphia; died 22 Dec 1966, Drums, Luzerne, Pennsylvania.

563.   ii.   HELEN ELIZABETH WYETH, born 22 Feb 1885, Philadelphia;[1368] married JOSEPH OTIS PIERCE there, 07 Oct 1907.[1369] Helen, a musician, was struck by an auto and died, 14 Jan 1961, Philadelphia.

301. **ABIEL AUGUSTUS⁷ WYETH** (Benjamin Francis⁶, Captain Job⁵, Noah⁴ Sr., Ebenezer³ Sr., John², Nicholas¹) was born on 21 Nov 1843 in Cambridge, Middlesex, Massachusetts. From 28 Jul 1862 to 25 May 1864, he served in Co. F of the 1ˢᵗ Mass. Infantry Regiment. He was a clerk in Cambridge at his enlistment. On 06 Apr 1865, in Boston, Abiel re-enlisted in the military with the 62ⁿᵈ Mass. Infantry. He was promoted to corporal shortly before mustering out on 05 May 1865.[1370] Abiel married **ALICE SNOW HODGES** on 13 Sep 1876 in Chelsea, Suffolk, Massachusetts. Alice, daughter of William Grey Hodges and Lydia Presbrey, was born on 31 May 1854 in Taunton, Bristol, Massachusetts. Abiel died on 18 Oct 1895. His funeral was held at his home at 51 Ellery St. in Cambridge.[1371] Alice married Edward White and died in Cambridge on 26 Mar 1948.

Abiel Augustus Wyeth and Alice Snow Hodges had the following children:

564.   i.   GRACE EMELINE⁸ WYETH, born 12 Jul 1877, Cambridge; married Dr. ALBERT PERLEY NORRIS there, 12 Jan 1911; died 02 Jan 1971, Cambridge.

         ii.   NORMAN AUGUSTUS WYETH, born 22 Sep 1880, Cambridge; billed as the boy soprano, Norman performed for many Boston audiences in 1896;[1372] enlisted in the U.S. Army, 10 Nov 1901, fought in the Philippine-American War, discharged 28 Oct 1904, Angel Island, California; re-enlisted 28 Nov 1904, Presidio of San Francisco Military Base; had some legal troubles;[1373] moved to Florida for his health; while working there for the East Coast Line Canal, he was bitten by a rattlesnake near Delray on 18 Aug 1911. Sadly, the news reported, "…the deadly poison had too much time to do its work and he passed away at 9:30 that night. Mr. Wyeth was about 30 or 32 years of age, and a man of good birth and breeding. The courage with which he bore his suffering was nothing short of phenomenal. His main regret seemed to be that his mother could not be with him. The body will be sent back to his home in Cambridge for burial."[1374]

302. **BENJAMIN FRANKLIN⁷ WYETH SR.** (Benjamin Francis⁶, Captain Job⁵, Noah⁴ Sr., Ebenezer³ Sr., John², Nicholas¹) was born on 27 Dec 1845 in Cambridge, Middlesex, Massachusetts. He mustered in as a 90-day man in the 12ᵗʰ Mass. Infantry at Readville. His service during the Civil War was at Long's Point on the tip of Cape Cod until 15 Aug 1864.[1375] Benjamin married **CAROLINE ELIZABETH BIRD** on 12 Oct 1876 in Watertown, Middlesex, Massachusetts. Caroline, daughter of Joseph Bird and Ann Elizabeth Warland, was born there on 13 Mar 1850. From his father's business, in 1890, Benjamin formed the Wyeth Brothers

Benjamin F. Wyeth from
Samuel Atkins Eliot's
1913 *History of
Cambridge, Mass.*, p. 265.

Funeral Service with his brother, Henry Alonzo Wyeth. Benjamin also took over his father's duties as sexton of the First Church Congregational in Harvard Square.[1376] He died on 07 Aug 1909 in Cambridge. Caroline died there on 04 Oct 1926.

Benjamin Franklin Wyeth Sr. and Caroline Elizabeth Bird had the following children:[1377]

Henry Dunton Wyeth - photo from the HUP Collection, courtesy Harvard University Archives.

     i. MARION BIRD[8] WYETH, born 16 Aug 1877, Cambridge; died there unmarried on 20 Apr 1949.

565. ii. HERBERT FRANCIS WYETH, born 27 Jun 1878, Cambridge; married ETHEL LORIMER SQUIRE there, 07 Dec 1902; died 11 Jun 1917, Cambridge.

566. iii. BENJAMIN FRANKLIN "FRANK" WYETH JR., born on 25 Nov 1879, Cambridge; married EFFIE HARPER CURRIE, 27 Oct 1910, Milwaukee, Wisconsin;[1378] died 22 May 1968, Lexington, Middlesex, Massachusetts.

     iv. HENRY DUNTON WYETH was born 22 Jul 1881 in Cambridge; graduated Harvard, 1909; a classically trained pianist; during World War I, he served as a private in Co. B of the Harvard unit of the Students' Army Training Corps (SATC); Henry managed the Wyeth Funeral Service until age 84 in Cambridge; he died there unmarried on 17 Oct 1975 at age 94.[1379]

303. **AMELIA ANNIE**[7] **WYETH** (Andrew Newell[6], Captain Job[5], Noah[4] Sr., Ebenezer[3] Sr., John[2], Nicholas[1]) was born on 04 Jan 1846 in the oldest dwelling now standing in Cambridge, the Cooper-Austin House at 21 Linnaean St. Amelia married **JOHN BARKER** in Cambridge on 08 Apr 1869. John, son of Joseph Downe Barker and Mary Catherine Benner, was born on 15 Jul 1845 in West Cambridge (Arlington). Amelia died 06 Oct 1903 in Cambridge. John died there on 20 Jun 1932. They are buried near her parents in Cambridge Cemetery.[1380]

John Barker and Amelia Annie Wyeth had the following children:

567. i. JOHN HERBERT[8] BARKER, born 21 Jun 1870, Cambridge; married there (1) EMILY JOSEPHINE BURDAKIN, 18 Jun 1902; married (2) MIRA EMMA KNIGHT, 20 Nov 1926, Cambridge; an avid Wyeth family researcher, John's handwritten manuscripts on the Wyeth family are now housed in Boston's New England Historic Genealogical Society; John died 23 Feb 1951, Cambridge.[1381]

    ii. NEWELL ALVIN BARKER, born 13 Nov 1872, Cambridge; graduated Harvard College, 1895; instructor St. John's Military School, Salina, Kansas; died unmarried 18 Aug 1947, Cambridge.[1382]

    iii. HARRINGTON BARKER, born 08 Mar 1875, Cambridge; graduated M.I.T., 1898; supervisory examiner U.S. Patent Office; married EMMA LAURA BISHOP, 18

Nov 1914, Washington, D.C.; died there, 26 Dec 1942.[1383]

iv. ANNIE LOUISE BARKER, born 28 Jan 1881, Cambridge; died unmarried 05 Oct 1980 at age 99 in Manchester, Hartford, Connecticut.

304. **ANDREW NEWELL[7] WYETH JR.** (Andrew Newell[6], Captain Job[5], Noah[4] Sr., Ebenezer[3] Sr., John[2], Nicholas[1]) was born on 02 Feb 1853 in Cambridge, Middlesex, Massachusetts. Andrew married **HENRIETTE "HATTIE" ZIRNGIEBEL** on 21 Dec 1881 in Needham, Norfolk, Massachusetts. Hattie, daughter of Denys Zirngiebel and Henrietta Zeller, was born on Raymond Street in Cambridge on 25 Dec 1857.[1384] Andrew owned a wholesale grain company in Charlestown, Suffolk, Massachusetts. Hattie died on 11 Aug 1925 in Needham. Andrew died there on 29 Jul 1929.[1385] They are buried in Needham Cemetery.

Andrew Newell Wyeth Jr. and Henriette "Hattie" Zirngiebel had the following children:

568.   i. NEWELL CONVERS "N.C."[8] WYETH, born 22 Oct 1882, Needham; married CAROLYN BRENNEMAN "CAROL" BOCKIUS, 16 Apr 1906, First Unitarian Church, Wilmington, New Castle, Delaware; an extraordinarily talented artist, he is considered one of America's foremost illustrators. N.C. and his namesake grandson were killed when a train struck their automobile on 19 Oct 1945 in Chadds Ford, Delaware, Pennsylvania.[1386]

569.   ii. EDWIN RUDOLPH WYETH, born 05 Dec 1886, Needham; graduated Harvard College, 1907; an agricultural science teacher; he married CLARA LOUISE MOELLER, 25 Dec 1913, Needham; died 02 Aug 1960, Dighton, Bristol, Massachusetts.

The Wyeth family, 1902. Standing: Convers, Edwin, and Nat. Seated: Stimson, Hatti and Andrew. Credit: Wyeth Family Archives, Chadds Ford, PA.

570.   iii. NATHANIEL "NAT" WYETH, born 29 May 1888, Needham; marriages: (1) GLADYS ELLA POND there, 25 Dec 1909; (2) C. CHRISTINE ROY, 05 Jun 1948, New Mexico; (3) MARIA TIBERTI, 24 Dec 1948, Napoleon, Henry, Ohio; (4) C. CHRISTINE ROY in Santa Barbara, California on 20 Mar 1954; Nat, a design engineer for the Ford Motor Co., died on 27 Oct 1954 when the car he was testing collided with a road roller near Oldport, Monroe, Michigan.[1387]

571.   iv. STIMSON "BABE" WYETH, born 29 May 1891, Needham; graduated Harvard College, 1913; served in World War I; married CONSTANCE LOUISE TWIGG, 18 Jun 1923, Needham First Unitarian Church;[1388] a teacher of modern languages; he died 13 Jun 1970, Boston.

305. **MARY H.[7] WYETH** (Nahum Sargent[6], Jonathan[5], Noah[4] Sr., Ebenezer[3] Sr., John[2], Nicholas[1]) was born on 17 Oct 1846 in Boston, Suffolk, Massachusetts. She married **ELI A. LITHGOW** on 23 May 1877 in Boston. Eli, son of John Lithgow and Mary Arthur, was born on 04 Nov 1852 in South Hadley Falls, Hampshire, Massachusetts. She died on 29 Jan 1901 in New

Haven, Connecticut. Eli died there on 05 Mar 1917.

Eli A. Lithgow and Mary H. Wyeth had the following child:

       i. ARTHUR WALLACE[8] LITHGOW, born 25 Dec 1883, New Haven; married JULIA SULLIVAN, 25 May 1911, Boston; died 29 Jun 1934, New Haven.

306. **ELLA CAROLINE[7] WYETH** (Hollis Nye[6], Jonathan[5], Noah[4] Sr., Ebenezer[3] Sr., John[2], Nicholas[1]) was born on 13 Aug 1847 in Stoneham, Middlesex, Massachusetts. Because her mother died in 1848, Ella was raised by her aunt Nancy Stiles Chamberlin in Middlesex, Washington, Vermont. Ella married **JAMES DAVID EVANS** on 01 Jan 1864 in Moretown, Washington, Vermont. James, son of Osgood Evans and Mary Bailey, was born on 08 Jun 1843 in Moretown. Ella died on 05 Feb 1918 in Watertown, Middlesex, Massachusetts. James died there on 28 Jan 1926.

James David Evans and Ella Caroline Wyeth had the following children:

       i. MARY ELLA[8] EVANS, born 17 Mar 1869, Moretown; died unmarried 13 Sep 1956, Waltham, Middlesex, Massachusetts.[1389]

572.   ii. MINA GERTRUDE EVANS, born 12 Dec 1875, Watertown; married HOMER FRANKLIN HUNT there, 14 Sep 1898; died 19 May 1960, Brookline Hospital; funeral First Parish Unitarian, Watertown; burial Mt. Auburn, Cambridge.[1390]

307. **WILLIAM IRVING[7] BLISS** (Martha Ann[6] Wyeth, Jonathan[5], Noah[4] Sr., Ebenezer[3] Sr., John[2], Nicholas[1]) was born on 23 Jul 1859 in Nottingham, Rockingham, New Hampshire. William married **MAMIE FRANCES KIMBALL** on 04 Jan 1881 in Steubenville, Jefferson, Ohio. Mamie was born 11 Jan 1860 in Malden, Middlesex, Massachusetts to Lafayette Kimball and Mary Grover. William, a clerk for the Nickle Plate Railroad, died of bronchial pneumonia on 20 Jun 1923 in Cleveland, Cuyahoga, Ohio. Mamie died there in Cleveland Heights on 07 Aug 1934.[1391] Their ashes rest in lot 24 on Glade Ave. in Sleepy Hollow Cemetery, Concord, Massachusetts.

William Irving Bliss and Mamie Frances Kimball had the following child:

       i. HOWARD CRAIG[8] BLISS, born 10 Aug 1886, Cleveland; served in WWI, 27 Nov 1917 to 08 Aug 1919 and in WWII as a major, 24 Jan 1942 to 13 Nov 1945; he married DOROTHY GARLICK, they had one daughter, Mary E. Bliss; Howard, a payroll guard, died in Cleveland Clinic after an accidental shooting on 03 Jun 1955.[1392] His ashes rest near his parents in Sleepy Hollow Cemetery.

Authors' Ridge, where William and Howard's distant cousins, Nathaniel and Sophia Peabody Hawthorne, are buried, is on the hill directly behind the Bliss monuments. Howard's grave, with the flag by it, is next to his parents' marker. Henry Bliss and Martha Ann Wyeth's grave is front left. Martha Ann's mother, Lucy Stiles Wyeth, is buried front right. Her stone says she is the wife of Jonathan Wyeth.

308. **WILLIAM⁷ RUSSELL** (Jason⁶ III, Jason⁵ Jr., Elizabeth⁴ Winship, Elizabeth³ Wyeth, John², Nicholas¹) was born on 06 Sep 1796 in Madison, Somerset, Maine. William married **ACHSA KELLEY** in Jan 1820 in Brighton, Somerset, Maine. Achsa was born on 07 Jul 1804 in Mayfield, Somerset, Maine. William, a farmer and a church deacon, died on 13 May 1864 in Athens, Somerset, Maine. She died there on 01 Oct 1864. They are buried in Lord's Hill Cemetery in Athens.

The children of William Russell and Achsa Kelley included:

573.   i.   WARREN CHESTER⁸ RUSSELL, born 25 Jan 1841, Athens; married SARAH ANN ROBBINS, 08 Sep 1866, Gardner, Worcester, Massachusetts; died 22 Jun 1908, Petersham, Worcester, Massachusetts.
          ii.   ELLEN ALZONIA RUSSELL, born Sep 1847, Athens; married HARRISON C. JUDKINS, 10 Mar 1863, Newport, Penobscot, Maine; died 04 Apr 1913, Augusta, Kennebec, Maine.

309. **RACHEL⁷ BLATCHFORD** (Anna⁶ Grover, Betty⁵ Gamage, Nathaniel⁴, Deborah³ Wyeth, William², Nicholas¹) was born in 1786 in the Sandy Bay area of Gloucester (Rockport), Essex, Massachusetts. Rachel married **FRANCIS HILTON** there on 17 Dec 1805. Francis, son of Francis Hilton Sr. and Sarah Allen, was baptized 17 Jul 1774 in Gloucester. He died in 1812 in Sandy Bay. At last report, in 1865, Rachel was living with her daughter in Cambridge, Middlesex, Massachusetts. [1393]

The children of Francis Hilton and Rachel Blatchford include:

          i.   FRANCIS⁸ HILTON III, born 1806, Gloucester; marriages there (1) MARY PEW, 07 Oct 1827; (2) SARAH TAPPAN, 18 Jun 1861; died 05 May 1891; Gloucester.
574.   ii.   SARAH ANN HILTON, born 12 Apr 1808, Gloucester; marriages (1) DAVID MELLEN JR., 20 Aug 1826, Boston; (2) JAMES MELLEN, 10 Sep 1837, Charlestown, Suffolk, Massachusetts; died 12 Feb 1908, just 60 days shy of age 100, in San Antonio, Bexar, Texas. [1394]

310. **NEHEMIAH⁷ GROVER IV** (Nehemiah⁶ III, Betty⁵ Gamage, Nathaniel⁴, Deborah³ Wyeth, William², Nicholas¹) was born in 1799 in the Sandy Bay area of Gloucester (Rockport), Essex, Massachusetts. Nehemiah married **ELECTA WHITLOCK** on 26 Sep 1818 in Cheshire Township, Gallia, Ohio. Electa, daughter of Benjamin Whitlock and Abiah Higley, was born circa 1801 in Danbury, Fairfield, Connecticut. Nehemiah died on 10 Oct 1862 in Springfield Township, Gallia, Ohio. Electa died in Morgan Township, Gallia, Ohio in Jan 1863.

The children of Nehemiah Grover IV and Electa Whitlock included:

575.   i.   NEHEMIAH⁸ GROVER V, born 04 May 1819, Morgan Township; marriages there (1) SARAH "SALLY" HILL, 12 Feb 1837; (2) AMARYLLIS EAGLE WALLACE, widow of John Potter, 24 Mar 1871; died 10 Oct 1889, Morgan Township.
576.   ii.   JOHN PERRY GROVER, born 05 Dec 1821, Morgan; married CATHERINE DENNEY there, 09 Jul 1846; died 06 Dec 1902, Porter, Gallia, Ohio. [1395]

577. iii. AURILIA ANN GROVER, born 18 May 1823, Morgan; married JOHN SEARLS there, 26 May 1842; died 16 Feb 1877, Cheshire Township.

311. **JOHN**[7] **GROVER** (Nehemiah[6] III, Betty[5] Gamage, Nathaniel[4], Deborah[3] Wyeth, William[2], Nicholas[1]) was born on 25 Dec 1800 in the Sandy Bay area of Gloucester (Rockport), Essex, Massachusetts. John married (1) **MARY BRYANT** on 02 Nov 1824 in Gloucester. Mary was born in Ireland on 26 Sep 1800. She died shortly after the birth of her fourth child, on 05 Oct 1832. John married (2) **JANE CUTLER** on 15 Jun 1837 in Darke County, Ohio. Jane, daughter of Abner Cutler and Mary Woten, was born on 15 Apr 1820 in Gallia County, Ohio. John died on 06 Oct 1863 in Wabash County, Indiana. Jane died in Goshen, Elkhart, Indiana on 30 Jan 1896.

The children of John Grover and Mary Bryant included:

  i. JOHN BRYANT[8] GROVER, born 17 Jun 1825, Gloucester; served in the Civil War in Co. D, 141st Ohio Infantry; married in Gallia County, (1) ELEANOR SWISHER, 10 Oct 1852, (2) ELIZA RUSK, widow of Abe Danner, 19 Dec 1871; John died of dropsy on 04 Feb 1897, Cheshire Township, Gallia, Ohio.[1396]
  ii. MARY BRYANT GROVER, born 22 Sep 1832, Gloucester; married ELIAS ROBY, 24 Apr 1851, Wabash County; died 26 Jan 1914, Treaty, Wabash, Indiana.

The children of John Grover and Jane Cutler included:

  i. LUCY JANE GROVER, born 09 Sep 1852, Wabash County; married JOSEPH W. WIGNER there, 26 Aug 1868; died on 02 Dec 1929, Wabash.
  ii. (DR.) ANNA MARTHA GROVER, born 28 Sep 1858, La Fontaine, Wabash, Indiana; married (1) ALBERT EVANS KAUFFMAN there, 12 Mar 1876; married (2) GEORGE WASHINGTON HATTLE, 21 May 1902, Goshen; married (3) WILLIAM HENRY KREAGER there, 30 Jul 1910; all three marriages ended in divorce; she had one child, Blanche Kaufman; Anna, a physician and surgeon, offered her services in World War I, she died 08 Dec 1940, Goshen.

312. **EBENEZER ROWE**[7] **GROVER** (Nehemiah[6] III, Betty[5] Gamage, Nathaniel[4], Deborah[3] Wyeth, William[2], Nicholas[1]) was born 14 May 1801 in the Sandy Bay area of Gloucester (Rockport), Essex, Massachusetts. Ebenezer, a teacher, married **NANCY SCOTT** in 1836 probably in Darke County, Ohio. Nancy was born on 22 Jun 1818 in Jackson County, Ohio and died circa 1855. Ebenezer died 18 Jul 1874 in Cheshire Township, Gallia, Ohio.

The children of Ebenezer Rowe Grover and Nancy Scott included:

578. i. JAMES ADDISON[8] GROVER, born 20 Dec 1837, Darke County, Ohio;[1397] married (1) FRANCES HANNAH GROVER, 17 Mar 1859, Meigs County, Ohio; served in the 141st Ohio Infantry during the Civil War; married (2) REBECCA GRISSOM, widow of John Day, 02 Sep 1866, Hamilton County, Indiana; married (3) AMANDA CHURCHILL, widow of Reuben Jeffrey, 01 Oct 1908, Huntington County, Indiana; died 09 Jan 1915, Indiana State Soldiers' Home, Lafayette, Tippecanoe, Indiana.

579.   iii. FRANCIS MARION GROVER, born 13 Jan 1840, Recovery Township, Mercer, Ohio; married JULIA HIGLEY, 09 Sep 1880, Gallia County; died 11 Nov 1934, Orlando, Orange, Florida.

    ii. JOHN FRANKLIN GROVER, born 19 Jun 1846, Recovery Township; served in the 91st Ohio infantry during the Civil War; married EMMA HOOVER, 01 Mar 1883, Westchester, Porter, Indiana; died on 12 Jan 1926, Austin, Mecosta, Michigan.

    iv. CATHERINE ESTHER GROVER, born 17 Dec 1849, Recovery Township; married DAVID H. KENT, 12 Feb 1869, Gallia County, Ohio; died there, 09 Feb 1924.

313. **MARY ESTHER⁷ GROVER** (Nehemiah⁶ III, Betty⁵ Gamage, Nathaniel⁴, Deborah³ Wyeth, William², Nicholas¹) was born about 1805 in the Sandy Bay area of Gloucester (Rockport), Essex, Massachusetts. She married (1) **ELISHA KENT** on 23 Oct 1828 in Gallia County, Ohio. Elisha, son of Samuel Kent and Mary Noble, was born on 05 Sep 1793 in Rupert, Bennington, Vermont. He died on 08 Jan 1833 in Salem Township, Meigs, Ohio. Esther married (2) **GEORGE ROBERT SMITH** on 03 Nov 1833 in Salem Township. George, son of Robert and Ann Smith, was born on 13 Sep 1792 in London, England and baptized there on 28 Jun 1795 at St. Leonard, Shoreditch.[1398] George arrived in America on 19 Oct 1829 with his step-daughter Elizabeth Catherine Weeks, who later married Esther's brother William Hoskins Grover, and his daughter Caroline Smith, who married Matilda Denney's brother Henry Denney. Esther died in childbirth on 01 Apr 1842 in Salem Township. George, a farmer and a teacher, last appeared in the census of 15 Jun 1860 when he lived near Ebenezer Rowe Grover in Cheshire Township, Gallia, Ohio. His obituary of 01 Mar 1861 says he died there. It calls him, "… a kind and indulgent father, a warm and sincere friend, loved and respected by all who knew him. From his youth up, he always tried to promote the good of others more than himself…"[1399]

St. Leonard's was Shakespeare's home church in London. On the day we visited, the altar was being set to stage Richard III.

Elisha Kent and Mary Esther Grover had the following children:

580.   i. HENRY ALLEN⁸ KENT, born 20 Dec 1829, Meigs County; married (1) MARY MARGARET MISNER, 13 Dec 1849, Athens County, Ohio; married (2) MATILDA DENNEY, 05 Oct 1854 Gallia; a corporal in Co. B of the 91st Ohio Infantry, Henry lost his left arm in battle near Lynchburg, Virginia on 18 Jun 1864; unable to return to his lumberman occupation, he studied law and had an eminent career as a judge in Meigs County. Henry died there, 21 Apr 1900.

581.   ii. ELISHA KENT, born 09 Jul 1832, Meigs County; married ELIZABETH GRATE (William Grate Wyeth's aunt) there, 07 Aug 1856; served in Co. C of the 194th Ohio Infantry; died 07 Feb 1896, Huntington Township, Gallia, Ohio.

George Robert Smith and Mary Esther Grover had the following children: [1400]

    i. ALFRED⁸ SMITH (twin), born 27 Mar 1836, Meigs County; served the Union's 1st Virginia Cavalry which was organized in West Virginia before it became a state.[1401] [1402] Alfred died in the service after peace was declared in Apr 1865.

582.   ii. JAMES T. SMITH (twin), born 27 Mar 1836, Meigs County; marriages there (1) SARAH LOWE, 20 Nov 1856; (2) RACHEL HAWK, widow of John Ewing, 17

Sep 1891; served in Co. B of the 91st Ohio Infantry; died 13 Aug 1915, Huntington Township.

583. iii. ESTHER A. OLIVE SMITH, born 17 Jun 1838, Salem Township; married JAHU GRATE there, 18 Feb 1858; died 18 Apr 1929, Salem Township.

584. iv. SARAH JANE SMITH, born 13 Jan 1840, Salem Township; married JOHN SCOTT, 12 Apr 1857, Ewington, Gallia, Ohio; died 22 May 1916, Salem Township.

v. GEORGE ROBERT SMITH JR., born about 01 Apr 1842, Salem Township; died after 1867.

Sarah Jane Smith, John Scott and granddaughter Blanche Butcher Tullis.

314. **EPHRIAM R.**[7] **GROVER** (Nehemiah[6] III, Betty[5] Gamage, Nathaniel[4], Deborah[3] Wyeth, William[2], Nicholas[1]) was born Jun 1807, in the Sandy Bay area of Gloucester (Rockport), Essex, Massachusetts. Ephriam married three times and little is known about his wives. He married (1) **MARY CLARK** on 22 Nov 1832 in Gallia County, Ohio; married (2) **SUSANNAH BRADBURY** on 14 Nov 1841 in Meigs County, Ohio; and married (3) **AMELIA MCCOY** on 07 Oct 1858 in Gallia County. Ephriam died on 22 Jun 1872 in Cheshire Township, Gallia, Ohio.[1403]

Ephriam R. Grover and Mary Clark had the following child:

i. MARY ESTHER[8] GROVER, born 1834, Gallia County; married JOHN WILLIAM DAVIS there, 08 Sep 1853; death unknown.

Ephriam R. Grover and Susannah Bradbury had the following children:

585. i. VESTA[8] GROVER, born Jun 1845, Meigs County, Ohio; married (1) ANDERSON CAMPBELL BLAKE, 12 Apr 1868, Gallia County; married (2) ERASTUS D. HANNAN, there on 21 Oct 1877; died circa 1911.

586. ii. ELECTA ELIZABETH GROVER, born Jun 1848, Gallia County; married WILLIAM HENRY MCCOY, there on 05 Nov 1867; died 30 Nov 1900, Hannan District, Mason, West Virginia.

587. iii. EPHRAIM "EFRON" GROVER, born Jul 1851, Gallia County; married MALINDA CHANDLER, 11 Jul 1874, Mason County, West Virginia; died 20 Jun 1929, High Coal, Boone, West Virginia.

iv. JABEZ R. GROVER, born Mar 1852, Gallia County; a grocer, he died unmarried 23 Apr 1921 in Huntington, Cabell, West Virginia.

v. PERRY JEFFERSON GROVER, born 02 Jul 1853, Gallia County; married LYDIA JANNEY, 1876; died 28 Dec 1936, Glenwood, Mason, West Virginia.

vi. JAMES ADDISON GROVER, born 06 Jun 1856, Gallia County; married MARTHA ERRETT, 21 May 1882, Mason County; died 06 Sep 1920, Charleston, Kanawha, West Virginia.

The children of Ephriam R. Grover and Amelia McCoy included:

588. i. JOSEPHINE[8] GROVER, born 1861, Gallia County; last name was "Gwyn" in her daughter Blanche Grover's marriage record; death unknown.

315. **ELISHA**[7] **GROVER** (Nehemiah[6] III, Betty[5] Gamage, Nathaniel[4], Deborah[3] Wyeth, William[2], Nicholas[1]) was born circa 1817 in the Sandy Bay area of Gloucester (Rockport), Essex, Massachusetts. Elisha married **HARRIET J. PETTINGILL** on 26 Dec 1850 in Gallia County, Ohio. Harriet, daughter of Allen Pettingill and Mary Higgins, was born 17 Apr 1831 in North Yarmouth, Cumberland, Maine. Elisha died in Gallia County between 21 Jan 1864, the date of his will, and 30 Jan 1864, the date it was taken for probate in Gallipolis. His will, left Ohio property in Gallia and Mercer counties to his daughter, Harriet Thankful Grover, who remained with him, and proceeds to the two younger children who lived in Massachusetts with their mother and her new husband, Edmond Fitzgerald. Harriet died on 09 Apr 1921 in Newburyport, Essex, Massachusetts.

Elisha Grover and Harriet J. Pettingill had the following children:

> i. HARRIET THANKFUL[8] GROVER, born 07 Nov 1851, Kyger, Gallia, Ohio; died at age 23 of consumption, 07 Sep 1875, Rockport, Essex, Massachusetts.
> ii. MARY ELLEN GROVER, born circa Apr 1853, Kyger; died 26 Mar 1874, at age 20, of consumption in Somerville, Middlesex, Massachusetts.
> iii. FRANK ELISHA GROVER, born 25 Nov 1854, Kyger; married LIZZIE HOYT, 22 Nov 1879, Rochester, New Hampshire; died 16 Aug 1927, Newburyport.

316. **WILLIAM HOSKINS**[7] **GROVER** (Nehemiah[6] III, Betty[5] Gamage, Nathaniel[4], Deborah[3] Wyeth, William[2], Nicholas[1]) was born on 02 Apr 1818 in the Sandy Bay area of Gloucester (Rockport), Essex, Massachusetts.[1404] William married (1) **ELIZABETH CATHERINE WEEKS** on 16 Mar 1837 in Meigs County, Ohio. Elizabeth daughter of John Thomas Weeks and Elizabeth Brandon, was born on 20 Dec 1812 in London, England and baptized there on 03 Jun 1813 at St. Leonard, Shoreditch.[1405] Elizabeth arrived in the port of New York with her step-father, George Robert Smith, on 19 Oct 1829. Her mother died during the crossing. Elizabeth died 03 Jun 1867 in Kyger, Gallia, Ohio and was buried there on the Grover farm in Cheshire Township. Her gravestone is the only one remaining on the plateau of a steep precipice that was stripped for coal.[1406] William married (2) **SARAH WILLIAMS**, the widow of Charles Higley, on 23 Jan 1868, Rutland Township, Meigs, Ohio. Sarah, daughter of Perry Williams and Eliza Harrison, was born on 13 Sep 1833 in New Haven, Connecticut.[1407] William died 18 Jan 1892 in Kyger.[1408] Sarah, last recorded in Topeka, Kansas on 19 Apr 1910, was living with her daughter Julia Higley and son-in-law, Francis Marion Grover.

William and Elizabeth Weeks Grover's children were born in Cheshire Township:[1409]

> 589. i. JOHN ROBERT[8] GROVER, born 17 Feb 1838; married MARIAH RIGGS, 31 Dec 1860, Meigs County; served 1861-1865 in Co. C of the 18th West Virginia Regiment; died 28 Nov 1901, Cheshire Township.
> ii. WILLIAM BRANDON GROVER, born Jun 1841; served in the 192nd Ohio Infantry, Co. F; married ALVIRA CLARK, 29 Sep 1869, Gallia County; died there on 09 Apr 1915 in Cheshire.
> iii. MARY M. GROVER, born May 1844; married JOSEPH WARREN CLARK, 05 Jul 1872, Cheshire Township; death unknown.
> iv. ELIZABETH CATHERINE GROVER, born 26 Mar 1847; married JOHN PRICE, 12 Jan 1868, Cheshire Township; died there, 05 Jan 1915.

590.   v.   SOPHIA ESTHER GROVER, born 31 Jan 1851; married (1) ANDREW J. MCCANN
              M.D. there, 01 May 1872; married (2) DAVID BOOTH WELLS, 28 Mar 1887,
              Wilkesville, Vinton, Ohio; died 21 Mar 1913, Gallia County.
          vi.   THOMAS EDWARD WATTON GROVER M.D., born 11 Jul 1853, married
              MARGARET WILHELM, 11 Oct 1894, Huntington, Cabell, West Virginia; died
              there, 28 May 1933.

William Hoskins Grover and Sarah Williams had the following child:

          i.   ELIZA ESTHER⁸ GROVER, born 11 Dec 1872, Cheshire Township; died young.

317. SARAH "SALLY"⁷ GAMAGE (Joshua⁶ Jr., Joshua⁵, Nathaniel⁴, Deborah³ Wyeth, William²,
      Nicholas¹) was baptized 26 Jul 1791 in the Sandy Bay area of Gloucester (Rockport),
      Essex, Massachusetts. She married MOSES BEAUJEAN ROGERS on 03 Jan 1811 in Bristol,
      Lincoln, Maine. He was born there circa 1789 to Moses Rogers and Thankful Freeman.
      Moses Beaujean Rogers died on 02 Nov 1856 in the Marine Hospital, Portland, Maine
      and she died the next day over 100 miles away in Gloucester.

The children of Moses Beaujean Rogers and Sarah "Sally" Gamage included:

          i.   JOHN⁸ ROGERS, born 1824, Bristol; married JANE GRANT, Gloucester, 06 Jun
              1851; a fisherman, he died 18 Dec 1880, Gloucester.
          ii.   CHARLES HENRY ROGERS, born Jun 1830, Bristol; a fisherman, married LYDIA
              BEAN, 22 Jan 1853, Gloucester; served in the 30ᵗʰ Mass. Infantry, Co. B; died
              in Soldiers' home, 24 Jun 1915, Togus, Kennebec, Maine.
          iii.   NANCY ROGERS, born 1841, Bristol; married SIMON BRAY, 13 Nov 1855,
              Gloucester; died of consumption on 24 Jan 1860, Gloucester.

318. HANNAH⁷ GAMAGE (Joshua⁶ Jr., Joshua⁵, Nathaniel⁴, Deborah³ Wyeth, William²,
      Nicholas¹) was born on 17 Dec 1801 in Bristol, Lincoln, Maine. Hannah married
      GEORGE MCFARLAND there on 12 Oct 1818. George, born in Bristol on 02 Apr 1799 to
      John McFarland and Jemima Gamage, may also be descended from Nicholas Wyeth
      through Jemima. After John was lost at sea, Jemima married Ebenezer Cleveland Pool.
      Hannah Gamage and George McFarland had 11 children.[1410] Some were not named at
      birth. Hannah died on 28 May 1872 in Bristol. George died there on 16 Nov 1873.

The children of George McFarland and Hannah Gamage include the following:

          i.   DEBORAH⁸ MCFARLAND, born 1828, Bristol; died there in 1833.
          ii.   ALBERT MCFARLAND, born 1833, Bristol; died there in 1834.
          iii.   HATTIE MCFARLAND, born 15 Sep 1840, Bristol; married HARVEY OLIVER
              there, circa 1878; died 1889, Bristol.
          vi.   ADDISON MCFARLAND, born 06 Jun 1844, Bristol; died there, 11 Aug 1864.

319. MARTHA⁷ GAMAGE (Joshua⁶ Jr., Joshua⁵, Nathaniel⁴, Deborah³ Wyeth, William²,
      Nicholas¹) was born on 30 Apr 1803 in Bristol, Lincoln, Maine. Martha married THOMAS
      THOMPSON there on 17 Nov 1825. Thomas, son of Joshua Thompson and Martha
      Coombs, was born on 19 Apr 1802 in Bristol. She died there on 11 Jun 1862. Thomas

died on 15 Feb 1883 in Bristol.

Thomas Thompson and Martha Gamage had the following children:

        i.   CORDELIA^8 THOMPSON, born 01 Jul 1828, Bristol; married STEPHEN FARROW, 09 Dec 1855, Bristol; died there, 14 Aug 1908.

591.   ii. OREN B. THOMPSON, born 01 Jul 1832, Bristol; married PHEBE ANN FARROW there, 19 Mar 1856; served in the 31st Maine Regiment during the Civil War; died 09 Jul 1915, South Bristol, Lincoln, Maine.

      iii. EDNA A. THOMPSON, born 17 Aug 1844, Bristol; married SAMUEL E. DAVIS there, 03 Dec 1866; died 16 Dec 1921, Portland, Cumberland, Maine.

320. (GENERAL) HENRY JACKSON^7 HUNT (Samuel Wellington^6, Thomas^5, Ruth^4 Fessenden, Martha^3 Wyeth, William^2, Nicholas^1) was born on 14 Sep 1819 in a military outpost of present-day Detroit, Wayne, Michigan. He married (1) EMILY CAROLINE DERUSSY, daughter of Brigadier General Rene Edward DeRussy and Harriet Elizabeth Taylor, on 18 Dec 1851, Fort Monroe, Old Point Comfort, Hampton, Virginia. She was born on 19 Aug 1831 in Brooklyn, Kings, New York (near present day DeRussy Drive on Dyker Heights). Emily died on 12 May 1857 in Fort Monroe from complications of the birth of her son two years earlier.[1411] Henry married (2) MARY BETHUNE CRAIG on 27 Dec 1860 in Washington, D.C. Mary was born in Watertown, Middlesex, Massachusetts on 10 Dec 1836 to Henry Knox Craig and Maria Bethune Hunt. Henry and Mary are second cousins since John Hunt and Ruth Fessenden are the great grandparents of both of them. General Henry Jackson Hunt died on 11 Feb 1889 at the Soldiers' Home in Washington, D.C. Mary died on 23 Jan 1911 at her residence, 1815 M St. NW., Washington, D.C.

Henry Jackson Hunt and Emily Caroline DeRussy had the following children:

        i.   EMILY DERUSSY^8 HUNT, born 17 Oct 1852, Fort Monroe; died 10 Mar 1873, at the residence of her aunt Mrs. W. A. Nichols, Fort Leavenworth, Kansas.[1412]

592.   ii. (LT.) HENRY JACKSON "HARRY" HUNT, born 10 Apr 1855, Ft. Aruckle, Indian Territory, Oklahoma; married HENRIETTA MARGARET "BLOSSOM" DRUM, 25 Jun 1883, Washington, D.C.; died there, 05 May 1886 at the Soldiers' Home.

Henry Jackson Hunt and Mary Bethune Craig had the following children:

        i.   CONWAY BETHUNE^8 HUNT, born 30 Sep 1861, Washington, D.C.; died there, unmarried on 20 Dec 1947.

      ii. MARIA BETHUNE HUNT, born 06 Nov 1862, D.C.; died there,15 Sep 1938.

    iii. JULIA HERRICK HUNT, born 23 Mar 1867, Washington, D.C.; worked for Herbert Hoover in an economic relief effort, died unmarried 07 Jun 1954, D.C.

    iv. (DR.) PRESLEY CRAIG HUNT, born 04 Mar 1871, Ft. Adams, Newport, Rhode Island; 1891, medical degree, Georgetown University, noted psychiatrist; died unmarried 15 Dec 1910, John Hopkins Hospital, Baltimore, Maryland.[1413]

     v. (COLONEL) JOHN ELLIOTT HUNT, born 19 Jan 1874, Ft. Adams; 1894 graduate of the U.S. Military Academy; married ALICE WALKER NORVELL, 16 Oct 1902, D.C.; died 20 Dec 1951, Chevy Chase, Montgomery, Maryland.[1414]

vi. JANE BETHUNE HUNT, born 28 Jun 1875, Ft. Adams; died 23 Jan 1921, Washington, D.C.

Notes for (Brig. General) Henry Jackson Hunt:

As Chief of Artillery in the Army of the Potomac, Brigadier General Henry Jackson Hunt was considered by his contemporaries to be the greatest artillery tactician and strategist of the Civil War. Even today, he is featured prominently in Civil War sagas such as the "what if" history, *Gettysburg: A Novel of the Civil War* by Newt Gingrich and William R. Forstchen.

Henry Jackson Hunt, like his uncle, the second mayor of Detroit, was named for his grandfather Colonel Thomas Hunt's 1777 regimental commander, Colonel Henry Jackson. Sadly, like his father, (Lt.) Samuel Wellington Hunt, Henry was orphaned and separated from his siblings at a young age. He was raised by his uncle General John Elliott Hunt in Toledo, Maumee, Ohio. [1415]

Through his uncle John's brother-in-law, General Lewis Cass, then President Jackson's Secretary of War, Henry Jackson Hunt, was appointed to the United States Military Academy in West Point, New York. He graduated in 1839 as a brevet second lieutenant in the 2nd U.S. Artillery. While serving in the Mexican War, he was made brevet captain for gallantry at the Battle of Churubusco on 20 Aug 1847. He was wounded twice at Molino del Rey and then promoted to brevet major on 13 Sep 1847 during the Battle of Chapultepec in Mexico City. [1416]

Hunt immersed himself in the study of gunnery. With William H. French and William F. Barry, Hunt wrote the manual, *Instruction for Field Artillery*. It was published by the War Department in 1861 and quickly became the definitive source for Union artillerists during the Civil War.

General Henry Jackson Hunt portrait by Mathew Brady or Levin C. Handy is courtesy of the Library of Congress.

Hunt's first engagement in that war came during the First Battle of Bull Run on 21 Jul 1861. His actions in covering the Union retreat with a four-gun battery, led to his appointment as chief of artillery in the Northeast Virginia department responsible for defending Washington, D.C.

Hunt understood concentrated massed artillery barrage was necessary to repel assaults. Nevertheless, he urged his cannon crews to fire slowly and deliberately at an average of one shot per minute. He believed quicker firing impaired accuracy and depleted ammunition faster than could be replenished. He once reprimanded a gunner of a fast-firing cannon, "Young man, are you aware that every round you fire costs $2.67?" [1417]

His courage and tactics greatly added to the success of the Army at the battles of Malvern Hill, Antietam, Fredericksburg, and Gettysburg. When his expertise was not used to best advantage, it too affected the Army's success. Maj. Gen. Joseph Hooker angrily took Hunt's command from him in May 1863. The resulting lack of coordination of the artillery forces contributed greatly to the Union defeat in the Battle of Chancellorsville.

Maj. Gen. George G. Meade had greater respect for Hunt than Hooker and gave him enormous latitude at the Battle of Gettysburg. Hunt's handling of the artillery was prominent in the repulse of Pickett's Charge on 03 Jul 1863. Hunt directed his cannons to cease fire slowly to create the illusion they were being destroyed one by one. This method of cannon fire fooled the Confederates into thinking Hunt's batteries were destroyed. It triggered their disastrous assault. Also, Hunt's concealed placement of Lt. Col. Freeman McGilvery's batteries north of Little Round Top, contributed significantly to the Confederate infantry losing that hill.

Henry was breveted major general both in the volunteers and in the Regular Army. From 09 Jun 1864 to 25 Mar 1865, Henry managed the siege operations during the nine months of trench warfare led by U.S. Grant in the Richmond–Petersburg Campaign.

No doubt he worked with his cousin Colonel Lewis Cass Hunt of the Ohio 67th who commanded the Sixth Offensive of the Siege of Petersburg, Virginia on 31 Oct 1864.[1418] As mentioned before, Henry's cousin and his brother, Brigadier General Lewis Cass Hunt, had the same name.[1419]

When the U.S. Army was reorganized in 1866, Hunt became colonel of the 5th U.S. Artillery. From 20 May 1869 to 10 Nov 1875, he served as the commanding officer of Fort Adams in Newport, Rhode Island. He held various commands until 1883, when he retired to become governor of the Soldiers' Home.[1420] The home, today called the Armed Forces Retirement Home, is located at 140 Rock Creek Church Road NW, Washington, D.C. At Henry's death there, he was buried in the nearby Soldiers' Home National Cemetery. His wife Mary Bethune Craig and many of his children rest near him.

321. **MARY TYLER[7] PEABODY** (Elizabeth "Eliza"[6] Palmer, Elizabeth "Betsy"[5] Hunt, Ruth[4] Fessenden, Martha[3] Wyeth, William[2], Nicholas[1]) was born on 16 Nov 1806 in Cambridgeport (Cambridge), Middlesex, Massachusetts. Mary Tyler Peabody, a gifted teacher and writer, married the Whig politician and the "father of American Public Education," Horace Mann, on 01 May 1843 in Boston, Suffolk, Massachusetts. **HORACE MANN**, son of Thomas Mann and Rebecca Stanley, was born on 04 May 1796 in Franklin, Norfolk, Massachusetts. While serving in the U. S. House of Representatives, he was nominated for governor of Massachusetts by the Free Soil Party. On that same day, he was chosen president of the newly established Antioch College at Yellow Springs, Greene, Ohio. Defeated in the election, he accepted Antioch's offer.[1421] Horace died from typhoid fever at his Ohio post on 02 Aug 1859. Mary died on 11 Feb 1887 on Lamartine St., Jamaica Plain, Suffolk, Massachusetts.

Horace Mann and Mary Tyler Peabody had the following children:

Benjamin Pickman Mann and Mary Tyler Peabody, public domain photo.

   i. HORACE[8] MANN JR., born 25 Feb 1844, Boston; a botanist credited with discovering more than 100 species in his young life;[1422] died from consumption on 11 Nov 1868 at age 24 in Cambridge.

   ii. GEORGE COMBE MANN, born 27 Dec 1845, Boston; graduated Harvard, 1867; married ESTHER WINSHIP LOMBARD, 22 Aug 1877, Cambridge; died 28 Jan 1921, Richmond, Berkshire, Massachusetts.

   iii. BENJAMIN PICKMAN MANN, born 29 Apr 1848, West Newton, Middlesex, Massachusetts; graduated Harvard,

1870; married LOUISA VAN DE SANDE, 12 Jul 1878 in Cambridge; died on 22 Mar 1926 in Washington, D.C.

322. **SOPHIA AMELIA**[7] **PEABODY** (Elizabeth "Eliza"[6] Palmer, Elizabeth "Betsy"[5] Hunt, Ruth[4] Fessenden, Martha[3] Wyeth, William[2], Nicholas[1]) was born on 21 Sep 1809 in Salem, Essex, Massachusetts. Sophia (long i) married **NATHANIEL HAWTHORNE** on 09 Jul 1842 in Boston, Suffolk, Massachusetts. Nathaniel Hawthorne, son of Nathaniel Hathorne and Elizabeth Clarke Manning, was born on 04 Jul 1804 in Salem. Nathaniel, one of the greatest writers of the 19th century, died on 19 May 1864 in Plymouth, Grafton, New Hampshire. His books the *Scarlet Letter* and the *House of the Seven Gables* are American classics. Sophia, a gifted artist and illustrator, died 26 Feb 1871 in London, England. After more than a century, on 26 Jun 2006, Sophia and daughter Una's remains were moved from London's Kensal Green Cemetery and reinterred near Nathaniel's on Authors' Ridge in Sleepy Hollow Cemetery, 129 Bedford St., Concord.[1423]

Sophia Peabody and Nathaniel Hawthorne, public domain photos.

The children of Nathaniel Hawthorne and Sophia Amelia Peabody were:

  i.   UNA[8] HAWTHORNE, born 03 Mar 1844, Concord, Middlesex, Massachusetts; died unmarried 10 Sep 1877; Clewer, Windsor, Berkshire, England.[1424]

  ii. JULIAN HAWTHORNE, born 22 Jun 1846, Boston; married (1) MARY ALBERTINA "MINNIE" AMELUNG, 15 Nov 1870; New York City; married (2) EDITH HELENE GARRIGUES, 06 Jul 1925, San Diego, California; earned his living as a journalist and writer; unwittingly became involved in a mail fraud scheme and served a term in the Atlanta Federal Penitentiary; died 14 Jul 1934 at age 88 in San Francisco, California; survived by seven of nine children.[1425]

593.   iii. ROSE HAWTHORNE, born 20 May 1851, Lenox, Berkshire, Massachusetts. Her father compared her to a book when he wrote to a friend: "Mrs. Hawthorne published a little work, two months ago, which still lies in sheets; but, I assure you, it makes some noise in the world, both by day and night."[1426] Rose married GEORGE PARSONS LATHROP, 11 Sep 1871, Saint Luke's Church, Chelsea, London, England. At age 45, after the death of her five-year-old son, Francis Hawthorne Lathrop, Rose trained as a nurse. Then after her husband's death, she became a Catholic sister. As Mother Mary Alphonsa, she founded the Dominican Sisters of Hawthorne. The order was Servants of Relief for Incurable Cancer. Mother Mary died on 09 Jul 1926 in Hawthorne, Westchester, New York. She is now being considered for sainthood by the Roman Catholic Church for her work in caring for impoverished cancer patients.[1427]

Sophia Peabody and Nathaniel Hawthorne's home, The Wayside, 455 Lexington Rd., Concord, Massachusetts.

424

APPENDIX 1: MORE ACKNOWLEDGMENTS

Over 40 years after Marion Sims Wyeth Sr. sent Jeff the information that is the basis of this book, we continue to receive resource materials from family members all over the United States and Canada. This appendix has been created in an effort to acknowledge these contributors. Jeff and I both are so very grateful for their beneficial input and valuable suggestions. Hopefully, we have not overlooked thanking anyone. If we did, please write us at WyethBaker6@gmail.com.

Family who have provided data forms, informative stories, descriptive photographs, helpful letters, Bible records, messages or emails include:

Eugene Miro Arroyo Sr.	John Wyeth Barkhausen	Joshua Buxton
Ethel Wyeth Canion	Judi Harms Edwards	Christine Bolt Flowers
June Carol Wyeth Fuller	Susan Wyeth Gentry	Jean-Marie Wyeth Gilstrap
Rosemary Hummel Goins	Joan Wyeth Greer	Sue Hummel Hill
Richard Laird Hoffman	Vickilyn Warburton Lallatin	Lynda Evans Levin
Marselle "Bunnie" Wyeth Margraff	Valory Wyeth Marsh	Trish Marti
Patricia Molitor	Amy Borst Ocker	Claire Wyeth Raimondo
John Thomas Slemons	France Griggs Sloat	Cindy Wyeth Strother
Donna Wyeth Thibodeau	Gary & Diana Wythe Totten	Jeanne Wyeth Wald
Charles Arthur and Jane Walker	Geri Wyeth Watson	Ed & Deborah Wyeth White
Deb Wyeth Wilkie	Julie Rowan Wolford	Barbara Edith Wyeth
Betsy James Wyeth	Brenton Irwin Wyeth	Duncan Orn Wyeth
Garland & Sandy Treble Wyeth	George Bullock Wyeth	Harmon Harold Wyeth Sr.
Huston Wyeth	James & Sheila Baum Wyeth	Jerry Alan Wyeth
Jerry Dean Wyeth	John Bound Wyeth	Joseph Robert Wyeth
Keith Lyon Wyeth	Leonard Jarvis "Trip" Wyeth	Marc Anthony Wyeth
Marian Gertrude Wyeth	Maureen Christensen Wyeth	Philip Martin Wyeth
Richard Eugene Wyeth	Richard Warren Wyeth	Robert Frank Wyeth
Scott Allen Wyeth	Sims Wyeth	Stuart McReynolds Wyeth Jr.
William "Max" Wyeth IV	Michael Reed Wythe	Debrah Wyeth Zimmer

A special shout out goes to one of our most prolific contributors, Ethel Ross "Rossie" Wyeth Canion. Rossie, granddaughter of Jackson Wyeth #398, has sent dozens of items through the years. Particularly wonderful are her family group photos. We encourage all of you who would like your family remembered in any new Wyeth / Wythe volumes, to email family group photos to me. As they depict many people in one photo, for size, group photos will have priority in future books. So photos are not lost in the shuffle, if you have sent Jeff photos in the past, expecting them to be in a book, please email me directly about them at WyethBaker6@gmail.com.

Baby Rossie on her father Leo Ross Wyeth's knee - sister Mary Jane, mom Ethel Maud Roberts, sister Alma Rachel and brother Jackson Wyeth in 1926.

Rossie joined the U.S. World War II Cadet Nursing Corps in 1943. A conservationalist and genealogist her whole life, today, at age 92, she continues to stay active.

Rossie greatly misses her husband of 63 years, Barney Canion. Her loving children, Gwen, Barney Ross and Rachel, together with her grandchildren and great grandchildren are her greatest blessings. Not only does her family keep Rossie very busy, but she enjoys so many activities at her retirement home in Temple, Texas, that she barely has a moment to spare.

"History remembers only the celebrated.

Genealogy remembers them all."

~ Laurence Overmire

APPENDIX 2: DETAILS OF ELIZABETH E. SMITH WYETH WIDOW'S PENSION

The following information with image numbers comes from Jonas Jr. and Elizabeth Wyeth's Revolutionary War pension file W14205 on Ancestry.com. Data with numbers are from the *Ledgers of Payments, 1818-1872, to U.S. Pensioners Under Acts of 1818 through 1858* (from Records of the Office of the Third Auditor of the Treasury.)

No.	Date	From	Detail of Letter or Document (most letters refer to Jonas Sr. as a very aged man)
n/a	1836/03/01	Pension Rolls	rolls show she got a pension for Jonas from Mar 1836 to Mar 1848
99	1836/03/04	Boston Pension Roll	Inscribed at $42.64 arrears from 04 Mar 1836 to 14 Aug 1855 (cert. sent LB True in 1855) *
101	1838/08/07	Pension Rolls #12082	From Certificate 19 Jul 1845
100	1843/03/03	Act of Congress	for Widow's pension and on 1844/06/17
105	1845/03/17	Jacob Wyeth, age 81	states he had three brothers in the Rev. War
116	1845/03/17	Elizabeth E. Smith Wyeth, age 73	to Secretary of Mass. for docs; said Jonas was at Ft. Ticonderoga (appears Clarke sent affidavit as to review on ship board)
102	1845/06/02	Mass. Secretary	Gives service, not on rolls of Bradley; on index a seaman on *Hague*
75	1845/06/20	Lucius Paige	certifies 8th day of Apr 1792 was marriage of Jonas Wyeth and Elizabeth Smith by A. Holmes
76	1845/06/20	James Monroe	age 70 and has always lived in Cambridge
79	1845/06/24	Elizabeth Smith Wyeth	Declaration to obtain benefits of the provision made by the Act of Congress passed July 7th, 1838 entitled an act granting half pay and pensions to certain widows. Also, the act of March 3rd 1843 and June 17th 1844 continuing pensions to certain widows; gives service from Alarm Apr 1775 to Navy on *Hague* 1781
104	1845/07/16	Elijah Clarke, JP	To JL Edwards, Comm. of Pensions: "I enclose to you herewith the claims and docs of Mrs. Elizabeth Wyeth of Cambridge for a pension agreeable to the act of 1838 and the subsequent act for widows."
n/a	1845/07/19	Elizabeth Smith Wyeth	Index record this date shows 07 Aug 1838 certificate suspended for authenticity that he was the specific Jonas in service on the *Hague*
149	1845/08/26	Elijah Clarke, JP re: Comm. of Pensions letter	Image 149 is a letter dated 30 Jan 1851 from Atty. Elijah Clark to Hon. Horace Mann referencing letters Comm. of Pensions wrote on 8/26/1845 and 31 Jan 1846 **wanting additional proof that Jonas is THE sailor** who served
96	1845/09/01	Lydia Francis Wyeth, age 67	"When I was nine years old, I was placed in the family of Ebenezer Wyeth of this town. At which time the said Ebenezer Wyeth has six sons living whose names were Ebenezer, Jonas, Joshua, Jacob, Gad and John. " (Lydia Francis married Job Wyeth)
118	1845/11/01	Samuel Sawin, age 82	from Maine; Jonas took Queen's arm (British flintlock musket) in the battle of Lexington and Concord
150	1845/12/06	Elijah Clarke, JP	to J. L. Edwards, Comm. of Pensions: I herewith enclose the additional evidence in support of the claims of Elizabeth Wyeth
149	1846/01/31	Elijah Clarke, JP re: Comm. of Pensions letter	Image 149 is a letter dated 30 Jan 1851 from Atty. Elijah Clark to Hon. Horace Mann referencing letters Comm. of Pensions wrote on 8/26/1845 and 31 Jan 1846 **wanting additional proof that Jonas is THE sailor** who served
n/a	1848/03/04	Pension Roll ends	rolls show she got a pension from Mar 1836 to Mar 1848
127	1850/02/04	Elizabeth Jarvis Wyeth	age 82; Her father, Nathaniel Jarvis, resided on the north side of the common; knew Jonas was repeatedly in the service of his country and was away in the naval service; talks about his brother Ebenezer Wyeth III receiving a pension in Ashby
142	1850/02/08	Elijah Clarke, JP	request to Mass. Secretary to re-examine records
141	1851/01/21	Mass. Secretary	Secretary has no more to add to Jonas' 02 Jun 1845 certificate
130	1851/01/27	Samuel Watson	age 82; Jonas resided within two miles of his residence
149	1851/01/30	Elijah Clarke, JP	To Hon. Horace Mann, Washington City, D.C. – agreeable to the letters of the Comm. of Pensions of date 26 Aug 1845 & 31 Jan 1846, we have made constant inquiry to hear of some aged person or a Rev. soldier who was a native of Cambridge who could identify Jonas Wyeth

149	1851/01/30	Elijah Clarke, JP	... Mr. Sawin whose affidavit is on file (supports it) ... I herewith enclose the additional evidence in support of the claims
155	1851/02/07	Rep. Horace Mann	to Comm. of Pensions enclosing Elijah Clark's application
132	1851/11/24	Nathan Watson, age 79 of Roxbury	Jonas was called Merchant Jonas; the well-known Courage and Firmness of the said Jonas Wyeth was often spoken of to his praise.
90	1852/06/26	Jacob Wyeth, age 87	states he is the son of Ebenezer and Mary Wyeth; Jonas was in the service at NY under Capt. Bradley of Charleston; that he had a fever in the service near NY, and on his way home stopped at his uncle Mannings in Norwich, CT, his father, Ebenezer went to Norwich to bring him home; Jonas was then a privateer seaman and then joined the Navy and was some of the time under Capt. Manley: my father had a brother, Jonas, but he was not the person who performed this type of service, but "my brother Jonas was of that character by which he was always ready to engage in any dangerous engagements."
148	1852/08/25	Rep. Ben Thompson	To Elijah Clarke; the congressman will call on Comm. of Pensions & personally hand him papers
154	1852/08/25	Rep. Ben Thompson	enclosed additional evidence
140	1852/09/23	Elijah Clarke, JP	To Rep. Ben Thompson "Mrs. Wyeth is now ... feeble as well as indigent and she cannot probably stay long. It will be an act of justice that her claim be allowed & paid to her while living."
84	1852/11/05	Susannah Monroe	age 60; daughter of Ebenezer Jr.'s sister, Sarah Wyeth Monroe
86	1852/11/05	Jacob Wyeth	age 87; states: I well recollect the Revolutionary War. That my said father (Ebenezer Jr.) with his oldest son and my two other brothers by the name of Jonas and Joshua were in the service of the Lexington and Concord Alarm on the 19th of Apr 1775. I think they belonged to Capt. Thatcher's Company in Cambridge.
82	1852/11/13	Jonas Wyeth 2d	Son of Major Jonas and his grandfather was Jonas, Sr.; "I never heard my father state he was in the Revolutionary War."
159	1852/11/18	Elijah Clarke, JP	The Comm. of Pensions lost Ben Thompson's hand delivered docs
112	1853/08/02	Elizabeth Smith Wyeth	Appoints L. Blanchard True her atty after "pension suspended for proof of identity that he was the very Jonas Wyeth as sailor who served on board Capt. Manly's vessel the Hauge"
109	1853/08/03	to LB True	Daniel Shed suspended case; wish to see papers (wrote to True after 8/2/1853 letter of Elizabeth E. Smith)
n/a	1853/09/12	Elizabeth died	rolls show she received a pension from Sep 1848 to Sep 1853 (died 12 Sep 1853 as shown on rolls paid in full 3rd quarter 1833.??)
134	1854/03/28	Solomon Hancock	age 79
138	1854/03/28	Samuel Hancock	age 78
152	1854/07/11	LB True	Says there is no problem just because the words "Jr." or "2nd" did not appear in records
124	1854/08/22	Susannah Wyeth	age 81; wife of Major Jonas Wyeth
121	1854/08/24	Royal Morse	age 76 (Morse is probably the illegitimate son of Royall Tyler)
136	1854/11/21	William E. Carter	States that before 1812, Jonas was called Jonas 2d
157	1854/12/21	Charles W. Upham	Wrote Comm. of Pensions; trying to help (wrote books on witchcraft)
144	1855/06/12	Atty. LB True	"I desire case reviewed with reference to allowing the case; a cloud of witnesses ... of his sea service they declare he served on board the same ship, the *Hague*, and under the same captain - Capt. Manly, as the records of Mass. show he did serve! How could this be, were it not so for the records of Mass. are a sealed book to all prior to the sworn application now on file in the case."
99	1855/08/14	Pension certificate	Arrears paid to the 4th of Sep ? semi-annual ending present 11 months and 10 days seaman and 21 days private $42.64 per annum is to commence on the 4th day of Mar 1836
156	1855/08/14	Comm. of Pensions	Approved from 03/4/1836 2 years excepted Adm 07 Jul 1838; $42.64 per annum cert to L. B. True*

APPENDIX 2: A THEORETICAL LINEAGE FOR SIGNER GEORGE WYTHE

It has long been a legend in the Wyeth / Wythe family that Declaration of Independence signer George Wythe's ancestor was brother to Nicholas Wyeth. The following tree is based on the theory that Richard Wyth, who appears in 17th century records of both Massachusetts[1428] and Virginia,[1429] is the brother of Nicholas Wyeth.

The Saxtead baptism, marriage and burial records in the following tree are from All Saints Church in Saxtead, Suffolk, England. For the most part, names are spelled as they appear in those records. Additionally, there are two English records for a Richard Wythe being the father of a Thomas Wythe. One record is from Suffolk County[1430] and the other from Norfolk County.[1431]

There is no proof either record is for the specific ancestor of George Wythe, but George's bookplate of three walking griffins does indeed directly connect him to the Wythe families in the eastern area of England.[1432] Burke's *Encyclopaedia of Heraldry* indicates griffins appear on the arms of the eastern counties of Cambridgeshire and Norfolk.[1433] Griffins also appear on Suffolk County heraldry as evidenced by a monument recognizing Vicar Thomas Wythe's service from 1779 to 1835 in the Church of St. Peter and St. Paul in Eye, Suffolk, England.[1434]

Some researchers believe Thomas Wayte (Waite), listed in Peter Wilson Coldham's book, *The Bristol Registers of Servants Sent to Foreign Plantations*, is George Wythe's first Virginia ancestor. However, of the 10,000 servants in the Bristol registers, almost all came from the West Country, the West Midlands, or from Wales. Since lions appear on the Wythe arms in counties on the western side of Great Britain, there is nothing connecting Thomas Wayte, who arrived in Virginia in 1667, to the griffins' heraldry on George Wythe's bookplate.[1435] Also, in the first mention of Thomas Wythe Sr. in Virginia, he is called a "gentleman" and thus he could not have been one of the servants listed on the Bristol registers.[1436]

As pointed out earlier in this book, another factor tying George Wythe to the descendants of Nicholas Wyeth is his facial profile and aquiline nose.[1437] The similarity of George Wythe's profile to Dr. John Allan Wyeth's profile started Dr. John's son, Marion Sims Wyeth (1889-1982), on the search detailed in his self-published pamphlet *Nicholas and George Wythe: An Account of a Search for Their English Antecedents*. Here is another side view comparison three generations beyond John Allan Wyeth. These photos compare my brother, Sidney James Wyeth, to George Wythe. It is also noteworthy that my father, Richard Caldwell Wyeth, but for a higher hairline and fuller lips, had an almost identical profile to his son, Sidney.

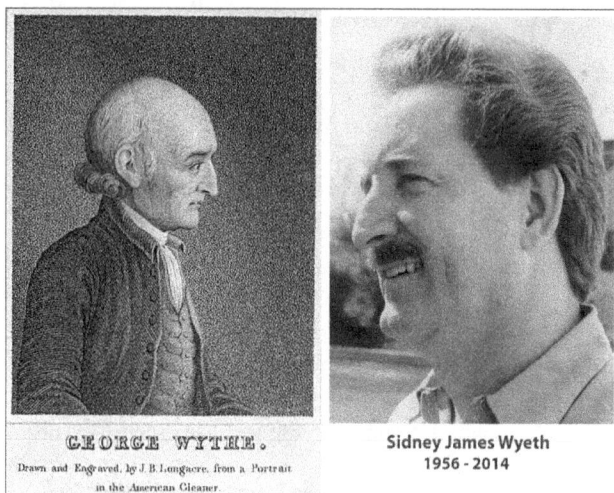

GEORGE WYTHE.
Drawn and Engraved by J. B. Longacre, from a Portrait in the American Gleaner.

Sidney James Wyeth
1956 - 2014

The James B. Longacre drawing of George Wythe is courtesy of the New York Public Library Digital Collections.

First Generation

1. **Thomas Wythe** was born about 1527 in either Norfolk or Suffolk County, England. His father may be Thomas Wyth who Marion Sims Wyeth pointed out was on a 1524 Suffolk County Subsistence Return. Researchers believe this Thomas Wythe married **Alice Gyrling** on 01 Apr 1553 in Frostenden, Suffolk, England. Thomas is definitely the father of John Wythe because his name appears on John's Saxtead marriage record.

Thomas Wythe and Alice Gyrling had the following children:

2   i. **John Wythe**, born abt 1561 in either Norfolk or Suffolk County, England; married Margaret Cutler (or Wyard), 27 Jan 1583, Saxtead, Suffolk, England; buried 22 Feb 1605, Saxtead, Suffolk, England.

3   ii. **Robert Wieth**, born abt 1562, in either Norfolk or Suffolk County, England; nuncupative will written 25 Jun 1617 in Saxtead, Suffolk, England.

2. **John Wythe** (Thomas[1]) was born about 1561 in either Norfolk or Suffolk County, England. John Wythe and **Margaret Cutler** (or Wyard) were married in Saxtead, Suffolk, England. Her name did not appear on the marriage record. It merely said, "John Wyeth the son of Thomas Wyethe was married the 27th of January Anno Domini 1583." John was buried on 22 Feb 1605 and Margaret on 12 Apr 1633 at All Saints Church in Saxtead, England.

It is likely John and Margaret Wythe had the following children:

4   i. **Laurance Wythe**, baptized 11 Oct 1584, Saxtead, Suffolk, England; married Margerie Wythe, abt 1607; married Frances Wythe, 14 Mar 1609, Saxtead; buried there 08 Aug 1671.
     ii. **Jane Withe**, baptized 30 Aug 1590, Saxtead, Suffolk, England; married Henry Cornish, 14 Oct 1624, Saxtead; death date unknown.
5   iii. **Richard Wyth**, born abt 1596 probably in Suffolk County, England; died in either Massachusetts or Virginia, death date unknown.
     iv. **Rose Wyeth** was baptized on 25 Mar 1599 in Saxtead, Suffolk, England; death date unknown.
     v. **Nicholas Wyth (Nicholas Wyeth)**, baptized 20 Jan 1600, Saxtead; married Margaret Clarke, abt 1630, Suffolk County, England; married Rebecca Parks Andrews, abt 1647, Cambridge, Middlesex, Massachusetts, died there, 19 Jul 1680.

3. **Robert Wieth** (Thomas[1]) was born about 1562 in either Norfolk or Suffolk County, England. On the "25th day of June Anno Domini – 1617 – Robert Wieth of Saxsted in the County of Suffolk yeoman did declare his will nuncupative." The will was proved at Tannington on 12th of July Anno Domini 1617. He left everything to his wife, Margerie.[1438] She was buried on 10 May 1623 in Saxtead, Suffolk County, England.

Robert and Margerie Wieth had the following children:

6   i. **William Wythe (William With)**, baptized 25 Mar 1593, Saxtead, Suffolk, England; a tailor, William married Elizabeth Wyard, 21 Sep 1617, All Saints Church, Saxtead, Suffolk, England.
7   ii. **Daniell Withe**, baptized 29 Oct 1604, Saxtead, Suffolk, England.
     iii. **Robert Wyeth II** was baptized on 20 Oct 1607 in Saxtead, Suffolk, England.
     iv. **Elizabeth Wyeth** was baptized on 18 Jun 1614 in Saxtead, Suffolk, England.

Third Generation

4. **Laurance Wythe** (John[2], Thomas[1]) was baptized on 11 Oct 1584 in Saxtead, Suffolk, England. In 1638 he was listed among the able men of Suffolk. Laurance was buried on 08 Aug 1671, at about the age of 86, in Saxtead, Suffolk, England. Laurance Wythe and **Margerie Wythe** were married about 1607.

Laurance and Margerie Wythe had the following children:

     i. **Thomas Wyeth** was baptized on 20 Feb 1609 in Saxtead, Suffolk, England.
     ii. **George Withe**, baptized on 08 Mar 1611 in Saxtead, Suffolk, England; buried on 04 Sep 1630, at age 19, in Saxtead, Suffolk, England.
     iii. **Robert Wythe** was baptized on 26 Jan 1616 in Saxtead, Suffolk, England.

Laurance Wythe and Frances Wythe were married on 14 Mar 1609 in Saxtead, Suffolk, England. **Frances Wythe** was born about 1585. She was buried on 23 Aug 1652 in Saxtead, Suffolk, England.

Laurance and Frances Wythe had the following child:

     i. Marie Withe was baptized on 17 Oct 1619 in Saxtead, Suffolk, England.

5. **Richard Wyth** (John[2], Thomas[1]) was born about 1596 probably in Suffolk County, England. Although he was not listed among the baptisms for children of John and Margaret Wyeth in Saxtead, it does not necessarily mean he

is not their child. Many dates were not recorded in those early times. On 06 Mar 1622 a Richard and Joane Wythe baptized their son Thomas in Aldringham, Suffolk, England.[1439] A Richard Wyth witnessed the will of Anna Clubb of Stradbroke (a town nine miles north of Saxtead) on 13 Dec 1626. A Richard and **Joane Wythe** baptized their son Thomas in Costessey, Norfolk, England on 25 Sep 1632.[1440] A Richard Wyth lived in Virginia in 1635.[1441] Richard also has a record in Cambridge, Middlesex, Massachusetts on 10 Jun 1649.[1442] Records also show his name as Richard Wythe, Richard Withe, and Rich Wyeth.

Richard Wyth and his wife Joane may have been parents to:

    8   i. **Thomas Wythe Sr.**, born abt 1622 or 1632 in either Norfolk or Suffolk County, England; could have been the Thomas Wythe who married Mrs. Ann Smith, abt 1663, Elizabeth City County, Virginia; died abt Mar 1694, Back River, Elizabeth City County, Virginia.

6. **William Wythe** (Robert[2], Thomas[1]) was baptized on 25 Mar 1593 in Saxtead, Suffolk, England. William Wythe and Elizabeth Wyard were married on 21 Sep 1617 in All Saints Church, Saxtead, Suffolk, England.

William Wythe and **Elizabeth Wyard** had the following children:

    i. **Elizabeth Wyeth** was baptized on 05 Jun 1622 in Saxtead, Suffolk, England.
    ii. **John Wyeth** was baptized on 22 Nov 1625 in Saxtead.
    iii. **Sarra Wyeth** was baptized on 16 Mar 1627 in Saxtead.
    iv. **Mearie Wyeth** was baptized on 17 Feb 1632 in Saxtead.

7. **Daniell Withe** (Robert[2], Thomas[1]) was baptized on 29 Oct 1604 in Saxtead, Suffolk, England. He married **Silvester Withe** about 1624.

Daniell and Silvester Withe had the following child:

    i. **Elizabeth Wyeth** was baptized on 29 Jan 1625 in Saxtead, Suffolk, England.

Fourth Generation

8. **Thomas Wythe Sr.** (Richard[3], John[2], Thomas[1]) may have been born of the Richard and Joane Wythe who had their son, Thomas, baptized on 06 Mar 1622 in Aldringham, Suffolk, England. Or he may have been baptized on 25 Sep 1632 in Costessey, Norfolk, England by a couple of the same name. Undoubtedly basing his claim on the arms of George Wythe's bookplate, John Bennett Boddie in *Virginia Historical Genealogies* wrote Thomas Wythe Sr. came from Norfolk County, England.[1443] However, as shown, those arms were also used in Suffolk County. Thomas' Back River land was first mentioned in 1676 in an Elizabeth City County, Virginia patent book.[1444] On 09 Jun 1680, Thomas was a member of the House of Burgesses from Elizabeth City County, Virginia. He purchased 204 acres from Edward Sweeney on 20 Mar 1691 in Elizabeth City County, Virginia. Thomas Sr. made his will on 14 Dec 1693, leaving his grandson Thomas III the land he bought from Mr. Sweeney. The will was probated in Elizabeth City County, Virginia on 19 Mar 1693/94 with son Thomas Jr. and grandson Thomas III as the executors.[1445]

Thomas Wythe Sr. and widow Mrs. Ann Smith were married about 1663, most likely in Elizabeth City County, Virginia. **Ann Smith's** birth circa 1641 is based on the date her son from her first marriage, William Smith, had his will probated. It was recorded on 18 Oct 1693 in Elizabeth City County, Virginia. In the will, Thomas Wythe Jr.'s age was given as 23. On 07 Sep 1695, Ann Smith Wythe married Thomas Harwood. She died after 19 Nov 1697 when she was party in a suit with her grandson, Thomas Wythe III, in Elizabeth City County, Virginia.[1446]

Thomas Wythe Sr. and Ann Smith had the following children:

    i. **Daughter Wythe**, born abt 1665, likely in Elizabeth City County, Virginia; died bef 1694, Elizabeth City County, Virginia. She was deceased at the time of her father's will, however, her husband, John Tomer, was mentioned in the will. Later their child, John Tomer Jr., was mentioned in the will of Thomas Wythe Jr.[1447]

9   ii.   **Ann Wythe**, born abt 1668, likely in Elizabeth City County, Virginia; married William Mallory, bef 1693, Virginia; died 1720, Elizabeth City County, Virginia.

10   iii. **Thomas Wythe Jr.**, born abt 1670, likely in Elizabeth City County, Virginia; married Anne Sheppard Gutherick, 1689, Elizabeth City County, Virginia; will probated 18 Sep 1694, Elizabeth City County, Virginia.

Fifth Generation

9. **Ann Wythe** (Thomas[4], Richard[3], John[2], Thomas[1]) was born about 1668 likely in Elizabeth City County, Virginia. Ann Wythe and William Mallory were married before 1693. On 02 May 1693, Ann Wythe Mallory, daughter of Thomas Wythe Sr. and wife of William Mallory, appointed her father-in-law, Captain Roger Mallory of King and Queen County, her attorney to relinquish her dower rights on property in Pomonky Necke, Virginia. Witnesses included her father Thomas Wythe Sr. **William Mallory**, son of Roger Mallory and Jane Holland, was born about 1668 in King William County, Virginia. He was a very active attorney in Elizabeth City County. She died circa 1719, as she was not mentioned in her husband's will. Ann Wythe Mallory did, however, give land to her son on 17 Sep 1718 in Elizabeth City County, Virginia. Her husband's will was probated on 15 Feb 1720 in Elizabeth City County, Virginia.[1448]

William Mallory and Ann Wythe had the following children:

11   i.   **Francis Mallory**, born 1694, Elizabeth City County, Virginia; married Ann Johnson Myhill, circa 1720, Elizabeth City County, Virginia; his will was probated 18 Jul 1744, Elizabeth City County, Virginia.

12   ii. **Mary Mallory**, born 1702, Elizabeth City County, Virginia; died 1736, Chesterfield County, Virginia.

        iii. **Ann Mallory**, born about 1704 in Elizabeth City County, Virginia; died unmarried after 1721 in Elizabeth City County, Virginia.[1449]

        iv. **William Mallory,** born circa 1706 in Elizabeth City County, Virginia; died before 20 Jul 1753 in Elizabeth City County, Virginia.[1450]

10. **Thomas Wythe Jr.** (Thomas[4], Richard[3], John[2], Thomas[1]) was born about 1670 likely in Elizabeth City County, Virginia. At the young age of 24, he died just a few months after his father. Thomas Jr.'s will was probated on 18 Sep 1694 in Elizabeth City County, Virginia.[1451]

Thomas Wythe Jr. and Anne Sheppard Gutherick were married in about 1689 in Elizabeth City County, Virginia. **Anne Sheppard**, daughter of John Sheppard and Elizabeth Jordan, was born about 1666 in Jamestown, James City County, Virginia. After Thomas' death, Anne married Rev. James Wallace. Her will was probated on 18 Feb 1740 in Elizabeth City County, Virginia.[1452]

Thomas Wythe Jr. and Anne Sheppard had the following children:

13   i.   **Thomas Wythe III**, born 1690, Elizabeth City County, Virginia; married Margaret Keith Walker, 1720, Elizabeth City County, Virginia; died circa 1729, Elizabeth City County, Virginia.

14   ii. **Anne Wythe**, born abt 1694, Elizabeth City County, Virginia; died 1735, York County, Virginia.

Sixth Generation

11. **Francis Mallory** (Ann[5] Wythe, Thomas[4], Richard[3], John[2], Thomas[1]) was born circa 1694 in Elizabeth City County, Virginia. Francis had his estate probated on 18 Jul 1744 in Elizabeth City County, Virginia. In it, he left a legacy to niece Elizabeth Reade and to son Johnson Mallory.[1453] Francis Mallory and Ann Johnson Myhill were married circa 1720 in Elizabeth City County, Virginia. **Ann Johnson**, daughter of Phillip Johnson and Winifred Proby, was born about 1683 in Elizabeth City County, Virginia.[1454] Her first husband, Edward Myhill, stated in his will that benefitted his daughter Elizabeth Myhill, "wife Ann did some years past elope and has lately borne a child, the said child and my wife are disbarred from inheriting any part of my estate." Nevertheless, Ann Myhill

administered Edward's will and Francis Mallory provided security when it was probated on 17 Jun 1719 in Elizabeth City County, Virginia.[1455] Ann died before Francis as she is not named in his will.[1456]
Francis Mallory and Ann Johnson Myhill had the following child:

15   i.   **Johnson Mallory**, born before 17 May 1721, Elizabeth City County, Virginia; married Diane Tabb, circa 1740, Elizabeth City County; died there before 05 May 1762.

12. **Mary Mallory** (Ann[5] Wythe, Thomas[4], Richard[3], John[2], Thomas[1]) was born in 1702 in Elizabeth City County, Virginia. She died in 1736 at age 34 in Chesterfield County, Virginia. **John Reade**, son of Thomas Reade and Anne Allen, was born in 1700 in Elizabeth City County. He died in Mar 1739 at age 39 in Chesterfield County, Virginia.

John and Mary Mallory Reade's children included:

     i.   **Elizabeth Reade** was born in 1730 in Elizabeth City County, Virginia. After her parents' deaths on 17 Nov 1742 in Elizabeth City County, she chose her uncle Francis Mallory as guardian. In Francis' will probated on 18 Jul 1744 in Elizabeth City County, he left her a legacy.[1457]
     ii. **Mary Reade** was born in 1734 in Elizabeth City County. She also had uncle Francis Mallory as guardian. On behalf of Mary, Francis brought suit against her stepmother, Elizabeth Reade Owen for monies due the children of John Reade. The case was settled at December Court 1745 when arbitrator Richard Randolph divided the money between the stepmother and Reade's children.[1458]

13. **Thomas Wythe III** (Thomas[5], Thomas[4], Richard[3], John[2], Thomas[1]) was born circa 1691 in Elizabeth City County, Virginia. His birth date is confirmed by the death of his mother's first husband, Quintillian Gutherick, in 1689. Thomas was a delegate to the house of Burgesses in 1718, 1723, and 1726. He was about age 39 at his death. His will, written 03 Nov 1728, was probated on 15 Oct 1729 in Elizabeth City County. Thomas Wythe III and Margaret Keith Walker were married in 1719 in Elizabeth City County, Virginia. **Margaret Keith Walker**, daughter of George Walker and Anne Keith, was born there about 1699. She died about 1745 in the Chesterville Plantation on the Back River, Elizabeth City County, Virginia.[1459] The county is now Hampton and NASA Langley Research Center sits on this land.[1460]

This painting of the Chesterville Plantation site was included in a 1976 marker designating George Wythe's birth place on the grounds of NASA Langley.

Thomas Wythe III and Margaret Keith Walker had the following children:

     i.   **Thomas Wythe IV** was born in 1721 in the Chesterville Plantation on the Back River, Elizabeth City County, Virginia. He wrote his will in 1754. Although the will indicated Thomas had a wife, Frances, he apparently did not have children because Thomas Wythe IV left his brother, George Wythe, the Chesterville Plantation. As his will was probated in 1755, Thomas died at age 34.
16   ii. **Ann Wythe**, born circa 1723, in the Chesterville Plantation on the Back River, Elizabeth City County, Virginia; married Charles Sweeney, 1744, Elizabeth City County, Virginia; she died before 27 Jul 1790, Sewells Point, Norfolk, Virginia.
17   iii. **George Wythe**, born 1726, in the Chesterville Plantation on the Back River, Elizabeth City County, Virginia; married Ann Lewis, 26 Dec 1747, Spotsylvania County, Virginia; married Elizabeth Eggleston Taliaferro, abt 1755, Williamsburg, James City County, Virginia; died 08 Jun 1806, Richmond, Virginia.

14. **Anne Wythe** (Thomas[5], Thomas[4], Richard[3], John[2], Thomas[1]) was born about 1694 in Elizabeth City County, Virginia. She married Matthew Ballard circa 1715. When the will of her husband was presented in court on 18 May 1719, Anne, after being first privately examined, relinquished her right of dower. She died in 1735 in York County, Virginia.[1461]

Matthew Ballard, son of Thomas Ballard and Catherine Hubbard, baptized about 1685, York Hampton Parish, York County, Virginia. His will bearing the date of 13 May 1719 was recorded in York County, Virginia on 18 May 1719.

Matthew Ballard and Anne Wythe had the following child:

> i. **Matthew Ballard Jr.** was born about 1716 in York County, Virginia. He was mentioned in his uncle Thomas Wythe Jr.'s Elizabeth City County, Virginia will in 1729. 11 years later he was mentioned in his grandmother Anne Sheppard Gutherick Wythe Wallace's Elizabeth City County, Virginia will. Matthew died at age 25 in York County, Virginia. Per York County records, book 18, page 8, his estate was probated on 18 May 1741 in York County, Virginia.

Seventh Generation

15. **Johnson Mallory** (Francis^6, Ann^5 Wythe, Thomas^4, Richard^3, John^2, Thomas^1), born before 17 May 1721 in Elizabeth City County, Virginia when his parents deeded a plantation into his name.[1462] His will was probated on 05 May 1762 in Elizabeth City County, Virginia.[1463]

Johnson Mallory and Diane Tabb were married circa 1740 in Elizabeth City County, Virginia. **Diane Tabb**, daughter of Col. John Tabb and Mary Sclater, was born there circa 1722. The legacy in her will, probated on 27 Jan 1785 in Elizabeth City County, Virginia, to grandson Augustine Moore connects her to daughter Ann Mallory.[1464]

Johnson and Diane Tabb Mallory's children included:

> i. **Col. Francis Mallory** was born circa 1741 in Elizabeth City County, Virginia. During the Revolutionary War, he commanded the militia guarding the Hampton area. He was killed in a running fight with the British on 08 Mar 1781 near Tompkins Bridge, Hampton, Virginia.[1465]
>
> 18   ii. **Ann Mallory**, born before 07 Jan 1742, Elizabeth City County; died there before 09 Feb 1801.
>
> iii. **Mary Mallory Moore** was born about 1743 in Elizabeth City County, Virginia.
>
> iv. **Margaret Mallory Goodwin** was born about 1748 in Elizabeth City County, Virginia.
>
> 19   v. **Edward Mallory** according to the OneWorldTree was born 1752, Elizabeth City County, Virginia; died about 1789, Elizabeth City County, Virginia.

16. **Ann Wythe** (Thomas^6, Thomas^5, Thomas^4, Richard^3, John^2, Thomas^1) was born circa 1723 at the Chesterville Plantation, Back River, Elizabeth City County, Virginia. Her will was probated on 27 Jul 1790 in Norfolk County, Virginia. Ann Wythe and Charles Sweeney were married circa 1744 in Elizabeth City County, Virginia. **Charles Sweeney**, son of Samuel Sweeney and Anne Armistad, was born about 1723 in Sewells Point, Norfolk, Virginia. He died after his daughter Euphan, circa 1775, in Sewells Point, Norfolk, Virginia.[1466]

Charles Sweeney and Ann Wythe had the following children:

> 20   i. **Anne Sweeney**, born abt 1745, Norfolk County, Virginia; married Arthur Boush, 08 Feb 1763, Norfolk County, Virginia; died abt 1782, Virginia.
>
> 21   ii. **Euphan Sweeney**, born 1747, Sewells Point, Norfolk, Virginia; married Thomas Claiborne, 13 Apr 1769, Norfolk County, Virginia; died bef 22 Dec 1775, Norfolk County, Virginia.
>
> iii. **Margaret Sweeney** was born about 1748 in Sewells Point, Norfolk, Virginia. She was named in her mother's will in 1790 in Norfolk County, Virginia.
>
> iv. **Elizabeth Sweeney** was born about 1750 in Sewells Point, Norfolk, Virginia. She was named in her mother's will in 1790 in Norfolk County, Virginia.
>
> 22   v. **Martha Sweeney**, born abt 1753, Sewells Point, Norfolk, Virginia; married Charles Sayer Boush, 06 May 1774, Sewells Point; died 17 Jun 1792, Virginia.
>
> 23   vi. **George Wythe Sweeney Sr.**, born abt 1758, Sewells Point; married Jane "Jeney" Moore, abt 1786, Norfolk County, Virginia; died 14 May 1805, Norfolk County, Virginia.[1467]

17. **George Wythe** (Thomas^6, Thomas^5, Thomas^4, Richard^3, John^2, Thomas^1) was born in 1726 in the Chesterville Plantation on the Back River, Elizabeth City County, Virginia. He was only three when his father died and left Chesterville to George's older brother. Without land, it was clear at an early age, that George would have to pursue another course to earn a living.

With public education limited, George was most fortunate to receive a classical education at his mother's knee. Margaret was the granddaughter of the intellectual and progressive Quaker minister, George Keith. Keith excelled in mathematics and Oriental studies at Scotland's Marischal College and Aberdeen University before his conversion to the Quaker philosophy. He strongly opposed slavery. In 1693, he denounced it some 34 years before the Friends as an organization attacked it. Rev. Keith also believed in educating women. At a time when women like George Wythe's paternal grandmothers signed their wills with an "x," compared to their peers, Keith's daughters and granddaughters, were well educated.[1468]

When George was about 15, Margaret sent her son to study law with her older sister Elizabeth's husband, Stephen Dewey, near Petersburg, Virginia. Although Dewey lacked teaching skills, in the spring of 1746, Wythe's appearance before examiners to procure his license to practice law in the county courts was successful. George's first job in the busy Spotsylvania County law firm of Zachary Lewis, had many benefits.[1469]

On 26 Dec 1747, Zachary gave George his 21-year-old daughter's hand in marriage. **Ann Lewis**, born on 30 Aug 1726 to Zachary Lewis and Mary Waller, spent her whole life in Spotsylvania County, Virginia. Just a few months after her wedding, Ann, not yet 22 years old, left George a widower on 08 Aug 1748. Desperate and lonely, George moved south to Williamsburg for a change of pace.[1470]

After a short stint as Virginia's attorney general in 1754, George married 15-year-old Elizabeth Taliaferro in Williamsburg, James City County, Virginia. **Elizabeth Eggleston Taliaferro**, daughter of Richard Taliaferro and Elizabeth Eggleston, was born in 1739 in the Powhatan Plantation, James City County, Virginia.[1471] Her architect father built this beautiful brick home on Palace Green Street in Williamsburg as a wedding gift for the couple. Now known as the George Wythe house, it is one of the most beautiful buildings in Colonial Williamsburg.[1472] Elizabeth Taliaferro Wythe died on 18 Aug 1787 at age 48 at the Palace Green house, Williamsburg, James City County, Virginia.[1473]

Rob Shenk's striking photograph of the George Wythe House was retrieved from Wikimedia Commons, the free media repository on 3 Mar 2017.

George Wythe and Elizabeth Eggleston Taliaferro had the following child:

> i. **Infant Wythe** was born about 1756 in Williamsburg, James City County, Virginia. The unnamed infant died there soon after birth.[1474]

Although George did not have children of his own, many friends and relatives named their children for him. He kept busy in a long and prosperous career in both Williamsburg and Richmond. From *Wythepedia*, a site devoted to George at the William & Mary Law School Library, here are a few of his career highlights.

- Mayor of the city of Williamsburg, Virginia, 30 Nov 1768 – 29 Nov 1769
- Member of the Virginia House of Burgesses, 1754 - 1775
- Thomas Jefferson's tutor, 1760 - 1767
- Delegate to the Second Continental Congress from Virginia, 11 Aug 1775 - 13 Jun 1776
- Signed the Declaration of Independence, 1776
- Professor of Law and Police, College of William & Mary, 04 Dec 1779 - 1789
- Judge, High Court of Chancery of Virginia, 14 Jan 1778 - 08 Jun 1806
- Chancellor of the Commonwealth of Virginia, 24 Dec 1788 - 23 Jan 1802
- Wythe held the novel view in America at the time that the Negro race was as intelligent as the white race and proved it by educating his black students in the same manner as his white students.[1475]

George Wythe Randolph, Thomas Jefferson's grandson,[1476] and George Wythe Sweeney Jr., sister Anne Wythe Sweeney's grandson, were two of the many individuals named for George Wythe.

Always the teacher, George brought his sister Anne's grandson into his Richmond home hoping to educate the young Sweeney in Latin and Greek alongside his mixed-race student, Michael Brown, a freed boy in the chancellor's household. The two boys along with two of Wythe's emancipated slaves, Lydia Broadnax and Benjamin, were named in his 1803 will.

However, by age 17, his namesake was stealing and selling the chancellor's valuable law books to cover gambling debts. Curiously, the chancellor overlooked Sweeney's behavior and added a codicil to his will dividing his bank stock equally between Sweeney and Michael Brown. This set in motion jealous Sweeney's desperate plan to gain access to all of the money by poisoning Michael, the chancellor, and the cook – Lydia Broadnax.[1477]

Of the three, only Broadnax survived. However, since Virginia race laws prohibited blacks from testifying against whites, she was unable to validate seeing Sweeney put a powder in their morning coffee. Although 14 witnesses did testify about the arsenic and Sweeney's forging his grand uncle's name on checks, Sweeney went free. The only known punishment he suffered, before disappearing into oblivion, was being disinherited by his grand uncle. Although racked with spasms, diarrhea and continuously vomiting blood and bile, when Wythe learned of Michael Brown's death on 01 Jun 1806, he remade his will to benefit Sweeney's siblings, Anne, Jane and Charles.[1478] [1479]

After two weeks of excruciating pain, George Wythe died on 08 Jun 1806, at age 80, in Richmond, Virginia. He was buried in the cemetery of St. John's Episcopal Church, 2401 East Broad Street, Richmond, Virginia. The great teacher and judge was mourned throughout the Commonwealth with "more column inches of eulogy than had been elicited in Virginia newspapers by the death of George Washington or by that of any other person."[1480] In 1922, the patriotic citizens of Virginia erected a marker at his gravesite. It reads: "This Tablet is Dedicated to Mark the Site Where Lie the Mortal Remains of **George Wythe**, Born 1726 — Died 1806; Jurist and Statesman; Teacher of Randolph, Jefferson and Marshall; First Professor of Law in the United States; First Virginia Signer of the Declaration of Independence."[1481]

Eighth Generation

18. **Ann Mallory** (Johnson[7], Francis[6], Ann[5] Wythe, Thomas[4], Richard[3], John[2], Thomas[1]) was born before 07 Jan 1742 in Elizabeth City County, Virginia. Her will was probated on 09 Feb 1801 in Elizabeth City County, Virginia. **Augustine Moore**, son of William Moore, was born circa 1736 in Virginia. His will was probated on 26 Jun 1795 in Elizabeth City County, Virginia.[1482]

Augustine Moore and Ann Mallory had the following children:

	i.	**William Moore**, born about 1760 in Virginia; died after 1801 in Virginia.
	ii.	**John Moore**, born about 1762 in Virginia; died after 1798 in Virginia.
	iii.	**Major Augustine Moore** was born about 1763 in Virginia. He died circa 1822, probably in Richmond, Virginia.
	iv.	**Merritt Moore** was born about 1764 in Virginia. His will was proved on 27 Dec 1798 in Elizabeth City County, Virginia.
	v.	**Ann Moore King** was born about 1765 in Virginia. She died after 1801 in Virginia.
24	vi.	**Jane "Jeney" Moore**, born abt 1766, Virginia; married George Wythe Sweeney Sr., abt 1786, Norfolk County, Virginia; died after 1806, Virginia.

19. **Edward Mallory** (Johnson[7], Francis[6], Ann[5] Wythe, Thomas[4], Richard[3], John[2], Thomas[1]) according to the OneWorldTree was born in 1752 in Elizabeth City County, Virginia. He died about 1789 in Elizabeth City County, Virginia. His wife **Rachel Goodwin,** daughter of James Goodwin and Elizabeth Chapman, was born in 1752 in Virginia. She died in Aug 1780 in North Carolina.

Edward and Rachel Goodwin Mallory's children included:

    i.   **Elizabeth Tabb Mallory**, born 01 Jan 1769, Elizabeth City County; died there circa 1807.
   ii. **Johnson Mallory**, born circa 1770, Elizabeth City County, Virginia; married Anne Wythe Boush, 13 Jul 1799, Sewells Point, Norfolk, Virginia; died Jul 1832, Norfolk County, Virginia.

20. **Ann Sweeney** (Ann[7] Wythe, Thomas[6], Thomas[5], Thomas[4], Richard[3], John[2], Thomas[1]) was born about 1745 in Norfolk County, Virginia. Ann Sweeney and Arthur Boush were married on 08 Feb 1763 in Norfolk County, Virginia. **Arthur Boush**, son of Samuel Boush and Frances Sayer, was born circa 1742 in Virginia. He died after 1790 in Norfolk County, Virginia.

Arthur Boush and Ann Sweeney had the following child:

    i.   **Ann Boush** was born about 1765 in Norfolk County, Virginia.

21. **Euphan Sweeney** (Ann[7] Wythe, Thomas[6], Thomas[5], Thomas[4], Richard[3], John[2], Thomas[1]) was born in 1747 in Sewells Point, Norfolk, Virginia. She died before 22 Dec 1775 at age 28 in Norfolk County, Virginia. She was also known as Upsher Sweaney. On 13 Apr 1769, she married **Thomas Claiborne**, son of Nathaniel Claiborne and Jane Cole, in Norfolk County, Virginia. He was born circa 1735 in Sweet Hall, King William County, Virginia and died in 1777 in Norfolk County, Virginia.

Thomas and Euphan Sweeney Claiborne's children included:

    i.   **Anne Claiborne Tarrant** was born about 1770; died after 1790 in Norfolk County, Virginia.
   ii. **George Wythe Claiborne** was born about 1772 in Virginia.

22. **Martha Sweeney** (Ann[7] Wythe, Thomas[6], Thomas[5], Thomas[4], Richard[3], John[2], Thomas[1]) was born about 1753 in Sewells Point, Norfolk, Virginia. She died on 17 Jun 1792 in Virginia. Martha Sweeney and Charles Sayer Boush were married on 06 May 1774 in Sewells Point, Norfolk, Virginia. **Charles Sayer Boush**, son of Samuel Boush and Frances Sayer, was born about 1742 in Norfolk County, Virginia. He died in Feb 1809 in Norfolk County, Virginia.

Charles Sayer Boush and Martha Sweeney had the following children:

    i.   **Anne Wythe Boush**, born 16 Feb 1775, Sewells Point, Norfolk, Virginia; married Johnson Mallory, 13 Jul 1799, Sewells Point; died 26 Sep 1831, Norfolk County, Virginia.
   ii. **Martha Sweeney Frances Sayer Boush**, born 23 Nov 1787, Sewells Point, Norfolk, Virginia; married Marshall Parks, 19 Nov 1817, Sewells Point, Norfolk, Virginia; died Oct 1846, Cedar Grove, Norfolk, Virginia.

23. **George Wythe Sweeney Sr.** (Ann[7] Wythe, Thomas[6], Thomas[5], Thomas[4], Richard[3], John[2], Thomas[1]) was born about 1758 in Sewells Point, Norfolk, Virginia. He died on 14 May 1805 at age 50 in Norfolk County, Virginia. George Wythe Sweeney and Jane Moore were married about 1786 in Norfolk County, Virginia. **Jane "Jeney" Moore**, daughter of Augustine Moore and Ann Mallory, was born about 1766 in Virginia. She is also #24 in this tree as her mother too is descended from Thomas Wythe Sr. Jane was mentioned in her mother's will on 09 Feb 1801 in Elizabeth City County, Virginia. There is no record of her after her son's 1806 trial.[1483]

George Wythe Sweeney Sr. and Jane "Jeney" Moore had the following children:

    i.   **Ann Wythe Sweeney**, born abt 1787, Norfolk County, Virginia; married John Cary Jr., 31 Mar 1808, Virginia; gave birth to nine children; died 24 Oct 1822, Hampton, Elizabeth City County, Virginia.[1484]
   ii. **George Wythe Sweeney Jr.** was born about 1789 in Norfolk County, Virginia. Before William Wirt became Sweeney's attorney for the murder of his great uncle George Wythe, Wirt wrote in a 10 Jun 1806 letter to James Monroe, "the little villain is only about 16 or 17." Particulars show below. Sweeney's death date is unknown since he disappeared after his murder trial.

iii. **Jane Sweeney**, born abt 1793, Norfolk County, Virginia. Before she married William Ross Jr., in 1816 in Hampton, Elizabeth City County, Virginia, Ross wrote a letter to one Colonel Edmundson on 20 Feb 1816. He announced to the colonel his imminent marriage "to a lady of Hampton. She has fortune sufficient to raise me above the frowns of the world say for 20 to 25 thousand dollars – in real estate in Richmond – bequeathed to her by the late Chancellor Wythe…" Jane Sweeney Ross gave birth to four children. She died 30 Jun 1865, Fairfield, Jefferson, Iowa.[1485]

iv. **Charles Sweeney** was born about 1796 in Norfolk County, Virginia. The last known record for Charles was in 1816.[1486] He was under age 21 at the time.

Sweeney timeline from William & Mary Law Library's Wythepedia: The George Wythe Encyclopedia:

George Wythe Sweeney is first mentioned in George Wythe's last will and testament of Apr 1803. Two years later, in 1805, Sweeney took books from his great uncle's library to sell at public auction to cover gambling and other debts. He was also suspected of selling a terrestrial globe that Wythe had intended to bequeath to Thomas Jefferson. Proving that Wythe was well aware of Sweeney's debts, he added a codicil, dated 19 Jan 1806, to his will specifying that the residuary estate left to Sweeney should be "charged with debts and demands."[1487]

A few months later, in Apr 1806, Sweeney forged his granduncle's name on six checks drawn on the Bank of Virginia. Perhaps intending to cover that crime with a greater crime, Sweeney purchased a large quantity of yellow arsenic in May 1806.

On Pentecostal Sunday morning, 25 May 1806, Sweeney poisoned the morning coffee of the chancellor, his student, Michael Brown and his cook, Lydia Broadnax. Although the poison first struck the chancellor three hours later, Michael Brown was first to die on June 1.[1488]

The best contemporary evidence of events come from a series of letters written by the executor of chancellor Wythe's will, William DuVal, to Thomas Jefferson, then President of the United States.[1489]

> "Worthy Sir,   Richmond June 4th 1806
>
> Geo W. Sweeny who lived with Mr. Wythe was committed to Gaol on the 27th of May last for forging Six Checks on the Bank of Virginia on the 25th of May. Mr. Wythe was taken with a Cholera Morbus on the 26 & 27 all the Rest of the Family were seized with the same violent disorder on the 27. We had no idea that Sweeny had poisoned the whole Family — On Sunday Morning June the first last Michael the Mulatto boy died — Yellow Arsenic was found in Sweeny's Room & many other strong Circumstances concurred to induce a beleive (sic) he had poisoned the whole Family — As a Magistrate I requested four eminent Physicians to open the body of the Boy — they did so, from the Inflamation in the Stomach & Bowels they said that it was the kind of Inflamation produced by Poison — Our Worthy Friend is still alive — he has suffered greatly — on Whitsunday Evening, he told me he never suffered more in his Life — That in the Morning he attended to his Official Duties, the Chancery Court being in Session, that he ate his Breakfast as usual, that about Nine O'Clock in the Morning he was attacked in the most violent Manner & had rose from his Bed Forty Times, to evacuate the Feces — I had Doctors McClurg, Currie & McCan to attend him — They pronounce his Death to be certain in a day or two — They say that his Constitution was remarkably Strong for a person of his age — Thus by the hands of a Youth, to whom he was kinder than a Father, is about to be taken from us the most virtuous and illustrious of our Citizens — one among the best of Men to whom even Death, can't terrify, or alarm.
>
>   I am Yr. mo. Obd. Servt
>   *Wm DuVal*"

In a letter dated 29 Jun 1806, Duval reported on Sunday, June 1, the chancellor was informed that Michael Brown had died that morning. "When Mr. Wythe heard of the untimely death of Michael the freed boy, he made a long breath — and pathetically said —'poor boy.'"

438

Wythe immediately called for his will that he might add a codicil to it. Apparently, he believed then he was the victim of a murderer. Five days later, on Thursday, June 5, as shown in the following letter, he roused himself to exclaim it out loud to those around the bedside, "I am murdered!" But he mentioned no name. He did not need to do so; the significant codicil to his will pointed a finger straight at George Wythe Sweeney.[1490]

"Sir,   Richmond June 8th 1806

Our venerable great and pious Friend departed this Life about half an hour after Nine of the Clock this Morning — Doctors Foushee, Currie Grunhow, McClurg & McCaw opened his Chest & Bowels, there was considerable in Flamation [sic] in the Stomach. It is strongly suspected that he & Michael Brown were poisoned with Yellow Arsenic by Geo W. Sweeny — On Thursday he said **I am murdered** but mentioned no name — The day before Yesterday he said Let me die righteous — he during his severe complaint displayed uncommon Patience & Fortitude — He called on the Lord Jesus Christ to have mercy on him —

The Governour & Council have desired that his Body shall be conveyed to the Capitol. Tomorrow at Four O'Clock in the Afternoon his Funeral Oration will be pronounced by Mr Wm. Montford who lived with Mr Wythe formerly, and is a Member of our Council of State. When Mr Wythe's Will shall be proven. I shall enclose you a Copy of the Will with the Codicils — I believe he inclosed to you a Copy of it.
I am, with great Respect yr obd. Servant
Wm DuVal"

On Wednesday, June 18, Sweeney, charged with the murder of Chancellor Wythe and Michael Brown, was brought for examination before Colonel Edward Carrington, Mayor of Richmond, and two magistrates. Witnesses were questioned for nearly five hours and the examiners unanimously decided Sweeney was guilty as charged.

He was thereupon remanded to the Richmond jail to await a special 23 Jun 1806 Court of Examination. "You may suppose," DuVal wrote to Jefferson, "that the Conduct of Sweeney has excited the most lively sympathy for the deceased and detestation against the supposed Culprit."[1491]

Julian P. Boyd, editor of *The Papers of Thomas Jefferson*, contributed to a special issue of *The William and Mary Quarterly* in October, 1955. Boyd gives the following details of Sweeney's hearings.[1492]

On 23 Jun 1806 bills were found on six charges: one for the murder of George Wythe, one for the murder of Michael Brown, and four for the forgery of Wythe's name on checks drawn on the Bank of Virginia. The trial of Sweeney on these charges was scheduled for the District Court at Richmond in September.[1493]

At his trial on Tuesday, 02 Sep 1806, Sweeney was represented by William Wirt and Edmund Randolph. The Virginia Attorney General, Philip N. Nicholas, was counsel for the prosecution. After an able and eloquent discussion, the jury retired, and in a short time brought in the verdict of *not guilty*. A similar indictment against Sweeny for poisoning Michael Brown was quashed without a trial. Despite this acquittal, Sweeney was convicted of forging checks in Wythe's name with a penalty of six months imprisonment in jail and one hour in the pillory. However, that sentence against him was never executed.[1494]

Shortly after the acquittal, on 09 Sep 1806, the *Richmond Enquirer* strongly hinted in an editorial comment that it had other views than those of the jury: "The pen yet lingers to add, that some of the strongest testimony exhibited before the called court and before the grand jury was kept back from the petit jury. The reason is, that it was gleaned from the evidence of negroes, which is not permitted by our laws to go against a white man."[1495]

Boyd added, "Lydia Broadnax, the cook, who was the chief witness, was not a slave but a freed woman. Yet, because of the texture of her skin, Virginia justice was unable to punish the murderer for a crime which the President of the United States, the attending doctors, the examining courts, and the victim himself believed to have been committed. Surely there is irony in the fact that the death of the great and benevolent chancellor, who believed that kindness and freedom for Negroes were for the best interests of his beloved Commonwealth, went unavenged by his native state in part because of this legal repression of Negro evidence."[1496]

ENDNOTES FOR SECTION TWO

(Sources without endnote numbers show in the Bibliography by their Ancestry.com citation.)

[1] Kimberly Powell, "Numbering Your Family Tree." *ThoughtCo.* https://www.thoughtco.com/numbering-your-family-tree-1420742 (accessed 11/1/2017).

[2] "Fire, water, ice destroy the 1890 Census," *The Ancestry Insider*, 25 Feb 2009, www.ancestryinsider.org/2009/02/fire-water-ice-destroy-1890-census.html (accessed 4/3/2019).

[3] Johni Cerny, "Births and Deaths in Public Records," *The Source: A Guidebook to American Genealogy* (1984, digitized by Ancestry.com in 2010) http://www.ancestry.com/wiki/index.php?title=Births_and_Deaths_in_Public_Records (accessed 11/2/2017).

[4] Dennis Freeborn, *From Old English to Standard English: A Course Book in Language Variation* (Ottawa, Ontario: University of Ottawa Press, 1998), 322.

[5] All Saints Church Registers, Saxtead, UK, 1546 to 1742, Suffolk Record Office, Ipswich, UK, transcribed by Muriel L. Kilvert, 12.

[6] G. Andrews Moriarity, Jr., "Genealogical Research in England," *New England Historical and Genealogical Register, Vol. LXXV* (Boston: New England Historic and Genealogical Society (NEHGS), 1921), 279. <https://books.google.com/books?id=88sUAAAAYAAJ&pg>

[7] National Society of Daughters of Founders and Patriots of America, *Founders and Patriots of America Index* (Baltimore, MD: Genealogical Publications, 1975), 254. <https://books.google.com/books?id=7dGPyld17G4C&printsec>

[8] Marion Sims Wyeth, *Nicholas and George Wythe: an account of a search for their English antecedents* (Palm Beach, FL: Unk., 1958), 17.

[9] All Saints Church Registers, Saxtead, UK, 1546 to 1742, Suffolk Record Office, Ipswich, UK, transcribed by Muriel L. Kilvert, 24.

[10] All Saints Church Registers, Saxtead, UK, 1546 to 1742, Suffolk Record Office, Ipswich, UK, transcribed by Muriel L. Kilvert, 25 and 67.

[11] All Saints Church Registers, Saxtead, UK, 1546 to 1742, Suffolk Record Office, Ipswich, UK, transcribed by Muriel L. Kilvert, 25 and 67.

[12] E. A. Wrigley, R. S. Schofield, *The Population History of England 1541-1871* (Cambridge, UK: Press Syndicate of the University of Cambridge, 1989), 96. <https://books.google.com/books?id=pV9SZS4WpjkC&pg>

[13] Marion Sims Wyeth, 27, referencing: oath in Gookin et al vs Danforth "Middlesex County, MA: Court Records, 1643-1674."

[14] All Saints Church Registers, Saxtead, UK, 1546 to 1742, Suffolk Record Office, Ipswich, UK, transcribed by Muriel L. Kilvert, 41.

[15] Cambridge (Mass.), *The Records of the Town of Cambridge (formerly New-towne) Massachusetts: 1630-1703. The Records of the Town Meetings, and of the Selectmen, Comprising All of the First Volume of Records, and Being Volume II, of the Printed Records of the Town.* (Cambridge, MA: The Council, 1901), 166. <https://books.google.com/books?id=p7N4AAAAMAAJ&pg=PP1&dq>

[16] J. Albert Holmes, "About Menotomy River," *Somerville Journal*, 28 Jan 1910, 12. <www.friendsofalewifereservation.org/1910_01_28_menotomyriver.pdf>

[17] *Find A Grave*, database and images (https://www.findagrave.com : accessed 14 April 2018), memorial page for Richard Park (1609–12 Jul 1665), Find A Grave Memorial no. 119613457, citing East Parish Burying Ground, Newton, Middlesex County, Massachusetts, USA; Maintained by Evelyn Park Blalock (contributor 47540842).

[18] G. Andrews Moriarity, Jr., 279.

[19] All Saints Church Registers, Saxtead, UK, 1546 to 1742, Suffolk Record Office, Ipswich, UK, transcribed by Muriel L. Kilvert, 5.

[20] All Saints Church Registers, Saxtead, UK, 1546 to 1742, Suffolk Record Office, Ipswich, UK, transcribed by Muriel L. Kilvert, 42.

[21] G. Andrews Moriarity, Jr., 279.

[22] Thomas Williams Bicknell, *The Story of John Clarke, the founder of the first free commonwealth of the world on the basis of "full liberty in religious concernment,"* (Providence, RI: the author, 1915), 209. <https://books.google.com/books?id=uO5YAAAAMAAJ&pg=PA216&dq>

[23] Louis F. Asher, *John Clarke (1609-1676): pioneer in American medicine, democratic ideals, and champion of religious liberty* (Paris, AK: Baptist Standard Bearer, 2004), 45, 82.

[24] Louis F. Asher, John Clarke, 4.

[25] Cambridge (Mass.), *The Records of the Town of Cambridge (formerly New-towne) Massachusetts: 1630-1703. The Records of the Town Meetings, and of the Selectmen, Comprising All of the First Volume of Records, and Being Volume II, of the Printed Records of the Town.* (Cambridge, MA: The Council, 1901), 83 (Richard Withe), 350 (Rich Wyeth), 55 (Brother Withe - Hog), 57 (Brother Withe – Barn) <https://books.google.com/books?id=p7N4AAAAMAAJ&pg=PP1&dq>

[26] Southworth Lancaster, "Fire in Cambridge read 24 Apr 1956 " *The Proceedings of the Cambridge Historical Society, Volume 36, 1955-1956*, 76. <http://cambridgehistory.org/wp-content/uploads/2017/08/Proceedings-Volume-36-1955-1956.pdf>

[27] Stephen Paschall Sharples, *First Church (Cambridge, Mass.) Records of the Church of Christ at Cambridge, in New England: 1632-1830* (Boston: Eben Putnam, 1906), 11-12. <https://books.google.com/books?id=RoLJh2dqZcgC&printsec>

[28] Mary Louise Marshall Hutton, National Society Colonial Dames XVII Century, *Seventeenth Century Colonial Ancestors of Members of the National Society Colonial Dames XVII Century, 1915-1975* (Madison, WI: Edwards Brothers, 1976), 290. <https://books.google.com/books?id=P0FlAAAAMAAJ&q>

[29] Laurence Clyde Andrew, *Thomas Andrew, Immigrant* (Portland, ME: Casco Printing Co., 1972), 3-5.

[30] Charles Edward Banks, *The Planters of the Commonwealth* (Boston: Riverside Press for Houghton Mifflin Company, 1930), 65-66.

[31] Charles Wentworth Upham, Volume 2, 384.

[32] Benjamin Ray and The Rector and Visitors of the University of Virginia, "SWP No. 81.6 - Petition of Rebecca Fox," *Salem Witch Trials Documentary Archive and Transcription Project*, http://salem.lib.virginia.edu/texts/tei/swp?div_id=n81#n81.1 (accessed 5/9/2016).

[33] William Henry Egle, *Pennsylvania Genealogies* (Harrisburg, PA: L. S. Hart, printer, 1886), 680. <https://books.google.com/books?id=d7_akH9VO_cC&pg>

[34] All Saints Church Registers, Saxtead, UK, 1546 to 1742, Suffolk Record Office, Ipswich, UK, transcribed by Muriel L. Kilvert, 24.

[35] Sydney V. James, *John Clarke and his Legacies* (University Park, PA: Pennsylvania State University Press, 1999), 186.

[36] Henry Bond, Horatio Gates Jones, *Genealogies of the families and descendants of the early settlers of Watertown, Massachusetts* (Boston: Little, Brown and Company, 1855), 210. <https://books.google.com/books?id=_oc6AQAAIAAJ&printsec>

[37] Charles Alexander Nelson, *Waltham, Past and Present* (Cambridge, MA: Moses King, 1882), 72, 5.

<https://books.google.com/books?id=axEIAAAAQAAJ&pg=PA5&dq>

[38] Harriet Ruth Cooke, *The Driver Family: A Genealogical Memoir of the Descendants of Robert and Phebe Driver* (New York: John Wilson and Son, 1889), 325. <https://books.google.com/books?id=zCNKAAAAMAAJ&pg=PA325&lpg=PA325&dq>

[39] Clarence Torrey, *U.S. and New England Marriages prior to 1700* (Baltimore, MD: Genealogical Publishing Co., 2004), 844.

[40] Lucius R. Paige, *History of Cambridge, Massachusetts, 1630-1877: with a genealogical register* (Boston: H.O. Houghton, 1877), 398-399. <https://books.google.com/books?id=Yc00AQAAMAAJ&pg=>.

[41] Benjamin Church, "Phillip [sic] alias Metacomet of Pokanoket," *Library of Congress Prints and Photographs Division.* Rights Advisory: No known restrictions on publication. *Reproduction #: LC-USZ62-96234* (b&w film copy neg.) Call #: BIOG FILE - Philip [item] [P&P]. http://www.loc.gov/pictures/item/89707293/ (accessed 10/28/17).

[42] George Madison Bodge, *Soldiers in King Philip's War* (Boston: The Rockwell and Churchill Press, 1906), 168-172, 474. <https://books.google.com/books?id=ewMOAAAAIAAJ&pg>

[43] Frederick Adams Virkus, *The abridged compendium of American genealogy, v.3.* (Chicago: F. A. Virkus & Co., 1928),184. <https://babel.hathitrust.org/cgi/pt?id=wu.89062959150;view=1up;seq=11>

[44] Lucius R. Paige, 703.

[45] Nicholas and William Wyeth, *Nicholas and William Wyeth papers (Mss 73),* R. Stanton Avery Special Collections, New England Historic Genealogical Society (NEHGS). (Timothy Salls, Mgr. of Manuscript Collections, approved use of documents in an email dated 6 May 2019.)

[46] Cambridge (Mass.), *The Records of the Town of Cambridge (formerly New-towne) Massachusetts*, 288, 296, 297, 321, 319, 329, 336.

[47] Lucius R. Paige, 12, 14.

[48] Andrew Henshaw Ward, 9.

[49] Andrew Henshaw Ward, *Ward Family; Descendants of William Ward: Who Settled in Sudbury, Mass., in 1639* (Boston: Samuel G. Drake, 1851), 9-10. <https://books.google.com/books?id=yHhZAAAAMAAJ&printsec>

[50] Andrew Henshaw Ward, 9, 48.

[51] Shepard Congregational Society (Cambridge, Mass.), *The Manual of The first Church in Cambridge (Congregational)* (Boston: Samuel Usher, 1900), 35. <https://books.google.com/books?id=ZN2M_zs8EBEC&pg=PA35&dq>

[52] Benjamin and William Richard Cutter, *History of the Town of Arlington, Massachusetts: Formerly the Second Precinct in Cambridge or District of Menotomy, afterward the town of West Cambridge, 1635-1879* (Boston: David Clapp & Son, 1880), 331. <https://books.google.com/books?id=ZPePzTEEhsYC&pg=PA16&dq>

[53] Lucius R. Paige, 703.

[54] William Henry Egle, *Pennsylvania Genealogies*, 681.

[55] Lucius R. Paige, 703.

[56] Angela B. Chrysler, "Grandparents of Kym Marie Chrysler Who Were Killed by Indians," *The Chrysler Family*, Excel spreadsheet http://thechryslerfamily.com/ (accessed 10/14/2017).

[57] Cambridge (Mass.), *The Records of the Town of Cambridge (formerly New-towne) Massachusetts*, 289, 292, 300, 315.

[58] Nicholas and William Wyeth, *Nicholas and William Wyeth papers (Mss 73).*

[59] Lucius R. Paige, 703.

[60] Lucius R. Paige, 703.

[61] Angela B. Chrysler, "Grandparents of Kym Marie Chrysler Who Were Killed by Indians," *The Chrysler Family*, Excel spreadsheet http://thechryslerfamily.com/ (accessed 10/14/2017).

[62] "Queen Anne's War," *Wikipedia*, https://en.wikipedia.org/wiki/Queen_Anne%27s_War (accessed 9/20/2017).

[63] "Northeast Coast Campaign (1703)," *everipedia,* https:// everipedia.org/wiki/ Northeast_Coast_Campaign _%281703%29 (accessed 9/20/2017).

[64] "Northeast Coast Campaign (1703)," *everipedia.*

[65] Samuel Adams Drake, *The Border Wars of New England* (New York, Charles Scribner's Sons, 1897), 153-161. <https://books.google.com/books?id=FhETAAAAYAAJ&pg=PA164&dq>

[66] Samuel Adams Drake, 169-170.

[67] Art and Picture Collection, The New York Public Library, "White captives driven to Canada by the Indians," *New York Public Library Digital Collections.* http://digitalcollections.nypl.org/items/510d47e0-f46e-a3d9-e040-e00a18064a999 (accessed 10/28/17).

[68] Samuel Adams Drake, 164.

[69] Charles M. Sullivan, *Memorandum to the Historical Commission*, 22 Feb 1995, 7.

[70] Christopher Hail, "Harvard/Radcliffe Online Historical Reference Shelf," *Cambridge Buildings and Architects,* https://wayback.archive-it.org/5488/20170330145544/http://hul.harvard.edu/lib/archives/refshelf/cba/g.html#gardenst (accessed 1/31/2019).

[71] David L. Greene, "Salem Witches II: George Jacobs," *The American Genealogist* (New Haven, CT: D. L. Jacobus, Apr 1982). (Online database. AmericanAncestors.org. New England Historic Genealogical Society). <http://www.americanancestors.org/databases/american-genealogist-the/image/?volumeId=12608&pageName=65&rId=143312247>

[72] Laurence Clyde Andrew, *Thomas Andrew, Immigrant* (Portland, ME: Casco Printing Co., 1972), 3.

[73] Charles Edward Banks, 65-66.

[74] Henry Bond, Horatio Gates Jones, 8, 978.

[75] Lucius R. Paige, 481.

[76] Myra Albert Wiggins, photographer. *"The Mother."* [1901] Image. *Library of Congress Prints and Photographs Division,* https://www.loc.gov/item/2004676339 (accessed 11/27/2016).

[77] Rebecca Beatrice Brooks, "Thomas Putnam: Ringleader of the Salem Witch Hunt?," *History of Massachusetts* (blog), 19 Nov 2013. <http://historyofmassachusetts.org/thomas-putnam-ringleader-of-the-salem-witch-hunt/>

[78] John V. Goff, *Salem's Witch House: A Touchstone to Antiquity* (Charleston, SC: History Press, 2009), 41. <https://books.google.com/books?id=CdGTvyHshBMC&pg>

[79] Marilynne K. Roach, 128.

[80] Charles Wentworth Upham, *Volume 2*, 187-188.

[81] Howard Pyle, Art and Picture Collection, The New York Public Library. "There Is A Flock Of Yellow Birds Around Her Head," *New York Public Library Digital Collections*, http://digitalcollections.nypl.org/items/510d47e1-0cb1-a3d9-e040-e00a18064a99 (accessed 10/28/2017).

[82] Charles Wentworth Upham, Volume 2, 384.

[83] John V. Goff, 41.

[84] Marilynne K. Roach, 561.

[85] Charles Wentworth Upham, *Salem Witchcraft: with an Account of Salem Village, and a History of Opinions on Witchcraft and Kindred Subjects, Volume 2* (Boston: Wiggin and Lunt, 1867), 466. <https://books.google.com/books?id=qiwLAAAAYAAJ&pg>

[86] Marilynne K. Roach, 243.

[87] Benjamin Ray and The Rector and Visitors of the University of Virginia, "SWP No. 172.10 - Petition of Phillip English," *Salem Witch Trials Documentary Archive and Transcription Project*, http://salem.lib.virginia.edu/texts/tei/swp?div_id=n172#n172.10 (accessed 10/30/2017).

[88] Rebecca Beatrice Brooks, "The Salem Witch Trials Victims: Who Were They?," *History of Massachusetts* (blog), 19 Aug 2015. <http://historyofmassachusetts.org/salem-witch-trials-victims>

[89] Henry Bond, Horatio Gates Jones, 210.

[90] Henry Bond, Horatio Gates Jones, 210.

[91] Harriet Ruth Cooke, 325.

[92] Lucius R. Paige, 703.

[93] Lucius R. Paige, 698.

[94] Roland Gray, "The William Gray House in Cambridge," *Cambridge Historical Society Publications XIV, Proceedings for the Year 1919* (Cambridge, MA: Cambridge Historical Society, 1926), 104. <https://books.google.com/books?id=558yAQAAMAAJ&pg>

[95] John Ward Dean, *The New England Historical and Genealogical Register for the year 1863, Vol. XVII* (Albany, NY: J. Munsell, 1863), 121-123. <https://books.google.com/books?id=BWsFAAAAQAAJ&pg>

[96] Lucius R. Paige, 703.

[97] Benjamin and William Richard Cutter, 334.

[98] Benjamin and William Richard Cutter, 334.

[99] Charles J. F. Binney, *The History and Genealogy of the Prentice Or Prentiss Family in New England, from 1631 to 1852* (Boston: Charles Binney, 1852), 74. <https://books.google.com/books?id=-RNYAAAAcAAJ&pg>

[100] Doris Birmingham, Editor, *Jason Russell House Tour Guide Manual*, (Arlington, MA: Arlington Historical Society, 2016-2017), 16. <https://arlingtonhistorical.org/wp-content/uploads/2017/07/JRHManualBody20164.pdf>

[101] Lucius R. Paige, 703.

[102] Benjamin Cutter, William Richard Cutter, *History of the town of Arlington, Massachusetts*, 325.

[103] Benjamin Cutter, William Richard Cutter, 696.

[104] Benjamin and William Richard Cutter, 256.

[105] Lucius R. Paige, 698.

[106] Lucius R. Paige, 698.

[107] Wyeth, Jonas. *Wyeth family records (Mss A 3058)*. R. Stanton Avery Special Collections, New England Historic Genealogical Society and www.americanancestors.org (accessed 8/24/2015.) (Timothy Salls, Mgr. of Manuscript Collections, approved use of NEHGS documents in an email dated 6 May 2019.)

[108] Stephen Paschall Sharples, *Records of the Church of Christ at Cambridge in New England, 1632-1830* (Boston: Eben Putnam, 1906), 48, 94. <https://books.google.com/books?id=uec5NeoICFUC&pg=PA499&dq>

[109] Stephen Paschall Sharples, 56.

[110] John Ward Dean, 114, 118, and 122-23.

[111] Lucius R. Paige, 703.

[112] Lucius R. Paige, 629, 703.

[113] Benjamin and William Richard Cutter, 326.

[114] Lucius R. Paige, 697.

[115] Doris Birmingham, 9.

[116] Doris Birmingham, 16.

[117] Clifford Kenyon Shipton, *Sibley's Harvard Graduates, Volume 14, the Classes of 1756–1760* (Boston: Massachusetts Historical Society, 1968) 676. <https://dcms.lds.org/delivery/DeliveryManagerServlet?dps_pid=IE7613052>

[118] Frederick Robinson, "How The First Parish In Cambridge Got A New Meetinghouse read 26 Jan 1937," *The Proceedings of the Cambridge Historical Society, Volume 24, 1936-1937*, 59. <http://cambridgehistory.org/wp-content/uploads/2017/08/Proceedings-Volume-24-1936-1937.pdf>

[119] Frederick Robinson, 676.

[120] John James Babson, *History of the Town of Gloucester* (Gloucester, MA: Procter Brothers, 1860), 355-356. <https://books.google.com/books?id=qEgWwCBGyCQC&printsec>

[121] John James Babson, 356.

[122] John James Babson, 357.

[123] Clifford Kenyon Shipton, 677.

[124] Clifford Kenyon Shipton, 677.

[125] Secretary of the Commonwealth, *Massachusetts Soldiers and Sailors of the Revolutionary War, Volume 17* (Boston: Wright & Potter Printing, 1908) 973. <https://archive.org/stream/masssoldiers17bostrich#page/972/mode/2up/search/wyeth>

[126] Clifford Kenyon Shipton, 677.

[127] Lucius R. Paige, 704.

[128] H. L. Peter Rounds, *Abstracts of Bristol County, Massachusetts Probate Records, 1687-1745, Volume IX 1737-1740* (Baltimore, MD: Genealogical Publishing Co., Inc., 1987), 272.

[129] Arabella Morton, *Descendants of John Gamage of Ipswich, Mass.* (Worcester, MA: Press of Charles R. Stobbs, 1906), 18.

<https://books.google.com/books?id=QidMAAAAMAAJ&pg>

[130] Arabella Morton, 18.

[131] Arabella Morton, 18.

[132] Arthur Meredyth Burke, *The Prominent Families of the United States of America* (London: The Sackville Press, 1908), 306.

[133] Arabella Morton, 11-12.

[134] Thomas P. Hughes, *American Ancestry of Americans whose Ancestors Settled in the United States Previous to the Declaration of Independence, Vol. IX* (Albany, NY: Joel Munsell's Sons, 1894), 71. <http://digital.cincinnatilibrary.org/cdm/pageflip/collection/p16998coll15/id/157566/type/compoundobject/filename/print/page/download/start/2 2/pftype/pdf>

[135] Massachusetts Daughters of the American Revolution, Hannah Winthrop Chapter, Cambridge, *An Historic Guide to Cambridge* (Cambridge, MA: N. S. D. A. R., 1907), 156. <https://books.google.com/books?id=ogwNrgEACAAJ&printsec>

[136] Arabella Morton, 18.

[137] Charles Hudson, *History of the Town of Lexington, Massachusetts, volume II* (Cambridge, MA: The Riverside Press, 1913), 203-204. <https://books.google.com/books?id=BEEOAAAAIAAJ&pg>

[138] Lucius R. Paige, 543.

[139] Lucius R. Paige, 516.

[140] Lucius R. Paige, 552.

[141] Stephen Paschall Sharples, 84.

[142] Lucius R. Paige, 542.

[143] Thomas Shepard; Michael MacGiffert, *God's plot: Puritan spirituality in Thomas Shepard's Cambridge* (Amherst, MA: Univ. of Massachusetts Press, 1994), 72-73.

[144] *Find A Grave*, database and images (https://www.findagrave.com : accessed 25 Oct 2017), memorial page for Mary Wigglesworth (29 Jan 1883–19 Dec 1884), Find A Grave Memorial no. 40308880, citing Mt. Auburn Cemetery, Cambridge, Middlesex County, Massachusetts, USA; Maintained by Kristin Jones (contributor 47028934).

[145] Henry Bond, Horatio Gates Jones, 458-459.

[146] Benjamin Cutter and William Richard Cutter, *A History of the Cutter Family of New England* (Boston: David Clapp & Son, 1871), 250-251. <https://books.google.com/books?id=MIxGAAAAMAAJ&pg>

[147] Benjamin and William Richard Cutter, *History of Arlington,* 216.

[148] Lucius R. Paige, 597.

[149] Florian Cajori, *The Teaching and History of Mathematics in the United States, Volumes 890-893* (Washington: Government Printing Office, 1890) 45. <https://books.google.com/books?id=g98FlwgbJyEC&pg>

[150] Clifford Kenyon Shipton, *Volume 16, 327.*

[151] Henry Bond, Horatio Gates Jones, 701.

[152] Henry Bond, Horatio Gates Jones, 701.

[153] Lucius R. Paige, 698.

[154] Lucius R. Paige, 632.

[155] Suzanne Ruth Thurman, *"O Sisters Ain't you Happy?": Gender, Family, and Community Among the Harvard and Shirley Shakers, 1781-1918* (Syracuse, NY: Syracuse University Press, 2002), 189. <http://books.google.com/books?id=zqgOwvtKlKUC&pg=PA66&lpg>

[156] "Eagle Scout Service project," *Restoration of the Shaker Cemetery, Harvard, MA,* Jun 1990. <https://historicharvard.files.wordpress.com/2016/03/eagle-scout-service-project-1990.pdf>

[157] Lucius R. Paige, 631, 632.

[158] Roben Campbell, *A Short Biography: Deborah Prentice, Harvard Shaker.*

[159] Charles J. F. Binney, 121.

[160] Charles M. Sullivan, 3.

[161] Suzanne Ruth Thurman, 26.

[162] Abraham Tomlinson, *The Military Journals of Two Private Soldiers* (Poughkeepsie, NY: Abraham Tomlinson, 1855), 106. <https://books.google.com/books?id=UmfU4HZV2n0C&pg>

[163] Doris Birmingham, 16.

[164] Lucius R. Paige, 698.

[165] William and Benjamin Cutter, 327.

[166] Lucius R. Paige, 698.

[167] Medford Historical Society, *The Medford Historical Register, Volume 6* (Medford, MA: J. C. Miller, Jr. 1903), 68-69. https://books.google.com/books?id=EY1QAAAAYAAJ&pg

[168] Patricia Law Hatcher, *Graves of Revolutionary Patriots, Vol. 4, S – Z* (Dallas, TX: Pioneer Heritage Press, 1988), 220.

[169] Benjamin and William Richard Cutter, *History of Arlington,* 217-218.

[170] Henry Bond, Horatio Gates Jones, 992.

[171] Roland Gray, 104-106.

[172] Henry Bond, Horatio Gates Jones, 992.

[173] "The Midnight Ride of Paul Revere," *Paul Revere,* 27 Apr 2015. <http://paulrevere.us/midnight-ride-of-paul-revere>

[174] Frank Warren Coburn, *The battle of April 19, 1775: in Lexington, Concord, Lincoln, Arlington, Cambridge, Somerville, and Charlestown, Massachusetts* (Boston: F. L. Coburn and Company, 1912), 104-105, 40-41 (muster rolls) <https://archive.org/details/battleofapril19100cobu>

[175] Frank Warren Coburn, 63 and 70.

[176] Frederick Adams Virkus, Vol. 3, 184.

[177] Eliphalet Newell, *Abstract of pay for Captain Newell's Company in Henry Knox's regiment* (Jan 1776), Gilder Lehrman Collection #: GLC02437.09497 <http://www.gilderlehrman.org/collections/ddef21d4-9296-4fd7-ab16-428856309333>

[178] Ancestry.com, Widow's Pension Application, No. W14205, Elizabeth Wyeth, Revolutionary War, RG 15; NA–Washington, image 96.

[179] Lucius R. Paige, 704.

[180] Jill Sinclair, *Fresh Pond: The History of a Cambridge Landscape* (Cambridge, MA: The MIT Press, 2009), 20.

[181] "Died," *The Democrat* (Boston, MA) 08 Feb 1806, 3.

[182] Dean Dudley, *The Dudley Genealogies and Family Records* (Boston: Dean Dudley, Publisher, 1848), 116-117 and 121.

[183] "Thomas Dudley," *Wikipedia*, https://en.wikipedia.org/wiki/Thomas_Dudley (accessed 8/20/2017).

[184] "John Cotton (minister)," *Wikipedia*, https://en.wikipedia.org/wiki/John_Cotton_(minister) (accessed 8/20/2017).

[185] Benjamin and William Richard Cutter, *History of Arlington*, 332.

[186] Jonas Wyeth, *Wyeth family records (Mss A 3058)*, R. Stanton Avery Special Collections, New England Historic Genealogical Society.

[187] Frank Warren Coburn, 104-105.

[188] Jonas Wyeth, *Wyeth family records (Mss A 3058)*, R. Stanton Avery Special Collections, New England Historic Genealogical Society.

[189] *Find A Grave*, database and images (https://www.findagrave.com : accessed 13 Feb 2017), memorial page for Susannah Wyeth Sawin (2 Mar 1734–23 Mar 1794), Find A Grave Memorial no. 28006515, citing Old Burying Place, Watertown, Middlesex County, Massachusetts, USA ; Maintained by Bill Boyington (contributor 46800933).

[190] *Find A Grave*, (https://www.findagrave.com : accessed 13 Feb 2017), memorial page for Susannah Wyeth Sawin no. 28006515.

[191] Frank Warren Coburn, 48.

[192] *Find A Grave*, (https://www.findagrave.com : accessed 13 Feb 2017), memorial page for Susannah Wyeth Sawin no. 28006515.

[193] Secretary of the Commonwealth, *Massachusetts Soldiers and Sailors in the War of the Revolution, Volume 13* (Boston: Wright & Potter Printing Co., 1896), 850-851. <https://archive.org/stream/masssoldiers13bostrich#page/848/mode/2up/search/sawin>

[194] Watertown (Mass.), *Watertown's military history*. Authorized by a vote of the inhabitants of the town of Watertown, Massachusetts. Published under the direction of a committee representing the Sons of the American revolution, and Isaac B. Patten post 81, Grand Army of the Republic (Boston: David Clapp & Son, 1907), 102. <https://books.google.com/books?id=WUyQkyv5eDgC&pg>

[195] Thomas E. Sawin and John Sawin, *Sawin: Summary Notes Concerning John Sawin and His Prosperity* (Wendell, MA: Rufus Putnam Printers, 1866), 22. <https://books.google.com/books?id=KrdXAAAAcAAJ&printsec>

[196] Thomas E. Sawin and John Sawin, 8.

[197] Thomas E. Sawin and John Sawin, 21-22.

[198] Thomas E. Sawin and John Sawin, 22.

[199] Thomas E. Sawin and John Sawin, 21.

[200] J. L. Bell, "The Man Who Named the Boston Tea Party," *Boston 1775 Blog*, 22 Dec 2010. <http://boston1775.blogspot.com/2010/12/man-who-named-boston-tea-party.html>

[201] Thomas E. Sawin and John Sawin, 22.

[202] Thomas E. Sawin and John Sawin, 22.

[203] Thomas E. Sawin and John Sawin, 24.

[204] *Find A Grave*, database and images (https://www.findagrave.com : accessed 13 Feb 2017), memorial page for Eunice Kendall (1784–23 Dec 1821), Find A Grave Memorial no. 126564214, citing Wendell Center Cemetery, Wendell, Franklin County, Massachusetts, USA; Maintained by James Bianco (contributor 47745493).

[205] Thomas E. Sawin and John Sawin, 22.

[206] Rensselaer Allston Oakes, *Genealogical and Family History of the County of Jefferson, New York, Volume 2* (New York: Higginson Book Company, 1905), 992. <https://books.google.com/books?id=T8kpAQAAMAAJ&dq>

[207] William Richard Cutter, *Genealogical and Personal Memoirs Relating to the Families of Boston and Eastern Massachusetts, Volume 2* (New York: Lewis Historical Publishing Co., 1908), 970. <https://books.google.com/books?id=kFoLBC2TwFYC&pg=PA970&dq>

[208] "Died," *Boston Patriot and Daily Chronicle* (Boston, MA), 7 Jan 1825, 3. (GenealogyBank.com)

[209] Stephen Paschall Sharples, 518.

[210] Henry R. Stiles, *Contributions toward a genealogy of the family of Stiles: descended from Robert, of Rowley, Mass., 1659-1860* (Albany, NY: J. Munsell, 1863), 32. (Ancestry.com, [database on-line] - Provo, UT: Ancestry.com Operations Inc., 2005.)

[211] Henry Fitz-Gilbert Waters, The New England Historical and Genealogical Register, Volume 55, (Boston: NEHGS, 1901), 402. <https://books.google.com/books?id=hcAg0OBzr1oC&pg>

[212] Secretary of the Commonwealth, *Volume 17*, 974.

[213] Lucius R. Paige, 704.

[214] Lucius R. Paige, 12, 14.

[215] Roger Gilman, 30.

[216] Christopher Hail, *Garden Street*.

[217] "Cambridge, July 13, 1791," *Herald of Freedom* (Boston, MA), 19 Jul 1791, 3.

[218] Lucius R. Paige, 704.

[219] Ancestry.com, Widow's Pension Application, No. W14205, Elizabeth Wyeth, Revolutionary War, RG 15; NA–Washington, image 96.

[220] John Goodwin Locke, *Book of the Lockes* (Boston and Cambridge, MA: James Munroe and Company, 1853), 66. <https://books.google.com/books?id=zxdYAAAAcAAJ&pg=PA112&dq>

[221] John Boynton Hill, *History of the Town of Mason, N.H.* (Boston, MA: Lucius A. Elliot & Co., 1858), 186.

[222] Georgiana I. Sluman, *The Russell Family*, a story found in the Mason, New Hampshire Historical Room, about 1985, page 1.

[223] Doris Birmingham, 10.

[224] Samuel Abbot Smith, *West Cambridge on the Nineteenth of April, 1775, an Address* (Boston: Alfred Mudge & Son, 1864) 37-39. <https://books.google.com/books?id=VMo_AAAAYAAJ&pg=PA4&dq>

[225] Samuel Abbot Smith, 37-39.

[226] Benjamin and William Richard Cutter, 70.

[227] Frank E. Shedd, "Daniel Shed Genealogy," *Ebenezer Shed [4:1726*, http://library.untraveledroad.com/Ch/Shedd/Daniel-Shed/Fourth/Ebenezer-1726.htm (accessed 4/11/2017).

[228] Arabella Morton, 18-19.

[229] Arabella Morton, 19.

[230] Stephen Paschall Sharples, 142.

[231] Stephen Paschall Sharples, 154.

[232] Stephen Paschall Sharples, 156.

[233] Stephen Paschall Sharples, 159.

[234] William Otis Sawtelle, *Daniel Gott, Mount Desert pioneer: his ancestors and descendants*, (Mt. Desert, ME: No publisher ID, 1926), 12-13. <https://dcms.lds.org/delivery/DeliveryManagerServlet?dps_pid=IE3997061>

[235] John James Babson, 336.

[236] Essex Society of Genealogists, *The Essex Genealogist, Volumes 12-13* (Lynnfield, MA: Essex Society, 1992), 188. <https://books.google.com/books?id=U2sjAQAAMAAJ&q>

[237] H. L. Peter Rounds, 272.

[238] Henry Bond, Horatio Gates Jones, 771.

[239] Essex Society of Genealogists, 188.

[240] Arabella Morton, 18.

[241] Duane Hamilton Hurd, *History of Essex County, Massachusetts, Volume II* (Philadelphia: JW Lewis & Co., 1888), 1360-1361. <https://books.google.com/books?id=k98_AQAAMAAJ&pg>

[242] Essex Society of Genealogists, 188.

[243] John James Babson, 340.

[244] "Gloucester, Massachusetts," *Wikipedia*, https://en.wikipedia.org/wiki/Gloucester,_Massachusetts (accessed 9/2/2017).

[245] Arabella Morton, 19.

[246] John James Babson, 119.

[247] Arabella Morton, 19.

[248] Direct Data Capture, comp., *U.S., War of 1812 Service Records, 1812-1815* [database on-line] (Provo, UT: Ancestry.com Operations, Inc., 1999). Original data: National Archives and Records Administration, *Index to the Compiled Military Service Records for the Volunteer Soldiers Who Served During the War of 1812,* citing the service of Nathaniel Gamage as a Private in the 2nd Regiment (Osgood's) Massachusetts Militia; Washington, D.C.: National Archives and Records Administration, Microfilm Publication: M602, Box 77.

[249] Arabella Morton, 22-23.

[250] Arabella Morton, 24.

[251] Arabella Morton, 24.

[252] Stephen Paschall Sharples, 167.

[253] Stephen Paschall Sharples, 104.

[254] Massachusetts Vital Records Project (Transcriber), *Town of Weston Records* (Boston: McIndoe Brothers, 1901), 20. <http://ma-vitalrecords.org/MA/Middlesex/Weston/Images/Weston_020.shtml>

[255] Massachusetts Vital Records Project, 131.

[256] Arabella Morton, 18.

[257] Massachusetts Vital Records Project, 62.

[258] Massachusetts Vital Records Project, 463.

[259] Bruce A. Ronda, *Elizabeth Palmer Peabody: A Reformer on Her Own Terms* (Cambridge, MA: Harvard University Press, 1999) 19. <https://books.google.com/books?id=_9-z8gVAqSkC&pg>

[260] Clifford Kenyon Shipton, *Volume 9*, 414-418. <https://dcms.lds.org/delivery/DeliveryManagerServlet?dps_pid=IE7664427&from=fhd&>

[261] Megan Marshall, *The Peabody Sisters* (Boston and New York: Houghton Mifflin Company, 2005) 23-24.

[262] "Elizabeth Peabody," *Wikipedia*, https://en.wikipedia.org/wiki/Elizabeth_Peabody (accessed 5/24/17).

[263] Megan Marshall, 23.

[264] William Richard Cutter, Edward Henry Clement, Samuel Hart, Mary Kingsbury Talcott, Frederick Bostwick, Ezra Scollay Stearns, *Genealogical and Family History of the State of Connecticut, Volume 4* (New York: Lewis Historical Publishing Co., 1911), 1743. <https://books.google.com/books?id=DNA4AQAAMAAJ&printsec>

[265] "Phineas Stearns," *Boston Tea Party Ships and Museum*, https://www.bostonteapartyship.com/phineas-stearns (accessed 6/2/2017).

[266] Clifford Kenyon Shipton, *Volume 16*, 327.

[267] Clifford Kenyon Shipton, *Sibley's Harvard Graduates, Volume 16* (Boston: Massachusetts Historical Society, 1968) 327. <https://dcms.lds.org/delivery/DeliveryManagerServlet?dps_pid=IE7613052>

[268] Clifford Kenyon Shipton, *Volume 16*, 327.

[269] "Revolutionary War Raids & Skirmishes in 1780," *American Revolutionary War,* http://www.myrevolutionarywar.com/battles/1780-skirmish/ (accessed 9/29/16).

[270] "We hear from Cambridge," *Boston Gazette* (Boston, MA), 09 Feb 1761, 3.

[271] Daniel V. Boudillion, "How the Shakers Invented Spiritualism - The Ecstatic Spirits of Holy Hill, Harvard Massachusetts," *Field Investigations*, 11 Aug 2002 & 30 May 2007 http://www.boudillion.com/holyhill/holyhill.htm

[272] Suzanne R. Thurman, 63, 22.

[273] Roben Campbell, *A Short Biography: Deborah Prentice, Harvard Shaker (1720-1811),* In Historic Harvard Town, 2016. https://historicharvard.wordpress.com/historic-places/highlight-our-historic-places/our-harvard-shakers-cemetery/a-biography-deborah-prentice-harvard-shaker/

[274] Suzanne R. Thurman, 64, 36.

[275] "Shaker Cemetery Burial Map," *In Historic Harvard Town*, https://historicharvard.wordpress.com/historic-places/highlight-our-historic-places/our-harvard-shakers-cemetery/comment-page-1/ (accessed 5/22/17).

[276] The Essex Institute, 325 (records of Westford spell his name Ebenezer Wythe).

[277] Pennsylvania Historical Survey of the Works Project Administration, *Port of Philadelphia, Maritime Records, Alphabetical List of*

Masters and Crews: 1798-1880 (Philadelphia: Works Project Administration, 1937), 11.

[278] Helen L. Harman, Herman Stephan, Vi P. Limric, *Silver Spring Presbyterian Church Marriages, 1814-30, Silver Spring Twp., Cumberland County, Pennsylvania*, 1959. <pagenweb.org/~cumberland/silspma.htm>

[279] "Died," *National Gazette* (Philadelphia, PA) 13 Apr 1840, 3.

[280] "Died," *Boston Courier* (Boston, MA) 9 Jun 1845, 2

[281] Henry Bond, Horatio Gates Jones, 992.

[282] Eliphalet Newell, Gilder Lehrman Collection #: GLC02437.09497.

[283] Ancestry.com, *U.S., Revolutionary War Pension and Bounty-Land Warrant Application Files, 1800-1900* [database on-line] (Provo, UT: Ancestry.com Operations, Inc., 2010). Original data: Application, 1819, Joshua Wyeth, Survivor's Pension Application File, No. S40734 (Private, Continental Army, First Massachusetts Regiment, Revolutionary War); "Revolutionary War Pension and Bounty-Land Warrant Application Files," NARA microfilm publication M804, Department of Veterans Affairs, Record Group 15, Roll No. 2654; National Archives, Washington, D.C., Image 169.

[284] Ancestry.com, *U.S., Revolutionary War Pension and Bounty-Land Warrant Application Files, 1800-1900* [database on-line] (Provo, UT: Ancestry.com Operations, Inc., 2010). Original data: Application, 1819, Ebenezer Wyeth, Survivor's Pension Application File, No. S34,576 (Private, Continental Army, First Massachusetts Regiment, Revolutionary War); "Revolutionary War Pension and Bounty-Land Warrant Application Files," NARA microfilm publication M804, Department of Veterans Affairs, Record Group 15, Roll No. 2654; National Archives, Washington, D.C., Image 56.

[285] Ernest Byron Cole, *The Winship family in America: giving the line of decent from Edward Winship, born in England in 1613, who came to Cambridge, Massachusetts, in 1635, to Jabez Lathrop Winship, born in Norwich, Conn., 1752, died in Brookville, Indiana, 1827, with the record of the families of his children and grandchildren, with their line of descent from William the Conqueror* (Indianapolis, IN: [Cole], 1905), 7. <https://books.google.com/books?id=F79bAAAAMAAJ&printsec>

[286] William S. Lawyer, *Binghamton: its settlement, growth, and development, and the factors in its history, 1800-1900* (Boston: Century Memorial Publishing Co., 1900), 617. <https://books.google.com/books?id=E9YwAQAAMAAJ&pg.>

[287] Benjamin and William Richard Cutter, *History of Arlington*, 332.

[288] Ancestry.com, *Massachusetts, Wills and Probate Records, 1635-1991* [database on-line] (Provo, UT: Ancestry.com Operations, Inc., 2015), 511. Original data: Massachusetts County, District and Probate Courts, Ebenezer Wyeth, case number: 25805.

[289] Henry Francis Walling, *Map of the City of Cambridge, Middlesex County, Mass.* (Boston : Geo. L. Dix, 1854). <http://ids.lib.harvard.edu/ids/view/10389750?buttons=y>

[290] Roland Gray, 104.

[291] The Essex Institute, *Vital Records of Westford, Massachusetts to the end of the year 1849* (Salem, MA: Newcomb & Gauss, 1915), 325.

[292] Lucius Paige, 705.

[293] Ancestry.com, Series T718: 1818 - 1872 04: Revolutionary War, 1833-1848, Image 90.

[294] Ancestry.com, Survivor's Pension Application File, No. S34,576, Ebenezer Wyeth, Rev. War, RG 15; NA–Washington, Image 60 and 69.

[295] "Died," *Cambridge Press* (Cambridge, MA), 10 Aug 1889, 3.

[296] "Old Cambridge," *Cambridge Chronicle* (Cambridge, MA), 17 Sep 1887, 5.

[297] "Mortgagees' Sale," *Cambridge Chronicle* (Cambridge, MA), 13 Nov 1909, 14.

[298] Christopher Hail, *Mt. Auburn Street.*

[299] John Herbert Barker, *Some notes on the Wyeth family 1595-1940 Giving eight generations of the Descendants of Nicholas Wyeth who came to America about 1645* (Cambridge, MA: Handwritten genealogy, 1940), 40.

[300] George C. Groce; David H. Wallace; New York Historical Society, *The New-York Historical Society's dictionary of artists in America: 1564 – 1860* (New Haven, CT: Yale Univ. Press, 1975), 707.

[301] Lucius Paige, 704-705.

[302] "Died," *Emancipator and Weekly Chronicle* (London, England), 25 Jun 1845, 36.

[303] Ancestry.com, Widow's Pension Application, No. W14205, Elizabeth Wyeth, Rev. War, RG 15; NA–Washington, image 149 and 118.

[304] Charles Winthrop Sawyer, *Firearms in American History, Volume 1* (Norwood, MA: Plimpton Press, 1910), 93. <https://books.google.com/books?id=FW_fAAAAMAAJ&pg>

[305] Secretary of the Commonwealth, *Massachusetts Soldiers and Sailors of the Revolutionary War, Volume 17*, 972-974.

[306] Eliphalet Newell, Gilder Lehrman Collection #: GLC02437.09497.

[307] Lucius Paige, 705.

[308] Ancestry.com, Widow's Pension Application, No. W14205, Elizabeth Wyeth, Revolutionary War, RG 15; NA–Washington, image 116.

[309] Ancestry.com, Widow's Pension Application, No. W14205, Elizabeth Wyeth, Revolutionary War, RG 15; NA–Washington, image 105.

[310] Eliphalet Newell, Gilder Lehrman Collection #: GLC02437.09497.

[311] Ancestry.com, Survivor's Pension Application File, No. S40734, Joshua Wyeth and No. S34,576, Ebenezer Wyeth, Revolutionary War, RG 15; NA–Washington, image 169 and 56.

[312] Ancestry.com, Survivor's Pension Application File, No. S34,576, Ebenezer Wyeth, Rev. War, RG 15; NA–Washington, Image 69.

[313] Ancestry.com, Widow's Pension Application, No. W14205, Elizabeth Wyeth, Revolutionary War, RG 15; NA–Washington, image 102.

[314] Ancestry.com, Widow's Pension Application, No. W14205, Elizabeth Wyeth, Revolutionary War, RG 15; NA–Washington, image 79-80.

[315] Ancestry.com, Widow's Pension Application, No. W14205, Elizabeth Wyeth, Revolutionary War, RG 15; NA–Washington, image 99.

[316] Ancestry.com, *U.S., Revolutionary War Pensioners, 1801-1815, 1818-1872* [database on-line] (Provo, UT: Ancestry.com Operations, Inc., 2007), images 136 and 159. Original data: "Ledgers of Payments, 1818-1872, to U.S. Pensioners Under Acts of 1818 Through 1858, From Records of the Office of the Third Auditor of the Treasury, 1818-1872," Citing Pension Payment Roll of Veterans of the Revolutionary War and the Regular Army and Navy for Elizabeth Wyeth; service of Jonas Wyeth (Navy, Massachusetts, Revolutionary War); NARA microfilm publication T718, Department of Veterans Affairs, Record Group 217, roll No. 19 (136) and 17 (159); National Archives, Washington, D.C.

[317] Jill Sinclair, 23.

[318] Susan E. Maycock, Charles M. Sullivan, *Building Old Cambridge* (Cambridge, MA: MIT Press, 2016), 238.

[319] Sandra Sutphin Olne, *Passengers on the "Lion" From England to Boston, 1632, and five generations of their descendants* (Westminster,

MD: Heritage Books, 2008), 90.

[320] "Report of deaths in the city of Cincinnati, for the week ending Wednesday, 28 Jan 1829," *Daily Cincinnati Republican* (Cincinnati, Ohio), 3 Feb 1829, 3.

[321] Horace E. Hayden, editor for the Wyoming Historical and Geological Society, *Proceedings and Collections, Volumes 7-8* (Wilkes-Barre, PA:, The E. B. Yordy Co.,1902), 228. <https://books.google.com/books?id=ZyFCAQAAMAAJ&printsec>

[322] Clement Ferdinand Heverly, *History of the Towandas 1776-1886* (Towanda, PA: Reporter-Journal Printing Co., 1886), 53. <https://books.google.com/books?id=aBkVAAAAYAAJ>

[323] Martha Helwagen, *Ohio Records and Pioneer Families,Vol. 9* (Mansfield, OH: The Ohio Genealogical Society, 1968), 87.

[324] Benjamin and William Richard Cutter, *History of Arlington*, 333.

[325] David Craft, 382.

[326] Benjamin and William Richard Cutter, *History of Arlington*, 333.

[327] Benjamin and William Richard Cutter, *History of Arlington*, 333.

[328] Benjamin and William Richard Cutter, *History of Arlington*, 333.

[329] Benjamin and William Richard Cutter, *History of Arlington*, 333.

[330] J. L. Bell, "The Man Who Named the Boston Tea Party," *Boston 1775 Blog*, 22 Dec 2010.

[331] Ray Raphael, *Founders: The People Who Brought You a Nation* (New York: New Press, 2009), 124. <https://books.google.com/books?id=toWzDnM9JDEC&pg>

[332] Isaiah Thomas, "Boston, April 23," The *Worcester Magazine Fourth week in April, 1787* (Worcester, MA), Apr, 1787, 50. <https://books.google.com/books?id=omoAAAAYAAJ&pg>

[333] Clement Ferdinand Heverly, 44.

[334] Clement Ferdinand Heverly, 43-44.

[335] David Craft, *History of Bradford County, Pennsylvania with Illustrations and Biographical Sketches of Some of its Prominent Men and Pioneers* (Philadelphia: L. H. Everts & Co., 1878), 382. <http://www.joycetice.com/craft/towanddc.htm>

[336] Ancestry.com, Survivor's Pension Application File, No. S40734, Joshua Wyeth, Rev. War, RG 15; NA–Washington, image 165, 169-170.

[337] "Gleanings," *The Long-Island Star* (Brooklyn, New York), 28 Sep 1826, 3.

[338] Benjamin and William Cutter, 332-333.

[339] Clement Ferdinand Heverly, 44.

[340] Benjamin and William Cutter, 332-333.

[341] Dorothy J. Clark, "Historically Speaking," *The Terre Haute Tribune* (Terre Haute, IN), 14 Dec 1975, 4.

[342] Timothy Flint, "Revolutionary Reminiscence July 1827," *The Western Monthly Review* (Cincinnati, OH: E.H. Flint, 1827), 147-149. <https://archive.org/details/westernmonthlyre01flin>

[343] "Obituary," *The Daily Cincinnati Gazette* (Cincinnati, OH), 23 Jan 1829, 1.

[344] Clement Ferdinand Heverly, *Pioneer and patriot families of Bradford County, Pennsylvania, 1800-1825, Volume II* (Towanda, Pa: Bradford Star Print, 1915), 439.

[345] Gen. Samuel F. Cary, *Record of Revolutionary Soldiers buried in Hamilton Co., Ohio* (Cincinnati, OH: Ohio Society of the Sons of the Revolution, 1895), 2.

[346] "Spring Grove Cemetery," *Genealogy Search Listing (Cenotaph Records)*, http://www.springgrove.org/cenotaph.aspx?id=2734&cemetery=SPRINGGROVE (accessed 4/26/2014).

[347] Jeff Suess, "Honoring America's original patriots." *The Cincinnati Enquirer* (Cincinnati, OH), 13 Apr 2014, AA14-15.

[348] Massachusetts Daughters of the American Revolution, Hannah Winthrop Chapter, Cambridge, 39.

[349] Lucius Paige, 705.

[350] Stephen Paschall Sharples, 204.

[351] Lucius Paige, 705.

[352] H. F. Kett and Company, *The History of Jo Daviess County, Illinois* (Chicago: H. F. Kett & Co., Times Building, 1878), 476. <https://books.google.com/books?id=0BIVAAAAYAAJ&pg>

[353] Robert Hanson, *Vital Statistics from Galena Newspapers, July 22, 1828 - November 19, 1850*, jodaviess.illinoisgenweb.org/vitals/VS1a.htm (accessed 7/25/17).

[354] Robert Hanson.

[355] Thomas M. Myers, *The Norris family of Maryland* (New York: William M. Clemens, 1916), 47-48. <https://babel.hathitrust.org/cgi/pt?id=wu.89069612463;view=1up;seq=3>

[356] Thomas M. Myers, 47-48.

[357] Mrs. Edwin C. Gibbons, Maryland Historical Society, *Vital records of the First Independent (now Unitarian) Church: Baltimore, Maryland, 1818-1921* (Westminster, MD: Heritage Books, 2007), 49.

[358] Joseph Gardner Bartlett, *Gregory Stone Genealogy: Ancestry and Descendants of Dea. Gregory Stone of Cambridge, Mass., 1320-1917* (Boston: Murray Printing Co., 1918), 360. <https://books.google.com/books?id=ZxsVAAAAYAAJ&pg>

[359] Jill Sinclair, 20.

[360] Joseph Palmer, *Necrology of Alumni of Harvard College, 1851-52 to 1862-63* (Boston: John Wilson and Son, 1864), 107-108.

[361] Joseph Palmer, 108.

[362] Chauncey Depew Steele, Jr., *A History of Inns and Hotels in Cambridge* (Cambridge, MA: Cambridge Historical Society, 1957), 34. <http://cambridgehistory.org/wp-content/uploads/2017/02/CHS-Index-to-Proceedings.pdf>

[363] Jill Sinclair, 21.

[364] Ancestry.com, *Massachusetts, Wills and Probate Records, 1635-1991*, Ebenezer Wyeth, case number: 25805.

[365] Jill Sinclair, 22.

[366] Lucius Paige, 705.

[367] Jill Sinclair, 23.

[368] Jill Sinclair, 30, 70, 75.

[369] Christopher Hail, *Fresh Pond Parkway*.

[370] "The Changing Face of Homelessness," *Heading Home*, http://www.headinghomeinc.org/ (accessed 6/17/2016).

[371] Chauncey Depew Steele, Jr., 34.

[372] "The Fresh Pond Hotel," *Wikipedia*, https://en.wikipedia.org/wiki/Fresh_Pond_Hotel (accessed 6/7/2016).

[373] Jill Sinclair, 36.

[374] Jill Sinclair, 33, 36.

[375] Samuel Atkins Eliot, *All Aboard the "Natwyethum!"* (Cambridge, MA: Cambridge Historical Society, 1942), 38.

[376] John B(ound) Wyeth, Benjamin Waterhouse, *Oregon, or, a Short History of a Long Journey* (Cambridge, MA: Printed for John B. Wyeth, 1833), 30, 63. <https://books.google.com/books?id=K2xZAAAAcAAJ&pg>

[377] Samuel Atkins Eliot, 39, 41, 46, 49.

[378] Samuel Atkins Eliot, 52-53.

[379] Nathaniel Jarvis Wyeth, *The Correspondence and Journals of Captain Nathaniel J. Wyeth, 1831-6* (Eugene, OR: University Press, 1899), 153-154. <https://books.google.com/books?id=5CIwAAAAYAAJ&printsec>

[380] Nathaniel Jarvis Wyeth, 243.

[381] "Nathaniel Jarvis Wyeth," *Wikipedia*, https://en.wikipedia.org/wiki/Nathaniel_Jarvis_Wyeth (accessed 2/16/2016).

[382] "Nathaniel Jarvis Wyeth," *Wikipedia*.

[383] Hubert Howe Bancroft, *History of the northwest coast. Vol. II. 1884-86* (San Francisco: A. L. Bancroft & Company, 1884), 598. <https://books.google.com/books?id=Ndg1AAAAIAAJ&pg>

[384] Jill Sinclair, 40, 43, 46.

[385] Daniel J. Boorstin, *The Americans: The National Experience* (New York: Vintage, 2010), 14. <https://books.google.com/books?id=YXVMTJMf9ZAC&pg>

[386] Edmund Burke, *List of Patents for Inventions and Designs, Issued by the United States from 1790 to 1847* (Washington: J. & G. S. Gideon, 1847), 170, 358, 209, 208, 102. <https://books.google.com/books?id=qnfPAAAAMAAJ&pg>

[387] Nathaniel Jarvis Wyeth, v.

[388] Licking County Genealogical Society, *Licking County, Ohio, 1982: a collection of historical sketches and family histories* (Defiance, OH: Hubbard Company, 1982), 31.

[389] Ancestry.com, *Massachusetts Vital Records to 1850, Wendell 1763 - 1893* [database on-line]. (Provo, UT: Ancestry.com Operations, Inc., 2011), 41. Original data: Town and City Clerks of Massachusetts. Massachusetts Vital and Town Records. Provo, UT: Holbrook Research Institute (Jay and Delene Holbrook).

[390] Lucy Snow Wyeth Hoffman, *Gad Wyeth Branch* (gives the vital statistics of all six of Gad's children and includes marriage dates from the Bible held by Augustus Greenleaf Wyeth), written circa 1990.

[391] Donald Elwyn Wyeth, research shared in person with Jeff Wyeth in Alliance, Ohio, 1984.

[392] David Kent Coy, Coles County Genealogical Society, Chapman Brothers, *Portrait and Biographical Album of Coles County, Ill.* (Chicago: Chapman Brothers, 1887), 467. <https://books.google.com/books?id=GE00AQAAMAAJ&pg>

[393] Mary Stiles (Paul) Guild, *The Stiles Family in America: Genealogies of the Massachusetts Family* (Albany, NY: Joel Munsell's Sons, 1892), 52. <https://books.google.com/books?id=BvEUAAAAYAAJ&printsec>

[394] Timothy Hopkins, *The Kelloggs in the Old World and the New, Vol. 1,* (San Francisco: Sunset Press, 1903), 295, 656. <https://archive.org/details/kelloggsinoldwor01hopk/page/n3>

[395] David Kent Coy, Coles County Genealogical Society, Chapman Brothers, 467.

[396] Timothy Hopkins, 295, 657.

[397] Stephen Paschall Sharples, 205.

[398] Thomas E. Sawin and John Sawin, 22.

[399] Rensselaer Allston Oakes, *Genealogical and Family History of the County of Jefferson, New York, Volume 2* (New York: Higginson Book Company, 1905), 992. <https://books.google.com/books?id=T8kpAQAAMAAJ&dq>

[400] Thomas E. Sawin and John Sawin, 22.

[401] Thomas E. Sawin and John Sawin, 22.

[402] *Find A Grave*, memorial page for Eunice Kendall (1784–23 Dec 1821), memorial no. 126564214.

[403] Benjamin and William Cutter, *History of the Town of Arlington, Massachusetts*, 333.

[404] Edwin M. P. Brister, *Centennial History of the City of Newark and Licking County, Ohio, Volume 2* (Chicago, IL: The S. J. Clarke Publishing Co., 1909), 865-866. <https://books.google.com/books?id=mNUyAQAAMAAJ&pg>

[405] The Licking County Genealogical Society, 31.

[406] "Obituary Communicated," *Washington Review and Examiner* (Washington, PA), 10 Jun 1822, 2.

[407] John A. Small, *History of the Harrisburg Cemetery Association, With Its Charter, By-Laws and Regulations, Together with a List of the Owners of Lots* (Harrisburg, PA: Telegraph Printing House, 1876), 35-67. Harrisburg Cemetery Lot Owners, Harrisburg, Dauphin County, PA, Contributed for use in the USGenWeb Archives by DBA. <http://files.usgwarchives.net/pa/dauphin/cemeteries/hburg-cem-assoc.txt>

[408] John Churchill Wyeth Jr., *Tree compiled for each of his children*. Jeff Wyeth received 31 Oct 2010 from Maureen Christensen Wyeth.

[409] William Henry Egle, *Pennsylvania Genealogies*, 762.

[410] Richard L. Arnold, *A Sesquicentennial Review of the Second Presbyterian Church, Carlisle Pennsylvania, 1833-1983* (Chambersburg, PA: Craft Press, 1982), 102-104.

[411] Simon J. Woelfly, *Swatara Collegiate Institute, Jonestown, Lebanon County, Pa. Paper read before the Lebanon County Historical Society*, 19 Apr 1907. Vol. IV, No. 2, Lebanon County Historical Society, Historical Papers and Addresses, Volumes 1-2 (Lebanon, PA: The Society, 1907), 40-45. <https://books.google.com/books?id=dyJCAQAAMAAJ&pg>

[412] "Fifty Years Ago In Harrisburg," *The Evening News* (Harrisburg, PA), 11 Aug 1939, 8.

[413] "The Man in the Dome: The Checkered Career of Samuel Douglass Wyeth," *St. Louis Globe-Democrat* (St. Louis, MO), 28 Jan 1881, 7.

[414] William Henry Egle, *Notes and queries historical, biographical, and genealogical, relating chiefly to interior Pennsylvania, Volume I* (Harrisburg, PA: Harrisburg Publishing Company, 1894), 376-377. <https://books.google.com/books?id=tCxBAQAAMAAJ&pg>

[415] William Henry Egle, *Pennsylvania Genealogies*, 685.

[416] William Henry Egle, *Pennsylvania Genealogies*, 685.

[417] Luther Reily Kelker, *History of Dauphin County, Volume II* (New York: The Lewis Publishing Co., 1907), 565. <https://books.google.com/books?id=wdU4AQAAMAAJ&printsec>

[418] William Henry Egle, *Notes and queries historical, biographical, and genealogical, relating chiefly to interior Pennsylvania, Volume II* (Harrisburg, PA: Harrisburg Publishing Company, 1896), 87. <https://books.google.com/books?id=d8IxAQAAMAAJ&pg>

[419] William Henry Egle, *Pennsylvania Genealogies*, 686.

[420] Russell Sanjek, *American Popular Music and its Business: The First Four Hundred Years, Volume II, From 1790 to 1909* (New York: Oxford University Press, 1988), 191. <https://books.google.com/books?id=7UbS22L6neQC&pg>

[421] "John Wyeth," *Center for Church Music Songs & Hymns*, http://www.songsandhymns.org/people/detail/john-wyeth (accessed 3/25/2016).

[422] Ross W. Ellison, "John Wyeth–Early American Tunebook Publisher" *North Carolina Music Teacher Magazine*, Oct 1974, 22-24.

[423] Ross W. Ellison, 22-24.

[424] Ross W. Ellison, 22-24.

[425] Irving Lowens, "Shape Notes, New England Music, and White Spirituals," *Etude Magazine*, January 1957, 15 and 64.

[426] John David Warren Steel, "Wyeth and the Development of Southern Folk Hymnody," *Music from the Middle Ages Through the 20th Century: Essays in Honor of Gwynn McPeek*, Carmelo P. Comberiati and Matthew C. Steel, eds. (London: Gordon & Breach, 1988), pp. 357-374. <http://home.olemiss.edu/~mudws/wyeth.html>

[427] Ross W. Ellison, 22-24.

[428] Ancestry.com. Pennsylvania, *Compiled Marriage Records, 1700-1821 [database on-line]*, (Provo, UT: Ancestry.com Operations Inc., 2011), Marriage Register of the Moravian Church, Philadelphia, Image, page 151. Original data: Pennsylvania Marriage Records. Harrisburg, PA: Pennsylvania Archives Printed Series, 1876. Series 2, Series 6.

[429] William Henry Egle, *Pennsylvania Genealogies*, 686.

[430] "At Harrisburg on Thursday last," *National Gazette (*Philadelphia, PA), 13 Apr 1840, 3.

[431] "Evangelical and Reformed Church," *Wikipedia*, https://en.wikipedia.org/wiki/Evangelical_and_Reformed_Church (accessed 8/25/2017).

[432] "Our Historic Roots," *The First Parish in Cambridge, Unitarian Universalist*, http://firstparishcambridge.org/welcome/our-historic-roots (accessed 3/25/2016).

[433] Harvard University Maps Archive, *First Parish Cambridge Pew Diagram*, G3764.c2:2F5 1865. P6.

[434] "Furness, William Henry, 1802-1896," *social networks and archival context - snac*, http://socialarchive.iath.virginia.edu/ark:/99166/w6cz387g (accessed 8/25/2017).

[435] Ancestry.com, *Historical Society of Pennsylvania; Historic Pennsylvania Church and Town Records; Reel: 847* (Provo, UT: Ancestry.com Operations, Inc., 2011), image 148.

[436] John Allan Wyeth, *With Sabre and Scalpel*, 529.

[437] Ancestry.com, *Pennsylvania, Wills and Probate Records, 1683-1993* (Provo, UT: Ancestry.com Operations, Inc., 2015), images 262-271.

[438] Henry Bond, Horatio Gates Jones, 179.

[439] "Livermore/Livermore Falls Historical Society," *photographs and maps*, package received 1/17/2018 from Muriel Bowerman, President of the Society.

[440] Israel Washburn, *Notes, historical, descriptive, and personal, of Livermore, in Androscoggin (formerly in Oxford) county, Maine* (Portland, ME: Bailey & Noyes, 1874), 31. <https://books.google.com/books?id=4i5AAAAAYAAJ&pg>

[441] Cora C. Briggs, "Historical Society welcomes portrait's return," *Sun Journal* (Lewiston, Maine), 27 Jun 1992, 12. <https://news.google.com/newspapers?nid=1914&dat=19920627&id=ojkpAAAAIBAJ&sjid=LGUFAAAAIBAJ&pg=1172,6457681&hl=en>

[442] "Livermore/Livermore Falls Historical Society," package from Muriel Bowerman.

[443] *Find A Grave*, database and images (https://www.findagrave.com : accessed 14 April 2018), memorial page for Lucy Wyeth Coolidge (7 Feb 1754–16 Oct 1850), Find A Grave Memorial no. 154298253, citing Alden Cemetery, Livermore, Androscoggin County, Maine, USA ; Maintained by Jacki, Weymouth Massachusetts (contributor 47755371).

[444] Jonas Wyeth, *Wyeth family records (Mss A 3058)*, R. Stanton Avery Special Collections, New England Historic Genealogical Society.

[445] Stephen Paschall Sharples, 277.

[446] Stephen Paschall Sharples, 278.

[447] Stephen Paschall Sharples, 476 and 508.

[448] Lucius Paige, 705.

[449] Secretary of the Commonwealth, *Massachusetts Soldiers and Sailors of the Revolutionary War, Volume 17*, 973.

[450] Ancestry.com, Widow's Pension Application, No. W14205, Elizabeth Wyeth, Revolutionary War, RG 15; NA–Washington, image 82.

[451] Ancestry.com, *War of 1812 Pension Application Files Index, 1812-1815*, [database on-line] (Provo, UT: Ancestry.com Operations, Inc., 2010). Original data: Jonas Wyeth (Private, Captain Samuel Child's Co. (Lt. Colonel Joseph Valentine's regiment), Massachusetts Militia, War of 1812); Widow: Elizabeth N. Wyeth Pension Number - #1: WO 17326, Pension Number - #2: WC 19788, "War of 1812 Pension Application Files Index, 1812-1815," NARA microfilm publication M313, Department of Veterans Affairs, Record Group 15, Roll No. 102; National Archives, Washington, D.C., Image 52.

[452] Jonas Wyeth, *Wyeth family records (Mss A 3058)*, R. Stanton Avery Special Collections, New England Historic Genealogical Society.

[453] Thomas E. Sawin and John Sawin, 24.

[454] Ancestry.com, *Massachusetts, Wills and Probate Records, 1635-1991* (Provo, UT: Ancestry.com Ops., Inc., 2015), images 655-660.

[455] Alice C. Allyn, *A History of Berkeley Street, Cambridge Massachusetts* (Cambridge: Cambridge Historical Society, 1931), 63-64. <http://cambridgehistory.org/wp-content/uploads/2017/08/Proceedings-Volume-21-1930-1931.pdf >

[456] Jonas Wyeth, *Wyeth family records (Mss A 3058)*, 6-7.

[457] Jonas Wyeth, *Wyeth family records (Mss A 3058)*, 2.

[458] Edward W. Gordon, "46 North Main Street, Dr. Tapley Wyeth house," *Sherbornma.org*, July 1981. <https://www.sherbornma.org/sites/sherbornma/files/uploads/northmain_046.pdf>

[459] Edward W. Gordon, *Sherbornma.org*.

[460] Edward W. Gordon, *Sherbornma.org.*

[461] Edward W. Gordon, *Sherbornma.org.*

[462] Town Clerk, "Dr. Tapley Wyeth, Bond for Smallpox Hospital," *Town of Sherborn,* 11 Sep 1792.

[463] Edward W. Gordon, *Sherbornma.org.*

[464] "Deaths," *Independent Chronicle* (Boston, MA), 23 Sep 1813, 3.

[465] Edward W. Gordon, *Sherbornma.org.*

[466] Edward W. Gordon, *Sherbornma.org.*

[467] Secretary of the Commonwealth, *Massachusetts Soldiers and Sailors in the War of the Revolution, Volume 13* (Boston: Wright & Potter Printing Co., 1896), 850-851. <https://archive.org/stream/masssoldiers13bostrich#page/848/mode/2up/search/sawin>

[468] Stephen Paschall Sharples, 243, 275, and 273.

[469] Thomas E. Sawin and John Sawin, 21.

[470] Thomas E. Sawin and John Sawin, 24.

[471] Thomas E. Sawin and John Sawin, 24.

[472] "New York, New York City Municipal Deaths, 1795-1949," database, *FamilySearch* (https://familysearch.org/ark:/61903/1:1:FD1F-NML : 20 March 2015), Isaac Wyeth, 01 Sep 1817; citing Death, Manhattan, New York, New York, New York Municipal Archives, New York; FHL microfilm 447,544.

[473] "New York, New York City Municipal Deaths, 1795-1949," *Andrew Weith,* 07 Sep 1835.

[474] "Deaths," *Haverhill Gazette* (Haverhill, MA), 11 Feb 1832, 3.

[475] "New York Marriages, 1686-1980," database, *FamilySearch* (https://familysearch.org/ark:/61903/1:1:F63H-BPR : 12 Dec 2014), John Hadly and Mary Wyeth, 03 Jun 1820; citing reference ; FHL microfilm 17,475.

[476] "Died," *New York Herald* (New York, NY), 22 Feb 1870, 9. (GenealogyBank.com)

[477] "Sales by George Hunter and Co.," *Daily Advertiser* (New York, NY), 02 Dec 1795, 3.

[478] "For Amsterdam," *Argus* (New York, NY), 28 Jan 1796, 1.

[479] Webster (1913), "Academic Dictionaries and Encyclopedias," *The Collaborative International Dictionary of English.* 2000. <en.academic.ru/dic.nsf/cide/163048/Snow>

[480] Lance Woodworth, *originally posted to Flickr as Brig Niagara full sail,* https://creativecommons.org/licenses/by/2.0/ Attribution 2.0 Generic (CC BY 2.0), this image, which was originally posted to Flickr.com, was uploaded to Commons using Flickr upload bot on 23:07, 30 Apr 2010 (UTC) by Niagara (talk). On that date, it was available under the license indicated. <https://commons.wikimedia.org/w/index.php?curid=10208096 (accessed 9/5/2017).

[481] "For Dublin," *New-York Gazette* (New York, NY), 16 Mar 1797, 1.

[482] "New York (Manhattan) Wards: Population & Density: 1800-2910," *Demographia.com,* http://www.demographia.com/nyward1800.jpg (accessed 9/6/2017).

[483] "From French Papers," *Commercial Advertiser* (New York, NY), 29 Jan 1802, 3.

[484] "Nutmegs and bandanna Hdkfs." *Commercial Advertiser* (New York, NY), 09 Sep 1801, 2.

[485] "Port of New York," *Mercantile Advertiser* (New York, NY), 3 Sep 1801, 2.

[486] "Gibraltar July 10," *Hudson Gazette (*Hudson, NY), 08 Sep 1801, 3.

[487] "Kingston, Jamaica, Oct. 8," *Chronicle Express* (New York, NY), 24 Nov 1803, 4.

[488] "Lang & Co's Marine and Commerical Lift. Arrivals at this Port," *New-York Gazette* (New York, NY), 05 Dec 1803, 2.

[489] Ancestry.com, *New York, Wills and Probate Records, 1659-1999 [database on-line]* (Provo, UT: Ancestry.com Operations, Inc., 2015), image 247. Original data: New York County, District and Probate Courts.

[490] "Died," *Greenleaf's New York Journal* (New York, NY), 08 Sep 1798, 2.

[491] "Married," *Constitutional Telegraph* (Boston, MA), 24 Apr 1802, 3.

[492] "Died," *Commercial Advertiser* (New York, NY), 15 Apr 1829, 2.

[493] Agnes M. Grousset, 82-84, 90.

[494] Agnes M. Grousset, 83.

[495] Secretary of the Commonwealth, *Massachusetts Soldiers and Sailors of the Revolutionary* War, Volume 11, 345. <https://archive.org/details/massachusettssolmpazmass>

[496] "Died," *Greenleaf's New York Journal* (New York, NY), 08 Sep 1798, 2.

[497] Agnes M. Grousset, 82.

[498] "Notice," *Daily Advertiser* (New York, NY), 04 Mar 1799, 1.

[499] "Died," *Commercial Advertiser* (New York, NY), 26 Dec 1811, 3.

[500] "Married," *Constitutional Telegraph* (Boston, MA), 24 Apr 1802, 3.

[501] "Died," *Commercial Advertiser* (New York, NY), 15 Apr 1829, 2.

[502] William H. Manning, *The Genealogical and Biographical History of the Manning Families of New England and descendants* (Salem, MA: Salem Press Company, 1902), 279-280.

[503] Stephen Paschall Sharples, 479, 511.

[504] Agnes M. Grousset, 23.

[505] Stephen Paschall Sharples, 511.

[506] John Herbert Barker, *Nicholas Wyeth of Cambridge, Mass., and some of his descendants.* Cambridge, MA: 1929, xiv.

[507] Ancestry.com, Widow's Pension Application, No. W14205, Elizabeth Wyeth, Revolutionary War, RG 15; NA–Washington, image 96.

[508] Christopher Hail, *Garden Street.*

[509] N. C. Wyeth, Betsy James Wyeth, Ed., *The Wyeths, The Intimate Correspondence of N. C. Wyeth, 1901-1945* (Boston: Gambit, 1971), 28.

[510] Bob Rowen, *American Privateers in The War Of 1812,* revised for web publication 2006-8. <http://bobrowen.com/nymas/warof1812paper/paperrevised2006.html>

[511] John B(ound) Wyeth, Benjamin Waterhouse, 14-18, 20.

[512] John B(ound) Wyeth, Benjamin Waterhouse, 23-30.

[513] John B(ound) Wyeth, Benjamin Waterhouse, iv, 44, 73-77.

[514] Nathaniel Jarvis Wyeth, 80-85.

[515] Aaron Sargent, John S. Sargent, *Sargent Genealogy* (Boston, MA: Aaron Sargent, 1895), 47 and 63. <https://books.google.com/books?id>

[516] Henry R. Stiles, 32.

[517] Ancestry.com, Widow's Pension Application, No. W14205, Elizabeth Wyeth, Revolutionary War, RG 15; NA–Washington, image 96.

[518] Ancestry.com, *Massachusetts, Death Records, 1841-1915* (Provo, UT: Ancestry.com Operations, Inc., 2013), image 550.

[519] Georgiana I. Sluman, *The Russell Family,* a story found in the Mason, New Hampshire Historical Room, about 1985, page 1.

[520] "Died," *Columbian Centinel* (Boston, MA), 02 Mar 1808, 1.

[521] John James Babson, 340.

[522] Sidney Perley, *The Essex Antiquarian, Vol. II* (Salem MA: Essex Antiquarian, 1898), 151-154, 156-157, 189-19. <https://books.google.com/books?id=k3jypar-2xgC&q>

[523] Gardner W. Pearson, 12.

[524] Stephen Paschall Sharples, 142.

[525] Secretary of the Commonwealth, *Massachusetts Soldiers and Sailors of the Revolutionary War, Volume 6*, 245.

[526] "Gloucester, Massachusetts," *Wikipedia*, https://en.wikipedia.org/wiki/Gloucester,_Massachusetts (accessed 9/2/2017).

[527] George Wharton Rice, *The shipping days of old Boothbay: from the Revolution to the World War, with mention of adjacent towns* (Portland, ME: Southworth-Anthoensen Press, 1938), 354.

[528] Arabella Morton, 28.

[529] Arabella Morton, 28.

[530] Gardner W. Pearson, 13.

[531] Arabella Morton, 28.

[532] Stephen Paschall Sharples, 156.

[533] "HMS Milford (1759)," *Wikipedia*, https://en.wikipedia.org/wiki/HMS_Milford_(1759) (accessed 9/27/2016).

[534] Thomas Nicholas, *Annals and antiquities of the counties and county families of Wales, Volume 2* (London: Longmans, Green, Read, and Co., 1872), 569. <https://books.google.com/books?id=Y1lBAAAAQAAJ&pg>

[535] Secretary of the Commonwealth, *Massachusetts Soldiers and Sailors of the Revolutionary War, Volume 6*, 245.

[536] Gardner W. Pearson, 12.

[537] William Otis Sawtelle, 12.

[538] Ancestry.com, *Massachusetts, Town and Vital Records, 1620-1988* [database on-line] (Provo, UT: Ancestry.com Operations, Inc., 2011), Original data: Births, Baptisms, Marriages, and Deaths from the Gloucester Church Records - 1877, page 515.

[539] *Find A Grave*, database and images (https://www.findagrave.com: accessed 28 Aug 2017), memorial page for William Gott (29 Sep 1771– 10 Jan 1859), Find A Grave Memorial no. 30682559, citing Lakeshore Cemetery, Wayne, Kennebec County, Maine, USA ; Maintained by amyinleeds (contributor 47399796).

[540] William Otis Sawtelle, 12-13.

[541] William Otis Sawtelle, 12.

[542] William Otis Sawtelle, 12.

[543] Henry Bond, Horatio Gates Jones, 631.

[544] Clarence Monroe Burton, William Stocking, Gordon K. Miller, editors, *The City of Detroit, Michigan, 1701-1922, Volume 2,* (Detroit: S. J. Clarke Publishing Co., 1922), 1443-1445. <https://books.google.com/books?id=8_E1AQAAMAAJ&pg>

[545] Francis S. Drake, *Memorials of the Society of the Cincinnati of Massachusetts* (Cambridge, MA: John Wilson and Son, 1873), 355. <https://books.google.com/books?id=CvJEg2jiPnsC&pg=PA355&dq>

[546] Clarence Monroe Burton, William Stocking, Gordon K. Miller, editors, 1444.

[547] Clarence Monroe Burton, William Stocking, Gordon K. Miller, editors, 1444.

[548] John Elliott Hunt; Richard J. Wright, *The John Hunt Memoirs, Early Years of the Maumee Basin* (Maumee, OH: Maumee Valley Historical Society, 1978?) 75.

[549] Clarence Monroe Burton, William Stocking, Gordon K. Miller, editors, 1445.

[550] Harvey Scribner; Western Historical Association, *Memoirs of Lucas County and the city of Toledo, from the earliest historical times down to the present, including a genealogical and biographical record of representative families* (Madison, Wis., Western Historical Association, 1910) 129-130. <https://books.google.com/books?id=C98yAQAAMAAJ&pg=PA129&dq>

[551] Edward G. Longacre, *The Man Behind the Guns: A Biography of General Henry Jackson Hunt, Chief of Artillery, Army of the Potomac* (Cranbury, NJ: A. S. Barnes and Co., 1977), 22. <https://books.google.com/books?id=kZ8BAAAAMAAJ&dq>

[552] Francis S. Drake, 355.

[553] Clarence Monroe Burton, William Stocking, Gordon K. Miller, editors, 1444.

[554] Clarence Monroe Burton, William Stocking, Gordon K. Miller, editors, 1445.

[555] Clarence Monroe Burton, William Stocking, Gordon K. Miller, editors, 1445.

[556] "Thomas Hunt (Soldier)," *Wikipedia*, https://en.wikipedia.org/wiki/Thomas_Hunt_(soldier) (accessed 9/29/2016).

[557] *Find A Grave*, database and images (https://www.findagrave.com : accessed 14 April 2018), memorial page for Col Thomas Hunt (17 Sep 1754–16 Aug 1808), Find A Grave Memorial no. 19242, citing Jefferson Barracks National Cemetery, Lemay, St. Louis County, Missouri, USA; Maintained by Find A Grave contributor Dan Keenan (49308762).

[558] Bert Joseph Griswold, Mrs. Samuel R. Taylor, *The Pictorial History of Fort Wayne, Indiana* (Chicago: Robert O. Law Co., 1917), 173. <https://books.google.com/books?id=2lI0AQAAMAAJ&pg>

[559] John Elliott Hunt; Richard J. Wright, 4.

[560] Horace S. Knapp, *History of the Maumee Valley: Commencing with Its Occupation by the French in 1680* (Toledo, OH: Glade Mammoth Printing and Publishing House, 1872), 562-566. <https://books.google.com/books?id=IT0VAAAAYAAJ&pg>

[561] John Elliott Hunt; Richard J. Wright, 55, 63-65.

[562] John Elliott Hunt; Richard J. Wright, 62.

563 John Elliott Hunt; Richard J. Wright, 63.

564 John Elliott Hunt; Richard J. Wright, 65.

565 "Lewis C. Hunt Col. 67th—Ohio," United States, [Between 1860 and 1870] Photograph, *Library of Congress Prints and Photographs Division*, https://www.loc.gov/item/cwp2003001394/PP/ (accessed 5/19/2018).

566 Brett Schulte, "Number 264. Petersburg Campaign Report of Capt. Lewis C. Hunt, Sixty-seventh Ohio Infantry, of operations Oct 27-28," and "67th Ohio Infantry," *The Siege of Petersburg Online*, http://www.beyondthecrater.com/ (accessed 5/19/2018).

567 John Eicher, David Eicher, *Civil War High Commands* (Stanford, CA: Stanford University Press, 2001), 310. <https://books.google.com/books?id=Fs0Ajlnjl6AC&pg>

568 Mary Palmer Tyler, *Grandmother Tyler's Book – the Recollections of Mary Palmer Tyler, 1775-1866*, ed. Frederick Tupper and Helen Tyler Brown, (New York: G. P. Putnam's Sons, 1925), 29.

569 Mary Palmer Tyler, 252.

570 Megan Marshall, 36-37.

571 Mary Palmer Tyler, 329.

572 Megan Marshall, 19, 28, 468.

573 Mary Palmer Tyler, 37, 204, 331.

574 Mary Palmer Tyler, 329.

575 "Deaths," *Daily Atlas* (Boston, MA), 13 Jan 1853, 2.

576 "Deaths," *Boston Daily Advertiser* (Boston, MA), 16 Jul 1813, 3.

577 *Find A Grave*, database and images (https://www.findagrave.com : accessed 14 April 2018), memorial page for John Hampden Palmer (22 Feb 1780–6 Jul 1813), Find A Grave Memorial no. 55256740; Maintained by Don Blauvelt (contributor 46932939).

578 Thomas St. John, "Edward Palmer's Drowning," *Nathaniel Hawthorne Studies in The House of the Seven Gables*, http://hawthornessevengables.com/ (accessed 9/30/2017).

579 Megan Marshall, 29.

580 Thomas St. John, "Judge Royall Tyler, Judge Jaffrey Pyncheon."

581 Megan Marshall,30.

582 "Married," *Repertory* (Boston, MA)15 Sep 1807, 2.

583 "Died," *New York Herald* (New York, NY), 10 Jan 1869, 9.

584 Thomas St. John, "Judge Royall Tyler, Judge Jaffrey Pyncheon."

585 "Mary Palmer Tyler," *Vermont Historical Society*, http://vermonthistory.org/research/vermont-women-s-history/database/tyler-mary (accessed 11/16/2017).

586 Mary Palmer Tyler, 6, 15.

587 Mary Palmer Tyler, 16, 18.

588 Betty Boyd Caroli, "Abigail Adams American First Lady," *Encyclopaedia Britannica*, last updated 9/8/2017. <https://www.britannica.com/biography/Abigail-Adams>

589 Mary Palmer Tyler, 83-84.

590 Mary Palmer Tyler, 75.

591 Letter from John Adams to Abigail Adams, 04 Feb 1783 [electronic edition], "Adams Family Papers: An Electronic Archive," *Massachusetts Historical Society*. <http://www.masshist.org/digitaladams/>

592 Thomas St. John, "Judge Royall Tyler, Judge Jaffrey Pyncheon."

593 "Mary Smith Cranch to Abigail Adams, 09 Oct 1786," *Founders Online, National Archives*, last modified 29 Jun 2017, http://founders.archives.gov/documents/Adams/04-07-02-0134. [Original source: The Adams Papers, Adams Family Correspondence, vol. 7, January 1786–February 1787, ed. C. James Taylor, Margaret A. Hogan, Celeste Walker, Anne Decker Cecere, Gregg L. Lint, Hobson Woodward, and Mary T. Claffey. Cambridge, MA: Harvard University Press, 2005, pp. 356–359.]

594 Mary Palmer Tyler, 98.

595 "Mary Smith Cranch to Abigail Adams, 24 Sep 1786," *Founders Online, National Archives*, last modified Jun 29, 2017, http://founders.archives.gov/documents/Adams/04-07-02-0129. [Original source: The Adams Papers, Adams Family Correspondence, vol. 7, January 1786–February 1787, ed. C. James Taylor, Margaret A. Hogan, Celeste Walker, Anne Decker Cecere, Gregg L. Lint, Hobson Woodward, and Mary T. Claffey. Cambridge, MA: Harvard University Press, 2005, pp. 341–344.]

596 Mary Palmer Tyler, 204, 207.

597 Mary Palmer Tyler, 106, 298.

598 Thomas St. John, "Judge Royall Tyler, Judge Jaffrey Pyncheon."

599 "Died," *The Reporter* (Brattleboro, VT), 12 Apr 1815, 3. (Genealogy Bank)

600 Henry Bond, Horatio Gates Jones, 520.

601 "Domestic Intelligence from the Lansingburgh Gazette," *Independent American* (Ballston Spa, New York) 21 Nov 1809, 2.

602 Avis Stearns Van Wagenen, *Genealogy and memoirs of Isaac Stearns and descendants* (Syracuse, NY: Courier Printing Co., 1901), 317.

603 "Arlington, Massachusetts," *Wikipedia*, https://en.wikipedia.org/wiki/Arlington,_Massachusetts (accessed 10/5/2017).

604 Henry Bond, Horatio Gates Jones, 701.

605 Ancestry.com, *Massachusetts Vital Records to 1850, Townsend 1726 - 1891* [database on-line]. (Provo, UT: Ancestry.com Operations, Inc., 2011), 6 (image 190). Original data: Town and City Clerks of MA. Holbrook Research Institute (Jay Mack Holbrook), Oxford, MA, 1984.

606 Seth Chandler, *History of the town of Shirley* (Shirley, MA: Seth Chandler, 1883), 663. <https://books.google.com/books?id=mBYQAwAAQBAJ&printsec>

607 Juanita Vogt Wyeth letter and Charles Leon Wyeth chart to Jeff Wyeth, 08 May 1988.

608 Levi Daniel Temple, *Some Temple pedigrees. A Genealogy of the known descendants of Abraham Temple, who settled in Salem, Mass, in 1636* (Boston: D. Clapp & son, 1900), 47. <https://archive.org/details/sometemplepedigr00temp>

609 Benjamin and William Cutter, 331.

610 "Tioga, New York," *Wikipedia*, https://en.wikipedia.org/wiki/Tioga_County,_New_York (accessed 10/27/2017).

453

[611] William Summer Lawyer, *Binghamton, Its Settlement, Growth and Development, and the factors in its history, 1800-1900* (Binghamton, NY: Century Memorial Publishing Co., 1900), 613, 617. <https://books.google.com/books?id=E9YwAQAAMAAJ&pg>

[612] Lucius Paige, 431.

[613] Christopher Hail, *Hilliard Place*.

[614] Susan E. Maycock, Charles M. Sullivan, 185.

[615] Thomas W. Baldwin, compiler, *Vital Records of Cambridge, Massachusetts, to the year 1850*, 787.

[616] Benjamin and William Cutter, 330, 334.

[617] "In Bankruptcy," *Boston Post* (Boston, MA), 30 Jun 1842, 1.

[618] "A list of Lands and Town Lots," *Meigs County telegraph* (Pomeroy, Ohio), 15 Dec 1857, 3. <http://chroniclingamerica.loc.gov/lccn/sn85038183/1857-12-15/ed-1/seq-3/>

[619] "Died," *Boston Courier* (Boston, MA), 9 Jun 1845, 2

[620] "100 years ago today," *Fitchburg Sentinel* (Fitchburg, MA), 18 May 1957, 6.

[621] "Hodgeman County History Collection," *Kansas Historical Society*, http://www.kshs.org/archives/40696 (accessed 11/16/2017).

[622] Boston Registry Dept., *Records Relating to the Early History of Boston, Volume 30* (Boston: Municipal Printing Office, 1903), 184. <https://books.google.com/books?id=8oA1AQAAMAAJ&pg>

[623] *Find A Grave*, database and images (https://www.findagrave.com : accessed 14 April 2018), memorial page for Eliphalet Jones (unknown–4 Dec 1811), Find A Grave Memorial no. 13656987, citing Copp's Hill Burying Ground, Boston, Suffolk County, Massachusetts, USA ; Maintained by Jan Franco (contributor 46625834) photo by Leigh Miller.

[624] "Married," *Columbian Centinel* (Boston, MA), 26 Apr 1834, 4.

[625] "Chelsea," *Boston Post* (Boston, MA), 28 Mar 1870, 3.

[626] "Deaths," *Boston Recorder* (Boston, MA), 02 Apr 1828, 55.

[627] "Marriages," *Cambridge Chronicle* (Cambridge, MA), 4 Sep 1858, 2.

[628] "Marriages," *Cambridge Chronicle* (Cambridge, MA), 4 Sep 1858, 2.

[629] Gardner W. Pearson, *Records of the Massachusetts volunteer militia called out by the Governor of Massachusetts* (Boston: Wright & Potter Printing, 1913), 97-98. <https://archive.org/stream/recordsofmassach00inmass>

[630] Jill Sinclair, 22.

[631] Jill Sinclair, 23.

[632] "Friends of Fresh Pond Reservation," *Cambridge, Massachusetts*, http://www.friendsoffreshpond.org/ (accessed 1/3/2018).

[633] Chauncey Depew Steele, Jr., 34.

[634] Lucius Paige, 706.

[635] "President Eliot Buys a House," *Cambridge Tribune*, Volume XXXI, Number 46 (Cambridge, MA), 16 Jan 1909, 1.

[636] Lucius Paige, 706.

[637] "Death of an Old Resident," *Cambridge Chronicle* (Cambridge, MA), 25 May 1895, 3.

[638] Benjamin Franklin Wyeth, *Wyeth Funeral Service records, 1904-1964 (Mss 223)*, New England Historic Genealogical Society.

[639] Lydia Nelson Hastings Buckminster, *The Hastings Memorial: A Genealogical Account of the Descendants of Thomas Hastings* (Boston: Samuel G. Drake, 1866), 167. <https://books.google.com/books?id=RFdKAAAAYAAJ&pg>

[640] John Herbert Barker, 40.

[641] "The John Wyeth House," *Wikipedia*, https://en.wikipedia.org/wiki/John_Wyeth_House (accessed 6/25/2016).

[642] "Auburn House," *Trumpet and Universalist Magazine* (Boston, MA), 16 Jul 1842, 3.

[643] John Ford, *The Cambridge Directory: Containing a General Directory of Citizens and a General Directory of Citizens* (Cambridge, MA: Chronicle Office, 1848), 59. <https://books.google.com/books?id=EqQtAAAAYAAJ&pg=PA59&dq>

[644] "Viennapedia," *The Encyclopedia of Vienna Township, Trumbull County, Ohio, Businesses Temperance House*, https://sites.google.com/a/viennahistory.org/viennapedia/business/temperance-house (accessed 01/23/2016).

[645] Virginia Wilhoit; Nelson Eddy; Wabash Valley Genealogical Society, *Cemeteries, Vigo County, Indiana, Volume III* (Terre Haute, IN: Wentz Printing, 1982), 7 (correction by Lucille Poindexter).

[646] Simona Lansaw, *Woodlawn Cemetery, Terre Haute, Vigo County, Indiana* (Owensboro, KY: Cook-McDowell Publications, 1980).

[647] "USS General Lyon (1860)," *Wikipedia*, https://en.wikipedia.org/wiki/USS_General_Lyon_(1860) (accessed 2/17/2019).

[648] Benjamin Johnson, "Boston Burning: the Fire of 1787," *Massachusetts Historical Society*, December 2006. <http://www.masshist.org/object-of-the-month/objects/boston-burning-the-fire-of-1787-2006-12-01>

[649] "Boston, April 23," *Maryland Journal* (Baltimore, Maryland), 08 May 1787, 2.

[650] Ancestry.com, "Samuel Gilbert Death Certificate," *Pennsylvania, Death Certificates, 1906-1944* (Provo, UT: Ancestry.com Operations, Inc., 2014).

[651] Clement Ferdinand Heverly, 44.

[652] Benjamin Cutter, William Richard Cutter, *History of the town of Arlington, Massachusetts*, 332.

[653] "Bradford County, Pennsylvania," *Wikipedia*, https://en.wikipedia.org/wiki/Bradford_County,_Pennsylvania (accessed 12/27/2017).

[654] Clement Ferdinand Heverly, *Pioneer and patriot families of Bradford County, Pennsylvania, 1800-1825, Volume I* (Towanda, Pa: Bradford Star Print, 1913), 288.

[655] "John E. Kent," *The Gleaner* (Wilkes-Barre, PA), 16 Jun 1809, 2.

[656] James H. Codding, *A History of Union Lodge No. 108, Free and Accepted Masons, Towanda, Pa. Held under a warrant from The Right Worshipful Grand Lodge of Pennsylvania and Masonic Jurisdiction Thereunto Belonging* (Towanda, PA: Reporter-Journal Printing Co., 1899), appendix H. Reprint publication on Tri-Counties Genealogy & History by Joyce M. Tice, 2004, http://www.rootsweb.com/~srgp/jmtindex.htm <http://www.joycetice.com/booksb/fam108d.htm>

[657] Kentucky State Historical Society, *Register of Kentucky State Historical Society* (Frankfort, KY: Kentucky State Historical Society, 1913), 34. <https://books.google.com/books?id=qfQxAQAAMAAJ&pg>

[658] "United States War of 1812 Index to Service Records, 1812-1815," Database with images, *FamilySearch*. Elisha Wythe / Elisha Witt (https://familysearch.org/ark:/61903/3:1:33S7-95Z1-YQJ?cc=1916219&wc=M6YX-HTG%3A203374801 : 11 March 2016), Wr - Ya > image

2365 of 3016; citing NARA microfilm publication M602 (Washington, D.C.: National Archives and Records Administration, n.d.).

[659] Hiram Williams Beckwith, *History of Vigo and Parke Counties, Together with Historic Notes on the Wabash Valley* (Chicago: H. H. Hill and N. Iddings, 1880), 404. <https://books.google.com/books?id=18lMAQAAMAAJ&q>

[660] Henry C. Bradsby, *History of Vigo County, Indiana* (Chicago: S. B. Nelson & Co., 1891), 1005. <https://books.google.com/books?id=p040AQAAMAAJ&q>

[661] Horace E. Hayden, 228.

[662] Clement Ferdinand Heverly, *Pioneer and patriot families of Bradford County, Pennsylvania, 1800-1825, Volume I*, 233.

[663] Ruth W. Brown, *My Wyeth Connection*, Flint Genealogical Quarterly, Vol. 21, No. 1, Jan. 1979.

[664] Joshua Wyeth Jr., *Bible records*, courtesy of Ethel Ross "Rossie" Wyeth Canion, 12 Feb 2004.

[665] Virginia Wilhoit; Nelson Eddy; Wabash Valley Genealogical Society, *Cemeteries, Vigo County, Indiana, Volume III* (Terre Haute, IN: Wentz Printing, 1982), 7 (correction by Lucille Poindexter).

[666] Benjamin and William Richard Cutter, *History of Arlington*, 332.

[667] Benjamin and William Richard Cutter, *History of Arlington*, 333.

[668] Hiram Williams Beckwith, *History of Vigo and Parke Counties, Together with Historic Notes on the Wabash Valley* (Chicago: H. H. Hill and N. Iddings, 1880), 404. <https://books.google.com/books?id=18lMAQAAMAAJ&q>

[669] Lillian Neisz, letter to Jeff Wyeth from West Lafayette, Indiana, August 1978.

[670] Lillian Neisz, letter.

[671] "Spring Grove Cemetery," *Genealogy Search Listing*, http://www.springgrove.org/stats/5913.tif.pdf (accessed 1/9/2018).

[672] "Barbados Burials, 1854-1885," database, *FamilySearch* (https://familysearch.org/ark:/61903/1:1:F23Y-V2L : 27 November 2014), Byton Cook Wyeth; citing , reference 690; FHL microfilm 1,157,975.

[673] "Green-Wood Cemetery," *Burial Search*, https://www.green-wood.com/burial_search/ (accessed 11/23/2014).

[674] Soldier's Pension Application File, 26 Oct 1870, service of Alexander R. Wyeth (Co. F&S, 6th Pennsylvania Cavalry, Civil War); soldier's pension application no. 160,817; Widow's Pension Application, 09 Feb 1877, Elizabeth Wyeth; widow's pension application no. 229,955; NA catalog title: Civil War and Later Pension Files; Dept. of Veterans Affairs Records; RG 15; National Archives, Washington, D.C.

[675] National Council of the Congregational Churches of the United States, Publishing Committee, *The Congregational Year-book, Volume 4* (Boston: Congregational Publishing Society, 1882), 36. <https://books.google.com/books?id=cAIRAAAAIAAJ&pg>

[676] "Fulton's Grandniece Dies at Great Age," *San Francisco Chronicle* (San Francisco, California), 9 Jun 1915, 13.

[677] Marilyn Johnson "Wyeth family in Evergreen." 5/5/16, email.

[678] "Died," *Washington Review and Examiner* (Washington, PA), 1 Nov 1828, 3.

[679] John H. Tice, *The Teacher and Western Educational Magazine, Volume 1* (St. Louis: Republican Office, 1854), 401. <https://books.google.com/books?id=ZVs9AQAAMAAJ&pg>

[680] *Find A Grave*, database and images (https://www.findagrave.com : accessed 14 Jan 2018), *memorial page for George M. Wyeth, Sr.* (1784–4 Jun 1844), Find A Grave Memorial no. 116336206, citing Old Manchester Cemetery, Manchester, Scott County, Illinois; Maintained by Ellen Fanning Coulter (contributor 47637781).

[681] Clement Ferdinand Heverly, *History of the Towandas 1776-1886*, 44.

[682] Benjamin and William Richard Cutter, *History of the Town of Arlington, Massachusetts*, 332.

[683] D.P. Robbins, *Popular history of Erie county, Pennsylvania* (Erie, PA: Advertising Printing Co., 1895), 162. <https://books.google.com/books?id=p9EPAwAAQBAJ&pg>

[684] "About The Monongahela expositor, and Williamsport weekly chronicle. (Williamsport, Washington County, Pa.) 1811-18??," *The Library of Congress*, https://chroniclingamerica.loc.gov/lccn/sn86081676/ (accessed 1/10/2018).

[685] United States Post Office Department, *Table of Post Offices in the United States* (Washington, D.C.: Post-Master General, 1813), 55. <https://books.google.com/books?id=Y_sCAAAAYAAJ&pg>

[686] United States Department of the Interior, *Official register of the United States, containing a list of officers and employees in the civil, military, and naval service on the 30th of Sep 1823* (Washington, Davis & Force, 1824), 80. <https://books.google.com/books?id=etg9AQAAMAAJ&pg>

[687] Post-Master General, *List of the post-offices in the United States: with the names of the post-masters, of the counties and states to which they belong, the distances from the city of Washington, and the seats of state governments, respectively; exhibiting the state of post-offices on the 1st of June, 1828* (Washington, D.C.: Way & Gideon, 1828) 90. <https://books.google.com/books?id=4iHiqHCs4ksC&pg>

[688] Postmaster General, *Table of the post offices in the United States, arranged by states and counties; as they were October 1, 1830* (Washington, D.C.: Duff Green, 1831), 105. <https://books.google.com/books?id=OE4ZAAAAYAAJ&pg>

[689] "Historical Sketch of the city of Monongahela," *city of monongahela - pa .gov*, http://www.cityofmonongahela-pa.gov/Historical_Sketch.html (accessed 1/10/2018).

[690] Earle R. Forrest, "History of Monongahela City, Pa." from: *A History of Washington County, Pennsylvania* (Chicago: The S. J. Clark Publishing Company, 1926). <http://history.rays-place.com/pa/wash-monongahela.htm>

[691] "Robert Fulton's Mother Lies in Unmarked Grave," *The Pittsburgh Press* (Pittsburgh, PA), 03 Oct 1909, 12.

[692] John Bennett Boddie, *Virginia Historical Genealogies* (Baltimore, MD: Reprinted for Clearfield by Genealogical Publishing Co., 2008), 124-125. <https://books.google.com/books?id=AyhusD7Hc2MC&pg=PA122&dq>

[693] "People of Monongahela, who Helped to Rule our Country," *Historical Magazine of Monongahela's Old Home Coming Week: Sept. 6-13, 1908*, 266. Historic Pittsburgh General Text Collection, http://documenting.pitt.edu/islandora/object/pitt%3A00z838213m/viewer#page/266/mode/2up (accessed 1/12/2018).

[694] Genevieve Wyeth Tuttle, "Statement from family Bible (of Francis S. Wyeth and Mary Hillman and Francis S. (sic) Wyeth and Margaret Carney marriages)," *Supplement to DAR application*, notarized 21 Dec 1938.

[695] Thomas Cushing, *History of Allegheny County, Pennsylvania, Volume II, Part I* (Chicago: A. Warner & Co., 1889), 353. <https://archive.org/stream/historyofalleghe1889cush#page/353/mode/2up/search/kearney>

[696] Chill W. Hazzard, *Centennial anniversary of the founding of Monongahela City, Pa.: celebrated August. 27th, 1892* (Monongahela City, PA: Chill W. Hazzard Publisher, 1895), 214.

[697] "List," *Washington Review and Examiner* (Washington, PA), 21 Nov 1829, 2.

[698] "For sale at this Office," *Washington Review and Examiner* (Washington, PA), 10 Apr Sep 1824, 4.

[699] "Just Published," *Washington Review and Examiner* (Washington, PA), 09 Sep 1826, 2.

[700] "The Church of Christ at Brush Run," *History of the Restoration Movement*, www.therestorationmovement.com/_states/wv/brushrun.htm (accessed 1/13/2018).

[701] "On these days in the American Restoration Heritage: March 29 – April 4," *Preachersmith a minister's musings in pics and text*, https://preachersmith.com/tag/peyton-c-wyeth/ (accessed 1/13/2018).

[702] "Washington, Feb. 4th, 1830," *Washington Review and Examiner* (Washington, PA), 06 Feb 1830, 3.

[703] "Voice Of Washington County Jackson Meeting." *Washington Review and Examiner* (Washington, PA), 11 Oct 1828, 2.

[704] Julie Rowan Wolford, "George and Eliza, merchant, of Donegal sold their land to a James Warrell in 1837." 8/13/16, email.

[705] Benjamin and William Richard Cutter, *History of Arlington*, 333.

[706] *Find A Grave*, database and images (https://www.findagrave.com : accessed 14 Jan 2018), *memorial page for George M Wyeth, Sr.* (1784–4 Jun 1844), Find A Grave Memorial no. 116336206, citing Old Manchester Cemetery, Manchester, Scott County, Illinois; Maintained by Ellen Fanning Coulter (contributor 47637781).

[707] George C. Groce; David H. Wallace; New York Historical Society, 707.

[708] "Shrewsbury Family images," Historic Madison, Inc., *Flickr*, https://www.flickr.com/photos/117251246@N06/albums/72157644429204591 (accessed 1/14/2018).

[709] Ancestry.com, "Samuel Gilbert Death Certificate."

[710] Horace E. Hayden, 212.

[711] Clement Ferdinand Heverly, *History of the Towandas 1776-1886*, 53.

[712] "Monroe," *Towanda Daily Review* (Towanda, PA), 14 Dec 1881, 5. (GenealogyBank.com)

[713] Elissa Sohl, "Pedigree Resource File," database, *FamilySearch* (https://familysearch.org/ark:/61903/2:2:3HQK-BPN: accessed 1/19/2018, entry for Nelson /Gilbert/.

[714] Clement Ferdinand Heverly, 43-44.

[715] David Craft, *History of Bradford County, Pennsylvania with Illustrations and Biographical Sketches of Some of its Prominent Men and Pioneers* (Philadelphia: L. H. Everts & Co., 1878). Retyped by Bruce Preston for Tri-Counties Genealogy & History by Joyce M. Tice. <http://www.joycetice.com/craft/towanddc.htm>

[716] David Craft, retyped by Bruce Preston for Tri-Counties Genealogy & History by Joyce M. Tice.

[717] Clement Ferdinand Heverly, History of the Towandas 1776-1886, 53.

[718] "Monroe," *Towanda Daily Review* (Towanda, PA), 14 Dec 1881, 5. (GenealogyBank.com)

[719] Joyce M. Tice, "Cole's Farm Cemetery, Towanda Township, Bradford County, Pennsylvania," Tri-Counties Genealogy & History by Joyce M. Tice, www.joycetice.com/cemb/coleobit.htm (accessed 1/18/2018).

[720] Genevieve Wyeth Tuttle, "Statement from family Bible," 1938.

[721] "Died," *Monongahela Valley Republican* (Monongahela, PA), 22 Feb 1877, 3. (Newspapers.com)

[722] State of Indiana, Monroe County Court of Common Pleas, *Francis Wyeth vs Mary Wyeth (Divorce)*, term of December 1865 (box 127, 9 pages, marriage is listed in book 4, p. 346), records housed Monroe County History Center, Bloomington, IN.

[723] State of Indiana, Monroe County Court of Common Pleas, *Elizabeth Wyeth vs Francis Wyeth (Divorce)*, term of December 1872 (box 163), records housed Monroe County History Center, Bloomington, IN.

[724] Kenneth A. White, Director, "Baptism records of St. Patrick Parish, Strip District, Pittsburgh, PA - Baptized 14 Nov 1826, Fidelia Anna, daughter of Francisci and Margaretha Wythe," *Archives & Records Center of the Roman Catholic Diocese of Pittsburgh*, letter of 25 Aug 2016 to Julie Rowan Wolford.

[725] Kenneth A. White, Director, "Register of Marriages of St. Paul's Cathedral, Pittsburgh - Married 27 Jun 1836 Simonem Shaeffer and Fediliam Anna Wyer." *Archives & Records Center of the Roman Catholic Diocese of Pittsburgh*, 25 Aug 2016 letter to Julie Rowan Wolford.

[726] "Died," *The Daily Republican* (Monongahela, PA) 06 Jan 1890, 1.

[727] Kenneth A. White, Director, "Register of Marriages of St. Paul's Cathedral, Pittsburgh - Married 28 Jun 1838 Joannes Finn and Margarita Wight." Archives & Records Center of the Roman Catholic Diocese of Pittsburgh, 16 Nov 2017 email from Julie Rowan Wolford.

[728] Genevieve Wyeth Tuttle, "Statement from family Bible," 1938.

[729] "St. Mary's Cemetery," (Jan 28. Francis S. Wyeth, 65) The Daily Republican (Monongahela, PA), 15 Jan 1889, 4.

[730] "Cemetery Listing," City of Terre Haute, Indiana, http://www.terrehaute.in.gov/departments/cemetery/cemetery-12-11-2012-formatted-for-printing.pdf (accessed 23 Jan 2018).

[731] "Indiana Digital Archives - Wyeth,Taylor" *Indiana Archives and Records Administration*, https://secure.in.gov/apps/iara/search/Home/Detail?rId=1199464 (accessed 21 Nov 2016).

[732] Adjutant General's Office, *Registers of Deaths of Volunteers, compiled 1861–1865*, ARC ID: 656639. Record Group 94 Indiana S-Z, National Archives Washington, D.C., 182-183.

[733] Benjamin and William Richard Cutter, *History of Arlington*, 332.

[734] "Mrs. Margaret Wyeth Finn," *The Pittsburgh Press* (Pittsburgh, PA), 31 Jan 1905, 4. (Newspapers.com)

[735] Benjamin and William Richard Cutter, *History of Arlington*, 333.

[736] "Saint Patrick (Strip) District," *Catholic Diocese of Pittsburgh*, https://diopitt.org/saint-patrick-strip-district (accessed 1/26/2018).

[737] Kenneth A. White, Director, "Baptism records of St. Patrick Parish," letter of 25 Aug 2016 to Julie Rowan Wolford.

[738] "Editor Dead," (Thompson has Wyeth and Kearney relatives in Monongahela) *The Daily Republican* (Monongahela, PA), 19 Jul 1882, 4.

[739] Thomas Cushing, *History of Allegheny County, Pennsylvania, Volume II, Part I* (Chicago: A. Warner & Co., 1889), 353. <https://archive.org/stream/historyofalleghe1889cush#page/353/mode/2up/search/kearney>

[740] "Editor Dead," *The Daily Republican* (Monongahela, PA), 19 Jul 1882, 4.

[741] "People of Monongahela, who Helped to Rule our Country," *Historical Magazine of Monongahela's Old Home Coming Week: Sept. 6-13, 1908*, 266. Historic Pittsburgh General Text Collection, http://documenting.pitt.edu/islandora/object/pitt%3A00z838213m/viewer#page/266/mode/2up (accessed 1/12/2018).

[742] Edna Evans, Lynda Levin, "John Francis Wyeth," *The Schroeder-Wyeth Newsletter*, Washington, PA, 4 Nov 1976.

[743] "Signed Declaration of Independence, Wyeth, Historical Figure, Has Area Descendants," *The Daily Republican* (Monongahela, PA), 14 Jun 1969, 5.

[744] "Francis Wyeth and wife to F. A. Shaffer and M. A. Burgan," *Washington County, PA Deed book 136*, recorded 13 Jul 1886, 477-478.

[745] "Mrs. Margaret Murray of the East End was blessed by seeing her great-great grand child come into this world on Friday morning." *Monongahela Valley Republican* (Monongahela, PA), 13 May 1875, 3.

[746] "United States Civil Records," *FamilySearch Research Wiki*, https://www.familysearch.org/wiki/en/United_States_Civil_Records (accessed 1/26/2018).

[747] Ancestry.com, *Ohio County Marriages, 1774-1993* (Lehi, UT: Ancestry.com Operations, Inc., 2016), Film #: 000344453, image 85.

[748] J. G. Olden, *Historical Sketches and Early Reminiscences of Hamilton County, Ohio* (Cincinnati, OH: H. Watkin, 1882), 162-163. <https://books.google.com/books?id=MtsyAQAAMAAJ&pg>

[749] "Complete List of Killed and Wounded of the 31st and 11th Regiments," *The Terre Haute Star* (Terre Haute, Indiana), 16 Apr 1862, 2.

[750] "Grantees (Buyers) Index," Monroe History PDF, page 691. <monroehistory.org/wp-content/uploads/2015/11/Combined_Deed_Book_A_to_Z_Index_for_Publication.pdf>

[751] State of Indiana, Monroe County Court of Common Pleas, *Francis Wyeth vs Mary Wyeth (Divorce)*.

[752] Soldier's Pension Application File, 07 Oct 1887, service of Henry E. Wyeth (Co. C, 31st Indiana Infantry, Civil War), soldier's pension application no. 625,054; Widow's Pension Application, 12 Sep 1904, Hannah Wyeth, widow's pension application no. 813,387; NA catalog title: Civil War and Later Pension Files; Dept. of Veterans Affairs Records; RG 15; National Archives, Washington, D.C.

[753] Ancestry.com, *U.S., Indexed County Land Ownership Maps, 1860-1918* [database on-line] (Provo, UT: Ancestry.com Ops., Inc., 2010), image 69. Original data: Various publishers of County Land Ownership Atlases. Microfilmed by the Library of Congress, Washington, D.C.

[754] State of Indiana, Monroe County Court of Common Pleas, *Elizabeth Wyeth vs Francis Wyeth (Divorce)*.

[755] State of Indiana, Monroe County Court of Common Pleas, *Francis Wyeth vs Elizabeth Wyeth (Divorce)*, term of August 1871 (box 144), records housed Monroe County History Center, Bloomington, IN.

[756] Vigo Atlas Map Co., *Standard atlas of Vigo County, Indiana: including a plat book of the villages, cities and townships of the county, map of state and United States and world* (Terre Haute, IN: Vigo Atlas Map Co, 1907) Map. Retrieved from the Library of Congress, https://www.loc.gov/item/2007626785/ (accessed 01/28/2018).

[757] Benjamin and William Richard Cutter, *History of Arlington*, 332.

[758] Clement Ferdinand Heverly, *Pioneer and patriot families of Bradford County, Pennsylvania*, 1800-1825, Volume II (Towanda, Pa: Bradford Star Print, 1915), 204.

[759] "Spring Township," *The Conneautville Courier* (Conneautville, PA), 05 Mar 1886, 1.

[760] Soldier's Pension Application File, 25 Aug 1871, service of Matthew W. Wyeth (Co. E, 128th Indiana Infantry, Civil War), soldier's pension application no. 168,330; Widow's Pension Application, 06 Aug 1909, Fanny Wyeth, widow's pension application no. 925,070; NA catalog title: Civil War and Later Pension Files; Dept. of Veterans Affairs Records; RG 15; National Archives, Washington, D.C.

[761] "Deaths," *The Conneautville Courier* (Conneautville, PA), 05 Mar 1891, 8.

[762] Ohio Deaths, *1908-1953*; https://familysearch.org/ark:/61903/3:1:S3HY-6SM3-X8H?cc=1307272&wc=MD9X-VM9%3A287601601%2C294454601

[763] Ancestry.com. *U.S. National Homes for Disabled Volunteer Soldiers, 1866-1938* [database on-line]. Provo, UT: Ancestry.com Operations Inc., 2007, Image 715 (George W. Wyeth.)

[764] Soldier's Pension Application File, 7 Aug 1890, service of George W. Wyeth (Navy and Co. F, Illinois 56th Infantry, Civil War); Navy pension certificate no. 27,895, soldier's application no. 842,320; National Archives catalog title: Civil War and Later Pension Files; Records of the Department of Veterans Affairs; Record Group 15; National Archives, Washington, D.C.

[765] Roster Commission, *Official roster of the soldiers of the State of Ohio in the War of the Rebellion, 1861-1865, Vols. 1-12* (Akron, OH: The Werner Company, 1893), 404. [Ancestry.com database on-line] image 209.

[766] "The Civil War Soldiers and Sailors Database - Wythe (Wyeth), Lafayette," *National Park Service*, https://www.nps.gov/civilwar/search-soldiers.htm?submitted=1&firstName=lafayette&lastName=wythe&warSideCode=U&battleUnitName= (accessed 10/26/2016).

[767] "Terrible Boiler Explosion – Three men killed," *The Elk County Advocate* (Ridgway, PA), 27 Aug 1864, 2.

[768] Benjamin and William Richard Cutter, *History of Arlington*, 332.

[769] Benjamin and William Richard Cutter, *History of Arlington*, 332.

[770] Donna Wyeth Thibodeau phone conversation with Jeff Wyeth, circa 1988.

[771] Donna Wyeth Thibodeau, "Charles Alonzo Wyeth Biography," 18 Nov 1986.

[772] "Charles A. Wyeth (born Cincinnati) and Joseph Morcatt Die at Veterans' Home," *Star Tribune* (Minneapolis, MN), 31 Mar 1915, 8.

[773] Benjamin and William Richard Cutter, *History of Arlington*, 333.

[774] Ancestry.com, Survivor's Pension Application File, No. S40734, Joshua Wyeth, Revolutionary War, RG 15; NA–Washington, image 165.

[775] Hamilton County Genealogical Society First Families of Hamilton County, *Ohio Records (Mss 1093), Application 131 Jerry D. Harrison*, Series 1: Applications, Box 10: Applications, Folder 14., received 8/4/17.

[776] Hamilton County Genealogical Society First Families of Hamilton County, *Ohio Records (Mss 1093)*.

[777] H. F. Kett and Company, 476.

[778] "Collegiate Record," *New Hampshire Patriot and State Gazette* (Concord, New Hampshire), 19 Sep 1825, 1.

[779] Robert Hanson, marriage in paper on 6/16/1834.

[780] Ancestry.com, *U.S., French Catholic Church Records (Drouin Collection) St-Louis; Baptemes 1814-1823* [database on-line] (Provo, UT: Ancestry.com Operations, Inc., 2007), page 69, Image 77.

[781] "Died," *Daily Atlas* (Boston, MA), 29 Sep 1841, 2.

[782] Ancestry.com, *Catalogue of the officers and students of Phillips Exeter Academy for the Academical Year 1868-69* showing past student Charles Jones Wyeth of Galena, Ill. (Cambridge, MA: John Wilson and son, 1869), 70. (Provo, UT: Ancestry.com Operations, Inc., 2012).

[783] Donna Valley Stuart, "Marriages of Christ Church, Detroit 1849-1879," *Detroit Society for Genealogical Research Magazine*, Spring 1979, 115.

[784] "Obituary," *Daily Arkansas Gazette* (Little Rock, Arkansas)13 Apr 1873, 1.

[785] Robert Hanson, death in paper on 11/13/1841.

[786] William Henry Egle, *Pennsylvania Genealogies*, 700.

[787] Lucius Paige, 705.

[788] H. F. Kett and Company, 476.

[789] "Jacob Wyeth (1820)," *Harvard College Library Clipping Sheet*, Harvard University Archives (various dates).

[790] "Commencement at Cambridge," *Boston Commercial Gazette* (Boston, MA), 01 Sep 1823, 2.

[791] John B(ound) Wyeth, Benjamin Waterhouse, 57.

[792] H. F. Kett and Company, 476.

[793] Robert Hanson, marriage in paper on 6/16/1834.

[794] Ancestry.com, *U.S., French Catholic Church Records (Drouin Collection) St-Louis; Baptemes 1814-1823*, page 69, Image 77.

[795] Michael C. O'Laughlin, *Missouri Irish: The Original History of the Irish in Missouri* (Kansas City, MO: Irish Genealogical Foundation, 2007), 87-91. <https://books.google.com/books?id=7OtFfyk3y3AC&pg>

[796] "Died," *Daily Atlas* (Boston, MA), 29 Sep 1841, 2.

[797] "Items of Interest from Various Localities," *American Gas Light Journal*, Volume 56 (New York City: A. M. Callender & Co. Publishers, 30 May 1892), 784. <https://books.google.com/books?id=-XtBAQAAMAAJ&pg=PA784&dq>

[798] Lucius Paige, 705.

[799] Mrs. Edwin C. Gibbons, 49.

[800] "Died," *The New York Times* (New York, NY), 17 Jan 1882, 5. (Newspapers.com)

[801] Mrs. Edwin C. Gibbons, 49.

[802] "New York Deaths and Burials, 1795-1952," database, *FamilySearch* (https://familysearch.org/ark:/61903/1:1:F691-VF2 : 10 Feb 2018), Mary Frances Wyeth, 12 Jan 1878; citing Newport, Newport, Rhode Island, reference pg 392; FHL microfilm 1,671,687

[803] "Leonard Jarvis Wyeth (1854)," *Harvard College Library Clipping Sheet*, Harvard University Archives (various dates).

[804] "Deaths and Burials," *The Baltimore Sun* (Baltimore, Maryland), 28 Jan 1891, 6. (GenealogyBank.com)

[805] "Dissolution," *National Advocate* (New York, NY), 13 Sep 1828, 3.

[806] "Co-Partnership," *American and Commercial Daily Advertiser* (Baltimore, Maryland), 28 Dec 1838, 1. (GenealogyBank.com)

[807] "At a Meeting of the Directors," *Commercial Advertiser* (New York, NY), 02 Mar 1839, 3.

[808] "Williamsburgh Fire Insurance Company," *Evening Post* (New York, NY), 14 Jun 1839, 3.

[809] "Died," *Evening Post* (New York, NY), 2 Feb 1855, 3.

[810] Lucius Paige, 705.

[811] "Interments Listed by Vault," *The New York City Marble Cemetery*, www.nycmc.org/intermentvaults.html (accessed 2/14/2018).

[812] "Green-Wood Cemetery," *Burial Search*, https://www.green-wood.com/burial_search/ (accessed 2/14/2018).

[813] "Real Property Records," City of Newport, https://i2f.uslandrecords.com/RI/Newport/D/Default.aspx (accessed 2/15/2018).

[814] "Newport," *Trulia*, https://www.trulia.com/p/ri/newport/58-ayrault-st-newport-ri-02840--1119370556 (accessed 2/15/18).

[815] Margaret B. Moore, *The Salem World of Nathaniel Hawthorne* (Columbia, MO: University of Missouri Press, 1998), 53. <https://books.google.com/books?id=rK_6EycRyFwC&pg>

[816] Margaret B. Moore, 53.

[817] "Circuit Court," *New York Daily Herald* (New York, NY), 21 Feb 1846, 2. (Newspapers.com)

[818] "Nathaniel J. and Ann C. Wyeth House," *Landmarks Preservation Commission*, 15 May 2007, 3. <http://s-media.nyc.gov/agencies/lpc/lp/2253.pdf>

[819] "Varieties," *Cincinnati Daily Gazette* (Cincinnati, Ohio), 09 Dec 1878, 7. (GenealogyBank.com)

[820] "Approved pension applications of widows and other dependents of Civil War veterans who served between 1861 and 1910," digital images, *Fold3* (http://www.fold3.com : accessed 20 Feb 2018), 1st Potomac Home Brigade Cavalry; pages: 13, 213-214 (Deposition of Charles Wyeth); veteran: James Clary; Company: G; Widow: Ellen Augusta Topman Clary, pension application no. 74,324; citing NARA catalog title: *Case Files of Approved Pension Applications of Widows and Other Veterans of the Army and Navy Who Served Mainly in the Civil War and the War With Spain, compiled 1861 - 1934, NARA Catalog Id: 300020, Record Group: 15, roll: WC147244-WC147259.*

[821] Thomas M. Myers, 47.

[822] "Died on Tuesday evening," *American and Commercial Daily Advertiser* (Baltimore, MD), 18 May 1843, 2. (GenealogyBank.com)

[823] Nicole Thompson, Adm. Assistant, *Green Mount Cemetery, Baltimore, Maryland*, email 2/20/2018 and phone conversation 2/26/2018.

[824] Mrs. Edwin C. Gibbons, 49.

[825] "Deaths and Burials," *The Baltimore Sun* (Baltimore, Maryland), 28 Jan 1891, 6. (GenealogyBank.com)

[826] Nicole Thompson, *Green Mount Cemetery Office*, 2/26/2018.

[827] Thomas M. Myers, 47-48.

[828] Mallory Herberger, Special Collections Archivist, *Maryland Historical Society*, emails dated 12/06/2018 and 12/07/2018.

[829] Nicole Thompson, *Green Mount Cemetery Office*, 2/26/2018.

[830] Nicole Thompson, *Green Mount Cemetery Office*, 2/26/2018.

[831] Thomas M. Myers, 48.

[832] "Obituary Notes," *New York Times* (New York, NY), 16 Apr 1890, 2. (ProQuest Historical Newspapers)

[833] Baltimore County, Maryland. *Marriage Cards, Court of Common Pleas (Marriage Index, Male) CM205*. State of Maryland, 1851-1855. reel No. 23.22, msa.maryland.gov/megafile/msa/coagserm/cm200/cm205/000000/000022/pdf/msa_cm205_000022.pdf (accessed 2/18/2018).

[834] Mallory Herberger, Special Collections Archivist, *Maryland Historical Society*, emails dated 12/06/2018 and 12/07/2018.

[835] "Deaths and Burials," *The Baltimore Sun* (Baltimore, Maryland), 28 Jan 1891, 6. (GenealogyBank.com)

[836] Maryland State Archives, "Session Laws, 1846, Volume 611, Page 256," *Archives of Maryland Online*, 31 Oct, 2014. <aomol.msa.maryland.gov/000001/000611/html/am611--256.html>

[837] "By Wm. Hamilton," *The Baltimore Sun* (Baltimore, Maryland), 7 Apr 1853, 3. (Newspapers.com)

[838] "Approved pension applications of widows and other dependents of Civil War veterans who served between 1861 and 1910," digital

images, *Fold3*, 1st Potomac Home Brigade Cavalry; pages: 13, 213-214 (Deposition of Charles Wyeth); entry for veteran: James Clary; Widow: Ellen Augusta Topman Clary.

839 "Trustees' Sale," *Baltimore Sun* (Baltimore, Maryland), 13 Nov 1893, 9. (GenealogyBank.com)

840 David Kent Coy, Coles County Genealogical Society, Chapman Brothers, 467.

841 Lula Browning, letter to Jeff Wyeth dated 31 Dec 1978.

842 Wallace H. Wyeth Sr. (1943-2012) personal records, phone conversations with Jeff Wyeth, 2009.

843 Gad Wyeth Jr., *Family Record*, courtesy of Sheila Baum and James Allen Wyeth, 27 Aug 2014.

844 Thomas E. Sawin and John Sawin, 22.

845 NNY Genealogy, *Stories in Stone*, Burial Collection - Gad Wyeth, nnygenealogy.com (accessed 2/27/2018).

846 Gad Wyeth Jr., *Family Record*, courtesy of Sheila Baum and James Allen Wyeth, 27 Aug 2014.

847 The Church of Jesus Christ of Latter-day Saints, "Ancestral File," database, *FamilySearch,* entry for Silas J. Wyeth (M1LP-6CQ), https://www.familysearch.org/tree/person/details/M1LP-6CQ (accessed 2/27/2018).

848 Soldier's Pension Application File, 08 May 1882, service of William H. Wyeth (Co. H, 1st New York Light Artillery, Civil War); soldier's pension application no. 448,961(confirms birth, marriage and death); National Archives catalog title: Civil War and Later Pension Files; Records of the Department of Veterans Affairs; Record Group 15; National Archives, Washington, D.C.

849 Charles E. Wyeth, *Family Records*, courtesy of Milton Dirst, 16 Aug 2001.

850 Augustus Greenleaf Wyeth Bible records furnished by Lucy Snow Wyeth Hoffman, circa 1990.

851 Donald Elwyn Wyeth, research shared in person with Jeff Wyeth in Alliance, Ohio, 1984.

852 "Approved pension applications of widows and other dependents of Civil War veterans who served between 1861 and 1910," digital images, *Fold3* (http://www.fold3.com : accessed 21 Nov 2016), 75th Illinois Infantry; Pages: 2, 5, 7, and 9; veteran: James M. Wyeth; Company: I; Widow: Almira Thompson Wyeth, pension application no. 7,841; citing NARA catalog title: *Case Files of Approved Pension Applications of Widows and Other Veterans of the Army and Navy Who Served Mainly in the Civil War and the War With Spain, compiled 1861 - 1934, NARA Catalog Id: 300020, Record Group: 15,* roll: WC118320-WC118350.

853 Wing Family, *The Owl - A Genealogical Quarterly Magazine, Vol. 22-25* (Kewaunee, WI: Wing Family of America, 1920-1924), 2282.

854 Benjamin and William Cutter, *History of the Town of Arlington, Massachusetts,* 333.

855 Henry R. Stiles, 41.

856 David Kent Coy, Coles County Genealogical Society, Chapman Brothers, 467.

857 Ceal Guilbault and Pam Richardson, "Gravestone Inscriptions/Wendell Cemeteries," *Wendell Massachusetts,* www.wendellmass.us/index.php/about-wendell/genealogy-reference (accessed 3/6/2018).

858 John Gresham, *Historical and Biographical Record of Douglas County, Illinois* (Logansport, IN: Wilson, Humphreys & Co., 1900), 149-151. <https://books.google.com/books?id=6XAUAAAAYAAJ&pg>

859 Timothy Hopkins, 657.

860 Timothy Hopkins, 657.

861 Augustus Greenleaf Wyeth Bible records furnished by Lucy Snow Wyeth Hoffman, circa 1990.

862 "International Genealogical Index (IGI)," *FamilySearch* (https://familysearch.org/ark:/61903/2:1:MS62-XZ4: accessed 12/16/ 2018).

863 Ceal Guilbault and Pam Richardson (accessed 3/6/2018).

864 Lucy Snow Wyeth Hoffman, *Gad Wyeth Branch*, written circa 1990

865 Wing Family, *The Owl - A Genealogical Quarterly Magazine, Vol. 22-25* (Kewaunee, WI: Wing Family of America, 1920-1924), 1677.

866 William Henry Egle, *Pennsylvania Genealogies*, 686.

867 John Churchill Wyeth Jr., *Tree compiled for each of his children.* Received 31 Oct 2010 from Maureen Christensen Wyeth.

868 "J. W. Douglas," *The Herald and Torch Light* (Hagerstown, Maryland), 12 May 1895, 4.

869 "Miss Louise W. Douglas," The Baltimore Sun (Baltimore, MD), 13 Oct 1910, 9. (Newspapers.com)

870 Frederick A. Canfield, *Descendants of Thomas Canfield and Matthew Camfield* (New Haven, CT: Tuttle, Morehouse & Taylor Press, 1897), 22. Republished by Canfield Family Association, 1 Jan 2006. <https://books.google.com/books?id=J1AZAQAAMAAJ&q>

871 Burton Alva Konkle, *The Life of Chief Justice Ellis Lewis, 1798-1871* (Philadelphia: Campion & Co., 1907), 89. <https://books.google.com/books?id=AAA9AAAAIAAJ&pg>

872 Patricia King Harms, *Family Tree*, Jeff furnished to Tina Wyeth Baker in 2015. (John Wyeth Jr. lived in Harrisburg for 1840 census.)

873 "Wyeth," *Harrisburg Telegraph* (Harrisburg, PA), 29 Mar 1923, 26.

874 Soldier's Pension Application File, 19 Dec 1904, service of John W. Wyeth (Co. E&L, 9th Pennsylvania Cavalry, Civil War), soldier's pension application no. 1,329,061; Widow's Pension Application, 27 Apr 1908, Frances A. Wyeth, widow's pension application no. 840,659; NA catalog title: Civil War and Later Pension Files; Dept. of Veterans Affairs Records; RG 15; National Archives, Washington, D.C.

875 "Deaths," *Patriot* (Harrisburg, PA), 02 Dec 1905; 11.

876 "Cuba -- Diplomatic Correspondence -- The Speakman and Wyeth Executions." *The Evening Telegraph* (Philadelphia, PA), 13 Jan 1870, 1. (Newspapers.com)

877 Richard L. Arnold, 102-104.

878 Bible records held in the care of William Maxwell "Max" Wyeth IV. (Susan was born in 1811 since she was baptized in January 1812.)

879 Bible records held in the care of William Maxwell "Max" Wyeth IV.

880 "Francis Wyeth Dead," *The Harrisburg Patriot* (Harrisburg, Pennsylvania), 3 Jul 1893. 2.

881 John A. Smull, 35-67. <http://files.usgwarchives.net/pa/dauphin/cemeteries/hburg-cem-assoc.txt>

882 "Francis Houston Wyeth," *The Churchman*, Volume 108 (New York City, NY), 12 Jul 1913, 64. <https://books.google.com/books?id=LZNOAQAAMAAJ&pg>

883 Bible records held in the care of William Maxwell "Max" Wyeth IV say birth was 15 Jun 1853 but all other records say 1854.

884 William Henry Egle, *History of the counties of Dauphin and Lebanon in the Commonwealth of Pennsylvania, biographical and genealogical* (Philadelphia: Everts & Peck, 1883), 605-606. (Ancestry.com)

885 "Fifty Years Ago in Harrisburg," *The Evening News* (Harrisburg, Pennsylvania), 28 Dec 1936, 10.

886 Simon J. Woelfly, 40-44. <https://books.google.com/books?id=dyJCAQAAMAAJ&pg>

[887] "Died," *Harrisburg Daily Independent* (Harrisburg, PA), 14 Oct 1884, 4. (Newspapers.com)

[888] "Chess and Checkers," *The Philadelphia Inquirer* (Philadelphia, PA),17 Nov 1918, 56.

[889] William Henry Egle, *History of the counties of Dauphin and Lebanon in the Commonwealth of Pennsylvania*, 599.

[890] Simon J. Woelfly, 40-44. <https://books.google.com/books?id=dyJCAQAAMAAJ&pg>

[891] George Black Stewart, "Address by Samuel H. Garland," *Centennial Memorial, English Presbyterian Congregation, Harrisburg, Pa.* (Harrisburg, PA: Harrisburg Publishing Co., 1894), 169. <https://books.google.com/books?id=2BgVAAAAYAAJ&pg>

[892] Lavone Johnson Anglen, "Biography: Louis Weiss Wyeth born 1812 with photograph," *Alabama Pioneers*, 2013-2015. <http://alabamapioneers.com/biography-louis-weiss-wyeth-born-1812/>

[893] *Find A Grave*, database and images (https://www.findagrave.com : accessed 14 April 2018), memorial page for Euphemia Allan Wyeth (16 Jul 1817–27 Dec 1895), Find A Grave Memorial no. 63347378 and memorial page for Louis W Wyeth (20 Jun 1812–7 Jun 1889), Find A Grave Memorial no. 63347379 citing Guntersville City Cemetery, Guntersville, Marshall County, Alabama; Maintained by Johnny Tidmore (contributor 47270806); Larry A. McCoy, photographer of tombstones that give birth and death dates and CSA military information.

[894] "Mrs. Wyeth, wife of the late Judge Louis Wyeth, of Marshall county, died last week," *The Scottsboro Citizen* (Scottsboro, AL), 9 Jan 1896, 2. (Newspapers.com)

[895] Lavone Johnson Anglen, *Alabama Pioneers*, 2013-2015.

[896] John A. Wyeth, "Cold Cheer in Camp Morton," 844. <https://babel.hathitrust.org/cgi/pt?id=coo.31924079633362>

[897] Roderick Davis, "John Allan Wyeth," *Encyclopedia of Alabama*, 05 Sep 2013. <http://www.encyclopediaofalabama.org/article/h-3522>

[898] "Dr. John A. Wyeth, 77, Noted Surgeon, Dies in His Office," *New York Herald* (New York, NY), 29 May 1922, 7.

[899] "Golden Wedding," *The Guntersville Democrat* (Guntersville, AL), 11 Apr 1889, 3. (Newspapers.com)

[900] A. Davis Smith and T. A. DeLand, *Northern Alabama Historical and Biographical* (Chicago: Donohue & Henneberry, 1888), 395-396. <https://books.google.com/books?id=Sp0IAwAAQBAJ&pg>

[901] Donna J. Siebenthaler, "Marshall County," *Encyclopedia of Alabama*, 03 Jul 2007, www.encyclopediaofalabama.org/article/h-1202 (accessed 4/12/2018).

[902] Treaty of New Echota, *Wikipedia*, https://en.wikipedia.org/wiki/Treaty_of_New_Echota (accessed 2/14/2019).

[903] Donna J. Siebenthaler, "Marshall County," *Encyclopedia of Alabama* (accessed 4/12/2018).

[904] John Allan Wyeth, *With Sabre and Scalpel: The Autobiography of a Soldier and Surgeon* (New York: Harper & Brothers, 1914), 3. <https://books.google.com/books?id=-ekRAAAAYAAJ>

[905] John Allan Wyeth, *With Sabre and Scalpel*, 3.

[906] Donna Siebenthaler, (accessed 4/12/2018).

[907] John Allan Wyeth, *With Sabre and Scalpel*, 530.

[908] John Allan Wyeth, *With Sabre and Scalpel*, 74, 53.

[909] *Dwayne Cox, "Manumission by Last Will in Antebellum Alabama," Auburn University Libraries*, www.lib.auburn.edu/archive/aghy/manumission/manu-txt.htm#1b (accessed 4/13/2018).

[910] John Allan Wyeth, *With Sabre and Scalpel*, 54.

[911] Louis Wyeth, "Letter from Louis Wyeth in Guntersville, Alabama, to Governor Robert Miller Patton," *Alabama Department of Archives and History* (Guntersville, Marshall County, Alabama, 2 Apr 1866). <digital.archives.alabama.gov/cdm/ref/collection/voices/id/2192>

[912] "The Starving People of Alabama," *Courier-Journal* (Louisville, Kentucky), 12 Apr 1866, 3.

[913] "Judge Louis Wyeth," *Harrisburg Telegraph* (Harrisburg, PA), 26 May 1876, 4. (Newspapers.com)

[914] James T. White, *The National Cyclopaedia of American Biography, Volume VI*, (New York: James T. White & Co., 1896), 74. <https://books.google.com/books?id=bnRMAAAAYAAJ&pg>

[915] "Cyclone rips through Alabama," *Chicago Tribune* (Chicago, Illinois) 10 Jun 1896, 1.

[916] Angela C. Otts, "Guntersville Museum & Cultural Center," *Encyclopedia of Alabama*, 23 May 2012. <www.encyclopediaofalabama.org/article//h-3255>

[917] "Beloved by All Classes," *The Guntersville Democrat* (Guntersville, Alabama), 08 Aug 1889, 1.

[918] Rhode Island USGenWeb Project, "The Record of Old Smithfield from 1730 To 1850, Vol. VIII, 1889, from Records in Town Clerk's Office, Lincoln," Rhode Island Reading Room, http://www.rootsweb.ancestry.com/~rigenweb/Smithfield13.html (accessed 10/31/2017).

[919] "The Man in the Dome: The Checkered Career of Samuel Douglass Wyeth," *St. Louis Globe-Democrat* (St. Louis, MO), 28 Jan 1881, 7.

[920] The Church of Jesus Christ of Latter-day Saints, "Ancestral File," database, *FamilySearch* (https://familysearch.org/ark:/61903/2:1:M1LL-3JY : accessed 4/16/2018), entry for George Wardwell Wyeth (3312-0RF); record merged from multiple submissions.

[921] "Died," *New York Daily Herald* (New York, NY), 23 Nov 1875, 8. (Newspapers.com)

[922] New York Death records," Rebecca Churchhill Wyith-Wardwell," database, *FamilySearch*, https://familysearch.org/ark:/61903/1:1:2WF7-6G7 (accessed 3/17/2017).

[923] The Church of Jesus Christ of Latter-day Saints, "Ancestral File," database, *FamilySearch* (https://familysearch.org/ark:/61903/2:1:M1LL-4CZ : accessed 4/16/2018), entry for Frances Jane Howe "Fanny" Wyeth (3312-430); record merged from multiple submissions.

[924] "Died," *New York Tribune* (New York, NY), 18 Sep 1891, 7.

[925] Robert F. Gist, "Rosedale Cemetery records," *Email*, 04 Apr 2014.

[926] Robert F. Gist, "Rosedale Cemetery records," *Email*, 04 Apr 2014.

[927] "Wyeth Waived Examination," *New York Tribune* (New York, NY), 25 Jan 1889, 3.

[928] "Wyeth Held in Heavy Bail," *The Evening World* (New York, NY), 24 Jan 1889, 2.

[929] "Died," *New York Herald* (New York, NY), 7 Sep 1891, 1. (GenealogyBank.com)

[930] Jonas Wyeth, *Wyeth family records (Mss A 3058)*, R. Stanton Avery Special Collections, New England Historic Genealogical Society.

[931] "Divorce Case in Cambridge," *Emancipator and Republican* (Boston, MA), 08 Dec 1848, 3.

[932] *File #211*, Scott County, Iowa District Court records.

[933] Scott County, Iowa Marriage Certificates and License Returns.

[934] *File #211*, Scott County, Iowa District Court records.

[935] David Michaelis, *N. C. Wyeth: A Biography* (New York: Alfred A. Knopf, 1998), 5-6.

[936] Jonas Wyeth, *Wyeth family records (Mss A 3058),* R. Stanton Avery Special Collections, New England Historic Genealogical Society.

[937] Jonas Wyeth, *Wyeth family records (Mss A 3058),* R. Stanton Avery Special Collections, New England Historic Genealogical Society.

[938] Jonas Wyeth, *Wyeth family records (Mss A 3058),* R. Stanton Avery Special Collections, New England Historic Genealogical Society.

[939] "Compiled Service Records of Volunteer Union Soldiers Who Served in Organizations from the State of Vermont," digital images, *Fold3* (http://www.fold3.com : accessed 23 Apr 2018), 4th Infantry, Pages: 14-15, veteran: Charles A. Read; Company: C,F&S; citing NARA catalog title: *Carded Records Showing Military Service of Soldiers Who Fought in Volunteer Organizations During the American Civil War, compiled 1890 - 1912, documenting the period 1861 - 1866, NARA Catalog Id: 300398, Record Group: 94, roll:* RG94-CMSR-VT-4INF-BX079.

[940] "New York Births and Christenings, 1640-1962," database, *FamilySearch* (https://familysearch.org/ark:/61903/1:1:FDRT-RY3 : 12 Dec 2014), Mary Kimble Wyeth, 12 Aug 1801; citing Broadway And Seventy First Street Christ Episcopal, New York, NY, reference ; FHL microfilm 532,976.

[941] The Church of Jesus Christ of Latter-day Saints, "Ancestral File," database, *FamilySearch,* John Spencer Hadley (K8HQ-VVJ) family tree, https://www.familysearch.org/tree/pedigree/landscape/K8HQ-VVJ (accessed 4/24/2018).

[942] "Died," *New York Tribune* (New York City, NY), 2 May 1864, 5.

[943] "New York, New York City Municipal Deaths, 1795-1949," database, *FamilySearch* (https://familysearch.org/ark:/61903/1:1:2WCW-Z3J : 10 February 2018), Eliza Jane Hadley in entry for Mary Louisa Hadley Risley, 26 Jun 1916; citing Death, Manhattan, New York, New York, United States, New York Municipal Archives, New York; FHL microfilm 1,322,393.

[944] The Church of Jesus Christ of Latter-day Saints, John Spencer Hadley (K8HQ-VVJ) family tree.

[945] The Church of Jesus Christ of Latter-day Saints, John Spencer Hadley (K8HQ-VVJ) family tree.

[946] "Died," *The New York Times* (New York, NY), 27 Sep 1913, 13.

[947] The Church of Jesus Christ of Latter-day Saints, John Spencer Hadley (K8HQ-VVJ) family tree.

[948] "Died," *New York Tribune* (New York City, NY), 22 Nov 1914, 11.

[949] The Church of Jesus Christ of Latter-day Saints, John Spencer Hadley (K8HQ-VVJ) family tree.

[950] "New York, New York City Municipal Deaths, 1795-1949," database, *FamilySearch* (https://familysearch.org/ark:/61903/1:1:2WWH-X3C : 11 February 2018), Henry Clay Hadley, 03 May 1905; citing Death, Brooklyn, Kings, New York, United States, New York Municipal Archives, New York; FHL microfilm 1,324,099.

[951] W. F. Brainard, *Who's who in New York City and State: a biographical dictionary of contemporaries* (Brooklyn, NY: Press of Wm. G. Hewitt, 1911), 416. (Ancestry.com)

[952] "New York Births and Christenings, 1640-1962," database, *FamilySearch* (https://familysearch.org/ark:/61903/1:1:V2C7-PWB : 12 Dec 2014), Mary Kemble Johnson, Sep 1808; citing Broadway and 71st Street Christ Episcopal New York.

[953] "Died," *New York Herald* (New York, NY), 22 Feb 1870, 9. (GenealogyBank.com)

[954] "Died," New York Daily Herald (New York, NY), 20 Feb 1875, 6.

[955] Ancestry.com, *New York and Vicinity, United Methodist Church Records, 1775-1949* (Lehi, UT: Ancestry.com Operations, Inc., 2016), image 48. Original data: Vol 203: NYC Forsyth Street Church: Baptisms 1837-1874.

[956] "New York, New York City Municipal Deaths, 1795-1949," database, *FamilySearch* (https://familysearch.org/ark:/61903/1:1:2W8F-736 : 10 Feb 2018), Mary Lucretia Levi, 22 Nov 1882; citing Death, Manhattan, New York, New York, United States, New York Municipal Archives, New York; FHL microfilm 1,322,632.

[957] Agnes Grousset, 22.

[958] "Died," *Commercial Advertiser* (New York, NY), 15 Apr 1829, 2.

[959] Agnes Grousset, 22.

[960] Agnes Grousset, 94.

[961] "Daniel F. Tiemann," *Wikipedia,* https://en.wikipedia.org/wiki/Daniel_F._Tiemann (accessed 04/26/2018).

[962] Stephen Paschall Sharples, 477.

[963] Edmund Burke, 312.

[964] John Herbert Baker, 42.

[965] John Herbert Baker, 43.

[966] "Compiled Service Records of Volunteer Union Soldiers Who Served in Organizations from the State of Massachusetts," digital images, *Fold3* (http://www.fold3.com : accessed 21 Nov 2016), MA 3rd Cavalry, veteran: Richard H. Wyeth; Company: D; Pages: 13, citing NARA catalog title Carded Records Showing Military Service of Soldiers Who Fought in Volunteer Organizations During the American Civil War, compiled 1890 - 1912, documenting the period 1861 - 1866, NARA Catalog Id: 300398, Record Group: 94, roll: RG94-CMSR-MA-3CAV-Bx0236

[967] "Compiled Service Records of Volunteer Union Soldiers Who Served in Organizations from the State of Massachusetts," digital images, *Fold3,* 1st Cavalry, Pages: 1-25, entry for William H. (Henry) Wyeth.

[968] Brett Schulte, "150 Years Ago Today: The Skirmish at Lee's Mill: July 30, 1864" *The Siege of Petersburg Online,* www.beyondthecrater.com/news-and-notes/siege-of-petersburg-sesquicentennial/150-years-ago-today/150-18640730-lees-mill/ (accessed 5/1/2018).

[969] "Compiled Service Records of Volunteer Union Soldiers Who Served in Organizations from the State of Massachusetts," digital images, *Fold3,* 1st Cavalry, Page: 18, entry for William H. (Henry) Wyeth.

[970] John Herbert Baker, 43.

[971] "History," *First Church in Cambridge,* http://www.firstchurchcambridge.org/about-us/first-church-history (accessed 3/25/2016).

[972] John Herbert Baker, 44.

[973] Soldier's Pension Application File, 30 Apr 1907, service of John B. Wyeth (Co. N/A, MA 12th Unattached Company, Militia Infantry, Civil War); soldier's pension app. no. 1,363,684; Widow's Pension Application, 01 Sep 1926, Emma E. Wyeth; application no. 1,552,850; NA catalog title: Civil War and Later Pension Files; Dept. of Veterans Affairs Records; RG 15; National Archives, Washington, D.C.

[974] "Andrew N. Wyeth Suddenly Expires," *Cambridge Chronicle* (Cambridge, MA), 14 Apr 1900.

[975] "Death Andrew N. Wyeth," *Cambridge Tribune* (Cambridge, MA), 21 Apr 1900, 7.

[976] "Miss Susan E. Wyeth Retires," *Cambridge Chronicle* (Cambridge, MA), 07 Jul 1917, 6. (Cambridge Public Library)

[977] "An Octogenarian," *Cambridge Chronicle* (Cambridge, MA), 01 May 1897, 1. (Cambridge Public Library)

[978] "Deaths," *The Boston Daily Atlas* (Boston, MA),19 Jun 1851, 2, 19th Century U.S. Newspapers. Web. 3 May 2018.

[979] John Lathrop, *Massachusetts Reports: Cases Argued and Determined in the Supreme Judicial Court of Massachusetts, January-June 1875* (Boston: Houghton, Mifflin and Co., 1875), 260. <https://books.google.com/books?id=VPhHAQAAMAAJ&q>

[980] William Burnham Stevens, *History of Stoneham, Massachusetts* (Stoneham, MA: F. L. & W. E. Whittier, 1891), 337. <https://books.google.com/books?id=0eeRuBfl U9EC&q>

[981] "Retrospective Glances. Central Square and Its Environs In the 1840s," *Stoneham Independent* (Stoneham, MA), 28 Aug 1931, 3. Community History Archive of the Stoneham Public Library, stoneham.advantage-preservation.com (accessed 5/5/2018).

[982] Henry R. Stiles, 32.

[983] "Mr. Hollis N. Wythe," *Stoneham Independent* (Stoneham, MA), 16 May 1896, 5. (http://stoneham.advantage-preservation.com/)

[984] Mary Stiles (Paul) Guild, 339.

[985] "Divorce Case in Cambridge," *Emancipator and Republican* (Boston, MA), 08 Dec 1848, 3.

[986] *File #211*, Scott County, Iowa District Court records.

[987] Alice C. Allyn, 63-64.

[988] Sidney Perley, 156.

[989] John Blatchford; Charles I. Bushnell, *The narrative of John Blatchford, detailing his sufferings in the revolutionary war, while a prisoner with the British. As related by himself* (New York: unknown, 1865), v and 112-113. <https://archive.org/stream/narrativeofjohnb00blat#page/n9/mode/2up>

[990] John Blatchford; Charles I. Bushnell, 113-115.

[991] Abigail Bliss, "New Old Sloop steeple takes shape," *Gloucester Daily Times*, 13 Sep 2017. <www.gloucestertimes.com/news/local_news/new-old-sloop-steeple-takes-shape/article_19e70a53-1938-53b6-bef5-a1e9a0ed87cc.html>

[992] Gardner W. Pearson, 10.

[993] Sidney Perley, 157.

[994] Sidney Perley, 189.

[995] Sidney Perley, 158.

[996] William Otis Sawtelle, 13.

[997] Sidney Perley, 191.

[998] Gardner W. Pearson, 12.

[999] The Church of Jesus Christ of Latter-day Saints, "Ancestral File," database, *FamilySearch*, entry for John Grover, cites sources; "Crawford-Osborn Family Tree 040918" file (2:2:2:MM6Z-WD1), submitted 9 Apr 2018 by JohnCrawford2, , https://familysearch.org/ark:/61903/2:2:3N5B-NLR (accessed 23 May 2018).

[1000] Arabella Morton, 27.

[1001] Gardner W. Pearson, 193.

[1002] Gardner W. Pearson, 42.

[1003] Gardner W. Pearson, 42.

[1004] Edward G. Longacre, *The Man Behind the Guns: A Biography of General Henry Jackson Hunt, Chief of Artillery, Army of the Potomac* (Cranbury, NJ: A. S. Barnes and Co., 1977), 22. <https://books.google.com/books?id=kZ8BAAAAMAAJ&dq>

[1005] Edward G. Longacre, 22.

[1006] Edward G. Longacre, 23.

[1007] Francis S. Drake, *Memorials of the Society of the Cincinnati of Massachusetts*, 355.

[1008] John Eicher, David Eicher, 310.

[1009] Brett Schulte, "Number 264. Petersburg Campaign Report of Capt. Lewis C. Hunt, Sixty-seventh Ohio Infantry, of operations Oct 27-28," and "67th Ohio Infantry," *The Siege of Petersburg Online*, http://www.beyondthecrater.com/ (accessed 5/19/2018).

[1010] "Lewis C. Hunt Col. 67th—Ohio," United States, [Between 1860 and 1870] Photograph, *Library of Congress Prints and Photographs Division*, https://www.loc.gov/item/cwp2003001394/PP/ (accessed 5/19/2018).

[1011] "Mrs. Julia Hunt Tompkins," *The Monmouth Inquirer* (Freehold, New Jersey), 11 Mar 1915, 1. (Newspapers.com)

[1012] "Deaths," *Daily Atlas* (Boston, MA), 13 Jan 1853, 2. (GenealogyBank.com)

[1013] "Raritan Bay Union and Eagleswood Military Academy Collection, 1809-1973, Mg 285," *The New Jersey Historical Society*, www.jerseyhistory.org/findingaid.php?aid=0285 (accessed 5/25/2018).

[1014] Selim H. Peabody, *Peabody (Paybody, Pabody, Pabodie) Genealogy*, (Boston, MA: Charles H. Pope, 1909), 85. <https://books.google.com/books?id=cIlJAAAAMAAJ&pg>

[1015] Megan Marshall, 43.

[1016] Maggie MacLean, "Elizabeth Peabody Founder of the First Public Kindergarten," *Civil War Women*, 7/16/2012. <www.civilwarwomenblog.com/elizabeth-peabody/>

[1017] "About Us," *The Elizabeth Peabody House*, 2016. <teph.org/about-us/>

[1018] "Dr. Lucius K. Russell," *Herald-Recorder* (Potsdam, NY), 8 Nov 1935, transcribed on 13 Jun 2009 by Karen E. Dau for the New York State Convention of Universalists. <nyscu.org/Archives/Universalist%20Memory%20Garden/Universalist%20Memory%20Garden%20Q-R/Russell,%20Lucius%201935.pdf>

[1019] "The Catahoula Parish Descendants of Dr. Nathaniel Bowman," *Roots From the Bayou*, 8 Dec 2012. <rootsfromthebayou.blogspot.com/2012/12/the-catahoula-parish-descendants-of-dr.html>

[1020] Seth Chandler, *History of the town of Shirley* (Shirley, MA: Seth Chandler, 1883), 663. <https://books.google.com/books?id=mBYQAwAAQBAJ&printsec>

[1021] Juanita Vogt Wyeth letter and Charles Leon Wyeth chart to Jeff Wyeth, 08 May 1988.

[1022] Ancestry.com, Ohio, Court of Common Pleas (Cuyahoga County), *Ohio, Wills and Probate Records, 1786-1998*, Estate of Joseph Wyeth filed 19 Feb 1845 - image 117, Provo, UT: Ancestry.com Operations Inc., 2010.

[1023] Soldier's Pension Application File, Walter H. Wyeth, No. 323,729; Widow: Frances E. Wyeth, No. 945,418; Civil War, RG 15; NA–

Washington. (Birth, marriage and death dates are all from this file as well as the spelling of Francies.)

[1024] "Michigan Death Certificate for William Wyeth," *Seeking Michigan*, 1915 (gives date of birth as 07 Mar 1840; died at 75 yrs. on 27 Aug 1915 - conflicts with tombstone date of 07 Mar 1835 that must be in error as it is far before parents' marriage) http://seekingmichigan.contentdm.oclc.org/cdm/ref/collection/p129401coll7/id/260920 (accessed 7/19/2018).

[1025] "From the 124th Ohio," *The Daily Cleveland Herald* (Cleveland, OH), 6 Oct 1863, 3.

[1026] "The Civil War Soldiers and Sailors Database - Wyeth, Jonathan," *National Park Service*, https://www.nps.gov/civilwar/soldiers-and-sailors-database.htm (accessed 10/26/2016) and U.S. National Cemetery Interment Control Forms, image 45 from Ancestry.com.

[1027] Ancestry.com, *State of Michigan, Berrien County, Return of a Marriage No.173,* Fales Edwin Wyeth, Residence: Laketon, age; 23, born; Cleveland, Ohio, (Lehi, UT: Ancestry.com Operations Inc., 2016).

[1028] Soldier's Pension Application File, George W. P. Wyeth, No. 24,713; Widow: Sarah Wyeth; No. 1,032,906; Civil War, RG 15; NA–D.C.

[1029] "Vital Statistics," *Fitchburg Sentinel* (Fitchburg, MA), 28 Jan 1930, 3. (Confirmed on 7/24/2018 by Townsend Town Clerk)

[1030] "Mrs. William Newton," *Fitchburg Sentinel* (Fitchburg, MA), 16 Nov 1949, 12. (Newspapers.com)

[1031] "Dr. Eliza E. Judson," *Cleveland Leader* (Cleveland, OH), 05 Feb 1880, 2. (Genealogybank.com)

[1032] "Slavery," *The Liberator* (Boston, MA), 06 Feb 1836, 1. (Newspapers.com)

[1033] "United States District Court," *Boston Post* (Boston, MA), 21 Apr 1842, 1. (Newspapers.com)

[1034] Old Residents' Historical Association, *Contributions of the Old Residents' Historical Association, Lowell, Mass., Volume 4* (Lowell, MA: Morning Mail Print, 1891), 116. <https://books.google.com/books?id=UIolAQAAMAAJ&pg>

[1035] "A list of Lands and Town Lots," *Meigs County telegraph* (Pomeroy, Ohio), 15 Dec 1857, 3. <http://chroniclingamerica.loc.gov/lccn/sn85038183/1857-12-15/ed-1/seq-3/>

[1036] Francis John Higginson, *Remarks on Slavery and Emancipation* (Boston: Hilliard, Gray and Co., 1834), 15. <https://books.google.com/books?id=r1wSAAAAIAAJ&pg>

[1037] "The John Hunt Morgan Heritage Trail." Salisbury Township, The Gauntlet, *HMdb.org the Historical Marker Database* https://www.hmdb.org/map.asp?markers=108278,122850,108185,108189,28495,28481,28479,28964,28970 and https://www.hmdb.org/Photos3/398/Photo398570o.jpg and https://www.hmdb.org/Photos4/443/Photo443946o.jpg (accessed 10 Sep 2018).

[1038] "Historical Sketch of Columbiana County," *Columbiana County, Lisbon, Ohio*, www.columbianacounty.org/history.htm (accessed 11 Sep 2018).

[1039] Hodgeman County, KS, *eReference Desk*, www.ereferencedesk.com/resources/counties/kansas/hodgeman.html (accessed 11 Sep 2018).

[1040] "Somerville," *The Boston Globe* (Boston, MA), 26 Apr 1915, 5. (Newspapers.com)

[1041] Docket - 1006, Joseph H. Wyeth of Boston, discharged 25 Sep 1868. *Record Group 21: Records of District Courts of the United States, 1685 – 2009* (Series: Bankruptcy Act of 1841 Case Files, 1842 - 1844), National Archives Identifier: 4659096.

[1042] "Local Varieties," *Boston Daily Advertiser* (Boston, MA), 1 Sep 1882; 4. (GenealogyBank.com)

[1043] Samuel Atkins Eliot, *A History of Cambridge, Massachusetts, 1630-1913* (Cambridge, MA: Cambridge Tribune, 1913), 266. <https://books.google.com/books?id=siPZKHPQ1rcC&pg>

[1044] "Marriages," *Cambridge Chronicle* (Cambridge, MA), 4 Sep 1858, 2.

[1045] "Death Notices," *Boston Herald* (Boston, MA), 11 Apr 1956, 18.

[1046] "Will go 9000 Miles to Get Married," *Boston Post* (Boston, MA) 29 Jun 1901, 5. (Newspapers.com)

[1047] John J. Wyeth, 5.

[1048] Diana Ballew, *Welcome to our Ballew Family Page*, www.oocities.org/heartland/plains/2805/ballew3.html (accessed 9/24/2018).

[1049] Henry C. Bradsby, 469.

[1050] Wanda Smith, *Grand Lodge of Indiana, Wyeth Masonic history*, email 11/2/2017.

[1051] "Wallace Mewhinney, formerly of this city, is foreman of a 45-hand cooper shop at Wyandotte, Kansas," *Terre Haute Saturday Evening Mail* (Terre Haute, IN), 04 Feb 1871, 5. (NewspaperArchive.com)

[1052] "Local Intelligence," *The Wyandotte Herald* (Kansas City, KS), 16 Dec 1875, 4. (Newspapers.com)

[1053] "Sheriff's Sale," (shows *Tressa* Wyeth as defendant) *Wyandotte Echo* (Wyandotte, KS), 06 Jan 1933, 2. (Death records for Flora Wangsness show her mother's name spelled "Tressa" as well.)

[1054] "Mrs. George O. Drake Dead," *The Black Hills Daily Times* (Deadwood, SD), 29 Jan 1897, 3.

[1055] Softschools.com, *Mexican-American War Timeline*, www.softschools.com/timelines/ (accessed 10/2/2018).

[1056] Henry C. Bradsby, 1005.

[1057] Kristin Rodgers, "St. Francis Hospital and Starling Medical College," *The Ohio State University Libraries*, 26 Nov 2012. <https://library.osu.edu/blogs/mhcb/2012/11/26/st-francis-hospital-and-starling-medical-college/>

[1058] Henry C. Bradsby, 1005.

[1059] Henry C. Bradsby, 1005.

[1060] "The Death of E. R. Wythe," *Daily Wabash Express* (Terre Haute, IN), 13 Dec 1888, 1.

[1061] Adjutant General's Office. Registers of Deaths of Volunteers, compiled 1861–1865, 152-153.

[1062] Ancestry.com, *U.S. Confederate Pensions, 1884-1958*, A. LaForge, application date 21 Apr 1915, pension file number 31117, Provo, UT: Ancestry.com Operations Inc., 2010.

[1063] Christina Stopka and Tony Black, "Partial List of Texas Ranger Company and Unit Commanders," *Texas Ranger Research Center*, edensfamily.com/geneology/raw/research/jim-linney-texas-rangers-shawnee-delaware.htm (accessed 10/5/2018).

[1064] Joshua Wyeth Jr., *Bible records*, courtesy of Ethel Ross "Rossie" Wyeth Canion, 12 Feb 2004.

[1065] Henry C. Bradsby, 859.

[1066] "The Civil War Soldiers and Sailors Database - Collins, John W.," *National Park Service*, https://www.nps.gov/civilwar/search-soldiers-detail.htm?soldierId=DF69188F-DC7A-DF11-BF36-B8AC6F5D926A (accessed 10/06/2018).

[1067] "State of Indiana, Vigo County, ss: Clarissa Mewhinney vs. John Mewhinney," *The Terre Haute Star* (Terre Haute, IN), 01 Jun 1861, 2. (Newspapers.com)

[1068] Robert B. Mewhinney Letters, *Vigo County Public Library*, Inventory. www.vigo.lib.in.us/archives/inventories/wars/civilwar/mewhinney.php (accessed 10/8/2018).

[1069] "Candy Manufacturer Dies," *The Indianapolis News* (Indianapolis, IN), 05 Jan 1918, 12. (Newspapers.com)

[1070] Pat Mathews, "Re: Wyeth Genealogy," webmail.peoplepc.com email 03/16/2007. (she discusses her ancestor George McHenry who married into the Wyeth family - https://www.genealogy.com/forum/regional/states/topics/in/vigo/74/)

[1071] Joshua Wyeth Jr., *Bible records*, courtesy of Ethel Ross "Rossie" Wyeth Canion, 12 Feb 2004.

[1072] Family Data Sheets, courtesy of Ethel Ross "Rossie" Wyeth Canion, 12 Feb 2004.

[1073] "Indiana Digital Archives -Willis B. Wyeth, Ref. # MEX3342," *Indiana Archives and Records Administration*, https://secure.in.gov/apps/iara/search/Home/Detail?rId=771265 (accessed 25 Oct 2016).

[1074] J. H. Beers and Co., *Commemorative Biographical Record of Washington County, Pennsylvania* (Chicago: J. H. Beers & Co., 1893), 893. Transcribed by Neil and Marilyn Morton of Oswego, Illinois as part of the Beers Project. Published January 1997 on the Washington County, PA USGenWeb. www.chartiers.com/beers-project/articles/winter-893.html.

[1075] Soldier's Pension App. File, Alexander R. Wyeth, No. 160,817; Widow: Elizabeth Wyeth, No. 229,955; Civil War, RG 15; NA-DC.

[1076] Lillian Neisz, letters to Jeff Wyeth and family tree, West Lafayette, Indiana, August 1978.

[1077] Reference, *What Is Death by Consumption?* https://www.reference.com/health/death-consumption-5614f844064455f8 (accessed 10/15/2018).

[1078] Ellen Coulter, *Scott and Morgan Counties, IL researcher*, email 01/14/18.

[1079] "Robert Fulton's Mother Lies in Unmarked Grave," *The Pittsburgh Press* (Pittsburgh, PA), 03 Oct 1909, 12. (Newspapers.com)

[1080] Lillian Neisz, letters to Jeff Wyeth and family tree, West Lafayette, Indiana, August 1978.

[1081] Soldier's Pension App. File, Alexander R. Wyeth, No. 160,817; Widow: Elizabeth Wyeth, No. 229,955; Civil War, RG 15; NA-DC.

[1082] National Council of the Congregational Churches of the United States, Publishing Committee, 36.

[1083] Ellen Coulter, *Scott and Morgan Counties, IL researcher*, email 01/14/18.

[1084] Ellen Coulter, *Scott and Morgan Counties, IL researcher*, email 01/14/18.

[1085] "Metcalf, Edwin T.," www.scattercreek.com/~normw/METCALF,EDWIN%20T,.pdf (accessed 10/16/2018).

[1086] "Fulton's Grandniece Dies at Great Age," *San Francisco Chronicle* (San Francisco, CA), 9 Jun 1915, 13.

[1087] "The Death of Mrs. M.E.C. Wyeth," *The Florida Times-Union* (Jacksonville, FL), 27 May 1887, page 8.

[1088] "Dr. Wyeth Dead," *The Florida Times-Union* (Jacksonville, FL), 16 Oct 1899, page 5.

[1089] Evergreen Cemetery, evergreenjax.com, email from Marilyn Johnsen, 5/5/2016.

[1090] "A Portrait of Raphael," *The Los Angeles Times* (Los Angeles, CA), 21 Sep 1913, 27. (Newspapers.com)

[1091] "Deaths," *The Florida Times-Union* (Jacksonville, FL), 9 Apr 1900, page 5.

[1092] Evergreen Cemetery, evergreenjax.com, phone conversation with Belinda (904) 353-3649, 10/19/2018.

[1093] "Wife Tried to Prevent His Swallowing Cyanide of Potassium, but Failed," *The Brooklyn Daily Eagle* (Brooklyn, NY), 3 Jun 1904, 1.

[1094] "Mrs. Virginia Bradley," *Oakland Tribune* (Oakland, CA), 20 Nov 1951, 13. (Newspapers.com)

[1095] Patrick Schroeder, "The Battles of Sailor's Creek," *Encyclopedia Virginia*, https://www.encyclopediavirginia.org/Sailor_s_Creek_Battles_of (accessed 10/20/2018).

[1096] Kenneth A. White, Director, "Register of Marriages of St. Paul's Cathedral, Pittsburgh - Married 27 Jun 1836 Simonem Shaeffer and Fediliam Anna Wyer." *Archives & Records Center of the Roman Catholic Diocese of Pittsburgh*, 25 Aug 2016 letter to Julie Rowan Wolford.

[1097] "Died," *The Daily Republican* (Monongahela, PA), 06 Jan 1890, 1. (Newspapers.com)

[1098] "Serious Accident," *The Pittsburgh Gazette* (Pittsburgh, PA), 19 Aug 1865, 1 (and St. Mary's cemetery records).

[1099] Kenneth A. White, Director, "Baptized 14 Nov 1826, Fidelia Anna Wythe," letter of 25 Aug 2016 to Julie Rowan Wolford.

[1100] Allegheny County (PA) Register of Wills, *Will of Charles Kenny written 20 Aug 1839*, Pennsylvania, Wills and Probate Records, 1683-1993, Allegheny County Will Packets, Vol 5-6, image 1226.

[1101] Julie Rowan Wolford "Re: Wythe," email 11/19/17.

[1102] "West Mifflin, Pennsylvania," *Wikipedia*, https://en.wikipedia.org/wiki/West_Mifflin,_Pennsylvania (accessed 10/21/2018).

[1103] Kenneth A. White, Director, "Register of Marriages of St. Paul's Cathedral, Pittsburgh" 16 Nov 2017 email from Julie Rowan Wolford.

[1104] "Mrs. Margaret Wyeth Finn," *The Pittsburgh Press* (Pittsburgh, PA), 31 Jan 1905, 4. (Newspapers.com)

[1105] Genevieve Wyeth Tuttle, "Statement from family Bible," 1938.

[1106] "St. Mary's Cemetery," (Jan 28. Francis S. Wyeth, 65) *The Daily Republican* (Monongahela, PA), 15 Jan 1889, 4.

[1107] "Mrs. Mary Wyeth," *Monongahela Valley Republican* (Monongahela, PA), 29 Nov 1894, 3.

[1108] Edna Evans, Lynda Levin, "John Francis Wyeth," *The Schroeder-Wyeth Newsletter*, Washington, PA, 4 Nov 1976.

[1109] "Died," *Monongahela Valley Republican* (Monongahela, PA), 12 Oct 1882, 3.

[1110] "Died," *The Daily Republican* (Monongahela, PA), 02 Aug 1884, 1.

[1111] "Prisoner Escaped," *The Daily Republican* (Monongahela, PA), 23 Jan 1896, 1.

[1112] "Court News," *The Daily Republican* (Monongahela, PA), 12 Jul 1904, 1, and 26 Oct 1905, 4.

[1113] "Ohio Deaths, 1908-1953," database with images, *FamilySearch* (https://familysearch.org/ark:/61903/3:1:S3HT-696Q-TQJ?cc=1307272&wc=MD96-L38%3A287598601%2C292620302 : 21 May 2014), 1924 > 08601-11500 > image 1318 of 3245.

[1114] "Sarver Surrendered Today," *The Daily Republican* (Monongahela, PA), 10 Oct 1911, 1.

[1115] Joshua "Jock" Wyeth news, *The Daily Republican* (Monongahela, PA), 11 Apr 1887; 06 Jul 1896; 24 Jun 1901, all articles on page 1.

[1116] "May be a Costly Chicken Dinner," *The Daily Republican* (Monongahela, PA), 06 Aug 1906, 1.

[1117] Soldier's Pension Application File, Henry E. Wyeth, No. 625,054; Record Group 15; National Archives, Washington, D.C.

[1118] "Complete List of Killed and Wounded of the 31st and 11th Regiments," *The Terre Haute Star* (Terre Haute, IN), 16 Apr 1862, 2.

[1119] "Letter Finds Father Dead," *Logansport Daily Reporter* (Logansport, IN), 2 Aug 1904, 8. (NewspaperArchive.com)

[1120] "A Fatal Accident," *The Republican Progress* (Bloomington, IN), 23 Apr 1884, 3. (NewspaperArchive.com)

[1121] Robert E. King, Doris Ruth Van Dusen Jones, *History of the King family in Flanders & America, 1300's-1980*, (Place not given: R.E. King, 1980), 138-139. <https://books.google.com/books?id=yRIZAQAAMAAJ&dq>

[1122] Widow's Pension Application File, Fanny Wyeth, No. 925,070 (service of Matthew W. Wyeth); Civil War, RG 15; NA–Washington.

[1123] "Deaths," *The Conneautville Courier* (Conneautville, PA), 05 Mar 1891, 8.

[1124] "Resolutions of Condolence," *The Conneautville Courier* (Conneautville, PA), 12 Mar 1891, 8. (Newspapers.com)

[1125] "Neighborhood News," *The Conneautville Courier* (Conneautville, PA), 24 Feb 1904, 5.

[1126] "Clayton E. Perkins Funeral Tomorrow," *Oakland Tribune* (Oakland, CA), 13 May 1947, 10. (Newspapers.com)

[1127] "Crushed by a Falling Tree," *The Conneautville Courier* (Conneautville, PA), 20 Dec 1894, 1. (Newspapers.com)

[1128] Ancestry.com, *U.S. National Homes for Disabled Volunteer Soldiers, 1866-1938* [database on-line]. Provo, UT: Ancestry.com Operations Inc., 2007, Image 715 (George W. Wyeth.)

[1129] Soldier's Pension Application File, George W. Wyeth, no. 842,320, Navy no. 27,895, Civil War, RG 15; NA–Washington.

[1130] "Tom Wyeth Murdered in Butte," *Santa Cruz Evening News* (Santa Cruz, CA), 24 Jan 1918, 1.

[1131] "Called by Death," *New Castle Herald* (New Castle, PA), 31 Jan 1912, 9.

[1132] "Approved pension applications of widows and other dependents of Civil War veterans who served between 1861 and 1910," digital images, *Fold3* (http://www.fold3.com : accessed 11 Nov 2018), 17th Ohio Light Artillery; veteran: Mathew Canady; Battery L.A.; Widow: Elvira Bailey Canady, pension application no. WC48933; citing NARA catalog title: *Case Files of Approved Pension Applications of Widows and Other Veterans of the Army and Navy Who Served Mainly in the Civil War and the War With Spain, compiled 1861 - 1934, NARA Catalog Id: 300020, Record Group: 15, roll: WC48933.*

[1133] "Approved pension applications of widows and other dependents of Civil War veterans who served between 1861 and 1910," digital images, *Fold3* (http://www.fold3.com : accessed 11 Nov 2018), 45th Ohio Infantry; veteran: William W. Canady; Company: B; Widow: Martha R. Bailey Canady Brown, pension application no. WC53766; citing NARA catalog title: Case Files of Approved Pension Applications of Widows and Other Veterans of the Army and Navy Who Served Mainly in the Civil War and the War With Spain, compiled 1861 - 1934, NARA Catalog Id: 300020, Record Group: 15, roll: WC53766.

[1134] "Ohio Deaths, 1908-1953," database with images, *FamilySearch* (https://familysearch.org/ark:/61903/3:1:33S7-9PVR-9NS1?cc=1307272&wc=MD9X-6M9%3A287600401%2C294383201 : 21 May 2014), 1909 > 26571-29262 > image 2053 of 2994.

[1135] "Compiled Service Records of Volunteer Union Soldiers Who Served in Organizations from the State of Ohio," digital images, *Fold3*, 45th Ohio Infantry; Pages: 120, entry for William W. Canady.

[1136] "Ohio, County Death Records, 1840-2001," database with images, *FamilySearch* (https://familysearch.org/ark:/61903/3:1:3QS7-99ZR-V98N-V?cc=2128172&wc=7DZ2-GYJ%3A1296071441%2C1296166484 : 30 September 2014), Auglaize > Death records, 1899-1938, vol 4-5 > image 28 of 454; county courthouses, Ohio.

[1137] "Ohio Deaths, 1908-1953," database with images, *FamilySearch* (https://familysearch.org/ark:/61903/3:1:33S7-9PKP-4HKT?cc=1307272&wc=MD9F-3PD%3A287598801%2C294602101 : 21 May 2014), 1942 > 50601-53500 > image 879 of 3231.

[1138] "Miss Cora Bailey," *Chillicothe Gazette* (Chillicothe, OH), 05 Nov 1953, 2. (Newspapers.com)

[1139] "Miss Mary Bailey," *The Circleville Herald* (Circleville, OH), 9 Feb 1952, 2. (Newspapers.com)

[1140] "Mr. James E. Bailey," *The Circleville Herald* (Circleville, OH), 1 Feb 1965, 2. (Newspapers.com)

[1141] "Will of W. A. Bailey," *Chillicothe Gazette* (Chillicothe, OH), 20 Jul 1936, 2. (Newspapers.com)

[1142] "Rev. John Hewson, Evangelist, Dies," *The Indianapolis Star* (Indianapolis, Indiana), 14 Jan 1940, 8. (Newspapers.com)

[1143] Donna Wyeth Thibodeau, "Charles Alonzo Wyeth biography," 18 Nov 1986.

[1144] "Colorado Statewide Divorce Index, 1900-1939," images, *FamilySearch* (https://familysearch.org/ark:/61903/3:1:3QS7-89WB-C8ZC?cc=2043439&wc=M612-XTG%3A348713701 : 26 June 2018), Wilson, Jennie B-Zizos, Ruth > image 1107 of 1808; Colorado State Archives, Denver. https://www.familysearch.org/ark:/61903/3:1:3QS7-89WB-C8ZC?i=1106&wc=M612-XTG%3A348713701&cc=2043439

[1145] "Colorado Statewide Divorce Index, 1900-1939," images, *FamilySearch* (https://familysearch.org/ark:/61903/3:1:3QS7-99WB-CD3G?cc=2043439&wc=M612-XTG%3A348713701 : 26 June 2018), Wilson, Jennie B-Zizos, Ruth > image 1105 of 1808; Colorado State Archives, Denver. https://www.familysearch.org/ark:/61903/3:1:3QS7-99WB-CD3G?i=1104&wc=M612-XTG%3A348713701&cc=2043439

[1146] "Colorado Statewide Divorce Index, 1900-1939," images, *FamilySearch* (https://familysearch.org/ark:/61903/3:1:3QS7-L9WB-C8JR?cc=2043439&wc=M612-XTG%3A348713701 : 26 June 2018), Wilson, Jennie B-Zizos, Ruth > image 1106 of 1808; Colorado State Archives, Denver. https://www.familysearch.org/ark:/61903/3:1:3QS7-L9WB-C8JR?i=1105&wc=M612-XTG%3A348713701&cc=2043439

[1147] "Charles A. Wyeth (born Cincinnati) and Joseph Morcatt Die at Veterans' Home," *Star Tribune* (Minneapolis, MN), 31 Mar 1915, 8.

[1148] Donna Wyeth Thibodeau, "Charles Alonzo Wyeth biography and family data sheets," 18 Nov 1986.

[1149] Helen Fitzgerald Sanders, *A History of Montana Vol. III* (Chicago; New York: Lewis Publishing Co., 1913), 1818.

[1150] "Appendicitis ends 5-day Honeymoon," *Denver Post* (Denver, CO), 2 Jun 1915, 15.

[1151] Donna Wyeth Thibodeau, "Charles Alonzo Wyeth biography and family data sheets," 18 Nov 1986.

[1152] Donna Wyeth Thibodeau, "Charles Alonzo Wyeth biography and family data sheets," 18 Nov 1986.

[1153] Joan Wyeth Carpenter, letter to Jeff Wyeth, 28 Feb 1986.

[1154] "Ethel Kubicek," *Argus-Leader* (Sioux Falls, Minnehaha, SD), 23 Sep 2001, 27. (Newspapers.com)

[1155] Ballenger & Richards, *Annual Denver City Directory*, (Denver, CO: Ballenger & Richards, 1882), 204 (Drake), 610 (Wyeth).

[1156] "Colorado State Census, 1885," database with images, *FamilySearch* (https://familysearch.org/ark:/61903/3:1:939N-8Y7C-H?cc=1807096&wc=M83M-BMS%3A149195601%2C149208301%2C149200101 : 1 April 2016), Arapahoe > Denver > Population > image 430 of 598; citing NARA microfilm publication M158 (Washington, D.C.: National Archives and Records Administration, n.d.).

[1157] "T. R. Look Here," *Mount Carmel Item* (Mount Carmel, PA), 27 Mar 1915, 3.

[1158] "Funeral of Charles A. Wyeth," *Star Tribune* (Minneapolis, MN), 05 Apr 1915, 9. (Newspapers.com)

[1159] Ancestry.com. U.S. National Homes for Disabled Volunteer Soldiers, 1866-1938 [database on-line]. Provo, UT: Ancestry.com Operations Inc., 2007, Image 284 (George N. Wyeth.)

[1160] Captain Harold E. Wyeth, letter to Jeff Wyeth, 11 Mar 1979, from Coco Solo, Panama Canal Zone.

[1161] Hamilton County Genealogical Society First Families of Hamilton County, *Ohio Records (Mss 1093).*

[1162] "Spring Grove Cemetery," *Genealogy Search Listing (section 53, lot 87),* www.springgrove.org/geneology-listing.aspx?garden=LN&section=53&lot=87&cemetery=SPRINGGROVE (accessed 2/10/2018).

[1163] "Spring Grove Cemetery," *Genealogy Search Listing (section 53, lot 87).*

[1164] Ancestry.com, *Catalogue of the officers and students of Phillips Exeter Academy for the Academical Year 1868-69*, 70.

[1165] Donna Valley Stuart, 115.

[1166] "Obituary," *Daily Arkansas Gazette* (Little Rock, AR), 13 Apr 1873, 1.

[1167] "Mrs. Julia Elizabeth Willcox, Widely Known Here, is Dead in New York," *Denver Post* (Denver, CO), 9 Feb 1923, 5.

[1168] "Died." *Daily Inter Ocean* (Chicago, IL), 05 Oct 1866, 7. (Genealogybank.com)

[1169] "Commencement Exercises Next Week at Columbian University," *Evening Star* (Washington, D.C.), 25 May 1900, 8.

[1170] Alan J. Stein, "Denny, Orion O. (1853-1916)," *HistoryLink.org*, posted 11/24/2002. <www.historylink.org/File/4026>

[1171] "Wealthy Widow Commits Suicide," *Morning Oregonian* (Portland, OR), 10 Mar 1922, 1.

[1172] Ancestry.com. *U.S. National Homes for Disabled Volunteer Soldiers, 1866-1938* [database on-line]. Provo, UT: Ancestry.com Operations Inc., 2007, Image 1746 (Leonard J. Wyeth.)

[1173] "Nathan C. Wyeth," *Wikipedia*, https://en.wikipedia.org/wiki/Nathan_C._Wyeth (accessed 11/17/2018).

[1174] "Items of Interest from Various Localities," *American Gas Light Journal*, 784.

[1175] "Interments Listed by Vault," *The New York City Marble Cemetery*, www.nycmc.org/intermentvaults.html (accessed 11/17/2018).

[1176] "Green-Wood Cemetery," *Burial Search* (under Carpenter), https://www.green-wood.com/burial_search/ (accessed 11/17/2018).

[1177] "Died," *New York Times* (New York, NY), 17 Dec 1940, 25. (ProQuest Historical Newspapers)

[1178] "Leonard Jarvis Wyeth (1854)," *Harvard College Library Clipping Sheet*, Harvard University Archives (various dates).

[1179] "Died," *New York Times* (New York, NY), 09 Oct 1923, 21.

[1180] "Bequests to Charities in Mrs. F. S. Welles' Will," *The Brooklyn Daily Eagle* (Brooklyn, NY), 2 Apr 1911, 39. (Newspapers.com)

[1181] Mallory Herberger, Special Collections Archivist, *Maryland Historical Society*, emails dated 12/06/2018 and 12/07/2018.

[1182] "New York City," *New York Tribune* (New York, NY), 29 Oct 1874, 8. (chroniclingamerica.loc.gov)

[1183] "Other deaths," *Baltimore Sun* (Baltimore, MD), 23 Mar 1885, 4. (GenealogyBank.com)

[1184] New York City Municipal Archives record #9550, housed 31 Chambers Street, New York, NY 10007.

[1185] "Obituary," *Little Falls Herald* (Little Falls, NJ), 24 Feb 1944, 6. (fultonhistory.com)

[1186] "Nathaniel J. and Ann C. Wyeth House," *Landmarks Preservation Commission*, 1.

[1187] New York City Municipal Archives record #14807, housed 31 Chambers Street, New York, NY 10007.

[1188] National Biographical Publishing Co., *Biographical Cyclopedia of Representative Men of Maryland* (Baltimore: National Biographical Publishing Co., 1870), 104.

[1189] Thomas M. Myers, 48.

[1190] Mallory Herberger, Special Collections Archivist, *Maryland Historical Society*, emails dated 12/06/2018 and 12/07/2018.

[1191] "Obituary Notes," *New York Times* (New York, NY), 16 Apr 1890, 2. (ProQuest Historical Newspapers)

[1192] "Death of Mrs. W. N. Wyeth," *The Baltimore Sun* (Baltimore, MD), 18 Mar 1898, 10.

[1193] Mallory Herberger, Special Collections Archivist, *Maryland Historical Society*, emails dated 12/06/2018 and 12/07/2018.

[1194] "Charles M. Wyeth Dies," *The Star-Democrat* (Easton, MD), 11 Feb 1944, 12.

[1195] "Goodwin-Wyeth," *The Baltimore Sun* (Baltimore, MD), 23 Feb 1898, 10.

[1196] "The Alumni," *The Princeton Alumni Weekly*, Vol. XXIV, No. 24, (Princeton, NJ), 26 Mar 1924, 516. <https://books.google.com/books?id=SRJbAAAAYAAJ&pg>

[1197] Mallory Herberger, Special Collections Archivist, *Maryland Historical Society*, emails dated 12/06/2018 and 12/07/2018.

[1198] Baltimore County, Maryland. *Marriage Cards, Court of Common Pleas (Marriage Index, Male) CM205*. State of Maryland, 1851-1855. reel No. 23.22, msa.maryland.gov/megafile/msa/coagserm/cm200/cm205/000000/000022/pdf/msa_cm205_000022.pdf (accessed 2/18/2018).

[1199] National Biographical Publishing Co., 104.

[1200] "The Sunday afternoon Accident in Druid Hill Park," *The Baltimore Sun* (Baltimore, MD), 09 Jul 1873, 1.

[1201] Nicole Thompson, *Green Mount Cemetery Office*, emails, phone conversations, and visits 2/20/2018, 2/26/2018 and 6/5/2018.

[1202] Lula Browning, letter to Jeff Wyeth dated 31 Dec 1978.

[1203] Wallace H. Wyeth Sr. (1943-2012) personal records and phone conversations with Jeff Wyeth, 2009.

[1204] Widow's Pension Application File, Amelia L. Wyeth, No. 380,667 (service of Norman D. Wyeth); Civil War, RG 15; NA–Washington.

[1205] The Church of Jesus Christ of Latter-day Saints, "Ancestral File," database, *FamilySearch*, entry for Silas J. Wyeth (M1LP-6CQ) https://www.familysearch.org/tree/person/details/M1LP-6CQ (accessed 2/27/2018).

[1206] Marvel June Wyeth Ucen letter to Jeff Wyeth dated 5 Aug 1986.

[1207] NNY Genealogy, *Stories in Stone*, Marriage Records, nnygenealogy.com (accessed 10/15/2018).

[1208] Gad Wyeth Jr., *Family Record*, courtesy of Sheila Baum and James Allen Wyeth, 27 Aug 2014.

[1209] Terry Mandigo, *Flower Memorial Library Genealogy Dept.*, Watertown, NY, email 12/1/2018.

[1210] "Sudden Death at Great Bend," *Watertown Daily Times* (Watertown, NY), 15 Apr 1897, 5. (fultonhistory.com)

[1211] Terry Mandigo, *Flower Memorial Library Genealogy Dept.*, Watertown, NY, email 12/1/2018.

[1212] "Died," *The Watertown Herald* (Watertown, NY), 9 Jul 1898, 6. (nyshistoricnewspapers.org)

[1213] "Thaddeus Olds, 80, Succumbs at Granby," *Oswego Palladium-Times* (Oswego, NY), 01 Feb 1934, 1?. (fultonhistory.com)

[1214] Gad Wyeth Jr., *Family Record*, courtesy of Sheila Baum and James Allen Wyeth, 27 Aug 2014.

[1215] NNY Genealogy, *Stories in Stone*, Burial Collection – Abby Jane Wyeth, nnygenealogy.com (accessed 12/2/2018).

[1216] Terry Mandigo, *Flower Memorial Library Genealogy Dept.*, Watertown, NY, email 12/13/2018.

[1217] Anna May Souva Wyeth, *family data sheets* with letter to Jeff Wyeth dated 30 Dec 1984.

[1218] "Married," *Jefferson County Journal* (Adams, NY), 16 Jun 1875, 2. (fultonhistory.com)

[1219] NNY Genealogy, *Stories in Stone*, Burial Collection - Floretia White, nnygenealogy.com (accessed 11/29/2018).

[1220] *Find A Grave*, database and images (https://www.findagrave.com : accessed 30 November 2018), memorial page for Floretia White (unknown–28 Mar 1879), Find A Grave Memorial no. 48416157, citing Woods Mill Cemetery, North Wilna, Jefferson County, New York, USA ; Maintained by Old Ironsides (contributor 47198346) .

[1221] "Castorland," *The Journal and Republican* (Lowville, NY), 24 Jun 1897, 8. (nyshistoricnewspapers.org)

[1222] George Fisher and Co., *Biographical Directory of the Voters and Tax-payers of Kendall County* (Chicago: Geo. Fisher & Co., 1870), 72. https://books.google.com/books?id=5o3VN2ZX6K8C&pg

[1223] Soldier's Pension Application File, William H. Wyeth, no. 448,961, Civil War, RG 15; NA–Washington.

[1224] South Berwick, Maine Town Hall, phone conversation with Barbara, 12/10/18.

[1225] Elmer Dickson's *"Kendall County, Illinois Genealogy,"* http://kendallkin.org/databases/945/A,showall/131.html (accessed 12/10/2018).

[1226] Gad Wyeth Jr., *Family Record*, courtesy of Sheila Baum and James Allen Wyeth, 27 Aug 2014.

[1227] Charles E. Wyeth, *Family Records*, courtesy of Milton Dirst, 16 Aug 2001.

[1228] "Obituaries," *The Aurora Beacon-News* (Aurora, IL), 7 Dec 1949, 4.

[1229] "Approved pension applications of widows and other dependents of Civil War veterans who served between 1861 and 1910," digital images, *Fold3*, 75th Illinois Infantry, Pages: 2, 5, 7, and 9, entry for veteran: James M. Wyeth; Widow: Almira Thompson Wyeth.

[1230] "Approved pension applications of widows and other dependents of Civil War veterans who served between 1861 and 1910," digital images, *Fold3*, 75th Illinois Infantry, page 5 gives daughter's names and birthdates, entry for veteran: James M. Wyeth.

[1231] William Richard Cutter, *Genealogical and family history of Northern New York* (New York: Lewis Historical Pub., 1910), 1157-1158.

[1232] Donald Elwyn Wyeth, research shared in person with Jeff Wyeth in Alliance, Ohio, 1984.

[1233] Wing Family, *The Owl - A Genealogical Quarterly Magazine, Vol. 22-25* (Kewaunee, WI: Wing Family of America, 1920-1924), 2282.

[1234] "Wythe," *Herald Democrat* (Leadville, CO), 5 Dec 1921, 4.

[1235] John Gresham, 149-151.

[1236] Tuscola cemetery records, page 145.

[1237] David Kent Coy, Coles County Genealogical Society, Chapman Brothers, 467.

[1238] John Gresham, 165.

[1239] "Interest Taken in Landmarks," *The Newark Advocate* (Newark, OH), 02 Oct 1930, 21.

[1240] John Gresham, 149-151 and 188-189.

[1241] "Committal Service for Mrs. Brinton," *Dixon Evening Telegraph* (Dixon, IL), 05 Apr 1932, 1.

[1242] Ancestry.com. *Massachusetts, Town and Vital Records, 1620-1988*. n.p: Online publication - Provo, UT: Ancestry.com Operations, Inc., 2011. Original data – handwritten Wendell town clerk record, page 82.

[1243] Illinois Military and Naval Dept; Reece, Jasper N; Elliott, Isaac Hughes, *Report of the adjutant general of the state of Illinois, Volume 7* (Springfield, IL: Phillips Bros., 1900), 203. <http://www.archive.org/stream/reportofadjutant07illi1#page/193/mode/1up>

[1244] Timothy Hopkins, 657.

[1245] David Kent Coy, Coles County Genealogical Society, Chapman Brothers, 468.

[1246] David Kent Coy, Coles County Genealogical Society, Chapman Brothers, 468.

[1247] "James Wyeth …departed Weds for California," *Mattoon Gazette* (Mattoon, IL), 10 Dec 1897, 5.

[1248] Donna Stewart, *Coles County IL Genealogical Society*, email 12/27/2018 saying James had measles, returned from CA and died in IL.

[1249] "Laid to Rest," *Charleston Daily Courier* (Charleston, IL), 21 Dec 1897, 1. (Coles County IL Genealogical Society)

[1250] "Thomas Wyeth Will," *Journal Gazette* (Mattoon, IL), 03 Jun 1905, 6.

[1251] "Mrs. Cofer Dies," *Decatur Daily Review* (Decatur, IL), 9 Sep 1924, 4.

[1252] "John S. Cofer a Douglas County citizen about 50, committed suicide," *The Pantagraph* (Bloomington, IL), 12 Feb 1886, 1.

[1253] "Mrs. Merle H. Eckman," *The Decatur Herald* (Decatur, IL), 05 Jun 1963, 8.

[1254] "Mrs. Lucy Smith died on Saturday," *The Union County Journal* (Marysville, OH),16 Jul 1938, 2.

[1255] "Mrs. Sarah P. Baldwin," *The Union County Journal* (Marysville, OH), 16 Sep 1935, 4.

[1256] "David V. Wyeth dies at Broadway Home," *Richwood Gazette* (Richwood, OH), 19 Aug 1926, 1.

[1257] Margaret Main Bouic, "Bouic Index," *Mid-Ohio Genealogy Database*, www.midohiogen.org (accessed 1/3/2019).

[1258] "Hard Struggles of the Pioneers," *Marysville Tribune* (Marysville, OH), 09 Jan 1901, 1.

[1259] Amy Adeline Smith, *Memorials for funerals of Parker Judson Wyeth and Amy Nash Wyeth*, 1908 and 1923.

[1260] Timothy Hopkins, 657.

[1261] "International Genealogical Index (IGI)," *FamilySearch* (https://familysearch.org/ark:/61903/2:1:MS62-XZ4: accessed 12/16/ 2018).

[1262] Timothy Hopkins, 657 (says Rachel b. Woodland, NY but must mean Woodhull as her father there in 1840 census.)

[1263] "Northwestern Patents," *Chicago Tribune* (Chicago, IL), 03 Apr 1862, 1.

[1264] B. Homans, Jr., editor, *The Merchants' and Bankers' Almanac & Register* (New York: I. S. Homans, 1875), 102. <https://books.google.com/books?id=kG1QAQAAMAAJ>

[1265] "Inventor Dead Who Had Long Lived Here," *The Salt Lake Tribune* (Salt Lake City, UT), 05 Aug 1911, 14.

[1266] Welcome to our Davis County, Iowa Cemetery Project, http://baseportal.com/cgi-bin/baseportal.pl?htx=/bhoffman_7/Combined&cmd=list&range=1050,30&Last~=W&cmd=all&Id=14745 (accessed 12/14/2018).

[1267] Arthur Wyeth's handwritten 1922 notes and Ohio death records both show Libbie Wright died on 30 Oct 1912.

[1268] Stillman Samuel Wyeth, *Bible records*, birthdates courtesy of Charles Arthur "Chuck" Walker, 25 Mar 2016.

[1269] "Illinois, County Marriages, 1810-1940," database, *FamilySearch* (https://familysearch.org/ark:/61903/3:1:939Z-Y69L-9L?cc=1803970&wc=3268-K68%3A145956401 : 3 March 2016), 0338047 (004539312) > image 412 of 814; county offices, Illinois.

[1270] "Tolono Woman Dies in Daughter's Home," *Decatur Herald* (Decatur, IL), 27 Oct 1925, 9. (Newspapers.com)

[1271] Timothy Hopkins, 657.

[1272] Page County, Iowa obituaries transcribed by Pat O'Dell iagenweb.org/page/obituaries/oldfiles/Ru.html (accessed 1/4/2019).

[1273] Johnson Brigham, *Iowa, Its History and Its Foremost Citizens, Vol. 2* (Chicago: S. J. Clarke Publishing Co., 1915), 575-576. <https://books.google.com/books?id=CeE_AQAAMAAJ&pg>

[1274] Augustus Greenleaf Wyeth Bible records furnished by Lucy Snow Wyeth Hoffman, circa 1990.

[1275] Timothy Hopkins, 657.

[1276] "Dr. W. N. Wyeth," *Granville Times* (Granville, Ohio), 26 Oct 1899.

[1277] "Celebrated Golden Wedding Anniversary on Wednesday," *Newark Advocate* (Newark, OH), 5 Apr 1912, 1.

[1278] Edwin M. P. Brister, 528.

[1279] Lucy Snow Wyeth Hoffman, *Gad Wyeth Branch*, written circa 1990.

[1280] "Stricken in Chair, Wright David Wyeth, last of Wyeth-Scott Founders, Dead," *The Newark Advocate* (Newark, OH), 22 Jun 1956, 1.

[1281] "Hard Struggles of the Pioneers," *Marysville Tribune* (Marysville, OH), 09 Jan 1901, 1.

[1282] Wing Family, *The Owl - A Genealogical Quarterly Magazine*, Vol. 22-25 (Kewaunee, WI: Wing Family of America, 1920-1924), 1677.

[1283] Timothy Hopkins, 658.

[1284] Grace Wing Barnes, editor, *Annals of the Wing Family of America Incorporated, Vol. 54* (Des Moines, IA: Wing Family of America, 1954), 3807, 3835, 3836. <https://books.google.com/books?id=rG8dAQAAMAAJ&q>

[1285] Timothy Hopkins, 658.

[1286] Edwin M. P. Brister, 528.

[1287] "A. G. Wyeth dies Suddenly at Granville Street Home Upon Return from Drive," *Newark Advocate* (Newark, OH), 20 Jun 1914, 1.

[1288] "Ralph S. Wyeth, Bank Director and Ex-manufacturer, is Dead," *Newark Advocate* (Newark, OH), 24 Oct 1952, 1.

[1289] "$100,000 Given to Help County College Students," *Newark Advocate* (Newark, OH), 06 Jul 1965, 2.

[1290] "Senior Awards and Scholarships," *Newark Advocate* (Newark, OH), 14 Jun 2018, D7.

[1291] "Read First News of Death in the Age," *Coshocton Daily Age* (Coshocton, OH), 15 Apr 1907, 1.

[1292] "Mrs. Gertrude W. Shunk died at her City Home," *Harrisburg Telegraph* (Harrisburg, PA), 12 Dec 1912, 13.

[1293] "Miss Mary D. Shunk," *Harrisburg Telegraph* (Harrisburg, PA), 30 May 1905, 6.

[1294] "Parker-Shunk, Fashionable Wedding at St. Stephen's Church," *Patriot* (Harrisburg, PA), 02 Jun 1882, 1. (Genealogybank.com)

[1295] "Obituary," *The Morning Journal-Courier* (New Haven, CT), 31 Jan 1885, 2. (Newspapers.com)

[1296] "Col. Francis R. Shunk," *Boston Herald* (Boston, MA), 09 Jan 1925, 10.

[1297] "Lonely Widow ends life in a Hotel," *The New York Times* (New York, NY), 7 May 1917, 7.

[1298] Patricia King Harms, Family Tree, Jeff furnished to Tina Wyeth Baker in 2015. (John Wyeth Jr. lived in Harrisburg for 1840 census.)

[1299] Historical Data Systems, comp. *U.S., Civil War Soldier Records and Profiles, 1861-1865* [database on-line]. Provo, UT, USA: Ancestry.com Operations Inc., 2009.

[1300] "Marriage Licenses have been issued," *National Republican* (Washington, D.C.), 19 Jun 1876, 4.

[1301] "Agency Makes an Assignment," *Democrat and Chronicle* (Rochester, New York) 14 Oct 1905, 12. (Article says Mrs. Wyeth, the bankrupt's [John Louis Wyeth] mother [Abby Rogers Wyeth], claiming it as her property, being the discovery of her late husband [in reality her husband Louis Wyeth is not dead], although it was prepared by her son as his own.)

[1302] "Wyeth," Harrisburg *Telegraph* (Harrisburg, PA), 29 Mar 1923, 26.

[1303] Death Certificate attached to an email on 1/10/2019 by Wanda Wade, Research Volunteer, Wyoming State Archives.

[1304] "Wyeth Chemical Bankruptcy," *American Druggist and Pharmaceutical Record* (New York, NY), 25 Dec 1905, 358.

[1305] Judi Harms Edwards, message on 1/10/2019, Dorothy died in a hospital in Bremerton, but she lived in Port Orchard.

[1306] Marriage Certificate attached to an email on 1/10/2019 by Wanda Wade, Research Volunteer, Wyoming State Archives.

[1307] "Boehme-Wyeth Marriage Friday," *Branding Iron* (University of Wyoming, Laramie, WY), 14 Aug 1941, 4. <http://uwdigital.uwyo.edu/islandora/object/wyu%3A321368/datastream/OCR/view>

[1308] Laurabelle Boehme Wyeth, letter to Jeff Wyeth from Cheyenne, WY, dated 13 Mar 1978.

[1309] "The Sudden Death of a Former Chambersburger," *Valley Spirit* (Chambersburg, PA), 26 Oct 1887, 3.

[1310] "Lieut. J. S. Kennedy Dies," *Evening Star* (Washington, D.C.), 08 Oct 1916, 14. (Newspapers.com)

[1311] Bartlett Boder, *Museum Graphic*, 6.

[1312] "Mrs. Eliza Renick Wyeth," *Chillicothe Gazette* (Chillicothe, OH), 16 Nov 1920, 5.

[1313] William "Max" Wyeth IV, *William and Eliza Renick Wyeth and children's data*, email 07/10/2017.

[1314] "England Marriages, 1538–1973," database, FamilySearch (https://familysearch.org/ark:/61903/1:1:NVJV-2TF : 10 February 2018), Charles William Wyndham and Maud Wyeth Smith, 12 Nov 1892; citing Saint Martin In The Fields,Westminster,London,England, reference , index based upon data collected by the Genealogical Society of Utah, Salt Lake City; FHL microfilm 1,468,962.

[1315] "Huston Wyeth," *Wikipedia*, https://en.wikipedia.org/wiki/Huston_Wyeth (accessed 01/11/2019).

[1316] Bible records held in the care of William Maxwell "Max" Wyeth IV.

[1317] New York City Municipal Archives record #32750, housed 31 Chambers Street, New York, NY 10007.

[1318] Dan Flanagan, "John Wyeth & Brother: A Family Legacy in the History of Pharmacy." *The Bulletin* (Philadelphia, PA), Summer 2014, 7. <https://usciencesblogs.typepad.com/bulletin_102_1/john-wyeth-brother-a-family-legacy-in-the-history-of-pharmacy.html>

[1319] Bible records held in the care of William Maxwell "Max" Wyeth IV.

[1320] John McGill, *The Beverley family of Virginia; descendants of Major Robert Beverley, 1641-1687, and allied families* (Columbia, SC: R.L. Bryan Co., 1956), 90.

[1321] "Meet Mr. Wyeth," *American Professional Pharmacist*, Manhasset, NY: April 1958, 326.

[1322] New York City Municipal Archives record #12513, housed 31 Chambers Street, New York, NY 10007.

[1323] Yale University, *Vicennial record the Class of 1886 in Yale College* (New Haven, CT: Tuttle, Morehouse & Taylor Press, 1906), 115. <https://www.google.com/books/edition/Vicennial_Record/QisEAAAAYAAJ?hl>

[1324] John McGill, 90.

[1325] NavSource Online: Section Patrol Craft Photo Archive, *Emerald (SP 177)*, Commanding Officers 1. Lt. Maxwell Wyeth, USNRF - Awarded the Navy Cross (1918) 23 Jul 1917 - 12 Dec 1918, http://www.navsource.org/archives/12/170177.htm (accessed 2/13/2019).

[1326] Frederic A. Godcharles, *Encyclopedia of Pennsylvania Biography, Vol. xxiii*, (New York, Lewis Historical Pub. Co., 1938), 118-119.

[1327] Bible records held in the care of William Maxwell "Max" Wyeth IV say birth was 15 Jun 1853 but all other records say 1854.

[1328] John McGill, 87-88.

[1329] New York City Municipal Archives record #15633, housed 31 Chambers Street, New York, NY 10007.

[1330] New York City Municipal Archives record #30322, housed 31 Chambers Street, New York, NY 10007.

[1331] "Deaths Here," *The Philadelphia Inquirer* (Philadelphia, PA), 14 May 1981, 20.

[1332] B.J. Omanson, "The War Poetry of John Allan Wyeth," *blogspot.com*, http://johnallanwyeth.blogspot.com/p/about-john-allan-wyeth.html (accessed 10/30/2017).

[1333] John Allan Wyeth, *With Sabre and Scalpel*, 161, 166, 177, 197, 255-256.

[1334] John Allan Wyeth, *With Sabre and Scalpel*, 257, 280-289, 304, 306.

[1335] Roderick Davis, "John Allan Wyeth," *Encyclopedia of Alabama*, 05 Sep 2013. <http://www.encyclopediaofalabama.org/article/h-3522>

[1336] Roderick Davis, "John Allan Wyeth," *Encyclopedia of Alabama*, 05 Sep 2013. <http://www.encyclopediaofalabama.org/article/h-3522>

[1337] "Polyclinic Hospital," *Cursum Perficio*, Ficowww.cursumperficio.net/FicheAP16.html (accessed 1/14/2019).

[1338] John Allan Benedict Wyeth, *This Man's Army: A War in Fifty-Odd Sonnets* (New York: Harold Vinal, Ltd., 1928), 54.

[1339] B.J. Omanson (accessed 10/30/2017).

[1340] "Wyeth-Ginter," *The Baltimore Sun* (Baltimore, MD), 20 Sep 1917, 4. (Newspapers.com)

[1341] New York Municipal Archives record # 7168 states her mother's last name was "Scott" born MD and her father Juiter? Ginter? born PA.

[1342] "Will Wed this Afternoon," *Elizabeth Daily Journal* (Elizabeth, NJ), 11 Sep 1909, 5.

[1343] Rosedale Cemetery lot cards, picked up personally on 17 Aug 2016.

[1344] New York City Municipal Archives record #2420, housed 31 Chambers Street, New York, NY 10007

[1345] Rosedale Cemetery lot cards, picked up personally on 17 Aug 2016.

[1346] "Lieut. Col. Wyeth Dies," *Evening Star* (Washington, D.C.) 17 May 1924, 14. (Genealogybank.com)

[1347] "Lieut. Wyeth Takes Bride," *The New York Times* (New York, NY), 17 Feb 1917, 11. (Newspapers.com)

[1348] Jonas Wyeth, *Wyeth family records (Mss A 3058)*, R. Stanton Avery Special Collections, New England Historic Genealogical Society.

[1349] The Church of Jesus Christ of Latter-day Saints, "Ancestral File," database, *FamilySearch*, John Spencer Hadley (K8HQ-VVJ) family tree, https://www.familysearch.org/tree/pedigree/landscape/K8HQ-VVJ (accessed 4/24/2018)

[1350] "Obituary Record," *Asbury Park Press* (Asbury Park, NJ), 18 Jun 1898, 1.

[1351] "Died," *The New York Times* (New York, NY), 27 Sep 1913, 13.

[1352] The Church of Jesus Christ of Latter-day Saints, John Spencer Hadley (K8HQ-VVJ) family tree (accessed 4/24/2018).

[1353] "New York, New York City Births, 1846-1909," database, *FamilySearch* (https://familysearch.org/ark:/61903/1:1:27YV-BB8 : 11 February 2018), Charles Whitfield, 10 May 1858; citing Manhattan, New York, New York, United States, reference v 5 p 529 New York Municipal Archives, New York; FHL microfilm 1,315,313.

[1354] "Obituary," *Tampa Bay Times* (St. Petersburg, FL), 23 Aug 1921, 3.

[1355] The Church of Jesus Christ of Latter-day Saints, John Spencer Hadley (K8HQ-VVJ) family tree (accessed 4/24/2018).

[1356] "New York, New York City Municipal Deaths, 1795-1949," database, *FamilySearch* (https://familysearch.org/ark:/61903/1:1:2WWH-X3C : 11 Feb 2018), Henry Clay Hadley, 03 May 1905; citing Death, Brooklyn, Kings, New York, United States, New York Municipal Archives, New York; FHL microfilm 1,324,099.

[1357] "Mrs. Fannie Elton Hadley," *New York Tribune* (New York, NY), 26 Jul 1920, 7.

[1358] The Church of Jesus Christ of Latter-day Saints, John Spencer Hadley (K8HQ-VVJ) family tree (accessed 4/24/2018).

[1359] W. F. Brainard, 416.

[1360] Agnes McClellan Grousset, 107-108, 168-169 and 199-203.

[1361] Agnes McClellan Grousset, 108-109.

[1362] Agnes McClellan Grousset, 119-122, 124 and 129.

[1363] "Amid the Many Toils and Dangers: The Civil War Letters of William Francis "Frank" Tiemann," *New York State Military Museum*, dmna.ny.gov/historic/reghist/civil/infantry/159thInf/Tiemann/159thInfTiemannIndex.htm (accessed 1/18/2019).

[1364] John Herbert Baker, 42.

[1365] "School Teachers," *Cambridge Chronicle* (Cambridge, MA), 20 Jul 1872, 1.

[1366] John Herbert Baker, 44.

[1367] Soldier's Pension App. File, John B. Wyeth, No. 1,363,684; Widow: Emma E. Wyeth, No. 1,552,850; Civil War, RG 15; NA–DC.

[1368] Soldier's Pension App. File, John B. Wyeth, No. 1,363,684; Widow: Emma E. Wyeth, No. 1,552,850; Civil War, RG 15; NA–DC.

[1369] John Herbert Baker, 56.

[1370] Widow's Pension Application File, Alice S. Wyeth, No. 622,670 (service of Abiel Wyeth); Civil War, RG 15; NA–Washington.

[1371] "Funeral of A. A. Wyeth," *Boston Post* (Boston, MA), 21 Oct 1895, 6. (Newspapers.com)

[1372] "Undenominational," *Boston Post* (Boston, MA) 15 Aug 1896, 4. (Newspapers.com)

[1373] "Weepingly Admits Robbing Benefactor," *Los Angeles Herald* (Los Angeles, CA), 24 Mar 1910, 16. (Newspapers.com)

[1374] "Dies of Snakebite," *The Tampa Tribune* (Tampa, FL), 22 Aug 1911, 3.

[1375] Soldier's Pension Application File, Caroline E. Wyeth, No. 926,344; (service of Benjamin Wyeth); Civil War, RG 15; NA–Washington.

[1376] Samuel Atkins Eliot, *A History of Cambridge, Massachusetts, 1630-1913*, 265-266.

[1377] John Herbert Baker, 57, 62.

[1378] "Cambridge Man Takes Milwaukee Girl as His Bride," *Boston Globe* (Boston, MA), 28 Oct 1910, 8. (Newspapers.com)

[1379] "Henry D. Wyeth, Funeral Director," *The Boston Globe* (Boston, MA), 19 Oct 1975, 79. (Newspapers.com)

[1380] John Herbert Baker, 57-60, 62-68.

[1381] "Morning Death Notices," *The Boston Globe* (Boston, MA), 23 Feb 1951, 49. (Newspapers.com)

[1382] "Morning Death Notices," *The Boston Globe* (Boston, MA), 20 Aug 1947, 28. (Newspapers.com)

[1383] "Harrington Barker, Ex-Patent Office Aide, Succumbs at 67," *Sunday Star* (Washington D.C.), 27 Dec 1942, 14. (GenealogyBank.com)

[1384] David Michaelis, *N. C. Wyeth: A Biography* (New York: Alfred A. Knopf, 1998), 5-6.

[1385] N. C. Wyeth, Betsy James Wyeth, Ed., xiv, 5-8.

[1386] "N. C. Wyeth Dies in Train Crash," *The Philadelphia Inquirer* (Philadelphia, PA), 20 Oct 1945, 1, 10 and 22. (Newspapers.com)

[1387] "Nathaniel Wyeth, 66, of 1704 Walnut, Dearborn, was Killed," *Detroit Free Press* (Detroit, MI), 28 Oct 1954, 17. (Newspapers.com)

[1388] "Miss Constance Twigg to Wed Harvard Grad," *Boston Post* (Boston, MA), 13 Apr 1921, 24. (Newspapers.com)

[1389] "Death Notices," *Boston Herald* (Boston, MA), 14 Sep 1956, 37. (GenealogyBank.com)

[1390] "Mrs. Mina G. Hunt Funeral Tomorrow," *The Boston Globe* (Boston, MA), 21 May 1960, 24. (Newspapers.com)

[1391] "Ohio Deaths, 1908-1953," database with images, *FamilySearch* (https://familysearch.org/ark:/61903/3:1:33SQ-GPK6-D72?cc=1307272&wc=MD9F-7ZQ%3A287600301%2C294611601 : 21 May 2014), 1934 > 47401-50400 > image 418 of 3313.

[1392] "Own Gun Falls, Kills Pay Guard," *Plain Dealer* (Cleveland, OH), 04 Jun 1955, 1. (GenealogyBank.com)

[1393] John Blatchford; Charles I. Bushnell, 113-115.

[1394] "From all over Texas," *The Marshall Messenger* (Marshall, TX), 21 Feb 1908, 5. (Newspapers.com)

[1395] "Personal Notes," *Gallipolis Daily Tribune* (Gallipolis, OH), 13 Dec 1902, 1. (research of RThomassin)

[1396] Gallia County Newspaper Obituaries for Civil War Veterans, obituary from Gallipolis Bulletin, 13 Feb 1897 transcribed by Irene Blamer, www.galliagenealogy.org/Civil%20War/CW_obits/cwobits_d-g.htm#JohnWGrover

[1397] "Indiana Marriages, 1811-2007," database with images, *FamilySearch* (https://familysearch.org/ark:/61903/3:1:S3HT-DZ57-3Q9?cc=1410397&wc=Q83F-C8C%3A962973901%2C963005401 : 21 Jan 2016), Huntington > 1908-1908 Volume R > image 27 of 60; County clerk offices, IN. (Record detailed by James Grover himself says he was born in Darke County and his mother in Jackson County, OH)

[1398] Ancestry.com Operations, Inc., *London, England, Church of England Baptisms, Marriages and Burials, 1538-1812*, Hackney, St. Leonard, Shoreditch records 1791-1797 (Provo, UT: Ancestry.com, 2010).

[1399] "Died," *Pomeroy Weekly Telegraph* (Pomeroy, OH), 01 Mar 1861, 4. (GenealogyBank.com)

[1400] Marselle Allen Wyeth, *Genealogy of Scott Family of America*, privately published circa 1947, 15.

[1401] "Private Alfred Smith," *Gallipolis Journal* (Gallipolis, OH), 22 May 1862, 3.

[1402] "The Civil War Soldiers and Sailors Database - Smith, Alfred C.," *National Park Service*, https://www.nps.gov/civilwar/search-soldiers-detail.htm?soldierId=A5A4EBD1-DC7A-DF11-BF36-B8AC6F5D926A (accessed 01/27/2019).

[1403] "Ohio, County Death Records, 1840-2001," database with images, *FamilySearch* (https://familysearch.org/ark:/61903/3:1:3QS7-89ZY-5S6K?cc=2128172&wc=7DZ2-G5X%3A1296035701%2C1296035702 : 30 Sep 2014), Gallia > Death records, 1867-1899, vol 1 > image 80 of 497; county courthouses, Ohio.

[1404] H. H. Hardesty & Co., *History of Gallia County*, reprinted from the 1882 history, (Gallipolis, OH: St. Peter's Episcopal Church, 1976), 15. <https://books.google.com/books?id=DmxNAQAAMAAJ&q>

[1405] Ancestry.com Operations, Inc., *London, England, Church of England Baptisms, Marriages and Burials, 1813-1906*, Baptisms solemnized in the parish of St. Leonard, Shoreditch in the County of Middlesex in the year 1813 (Provo, UT: Ancestry.com, 2010), 90.

[1406] Charles A. Murry, "Post-Civil War Era Grave Recorded in Cheshire Township," *Gallia County Glade*, Vol. 18, No. 1 (Spring 1993) from the Mary Lee Davis Marchi email of 05 Oct 2000 to Joyce Ward and Bob Rainsberger.

[1407] H. H. Hardesty & Co., 15.

[1408] "Ohio, County Death Records, 1840-2001," database with images, *FamilySearch* (https://familysearch.org/ark:/61903/3:1:3QSQ-G9ZY-59N3?cc=2128172&wc=7DZ2-G5X%3A1296035701%2C1296035702 : 30 Sep 2014), Gallia > Death records, 1867-1899, vol 1 > image 195 of 497; county courthouses, Ohio.

[1409] H. H. Hardesty & Co., 15.

[1410] McFarland Family Bible, courtesy Deborah DeForest, shared online, 14 Jun 2014.

[1411] Edward G. Longacre, 62, 69.

[1412] "Died," *Evening Star* (Washington, D.C.), 18 Mar 1873, 3. (GenealogyBank.com)

[1413] "Dr. P. C. Hunt Buried," *The Baltimore Sun* (Baltimore, MD), 18 Dec 1910, 5. (GenealogyBank.com)

[1414] "Col. John Elliott Hunt, Retired Army Officer," *Evening Star* (Washington, D.C.), 22 Dec 1951, 5. (GenealogyBank.com)

[1415] Edward G. Longacre, 24.

[1416] Francis S. Drake, *Memorials of the Society of the Cincinnati of Massachusetts*, 356.

[1417] "Henry Jackson Hunt," *Wikipedia*, https://en.wikipedia.org/wiki/Henry_Jackson_Hunt (accessed 11/27/2016).

[1418] Brett Schulte, "Number 264. Petersburg Campaign Report of Capt. Lewis C. Hunt, Sixty-seventh Ohio Infantry, of operations Oct 27-28," and "67th Ohio Infantry," *The Siege of Petersburg Online*, http://www.beyondthecrater.com/ (accessed 5/19/2018).

[1419] "Henry Jackson Hunt," *Wikipedia*, https://en.wikipedia.org/wiki/Henry_Jackson_Hunt (accessed 11/27/2016).

[1420] "Henry Jackson Hunt," *Wikipedia*, https://en.wikipedia.org/wiki/Henry_Jackson_Hunt (accessed 11/27/2016).

[1421] "Horace Mann," *Wikipedia*, https://en.wikipedia.org/wiki/Horace_Mann (accessed 4/8/2018).

[1422] "Horace Mann Jr.," *Wikipedia*, https://en.wikipedia.org/wiki/Horace_Mann_Jr. (accessed 4/8/2018).

[1423] "Re-interment of Sophia and Una Hawthorne," *Hawthorne in Salem*, http://www.hawthorneinsalem.org/page/11853 (accessed 4/8/2018).

[1424] "Death of Una Hawthorne," *The Baltimore Sun* (Baltimore, Maryland), 12 Sep 1877, 1. (Newspapers.com)

[1425] "Julian Hawthorne Passes Away After Illness of Weeks," *The Oshkosh Northwestern* (Oshkosh, WI), 14 Jul 1934, 4.

[1426] "Mother Mary Alphonsa," *Wikipedia*, https://en.wikipedia.org/wiki/Mother_Mary_Alphonsa (accessed 10/24/2017).

[1427] "Servant of God, Rose Hawthorne," *Dominican Sisters of Hawthorne*, www.hawthorne-dominicans.org/rose-hawthorne.html#canonizationprocess (accessed 5/27/2017).

[1428] Cambridge (Mass.), *The Records of the Town of Cambridge (formerly New-towne) Massachusetts: 1630-1703. The Records of the Town Meetings, and of the Selectmen, Comprising All of the First Volume of Records, and Being Volume II, of the Printed Records of the Town.* (Cambridge, MA: The Council, 1901), 83 (Richard Withe), 350 (Rich Wyeth). <https://books.google.com/books?id=p7N4AAAAMAAJ&pg=PP1&dq>

[1429] George Cabel Greer, *Early Virginia Immigrants 1623-1666.* (Richmond, VA: W. C. Hill Printing Co., 1912), 374.

[1430] Ancestry.com, *England, Select Births and Christenings, 1538-1975* (Provo, UT: Ancestry.com Operations, Inc., 2014).

[1431] Ancestry.com, Northamptonshire Record Office; Northampton, England, *Norfolk, England, Church of England Baptism, Marriages, and Burials, 1535-1812* (Provo, UT: Ancestry.com Operations, Inc., 2014).

[1432] *Coat of Arms of George Wythe*, https://commons.wikimedia.org/wiki/File:Coat_of_Arms_of_George_Wythe.svg (accessed 01/23/2016).

[1433] John Burke and John Bernard Burke, *Encyclopaedia of heraldry, or General armory of England, Scotland, and Ireland, comprising a registry of all armorial bearings from the earliest to the present time, including the late grants by the College of Arms* (London: Bohn, 1844), Withe, Wyth, Wythe. <https://books.google.com/books?id=Y11BAAAAYAAJ>

[1434] Henry Creed, *Proceedings of the Suffolk Institute of Archaeology, Volume 2* (Lowestoft, UK: Samuel Tymms, 1859), 144. <https://books.google.com/books?id=q-oGAAAAYAAJ&pg>

[1435] "Wythe [Worcestershire]," *Coats of Arms*, http://www.heraldry.ws/html/wythe-worcestershire.html (accessed 01/23/2016).

[1436] Imogene E. Brown, *American Aristides* (Rutherford, NJ: Fairleigh Dickinson University Press, 1981), 15.

[1437] Henry W. and Albert A. Berg Collection of English and American Literature, *The New York Public Library*, "George Wythe. (Drawn and engraved by J.B. Longacre from a portrait in the American Gleaner.)" New York Public Library Digital Collections, http://digitalcollections.nypl.org/items/510d47db-c6dd-a3d9-e040-e00a18064a99 (accessed 28 Feb 2017).

[1438] Robert Wieth, *Original Will [IC/AA1/53/164]*, Saxtead, 1617, from the archives of the Suffolk Records Office, Ipswich, UK. (Translated by Claire Barker of the Suffolk Records Society.)

[1439] Ancestry.com, *England, Select Births and Christenings*, 1538-1975.

[1440] Ancestry.com, *Northamptonshire Record Office; Northampton, England, Norfolk, England, Church of England Baptism, Marriages, and Burials, 1535-1812.*

[1441] George Cabel Greer, 374.

[1442] Cambridge (Mass.), 83 (Richard Withe), 350 (Rich Wyeth).

[1443] John Bennett Boddie, *Virginia Historical Genealogies* (Baltimore, MD: Reprinted for Clearfield by Genealogical Publishing Co., 2008), 122. <https://books.google.com/books?id=AyhusD7Hc2MC&pg=PA122&dq>

[1444] Joyce Blackburn, *George Wythe of Williamsburg* (New York: Harper & Row, 1975), 1.

[1445] John Bennett Boddie, 122.

[1446] John Bennett Boddie, 122.

[1447] Blanche Adams Chapman, *Wills & Administrations of Elizabeth City County, VA 1688-1800* (Baltimore, MD: Clearfield, 1980), 107.

[1448] John Bennett Boddie, 117-119.

[1449] John Bennett Boddie, 119.

[1450] John Bennett Boddie, 120.

[1451] Blanche Adams Chapman, 107.

[1452] John Bennett Boddie, 124.

[1453] John Bennett Boddie, 120.

[1454] John Bennett Boddie, 119.

[1455] Blanche Adams Chapman, 63.

[1456] Blanche Adams Chapman, 54.

[1457] John Bennett Boddie, 119-120.

[1458] John Bennett Boddie, 120.

[1459] Imogene E. Brown, 22.

[1460] "Langley Research Center," *NASA Cultural Resources* (Government-produced materials are not copyright protected.) https://crgis.ndc.nasa.gov/historic/Langley_Research_Center (accessed 2/19/2016).

[1461] John Bennett Boddie, 124.

[1462] John Bennett Boddie, 119.

[1463] Blanche Adams Chapman, 54.

[1464] Blanche Adams Chapman, 54.

[1465] Ancestry.com, *North America, Family Histories, 1500-2000* (Ancestry.com Operations, Inc.: Provo, UT: 2016), Book Title: Lineage Book of the Charter Members of the DAR Vol 028.

[1466] Steve Henkel, "Murder in the Family," *The American Genealogist, Vol. 78, No. 2* (New Haven, CT: D. L. Jacobus, Apr 2003), 94-95.

[1467] Steve Henkel, 93.

[1468] Imogene E. Brown, 17-21.

[1469] Imogene E. Brown, 21-25.

[1470] Imogene E. Brown, 24-25.

[1471] "Wythepedia W&M Law Library," *Wythepedia: The George Wythe Encyclopedia*, http://lawlibrary.wm.edu/wythepedia/index.php/Main_Page (accessed 10/27/2016).

[1472] Rob Shenk, "The George Wythe House," *Wikimedia Commons, the free media repository*, 22 Sep 2012. <https://commons.wikimedia.org/wiki/File:The_George_Wythe_House_(8017084861).jpg>

[1473] "Wythepedia W&M Law Library," Elizabeth Taliaferro Wythe, (accessed 3/2/2017).

[1474] Frederick Wallace Pyne, *Descendants of the Signers of the Dec. of Independence, Volume 6*, VA (Rockport, ME: Picton Press, 1997), 6.

[1475] "Wythepedia W&M Law Library," George Wythe and Slavery, (accessed 5/7/2019).

[1476] Thomas Jefferson Foundation, "George Wythe Randolph, Jefferson's grandson," *The Monticello Classroom*, 2007. <http://classroom.monticello.org/kids/resources/profile/257/George-Wythe-Randolph-Jeffersons-grandson/>

[1477] Joyce Blackburn, 132-136.

[1478] Joyce Blackburn, 137-138.

[1479] Steve Henkel, 88-95.

[1480] W. Edwin Hemphill, "Examinations of George Wythe Swinney for Forgery and Murder: A Documentary Essay," *The William and Mary Quarterly*, 3rd Ser., 12, no. 4 (Oct., 1955), 545.

[1481] "Wythepedia W&M Law Library," Death of George Wythe, (accessed 3/2/2017).

[1482] Blanche Adams Chapman, 54, 61.

[1483] Steve Henkel, 94.

[1484] Steve Henkel, 95.

[1485] Steve Henkel, 94-95.

[1486] Steve Henkel, 95.

[1487] "Wythepedia W&M Law Library," Michael Brown, (accessed 3/2/2017).

[1488] "Wythepedia W&M Law Library," Chancellor Wythe's Death, (accessed 3/2/2017).

[1489] "Wythepedia W&M Law Library," Jefferson-DuVal Correspondence, (accessed 3/2/2017).

[1490] "Wythepedia W&M Law Library," Murder of George Wythe, (accessed 3/2/2017).

[1491] "Wythepedia W&M Law Library," Jefferson-DuVal Correspondence, 19 Jun 1806, (accessed 3/2/2017).

[1492] "Wythepedia W&M Law Library," Murder of George Wythe, Julian P. Boyd article, (accessed 3/2/2017).

[1493] "Wythepedia W&M Law Library," Murder of George Wythe, Julian P. Boyd article, page 539 (accessed 3/2/2017).

[1494] "Wythepedia W&M Law Library," George Wythe Sweeney, (accessed 3/2/2017).

[1495] "Wythepedia W&M Law Library," Murder of George Wythe, Julian P. Boyd article, page 539, (accessed 3/2/2017).

[1496] "Wythepedia W&M Law Library," Murder of George Wythe, Julian P. Boyd article, page 539, (accessed 3/2/2017).

BIBLIOGRAPHY

"About Harvard/Harvard at a Glance: History." *Harvard University*. http://www.harvard.edu/about-harvard/harvard-glance/history (accessed 3/12/2016).

"About Natalie Wyeth Earnest." *U.S. Department of the Treasury*. https://www.treasury.gov/about/organizational-structure/Pages/natalie-e.aspx (accessed 3/25/2016).

"About the Monongahela expositor, and Williamsport weekly chronicle. (Williamsport, Washington County, PA) 1811-18??." *The Library of Congress*. https://chroniclingamerica.loc.gov/lccn/sn86081676/ (accessed 1/10/2018).

"About the White House." *The Oval Office*. http://whitehousegiftsandapparel.com/ovaloffice.html (accessed 3/26/2016).

"About Us." *The Elizabeth Peabody House*, 2016. teph.org/about-us/.

"Account by Joshua Wyeth." *Boston Tea Party Historical Society*. http://www.boston-tea-party.org/account-Joshua-Wyeth.html (accessed 3/26/2016).

Adams, John. Letter to Abigail Adams, 04 Feb 1783 [electronic edition]. Adams Family Papers: An Electronic Archive. *Massachusetts Historical Society*. http://www.masshist.org/digitaladams/.

Adjutant General's Office. *Registers of Deaths of Volunteers, compiled 1861-1865,* ARC ID: 656639. Record Group 94 Indiana S-Z, National Archives Washington, D.C.

"Agency Makes an Assignment." *Democrat and Chronicle* (Rochester, NY), 14 Oct 1905.

Alexander, Magnus. "Research Department Report Series no. 106-2007." *Framlingham Castle, Suffolk, The Landscape Context Desk-Top Assessment*. http://services.english-heritage.org.uk/ResearchReportsPdfs/106_2007WEB.pdf (accessed 2/28/2016).

All Saints Church Registers, Saxtead, Suffolk County, England, 1546 to 1742, Suffolk Record Office, Ipswich, UK, transcribed by Muriel L. Kilvert.

"All Saints, Saxtead." *The Suffolk Churches Site*. www.suffolkchurches.co.uk/saxtead.html (accessed 12/20/16).

Allegheny County (PA) Register of Wills. *Will of Charles Kenny written 20 Aug 1839*. Pennsylvania, Wills and Probate Records, 1683-1993, Allegheny County Will Packets, Vol 5-6.

Allen, Marion E. and Nesta R. Evans. *Wills from the Archdeaconry of Suffolk: 1629-1636*. Boston: New England Historic Genealogical Society, 1986.

Allen, Marion E. and Suffolk Records Society. *Wills of the Archdeaconry of Suffolk: 1620-1624*. Woodbridge, UK: The Boydell Press, 1989.

Allyn, Alice C. *A History of Berkeley St., Cambridge MA*. Cambridge, MA: Cambridge Historical Society, 1931.

"The Alumni." *The Princeton Alumni Weekly*, Vol. XXIV, No. 24, (Princeton, New Jersey), 26 Mar 1924.

"American Home Products - Company Profile, Information, Business Description, History, Background Information on American Home Products." *Reference for Business*. ww.referenceforbusiness.com/history2/64/American-Home-Products.html#ixzz4DEaz5KpG (accessed 1/1/2017).

"Amid the Many Toils and Dangers: The Civil War Letters of William Francis "Frank" Tiemann," *New York State Military Museum*, dmna.ny.gov/historic/reghist/civil/infantry/159thInf/Tiemann/159thInfTiemannIndex.htm (accessed 1/18/2019).

Ancestry.com and Ohio Department of Health. *Ohio, Deaths, 1908-1932, 1938-2007*. Provo, UT: Ancestry.com Operations Inc., 2010.

Ancestry.com and The Church of Jesus Christ of Latter-day Saints. *1880 United States Federal Census*. n.p: Online publication - Provo, UT: Ancestry.com Ops. Inc., 2010. 1880 U.S. Census Index provided by The Church of Jesus Christ of Latter-day Saints. Original data: Tenth Census of the United States, 1880. (NARA microfilm publication T9, 1,454 rolls). Records of the Bureau of the Census, Record Group 29. National Archives, Washington, D.C.

Ancestry.com and The Church of Jesus Christ of Latter-day Saints. *1881 Census of Canada*. Provo, UT: Ancestry.com Operations Inc., 2009.

Ancestry.com. *1790 United States Federal Census*. Provo, UT: Ancestry.com Operations, Inc., 2010.

Ancestry.com. *1800 United States Federal Census*. Provo, UT: Ancestry.com Operations Inc., 2010.

Ancestry.com. *1810 United States Federal Census*. n.p: Online publication - Provo, UT: Ancestry.com Operations, Inc., 2010. Images reproduced by FamilySearch. Original data - Third Census of the United States, 1810. (NARA microfilm publication M252, 71 rolls). Bureau of the Census, Record Group 29, n.d.

Ancestry.com. *1820 United States Federal Census*. n.p: Online publication - Provo, UT: Ancestry.com Operations, Inc., 2010. Images reproduced by FamilySearch. Original data - Fourth Census of the United States, 1820. (NARA microfilm publication M33, 142 rolls). Records of the Bureau of the Census, n.d.

Ancestry.com. *1830 United States Federal Census*. n.p: Online publication - Provo, UT: Ancestry.com Ops., Inc., 2010. Images reproduced by FamilySearch. Original data - Fifth Census of the United States, 1830. (NARA microfilm publication M19, 201 rolls). Records of the Bureau of the Census, Record Gr, n.d.

Ancestry.com. *1840 United States Federal Census*. n.p: Online publication - Provo, UT: Ancestry.com Operations, Inc., 2010. Images reproduced by FamilySearch. Original data - Sixth Census of the United States, 1840. (NARA microfilm publication M704, 580 rolls). Records of the Bureau of the Census, n.d.

Ancestry.com. *1850 U.S. Federal Census - Slave Schedules* [database on-line]. Alabama, Marshall, District 22. Provo, UT: Ancestry.com Operations Inc. 2004.

Ancestry.com. *1850 United States Federal Census*. Provo, UT: Ancestry.com Operations, Inc., 2009.

Ancestry.com. *1851 England Census*. Provo, UT: Ancestry.com Operations Inc., 2005.

Ancestry.com. *1860 U.S. Federal Census - Slave Schedules* [database on-line], Alabama, Marshall, Western Division. Provo, UT: Ancestry.com Operations Inc., 2010.

Ancestry.com. *1860 United States Federal Census*. Provo, UT: Ancestry.com Operations, Inc., 2009.

Ancestry.com. *1870 United States Federal Census*. n.p: Online publication - Provo, UT: Ancestry.com Operations, Inc., 2009. Images reproduced by FamilySearch. Original data - 1870 U.S. census, population schedules. NARA microfilm publication M593, 1,761 rolls. Washington, D.C.: National Archives, n.d.

Ancestry.com. *1890 Veterans Schedules*. Provo, UT: Ancestry.com Operations Inc., 2005.

Ancestry.com. *1900 United States Federal Census*. n.p: Online publication - Provo, UT: Ancestry.com Operations Inc., 2004. Original data - United States of America, Bureau of the Census. Twelfth Census of the United States, 1900. Washington, D.C.: National Archives and Records Administration, 1900. T623, 18, n.d.

Ancestry.com. *1901 Census of Canada*. Provo, UT: Ancestry.com Operations Inc., 2006.

Ancestry.com. *1910 United States Federal Census*. Provo, UT: Ancestry.com Operations Inc., 2006.

Ancestry.com. *1911 Census of Canada*. Provo, UT: Ancestry.com Operations Inc., 2006.

Ancestry.com. *1920 United States Federal Census*. n.p: Online publication - Provo, UT: Ancestry.com Operations Inc., 2010. Images reproduced by FamilySearch. Original data - Fourteenth Census of the United States, 1920. (NARA microfilm publication T625, 2076 rolls). Records of the Bureau of the Census, n.d.

Ancestry.com. *1930 United States Federal Census*. Provo, UT: Ancestry.com Operations Inc., 2002.

Ancestry.com. *1940 United States Federal Census*. Provo, UT: Ancestry.com Operations, Inc., 2012.

Ancestry.com. *Alabama, Marriage Collection, 1800-1969*. Provo, UT: Ancestry.com Operations Inc., 2006.

Ancestry.com. *Alabama, Marriages, Deaths, Wills, Court, and Other Records, 1784-1920*. Provo, UT: Ancestry.com Operations, Inc., 2011.

Ancestry.com. *Alabama, Select Marriages, 1816-1957*. Provo, UT: Ancestry.com Operations, Inc., 2014.

Ancestry.com. *American Marriages Before 1699*. Provo, UT: Ancestry.com Operations Inc., 1997.

Ancestry.com. *American Revolutionary War Rejected Pensions*. Provo, UT: Ancestry.com Operations Inc., 2000.

Ancestry.com. *Ancestry Family Trees*. n.p: Online publication - Provo, UT: Ancestry.com. Original data: Family Tree files submitted by Ancestry members., n.d.

Ancestry.com. *Andersonville Prisoners of War*. Provo, UT: Ancestry.com Operations Inc., 1999.

Ancestry.com. *Arkansas, County Marriages Index, 1837-1957*. Provo, UT: Ancestry.com Operations, Inc., 2011.

Ancestry.com. *Border Crossings: From Canada to U.S., 1895-1956*. Provo, UT: Ancestry.com Ops., Inc., 2010.

Ancestry.com. *Boston, 1821-1850 Passenger and Immigration Lists*. Provo, UT: Ancestry.com Ops., Inc., 2003.

Ancestry.com. *Boston, Massachusetts, Birth Index, 1700-1800*. Provo, UT: Ancestry.com Operations, Inc., 1997.

Ancestry.com. *Boston, Massachusetts, Marriages, 1700-1809*. Provo, UT: Ancestry.com Operations Inc., 2000.

Ancestry.com. *Boston, Passenger and Crew Lists, 1820-1954*. Provo, UT: Ancestry.com Operations, Inc., 2006.

Ancestry.com. *California, Biographical Index Cards, 1781-1990*. Provo, UT: Ancestry.com Ops., Inc., 2011.

Ancestry.com. *California, Death Index, 1905-1939*. Provo, UT: Ancestry.com Operations, Inc., 2013.

Ancestry.com. *California, Death Index, 1940-1997*. Provo, UT: Ancestry.com Operations Inc., 2000.

Ancestry.com. *California, Voter Registrations, 1900-1968*. Provo, UT: Ancestry.com Operations Inc., 2008.

Ancestry.com. *Catalogue of the officers and students of Phillips Exeter Academy for the Academical Year 1868-69* (with a prefatory notice of the history.) Cambridge, MA: John Wilson and son, 1869. Provo, UT: Ancestry.com Operations, Inc., 2012.

Ancestry.com. *Colorado State Census, 1885*. Provo, UT: Ancestry.com Operations Inc., 2006.

Ancestry.com. *Colorado, Divorce Index, 1851-1985*. Provo, UT: Ancestry.com Operations, Inc., 2015.

Ancestry.com. *Connecticut Town Birth Records, pre-1870 (Barbour Collection)*. Provo, UT: Ancestry.com Operations Inc., 2006.

Ancestry.com. *Connecticut, Deaths and Burials Index, 1650-1934*. Provo, UT: Ancestry.com Ops., Inc., 2011.

Ancestry.com. *Connecticut, Hale Cemetery Inscriptions, 1675-1934*. Provo, UT: Ancestry.com Ops., Inc., 2012.

Ancestry.com. *Connecticut, Town Marriage Records, pre-1870 (Barbour Collection)*. Provo, UT: Ancestry.com Operations Inc., 2006.

Ancestry.com. *Cook County, IL, Deaths Index, 1878-1922*. Provo, UT: Ancestry.com Operations, Inc., 2011.

Ancestry.com. *Cook County, IL, Marriage and Death Indexes, 1833-1889*. Provo, UT: Ancestry.com Operations, Inc., 2011.

Ancestry.com. *Cuyahoga County, Ohio, Marriage Records and Indexes, 1810-1973*. n.p: Online publication - Provo, UT: Ancestry.com Operations, Inc., 2010. Original data - Cuyahoga County, Ohio, Marriage Records, 1810-1973. Microfilm publication, 137 rolls. Reels 1-110. Cuyahoga, Ohio. Original data: Cuyahoga County, Ohio, Marriage Records, n.d.

Ancestry.com. *Cuyahoga County, Ohio, Tax Lists, 1819-1869*. Provo, UT: Ancestry.com Operations, Inc., 2010.

Ancestry.com. *Delaware Death Records, 1811-1933*. Provo, UT: Ancestry.com Operations, Inc., 2010.

Ancestry.com. *District of Columbia, Select Deaths and Burials, 1840-1964*. Provo, UT: Ancestry.com Ops., 2014.

Ancestry.com. *District of Columbia, Select Marriages, 1830-1921*. Provo, UT: Ancestry.com Ops., Inc., 2014.

Ancestry.com. *Early Members of the Reorganized Church of Jesus Christ of Latter Day Saints*. Provo, UT: Ancestry.com Operations, Inc., 2013.

Ancestry.com. *England, Select Births and Christenings, 1538-1975*. Provo, UT: Ancestry.com Ops., Inc., 2014.

Ancestry.com. *Florida Death Index, 1877-1998*. Provo, UT: Ancestry.com Operations Inc., 2004.

Ancestry.com. *Florida, State Census, 1867-1945*. Provo, UT: Ancestry.com Operations Inc., 2008.

Ancestry.com. *Florida, State Census, 1885*. Provo, UT: Ancestry.com Operations Inc., 2005.

Ancestry.com. *Georgia, Marriage Records from Select Counties, 1828-1978*. Provo, UT Ancestry.com Ops., 2013.

Ancestry.com. *History of the Roseville Methodist Episcopal Church of the Methodist Episcopal Church, Newark, New Jersey*. Provo, UT: The Generations Network, Inc., 2004.

Ancestry.com. *Illinois, Deaths and Stillbirths Index, 1916-1947*. n.p: Online publication - Provo, UT: Ancestry.com Operations, Inc., 2011. Original data – "Illinois Deaths and Stillbirths, 1916-1947." Index. FamilySearch, Salt Lake City, Utah, 2010. Index entries derived from digital copies of original records, n.d.

Ancestry.com. *Illinois, Marriage Index, 1860-1920*. Provo, UT: Ancestry.com Operations, Inc., 2015.

Ancestry.com. *Illinois, State Census Collection, 1825-1865*. Provo, UT: Ancestry.com Operations Inc., 2008.

Ancestry.com. *Illinois, Wills and Probate Records, 1772-1999*. Provo, UT: Ancestry.com Operations, Inc., 2015.

Ancestry.com. *Indiana Deaths, 1882-1920*. n.p: Online publication - Provo, UT: Ancestry.com Operations Inc., 2004. Original data - Various Indiana county death records indexed by the Indiana Works Projects Administration. Indiana: circa 1938-1941.

Ancestry.com. *Indiana, Civil War Soldier Database Index, 1861-1865*. Provo, UT: Ancestry.com Operations, Inc. 2015. https://secure.in.gov/apps/icpr/search/Home/Detail?rId=1199463.

Ancestry.com. *Indiana, Marriage Collection, 1800-1941*. Provo, UT: Ancestry.com Operations Inc., 2005.

Ancestry.com. *Indiana, Wills and Probate Records, 1798-1999*. Provo, UT: Ancestry.com Operations, Inc., 2015.

Ancestry.com. *International, Find A Grave Index for Select Locations, 1300s-Current*. Provo, UT: Ancestry.com Ops., 2012.

Ancestry.com. *Iowa, Cemetery Records, 1662-1999*. Provo, UT: Ancestry.com Operations Inc., 2000.

Ancestry.com. *Iowa, Select Deaths and Burials, 1850-1990*. Provo, UT: Ancestry.com Operations, Inc., 2014.

Ancestry.com. *Iowa, Select Marriages, 1809-1992*. Provo, UT: Ancestry.com Operations, Inc., 2014.

Ancestry.com. *Iowa, State Census Collection, 1836-1925*. Provo, UT: Ancestry.com Operations Inc., 2007.

Ancestry.com. *Jacksonville, Florida Directories, 1888-93*. Provo, UT: Ancestry.com Operations Inc., 2000.

Ancestry.com. *Kansas State Census Collection, 1855-1925*. Provo, UT: Ancestry.com Operations Inc., 2009.

Ancestry.com. *Maine, Birth Records, 1621-1922*. Provo, UT: Ancestry.com Operations, Inc., 2010.

Ancestry.com. *Maine, Death Records, 1617-1922*. n.p: Online publication - Provo, UT: Ancestry.com Operations, Inc., 2010. Original data: Maine Death Records, 1617-1922. Augusta, Maine: Maine State Archives., n.d.

Ancestry.com. *Maine, Wills and Probate Records, 1584-1999*. Provo, UT: Ancestry.com Operations, Inc., 2015.

Ancestry.com. *Maryland, Births and Christenings Index, 1662-1911*. Provo, UT: Ancestry.com Ops., Inc., 2011.

Ancestry.com. *Massachusetts Death Index, 1970-2003*. n.p: Online publication - Provo, UT: Ancestry.com Operations Inc., 2005. Original data - State of MA. Massachusetts Death Index, 1970-2003. Boston, MA: Commonwealth of Massachusetts Department of Health Services, 2005. Original data: State of MA, n.d.

Ancestry.com. *Massachusetts Soldiers and Sailors in the Revolutionary War* (Images Online). Provo, UT: Ancestry.com Operations Inc., 2004.

Ancestry.com. *Massachusetts soldiers, sailors, and marines in the Civil War*. Provo, UT: Ancestry.com Ops., 2005.

Ancestry.com. *Massachusetts, Birth Records, 1620-1850 and 1840-1915*. n.p: Online publication - Provo, UT: Ancestry.com Operations, Inc., 1999 and 2013. Original data - Massachusetts Vital Records, 1840-1911. New England Historic Genealogical Society, Boston, MA. Massachusetts Vital Records, 1911-1915. New England Historic Genealogical Society, n.d.

Ancestry.com. *Massachusetts, Death Index, 1901-1980*. Provo, UT: Ancestry.com Operations, Inc., 2013.

Ancestry.com. *Massachusetts, Death Records, 1841-1915*. n.p: Online publication - Provo, UT: Ancestry.com Operations, Inc., 2013. Original data - Massachusetts Vital Records, 1840-1911 and 1911-1915. New England Historic Genealogical Society, Boston, MA.

Ancestry.com. *Massachusetts, Marriage Index, 1784-1840*. Provo, UT: Ancestry.com Operations Inc., 1998.

Ancestry.com. *Massachusetts, Marriage Records, 1840-1915*. n.p: Online publication - Provo, UT: Ancestry.com Ops., Inc., 2013. Original data - MA Vital Records, 1840-1911 and 1911-1915. New England Historic Genealogical Society, Boston, MA.

Ancestry.com. *Massachusetts, Mason Membership Cards, 1733-1990*. n.p: Online publication - Provo, UT: Ancestry.com Operations, Inc., 2013. Original data - Massachusetts Grand Lodge of Masons Membership Cards 1733-1990. New England Historic Genealogical Society, Boston, Massachusetts.

Ancestry.com. *Massachusetts, State Census, 1855*. Provo, UT: Ancestry.com Operations, Inc., 2014.

Ancestry.com. *Massachusetts, State Census, 1865*. Provo, UT: Ancestry.com Operations, Inc., 2014.

Ancestry.com. *Massachusetts, Town and Vital Records, 1620-1988*. n.p: Online publication - Provo, UT: Ancestry.com Operations, Inc., 2011. Original data - Town and City Clerks of Massachusetts. Massachusetts Vital and Town Records. Provo, UT: Holbrook Research Institute (Jay and Delene Holbrook), n.d.

Ancestry.com. *Massachusetts, Wills and Probate Records, 1635-1991* [database on-line]. Provo, UT: Ancestry.com Operations, Inc., 2015. (Will of Mary Wyeth transcribed by Claire Barker, Secretary, Suffolk Records Society, Westhorpe Lodge, Westhorpe, Stowmarket, Suffolk, England, IP14 4TA.)

Ancestry.com. *Massachusetts, Wills and Probate Records, 1635-1991*. Provo, UT: Ancestry.com Ops., Inc., 2015.

Ancestry.com. *Michigan, Births and Christenings Index, 1867-1911*. n.p: Online publication - Provo, UT: Ancestry.com Operations, Inc., 2011. Original data - "Michigan Births and Christenings, 1775-1995." Index. FamilySearch, Salt Lake City, Utah, 2009, 2010. Index entries derived from digital copies of original and compiled records, n.d.

Ancestry.com. *Michigan, Death Records, 1897-1920*. n.p: Online publication - Provo, UT: Ancestry.com Operations, Inc., 2010. Original data - Michigan Death Records, 1897-1920. Microfilm publication, 302 rolls. Library of Michigan. Lansing, Michigan. http://seekingmichigan.org.

Ancestry.com. *Michigan, Deaths and Burials Index, 1867-1995*. n.p: Online publication - Provo, UT: Ancestry.com Operations, Inc., 2011. Original data - "Michigan Deaths and Burials, 1800-1995." Index. FamilySearch, Salt Lake City, Utah, 2009, 2010. Index entries derived from digital copies of original and compiled rec, n.d.

Ancestry.com. *Minnesota, Death Index, 1908-2002*. Provo, UT: Ancestry.com Operations Inc., 2001.

Ancestry.com. *Minnesota, Marriages Index, 1849-1950*. Provo, UT: Ancestry.com Operations, Inc., 2011.

Ancestry.com. *Missouri Marriage Records, 1805-2002*. n.p: Online publication - Provo, UT: Ancestry.com Ops., Inc., 2007. Original data - Missouri Marriage Records. Jefferson City, MO: Missouri State Archives. Microfilm, n.d.

Ancestry.com. *Missouri, Death Records, 1834-1910*. Provo, UT: Ancestry.com Operations, Inc., 2008.

Ancestry.com. *Missouri, Wills and Probate Records, 1766-1988*. Provo, UT: Ancestry.com Ops., Inc., 2015.

Ancestry.com. *New Hampshire, Birth Records, 1659-1900*. n.p: Online publication - Provo, UT: Ancestry.com Operations. Inc., 2013. Original data - "New Hampshire, Birth Records, through 1900." Online index and digital images. New England Historic Genealogical Society. Citing NH Bureau of Vital Records, n.d.

Ancestry.com. *New Hampshire, Births and Christenings Index, 1714-1904*. n.p: Online publication - Provo, UT: Ancestry.com Ops., Inc., 2011. Original data - "New Hampshire Birth Records, early to 1900." Index. FamilySearch, Salt Lake City, Utah, 2009. NH Registrar of Vital Statistics. "Index to births, early to n.d."

Ancestry.com. *New Hampshire, Death and Burial Records Index, 1654-1949*. n.p: Online publication - Provo, UT: Ancestry.com Operations, Inc., 2011. Original data - "New Hampshire Death Records, 1654-1947." Index. FamilySearch, Salt Lake City, Utah, 2010. New Hampshire Bureau of Vital Records. "Death Records, 1654-1947." Bureau of Vital Records, n.d.

Ancestry.com. *New Hampshire, Death and Disinterment Records, 1754-1947*. n.p: Online publication - Provo, UT: Ancestry.com Operations, Inc., 2013. Original data - "New Hampshire, Death and Disinterment Records, 1754-1947." Online index and digital images. New England Historic Genealogical Society. Citing New Hampshire Bureau, n.d.

Ancestry.com. *New Hampshire, Marriage and Divorce Records, 1659-1947*. n.p: Online publication - Provo, UT: Ancestry.com Operations, Inc., 2013. Original data - "New Hampshire, Marriage and Divorce Records, 1659-1947." Online index and digital images. New England Historic Genealogical Society. Citing New Hampshire Bureau of Vital Records, n.d.

Ancestry.com. *New Hampshire, Marriage Records Index, 1637-1947*. n.p: Online publication - Provo, UT: Ancestry.com Operations, Inc., 2011. Original data - "New Hampshire Marriage Records 1637-1947." Index. FamilySearch, Salt Lake City, Utah, 2011. "New Hampshire Statewide Marriage Records 1637-1947," database, FamilySearch, n.d.

Ancestry.com. *New Hampshire, Wills and Probate Records, 1643-1982*. Provo, UT: Ancestry.com Ops., 2015.

Ancestry.com. *New Jersey, Abstract of Wills, 1670-1817*. Provo, UT: Ancestry.com Operations, Inc., 2011.

Ancestry.com. *New Jersey, Births and Christenings Index, 1660-1931*. Provo, UT: Ancestry.com Ops., Inc., 2011.

Ancestry.com. *New Jersey, Deaths and Burials Index, 1798-1971.* Provo, UT: Ancestry.com Ops., Inc., 2011.

Ancestry.com. *New York Marble Cemetery Records, New York City, NY, 1830-1937.* Provo, UT: Ancestry.com Operations, Inc., 2000.

Ancestry.com. *New York, Abstracts of World War I Military Service, 1917-1919.* Provo, UT: Ancestry.com Operations, Inc., 2013.

Ancestry.com. *New York, Compiled Census and Census Substitutes Index, 1790-1890.* Provo, UT: Ancestry.com Operations Inc., 1999.

Ancestry.com. *New York, Death Newspaper Extracts, 1801-1890* (Barber Collection). Provo, UT: Ancestry.com Operations Inc., 2005.

Ancestry.com. *New York, Genealogical Records, 1675-1920.* Provo, UT: Ancestry.com Operations Inc., 2004.

Ancestry.com. *New York, Marriage Newspaper Extracts, 1801-1880 (Barber Collection).* Provo, UT: Ancestry.com Operations Inc., 2005.

Ancestry.com. *New York, New York, Birth Index, 1878-1909.* Provo, UT: Ancestry.com Operations, Inc., 2014.

Ancestry.com. *New York, New York, Death Index, 1862-1948.* Provo, UT: Ancestry.com Operations, Inc., 2014.

Ancestry.com. *New York, New York, Marriage Indexes 1866-1937.* Provo, UT: Ancestry.com Ops., Inc., 2014.

Ancestry.com. *New York, Passenger Lists, 1820-1957.* Provo, UT: Ancestry.com Operations, Inc., 2010.

Ancestry.com. *New York, State Census, 1855.* Provo, UT: Ancestry.com Operations, Inc., 2013.

Ancestry.com. *New York, State Census, 1865.* Provo, UT: Ancestry.com Operations, Inc., 2014.

Ancestry.com. *New York, State Census, 1875.* Provo, UT: Ancestry.com Operations, Inc., 2013.

Ancestry.com. *New York, State Census, 1892.* n.p: Online publication - Provo, UT: Ancestry.com Operations, Inc., 2012. Original data - New York State Education Department, Office of Cultural Education, n.d. 1892 New York State Census. Albany, NY: New York State Library.

Ancestry.com. *New York, State Census, 1905.* Provo, UT: Ancestry.com Operations, Inc., 2014.

Ancestry.com. *New York, State Census, 1915.* Provo, UT: Ancestry.com Operations, Inc., 2012.

Ancestry.com. *New York, State Census, 1925.* Provo, UT: Ancestry.com Operations, Inc., 2012.

Ancestry.com. *New York, State Censuses, 1880, 1892, 1905.* Provo, UT: Ancestry.com Operations Inc., 2005.

Ancestry.com. *New York, Wills and Probate Records, 1659-1999.* Provo, UT: Ancestry.com Ops., Inc., 2015.

Ancestry.com. *North America, Family Histories, 1500-2000.* Provo, UT: Ancestry.com Operations, Inc., 2016.

Ancestry.com. Northamptonshire Record Office; Northampton, England. *Norfolk, England, Church of England Baptism, Marriages, and Burials, 1535-1812.* Provo, UT: Ancestry.com Operations, Inc., 2016.

Ancestry.com. *Ohio 1910 Census Miracode Index.* Provo, UT: Ancestry.com Operations Inc., 2000.

Ancestry.com. *Ohio Military Men, 1917-18.* n.p: Online publication - Provo, UT: Ancestry.com Operations Inc., 2000. Original data - Official Roster of Ohio Soldiers, Sailors and Marines in the World War, 1917-1918. Columbus, OH: F. J. Heer Printing Co., 1926. Original data: Official Roster of Ohio, n.d.

Ancestry.com. *Ohio Obituary Index, 1830s-2011, Rutherford B. Hayes Presidential Center.* n.p: Online publication - Provo, UT: Ancestry.com Operations, Inc., 2010. Original data - Hayes Presidential Center Obituary Indexers and Volunteers. "Ohio Obituary Index." Database. Rutherford B. Hayes Presidential Center. http://index.rbhayes.org/hayes/in, n.d.

Ancestry.com. *Ohio, Births and Christenings Index, 1800-1962.* Provo, UT: Ancestry.com Operations, Inc., 2011.

Ancestry.com. *Ohio, Compiled Census and Census Substitutes Index, 1790-1890.* Provo, UT: Ancestry.com Operations Inc., 1999.

Ancestry.com. *Ohio, Wills and Probate Records, 1786-1998.* Provo, UT: Ancestry.com Operations, Inc., 2015.

Ancestry.com. *Oregon, Death Index, 1898-2008.* n.p: Online publication - Provo, UT: Ancestry.com Ops., Inc., 2000. Original data - State of Oregon. Oregon Death Index, 1903-1998. Salem, OR: Oregon State Archives and Records Center. Oregon Death Indexes, 1903-1970.

Ancestry.com. *Pennsylvania 1910 Miracode Index.* Provo, UT: Ancestry.com Operations Inc., 2000.

Ancestry.com. *Pennsylvania, Church and Town Records, 1708-1985*. Provo, UT: Ancestry.com Ops., Inc., 2011.

Ancestry.com. *Pennsylvania, Civil War Muster Rolls, 1860-1869.* Provo, UT: Ancestry.com Ops., 2015.

Ancestry.com. *Pennsylvania, Death Certificates, 1906-1944*. Provo, UT: Ancestry.com Operations, Inc., 2014.

Ancestry.com. *Pennsylvania, Land Warrants and Applications, 1733-1952*. Provo, UT: Ancestry.com Ops., 2012.

Ancestry.com. *Pennsylvania, Marriage Records, 1700-1821*. Provo, UT: Ancestry.com Operations Inc., 2011.

Ancestry.com. *Pennsylvania, Marriages, 1852-1854*. Provo, UT: Ancestry.com Operations, Inc., 2011.

Ancestry.com. *Pennsylvania, U.S. Direct Tax Lists, 1798*. Provo, UT: Ancestry.com Operations, Inc., 2012.

Ancestry.com. *Pennsylvania, Veterans Burial Cards, 1777-1999*. Provo, UT: Ancestry.com Ops., Inc., 2010.

Ancestry.com. *Pennsylvania, Wills and Probate Records, 1683-1993*. Provo, UT: Ancestry.com Ops., Inc., 2015.

Ancestry.com. *Philadelphia City Directory, 1890*. Provo, UT: Ancestry.com Operations Inc., 1998.

Ancestry.com. *Philadelphia, PA, Death Certificates Index, 1803-1915*. Provo, UT: Ancestry.com Ops., 2011.

Ancestry.com. *Philadelphia, PA, Marriage Index, 1885-1951*. Provo, UT: Ancestry.com Operations, Inc., 2011.

Ancestry.com. *Public Member Trees*. n.p. Provo, UT: Ancestry.com Operations, Inc., 2006.

Ancestry.com. *Puerto Rico, Passenger and Crew Lists, 1901-1962*. Provo, UT: Ancestry.com Ops., Inc., 2012.

Ancestry.com. *Rhode Island, State Censuses, 1865-1935*. n.p: Online publication - Provo, UT: Ancestry.com Operations, Inc., 2013. Original data - Rhode Island State Census, 1865. Microfilm. New England Historic Genealogical Society, Boston, MA, n.d. Rhode Island State Census, 1875. Microfilm.

Ancestry.com. *Rhode Island, Vital Extracts, 1636-1899*. Provo, UT: Ancestry.com Operations, Inc., 2014.

Ancestry.com. *Salt Lake City, Utah, Cemetery Records, 1848-1992*. Provo, UT: Ancestry.com Ops., Inc., 2004.

Ancestry.com. *Salt Lake County, Utah, Death Records, 1908-1949*. Provo, UT: Ancestry.com Ops., Inc., 2014.

Ancestry.com. *Selected U.S. Federal Census Non-Population Schedules, 1850-1880*. Provo, UT: Ancestry.com Operations, Inc., 2010.

Ancestry.com. *Social Security Death Index*. Provo, UT: Ancestry.com Operations Inc., 2011.

Ancestry.com. *Tennessee, Death Records, 1908-1958*. Provo, UT: Ancestry.com Operations, Inc., 2011.

Ancestry.com. *Tennessee, Deaths and Burials Index, 1874-1955*. Provo, UT: Ancestry.com Ops., Inc., 2011.

Ancestry.com. *Texas Death Index, 1903-2000*. n.p: Online publication - Provo, UT: Ancestry.com Operations Inc., 2006. Original data - Texas Department of Health. Texas Death Indexes, 1903-2000. Austin, TX: Texas Department of Health, State Vital Statistics Unit, n.d.

Ancestry.com. *The New England Historical and Genealogical Register, 1847-2011*. n.p: Online publication - Provo, UT: Ancestry.com Operations, Inc., 2011. Original data: New England Historic Genealogical Society. Boston: New England Historic Genealogical Society, n.d.

Ancestry.com. *U.S. and Canada, Passenger and Immigration Lists Index, 1500s-1900s*. Provo, UT: Ancestry.com Operations, Inc., 2010.

Ancestry.com. *U.S. Army, Register of Enlistments, 1798-1914*. n.p: Online publication - Provo, UT: Ancestry.com Ops., Inc., 2007. Original data - Register of Enlistments in the U.S. Army, 1798-1914; (National Archives Microfilm Publication M233, 81 rolls); Records of the Adjutant General's Office, 1780's-1917, Rec, n.d.

Ancestry.com. *U.S. Census Mortality Schedules, New York, 1850-1880*. Provo, UT: Ancestry.com Ops., 2010.

Ancestry.com. *U.S. City Directories, 1821-1989 (Beta)*. n.p: Online publication - Provo, UT: Ancestry.com Operations, Inc., 2011. Original data - Original sources vary according to directory.

Ancestry.com. *U.S. Confederate Pensions, 1884-1958*. Provo, UT: Ancestry.com Operations Inc., 2010.

Ancestry.com. *U.S. Federal Census - 1880 Schedules of Defective, Dependent, and Delinquent Classes*. Provo, UT: Ancestry.com Operations, Inc., 2010.

Ancestry.com. *U.S. Federal Census Mortality Schedules, 1850-1885*. n.p: Online publication - Provo, UT: Ancestry.com Ops., Inc., 2010. A portion of this collection indexed by Ancestry World Archives Project contributors. Original data: State Citation U.S. Federal Mortality Census Schedules, 1850-1880 (f, n.d.)

Ancestry.com. *U.S. General Land Office Records, 1796-1907.* Provo, UT: Ancestry.com Operations Inc., 2008.

Ancestry.com. *U.S. IRS Tax Assessment Lists, 1862-1918.* n.p: Online publication - Provo, UT: Ancestry.com Operations Inc., 2008. Original data: National Archives (NARA) microfilm series: M603, M754-M771, M773-M777, M779-M780, M782, M784, M787-M789, M791-M793, M795, M1631, M1775-M1776, T227, T1208-T1209. For comp, n.d.

Ancestry.com. *U.S. National Cemetery Interment Control Forms, 1928-1962.* Provo, UT: Ancestry.com Ops., 2012.

Ancestry.com. *U.S. National Homes for Disabled Volunteer Soldiers, 1866-1938* [database on-line]. Provo, UT: Ancestry.com Operations Inc. 2007.

Ancestry.com. *U.S. Navy Pensions Index, 1861-1910.* Provo, UT: Ancestry.com Operations Inc., 2008.

Ancestry.com. *U.S. Passport Applications, 1795-1925.* Provo, UT: Ancestry.com Operations, Inc., 2007.

Ancestry.com. *U.S. Revolutionary War Rolls, 1775-1783.* Provo, UT: Ancestry.com Operations Inc., 2007.

Ancestry.com. *U.S. School Yearbooks.* Provo, UT: Ancestry.com Operations, Inc., 2010.

Ancestry.com. *U.S., Adjutant General Military Records, 1631-1976.* Provo, UT: Ancestry.com Ops., Inc., 2011.

Ancestry.com. *U.S., Atlantic Ports Passenger Lists, 1820-1873 and 1893-1959.* Provo, UT: Ancestry.com Operations Inc., 2010.

Ancestry.com. *U.S., Burial Registers, Military Posts and National Cemeteries, 1862-1960.* Provo, UT: Ancestry.com Operations, Inc., 2012.

Ancestry.com. *U.S., Civil War Draft Registrations Records, 1863-1865.* Provo, UT: Ancestry.com Ops., 2010.

Ancestry.com. *U.S., Civil War Pension Index: General Index to Pension Files, 1861-1934.* n.p: Online publication - Provo, UT: Ancestry.com Operations Inc., 2000. Original data: General Index to Pension Files, 1861-1934. Washington, D.C.: National Archives and Records Administration. T288, 546 rolls.

Ancestry.com. *U.S., College Student Lists, 1763-1924.* Provo, UT: Ancestry.com Operations, Inc., 2012.

Ancestry.com. *U.S., Department of Veterans Affairs BIRLS Death File, 1850-2010.* n.p: Online publication - Provo, UT: Ancestry.com Operations, Inc., 2011. Original data - Beneficiary Identification Records Locator Subsystem (BIRLS) Death File, n.d. U.S. Department of Veterans Affairs, Washington, D.C.

Ancestry.com. *U.S., Federal Census Mortality Schedules Index, 1850-1880.* Provo, UT: Ancestry.com Ops., 1999.

Ancestry.com. *U.S., Find A Grave Index, 1600s-Current.* Provo, UT: Ancestry.com Operations, Inc., 2012. (See endnotes for details.)

Ancestry.com. *U.S., French Catholic Church Records (Drouin Collection) St-Louis; Baptemes 1814-1823* [database on-line]. Provo, UT: Ancestry.com Operations, Inc., 2007.

Ancestry.com. *U.S., Headstone Applications for Military Veterans, 1925-1963.* n.p: Online publication - Provo, UT: Ancestry.com Operations, Inc., 2012. Original data - Applications for Headstones for U.S. Military Veterans, 1925-1941. Microfilm publication M1916, 134 rolls. Records of the Office of the Quartermaster General, n.d.

Ancestry.com. *U.S., High School Student Lists, 1821-1923.* Provo, UT: Ancestry.com Operations Inc., 2012.

Ancestry.com. *U.S., Indexed County Land Ownership Maps, 1860-1918.* n.p: Online publication - Provo, UT: Ancestry.com Operations, Inc., 2010. Original data - Various publishers of County Land Ownership Atlases, n.d. Microfilmed by the Library of Congress, Washington, D.C.

Ancestry.com. *U.S., National Cemetery Interment Control Forms, 1928-1962.* Provo, UT: Ancestry.com Operations, Inc., 2012.

Ancestry.com. *U.S., New England Marriages Prior to 1700.* n.p: Online publication - Provo, UT: Ancestry.com Operations Inc., 2012. Original data - Torrey, Clarence A. *New England Marriages Prior to 1700.* Baltimore, MD: Genealogical Publishing Co., 2004.

Ancestry.com. *U.S., Newspaper Extractions from the Northeast, 1704-1930.* Provo, UT: Ancestry.com Ops., 2014.

Ancestry.com. *U.S., Quaker Meeting Records, 1681-1994.* Provo, UT: Ancestry.com Operations, Inc., 2014.

Ancestry.com. *U.S., Registers of Deaths of Volunteers, 1861-1865.* Provo, UT: Ancestry.com Ops., Inc., 2012.

Ancestry.com. *U.S., Revolutionary War Pension and Bounty-Land Warrant Application Files, 1800-1900 [database on-line].* Provo, UT: Ancestry.com Operations, Inc., 2010. Original data: "Revolutionary War Pension and

Bounty-Land Warrant Application Files." NARA microfilm publication M804. Records of the Dept. of Veterans Affairs, Record Group 15. National Archives, Washington, D.C.

Ancestry.com. *U.S., Revolutionary War Pensioners, 1801-1815, 1818-1872* [database on-line]. Provo, UT: Ancestry.com Operations, Inc., 2007. Original data: "Ledgers of Payments, 1818-1872, to U.S. Pensioners Under Acts of 1818 Through 1858, From Records of the Office of the Third Auditor of the Treasury, 1818-1872." Department of Veterans Affairs, Record Group 217; National Archives, Washington, D.C.

Ancestry.com. *U.S., School Catalogs, 1765-1935.* Provo, UT: Ancestry.com Operations, Inc., 2012.

Ancestry.com. *U.S., Seamen's Protection Certificates, 1792-1869.* Provo, UT: Ancestry.com Ops., Inc., 2010.

Ancestry.com. *U.S., Sons of the American Revolution Membership Applications, 1889-1970.* Provo, UT: Ancestry.com Operations, Inc., 2011.

Ancestry.com. *U.S., The Pension Roll of 1835* [database on-line]. Provo, UT: Ancestry.com Operations, Inc., 2014. (Original data: United States Senate. The Pension Roll of 1835. 1968 Reprint, with index. Baltimore: Genealogical Publishing Company, 1992, Vol. 4.)

Ancestry.com. *U.S., The Pension Roll of 1835.* Provo, UT: Ancestry.com Operations, Inc., 2014.

Ancestry.com. *U.S., World War I Draft Registration Cards, 1917-1918.* Provo, UT: Ancestry.com Ops., 2005.

Ancestry.com. *U.S., World War II Draft Registration Cards, 1942.* Provo, UT: Ancestry.com Ops., Inc., 2010.

Ancestry.com. *US, Register of Civil, Military, and Naval Service, 1863-1959.* Provo, UT: Ancestry.com Ops., 2014.

Ancestry.com. *Utah Death Registers, 1847-1966.* Provo, UT: Ancestry.com Operations Inc., 2010.

Ancestry.com. *Utah, Death and Military Death Certificates, 1904-1961.* Provo, UT: Ancestry.com Ops., 2014.

Ancestry.com. *Vermont, Vital Records, 1720-1908.* Provo, UT: Ancestry.com Operations, Inc., 2013.

Ancestry.com. *Virginia, Select Marriages, 1785-1940.* Provo, UT: Ancestry.com Operations, Inc., 2014.

Ancestry.com. *War of 1812 Papers, 1789-1815.* Provo, UT: Ancestry.com Operations Inc., 2007.

Ancestry.com. *War of 1812 Pension Application Files Index, 1812-1815.* Provo, UT: Ancestry.com Ops., 2010.

Ancestry.com. *Washington Death Index, 1940-1996.* Provo, UT: Ancestry.com Operations Inc., 2002.

Ancestry.com. *Washington, D.C., Wills and Probate Records, 1737-1952.* Provo, UT: Ancestry.com Ops., 2015.

Ancestry.com. *Washington, Deaths, 1883-1960.* Provo, UT: Ancestry.com Operations Inc., 2008.

Ancestry.com. *Washington, Select Death Certificates, 1907-1960.* Provo, UT: Ancestry.com Ops., Inc., 2014.

Ancestry.com. *Watertown, Massachusetts Genealogies and History.* Provo, UT: Generations Network, Inc., 2003.

Ancestry.com. *Web: Allen County, Indiana, Obituary Index, 1841-2010.* Provo, UT: Ancestry.com Ops., 2010.

Ancestry.com. *Web: Brooklyn, New York, Green-Wood Cemetery Burial Index.* Provo, UT: Ancestry.com Operations, Inc., 2011.

Ancestry.com. *Web: Columbus, Ohio, Green Lawn Cemetery Index, 1780-2010.* n.p: Online publication - Provo, UT: Ancestry.com Operations, Inc., 2012. Original data n.d.- Green Lawn Cemetery Burials. Joe and Dick Fleshman. http://greenlawn.delaohio.com/greenlawn/Greenlawn/index.htm.

Ancestry.com. *Web: Columbus, Ohio, Union Cemetery Index, 1847-2012.* Provo, UT: Ancestry.com Ops., 2012.

Ancestry.com. *Web: Gallia County, Ohio, Burial Index, 1811-2011.* Provo, UT: Ancestry.com Ops., Inc., 2013.

Ancestry.com. *Web: Indiana, Marion Public Library Death Index, 1812 -2011.* Provo, UT: Ancestry.com Operations, Inc., 2013.

Ancestry.com. *Web: Indiana, Marion Public Library Marriage Index, 1831-2008.* Provo, UT: Ancestry.com Operations, Inc., 2013.

Ancestry.com. *Web: Missouri, Death Certificates, 1910-1962.* Provo, UT: Ancestry.com Operations, Inc., 2015.

Ancestry.com. *Web: Obituary Daily Times Index, 1995-2012.* Provo, UT: Ancestry.com Operations, Inc., 2012.

Ancestry.com. *Web: Western States Marriage Index, 1809-2011.* Provo, UT: Ancestry.com Ops., Inc., 2011.

Ancestry.com. *West Virginia, Deaths Index, 1853-1973.* Provo, UT: Ancestry.com Operations, Inc., 2011.

Ancestry.com. *West Virginia, Marriages Index, 1785-1971.* Provo, UT: Ancestry.com Operations, Inc., 2011.

Ancestry.com. *West Virginia, Wills and Probate Records, 1724-1978*. Provo, UT: Ancestry.com Ops., Inc., 2015.

Ancestry.com. *Wisconsin Deaths, 1820-1907*. Provo, UT: Ancestry.com Operations Inc., 2000.

Ancestry.com. *Wisconsin, State Censuses, 1895 and 1905*. Provo, UT: Ancestry.com Operations Inc., 2007.

Anderson, Richard B. *Harvard Square Old Burying Ground Map and Index*. Cambridge, MA: Cambridge Historical Commission, 2000.

Andrew, Laurence Clyde. *Thomas Andrew, Immigrant*. Portland, ME: Casco Printing Co., 1972.

Anglen, Lavone Johnson. "Biography: Louis Weiss Wyeth born 1812 with photograph." *Alabama Pioneers*. 2013-2015. http://alabamapioneers.com/biography-louis-weiss-wyeth-born-1812/.

Armstrong, Amy, comp. *Boston, Massachusetts, 1913 Harvard University Alumni Directory*. Provo, UT: The Generations Network, Inc., 2001.

Arnold, Richard L. *A Sesquicentennial Review of the Second Presbyterian Church, Carlisle Pennsylvania, 1833-1983*. Chambersburg, PA: Craft Press, 1982.

Art and Picture Collection, The New York Public Library. "White captives driven to Canada by the Indians." *New York Public Library Digital Collections*. http://digitalcollections.nypl.org/items/510d47e0-f46e-a3d9-e040-e00a18064a99 (accessed 10/28/2017).

Asher, Louis F. *John Clarke (1609-1676): pioneer in American medicine, democratic ideals, and champion of religious liberty*. Paris, AK: Baptist Standard Bearer, 2004.

"Auburn House." *Trumpet and Universalist Magazine* (Boston, MA), 16 Jul 1842.

Babson, John James. *History of the Town of Gloucester*. Gloucester, MA: Procter Brothers, 1860.

Baldwin, Thomas W. *Vital Records of Cambridge, Massachusetts, to the year 1850*. Boston: Wright & Potter Printing Company, 1914.

Ballenger & Richards. *Annual Denver City Directory*. Denver, CO: Ballenger & Richards, 1882.

Ballew, Diana. *Welcome to our Ballew Family Page* www.oocities.org/heartland/plains/2805/ballew3.html (accessed 9/24/2018).

Baltimore County, Maryland. *Marriage Cards, Court of Common Pleas (Marriage Index, Male) CM205*. State of Maryland, 1851-1855.

Bancroft, Hubert Howe. *History of the Northwest Coast. Vol. II. 1884-86*. San Francisco: A. L. Bancroft & Company, 1884.

"Bankruptcy files Wyeth, Stephen and Wyeth, Joseph Henry." *Record Group 21: Records of District Courts of the United States, 1685 – 2009. Series: Bankruptcy Act of 1841 Case Files, 1842 - 1844*. National Archives Identifier: 4659096. https://research.archives.gov/. National Archives Building, Waltham, Massachusetts.

Banks, Charles Edward. *Planters of the Commonwealth*. Boston: Riverside Press/Houghton Mifflin Co., 1930.

Bankston III, Carl L. *History of immigration, 1620-1783*. http://immigrationtounitedstates.org/548-history-of-immigration-1620-1783.html (accessed 2/25/2016).

Barker, H. R. *West Suffolk, Illustrated*. Bury St. Edmund's, UK: F.G. Pawsry and Co., Ltd., 1907.

Barker, John Herbert. *Nicholas Wyeth of Cambridge, Mass., and some of his descendants*. Cambridge, MA: 1929.

Barker, John Herbert. *Some notes on the Wyeth family 1595-1940, Giving eight generations of the Descendants of Nicholas Wyeth who came to America about 1645*. Cambridge, MA: Handwritten genealogy, 1940.

Barnes, Grace Wing, editor. *Annals of the Wing Family of America Incorporated, Vol. 54*. Des Moines, IA: Wing Family of America, 1954.

Bartlett, Joseph Gardner. *The English Ancestral Homes of The Founders of Cambridge*. Cambridge, MA: Cambridge Historical Society. Apr, 1919.

Bartlett, Joseph Gardner. *Gregory Stone Genealogy: Ancestry and Descendants of Dea. Gregory Stone of Cambridge, Mass., 1320-1917*. Boston, MA: Murray Printing Co., 1918.

Bartlett, Joseph Gardner. "Marriages from Sources not in the Line of a Direct Search." *The Genealogical Bulletin, Volume 1, No. 23*. Boston, MA: The Research Publication Company, 16 Jul 1904.

"Battle of White Plains." *BritishBattles.com.* www.britishbattles.com/white-plains.htm (accessed 10/13/2016).

Beckwith, Hiram Williams. History of Vigo and Parke Counties, Together with Historic Notes on the Wabash Valley. Chicago: H. H. Hill and N. Iddings, 1880.

Beers, J. H. and Co. *Commemorative Biographical Record of Washington County, Pennsylvania.* Chicago: J. H. Beers & Co., 1893. Transcribed by Neil and Marilyn Morton of Oswego, Illinois as part of the Beers Project. Published Jan 1997 on the Washington County, PA USGenWeb. www.chartiers.com/beers-project/articles/winter-893.html.

Bell, J. L. "The Man Who Named the Boston Tea Party." *Boston 1775 Blog.* 22 Dec 2010. http://boston1775.blogspot.com/2010/12/man-who-named-boston-tea-party.html.

"Benson Family: Putting 'Benson' in Bensonhurst." *Wandering NYC.* 12 Dec 2010. https://wanderingbrooklyn.wordpress.com/2010/12/12/the-benson-family-putting-the-benson-in-bensonhurst.

Benson, Arthur W. "Brooklyn, NY Deposition to Lawrence Marcellus." *File #211.* Scott County, Iowa District Court records. 19 May 1857.

Benson, Arthur W. "Last Will and Testament*." New York Wills, Volume 0142-0144.* 1889-1890.

Berg, Henry W. and Albert A. Collection of English and American Literature. *The New York Public Library.* "George Wythe. (Drawn and engraved by J.B. Longacre from a portrait in the American Gleaner.)" New York Public Library Digital Collections. http://digitalcollections.nypl.org/items/510d47db-c6dd-a3d9-e040-e00a18064a99 (accessed 2/28/2017).

Bible and Family Data Records, courtesy of Ethel Ross "Rossie" Wyeth Canion, Lucy Snow Wyeth Hoffman, Lillian Neisz, Donna Wyeth Thibodeau, Marvel June Wyeth Ucen, Juanita Vogt and Charles Leon Wyeth, Charles Arthur "Chuck" Walker, Anna May Souva Wyeth, Donald Elwyn Wyeth, Sheila Baum and James Allen Wyeth, William "Max" Wyeth IV and others.

Bicknell, Thomas Williams. *The Story of John Clarke, the founder of the first free commonwealth of the world on the basis of "full liberty in religious concernment."* Providence, RI: the author, 1915.

"Bing Russell, Father of Kurt Russell." *Find-a-Death.com.* www.findadeath.com/forum/showthread.php?20681-Bing-Russell-Father-of-Kurt-Russell (accessed 3/26/2016).

Binney, Charles J. F. *The History and Genealogy of the Prentice or Prentiss Family in New England, from 1631 to 1852.* Boston: Charles Binney, 1852.

Birmingham, Doris (Editor). *Jason Russell House Tour Guide Manual.* Arlington, MA: Arlington Historical Society, 2016-2017.

Blackburn, Joyce. *George Wythe of Williamsburg.* New York: Harper & Row, 1975.

Blatchford, John; Charles I. Bushnell. *The narrative of John Blatchford, detailing his sufferings in the revolutionary war, while a prisoner with the British. As related by himself.* New York: private printing, 1865.

Bliss, Abigail. "New Old Sloop steeple takes shape." *Gloucester Daily Times,* 13 Sep 2017.

Boddie, John Bennett. *Virginia Historical Genealogies.* Baltimore, MD: Reprinted for Clearfield by Genealogical Publishing Co., 2008.

Boder, Bartlett. "William Wyeth and His Times." *Museum Graphic* magazine published by the St. Joseph Museum (Saint Joseph, MO), Summer 1956.

Bodge, George Madison. *Soldiers in King Philip's War.* Boston: The Rockwell and Churchill Press, 1906.

Bond, Henry, Horatio Gates Jones. *Genealogies of the Families and Descendants of the Early Settlers of Watertown, Massachusetts, Including Waltham and Weston: to which is Appended the Early History of the Town.* Boston: Little Brown and Company, 1855.

Boorstin, Daniel J. *The Americans: The National Experience.* New York: Vintage, 2010.

Booth, John. *Nicholas Danforth and his Neighbours, Framlingham and Saxtead in the 17th Century with Introductory Paper, Nicholas Danforth, the Puritan Layman by John M. Merriam.* Framingham, MA: Lakeview Press, 1935.

Booth, John. *The Home of Nicholas Danforth in Framlingham, Suffolk, England in 1635.* Framingham, MA: Framingham Historical and Natural History Society, 1954.

Boston Registry Dept. *Records Relating to the Early History of Boston, Volume 30*. Boston: Municipal Printing Office, 1903.

Boucher, Jack E. "7. April 1967 East (Front) Elevation from Southeast - Mar-a-Lago, 1100 South Ocean Boulevard, Palm Beach, Palm Beach County, FL" photograph. *Library of Congress Prints and Photographs Division*, under the digital ID hhh.fl0181. Image courtesy of federal HABS—Historic American Buildings Survey in Florida project. http://www.loc.gov/pictures/item/fl0181.photos.053242p/ (accessed 3/25/2016).

Boucher, Jack E. "South (Front) Elevation from Southeast and Pre-Shaker Staircase, Showing Wood Wainscoting and Newel Post - Shaker Church Family Square House, Shaker Road, Harvard, Worcester, MA, photograph." *Library of Congress Prints and Photographs Division*, Washington, D.C., Apr 1963. http://www.loc.gov/pictures/resource/hhh.ma0562.photos.077061p/ (accessed 3/25/2016).

Boudillion, Daniel V. "How the Shakers Invented Spiritualism - The Ecstatic Spirits of Holy Hill, Harvard Massachusetts." *Field Investigations*: 11 Aug 2002 & 30 May 2007. http://www.boudillion.com/holyhill/holyhill.htm.

Bouic, Margaret Main. "Bouic Index." *Mid-Ohio Genealogy Database*. www.midohiogen.org (accessed 1/3/2019).

Boussel, Patrice, Henri Bonnemain, and Frank J. Bové; translated into English by James Desmond and Frank J. Bové, History *of Pharmacy and the Pharmaceutical Industry*. Paris: Asklepios Press, 1982.

Bowditch, Nathaniel Ingersoll. *Suffolk Surnames*. London: Trübner and Company, 1861.

Boyer, Paul and Stephen Nissenbaum. Revised, corrected, and augmented by Benjamin C. Ray and Tara S. Wood. *The Salem Witchcraft Papers*, used with permission of Benjamin Ray. The Rector and Visitors of the University of Virginia, 2002. SWP No. 81.1. http://salem.lib.virginia.edu/texts/tei/swp?div_id=n81.

Boyer, Paul and Stephen Nissenbaum. *Salem Possessed*. Cambridge, MA: Harvard University Press, 1974.

Bradsby, Henry C. *History of Vigo County, Indiana*. Chicago: S. B. Nelson & Co., 1891.

Brady, Mathew or Levin C. Handy. "Gen. H.J. Hunt, U.S.A. [between 1860 and 1865], photograph." *Library of Congress Prints and Photographs Division*. Brady-Handy Photograph Collection. http://hdl.loc.gov/loc.pnp/cwpbh.03181. LC-BH831- 957[P&P].

Brainard, W. F. *Who's who in New York City and State: a biographical dictionary of contemporaries*. Brooklyn, NY: Press of Wm. G. Hewitt, 1911.

Briggs, Cora C. "Historical Society welcomes portrait's return." *Sun Journal* (Lewiston, Maine), 27 Jun 1992.

Brigham, Johnson. *Iowa, Its History and Its Foremost Citizens, Vol. 2*. Chicago: S. J. Clarke Publishing Co., 1915

Brister, Edwin M. P. *Centennial History of the City of Newark and Licking County, Ohio, Vol. 2*. Chicago: S. J. Clarke Publishing Co., 1909.

Brooks, Charles, William Whitmore and James Usher, *The History of the Town of Medford, Middlesex County, Mass*. Boston: Rand, Avery, 1886.

Brooks, Rebecca Beatrice. "17th Century Massachusetts." *History of Massachusetts blog*. 2011-2018. http://historyofmassachusetts.org/.

Brown, Imogene E. *American Aristides*. Rutherford, NJ: Fairleigh Dickinson University Press, 1981.

Brown, Ruth W. *My Wyeth Connection*. Flint Genealogical Quarterly, Vol. 21, No. 1, Jan. 1979.

Buckminster, Lydia Nelson Hastings. *The Hastings Memorial: A Genealogical Account of the Descendants of Thomas Hastings*. Boston: Samuel G. Drake, 1866.

Burke, Arthur Meredyth. *Prominent Families of the United States of America*. London: Sackville Press, 1908.

Burke, Edmund. *List of Patents for Inventions and Designs, Issued by the United States from 1790 to 1847*. Washington: J. & G. S. Gideon, 1847.

Burke, John and John Bernard Burke. *Encyclopaedia of heraldry, or General armory of England, Scotland, and Ireland, comprising a registry of all armorial bearings from the earliest to the present time, including the late grants by the College of Arms*. London: Bohn, 1844.

Burns, M. "Statement of Daniel Andrew, Peter Cloyce, Israel & Elizabeth Porter for Rebecca Nurse." *A Guide to the On-line Primary Sources of the Salem Witchcraft Trials*. www.17thc.us/primarysources/document.php?id=31 (accessed 8/27/16).

Burr, George Lincoln. *Narratives of the New England Witchcraft Cases*. Mineola, New York: Dover Publications, 2002.

Burton, Clarence, Monroe William Stocking, Gordon K. Miller, editors. *The City of Detroit, Michigan, 1701-1922, Volume 2*. Detroit: S. J. Clarke Publishing Co., 1922.

Cajori, Florian. *The Teaching and History of Mathematics in the United States, Volumes 890-893*. Washington: Government Printing Office, 1890.

Caldwell, D. S. *Incidents of War and Southern Prison Life*. Dayton, OH: United Brethen Printing Est., 1864.

Calef, Robert. *More Wonders of the Invisible World*. London: Hillar & Collyer, 1700.

Cambridge Historical Society. *Publications I Proceedings 19 Jun 1905-24 Apr 1906*. Cambridge, MA: University Press, 1906.

Cambridge, Mass. *The Register Book of the Lands and Houses in the "New Towne" and the Town of Cambridge with the Records of the Proprietors of the Common Lands being the records generally called "The Proprietors' Records."* Cambridge: University Press - John Wilson and Son, 1896.

Cambridge, Mass. *The Records of the Town of Cambridge (formerly New-towne) Massachusetts: 1630-1703. The Records of the Town Meetings, and of the Selectmen, Comprising All of the First Volume of Records, and Being Volume II, of the Printed Records of the Town*. Cambridge, MA: The Council, 1901.

Cambridge, Mass. City Engineer. *Map of the city of Cambridge*. Cambridge, MA: City Engineer, 1894.

Campbell, Roben. "A Short Biography: Deborah Prentice, Harvard Shaker (1720-1811)." *In Historic Harvard Town*, 2016. https://historicharvard.wordpress.com/historic-places/highlight-our-historic-places/our-harvard-shakers-cemetery/a-biography-deborah-prentice-harvard-shaker/

Canfield, Frederick A. *Descendants of Thomas Canfield and Matthew Camfield*. New Haven, CT: Tuttle, Morehouse & Taylor Press, 1897. Republished by Canfield Family Association, 1 Jan 2006.

Caroli, Betty Boyd. "Abigail Adams American First Lady." *Encyclopaedia Britannica,* last updated 9/8/2017. https://www.britannica.com/biography/Abigail-Adams.

Carp, Benjamin L. *Defiance of the Patriots*. New Haven, CT: Yale University Press, 2010.

Cary, Gen. Samuel F. *Record of Revolutionary Soldiers buried in Hamilton Co., Ohio*. Cincinnati, OH: Ohio Society of the Sons of the Revolution, 1895.

Cascone, Sarah. "JFK Portrait by Jamie Wyeth Lands at MFA Boston." *artnet news.* 08 Jul 2014. https://news.artnet.com/art-world/jfk-portrait-by-jamie-wyeth-lands-at-mfa-boston-57402.

"The Catahoula Parish Descendants of Dr. Nathaniel Bowman." *Roots from the Bayou*. 8 Dec 2012. rootsfromthebayou.blogspot.com/2012/12/the-catahoula-parish-descendants-of-dr.html.

Caveler, William. *The ecclesiastical and architectural topography of England*. London: John Henry and James Parker, 1855.

"Cemetery Listing." *City of Terre Haute, Indiana.* http://www.terrehaute.in.gov/departments/cemetery/cemetery-12-11-2012-formatted-for-printing.pdf (accessed 1/23/2018).

Cerny, Johni. "Births and Deaths in Public Records." *The Source: A Guidebook to American Genealogy.* 1984, digitized by Ancestry.com in 2010.

Chandler, Seth. *History of the town of Shirley*. Shirley, MA: Seth Chandler, 1883.

"The Changing Face of Homelessness." *Heading Home-ending homelessness for good.* 2016. http://www.headinghomeinc.org/ (accessed 6/17/2016).

Chapman, Blanche Adams. *Wills and Administrations of Elizabeth City County, Virginia 1688-1800*. Baltimore, MD: Clearfield, 1980.

"Christ Church Cambridge History." *Christ Church Cambridge.* http://cccambridge.org/about/history (accessed 3/25/2016).

Christine Leigh, Heyrman. "Puritanism and Predestination." *Divining America, TeacherServe©*, National Humanities Center. http://nationalhumanitiescenter.org/tserve/eighteen/ekeyinfo/puritan.htm (accessed 3/3/2016).

Church, Benjamin. "Phillip [sic] alias Metacomet of Pokanoket, illustration." *Library of Congress Prints and Photographs Division*. Reproduction Number: LC-USZ62-96234 (b&w film copy neg.). http://www.loc.gov/pictures/item/89707293/.

"Church of Christ at Brush Run." *History of the Restoration Movement.* www.therestorationmovement.com/_states/wv/brushrun.htm (accessed 1/13/2018).

The Church of Jesus Christ of Latter-day Saints. *Various FamilySearch databases.* https://www.familysearch.org (accessed 2014-2019).

Church, William Conant, Editor. *The Galaxy, Volume 19.* New York: Sheldon & Company, 1875.

Chrysler, Angela B. "Grandparents of Kym Marie Chrysler Who Were Killed by Indians." *The Chrysler Family.* Excel spreadsheet. http://thechryslerfamily.com (accessed 10/14/2017).

Cillizza, Chris and Jon Cohen. "President Obama and the white vote? No problem." *The Washington Post* (Washington, D.C.), 08 Nov 2012. https://www.washingtonpost.com/news/the-fix/wp/2012/11/08/president-obama-and-the-white-vote-no-problem/?utm_term=.73b8a75cfe1c

"Civil War Service Records, Union Records." Digital images. *Fold3.* http://www.fold3.com (accessed 2016-2018).

"Civil War Soldiers and Sailors Database." *National Park Service.* https://www.nps.gov/civilwar/soldiers-and-sailors-database.htm (accessed 2016-2018).

Clark, Dorothy J. "Historically Speaking." *The Terre Haute Tribune* (Terre Haute, IN), 14 Dec 1975.

Clark, Ross. "The Long and Winding Road." *The Telegraph* (London, UK), 12 Apr 2003. http://www.telegraph.co.uk/motoring/2721693/The-long-and-winding-road.html.

Clarkin, William. *Serene Patriot: A Life of George Wythe.* Albany, NY: Alan Publications, 1970.

Coat of Arms of George Wythe. https://commons.wikimedia.org/wiki/File:Coat_of_Arms_of_George_Wythe.svg (accessed 01/23/2016).

Coburn, Frank Warren. *The battle of April 19, 1775: in Lexington, Concord, Lincoln, Arlington, Cambridge, Somerville, and Charlestown, Massachusetts.* Boston: F. L. Coburn and Company, 1912.

Codding, James H. *A History of Union Lodge No. 108, Free and Accepted Masons, Towanda, Pa. Held under a warrant from The Right Worshipful Grand Lodge of Pennsylvania and Masonic Jurisdiction Thereunto Belonging.* Towanda, PA: Reporter-Journal Printing Co., 1899. Reprint publication on Tri-Counties Genealogy & History by Joyce M. Tice, 2004.

Cole, Ernest Byron. *The Winship family in America.* Indianapolis, IN: [Cole], 1905.

Colonial Society of Massachusetts. *Publications of the Colonial Society of Massachusetts Transactions 1913-1914.* Cambridge, MA: University Press - John Wilson and Son, 1915.

Connecticut Department of Health. *Connecticut Death Index, 1949-2001.* Provo, UT: Ancestry.com Operations Inc., 2003.

Cooke, Harriet Ruth. *The Driver Family: A Genealogical Memoir of the Descendants of Robert and Phebe Driver.* New York: John Wilson and Son, 1889.

Copinger, Walter Arthur. *The Manors of Suffolk: The hundreds of Babergh and Blackbourn.* London: T. Fisher Unwin, 1905.

Cox, Dwayne. "Manumission by Last Will in Antebellum Alabama." *Auburn University Libraries.* www.lib.auburn.edu/archive/aghy/manumission/manu-txt.htm#1b (accessed 4/13/2018).

Coy, David Kent for Coles County Genealogical Society, Chapman Brothers. *Portrait and Biographical Album of Coles County, Ill.* Chicago: Chapman Brothers, 1887. Coles County Genealogical Society reprint.

Craft, David. *History of Bradford County, Pennsylvania with Illustrations and Biographical Sketches of Some of its Prominent Men and Pioneers.* Philadelphia: L. H. Everts & Co., 1878. Retyped by Bruce Preston for Tri-Counties Genealogy & History by Joyce M. Tice. http://www.joycetice.com/craft/towanddc.htm.

Cranch, Mary Smith. "Mary Smith Cranch to Abigail Adams, 24 Sep 1786" and "Mary Smith Cranch to Abigail Adams, 09 Oct 1786," *Founders Online, National Archives,* last modified 29 Jun 2017, http://founders.archives.gov/documents/Adams/04-07-02-0129 and 04-07-02-0134. [Original source: The Adams Papers, Adams Family Correspondence, vol. 7, Jan 1786-Feb 1787, ed. C. James Taylor, Margaret A.

Hogan, Celeste Walker, Anne Decker Cecere, Gregg L. Lint, Hobson Woodward, and Mary T. Claffey. Cambridge, MA: Harvard University Press, 2005, pp. 341–344 and pp. 356-359.]

Creed, Henry. *Proceedings of the Suffolk Institute of Archaeology, Vol 2.* Lowestoft, UK: Samuel Tymms, 1859.

Culpeper, Va. "Generals of the Army of the Potomac: Gouverneur K. Warren, William H. French, George G. Meade, Henry J. Hunt, Andrew A. Humphreys, George Sykes, Sep 1863, photograph." *Library of Congress Prints and Photographs Division.* Call #LC-B817- 7329. www.loc.gov/item/cwp2003000220/PP/ (accessed 11/27/2016).

Cushing, Thomas. *History of Allegheny County, Pennsylvania, Volume II, Part I* (Chicago: A. Warner & Co., 1889), 353. https://archive.org/stream/historyofalleghe1889cush#page/353/mode/2up/search/kearney.

Cutler, Nahum S. *A Cutler memorial and genealogical history.* Greenfield, MA: E. A. Hall & Co., 1889.

Cutter, Benjamin and William Cutter. *A History of the Cutter Family of New England.* Boston: David Clapp & Son, 1871.

Cutter, Benjamin and William Cutter. *History of the Town of Arlington, Massachusetts: Formerly the Second Precinct in Cambridge or District of Menotomy, afterward the town of West Cambridge, 1635-1879.* Boston: David Clapp & Son, 1880.

Cutter, William Richard. *Genealogical and Personal Memoirs Relating to the Families of Boston and Eastern Massachusetts, Volume 2.* New York: Lewis Historical Publishing Co., 1908.

Cutter, William Richard, Edward Henry Clement, Samuel Hart, Mary Kingsbury Talcott, Frederick Bostwick, Ezra Scollay Stearns. *Genealogical and Family History of the State of Connecticut, Volume 4.* New York: Lewis Historical Publishing Co., 1911.

Cutter, William Richard. *Genealogical and Family History of Northern New York.* New York: Lewis Historical Publishing Co., 1910.

Davis, Roderick. "John Allan Wyeth." *Encyclopedia of Alabama.* 05 Sep 2013; www.encyclopediaofalabama.org/article/h-3522 (accessed 10/20/2016 and 04/13/2018).

Dean, John Ward. *The New England Historical and Genealogical Register for the year 1863, Vol. XVII.* Albany, NY: J. Munsell, 1863.

Deeben, John. "Family Tree Friday: Artificers in the Revolutionary War." *The National Archives Narations.* 15 Oct 2010. https://narations.blogs.archives.gov/2010/10/15/family-tree-friday-artificers-in-the-revolutionary-war/.

Dickson, Elmer. *Kendall County, Illinois Genealogy.* http://kendallkin.org/databases/945/A,showall/131.html (accessed 12/10/2018).

Direct Data Capture, Co. *U.S., War of 1812 Service Records, 1812-1815.* Provo, UT: Ancestry.com Ops. Inc., 1999.

Dixon, Mike. *Norfolk Stained Glass, St. Martin at Palace Norwich.* http://www.norfolkstainedglass.co.uk/St_Martin_at_Palace/home.shtm (accessed 2/2/2014).

Dodd, Jordan R., comp. *Alabama Marriages, 1809-1920 (Selected Counties).* Provo, UT: Ancestry.com Operations Inc., 1999.

Dodd, Jordan, Liahona Research, comp. *Illinois Marriages, 1790-1860. Indiana Marriages, 1802-1892. Maryland Marriages, 1655-1850.* Provo, UT: Ancestry.com Operations Inc., 2004.

Dodd, Jordan, Liahona Research, comp. *Massachusetts, Marriages, 1633-1850.* Provo, UT: Ancestry.com Operations Inc., 2005.

Dodd, Jordan, Liahona Research, comp. *Michigan Marriages, 1851-1875.* Provo, UT: Ancestry.com Operations Inc., 2000.

Dodd, Jordan. *Illinois Marriages to 1850.* Provo, UT: Ancestry.com Operations Inc., 1997.

Dodd, Jordan. *Indiana Marriages to 1850.* n.p: Online publication - Provo, UT: Ancestry.com Operations Inc., 1997. Original data - Electronic transcription of marriage records held by the individual counties in Indiana. Original data: Electronic transcription of marriage records held by the individual, n.d.

Dodd, Jordan. *Kentucky Marriages, 1802-1850.* Provo, UT: Ancestry.com Operations Inc., 1997.

"Domestic Intelligence from the Lansingburgh Gazette." *Independent American* (Ballston Spa, New York), 21 Nov 1809.

Drake, Francis S. *Memorials of the Society of the Cincinnati of Massachusetts*. Cambridge, MA: John Wilson and Son, 1873.

Drake, Francis S. *Tea Leaves: Being a Collection of Letters and Documents*. Boston: A. O. Crane, 1884.

Drake, Samuel Adams. *The Border Wars of New England*. New York, Charles Scribner's Sons, 1897.

Dudley, Dean. *The Dudley Genealogies and Family Records*. Boston: Dean Dudley, Publisher, 1848.

Duffee, Mary Marshall. "Your Last Name." *The Evening Journal* (Wilmington, Delaware), 08 Feb 1928.

Dunton, John. *The Publications of the Prince Society: John Dunton's Letters from New-England*. Boston: T. R. Marvin & Son, 1867.

"Eagle Scout Service project." *Restoration of the Shaker Cemetery, Harvard, MA*. Jun 1990. https://historicharvard.files.wordpress.com/2016/03/eagle-scout-service-project-1990.pdf.

Edmund West, comp. *Family Data Collection - Births*. n.p: Online publication - Provo, UT: Ancestry.com Operations Inc., 2001., n.d.

Edmund West, comp. *Family Data Collection - Deaths*. Provo, UT: Ancestry.com Operations Inc., 2001.

Edmund West, comp. *Family Data Collection - Individual Records*. n.p: Online publication - Provo, UT: Ancestry.com Operations Inc., 2000., n.d.

Egle, William Henry. *History of the counties of Dauphin and Lebanon in the Commonwealth of Pennsylvania, biographical and genealogical*. Philadelphia: Everts & Peck, 1883.

Egle, William Henry. *Notes and queries historical, biographical, and genealogical, relating chiefly to interior Pennsylvania, Volume I*. Harrisburg, PA: Harrisburg Publishing Company, 1894.

Egle, William Henry. *Notes and queries historical, biographical, and genealogical, relating chiefly to interior Pennsylvania, Volume II*. Harrisburg, PA: Harrisburg Publishing Company, 1896.

Egle, William Henry. *Pennsylvania Genealogies*. Harrisburg, PA: L. S. Hart, printer, 1886.

Eicher, John and David Eicher. *Civil War High Commands*. Stanford, CA: Stanford University Press, 2001.

Eldredge, Donna. "Harvard Law School Wyeth Hall Dormitory." *Nor'East Architectural Antiques*. 2014. Photo courtesy of the Co-Owner of Nor'East Architectural Antiques, llc., 16 Exeter Rd., South Hampton, NH. http://www.noreast1.com/harvard1.html.

Eliot, Samuel Atkins. *All Aboard the "Natwyethum!"* Cambridge, MA: Cambridge Historical Society, 1942.

Eliot, Samuel Atkins. *A History of Cambridge, MA, 1630-1913*. Cambridge, MA: Cambridge Tribune, 1913.

Ellis, Joe. "Battle of Long Island with video from Mount Vernon on Vimeo." *George Washington's Mount Vernon*. www.mountvernon.org/digital-encyclopedia/article/battle-of-long-island/ (accessed 10/13/2016).

Ellison, Ross W. "John Wyeth – Early American Tunebook Publisher." *North Carolina Music Teacher Magazine*, Oct 1974.

Emery, Tom. "'Hundred-days' men left checkered Civil War legacy." *Dispatch-Argus QCOnline.com*. Moline, IL. 29 Sep 2012. http://www.qconline.com/life/hundred-days-men-left-checkered-civil-war-legacy/article_dcfafd2d-2517-563d-9c85-ff7c3cdcfe15.html.

Emmerton, James A. *A Record of the 23rd Regiment Mass. Vol. Infantry in the War of the Rebellion, 1861-1865: With Alphabetical Roster, Company Rolls, Portraits, Maps, Etc*. Salem, MA: Salem Press, 1886.

Epidemics in U.S. – 1633-1952. (sources: South Bend, IN Area Genealogical Society, Apr 1996, *Encyclopedia of Plague and Pestilence*, edited by George C. Kohn, published by Facts on File, Inc., 1995 and The Family Education Network.) http://www.rootsweb.ancestry.com/~wijuneau/Epidemics.htm.

Essex Institute. *Vital Records of Westford, Massachusetts to the end of the year 1849*. Salem, MA: Newcomb & Gauss, 1915.

Essex Society of Genealogists. *The Essex Genealogist, Vols. 12-13*. Lynnfield, MA: Essex Society, 1992.

Evans, Edna and Lynda Levin. "John Francis Wyeth." *Schroeder-Wyeth Newsletter*. Washington, PA: 11/4/1976.

"Fire, water, ice destroy the 1890 Census." *The Ancestry Insider*. 25 Feb 2009. www.ancestryinsider.org/2009/02/fire-water-ice-destroy-1890-census.html.

"First Church History." *First Church in Cambridge - Congregational, United Church of Christ.* http://www.firstchurchcambridge.org/about-us/first-church-history (accessed 3/25/2016).

"First Inoculation in America." *Celebrate Boston.* www.celebrateboston.com/first/inoculation.htm (accessed 6/1/2016).

Fisher, George and Co. *Biographical Directory of the Voters and Tax-payers of Kendall County.* Chicago: Geo. Fisher & Co., 1870.

Flanagan, Dan. "John Wyeth & Brother: A Family Legacy in the History of Pharmacy." *The Bulletin* (Philadelphia, PA), Summer 2014.

Flint, James, comp. *Middlesex County, Massachusetts Probate Index, 1648-1870.* Provo, UT: The Generations Network, Inc., 2000.

Flint, James, comp. Worcester County, MA, Probate Index, Vol. 1 & 2 A - Z, July 1731-1881. Provo, UT: The Generations Network, Inc., 2000.

Flint, James, editor. *Lexington, Massachusetts Cemetery Records.* Provo, UT: Ancestry.com Ops., Inc., 1999.

Flint, Timothy. "Revolutionary Reminiscence, July 1827." *The Western Monthly Review.* Cincinnati, OH: E.H. Flint, 1827. https://archive.org/details/westernmonthlyre01flin.

Forbes, Esther. *Paul Revere and the World He Lived In.* Boston: Houghton-Mifflin, 1969.

Ford, John. *The Cambridge Directory: Containing a General Directory of Citizens and a General Directory of Citizens.* Cambridge, MA: Chronicle Office, 1848.

Forrest, Earle R. "History of Monongahela City, Pa." from: *A History of Washington County, Pennsylvania.* Chicago: The S. J. Clark Publishing Company, 1926. http://history.rays-place.com/pa/wash-monongahela.htm.

Foster, F. Apthorp, Editor. *The New England Historical and Genealogical register, Volume LXIV.* Boston: The New England Historic and Genealogical Society, 1910.

"Framlingham Castle." *CastlesFortsBattles.co.uk.* www.castlesfortsbattles.co.uk/framlingham_castle.html (accessed 2/24/2016).

"Francis Houston Wyeth." *The Churchman,* Volume 108 (New York City, NY), 12 Jul 1913.

"Francis Parkman." *Brandywine River Museum: N. C. Wyeth Catalogue Raisonne'.* http://brandywine.doetech.net/Detlobjps.cfm?ParentListID=135094&ObjectID=1532125&rec_num=5 (accessed 7/26/15).

"Francis Wyeth and wife to F. A. Shaffer and M. A. Burgan." *Washington County, PA Deed book 136.* Recorded 13 Jul 1886.

Freeborn, Dennis. *From Old English to Standard English: A Course Book in Language Variation.* Ottawa, Ontario: University of Ottawa Press, 1998.

"Friends of Fresh Pond Reservation." *Cambridge, MA.* http://www.friendsoffreshpond.org/ (accessed 1/3/2018).

Fung, Abby Y. "Cambridge Residents Oppose Expanding Sheraton Parking." *The Harvard Crimson* (Cambridge, MA), 20 Oct 1995. http://www.thecrimson.com/article/1995/10/20/cambridge-residents-oppose-expanding-sheraton-parking.

"Furness, William Henry, 1802-1896." *social networks and archival context – snac.* http://socialarchive.iath.virginia.edu/ark:/99166/w6cz387g (accessed 8/25/2017).

Gamage, Daniel. Massachusetts Probate Court, Suffolk County. *Suffolk County (Massachusetts) Probate Records, Volumes 91-92.* Suffolk, MA: Probate Court, 1792-1793.

Gaskill, Malcolm. *Between Two Worlds: How the English Became Americans.* New York: Basic Books, 2014.

Gayley, Alice J. and Valerie Little-Vaughn, "Civil War Hospitals." *Pennsylvania in the Civil War.* http://www.pa-roots.com/pacw/hospitals/hospitallist.htm (accessed 11/10/2016).

Genealogical Research Library, comp. *New York City, Marriages, 1600s-1800s.* Provo, UT: Ancestry.com Operations Inc., 2005.

"George Wythe Founding Father." *Red Oak School District Social Studies*. http://www.redoakschooldistrict.com/vnews/display.v/ART/4e5673f8946c4?template=m (accessed 2/22/2016).

Gibbons, Mrs. Edwin C., Maryland Historical Society. *Vital records of the First Independent (now Unitarian) Church: Baltimore, Maryland, 1818-1921*. Westminster, MD: Heritage Books, 2007.

Gilman, Roger. *The Wyeth Background*. Cambridge, MA: Cambridge Historical Society, 1942.

Gist, Robert F. "Rosedale Cemetery records." *Email*, 04 Apr 2014 and cards picked up personally, 17 Aug 2016.

Godcharles, Frederic A. *Encyclopedia of Pennsylvania Biography, Vol. xxiii*. New York: Lewis Historical Pub. Co., 1938.

Godfrey Memorial Library, comp. *American Genealogical-Biographical Index (AGBI)*. n.p: Online publication - Provo, UT: Ancestry.com Operations Inc., 1999. Original data - Godfrey Memorial Library. American Genealogical-Biographical Index, Middletown, CT.

Goff, John V. *Salem's Witch House: A Touchstone to Antiquity*. Charleston, SC: History Press, 2009.

Gordon, Edward W. "46 North Main Street, Dr. Tapley Wyeth house." *Sherbornma.org*. Jul 1981. https://www.sherbornma.org/sites/sherbornma/files/uploads/northmain_046.pdf.

Gough, Henry and James Parker. *A Glossary of Terms Used in Heraldry*. Oxford, England: James Parker and Company, 1894. www.heraldsnet.org/saitou/parker/index.htm. code by Karl Wilcox, Jim Trigg and "Saitou".

"Grantees (Buyers) Index." Monroe County, Indiana, History PDF, page 691. monroehistory.org/wp-content/uploads/2015/11/Combined_Deed_Book_A_to_Z_Index_for_Publication.pdf.

Gray, Jr., Horace. *Reports of Cases Argued and Determined in the Supreme Judicial Court of Massachusetts, Volume 9*. Boston: Little, Brown and Company, 1864.

Gray, Roland. "The William Gray House in Cambridge." *Cambridge Historical Society Publications XIV, Proceedings for the Year 1919*. Cambridge, MA: Cambridge Historical Society, 1926.

"Green-Wood Cemetery." *Burial Search*. https://www.green-wood.com/ (accessed 2014 and 2018).

Greene, David L. "Salem Witches II: George Jacobs." *The American Genealogist*. New Haven, CT: D. L. Jacobus, Apr 1982. (Online database. AmericanAncestors.org. NEHGS).

Greer, George Cabel. *Early Virginia Immigrants 1623-1666*. Richmond, VA: W. C. Hill Printing Co., 1912.

Gresham, John. *Historical and Biographical Record of Douglas County, Illinois*. Logansport, IN: Wilson, Humphreys & Co., 1900.

Grimwade, M. E. *Index of the Probate Records of the Court of the Archdeacon of Suffolk, 1444-1700*. Keele, Staffordshire, UK: The British Record Society, 1980.

Griswold, Bert Joseph and Mrs. Samuel R. Taylor. *The Pictorial History of Fort Wayne, Indiana*. Chicago: Robert O. Law Co., 1917.

Groce, George C., David H. Wallace, New York Historical Society. *The New-York Historical Society's dictionary of artists in America: 1564-1860*. New Haven, CT: Yale Univ. Press, 1975.

Grousset, Agnes McClellan. *Horns A'Plenty*. Baltimore, MD: Gateway Press, Inc., 1980.

Guilbault, Ceal and Pam Richardson. "Gravestone Inscriptions/Wendell Cemeteries." *Wendell Massachusetts*. www.wendellmass.us/index.php/about-wendell/genealogy-reference (accessed 3/6/2018).

Guild, Mary Stiles (Paul). *The Stiles Family in America: Genealogies of the Massachusetts Family*. Albany, NY: Joel Munsell's Sons, 1892.

Hafner, Arthur Wayne, ed. *Directory of Deceased American Physicians, 1804-1929*. Chicago: American Medical Association, 1993.

Hail, Christopher. *Cambridge Buildings and Architects*. https://wayback.archive-it.org/5488/20170330145608/http://hul.harvard.edu/lib/archives/refshelf/cba/ (accessed 1/31/2016).

Hamilton County Genealogical Society First Families of Hamilton County. *Ohio Records (Mss 1093), Application 131 Jerry D. Harrison*. Series 1: Applications, Box 10: Applications, Folder 14, received 8/4/17.

Hanson, Robert. *Vital Statistics from Galena Newspapers, July 22, 1828 - November 19, 1850.* jodaviess.illinoisgenweb.org/vitals/VS1a.htm (accessed 7/25/17).

Harman, Helen L., Herman Stephan, Vi P. Limric, *Silver Spring Presbyterian Church Marriages, 1814-30*, Silver Spring Twp., Cumberland County, Pennsylvania, 1959. pagenweb.org/~cumberland/silspma.htm.

Harms, Patricia King. *Family Tree.* Received by author of this book in 2015.

Harper, R. J., John Caley and W. Minchin. *Ducatus Lancastriae Calendar to Pleadings, Depositions, etc.* London: Record Commission, 1823-1834.

Harris & Ewing, Inc. photographer. "White House President's Office" [between 1905 and 1945] photograph. *Library of Congress Prints and Photographs Division.* Harris & Ewing LC-H25- 3880-BM [P&P], LC-DIG-hec-14832. www.loc.gov/pictures/item/hec2009001530/ (accessed 5/30/2016).

Harvard University Archives. *HUP Collection.* HUP Wyeth, Alice (1); HUP Wyeth, Henry Dunton (1); HUP Wyeth, Leonard Jarvis (1); HUP Wyeth, Nathaniel J. (1); HUP Wyeth, Stuart (1).

Harvard University Archives. *Wyeth Hall Photographs.* Wyeth Hall: UAV 605 Box 88 (GS 44) and UAV 605 Box 88 (GS 45).

Harvard University Maps Archive. *First Parish Cambridge Pew Diagram.* 1865. G3764.c2:2F5 1865. P6.

Hatcher, Patricia Law. *Abstract of Graves of Revolutionary Patriots* [database on-line]. Provo, UT: Ancestry.com Operations Inc., 1999.

Hatcher, Patricia Law. *Graves of Revolutionary Patriots, Vol. 4, S – Z.* Dallas, TX: Pioneer Heritage Press, 1988.

Hay, Brenda Smelser. "Belle Isle Civil War Prison." *CensusDiggins.com.* 2002-2008. http://www.censusdiggins.com/prison_bellisle.html.

Hayden, Horace E., editor for the Wyoming Historical and Geological Society. *Proceedings and Collections, Volumes 7-8.* Wilkes-Barre, PA: The E. B. Yordy Co., 1902.

Hazzard, Chill W. *Centennial anniversary of the founding of Monongahela City, Pa.: celebrated August. 27th, 1892.* Monongahela City, PA: Chill W. Hazzard Publisher, 1895.

Heldler, David and Jeanne "War of 1812, United Kingdom-United States History." *Encyclopaedia Britannica*, 2016. https://www.britannica.com/event/War-of-1812.

Hemphill, W. Edwin. *Examinations of George Wythe Swinney for Forgery and Murder: A Documentary Essay.* The William and Mary Quarterly, Vol. XII, No. 4. Williamsburg, VA: Omohundro Institute of Early American History and Culture, Oct., 1955.

Henkel, Steve. "Murder in the Family." *The American Genealogist, Vol. 78.* New Haven, CT: D. L. Jacobus, Apr 2003.

Heritage Consulting. *Millennium File.* n.p: Online publication - Provo, UT: Ancestry.com Operations Inc., 2003. Original data - Heritage Consulting. The Millennium File. Salt Lake City, UT: Heritage Consulting, n.d.

Helwagen, Martha. *Ohio Records and Pioneer Families, Vol. 9.* Mansfield, OH: Ohio Genealogical Society, 1968.

Heverly, Clement F. *History of the Towandas 1776-1886.* Towanda, PA: Reporter-Journal Printing Co., 1886.

Heverly, Clement F. *Pioneer and Patriot Families of Bradford County, Pennsylvania, 1770-1800, Volume I.* Towanda, Pa: Bradford Star Print, 1913.

Heverly, Clement F. *Pioneer and Patriot Families of Bradford County, Pennsylvania, 1800-1825, Volume II.* Towanda, Pa: Bradford Star Print, 1915.

H. H. Hardesty & Co. *History of Gallia County.* Reprinted from the 1882 history. Gallipolis, OH: St. Peter's Episcopal Church, 1976.

Higginson, Francis John. *Remarks on Slavery and Emancipation.* Boston: Hilliard, Gray and Co., 1834.

Highsmith, Carol M. "Statue of John Allan Wyeth on the grounds of the Alabama State Capitol, photograph." From the George F. Landegger Collection of Alabama Photographs in America. *Library of Congress Prints and Photographs Division.* Published 22 Feb 2010. https://lccn.loc.gov/2010637478.

Hill, Frances. *Delusion of Satan.* New York: Da Capo Press, 2002.

Hill, John Boynton. *History of the Town of Mason, N.H.* Boston, MA: Lucius A. Elliot & Co., 1858.

Historical Data Systems, comp. *American Civil War Soldiers*. n.p: Online publication - Provo, UT: Ancestry.com Operations Inc., 1999. Original data - Data compiled by Historical Data Systems of Kingston, Copyright 1997-2000, Historical Data Systems, Inc., PO Box 35, Duxbury, MA, Orig, n.d.

Historical Data Systems, comp. *U.S., Civil War Soldier and Profiles, 1861-1865*. n.p: Online publication - Provo, UT: Ancestry.com Operations Inc., 2009. Original data compiled by Historical Data Systems of Kingston, MA, PO Box 35, Duxbury, MA 02331. Copyright 1997-2009, Orig, n.d.

Historical Data Systems, comp. *U.S., American Civil War Regiments, 1861-1866* [database on-line]. Provo, UT: Ancestry.com Operations Inc., 1999.

"Historical Sketch of Columbiana County." *Columbiana County, Lisbon, Ohio.* www.columbianacounty.org/history.htm (accessed 11 Sep 2018).

"Historical Sketch of the city of Monongahela." *City of Monongahela - Pa.gov.* http://www.cityofmonongahela-pa.gov/Historical_Sketch.html (accessed 1/10/2018).

"Hodgeman County History Collection." *Kansas Historical Society.* http://www.kshs.org/archives/40696 (accessed 11/16/2017).

Holmes, J. Albert. "About Menotomy River." *Somerville Journal*, 28 Jan 1910.

Homans, B. Jr., editor. *The Merchants' and Bankers' Almanac & Register*. New York: I. S. Homans, 1875.

Hopkins, Timothy. *The Kelloggs in the Old World and the New, Vol. 1*. San Francisco: Sunset Press, 1903.

Howe, Lois Lilley. *The History of Garden Street*. Cambridge, MA: Cambridge Historical Society, 1953.

Hudson, Charles. *History of the Town of Lexington, Massachusetts, Vol. II*. Cambridge, MA: Riverside Press, 1913.

Hunt, John Elliott; Richard J. Wright. *The John Hunt Memoirs, Early Years of the Maumee Basin*. Maumee, OH: Maumee Valley Historical Society, 1978?

Hughes, Thomas P. *American Ancestry of Americans whose Ancestors Settled in the United States Previous to the Declaration of Independence, Vol. IX*. Albany, NY: Joel Munsell's Sons, 1894.

"Humphrey Wyeth, 1600-1635." Ancestry.com. http://www.ancestry.com/genealogy/records/humphrey-wyeth_20458468 (accessed 2/24/2016).

Hurd, Duane Hamilton. *History of Essex County, Massachusetts, Vol. II*. Philadelphia: JW Lewis & Co., 1888.

Hurd, Duane Hamilton. *History of Middlesex County, Massachusetts*. Philadelphia: JW Lewis & Co., 1890.

Hutchinson, Thomas. *The History of the Province of Massachusets-Bay, from the Charter of King William and Queen Mary, in 1691, until the year 1750*. Boston: Thomas & John Fleet, 1767.

Hutton, Mary Louise Marshall and National Society Colonial Dames XVII Century. *Seventeenth Century Colonial Ancestors of Members of the National Society Colonial Dames XVII Century, 1915-1975*. Madison, WI: Edwards Brothers, 1976.

"Illinois Civil War Muster and Descriptive Rolls Detail Report, Illinois State Archives." *Office of the Illinois Secretary of State.* https://www.ilsos.gov/isaveterans/civilmustersrch.jsp (accessed 2016-2018).

Illinois Military and Naval Dept; Reece, Jasper N; Elliott, Isaac Hughes. *Report of the adjutant general of the state of Illinois, Volume 7*. Springfield, IL: Phillips Bros., 1900.

"Indiana Digital Archives." *Indiana Archives and Records Administration.* https://secure.in.gov/apps/iara/search/ (accessed 2016-2018).

"Items of Interest from Various Localities." *American Gas Light Journal*, Vol. 56. New York City: A. M. Callender & Co. Publishers, 30 May 1892.

"Interments Listed by Removal." *The New York City Marble Cemetery*, accessed 2018. www.nycmc.org/intermentremovals.html.

Jackson, Ronald V., Accelerated Indexing Systems, comp. *New Hampshire Census, 1790-1890*. Provo, UT: Ancestry.com Operations Inc., 1999.

"James Wilson Grimes." *National Governors Association.* 2015. http://www.nga.org/cms/home/governors/past-governors-bios/page_iowa/col2-content/main-content-list/title_grimes_james.default.html.

James, Sydney V. *John Clarke and his Legacies*. University Park, PA: Pennsylvania State University Press, 1999.

"The John Hunt Morgan Heritage Trail." *HMdb.org the Historical Marker Database* (accessed 10 Sep 2018).

"John Wyeth." *Center for Church Music Songs and Hymns.* http://www.songsandhymns.org/people/detail/john-wyeth (accessed 3/25/2016).

"John Wyeth." *NNDB Tracking the entire world.* http://www.nndb.com/people/515/000206894/ (accessed 11/2/8/2016).

Johnson, Benjamin. "Boston Burning: The Fire of 1787." *Massachusetts Historical Society*, Dec 2006. http://www.masshist.org/object-of-the-month/objects/boston-burning-the-fire-of-1787-2006-12-01.

Johnson, Sarah Benson Wyeth. "Divorce Petition." *File #211*, Scott County, Iowa District Court records.

Jordan Dodd and Liahona Research, comp. *Illinois, Marriages, 1851-1900.* n.p: Online publication - Provo, UT: Ancestry.com Ops. Inc., 2005. Original data - Index compiled from county marriage records on microfilm at the Family History Library in Salt Lake City, Utah by Jordan Dodd of Liahona Research (P.O. Box 740, n.d.)

Jordan Dodd, Liahona Research. *Ohio, Marriages, 1803-1900.* Provo, UT: Ancestry.com Operations Inc., 2001.

Kelker, Luther Reily. *History of Dauphin County.* New York: The Lewis Publishing Co., 1907.

Kentucky State Historical Society. *Register of Kentucky State Historical Society.* Frankfort, KY: Kentucky State Historical Society, 1913.

Kett, H. F. and Company. *The History of Jo Daviess County, Illinois.* Chicago: H. F. Kett & Co., 1878.

"King Philip's War." *History of the USA.* http://www.usahistory.info/NewEngland/King-Philips-War.html (accessed 6/6/2016).

King, Robert E. and Doris Ruth Van Dusen Jones. *History of the King family in Flanders & America, 1300's-1980.* Place not given: R.E. King, 1980.

King, Clennon L. "Student directories reveal Michelle Obama's Cambridge address." *Somerville Times* (Somerville, MA), 19 May 2013. http://www.thesomervilletimes.com/archives/38316.

Knapp, Horace S. *History of the Maumee Valley: Commencing with Its Occupation by the French in 1680.* Toledo, OH: Glade Mammoth Printing and Publishing House, 1872.

Knoles, Georgeann Malowney. "George T. Work." *Irishgenealogy.com.* www.irishgenealogy.com/us/pa/default.htm (accessed 10/24/2016).

Konkle, Burton Alva. *The Life of Chief Justice Ellis Lewis, 1798-1871.* Philadelphia: Campion & Co., 1907.

Krohnke, Duane W. "dwkcommentaries." *The American Revolutionary War's Campaign for New York and New Jersey, Mar 1776-Jan 1777.* https://dwkcommentaries.com/2012/08/13/the-american-revolutionary-wars-campaign-for-new-york-and-new-jersey-march-1776-january-1777/ (accessed 10/13/2016).

"Kurt Russell Biography." *IMDb.* http://www.imdb.com/name/nm0000621/bio?ref_=nm_ov_bio_sm (accessed 3/25/2016).

Lancaster, Southworth. "Fire in Cambridge read 24 Apr 1956 " *The Proceedings of the Cambridge Historical Society, Volume 36*, 1955-1956.

"Langley Research Center." *NASA Cultural Resources.* https://crgis.ndc.nasa.gov/historic/Langley_Research_Center (accessed 2/19/2016).

Lansaw, Simona. *Woodlawn Cemetery, Terre Haute, Vigo County, Indiana.* Owensboro, KY: Cook-McDowell Publications, 1980.

Lathrop, John. *Massachusetts Reports: Cases Argued and Determined in the Supreme Judicial Court of Massachusetts, Jan-Jun 1875.* Boston: Houghton, Mifflin and Co., 1875.

Lawyer, William S. *Binghamton: its settlement, growth, and development, and the factors in its history, 1800-1900.* Boston: Century Memorial Publishing Co., 1900.

Le Strange, Hamon. *Norfolk Official Lists from the Earliest Period to the Present Day.* Norwich, UK: Agas H. Goose, 1890.

Legere, Lyn, comp. *Massachusetts: Middlesex County, Cambridge, Mt. Auburn Cemetery.* n.p: Online publication - Provo, UT: Ancestry.com Operations Inc., 2004. Original data - Information extracted from the cemetery headstones at Mt. Auburn Cemetery, Middlesex County, Massachusetts by Lyn Legere.

Leggett, Conaway & Co. *The History of Wyandot County, Ohio containing a history of the county; its townships, towns, churches, schools, etc.* Chicago: Leggett, Conaway & Co., 1884.

"Lewis C. Hunt, Col. 67th—Ohio." United States, [Between 1860 and 1870] Photograph. *Library of Congress Prints and Photographs Division.* https://www.loc.gov/item/cwp2003001394/PP/(accessed 5/19/2018).

Licking County Genealogical Society. *Licking County, Ohio, 1982: a collection of historical sketches and family histories.* Defiance, OH: Hubbard Company, 1982.

Locke, John Goodwin. *Book of the Lockes.* Boston and Cambridge, MA: James Munroe and Company, 1853.

Long, William J. *America, A History of Our Country.* Boston: Ginn & Co., 1923. N. C. Wyeth illustration painted circa 1919 from http://www.sothebys.com/en/auctions/ecatalogue/2013/american-art-n09048/lot.14.html (accessed 5/14/2018).

Longacre, Edward G. *The Man Behind the Guns: A Biography of General Henry Jackson Hunt, Chief of Artillery, Army of the Potomac.* Cranbury, NJ: A. S. Barnes and Co., 1977.

Lowens, Irving. "Shape Notes, New England Music, and White Spirituals." *Etude Magazine,* January 1957.

Lyte, H.C. Maxwell. *Calendar of the Patent rolls preserved in the Public record office.* London: H.M. Stationery Office by Eyre and Spottiswoode, 1891-1916.

MacLean, Maggie. "Elizabeth Peabody Founder of the First Public Kindergarten." *Civil War Women,* 16 Jul 2012. www.civilwarwomenblog.com/elizabeth-peabody/.

Maine Historical Society. *Documentary History of the State of Maine, Volume 20.* Portland, ME: Lefavor-Tower Company, 1914.

Manning, William H. *The Genealogical and Biographical History of the Manning Families of New England and descendants.* Salem, MA: Salem Press Company, 1902.

Marshall, Megan. *The Peabody Sisters.* Boston and New York: Houghton Mifflin Company, 2005.

Marston, James "Do you know Suffolk's county town?" *Ipswich Star* (Ipswich, UK), 29 Jan 2007. http://www.ipswichstar.co.uk/news/do_you_know_suffolk_s_county_town_1_113090.

"Mary Palmer Tyler." *Vermont Historical Society.* http://vermonthistory.org/research/vermont-women-s-history/database/tyler-mary (accessed 11/16/2017).

Maryland State Archives, "Session Laws, 1846, Vol. 611, Page 256," *Archives of Maryland Online,* 31 Oct 2014.

Massachusetts Court System. *The Supreme Judicial Court.* 2016. http://www.mass.gov/courts/court-info/sjc/about.

Massachusetts Daughters of the American Revolution, Hannah Winthrop Chapter, Cambridge. *An Historic Guide to Cambridge.* Cambridge, MA: N. S. D. A. R., 1907.

"Massachusetts Regiment of Artillery, 1775-1776 (Knox's Artillery)." *Uniforms of the American Revolution.* http://www.srcalifornia.com/uniforms/p13.htm (accessed 10/14/2016).

Massachusetts Vital Records Project (Transcriber). *Town of Weston Records.* Boston: McIndoe Brothers, 1901.

Mather, Cotton. *Magnalia Christi Americana.* Hartford, CT: Silas Andrus & Son, 1858.

Mathews, Pat. "Re: Wyeth Genealogy." 03/16/2007 webmail.peoplepc.com email.

"Matt Franco." *Baseball-Reference.com.* http://www.baseball-reference.com/bullpen/Matt_Franco (accessed 3/25/2016).

Matteson, Tompkins Harrison. "The Trial of George Jacobs 05 Aug 1692." 1855. *Rulers and Leaders Free Area,* http://rulersandleaders.com/historic_paintings/hp_trial_georgejacobs.htm.

May, John Joseph. *Danforth Genealogy.* Boston: Charles H. Pope, 1902.

Maycock, Susan E., Charles M. Sullivan. *Building Old Cambridge.* Cambridge, MA: MIT Press, 2016.

McGill, John. *The Beverley family of Virginia; descendants of Major Robert Beverley, 1641-1687, and allied families.* Columbia, SC: R.L. Bryan Co., 1956.

Medford Historical Society. *The Medford Historical Register, Volume 6.* Medford, MA: J. C. Miller, Jr. 1903.

"Meet Mr. Wyeth." *American Professional Pharmacist.* Manhasset, NY: April 1958.

"Metcalf, Edwin T." www.scattercreek.com/~normw/METCALF,EDWIN%20T,.pdf (accessed 10/16/2018).

Michaelis, David. *N. C. Wyeth: A Biography.* New York: Alfred A. Knopf, 1998.

"Midnight Ride of Paul Revere." *Paul Revere.* 27 Apr 2015. http://paulrevere.us/midnight-ride-of-paul-revere.

Miller, Arthur. *The Crucible a Play in Four Acts.* New York: Viking Press, 1953.

Moore, John Bassett. *A Treatise on Extradition and Interstate Rendition.* Boston: The Boston Book Co., 1891.

Moore, Margaret B. *The Salem World of Nathaniel Hawthorne.* Columbia, MO: University of Missouri Press, 1998.

Morgan, Philip D. "Interracial Sex in the Chesapeake." in *Sally Hemings and Thomas Jefferson: History, Memory and Civic Culture,* ed. J.E. Lewis and P.S. Onuf. Charlottesville, VA: University Press of Virginia, 1999.

Moriarity, Jr., G. Andrews. "Genealogical Research in England." *New England Historical and Genealogical Register, Volume LXXV.* Boston: The New England Historic and Genealogical Society, 1921.

Mortlock, D. P. *The Guide to Suffolk Churches.* Cambridge, UK: Lutterworth Press, 2009.

Morton, Arabella. *Descendants of John Gamage of Ipswich, Mass.* Worcester, MA: Charles R. Stobbs, 1906.

Moynihan, Daniel Patrick. "The Negro Family: The Case for National Action." *United States Department of Labor, Office of the Assistant Secretary for Administration and Management.* Mar 1965.

Murry, Charles. "Post-Civil War Era Grave Recorded in Cheshire Township." *Gallia County Glade* (Spring 1993).

Musgrave, Zelotes A. *Diary of Zelotes A. Musgrave.* 1862-1865. Copied by William Frank Musgrave and Daniel L. Musgrave. 1914 and 1993. http://ohio45.homestead.com/musgrave.html.

Muskett, Joseph James, Editor. *Suffolk Manorial Families, Vol. II.* Exeter, UK: Wm. Pollard & Co., Ltd., 1908.

Myers, Thomas M. *The Norris Family of Maryland.* New York: William M. Clemens, 1916.

"Natalie Wyeth Earnest – White House Press Secretary Josh Earnest's wife." *Daily Entertainment News.* http://dailyentertainmentnews.com/breaking-news/natalie-wyeth-earnest-white-house-press-secretary-josh-earnests-wife/ (accessed 3/25/2016).

"Nathaniel J. and Ann C. Wyeth House." *Landmarks Preservation Commission,* 15 May 2007. http://s-media.nyc.gov/agencies/lpc/lp/2253.pdf.

National Biographical Publishing Co. *Biographical Cyclopedia of Representative Men of Maryland.* Baltimore: National Biographical Publishing Co., 1870.

National Cemetery Administration. *U.S. Veterans Gravesites, ca.1775-2006.* n.p: Online publication - Provo, UT: Ancestry.com Operations Inc., 2006. Original data - National Cemetery Administration. Nationwide Gravesite Locator. Original data: National Cemetery Administration. Nationwide Gravesite Locator, n.d.

National Council of the Congregational Churches of the United States, Publishing Committee. *The Congregational Year-book, Volume 4.* Boston: Congregational Publishing Society, 1882.

National Park Service, U. S. Dept. of the Interior. *Minute Man National Historical Park brochure and Parker's Revenge lecture* given by Rick Lawson, Park Ranger.

National Society of Daughters of Founders and Patriots of America. *Founders and Patriots of America Index.* Baltimore, MD: Genealogical Publications, 1975.

NavSource Online. *Emerald (SP 177).* http://www.navsource.org/archives/12/170177.htm (accessed 2/13/2019).

Nelson, Charles Alexander. *Waltham, Past and Present.* Cambridge, MA: Moses King, 1882.

"New York (Manhattan) Wards: Population & Density: 1800-2910." *Demographia.com.* http://www.demographia.com/nyward1800.jpg (accessed 9/6/2017).

Newell, Eliphalet. *Abstract of pay for Captain Newell's Company in Henry Knox's Regiment.* Jan 1776. Gilder Lehrman Collection #: GLC02437.09497.

Newspaper births, marriages, deaths, and other items (see endnotes for details) from 19th Century U.S. Newspapers, fultonhistory.com, galegroup.com, genealogybank.com, newspaperarchive.com, newspapers.com, nyshistoricnewspapers.org and more include: *American and Commercial Daily Advertiser* (Baltimore, MD); *Anti-slavery Bugle* (Salem, OH); *Argus* (New York City); *Argus-Leader* (Sioux Falls, Minnehaha, SD); *Asbury Park Press* (Asbury Park, NJ); *The Ashland Union* (Ashland, OH); *The Aurora Beacon-News* (Aurora, IL); *The Boston Daily Atlas* (Boston, MA); *The Baltimore Sun* (Baltimore); *Baton-Rouge Gazette* (Baton Rouge, LA); *The Black Hills Daily Times* (Deadwood, SD); *Boston Commercial Gazette* (Boston,

MA); *Boston Courier* (Boston); *Boston Daily Advertiser* (Boston); *Boston Gazette* (Boston, MA); *Boston Globe* (Boston); *Boston Herald* (Boston); *Boston Patriot and Daily Chronicle* (Boston, MA); *Boston Post* (Boston, MA); *Boston Recorder* (Boston); *Branding Iron* (University of Wyoming, Laramie, WY); *The Brooklyn Daily Eagle* (Brooklyn, NY); *Brooklyn Life* (Brooklyn, NY); *Cambridge Chronicle* (Cambridge, MA); *Cambridge Press* (Cambridge, MA); *Cambridge Tribune* (Cambridge, MA); *The Carthage Republican* (Carthage, NY); *Charleston Daily Courier* (Charleston, IL); *Chicago Tribune* (Chicago, IL); *Chillicothe Gazette* (Chillicothe, OH); *Chronicle Express* (New York City); *Circleville Herald* (Circleville, OH); *Cleveland Leader* (Cleveland, OH); *Colorado Transcript* (Golden, CO); *Columbian Centinel* (Boston); *Commercial Advertiser* (New York City); *The Conneautville Courier* (Conneautville, PA); *Constitutional Telegraph* (Boston); *Coshocton Daily Age* (Coshocton, OH); *Courier-Journal* (Louisville, KY); *Daily Advertiser* (New York, NY); *Daily Arkansas Gazette* (Little Rock, AR); *Daily Atlas* (Boston); *The Daily Cincinnati Gazette* (Cincinnati, OH); *Daily Cincinnati Republican* (Cincinnati, OH); *The Daily Cleveland Herald* (Cleveland, OH); *The Daily Republican* (Monongahela, PA); *Daily Inter Ocean* (Chicago, IL); *Daily Wabash Express* (Terre Haute, IN); *Decatur Daily Review* (Decatur, IL); *The Decatur Herald* (Decatur, IL); *The Democrat* (Boston); *Denver Post* (Denver, CO); *Denver Republican* (Denver, CO); *Detroit Free Press* (Detroit, MI); *Deutsche Correspondent* (Baltimore, MD); *Dixon Evening Telegraph* (Dixon, IL); *The Elk County Advocate* (Ridgway, PA); *Emancipator and Republican* (Boston, MA); *Emancipator and Weekly Chronicle* (London, England); *The Evening News* (Harrisburg, PA); *Evening Post* (New York City); *Evening Star* (Washington, D.C.); *Evening Telegraph* (Philadelphia, PA); *Evening World* (New York, NY); *Fitchburg Sentinel* (Fitchburg, MA); *The Florida Times-Union* (Jacksonville, FL); *Gallipolis Bulletin* (Gallipolis, OH); *Gallipolis Daily Tribune* (Gallipolis, OH); *Gallipolis Journal* (Gallipolis, OH); *The Gleaner* (Wilkes-Barre, PA); *Granville Times* (Granville, OH); *Greenleaf's New York Journal* (New York City); *The Guntersville Democrat* (Guntersville, AL); *Harrisburg Daily Independent* (Harrisburg, PA); *The Harrisburg Patriot* (Harrisburg); *Harrisburg Telegraph* (Harrisburg, PA); *Haverhill Gazette* (Haverhill, MA); *The Herald and Torch Light* (Hagerstown, MD); *Herald Democrat* (Leadville, CO); *Herald of Freedom* (Boston, MA); *Herald-Recorder* (Potsdam, NY); *Hudson Gazette* (Hudson, NY); *Independent Chronicle* (Boston); *The Indianapolis News* (Indianapolis, IN); *The Indianapolis Star* (Indianapolis, IN); *Jefferson County Journal* (Adams, NY); *The Journal and Republican* (Lowville, NY); *Journal Gazette* (Mattoon, IL); *The Liberator* (Boston, MA); *Little Falls Herald* (Little Falls, NJ); *Logansport Daily Reporter* (Logansport, IN); *The Long-Island Star* (Brooklyn, NY); *The Los Angeles Times* (Los Angeles, CA); *Lowell Daily Citizen and News* (Lowell, MA); *The Marshall Messenger* (Marshall, TX); *Maryland Journal* (Baltimore, MD); *Marysville Tribune* (Marysville, OH); *Mattoon Gazette* (Mattoon, IL); *Meigs County telegraph* (Pomeroy, Ohio); *Mercantile Advertiser* (New York, NY); *Monongahela Valley Republican* (Monongahela, PA); *The Monmouth Inquirer* (Freehold, New Jersey); *The Morning Journal-Courier* (New Haven, CT); *Morning Oregonian* (Portland, OR); *Mount Carmel Item* (Mount Carmel, PA); *National Advocate* (New York City); *National Gazette* (Philadelphia, PA); *National Republican* (Washington, D.C.); *New Castle Herald* (New Castle, PA); *New Hampshire Patriot and State Gazette* (Concord, New Hampshire); *New York Daily Herald* (New York City); *New York Daily Tribune* (New York City); *New-York Gazette* (New York City); *New York Herald* (New York City); *The New York Times* (New York City); *New York Tribune* (New York City); *Newark Advocate* (Newark, OH); *Oakland Tribune* (Oakland, CA); *The Oshkosh Northwestern* (Oshkosh, WI); *Oswego Palladium-Times* (Oswego, NY); *The Pantagraph* (Bloomington, IL); *Page County Democrat* (Clarinda, IA); *Patriot* (Harrisburg, PA); *The Philadelphia Inquirer* (Philadelphia, PA); *Pittsburgh Daily Post* (Pittsburgh, PA); *The Pittsburgh Gazette* (Pittsburgh, PA); *The Pittsburgh Press* (Pittsburgh, PA); *Plain Dealer* (Cleveland, OH); *Pomeroy Weekly Telegraph* (Pomeroy, OH); *Repertory* (Boston); *The Reporter* (Brattleboro, VT); *The Republican Progress* (Bloomington, IN); *Richwood Gazette* (Richwood, OH); *Rocky Mountain News* (Denver, CO); *Salt Lake Tribune* (Salt Lake City, UT); *San Francisco Chronicle* (San Francisco, CA); *Santa Cruz Evening News* (Santa Cruz, CA); *Scottsboro Citizen* (Scottsboro, AL); *St. Louis Globe-Democrat* (St. Louis, MO); *The Star-Democrat* (Easton, MD); *Star Tribune* (Minneapolis, MN); *Stoneham Independent* (Stoneham, MA); *Sunday Star* (Washington D.C.); *Tampa Bay Times* (St. Petersburg, FL); *The Tampa Tribune* (Tampa, FL); *Terre Haute Saturday Evening Mail* (Terre Haute, IN); *The Terre Haute Star* (Terre Haute, IN); *Towanda Daily Review* (Towanda, PA); *The Union County Journal* (Marysville, OH); *Valley Spirit* (Chambersburg, PA); *Washington Review and Examiner* (Washington, PA); *Watertown Daily Times* (Watertown, NY); *The Watertown Herald* (Watertown, NY); *Wyandotte Echo* (Wyandotte, KS); *The Wyandotte Herald* (Kansas City, KS).

Newsweek Staff. "Transition: Andrew Wyeth, 91, Artist." *Newsweek.* 16 Jan 2009. http://www.newsweek.com/transition-andrew-wyeth-91-artist-78451.

Nicholas, Thomas. *Annals and antiquities of the counties and county families of Wales, Volume 2.* London: Longmans, Green, Read, and Co., 1872.

NNY Genealogy. *Stories in Stone.* www.nnygenealogy.com (accessed 2018).

Oakes, Rensselaer Allston. *Genealogical and Family History of the County of Jefferson, New York, Volume 2.* New York: Higginson Book Company, 1905.

Obama, Barack. "President Barack Obama's State of the Union Address." *The White House, Office of the Press Secretary.* 28 Jan 2014. https://obamawhitehouse.archives.gov/the-press-office/2014/01/28/president-barack-obamas-state-union-address.

O'Laughlin, Michael C. *Missouri Irish: The Original History of the Irish in Missouri.* Kansas City, MO: Irish Genealogical Foundation, 2007.

Old Residents' Historical Association. *Contributions of the Old Residents' Historical Association, Lowell, Mass., Volume 4.* Lowell, MA: Morning Mail Print, 1891.

Olden, J. G. *Historical Sketches and Early Reminiscences of Hamilton County, Ohio.* Cincinnati: H. Watkin, 1882.

Olne, Sandra Sutphin. *Passengers on the "Lion" From England to Boston, 1632, and five generations of their descendants.* Westminster, MD: Heritage Books, 2008.

Omanson, B.J. "The War Poetry of John Allan Wyeth." *blogspot.com,* http://johnallanwyeth.blogspot.com/p/about-john-allan-wyeth.html (accessed 10/30/2017).

"On these days in the American Restoration Heritage: Mar 29 – Apr 4." *Preachersmith a minister's musings in pics and text.* https://preachersmith.com/tag/peyton-c-wyeth/ (accessed 1/13/2018).

Otts, Angela C. "Guntersville Museum & Cultural Center." *Encyclopedia of Alabama.* 23 May 2012; www.encyclopediaofalabama.org/article//h-3255 (accessed 04/14/2018).

"Our Historic Roots." *The First Parish in Cambridge, Unitarian Universalist.* http://firstparishcambridge.org/welcome/our-historic-roots (accessed 3/25/2016).

"Our History: Education Gets Physical." *BU College of Health & Rehabilitation Sciences: Sargent College.* http://www.bu.edu/sargent/about-us/our-history/ (accessed 7/2/16).

Page, Augustine and John Kirby. *A Supplement to the Suffolk Traveller, or, Topographical and Genealogical Collections: Concerning that County.* Ipswich, England: Joshua Page, 1844.

Paige, Lucius R. *History of Cambridge, Massachusetts, 1630-1877: with a genealogical register.* Boston: H.O. Houghton, 1877.

Paige, Lucius R. and Mary Isabella Gozzaldi. *History of Cambridge, Massachusetts, 1630-1877: with a genealogical register–Supplement and Index.* Cambridge, MA: The Cambridge Historical Society, 1930.

Paine, Thomas. *The American Crisis.* London: R. Carlile, 1819.

Palmer, Joseph. *Necrology of Alumni of Harvard College, 1851-52 to 1862-6.* Boston: John Wilson & Son, 1864.

Peabody, Selim H. *Peabody (Paybody, Pabody, Pabodie) Genealogy.* Boston, MA: Charles H. Pope, 1909.

Pearson, Gardner W. *Records of the Massachusetts Volunteer Militia.* Baltimore, MD: Clearfield Company, 1993 / 1913. http://interactive.ancestry.com/1873/32501_1220702381_0128-00031.

Pearson, Gardner W. *Records of the Massachusetts Volunteer Militia called out by the Governor of Massachusetts.* Boston: Wright & Potter Printing, 1913.

Pennsylvania Historical Survey of the Works Project Administration. *Port of Philadelphia, Maritime Records, Alphabetical List of Masters and Crews: 1798-1880.* Philadelphia: Works Project Administration, 1937.

"Pension application files based upon service in the Civil War and Spanish-American War." *Case Files of Approved Pension Applications of Veterans Who Served in the Army and Navy Mainly in the Civil War, 1861-1865.* Civil War and Later Pension Files; Records of the Department of Veterans Affairs, Record Group 15; National Archives Building, Washington, D.C.

"People & Events: John White Webster (1793-1850)." *Murder at Harvard.* http://www.pbs.org/wgbh/amex/murder/peopleevents/p_webster.html (accessed 6/26/2016).

"People in the Collections / Duke, Doris, 1912-1993." *Duke University Libraries.* http://library.duke.edu/rubenstein/collections/people/dorisduke/ (accessed 3/28/2016).

"People of Monongahela, who Helped to Rule our Country." *Historical Magazine of Monongahela's Old Home Coming Week: Sept. 6-13, 1908*, 266. Historic Pittsburgh General Text Collection. (accessed 1/12/2018. http://documenting.pitt.edu/islandora/object/pitt%3A00z838213m/viewer#page/266/mode/2up.

Perley, Sidney. *The Essex Antiquarian, Vol. II.* Salem MA: Essex Antiquarian, 1898.

Philips, Beth, comp. *Massachusetts Deaths, 1844: Vol. 8, Barnstable to Hampshire; Volume 9, Middlesex to Worcester.* Provo, UT: Ancestry.com Operations Inc., 2001.

"Phineas Stearns." *Boston Tea Party Ships and Museum.* https://www.bostonteapartyship.com/phineas-stearns (accessed 6/2/2017).

PineTree Productions. "Shaker Music." *AmericanMusicPreservation.com.* 2016. http://www.americanmusicpreservation.com/TheHumbleHeart.htm.

Pope, Charles. *The pioneers of Massachusetts: a descriptive list, drawn from records of the colonies, towns, and churches, and other contemporaneous documents.* Baltimore : Genealogical Pub. Co., 1991.

Post-Master General. *List of the post-offices in the United States: with the names of the post-masters, of the counties and states to which they belong, the distances from the city of Washington, and the seats of state governments, respectively.* Washington, D.C.: Way & Gideon, 1828.

Postmaster General. *Table of the post offices in the United States, arranged by states and counties; as they were October 1, 1830.* Washington, D.C.: Duff Green, 1831.

Powell, Kimberly. "Numbering Your Family Tree." *ThoughtCo.* https://www.thoughtco.com/numbering-your-family-tree-1420742 (accessed 11/1/2017).

Powers, Edwin. *Crime and Punishment in Early Massachusetts, 1620-1692: A Documentary History.* Boston: Beacon Press, 1966.

"Property Database." *City of Cambridge.* http://www.cambridgema.gov/propertydatabase (accessed 7/5/2016).

Pyle, Howard. Art and Picture Collection, The New York Public Library. "There is a Flock of Yellow Birds Around Her Head." *New York Public Library Digital Collections.* http://digitalcollections.nypl.org/items/510d47e1-0cb1-a3d9-e040-e00a18064a99 (accessed 10/28/ 2017).

Pyne, Frederick Wallace. *Descendants of the Signers of the Declaration of Independence, Volume 6, Virginia.* Rockport, Maine: Picton Press, 1997.

"Raritan Bay Union and Eagleswood Military Academy Collection, 1809-1973, Mg 285." *The New Jersey Historical Society.* www.jerseyhistory.org/findingaid.php?aid=0285 (accessed 5/25/2018).

Raphael, Ray. *Founders: The People Who Brought You a Nation.* New York: New Press, 2009.

Ray, Benjamin and The Rector and Visitors of the University of Virginia. "SWP No. 172.10 - Petition of Phillip English." "SWP No. 81.6 - Petition of Rebecca Fox." *Salem Witch Trials Documentary Archive and Transcription Project.* http://salem.lib.virginia.edu/texts (accessed 10/30/2017 and 5/9/2016).

"Real Property Records." *City of Newport,* accessed 2/15/2018. https://i2f.uslandrecords.com/RI/Newport/.

"Reeves Hall, Hepworth." *British Listed Buildings.* http://www.britishlistedbuildings.co.uk/en-284272-reeves-hall-hepworth-suffolk#.VahW1PlViko (accessed 7/15/2015).

"Region Fiche." *Country: England, County: Norfolk and Suffolk.* Jul 1984.

Reid, Robert. *Boston Tea Party - photograph of a mural signed "Robert Reid, 1904, asst. E. Trumbull."* Detroit: Thistle Publications, 1912. http://www.loc.gov/pictures/item/det1994023444/PP/.

"Re-interment of Sophia and Una Hawthorne." *Hawthorne in Salem,* accessed 4/8/2018. http://www.hawthorneinsalem.org/page/11853/.

"Retrospective Glances." *Stoneham Independent* (Stoneham, MA), 28 Aug 1931. Community History Archive of the Stoneham Public Library, stoneham.advantage-preservation.com (accessed 5/5/2018).

"Rettig, R. "National Register Criteria Statement." *Cambridge Historical Commission* (1969, 1980).

"Revolutionary War Commander Artemas Ward Dies October 28, 1800." *Mass Moments.* http://massmoments.org/moment.cfm?mid=311 (accessed 3/25/2016).

"Revolutionary War Raids & Skirmishes in 1780." *American Revolutionary War.* http://www.myrevolutionarywar.com/battles/1780-skirmish/ (accessed 9/29/16).

Rhode Island USGenWeb Project. "The Record of Old Smithfield from 1730 To 1850, Vol. VIII, 1889, from Records in Town Clerk's Office, Lincoln." *Rhode Island Reading Room.* http://www.rootsweb.ancestry.com/~rigenweb/Smithfield13.html (accessed 10/31/2017).

Rice, George Wharton. *The shipping days of old Boothbay: from the Revolution to the World War, with mention of adjacent towns.* Portland, ME: Southworth-Anthoensen Press, 1938.

Roach, Marilynne K. *The Salem Witch Trials–Day-by-Day Chronicle of a Community Under Siege.* New York: Cooper Square Press, 2002.

Robbins, D.P. *Popular history of Erie county, Pennsylvania.* Erie, PA: Advertising Printing Co., 1895.

Robert B. Mewhinney Letters. *Vigo County Public Library.* Inventory. www.vigo.lib.in.us/archives/inventories/wars/civilwar/mewhinney.php (accessed 10/8/2018).

Robinson, Frederick. "How the First Parish in Cambridge Got a New Meetinghouse read 26 Jan 1937," *The Proceedings of the Cambridge Historical Society, Volume 24, 1936-1937.*

Rode, C.R. *1846 and 1847 Doggett's New York City Directory.* New York: John W. Doggett, Jr., 1847.

Rodgers, Kristin. "St. Francis Hospital and Starling Medical College." *The OSU Libraries Blog*, 26 Nov 2012.

Rogers, David. "Marion Sims Wyeth leaves legacy of varied architectural styles, says architect Dragisic." *Palm Beach Daily News* (Palm Beach, FL), 23 Dec 2010.

Ronda, Bruce A. *Elizabeth Palmer Peabody: A Reformer on Her Own Terms.* Cambridge, MA: Harvard University Press, 1999.

Ross, David. "British Express." *Passionate about British Heritage.* www.britainexpress.com/counties/suffolk/Framlingham_Castle.htm (accessed 7/28/2015).

Roster Commission. *Official roster of the soldiers of the State of Ohio in the War of the Rebellion, 1861-1865, Vols. 1-12.* Akron, OH: The Werner Company, 1893.

Rounds, H. L. Peter. *Abstracts of Bristol County, Massachusetts Probate Records, 1687-1745, Volume IX 1737-1740.* Baltimore, MD: Genealogical Publishing Co., Inc., 1987.

Rowen, Bob. *American Privateers in The War Of 1812.* Revised for web publication 2006-8. http://bobrowen.com/nymas/warof1812paper/paperrevised2006.html.

Royal Commission on Historical Manuscripts, *Manuscripts of the House of Lords, 1678-1688.* London: H.M. Stationery Office by Eyre & Spottiswoode, 1887.

"Saint Patrick (Strip) District." *Catholic Diocese of Pittsburgh.* https://diopitt.org/saint-patrick-strip-district (accessed 1/26/2018).

Sanders, Helen Fitzgerald. *A History of Montana Vol. III.* Chicago; New York: Lewis Publishing Co., 1913.

Sanjek, Russell. *American Popular Music and its Business: The First Four Hundred Years, Volume II, From 1790 to 1909.* New York: Oxford University Press, 1988.

"Sarah Towne Clayes (Cloyes)." *Framingham History Center.* http://www.framinghamhistory.org/wp-content/uploads/2015/04/Sarah-Towne-Clayes-Cloyes.pdf (accessed 5/16/2016).

Sargent, Aaron and John S. Sargent. *Sargent Genealogy.* Somerville, MA: Aaron Sargent, 1895.

Sawin, Thomas E. and John Sawin. *Sawin: Summary Notes Concerning John Sawin and His Prosperity.* Wendell, MA: Rufus Putnam Printers, 1866.

Sawtelle, William Otis. *Daniel Gott, Mount Desert pioneer: his ancestors and descendants.* Mt. Desert, ME: No publisher ID, 1926.

Sawyer, Charles Winthrop. *Firearms in American History, Volume 1.* Norwood, MA: Plimpton Press, 1910.

"Saxtead, All Saints, Saxtead." *The Church of England*. www.achurchnearyou.com/saxtead-all-saints/ (accessed 1/4/2017).

Schulte, Brett. *The Siege of Petersburg Online*. www.beyondthecrater.com (accessed 5/1/2018 and 5/19/2018).

Scott County District Court. *Criminal Case Number 1*. Scott County, IA. May 1856 to Jun 1858.

Scribner, Harvey, Western Historical Association. *Memoirs of Lucas County and the city of Toledo, from the earliest historical times down to the present, including a genealogical and biographical record of representative families*. Madison, Wis., Western Historical Association, 1910.

Secretary of the Commonwealth. *Massachusetts Soldiers and Sailors of the Revolutionary War, Volumes 3,4,6,8,11,12,13,14, 17*. Boston: Wright & Potter Printing Co., State Printers, 1896 and 1903.

Secretary of the Commonwealth. *Massachusetts Soldiers and Sailors of the Revolutionary War, Volume 17*. Boston: Wright & Potter Printing, 1908.

"Servant of God, Rose Hawthorne." *Dominican Sisters of Hawthorne*. www.hawthorne-dominicans.org/rose-hawthorne.html#canonizationprocess (accessed 5/27/2017).

"Shaker Cemetery Burial Map." *In Historic Harvard Town*. https://historicharvard.wordpress.com/historic-places/highlight-our-historic-places/our-harvard-shakers-cemetery/comment-page-1/ (accessed 5/22/17).

Sharples, Stephen Paschall. *First Church (Cambridge, Mass.) Records of the Church of Christ at Cambridge, in New England: 1632-1830*. Boston: Eben Putnam, 1906.

Shedd Frank E. "Daniel Shed Genealogy." *Ebenezer Shed [4:1726]*. http://library.untraveledroad.com/Ch/Shedd/Daniel-Shed/Fourth/Ebenezer-1726.htm (accessed 4/11/2017).

Shenk, Rob. "The George Wythe House." *Wikimedia Commons, the free media repository*. 22 Sep 2012. https://commons.wikimedia.org/wiki/File:The_George_Wythe_House_(8017084861).jpg.

Shepard Congregational Society, Cambridge, Mass. *The Manual of the first Church in Cambridge (Congregational)*. Boston: Samuel Usher, 1900.

Shepard, Thomas and Michael MacGiffert. *God's plot: Puritan spirituality in Thomas Shepard's Cambridge*. Amherst, MA: Univ. of Massachusetts Press, 1994.

"Shrewsbury Family Images." Historic Madison, Inc., *Flickr*. https://www.flickr.com/photos/117251246@N06/albums/72157644429204591 (accessed 1/14/2018).

Shipton, Clifford Kenyon. *Sibley's Harvard Graduates, Volume 9, 16 and 18*. Boston: Massachusetts Historical Society, 1968.

Siebenthaler, Donna J. "Marshall County," *Encyclopedia of Alabama*. 03 Jul 2007; www.encyclopediaofalabama.org/article/h-120 (accessed 4/12/2018).

Sinclair, Jill. *Fresh Pond: The History of a Cambridge Landscape*. Cambridge, MA: The MIT Press, 2009.

Sluman, Georgiana I. *The Russell Family*. A story found in the Mason, NH, Historical Room. About 1985.

Smith, Amy Adeline. *Memorials for funerals of Parker Judson Wyeth and Amy Nash Wyeth*, 1908 and 1923.

Smith, A. Davis and T. A. DeLand. *Northern Alabama Historical and Biographical*. Chicago: Donohue & Henneberry, 1888.

Smith, Samuel Abbot. *West Cambridge on the 19th of April, 1775, an Address*. Boston: Alfred Mudge & Son, 1864.

Smith, Samuel Francis. *History of Newton, Massachusetts*. Boston: The American Logotype Company, 1880.

Smull, John A. *History of the Harrisburg Cemetery Association, With Its Charter, By-Laws and Regulations, Together with a List of the Owners of Lots*. Harrisburg, PA: Telegraph Printing House, 1876. Harrisburg Cemetery Lot Owners, Harrisburg, Dauphin County, PA. Contributed for use in the USGenWeb Archives by DBA. http://files.usgwarchives.net/pa/dauphin/cemeteries/hburg-cem-assoc.txt.

Softschools.com. *Mexican-American War Timeline*. www.softschools.com/timelines/ (accessed 10/2/2018).

Sós, R. "The Puritans Leave England for America." *The Historic Present blog*. 17 Sep 2008. "Christmas in Puritan New England, Or Not." 19 Dec 2013. thehistoricpresent.wordpress.com.

Souza, Pete. "Jan 2016: Photo of the Day." *The White House President Barack Obama*, 21 Jan 2016. https://obamawhitehouse.archives.gov/photos-and-video/photogallery/january-2016-photo-day.

Spalding, Ph.D., Matthew. "How to Understand Slavery and the American Founding." *The Heritage Foundation White Paper #138.* 26 Aug 2002. www.heritage.org/research/reports/2002/08/how-to-understand-slavery-and-americas.

Speicher, Tom. "Where are They Now: Fred Cox." *Minnesota Vikings*, 23 Jun 2011. http://www.vikings.com/news/article-1/Where-Are-They-Now-Fred-Cox/28a2116f-76f0-4e7f-b1ee-5cf12634e915.

"Spring Grove Cemetery." *Genealogy Search Listing.* http://www.springgrove.org/ (accessed 2014 and 2018).

St. John, Thomas. *Nathaniel Hawthorne Studies in The House of the Seven Gables.* http://hawthornessevengables.com/ (accessed 30 Sep 2017).

St. Louis Genealogical Society, comp. *St. Louis, Missouri Marriages, 1804-76.* Provo, UT: Ancestry.com Operations Inc., 2000.

State of Illinois. *Illinois, Public Land Purchase Records, 1800-1990.* Provo, UT: Ancestry.com Ops., Inc., 1999.

State of Indiana, Monroe County Court of Common Pleas, *Francis Wyeth vs Mary Wyeth (Divorce),* term of December 1865 (box 127, 9 pages, marriage is listed in book 4, p. 346). *Francis Wyeth vs Elizabeth Wyeth (Divorce),* term of Aug 1871 (box 144). *Elizabeth Wyeth vs Francis Wyeth (Divorce),* term of December 1872 (box 163). Records housed Monroe County History Center, Bloomington, IN.

"State of Iowa, Des Moines County, ss. District Court of Des Moines County Jonas Wyeth vs. Mary Torrey Wyeth late Mary Torrey Hancock." *Burlington Hawk Eye* (Burlington, IA), 02 Oct 1851.

Stazesky, Richard C. "George Washington, Genius in Leadership." *Washington Papers*, 22 Feb 2000. gwpapers.virginia.edu/history/articles/george-washington-genius-in-leadership/.

Steel, John David Warren. "Wyeth and the Development of Southern Folk Hymnody." *Music from the Middle Ages Through the 20th Century: Essays in Honor of Gwynn McPeek.* Carmelo P. Comberiati and Matthew C. Steel, eds. London: Gordon & Breach, 1988.

Steele, Jr., Chauncey Depew. *A History of Inns and Hotels in Cambridge.* Cambridge, MA: Cambridge Historical Society, 1957.

Stein, Alan J. "Denny, Orion O. (1853-1916)." *HistoryLink.org*, posted 11/24/2002. www.historylink.org/File/4026.

Stephens, H. L. *"The Parting – Buy us too."* Illustration made circa 1863. *Library of Congress Prints and Photographs* Division. https://www.loc.gov/item/93503990/ (accessed 12/6/2016).

Stern, Kenneth. "Duncan Wyeth." *My Child at CerebralPalsy.org.* 2016. www.cerebralpalsy.org/inspiration/athletes/duncan-wyeth.

Stevens, William Burnham. *History of Stoneham, Massachusetts.* Stoneham, MA: F. L. & W. E. Whittier, 1891.

Stewart, George Black. "Address by Samuel H. Garland." *Centennial Memorial, English Presbyterian Congregation, Harrisburg, Pa.* Harrisburg, PA: Harrisburg Publishing Co., 1894.

Stiles, Henry R. *Contributions toward a genealogy of the family of Stiles.* Albany, NY: J. Munsell, 1863.

Stopka, Christina and Tony Black. "Partial List of Texas Ranger Company and Unit Commanders." *Texas Ranger Research Center.* edensfamily.com/geneology/raw/research/jim-linney-texas-rangers-shawnee-delaware.htm (accessed 10/5/2018).

Strong, Ted. "Civil War expert: North fought to preserve Union." *The Daily Progress* (Charlottesville, VA), 21 Feb 2011.

Stuart, Donna Valley. "Marriages of Christ Church, Detroit 1849-1879." *Detroit Society for Genealogical Research Magazine*, Spring 1979.

Suess, Jeff. "Honoring America's original patriots." *The Cincinnati Enquirer* (Cincinnati, OH), 13 Apr 2014.

Suess, Jeff. "Honoring America's original patriots." *Cincinnat!com* (Cincinnati, OH), 13 Apr 2014. http://www.cincinnati.com/story/news/history/2014/04/13/honoring-americas-original-patriots/7666783/.

Suffolk Institute of Archaeology. *The Proceedings of the Suffolk Institute of Archaeology, Volume 10.* Ipswich, England: Ancient House Press, 1900.

Sullivan, Charles M. *Memorandum to the Historical Commission*, 22 Feb 1995.

Temple, Josiah Howard. *History of Framingham, Massachusetts, Early Known as Danforth's Farms*. Framingham, MA: Town of Framingham, 1887.

Temple, Levi Daniel. *Some Temple pedigrees. A Genealogy of the known descendants of Abraham Temple, who settled in Salem, Mass, in 1636.* Boston: D. Clapp & son, 1900.

Thibodeau, Donna Wyeth. "Charles Alonzo Wyeth Biography and family data sheets." 18 Nov 1986.

Thomas, Isaiah. "Boston, April 23." *Worcester Magazine Fourth week in April, 1787* (Worcester, MA), Apr, 1787.

Thomas Jefferson Foundation. "George Wythe Randolph, Jefferson's grandson." *The Monticello Classroom.* 2007. http://classroom.monticello.org.

Thurman, Suzanne Ruth. "O *Sisters Ain't you Happy?": Gender, Family, and Community Among the Harvard and Shirley Shakers, 1781-1918.* Syracuse, NY: Syracuse University Press, 2002.

Tice, John H. *The Teacher and Western Educational Magazine, Volume 1.* St. Louis: Republican Office, 1854.

Tice, Joyce M. "Cole's Farm Cemetery, Towanda Township, Bradford County, Pennsylvania." *Tri-Counties Genealogy & History.* www.joycetice.com/cemb/coleobit.htm (accessed 1/18/2018).

Tomlinson, Abraham. *The Military Journals of Two Private Soldiers.* Poughkeepsie, NY: A. Tomlinson, 1855.

Town Clerk. "Dr. Tapley Wyeth, Bond for Smallpox Hospital." *Town of Sherborn, MA.* 11 Sep 1792.

Tuttle, Genevieve Wyeth. "Statement from family Bible (of Francis Wyeth and Mary Hillman and Francis Wyeth and Margaret Carney marriages)." *Supplement to DAR application*, notarized 21 Dec 1938.

Tyler, Mary Palmer. *Grandmother Tyler's Book – the Recollections of Mary Palmer Tyler, 1775-1866.* Editors: Frederick Tupper and Helen Tyler Brown, New York: G. P. Putnam's Sons, 1925.

"United States Civil Records." *FamilySearch Research Wiki.* https://www.familysearch.org/wiki/en/United_States_Civil_Records (accessed 1/26/2018).

United States Department of the Interior. *Official register of the United States, containing a list of officers and employees in the civil, military, and naval service on the 30th of Sep 1823.* Washington, Davis & Force, 1824.

United States Post Office Department. *Table of Post Offices in the United States.* Washington, D.C.: Post-Master General, 1813.

"Universities earn big bucks as Harvard's stunt double." *The Harvard Law Record* (Cambridge, MA), 11 Dec 2002.

Upham, Charles Wentworth. *Salem Witchcraft: with an Account of Salem Village, and a History of Opinions on Witchcraft and Kindred Subjects, Volume 1.* New York: Frederick Ungar Publishing Co., 1867.

Upham, Charles Wentworth. *Salem Witchcraft: with an Account of Salem Village, and a History of Opinions on Witchcraft and Kindred Subjects, Volume 2.* Boston: Wiggin and Lunt, 1867.

Utah State Historical Society, comp. *Utah Cemetery Inventory.* Provo, UT: Ancestry.com Operations Inc., 2000.

Van Wagenen, Avis Stearns. *Genealogy and memoirs of Isaac Stearns and his descendants.* Syracuse, NY: Courier Printing Co., 1901.

"Viennapedia." *Encyclopedia of Vienna Township, Trumbull County, OH, Businesses Temperance House.* https://sites.google.com/a/viennahistory.org/viennapedia/business/temperance-house (accessed 1/23/2016).

Vigo Atlas Map Co. *Standard atlas of Vigo County, Indiana: including a plat book of the villages, cities and townships of the county, map of state and United States and world.* Terre Haute, IN: Vigo Atlas Map Co., 1907. Map. Retrieved from the Library of Congress, https://www.loc.gov/item/2007626785/ 01/28/2018.

Virkus, Frederick A. *The Abridged Compendium of American Genealogy, v.3.* Chicago: F. A. Virkus & Co., 1928.

Walling, Henry Francis. *Map of the City of Cambridge, Middlesex County, Mass.* Boston: Geo. L. Dix, 1854.

Ward, Andrew Henshaw. *Ward Family; Descendants of William Ward: Who Settled in Sudbury, Mass., in 1639.* Boston: Samuel G. Drake, 1851.

Washburn, Israel. *Notes, historical, descriptive, and personal, of Livermore, in Androscoggin (formerly in Oxford) County, Maine.* Portland, ME: Bailey & Noyes, 1874.

"Wasserstein Hall." *CPCI.ca Project of the Month*, 02 Jul 2016. http://www.cpci.ca/en/about_us/project_month/october_2012/.

Waters, Henry Fitz-Gilbert. *The New England Historical & Genealogical Register, Vol. 55.* Boston: NEHGS, 1901.

Watertown, Mass. Historical Society. *Watertown Records: The First and Second Books of Town Proceedings with the Lands, Grants and Possessions also the Proprietors' Book and the First Book and Supplement of Births, Deaths, and Marriages.* Watertown, MA: Press of Fred G. Barker, 1894.

Watertown, Mass. Historical Society. *Watertown Records: The third book of town proceedings, and the second book of Births, Marriages and Deaths to End of 1737.* Watertown, MA: Fred G. Barker, 1900.

Watertown Mass. *Watertown's military history.* Authorized by a vote of the inhabitants of the town of Watertown, Massachusetts. Published under the direction of a committee representing the Sons of the American revolution, and Isaac B. Patten post 81, Grand Army of the Republic. Boston: David Clapp & Son, 1907.

Web: Wabash Valley, *Indiana Obituaries, 1900-2010.* n.p: Vigo County Public Library, n.d.

Webster (1913). "Academic Dictionaries and Encyclopedias." *The Collaborative International Dictionary of English.* 2000.

Wermuth, James. "The Forgotten Patriot." *The Boston Globe* (Boston, MA), 28 Apr 2011. Boston.com. http://archive.boston.com/bostonglobe/editorial_opinion/oped/articles/2011/04/28/the_forgotten_patriot/.

White, James T. *National Cyclopaedia of American Biography, Vol. VI.* New York: James T. White & Co., 1896.

White, Kenneth A. "Records from Baptism and Marriage Registers." *Archives & Records Center of the Roman Catholic Diocese of Pittsburgh.* 3 Sep 2016 and 16 Nov 2017 emails from Julie Rowan Wolford.

White, William. *History, Gazetteer, and Directory of Suffolk.* Sheffield, England: Robert Leader, 1855.

Wieth, Robert. *Original Will [IC/AA1/53/164] Saxtead, 1617* from the archives of the Suffolk Records Office, Ipswich, UK. (Translated by Claire Barker of the Suffolk Records Society.)

Wiggins, Myra Albert, photographer. *"The Mother"* [1901] Image. *Library of Congress Prints and Photographs Division.* https://www.loc.gov/item/2004676339 (accessed 11/27/2016).

Wikipedia, the Free Encyclopedia. https://en.wikipedia.org/wiki/ (accessed various dates 2016-2019 - see endnotes).

Wilhoit, Virginia; Nelson Eddy; Wabash Valley Genealogical Society. *Cemeteries, Vigo County, Indiana, Volume III.* Terre Haute, IN: Wentz Printing, 1982.

Williams, Alicia Crane. *Early Families of New England.* Original Online Database: AmericanAncestors.org, New England Historic Genealogical Society. 2013. http://www.americanancestors.org/databases/early-new-england-families-1641-1700/image/?volumeId=13908&pageName=1&rId=250755076.

Williams, Heather Andrea. "Slavery Affected African American Families." *Freedom's story, Teacherserve©, National Humanities Center.* http://nationalhumanitiescenter.org/tserve/freedom/1609-1865/essays/aafamilies.htm (accessed 11/26/16).

Williams, Walter. *A History of Northwest Missouri, Volume 3.* Chicago: Lewis Publishing Company, 1915.

Wing Family. *The Owl, Vol. 22-25.* Kewaunee, WI: Wing Family of America, 1920-1924.

Woelfly, Simon J. *Swatara Collegiate Institute, Jonestown, Lebanon County, Pa. Paper read before the Lebanon County Historical Society,* 19 Apr 1907. Vol. IV, No. 2, Lebanon County Historical Society, Historical Papers and Addresses, Volumes 1-2. Lebanon, PA: The Society, 1907.

Wolford, Julie Rowan. "Re: Wyeths (Wythe)." 8/13/16, 8/7/17 and 11/19/17 emails.

Wrigley, E. A. and R. S. Schofield. *The Population History of England 1541-1871.* Cambridge, UK: Press Syndicate of the University of Cambridge, 1989.

Wyeth, Andrew. "My Father," Wyeth, N. C. (1882-1945). *The digital library of Unitarian Universalism.* http://www.harvardsquarelibrary.org/biographies/n-c-wyeth/ (accessed 9/25/2017).

Wyeth, Benjamin Franklin. *Wyeth Funeral Service records, 1904-1964 (Mss 223).* New England Historic Genealogical Society.

Wyeth, Harold E. Letter dated 11 Mar 1979 from Coco Solo, Panama Canal Zone.

Wyeth, John Allan. "Cold Cheer in Camp Morton." *Century Monthly Magazine,* Apr 1891.

Wyeth, John Allan. *With Sabre and Scalpel: The Autobiography of a Soldier and Surgeon.* New York, NY: Harper & Brothers Publishers, 1914.

Wyeth, John Allan Benedict. *This Man's Army: A War in Fifty-Odd Sonnets*. New York: Harold Vinal, Ltd., 1928.

Wyeth, John B(ound) and Benjamin Waterhouse. *Oregon, or, a Short History of a Long Journey.* Cambridge, MA: Printed for John B. Wyeth, 1833.

Wyeth, John Churchill. *Tree compiled for his children*. Received 31 Oct 2010 from Maureen Christensen Wyeth.

Wyeth, John J. *Leaves from a Diary Written While Serving in Co. E, 44 Mass., Dep't of No. Carolina, from September 1862 to June 1863.* Boston: L.F. Lawrence & Company, 1878.

Wyeth, Jonas. *Wyeth family records (Mss A 3058).* R. Stanton Avery Special Collections, New England Historic Genealogical Society (NEHGS) and www.americanancestors.org (accessed 8/24/2015.) (Timothy Salls, Manager of NEHGS Manuscript Collections, approved use of documents in an email dated 06 May 2019.)

Wyeth, Jonas 2^d. "Letter to Arthur Benson." File #211, Scott County, Iowa District Court records. 23 Jun 1855.

Wyeth, Louis. "Letter from Louis Wyeth in Guntersville, Alabama, to Governor Robert Miller Patton." *Alabama Department of Archives and History* (Guntersville, Marshall County, Alabama, 2 Apr 1866). digital.archives.alabama.gov/cdm/ref/collection/voices/id/2192 (accessed 4/15/2018).

Wyeth, Marion Sims. *Nicholas and George Wythe: an account of a search for their English antecedents.* Palm Beach, FL: unknown, 1958.

Wyeth, Marselle Allen, *Genealogy of Scott Family of America*, privately published circa 1947.

Wyeth, Nathaniel Jarvis. *The Correspondence and Journals of Captain Nathaniel J. Wyeth, 1831-6.* Eugene, OR: University Press, 1899.

Wyeth, N. C., Betsy James Wyeth, editor. *The Wyeths, The Intimate Correspondence of N. C. Wyeth, 1901-1945.* Boston: Gambit, 1971.

Wyeth, Nicholas and William. *Nicholas and William Wyeth papers (Mss 73).* R. Stanton Avery Special Collections, New England Historic Genealogical Society (NEHGS). (Timothy Salls, Manager of NEHGS Manuscript Collections, approved use of documents in an email dated 06 May 2019.)

"Wyeth Brickyard Superintendent's House." *digplanet.com.* 2016. http://www.digplanet.com/wiki/Wyeth_Brickyard_Superintendent%27s_House.

"Wyeth Cambridge." *Facebook.* https://www.facebook.com/TheWyethCambridge (accessed 7/1/2016).

"Wyeth Chemical Bankruptcy." *American Druggist and Pharmaceutical Record* (New York, NY), 25 Dec 1905.

"Wyeth Hall First University Dorm Open to Women." *The Harvard Crimson* (Cambridge, MA), 29 Sep 1958. http://www.thecrimson.com/article/1958/9/29/wyeth-hall-first-university-dorm-open/.

"Wythe [Worcestershire]." *Coats of Arms.* http://www.heraldry.ws/html/wythe-worcestershire.html (accessed 01/23/2016).

"Wythepedia W&M Law Library." *Wythepedia: The George Wythe Encyclopedia.* http://lawlibrary.wm.edu/wythepedia/index.php/George_Wythe (accessed 10/27/2016 and 3/2/2017).

Yale University. *Vicennial record the Class of 1886 in Yale College.* New Haven, CT: Tuttle, Morehouse & Taylor Press, 1906.

"Yale Indian Papers Project – Danforth, Thomas, 1623-1699 and Gookin, Daniel, 1612-1687." *Yale University.* http://yipp.yale.edu/bio/bibliography/danforth-thomas-1623-1699 (accessed 3/30/2016). http://yipp.yale.edu/bio/bibliography/gookin-daniel-1612-1687 (accessed 3/30/2016).

Yates Publishing. *U.S. and International Marriages, 1560-1900.* Provo, UT: Ancestry.com Ops., Inc., 2004.

Zombek, Angela M. "Libby Prison." *Encyclopedia Virginia.* 23 Jan 2014. http://www.encyclopediavirginia.org/Libby_Prison#start_entry.

INDEX TO NAMES OF RELATED PERSONS

Douglas
Louisa W., 302
Mary J., 302
Mary McKinley, 302
Samuel, 226, 301, 302

Dover
Elizabeth (Chandler), 212, 282, 287

Downing
John Jackson, 365

Doyle
Richard, 283

Drabenstott
Frederick R., 283, 358

Drake
Charles J., 298
George O., 344, 366, 367, 368

Drum
Henrietta Margaret "Blossom", 421

Dubre
Bashelon Ellen, 341

Dudley
Anne, 181
Thomas, 181

Duffy
Annie F., 401

Duncan
Mary Louisa, 302

Dunk
Walter Menijay, 399

Dunton
Hepzibah, 159
Rhodes, 314
Zoa Ann, 241, 314

Durant
Hannah, 203

Durnell
Mary Valko, 396

Earnest
Josh, 96

Easter
John H., 342

Eaton
Ezra Oliver, 336
Ruth Jane, 267, 336

Eccles
Martha, 152

Eckman
Merle, 387

Edwards
Aaron, 250
Abraham (Dr.), 250, 252
Euretta Lanphear, 382
Judi Harms, 425

Einwechter
Emma Rebecca, 314, 410, 411
Harry, 410
Henry, 410

Eldridge
James Ormel "Pops", 367

Ellars
Jessie, 386

Elliott
Sophronia, 330

Elton
Frances "Fannie", 311, 407, 408
Robert Henry, 407

Endicott
Mary, 152

Ensign
Hannah, 148

Enyart
Martha, 291

Errett
Martha, 418

Ervin
Nathaniel Gratton, 386

Esler
Anna Beatrice, 343

Evans
Darius Oscar, 329
James David, 317, 414
Lynda (Levin), 357, 425
Martha Ann, 355
Mary Ella, 414
Mina Gertrude, 414
Osgood, 414

Ewing
John, 417

Fairing
John Walker, 393

Farnsworth
Charles, 259

Farnum
Edgar, 241

Herman, 241
Joshua, 240
Sylvania Lowell, 241

Farran
Michael, 359
Secelia "Celia", 288, 359

Farrell
Irene Elizabeth, 371

Farrow
Phebe Ann, 421
Stephen, 421

Faubert
Emma Adelima, 330

Fawcett
Catharine Elizabeth, 239
Charles Newell, 239
Simeon, 187, 239, 240

Felter
Elizabeth (Patmore), 212, 282, 283, 286
Elsie, 286
William, 286

Felton
Susannah, 299, 300

Ferguson
Ann, 396

Fessenden
Benjamin, 169
Benjamin II, 169
Charles Franklin, 261, 331
Charles Newton, 331
Margaret, 169
Martha, 169, 197
Nathan, 176, 203
Nathan Jr., 203, 261
Nicholas, 168, 169
Ruth, 169, 196, 197, 254, 421
Thomas III, 58, 176, 177
Thomas Jr., 159, 176
Thomas Sr., 176
William, 148, 168, 169, 170
William (Rev.), 169

Fillebrown
Edward, 313
Hannah, 159, 177
Harrison Everett, 88
Isaac, 177

Gamage
Joshua III, 73, 321
Joshua Jr., 248, 321
Joshua Sr., 148
Martha, 167, 196, 321, 420, 421
Mary, 167, 193
Nancy E. (Mills), 249
Nathaniel, 60, 72, 73, 167, 193, 194, 248
Nathaniel Jr., 193
Rebecca, 167, 193
Ruth, 167, 193, 248
Samuel, 60, 195, 248, 321
Samuel G., 249
Samuel Gott, 73, 249
Sarah, 167, 193, 195, 249, 250, 319
Sarah "Sally", 321, 420
Stephen, 73, 248
Thomas, 73, 168, 321
Webster, 321
William, 57, 73, 167, 194, 248, 321
William (Dr.), 73, 194
William Dick, 195

Gamble
William C., 387

Gann
Grace (Wyeth), ix

Gard
Robert, 391

Gardner
Mariah, 366
Mary, 239

Garlick
Dorothy, 414

Garrigues
Edith Helene, 424

Garten
Alvin, 381

Garwood
Anderson, 289

Gemeny
Naomi, 376

Geoghegan
Michael, 160, 177
Prudence, 177

Gibson
James Anderson, 354
Mabel (Holt), 354

Gilbert
Daniel, 212, 214, 281, 282
Delphine Irene, 355
Elijah B., 355
Elizabeth, 281
George Milton, 355
Helen Mae, 355
Ida, 355
John W., 281
Mary Elizabeth, 355
Nelson, 281, 355
Oliver T., 355
Perry N., 355
Rosetta, 355
Samuel, 281

Gill
H. Louise, 337

Gilman
Sarah, 173

Gilmore
Edward, 399
Eleanor Elizabeth, 398

Ginter
Anna R., 308, 404
Francis, 404

Gleason
Joseph, 251

Gleeson
Adaline, 288

Goddard
Thomas, 175
Thomas Sr., 175

Goodrich
Jane, 203, 261

Goodridge
Charlotte Grosvenor, 374
Joshua, 171
Philip, 261

Goodwin
Adeline, 361
Charles Jr., 376
Edward, 177
Elvira, 361
George Kittredge, 272

James, 436
Rachel, 436, 437
Ransom, 361
Silas, 288, 360, 361
William, 360

Gordon
Hannah, 195
John Lee, 344

Gorham
Mary Olive, 328

Goss
Judith, 164, 192
Thomas, 192

Gott
Anna, 193, 248, 249
Betsey (Sadler), 320
Hannah T., 320
Honor, 249
James, 320
Jane, 320
John, 193, 320
Martha, 320
Mary, 320
Nathan E., 320
Patty, 320
Sarah, 249, 320
William IV, 248, 249
William Jr., 249, 319
William V, 193, 249, 250, 319
William VI, 247, 249, 250, 319, 320
William VII, 320

Goulding
Curtis, 298
Cyntha, 224, 298

Gove, 262
Hannah, 175
Keziah, 246

Grafton
Mary Ella, 314

Grant
Jane, 420
Lucy Weston, 373
Sarah, 195

Grate
Elizabeth, 417
Jahu, 418

Joshua Brackett, 406

Josiah, 171

Josiah Jr., 199

Josiah Sr., 199

Lucy, 325

Lucy Bemis, 406

Lydia, 171

Mary Sarah, 257

Nancy, 325

Noah, 178

Peter, 171

Phinehas (Captain), 57, 60, 199, 231

Polly, 257

Relief, 257

Samuel, 171, 257

Sarah, 148

Submit, 257

Susan, 101, 183, 199, 231, 318

Susanna, 199, 257

William, 171

William Brackett, 309, 406

William Brackett Jr., 406

Stephenson
James, 408, 409

Jane Waugh, 312, 409

John, 312, 408, 409

Stuart Augustus Sr., 409

Stewart
Helen V. "Nellie", 372

John H., 397

Sarah Bell "Sadie", 304, 397, 398

William, 372

Stiles
Benjamin, 299

Elijah H., 299

George F., 299

Hannah K., 299

Lucy, 187, 243, 244, 317

Mary H., 299

Mary Jane, 244, 316, 317

Nancy (Chamberlin), 317, 414

Parker W., 299

Peleg Stearns, 243, 317

Silas D., 224, 225, 299

William P., 299

Stimson
Amelia Hepzibah Bigelow, 242, 315, 316

Royal, 243, 315

Stinson
Fanny, 192

Indiana, 192

John Winship, 192

Robert, 164, 192

Robert (Deacon), 192

Thankfull, 192

Thomas, 192

Stockbridge
Marcia, 258, 325, 326

William, 325

Stone
Harry Ellery, 362

Howard L., 267

Kendall, 267

Phineas, 219, 220

Stonerook
Simon Burget, 392

Straughan
Alice F., 301, 394

Emma Pearl, 301, 394

Jesse Rittenhouse, 394

Strippel
Nicholas, 239

Stuart
Grace, 408, 409

Mary, 361

Stubecke
Anna Gertrude, 311

Sturdevant
Rhoda Brown, 363

Sullivan
Jane Frances "Jennie", 330

Julia, 414

Sumacher
Ann, 310

Sutton
Vickie (Bays), 287

Swan
Benjamin, 374

Ellen Aurline, 328

Frances Wyeth, 295, 374

Frederick George, 294, 374

Swanson
James, 380

Sweaney
Upsher, 437

Sweeney
Ann, 437

Ann Wythe, 437

Charles, 433, 434, 438

Euphan, 434, 437

George Wythe, 14, 15, 285, 436, 437, 438, 439

George Wythe Sr., 434, 436, 437

Jane, 438

Martha, 434, 437

Swinford
Sarah, 360

Swisher
Eleanor, 416

Symonds
Dorothy, 143

Tabb
Diane, 433, 434

John, 434

Taintor
Elizabeth, 219

Taliaferro
Elizabeth, 14, 435

Elizabeth Eggleston, 433, 435

Tallmage
Jennie L. "Jane, 299, 382

Tankersley
Charles, 342

Dorcas Tabitha, 74, 136, 274, 342

Tapley
Isaac, 187

John, 187, 236

John Mansfield, 236

Mansfield Jr., 162, 186, 187, 235

Mansfield Sr., 186

Mary "Polly", 187

Samuel Tufts, 236

Sarah, 187

Tappan
Sarah, 415

Tarbell
Anna Isabella, 260, 330

John, 330

529

Turner
Delphem Elvira, 327
John, 193
Lucy Moulton (Todd), 332
William H., 343

Twigg
Constance Louise, 413

Tyler
Royall, 253, 254, 255, 256, 428

Vail
Owens B., 369

Van De Sande
Louisa, 424

Vanderbilt
Cornelius, 103

Vernon
Martha Esther, 298, 380
Varnan, 380

Vesey
William, 18

Vogt
Juanita (Wyeth), ix, 399

Wade
Abigail, 192

Wagstaff
Alfred Inskipp, 268

Wait
Isabella Emeline, 301, 391
John Heaton, 391
Jonathan, 261
Zeruah, 204, 261

Walbridge
Anna, 317

Walker
Charles Arthur "Chuck", 225, 300, 389, 390, 393, 394, 425
Eugenie, 283
George, 433
Grace, 283
Jane, 389, 390, 394, 425
John Adams, 336
John D., 283
Josephine, 283
Leaffa Relief, 315
Margaret, 13, 14
Margaret Keith, 432, 433
Mary Anna, 360
Mattie A., 329

Millie, 314
Susanna, 336

Wallace
Amaryllis Eagle, 415
James Rev., 14, 432

Walsh
Charles E., 361
Theresa, 375

Wangsness
John A., 366

Wanson
Elizabeth, 248, 249

Warburton
Vickilyn (Lallatin), 388, 389, 390, 391, 392, 393, 425

Ward
Artemas, 93, 140, 148
Deborah Jackson, 140, 145, 148, 152
John "the turner", 145, 148
William, 148

Wardwell
Allen, 308
Caroline "Carrie" Churchill, 227, 229, 308
George Smith, 308
Margaret Louise Wilkeson, 308, 399
William T., 309
William Taylor, 308

Ware
Abigail, 159
Ephraim (Dr.), 194
Joseph, 159

Warland
Ann Elizabeth, 411
John Henry, 338
Maria Carter, 269, 338

Warner
Jacob, 239

Warren
Elizabeth "Betsy", 201, 259
Ephraim, 259
Francies Eliza, 326
Lydia, 331
Mary Ann Gillam, 339
Sarah, 190

Warren (Onion)
George, 272

Waterman
Emily (Dr.), 301, 391
Richard, 391

Watson
Frederick A., 340
Isaac, 218
Lucy, 194
Mary "Polly", 218
Nancy, 218
Priscilla, 218
Susanna Wyeth "Sukey", 218, 292
William Jr., 218
William Sr., 179, 218

Waugh
Jacob, 287

Wayne
Nancy, 187

Webb
Henry, 185
Sarah, 185

Webber
Jotham (Deacon), 190

Webster
Sarah, 248, 321
Thomas, 321

Weeks
Elizabeth Catherine, 321, 417, 419
John Thomas, 419

Weishaar
Lizzie, 366

Weiss
Louisa, 180, 226, 227
Wilhelm Ludwig "Lewis", 226, 229

Welch
Susannah, 349

Welles
Benjamin Sumner Jr., 374

Welling
Claudine, 409

Wellington
Eunice, 197, 250
Mary, 199, 231
Samuel, 250

Wells
David Booth, 420
Esther, 155
Sarah, 325

Wendell
Alice Hunt (Curtis), 251
Tunis, 251

Werker
Martin, 370

West
Elijah, 288
Emiline, 212, 288, 289
Emma Frances, 410
Levi H., 314, 410
Samuel, 410

Whallon
Maria J., 348

Wheeler
Elvira, 259, 326
Jonathan, 326
Nettie, 371
Sarah, 406

Whipple
Elizabeth, 236

Whitcomb
George Lillis, 329

White
Abigail, 171, 199
Andrew, 199
Ed, 425
Edward, 411
Elizabeth, 277
Oren Hamilton, 378

Whitfield
Alfred L., 407
Charles H., 310, 407
Charles H. Jr., 407
George, 407
George Buckmaster, 407
Mary Elizabeth, 396

Whitlock
Benjamin, 415
Electa, 320, 415

Whitmore
Anna, 179, 180, 181, 182, 265

Whitney
Abigail, 200

Benjamin, 155, 157
Joseph, 155
Rebecca, 410
Tabitha, 196

Whittemore
Elizabeth, 218

Whittle
Hannah Folsom, 259

Wieth
Margerie, 430
Robert, 12, 13, 429, 430

Wigner
Joseph W., 416

Wilbur
Frances "Fannie", 313

Wilder
Oscar Sylvester, 386
Walter Erwin, 329

Wilhelm
Margaret, 420

Wilivier
Amelia Louise, 377

Wilkinson
John W., 355

Willard
Carrie Louisa, 339
Charles Chester, 340
Edgar Lincoln, 339
Ellen Maria, 272
Emma Carrie, 339
Francis Oren, 271, 339
George Otis, 271, 339, 340
George Summer, 339
Hannah Augusta, 271
Ida Lucy, 339
Lulu C., 339
Lyman, 221, 270, 271
Mary Ann, 272, 339, 340
Mary Wyeth Perry, 339, 340
Oren, 207, 271
Reuben, 196
Sarah Elizabeth, 272
Simon, 271
Susan Annette, 340
Susan Louisa, 271, 340

Willcox
Orlando B., 372, 373

Williams
Arthur Franklin, 404
Harvey, 287
Martha, 361
Perry, 419
Sarah, 157, 321, 419, 420
William Stephen, 360

Willoughby
Emily, 267

Wilson
Abigail, 408
Andrew, 174
Sarah, 158, 174, 201

Winchester
Emeline Robbins, 330
Hosea Dana, 260, 330
Hosea Dana Jr., 330

Wing
Caroline Nye Freeman, 299, 382
Clifton, 382

Winship
Aaron, 161, 174
Abigail, 161, 178, 179
Alice Shepherd, 254
Benoni, 161
Caleb, 174
Deborah, 161
Edward Jr., 159, 161, 163
Elizabeth, 58, 59, 164, 179, 190, 203, 205, 264
Ephraim Sr., 158, 173
Hannah, 158, 173, 200
Isaac, 203
Jason III, 59, 160, 178, 191
Jason Jr., 57, 59, 160, 164, 177, 178, 191
Jason Sr., 146, 159, 160, 163
Joanna, 161
John, 163
John (Deacon), 94, 146, 163, 164
John II, 164
John III, 164
John IV, 164
Joseph, 148, 179, 180
Joseph (Captain), 203
Joseph Sr., 148
Josiah (Rev.), 164, 192

Wyeth

Armenta Demaris "Minnie", 370

Arthur E., 390

Arthur Walter, 399

Audra, 370

Augustus, 98, 107, 183, 231, 233, 234

Augustus Greenleaf "A.G.", 79, 225, 301, 392, 394

Barbara Edith, 425

Benjamin E., 357

Benjamin Francis, 40, 241, 314

Benjamin Franklin "Frank" Jr., 412

Benjamin Franklin Sr., 79, 107, 314, 411, 412

Bertha May, 367

Bessie Wright, 392

Betsey Ann, 298

Betsy A., 289

Brenton Irwin, 425

Burnham Nathan Francis "Burnie", 400

Burton Riley, 390

Carol, 405

Carole (Scott), 109

Caroline A., 294

Caroline E., 269

Carolyn Bockius, vii, 89

Carrie Ella, 375

Carrie Olive, 370

Catharine Baker, 268, 337

Catharine Margaret, 261

Catherine, 286

Catherine W., 204, 264, 267

Charles, 213, 219, 226, 295, 296, 297, 313

Charles Alonzo, 79, 291, 344, 366, 367, 368

Charles Augustus (Rev.), 204, 227, 230, 305

Charles Austin, 366, 367

Charles Carson, 304

Charles E., 298, 380

Charles Edwin, 385

Charles Eugene "Charlie", 91

Charles H., 259

Charles Jarvis, 295, 374

Charles Jones, 292, 293, 371, 372, 373

Charles L., 375

Charles Leon, ix, 326, 399, 405

Charles Lewis, 343

Charles Lewis "Charley" (Dr.), 390

Charles Maynard, 376

Charles McReynolds, 372

Charles Nathaniel, 375

Charles Sheafer, 79, 305, 400

Charlotte Grosvenor, 3

Charlotte Hoffman "Daisy", 295, 374

Christina "Tina" (Baker), xiii, 5, 108, 113, 335

Christopher, 289

Cindy (Strother), 425

Claire (Raimondo), 425

Clara, 383

Clara (Emmons), ix

Clara Josephine, 357

Clarence Leonard, 383

Clarissa, 276, 347, 348

Clay Monroe, 382

Clifford Austin, 367

Clinton Earl, 389

Clinton R., 375

Cora Ann, 384

Cynthia A., 329

Daisy Fay, 384

Daniel, 291, 371

Daniel S., 370

David G., 224, 300, 301

David Goddard, 224, 225, 301, 392

David Vinson, 387

Deb (Wilkie), 95, 404, 425

Deborah, xii, 39, 40, 57, 60, 85, 107, 138, 145, 148, 152, 157, 158, 161, 167, 169, 175, 178, 194, 202, 231, 250, 425

Debrah (Zimmer), 425

Delilah Jane, 300

Donald Elwyn, ix, 382

Donald Harrison "Donny", 108

Donna (Thibodeau), 367, 425

Dorcas, 187

Dorothy Lucia, 405

Dorothy Lucille "Dottie", 108

Douglas R., 305

Duncan Orn, 95, 425

Ebenezer III, 14, 39, 62, 63, 66, 69, 70, 104, 179, 180, 203, 204, 206, 207, 229, 264, 274, 427

Ebenezer IV, 70, 203, 206

Ebenezer Jr., 11, 14, 58, 62, 67, 68, 72, 93, 94, 104, 107, 138, 162, 163, 179, 180, 181, 182, 189, 205, 220, 242, 245, 264, 427

Ebenezer Sr., xii, 14, 98, 104, 135, 146, 161, 162, 163, 183, 234

Edgar Alan, 337

Edward, 303

Edward A., 338

Edward Cazneau, 336

Edward Francis, 313

Edward Orbin, 370

Edwin Augustus, 100, 101, 103, 309, 318, 406, 407

Edwin Rudolph, 413

Effie May (Winn), ix

Eleanor Maynard, 376

Eliphalet J., 268

Elisa Rebecca, 227

Elisha, 211, 273, 274, 275, 286

Eliza, 241, 261, 274, 331, 343

Eliza Brewer, 276, 346

Eliza Jane, 212, 287, 288, 361

Eliza Phillipa, 259

Elizabeth, xi, 94, 145, 146, 163, 164, 165, 180, 187, 201, 204, 227, 239, 241, 261, 262, 311, 430, 431

Elizabeth "Eliza" Fiske, 234

Elizabeth E., 207

Elizabeth Flagg, 338

Elizabeth H., 299

Elizabeth Jarvis, 294, 295, 373

Elizabeth Jarvis I, 293

Elizabeth Norris, 374

535

Wyeth

ABOUT THE AUTHOR

Since a high school teacher ignited a fascination with American history for her, Christina Wyeth "Tina" Baker greatly enjoys researching and studying the past as well as traveling to historic locales. These interests combined well into Tina's vocation for genealogy investigation and writing. She has spent thousands of hours online and at sites in the United States, Italy and England carefully documenting her family tree.

Tina developed her writing skills in a variety of communications courses at Otterbein University where she earned her B. A. degree, magna cum laude, as an adult student while working full time. After a career in business, Tina switched gears to help at an urban literacy mission in Central Ohio. Now retired and living a quiet life in the country north of Columbus, Tina still volunteers for the mission via Skype as an ESL tutor.

Tina has been married for 45 years to her dear husband. She is the proud mother of two daughters and the happy grandmother of two grandsons.

BLOG: wyeth-wythe.blogspot.com

EMAIL: WyethBaker6@gmail.com

www.ingramcontent.com/pod-product-compliance
Lightning Source LLC
Chambersburg PA
CBHW052129020426
42334CB00023B/2656

* 9 7 8 0 7 8 8 4 5 8 9 7 2 *